WHERE *to* SKI
AND *Snowboard* 2010

Published in Great Britain by
NortonWood Publishing
The Oaks, Bath Road
Norton St Philip
Bath BA2 7LW
United Kingdom

tel 0844 9911 123
email w14@wtss.co.uk

Editors Chris Gill and Dave Watts
Assistant editors Mandy Crook,
Wendy-Jane King, Chris Allan,
Sheila Reid, Rebecca Miles
Pacific editor Bronwen Gora
Parks/boarding Les Seddon-Brown
Contributors Minty Clinch,
Alan Coulson, Nicky Holford,
James Hooke, Eric Jackson,
Tim Perry, Ian Porter, Adam Ruck,
Helena Wiesner, Fraser Wilkin

Advertising manager
Dave Ashmore

Design by Val Fox
Production by Guide Editors
Contents photos generally
by Snowpix.com / Chris Gill
Production manager Ian Stratford
Proofreader Lynda Watson
Printed and bound in the UK
by St Ives Web Ltd

10 9 8 7 6 5 4 3 2 1

ISBN-13: 978–0–9558663–1–9

A CIP catalogue entry for this book
is available from the British Library.

Book trade sales are handled by
Portfolio Books Ltd
2nd Floor, Westminster House
Kew Road
Richmond
TW9 2ND

tel 020 8334 1730
fax 020 8334 1609

email sales@portfoliobooks.com

**Individual copies of the book can be
bought (for delivery anywhere in the
world) at a discount price by going to
our website – www.wtss.co.uk**

WHERE *to* SKI
AND *SnoWboard* 2010

The Definitive Guide
to the 1,000 Best Winter Sports Resorts in the World

Edited by
Chris Gill
and
Dave Watts

NortonWood

Contents 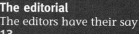 1

About this book
Why it's simply the best
10

The editorial
The editors have their say
13

WTSS online
What we're up to with
www.wtss.co.uk
22

What's new?
New lifts and other major
resort developments
24

Price survey
Our new Resort Price Index
figures explained
31

Snow business
Just how good was that season?
36

Pick the right lift pass
The choice gets ever wider
40

Jobs in the mountains
Live that dream: do a season
42

Gap year courses
Fill it, don't spill it
44

New gear for 2010
All the new kit for
next season
46

Smart apartments
Independence with comfort
50

Luxury chalets
Is there a better holiday?
54

Luxury hotels
Service with style and a smile
57

A home in the snow
Make buying painless
59

Family holidays
Our new ratings explained
63

Corporate ski trips
Motivate your staff and clients
69

Short breaks
A quick fix of the white stuff
72

Flying to the snow
More and more choice
74

Travelling by rail
Make tracks to the mountains
77

Drive to the Alps
Ski where you please
80

Drive to the French Alps
To make the most of them
85

That's the start of it – turn the page for the heart of it ...

www.wtss.co.uk

Our website is designed to complement this book. We like to think it's one of the best in the ski business, and it is being revamped to make it even better from this autumn – there's more about this on page 22.

On the site you'll find:

– twice-weekly news and updates on all the resorts in this book throughout the season

– full editors' ratings for 200 resorts – three times the number we can fit into the book

– interactive resort shortlist builder – you plug in what you want most from a resort (eg village charm, extensive slopes, convenient lodgings) and up pops a shortlist to suit you

– snow reports and resort weather forecasts

– free competitions with great prizes

– special holiday offers from leading tour operators

– links to thousands of useful sites such as resorts, tour operators, hotels, ski schools, airlines, transfer companies

– blogs from the editors on their winter travels

– dozens of background feature articles (eg for families)

– forums where you can exchange views, seek advice, give vent to those grumbles

– a resort reporting system, where you can file a report and maybe win next year's edition of the book

– a signup for monthly e-newsletters (essential reading for all keen skiers and boarders)

You know how good the book is. Don't miss the site.
Visit today and sign up for our e-newsletters.

Contents 2

Choosing your resort
Get it right first time
88

Resort ratings at a glance
All the big resorts evaluated
91

Resort shortlists
To help you spot resorts that
will suit you and your party
97

Our resort chapters
How to get the best out of them
100

RESORTS IN DETAIL
The heart of the book:
600+ pages of information,
analysis and evaluation;
chapter list over the page
102

Ski business directory
Tour operators, ski travel agents
and others
736

Ski retailers
The best ski/board equipment
emporia in the country
741

Resort directory / index
Page references for 400 major
resorts, at a glance summaries
of 700+ minor ones
742

Resort chapters

ANDORRA 102

Excellent British-oriented ski schools, but charmless villages – and no longer such a great bargain

Arinsal	105
Pas de la Casa	107
Soldeu	109

FRANCE 230

Unrivalled for big, high, snow-sure ski areas with convenient lodgings – but be prepared for high prices in the best-known ones

Alpe-d'Huez	234	Megève	305	Serre-Chevalier	360
Les Arcs	244	Les Menuires	312	Ste-Foy-Tarentaise	369
Avoriaz 1800	253	Méribel	316	St-Martin-de-B'ville	371
Chamonix	258	Montgenèvre	327	Les Sybelles	373
Châtel	268	Morzine	331	La Tania	378
La Clusaz	273	Paradiski	337	The Three Valleys	382
Les Contamines	275	La Plagne	339	Tignes	384
Courchevel	277	Portes du Soleil	349	Val d'Isère	393
Les Deux-Alpes	288	Puy-St-Vincent	350	Valmorel	404
Flaine	294	Risoul / Vars	352	Val Thorens	406
Les Gets	301	La Rosière	355	French Pyrenees	413
La Grave	303	Samoëns	358		

8

AUSTRIA 114

Charming villages, lively après-ski, friendly locals and modest prices – but beware low altitudes and poor snow as a result

Alpbach	120	Saalbach-H'glemm	179
Bad Gastein	123	Schladming	186
Bad Kleinkirchheim	126	Sölden	190
Ellmau	129	Söll	193
Hintertux	132	St Anton	200
Hochkönig	138	Stubai valley	210
Innsbruck	140	Vorarlberg	212
Ischgl	144	Vorarlberg –	
Kitzbühel	151	Bregenzerwald	213
Lech	158	Montafon	217
Mayrhofen	167	Westendorf	220
Obergurgl	172	Zell am See	222
Obertauern	177	Zugspitz Arena	227

ITALY 418

Jolly villages, up-to-the-minute lift systems and snowmaking, and modest prices – but few extensive ski areas to rival those of France

Aosta valley	422	Passo Tonale	454
Bormio	426	Sauze d'Oulx	456
Cervinia	428	Sella Ronda	461
Cortina d'Ampezzo	434	Selva	468
Courmayeur	439	Sestriere	475
Livigno	444	La Thuile	477
Madonna di C'o	448	Trentino	479
Monterosa Ski	450	Val di Fassa	483

GERMANY — 414

Has a great deal in common with Austria, over the border. There is one first-division resort, and dozens of minor ones

Garmisch-Partenkirchen	416

SWITZERLAND — 484

Some uniquely cute villages and spectacular scenery; slightly cheaper than France at current rates, but no match for Austria and Italy

Adelboden	491	Laax	518
Andermatt	493	Meiringen	520
Anzère	495	Mürren	523
Arosa	496	Saas-Fee	527
Champéry	498	St Moritz	532
Crans-Montana	501	Val d'Anniviers	539
Davos	503	Verbier	543
Engelberg	510	Villars	555
Grindelwald	512	Wengen	557
Klosters	516	Zermatt	562

USA — 572

Great service, mostly crowd-free slopes, frequent snow and safe, steep runs not found in Europe

California	**576**	**Utah**	**626**
Heavenly	577	Alta	627
Mammoth	582	The Canyons	629
Squaw Valley	587	Deer Valley	631
Colorado	**589**	Park City	633
Aspen	590	Snowbird	638
Beaver Creek	597	**Rest of the West**	**640**
Breckenridge	599	Big Sky	641
Copper Mountain	604	Jackson Hole	646
Keystone	606	**New England**	**651**
Snowmass	608	Killington	652
Steamboat	610	Stowe	656
Telluride	613		
Vail	615		
Winter Park	622		

CANADA — 658

A lot in common with the USA, but with some very distinctive resorts and grand scenery

Western Canada	**660**	**Eastern Canada**	**700**
Banff	661	Tremblant	701
Big White	668		
Fernie	671		
Kicking Horse	676		
Lake Louise	678		
Panorama	683		
Revelstoke	685		
Silver Star	687		
Sun Peaks	689		
Whistler	691		

THE REST

Spain	**703**	EASTERN EUROPE		FAR EAST	
Baqueira-Beret	704	**Bulgaria**	**715**	**Japan**	**721**
		Bansko	716		
SCANDINAVIA		**Romania**	**718**	SOUTHERN H'SPHERE	
Finland	**706**	**Slovenia**	**719**	**Australia**	**723**
Norway	**708**			**New Zealand**	**725**
Hemsedal	710	UK		Queenstown	728
Sweden	**712**	**Scotland**	**720**	**Argentina**	**732**
Åre	713			**Chile**	**733**

About this book

It's simply the best

Dave Watts

Where to Ski and Snowboard – Britain's only long-established annual guide to ski resorts worldwide – is the best guide you can buy. Here's why:

- With every new edition we introduce **improvements and innovations**. This year, we publish Resort Price Index figures, based on the most comprehensive survey of resort prices ever undertaken; our resort chapters all have several new sections; for major resorts we've upped the number of star ratings we give by 50%; we have new chapters on areas in Austria, Italy, Switzerland and Canada; and for the first time we cover Germany.

- By making the most of technology we are able to publish at the right time while going to press very late by conventional book publishing standards – so we can include the late-breaking news that makes the book **up to date for the season ahead**. The earliest editions of this book went to press in June; this year, it's 3 August, only a month ahead of publication day.

- We work hard to make our information **reader-friendly**, with clearly structured text, comparative ratings and no-nonsense verdicts for the main aspects of each resort.

Chris Gill

- We don't hesitate to express **critical views**. We learned our craft at Consumers' Association, where Chris became editor of *Holiday Which?* magazine and Dave became editor of *Which?* itself – so a consumerist attitude comes naturally to us.

- Our resort chapters give an **unrivalled level of detail** – including scale plans of each major resort, so that you get a clear idea of size – and all the facts you need.

- The book benefits enormously from the **hundreds of reports** that readers send in on the resorts they visit. (Every year, the 100 best reports are rewarded by a free copy of the book, and many of our best regular reporters get a free week's lift pass; prove your worth by sending us useful reports, and you could ski for free.)

- We use **colour printing** fully – we include not only piste maps for every major resort but also scores of photographs, carefully chosen so that you can see for yourself what the resorts are like.

Our ability to keep on investing in *Where to Ski and Snowboard* is largely due to the support of our advertisers – many of whom have been with us since the first edition in 1994. We are grateful for that support, and hope readers will in turn support our advertisers. It also helps if you tell them that you saw their ads in these pages: we know advertising in the book works, but advertisers can't be reminded too often.

We are absolutely committed to helping you, our readers, to make an informed choice; and we're confident that you'll find this edition the best yet. Enjoy your skiing and riding this season.

Chris Gill and Dave Watts
Norton St Philip, 3 August 2009

GET YOUR MONEY BACK
when you book a holiday

You can reclaim the price of Where to Ski and Snowboard when you book a winter sports holiday for the 2009/10 or 2010/11 seasons. All you have to do is book the holiday through the specialist ski travel agency Ski Solutions.

Ski Solutions is Britain's original and leading ski travel agency. You can buy whatever kind of holiday you want through them.

Ski Solutions sells the package holidays offered by all the bonded tour operators in Britain (apart from the very few who are direct-sell only). And if that isn't enough choice, they can tailor-make a holiday, based on any form of travel and any kind of accommodation. No one is better placed to find you what you want than Ski Solutions.

Making a claim

Claiming your refund could not be easier. When you make your definite booking, tell Ski Solutions that you want to take up this offer and claim the refund. They will deduct the price of the book from your bill.

Phone Ski Solutions on
020 7471 7700

Get next year's edition free
by reporting on your holiday

There are too many resorts for us to visit them all every year, and too many hotels, bars and mountain restaurants for us to see. So we are very keen to encourage more readers to send in reports on their holiday experiences. As usual, we'll be giving 100 copies of the next edition to the writers of the best reports.

There are five main kinds of feedback we need:

- what you particularly **liked and disliked** about the resort
- what aspects of the resort came as a **surprise** to you
- your other suggestions for **changes to our evaluation** of the resort – changes we should make to the ratings, verdicts, descriptions etc
- your experience of **queues** and other weaknesses in the lift system, and the **ski school** and associated childcare arrangements (please take care to name the school)
- your feedback on **individual facilities** in the resort – the hotels, bars, restaurants (including mountain restaurants), nightspots, equipment shops, sports facilities etc.

We now store reports in a central database where our editors can easily access them, which means that we much prefer to receive them in digital form.

Ideally, we'd like you to use our online form at
www.wheretoski.co.uk/reportform
but if you prefer you can send an email to
reports@wtss.co.uk

It's vital that you give us the date of your trip so that we can interpret your report sensibly. And include your phone number and postal address, in case we have trouble reaching you by email.

If you prefer, you can file short reports on our website:
www.wtss.co.uk
You can see other readers' reports there, too.

Consistently helpful reporters are invited to become 'resort observers', which means that when possible we'll arrange free lift passes in your holiday resorts, in exchange for detailed reports on those resorts.

The editorial

The editors have their say

THE ONLY GUIDE TO BUY

When we started *Where to Ski* (as it then was) in 1994 we were the upstart competitor, trailing in the wake of *The Good Skiing Guide*, published by *Which?* (and edited from its first edition in 1985 to 1992 by your current editor Gill). With the support of our advertisers we were able to invest in content and in colour printing that enabled us gradually to take over as market leader, and in 2005 *Which?* threw in the towel. A lookalike *Great Skiing and Snowboarding Guide* emerged from the ashes, and last season was renamed *Hardy's Guide*; no new edition of that is being published this year. Which leaves us with no major competitor. Don't worry; we will not rest on our laurels; we will continue to improve and develop, as we have this year (see 'About this book', page 10).

We'd like to thank the readers who support the book and our advertisers – particularly the many who have stayed with us over the years. We're well aware that measuring the effectiveness of printed advertising is difficult. But we're also aware that advertising in this book works. A visible presence in 'the skier's bible' makes commercial sense for anyone selling holidays, whether as agents or operators. If you contact an advertiser because you've seen an ad in this book, please make that clear so that the advertiser gets evidence that the ads in this book are working.

KEEPING TRACK

If you spent time in central or eastern Austria this season, there's a good chance you were able to plug into a new system (Skiline) that exploits the data collected by lift pass systems to produce lift-by-lift, run-by-run logs of your days on the hill. The log shown below represents a day we did in the SkiWelt in January.

Before we go any further, we should make it clear that the conspicuous stationary period between 1230 and 1415 was largely taken up by an extended interview with the head of the Scheffau ski school. Lunch at Tanzbodenalm took hardly any time at all.

As well as SkiWelt, the service currently operates in Schladming and most of the other Ski Amadé resorts, Saalbach-Hinterglemm-Leogang, Zell am See, the Zillertal (Mayrhofen etc) and lots of other small resorts. Outside Austria, it is currently confined to Zermatt-Cervinia, Nendaz, Courmayeur, and Fichtelberg in Germany.

This sort of log doesn't have quite the fascination of a GPS-based system, as offered in some American resorts, which of course logs

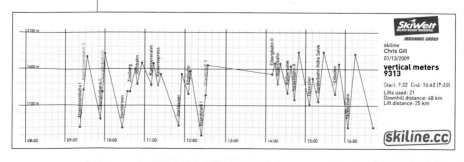

83% of the pistes are served by snow machines!

KATSCHBERG

GRAZ-TAMSWEG

MAUTERNDORF

VILLACH-KLAGENFURT
ST. MICHAEL I. L.

OBERTAUERN

GAMSKOGEL 2188 m

GALSTERBERGALM 1986 m

HAUSER KAIBLING 2015 m

PLANAI 1894 m

ZAUCHENSEE 1350 m

HOCHWURZEN 1850 m

REITERALM 1860 m

FAGERALM 1885 m

KEMAHÖHÖHE 1871 m

GRAZ-WIEN

ÖBLARN

PRUGGERN 660 m

GRÖBMING 776 m

AICH 750 m

ROHRMOOS

STODERZINKEN 2045 m

HAUS/ENNSTAL 752 m

SCHLADMING 745 m

FORSTAU 930 m

ALTENMARKT 856 m

PICHL 800 m GLEIMINGBERG

RADSTADT 862 m

MANDLING 840 m

RAMSAU AM DACHSTEIN 1100 1300 m

RITTISBERG 1582 m

ROSSBRAND 1600 m

TANNKOPPEN 1678 m

DACHSTEINGLETSCHER 2700 m

FILZMOOS 1057 m

NEUBERG

BISCHOFSMÜTZE

SCHLADMING-DACHSTEIN
Tel. +43 (0) 3687/23310, info@schladming-dachstein.at

FLACHAU, WAGRAIN, ST. JOHANN/ALPENDORF, ZAUCHENSEE, FLACHAUWINKL, KLEINARL, RADSTADT, ALTENMARKT, FILZMOOS
Tel. +43 (0) 6457/2929, info@salzburgersportwelt.com

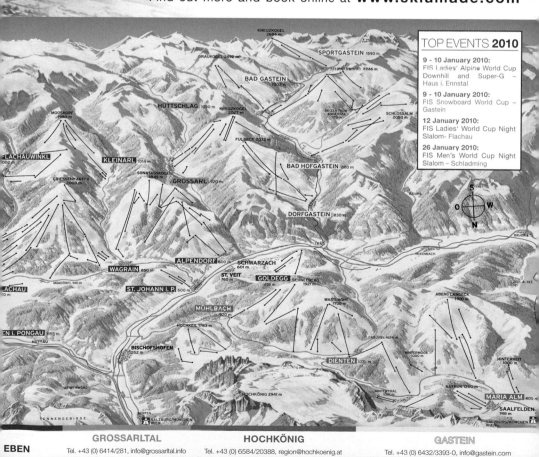

your actual track down the mountain as well as your lift-rides up it. But it's free, and doesn't involve carrying kit around with you. In some resorts you can print your log at the lift base station; in others, you use the Skiline website.

Currently, the website includes for each resort a list of the top 100 verticals skied in a day. Obviously, this will have to be stopped, to prevent nutters racing down the mountain all day, trying to set new records. But we can't deny a certain interest in the figures. The current record for the SkiWelt is a fairly amazing 33,609m, which makes our 9,313m look a bit puny. But then we did spend two hours conducting an interview.

QUAD-SPEED DOUBLES
We're intrigued to note that a new high-speed double chair is to be installed at Mürren, to serve an area at Allmendhubel. We're aware of only one other fast double, on Aspen Mountain in Colorado. Let's have more of them. The Alps are littered with slow old double chairs in positions where the capacity of a quad isn't needed but the ride-time of a slow chair is an irritant. Usually they are on shaded slopes, and on a January morning you spend 20 minutes getting gradually chilled to the marrow when a fast chair would whisk you up in a quarter of the time.

US LIFT PASS PRICES: WHY SO HIGH?
North American lift passes, and US ones especially, are reaching stratospheric heights. A single day ticket in Vail last year was $97 (around £65 at July exchange rates). This compares with a typical cost of 44 euros (£40) for a day in a top Euro resort such as Val d'Isère, Courchevel or St Anton. And you don't get much discount for buying a six-day pass in North America; in Vail you don't get any, so a six-day pass at the ticket office costs you getting on for £400, compared with around £190 for a six-day pass in Europe.

You can sometimes save by buying in advance or through a UK tour operator. Or even, bizarrely, by buying at local stores rather than at the ticket office window. But a week's skiing will still cost at least £250 to £300 in North America. To add to the injury, the lifts often close at 3pm (and some may close as early as 1.30pm in early season). The only explanation we've heard for these excessive prices is that the resorts face high insurance premiums to protect them from potential personal injury law suits. We're not convinced.

AIR FARE EXTRAS CONTINUE TO MOUNT
The extras being added to many so-called budget airlines' fares are reaching mind-numbing levels. Just taking your skis or snowboard with Ryanair adds a staggering £80 to your return fare, £60 if you book them in online. EasyJet's charges are appreciably lower, but still penal: £52 if you just pitch up with them, £37 if you book them in online.

But that's not all. Most budget airlines now charge for each piece of 'normal' baggage you check in (with no increase in the 15kg or 20kg weight limit, no matter how many bags you pay for); some charge a fee for checking in, some for booking; most charge a fee for paying by credit card (a sensible thing to do, because the credit card company has to refund you if the airline goes bust); most offer travel insurance (which may not adequately cover winter sports) and some sort of priority check-in or boarding – you will need to be

careful if you want to avoid these extras.

We looked at the cost of a flight to Salzburg for mid-March with one of the budget airlines. The initial basic air fare came to a very reasonable £42.98. But once you'd added on 'taxes and fees', paid for one piece of hold luggage plus skis and the credit card and booking or check-in fee, the cost had rocketed to almost £200.

SKI ROUTE NONSENSE

There doesn't seem to be much doubt that we are failing to hold back the tide of ski routes. But we'll keep plugging away, in the faint hope that someone running the dozens of affected resorts will pay attention. Why are we against them? Read on.

There are several problems with ski routes, or itinéraires. Much the most important is that skiers don't know what they are: they are hardly ever explained on mountain maps or on mountains. The most common meaning is that the runs are protected from avalanches, marked on the ground to some degree (but with fewer markers than a piste), not patrolled and not groomed. But in Austria, we're told, the rules say they may or may not be patrolled or groomed. And, indeed, we've repeatedly found ski routes that are groomed. This simply adds to the confusion, and confusion is dangerous. It opens up the bizarre possibility that you might descend a groomed run that is not patrolled. Madness.

Because ski routes are not patrolled, or potentially not patrolled, they are much less valuable to lone skiers and riders. If the run is quiet, or it's late in the day, the risk of finding yourself injured and alone on such a run is not one to take lightly. The next problem is that 'fewer markers' means 'no use in bad weather'. Very often there is no definition of the edge of the run, and in bad visibility you can't see from one marker to the next. And finally, the ski route designation usually gives no clue to difficulty (though some resorts have black, red and even blue ski routes). The result is that those not confident on genuine blacks usually have to avoid these runs, when many of them would be very rewarding for intermediates.

DIFFERING APPROACHES TO OFF-PISTE

Off-piste skiing in Italy, or the regulation of it, is in a mess. When we were in Bormio, Santa Caterina and Livigno last season, there were signs all over the mountains saying off-piste was not allowed. We saw people skiing off-piste unhindered, but we also heard of people being caught and fined on the spot by the police. When we tried to get to the bottom of it we were met with typical Italian confusion. The reason for the ban seems to be that the authorities are concerned that people going off-piste might set off avalanches that threaten people on the piste. A tourist office contact in Livigno told us that off-piste was banned throughout Italy by a national law. Other resorts told us there were no restrictions on off-piste. And in the Monterosa region a new cable car is due to open that serves only off-piste terrain. Make of all this what you will.

Adelboden – no wonder people keep coming back

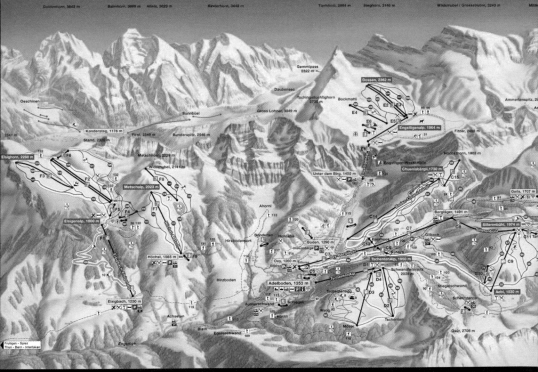

- 210 km superbly-prepared pistes
- 72 lift facilities
- 36 ski huts and après-ski bars
- Host of the FIS Ski World Cup 9./10.01.2010
- Family-friendly
- Snow secure from December to April with ski mountains up to 8000 ft. in height

- First accredited Alpine Wellness Holiday destination in Switzerland
- Highlight: Tropenhaus Frutigen (Tropical House, opening on 21 November 2009)
- 1 hour drive from Berne airport
- Direct flights to Berne airport from Birmingham, London Gatwick, Manchester and Southampton
(subject to schedule changes)

Further information: **www.adelboden.ch**

Meanwhile, in the French resort of Risoul, a much more constructive approach has developed, with echoes of the way American resorts manage their 'steep and deep' terrain (see page 573). Risoul divides off-piste terrain within the lift network into different categories, including controlled areas accessed through gates that are closed when there is avalanche risk. An excellent development, which should be copied elsewhere.

CAN THEY BE SERIOUS?

Remember the Segway human transporter, revealed to an astonished world in 2001? It's an electrically powered two-wheeled device that saves you the effort of walking or cycling, and it was going to replace the car, at least in cities. It hasn't done that, quite, but it still exists, and visitors to Méribel next season will find a fleet of off-road versions to play with. 'These innovative machines can tackle hills and snow. Silent and easy to use, the Segway is a new eco-friendly and fun way to discover the resort in summer and winter.' Well, that's what it says here. We can't wait.

CAR RENTAL RIP-OFFS

Car rental insurance routinely involves huge excesses – amounts you have to pay towards any damage. £750 to £1,000 seems fairly typical. You can pay extra to reduce or eliminate the excess, but we frequently found ourselves paying up to £100 or more to reduce the excess for a ten-day trip. And the reduction doesn't normally apply to windows, tyres, roof, undercarriage or built-in satnav equipment. So last season we bought year-round excess waiver cover, which really does reduce the excess to zero and has no important exclusions. The cost? £49 for European cover, £65 for worldwide; for a year, not a week. See www.insurance4carhire.com.

Then there's the winter equipment scam. You turn up in Munich; they ask you where you're headed; if it's Austria (of course it's Austria), you must have winter tyres. That'll be 20 euros extra; 20 euros per day, that is – more than the original rental cost. The cars already have winter tyres fitted, of course. It is a scam, pure and simple. And of course when booking online, particularly through a broker, you get no information about these extras, so you can't make an informed choice.

NOT REMOTELY INTERESTED

Another thing the discount rental brokers don't make clear is that some rental companies are located off the airport, several km away, which makes the whole pickup and dropoff process more protracted. We've had this in Innsbruck and Munich recently. But then Lyon and Geneva airports have moved their entire car rental facilities away from the terminal – a real backward step.

NO MORE SECONDARY SMOKING ... WE HOPE

French and Italian resort restaurants have been delightfully smoke-free for a few years now. But in Austria and Switzerland smoking has remained the norm almost everywhere. Things should change for this coming season. Nearly every Swiss canton containing major ski resorts has banned smoking except in dedicated smoking rooms, and all hotels, restaurants and bars will have smoke-free areas. In Austria, the situation is a bit less clear-cut and is spelled out on page 116; reports welcome on how effective the new Austrian laws are.

STILL ON COLLISION COURSE

We and many readers continue to be worried by the increasing frequency of collisions or near collisions on the pistes of the Alps. One regular reporter who had a series of incidents last season said: 'Usually, the other party said, "But you turned in front of me." It seems many people simply don't know the cardinal rule that the uphill skier must avoid the downhill skier. What's to be done?'

Well, one thing that might be done is to drop the absurdly fussy ten commandments put out by the FIS, and focus on four simple rules that could be widely publicised in several languages:
You must always:
Retain control, so that you can stop safely when necessary
Keep well clear of people below you, whatever their actions
Go to the side of the run when stopping or walking
Avoid the path of others when moving off

THE WRITE STUFF

We're eternally grateful for the annual flood of reports from readers about the resorts you've visited. But it has to be said that making use of them can be hard work. You pack them with so many facts, judgements, suggestions, complaints, recommendations; it's all pretty serious stuff. Or nearly all. One reader's view of Vars raised a titter: 'The only redeeming feature of the many draglifts is that they are quicker than the glacially slow chairlifts. The Mayt chair is so slow it's tempting to stay put at the bottom and simply wait for erosion to take its course.' Simon Lambert wins a copy of this edition for brightening an editorial day. Please keep the reports coming, with or without novel ways of quantifying lift speed.

PHOTO FINISH

Many thanks to the dozens of readers who submitted resort photos for this year – we've used about 20. The prize goes to Alan Liptrot for his picture in the Sella Ronda chapter. Alan wins a day's sailing on a splendid yacht in the Solent – with the WTSS editorial team, if he's very lucky. Please keep sending photos to photos@wtss.co.uk; there will again be a prize for the best of the bunch.

OUR ANNUAL AWARDS

This year's winners are:
Best European Resort Development – Saalbach-Hinterglemm, Austria
With the installation this year of a further three fast chairlifts, the number of fast chairs and gondolas here rises to over 80% of the total lift network, putting the resort comfortably at the top of our fast lifts league table. Compare that with bottom-of-the-league Les Sybelles – one of France's biggest lift networks – which has fewer than one fast lift in ten.
Best North American Resort Development – Jackson Hole, USA
This award is for sustained improvement over the last decade, in particular. When we first visited back in the early 1990s, we found long queues for the Tram, nowhere decent for lunch on the mountain and very limited options at the foot of the slopes. In the last few years the place has changed amazingly: there's a new Tram with a doubled hourly capacity, a smart new table-service mountain restaurant and a bunch of smooth upmarket hotels at the base. Many locals will tell you the place is losing its soul, going soft, selling out. Maturing nicely, we'd say.

WTSS online

Changes afoot at www.wtss.co.uk

by **Chris Gill**

Well, another year of the ongoing digital revolution has gone by and digital media haven't entirely displaced print yet, we're happy to say. For many purposes, books and magazines are still a pretty cute way of presenting a stack of information in a portable and accessible way. Of course, these newfangled e-book reader thingies are complicating things even further: just when we were all getting used to the clear choice between sitting at our keyboard/screen or lounging about with a book, we now have the option of lounging about with an e-book.

We'll get around to thinking about such things more seriously before long, no doubt. For now, we've got our hands full with a full-blown revamp of our website. It's four or five years since our current site was built, and it's time for a rethink/redesign/rebuild. What follows is a short tour of what we're up to. Whether we'll have it all working by the time this edition hits the bookshelves, the gods perhaps know.

ADAPT OR DIE

If there is one thing we've learned in the last five years about the construction of websites, it's that you need to be able to change things – add new elements, drop tired ones, change the prominence of things. So we're moving to a software system that will allow us to do that sort of stuff without triggering major delays and major bills. The practical result? We hope you'll find the site much more dynamic – continually expanding and changing to reflect new ideas and demands.

RESORT INFORMATION IS US

We're well aware that the key thing we need to do with the site is provide resort information that complements what we present in this book. (If we were in any doubt, the poll we ran over the summer on the home page – reproduced here – made things pretty clear.) The site can complement the book in two ways: by adding information that we can't fit into the book (there is, after all, no limit to the depth of information we can provide online); and by providing user interaction. We're working on both angles.

A key feature of the old site is the 'expert system' that you can use to get your own personal resort shortlist, and we're working on improvements to this. This system basically uses our resort ratings to build your shortlist. The first step towards a better interactive system is that we have created more ratings. As you'll see in our major resort chapters, we have now given these resorts 18 star ratings

The results of the poll we ran on our home page over the summer; no big surprises, but it's good to have our instincts confirmed →

GIVE US YOUR VIEWS

Once you've voted, you'll see the current poll results

What on the site would you most like to see developed further?

Resort info/chooser
35%

News and blogs
18%

Features and travel
13%

Snow reports/forecasts
23%

Forum/reader reviews
12%

instead of the 12 they have had up to now. On the new website, there will be 200 resorts in the system with these 18 ratings. But we're also working on adding other factors to the system, using factual data as well as our ratings – the airport transfer time, for example, or the distance from Calais.

There are three main ways in which we are adding depth to the resort information on the site – links, pictures and features. We already have a substantial database of hotel links for our own use, for example, and we'll be publishing that on the site as well as the links to tour operators etc that we have had for some time. Similarly, over our 15 years of operation we have accumulated a big collection of resort photos that will help visitors get a clear idea of the style of a resort, once it is put online. And we have a fat file of features on resorts waiting to be rolled out on to the site.

SNOW BUSINESS

You'll see from the poll results that snow reports and forecasts are next on visitors' lists of priorities. For the last two seasons we've posted weekly summaries of snow conditions in the main skiing regions, plus forecasts produced by our friends at Ski Solutions. We continue to get a good response to these, so we'll carry on doing them once the snow starts arriving.

We've also been finding out about sources of resort-specific snow data that we might feed into the site without human intervention. But having spent a season observing some of the detailed snow reports already published on the web, we have reservations about that very lack of human intervention. Some very strange figures can result at times. We're still working on this angle, and on acquiring an automatic feed of snow forecast information.

We may at the same time develop in the opposite direction, and construct further systems involving snow reports produced by people rather than databases. We're particularly attracted to the idea of a system that allows readers to post short snow reports by text or email from their mobile phones. In the end, the views of paying holidaymakers are worth more than the views of anyone with a commercial stake in promotion of a resort.

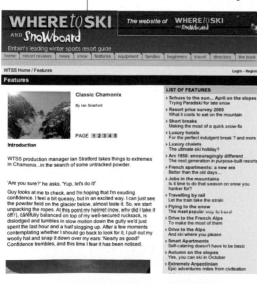

NEWS AND BLOGS
This heading came third on site visitors' agenda – and here we're fairly confident of making progress. Our new software system will allow us to have as many separate blogs as we like, and is much slicker from the point of view of posting items to both the blogs and the news system – so we'll be able to keep the site up to date more easily while travelling. We even entertain hopes of training editor Watts to post his own blog entries from the Alps and Rockies without requiring support from head office. Well, there's no harm in hoping.

New lifts and other major developments in top resorts

In this chapter we summarise major developments in ski resorts last season and those planned for 2009/10. Each major resort chapter has a 'News' panel near the start; you'll find many more news items in those panels. To keep up to date with resort developments, go to our website at www.wtss.co.uk and sign up for our email newsletters; you'll also find a flow of news on the opening page of the site.

ANDORRA

ARINSAL NOW HAS TWO SERIOUS LIFT BASES

Last season, a six-pack replaced the double chair from the valley at Cota. With improved snowmaking on the run down, this is now a viable alternative to the main lift base in the village centre.

AUSTRIA

BAD GASTEIN'S STUBNERKOGEL GETS THE TREATMENT

Last season, an eight-seat gondola was installed from Angertal up to Stubnerkogel – serving new blue and red runs. For 2009/10 the gondola out of Bad Gastein is being upgraded to an eight-seater.

ANOTHER FAST LIFT AT ELLMAU

For 2009/10 a new six-pack (Ellmi's) is planned for the top half of the mountain above Scheffau to Hartkaiser.

HIGHER CAPACITY AT HINTERTUX / TUX VALLEY

For 2009/10 the Lattenalm double chair on Eggalm is due to be replaced by a six-pack. Last season, a 24-person gondola replaced the smaller of the two access gondolas up to the Hintertux glacier.

NEW FAST CHAIR FOR HOCHKÖNIG – HIGH KING MOUNTAIN

For 2009/10 a six-pack is planned to replace the old double chair out of Hintermoos to Aberg.

FAST CHAIRS GALORE AT SAALBACH-HINTERGLEMM

For 2009/10 a six-pack is planned to replace the Turm draglift, on the lower slopes of Kohlmaiskopf at Saalbach. Above Hinterglemm, an eight-seat chair is expected to replace the quad to Hasenauer Köpfl. And at Leogang, a fast quad is due to replace the Almlift T-bar below the gondola mid-station. This is now the top-ranked major ski area in the world for fast lifts.

SCHLADMING PLANS AN EIGHT-PACK

For 2009/10 an eight-seat chairlift is planned to replace a T-bar near the top of Planai.

SÖLDEN TRIPLE CHAIR REPLACED, NEW RUN CREATED

Last season an eight-seat chairlift replaced an old triple chair at Giggijoch, and the ski route from the glacier became a blue piste.

TWO MORE FAST LIFTS ABOVE SÖLL

The Siller-Keat six-pack replaced a slow chair towards Zinsberg. Above Hopfgarten a gondola was built from the mid-station to Hohe Salve.

ST ANTON IMPROVES ACCESS TO RENDL

For 2009/10, a new eight-seat gondola is to replace the old one to Rendl, starting close to the town centre and with a piste back.

Vorarlberg – Bregenzerwald gets better connected
For 2009/10 Damüls (already the biggest ski area in Bregenzerwald) will be linked to Mellau by an eight-seat gondola and a new red piste – creating a linked piste network totalling 92km/57 miles.

Vorarlberg – Montafon: T-bars to go
For 2009/10 above St Gallenkirch, an eight-pack with covers and heated seats is due to replace the Gampabing T-bars at Valisera. But the tiny ski area above Tschagguns, Grabs, has closed.

Westendorf affirms connection
Westendorf is now properly linked to the SkiWelt by a gondola from Brixen to Choralpe and a piste back down. Another new gondola to Choralpe has improved access to there from the Westendorf slopes.

Zell am See plans a six-pack
For 2009/10 a six-pack is to replace the Gipfelbahn triple chair on the back of Schmittenhöhe; the Kettinglift draglift will also be removed.

New lift for the Zugspitz Arena
There are plans to install a new lift, Gamsalmbahn, in Ehrwald's Wetterstein sector for 2009/10.

Zürs ditches double chair for six-pack
For 2009/10 a heated and covered six-pack will replace the double chair to Muggengrat.

France

Alpe-d'Huez to replace gondola with chair
For 2009/10 a six-pack with covers is planned to replace the first stage of the Marmottes gondola. A new blue slope from the arrival point will run across to the mid-station of the DMC gondola.

Two old chairs to go at Les Arcs
For 2009/10 a six-pack is planned to replace the Arpette and Col des Frettes chairs above Arc 1600 and Arc 1800.

Fewer queues at Chamonix
A 10-person gondola has replaced the old smaller access lift to Le Brévent, easing queues to return to the valley as much as queues to go up. A new quad is to be installed at the Planards beginner area.

Châtel to replace old Linga double
For 2009/10 a new six-pack is due to replace the Linga double chair to Tête du Linga, starting from a lower point.

Speedy connection to Courchevel 1650
For 2009/10 a six-pack will replace the two double chairs from Prameruel to the slopes above 1650 – speeding up access from 1850. Six 1850 hotels have been elevated to the new 5-star classification.

Faster navigation around the Grand Massif
For 2009/10 a much-needed new six-pack is replacing two old chairs and a drag between Samoëns 1600 and Tête des Saix. Another six-pack is due above Les Molliets, improving the links from the Les Carroz sector.

Les Menuires to replace four lifts with one
For 2009/10 a six-pack is due to replace three chairs (Arcosses, Sapinière and Etelè) and a draglift at Reberty.

WITHOUT DOUBT, ONE OF THE WORLD'S BIGGEST SKI AREAS. BEYOND DOUBT, THE CLOSEST TO YOU.

EXCEPTIONAL SKIING

5 connected resorts, the Grand Massif, 4th biggest ski area in France, offers 265 km of pistes for all levels, from 720 to 2500 m in altitude, with panoramic views of the Mont Blanc range.

NEW SIX-PACKS… HIGH TECH

This Xmas, the Grand-Massif ski area will introduce 2 new fast six-packs: Chariande Express and Molliets Express.
Experience… Direct access to the ski area, capacity doubled, 3 times faster for even more ski time!
Enjoy… A preserved environment: several old lifts removed and replaced by 2 high performance chairlifts. Hand's free ski pass, renewable online, free ski buses and car parks.

RECORD SNOWFALLS!

4,85 m of snow- average annual snowfall - at 1650 m on the Grand Massif ski area, over the last 5 seasons.

Savoie Mon Blanc

MÉRIBEL INCREASES GONDOLA CAPACITY, PLANS A FAST QUAD

Last season, capacity on the Tougnète gondola was increased. For 2009/10 a fast quad is to replace the old Golf chairlift from Méribel-Village up to the Altiport area.

MONTGENÈVRE INSTALLS TWO HYBRIDS

A chondola now serves Les Gondrans, and another one accesses the Chalvet sector – opening up new slopes there.

LA PLAGNE HAS A RESHUFFLE

For 2009/10 a six-pack is due at Plagne Soleil, replacing a drag at Plagne-Villages and a chair below it. This chair will be moved to Plagne 1800, for direct access towards Bellecôte without passing through Plagne Centre. The old Vega chairlift above Plagne Centre will also be removed.

SERRE-CHEVALIER OPENS SMART SPA, NEW HOTEL

Last season a smart thermal spa centre opened in Le Monêtier. And the resort's first 4-star hotel opened in Chantemerle.

LES SYBELLES STICKS WITH DRAGS

For 2009/10 two additional draglifts are planned to reduce the peak season queues for the existing drags at Pte de L'Ouillon, the hub of the Les Sybelles ski area.

BETTER ACCESS FROM TIGNES TO VAL D'ISÈRE

For 2008/09 a six-pack replaced the Tufs chairlift from Val Claret to Tovière.

VAL D'ISÈRE CHAIR UPGRADED

A six-pack has replaced the triple Marmottes chair above La Daille. For 2009/10 a big new sports centre is due to open.

ITALY

ANOTHER FAST CHAIR FOR CERVINIA

For 2009/10 the slow chairlifts above Plan Torrette are to be replaced by one fast chair, removing the one remaining weakness in the lift system.

CORTINA D'AMPEZZO ADDS CHAIR AND PISTE LINK

A chair and piste have created linked access from Fedare on the back side of the Cinque Torre area to the Col Gallina area (and the cable car from Passo Falzarego to Lagazuoi).

SMART NEW SPA FOR LIVIGNO

For 2009/10 a thermal spa and wellness centre is expected to open.

MONTEROSA SKI CABLE CAR REPLACEMENT AT LAST?

A new cable car to replace the ancient Punta Indren lift (removed in 2007) should be in place for 2009/10. The lift restores access to some excellent off-piste routes back towards Gabiet and Stafal.

SAUZE D'OULX AND SESTRIERE CHANGE EVERYTHING

For 2009/10 major changes are planned for the lifts around M Fraiteve, radically changing routes between Sauze, Sansicario and Sestriere. It's all too complicated to explain here ...

SELLA RONDA DOUBLE CHAIR TO BECOME A SIX-PACK

For 2009/10 a six-pack will replace the Ciampai double chairlift to Piz Sorega above San Cassiano.

SELVA / VAL GARDENA TO SWAP SINGLE SEAT FOR CHONDOLA

For 2009/10 a hybrid chairlift/gondola will replace the old Bullaccia single chairlift on Alpe di Siusi – one of the most radical lift upgrades we've come across.

Micro-fun at La Thuile

Last season the Maison Blanche 'micro ski area' was created above the base, with a fast quad chair, new blue and red pistes. A black will open for 2009/10.

Trentino shares in World Heritage

This year nine groups of Dolomite mountains spread across Trentino and four other provinces – were declared a UNESCO World Heritage Site.

Switzerland

Champéry plans another upgrade

For 2009/10, the Grande Conche chairlift from Les Crosets is to be upgraded to a six-pack. A key lift above Champoussin was out of action all last season; we are assured it will run in 2009/10.

Crans-Montana gets smart new restaurant

For 2009/10 a stylish mountain restaurant and hotel, including a lounge bar and three terraces, will replace the former Chetzeron building.

Engelberg revamps cable car

For 2008/09 the cable car to Brunni was upgraded and its base station moved to the nursery area at Klostermatte.

Six-pack for Grindelwald/Wengen

For 2009/10 there are plans to replace the Salzegg drag to Eigergletscher with a six-pack.

Laax rocks on

The first phase of the huge Rocksresort complex opened at Laax in 2008. By the end of 2009, most of it will be open.

Mürren makes it two new chairs

For 2009/10 a fast quad will replace the double chairlift from Winteregg to Maulerhubel. And a new high-speed double chair – a rare animal – will form a new link to go on from below Maulerhubel to Allmendhubel.

St Moritz's new double

A double chair has been installed from Rabgiusa to Curtinella on Corvatsch, and the top cable car from Murtèl to Corvatsch has been upgraded.

Verbier cable car goes large

For 2009/10 the Tortin-Gentianes cable car above Siviez is to get new jumbo cabins. But the chondola planned to access Savoleyres from the nursery slopes won't now be built before 2010.

Yet another new lift for Zermatt

For 2009/10 the modern gondola from Zermatt up to Schwarzsee via Furi will be extended by a third stage to Trockener Steg, creating a hassle-free alternative route to the glacier area.

USA – Colorado

Breckenridge peaks at 7

The Peak 7 base opened last season, including the Crystal Peak lodge and gondola mid-station.

All blacks at Copper Mountain

Last season a double black diamond glade – Black Bear – opened above East Village.

Keystone opens smart new gondola
The River Run gondola has been replaced by an eight-seat version, including a mid-station and easier village access.

Sheer bliss at Snowmass
A fast quad replaced the Sheer Bliss double chair.

Telluride reveals new terrain and quad
A new quad chairlift has opened on the back of the summit ridge, serving Revelation Bowl and accessing another expert chute on the front side.

USA – Utah
Fast new quad at Park City
A fast quad now serves King Con Ridge from the base.

USA – Rest of the West
Big Sky removes lift
The gondola out of the village has been removed, and plans to replace it have been put on the back burner for the moment.

Jackson Hole boasts new tram
The new Tram (cable car) to Rendezvous Mountain opened in December 2008; it is not big, but has more than double the hourly capacity of the old tram.

Canada – Western Canada
Revelstoke keeps growing
Last season the gondola was extended (giving the resort the biggest lift-served vertical in North America), the Ripper fast quad chair opened, and the size of the ski area doubled. The first accommodation at the base has opened in Nelsen Lodge.

Whistler goes for gold and a gondola
A gondola, Peak 2 Peak, now links Whistler and Blackcomb at altitude. And the resort plays host to the 2010 Vancouver Winter Olympic games in February and Paralympics in March.

Canada – Eastern Canada
Tremblant gondola
For 2009/10 a new eight-seat gondola is due to link the village to the Versant Soleil area.

Bulgaria
Pamporovo gets Bulgaria's first six-pack
A six-seat chairlift opened for 2008/09, serving new pistes on a newly developed flank of the main mountain. This appears to be the first phase of a long-heralded plan to expand the ski area.

Sweden
New lift and restaurant at Vemdalen
A six-pack was installed at the Klövsjö area and a mountain restaurant opened at Vemdalsskalet for 2008/09.

Åre revamps chairs
Two chairlifts in the central sector of the ski area have been given a capacity boost.

Cutting your costs

Resort prices in the Alps vary by a factor of two

by **Chris Gill**

It was on arrival at a modest 3-star hotel in Courchevel 1850, in January 2009, that we realised we had to do something about Alpine resort prices. We had made the elementary mistake of buying a few euros at the airport on the way out, at a net rate of almost exactly one euro to the pound, so we had no trouble working out what drinks in the bar were costing. A coke was £4.50; a coffee was £5; a large beer was £7. Ouch.

Six months on, we know that those prices were 40% to 50% above the Alpine norm, and (not surprisingly) also well above what you pay in other big French resorts (including cheaper parts of Courchevel). We know because, during the rest of the season, we and our faithful readers recorded over 2,500 prices in the bars and restaurants of the Alps – the biggest such survey ever conducted, we believe. We have since slaved away to analyse the data, and the result is our new Resort Price Index figures, attached to all the major resort chapters in the book and many of the minor ones. We think you'll find some of them surprising, and we hope you'll find them useful in making your holiday choices for the coming season. This chapter takes a general view of the results, and also gives an update on the costs of the other key components of a holiday – package holidays and lift passes.

£120
RESORT PRICE INDEX

£100
RESORT PRICE INDEX

£80
RESORT PRICE INDEX

FRENCH VAT

In the summer, the French cut the VAT rate on restaurant sales of food and non-alcoholic drinks from 19.6% to 5.5%.

If passed on to customers in full, this would result in price reductions of over 11%. The cut will be a great help to those proprietors who see the need to compete with the Austrians and the Italians. But there is talk about the need to employ more staff and to bolster profit margins, so we may not see the full reduction in practice.

Our Resort Price Index (RPI) figures give a simple guide to bar and restaurant prices in each resort. An 'average' resort has an RPI of 100. The range in the Alps runs from 70 (the cheapest) to 145 (the most expensive). There are lower figures for one or two places outside the Alps. At the end of the chapter are tables listing all the RPIs we've arrived at.

The figures for individual resorts are given on the first page of each major resort chapter (and of the minor resort chapters where we have enough information). As shown in the margin here, high figures are coloured red, low ones green. We've placed a £ sign in front of the RPI figures to make them seem more immediate, although we carried out the analysis entirely in euros (see 'Our survey', over the page). For these amounts in £££, a couple could have a pretty indulgent day, from coffee mid-morning through lunch with beers, vin chaud before that last run, more beers at close of play, then dinner with wine and dessert.

THE RPI PICTURE BY COUNTRY

Not surprisingly, there are clear national differences; but in most countries there is also a wide range. Crudely, you can divide the Alps into two halves. Italy has the reputation of being the Alps' bargain basement, but in fact it is more or less matched by Austria: both countries have resorts ranging from the average score of 100 down to 70. Only Austria's super-smart Lech and Zürs are above average, at 115. Then you have France and Switzerland. The cheapest resorts in both countries are just below the 100 mark – matching the priciest resorts in Austria and Italy; the great bulk of resorts are in the range 105 to 115; and there are just a notorious few scoring 120 to 145.

Outside the Alps, prices are lower. Duty-free Andorra, once

OUR SURVEY

Every price gathered was categorised, and compared to the median price for its category (a bit like the average, but not quite: it's the price with as many figures above it as below it).

So all large beer prices were compared to the median pint (€5, since you ask – based on 250 pints) to get an index for each of those prices. All dessert prices were compared to the median dessert price, and so on. Prices from countries such as Switzerland and the USA were first converted to euros at rates applying in mid-summer – so the value of the pound doesn't really matter.

Then for each resort we averaged all the index figures to get our Resort Price Index. An RPI of 100 means you are looking at what you might loosely call an average resort. The lowest RPI in the Alps is 70, and the highest is 145 – so over twice as expensive.

synonymous with low prices, is now close to average. Bulgaria (the only eastern European country we have data for) is still seriously cheap, particularly for certain items.

Across the pond, comparisons were complicated by many cultural differences. Beer comes in fl oz. Coffee comes in pint-sized styrofoam cups (and is undrinkable, but that's another matter). Coke comes from a tap. Pizza comes in slices. Soup comes with salad. However: at mid-summer dollar-euro exchange rates, the USA was clearly cheap – even Aspen and Vail were below the Alpine average. And Canada was consistently very cheap: amazingly, all western resorts produced exactly the same RPI of 75.

THE DETAIL

It's interesting to look at the most common items for which we gathered prices – and it may be helpful if you tend to consume a lot of coffee, say. Or beer. The bold prices at the start of each paragraph are the medians for that item – see margin.

Cheap eats (pasta/pizza) €10 In top Swiss as well as French resorts, a simple plate of pasta was often €12 or €13, and it wasn't difficult to pay €20. In Söll, in Austria, we found spaghetti bolognese for €5; lots of places had pasta for €7 to €9 in all Alpine countries except Switzerland, where cheap meals are not easy to find.

Proper meals, eg plat du jour €15 As soon as you take a step up from pasta and pizza, things get complicated. But it's clear that the plat du jour concept makes it possible to eat well in France without breaking the bank – we found pdj examples at well below average prices in Les Arcs, Val Thorens, even Méribel – whereas most of the entrecôte steaks we found were €20 or more.

Coke – small €3 Paying £4 for a can of coke is a parent's nightmare, and it came true in top French resorts last season – and even in Les Menuires (distinctly the best value of French mega resorts) the standard price was around €3. Cheapest Alpine cokes, mainly in Austria, were around €2. In North America, coke was typically half the Alpine price.

Beer – large €5 Perhaps surprisingly, it wasn't difficult to find a 'pint' in the Alps for less than in your local – in unpretentious Austrian resorts such as Söll, it was not uncommon to pay only €2.50. In the top French resorts, people were routinely paying twice

KEEPING COSTS DOWN

One way of avoiding the full impact of high resort restaurant prices is to go on a catered chalet holiday. With chalet holidays you get a big cooked breakfast and afternoon tea, as well as a substantial dinner. And, crucially, you get unlimited wine included with dinner. Hotel holidays are normally half-board, but buying wine in hotel restaurants can really bump up the cost of the holiday. The cost of other drinks can mount up, too. In a chalet, you can organise your own aperitifs, or there may be beer and mixers available at modest cost. So the main additional expense you are left with is lunch, if you want it. Some tour ops (such as Ski Total) are tackling this by offering 'piste picnic' packed lunches for an extra sum.

Fortunately, all the priciest resorts in our table (except St Moritz and Zürs) have lots of chalet options offered by UK tour operators. And you'll find no shortage of tour operators advertising their wares in these and other chapters of this book. The obvious alternative is to go to an apartment and cater for yourselves – if you drive, you can take food and drink with you or stock up in the valley on the way to avoid high in-resort supermarket prices.

A few tour operators such as Ski 2 offer 'all inclusive deal' options quoting a price that includes half-board, vouchers for lunch at mountain restaurants, lift pass, plus more.

We worked out average package prices (with flights and transfers) for March 2010.

Inghams, Crystal, First Choice, Neilson and Thomson gave us advance price information – our thanks to them; contact details are in our ski business directory at the back of the book and on our website www.wtss.co.uk.

Prices are based on two people sharing a room for a week; European prices are for half board; North American prices exclude any food.

Lift pass prices are for six days, and are 2009 prices converted at exchange rates current in July 2009.

PACKAGE AND PASS PRICES		3* hotel £	4* hotel £	Lift pass £
EUROPE				
Courchevel 1850	France	1380	1580	205
Val d'Isère	France	900	1240	190
Zermatt	Switzerland	850	900	210
Verbier	Switzerland	810	1060	200
Alpe-d'Huez	France	770	910	185
St Anton	Austria	755	870	185
Obergurgl	Austria	730	810	195
Cervinia	Italy	660	860	175
Serre-Chevalier	France	650	–	170
Wengen	Switzerland	640	770	180
Courmayeur	Italy	580	810	180
Söll	Austria	570	640	165
Sauze d'Oulx	Italy	540	670	165
Soldeu	Andorra	520	580	195
Poiana Brasov	Romania	430	570	60
Bansko	Bulgaria	400	480	85
NORTH AMERICA				
Whistler	Canada	890	950	265
Breckenridge	USA	850	910	360
Vail	USA	850	1010	380
Banff	Canada	730	930	285
Jackson Hole	USA	720	990	320

Cutting your costs

33

Interactive resort shortlist builder at **www.wtss.co.uk**

as much, and often more – lots of people recorded prices of €7 or €7.50. Top slot this time goes to Courchevel, at €12.

Wine – 50cl carafe €8.50 Range €3.50 to €20. This is one area where Austria doesn't do well – even in modest resorts wine tends to be pricey. Most of the bargains were in Italy.

Wine – bottle €19 Alpine range €11 to €40. Tricky one this, for obvious reasons – what bottle are you buying? Swiss resorts take top slot, not surprisingly – cheap wine is notoriously difficult to find in Switzerland. But you can get affordable and drinkable wine even in the most expensive French resorts. The house red at Bel Air above Courchevel 1650 is the cheapest bottle we found in the Alps: €11.

Cappuccino/hot chocolate/glühwein €3 to €3.40 Alpine range €2 to €6. No national patterns discernible here.

PACKAGES AND PASSES

The table on the previous page shows average hotel-based package prices for a range of resorts. If you treasure a copy of our first edition, you'll find a similar table there and you'll see that, 15 years on, very little has changed in the relative costs you confront. Courchevel 1850 remains in splendid isolation at the summit of European cash-guzzling resorts. Val d'Isère and Zermatt follow quite some distance behind. The Romanian and Bulgarian resorts are still firmly planted in the bargain basement camp.

Although the top French and Swiss resorts remain in a league of their own, there are more reasonable options available in both countries. For example, we found that a week's stay in low season at a 3-star hotel in Serre-Chevalier will cost you nearly 30% less than a week in Val d'Isère. A week in Wengen works out around 25% less than a week in Zermatt. But the big savings result from switching to other countries. The top Austrian and Italian resorts offer relatively cheap alternatives. A week in a St Anton 3-star will cost around 45% less than a week in Courchevel 1850.

With the USA and Canada, price differences between resorts are less noticeable. This is because the air fare is a high fixed cost which forms a much higher proportion of the total price. The cost of lift passes there is much higher than in Europe. But the prices we give here are what you'd pay if you bought at the resort lift pass office – you can often make savings by buying in advance through a UK tour operator or on the internet.

Of course, when you go affects the cost. The price gap between high and low season is huge. For example, we found that if you can avoid the February half-term week and go away in low season March, you'll save around 33% on the price of a 3-star hotel holiday in many resorts.

The two tables contain the same information ordered differently:
on the left, the resorts are grouped by country then ordered by RPI;
on the right, all resorts are in a single list, ordered by RPI.

Country	Resort	RPI
Andorra	Soldeu	95
Austria	Scheffau	70
Austria	Hochkönig	75
Austria	Bad Gastein	80
Austria	Ellmau	80
Austria	Schladming	80
Austria	Söll	80
Austria	Zell am See	85
Austria	Mayrhofen	90
Austria	Obergurgl	90
Austria	Saalbach-Hinterglemm	90
Austria	Sölden	90
Austria	Kitzbühel	95
Austria	St Anton	95
Austria	Ischgl	100
Austria	Lech	115
Austria	Zürs	115
Bulgaria	Bansko	40
Canada	Banff	75
Canada	Fernie	75
Canada	Lake Louise	75
Canada	Whistler	75
Canada	Tremblant	80
France	Montgenèvre	95
France	Les Menuires	100
France	St-Martin-de-Belleville	100
France	Alpe-d'Huez	105
France	Les Arcs	105
France	Avoriaz	105
France	Châtel	105
France	Les Deux-Alpes	105
France	Les Gets	105
France	Morzine	105
France	Serre-Chevalier	105
France	Flaine	110
France	Chamonix	115
France	La Plagne	115
France	Tignes	115
France	Val Thorens	120
France	Megève	125
France	Méribel	125
France	Val d'Isère	125
France	Courchevel	145
Italy	Bormio	75
Italy	Livigno	80
Italy	Monterosa	85
Italy	Sauze d'Oulx	85
Italy	Selva	85
Italy	Cervinia	90
Italy	Cortina d'Ampezzo	95
Italy	Courmayeur	95
Switzerland	Grindelwald	90
Switzerland	Mürren	90
Switzerland	Wengen	90
Switzerland	Villars	95
Switzerland	Laax	100
Switzerland	Saas-Fee	100
Switzerland	Davos	110
Switzerland	Zermatt	115
Switzerland	St Moritz	125
Switzerland	Verbier	125
USA	Big Sky	65
USA	Breckenridge	70
USA	Killington	70
USA	Jackson Hole	75
USA	Winter Park	80
USA	Mammoth Mountain	85
USA	Park City	85
USA	Heavenly	90
USA	Vail	90
USA	Aspen	95

Country	Resort	RPI
Bulgaria	Bansko	40
USA	Big Sky	65
USA	Breckenridge	70
USA	Killington	70
Austria	Scheffau	70
Canada	Banff	75
Italy	Bormio	75
Canada	Fernie	75
Austria	Hochkönig	75
USA	Jackson Hole	75
Canada	Lake Louise	75
Canada	Whistler	75
Austria	Bad Gastein	80
Austria	Ellmau	80
Italy	Livigno	80
Austria	Schladming	80
Austria	Söll	80
Canada	Tremblant	80
USA	Winter Park	80
USA	Mammoth Mountain	85
Italy	Monterosa	85
USA	Park City	85
Italy	Sauze d'Oulx	85
Italy	Selva	85
Austria	Zell am See	85
Italy	Cervinia	90
Switzerland	Grindelwald	90
USA	Heavenly	90
Austria	Mayrhofen	90
Switzerland	Mürren	90
Austria	Obergurgl	90
Austria	Saalbach-Hinterglemm	90
Austria	Sölden	90
USA	Vail	90
Switzerland	Wengen	90
USA	Aspen	95
Italy	Cortina d'Ampezzo	95
Italy	Courmayeur	95
Austria	Kitzbühel	95
France	Montgenèvre	95
Andorra	Soldeu	95
Austria	St Anton	95
Switzerland	Villars	95
Austria	Ischgl	100
Switzerland	Laax	100
France	Les Menuires	100
Switzerland	Saas-Fee	100
France	St-Martin-de-Belleville	100
France	Alpe-d'Huez	105
France	Les Arcs	105
France	Avoriaz	105
France	Châtel	105
France	Les Deux-Alpes	105
France	Les Gets	105
France	Morzine	105
France	Serre-Chevalier	105
Switzerland	Davos	110
France	Flaine	110
France	Chamonix	115
Austria	Lech	115
France	La Plagne	115
France	Tignes	115
Switzerland	Zermatt	115
Austria	Zürs	115
France	Val Thorens	120
France	Megève	125
France	Méribel	125
Switzerland	St Moritz	125
France	Val d'Isère	125
Switzerland	Verbier	125
France	Courchevel	145

Snow question

Just how good was 2008/09?

by **Fraser Wilkin**
and **Chris Gill**

An excellent season for snow? Certainly. One of the great seasons? Up to a point. The season 2008/09 will probably be remembered as one of the great Alpine winters, but in most areas that's more to do with when the snow arrived than how much arrived all in all. High season was remarkable, with a record base in place on the south side of the Alps and heavy falls on the north side – so everyone was happy.

We've assembled over the page an overview of how the season panned out in different areas of the Alps. But first, a general summary of how the season progressed.

Over the whole season it was basically resorts on the south side of the Alps that saw their snowfall records broken; but in many parts of the Alps there were some very snowy spells, and as a whole the Alps had one of their most satisfying winters in some years.

Slow starts had become the norm in recent years, but the last two seasons have seen plentiful early snow. Northern Austria didn't do particularly well at the start – even the super-snowy Bregenzerwald was below average in early season – but elsewhere winter came early, and in the southern Alps dump after dump arrived through November and December.

The most spectacular falls were recorded in the relatively unknown resort of Isola 2000, way down south near the Mediterranean coast. It saw over 3m of snow fall in December alone and was cut off for the first of many times during the season – the heavy falls continued into January. Many other resorts on the south side of the Alps had a share in this action, from Montgenèvre in France, close to the Italian border, through Italy's Monterosa (close to the Swiss border), to the resorts of the Dolomites, close to the Austrian border – one of Italy's least reliable areas for natural snow, and entirely used to relying on its excellent snowmaking.

Further north, conditions in January were basically good, without breaking records – we had good snow off-piste in Les Menuires and Val Thorens, for example. But in February a radical change in weather patterns brought major dumps to northern areas, especially Austria. Low resorts in the Tirol and Salzburgland, where snow quality is often a concern, had great conditions through February into March. With the weather coming from the north, February was quiet in Italy, but in such a mega-snowfall year this was of little consequence. Alagna in the Monterosa area, for example, reported a snow base of 4m-plus throughout the season.

For a few remarkable weeks mid-season, every resort in the Alps reported excellent conditions – something of a rarity. And that, probably, is the key to understanding the memorable impression created by a season that broke few records in the northern Alps: at the time when it mattered, the snow was there.

March was unsettled, with further snow at times for all regions, and although April began with more snow for the south, it did not really live up to expectations – Avoriaz's paltry 12cm of snowfall was typical of the dry, mild month.

The good snow wasn't confined to the Alps. In particular, the Pyrenees – after two rather lean years – had an excellent season. It

BRITAIN'S BEST SELLING SNOWSPORTS MAGAZINE

Published monthly from October to March, *DMS&S* has everything you need for an action packed winter season:

- Resort reviews
- Gear tests
- Technique tips
- Holiday offers
- Amazing pics
- Plus loads more

FREE GOODY BAG worth £70*

SUBSCRIBE NOW!

Subscribe to the UK's best selling snowsports magazine *Daily Mail Ski & Snowboard* and receive a Salomon backpack (worth £25), Pop Yer Bottlez! action dvd (£20), Metrosnow t-shirt (£15) and Metrosnow beanie (£10) all for free.

Subscribe today for £47.40 and enjoy 12 issues delivered straight to your door. Europe £88, rest of the world £98.

Visit www.subscription.co.uk/dmski/sko8 or call 01858 438831 and quote SKo9

* Offer applies to Direct Debit payments only, and is subject to availability

FOR UP-TO-DATE SNOW REPORTS VISIT metrosnow.co.uk

got off to a cracking start: resorts in Spain and Andorra opened well ahead of schedule in November. But it was also sustained: Spain's Baqueira-Beret clocked a record 11.5m of snow for the season, an amazing 230% of its modest 5m annual average.

And 2008/09 ended up another good season for North America, partly due to good falls in the latter part of it. Only western Canada fell well below par. After a shaky start conditions did improve in Whistler, but a total of 8.9m of snowfall for the season is still 15% below average. Further south in the United States, Jackson Hole

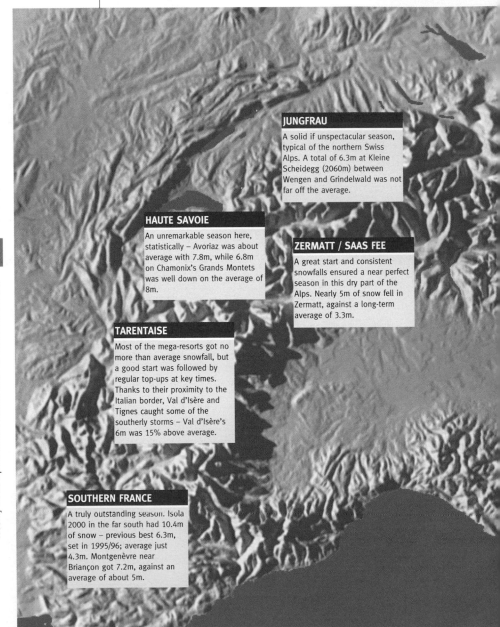

JUNGFRAU

A solid if unspectacular season, typical of the northern Swiss Alps. A total of 6.3m at Kleine Scheidegg (2060m) between Wengen and Grindelwald was not far off the average.

HAUTE SAVOIE

An unremarkable season here, statistically – Avoriaz was about average with 7.8m, while 6.8m on Chamonix's Grands Montets was well down on the average of 8m.

ZERMATT / SAAS FEE

A great start and consistent snowfalls ensured a near perfect season in this dry part of the Alps. Nearly 5m of snow fell in Zermatt, against a long-term average of 3.3m.

TARENTAISE

Most of the mega-resorts got no more than average snowfall, but a good start was followed by regular top-ups at key times. Thanks to their proximity to the Italian border, Val d'Isère and Tignes caught some of the southerly storms – Val d'Isère's 6m was 15% above average.

SOUTHERN FRANCE

A truly outstanding season. Isola 2000 in the far south had 10.4m of snow – previous best 6.3m, set in 1995/96; average just 4.3m. Montgenèvre near Briançon got 7.2m, against an average of about 5m.

could not match its record-breaking exploits of 2007/08, but 10.4m of snow is still above normal and impressive enough by most standards. Colorado resorts also fared well, with nearly 11m for Vail (average 9m) and 11.9m for Steamboat, a quarter up on what it would expect. In California, Mammoth finished with 12.2m, 38% above normal. In the famously snowy state of Utah, even more famously snowy Alta had a stonking season, recording snowfall of 17.7m, some 30% up on a figure that is already the highest snowfall average of any major US resort.

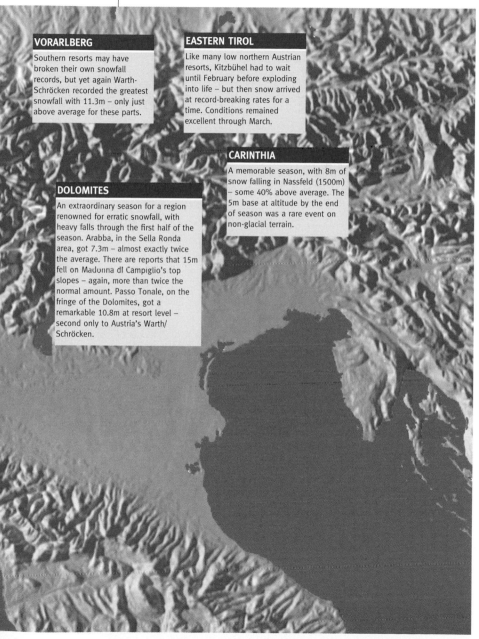

VORARLBERG

Southern resorts may have broken their own snowfall records, but yet again Warth-Schröcken recorded the greatest snowfall with 11.3m – only just above average for these parts.

EASTERN TIROL

Like many low northern Austrian resorts, Kitzbühel had to wait until February before exploding into life – but then snow arrived at record-breaking rates for a time. Conditions remained excellent through March.

CARINTHIA

A memorable season, with 8m of snow falling in Nassfeld (1500m) – some 40% above average. The 5m base at altitude by the end of season was a rare event on non-glacial terrain.

DOLOMITES

An extraordinary season for a region renowned for erratic snowfall, with heavy falls through the first half of the season. Arabba, in the Sella Ronda area, got 7.3m – almost exactly twice the average. There are reports that 15m fell on Madonna di Campiglio's top slopes – again, more than twice the normal amount. Passo Tonale, on the fringe of the Dolomites, got a remarkable 10.8m at resort level – second only to Austria's Warth/Schröcken.

Pick the right lift pass

The choice is wider than ever

by **Wendy King**

Choosing and buying a lift pass for your skiing holiday used to be simple: in most resorts, there was only the one weekly pass, with a discounted variant for kids and the option of a pass covering a broader linked area (the Three Valleys, for example). Take a closer look now and you'll find passes covering just a few hours, passes better suited to novices, increasing numbers of regional options .... We highlight some of the best deals.

These days most lift passes are electronic, containing 'chips', and normally hands-free. This means the lift companies can track which lifts you ride when, and effectively maintain an 'account' associated with your pass. You can often buy or recharge them online, and make a small saving, even if the pass is the one-resort one-week kind. But their real value becomes clear when they offer the facility to debit your account according to usage. All of this will seem familiar to anyone with an Oyster card for use on London's tubes and buses. In some cases, though, the lift company charges your credit or debit card retrospectively.

Smart passes are potentially of most value to people making multiple visits to an area, so they are most often offered by regions or resort conglomerates. Last season the Compagnie des Alpes, which runs the lifts in a very high proportion of France, introduced Holiski. This covers about six ski areas (Les Arcs, La Plagne, Méribel, Les Menuires, Flaine/Grand Massif and Serre-Chevalier); you pay an annual subscription of €32, and the pass charges your credit card according to usage. There are several Compagnie des Alpes lift companies not covered by the Holiski pass, but one offers its own single-area equivalent – the Carte Club pass, covering Verbier and the 4 Valleys.

Regional passes can cover huge numbers of resorts, which may be within striking distance from a single base or may make an interesting tour from place to place. The advantages over buying separate passes are obvious: lower cost, and no repeated queueing.

AUSTRIA

There are some splendid options here, particularly in and around Salzburger Land, to the east of the Tirol. **Ski Amadé** covers 270 lifts and is described in the introduction to Austrian resorts, later in the book. **Salzburg Super Ski Card** covers all of that territory plus a further 300 lifts. We've enjoyed an excellent short tour with this pass, skiing Zell-Königsleiten (Zillertal Arena), Saalbach, Zell am See, Kaprun and Kitzbühel. **AllStar Card** covers seven regions around Kitzbühel and the SkiWelt, and including Alpbach, Saalbach, Zell am See and Wildschönau. There are consecutive-day passes (eg six days €211) and a non-consecutive six-day pass. **Innsbruck Super Ski Pass** covers nine resorts around the city, plus the Stubai glacier and a day each in the Arlberg and Kitzbühel. Five days cost €213 last season. **Tirol's 'White 5' Glacier Pass** is useful for an early/late season break if the snow's poor elsewhere; it gives you 10 days' non-consecutive access to Austria's best glacier slopes (Hintertux, Stubai, Pitztal, Kaunertal and Sölden).

BEGINNERS

In some resorts, beginners have to buy a full week's pass – a big expense when you're likely to be confined to the nursery slopes. Usually, these resorts have their nursery slopes at mid-mountain rather than village level: Ischgl, Mayrhofen and Châtel, for example.

A more common arrangement is the points card – where each lift has a fare expressed in points; you prepay for a number of points, which get deducted each time you ride.

Quite a few French resorts have free lifts – this year Alpe-d'Huez made four of its lifts free for beginners. And the new Premier Glisse pass there covers 27 lifts that access suitable novice terrain. Courchevel has both free lifts and a minipass that covers ten other lifts.

A common deal in North America is to purchase a beginner package: lessons and ski pass together.

HOTLINKS

Hotlinks to sites with information about all these passes are on our own site at **www.wtss.co.uk**.

ITALY

Dolomiti Superski is the original and still one of the most impressive regional passes, covering 450 lifts and 1220km of pistes in 12 areas. The **Aosta Valley Pass** covers 20 resorts, including La Rosière in France. The main ones are Cervinia, Courmayeur, La Thuile, Monterosa and Pila – but there are lots of smaller places too (see our new chapter on the valley). A six-day pass starts at €242 and also allows two days in Zermatt.

FRANCE

The Chamonix region is covered by two valuable passes, especially good if you are exploring by car. The **Mont Blanc Unlimited** pass includes the whole Chamonix valley, plus Courmayeur in Italy and – new for 2009/10 – Verbier. The **Mont Blanc Skipass** covers the Chamonix valley too, but also Megève, Les Contamines and Courmayeur – oddly not Verbier though. And if this year's good snowfall has prompted plans for a trip to the Pyrenees, the **Catalan Snows** pass allows you to ski eight resorts in the region.

SWITZERLAND

Regional passes are not as common, but the **Valais SkiCard** covers over 40 resorts (including the Franco-Swiss Portes du Soleil area). The pass is prepaid and activated at the first lift you use; it is then valid for two years. But it was primarily designed for Swiss residents, and when we used this pass last season, we found difficulties in topping up points because the system didn't accept our postcode.

PASSES FOR PART-TIMERS

Until recently, the classic solution for fair-weather skiers and boarders has been the half-day (morning or afternoon) lift pass. But a few resorts now offer a more flexible choice such as 'any four hours', which allows you to choose when you start/finish – La Plagne for example. Courchevel and Méribel similarly offer passes of this kind for three hours. And St Anton has a graduated price scheme on day passes, whereby you receive a refund on unused time – particularly good if you fancy a short ski on departure day. Less widely known are non-consecutive passes, whereby you can pick and choose which days to ski – available on some of the regional passes.

NORTH AMERICAN PASSES

In North America non-consecutive passes are the norm; you will often buy a pass valid for six days in eight, for example. These passes are very expensive, but there are usually ways to avoid paying the full fare. You can usually get a good deal by booking in advance or through a UK tour operator – try the US specialist operators listed in our resort chapters, or on our website. 'Free' days are often included as part of an early booking deal – such as 14 days for the price of 10. Lift pass only deals are available for Utah, Vail Resorts and Winter Park; a typical example we looked at offered a 45% reduction on a six-day Breckenridge pass for mid-February 2010 and 30% off the equivalent Vail pass. For deals to other resorts, you may need to book lodging through the operator too. There are a few resorts that don't offer much of a saving via tour operators, such as Banff or Whistler, so in these cases it may best to look for smaller savings available by booking direct.

Jobs in the mountains

Is it time to do that season on snow you hanker for?

by **Wendy King**

Working a season is a dream many winter sports fans share: endless days on the snow, new friends, fun and partying – with a little work thrown in to pay for it. The reality isn't quite like that, but there is no denying it can be a very rewarding experience. Every winter, seasonal workers take up jobs in ski resorts; most love it and many return for more. But success often depends on careful planning and realistic expectations. We hope this short article will help.

SOME MYTHS

Myth
You need to be in your 20s
Fact
You're never too old
Myth
You have to be a chalet host
Fact
There are lots of alternatives
Myth
It's just for singles
Fact
Couples are employed too
Myth
It's an easy life
Fact
Seasonal work can be tough
Myth
It is for the whole season
Fact
Part-time placements are available

CHOOSING A JOB

The traditional winter job has always been for chalet hosts or tour operator resort representatives, but these days there are lots of other possibilities. Businesses often have administration and reception roles; many need maintenance people or bar staff too. Some employers need cover during peak weeks, such as school holidays, or when vacancies arise due to staff drop-out, illness or injury. School specialists such as PGL and TOPS have part-time placements for reps and instructors. Earnings vary widely, depending on the level of responsibility; expect £50 to £250 per week, plus season pass, accommodation and insurance.

WHERE TO FIND ONE

Major French resorts are the obvious starting point for chalet work. Swiss, Austrian and North American resorts are generally better suited to hotel, leisure or rep work. In North America one company usually runs the whole resort infrastructure – lifts, ski school, ski shops, kindergarten – so it can be simpler to look for casual work there. You'll need a visa to work in Switzerland or North America.

WHEN TO APPLY

Recruitment generally takes place between July and October, with a second intake in November. You'll normally head out to the resort in December. But you could wait until mid-season to take advantage of drop-out vacancies.

HOW TO GO

You need to decide whether you want a 'packaged' job with a tour operator or to look for work independently. If you head out independently, Alpservice can help you find cheap accommodation – and people to share with if you need them – for the season or for just a few weeks in several resorts in France, Canada and the US. If you prefer the security of working for a tour operator, you will normally be provided with accommodation and things like a lift pass and insurance; major companies generally have the most vacancies to fill, but smaller outfits can offer a more individual and personal approach.

KEEPING INFORMED

Web-based agencies are a great source of information. They can notify you of suitable vacancies and put your CV out to potential employers. BUNAC (British Universities North America Club) is an excellent starting point if you fancy the States or Canada, although its scope is considerably wider than that. Recruitment fairs or workshops, such as those arranged by Natives, are worth a look. They generally cover what you'll need to know, and you can put your questions to the experts.

WHAT ABOUT QUALIFICATIONS AND TRAINING?

Previous experience and/or relevant qualifications will almost certainly be required in some form. Some posts necessitate a formal qualification – an NNEB certificate to work with children, for example. Instructors must also be certified. Foreign language skills are helpful, but essential only for resort reps. Of course, being able to communicate effectively will make settling into resort life easier and help you to establish a better rapport with the locals. If you are hoping to improve your language skills, make sure you go to a resort where English doesn't dominate. Companies often provide pre-season training, perhaps in hygiene or customer service, or you can sign up for one of the proper courses offered, such as cookery classes or ski technician training.

DOES THE DREAM MATCH REALITY?

Reports suggest 30-40% of workers do more than one season. But seasonal work is tough, often juggling late nights and early starts. Key factors for survival seem to be developing a sensible routine and maintaining the correct attitude. If you go expecting a full-on party and not much work, you are likely to be disappointed. If you go with an open mind, a strong work ethic and the determination to enjoy the experience, you are likely to end the season planning the next. For more feedback from those who know, take a look at the Natives website.

TOP TEN TIPS FOR THE PERFECT SEASON

- *Consider the options: what type of work you would enjoy most given the skills you possess.*
- *Think about where you would like to be based: resorts vary enormously in character and size – remember you'll be spending the whole season there. But ...*
- *Don't limit your choices too much; it's much harder to find something suitable if you do.*
- *Ask around: while you are on holiday, chat to your local host or rep for advice. They might be able to put you in touch with their employer.*
- *Go to a jobs fair or a workshop such as those arranged by Natives: they generally cover what you'll need to know and you can put your questions to the experts.*
- *Join an agency: web-based agencies are a great source of information. They can notify you of suitable vacancies and put your CV out to potential employers.*
- *Apply early, to get the pick of jobs and resorts. Or head out mid-season to take advantage of drop-out vacancies.*
- *Make a plan: should things go wrong, it's worth having some savings – especially if travelling independently.*
- *Acquire more skills: look out for one of the basic courses offered, such as cookery classes or ski technician training.*
- *Be realistic: seasonal work is tougher than most people expect.*

Gap year courses

by **Rebecca Miles**

Growing numbers of 18-year-olds, career-breakers and even early retirees are going on gap year instructor courses. Many want to become instructors. But many simply want to spend several weeks on the slopes and feel by the end of it that they've had a good time and achieved something as well as improving their skiing or snowboarding.

It used to take years to qualify as an instructor, slowly working your way through the different levels. But now there are lots of gap year course providers offering you the chance to get the first stage or two in the bag in a season; a course designed to do that typically lasts 10 or 11 weeks. And each year, around 1,000 Brits take such courses leading to a British (BASI), Canadian (CSIA) or New Zealand (NZSI) qualification, the three most popular for UK gappers. It is estimated that between 25% and 50% of pupils go on to work in the snow-sports industry – the rest return to their job, make a career change or go to university. Tom Saxlund, a director of New Generation, says, 'Our gappers really like skiing, want to improve and want to devote more time to doing it.' Matt Cooke, New Gen's marketing manager, adds, 'We really welcome those who want to make a career of it – we have a number of people who've trained with us and then gone on to teach with us, which is great for New Gen.'

On most courses, around two-thirds of pupils will be either pre- or immediately post-university; the other third will be made up of late-20s to 60-somethings. In the current economic climate, a lot of bookings are coming from recent graduates who have been told by their employers to delay starting work by a year and from people who have been encouraged to take sabbaticals to cut wage bills.

Some providers, such as Base Camp, offer the option of shorter courses too – eg of four weeks – leading to the level 1 exam (see below). Base Camp also offers improvement camps run in parallel with instructor training ('good for people who don't want the hassle of taking an exam', says Base Camp's Alex Berman).

WHAT DO YOU DO AFTERWARDS?

How easy is it to work as an instructor after doing a gap year course? The snowsports instruction industry is a political minefield, and despite valiant efforts by BASI (including a new recruitment partnership with the ESF) and others to make it possible for Brits to work in, say, France, it's just not that easy.

Thirty-seven countries are members of the International Ski Instructors Association (ISIA), a political body that recognises national qualifications and sets minimum standards. In theory, if you have an ISIA qualification you can teach in any of the ISIA member countries. In practice, this isn't possible because some countries specify further qualifications to reach the top level within their governing body. So, for example, to be a fully qualified ski instructor in France, you do need to pass the notorious speed test.

BASI has a four-level system starting at instructor (two levels) and progressing to ski teacher ISIA and then international ski teacher diploma. If you pass at the end of a 10- or 11-week course, you qualify as a BASI Alpine Instructor level 2 (formerly BASI 3).

This entitles you to teach in the UK, Canada, USA, Germany, Austria, Italy, Andorra, Spain, eastern Europe, Australia and New Zealand. The 10- or 11-week course includes the BASI Alpine Instructor level 1 (formerly BASI trainee): this is done over the first week, includes first aid and child protection modules and an exam. With a level 1 qualification, you can teach on UK dry slopes.

The Canadian system has four levels, 1 being the lowest, 4 the highest. On a gap year course, you could expect to pass level 1 and some people reach level 2. With level 1, you would be able to teach beginners, with level 2, up to blue runs. With a level 1 you can teach in Canada, USA, New Zealand, Australia and South America. To teach in most European countries, you would need to be level 4.

New Zealand also has four stages. On a typical gap year course, you would work towards the first two: the certificate in ski or snowboard instruction (CSI), which allows you to teach advanced beginners, and stage 1, which allows you to teach advanced intermediates. A CSI certificate entitles you to teach in New Zealand; stage 1 broadens your choice to include USA, Canada, Australia, Japan, Andorra, Switzerland, Austria and Italy.

HOW MUCH DOES IT COST?

The average 10-week gap year course costs around £6,900, which includes tuition (the norm is five days a week), accommodation (the norm is with five or six evening meals a week, but it may be self-catering) and a season lift pass. Lunches aren't usually included, and spending money of around £100 a week is recommended. It's worth checking that all your exam fees and necessary modules are included. Courses typically run from January to March.

New gear for 2010

The latest kit means more fun for less effort

Versatility, ease of use and comfort. These are what innovations in the ski and snowboard equipment market for the coming season are designed to improve. The main stories are that skis are still getting wider, boots are getting comfier, a custom fit helmet has been launched and snowboard technology is bounding ahead. Clothing is getting brighter too, at least for men.

Ten years ago Rossignol Vipers were among the best-selling skis on the market and were 68mm underfoot and 111mm at the front. Now the norm is more like 78mm underfoot and 120mm at the widest point. Wider skis are more stable, easier to ski and more versatile – they float a lot more easily through powder and crud as well as still turning easily because of the greater sidecut. The versatility of wider skis is also improved by the more widespread use of 'reverse camber' or 'rocker technology' that was introduced on a small scale last season. Basically, this means that the tips of the skis are lifted up from the snow, and this has a twofold effect: first, it improves floatation in powder and crud (and makes landing jumps easier too); and second, it makes turning easier (on-piste as well as off) because less of the ski is in contact with the snow and so pressure is concentrated in the centre section of the ski.

Snow + Rock now divides its skis into four main groups based on the width underfoot: On piste 63mm to 73mm; All Mountain 70mm to 79mm; Freeride 80mm to 98mm; Big Mountain 99mm or more. Last March I went on a week-long test of all the new skis for 2009/10 organised by the Snowsports Industries of Great Britain (a trade body of ski distributors and retailers), and I tested skis in all these categories.

Of the piste skis aimed at decent skiers, the Scott Wind and Rossignol Zenith 4.5 Carbon did well – with the former a little more stable and the latter needing to be skied more elegantly to get the most out of it. First-time buyers should take a look at the Salomon Aeromax Ti, Dynastar Booster 10 and Fischer Viron 2.2. Snow + Rock is offering a special package aimed at first-time buyers – selling the Fischer plus binding, poles, ski

bag and a pair of Salomon ski boots for just £299, an amazing bargain compared with the £499 it would cost to buy them all separately (the ski and binding alone normally sell for £320).

With all-mountain skis (designed to be skied off-piste as well as on), I loved the Salomon X-Wing Tornado Ti and Fischer Watea 78; both these turned really powerfully on the piste and floated fabulously in the powder. The Grizzly from Volkl was fabulous too (as it should be when it sells for £850 including bindings, compared with £400 for the Fischer and £550 for the Salomon). It also has a 'Power Switch' system, operated by a dial, which you can twist to activate two carbon rods that run along the length of the ski, 'loading or unloading them with power to control the ski's characteristics and energy'. There are three settings: 'cruise', 'dynamic' and 'power'. I tried it and really noticed the difference between the two extremes.

With the freeride skis (designed for people who want to spend most of their time off-piste but some on as well), top performers included the Rossignol Bandit SC80 (my personal favourite), Scott Mission, Salomon Lord, Volkl Mantra, Fischer Watea 84 and K2 Apache Explorer. Big, heavy skiers (more like editor Gill than me!) really enjoyed the Volkl AC30 as well. The big mountain category is really designed for people who spend a lot of time in the mountains and want a great ski for powder days. Among others, the K2 Coomback, Salomon Shogun and Volkl Katana all did well.

Kästle skis were not on the test. But Snow + Rock got to try some and was so impressed that it decided to sell them and has an exclusive deal to be the only Kästle stockist in the UK. 'Their new Hollowtech technology ensures a smooth ride and consistent edge tracking,' says Ross McCloy, Snow + Rock's ski equipment buyer.

WOMEN'S SKIS: A BOOMING MARKET

Nearly every manufacturer now produces a range of skis designed specifically for women (from novice to expert), taking account of their different physical make-up to men. In general, women tend to be lighter and less powerful, so manufacturers give their women's skis a different construction, flex and shape. All this makes for skis that are easier to turn. Favourites include, in the on-piste category: K2 Tru Luv, Fischer Koa 73, Dynastar Exclusive Active, Volkl Estrella and Salomon Origins Amber. All-mountain: K2 Burnin' Luv, Fischer Koa 78, Rossignol Attraxion 6 and Volkl Fuego. Freeride: K2 Lotta Luv, Rossignol Bandit W80, Salomon Lady, Scott Rosa and Volkl Aura. Big mountain: K2 MissBehaved, Salomon Geisha, Volkl Kiku.

BOOTED AND SUITED

The big news in boots this season is that Salomon is rolling out to ten of its models the Custom Shell concept that it introduced in one boot last year. This is good news because I have heard great feedback about it. Before this innovation, customised fit focused on the liner of your boot. But now the shell can be customised too.

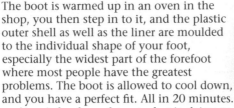

The boot is warmed up in an oven in the shop, you then step in to it, and the plastic outer shell as well as the liner are moulded to the individual shape of your foot, especially the widest part of the forefoot where most people have the greatest problems. The boot is allowed to cool down, and you have a perfect fit. All in 20 minutes.

Atomic has brought out what it claims to be 'the world's first carbon negative, planet positive ski boot', the Renu. The shell is made from 'organic bio plastic from Castor plants' and is also recyclable. And the liner is made from recycled foam and bamboo. It is a high-performance boot and very light – 'good for the lighter expert skier', says Ross McCloy.

There's been innovation in products for the other end of your body too. Your head can now be protected by Salomon's new Custom Air helmet. This comes with a built-in pump that you can use to inflate the lining of the helmet for a custom fit. It has the added benefit of giving extra warmth as well.

On the clothing front, women's clothing this season majors on the colours of a summer garden: soft greens, fuchsia and lemon through to deep purples, rich reds and aqua. They are used in a mix of busy-on-the-eye plaids, stripes and graphic prints interspersed with solid block colours. Men's colours are bright and bold, often mixing clashing colours for jacket and pants such as royal blue with red, green or yellow. Kjus clothing flew off the Snow + Rock shelves last year and is expected to again – Claire Collins of Snow + Rock says, 'Their fully technical range oozes style in every detail, even down to their 'K' logo, which has taken four years to perfect.'

GET ON BOARD

As with skis, this season sees a flood of reverse camber snowboards coming to the market following last season's trendsetting success of Lib Tech's Skate Banana and K2's rocker technology. K2 now offers three rocker types, the most versatile of which is the All Terrain Rocker available on the Turbo Dream; this works by lifting the tip and tail contact points slightly for a catch-free yet controlled feel that works well across all conditions. This season K2 also launches a new Flatline technology, available on the Believer, Slayblade and women's Ecopop boards. This is essentially a camberless board that works to distribute pressure evenly along the entire length of the contact edge, giving you optimum control. It also gives you a consistent and reliable feel under your feet whether you're in the park, pipe, trees or on a groomed run.

Nitro has taken a cue from the reverse camber revolution and developed Gullwing Technology, available on the Team and Sub Zero snowboards. This combines reverse camber in the middle of the board for exceptional powder floatation with regular camber

WINTER
09/10

↑ This season's colours: bright and clashing for men, the colours of a summer garden for women. And ski tests are hard work, honest!

Lib Tech Skate Banana
K2 Turbo Dream
Nitro Sub Zero
Burton Joystick
Burton Lipstick ↓

underneath both feet for extra stability, drive through the turns, and pop in the tail. Burton has also introduced reverse camber into its line-up in the form of V-Rocker available on the brand new Joystick, a three-stage design that places a rocker between your feet and two additional rockers in front of your feet. This works in the same way as the Lib Tech and K2 reverse camber boards, giving you more control at your feet and ultimately more fun. Burton also incorporates PDE (pressure distribution edges) to add additional grip under your feet for a more confident feel in the turns. This reverse camber technology is available on the brand new women's Burton Lipstick board, an all-terrain board with the ICS (infinite channel system) that has been developed to work in harmony with EST (extra sensory technology) bindings. This system has been designed to give you enhanced board feel, way more cushioning to take the sting out of harsh terrain and a system that is much easier to set up, making the ICS channel and EST bindings the ultimate board-to-binding combination.

More and more snowboard companies are now joining in with the likes of Lib Tech, K2 and Arbor to produce more environment-friendly equipment using fewer harmful materials and greater recycled content. Burton now uses re-ground materials in some of its bindings, and 60% recycled steel edges in its boards.

On the binding front, Ride has developed new Wedgie footbeds that use subtle angles to align the ankles and knees to a more natural and comfortable position. This effectively eases the pressure on your ankles and knees and also gives you more leverage for extra pop when you ollie. The Ride NRC bindings feature an adjustable footbed, so you can determine the angle that suits you best, and a Custom flex ankle strap that also allows you to adjust the flex of your binding strap so you can decide if you prefer it stiffer or softer.

New gear for 2010

49

Interactive resort shortlist builder at **www.wtss.co.uk**

Smart apartments

Enjoy full independence in comfortable surroundings

by **Dave Watts**

ERNA LOW / TRISTAN SHU

Many of the smart
new apartment
buildings have good
leisure facilities; this
is Montsoleil in Flaine
↓

Apartment holidays used to be the budget option for most people – at least on holidays to France. Shoehorn six people into a studio advertised for six and you'd have a cheap but not very comfortable time. Now things have changed. Even in France, traditional home of the cramped apartment, smart, reasonably spacious apartments are now widely available. Most have dishwashers and many share a pool, sauna, steam room and gym to add to the pampering. Some even have comfortable furniture to relax in too. Sure, the budget option still exists, but now you can have a comfortable apartment holiday with all the other advantages that it brings (see below). We've looked for smart apartments to recommend throughout the Alps and included them in the resort chapters. And opposite is a table summarising some of what's on offer.

I've been taking my annual ski holiday with my wife and a couple of friends in apartments ever since 1992. That's because we value the freedom an apartment gives you. You don't have to stick to meal times (and meals) dictated by the hotel or chalet staff; you can slob around in whatever clothes you want; you can go out and come back in whenever you choose. And, crucially in our case, you are free to have a big lunch up the mountain without worrying about having to eat a huge meal – which your chalet staff or hotel will have prepared for you – in the evening; if you lack the appetite

for a full meal in the evening,
you can buy snacks such as
oysters, smoked salmon, pâté
and local cheeses along with a
good bottle of wine or two from
the supermarket. If you are
hungry, you can go out to a
restaurant to eat. Staying in an
apartment doesn't mean having
to cook big meals – not for us
anyway.

When we started this
apartment lark, we couldn't find the sort of thing we were looking
for in tour operators' brochures – all the apartments were of the
cram-'em-in-and-make-it-cheap variety. So we ended up booking
independently, through agents in resorts and direct with apartment
owners. But it was hard work doing the research – especially as it
was before the internet took off.

Now, at least in France – the country that used to have the
smallest, most sordid apartments – a few tour operators (notably
those advertising in this chapter) offer some really smart and
spacious places. The French smart apartment concept was kick-
started by apartments built by or opened in the Montagnettes and
MGM names. Now they've been joined by other brands, such as
Lagrange Prestige and Intrawest. Many properties constructed by
MGM are now operated by other companies, such as CGH.

What can you expect in one of the places we feature in our
table? First, you get more space than in your average French

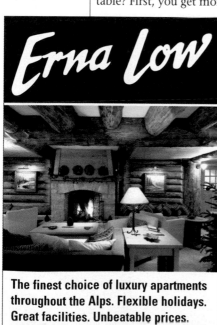

↑ Comfy sofas and armchairs like this that you can sink into are not the norm. If they are important to you, check carefully before you book

ERNA LOW

apartment – but not as much as you'd get as standard in North America. (Note that we haven't put any Canadian or US apartments in our table because, in our experience, they are nearly all smart.) You still need to check the space is enough to meet your expectations – I reckon an apartment for four adults needs to be at least 50m². And check whether the number it's advertised for involves anyone sleeping in the living room, in bunk beds, on a mezzanine or in a cabin (which can mean an alcove or an area separated by a curtain or sliding door but maybe with no window).

You might also be disappointed by the amount of hanging and storage space, especially for wet ski gear and storing suitcases. Also check the bathroom and toilet facilities. We find that even with a group of just four, it's best to have two bathrooms (or at least one bathroom and a shower room) and two loos.

Second, most of the apartments we list here come with a modern design and smartish furniture (but we're sometimes disappointed by the lack of really comfy sofas and easy chairs you can sink into and relax – often because sofas double up as beds and are more comfortable to sleep in than sit on). Third, many new smart apartments now include leisure facilities such as a pool, sauna, steam room and gym (but check if there is a charge for using these; sadly, there often is). Fourth, a lot of them also have smart reception areas with comfy furniture and log fires. Personally, we think this is a bit of a waste of space; we'd prefer the extra space, comfy furniture and log fires to be in the living rooms. Fifth, many new apartments come with dishwashers; but separate kitchens are rare – most places

that we've seen have small open-plan kitchen areas forming part of the living room.

You'll gather from the above that these places aren't perfect. We'd prefer to stay in a smart North American condo with loads of space, comfortable furniture and a private hot tub on our own balcony. But they are a vast improvement on what was on offer ten years ago. And if you quiz the tour operator you are booking through and tell them what you want, they will point you towards the best places for you – those advertising in this chapter don't pretend everything is perfect and don't want dissatisfied clients.

Sadly, although there are luxurious apartments to be found in the other Alpine countries (Switzerland especially), few of them are featured by UK tour operators. (Why not? we ask. There must be a market opportunity there.) Exceptions listed in our table include the places in Champéry and Laax (bookable through Erna Low) and Grimentz in Val d'Anniviers (bookable through Mountain Heaven). But in many cases (such as with Alpin Resort in Kühtai near Innsbruck) you have to book independently.

SMART APARTMENTS MENTIONED IN THE CHAPTERS

Alpe-d'Huez	**Oz-en-Oisans**: Chalet des Neiges
Les Arcs	Arc 1950, Chalet des Neiges, Chalet Altitude, Alpages de Chantal **Peisey-Vallandry**: L'Orée des Cimes
Chamonix	Balcons du Savoy, Ginabelle **Vallorcine**: L'Ours Bleu **Les Houches**: Le Hameau de Pierre Blanche
Champéry	The Lodge
Courchevel	Chalets les Montagnettes, Chalets du Forum
Les Deux-Alpes	Alba, Alpina Lodge, Cortina, Goleon, Val Ecrin
Flaine	Montsoleil **Les Carroz**: Les Fermes du Soleil, Les Chalets de Jouvence
Innsbruck	**Kühtai**: Alpin Resort
Megève	Chateau & Residence Megève
Les Menuires	Residence Montalys, Chalets les Montagnettes, Les Alpages, Chalets du Soleil, Les Chalets de l'Adonis, Les Clarines
Méribel	Les Fermes de Méribel
Morzine	L'Aiglon
Laax	Rocksresort
La Plagne	Chalets les Montagnettes, Les Hauts Bois, Pelvoux, Les Granges du Soleil, Chalets Edelweiss **Montalbert**: Chalets de Montalbert, Les Granges **Les Coches**: Les Chalets de Wengen **Champagny-en-Vanoise**: Les Alpages de Champagny
Puy-St-Vincent	Gentianes
La Rosière	Cîmes Blanche, Balcons, Chalet Altitude
Samoëns	Fermes de Samoëns, Chalet la Ferme des Fontany, La Reine des Prés
Serre-Chevalier	Hameau du Rocher Blanc, Best Western Premier
Ste-Foy-Tarentaise	Les Fermes de Ste-Foy
St-Martin	Les Chalets du Gypse
Les Sybelles	**La Toussuire**: Les Hauts de Comborcière
Tignes	L'Ecrin des Neiges, Residence Village Montana, Telemark, Ferme du Val Claret, Nevada **Les Brévières**: Le Belvedere
Val d'Anniviers	**Grimentz**: Les Vieux Chalets
Val d'Isère	Chalets du Jardin Alpin, Chalets du Laisinant
Val Thorens	Too many to list – see resort chapter, pages 411-12

Luxury chalets

The ultimate ski holiday?

by **Chris Gill** | This annual review of the top of the chalet market – places that rival good hotels for comfort and cuisine – grows in scope every year. The catered chalet concept (explained for the benefit of newcomers in the panel below) goes from strength to strength, with ever expanding programmes from the established operators and ever increasing numbers of competitors. And every year we find more suitable chalets in more resorts. But there is no threat to the ruling trio of top chalet resorts – Méribel and Val d'Isère in France, and Verbier in Switzerland.

As the choice gets wider, it makes choosing harder work of course. Some helpful websites have been set up by agents, allowing you to sift out chalets that might suit you from the hundreds on the market; some advertise in this chapter, or elsewhere in the book.

The greatest concentration of smart chalets is found in **Méribel**. Long-time local specialist Meriski exemplifies the transformation of the chalet business over the last two decades. In the 1980s it was a run-of-the-mill operation, but then it successfully repositioned itself upmarket. The company has changed hands a couple of times recently, but it still has a wide range of impressive chalets.

Purple Ski has impressive places with all the trimmings in every part of the resort, including the lovely Iamato in Village and the swanky Lapin Blanc, in a great piste-side location. Ski Olympic took a big step into the luxury market a couple of years back with the

THE EVOLUTION OF THE CHALET HOLIDAY

The catered chalet holiday is a uniquely British idea. Tour operators install their own cooks and housekeepers in chalets that they take over for the season, then sell packages of half-board in these chalets with travel from the UK.

Dinner is a no-choice affair at a communal table, including wine unlimited in quantity but often severely limited in quality. You can either book a whole chalet (the smallest typically sleep six or eight) or share a larger chalet with others.

In its early days, in the 1960s and 1970s, the chalet business didn't do luxury. Chalet holidays meant creaky old buildings, with spartan furniture and paper-thin walls, and with six or more people sharing a bathroom. And the chalet girl – always a girl, back then – was often straight out of college or finishing school, and mainly intent on having a fun season.

Then, in the late 1980s, one or two companies realised that people would pay a lot more for comfortable and stylish accommodation, good food and wine, and just enough personal service to make the customer feel valued rather than neglected. The new formula worked, probably better than anyone could have expected.

acquisition of the 24-bed Parc Alpin, formerly run as a boutique hotel. Alpine Action has four smart-looking chalets, most with saunas and hot tubs; best is the central 14-bed chalet de Launey. Several of Ski Total's properties here deserve to be considered. Descent has three or four very swish properties. Snowline's seven chalets include some lovely places, the very attractive Mira Belum now among them. Upscale sister company VIP has six impressive chalets, including adjacent Taiga Lodge and Indiana Lodge, splendid properties close to the piste and lift base.

Courchevel 1850 is well established as the 'smartest' resort in France, with the highest prices and the swankiest hotels. It now also has a growing number of smart chalets on the UK package market. The resort is at the heart of the Supertravel programme; some properties are apartments, but some are proper chalets, including the firm's flagship Montana. Kaluma has the richly traditional Anemone and the modern Totara (driver and butler included). Descent has the 'intensely private' 10-bed Hermine in the exclusive Hameau du Cospillot enclave. Scott Dunn's properties include one of its two flagship chalets, Aurea – complete with dinky swimming pool. In **Courchevel 1650**, Le Ski's range continues to slide upmarket with recently built properties boasting trimmings such as saunas and hot tubs. One of Ski Olympic's two flagship Gold Collection chalets is here – chalet Monique, with flat-screen TVs in the rooms and an outdoor hot tub. **La Tania**, not far away on the road towards Méribel, has developed quite a range of comfortable chalet properties, including the best of the Ski Amis range, the 14-bed Balkiss. Le Ski has some neat-looking properties with en suite bedrooms and the usual trimmings here.

Val d'Isère is the great rival to Méribel in the French chalet business. The local specialist, YSE, doesn't operate at the very top of the market, but the company's ancient Mountain Lodges are old favourites, offering no picture windows but atmospheric and comfortable living rooms, with stone walls and ample leather sofas. Apartments apart, their top place is the newly built chalet de Pierre in Le Laisinant, with sauna and gym. Scott Dunn's impressive portfolio here is dominated by the 12-bed Eagle's Nest – an extraordinary place, with an indoor jet-stream pool. Le Chardon Mountain Lodges has an enclave of four modern chalets at the southern extremity of the resort. Descent's extensive portfolio now includes Le Rocher, with jet-stream pool. At the top end of the Le Ski programme are two very attractive places sharing a hot tub – La Bouclia and La Pierre de Complia. VIP has some very smart places, including 12 spacious, stylish chalet apartments in its flagship Aspen Lodge on the main street – a novel concept in chalets, with a

reception desk, lounge area and coffee bar. Their Farmhouse is something else – a beautifully converted, er, 200-year-old farmhouse.

The other great French mega-area, Paradiski, offers lots of chalets in **La Plagne** and growing numbers at **Peisey-Vallandry**, on the Les Arcs side of the cable car link from La Plagne. Few really deserve a mention here; start with the Ski Amis and Ski Beat brochures.

La Rosière is a recent entrant into this chapter. As well as Mountain Heaven's smart-looking Penthouse, with grand top-floor living space and outdoor hot tub, Ski Olympic has two chalets in a new development with its own pool, sauna and hot tub.

The small-but-growing resort of **Ste-Foy** contains some very comfortable places offered by Gite de Sainte Foy and Première Neige. The swanky chalet Yellowstone is now in the Descent stable.

Morzine is known mainly for cheap-and-cheerful properties, but Snowline has several interesting possibilities, including an impressive cluster of 'town house' properties right in the centre and the newly renovated, contemporary-style Alaska Lodge. Up at **Les Gets**, seductively converted farmhouses are not hard to find. Descent has the Ferme de Moudon, as seen on Channel 4. The Ferme de Montagne is a beautifully renovated old chalet.

In Switzerland, **Verbier** is the chalet capital, and Ski Verbier the dominant supplier to the UK market. Its portfolio includes several glorious properties, topped by the swanky Septième Ciel – high on the Savoleyres side of the resort – plus the recently built Cheyenne and Sorojasa – with cinema and private pool. Ski Verbier also has more modest places including smaller apartments. Descent's new chalet Pierre Avoi is furnished in cool, modern style. Ski Total's acquisition of the hotel Rosalp is an intriguing development.

Zermatt, curiously, has never been a great chalet resort. Scott Dunn has long been the main source, but its offerings are all in apartments. But real chalets do exist. Descent has the cool chalet Maurice and chalet Grace, said to be Zermatt's best. VIP has a newly converted house in a central location as well as two apartment-based chalets. Ski Total's handful of properties here includes the Génépy, stylishly created within a lovely old wooden building.

Elsewhere in Switzerland, Descent has some fabulous places in **Klosters** and now in **Davos** too. Possibly even more remarkable is the company's palatial Chesa Albertini in hotel-dominated **St Moritz** – 'more a mansion than a chalet'. In cute little **Grimentz** (covered in our Val d'Anniviers chapter), Mountain Heaven has the very smooth Cole Ridge, with outdoor hot tub.

In Austria, luxury chalets are now easy to find in **St Anton**, where Kaluma's Montfort made a welcome debut two seasons back – stylish and comfortable. Scott Dunn added four swanky units about the same time, in a single building in the Stadle area – all in modern style, with some notably spacious bedrooms – and also offers the super-cool Artemis in Nasserein. Descent has the starkly modern chalet Katharina. Supertravel has a handful of places, including the minimalist Chiara, and the renovated Narnia.

Luxury hotels

For the perfect indulgent break – and more

by **Chris Gill**

Can you luxuriate in a room composed mainly of pale hardwood, slate, steel and glass? It's a question we find ourselves asking with increasing frequency as we find ourselves billeted in what are called (in some parts of the Alps) design-hotels – probably better known in the English-speaking universe as hip hotels. The answer we find ourselves giving is generally 'Yes', and now that the breed is becoming more widespread we're planning to take more of an interest in it – look out for developments in the resort chapters next year. For the moment, some pointers to notable places are included below.

One of the reasons stark, shiny surroundings can be luxurious is that a key component of luxury in lodgings is space, and cool design with minimal clutter tends to make the most of whatever space is available. Hotels in general are more spacious than chalets and apartments, giving them a head start in competition with those forms of lodging. Hotels may not offer the privacy of your own chalet or apartment, but in other respects – service, food, facilities – the best of the breed take some beating.

No one who has an appetite for luxurious ski hotels (and an inclination towards letting a tour operator make the arrangements) should fail to get hold of a copy of the Inghams Ski Luxury brochure, containing scores of difficult-to-resist places in North America and the Alps (plus a handful elsewhere – Andorra and Norway, for example).

If you like to be guided by star ratings when comparing hotels – and there is no doubt the system offers a useful short cut, whatever its imperfections – you'll be pleased to hear that the French now do five stars, instead of topping off their range with the '4-star luxe' category. In a coup that doubtless enraged top hotel managers elsewhere in France, Courchevel managed to get six of its top hotels included in the initial batch of a dozen 5-stars announced in June.

HIP HOTELS

The Madlein in Ischgl claims to have been the first 'design-hotel' in the Alps, and Austria does seem to be setting the pace. Last season we greatly enjoyed staying at the Sonne Lifestyle in Mellau (in the Vorarlberg-Bregenzerwald region) and at the Josl in Obergurgl – completely rebuilt in 2006, with modish glass walls to the bathrooms and so on. The top floor is given over to spa facilities including relaxing areas with floor-to-ceiling windows.

Spas are often a key feature of these cool new hotels, and nowhere more so than in the award-winning Mavida Balance hotel in Zell am See; in the same resort is another cool place, Living Hotel Max. It probably sounds better in German.

Zermatt in Switzerland is something of an Alpine design

hot spot, partly due to the influence of artist/designer Heinz Julen. The glass-walled Matterhorn Focus is one of his projects. He also played a part in the precursor of the key hip hotel, the Omnia, perched on a rock above the village. At Laax, the resort formerly known as Flims, the big new Rocksresort development incorporates the very cool hotel Signina. In sleepy old Andermatt, the delectable Riverhouse has made great modern use of a substantial 18th-century house. The 100-year old Belvedere in Grindelwald is not really cool, but has hip touches such as an outdoor salt-water hot tub, and a 'pillow bar' offering seven different types of pillow.

French resort hotels are not renowned for cutting-edge design. Two exceptions in Courchevel are the swanky Mélézin in 1850 and the much more modest but very stylish Seizena in 1650. In Tignes, the Ski d'Or is more than averagely cool.

We've spotted precious few hip places in Italy. One is the hotel Nives in Selva – this is a stylish offshoot of the very well run hotel Linder, so we have high expectations. On our next visit to Andorra we'll be keen to check out the Palomé in Arinsal (of all places).

PERSONAL FAVOURITES
Many of my favourite hotels are in Italy, where they manage to achieve a great blend of comfort and service with informality. The Rosa Alpina, in San Cassiano, in the Dolomites, offers a great combination of relaxed ambience, well-furnished rooms and superb food. At Champoluc in the Monterosa area, the Breithorn is a beautifully furnished, welcoming place – all wooden beams and panelling – with a choice of excellent restaurants. UK operator Ski 2 can fix a holiday in these and other compelling places.

In Switzerland, you can keep the glitz of St Moritz. I'll settle for the Alpina in Klosters, or the peaceful Chalet d'Adrien in Verbier. In Zermatt, take me to the impeccable Riffelalp, up the mountain.

In Austria, luxury generally comes with a softening rustic edge. Lech and neighbouring Zürs are the leaders. They offer an exceptional six 5-star places – but there is also a handsome range of 4-star options, both in the main village and up at Oberlech – check out our Lech chapter (which covers Zürs). Over the hill in St Christoph are the very welcoming Maiensee and the historic Hospiz.

In France, Courchevel's raft of 5-star places (explained above) leave me cold. Megève, where the old money still goes, excels in the rustic chic that seems to elude Courchevel – places like the Chalet du Mont d'Arbois, Fer à Cheval and Ferme Hôtel Duvillard come close to perfection. In Méribel, the Grand-Coeur, Altiport and three-star Allodis vie for editorial affections. In Val d'Isère the Barmes de l'Ours is very compelling, although the more central Christiania and Blizzard have attractions.

Luxury hotels

Weekly news updates and resort links at **www.wtss.co.uk**

A home in the snow

Make your dream of a bolt-hole in the snow come true

by **Dave Watts**

Buying a place in a ski resort has been many people's ambition for years. The recession is not hitting the Alpine property market in the way it has hit the UK and US, though fewer sales are going through than last year. So now may be a good time to buy. Despite restrictions on new building in many parts of the Alps and on foreigners buying property in parts of Switzerland and Austria, there are still plenty of attractive new developments on offer, as well as resale properties.

CONTACTS

Erna Low Property
020 7590 1624
www.ernalowproperty.
co.uk

Investors in Property
020 8905 5511
www.investorsin
property.com

Simon Malster, managing director of Investors in Property, has been selling property in the Alps for over 20 years. He says, 'Obviously, the market has slowed down compared with a couple of years ago. But there is still some extremely attractive property available – especially in Switzerland and Austria. These countries have traditionally restricted sales to foreigners and so prices have not been forced up to the inflated levels they reached in some other countries. What we are seeing now is that prospective purchasers are being much more cautious. They are reluctant to buy into a big development off-plan because of the fear that it might not come to fruition. Small is beautiful these days, with people preferring to look at modest-sized building projects, ideally with properties already built or at least with some of them built so that they can see exactly what they'll be getting for their money.'

Investors in Property has some ski-in/ski-out chalets at 1800m in Les Collons, part of the 4 Valleys ski area in Switzerland that also includes Verbier. They were built around 10 to 20 years ago and are now undergoing complete refurbishment and are 'the best value in Switzerland' says Malster. They sell for around £370,000 for a 4-bedroom chalet or £170,000 for a 2-bedroom apartment. All have fabulous views and come with a guaranteed rental income of around 6% of the purchase cost. As part of the deal with the Valais authorities to allow permits for foreigners to purchase them, you have to agree that for 15 years you will rent out your property when you are not using it. Investors in Property has a development of 25 brand new luxury chalets in Lenzerheide – also in Switzerland

INVESTORS IN PROPERTY

These chalets at Les Collons (linked to the Verbier ski area) are being refurbished and are 'the best value in Switzerland' says Simon Malster of Investors in Property
↓

↑ Arc 1950 is an attractive mini-resort with its own shops, bars and restaurants and ski-in/ski-out access to the whole of the Les Arcs ski area

ERNA LOW PROPERTY

and where tennis star Roger Federer has just bought a place. The 4- and 5-bedroom chalets are 10 minutes' walk from the slopes, have spacious living rooms with fireplace and double-height ceilings, and cost from around £630,000. Malster also likes Villars. He says, 'We sell more property there than in any other resort as it is attractive in both summer and winter and less than 90 minutes from Geneva airport, so it's easy to visit for the weekend. We have a good selection of resale apartments, and you can expect to pay around £425,000 for a 2-bedroom apartment in a prime position, £600,000 for a 3-bed.'

Investors in Property also has attractive property in Austria and is delighted to be able to sell places in the Tirol at last. Until recently, you could buy a property there only if it was going to be your main home, but now some developments have been approved for a mixture of 'holiday apartments' (owners agree to make them available for rental when not using them themselves) and 'second homes' (owners are not obliged to rent them out). These include luxury apartments in the Alpin Resort development in Kühtai (also featured in our 'Smart apartments' chapter), which is set at over 2000m/6,560ft (so it's very snow-sure) and is only just over 30 minutes from Innsbruck airport. These sell from about £400,000 for a 2-bedroom property to £425,000 for 3-beds. Investors in Property is also hoping to have apartments for sale this autumn in Wald am Arlberg, close to St Anton and Lech and at the foot of the Sonnenkopf ski area (covered by the Arlberg ski pass).

But France remains the favourite place for British skiers and boarders to buy property. Joanna Yellowlees-Bound, CEO of Erna Low Property, agrees with Malster that people are now reluctant to buy into new developments off-plan and says, 'We have a lot of people interested in buying existing apartments in Arc 1950, which was Canadian developer Intrawest's first project in the Alps.' Arc 1950 was built in

↑ Many new and refurbished properties are sold fully furnished; check you like the style before committing to this
INVESTORS IN PROPERTY

the early to mid-2000s and is a traffic-free, ski-in/ski-out complete mini-resort with attractive buildings, outdoor pools and hot tubs, restaurants, bars, shops and ski school. Yellowlees-Bound says, 'Some of the original buyers find their circumstances have changed and now need to sell. Current prices are much the same as the original sale prices, so they are a bargain for purchasers, and UK sellers are still making a profit in £ terms because of the exchange rate change. We now have an office in Arc 1950 and currently have around 80 apartments on our books, selling for around £160,000 for 1-bedroom, £250,000 for 2-beds. We also have a few apartments available in Intrawest's Montsoleil development in Flaine, starting at around £130,000 for 1-bed, £180,000 for 2-beds. And we will have another phase of apartments for sale in La Schappe, a marvellous conversion of a former silk mill that dates back to the 1840s in Briançon (part of the Serre-Chevalier ski area), which has a medieval walled citadel that is now a UNESCO World Heritage Site. Expect prices to start at around £130,000 for a 33m² studio.'

Erna Low will also be selling apartments in a converted art deco former health retreat that was popular in the 1930s. This is at Passy, around 15 minutes from St-Gervais and less than 30 minutes from Chamonix and Megève.

Investors in Property has apartments for sale in Les Gets in France. These are being built in the grounds of one of our favourite luxury chalets/small hotels – the Ferme de Montagne. Each will have its own hot tub on the balcony, and there will also be a pool, spa and restaurant in the apartment building. Half the apartments have already been sold to people who have stayed at the Ferme.

WHAT TO LOOK FOR WHEN BUYING A HOME IN THE SNOW

First, you need to decide whether you want somewhere just for the skiing or whether you want a place in a resort that is attractive in the summer as well. Many French resorts developed after the 1950s can be deadly dull in summer, whereas most of those featured here are attractive for summer as well as winter use. Second, if you want the place primarily for skiing and snowboarding, you will want reliable snow. And with global warming likely to continue, that means going for somewhere with access to high, snow-sure slopes. Third, if you intend to use the place frequently yourself, you will probably want somewhere within a couple of hours of an easily accessible airport. Fourth, make sure you understand the legal and taxation aspects – buying and running costs, all types of taxes and any resale restrictions. It is highly advisable to get professional advice on these. Fifth, make sure you understand any arrangements that you may be offered for 'sale and leaseback' or 'guaranteed return' from renting it out – these can vary enormously and in France enable you to save VAT on the purchase price in some circumstances. Sixth, if you are intending to rent the property out yourself, don't overestimate the income you will get from it.

Family holidays

Resorts rated, at last – worth the wait?

by **Chris Gill**

To be honest, we can't remember how it came about. But when we produced the first edition of Where to Ski and Snowboard, an astonishing 15 years ago, we settled on a set of resort star ratings that did not include 'suitability for families'. The best explanation we can come up with is that we thought such a rating would be an over-simplification of a complex, many-faceted thing. Sounds plausible, eh? The more likely explanation is that because suitability for families undoubtedly is a many-faceted thing, we just couldn't summon up the energy to tackle the issue.

Well, 15 years on, we've recognised the error of our early ways. In the major resort chapters in the book where we have sufficient space, this year we've expanded the ratings from 12 to 18 in number, and have included a Families rating. (On our website – if all goes to plan, fully revamped to coincide with publication of this edition – you'll find a Families rating for many more resorts.)

So now choosing a resort for your family hols is a doddle – you just focus on the resorts that get four or five stars (there are over 20 major ones flagged in the book). Or is it? Not really. We know from personal experience that you can have very satisfactory family holidays in resorts that rate two stars, and maybe even one – we've done so in Chamonix, for heaven's sake. The point about high-rated resorts is that they improve your chances of success. And what constitutes a high-rated resort? Read on.

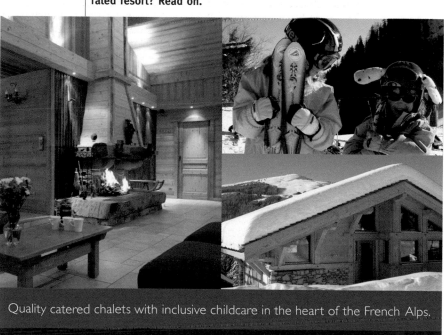

WHAT WE LOOKED FOR

Families differ. Children differ, parents differ, and the requirements of children and parents change over time, as the children get older and more competent at skiing. So it's obvious that there is no perfect family resort. But to suit the widest range of needs ...

- The resort should be easy to get to, without protracted ascents on winding roads, whether you are driving to the place or transferring from an airport. Transfers of more than two or three hours will present problems for many young children.
- The village should be easy to get around – compact, with your lodgings close to the slopes and close to the ski school meeting point or other institutions that your week will revolve around. It should be without intrusive traffic or other obstacles to safe, relaxed progress from A to B.
- The resort should offer things to do other than skiing, and in particular should make it possible for kids to play safely on the snow. Even kids who enjoy skiing will also get a lot out of other activities such as tobogganing and tubing, and the holiday will be more successful as a result.
- There should be one or more jolly, convenient and safe dedicated kids' nursery slopes (or 'snow gardens'). The main nursery slopes should be gentle, and free of through-traffic. There should be plenty of longer easy runs to progress to. All of these runs should get sun even in midwinter, without getting so much sun that snow conditions are routinely rubbish.
- The ski school or kindergarten should be well run and highly regarded, with English widely and well spoken. Large numbers of fellow English-speaking pupils is a great help.

THE PERFECT FAMILY HOLIDAY? THE LOW-DOWN ON CHALET HOTELS

The catered chalet holiday is as popular as ever, especially with families. Since en suite bathrooms and comfy sofas became the norm rather than the exception, the attractions of the chalet – more private and less formal than hotels – have increased considerably. Now, more people are discovering the merits of the chalet's bigger cousin, the chalet hotel.

Chalet operators have for years set the pace in childcare. It was a natural extension of hiring British gels as cooks and housekeepers to hire a few as nannies, too; then all they had to do was identify a suitable room in a suitable chalet, and bingo – a crèche was born. For British parents reluctant to submit their beloved to the brutality of French nurseries, the chalet was the obvious solution.

Chalet hotels are a larger version of the same thing, with some additional advantages. Some are purpose-built, but usually they are based on buildings that have operated as proper hotels. As a result, bedrooms typically are more generous than in chalets. Facilities are often better – there is likely to be a bar (with moderate prices if you're lucky), and there may be a swimming pool, spa or gym, for example. There may be a menu choice at dinner.

Two of the most long-established chalet operators dominate the family chalet hotel market, between them offering a wide range of top resorts. Mark Warner has always focused on chalet hotels, and has crèches in 9 of their 14 properties. Esprit Ski was the original family chalet specialist. Its programme is still dominated by chalets, but it now includes seven chalet hotels.

Moira Clarke, Esprit's head of marketing, says chalet hotels are proving increasing popular with their guests. 'This is not only because of the better facilities but also because of the communal versus private balance. Guests can choose to be as sociable or as private as they wish, either dining with other guests or just by themselves, or with their own friends. In traditional chalets, guests do have to all get along together, and this doesn't suit everyone.' Esprit's flagship chalet hotel is the super-cool Deux Domaines at Belle-Plagne, which we had a wander around just after it opened for the 2008 season. It has a decent pool and spa (young children not allowed in the latter), and a good ski-in/ski-out location on the edge of the village.

USING OUR RATINGS

We suggest you view our ratings as nothing more than a starting point in your search for a suitable resort. Very often, the key to success lies in the details of your holiday arrangements – exactly where your lodgings are, in particular. We've noted in the introduction that it is perfectly possible to have good family holidays in resorts that we rate only two stars. We have had reports from families who have had satisfactory holidays even in Kitzbühel, the one major resort to get only one star (a distinction it owes to a combination of poor beginner amenities, inconvenient layout and traffic).

There is an obvious reservation to be born in mind about the North American resorts that get high ratings: impressive though they are in the way they deal with kids, they have clear general drawbacks – not only the cost, time and hassle involved in getting there from Britain but also the high cost of childcare or full-time tuition, if that's what you have in mind. And one further reservation about Breckenridge, in particular: the altitude. Don't go there from the UK without a couple of nights at an intermediate altitude on the way (eg Denver).

We fully expect – no, we actively want – a lot of vigorous feedback from readers on the initial selection of resorts that we rate above average for families.

THE BEE'S KNEES?

We've given four stars to about 25 major resorts, and just one resort gets five stars: Lech, in Austria's Vorarlberg. Lech itself it not a bad spot for a family holiday, but our rating is actually based on staying up at Oberlech, an entirely car-free satellite mini-resort, where the hotels are grouped around a gentle snowy slope. The idea is that you get there from Lech by cable car, and your bags get relayed to your hotel through a system of tunnels under the slope. The place is busy during the day – not surprisingly, it's a popular place to have lunch – but once the lifts close it's the preserve of residents and a few après-skiers. A toboggan run down to Lech starting here is a key ingredient in the family formula. Residents get free use of the local snow garden.

Drawbacks? Well, clearly, there are easier places to get to, where you don't have to ascend by cable car. And it's a limited little place, with nothing to do outside the closed world of your hotel unless you ride the cable car down to the bright lights of Lech (yes, it does run in the evening). But probably the main negative is that it's not cheap: the hotels here know they are in a prime spot, and don't fail to make the most of it.

AN ALTERNATIVE APPROACH

We've stressed already that, in the end, the details of your holiday arrangements may matter more than the choice of your resort. Even in Kitzbühel, there will be lodgings conveniently located on snow, well away from traffic. The aspect of your arrangements where this is most emphatically true is that of childcare. We take account of resort childcare facilities in arriving at our ratings, but we are well aware that the majority of British families wanting childcare prefer to rely on their British tour operator to provide it. And it makes perfect sense – we've done it successfully ourselves, many times – to start by deciding which tour operators you like the look of, and then considering which resorts they go to.

Plugging in to tour operator childcare has many advantages. It isn't only that you can be confident that your kids will be in the care of trained, English-speaking nannies. It's also that these operators will usually relieve you of all kinds of burdens – getting kids of skiing age to and from ski school, for example.

Happily, the operators advertising in this chapter include most of the big names in family package holidays, so you don't need to look any further. And to save you the work, below are lists of the resorts each of them goes to. Note that some of these operators are less specialised in family holidays than others, and don't have full childcare facilities in every resort.

Family holidays

67

Interactive resort shortlist builder at **www.wtss.co.uk**

Esprit Ski Austria: Kaprun, Obergurgl, St Anton; France: Alpe d'Huez, Les Arcs, Chamonix, Les Gets, Méribel, Peisey-Vallandry (Les Arcs), La Plagne, La Rosière, Tignes, Val d'Isère; Italy: Selva. Switzerland: Saas Fee

Family Ski Company France: Ardent (Avoriaz), Les Coches (La Plagne), Les Menuires; Switzerland: Saas Fee

Ski Famille France: Les Gets, Les Menuires

Ski Amis France: Les Arcs, Courchevel, Les Menuires, Méribel, Montalbert (La Plagne), La Plagne, La Rosière, La Tania, Tignes, Val d'Isère, Val Thorens

Ski 2 Italy: Champoluc (Monterosa Ski), San Cassiano (Sella Ronda)

Snowbizz France: Puy-St-Vincent

Mountain Heaven: Montalbert (La Plagne), La Plagne, La Rosière, Les Sept Laux; Switzerland: Grimentz

Premiere Neige Ste-Foy

Most of these operators are focused on catered chalet holidays. (If that doesn't mean much to you, check out our chapter on Luxury chalets, on page 54, which includes an explanation of this uniquely British concept.) Elsewhere in this chapter is a feature box on chalet hotels, or jumbo chalets – hotels operated along chalet lines. If the chalet formula sounds a bit claustrophobic for your taste, the chalet hotel may be the solution.

Of course, there are plenty of other operators offering childcare. Last time we checked, there were 44 UK firms doing it; there's a list in the families section of our website at www.wtss.co.uk – with links to all their websites.

CHRIS GILL / SNOWPIX.COM
If she gets the required grades, little Laura will be starting a degree course in philosophy and English shortly after publication of this edition ↘

Corporate ski trips

A great way to motivate your staff and clients

by **Dave Watts**

MOMENTUM SKI

020 7371 9111
www.momentumski.com

For a whole variety of reasons many companies choose to get groups of staff and/or clients together out of the office occasionally. Team building, rewarding performance, bonding with clients, launching new products, problem solving and planning future strategy are examples. Getting together in another boring UK hotel can seem a bit tedious – but getting together in a splendid ski resort environment most certainly will not be. That's why many firms are still doing that, despite the recession.

You might have thought that the recession would have meant the end of corporate freebie trips. But apparently not. Amin Momen of Momentum Ski, which does a lot of corporate business, says, 'Last season, nearly all my regular clients except the bankers carried on with their corporate trips but tended to cut down a bit on the numbers going to keep costs down. And some economised further by trading down from, say, 4-star accommodation to 3-star. And we're also finding that firms that used to organise a trip purely for bonding purposes are now making them more business-focused, incorporating half a day of themed meetings into the programme.'

Roger Walker of Ski 2 agrees that corporate clients are continuing to go to the mountains. He says, 'Last season we had a good number of corporate groups, and most are saying they'll go again this year. I think if they cut some corporate freebies out, they are more likely to cut the UK-based ones. They say a weekend on the slopes and in the mountains is a lot more memorable for their clients than a day out at Ascot or Henley.'

And that's a good point. The perceived status of ski resorts is high – whoever you invite, they will be in no doubt that they are being given a treat (as will their friends and business colleagues). And the clear fresh air, the sun and the snowy, dramatic mountain scenery have a huge and immediate impact on people arriving from the European lowlands and their dreary winters. There is a great sense of fun and liberation, and people are happy to relax and enjoy themselves.

HOW LONG FOR AND HOW BIG A GROUP?

Corporate trips of a few days are the norm – Thursday to Sunday, say. In principle, your group can be any size you like; but with really small groups, be aware that the social success of the trip is going to depend on how the individuals mesh. Charlie Paddock of The Corporate Ski Company says that the groups they work with vary in number from 15 to several hundred but that generally the average size is between 30 and 50. Momentum Ski organises groups of all sizes from 15 to 1500, 'and small groups can be just as complicated to arrange as big ones', says Amin Momen. Ski 2's groups tend to be in the 10-to-30-people range.

HOW MUCH HASSLE IS IT TO ORGANISE?

Organising the whole thing yourself is a real hassle. People based in different areas of the country are likely to want to fly from different airports and at different times of day. And many hotels in the Alps

This season will see the 11th annual City Ski Championships held in Courmayeur in Italy's Aosta valley and organised by Momentum Ski. Among the attractions is the array of celebrities who turn up. For 2010 Lawrence Dallaglio, Eddie the Eagle and Heston Blumenthal are all set to attend, and Marcus Brigstocke is lined up to MC the prize-giving event. A new addition this year is Warren Smith, who will run pre-race coaching clinics with his team of instructors. Around 200 skiers from 40 City firms are expected to take part.

The Saturday GS race is the main event. But two other races are held on the Friday: the Accenture parallel slalom and the Columbia Radar Trap Challenge (speed skiing). On both days there's a raceside buffet. On the Friday evening there's a welcome drinks party and on the Saturday a Mumm champagne reception followed by a gala presentation dinner with all sorts of prizes – for the fastest men, women, single sex and mixed teams, over-50s, best wipe-out, slowest time ... and then ... clubbing till dawn. Sunday is free for skiing or sleeping.

The 2010 event will be held from 18 to 21 March. For more details contact Momentum Ski on 020 7371 9111 or City Championships on 020 7863 8813 – or visit www.momentumski.com.

70

don't want to take bookings for just a few days, or to provide the number of single rooms that you might want. Numbers are likely to change as people drop out for various reasons. Your group is likely to have skiers and boarders of widely differing ability and maybe some complete beginners or non-slope users, so you need to organise ski instructors or guides to teach or lead different groups. You need to organise equipment (and maybe clothing) rental and lift passes. You might want to organise jollies such as dinner up the mountain and a torchlit descent back or a lunchtime BBQ on the piste or a 'treasure hunt' event for teams on the slopes. And you might need rooms to hold business meetings in.

But that's what you use a tour operator or event organiser for – to deal with all the hassle and organise things on your behalf. And the great thing is that they don't charge you any extra for doing all that – it's part of the business to them. They'll cost out what you want and give you a price, then it's up to them to stick within that budget – the cost of drink, though, is likely to be a variable in many cases.

Simon Brown of Ski 2 lives all winter in Champoluc in the Monterosa region of Italy, where nearly all of Ski 2's corporate groups go. He says: 'Most of our groups are office jollies organised for bonding purposes, and we'll lay on anything they want – maybe ski instructors for beginners (we've got our own British Ski School and can organise fast-track learning so that even complete beginners will be able to get up the mountain and meet for a lunchtime BBQ on the third day) and heli-skiing for the good skiers, a night out at Milan's San Siro stadium to watch the soccer, a trip to the casino in Chamonix, an evening having dinner in an old restaurant up the

mountain reached by snowcat. Anything's possible.' Ski 2 also organises private transfers to meet any flight arriving at any of six airports within striking distance, including Geneva, Milan and Turin, and it doesn't cost any extra – that's a huge saving when you consider a private taxi transfer might cost £500 or more return from Geneva airport.

Amin Momen says, 'Our groups want widely different things. Each year we take a group out for Ford, combining the trip with the Geneva Motor Show; then we organise a route from Geneva to the mountains enabling them to test drive the cars on suitable roads (and maybe even ice-driving circuits for 4x4s). And Lambert Smith Hampton runs an annual ski race for the UK property industry with around 250 people attending. This year it is going to be focused around a business forum with guest speakers and a state of the industry discussion. So we are fixing all that for them.'

WHERE TO GO?

If the group is UK or European based, the Alps would be best. Because corporate trips tend to be short, you'll want to keep the travel time to the minimum. Transfer times from airports to resorts generally range from one to four hours, and you'll probably want to operate at the lower end of that range if you can.

Shelley Cunningham of Ski Verbier says: 'We deal with a large number of corporate groups who are looking to exploit the joys of a 100-minute transfer time from Geneva to Verbier, combined with world-class skiing and a very lively nightlife. Our two boutique hotels (15 rooms each) cater perfectly for groups that want a property exclusively to themselves, combining chalet-style accommodation with a five-star service. And our flexible booking policy allows groups to go for long weekends or midweek breaks.'

Amin Momen of Momentum Ski says, 'We use Courmayeur in Italy a lot because it has great accommodation and restaurants and is less than two hours from Geneva airport. But we also send a lot of groups to Engelberg in Switzerland and to Garmisch in Germany. Garmisch can be especially good fun because we can organise your own private train carriage all the way to the glacier to ski and back again and then a fun "Bavarian slap dancing evening" in a lovely old restaurant with traditional local music and guys in lederhosen.'

Whatever you do, choose a resort with a good snow record and/ or extensive snowmaking. You don't want to invite people on a skiing break to find that there's no snow. Avoid early season for the same reason. A March trip to a high resort will mean good snow, and it should mean strong sunshine, too. Don't get hung up on size – with only a couple of days to spend on the slopes, almost any resort has plenty of terrain, especially with good local guides to help you make the most of it.

Short breaks

Making the most of a quick snow-fix

Taking short-break ski trips can give you three refreshing days on the slopes and leave you with the feeling of having been away for ages. The growth in budget airlines and greater choice of airports to fly from and to mean more of us are discovering the joys of short breaks and trying a wider range of resorts. The classic short breaks are weekends, but if you can get away midweek, there are many advantages. Flights and accommodation can be cheaper and popular weekend resorts can be very quiet, especially in low season.

Using a specialist tour operator or travel agent such as those advertising in this chapter makes sense if you don't want to make your own arrangements, or don't have the time. They have special deals with hotels and can organise lift passes and rental equipment. In some cases, arrival/departure airports and dates are flexible. Around 50% of Ski 2's business is short breaks to Champoluc (Italy), and they include private transfers from any of six airports within striking distance and will meet any flight – all included in their prices. Ski Weekends is a weekend specialist that features several resorts and offers overnight coach travel as well as flight options.

If you fly, to maximise your slope time, it's best to catch early or late flights. An early flight can put you on the slopes before lunch, and a late flight back can mean a full day before you have to leave. We try to avoid travelling back on Sunday evenings as traffic can be horrendous with locals going home after the weekend.

CHOOSING AND GETTING TO THE RESORT

Book a transfer or rental car in advance; it's often cheaper and saves time the other end. And it's worth considering a different car hire company from the one your airline promotes – so you avoid queuing with everyone else from your flight. Taxis are generally very expensive. In our experience, public transport times between airports are rarely convenient for short trips, though there are pretty good rail connections in Switzerland.

Resorts near to your arrival airport may seem the obvious choice, but if you're going for the weekend, the last thing you want is to be joined by hordes of local visitors. A little extra transfer time may be worth it for quieter slopes. Of course, midweek and early or late season trips can be a good way to enjoy blissfully empty runs. And as you will only be there for a few days, you could try some smaller resorts that you might not consider visiting for a whole week.

From Geneva, the classic destination

is Chamonix, just over an hour away. Similarly, Megève, Flaine, Morzine, Courmayeur (Italy) and Villars (Switzerland) are close by. Allow two and a half hours for Verbier and Crans-Montana and up to three hours for Tarentaise resorts. Smaller resorts to consider include the Val d'Anniviers resorts and Anzère (opposite and next to Crans-Montana respectively).

From Zürich, Laax, Davos and Klosters are the nearest big resorts; Engelberg and Andermatt are within easy reach. Or you could try the less well-known Arosa or (in Austria) the Montafon.

From Innsbruck, there's lots of choice, from the smaller resorts surrounding the city to St Anton and Lech (also reached from Friedrichshafen), and Mayrhofen – and even the Italian Dolomites. Less well-known resorts include those of the Zugspitz Arena.

From Salzburg, lots of resorts, such as Schladming, Bad Gastein and Hochkönig, are less than two hours away.

From Turin, Sauze d'Oulx, Sestriere, Courmayeur and La Thuile and (in France) Montgenèvre and Serre-Chevalier are less than two hours. Or you could try less well-known Champoluc or Pila.

For the Dolomites, consider Verona or Bergamo. Beware of Treviso – foggy weather is common and can mean cancelled flights.

Unless you can book at short notice, avoid low resorts where snow may be unreliable and very high resorts where the skiing is entirely above the treeline and may close in bad weather.

WHERE TO STAY
In some resorts it can be difficult to find accommodation for short-stay bookings except in very low season. But it's normally fairly easy in resorts that have a lot of accommodation because of big summer business – Chamonix and Morzine, for example. You could consider staying in Salzburg or Innsbruck and taking the daily shuttles to different resorts. If you have a car, you could stay in a valley town such as Chur in Switzerland, Aosta in Italy or Radstadt in Austria and visit nearby resorts each day.

WHAT ABOUT PRICE?
Costs vary enormously. Airlines normally release their winter flights in July, with lower fares to early bookers. Ski 2 quoted us a price of from £434 for return transfers, three nights' B&B in a 3-star hotel in Champoluc, a three-day lift pass and lunches (eg pasta and a drink); you book your own flights. Momentum quoted from £398 for flights, car hire or transfers, and three nights' B&B in a 3-star hotel in Courmayeur; lift passes and lunches not included. Consider renting equipment rather than taking your own: airlines can charge hefty fees for ski/board carriage (see 'Flying to the snow' chapter).

Short breaks

73

Inte-active resort shortlist builder at **www.wtss.co.uk**

Flying to the snow

Flights and transfers for independent travellers

by **Wendy King**

The choice of flights to the Alps is greater than ever. The number of companies offering affordable transfers to resorts has risen too. Sadly, the cost of extras to basic air fares continues to rocket; as well as sky-high charges for taking skis, there are lots of other extras. One return flight we looked at started off at £42.98 for the basic flight costs and ended up at over £216.

ONLINE BOOKING

Most budget airlines expect you to make your booking online, and many charge less if you book such 'extras' as hold baggage and ski carriage online too. The web addresses of the airlines we list are given as links on our own website at www. wtss.co.uk.

Budget airlines operate from many UK airports. And they fly to a wide range of airports suitable for most resorts – some of which you might not have previously considered. But national carriers have become increasingly competitive too, both on destination and cost, so they shouldn't be overlooked when planning a trip.

Our map shows the arrival airports dotted around the Alps, so you can see which are likely to work for which resorts. But there are also flights that get you closer to Andorra and the Pyrenees, Sierra Nevada and Bulgaria. Note that some winter routes may stop operating before the end of the season.

CHECK OUT SOME OF THE OPTIONS

EasyJet flies from various airports around the UK and has by far the biggest range of flights to Geneva. Options from London Gatwick have grown too; you can now fly to Zürich, Munich, Basel, Innsbruck and Salzburg from there.

Ryanair operates mainly from Stansted, with a few flights from other UK airports. Noteworthy alternatives to the major gateways include Friedrichshafen (handy for German resorts, the Vorarlberg and eastern Switzerland). But as we went to press, the airline announced that a number of winter flights from Stansted would be scrapped – it was unclear which routes would be affected.

Jet2.com has flights from Manchester, Leeds/Bradford, Blackpool, Newcastle, Edinburgh and Belfast, and serves Geneva, Salzburg and Chambéry (a more appealing arrival spot than Lyon). Their dedicated ski website also offers a useful way of pre-booking extras, including rental equipment in various resorts.

Flybe serves Geneva, Salzburg, Berne, Milan, Chambéry and, unusually, Stuttgart (handy for western Austrian and German resorts) from various airports – mainly Exeter and Southampton, but also Birmingham and Norwich.

Bmibaby flies from Cardiff, Manchester, Birmingham and East Midlands to Geneva and Grenoble; from Birmingham and East Midlands to Nice; from Manchester to Toulouse; and from Edinburgh to Zürich.

British Airways goes to lots of relevant airports from a variety of UK ones. New this year is Innsbruck. **Swiss** has flights from Heathrow, London City, Manchester and Birmingham, with lots of flights to Zürich, fewer to Geneva and Basel.

Charter flights are also sometimes sold on a seat-only basis: **Inghams** has various routes, such as Innsbruck and Brescia from £199 return. And new last winter, **Monarch** introduced a weekend route between Gatwick and Huesca, Spain (for Formigal). **Snowjet** has weekend flights from Bristol, Gatwick, Stansted and Manchester

to Chambéry. And from December you can fly from Stansted to Sion, Switzerland – from where it's less than 30 minutes up to the 4 Valleys and good for other Valais resorts such as Zermatt (1hr30).

WHAT ABOUT THOSE HIDDEN EXTRAS?

See left for example costs of extras, which can mount up alarmingly. Most budget airlines now charge for checking in bags. And charges for carrying skis/boards have soared. Charges and rules vary between airlines and change frequently – so it's important to check the detail carefully. In July 2009, we looked at March 2010 flights to Salzburg and found a return flight from one budget airline that started off at a very reasonable £42.98. But once you'd added on various extras, the cost had rocketed to almost £200. Now BA is effectively charging for skis; it allows one checked-in bag free up to 23kg; additional bags for European flights cost £70 return each if you just show up with them at the airport; so pack your boots with other stuff. Swiss allows a bag up to 20kg plus skis and boots free.

GETTING TO THE RESORT

Renting a car can be cost-effective for a short break or with a group – but again watch for hidden extras. Public transport is easier than it used to be, and independent travel has brought with it a rapid expansion in the private transfer market too. Most Swiss and Austrian airports have good rail and bus links to lots of places. It might be cheaper to get a special rail pass than a return ticket; it often covers some bus connections too. Try the Swiss Travel Centre (www.stc.co.uk), for example. Buses run to the Dolomites from Verona and to the Aosta valley from Turin. Public transport to and from French resorts is slightly trickier, but private minibus transfers are now plentiful. You can either book a seat on a shared transfer, maybe having to wait for other flights, or reserve a whole minibus. Ski Shuttles (www.skishuttles.com) is one of the largest organisers; it covers over 400 resorts from 15 or so major airports, using taxis, minibuses or shared shuttle-buses. For example, a shared shuttle-bus between Geneva and Chamonix starts at £33 per person (one way). You will find a comprehensive list of airlines, transfers etc and their relevant links on our website: www.wtss.co.uk.

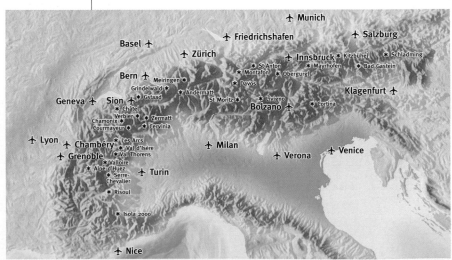

Make tracks to the snow (greener ones)

by **Wendy King**

So why the growing interest in rail travel? And what options are there? Well, for starters, letting the train take you to the snow can be a great way to enjoy more time on the slopes, and it avoids overcrowded airports and congested roads. With better high-speed links, travel by train is worth considering even for destinations beyond the obvious French ones. And with shorter journey times between London and the Channel tunnel, getting to the mountains is quicker than ever, too. Travel overnight and you could be on the snow before lunchtime, and daytime services can take as little as 7.5 hours (with Eurostar direct). We take a look at some of the options providing the quickest routes to the Alps.

The starting point of most European rail trips is likely to be the Eurostar high-speed trains from London St Pancras, Ashford (direct ski train) and Ebbsfleet in Kent stations (www.eurostar.com).

DIRECT SERVICES TO THE FRENCH ALPS

The fastest way to France is Eurostar's direct services to the Tarentaise region – to Moûtiers (for the Three Valleys), Aime (for La Plagne) and Bourg-St-Maurice (for Les Arcs, La Rosière, Ste-Foy, Tignes and Val d'Isère). There are overnight services that allow you eight days on the slopes, and daytime services that get you only the regular six days that you would expect when travelling by air.

Overnight trains depart from London every Friday night from 19 December 2009 until 10 April 2010. These will get you into Bourg at 6.30am. Return services leave Bourg at 10.15pm on Saturdays. There are no special sleeping arrangements – you just doze (or not) in your seat. The daytime services run on Saturdays at 10.00am, getting you to Bourg by early evening. The first train out next season is on 1 January. Generally allow an hour or so for the onward bus transfers, depending on the resort – though Moûtiers to Méribel takes a lot less.

Ticket prices have been reduced from last season: a standard adult return now costs from £149 (a saving of £30). For £229 you can get a Leisure Select ticket (non-flexible), which gets you a bigger seat pitch and meals. Seats can also be booked as part of a package holiday. There are usually discounts for the under-25s and over-60s.

INDIRECT SERVICES TO THE FRENCH ALPS

One of the most popular choices among skiers heading for the French Alps by train had been Rail Europe's Snow Train – a sleeper service timed to meet Eurostar arrivals in Paris on a Friday night, and popular for it's lively bar/disco carriage. Sadly, it is no more – at least not for 2009/10. The service has been axed for the moment, and its future is uncertain.

The French regular rail network (SNCF) can get you to places such as Chambéry, Briançon or Grenoble for onward buses to more southerly resorts. Or you could, for example, take the overnight train from Paris Austerlitz, arriving in St-Gervais and Chamonix next morning. Travelling via Lille instead avoids changing stations. SNCF has saver cards for young and older travellers – such as the Carte 12-25 that entitles you to 25% or 50% discount, depending on times/days and peak periods. The cards cost about £40.

HIGH-SPEED TO SWITZERLAND

Reaching Swiss resorts by rail is relatively straightforward. New high-speed trains from Paris have cut journey times, and morning departures from London can get you to many resorts by early evening. The time to Zermatt is an hour shorter than it used to be, for example; and resorts such as Engelberg, Grindelwald or Meiringen (with local railway stations) are easily accessible from Basel and Zürich. Eurostar now offers connecting fares to 18 Swiss destinations, including the main hubs of Geneva, Zürich and Basel. Also bookable are journeys to Chur, Sion and Visp – all excellent bases in themselves for visiting more than one ski area.

Allow an overall travel time of 10–12 hours from London. A 9am train from London puts you in Geneva by 4.30pm, with just the one change in Paris. For Verbier, onward trains go as far as Le Châble (with a change at Martigny), from where there is a bus (or gondola if you arrive early enough). Return fares start at £90 for Geneva and £112 for Zürich. Eurostar's Leisure Select fares also apply to Swiss routes.

It might be worth getting a Swiss Transfer ticket (from £75), which allows one return journey from the point of entry to any other station in the country, regardless of distance. You will need to buy it before you travel.

AUSTRIA AND GERMANY

In Austria, lots of resorts are on the rail network and often with their own central stations. But getting there requires several changes. Last winter a special overnight sleeper service, the Bergland Express, served Austria's Tirol region from various points including Aachen in Germany. As we go to press, it is unclear whether this service will operate again for 2009/10, but there are similar options. Make an early start and you could be partying in St Anton 12 hours later if you travel via Paris and Munich. City Night Line is part of a large network

of European rail services, with sleeper trains departing from Paris, Amsterdam and Munich. Services from Paris Est include nightly trains to Salzburg or Innsbruck, via Munich, arriving late morning. Lots of resorts are accessible from these two cities. From Munich, there are overnight connections with Italian cities – passing close enough to the Dolomites to make that worth considering. Adult fares start at £95 return (from Paris). Check out www.bahn.de/citynightline for more details. From Munich it's an easy hop to Garmisch-Partenkirchen – once there, a new service (Schnee Express) will get you around both the German and Austrian parts of the Zugspitze area (free with a guest card).

THE ITALIAN JOB
Most Italian resorts are hard work to reach, but there are exceptions. The Dolomites are close to the line through Trento and Bolzano, reachable from Innsbruck to the north or Verona to the south. Three trains a day run from Paris to Turin and Milan, stopping at Bardonecchia – a resort that held some of the Olympic events in 2006 – and Oulx. From Oulx, it is a 15-minute bus ride up to Sauze d'Oulx. Check out www.artesia.eu for more details.

PLANNING AND BOOKING
Rail fares have the advantage of few hidden charges, such as baggage fees, weight excesses or extra taxes. But like air fares, the cheapest fares are often secured in advance. Booking is normally up to 90 days in advance. Try Rail Europe (www.raileurope.co.uk), Swiss railways (www.sbb.ch/en) or Austrian railways (www.oebb.at). Some local lines such as Martigny to Le Châble (for Verbier) and Bex up to Villars may have to be organised separately. Helpful general websites include www.seat61.com and perhaps www.snowcarbon.co.uk (launching in September 2009).

ROUTES TO SOME ACCESSIBLE RESORTS

Resort	Route	Arrival	Fare from
Austria			
Innsbruck	Paris Est, Zürich	21:21	£218
St Anton	Paris Est, Zürich	20:10	£194
France			
Briançon*	Paris Austerlitz	08:32	£124
Chamonix*	Paris Austerlitz, St-Gervais	10:13	£142
Italy			
Bardonecchia	Paris Lyon	18:45	£70 (Paris)
Switzerland			
Andermatt	Paris Est, Basel, Göschenen	19:03	£174
Arosa	Paris Est, Zürich, Chur	20:09	£176
Engelberg	Paris Est, Basel, Luzern	18:12	£230
Klosters	Paris Est, Zürich, Lanquart	18:39	£182
St Moritz	Paris Est, Basel, Chur	20:58	£203
Verbier	Paris Est, Lausanne, Martigny, Le Châble	20:15	£133
Villars	Paris Lyon, Lausanne, Bex	19:30	£107
Zermatt	Paris Est, Basel, Visp	19:14	£229

Evening arrivals assume you get a train from Paris departing around noon
* by overnight sleeper train. Most fares from Rail Europe.

Drive to the Alps

And ski where you please

by **Chris Allan**

More and more people from Britain are doing what the French, the Germans and the Dutch have done for years: driving to their Alpine resorts. It has various advantages, even for those going on a pretty standard week in the Alps. For many people, it's just less hassle than checking in at dawn for a flight from Gatwick, and less tedious than sitting around waiting for a delayed charter plane that's stuck in Majorca. For families (especially those going self-catering), it simplifies the job of moving half the contents of your house to the Alps. If there are four or five people in your party, the cost can be low.

If you fancy something a bit more adventurous, taking a car opens up the exciting possibility of touring around several resorts in one trip, and even making up your plans as you go, to follow the snow.

Cross-Channel ferries are faster and more pleasant than ever, with the possibility of a seriously good lunch on short crossings as an alternative to the quicker shuttle-trains through the tunnel. And the motorway networks in north-eastern France and on the approaches to the Alps have improved immensely in recent years. You can now get to most resorts easily in a day from south-east England, in some cases using motorways virtually all the way.

Another plus point is that you can extend the standard six-day holiday. Spending a full day on the slopes on the final Saturday and then driving for a few hours before stopping for the night means you won't find Sunday's journey too demanding, and you may even have time for a traditional French Sunday lunch. You might even like to take the Friday off work and drive down then, enabling you to spend the first Saturday of your trip on the slopes too (and bear in mind that Saturday is a good day to be skiing or boarding rather than driving because it is changeover day, which means the slopes are relatively quiet and the roads can be horrendously busy).

For us, the freedom is also a key factor. If the snow in your resort isn't too good, if the lift queues are bad, or if the resort you've plumped for turns out to be a let-down, you don't have to grin and bear it – if you have a car, you can try somewhere else. There was one famous New Year in the past when the Méribel snow was poor, but because we'd driven down, we were able to drive to Val Thorens on a couple of days and step straight on to great snow.

AS YOU LIKE IT

If you fancy visiting several resorts, you can do it in three ways: use one resort as a base and make day trips to others; use a strategically placed valley town as a base, and make resort visits from there; or embark on a tour, moving on every day or two. The separate chapter on lift passes describes some notable regional passes that might form the basis of a trip.

AROUND THE ALPS IN SEVEN DAYS

The most rewarding although the least relaxing approach to exploring the Alps is to go touring, moving every day or two to a different resort and enjoying the complete freedom of going where you want, when you want. We routinely do this when we are inspecting resorts for this book. Out of high season there's no need to book accommodation before your trip, so you can decide at the last minute where to go. A touring holiday doesn't mean you'll be spending more time on the road than on the piste – provided you plan your route carefully. An hour's drive after the lifts have shut is all it need take. It does eat into your après-ski time, of course.

The following chapter has some suggestions for a trip to France. Austria offers lots of possibilities. In the west, you could take in the best skiing the country has to offer, by combining the Arlberg resorts with Ischgl, and maybe Sölden. Or, as we did last winter, you could visit the unspoiled resorts of Vorarlberg's Bregenzerwald region and then move on to the Zugspitz Arena resorts and visit Garmisch, over the border in Germany. Further east, there are scores of resorts you could visit. It is easy to combine Hintertux and Mayrhofen with the SkiWelt resorts and Kitzbühel. And the Ski Amadé lift pass makes it great value to combine the Gastein valley with Hochkönig and Schladming. If you fancy a city-based holiday, you could consider staying in Innsbruck or Salzburg – both beautiful old places – and driving to a different resort each day.

In Italy you can stay in the beautiful old city of Aosta and visit a different resort in the Aosta valley (such as Courmayeur, Cervinia and the Monterosa resorts) each day – see our new Aosta valley chapter. Elsewhere in Italy, many resorts are far more suitable for tourers than day trippers, provided you're prepared to put up with some slow drives on winding passes. For example, you could start in Livigno, drive to Bormio and then to the Dolomites, visiting Madonna di Campiglio and Selva, and finish your Italian expedition in Cortina.

Switzerland also offers lots of possibilities. In the west, you could combine Verbier with Val d'Anniviers, Anzère and Crans-Montana – either moving between resorts or basing yourself in Sierre or Sion. You could even combine this Valais region with the Jungfrau resorts of Wengen, Grindelwald and Mürren by putting your car on the train through the Lötschberg tunnel. Further east, you could start in Davos/Klosters, take in Lenzerheide and Arosa and end up in Flims. You could even include St Moritz.

There's no need to confine yourself to one country. You could imitate the famous Haute-Route by starting in Argentière in France and ending up in Switzerland's Saas-Fee, via Verbier and Zermatt.

The major thing that you have to watch out for with a touring holiday is the cost of accommodation. Checking into a resort hotel for a night or two doesn't come cheap, and can be a bit of a rip-off. But valley hotels often offer very good value.

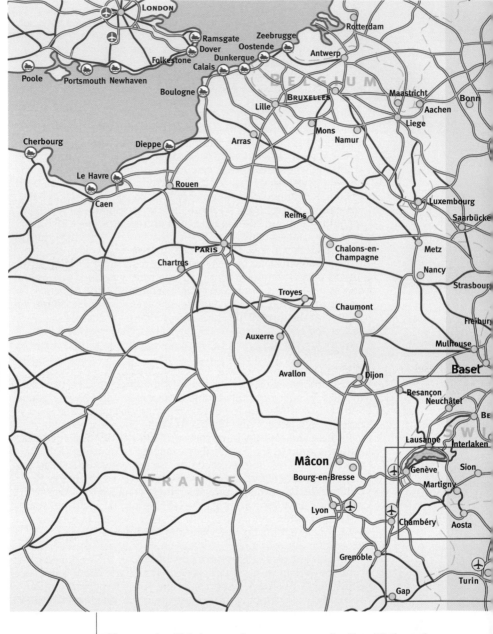

This map should help you plan your route to the Alps. All the main routes from the Channel and all the routes up into the mountains funnel through (or close to) three 'gateways', picked out on the map in larger type – Mâcon in France, Basel in Switzerland and Ulm in Germany.

Decide which gateway suits your destination, and pick a route to it from your planned arrival port at the Channel. Occasionally, using different Channel ports will lead you to use different gateways.

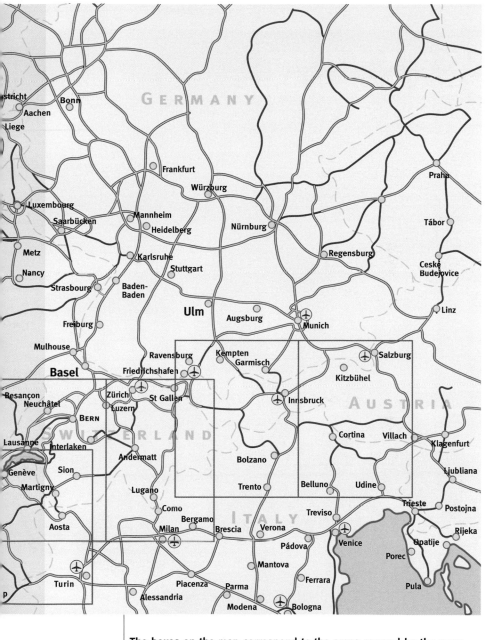

The boxes on the map correspond to the areas covered by the more detailed maps at the start of the sections of the book devoted to the four main Alpine countries:

Austria page 114
France page 230
Italy page 418
Switzerland page 484

Interactive resort shortlist builder at **www.wtss.co.uk**

Drive to the French Alps

To make the most of them

by **Chris Gill**

If you've read the preceding chapter, you'll have gathered that we are keen on driving to the Alps in general. But we're particularly keen on driving to the French Alps. The drive is a relatively short one, whereas many of the transfers to major French resorts from Geneva airport are relatively long. And the route from the Channel is through France rather than Germany, which for Francophiles like us means it's a pleasant prospect rather than a vaguely off-putting one.

TRAVEL TIME

The French Alps are the number-one destination for British car-borne skiers. The journey time is surprisingly short, at least if you are starting from south-east England. From Calais, for example, you can comfortably cover the 900km/560 miles to Chamonix in about nine hours plus stops – with the exception of the final few miles, the whole journey is on motorways. And except on peak weekends the traffic is relatively light, if you steer clear of Paris.

With some exceptions in the southern Alps, all the resorts of the French Alps are within a day's driving range, provided you cross the Channel early in the day (or overnight). Saturday is still the main changeover day for resorts, and traffic into and out of many can be heavy. This is especially true between Albertville and the Tarentaise resorts (from the Three Valleys to Val d'Isère); things are nothing like as bad as they were 20 years ago, before road improvements for the 1992 Olympics, but on peak-season Saturdays you can encounter serious queues around Moûtiers. There are traffic lights placed well away from the town, to keep the queues and associated pollution away from Moûtier's tightly enclosed setting.

DAY TRIP BASES

As we explained in the previous chapter, a car opens up different kinds of holiday for the adventurous holidaymaker. Day tripping from a base resort, for example.

In the southern French Alps, Serre-Chevalier and Montgenèvre are ideal bases for day tripping. They are within easy reach of one another, and Montgenèvre is at one end of the Milky Way lift network, which includes Sauze d'Oulx and Sestriere in Italy – you can drive on to these resorts, or reach them by lift and piste. On the French side of the border, a few miles south, Puy-St-Vincent is an underrated resort that is well worth a visit for a day – as is Risoul, a little further south. The major resorts of Alpe-d'Huez and Les Deux-Alpes are also within range, as is the cult off-piste resort of La Grave. Getting to them involves crossing the high Col du Lautaret, but it's a major route and is kept open pretty reliably.

The Chamonix valley is an ideal destination for day tripping. The Mont Blanc Unlimited lift pass covers all the Chamonix areas, plus Courmayeur in Italy (easily reached through the Mont Blanc tunnel) and, new for 2009/10, Verbier in Switzerland (easily reached if the intervening passes are open). Megève and Les Contamines are close by, and Flaine and its satellites are fairly accessible. You could stay in a valley town such as Cluses, to escape resort prices – but Chamonix itself is not an expensive town.

MOVING ON

A look at the map on the page opposite shows that a different approach will pay dividends in the Tarentaise region of France. Practically all the resorts here – from Valmorel to Val d'Isère – are found at the end of long winding roads up from the main valley. You could visit them all from a base such as Aime or Bourg-St-Maurice, but it would be pretty hard work. If instead you stayed in a series of different resorts for a day or two each, moving on from one to the next in the early evening, you could have the trip of a lifetime. You might want to consider using the Holiski lift pass offered by Compagnie des Alpes, described in our chapter on lift passes. This company owns the lift systems in practically all the big-name resorts of this area, with the conspicuous exceptions of Courchevel and Val Thorens.

GETTING THERE

There are three 'gateways' to the different regions of the French Alps. For the northern Alps – Chamonix valley, Portes du Soleil, Flaine and neighbours – you want to head for Geneva. If coming from Calais or another short-crossing port, you no longer have to tangle with the busy A6 from Paris via Beaune to Mâcon and Lyon. The relatively new A39 autoroute south from Dijon means you can head for Bourg-en-Bresse, well east of Mâcon.

For the central Alps – the mega-resorts of the Tarentaise, from Valmorel to Val d'Isère, and the Maurienne valley – you want to head for Chambéry. For the southern Alps – Alpe-d'Huez, Les Deux-Alpes, Serre-Chevalier – you want to head for Grenoble. And for either of these gateways first head for Mâcon and turn left at Lyon.

If you are taking a short Channel crossing, there are plenty of characterful towns for an overnight stop between the Channel and Dijon – Arras, St-Quentin, Laon, Troyes, Reims. All have plenty of choice of budget hotels, some of them in central locations where you can easily enjoy the facilities of the town, others on bleak estates on the outskirts.

From the more westerly Channel ports of Le Havre or Caen, your route to Geneva or Mâcon sounds dead simple: take the A13 to Paris then the A6 south. But you have to get through or around Paris in the process. The most direct way around the city is the notorious périphérique – a hectic, multi-lane urban motorway close to the centre, with exits every few hundred yards and traffic that is either worryingly fast-moving or jammed solid. If the périphérique is jammed, getting round it takes ages. The more reliable alternative is to take a series of motorways and dual carriageways through the south-west fringes of Greater Paris. The route is not well signed, so it's a great help to have a competent navigator.

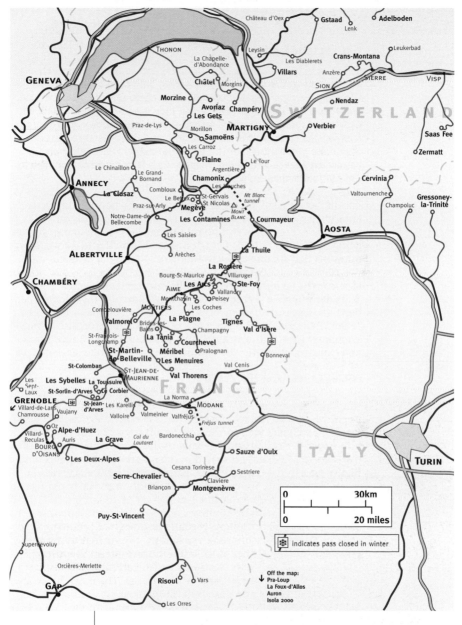

Off the map:
↓ Pra-Loup
La Foux-d'Allos
Auron
Isola 2000

0   30km
0   20 miles

❄ indicates pass closed in winter

Pick the right gateway – Geneva, Chambéry or Grenoble – and you can
hardly go wrong. Generally, there are no mountain passes involved.
The exception is the approach to Serre-Chevalier and Montgenèvre,
which involves the 2060m/6,760ft Col du Lautaret; the road is a major
one and is ploughed frequently, but we have felt the need for chains
here on one occasion. Crossing the French-Swiss border between
Chamonix and Verbier involves two closure-prone passes – the Montets
and the Forclaz. When necessary, one-way traffic runs beside the
tracks through the rail tunnel beneath the passes.

Choosing your resort

Get it right first time

Most people get to go skiing or boarding only once or twice a year, so choosing the right resort is crucially important. Chamonix, Châtel and Courchevel are all French resorts, but they are as similar as chalk and Camembert. Start to consider resorts in other countries – Alpbach in Austria, say, or Zermatt in Switzerland – and the differences become even more pronounced. For the benefit of readers with relatively narrow experience of different resorts, here is some advice on how to use our information to best effect.

Lots of factors need to be taken into account when making your choice. The weight you attach to each of them depends on your own personal preferences, and on the make-up of the group you are going on holiday with. Starting on page 97 you'll find 21 shortlists of resorts that we rate as outstanding in various key respects. And you can get your own shortlist built for you by going to our website at www.wtss.co.uk, and choosing the resort reviews page.

Minor resorts and regions not widely known in the UK are described in short chapters of two or three pages. Major resorts get more detail, and more pages. Each resort chapter is organised in the same way. This short introduction takes you through the structure and explains what you will find under each heading we use.

GETTING A FEEL FOR THE PLACE

We start each chapter with a two-line verdict, in which we aim to sum up the resort in a few words. If you like the sound of it, you might want to go next to our new Resort Price Index, in the margin. Explained fully in the chapter on page 31, this tells you how expensive eating and drinking in the resort is; figures around the average of 100 are presented in blue, lower ones in green, higher ones in red. Then, in the 'Ratings' section, we rate each resort from various points of view – the more stars the better. Longer chapters have a newly expanded set of 18 ratings, but in shorter chapters we have room for only the 10 most important. (All these star ratings are brought together in one chart following this chapter, so that you can easily track down resorts that might suit you.) Still looking at the information in the margin, in most chapters we have a 'News' section; this is likely to be of most use and interest in resorts you already know from past visits.

For major resorts, the next things to look at are our lists of the main good and bad points about the resort and its slopes, picked out with ■ and ■. These lists are followed by a summary in **bold type**, in which we've aimed to weigh up the pros and cons, coming off the fence and giving our view of who might like the resort. These sections should give you a good idea of whether the resort is likely to suit *you*, and whether you should read our detailed analysis of it or move on to another resort.

You'll know by now, for example, whether this is a high, hideous, convenient, purpose-built resort with superb, snow-sure, challenging slopes but absolutely no nightlife; or a pretty, traditional village with gentle wooded slopes, ideal for beginners if only it had some decent snow.

THE RESORT

In this first section of each chapter, we try to sort out the character of the place for you. Later, in the 'Staying there' section, we tell you more about the hotels, restaurants, bars and so on. Resorts vary enormously in some key respects. We have always published ratings for resort charm, convenience and scenery, but this year we have introduced separate sections for each of these headings.

01799 531888

THE SKI HOLIDAY CONSULTANCY
with over 25 years experience
in Europe's Top Resorts, the USA & Canada

The service is friendly, the information
is accurate and the advice is free

Just one call away from your ideal holiday

01799 531888

Charm At the extremes of the range are the handful of really hideous modern apartment-block resorts thrown up in France in the 1960s, and the ancient, captivating, traffic-free mountain villages of which Switzerland has an unfair number. But it isn't simply a question of old versus new. Some purpose-built places can have a much friendlier feel than some long-established resorts with big blocky buildings. Some places are working towns as well as ski resorts. Some are full of bars, discos and shops; others are peaceful backwaters. Traffic may choke the streets; or the village may be traffic-free.

Convenience Some places can be remarkably strung out, whereas others are surprisingly compact; our village plans are drawn to a standard scale, to help you gauge this. And of course proximity of lodgings to pistes determines how much walking or bussing you do.

Scenery Mountains are of course generally scenic, but there are differences, from the routinely hilly to the jaw-droppingly marvellous scenery of the Italian Dolomites and the Swiss Jungfrau region, to name two favourites.

THE MOUNTAINS

The slopes Some mountains and lift networks are vast and complex, while others are much smaller and lacking variety.

Fast lifts Gondolas and fast chairlifts travel at three times the speed of slow chairlifts – cable cars and funicular railways even faster; these lifts offer short ride times, and most shift queues quickly. We summarise the kinds of lifts you'll spend your time on. On our piste maps, we use a chair symbol to identify only fast chairs; lifts not marked with a symbol are slow chairs or draglifts.

Queues Monster queues are largely a thing of the past, but it still pays to avoid the resorts with the worst queues, especially in high season. Crowding on the pistes is more of a worry in many resorts, and we mention problems of this kind under this heading.

Terrain parks We summarise here the specially prepared fun parks and other terrain features most resorts now arrange for freestylers.

Snow reliability This is a crucial factor for many people, and one that varies enormously. In some resorts you don't have to worry at all about a lack of snow, while others (including some very big names) are notorious for treating their paying guests to ice, mud and slush. Whether a resort is likely to have decent snow on its slopes normally depends on the height, the direction most of the slopes face (north good, south bad), its snow record and how much snowmaking it has. But bear in mind that in the Alps high resorts tend to have rocky terrain, where the runs will need more snow than those on the pasture land of lower resorts. Many resorts have increased their snowmaking capacity in recent years; in the 'Key facts' section we list the latest amount they claim to have, and comment on it in the snow reliability text.

For experts, intermediates, beginners Most (though not all) resorts have something to offer beginners, but relatively few will keep an expert happy for a week's holiday. As for intermediates, whether a resort will suit you really depends on your standard and inclinations. Places such as Cervinia and Obergurgl are ideal for those who want easy cruising runs, but have little to offer intermediates looking for more challenge. Others, such as Sölden and Val d'Isère, may intimidate the less confident intermediate who doesn't know the area well. Some areas linking several resorts, such as the Trois Vallées and Portes du Soleil, have vast amounts of terrain, so you can cover different ground each day. But some other well-known names, such as Alpbach and Courmayeur, and many North American resorts, have surprisingly small areas.

For cross-country We don't pretend that this is a guide for avid cross-country skiers. But we do try to help.

Mountain restaurants Here's a subject that divides people clearly into two opposing camps. To some, having a decent lunch in civilised surroundings – either in the sun, contemplating amazing scenery, or in a cosy hut, sheltered from the elements – makes or breaks their holiday. Others regard a prolonged midday stop as a waste of valuable skiing time, as well as valuable spending money. We are firmly in the former camp. We get very disheartened by places with miserable restaurants and miserable food (eg many resorts in America); and there are some resorts that we go to regularly partly because of the cosy huts and excellent cuisine (eg Zermatt).

Schools and guides This is an area where we rely heavily on readers' reports of their own or their friends' experiences.

For families We sum up the merits of the resort, where possible evaluating the childcare arrangements. But, again, to be of real help we need first-hand reports from people whose children have actually used the facilities.

STAYING THERE

How to go The basic choice is between catered chalets, hotels and self-catering accommodation. Some resorts have few hotels or few chalets. Note that we now have feature chapters on notably good hotels, as well as chalets and apartments. If there are interesting options for staying in isolation on the slopes above the resort village, or in valley towns below it, we pick them out at the end of this section.

Eating out The range of restaurants varies widely. Even some big resorts, such as Les Arcs, may have little choice because most of the visitors stay in their apartments. Most US resorts offer lots of choice.

Après-ski Tastes and styles vary enormously. Most resorts have pleasant places in which to have an immediate post-skiing beer or hot chocolate. Some then go dead. Others have noisy bars and discos until the early hours.

Off the slopes This is largely aimed at assessing how suitable a resort is for someone who doesn't intend to use the slopes, such as a non-skiing spouse. But of course it is also of interest to anyone who wants some variety of evening entertainment.

Resort ratings at a glance

ANDORRA / AUSTRIA

	Arinsal	Pas de la Casa	Soldeu		Alpbach	Bad Gastein	Bad Klein-Kirchheim	Ellmau
Page	105	107	109		120	123	126	129
Extent	*	***	***		*	****	**	****
Fast lifts	**	**	**		***	***	**	***
Queues	***	***	***		***	***	****	****
Snow	****	****	***		**	***	***	**
Expert	*	*	*		*	***	**	*
Intermediate	**	***	***		**	****	***	****
Beginner	***	****	****		****	**	**	****
Charm	*	*	*		*****	***	**	***
Convenience	***	****	***		**	**	***	***
Scenery	***	***	***		***	***	***	***

	Hintertux	Hochkönig	Ischgl	Kitzbühel	Lech	Mayrhofen	Obergurgl	Obertauern
Page	132	138	144	151	158	167	172	177
Extent	***	***	****	***	****	***	**	**
Fast lifts	**	**	*****	***	****	****	*****	*****
Queues	***	****	****	***	****	*	*****	****
Snow	*****	***	****	**	****	***	*****	****
Expert	***	**	***	***	****	**	**	***
Intermediate	***	****	****	****	****	***	***	****
Beginner	**	***	**	**	****	**	****	****
Charm	***	***	***	****	****	***	****	**
Convenience	**	**	***	**	***	*	****	****
Scenery	***	***	***	***	***	***	***	***

	Saalbach-Hinterglemm	Schladming	Sölden	Söll	St Anton	Stubai Valley	Westendorf	Zell am See
Page	179	186	190	193	200	210	220	222
Extent	***	***	***	****	****	***	****	**
Fast lifts	*****	****	****	***	***	**	***	****
Queues	***	****	***	***	***	***	****	***
Snow	**	****	*****	**	****	*****	**	**
Expert	**	**	***	*	*****	***	**	**
Intermediate	****	****	****	****	***	***	***	***
Beginner	***	***	**	**	*	**	***	***
Charm	****	***	**	***	****	****	****	****
Convenience	****	***	**	**	***	**	***	***
Scenery	***	***	***	***	***	****	***	***

Want to see the full set?

Major resort chapters in the book have an additional eight ratings shown at the start of the chapter. And you can see the full set of ratings for 200 resorts on our website.

www.wtss.co.uk

	Alpe-d'Huez	Les Arcs	Avoriaz	Chamonix	Châtel	La Clusaz	Les Contamines	Courchevel
Page	234	244	253	258	268	273	275	277
Extent	****	***	*****	***	*****	***	***	*****
Fast lifts	**	***	****	***	**	**	**	****
Queues	****	****	***	**	***	***	***	****
Snow	****	****	***	****	**	**	****	****
Expert	****	*****	***	*****	***	***	***	****
Intermediate	****	****	****	**	****	****	****	*****
Beginner	*****	***	****	**	***	****	**	****
Charm	**	*	**	****	***	****	***	**
Convenience	****	****	*****	*	**	***	**	****
Scenery	****	***	***	*****	***	***	****	***

	Les Deux-Alpes	Flaine	Les Gets	La Grave	Megève	Les Menuires	Méribel	Mont-Genèvre
Page	288	294	301	303	305	312	316	327
Extent	***	****	*****	*	*****	*****	*****	**
Fast lifts	**	**	**	*		****	*****	**
Queues	**	***	***	****	****	****	****	***
Snow	****	****	**	***	**	****	***	****
Expert	****	****	***	*****	**	****	****	**
Intermediate	**	*****	****	*	****	*****	*****	****
Beginner	***	*****	****	*	***	***	****	*****
Charm	**	*	****	***	****	*	***	***
Convenience	***	*****	***	***	**	*****	***	***
Scenery	****	****	***	****	*****	***	***	***

	Morzine	La Plagne	Puy-St-Vincent	Risoul / Vars	La Rosière	Samoëns	Serre-Chevalier	Ste-Foy-Tarentaise
Page	331	339	350	352	355	358	360	369
Extent	*****	****	**	***	***	****	****	*
Fast lifts	**	**	**	*	*	**	**	**
Queues	***	***	***	****	***	****	***	*****
Snow	**	****	***	***	***	***	***	***
Expert	***	****	***	**	**	****	***	****
Intermediate	****	*****	***	****	***	*****	****	***
Beginner	***	****	***	****	*****	**	****	**
Charm	***	**	**	**	***	****	***	***
Convenience	**	*****	*****	****	***	*	***	***
Scenery	***	***	****	***	***	****	***	***

Want a shortlist shortcut?

Our website will build a shortlist for you: you specify your priorities, and the system will use our resort ratings to draw up a shortlist – confined to one area or country, if you like.

www.wtss.co.uk

	St-Martin-de-Belleville	Les Sybelles	La Tania	Tignes	Val d'Isère	Valmorel	Val Thorens	
Page	371	373	378	384	393	404	406	
Extent	*****	*****	*****	*****	*****	***	*****	
Fast lifts	****	*	****	***	****	**	****	
Queues	****	****	****	****	****	***	***	
Snow	***	***	***	*****	*****	**	*****	
Expert	****	**	****	*****	*****	**	****	
Intermediate	*****	***	*****	*****	*****	****	*****	
Beginner	**	****	***	**	***	*****	****	
Charm	****	***	***	*	***	****	**	
Convenience	***	***	****	****	***	*****	*****	
Scenery	***	***	***	***	***	***	***	

	Garmisch-Partenkirchen		Bormio	Cervinia	Cortina d'Ampezzo	Courmayeur	Livigno	Madonna di Campiglio
Page	416		426	428	434	439	444	448
Extent	*		**	***	***	**	**	***
Fast lifts	**		****	****	***	****	****	***
Queues	***		***	****	****	****	****	****
Snow	***		***	*****	***	****	****	***
Expert	****		*	*	**	***	*	**
Intermediate	***		***	****	***	****	***	****
Beginner	*		**	*****	*****	**	****	****
Charm	***		****	**	****	****	***	***
Convenience	**		***	***	*	*	**	***
Scenery	****		***	****	*****	****	***	****

	Monterosa Ski	Passo Tonale	Sauze d'Oulx	Sella Ronda	Selva / Val Gardena	Sestriere	La Thuile
Page	450	454	456	461	468	475	477
Extent	***	**	****	*****	*****	****	***
Fast lifts	*****	****	***	****	***	***	***
Queues	****	****	***	***	***	***	****
Snow	****	****	**	****	****	****	****
Expert	****	*	**	**	***	***	**
Intermediate	****	***	****	*****	*****	****	****
Beginner	**	*****	*	****	***	***	****
Charm	***	*	**	***	***	*	***
Convenience	***	***	**	***	***	***	***
Scenery	****	***	***	*****	*****	***	***

Resort ratings at a glance

93

Interactive resort shortlist builder at **www.wtss.co.uk**

Want to keep up to date?

Our website has weekly resort news throughout the year, and you can register for our monthly email newsletter – with special holiday offers, as well as resort news highlights.

www.wtss.co.uk

	Adelboden	Andermatt	Anzère	Arosa	Champéry	Crans-Montana	Davos
Page	491	493	495	496	498	501	503
Extent	***	*	*	*	*****	***	*****
Fast lifts	***	*	*	***	*	****	***
Queues	***	**	****	****	****	***	***
Snow	***	****	**	***	**	**	****
Expert	**	****	**	**	***	**	****
Intermediate	***	**	***	***	****	****	*****
Beginner	****	*	***	****	**	***	**
Charm	****	****	***	**	****	**	**
Convenience	**	***	***	**	*	**	**
Scenery	****	***	****	***	****	****	****

	Engelberg	Grindel-wald	Klosters	Laax	Meiringen	Mürren	Saas-Fee
Page	510	512	516	518	520	523	527
Extent	**	***	*****	****	*	*	**
Fast lifts	***	***	***	****	****	****	****
Queues	**	**	**	****	****	***	***
Snow	***	**	****	***	***	***	*****
Expert	****	**	****	***	*	***	**
Intermediate	***	****	*****	*****	***	***	****
Beginner	**	***	***	****	****	**	*****
Charm	**	****	****	***	***	*****	*****
Convenience	*	**	**	***	***	***	**
Scenery	****	*****	****	***	****	*****	****

	St Moritz	Val d'Anniviers	Verbier	Villars	Wengen	Zermatt	
Page	532	539	543	555	557	562	
Extent	*****	**	*****	***	***	****	
Fast lifts	****	*	****	**	***	*****	
Queues	***	****	***	***	***	***	
Snow	****	****	***	**	**	****	
Expert	****	****	*****	**	**	****	
Intermediate	****	***	***	***	****	****	
Beginner	**	***	**	****	***	**	
Charm	**	*****	***	***	*****	*****	
Convenience	*	**	**	**	***	**	
Scenery	****	****	****	***	*****	*****	

Want a shortlist shortcut?

Our website will build a shortlist for you: you specify your priorities, and the system will use our resort ratings to draw up a shortlist – confined to one area or country, if you like.

www.wtss.co.uk

	CALIFORNIA			COLORADO	Beaver Creek	Brecken-ridge	Copper Mountain	Keystone
	Heavenly	Mammoth Mountain	Squaw Valley	Aspen				
Page	577	582	587	590	597	599	604	606
Extent	★★★	★★★	★★★	★★★★	★★	★★	★★	★★★
Fast lifts	★★★★	★★★★	★★★	★★★★	★★★★★	★★★	★★	★★★★★
Queues	★★★★	★★★★	★★★★	★★★★	★★★★★	★★★★	★★★★	★★★★
Snow	★★★★	★★★★	★★★★	★★★★★	★★★★★	★★★★★	★★★★★	★★★★★
Expert	★★★	★★★★	★★★★	★★★★★	★★★★	★★★★	★★★★	★★★
Intermediate	★★★★	★★★★	★★	★★★★★	★★★★	★★★★	★★★★	★★★★
Beginner	★★★★	★★★★	★★★★	★★★★★	★★★★★	★★★★★	★★★★	★★★★
Charm	★	★★	★★★	★★★★	★★	★★★	★★	★★
Convenience	★	★★	★★★★	★★	★★★★	★★★	★★★★	★★
Scenery	★★★★	★★★	★★★	★★★	★★★	★★★	★★★	★★★

					Winter Park	UTAH	The Canyons	
	Snowmass	Steamboat	Telluride	Vail		Alta		
Page	608	610	613	615	622	627	629	
Extent	★★★★	★★★	★★	★★★★	★★★	★★★	★★★	
Fast lifts	★★★★★	★★★	★★★★	★★★★★	★★★★	★★★★	★★★	
Queues	★★★★	★★★★	★★★★★	★★	★★★★	★★★	★★★★	
Snow	★★★★★	★★★★	★★★★	★★★★★	★★★★★	★★★★★	★★★★	
Expert	★★★★★	★★★	★★★★	★★★★	★★★★	★★★★★	★★★★	
Intermediate	★★★★★	★★★★	★★★	★★★★★	★★★★	★★★	★★★★	
Beginner	★★★★★	★★★★★	★★★★★	★★★	★★★★★	★★★	★★	
Charm	★★	★★	★★★★	★★★	★★	★★	★★	
Convenience	★★★★	★★★	★★★★	★★★	★★★	★★★★	★★★★	
Scenery	★★★★	★★★	★★★★	★★★	★★★	★★★	★★★	

				REST OF THE WEST	Jackson Hole	NEW ENGLAND	Stowe	
	Deer Valley	Park City	Snowbird	Big Sky		Killington		
Page	631	633	638	641	646	652	656	
Extent	★★	★★★	★★★	★★★★	★★★	★	★	
Fast lifts	★★★★	★★★	★★★★	★★	★★★	★★★	★★★	
Queues	★★★★	★★★★	★★★	★★★★★	★★★	★★★★	★★★★	
Snow	★★★★	★★★★	★★★★★	★★★★★	★★★★	★★★	★★★	
Expert	★★★	★★★★	★★★★★	★★★★	★★★★★	★★★	★★★	
Intermediate	★★★★	★★★★	★★★	★★★★	★★	★★★	★★★★	
Beginner	★★★★	★★★★	★★	★★★★★	★★★	★★★★	★★★★	
Charm	★★★	★★★	★	★	★★★	★	★★★★	
Convenience	★★★★	★★	★★★★★	★★★★	★★★	★	★	
Scenery	★★★	★★★	★★★	★★★	★★★	★★★	★★★	

Resort ratings at a glance

Interactive resort shortlist builder at www.wtss.co.uk

Want to see the full set?

Major resort chapters in the book have an additional eight ratings shown at the start of the chapter. And you can see the full set of ratings for 200 resorts on our website.

www.wtss.co.uk

| | WESTERN CANADA | | | | | |
	BANFF	BIG WHITE	FERNIE	KICKING HORSE	LAKE LOUISE	PANORAMA
Page	661	668	671	676	678	683
Extent	***	***	***	***	***	**
Fast lifts	****	****	*	***	****	***
Queues	****	*****	****	****	****	*****
Snow	****	*****	*****	****	***	***
Expert	****	***	*****	****	****	****
Intermediate	****	****	**	***	****	***
Beginner	***	****	****	***	***	****
Charm	***	**	**	**	***	**
Convenience	*	****	****	****	*	****
Scenery	****	***	***	***	****	***

| | | | | | EASTERN CANADA | |
	REVELSTOKE	SILVER STAR	SUN PEAKS	WHISTLER	TREMBLANT	
Page	685	687	689	691	701	
Extent	***	***	***	****	*	
Fast lifts	*****	****	**	*****	*****	
Queues	*****	*****	*****	***	***	
Snow	*****	****	****	****	****	
Expert	*****	****	***	*****	**	
Intermediate	**	***	****	*****	***	
Beginner	*	****	****	***	****	
Charm	**	***	***	***	****	
Convenience	*	*****	****	****	****	
Scenery	****	***	***	***	***	

| | SPAIN | NORWAY | SWEDEN | BULGARIA | NEW ZEALAND | |
	BAQUEIRA	HEMSEDAL	ÅRE	BANSKO	QUEENSTOWN	
Page	704	710	713	716	728	
Extent	**	*	**	*	*	
Fast lifts	***	***	*	*****	***	
Queues	****	****	****	***	***	
Snow	***	****	***	***	**	
Expert	***	**	**	**	***	
Intermediate	****	****	****	****	***	
Beginner	**	***	****	***	***	
Charm	**	**	***	**	**	
Convenience	***	**	***	**	*	
Scenery	***	**	***	***	****	

Want to get other views?

Our website has an active forum, where readers swap experiences and views on resorts. The WTSS editors join in, when they have time, so it's a good way to get their views.

www.wtss.co.uk

Resort shortlists

To help you spot resorts that will suit you

To streamline the job of spotting the ideal resort for your own holiday, here are lists of the best ten or so resorts for 21 different categories. Some lists embrace European and North American resorts, but many we've confined to Europe, because the US has too many qualifying resorts (eg for beginners) or because the US does things differently, making comparisons invalid (eg for off-piste).

SOMETHING FOR EVERYONE
Resorts with everything from reassuring nursery slopes to real challenges for experts
Alpe-d'Huez, France 234
Les Arcs, France 244
Aspen, Colorado 590
Courchevel, France 277
Flaine, France 294
Mammoth, California 582
Vail, Colorado 615
Val d'Isère, France 393
Whistler, Canada 691
Winter Park, Colorado 622

INTERNATIONAL OVERSIGHTS
Resorts that deserve as much attention as the ones we go back to every year, but don't get it
Alta, Utah 627
Andermatt, Switzerland 493
Bad Gastein, Austria 123
Big Sky, Montana 641
Les Contamines, France 275
Copper Mountain, Colorado 604
Laax, Switzerland 518
Monterosa Ski, Italy 450
Risoul, France 352
Telluride, Colorado 613
Val d'Anniviers, Switzerland 539

HIGH-MILEAGE PISTE-BASHING
Extensive intermediate slopes with big lift networks
Alpe-d'Huez, France 234
Davos/Klosters, Switz 503/516
Laax, Switzerland 518
Milky Way: Sauze d'Oulx (Italy), Montgenèvre (France) 456/327
Paradiski, France 337
Portes du Soleil, France/Switz 349
Sella Ronda, Italy 461
Selva, Italy 468
SkiWelt/Kitzbühel, Austria 129/151/193/220
Les Sybelles, France 373
Three Valleys, France 382
Val d'Isère/Tignes, France 393/384
Whistler, Canada 691

RELIABLE SNOW IN THE ALPS
Alpine resorts where snow is rarely in short supply
Bregenzerwald, Austria 213
Chamonix, France 258
Cervinia, Italy 428
Courchevel, France 277
Hintertux, Austria 132
Lech/Zürs, Austria 158
Obergurgl, Austria 172
Obertauern, Austria 177
Saas-Fee, Switzerland 527
Sölden, Austria 190
Val d'Isère/Tignes, France 393/384
Val Thorens, France 406
Zermatt, Switzerland 562

OFF-PISTE WONDERS
Alpine resorts where, with the right guidance and equipment, you can have the time of your life
Alpe-d'Huez, France 234
Andermatt, Switzerland 493
Chamonix, France 258
Davos/Klosters, Switz 503/516
La Grave, France 303
Lech/Zürs, Austria 158
Monterosa Ski, Italy 450
St Anton, Austria 200
Val d'Isère/Tignes, France 393/384
Verbier, Switzerland 543

DRAMATIC SCENERY
Resorts where the mountains are not just high and snowy, but spectacularly scenic too
Chamonix, France 258
Cortina, Italy 434
Courmayeur, Italy 439
Heavenly, California 577
Jungfrau resorts
    (Grindelwald, Mürren, Wengen), Switzerland 512/523/557
Lake Louise, Canada 678
Megève, France 305
Sella Ronda, Italy 461
Selva, Italy 468
St Moritz, Switzerland 532
Zermatt, Switzerland 562

Resort shortlists

BACK-DOOR RESORTS
Cute little Alpine villages linked to big, bold ski areas, giving you the best of two different worlds
Les Brévières (Tignes), France 384
Champagny (La Plagne), France 339
Leogang (Saalbach), Austria 179
Montchavin (La Plagne), France 339
Peisey (Les Arcs), France 244
Le Pré (Les Arcs), France 244
Samoëns (Flaine), France 294
St-Martin (Three Valleys), France 371
Stuben (St Anton), Austria 200
Vaujany (Alpe-d'Huez), France 234

VILLAGE CHARM
Resorts with traditional character – from mountain villages to mining towns
Alpbach, Austria 120
Champéry, Switzerland 498
Courmayeur, Italy 439
Lech, Austria 158
Mürren, Switzerland 523
Saas-Fee, Switzerland 527
Telluride, Colorado 613
Val d'Anniviers, Switzerland 539
Wengen, Switzerland 557
Zermatt, Switzerland 562

BLACK RUNS
Resorts with steep, moguly, lift-served slopes within the safety of the piste network
Alta/Snowbird, Utah 627/638
Andermatt, Switzerland 493
Argentière/Chamonix, France 258
Aspen, Colorado 590
Beaver Creek, Colorado 597
Courchevel, France 277
Jackson Hole, Wyoming 646
Whistler, Canada 691
Winter Park, Colorado 622
Zermatt, Switzerland 562

POWDER PARADISES
Resorts with the snow, the terrain and (ideally) the lack of crowds that make for powder perfection
Alta/Snowbird, Utah 627/638
Andermatt, Switzerland 493
Big Sky, Montana 641
Big White, Canada 668
Fernie, Canada 671
La Grave, France 303
Jackson Hole, Wyoming 646
Kicking Horse, Canada 676
Monterosa Ski, Italy 450
Revelstoke, Canada 685
Ste-Foy, France 369

CHOPAHOLICS
Resorts where you can have a day riding helicopters or cats
Aspen, Colorado 590
Courmayeur, Italy 439
Fernie, Canada 671
Lech/Zürs, Austria 158
Monterosa Ski, Italy 450
Panorama, Canada 683
La Thuile, Italy 477
Verbier, Switzerland 543
Whistler, Canada 691
Zermatt, Switzerland 562

TOP TERRAIN PARKS
Alpine resorts with the best parks and pipes for freestyle thrills
Les Arcs, France 244
Avoriaz, France 253
Cervinia, Italy 428
Davos, Switzerland 503
Les Deux-Alpes, France 288
Ischgl, Austria 144
Laax, Switzerland 518
Lech, Austria 158
Livigno, Italy 444
Mayrhofen, Austria 167
Méribel, France 316
La Plagne, France 339
Saalbach-Hinterglemm, Austria 179
Saas Fee, Switzerland 527
St Moritz, Switzerland 532
Zermatt, Switzerland 562

WEATHERPROOF SLOPES
Alpine resorts with fairly snow-sure slopes if the sun shines, and trees in case it doesn't
Les Arcs, France 244
Courchevel, France 277
Courmayeur, Italy 439
Laax, Switzerland 518
Schladming, Austria 186
Selva, Italy 468
Serre-Chevalier, France 360
Sestriere, Italy 475
La Thuile, Italy 477

MICHAEL MARLAIS
Zürs is one of the snowiest resorts in the Alps ↓

MOTORWAY CRUISING
Long, gentle, super-smooth pistes to bolster the frail confidence of those just off the nursery slope
Les Arcs, France 244
Breckenridge, Colorado 599
Cervinia, Italy 428
Cortina, Italy 434
Courchevel, France 277
Megève, France 305
La Plagne, France 339
Snowmass, Colorado 608
La Thuile, Italy 477
Vail, Colorado 615

RESORTS FOR BEGINNERS
European resorts with gentle, snow-sure nursery slopes and easy, longer runs to progress to
Alpe-d'Huez, France 234
Cervinia, Italy 428
Courchevel, France 277
Flaine, France 294
Montgenèvre, France 327
Passo Tonale, Italy 454
La Plagne, France 339
La Rosière, France 355
Saas-Fee, Switzerland 527
Soldeu, Andorra 109

SPECIALLY FOR FAMILIES
Alpine resorts where you can easily find accommodation surrounded by snow, not by traffic and fumes
Les Arcs, France 244
Avoriaz, France 253
Flaine, France 294
Lech, Austria 158
Montchavin (La Plagne), France 339
Mürren, Switzerland 523
Puy-St-Vincent, France 350
Risoul, France 352
Saas-Fee, Switzerland 527
Les Sybelles, France 373
Valmorel, France 404
Wengen, Switzerland 557

SNOW-SURE BUT SIMPATICO
Alpine resorts with high-rise slopes, but low-rise, traditional-style buildings
Andermatt, Switzerland 493
Arabba (Sella Ronda), Italy 461
Argentière (Chamonix), France 258
Les Contamines, France 275
Ischgl, Austria 144
Lech/Zürs, Austria 158
Monterosa Ski, Italy 450
Obergurgl, Austria 172
Saas-Fee, Switzerland 527
Val d'Anniviers, Switzerland 539
Zermatt, Switzerland 562

SPECIAL MOUNTAIN RESTAURANTS
Alpine resorts where mountain restaurants can really add an extra dimension to your holiday
Alpe-d'Huez, France 234
La Clusaz, France 273
Cortina d'Ampezzo, Italy 434
Courmayeur, Italy 439
Kitzbühel, Austria 151
Megève, France 305
La Plagne, France 339
Saalbach, Austria 179
Selva, Italy 468
Zermatt, Switzerland 562

MODERN CONVENIENCE
Alpine resorts where there's plenty of slope-side accommodation where you can ski from the door
Les Arcs, France 244
Avoriaz, France 253
Courchevel, France 277
Flaine, France 294
Les Menuires, France 312
Obertauern, Austria 177
La Plagne, France 339
Puy-St-Vincent, France 350
La Tania, France 378
Tignes, France 384
Valmorel, France 404
Val Thorens, France 406

LIVELY NIGHTLIFE
European resorts where you'll have no difficulty finding somewhere to boogie
Chamonix, France 258
Ischgl, Austria 144
Kitzbühel, Austria 151
Méribel, France 316
Pas de la Casa, Andorra 107
Saalbach, Austria 179
Sauze d'Oulx, Italy 456
Sölden, Austria 190
St Anton, Austria 200
Val d'Isère, France 393
Verbier, Switzerland 543
Zermatt, Switzerland 562

OTHER AMUSEMENTS
Alpine resorts where those not interested in skiing or boarding can still find plenty to do
Bad Gastein, Austria 123
Chamonix, France 258
Cortina, Italy 434
Davos, Switzerland 503
Innsbruck, Austria 140
Kitzbühel, Austria 151
Megève, France 305
St Moritz, Switzerland 532
Zell am See, Austria 222

Resort shortlists

99

Interactive resort shortlist builder at www.wtss.co.uk

FINDING A RESORT

The bulk of the book consists of the chapters listed on the facing page, devoted to individual major resorts, plus minor resorts that share the same lift system. Sometimes we devote a chapter to an area not dominated by one resort, in which case we use the area name (eg Les Sybelles, Monterosa Ski).

Chapters are grouped by country: first, the six major European countries (now including Germany); then the US and Canada (where resorts are grouped by states or regions); then minor European countries; then Japan; and lastly, countries in the southern hemisphere. Within each group, resorts are ordered alphabetically. Bregenzerwald and Montafon now follow an introductory chapter on their 'land', Vorarlberg.

Short cuts to the resorts that might suit you are provided (on the pages preceding this one) by a table of comparative **star ratings** and a series of **shortlists** of resorts with particular merits.

At the back of the book is an **index** to the resort chapters, combined with a **directory** giving basic information on hundreds of other minor resorts. If the resort you are looking up is covered in a chapter devoted to a bigger resort, the page reference will be to the start of the chapter, not to the exact page on which the minor resort is described.

There's further guidance on using our information in the chapter on 'Choosing your resort', on page 88 – designed to be helpful particularly to people with little or no experience of ski resorts, who may not appreciate how big the differences between one resort and another can be.

READING A CHAPTER

This year we have introduced new Resort Price Index figures, based on prices of food and drink in each resort – explained in detail in the chapter on page 31. Figures close to the average figure of £100 are shown in blue, lower ones in green, higher ones in red.

£105
RESORT PRICE INDEX

Star ratings summarise our view of the resort, including its suitability for different standards of skier/boarder. The more stars, the better. In major resort chapters we now give an expanded set of 18 ratings.

We give phone numbers and internet addresses of the **tourist office** (in North America, the ski lift company) and phone numbers for recommended **hotels**. We give star ratings for hotels – either official ones or ones awarded by major tour operators. The UK tour operators offering **package holidays** in major resorts are listed in the chapter margins. For minor resorts they are listed in the directory at the back of the book.

Our **mountain maps** show the resorts' own classification of runs. On some maps we show black diamonds to mark expert terrain without defined runs. We do not distinguish single diamond terrain from the steeper double diamond.

We include on the map any lifts definitely planned for construction for the coming season.

We use the following symbols to identify **fast lifts**:

 fast chairlift

 gondola

 chondola – chair/gondola

 cable car

 railway/funicular

THE WORLD'S BEST WINTER SPORTS RESORTS

To find a minor resort, or if you are not sure which country you should be looking under, consult the index/directory at the back of the book, which lists all resorts alphabetically.

ANDORRA	**102**
Arinsal	105
Pas de la Casa	107
Soldeu	109

AUSTRIA	**114**
Alpbach	120
Bad Gastein	123
Bad Kleinkirchheim	126
Ellmau	129
Hintertux	132
Hochkönig	138
Innsbruck	140
Ischgl	144
Kitzbühel	151
Lech	158
Mayrhofen	167
Obergurgl	172
Obertauern	177
Saalbach-H'glemm	179
Schladming	186
Sölden	190
Söll	193
St Anton	200
Stubai valley	210
Vorarlberg	212
– Bregenzerwald	213
– Montafon	217
Westendorf	220
Zell am See	222
Zugspitz Arena	227

FRANCE	**230**
Alpe-d'Huez	234
Les Arcs	244
Avoriaz	253
Chamonix	258
Châtel	268
La Clusaz	273
Les Contamines	275
Courchevel	277
Les Deux-Alpes	288
Flaine	294
Les Gets	301
La Grave	303
Megève	305
Les Menuires	312
Méribel	316
Montgenèvre	327

Morzine	331
Paradiski	337
La Plagne	339
Portes du Soleil	349
Puy-St-Vincent	350
Risoul	352
La Rosière	355
Samoëns	358
Serre-Chevalier	360
Ste-Foy-Tarentaise	369
St-Martin-de-B'ville	371
Les Sybelles	373
La Tania	378
The Three Valleys	382
Tignes	384
Val d'Isère	393
Valmorel	404
Val Thorens	406
French Pyrenees	413

GERMANY	**414**
Garmisch-Parten'n	416

ITALY	**418**
Aosta valley	422
Bormio	426
Cervinia	428
Cortina d'Ampezzo	434
Courmayeur	439
Livigno	444
Madonna di C'glio	448
Monterosa Ski	450
Passo Tonale	454
Sauze d'Oulx	456
Sella Ronda	461
Selva	468
Sestriere	475
La Thuile	477
Trentino	479
Val di Fassa	483

SWITZERLAND	**484**
Adelboden	491
Andermatt	493
Anzère	495
Arosa	496
Champéry	498
Crans-Montana	501
Davos	503

Engelberg	510
Grindelwald	512
Klosters	516
Laax	518
Meiringen	520
Mürren	523
Saas-Fee	527
St Moritz	532
Val d'Anniviers	539
Verbier	543
Villars	555
Wengen	557
Zermatt	562

USA	**572**

CALIFORNIA	**576**
Heavenly	577
Mammoth	582
Squaw Valley	587

COLORADO	**589**
Aspen	590
Beaver Creek	597
Breckenridge	599
Copper Mountain	604
Keystone	606
Snowmass	608
Steamboat	610
Telluride	613
Vail	615
Winter Park	622

UTAH	**626**
Alta	627
The Canyons	629
Deer Valley	631
Park City	633
Snowbird	638

REST OF WEST	**640**
Big Sky	641
Jackson Hole	646

NEW ENGLAND	**651**
Killington	652
Stowe	656

CANADA	**658**

WESTERN CANADA	**660**
Banff	661
Big White	668
Fernie	671
Kicking Horse	676
Lake Louise	678
Panorama	683
Revelstoke	685
Silver Star	687
Sun Peaks	689
Whistler	691

EASTERN CANADA	**700**
Tremblant	701

THE REST	
SPAIN	**703**
Baqueira-Beret	704
FINLAND	**706**
NORWAY	**708**
Hemsedal	710
SWEDEN	**712**
Åre	713
BULGARIA	**715**
Bansko	716
ROMANIA	**718**
SLOVENIA	**719**
SCOTLAND	**720**
JAPAN	**721**
AUSTRALIA	**723**
NEW ZEALAND	**725**
Queenstown	728
ARGENTINA	**732**
CHILE	**733**

Our resort chapters

101

Interactive resort shortlist builder at **www.wtss.co.uk**

Andorra

Andorra is a highly distinctive destination. Or, to put it another way, a bit strange. It is a tiny state – almost entirely mountainous and sandwiched between France and Spain – that has built its prosperity on the twin pillars of tax-haven status and low-cost tourism – particularly winter tourism, and particularly in the UK market. Andorra used to be seen primarily as a cheap and cheerful holiday destination, attracting younger singles and couples looking for a good time in the duty-free bars and clubs, as well as learning to ski or snowboard. But the place has changed radically over the last 25 years.

Even in our first edition, published 15 years ago, we noted that rising package prices meant you could get holidays to Italy for less than you paid to go to Andorra (though on-the-spot prices were higher). We applauded heavy investment in snowmaking, but noted a lack of investment in lifts, which we described as 'antiquated'. So we viewed the place as a bit backward, and dealt with it at the back of the book, along with eastern Europe.

Then, over the next decade, the lift systems and piste-grooming fleets were transformed, making the skiing much more appealing to intermediates as well as beginners. Upmarket hotels were built (though they often resembled Spanish summer package hotels, with self-service buffet meals). Prices continued to rise, but the rises seemed justified by improvements that put the resorts – Soldeu and its neighbours, in particular – in the same league as many Alpine resorts. Six years ago, we recognised that Andorra had arrived: we moved it from the back of the book into the main sequence of European skiing countries, along with the Alpine big four.

We really had no choice: at that stage, Andorra was the fourth most popular winter sports destination for Brits, and threatened to overtake Italy, in third place. Industry estimates were that Andorra had an amazing 14% of the UK skiing package market – more than Switzerland, the USA and Canada combined. And practically all these people were going to three resorts – the three resorts we cover in the following chapters.

Now, the bubble may have burst. Andorra's prices have continued to rise, and its market share has declined sharply. The latest *Crystal Ski Industry Report* puts Andorra's share of the package holiday market at only 5%, pushing it back to fifth place (sixth if you treat the USA and Canada as one, which many observers do).

We're not surprised: our new Resort Price Index for Soldeu, based on bar and restaurant prices in the resort, puts Soldeu alongside big-name resorts in Austria and the most expensive resorts in Italy. Frankly, Soldeu is not in the same league as these resorts. Even more surprising is the pricing of lift passes. A six-day pass for the Grandvalira area (centred on Soldeu) cost 213 euros last season, making it one of the most expensive in Europe. You can get a pass covering 350 lifts and 1000km of pistes around Kitzbühel for less. What's more, Soldeu beginners have to go up the mountain even to start skiing, and the resort does not sell special beginner passes.

So where does this leave Andorra as a holiday destination for skiing Brits? Well, Pas de la Casa and Arinsal are cheaper than

GRANDVALIRA

← The steep-sided valleys of Andorra have been heavily developed wherever the opportunity arises. This is Canillo, which is one of four main points of access to the Soldeu slopes

LIFT PASSES

Ski Andorra
The Ski Andorra pass covers all Andorran areas and allows skiing at any single one of them each day: €187 for five non-consecutive days

Phone numbers
From abroad use the prefix +376

TOURIST OFFICES

Ski Andorra
t 805200
skiandorra@ski andorra.ad
www.skiandorra.ad

Arcalis
t 739600
info@vallnordturisme. com
www.vallnord.com

Soldeu, particularly for beginners. Look first at them. But if you are looking at holidays anywhere in Andorra, it now makes obvious sense to look at Italy and Austria too.

STAYING DOWN THE VALLEY

Several valley towns can be used as alternative bases to the main resorts. **Encamp** has a powerful 18-seat gondola giving a quick way into the Grandvalira ski area shared by Soldeu and Pas de la Casa. It is cheap, but plagued by its situation on the traffic-choked main road. **La Massana** is a more appealing town, and is linked by gondola to the Pal-Arinsal ski area. It is also fairly convenient for trips to Arcalis (covered by the lift pass). **Ordino** is nearer still to Arcalis, and pleasantly rustic, but it has no direct access to slopes.

The capital, **Andorra la Vella**, is not far down the valley from Encamp and also choked by traffic and fumes. There are plenty of high-quality hotels and restaurants, plus bars and nightclubs and duty-free shopping. The clientele is mainly Spanish. At Escaldes-Engordany, just outside the centre, the splendid Caldea spa has a fantastic array of pools, baths and treatments.

OUTINGS TO ARCALIS

Arcalis is the most remote area of slopes in Andorra, tucked away at the head of a long valley, and most British visitors to Soldeu or Pas de la Casa never hear about it. But it makes a very worthwhile day trip, particularly from Arinsal and Pal. The terrain is varied and scenic, the slopes are usually deserted except at weekends (when locals pour in), and the snow is usually the best around. There is excellent intermediate and beginner terrain, but what marks it out is the expert terrain, including lots of off-piste between the marked runs. 'A real jewel – the boarder in our group was in heaven,' said a recent reporter. There is no accommodation at the mountain.

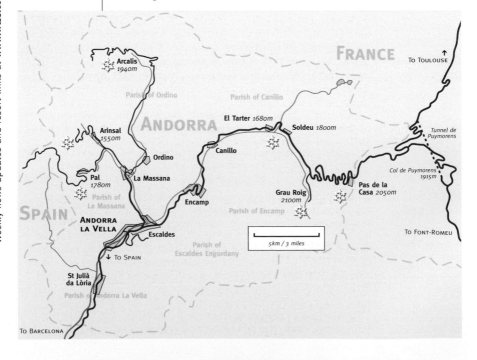

PAL-ARINSAL RESORT

Arinsal

Cheap, lively base that suits beginners best; La Massana is better if you also want to explore Arcalis (covered by the Vallnord lift pass)

- ✚ Lively bars
- ✚ Ski school geared to British needs
- ✚ Cable car link with Pal and shared Vallnord lift pass with Arcalis
- ✚ Pretty, treelined slopes in Pal

- ➖ Local Arinsal slopes are bleak and confined – though this means children can't stray far
- ➖ Run to village doesn't go to centre
- ➖ Long, dour village with no focus
- ➖ Poor bus link to Arcalis

TOP 10 RATINGS

Extent	★
Fast lifts	★★
Queues	★★★
Snow	★★★★
Expert	★
Intermediate	★★
Beginner	★★★
Charm	★
Convenience	★★★
Scenery	★★★

NEWS

For 2008/09 in Arinsal, a six-pack replaced the double chair from the valley at Cota. Snowmaking was increased, in particular on the blue piste back to Cota. The aim is to have 100% snowmaking within the next few seasons. In Pal, the Del Camí Inferior trail from Coll de la Botella up to Planell was widened and a new freestyle area built for beginners.

KEY FACTS

Resort	1470m
	4,820ft
Slopes	1550-2560m
	5,090-8,400ft
Lifts	31
Pistes	63km
	39 miles
Green	12%
Blue	38%
Red	38%
Black	12%
Snowmaking	41%

Arinsal is the most British-dominated resort in Andorra, largely because British tour operators are able to offer packages here at tempting prices. The resort attracts mainly first-time skiers and riders; reports suggest that Arinsal, like the rest of Andorra, is managing to attract more families and fewer binge drinkers.

THE RESORT

Arinsal sits near the head of a steep-sided valley north of Andorra la Vella. Development in recent years has been rapid. Pal has a more open setting in another valley. The two were linked a few years back by cable car.

You can also stay in the lower town of La Massana (with a gondola up to Pal's slopes). La Massana is better placed if you want to visit the very worthwhile slopes of Arcalis (covered by the Vallnord lift pass – see the Andorra introduction. It's closer and has a better bus service.

Village charm The resort is a long, narrow village of grey, stone-clad buildings – with some rustic appeal. Reporters have commented on the friendliness of the locals.

Convenience The gondola from the village centre is the main way to and from the slopes, and staying close to it is convenient; the alternative chairlift, 1km/0.5 miles out of town, is much more relevant now that it has been upgraded to a six-pack, with improved snowmaking on the run down. You can also drive to the top of the gondola. Pal is a bus ride from its several lift bases.

Scenery Shady valleys and nicely wooded slopes dominate. Pic Negre gives a decent viewpoint.

THE MOUNTAINS

The area above Arinsal is an open, east-facing bowl, whereas Pal has the most densely wooded slopes in Andorra. Most face east; those down to the link with Arinsal face north. Reporters note good signposting.

Slopes Arinsal's slopes consist essentially of a single, long, narrow bowl above the upper gondola station at Comallempla, served by a network of chairs and drags, including a quad and a six-pack. Almost at the top is the cable car link with Pal. Pal's slopes are widely spread around the mountain, with four main lift bases, all reachable by road. The main one, La Caubella, at the opposite extreme from the Arinsal link, is the arrival point of the gondola from La Massana.

Fast lifts Access has improved with new fast chairs. More needed high up.

Queues At peak times queues can build up at Arinsal's gondola to return to the village. The cable car link with Pal can close if the wind is high.

Terrain parks Arinsal's big freestyle area has its own lift, a huge half-pipe, a big jump, a terrain park with rails and jumps, a boardercross and a chill-out area. There is a Junior Rails Zone for beginners. Pal also has a beginners' park.

Snow reliability With most runs above 1950m/6,400ft, the north-easterly orientation and a decent amount of snowmaking, snow is relatively assured. There are plans to have 100% snowmaking on the slopes within the next few seasons. Grooming is good.

Experts This isn't a great area for experts, but there are off-piste freeride areas marked on the map in both Arinsal and Pal – the latter offering some great tree skiing. Arcalis has more to offer.

Intermediates Arinsal offers a fair range of difficulty, but decent intermediates will want to explore the much more interesting, varied and extensive Pal and Arcalis slopes.

The rolling wooded slopes of Pal are reminiscent of many American resorts →
EMAP (ESTACIONS DE MUNTANYA DÍ ARINSAL-PAL)

UK PACKAGES

Crystal, Directski.com, First Choice, Inghams, Neilson, Simply Alpine, Ski McNeill, Skitracer, STC, Thomson

Phone numbers
From abroad use the prefix +376

TOURIST OFFICES

Arinsal and Pal
t 737020
info@vallnordturisme.com
www.vallnord.com

Beginners Around half the guests here are beginners. Arinsal and Pal both have gentle nursery slopes set apart from the main runs, but they can get crowded at peak times. There are long easy runs to progress to, as well.

Snowboarding Over half the lifts are drags, and some of them are vicious. There are some flat sections in Pal.

Cross-country There isn't any.

Mountain restaurants These are mainly self-service snackeries, and crowded; the Bella Italia in Pal does 'tasty pizzas'. There is said to be a BBQ at Comallempla when weather permits.

Schools and guides Over half the instructors are native English speakers. The reports we have are nearly all positive – 'one of the best'; 'first class'. But groups can be large – 'average of 15' says a recent reporter. Another visitor liked his instructor's 'laid back approach', but a friend's beginner wife was 'left on the mountain to make her own way down'.

Families There are themed ski kindergartens for four to eight year olds and nurseries for children one to four at both Pal and Arinsal.

STAYING THERE

There is a wide choice of hotel and self-catering packages.

Hotels The Princesa Parc (736500), a big, glossy 4-star place a walkable distance from the gondola, with a swanky spa and a bowling alley, gets good reviews – 'good quality food; helpful, polite staff; room was palatial'. Rooms in the hotel Arinsal (835640) are not large, but it is well run, ideally placed and has a pleasant bar. The Xalet Verdú (737140) is a smooth little 3-star. The Micolau (835052) is a characterful stone house near the centre with a jolly, beamed restaurant. The 3-star Crest (835866) at the bottom of the valley run is more attractive now that there is a fast chair up to the main slopes.

Self-catering There is a reasonable choice of places.

Eating out The Surf disco-pub and the Rocky Mountain do good steaks. El Cisco is a Tex-Mex place in a lovely wood and stone building. El Rusc and Micolau do good food. Quo Vadis is recommended for pizza.

Après-ski Arinsal has plenty of lively bars and discos. We hear most about Quo Vadis ('great fun'). Others include El Cau, Surf, Rocky Mountain and El Cisco. El Derby is heaving on karaoke night. For a quiet drink, head for the bar of the hotel Arinsal.

Off the slopes There are helicopter rides, dog sledding, snowmobiling and snowshoeing, but a past reporter felt that family entertainment was limited in the evenings. Andorra la Vella is half an hour away by infrequent bus or inexpensive taxi.

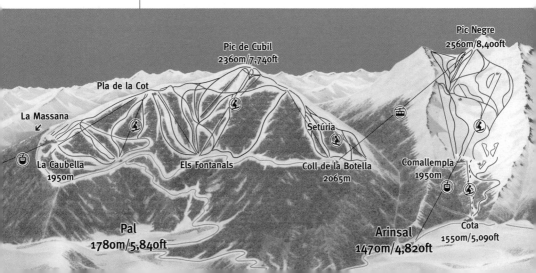

Pic Negre 2560m/8,400ft
Pic de Cubil 2360m/7,740ft
Pla de la Cot
La Massana
Setúria
La Caubella 1950m
Els Fontanals
Coll de la Botella 2065m
Comallempla 1950m
Pal 1780m/5,840ft
Arinsal 1470m/4,820ft
Cota 1550m/5,090ft

Pas de la Casa

Andorra's liveliest resort – great if you like that kind of thing; we prefer to ski the extensive Grandvalira ski area from a quieter base

➕ Grandvalira area including Soldeu rivals major Alps resorts for size

➕ Some conveniently placed hotels

➕ Andorra's liveliest nightlife

➕ Attractive hotel at Grau Roig

➖ Pas is an eyesore and suffers from traffic (and fumes)

➖ Weekend crowds from France

➖ Very few woodland slopes – unpleasant in bad weather

TOP 10 RATINGS

Extent	★★★
Fast lifts	★★
Queues	★★★
Snow	★★★★
Expert	★
Intermediate	★★★
Beginner	★★★★
Charm	★
Convenience	★★★★
Scenery	★★★

NEWS

For 2008/09 new ice bars opened at the foot of the slopes in Pas de la Casa and in Grau Roig – a new igloo hotel opened here, too, and the Grau Roig hotel opened an exclusive little restaurant focusing on great wines. New ice rinks opened at Pas de la Casa and Grau Roig.

GRANDVALIRA

Pas has a bleak setting, but its treeless slopes link over the pass to the mixed terrain of Grau Roig and Soldeu ↓

The tour op brochures (and the few readers' reports we get) all say that Pas is Andorra's wildest party resort, and we don't doubt it. Having driven through it and skied down to it, we are quite happy to stay over the hill in Soldeu – or, for doorstep access to the Grandvalira slopes, at secluded Grau Roig.

THE RESORT

Sited right on the border between Andorra and France, Pas de la Casa owes its development as much to duty-free sales to the French as to skiing. The resort attracts a lot of French and Spanish families, as well as Brits on a budget. The slopes extend over a ridge to the mini-resort of Grau Roig (pronounced 'Rosh') with links over further ridges to Soldeu – the whole are operating under the name Grandvalira. You can now drive to central Andorra via a toll tunnel, which avoids the high Port d'Envalira pass.

Village charm The resort is a sizeable collection of dreary concrete-box-style apartment blocks and hotels, a product of the late 1960s and early 1970s. One reporter draws attention to 'loads of restaurants with plastic-covered faded images of burgers and chips'. Yum. The central area at the base of the slopes is now traffic-free, but elsewhere traffic and fumes are intrusive. Grau Roig is completely different – an isolated hotel in attractively wooded setting.

Convenience Most accommodation is conveniently placed near the lift base and slopes. There are plenty of shops and bars, as well as a sports centre.
Scenery Pas has a bleak position near the top of a high mountain pass, but there are fine views from the ridges.

THE MOUNTAINS

The Grandvalira ski area offers an extensive 193km/120 miles of pistes – comparable to big-name Alpine resorts such as Kitzbühel and Les Deux-Alpes. With the exception of a couple of attractively wooded slopes in the central valley, the slopes above Pas are all open, and vulnerable to bad weather. Soldeu is more sheltered.
Slopes The home slopes, facing northeast, descend from a high, north–south ridge; lifts go up to it at four points. Runs on the far side of the ridge converge on Grau Roig, where there is some wooded terrain at the head of the valley. And a single lift goes on further west to the bowl of Llac del Cubill and the rest of the Grandvalira ski area. On the far side of this bowl is the arrival station of the 6km/4 mile gondola up from Encamp. In the opposite direction out of Pas, a newish six-pack is the start of expansion over the French border – on the left side of our map – called Porte des Neiges. The final plan is to have three chairlifts, a gondola, 50km/31 miles of slopes, 12 runs and the largest beginner area in the Pyrenees.
Fast lifts Pas has just three fast chairs.
Queues Queues are rarely serious during the week. But at weekends and French school holidays some can develop, especially at Grau Roig – confirmed by a recent visitor.

KEY FACTS

Resort	2100m 6,890ft
Grandvalira (Soldeu/ El Tarter/Pas/Grau Roig)	
Slopes	1710-2560m 5,610-8,400ft
Lifts	67
Pistes	193km 120 miles
Green	16%
Blue	35%
Red	29%
Black	20%
Snowmaking	43%

UK PACKAGES

Crystal, Directski.com, First Choice, Independent Ski Links, Inghams, Neilson, Simply Alpine, Ski McNeill, Skitracer, Thomson

Phone numbers
From abroad use the prefix +376

Central reservations phone number
For all resort accommodation call 801074

TOURIST OFFICE

t 871900
info@grandvalira.com
www.grandvalira.com

Terrain parks There's a slope-style area with jumps at Grau Roig, the Isards terrain park and a boardercross at Pas.
Snow reliability The combination of height and lots of snowmaking means good snow reliability and a season that often lasts until late April. But on both our visits the snow has been better in the Soldeu sector.
Experts There are few challenges on-piste – the black runs are rarely of serious steepness, and moguls are sparse. But there seem to be plenty of off-piste slopes inviting exploration – above Grau Roig, in particular.
Intermediates The local slopes cater for confident intermediates best, with plenty of top-to-bottom reds on the main ridge; they lack variety – and can be tricky for more timid intermediates, for whom Soldeu makes a better base.
Beginners There are beginner slopes in Pas and Grau Roig. The Pas area is a short but inconvenient bus ride out of town. Progression to longer runs is easier in the Grau Roig sector.
Snowboarding Boarding is popular with the young crowd the resort attracts. Drags are usually avoidable.
Cross-country There are loops totalling 13km/8 miles near Grau Roig.
Mountain restaurants There are routine places on the ridge above Pas and the top of the gondola from Encamp but also a couple of small places labelled 'restaurants with charm'. The Rifugi dels Llacs dels Pessons at the head of the Grau Roig bowl is a cosy, beamed table-service place with excellent food.
Schools and guides The ski school has a high reputation – good English.

Families There are ski kindergartens at Pas and Grau Roig, and a non-ski one at the latter.

STAYING THERE

There are lots of hotels and apartments and a few chalets.
Hotels Himàlaia-Pas (735 515) is the place we hear most about: 'good position, nice bar, reasonable food, comfy rooms'; and a pool. Beware of hotels catering for the 18-30 crowd. The Grau Roig hotel (755 556) is in a league of its own.
Apartments The Frontera Blanca are simple, but at the foot of the slopes.
Eating out It's not a resort for gourmets – though we've had reports of 'good charcuterie and paella' and 'quail and foie gras'. Local tips include Cal Padrí (Catalan food), KSB (good grills), Tagliatelle (pizza and pasta) and Chez Paulo (French cuisinc). One reader was impressed by the 'friendly and welcoming' attitude of staff.
Après-ski Après-ski is very lively, at least at peak holiday times (a March visitor found the resort 'quite quiet'). The Grandvalira website has a very helpful page describing about eight clubs and bars – and listing a smaller number with 'a very British feel'. Then there's Paddy's Irish Pub.
Off the slopes You can go dog sledding, snowmobiling and snowshoeing; otherwise there's visiting the leisure centre, shopping (check out that website again), or taking a trip to Andorra la Vella for more serious and stylish shopping.

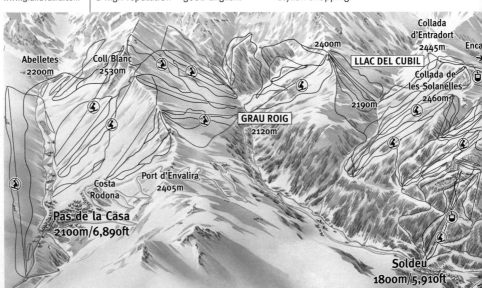

SNOWPIX.COM / CHRIS GILL

Soldeu

Our favourite place to stay in Andorra: a reasonably pleasant village, centrally placed in the impressive Grandvalira ski area

£95
RESORT PRICE INDEX

RATINGS

The mountains

Extent	★★★
Fast lifts	★★
Queues	★★★
Terrain p'ks	★★★★
Snow	★★★
Expert	★
Intermediate	★★★
Beginner	★★★★
X-country	★
Restaurants	★★
Schools	★★★★★
Families	★★

The resort

Charm	★
Convenience	★★★
Scenery	★★★
Eating out	★★★
Après-ski	★★★★
Off-slope	★

GRANDVALIRA

Dense forest above El Tarter; the main piste you can see is a black, but doesn't deserve to be ↓

- ➕ Grandvalira area including Pas de la Casa rivals major Alps resorts in terms of size
- ➕ Not as rowdy as it once was
- ➕ Excellent beginner and early intermediate terrain
- ➕ Ski school has excellent British-run section for English-speaking visitors

- ➖ Slopes can get very crowded
- ➖ Very little to interest experts
- ➖ Intrusive through traffic
- ➖ No longer cheap – and the lift pass is one of the dearest in Europe
- ➖ Some hotels are way out of town
- ➖ Not much to do off the slopes

If we were planning a holiday in Andorra, it would be in Soldeu (or the isolated hotel at Grau Roig, up the road – covered in the Pas de la Casa chapter). It is in the best position to make full use of the extensive Grandvalira area shared with neighbouring Pas de la Casa; with 193km/120 miles of pistes, this is only just outside our ★★★★ category. And it has some attractive central hotels. But it no longer offers a cheap holiday, especially for beginners.

THE RESORT

Soldeu is set on a steep hillside lining the busy road that runs down the valley from France to Andorra la Vella and on to Spain, facing the ski area across the valley. El Tarter, a few miles down the valley, and Canillo, a few miles further, are alternative bases with major lifts. The slopes link with Pas de la Casa via Grau Roig – see separate chapter – to form the Grandvalira area. Outings to other resorts in Andorra are possible, and Arcalis in particular is worth the trip, but it's easiest by car.

VILLAGE CHARM ★
Mainly hotels

The village is an ever-growing ribbon of modern buildings with traditional stone cladding; there is little focus or atmosphere, and traffic on the through-road is heavy and sometimes fast. Most buildings are hotels, apartments or bars, with the occasional shop.

CONVENIENCE ★★★
Hill start

A steep hillside leads down from the village to the river, and the slopes are on the opposite side. A gondola or a

For 2008/09 at Encamp a new service building opened at the base of the gondola, containing a ski school, a kids' snow garden and equipment rental shops. A new beginner area was opened at Encamp too. A terrain park-only lift pass was introduced, though it's not exactly cheap.

six-pack takes you to the heart of the slopes at Espiolets, and a wide bridge across the river forms the end of the piste home, with elevators to take you up to the gondola. A lot of people leave their skis, boots and boards at the bottom or top of the gondola. Along the road down to El Tarter, hotels and apartments are being built and sold under the Soldeu banner – so check where your proposed accommodation is if you want to avoid long walks or lots of bus rides. There is a timetabled valley bus covered by the pass, but it is neither frequent nor reliable.

SCENERY ★★★ ★★
Unremarkable

Soldeu sits in a long, quite attractively wooded valley – more hospitable than Pas de la Casa's setting – and from the slopes there are wide mountain views, but they don't include much of a dramatic nature.

THE MOUNTAINS

Soldeu's main local slopes are on open mountainsides above the woods; there are runs in the woods back to most of the lift bases, but they can be challenging especially when conditions are not particularly good.

EXTENT OF THE SLOPES ★★★ ★★
Pleasantly varied but crowded

The gondola rises over wooded, north-facing slopes to **Espiolets**, a broad shelf that is virtually a mini-resort – the ski school is based here, and there are extensive nursery slopes. From Espiolets, a gentle run to the east takes you to an area of long, easy runs served by a six-pack. Beyond that is an extensive area of more varied slopes that links with the Pas de la Casa area. Going west from Espiolets takes you to the open bowl of **Riba Escorxada** and the arrival point of the gondola up from El Tarter. From here,

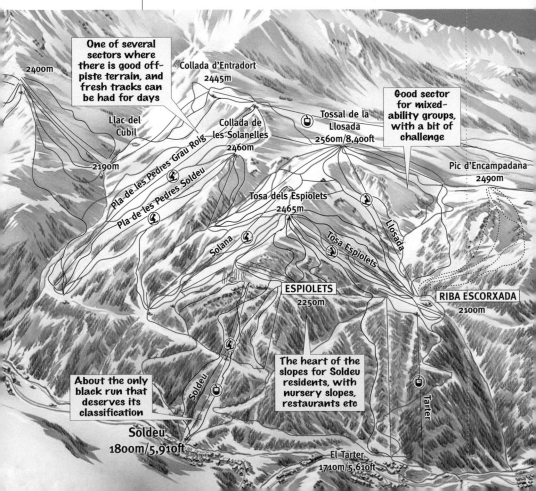

KEY FACTS

Resort	1800m
	5,910ft

Grandvalira (Soldeu/
El Tarter/Pas/Grau
Roig)

Slopes	1710-2560m
	5,610-8,400ft
Lifts	67
Pistes	193km
	120 miles
Green	16%
Blue	35%
Red	29%
Black	20%
Snowmaking	43%

another six-pack serves sunny slopes on Tosa dels Espiolets and a fourth goes to the high point of Tossal de la Llosada and the link with **El Forn** above Canillo.

FAST LIFTS ★★☆☆☆
Fine access but ...
Most of Grandvalira's key lifts are high-speed chairs or gondolas, but there are a lot of slow lifts too, particularly up at altitude.

QUEUES ★★★☆☆
Crowds more of a problem
The lift system generally copes. There can be morning queues for the gondola but the next-door chair offers a choice. Up the mountain, the chairlifts in both directions out of Grau Roig are the main bottleneck. More of a problem than queues are the crowds on the blue slopes (including lots of school classes snaking along) – the reds and blacks are much quieter.

TERRAIN PARKS ★★★★☆
A good one
The terrain park situated just above Riba Escorxada is fast gaining a good reputation. The shaping crew service it daily, as well as organising frequent events there. In 2009 a freestyle day pass was introduced. The triple line of kickers that ranges between 8m and 16m (26ft and 52ft) is well maintained. A huge gap jump to a jib feature is now a regular feature in the park, as is the giant air bag, where you can test new tricks out before you take them to the steep landings. There is a great selection of rails including a big rainbow rail and wave-box and two wall rides. For beginners there are three small jumps culminating in a 5m/16ft medium jump and a couple of fun boxes. The half-pipe is touch-and-go depending on snowfall. A draglift services the park, but there is also a speedy quad that takes you slightly higher up the hill.

Pic d'Encampadana
2490m

Pic de la Portella
2465m

Refreshingly quiet slopes, and the black could easily be a red

Funicamp

Portella

Encamp
1300m/4,270ft

Junior

RIBA ESCORXADA
2100m

If you're lucky you may find a snowcat giving rides up to the top of these off-piste routes

EL FORN
2000m

Encamp is a cheap base, and the gondola ride – though long – isn't quite as long as it looks here

Canillo

Tarter

Canillo
1500m/4,920ft

LIFT PASSES

Grandvalira

Prices in €

Age	1-day	6-day
under 12	31	148
12 to 64	44	214
over 65	18	108

Free under 6, over 70
Beginner pass in each sector for beginners' area €25 per day

Notes
Covers all lifts in Soldeu, El Tarter, Canillo, Grau Roig and Pas de la Casa; pedestrian and local day and half-day passes available

Alternative passes
The Ski Andorra pass covers all Andorran areas and allows skiing at any single one of them each day; €187 for five non-consecutive days

UK PACKAGES

Crystal, Directski.com, Elegant Resorts, First Choice, Independent Ski Links, Inghams, Neilson, Simply Alpine, Ski McNeill, Skitracer, STC, Thomson
El Tarter *First Choice, Inghams, Neilson*

boarding

Soldeu has become the home of snowboarding in the Pyrenees. This is a perfect place for beginners to learn on wide, gentle slopes served mainly by chairs not drags. For the more advanced, Soldeu offers some good off-piste, steeper areas and the best snow park in the Pyrenees. However, true backcountry enthusiasts should head to Arcalis, which has the steepest terrain and heli-boarding, or to Pal. Soldeu's snowboard shop Loaded, run by British pro and Andorran resident Tyler Chorlton, is a real hub in the area, and the staff will give you plenty of pointers.

SNOW RELIABILITY ★★★
Much better than people expect
Despite its name (Soldeu means Sun God) the slopes generally enjoy reliable snow. Most slopes are north-facing, with a good natural snow record (though they've recently had a couple of poor years) and there's snowmaking on 43% of the pistes. The generally excellent grooming helps maintain good snow. But last year and this we have had complaints about poor conditions on the lower slopes.

FOR EXPERTS ★
Hope for good snow off-piste
It's a limited area for experts, at least on-piste. The improved Avet black run down to Soldeu deserves its grading, but most of the other blacks would be no more than reds (or even blues) in many resorts. The blacks on Tosa dels Espiolets are indistinguishable from the neighbouring (and more direct) red and blue, for example. And don't go looking for moguls – the grooming is too thorough. But there is plenty of off-piste potential – notably in the bowl above Riba Escorxada, in the Espiolets and Solanelles areas (we had a great time there in fresh powder on our last visit), and above El Forn. And the off-piste remains untouched for days because most visitors are beginners and early intermediates. When conditions permit at weekends, a snowcat takes people up to Pic d'Encampadana, from where four off-piste routes (dotted on our map) descend to Riba Escorxada.

FOR INTERMEDIATES ★★★
Explore Grandvalira
There is plenty to amuse all but the very keenest intermediates. The area east of Espiolets is splendid for building confidence, and those already confident will be able to explore the whole mountain. Riba Escorxada is a fine section for mixed-ability groups. The Canillo/El Forn sector has an easy, little-used blue run along the ridge

with excellent views all the way to Pal and Arinsal and an easy black in the valley. Many of the blues and reds have short steeper sections, preceded by a 'slow' sign and netting in the middle of the piste to slow you down.

FOR BEGINNERS ★★★★
One of the best
In some respects this is an excellent place to start, particularly because of the school. But it's not ideal: you have to go up the mountain to the nursery slopes, which is not only inconvenient but also expensive. The beginner passes are not cheap, and our current understanding is that they are not sold on the spot, but must be bought in the UK, through tour operators. One reporter had no alternative but to buy a full weekly pass, which is a huge waste of money for a beginner. Soldeu's Espiolets nursery area is vast, and there's a smaller area at Riba Escorxada, above El Tarter (which one reader reckons is better) – both with a moving carpet. They are relatively snow-sure, and there are numerous easy pistes to move on to (though the crowds can be off-putting). The runs to resort level can be quite challenging, though, because of crowds and snow conditions, and novices are often better off riding a lift down.

FOR CROSS-COUNTRY ★
Er, what cross-country?
There are loops not far away at Grau Roig (see the Pas de la Casa chapter), reachable by bus.

MOUNTAIN RESTAURANTS ★★
Not a highlight
The mountain restaurants are generally crowded and monotonous but there are increasing numbers of exceptions. A reporter rates the table-service section of Pi de Migdia at the top of the El Tarter gondola 'worth the extra cost' for its 'relaxed atmosphere and courteous staff'. Not far away the Riba Escorxada restaurant has been

Soldeu

SCHOOLS

Soldeu
t 753191

Classes
15hr: €115

Private lessons
€75 for 1hr for 1 person; €6 extra per additional person

CHILDCARE

Nurseries run by ski school
Ages 1 to 4; 2hr €18

Snow gardens run by ski school
Ages 3 to 7; five days €148

Ski school
For ages 6 to 11; 15hr: €105

GETTING THERE

Air Toulouse 170km/110 miles 2hr45)

Rail L'Hospitalet-Près-L'Andorre (25km/16 miles); buses and taxis to Soldeu

ACTIVITIES

Indoor Thermal spas, bowling (at Pas), leisure centre (pools, hot tub, gym)

Outdoor Helicopter rides, snowmobiling, dog sledding, snowshoeing, paragliding, paintballing, archery, igloo building

Phone numbers
From abroad use the prefix +376
Central reservations phone number
Call 801074

TOURIST OFFICE

t 890500
info@grandvalira.com
www.grandvalira.com

revamped to include a 'light and airy' trattoria-pizzeria with a neat little terrace. At Espiolets, there is table service at Gall de Bosc.

SCHOOLS AND GUIDES ★★★★★
One of the best for Brits
The school is well set up to deal with the huge numbers of beginner Brits, with a dedicated team of mostly native English-speaking instructors led by an Englishman. This year's reporters include one who was 'unimpressed', but we also had two of the usual endorsements: 'could not praise the school enough'; 'by the end of the week our two beginners were skiing parallel on red runs'.

FOR FAMILIES ★★★★★
Unconvincing
Soldeu doesn't strike us as a great place for families, with its busy through-road and remote slopes. Whether skiing or not, children are looked after at the mid-mountain stations. There are nurseries and snow gardens at various points, and a kids' circuit with themed runs at Riba Escorxada above El Tarter.

STAYING THERE

A wide range of UK tour operators offer packages here, mainly in hotels but with some apartments and chalets.
Hotels The best hotels are of a far better standard than a decade ago.
★★★★★Sport Hotel Hermitage (870550) Newish, at the foot of the slopes; all bedrooms are suites with mountain views. A huge spa is part of the hotel.
★★★★Sport Hotel Village (870500) Right by the Hermitage. Stylish public areas – comfortable chairs and sofas, high ceilings, beams and picture windows.
★★★★Sport (870600) Over the road from the other two Sports. Lively, comfortable bar and a popular disco-bar. But dull buffet-style food.
★★★★Piolets Park (871787) Right next to the gondola, with a pool. 'Good buffet-style food.'
★★★★Himàlaia (878515) Refurbished, central, with sauna, steam and hot tub. A reporter is 'very impressed – excellent food, helpful staff'.

EATING OUT ★★★★★
Some atmospheric places
We lack recent reports, but we've enjoyed meals in two atmospheric old restored buildings: British-run Fat

Albert's (steaks, fish, burgers), and Borda del Rector (Andorran-run and with authentic Andorran cuisine), nearer to El Tarter than Soldeu. Check out the Grandvalira website.

APRES-SKI ★★★★★
Lively
There isn't a great Austrian-style end-of-day après-ski scene – no umbrella bars at the foot of the slopes. But before long the many bars with happy hours quickly fill up, and a 'lively but not loutish' evening ensues. Fat Albert's often has a live band, and is very popular – too much so for one reporter, who thought it hazardous. The Piccadilly, under the Sport hotel, is popular, with 'friendly staff and live bands'. The Aspen and the next-door Avalanche attract a younger crowd. A trusted reporter endorses our liking for the Villager – 'spacious, airy, convivial but not such a young clientele'. Expect noise in the streets late at night.

OFF THE SLOPES ★★★★★
Head downhill
One group reports a 'wonderful evening sliding around on tubes and sledges' at Riba Escorxada. There is the spa in Soldeu itself. Down in Canillo is the Palau de Gel; in Escaldes-Engordany, there's the impressive Caldea thermal spa; and in Andorra la Vella serious shopping.

El Tarter 1710m/5,610ft

El Tarter has grown over recent years and is rather sprawling, with no real centre. It is 'dull at night'.

Canillo 1500m/4,920ft

This acceptably pleasant spot has no runs to valley level, but has the impressive Palau de Gel – an Olympic ice rink plus pool, gym, tennis etc.

Austria

Austria's holiday recipe is quite distinctive. It doesn't suit everybody, but for many holidaymakers nothing else will do; in particular, France won't do. Austria is the land of cute little villages clustered around onion-domed churches – there are no monstrous, purpose-built, apartment blocks here. It's the land of friendly wooded mountains, reassuring to beginners and timid intermediates in a way that bleak snowfields and craggy peaks will never be. It's the land of friendly, welcoming people who speak good English. And it's the land of jolly, alcohol-fuelled après-ski action – in many resorts starting in mid-afternoon with dancing in mountain restaurants and going on as long as you have the legs for it. It's also great value for money – in our eating and drinking price survey, with the sole exception of upmarket Lech, every other Austrian resort came out as average or below average for prices.

In general, Austria isn't the first place you'll want to consider if reliably good snow is your top priority – though there are some wonderful exceptions to this rule, including some of the world's best glacier areas (such as those at Hintertux, Kaprun and in the Stubai valley), high snow-sure ski areas (such as Obergurgl, Ischgl and Obertauern) and areas that get huge amounts of snow (such as Bregenzerwald, Lech and Zürs). But most resorts are relatively low, and conditions are more likely to be problematic here than in higher places. However, most low resorts have radically increased their snowmaking capacity in the last decade. In midwinter, especially, lack of snow generally coincides with low night-time temperatures, even at low altitudes, and snowmaking comes into its own. And recent seasons have included some bumper natural snow years for much of Austria.

It's the après-ski that strikes most first-time visitors as being Austria's unique selling point. Huge quantities of beer and schnapps are drunk, German is the predominant language, and German drinking songs are common. So is loud Europop music. People pack into mountain restaurants well before the end of the day and gyrate in their ski boots on the dance floor, on the tables, on the bar. There are open-air ice bars, umbrella bars and countless transparent 'igloo' bars in which to shelter from bad weather. In many resorts the bands don't stop playing until darkness falls, when the happy punters slide off in the general direction of the village to find another watering hole. After dinner the drinking and dancing starts again – for those who pause for dinner, that is.

Of course, not all resorts conform to this image. Lech and Zürs, for example, are full of rich, cool, 'beautiful' people enjoying the comfort of 4- or 5-star hotels. And resorts such as Westendorf and Alpbach are pretty, quiet, family resorts. But lots of big-name places with the best and most extensive slopes are also big party towns – notably St Anton, Saalbach-Hinterglemm, Ischgl and Sölden.

Nightlife is not limited to drinking and dancing. There are lots of floodlit toboggan runs, and UK tour operator reps organise Tirolean, bowling, fondue, karaoke and other evenings.

One thing that all Austrian resorts have in common is reliably

SNOWPIX.COM / CHRIS GILL

← Austria has some of the best glaciers in the Alps, as well as hundreds of low, woodland resorts. This is Kaprun's Kitzsteinhorn, seen from Zell am See

comfortable accommodation – whether it's in 4- or 5-star hotels with pools, saunas and spas or in great-value, family-run guest houses, of which Austria has thousands. Catered chalets and self-catering apartments are in general much less widely available.

The Germanic aversion to credit cards causes problems for many of our reporters. Many establishments do not accept cards – even quite upmarket hotels, as well as many ski lift companies. So check well in advance, and be prepared to pay in cash.

Austrian resorts are now easier to get to independently using cheap flights. The standard arrival airports are Munich, Salzburg, Innsbruck and, for western resorts, Zürich. But don't overlook less well-known airports such as Klagenfurt in Carinthia and Friedrichshafen, just over the German border and handy for resorts in western Austria such as St Anton, Lech and Ischgl.

↑ For medieval town charm, Kitzbühel takes some beating

TVB KITZBÜHEL / M MITTERER

A SHAMBLES: SMOKING LAWS AND SKI ROUTES

Since the start of 2009, smoking restrictions have at last applied to bars, night clubs, restaurants and hotels. The general rules are that in 'multiple room establishments' the 'main room' has to be non-smoking. In places with only one room, if it's under 50m² the owner can decide whether or not smoking is allowed; if it's over 80m², it must be no-smoking, although owners have until June 2010 to build a separate room for smokers, and until then smoking can continue. Between 50m² and 80m², it's more complicated. Reports welcome on what happens this winter!

With ski routes, things are also shambolic. If the piste map explains what a ski route is (and some don't), it often says a ski route is marked, avalanche controlled but not groomed or patrolled. And some we skied on the Stubai glacier in January were certainly not groomed. But those we skied in Bregenzerwald in January were all groomed (and many had more people on them than on normal pistes). And those we skied in St Anton and Lech in April were groomed; but we were told by locals that other ski routes were never groomed. So we looked into it and were told that the rule throughout Austria is that a ski route is 'marked, protected against avalanche hazards (but not other hazards) and can be (but doesn't have to be) groomed and patrolled'. Well, that's great – so the official answer is you can never be sure whether a ski route is going to be groomed or patrolled, so you don't know whether you can safely ski it alone or not; and it opens up the insane possibility that you might descend a groomed run that is not patrolled. Madness.

Salzburgerland's Ski Amadé lift pass is one of the world's biggest in terms of the amount of terrain and number of lifts covered. What's more, with a car you really could aim to get around most of the resorts it covers – they are clustered close together, no high passes are involved in getting from one resort to another, and many areas are geared to people arriving by car, with out-of-town lifts and serious car parks. (They are also conveniently close to Salzburg airport – we have taken early flights and been on the slopes before lunchtime; come departure day, we have skied until the end of the day, had a leisurely drive to the airport and still had time to kill before a late flight home.)

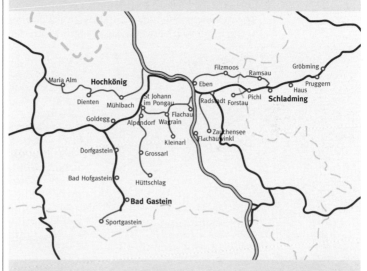

Some of the major resorts covered by the pass have their own chapters in the pages that follow. In the Schladming chapter we also cover the smaller linked resorts of Haus in Ennstal and Pichl, as well as Schladming's elevated outpost of Rohrmoos. Also close to Schladming is Ramsau in Dachstein, which has slopes at village level but also a lift up to the lip of the Dachstein glacier. In the Bad Gastein chapter we cover not only the resorts in the Gastein valley but also the next-door valley of Grossarl, which is linked over the hill to Dorfgastein.

We also have a chapter on the major area of Hochkönig. This is now being marketed as High King Mountain to the British market and has an extensive network of runs linking Mühlbach, Dienten and Maria Alm.

Another big region is the Salzburger Sportwelt. The largest linked area here is the 200km/124 mile three-valley system linking Wagrain to Flachau (home of Hermann Maier) in one direction and Alpendorf/St Johann im Pongau in the other. This area also embraces an extensive lift network linking Zauchensee, Flachauwinkl and Kleinarl, plus more modest lift systems at Filzmoos, Radstadt-Altenmarkt, Eben and Goldegg. We skied the Zauchensee and Flachauwinkl slopes for a day and enjoyed it in excellent snow (Zauchensee often has the best snow in the region because of its height and north-facing slopes).

Considering the extent of the lift networks it covers (and the generally impressive efficiency of the lifts) the Ski Amadé pass is not expensive – 196 euros in high season. Prices on the spot are cheap as well. In our eating and drinking price survey, resorts in the Ski Amadé region came out among the cheapest in the Alps – with prices some 20 or 25 per cent cheaper than the average resort.

Introduction

117

Interactive resort shortlist builder at **www.wtss.co.uk**

GETTING AROUND THE AUSTRIAN ALPS

Austria presents few problems for the car-borne visitor, because practically all the resorts are valley villages, which involve neither steep approach roads nor high altitude.

The dominant feature of Austria for the ski driver is the thoroughfare of the Inn valley, which runs through the Tirol from Landeck via Innsbruck to Kufstein. The motorway along it extends, with one or two breaks, westwards to the Arlberg pass and on to Switzerland. This artery is relatively reliable except in exceptionally bad conditions – the altitude is low, and the road is a vital transport link that is kept open in virtually all conditions.

The Arlberg – which divides Tirol from Vorarlberg, but which is also the watershed between Austria and Switzerland – is one of the

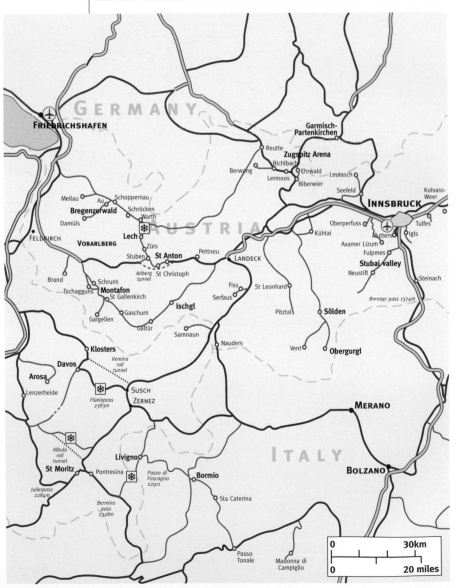

few areas where driving plans are likely to be seriously affected by snow. The east–west Arlberg pass itself has a long tunnel underneath it; this isn't cheap, and you may want to take the high road when it's clear, through Stuben, St Christoph and St Anton. The Flexen pass road to Zürs and Lech (which may be closed by avalanche risk even when the Arlberg pass is open) branches off just to the west of the Arlberg summit.

At the eastern end of the Tirol, the Gerlos pass road from Zell im Zillertal over into Salzburg province can be closed. Resorts in Carinthia, such as Bad Kleinkirchheim, are usually reached by motorway, thanks to the Tauern and Katschberg tunnels. The alternative is the Radstädter Tauern pass through Obertauern, or the car-carrying rail service from Böckstein to Mallnitz.

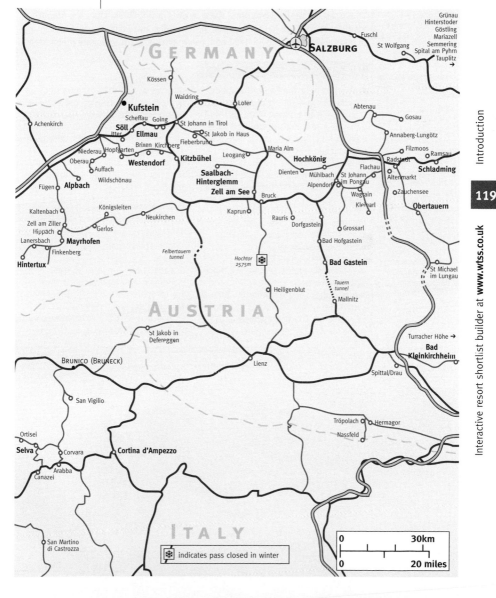

❄ indicates pass closed in winter

0 ———— 30km

0 ———— 20 miles

Alpbach

Small but perfectly formed: it's the pretty village rather than the extent of the slopes that have attracted generations of Brits

➕ Charming, traditional, relaxed village – great for young children

➕ Handy, central nursery slopes

➕ Several other worthwhile resorts within day-trip distance

➕ Good, intermediate terrain, not without challenges, but ...

➖ Slopes limited in extent and variety

➖ Main slopes are a shuttle-bus-ride away (efficient service, though)

➖ Few long easy runs for beginners to progress to

➖ Lower slopes can suffer from poor snow, despite snowmaking help

TOP 10 RATINGS

Extent	★☆☆☆☆
Fast lifts	★★★☆☆
Queues	★★★☆☆
Snow	★★☆☆☆
Expert	★☆☆☆☆
Intermediate	★★☆☆☆
Beginner	★★★★☆
Charm	★★★★★
Convenience	★★☆☆☆
Scenery	★★★☆☆

NEWS

For 2009/10 the free guest card, the Saanland, is being improved – giving free use of the public pool, bus, two nursery lifts for kids up to 15 years old and various other incentives.

For 2008/09 a new mid-station was added to the gondola up from Inneralpbach. And there's now night skiing at Reith three times a week.

This is an old British favourite – there is even a British ski club, the Alpbach Visitors. The village is small, pretty and friendly, and inspires great loyalty in regular visitors – one who has been going since 1983 claims only junior status.

THE RESORT

Alpbach is near the head of a valley, looking south across it towards the slopes of Wiedersbergerhorn. The Inn valley is a few miles north, and trips east to Kitzbühel or west to Innsbruck are possible. The Hintertux and Stubaier glaciers are within reach. If you are planning a tour, bear in mind that the Kitzbüheler Alpen All Star pass covers Alpbach and six other regions including the Ski Welt (Söll, Ellmau etc) and Kitzbühel. The local free guest card is worth picking up from your hotel too (see 'News').

Village charm Alpbach is an exceptionally pretty, captivating place; traditional chalets crowd around the pretty church, and the friendly nursery slopes are only a few steps away.

Convenience The main village is the place to stay for atmosphere and après-ski, but it involves using a free shuttle-bus to and from Achenwirt, a mile away, where a gondola goes up to Hornboden – though reporters seem happy with the service. The backwater hamlet of Inneralpbach is more convenient for the slopes, with its own gondola up the mountain.

Scenery Alpbach's pretty valley and low, partly wooded ridges are picture-postcard Tirol.

THE MOUNTAINS

Alpbach's slopes, on two flanks of the Wiedersbergerhorn, are small and simple.

Slopes The two gondolas from Achenwirt and Inneralpbach take you up to open, north-facing slopes above the treeline, served by chairs and drags. The runs are mostly of 200m to 400m (660ft to 1,310ft) vertical, but

WIEDERSBERGERHORN
2025m/6,640ft

Gmahkopf 1900m

Hornboden 1850m

Inneralpbach
1050m/3,440ft

1230m

Böglalm

REITH
1280m/4,200ft

1345m

Wölzenberg

Alpbach
1000m/3,280ft

Achenwirt
830m

Reith im Alpbachtal
670m/2,200ft

KEY FACTS	
Resort	1000m
	3,280ft
Slopes	670-2025m
	2,200-6,640ft
Lifts	21
Pistes	54km
	32 miles
Blue	27%
Red	63%
Black	10%
Snowmaking	71%

you can get more by descending to the bottom of the gondolas when snow is good down to valley level. Behind Gmahkopf is a short west-facing slope. A tiny separate area at Reith is on the lift pass and is 'well worth a morning's visit – well groomed and deserted', says a reporter. Access is by an eight-seat gondola. There's night skiing three times a week.

Fast lifts The only fast lifts are the two access gondolas – otherwise, it's all slow chairs and draglifts. A third gondola serves Reith.

Queues The gondolas make light work of any queues.

Terrain parks There's a half-pipe near the top of the Achenwirt gondola.

Snow reliability Alpbach cannot claim great snow reliability, but at least most of the Wiedersbergerhorn faces north, and 71% of the pistes are covered by snowmaking. The resort says this has helped to keep the runs to the valley open even in a poor snow year. The Inneralpbach gondola developed a mid-station last year, which you might think would facilitate skiing on the upper mountain there; but there is no news of a piste to the mid-station. Piste grooming is excellent.

Experts Alpbach isn't ideal, but the reds and the three blacks (often groomed) are not without challenge, and runs of 1000m/3,300ft vertical (when snow is good) are not to be sniffed at. There are a few off-piste routes to the valley, and the schools take the top classes off-piste. One reporter 'skied with a guide for three hours in untracked powder'.

Intermediates There is fine intermediate terrain; the problem is that there's not much of it. This resort is for practising technique on familiar slopes, not high mileage.

Beginners Beginners love the sunny nursery slopes beside the village. But

Weekly news updates and resort links at **www.wtss.co.uk**

↑ The slopes of Inneralpbach are only an off-piste run from the top of Auffach, from which point this shot was taken

DAVID MAXWELL-LEES

UK PACKAGES

Alpine Answers, Crystal, Inghams, Interhome, Simply Alpine, Skiing Austria

Phone numbers

From elsewhere in Austria add the prefix 05336; from abroad use the prefix +43 5336

TOURIST OFFICE

t 200941
alpbach@alpbachtal.at
www.alpbachtal.at

the main slopes are not ideal for confidence-building as most of them are classified red and there are only a few blues.

Snowboarding There's some good freeriding terrain.

Cross-country There are 20km/12 miles of pretty cross-country trails that rise up beyond Inneralpbach.

Mountain restaurants There are several mountain restaurants – each worth a visit. Reporters recommend the Böglalm and 'great food and service' at the Dauerstoa Alm.

Schools and guides We've had good reports in the past on both main schools, Alpbach and Alpbach Aktiv; the head of the Alpbach school is qualified to teach people with disabilities (and he himself has a disability).

Families Reporters find the compact, relaxed village and adjacent nursery slopes very child-friendly, with good ski kindergartens; babysitters can be arranged by the tourist office.

STAYING THERE

Hotels and pensions dominate in UK packages.

Hotels Of the smart 4-star places, the Alpbacherhof (5237) ('superb food and excellent service'), Alphof (5371) ('excellent, with friendly and welcoming staff') and ancient

Böglerhof (5227) get most votes. The Berghof (5275) has been praised as 'an excellent 3-star; only 20 metres from the nursery slopes'. The 3-star Post (5203) is 'better than a lot of 4-stars'. The simpler Haus Thomas (5944), Haus Angelika (5339) and Haus Theresia (5386) have also been recommended. Pension Edelweiss (5268) is close to the nursery slopes and offers B&B and 'clean, spacious, good value apartments'.

Apartments There are quite a few to choose from, easily bookable through the tourist office website.

Eating out The popular Post and Alphof have been recommended by a reporter, who also favoured the 'superb' Jakober. Wiedersbergerhorn in Inneralpbach has been recommended, as has the Rossmoos Inn for its lively Tirolean evenings, 'superb' food and the toboggan run back to the resort.

Après-ski At peak times this is typically Tirolean, with lots of noisy teatime beer swilling in the bars of central hotels such as the Jakober and the Post. The latter has regular live music. Joe's Salett'l is at Inneralpbach.

Off the slopes There are pretty walks, and trips to Innsbruck and Salzburg are possible. There is also an indoor swimming pool (free with the guest card) and an indoor ice rink (at Reith). The ski schools put on a 'ski show' once a week.

Bad Gastein

If you fancy 'taking the cure', there are few better resorts; even if you don't, you're likely to be impressed by the slopes

£80
RESORT PRICE INDEX

TOP 10 RATINGS

Extent	★★★★
Fast lifts	★★★
Queues	★★★
Snow	★★★
Expert	★★★
Intermediate	★★★★
Beginner	★★
Charm	★★★
Convenience	★★
Scenery	★★★

KEY FACTS

Resort	1080m
	3,540ft

The Gastein valley and Grossarl areas

Slopes	840-2685m
	2,760-8,810ft
Lifts	44
Pistes	201km
	125 miles
Blue	30%
Red	58%
Black	12%
Snowmaking	
	537 guns

Bad Gastein and Bad Hofgastein only

Slopes	860-2685m
	2,820-8,810ft
Lifts	26
Pistes	121km
	75 miles

Angertal is in many respects the focal point of the local slopes, with the best nursery slopes ↓

- ➕ Extensive, varied, often quiet slopes
- ➕ Excellent, testing long runs for confident intermediates
- ➕ More reliable snow than in most low-altitude Austrian resorts
- ➕ Lots of good, atmospheric, traditional mountain restaurants
- ➕ Excellent thermal spas, but ...

- ➖ Main resorts are spa towns, lacking the usual Austrian resort ambience
- ➖ Bad Gastein itself has a steep, confined setting and narrow streets
- ➖ Valley slopes are split into five areas, and having a car helps
- ➖ Timid intermediates and beginners are better off elsewhere

The Gastein valley is attracting more Brits and reporters seem impressed by what they find too. Rightly so – the slopes form one of Austria's bigger, more varied and more snow-sure areas. Steeply tiered Bad Gastein itself is a difficult place to like; we much prefer rustic Dorfgastein or spacious Bad Hofgastein – described here.

THE RESORT

Bad Gastein is an old spa town near the head of the Gastein valley. At its heart is the original spa area, laid out in a compact horseshoe on steep slopes. Above this, at the level of the railway, is a modern suburb with more of a ski resort feel.

The Stubnerkogel slopes above the town link with Bad Hofgastein, down the valley. Beyond that, a separate area of slopes above Dorfgastein links with Grossarl in the next valley. Up the valley is another separate area at Sportgastein. Various ski-bus routes connect the villages and lift stations, and these days are reportedly efficient – though some services stop early (eg Dorfgastein). Taxis are affordable. Lots of resorts in this region are covered by the Ski Amadé lift pass.

Village charm The core is a bizarre mix of towny buildings – some grand, some modest. Away from here, the more modern hotels and guest-houses have been built in chalet style.

Convenience The modern part has developed around the Stubnerkogel gondola, but the resort as a whole spreads widely. Across town, the double chair to the separate Graukogel area is a taxi ride from the centre.

Scenery The resort is set in virtually a gorge, steeply tiered and wooded. The mountains are higher than many Austrian resorts (particularly at Sportgastein), with good views.

THE MOUNTAINS

Most of the runs in the main area are on the open slopes above the treeline. This is a quite exposed part of the Alps, and wind can affect both the snow and the lifts. Sportgastein is entirely open, and higher, so more vulnerable. Graukogel is wooded.

Slopes A gondola (being upgraded for 2009/10) goes up to Stubnerkogel, where there are runs in several directions. There is a long blue run back to base, but most runs end up in Angertal, which links with the slopes of Bad Hofgastein. Graukogel is much smaller, but attractively quiet. We cover the slopes above Bad Hofgastein and Dorfgastein later in the chapter.

NEWS

For 2009/10 the Stubnerkogel gondola from Bad Gastein is to be replaced; eight-seat cabins will result in increased capacity. At Angertal snowmaking is being improved and the terrain park is being expanded.

At Dorfgastein, a six-pack is planned to replace the Fulseck T-bar.

For 2008/09 a two-stage, eight-seat gondola was installed from Angertal up to Stubnerkogel. A new red run opened there and a short blue from the mid-station down to Angertal – work will improve this blue for 2009/10, but a new black run being cut from Schlossalm to Angertal won't be ready in time.

Fast lifts New gondolas are improving access to Stubnerkogel (see 'News'). There are still quite a few draglifts, but most can be avoided.

Queues There are few major problems. The new gondola at Angertal has 'made a huge difference'.

Terrain parks There is a newish park; it's quiet and well-run, say reporters.

Snow reliability The area is higher than many Austrian rivals, and there is snowmaking on crucial sections. Grooming is fine.

Experts The few black runs are not severe, but many reds are long and satisfying. Graukogel has some of the most testing slopes. The other sectors have plenty of opportunity for off-piste. Sportgastein is worth the trip – notably for its long ski-route.

Intermediates Confident intermediates, will find long, leg-sapping runs throughout the valley. The timid are better off at Bad Hofgastein.

Beginners The main nursery area at Angertal is fine. But Bad Gastein Is not the best place for beginners: the local nursery slope is too steep and there are no free lifts. And the few easy runs to progress to are often boring paths.

Snowboarding The valley hosts snowboard events and there is good freeriding. Draglifts are dotted around.

Cross-country There are 90km/56 miles of trails, but they are all low down.

Mountain restaurants There are lots of pleasant huts; but they can get crowded. The Hirschenhütte just above Angertal on Stubnerkogel is said to be quieter. Jungerstube is still 'very good'. By contrast, the Stubnerkogelgipfel self-service is charmless, but has great views and 'decent food'.

Schools and guides Past reports on the school have been favourable, for both group and private lessons.

Families Facilities are quite good. Angertal has the school and a snow adventure park. Many of the huts have play areas too. There's also a kids 'Fun Centre' at the top of the Stubnerkogel gondola, with playstations and other activities. Day care is available.

STAYING THERE

Most lodging is hotel-based.

Hotels There are lots of smart 4- and 3-star hotels with spa facilities. The quite grand 4-star Elizabeth Park (25510) has been recommended. The Mozart (26860) is 'quirky, friendly with a brilliant chef'.The Grüner Baum (25160) is a lovely retreat, but wildly inconvenient except for langlauf (though they do have a hotel bus).

Eating out Choice is reasonable. The traditional Jägerhäusl is near the old town and has 'lovely food, large portions and helpful staff'. The Landhausstube Sonnenschein is new.

Après-ski The bars are lively at close

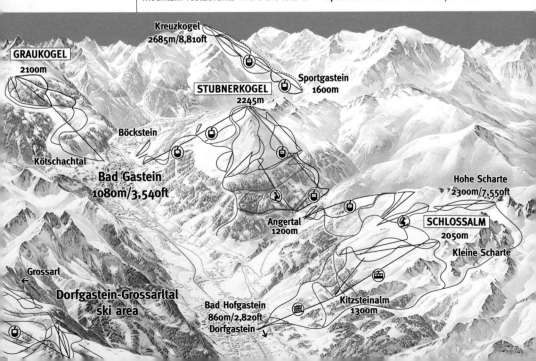

Alpine Answers,
Crystal, Crystal Finest,
Directski.com, Made to
Measure, Simply
Alpine, Skiing Austria,
Ski Line, Ski McNeill,
Ski Miquel, STC, White
Roc
Bad Hofgastein *Crystal,*
Crystal Finest, Inghams,
Kuoni, Skiing Austria,
Ski Line, Skitracer, STC

of play; evenings are more subdued. The Silver Bullet has 'excellent' live bands and 'a great atmosphere'. Haeggbloms is similarly popular. Places for a quiet late drink include the smart Bellini bar and the Ritz cocktail bar. There are a couple of discos and a casino.

Off the slopes The thermal spa facilities are excellent and extensive – and excursions to Salzburg are possible.

Bad Hofgastein

860m/2,820ft

THE RESORT

Bad Hofgastein is a sizeable, spacious, quiet spa village set on flat ground in the widest part of the valley.

Village charm The pedestrianised centre is compact and pleasant enough to stroll around, with lots of shops and restaurants. But there's little traditional Austrian rustic charm.

Convenience The resort spreads widely; much of the lodging is a long walk or shuttle-bus ride away from the funicular to the slopes at Kitzsteinalm. It's a longer bus ride to Angertal.

Scenery Bad Hofgastein is more spacious than its neighbour, with good valley views.

THE MOUNTAINS

Schlossalm is a broad, open bowl, with runs through patchy woods both to Bad Hofgastein and Angertal. As at Stubnerkogel, wind can be a problem.

Slopes Schlossalm is the valley's gentlest area, with sunny open blue and red slopes. The Kleine Scharte cable car serves a serious 750m/ 2,460ft vertical, with a splendid long red to the valley floor.

Fast lifts Getting up the mountain can be slow, and a few old chairs remain.

Queues The funicular and cable car are queue-prone at peak times – and the cable car can be closed by wind.

Terrain parks There isn't one.

Snow reliability Snowmaking is fairly extensive, but snow-cover down to the bottom is unreliable, especially on the sunny Angertal slopes.

Experts There are no real challenges on the local pistes but there is ample opportunity to go off-piste.

Intermediates All Intermediates will enjoy the Schlossalm slopes – and the more confident can go further afield.

Beginners You have to catch a bus to the nursery area at Angertal.

Phone numbers
From elsewhere in Austria add the prefix 06434 (Bad Gastein), 06432 (Bad Hofgastein), 06433 (Dorfgastein); from abroad use the prefix +43 and omit the initial '0'

TOURIST OFFICES

For all resorts in the Gastein valley contact
t 06432 33930
info@gastein.com
www.gastein.com
Bad Gastein
t 06432 3393-539
info@badgastein.at
Bad Hofgastein
t 06432 3393-223
info@badhofgastein. com
Dorfgastein
t 06432 3393-413
engl@dorfgastein.com

Snowboarding Good freeriding. Draglifts are dotted around.

Cross-country Bad Hofgastein makes a fine base for cross-country when its lengthy valley-floor trails have snow.

Mountain restaurants Reader tips are the 'quieter' Haitzingalm, the self-service Aeroplanstadl for 'good value home cooking' and the Bärsteinalm for 'pleasant' table-service.

Schools and guides 'Friendly and very professional', says a 2009 reporter.

Families See Bad Gastein.

STAYING THERE

Mostly hotels.

Hotels Readers recommend the 4-star St Georg (61000; '200m to lift, spa, sauna, quite good food'), the Palace (67150; 'large rooms') and the Tirol (63940; 'great spa').

Apartments The new Alpenparks resort is 'excellent', says a 2009 visitor.

Eating out There's plenty of choice. Piccola Italia does 'simple, tasty, good value' food. The Wintergarten is an intimate restaurant, the Maier one of the better informal places.

Après-ski Quiet by Austrian standards. The Aeroplanstadl on the hill and central Piccolo ice bar are popular at close of play. Head to Cafe Weitmoser, a historic little castle, for cakes. There are said to be a couple of disco bars, but reporting teenagers found none.

Off the slopes The huge Alpen Therme Gastein spa has excellent pools etc. Other amenities include good shops, walking and ice skating.

Dorfgastein 830m/2,720ft

Dorfgastein is a quiet, rustic village. It has its own extensive slopes, shared with Grossarl in the next valley. A two-stage gondola or chairlifts start a little way outside the village. Much of the front side is below the treeline, and good for bad weather days. The long, varied runs are ideal for beginners and intermediates; many are gentle cruises. Grooming is fine. The low nursery slopes can be icy though. The resort also has a terrain park. There are pleasant huts. The table-service Wengeralm is repeatedly praised: 'outstanding', 'best lunch of the week', The Dorf Aktiv school gets good reviews. Off-slope amenities are limited, but there's a pool. Evenings are quiet. Reporters love the 4-star Römerhof hotel (7777) – 'friendly, superb food, excellent pool/spa'.

Interactive resort shortlist builder at **www.wtss.co.uk**

Bad Kleinkirchheim

Large resort tucked away in Carinthia, with marvellous spa facilities and a ski area best suited to intermediates

- ➕ Mainly intermediate slopes
- ➕ Virtually 100% snowmaking
- ➕ Two superb thermal spas
- ➕ Plenty to do off the slopes
- ➖ Spread-out town
- ➖ Still a lot of T-bars
- ➖ No terrain park or half-pipe

NEWS

The Thermal Römerbad spa opened two seasons ago after complete renovation. The 12,000 square metre centre is on three levels and offers 13 different types of sauna and steam rooms, indoor and outdoor pools, relaxation areas, a large adults-only section and a children's area.

KEY FACTS

Resort	1090m
	3,580ft
Slopes	1090-2055m
	3,580-6,740ft
Lifts	25
Pistes	103km
	64 miles
Blue	17%
Red	75%
Black	8%
Snowmaking	97%

BKK, as the locals call it, is downhill race hero Franz Klammer's favourite ski area – he learned to ski here and there's a World Cup downhill run bearing his name. (What? Franz who, did you say? Oh come on! Arguably the best downhill racer ever? Innsbruck Olympics, 1976? Honestly, the young people of today …)

Given Klammer's endorsement, it's no surprise that the resort has some serious skiing: 75% of its slopes are classified red. It is perhaps a surprise then that there are few real challenges for experts. So the resort suits confident intermediates best. It's a traditional spa town (with two excellent thermal spas) but, unlike many of those, it has mainly easy-on-the-eye chalet-style buildings.

THE RESORT

BKK is tucked away on the edge of the Nock Mountain National Park in Carinthia, in the far south-east of Austria, near the Italian and Slovenian borders. The nearest airports are Klagenfurt (around 50 minutes away) and Ljubljana (90 minutes). Salzburg is less than two hours away.

The lift pass covers St Oswald, a smaller village at the far end of the shared ski area, and all the resorts in Carinthia – useful for visiting other resorts if you have a car.

BKK's spa facilities are excellent, with indoor and outdoor thermal pools (with temperatures of between 28° and 34°C), different types of sauna – including a tepidarium (a sauna with a lower temperature so you can sit there longer) and steam rooms, solariums, hot tubs, massage and therapy rooms. There are also water slides, waterfalls and massage jets in the pools. 'We found the spas superb,' says a reporter. 'They are a great way to unwind after skiing and mean there's plenty to do if the snow is limited.' The new Thermal Römerbad opened two seasons ago – see 'News'. We tried it and thought it was superb; we could happily have spent days there.

And for the benefit of devotees … Franz Klammer, 1976 Olympic downhill gold medallist and winner of a record 25 World Cup Downhills, was born in Mooswald, near Bad Kleinkirchheim. His mother runs a gasthaus with his brother and sister-in-law in Fresach,

about 20km/12 miles from BKK. He learned to ski at BKK, and it remains his favourite resort.

Village charm The mainly chalet-style buildings with sloping roofs are rather more appealing than the austere blocks of some ski resorts.

Convenience The town is very spread out along the valley, and the most convenient place to stay is near one of the main lifts out. A ski-bus links all the main lift stations, and some buses also go to St Oswald.

Scenery The scenery you gaze at from the spa pools is of gently rounded, rather than dramatic, mountains.

THE MOUNTAINS

BKK has shady home slopes and sunnier ones shared with St Oswald. Throughout, they are mainly wooded and of intermediate standard (75% are classified red). The piste map usefully marks the mountain restaurants; it also marks 'Römer Lounges' and 'Hits am Lift' – see overleaf.

Slopes BKK's main home slopes are reached by lifts from two different parts of the village. A two-stage gondola goes up to the area's high point, Kaiserburg, at one end of the ski area, where a couple of T-bars serve the highest slopes. And a fast quad chair takes you to the other end of the same mountain face at Maibrunn. Pistes go down from both peaks to the gondola mid-station, and a double chair takes you back to above Maibrunn.

Phone numbers
From elsewhere in Austria add the prefix 04240; from abroad use the prefix +43 4240

BAD KLEINKIRCHHEIM TOURIST OFFICE

The Thermal Römerbad is superb. There are lots of different saunas, steam rooms and indoor pools to try as well as lounging around outside, admiring the views ↓

From the same end of the village as the Maibrunn quad, successive old double chairs and a drag take you up the other side of the valley to the Nockalm slopes, which link in with St Oswald's slopes further along the valley. This area can also be accessed by a gondola midway between BKK and St Oswald, which can be reached by ski-bus. At St Oswald a gondola goes up to Brunnach, at the far end of the shared ski area.

Two quads link the Nockalm and St Oswald slopes, and most of the other upper lifts are drags.

Fast lifts There is one for each sector. But lots of slow lifts remain.

Queues We have no reports of lift queues being much of a problem.

Terrain parks There isn't one.

Snow reliability Being south of the Tauern mountain range, BKK can have completely different weather from the rest of Austria. So snow reliability can be better or worse, depending on the season. In general, BKK's main home slopes are north-facing and keep their snow best. The Nockalm-St Oswald slopes are more sunny. The resorts now have 800 snow-guns and virtually all the pistes (97%) are covered.

Experts BKK has little to keep experts interested for a week. The best and most challenging black is the Franz Klammer World Cup run, which goes from Strohsack to the gondola base (the short top section is very steep and often closed). There are two short black runs below Kaiserburg and another under the Wiesernock quad. Off-piste tours that involve some hiking can be arranged (eg to the Mallnock and Klomnock mountains from the top of the gondola from St Oswald and on Falkert mountain, reached by taxi from BKK and then a T-bar followed by a hike).

Intermediates Virtually all the slopes in both BKK and St Oswald are ideal for good intermediates as three-quarters of the slopes are classified red and many are long (up to 1000m/3,280ft vertical), wide and flattering. One of the most beautiful runs is the FIS K70 downhill run, classified red, which goes from top to bottom of the mountain away from all the lifts and through the trees in the lower section – on the extreme left-hand side of our piste map. It is almost 5km/3 miles long (and rarely groomed, says a local). There are two other long top-to-

KAISERBURG 2055m/6,740ft — Strohsack 1905m — MAIBRUNN 1760m/5,775ft — Priedröf 1965m/6,445ft — NOCKALM — Wieser Nock 1970m/6,46oft — Brunnach 1910m/6,270ft

1370m — 1025m — 1280m — St Oswald

Bad Kleinkirchheim 1090m/3,58oft

Feldkirchen ↓

RÖMER LOUNGES & HITS AM LIFT

What are these things marked on the piste map, we wondered?

A 'Römer Lounge' is an area with a red sofa designed to encourage you to take a rest and soak up the sun while admiring the panorama in a kind of sitting room complete with a TV set and Roman-style columns and mosaics on the back wall, meant to be in keeping with the new Thermal Römerbad. There's no roof, two side walls come up halfway, and the front is open to the view. There are four on the slopes, and we found them comfortable, relaxing and with great views.

Hits am Lift? Yes, you guessed it: at the bottom of certain lifts different music (eg Austrian folk music, Rock and Roll, Italian, Evergreen) is pumped out to keep visitors amused while waiting for the lift. It works surprisingly well.

TOURIST OFFICE

t 8212
office@
badkleinkirchheim.at
www.
badkleinkirchheim.at

bottom red runs in this area too, as well as the Franz Klammer black. The Nockalm and St Oswald sectors also have long red runs, which are mostly easier than those in the Kaiserburg-Maibrunn sector; so this area is better for early intermediates and families.

Beginners There are nursery slopes and draglifts for beginners at both BKK and St Oswald – the St Oswald ones are at the top of the Nockalm gondola and much warmer and sunnier in midwinter, when the low BKK ones are in the shade. Once off the nursery slopes, there is a long blue the length of the gondola here.

Snowboarding Although the main lifts are all gondolas or chairs, there are a lot of T-bars, which less experienced boarders may not like. And there's no terrain park or half-pipe.

Cross-country BKK takes cross-country seriously, with 54km/34 miles of tracks, some as high as 1900m/6,230ft at the top of the Nockalm.

Mountain restaurants There are 22 mountain restaurants and huts. The most recent addition is the panoramic Nock IN at the top of Brunnach above St Oswald. You might meet Franz Klammer himself having lunch at the Kaiserburg at the top of the gondola of that name; he is always happy to have a chat and sign autographs. We also enjoyed the cosy Brentlerhütte (excellent ham) on the way down from Nockalm to the valley and Zum Weltcup Poldl above St Oswald.

Schools and guides There are four schools to choose from, three based in BKK and one in St Oswald. Style Check is a twice-weekly concept, offering slope-side tips in specially marked areas from instructors to help polish

your technique (five euros).

Families There's a non-skiing kindergarten for children from age two upwards at the foot of the gondola from BKK. First Steps takes children from two and a half, where they can learn to ski while playing.

STAYING THERE

Hotels There are two 5-stars, 21 4-stars, several 3-stars and lots of gasthofs too. BKK boasts 21 hotels with swimming pools and 50 saunas. The two 5-star hotels, the Pulverer (744) and the Thermenhotel Ronacher (282), are both near the high-speed chair and have excellent spa facilities. St Oswald (591), near the gondola to Brunnach, has very comfortable rooms and suites, a smart spa and an excellent wine cellar.

Apartments There are lots of self-catering apartments to rent.

Eating out There is plenty of choice, including a lot of hotel restaurants. We loved the atmospheric old Loystub'n in the hotel Pulverer.

Après-ski Near the BKK gondola base are several popular places: the Almstube, Viktoria Pub, Club MC 99 and the Take Five Dancing Club.

Off the slopes You can buy lift tickets that include the use of the thermal spas. There are also some good walks (including the Spa Boulevard at the top of the gondola from St Oswald), a tennis centre, squash courts, outdoor ice rink, curling, tubing, snowshoeing, horse riding, sleigh rides and a 4km/2.5 mile floodlit toboggan run. Those with cars can visit Villach 36km/ 22 miles away for a shopping spree or carry on across the border into Italy.

Ellmau

A decent base on the extensive SkiWelt circuit, combining charm with reasonable convenience – good value too

£80
RESORT PRICE INDEX

TOP 10 RATINGS

Extent	★★★★
Fast lifts	★★★
Queues	★★★★
Snow	★★
Expert	★
Intermediate	★★★★
Beginner	★★★★
Charm	★★★
Convenience	★★★
Scenery	★★★

KEY FACTS

Resort	800m
	2,620ft

Entire SkiWelt	
Slopes	620-1890m
	2,030-6,200ft
Lifts	91
Pistes	279km
	173 miles
Blue	44%
Red	46%
Black	10%
Snowmaking	75%

+ Part of the SkiWelt, Austria's largest linked ski and snowboard area

+ Excellent nursery slopes

+ Quiet, charming family resort – more appealing than Söll

+ Cheap, even by Austrian standards

+ Snowmaking is now more extensive and well used; even so ...

- Low altitude can mean poor snow

- Main lift a bus ride from village – though reachable via a draglift

- Mostly short runs in the local sector

- Little to challenge decent riders

- Limited range of nightlife

- The SkiWelt slopes can get crowded

- Appallingly inadequate piste map

If you like the sound of the large, undemanding SkiWelt circuit, Ellmau has a lot to recommend it as your base – quieter than Söll, but with more amenities than other neighbours such as Scheffau (covered in the Söll chapter). But consider Westendorf as a base too – see separate chapter.

THE RESORT

Ellmau sits at the north-eastern corner of the SkiWelt – an area of linked slopes that's an impressive 15km/9 miles across. The SkiWelt pass also covers Westendorf, linked by a new gondola from Brixen; from there you can also progress to the Kitzbühel slopes – see the Westendorf chapter. These, along with Waidring, Fieberbrunn and St Johann, are possible day trips covered by the Kitzbüheler Alpen All Star skipass.
Village charm Although sizeable, the village remains quiet, with traditional chalet-style buildings, welcoming bars and shops, and a pretty church.

Convenience Ellmau has a compact centre, but accommodation is scattered – so the buses around the resort are important (and now quite well organised). There is accommodation out by the funicular to the main slopes, but we prefer to stay near the heart of the village.
Scenery The craggy Wilder Kaiser and the long SkiWelt ridge make a fine backdrop to the village.

THE MOUNTAINS

The SkiWelt is the largest mountain circuit in Austria, linking eight resorts. The piste map is hopelessly over-ambitious in trying to show the whole

← Ellmau is prettily set away from the main road and with the Wilder Kaiser mountain as a spectacular backdrop
SNOWPIX.COM / CHRIS GILL

Fast lifts The main access lift is a fast funicular. There is a growing number of fast chairs on the upper slopes but still a lot of slow ones around too.

Queues Lift upgrades have greatly improved this once queue-prone area and 2009 reporters found few queues. But there are several bottlenecks at slow chairs around the mountain, and when snow is poor the links between Zinsberg and Eiberg get crowded.

Terrain parks Ellmau has its own terrain park, the Kaiser-Park, with beginner and expert boxes, rails and kickers, as well as a chill-out zone.

Snow reliability With a low average height, and important links that get a lot of sun, the snowmaking that the SkiWelt has installed is essential; the Ellmau-Going sector now claims almost all its slopes are covered. Snowmaking can, of course, only be used when temperatures are low enough. The north-facing Eiberg area above Scheffau holds its snow well. Grooming is reported to be 'excellent', and reports have praised 'ace' snowmaking.

Experts There are steep plunges off the Hohe Salve summit, a ski route from Brandstadl down to Scheffau and a little mogul field between Brandstadl and Neualm, but the area isn't really suitable unless you go off-piste.

Intermediates With good snow, the SkiWelt is a paradise for those who love easy cruising. There are lots of blue runs and many of the reds deserve a blue classification. It is a big area and you get a feeling of travelling around. The main challenge is when the snow isn't perfect – ice and slush can make even gentle lower slopes seem tricky. For timid intermediates the easy slopes of Astberg are handy. More adventurous ones should head for Westendorf.

Beginners Ellmau has an array of good nursery slopes covered by snowmaking. The main ones are at the Going end, but there are some by the road to the funicular. The Astberg chair opens up a more snow-sure plateau at altitude. The Brandstadl area has a section of short easy runs.

Snowboarding Ellmau is a good place to learn as its local slopes are easy.

Cross-country There are long, quite

NEWS

For 2009/10 a new six-pack (Ellmi's) is planned for the top half of the mountain above Scheffau to Hartkaiser.

For 2008/09 the Siller-Keat six-pack replaced a triple chair, improving the return to Ellmau from Söll.

Above Hopfgarten a gondola with heated seats was built from the mid-station to Hohe Salve, replacing the single chairlift at Rigi. A new terrain park was built below Hochsöll and is the SkiWelt's first to be open at night.

Westendorf was at last properly connected to the rest of the SkiWelt via Brixen. And a new Skiline system to track your progress around the SkiWelt was introduced. See Westendorf chapter.

area in a single view – see Söll chapter. Most runs are easy, and short – which means that getting around the area can take time, despite increasing numbers of fast lifts.

Slopes The funicular railway on the edge of the village takes you up to Hartkaiser, from where a fine long red leads down to Blaiken (Scheffau's lift base station). Here, one of two gondolas takes you up to Brandstadl. Immediately beyond Brandstadl, the slopes become rather bitty; an array of short runs and lifts link Brandstadl to Zinsberg. From Zinsberg, long, south-facing pistes lead down to Brixen, where a new gondola goes up to Choralpe in Westendorf's area and a lovely north-facing red piste comes back down. Part-way down to Brixen you can head towards Söll, and if you go up Hohe Salve, you get access to a long, west-facing run to Hopfgarten.

Ellmau and Going share a pleasant little area of slopes on Astberg, slightly apart from the rest of the area, and well suited to the unadventurous and families. One piste leads to the funicular for access to the rest of the SkiWelt. The main Astberg chair is rather inconveniently positioned, midway between Ellmau and Going.

LIFT PASSES

SkiWelt Wilder Kaiser-Brixental

Prices in €

Age	1-day	6-day
under 16	19	91
16 to 17	30	146
over 18	36	182

Free under 7
Senior no deals
Beginner points cards

Notes
Covers Wilder Kaiser-Brixental area from Going to Westendorf, and the ski-bus; single ascent and part-day options; family discounts

ON YOUR OWN?

You can team up with other skiers/boarders by turning up at 10am or 1pm at one of seven designated points in the SkiWelt; there are stickers to identify participants, and even a website forum for making prior arrangements.

UK PACKAGES

Crystal, First Choice, Inghams, Interhome, Neilson, Simply Alpine, Ski Line, Skiing Austria, Skitracer, STC, Thomson
Going *Skiing Austria*

Phone numbers
From elsewhere in Austria add the prefix 05358; from abroad use the prefix +43 5358

TOURIST OFFICES

WILDER KAISER
(Ellmau, Söll, Scheffau, Going)
t 505
www.wilderkaiser.info

Ellmau
ellmau@wilderkaiser.info

Going
going@wilderkaiser.info

SkiWelt
www.skiwelt.at

challenging trails (the SkiWelt area has a total of 170km/106 miles), but trails at altitude are lacking.

Mountain restaurants The smaller places are fairly consistent in providing good-value food in pleasant surroundings. The Rübezahlalm above Ellmau is one of our favourites in the whole SkiWelt – a lovely old hut with good food (the rack of ribs has been recommended) and lots of different rooms and areas which make it very cosy; but it gets very busy. Other reporter recommendations include: the Jagerhütte (below Hartkaiser) for 'home-made strudel' and 'a drinks stop' before enjoying the 'quiet and pleasant' home-run, and the Hartkaiser for 'food quality and ambiance, and escalators to the loos'. The Bergkaiser also has 'quick service and good food'. The Blattlalm on Astberg has 'super views'. The larger self-service restaurants are functional (the Jochstuben at Eiberg is a pleasant exception) and generate queues at times.

Schools and guides The four schools (includes one at Going) have good reputations – except that classes can be very large. Top is highly rated for children's lessons – 'All our children had a great time in different classes with Top, who made sure they were in English-only speaking groups. It was a very busy week, but only our youngest was in the maximum class size of 12.'

Families Ellmau is an attractive resort for families, described by a regular visitor as 'so child-friendly'. Top ski school is praised (see 'Schools'). Kindergartens seem to be satisfactory and include fun ideas such as a mini train to the lifts. Top's Kinderland has its own fun park and play areas. But we lack reports.

STAYING THERE

Ellmau is essentially a hotel and pension resort, though there are apartments that can be booked locally.
Hotels The Bär (2395) is an elegant, relaxed luxury place. 'It was friendly and welcoming, with a very good wellness centre,' wrote a reporter. 'Luxury without pretensions,' said another. The Kaiserhof (2022) is another luxury option ('very comfortable and friendly, and with amazing food'). The Hochfilzer (2501) is central, well equipped (with outdoor hot tub) and popular with reporters

(as is the simpler Pension Claudia, which it owns – use of hotel facilities allowed). Kaiserblick (2230), with good spa facilities and right by the piste, is recommended by a regular visitor, who went with six families including 12 children.

Apartments There is a wide variety. The Landhof apartments continue to impress a regular visitor – 'spacious, immaculately clean, well equipped' – with pool, sauna and steam room. The supermarket on the way out of town towards Going is also rated as 'excellent'.

Eating out The jolly Gasthof Lobewein is a splendid, big, central chalet, with cheerful service in countless rooms and excellent food. The Ellmauer Alm is also recommended (see below).

Après-ski Bettina is good for coffee and cakes. Memory (which has internet facilities) is the early-evening riotous party pub. Pub 66 and Ötzi have regular events such as karaoke and 'erotic dancers'. The Ellmauer Alm at the Going end of the village has fun, live entertainment and is 'always good'. Tour operator reps organise events such as sleigh rides and tubing, and bowling and Tirolean folklore evenings in Söll. There's an Instructors' Ball and ski displays with 'a party atmosphere' each week, and the toboggan run from the Astberg lift is recommended.

Off the slopes A guest card entitles you to various discounts, including entry to the KaiserBad leisure centre. There are many excursions available, including ones to Salzburg and Vitipeno. Valley walks are spoiled by the busy main road. Heading up to Hartkaiser by funicular railway to relax on the terrace 'was a highlight for our non-skiers', writes a reporter.

Going 775m/2,540ft

Going is a tiny, attractively rustic village, ideal for families looking for a quiet time. It is well placed for the limited but quiet slopes of the Astberg and for the vast area of nursery slopes between here and Ellmau. Prices are low, but it's not an ideal base for covering the whole of the SkiWelt on the cheap unless you have a car for quick access to Scheffau and Söll. The Lanzenhof (2428) is a cosy central pension doing excellent traditional food in its woody dining rooms. Wellness centre includes a sauna.

Hintertux / Tux valley

Small, unspoiled, traditional villages, high snow-sure glacier slopes and lots of other areas covered by the valley lift pass

+ Hintertux has one of the best glaciers in the world, open summer as well as winter

+ Lanersbach's ski area is linked to Mayrhofen and Finkenberg; and several other areas are covered by the area lift pass and free buses

+ Some excellent off-piste opportunities

+ A choice of quiet, unspoiled, traditional villages to stay in

− Not for those who want a huge choice of shops and throbbing nightlife on their doorstep

− Not ideal for beginners or timid intermediates, with few easy runs to valley level

− Glacier can be cold and bleak in midwinter, and there are lots of T-bars and slow chairs

NEWS

For 2009/10 the Lattenalm double chair on Eggalm is due to be replaced by a six-pack. And more snowmaking is due to be installed on Rastkogel.

For 2008/09 a 24-person gondola, Gletscherbus I, replaced the smaller of the two gondolas from the Hintertux glacier base area up to Sommerbergalm.

The main attraction of Hintertux is obvious: its glacier. It is not only extensive; it arguably has the most challenging and interesting runs of any lift-served Alpine glacier. For guaranteed good snow, Hintertux is simply one of the best places to go. But the Tux valley has broader appeal: the quieter, friendlier, non-glacial slopes above Lanersbach and its nearby twin, Vorderlanersbach are linked by fast lifts with those above Mayrhofen and Finkenberg. Together, they form a fair-sized circuit. With the glacier only 15 to 20 minutes away by bus, these quiet, unspoiled, traditional villages are attractive bases – for many people, more attractive than either higher Hintertux or lower Mayrhofen (covered in its own chapter). There are other areas further down the Zillertal that are worth a day trip (see the end of the Mayrhofen chapter).

Gefrorene Wand 3250m/10,66oft

Grosser Kaserer 3220m

GLACIER 3030m

3050m

Tuxer Fernerhaus 2660m

Tuxer Joch 2460m

Sommerbergalm 2100m

Beil 2300m/7,55oft

Hintertux 1500m/4,920ft

EGGALM

Madseit

Juns

1680m

1850m

Lanersbach 1300m/4,270ft

2150m

Finkenberg

Vorderlanersbach

Penken

↙ Mayrhofen

Wanglspitz 2420m

2050m

RASTKOGEL

↑ The glacier is Hintertux's huge asset: snow-sure, extensive and with challenging and interesting runs
TVB TUX / JP FANKHAUSER

Interactive resort shortlist builder at www.wtss.co.uk

KEY FACTS

Resort	1500m
	4,920ft

Ski and Glacier World Zillertal 3000

Slopes	630-3250m
	2,070-10,660ft
Lifts	59
Pistes	225km
	140 miles
Blue	26%
Red	58%
Black	16%
Snowmaking	66%

Hintertux only

Slopes	1500-3250m
	4,920-10,660ft
Lifts	21
Pistes	86km
	53 miles

For Ziller valley

Slopes	630-3250m
	2,070-10,660ft
Lifts	174
Pistes	646km
	401 miles

The Tux valley, an extension of Mayrhofen's Zillertal, has a variety of small villages, linked by frequent free ski-buses. A cheap (one euro) night-bus also runs until 2am. At the top of the valley, directly below the glacier, is **Hintertux**; a 15-minute bus ride down the valley, the major resorts are **Lanersbach** and **Vorderlanersbach**. Lower down still – actually in the Zillertal, and much less well served by buses – is **Finkenberg**. There is also accommodation in Juns and Madseit.

There are some good rustic restaurants and bars and a few places along the valley with discos or live music. But nightlife tends to be quieter than in many bigger Austrian resorts (Mayrhofen, for example).

All the major resort villages have gondola links into the local slopes: the Finkenberg gondola goes up to the Penken slopes shared with Mayrhofen; the Vorderlanersbach one goes to Rastkogel, which is linked with the Penken slopes; and the Lanersbach one goes to Eggalm, from which you can ski to Vorderlanersbach.

The Tux valley and Mayrhofen lifts now form what is called the Ski and Glacier World Zillertal 3000. Lift passes for four days or more also cover the other resorts in the Ziller valley (see the end of the Mayrhofen chapter).

Hintertux 1500m/4,920ft

THE RESORT
Tiny Hintertux is set at the end of the Tux valley.
Village charm The resort is little more than a small collection of hotels and guest houses.
Convenience There is a smaller group of hotels near the lifts, which lie a 15-minute walk away from the village, across a car park that fills with day-visitors' cars and coaches, especially when snow is poor in lower resorts.
Scenery The glacier is high and there are fabulous views from the top lifts.

THE MOUNTAINS
Hintertux's slopes are fairly extensive and, for a glacier, surprisingly challenging. The glacier is one of the best in the world, with varied terrain that attracts national ski teams for summer training.
Slopes A series of three speedy gondolas (all with 24-person cabins) takes you up from the base to the top of the glacier (vertical rise 1750m/ 5,740ft) in around 30 minutes. The first of these was new for 2008/09, replacing one of the two parallel access lifts up to Sommerbergalm; the increased capacity pleased 2009 reporters ('really speeded getting up the glacier' and 'the real improvement is in coming down, we didn't queue once'). The second and third stages are linked by a short slope at Tuxer Fernerhaus. A fast quad chair from Sommerbergalm serves short, easy slopes below Tuxer Joch; from the top of this sector, the excellent secluded Schwarze Pfanne ski route goes down to the base station. Between the top of the glacier and Tuxer Fernerhaus there are further chairs and draglifts to play on and links across to another

LIFT PASSES

Zillertaler Superskipass

Prices in €

Age	1-day	6-day
under 15	19	88
15 to 18	32	149
over 19	39	186

Free under 6
Senior no deals
Beginner no deals

Notes
1-, 2- or 3-day passes cover Hintertux glacier, Eggalm, Rastkogel and Penken areas; 4-day and over passes include all Ziller valley lifts; part-day and pedestrian passes available

SCHOOLS

Tuxertal
t 87755

Luggis
t 86808

Tux 3000
t 86112

Classes
(Tuxertal prices)
6 days (2hr am and pm) €129

Private lessons
€49 for 1hr; each additional person €15

CHILDCARE

Guest kindergarten
t 87755
Ages 1 to 3

Ski school
All the ski schools run children's classes. Tuxertal school takes children from 10am to 3pm (5 days including lunch €177)

1000m/3,300ft-vertical chain of lifts below Grosser Kaserer on the west. Behind Gefrorene Wand is the area's one sunny piste, served by a triple chair. Descent to the valley involves a short ascent to Sommerbergalm on the way, achieved by a six-seater chairlift.

Fast lifts There are high-capacity gondolas all the way to the top, but a lot of the shorter lifts are T-bars.

Queues There used to be huge queues at Hintertux when snow was poor elsewhere. Improved lifts have largely solved this problem and the new gondola from the valley has cut queues for going down as well as going up. But the main runs can get crowded, and then it is best to head over to the quieter Kaserer areas.

Terrain parks Europe's highest World Cup half-pipe is on the glacier (a popular hang-out throughout the summer), and there is a terrain park for all levels with jumps, fun boxes and rails.

Snow reliability Snow does not come more reliable than this. Even off the glacier, the other slopes are high and face north, making for very reliable snow-cover. The runs from Tuxer Fernerhaus and Tuxer Joch down to Sommerbergalm have snowmaking, as does the Schwarze Pfanne ski route.

Experts There is more to amuse experts here than on any other glacier, with a couple of serious black runs at glacier level and steep slopes and ungroomed ski routes beneath. A lot of the off-piste is little used and one reporter said, 'We found untracked snow not far from the lifts two weeks after the last snowfall.'

Intermediates The area particularly suits good, confident intermediates. The long runs down from Gefrorene Wand and Kaserer are fun. And there is a pleasant, treelined ski route to the valley from Sommerbergalm and another from Tuxer Joch. Moderate intermediates will love the glacier.

Beginners There is a nursery slope at valley level, but the glacier isn't the ideal place to progress to.

Snowboarding There are some great off-piste opportunities, but boarders complain about the number of T-bars.

Cross-country See the Lanersbach information later in the chapter.

Mountain restaurants The mountain restaurants tend to get very crowded and the big self-service places lack charm – 'the food is better at Tuxer Fernerhaus than at Sommerbergalm'

says a 2009 reporter. One exception is the out-of-the-way Tuxer Joch Haus – 'stunning views', says a 2009 visitor. Another is the almost-100-year-old Spannagelhaus – 'good traditional Austrian food', 'fun atmosphere'. There are great views from 'friendly' Gletscherhütte, at the top.

Schools and guides There are three schools, which serve all the resorts in Tux, but we lack reports on them. Tux 3000 has special guiding, touring and freeriding programmes.

Families Most of the ski schools run classes for children aged three to 14, and lunch is provided. There's a children's fun area on the glacier.

STAYING THERE

Most hotels are large and comfortable and have spa facilities, but there are also more modest pensions.

Hotels Close to the lifts are the 4-star Vierjahreszeiten (8525) and Neuhintertux (8580) in which a 2009 reporter found 'a good wine list' and enjoyed the large pool, saunas, steam baths and modern spa. Reporters also recommend the 4-star Berghof (8585) with its 'good service and spa' and the Thermal Badhotel Kirchler (8570) for its good food and 'welcoming bar' (but it was a good 20 minute walk to the lifts, and buses were not frequent in May/June when we were there). The 4-star Alpenhof (8550) has also been praised and we have enjoyed staying in the 3-star Hintertuxerhof (8530): good food, sauna and steam room. Pensions Kössler (87490) – 3-star – and the 2-star Willeiter (87492) are in the heart of the village.

Apartments There are plenty of self-catering apartments.

Eating out Restaurants are mainly hotel-based. The Vierjahreszeiten is pleasant and informal.

Après-ski There can be a lively après-ski scene both at mid-mountain (Sommerbergalm) and at the base; the Hohenhaus Tenne has several different bars and 'is great fun and the dance floor gets packed', the Rindererhof has a popular tea dance, and there are a couple of local bars. The cheap (one euro) night-bus gets you to and from the other villages until 2am, but this is not the place for keen clubbers.

Off the slopes The spa facilities are excellent, including a thermal indoor pool, but there are many more options in Mayrhofen.

100% SNOW GUARANTEE

picture: marcotonolo.com

www.tux.at

GETTING THERE

Air Salzburg
195km/120 miles
(3hr); Munich
210km/130 miles
(3hr30); Innsbruck
90km/55 miles
(1hr45)

Rail Local line to
Mayrhofen; regular
buses from station

Lanersbach 1300m/4,270ft

THE RESORT
Lanersbach and neighbouring
Vorderlanersbach have long been
attractive bases for exploring the
resorts of the Zillertal and Tuxertal.
Since their ski areas were linked with
Mayrhofen's slopes, their attractions
are greatly reinforced. And prices are
relatively low.

Village charm Lanersbach is small,
attractive, spacious and traditional.
The quiet centre near the pretty church
is delightfully unspoiled and is
bypassed by the busy road up to
Hintertux that passes the main lift. It
has all you need in a resort.
Vorderlanersbach is even smaller and
quieter.

Convenience The centre of Lanersbach
is within walking distance of the
gondola up to Eggalm.
Vorderlanersbach has its own gondola
up to the Rastkogel area.

Scenery These are attractive villages in
a long, pretty and varied valley.

THE MOUNTAINS
Slopes The slopes of Eggalm, accessed
by the gondola from Lanersbach, offer
a small network of pleasantly varied,
intermediate pistes, usually delightfully
quiet. You can descend on red or blue
runs back to the village or to
Vorderlanersbach, where a gondola
goes up to the higher, open Rastkogel
slopes; here, two fast chairlifts – one a
covered eight-seater – serve some very
enjoyable long red and blue runs and
link with Mayrhofen's slopes. The
linking run is classified red but can get
very mogulled and many people opt to
ride the 150-person cable car down; a
short rope-tow cuts out the need to
hike up to the top station. The lower

half of the run back from Rastkogel to
Eggalm is now a ski route, but is really
quite easy and is served by
snowmaking. The alternative is to ride
the gondola down to Vorderlanersbach
(there are no pistes to the village) and
catch the bus to Lanersbach.

Fast lifts Gondolas are the access lifts
and another fast chair is planned for
Eggalm for 2009/10.

Queues We have no reports of any
problems. Indeed, Eggalm can be
delightfully quiet.

Terrain parks The Mayrhofen and
Hintertux pipes and parks are easily
accessed.

Snow reliability Snow conditions are
usually good, at least in early season;
by Austrian standards these are high
slopes and snowmaking covers some
runs on both Eggalm and Rastkogel.
But Rastkogel is basically south-facing,
so snow quality can suffer.

Experts There are no pistes to
challenge experts, but there is a fine
off-piste route starting a short walk
from the top of the Eggalm slopes and
finishing at the village.

Intermediates The local slopes suit
intermediates best – and you have
Mayrhofen's slopes to explore too.

Beginners Lanersbach has a nursery
slope (as do Madseit and Juns) but
there are few ideal progression slopes
– most of the easy runs are on the
higher lifts of the Rastkogel sector.

Snowboarding The area isn't great for
novices – there are draglifts dotted
around, some in key places.

Cross-country There are 14km/9 miles
of cross-country trails, alongside the
Tux creek, between Madseit and
Vorderlanersbach, and a 14km/9 miles
skating track in Juns/Madseit.

Mountain restaurants There's no
shortage but most, though fairly rustic,
are self-service with simple food; the
small Lattenalm on Eggalm is a table-
service exception with a terrace that
has splendid views of the Tux glacier.

Schools and guides There are three
schools in the valley, but we lack
recent reports on them.

Families The non-ski nursery takes
children aged from one to three, and
most of the schools take children from
four upwards. There's a children's
garden, including a carousel and a
bob-run, on Eggalm.

STAYING THERE
Both villages are essentially hotel-
based resorts.

Hintertux 'village' is
little more than a
small collection of
hotels and guest
houses a 15-minute
walk from the lifts ↓

Ski the five resorts of 'High King Mountain'

HKM

One of Austria's biggest undiscovered ski areas!

www.HighKingMountain.com

0845 643 9424

ACTIVITIES

Indoor Bowling, squash, saunas, fitness rooms and pools in hotels open to public

Outdoor Ice rinks, curling, winter hiking trails, paragliding, tobogganing, snowshoe tours, ice climbing

TOURIST OFFICE

Tux-Finkenberg
t 8506
info@tux.at
www.tux.at
www.finkenberg.at

Hotels The better places tend to be on the main road, but readers tell us noise is no problem. The Lanersbacherof (87256) is a good 4-star with pool, sauna, steam and hot tub close to the lifts ('friendly, the food and wine are outstanding' says a regular visitor). The 3-star Pinzger (87541) and Alpengruss (87293) are cheaper alternatives. In Vorderlanersbach the 3-star Kirchlerhof (8560) is repeatedly recommended – 'welcoming, with good food, comfortable rooms'; good spa.

Apartments Quite a lot are available.

Eating out Restaurants are mainly hotel-based, busy, and geared to serving dinner early. The Forelle has been recommended for 'delicious trout'.

Après-ski Nightlife is generally quiet by Austrian standards, which suits us. We enjoyed the jolly Hühnerstall in Lanersbach (an old wooden building with traditional Austrian music). Gletscherspalte is a disco.

Off the slopes Facilities are fairly good for small resorts. Some hotels have pools, hot tubs and fitness rooms open to non-residents. Innsbruck and Salzburg are possible excursions.

Finkenberg 840m/2,760ft

THE RESORT
Finkenberg is a small, quiet village with a gondola into the Penken slopes shared with Mayrhofen.

Village charm The resort is no more than a collection of traditional-style hotels, bars, cafes and private homes. There is a pretty central area around the church.

Convenience Most of the buildings (and hotels) are spread along the busy, steep, winding main road up to Lanersbach. Beware slippery pavements. Some hotels are within walking distance of the gondola, and many of the more distant ones run their own minibuses; there is also an inefficient village minibus service.

Scenery Steep mountainsides rise up on both sides.

THE MOUNTAIN
Finkenberg shares Mayrhofen's main Penken slopes.

Slopes A two-stage gondola gives direct access to the Penken slopes – and in good conditions you can ski back to the village on a ski route (though it is often closed).

Fast lifts See Mayrhofen.

Queues Few problems reported. The gondola to and from the Penken may have queues at peak times.

Terrain parks The Mayrhofen park is easily accessed.

Snow reliability The local slopes are not as well-endowed with snowmaking as those on Mayrhofen's side.

Experts Not much challenge, except off-piste and the Harakiri piste.

Intermediates The whole area opens up from the top of the gondola.

Beginners There are nursery areas at the top of the gondola, on Penken, but Mayrhofen is a more suitable base.

Snowboarding See Mayrhofen.

Cross-country Cross-country skiers have to get a bus up to Lanersbach.

Mountain restaurants See the Mayrhofen chapter.

Schools and guides The Finkenberg school has a good reputation.

Families The Finkenberg school takes children from age four.

STAYING THERE
Hotels The Sporthotel Stock (6775), owned by the family of former downhill champion Leonard Stock, is near the gondola station, and has great spa facilities. The Eberl (62667) has been recommended ('attentive staff, excellent food – but avoid the annexe rooms'), and the Kristall (62840) is 150m/490ft from the gondola ('superb wellness spa'). All these are 4-stars.

Eating out Mainly in hotels, notably the Eberl.

Après-ski The main après-ski spots are the lively Laterndl Pub at the foot of the gondola and Finkennest ('welcoming, cosy, weird decor', but 'more civilised than the Laterndl').

Off the slopes OK for the active: curling, ice skating, swimming and good local walks.

Hochkönig (High King Mountain)

An unusual combination: small unspoiled villages and a large uncrowded ski area, virtually unknown on the British market

£75
RESORT PRICE INDEX

- ➕ Traditional quiet villages
- ➕ Very good value for money
- ➕ Plenty of uncrowded terrain

- ➖ Little for experts except off-piste
- ➖ Buses needed in parts, and there are some slow chairs and T-bars

TOP 10 RATINGS

Extent	★★★
Fast lifts	★★
Queues	★★★★
Snow	★★★
Expert	★★
Intermediate	★★★★
Beginner	★★★
Charm	★★★
Convenience	★★
Scenery	★★★

Phone numbers

From elsewhere in Austria use the prefix 06584 (Maria Alm and Hinterthal), 06461 (Dienten), 06467 (Mühlbach); from abroad use the prefix +43 and omit the initial '0'

AUSTRIA!
Ski Chalets
www.ElevationHolidays.com
0845 6443578

The picturesque Salzburgerland villages of Maria Alm, Hintermoos, Hinterthal, Dienten and Mühlbach combine to provide a sizeable ski area, best suited to intermediates and beginners. The lift system is not completely linked, so you'll have to drive or catch the ski-buses to explore it all.

THE RESORT

The resort is a collection of several small unspoiled villages below a sizeable ski area. Prices are low – it was one of the cheapest resorts in our eating and drinking price survey.

Village charm Maria Alm, though small and pretty, is one of the two largest villages. Hinterthal, the next real village up the valley, is even smaller – little more than a few hotels and chalets and a couple of ski shops and bars. Further up the road and over a pass is Dienten, a tiny, picturesque village with a handful of traditional hotels and guest houses. Mühlbach, at the eastern end of the ski area, is a similar size to Maria Alm; it sprawls along the main road – unlike the other villages, which are set off it.

Convenience The Mühlbach gondola is a bus ride from the village centre, Most people take a bus to and from the main slopes at Maria Alm too (though you can reach them from the small Natrun area in the centre of the village). You can ski directly from Hinthertal and Dienten.

Scenery The spectacular Hochkönig (which means 'High King') massif, from which the region gets its name, can be seen from many of the slopes, but it is not part of the ski area.

THE MOUNTAINS

There are 150km/93 miles of pistes, on a par with well-known names such as Kitzbühel and Mayrhofen.

Slopes The main slopes spread along several small mountains running east along the valley from Maria Alm to Mühlbach. Many of the runs are north-facing. Just to the west of Maria Alm is the tiny little area of Hinterreit, where international ski teams train. Maria Alm has its own small ski area – Natrun – and a red run leads off the back to the main local Aberg-Langeck mountain served by a gondola. You need a bus from Aberg to the rest of the main ski area, starting at Hinterthal – but you can ski from Hinterthal to Aberg (this is a flattish track but a new piste is planned). From Hinterthal you can go via Dienten to Mühlbach.

Bischofshofen ↙

HOCHKEIL 1785m/5,86oft

Mühlbach 855m/281oft

1560m

SCHNEEBERG 1820m/5,97oft

Sunnhütte 1750m/5,74oft

WASTLHÖHE 1730m/5,68oft

Dienten 1070m/3,510ft

NEWS

For 2009/10 a six-pack is planned to replace the old double chair out of Hintermoos to Aberg. A new piste is planned from Hochmais to Hintermoos.

For 2008/09 an eight-seat gondola replaced T-bars at Sunnhütte, between Mühlbach and Dienten. Snowmaking was increased.

KEY FACTS

Resorts	800-1070m
	2,620-3,510ft
Slopes	800-1900m
	2,620-6,230ft
Lifts	34
Pistes	150km
	93 miles
Blue	35%
Red	55%
Black	10%
Snowmaking	80%

UK PACKAGES

Maria Alm *Elevation Holidays, Interhome, Neilson, Skiing Austria*
Dienten *Made to Measure*
Hinterthal, Hintermoos *Elevation Holidays*

TOURIST OFFICE

info@highking
mountain.com
www.highking
mountain.com
t UK 0845 643 9424

Fast lifts Mühlbach and Dienten are now generally well linked by fast lifts. And the new six-pack due for 2009/10 is part one of a plan to link Aberg and Hochmais properly from Hintermoos.

Queues Not usually a problem.

Terrain parks There are several; the best are on Aberg and Sunnhütte (the new Kings Park is near the gondola).

Snow reliability The region is in a snow pocket, so it tends to have good conditions for its height. Snowmaking covers 80% of the pistes.

Experts There are several ungroomed ski routes, the best of which is in a huge off-piste bowl behind the Aberg ridge. It's not well marked, and having a guide is useful; a local says, 'There are lots of ways in and it's better than Vail's back bowls.' With a guide you can explore other excellent off-piste too, including tree skiing. There's one genuinely steep black piste on Aberg.

Intermediates The area between Hinterthal and Mühlbach is best for adventurous intermediates, with mainly challenging red runs. You really get a feeling of travelling around here. There are a few easy cruising blue runs in the centre of this area, served by fast lifts, and on Aberg.

Beginners All the villages have good nursery slopes, and there are good progression runs in each sector.

Snowboarding Good for beginners and intermediates, but there are draglifts.

Cross-country There are over 40km/25 miles of prepared tracks.

Mountain restaurants Lots of pleasant huts. Reporters praise Bergstadl and Tischlerhutte (Aberg), Thoraualm (Hintermoos), Burgalm and Almhäusl (Dienten), Tiergartenalm (Sunnhütte).

Schools and guides All four main villages have schools, and many instructors speak good English. Maria Alm's school was 'great and catered for all our different levels'.

Families The kindergartens take children from age two, the schools from age four. Babysitting is available by prior arrangement.

STAYING THERE

Hotels There are plenty of good 3- and 4-star hotels, many with spa facilities, especially in Maria Alm. In Hinterthal Haus Salzburg (23497) is a chalet hotel run by an English couple (Carl is a ski instructor who guides his guests on the Hinterthal-Mühlbach 'safari'), and the 4-star Urslauerhof (8164) has a 'really impressive' spa. In Dienten the 4-star Vital Hotel Post (2030) was 'superb; first-class food, spa, friendly'.

Eating out In Maria Alm the 'friendly' Wirtshausl, the Almerwirt, Alpenland Sporthotel and the Dorfcafe have been recommended. In Hinterthal, Haus Salzburg (see 'Hotels') serves international rather than traditional Austrian food. In Hintermoos, the restaurant at the hotel Handlerhof has 'great food, good service.'

Après-ski Maria Alm is by far the most animated village. The Bachwirt and Dengl Alm are jolly, traditional bars. Almer Tenne has live music and a disco. Orgler Keller is good for a quieter time. The Almbar in Hinterthal can be lively and opens till late, as does the Haus Salzburg bar. Saustall is a decent 'pub' in Mühlbach.

Off the slopes Maria Alm has tobogganing, sleigh rides and nice walks. There are KTrack bikes (with a caterpillar track back wheel and a ski on the front) in Hinterthal. Several hotel pools are open to the public.

Hochkönig (High King Mountain)

139

ABERG-LANGECK
1900m/6,230ft

TLHÖHE
m/5,68oft

Gabühel
1635m/5,36oft

HINTERREIT

Saalfelden

Hintermoos

NATRUN
1100m

Dienten
1070m/3,51oft

HOCHMAIS

Maria Alm
800m/2,62oft

Hinterthal

Innsbruck

Stay in a small, historic, cultured city and visit a different ski area every day, including one of Austria's best glacier areas

Innsbruck is not a ski resort in the usual sense. It is a historic university city of around 140,000 inhabitants, with a vibrant cultural life, and is a major tourist destination in summer. The city has twice hosted the Olympic Winter Games, and is surrounded by several ski areas that share a lift pass and are accessible by efficient bus services. Among them are a glacier that is one of the best in the world, the Stubaier Gletscher (see Stubai valley chapter) and one of Austria's highest, most snow-sure non-glacier areas, Kühtai (2020m/6,630ft).

NEWS

For 2008/09 in Kühtai, an eight-seat gondola replaced a draglift from the valley to the top of Schwarzmoos.

In Oberperfuss, snowmaking was increased to cover 75% of the slopes.

In Igls, a new restaurant opened at the top of the cable car, with a large sun terrace and indoor seating for 150. And there's a new children's area near the base station – due to be improved for 2009/10.

140

KEY FACTS

Resort	575m
	1,890ft
Slopes	800-3210m
	2,620-10,530ft
Lifts	78
Pistes	282km
	175 miles
Blue	32%
Red	49%
Black	19%
Snowmaking	71%

The Inn valley is a broad, flat-bottomed trench here, but Innsbruck manages to fill it from side to side. It is a sizeable city, and as you would expect from its Olympic background, it has an excellent range of winter sports facilities, as well as a captivating car-free medieval core. It has smart, modern, shopping areas, trendy bars and restaurants, museums (including one devoted to the Olympics), concert halls, theatres, a zoo and other attractions that you might seek out on a summer holiday, but wouldn't expect to find when going skiing.

Winter diversions off the slopes include 117km/73 miles of cross-country trails (some at valley level but others appreciably above it), curling and skating at the Olympic centre, several toboggan runs totalling 100km/62 miles (the longest – above Birgitz – an impressive 11km/7 miles) and rides on a four-man bob at Igls.

There are hotels, inns and B&Bs of every standard, with 3-star and 4-star hotels forming the nucleus. Among the more distinctive hotels in the central pedestrian zone are the grand 5-star Europa Tyrol (59310), the ancient Goldener Adler (571111), the Schwarzer Adler (587109), the Grauer Bär (5924) – all 4-stars – and the 3-star Weisses Kreuz (59479).

As well as traditional Austrian restaurants there are several Italian ones, plus a smattering of more exotic alternatives, from Mexican to Japanese.

There is an impressive 1400m/ 4,590ft vertical of slopes on the south-facing slopes of **Nordpark-Seegrube**, reached by a funicular from the fringe of the city centre to the base of the access cable car at Hungerburg. Although there are red runs to the valley, the snow is not reliable. You go up here expecting to ski the red run/ski routes of 370m/1,210ft vertical

below Seegrube, served by a chairlift. A further stage of the cable car rises 350m/1,150ft to access the Karinne ski route, which is said to be very steep.

But for visitors, if not for residents, skiing usually means heading for the opposite side of the Inn trench. The runs on **Glungezer**, above Tulfes, are on north-facing slopes. The chairlift from the bottom serves red and blue runs and another chair up to the treeline serves a red run. This in turn leads to a drag and a chairlift serving open red runs from the top at 2305m/7,560ft – almost 1400m/4,590ft above the village. All the lifts are slow.

The standard Innsbruck lift pass covers the lifts in all the resorts dealt with here, plus the slopes of Schlick

GLUNGEZER
2305m

2245m

Tulfes
920m

Hall in Tirol

LIFT PASSES

Innsbruck Gletscher Skipass

Prices in €

Age	1-day	6-day
under 15	14	105
15 to 18	22	140
19 to 59	27	175
over 60	22	140
Free under 7		
Beginner no deals		

Notes
Day pass is price for Nordpark area only

Alternative passes
Day passes for individual areas; Super Ski pass also covers days in the Arlberg (St Anton) and Kitzbühel

2000 above Fulpmes (see the Stubai valley chapter later in the book). The Innsbruck resort information makes more use of ski area names than village names, so where relevant we show both names.

Free ski-bus services run to and from all the lift-pass-covered areas, but only at the beginning and end of the day. A car makes life more convenient, especially if you are staying outside downtown Innsbruck.

There are terrain parks at Seegrube, Axamer Lizum, the Stubaier Gletscher, Kühtai and Oberperfuss.

A major road runs southwards from Innsbruck over the Brenner pass to Italy – opening up the possibility of excursions to resorts in the Dolomites.

Igls 900m/2,950ft

PATSCHERKOFEL

Igls seems almost a suburb of Innsbruck – the city trams run out to the village – but it is a small resort in its own right. Its famous downhill race course is an excellent piste.

The village of Igls is small and quiet, with not much in the way of diversions apart from the beautiful walks, an outdoor ice rink, the Olympic bob run and the tea shops. You can stay in Igls, and a few UK operators sell

packages there. Most hotels are small and in the centre of the village, a bit of a walk from the cable car station. An exception is the family-run 4-star Sporthotel (377241), which occupies the prime site between the tram and the cable car stations ('excellent facilities and bar').

The skiing on Patscherkofel is very limited and revolves around the excellent, varied, long red run that formed the men's downhill course in 1976, when Franz Klammer took ski racing (and the Olympic gold medal) by storm. There is a blue-run variation on this run, but few other pistes. A cable car rises 1050m/3,440ft from the village (and you can take it down if the lower runs are poor or shut). At the top, a chair rises a further 275m/900ft to the summit offering wonderful views over Innsbruck and ski routes back down. Two fast quads and a couple of drags serve the other slopes. There is a short beginner lift at village level, and another a short bus-ride up the hill. There are half a dozen restaurants (including the new Panorama), children's area and a race training centre. We have received mixed reports on grooming.

Après-ski is quiet. The resort suits families but others might prefer to stay in Innsbruck.

Innsbruck

STUBAIER GLETSCHER
3210m/10,530ft

Hoadl
2340m/7,680ft

Pleisen

Mutterberg

Birgitzköpfl
2100m

245m

PATSCHERKOFEL

Neustift

1800m

Schlick
2000

Fulpmes

Kühtai

AXAMER LIZUM
1580m

RANGGER KÖPFL

Mutters
830m

MUTTERERALM

Igls
900m

Götzens
870m

Axams

Oberperfuss
815m

Innsbruck
575m/1,890ft

Seefeld

Hungerburg

NORDPARK-SEEGRUBE   2255m

UK PACKAGES
Innsbruck *Simply Alpine*
Igls *Inghams, Lagrange, Made to Measure, Simply Alpine, Skiing Austria*
Axamer Lizum *First Choice, Skiing Austria*
Götzens *Lagrange*
Kühtai *Crystal, Inghams, Skiing Austria*
Mutters *Skiing Austria*

Phone numbers
Calling long-distance
Add the prefix given below for each resort; when calling from abroad use the country code 43 and omit the initial '0'.

Innsbruck, Igls, Mutters
0512

Axamer Lizum
05234

Oberperfuss
05232

Kühtai
05239

INNSBRUCK TOURISM

Great views of the city and mountains beyond from sunny Nordpark-Seegrube ↓

Axamer Lizum

1580m/5,180ft

The mountain outpost of the Inn-side village of Axams is a ski station and nothing more, but it does have some good slopes and reliable snow conditions – and, as a reporter says, 'You feel as if you are in a wilderness.'
Axamer Lizum could scarcely provide a sharper contrast to Igls. It offers much more varied slopes and a network of lifts, with the base station at a much higher altitude. The slopes here hosted all the Olympic Alpine events in 1976 except the men's downhill, and this is the standard local venue for weekends – hence the huge car park at the base.

The main slopes are blues and reds, almost entirely above the trees but otherwise nicely varied, and there is scope to 'play in gullies and bumps, as well as true off-piste', says a reporter. The vertical of the main east-facing slopes above the main lift station is 700m/2,300ft and there is the possibility (given good snow conditions) of a 1300m/ 4,260ft descent at the end of the day from Pleisen to the outskirts of Axams – an easy 6.5km/4 mile black. On the opposite side of the valley, a chairlift serves a fairly easy black slope. Beyond it are the slopes of Mutters, which were closed for a few years, but have reopened. Snowmaking covers 75% of the slopes and there is a large restaurant with panoramic views on Hoadl. There are two good nursery lifts, and two ski schools.

You can stay up here – there is a 4-star hotel, the Lizumerhof (68244) at the lift base – 'nice rooms and decent modern Austrian cuisine' – and a couple of other hotels too. But there's little in the way of après-ski apart from a couple of bars – the Almbar Löchle is the most atmospheric – and you have to eat in your hotel or go down to Axams.

There is also accommodation not far away at lower altitude in Axams – including three 3-star hotels – and nearby villages such as Birgitz and Götzens (see below) on the road to Mutters.

Mutters / Götzens

830m/2,720ft / 870m/2,850ft
MUTTERERALM

Almost as close to Innsbruck as Igls, Mutters and Götzens are charming rustic villages on an elevated shelf at the foot of long slopes on Muttereralm.
Mutters makes an attractive base for beginners and particularly families: the eight-seat gondola from the village serves a long blue piste and an equally long toboggan run. There is a nursery draglift up the hill. Above that a high-speed quad takes you to the summit at 1800m/5,910ft and serves its own red run. From the top a long and challenging red run goes down to Götzens along the valley, with another gondola back up. There's snowmaking on both these valley runs. Götzens has another good toboggan run, and skating and curling; there are cross-

country loops between the villages, more directly accessed from Mutters.

Mutters has a slightly better choice of lodgings than Götzens, with a couple of 4-star hotels as well as more modest places.

Oberperfuss 815m/2,670ft

RANGGER KÖPFL

A small resort with a small ski hill, covered by the Innsbruck lift pass.
The hill is a very limited one, with five lifts, including a newish eight-seat gondola, in a largely linear arrangement serving 17km/11 miles of slopes (a long blue and a few reds) – but an impressive vertical of 1200m/3,940ft. And 75% of the pistes have snowmaking. The village is small but self-sufficient; it has a big 3-star hotel, the Krone (81465) – with a new restaurant, M1. It is prettily rustic, and targets the family market with the aid of a moving carpet lift on the nursery slopes. There is night skiing and tobogganing on Tuesdays and Fridays.

Kühtai 2020m/6,630ft

A collection of comfortable hotels spread along a high road pass 25km/16 miles west of Innsbruck – higher and cheaper than equally snow-sure Obergurgl or Obertauern.
Glaciers apart, Kühtai's altitude means it is one of Austria's most snow-sure resorts. That is its main attraction, given the limited nature of the village.

A new eight-seat gondola, three fast quad chairs and several draglifts serve 37km/23 miles of mainly red cruisers of up to 500m/1,640ft vertical on either side of the road, plus some token blue and black runs (which may be easier than the reds because they

get less traffic). There is a good nursery slope, but no easy blues to graduate to. There's also a terrain park with kickers and rails. And on Wednesdays and Saturdays there's night skiing. The resort attracts families during school holidays and day trippers on fine weekends – especially if lower resorts are short of snow – but it is otherwise crowd- and queue-free. There are three mountain restaurants and three ski schools.

The village is quiet in the evening, but for its size has a reasonable selection of bars and restaurants – practically all in hotels. The 4-star hotels include the Jagdschloss (5201) – an old hunting lodge ('a gem of a hotel, great food, wonderful ambience'). Other visitors have recommended the 4-star Mooshaus (5207) – 'convenient, excellent service and food' – and the Elisabeth (5240) – 'very friendly, excellent food'. The Alpin Resort (7155510) has smart apartments from 1 to 4 bedrooms plus a fitness centre. Reporters say that English is not spoken everywhere.

Stubaier Gletscher

The Stubaier Gletscher is one of the best glacier ski areas in the world; it is open in summer as well as in winter and is covered in more detail in the Stubai valley chapter later in the book.
The glacier is accessed by two alternative two-stage gondolas from the huge car park at Mutterberg. A third gondola from Eisgrat at 2900m/9,510ft takes you right to the top of the slopes at over 3200m/10,500ft.

On the glacier a variety of chairs and draglifts (including three six-packs) allow fabulous high altitude cruising on blue and red runs.

Interactive resort shortlist builder at **www.wtss.co.uk**

TOURIST OFFICES

Innsbruck
t 53560
info@innsbruck.info
www.innsbruck.info

Igls
t 377101
igls@innsbruck.info
www.innsbruck.info/igls

Axamer Lizum
t 68178
axams@innsbruck.info
www.innsbruck.info/axams/

Mutters
t 548410
mutters@innsbruck.info
www.innsbruck.info/mutters

Oberperfuss
t 81489
oberperfuss@innsbruck.info
www.innsbruck.info/oberperfuss

Kühtai
t 5222
info@schneegarantie.at
www.schneegarantie.at

Ischgl

Ischgl is unique: high, snow-sure slopes, a superb lift system, and a traditional-style Tirolean village with extraordinary après-ski

£100
RESORT PRICE INDEX

RATINGS

The mountains

Extent	★★★★
Fast lifts	★★★★★
Queues	★★★★
Terrain p'ks	★★★★★
Snow	★★★★
Expert	★★★
Intermediate	★★★★
Beginner	★★
X-country	★★★
Restaurants	★★★★
Schools	★★★
Families	★★

The resort

Charm	★★★
Convenience	★★★
Scenery	★★★
Eating out	★★★★
Après-ski	★★★★★
Off-slope	★★★

144

NEWS

For 2009/10 snowmaking is again being increased, and several hotels and restaurants are being renovated and modernised. There are plans to replace the Pardatschgrat gondola – but not until 2010/11.

For 2008/09 the Gampenalp mountain restaurant was revamped and renamed Bistro Gampen. On the Swiss side a new hotel, the Smart Hotel, opened in Samnaun Ravaisch.

- ➕ Towny Tirolean village, with lots of upmarket hotels
- ➕ High slopes with reliable snow
- ➕ Broad area of slopes linked to Switzerland, with some long runs
- ➕ Superb modern lift system
- ➕ Après-ski that could be described as lively and uninhibited, or ...

- ➖ Après-ski that could be described as sordid and tacky
- ➖ Not ideal for beginners or timid intermediates, for various reasons
- ➖ Few seriously steep runs
- ➖ Very little wooded terrain to give shelter in bad weather

Judging by the number of reader reports we receive, Ischgl and neighbouring Galtür are at last becoming more popular with UK skiers and boarders. About time, too – we've been droning on about Ischgl for years. Its lift system is particularly impressive, near the top of our fast lifts league table. Unless cost is an obstacle, or you insist on lots of woodland runs with unreliable snow, put it on your Austrian shortlist. And the après-ski? Well, it's easy to avoid the pole dancing and lap dancing if that's not your scene, so it shouldn't cause anyone to stay away – except on principle. But it is part of a more general vulgarity about Ischgl that is less easy to pin down, and less easy to escape. You might prefer to stay in much quieter Galtür (a bus ride away) or Samnaun (linked to Ischgl's ski area but a duty-free village in Switzerland).

THE RESORT

Ischgl is a compact village tucked away south of St Anton in the long, narrow Paznaun valley, on the Swiss border; the ski area is shared with Samnaun in Switzerland. A regional pass is available covering Galtür further up the valley and Kappl and See down the valley, all described at the end of this chapter. All are worth a visit and would make cheaper, quieter bases. There are frequent ski-buses to all of them. A car makes trips to St Anton viable.

VILLAGE CHARM ★★★
More town than village
The buildings are predominantly traditional chalet style, with one or

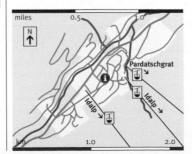

two modern exceptions, but this is no rustic backwater – the narrow streets give it a towny air, and the style is swanky and brash rather than tasteful. There's a selection of lively bars and an excellent sports centre; shops are mainly confined to winter sports. The narrow main street plus a couple of side streets are mostly traffic-free – the valley road up to Galtür bypasses the village.

CONVENIENCE ★★★
Beware of the bypass
The best location, overall, is on or near the main pedestrian street. At the western end is the main gondola to the mid-mountain focus of Idalp. On the eastern fringe of the village, over a low hill but reachable via an underground moving walkway, is another gondola to Idalp, and a third to Pardatschgrat, higher up. Beware of accommodation across the bypass road, a long way from the lifts.

SCENERY ★★★
Good at the top
The wooded flanks of the valley rise steeply from the village, which gets almost no sun in January. But above the treeline, the Silvretta range is revealed in all its glory.

KEY FACTS

Resort	1400m
	4,590ft
Slopes	1400-2870m
	4,590-9,420ft
Lifts	39
Pistes	215km
	134 miles
Blue	18%
Red	61%
Black	21%
Snowmaking	53%

TVB PAZNAUN-ISCHGL

Ideal intermediate cruising on open slopes served by lots of high-speed lifts; the only thing you need to worry about is crowds on the trails ↓

THE MOUNTAINS

Ischgl is a fair-sized, relatively high, snow-sure area. Practically all the slopes are above the treeline, the main exception being the steep lower slopes above the village and a couple of short runs low in the Fimbatal.

The piste map is good. But signposting can be 'a bit confusing' says a recent reporter and a 2009 visitor found the edge marking 'shocking and dangerous – my wife went over the edge in poor visibility and had a nasty fall'. Reporters generally find grooming 'excellent'.

EXTENT OF THE SLOPES ★★★★
Extensive cross-border cruising
The sunny **Idalp** plateau, reached by the 24-person Silvrettabahn and eight-seat Fimbabahn, is the hub of the slopes. It can be very crowded, especially at ski school meeting time, lunchtime and the end of the day. Pardatschgrat, reached by the third gondola, is about 300m/980ft higher, and offers testing runs of 1260m/4,130ft vertical to the village. From Idalp, lifts radiate to a wide variety of mainly north-west- and west-facing runs including over the border in Switzerland. The red runs back down to Ischgl provoke regular complaints. Neither is easy, conditions can be tricky, and beer-lubricated crowds don't help. Quite a few people ride the gondolas down; you can leave your skis and boots in lockers at Idalp if you wish. The wide, quiet piste down the pretty Velilltal is much more pleasant, but doesn't entirely avoid the steep bottom part of run 1A to the Pardatschgratbahn, which should probably be a black.

A short piste brings you from Idalp to the lifts serving the **Höllenkar** bowl, leading up to the area's south-western

extremity and high point at Palinkopf. Runs of 900m/2,950ft vertical from here lead down to the **Fimbatal**. On the Swiss side, the hub of activity is **Alp Trida**, surrounded by south- and east-facing runs with great views. From here a scenic red run goes down to Compatsch, where a short walk takes you to buses to Ravaisch – for the cable car back – and Samnaun. From Palinkopf there is a long, beautiful red run down an unspoiled valley to Samnaun-Dorf – not difficult, but excessively sunny in parts and prone to closure by avalanche risk. There is a long flat stretch at the end.

FAST LIFTS ★★★★★
One of the best
Ischgl is near the top of our fast league table. Around 75% of its lifts are fast; most are ultra-modern chairs that serve both sides of the border.

QUEUES ★★★★
OK up the mountain
The upgrade of the Fimbabahn gondola two seasons ago has helped relieve pressure on the other two gondolas, which have nearby car/coach parks and can build serious queues. None of our 2009 reporters mentioned any queue problems. Up the mountain, crowds on the runs are more of an issue, especially at Idalp and the easier runs on the Swiss side. We've found lots of people skiing too fast and too close to others.

TERRAIN PARKS ★★★★★
One of Europe's best
The huge SnowArt park above Idalp, served by three chairlifts including the Idjochbahn, is enough to draw freestylers to Ischgl. It is now 1600m/5,250ft long and is always well-shaped and maintained. The park is split into public/beginner, intermediate

Ischgl

145

LIFT PASSES

VIP Skipass

Prices in €

Age	1-day	6-day
under 17	25	116
17 to 59	43	193
over 60	38	164

Free under 8

Beginner no deals

Notes

Covers all lifts in Ischgl and Samnaun and local buses; half-day pass and non-skier pass available; 2-day-plus pass available only to those staying in Ischgl or Mathon on presenting a guest card

Alternative passes

Regional pass covers Ischgl, Samnaun, Galtür, Kappl and See

and king-size lines. New rails and boxes were added last season, as well as several good intermediate and entry-level kickers. The big pro line consists of several 15-17m/50-56ft kickers and three corner jumps in a row. Fluidity was vastly improved last season, allowing you to hit several obstacles in a row. The World Rookie fest finals are held here, which means the park set-ups are second to none around the event held in April. There is another small park on the Swiss side. 'Style on Art' weeks are held every January – where rails and wall rides get a makeover by local and national street artists.

SNOW RELIABILITY ★★★★☆
Very good

All the slopes, except the runs back to the resort, are above 1800m/5,910ft, and many of those on the Ischgl side

are north-west-facing. So snow conditions are generally reliable; we've always had good snow here, and we are not alone. There is snowmaking on a good proportion of the slopes, including the descents to Ischgl and Samnaun – due to be increased again this year. Piste grooming is good.

FOR EXPERTS ★★★☆☆
Not much on-piste challenge

Ischgl can't compare with St Anton for exciting slopes, and some of the runs marked black on the piste map would be red elsewhere. But by general Tirolean standards Ischgl serves experts quite well. None of the black runs is particularly steep, but all are genuine blacks and in combination with testing reds offer excellent, challenging descents. Head first for Palinkopf and Pardatschgrat – piste 4 is a favourite – but don't neglect

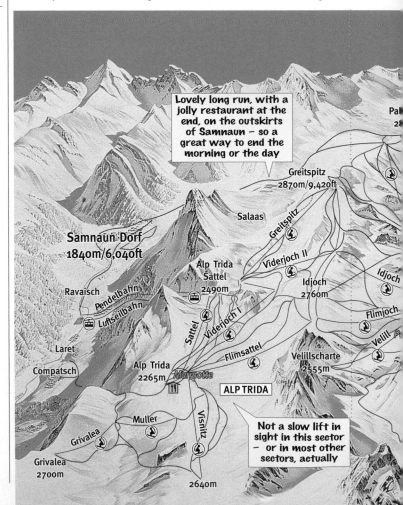

Lovely long run, with a jolly restaurant at the end, on the outskirts of Samnaun – so a great way to end the morning or the day

Not a slow lift in sight in this sector – or in most other sectors, actually

Greitspitz. The wooded lower slopes of the Fimbatal are delightful in a storm. There are off-piste opportunities around the pistes all over the place; there is plenty of serious off-piste to be found with a guide; and powder doesn't get tracked out quickly. There are also ski routes. Ski route 39 from Palinkopf is recommended to leave you 'suitably exhausted' after a testing 1000m/3,28oft descent.

FOR INTERMEDIATES ★★★★
Something for everyone

Most of the slopes are wide, forgiving and ideal for intermediates.

At the tough end of the spectrum our favourite runs are those from Palinkopf down to Gampenalp at the edge of the ski area, with great views of virgin slopes. There are also interesting and challenging black runs down the Höllspitz chair, and on Greitspitz. The reds from Pardatschgrat and Velillscharte down the beautiful Velilltal and the red from Greitspitz into Switzerland are great for quiet, high-speed cruising.

For easier motorway cruising, there is lots of choice, including those down to and around Alp Trida on the Swiss side – but these can get crowded. Timid intermediates should avoid the steep runs back to town.

FOR BEGINNERS ★★
Up the mountain

Beginners must buy a full lift pass and go up the mountain to Idalp, where there are good, sunny, snow-sure nursery slopes served by drags and a fast chair. The blue runs on the east side of the bowl offer pleasant progression for fast learners. Over at Alp Trida there are further easy expanses – you can return by lift.

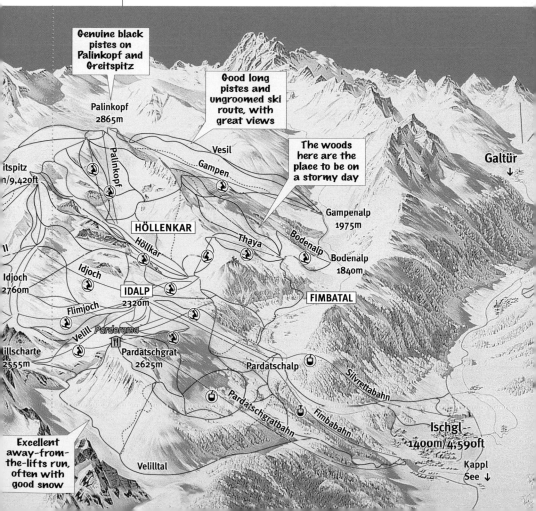

boarding

Ischgl has long been a popular spot for snowboarders, with its long, wide, well-groomed slopes served by snowboard-friendly gondolas and high-speed chairlifts. Although the off-piste terrain is less steep than in some other resorts, its above-the-treeline, easily accessible nature and good snow record makes for great riding for most ability levels. Ischgl is home to one of Austria's best terrain parks and Silvretta Sports and Intersport Mathoy are recommended snowboard shops.

FOR CROSS-COUNTRY ★★★
Plenty in the valley

There are 24km/15 miles of track in the valley between Ischgl, Galtür and Wirl. This tends to be shady, especially in early season, and is away from the main slopes, which makes meeting downhillers for lunch inconvenient.

MOUNTAIN RESTAURANTS ★★★★
New and improved

Mountain restaurants have tended to offer quite good quality, but inadequate capacity. But things have improved recently, with new places opening on both sides of the border. **Editors' choice** The Marmotte (+41 81 868 5221) at Alp Trida on the Swiss side wins no prizes for interior design but serves reliably good food in calm and comfortable surroundings. On the Austrian side, in the past we've had fabulous spicy prawns and ox fillet at the glass-sided Pardorama complex (606800) at the top of Pardatschgrat. **Worth knowing about** At Idalp the Alpenhaus has a choice of table- or self-service, and gets top marks from a reporter for its 'stunning' interior design, with a mention too for the barbecued steak. The Paznauner Thaya, above Bodenalp, has table- and self-service sections, and often has live bands or throbbing disco music. Some reporters prefer the quieter Bodenalpe, down in Fimbatal: 'service with a smile' and 'huge portions'. From Gampenalp you can be towed 5km/3 miles by snowmobile to the remote Heidelberger hütte – the way back is quite hard work, though.

On the Swiss side the newish Salaas is a spacious, sunny, glass-sided place just above Alp Trida Eck, with self-service and 'limited' table service. We've had mixed reviews but a 2009 visitor raved about the 'stunning views'. The woody Alp Bella is good value and a consistent favourite – 'fabulous rösti, delicious desserts'. The Skihaus Alp Trida and the Panorama Sattel have also been recommended, not least for the views.

SCHOOLS AND GUIDES ★★★
Best for late risers

The school meets up at Idalp and starts at 10am. A 2009 visitor found his lesson 'good' with his instructor speaking 'sufficient English' and the class smaller than the 10-12 that he noticed many others contained. The school also organises off-piste tours.

FOR FAMILIES ★★
High-altitude options

The childcare facilities are all up at Idalp. Small kids might be better off in Galtür or Kappl – see descriptions at the end of this chapter.

STAYING THERE

Hotels There is a good selection from luxurious and pricey to simple B&Bs. *******Trofana Royal** (600) One of Austria's most luxurious hotels, with prices to match. A celebrity chef runs the kitchen. Sumptuous spa facilities. ******Madlein** (5226) Convenient, 'hip', modern hotel. Pool, sauna, steam room. Nightclub and disco. ******Elisabeth** (5411) Right by the Pardatschgrat gondola, with lively après-ski. Pool, sauna and steam. ******Solaria** (5205) Near the Madlein and just as luxurious, with a 'friendly family atmosphere' and 'helpful staff'. ******Brigitte** (5646) Central, but quiet location. Pool. Highly recommended. ******Piz Tasna** (5277) Up hill behind church: 'Quiet, friendly, lovely views.' ******Goldener Adler** (5217) Central, smart, modern hotel, with 'outstanding food'. Sauna and whirlpool. ******Olympia** (5432) Family-run hotel with reportedly good-sized rooms. Bar and restaurant. Sauna and solarium. ******Jägerhof** (5206) 'Jewel of a hotel.' Friendly, good food, large rooms. Sauna, steam and whirlpool. ******Post** (5232) 'Excellent central position; very nice staff,' says a 2008 visitor. Wellness centre. ******Christine** (5346) Probably the best B&B in town. 'Huge rooms, nice views, near the lifts.' Sauna and steam.

****Dorfschmiede** (5769) Small, central B&B with 'friendly service'.
****Lamtana** (56095) Near the Silvrettabahn. 'Very good buffet breakfast; spacious, modern rooms.' Wellness area.
***Alpenglühn** (5294) Convenient, recently refurbished and good value. Recommended by a recent visitor.
Apartments Some attractive apartments are available. Recommendations include the Golfais by the Pardatschgrat gondola and the apartments in the hotel Solaria (with use of its spa).

EATING OUT ★★★★
Plenty of choice
Most of our reporters eat in their hotels. For lighter meals try the Nona, the Schatzi or the Trofana Alm ('good ribs'), which is as much a bar as a restaurant, and for fondue or ribs the Kitzloch, with its galleries over the dance floor. The Allegra and Salz & Pfeffer 'pasta and pizza' have been recommended. The Grillalm and Salnerhof are popular, 'traditional Austrian fare, huge portions'. A reporter pronounces the Nudelhimmel (hotel Solaria) his favourite – local dishes at reasonable prices. The Nevada has also been recommended: 'Excellent venison and duck.'

APRES-SKI ★★★★★
Very lively
Ischgl is one of the liveliest resorts in the Alps, from early afternoon on. Lots of people are still in ski boots late in the evening. Mountain restaurants such as Paznauner Thaya slide into après mode directly after lunch. When you manage to get back to the village, the obvious ports of call are the Trofana Alm near the Silvrettabahn or the Schatzi bar of the hotel Elisabeth by the Pardatschgratbahn – with scantily clad dancing girls. Niki's Stadl across the road is the place for a Tirolean knees-up, with DJs. The Kitzloch 'rocks', with dancing on the tables in ski boots. The Kuhstahl under the Sporthotel Silvretta and Feuer & Eis over the road are packed all evening. The bar at the hotel Sonne, the Höllboden and the Golden Eagle are 'good for live bands'. The Allegra livens up after dinner. There's lap dancing at the huge Trofana Arena and the Coyote Ugly at hotel Madlein. The Pacha nightclub (also in Ibiza and London) is a bit 'tacky', says a visitor.

The Living Room (Grillalm hotel) is allegedly 'more hands-on' than table dancing. And the club under hotel Post has an ancient Roman theme.

OFF THE SLOPES ★★★
No sun but a nice pool
The village gets little sun in the middle of winter, and the resort is best suited to those keen to hit the slopes. But there's no shortage of off-slope activities. There are lots of well-marked and maintained walking paths including many at altitude (the tourist office claims an astonishing 1140km/700 miles of walks in the whole Paznaun valley), a 7km/4 mile floodlit toboggan run and a splendid sports centre. And you can browse upmarket shops, which sell Versace and Bogner. It's easy to get around the valley by bus and the Smuggler's Pass for pedestrians enables them to use specially selected lifts.

Samnaun 1840m/6,040ft

Small, quiet duty-free Samnaun is in a corner of Switzerland more easily reached from Austria. It is virtually Brit-free. There are four small components, roughly 1km/0.5 mile apart: Samnaun-Dorf, prettily set at the head of the valley is the main focus, with some swanky hotels and duty-free shops; Ravaisch, where the cable car goes up; tiny Plan; and the hamlets of Laret and Compatsch, at the end of the main run down from the slopes. We've stayed happily on the edge of Dorf in the Waldpark B&B (8618310), and have eaten well at the Pasta in the hotel Montana (8619000). Reporters recommend the 4-star hotel Post (8619200) ('good food but pricey'), 4-star Muttler (8618130) ('very good spa and complimentary ski bus'), the Alpina ('exceptional value, traditional Swiss food, where the locals eat') and Des Alpes ('modern food and affordable'). There's a smart AlpenQuell spa-pool-fitness centre.

The Schmuggler Alm at the bottom of the long run from Palinkopf is a popular après-ski spot and does 'a good lunch'. A reporter also recommends a 'delicious amaretto hot chocolate' at the Almraus (hotel Cresta), at Compatsch.

Kappl 1260m/4,130ft

Kappl, a 15-minute bus ride down the valley from Ischgl, is worth a visit – we've had a great half-day there. Both the village and the slopes are family-oriented, and delightfully quiet compared with Ischgl. The village, with a couple of dozen hotels and guest-houses, sits on a shelf 100m/330ft above the valley floor. The Sunny Mountain area at the top of the access gondola has a big kindergarten and outside play area. There's a long toboggan run from here back to the village (floodlit twice a week).

There are 40km/25 miles of sunny, largely south-facing pistes going up to 2640m/8,660ft. The slopes – served by an access gondola from the roadside and fast quads above it – offer plenty of variety, with several tough reds, including the Lattenabfahrt down a deserted valley from the top – 8km/5 miles long, 985m/3,230ft vertical, more if you go on to the valley floor. Most of the slopes are open, but the run down the gondola offers some shelter for bad-weather days. Snow-guns cover all but the highest slopes.

See 1050m/3,440ft

See, a 10-minute bus ride further down the valley from Kappl, has 33km/21 miles of predominantly easy, largely north-facing slopes. It is worth a visit from Ischgl to get away from the crowds, if you don't mind the limited extent of the slopes.

We found great powder here on our recent April visit – excellent for making your first turns off-piste. There's a good nursery slope at the top of the access gondola, and easy runs to progress to. Piste 10 is a beautiful red run round the back of the mountain, away from all lifts, with spectacular views – a pleasant ski to start with and then a road you cruise along admiring the views. Bambini World offers childcare. There's a popular

toboggan run.

See is worth considering as a base for families – it's quieter and cheaper than Ischgl; but the village is not especially attractive and is rather spoiled by the main road through it. Accommodation is largely in 3-star roadside hotels and guest houses.

Galtür 1585m/5,200ft

Galtür is a charming, peaceful, traditional village clustered around a pretty little church, amid impressive mountain scenery at the head of the valley (and so unspoiled by through-traffic). Rebuilt and fortified after the devastating avalanche of 1999, the village is now home to the impressive Alpinarium, an avalanche-protection structure with an exhibition centre – 'worth a visit', says a reporter, despite the fact that it's all in German.

Sunnier, cheaper and much quieter than Ischgl, Galtür is a good base for families and mixed-ability groups – and the free buses to Ischgl are regular and quick, but they stop at around 6pm, 'so evening activities required a 20 euro taxi' says a 2009 visitor. There are good hotels, including the 4-star Almhof (8253), Flüchthorn (8202), Ballunspitze (8214) and 3-star Alpenrose (8201).

Galtür's own slopes rise to 2295m/7,530ft above a lift base at Wirl, a short bus ride from the village. The ski area has been re-branded Silvapark, with six 'sectors' (including one for kids with cartoon characters) to help guests make the most of the mountain. The slopes are not very challenging and can be bleak in poor weather; but the black runs are ideal for intermediates and there are fine nursery slopes. The area on the far right of the piste map, served by a slow double chair and a T-bar, has some good off-piste in a bowl and among well-spaced trees. There's a terrain park beside the Zeinislift drag. The school is 'excellent and well organised' and offers small classes. Kinderland has its own tow, carousel and moving carpet. Galtür has 74km/46 miles of cross-country loops, some quite testing. The cosy, wooden Wieberhimml mountain hut has waitresses in traditional costume.

Off-slope facilities are limited, but there's a sports centre with pool, tennis and squash. Night skiing and sledding are available on Wednesdays.

Phone numbers
Calling long-distance
Add the prefix given below for each resort; when calling from abroad use the country code +43 and omit the initial '0'
Ischgl
05444
Galtür
05443

Samnaun (Switzerland)
From elsewhere in Switzerland add the prefix 081; from abroad use the prefix +41 81

TOURIST OFFICES

Ischgl
t 05099 0100
info@ischgl.com
www.ischgl.com
Samnaun
(Switzerland)
t 868 5858
info@samnaun.ch
www.samnaun.ch
Kappl
t 05099 0300
kappl@kappl-see.com
www.kappl.at
See
t 05099 0400
see@kappl-see.com
www.see.at
Galtür
t 05099 0200
info@galtuer.com
www.galtuer.com

Kitzbühel

The extensive slopes are mostly pretty tame; the medieval town at the base, though, is something special – cute and lively

£95
RESORT PRICE INDEX

RATINGS

The mountains

Extent	★★★
Fast lifts	★★★
Queues	★★★
Terrain p'ks	★★★
Snow	★★
Expert	★★★
Intermediate	★★★★
Beginner	★★
X-country	★★★
Restaurants	★★★★
Schools	★★★★
Families	★

The resort

Charm	★★★★
Convenience	★★
Scenery	★★★
Eating out	★★★★
Après-ski	★★★★
Off-slope	★★★★★

NEWS

For 2008/09 the Ganslern fast quad was installed on the lower slopes, mainly to serve a race-training run but open to all. And a new 'south' terrain park aimed at advanced riders was built on the Hanglalm run in the Resterhöhe sector. Snowmaking facilities were improved again.

An ice bar and igloo village were created near the Sonnenrast chair at Ehrenbach-höhe.

An eight-seat gondola is planned for the separate Bichalm sector, but it won't be there for the 2009/10 season.

- ⊞ Large, attractive, varied slopes offering a sensation of travel
- ⊞ Beautiful medieval town centre
- ⊞ Vibrant nightlife
- ⊞ Lots to do off the slopes
- ⊞ Plenty of cheap lodging
- ⊞ Excellent mountain restaurants

- ⊟ Snow on the lower slopes is often poor (though there's now quite a bit of snowmaking)
- ⊟ Surprisingly little challenging terrain (though there's plenty of off-piste)
- ⊟ Disappointing nursery area
- ⊟ Some crowded pistes

Kitzbühel is one of the big names of the ski world, largely thanks to its Hahnenkamm downhill race course – the most spectacular on the World Cup circuit. And there is a lot to like about the resort – particularly the beautiful, traffic-free centre, complete with cobbled streets and lovely medieval buildings. Some of these contain elegant, upscale hotels. But there is a huge amount of inexpensive accommodation, which attracts low-budget visitors, many of whom are young and out to party in the resort's famous après-ski haunts.

The low altitude of the slopes is a real problem. In countless visits over a 20-year period we've rarely encountered good snow down to the village. Our advice is to book late, when you know the conditions are good.

THE RESORT

Kitzbühel is a large, animated town The beautiful walled medieval centre – with quaint church, cobbled streets and nicely painted buildings – is car-free and a compelling place to stay.

The Kitzbüheler Alpen All Star lift pass covers seven separate ski areas in the region – see 'Lift passes'. One of those – SkiWelt – is now accessible by the Ki-West gondola (a short bus ride from Skirast or Aschau).

VILLAGE CHARM ★★★★
A town in miniature
The car-free medieval centre is delightful. And many visitors love the sophisticated, towny ambience and

swanky shops and cafes. But the resort spreads widely, and busy roads surround the old town, reducing the charm factor somewhat. Visitors used to peaceful little Austrian villages are likely to be surprised by its urban feel.

CONVENIENCE ★★
Choose carefully
A gondola from the edge of the town goes up to the Hahnenkamm, start of the main area of slopes. Across town, close to the railway station but some way from the centre, another gondola accesses the much smaller Kitzbüheler Horn sector. The size of Kitz makes choice of location important. Many visitors prefer to be close to the Hahnenkamm gondola. Beginners

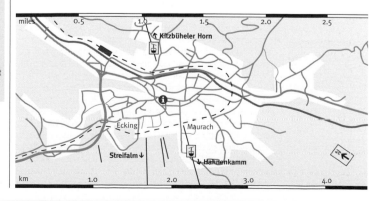

↑ The top of the Hahnenkamm, with the Horn across the valley; if the snow was always this good, Kitzbühel would be a great place to go

BERGBAHN AG KITZBÜHEL

should bear in mind that the Hahnenkamm nursery slopes are often lacking in snow, and then novices are taken up the Horn. Some reporters say the buses around town get overcrowded. But the post bus service is said to be 'cheap and efficient'.

SCENERY ★★★☆☆
Attractive valley views
Kitzbühel is set at a junction of broad, pretty valleys, among partly wooded mountains. There are good views from Pengelstein along both valleys and to the SkiWelt and beyond.

THE MOUNTAINS

Kitzbühel's extensive slopes – shared with Kirchberg and other villages – offer a mixture of entirely open runs higher up and patchy forest lower down. Most face north-east or north-west. The piste map is praised as 'very clear and easy to use'.

EXTENT OF THE SLOPES ★★★☆☆
Big but bitty
The slopes can be divided into several identifiable areas, most linked.

The **Hahnenkamm** gondola takes you to the bowl of Ehrenbachgraben, a major lift bottleneck in the past but now transformed by installation of not only a six-pack to Ehrenbachhöhe, the arrival point of lifts from Kirchberg, but also a newish eight-pack to the high-point of Steinbergkogel. Suddenly, this is a place you might want to do laps.

Beyond is the slightly lower peak of **Pengelstein**, from where several long west-facing runs go down to Skirast, where there is a gondola back up, or Aschau. Ski buses from these points will take you to the Ki-West gondola towards Westendorf and to Kirchberg. It takes up to an hour to reach the heart of the Westendorf slopes,

including the bus connection.

Pengelstein is also the start of the impressive 30-person cross-valley 3S gondola to **Wurzhöhe** above Jochberg. This peak-to-peak link has fabulous views (especially if you hit the cabin with the partial glass floor) and is worth the ride just for scenery.

Further lifts then take you to the **Resterhöhe** sector above Pass Thurn – well worth the excursion, for better snow and fewer crowds. There is a long, scenic, sunny red run to Breitmoos, mid-station of the gondola up from the valley to the south of Pass Thurn. Runs are otherwise short, but mostly served by fast chairs.

The **Kitzbüheler Horn** gondola second stage leads to the sunny Trattalm bowl, with an alternative cable car taking you up to the summit of the Horn, from where a fine, solitary piste leads down into the Raintal on the east side. There's a blue piste and two ski routes back towards town.

There's floodlit skiing on Thursday and Friday on **Gaisberg**, a small area of slopes at Kirchberg, across the resort from the main ski area.

The separate **Bichlalm** area, which used to offer lift-served off-piste, has reopened for guided snowcat skiing. A new lift is planned, but not imminent.

FAST LIFTS ★★★☆☆
Swanky new chairs help
Gondolas provide access from the town, and recent upgrades have introduced fast chairs at key points. More would be good though.

QUEUES ★★★☆☆
Major improvements
Queues to get out of the town have almost been forgotten, and the chair upgrades at Ehrenbachgraben – a six-pack and an eight-pack – have solved the main problem on the mountain.

KEY FACTS

Resort	760m
	2,490ft
Slopes	800-2000m
	2,620-6,560ft
Lifts	55
Pistes	168km
	104 miles
Blue	40%
Red	46%
Black	14%
Snowmaking	59%

LIFT PASSES

Kitzbühel

Prices in €

Age	1-day	6-day
under 16	21	94
16 to 18	33	150
over 19	41	187

Free under 7

Senior 60+: day pass €21 on Tue only; 80+: season pass €20

Beginner seven free lifts (three in Kitzbühel)

Notes

Covers all lifts in Kitzbühel, Kirchberg, Jochberg, Pass Thurn, Mittersill/Hollersbach; 50% reduction on pool entry and passes for 2 days or more; single ascent, hourly and pedestrian tickets; family reductions

Alternative passes

Kitzbüheler Alpen All Star Card covers seven ski areas – Kitzbühel, Schneewinkel (St Johann), Ski Welt, Alpbach, Wildschönau, Skicircus Saalbach, Zell-Kaprun; Salzburg Super Ski Card covers 22 ski areas in the Salzburg province

The slow Maierl chairs out of Kirchberg are still tiresome. But we have had reports of bearable queues at half-term, and queue-free weeks at other times. Both the Horn and the Hahnenkamm can have crowded pistes – though the gondola to Wurzhöhe has helped to spread the traffic.

TERRAIN PARKS ★★★
Double the fun

A brand new 'south' park opened in 2008/09, designed by Q parks and aimed at advanced riders. It is situated on the Hanglalm run in the Resterhöhe sector. The new park has several kicker lines, from big to huge, as well as advanced rails, a plethora of butter boxes and a visually pleasing wooden obstacle section. The existing 'north' park on the Kitzbüheler Horn, under the Alpenhaus ski lift is now a beginner specific area, full of ride-on boxes and smaller jumps. Local ski schools use this park to introduce novices to freestyle. If the park gets crowded, there are plenty of good kicker spots easily accessible on the nearby ungroomed terrain. The park in Westendorf is excellent – worth the trip for freestyle aficionados.

SNOW RELIABILITY ★★
More snowmaking now

The problem is that Kitzbühel's slopes have one of the lowest average heights in the Alps. To make matters worse, the Horn is also sunny. Even in an exceptionally good snow year some reporters complain of worn patches, ice and slush on the lower slopes. In a normal year, the lower slopes can be very tricky or bare at times (though the snow at the top is often OK). The expansion of snowmaking has improved matters when it's cold enough to make snow – runs down to Kitzbühel, Kirchberg, Klausen and Jochberg are covered. But many slopes still remain unprotected. If snow is poor, head for Resterhöhe.

FOR EXPERTS ★★★
Plan to go off-piste

Steep slopes – pistes and off-piste terrain – are mostly concentrated in the Steinbergkogel-Ehrenbachgraben area, now equipped with two fast chairs. Direttissima is seriously steep, but sometimes groomed – fabulous. The other blacks dotted around are easier. There are plenty of long, challenging reds. When conditions allow, there is plenty of gentler off-piste potential to be found – some of it safely close to pistes, some requiring a guide. And the long ski route from Pengelstein towards Jochberg is fabulous in good snow.

FOR INTERMEDIATES ★★★★
Lots of alternatives

The Hahnenkamm area is prime terrain but can get crowded. Good intermediates will want to do the World Cup downhill run, of course (see the feature panel). And the long blues of around 1000m/3,300ft vertical to Klausen and to Skirast are satisfying. The black to Aschau is not difficult, and a lovely way to end the day (check bus times first). The Wurzhöhe runs are good for mixed abilities, and the short, high runs at Resterhöhe are ideal if you are more timid. There are easy reds down to Pass Thurn and Jochberg. The whole of this area tends to be much quieter than Hahnenkamm and Pengelstein. Much of the Horn is good cruising and the east-facing Raintal run on the Horn is excellent.

FOR BEGINNERS ★★
Not ideal

The Hahnenkamm nursery slopes are no more than adequate, and prone to poor snow conditions. The Horn has a high, sunny, nursery-like section, and quick learners will soon be cruising home from there on the long Hagstein piste. There are some easy runs to progress to if the snow is OK. But there are better resorts to learn in.

boarding

Kitzbühel was never known as a snowboarders' hub, but it's growing in popularity, year on year. In order to attract a more freestyle-orientated clientele, Q parks was hired to build a new park. The Q team designs no fewer than 10 Austrian parks in areas such as Silvretta Nova (in the Montafon) and Sölden, so the resort is in good hands. Kitzbühel now boasts two decent terrain parks built for all levels, as well as a boardercross. There are some good off-piste runs and fun natural obstacles on the Hahnenkamm and around Pengelstein. All major lifts are gondolas and chairlifts – the area suits beginners and intermediates well.

FOR CROSS-COUNTRY ★★★
Plentiful but low
There are around 40km/25 miles of
trails scattered around, but all are at
valley level and prone to lack of snow.

MOUNTAIN RESTAURANTS ★★★★
A highlight
There are many attractive restaurants
(over 50 handily numbered and
marked on the piste map) – 'one of
the reasons we keep going back', says
one of our Kitz regulars.

Editors' choice On our 2009 visit, we
had a delicious lunch of oriental beef
strip salad and crispy pork ribs at
Bärenbadalm (0664 8557994), halfway
to Resterhöhe. This is a newish hut
with a cool, modern bar area with flat
screen TVs, a roaring log fire and
comfy armchairs and sofas; you can
eat there or in various restaurant areas
which have a more rustic feel.
Seidlalm (63135), right by the lower
part of the downhill course, is
relatively quiet and delightfully rustic;

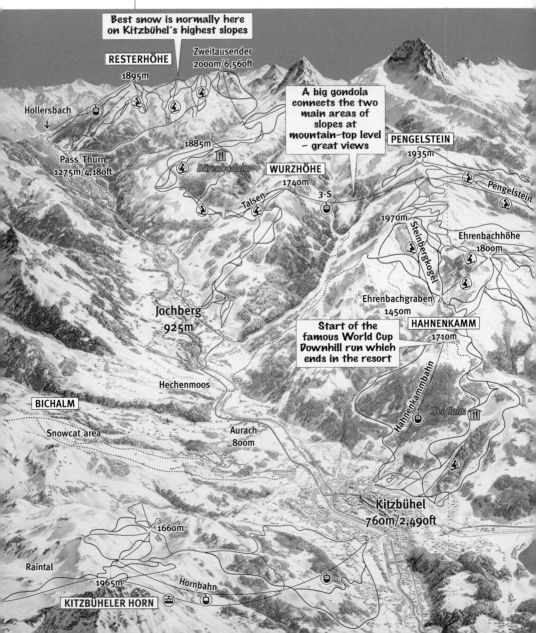

THE HAHNENKAMM DOWNHILL

Kitzbühel's Hahnenkamm Downhill race, held in mid-January each year, is the toughest as well as one of the most famous on the World Cup circuit. On the race weekend the town is packed and there is a real carnival atmosphere, with bands, people in traditional costumes and huge (and loud) cowbells everywhere. The race itself starts with a steep icy section before you hit the famous Mausfalle and Steilhang, where even Franz Klammer used to get worried. The course starts near the top of the Hahnenkamm gondola and drops 860m/2,820ft to finish amid the noise and celebrations right on the edge of town. The course is normally closed from the start of the season until after the race, but after the race weekend ordinary mortals can now try most of the course, if the snow is good enough – it's an unpisted ski route mostly. We found it steep and tricky in parts, even when going slowly – it must be terrifying at race speeds of 80mph or more.

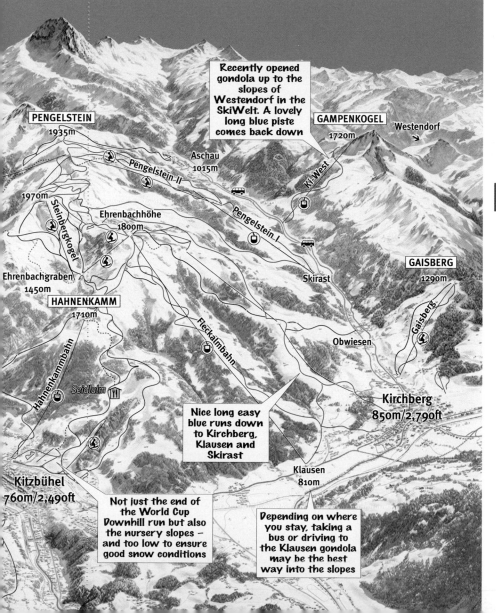

Recently opened gondola up to the slopes of Westendorf in the SkiWelt. A lovely long blue piste comes back down

Nice long easy blue runs down to Kirchberg, Klausen and Skirast

Not just the end of the World Cup Downhill run but also the nursery slopes – and too low to ensure good snow conditions

Depending on where you stay, taking a bus or driving to the Klausen gondola may be the best way into the slopes

PENGELSTEIN
1935m

Aschau
1015m

Pengelstein-II

1970m

Ehrenbachhöhe
1800m

Steinbergkogel

Pengelstein-I

Ehrenbachgraben
1450m

HAHNENKAMM
1710m

Fleckalmbahn

Hahnenkammbahn

Seidalm

Kitzbühel
760m/2,490ft

GAMPENKOGEL
1720m

Westendorf

Ki-West

GAISBERG
1290m

Gaisberg

Skirast

Obwiesen

Kirchberg
850m/2,790ft

Klausen
810m

SCHOOLS

Rote Teufel (Red Devil)
t 62500

Element3
t 72301

Classes
(Rote Teufel prices)
6 days (2hr am and pm) €170

Private lessons
€150 for 2hr

CHILDCARE

There is no non-ski nursery, but babysitters and nannies can be hired

Ski school
From age 3 (6 days €170 – Rote Teufel)

GETTING THERE

Air Salzburg 75km/ 45 miles (1hr30); Munich 165km/ 105 miles (2hr30); Innsbruck 95km/ 60 miles (1hr30)

Rail Mainline station in resort. Post bus every 15min from station

ACTIVITIES

Indoor Aquarena Centre (pools, slides, sauna, solarium, mud baths, aerated baths, underwater massage) – discounted entry with lift pass; tennis, fitness centre, beauty centre, indoor riding school, climbing wall, bowling, museums, casino, cinema

Outdoor Ice rink (curling and skating), tobogganing, ballooning, helicopter flights, paragliding, wildlife park, 65km/ 40 miles of cleared walking paths

regularly praised by reporters too. **Worth knowing about** In the Hahnenkamm sector we had a jolly meal at Berghaus Tyrol. Hockeckhütte has 'excellent food and atmosphere'. Melkalm 'is worth the effort of finding'. The Hochbrunn and the Schutzhütte Steinbergkogel are recommended. The expensive Hochkitzbühel at the top of the gondola has mixed reviews. A recent visitor enjoyed the 'bright and modern' Ehrenbachgraben. On Pengelstein, the Usterweis is a nice woody place with a limited menu and Schroll 'has good food and friendly service'. The Kasereckhütte on the ski route to Jochberg is 'brilliant'. At Wurzhöhe, Jägerwurzhütte is mentioned, as is Trattenbachalm; Hanglalm has 'great Kaiserschmarrn', and Panoramaalm great views. On the Horn, Hornköpfl-Hütte's good food and sunny terraces get praised. Alpenhaus 'does excellent self-service meals for great prices' but can get crowded; the quieter Gipfelhaus has 'super views'.

SCHOOLS AND GUIDES ★★★★
Good recent reviews
The Kitzbühel Rote Teufel (Red Devils) have absorbed several other local schools (including the Total school). Reports are favourable. A recent visitor 'learned more than ever before' in his week with them. The other schools emphasise their small scale. Element3 is an adventure company now offering ski/snowboard classes. Reports please.

FOR FAMILIES ★☆☆☆☆
Not an ideal choice
It's a spread-out resort for a family. Rote Teufel takes kids from age three.

STAYING THERE

Kitz is essentially a hotel resort, though a few tour operators run chalets and chalet hotels here.
Hotels There is an enormous choice, especially of 4-star and 3-star hotels.
★★★★★Tennerhof (63181) Luxurious former farmhouse, with renowned restaurant. Beautiful panelled rooms. Relais et Châteaux.
★★★★★Schloss Lebenberg (69010) Modernised 'castle' with smart wellness centre; inconvenient location but free shuttle-bus.
★★★★Golfhotel Rasmushof (652520) Right on the slopes by the finish area of the Hahnenkamm race, close to centre of town. 'Friendly, good service.

Book a room overlooking the slopes.'
★★★★Goldener Greif (64311) Elegant, historic inn; vaulted lobby-sitting area, panelled bar, sauna, steam.
★★★★Jägerwirt (6981) Modern chalet. Not ideally placed, but has been recommended.
★★★★Schwarzer Adler (6911) Traditional hotel, near centre, highly praised by a reporter. Pool.
★★★★Best Western Kaiserhof (75503) Next to the Hahnenkamm gondola. 'Great spa, indoor pool and excellent food – can't fault it,' says a reporter.
★★★★Schweizerhof (62735) Comfortable chalet right by Hahnenkamm gondola.
★★★Strasshofer (62285) Central location. 'Friendly, good with children, quiet rooms at back.' 'Excellent value.'
★★Mühlbergerhof (62835) Small, friendly pension in good position.
Apartments Many of the best are attached to hotels.

EATING OUT ★★★★
Something for everyone
There is a wide range of restaurants to suit all pockets, including pizzerias and fast-food outlets (even McDonald's). The Neuwirt in the Schwarzer Adler hotel is regarded as the best in town and wins awards in food guides; the Schwedenkapelle is also highly rated. Chizzo does fine-dining in one of the oldest buildings in Kitzbühel; recommended by a recent visitor. Good, cheaper places include the traditional Huberbräu-Stüberl, Eggerwirt and, a little out of town with great views, Hagstein. Goldene Gams has both traditional and modern dining rooms, plus a wide menu. Barrique does 'great pizza', as does Gallo. On Fridays and Saturdays you can dine at the top of the Hahnenkamm gondola (Hochkitzbühel). For something different take a taxi to Rosi's Sonnbergstub'n. Choose the speciality lamb or duck and expect to be serenaded by Rosi herself.

APRES-SKI ★★★★
A main attraction
Nightlife is one of Kitz's great selling points. There's something for all tastes, from throbbing bars full of teenagers to quiet places, nice cafes and smart spots for fur-coat flaunting.
Immediately after the slopes close, the town is jolly without being much livelier than many other Tirolean resorts. The Streifalm bar at the foot of the slopes is popular, with 'white

↑ The end of the famous Hahnenkamm downhill race course

© ALBIN NIEDERSTRASSER

Phone numbers
Kitzbühel
From elsewhere in Austria add the prefix 05356; from abroad use the prefix +43 5356
Kirchberg
From elsewhere in Austria add the prefix 05357; from abroad use the prefix +43 5357

pine and slate, open fire, widescreen TV and Europop music'. 'The outside bar at Chizzo was great fun,' says a 2009 reporter whose favourite bar was the Pavillion – 'great staff and a great party atmosphere'. Cafes Praxmair, Kortschak and Rupprechter are among the most atmospheric tea-time places for cakes and pastries. The lively Stamperl is 'classy and fun'. The Seidlalm has weekly Tirolean evenings (free) that reporters have enjoyed. Lichtl's (with thousands of lights hanging from the ceiling) has karaoke. The Londoner Pub is a famous drinking place, well summarised by visitors as: 'Very crowded, very noisy and great fun', but the bar staff can be 'rude and sulky'. The Fonda has been recommended for the 'younger generation'. The Python, Highways and Take Five are the main discos.

OFF THE SLOPES ★★★★★
Plenty to do
The lift pass gives a reduction for the pools in the impressive Aquarena leisure centre. The new Sports Park (with ice rink, ice hockey etc) is recommended. There's a museum, and there's a casino beside the Goldener Greif hotel. The railway makes excursions easy (eg Salzburg).

Kirchberg 850m/2,790ft

THE RESORT
Kirchberg makes a perfectly sensible alternative base – particularly if you are thinking of spending a lot of time at Resterhöhe (quick access from Skirast to Pengelstein and the linking 3S gondola) or the Ski Welt (quick access by bus to the Ki-West gondola).
Village charm The village is a large, spread-out place.
Convenience There are three ways into the slopes, all a bus ride away.
Scenery Like Kitzbühel, the village is

between two pretty valleys – the one to Aschau is quiet and scenic.

THE MOUNTAIN
Slopes The gondola from Skirast is the best choice, accessing fast chairs to Pengelstein which links to the gondola to Wurzhöhe. The Fleckalmbahn from Klausen to Ehrenbachhöhe can have queues. The alternative Maierl chairlifts are excruciatingly slow. The separate small Gaisberg ski area is on the other side of the valley.
Fast lifts Much improved with recent new lifts near Ehrenbachhöhe.
Queues There are some bottlenecks.
Terrain parks Head for Kitzbühel.
Snow reliability Kirchberg suffers from the same unreliable snow as Kitzbühel.
Experts Few challenging slopes.
Intermediates The main slopes back are easy cruises when snow is good.
Beginners There's a beginner lift and area on the Gaisberg side.
Snowboarding Kitzbühel has the edge, with the two terrain parks.
Cross-country There are lots of trails – but they can suffer from lack of snow.
Mountain restaurants There are some good local huts.
Schools and guides We lack recent reports on the local schools.
Families There are non-ski and ski kindergartens.

STAYING THERE
There's a wide choice of chalet-style hotels and pensions.
Hotels The 4-star Klausen (2128), close to the main gondola, and the Sporthotel Tyrol (2787), a bit out of the centre, have been recommended.
Apartments There are some available.
Eating out Mostly in hotels, but there's a pizzeria and a steakhouse too.
Après-ski There's a toboggan run on Gaisberg. Nightlife is very lively.
Off the slopes Some hotels have swimming pools and saunas.

Kitzbühel

157

Interactive resort shortlist builder at www.wtss.co.uk

Lech

If you can afford it, simply one of the best: a captivating blend of reliable snow, village charm and deeply comfortable hotels

£115
RESORT PRICE INDEX

RATINGS

The mountains

Extent	★★★★
Fast lifts	★★★★
Queues	★★★★
Terrain p'ks	★★★★
Snow	★★★★
Expert	★★★★
Intermediate	★★★★
Beginner	★★★★
X-country	★★★
Restaurants	★★★
Schools	★★★★
Families	★★★★★

The resort

Charm	★★★★
Convenience	★★★
Scenery	★★★
Eating out	★★★
Après-ski	★★★★
Off-slope	★★★

NEWS

For 2009/10 a new heated and covered fast six-pack will replace the double chair to Muggengrat.

For 2008/09 the former Aurelio hotel was renovated and became a 5-star luxury ski lodge and spa, with 19 rooms and two restaurants.

158

- ➕ Picturesque traditional village
- ➕ Sunny and usually uncrowded slopes with excellent snow record and extensive snowmaking
- ➕ Sizeable area of mainly intermediate pistes, plus good, extensive off-piste
- ➕ Easy access by bus to the slopes of St Anton and other Arlberg resorts
- ➕ Some very smart hotels, including ski-in/ski-out options at Oberlech
- ➕ Lots of lovely heated chairlifts
- ➕ Lively après-ski scene

- ➖ Pricey, especially by Austrian standards
- ➖ Surprising shortage, for a smart resort, of seductive shopping
- ➖ Few non-hotel bars or restaurants
- ➖ Local traffic intrudes on main street of Lech (and really spoils Zürs)
- ➖ Very few challenging pistes
- ➖ Nearly all slopes above treeline, and unpleasant in bad weather
- ➖ Blue runs back to Lech are rather steep for nervous novices
- ➖ Still a few slow, old lifts

Lech and its higher, linked neighbour Zürs are the most fashionable resorts in Austria, each able to point to a string of rich and celebrated regular visitors, and to pull in Porsche-borne Germans on an unmatched scale. But, like all such 'exclusive' resorts, they aren't actually exclusive in any real sense. A holiday here doesn't have to cost a lot more than in countless other international resorts in the Alps. We don't feel out of place here, and neither would you.

The real point about these resorts is that they offer a rare and attractive combination of impressive snowfall, traditional Alpine atmosphere and excellent hotels offering a truly personal service from their family owners. And they attract people who want to get out on the hill – they have few of the flash shopping opportunities of St Moritz or Cortina, for example.

THE RESORT

Lech is an old farming village set in a high valley that spent long periods of winter cut off from the outside world until the Flexen Pass road through Zürs was constructed at the end of the 19th century. (Even now, the road can be closed for days on end after an exceptional snowfall; a road tunnel is planned, but is not imminent.)

Not far from the centre is the cable car up to Oberlech: a small, traffic-free collection of 4-star hotels set on the mountainside, with an underground tunnel system under the central piste, linking the hotels and lift station –

used routinely to move baggage, and by guests in bad weather. The cable car works until 1am, allowing access to the mother resort's nightlife.

Zug is a hamlet 3km/2 miles from Lech, with a lift into the Lech slopes. The limited accommodation here is mostly B&B, with one pricey 4-star hotel. It's not ideal for sampling Lech's nightlife, but there is an evening bus service (see 'Après-ski')

Lech is linked by lifts and runs to higher Zürs, described at the end of this chapter. There is a free, regular but often very crowded ski-bus service between the two resorts. Buses (also crowded) run to St Anton, St Christoph and Stuben, too, all covered by the Arlberg pass. The post bus offers a less crowded option, but is not free.

The Sonnenkopf area at Klösterle, reached by ski-bus from Stuben, is also covered – 'worth a trip' for its combination of gondola rides and quiet, wide, woodland runs ('perfect for intermediates') not least in bad weather, say reporters.

SCENERY ★★★
In a bright spot
Lech is in a fairly sunny position at the junction of two attractive valleys, with adequately impressive scenery. It is high and open, with very few trees. From the top slopes, there are views to the Valluga above St Anton.

THE MOUNTAINS

Practically all the slopes are treeless, the main exception being the lower runs just above Lech. Most are quite sunny – very few are north-facing.

The toughest runs are classed as 'ski routes' or 'high-alpine touring runs'. The piste map says the former are marked, avalanche controlled but not groomed or patrolled and the latter are not marked or avalanche controlled either and an 'authorized guide' is recommended. We have no problem with the latter category – in other resorts, these off-piste runs would simply not appear on the piste map at all. But the ski route concept is used too widely, reducing the resort's responsibility for runs that are a key part of the area, and that should be patrolled pistes. Ski routes form the only ways down to Zug; the only way to complete the Lech-Zürs-Lech circuit; and most of the identified runs from Kriegerhorn. To add to the confusion, many (but not all) of these routes are groomed (they were when we visited in April 2009) and they even have signs on (some with lights) showing which are open and closed; and in practice most people ski them as if they were pistes. The introduction to the Austrian section of the book has more on this ludicrous situation.

The piste map, which covers the whole of the Arlberg region in one view is unclear and misleading in places – particularly around Oberlech. They should really have one piste map for Lech-Zürs and separate ones for St

VILLAGE CHARM ★★★★
Busy main street
The village is attractive, with upmarket hotels built in traditional chalet style, a gurgling river plus bridges, and a high incidence of snow on the streets. But don't expect a rustic backwater: away from the central area the place is fairly ordinary, and the appeal is somewhat dimmed by traffic on the main street, especially at weekends.

British visitors are outnumbered 10:1 by Germans and 3:1 by Austrians.

CONVENIENCE ★★★
It's a long village
The heart of the village is a short stretch of the main street beside the river; most of the main hotels are clustered here, along with the one serious emporium, Strolz. Right on this street is the base station of the Rüfikopf cable car, departure point for exploration of the Zürs slopes. A short walk away, across the river, are the Schlegelkopf chairlifts, leading up into Lech's main area of slopes. Chalets, apartments and pensions are dotted around the valley, and the village spreads along the main street for 2km/1.5 miles. Some of the cheaper accommodation is quite a walk from the lifts. The supermarket is 'excellent'.

KEY FACTS

Resort	1450m
	4,760ft

Arlberg region	
Slopes	1305-2650m
	4,280-8,690ft
Lifts	85
Pistes	276km
	172 miles
Blue	39%
Red	50%
Black	11%
Snowmaking	59%

For Lech-Zürs only	
Slopes	1450-2450m
	4,760-8,040ft
Lifts	33
Pistes	117km
	73 miles
Blue	39%
Red	48%
Black	13%

boarding

Lech's upper-crust image has not stood in the way of its snowboarding development. The jewel in the Arlberg crown has some of the best backcountry riding in Austria, and abundant snowfalls mean it is a popular destination for freeriders. If you have some money burning a hole in your snowboard pants, the Arlberg region is the only place in Austria where heli-boarding is available. Enquire at any ski school. Lech is also a regular stop on the Snowpark tour – a prestigious event on the freestyle calendar. A blend of impeccable piste grooming, modern chairlifts and few draglifts makes for nice learning conditions; but be careful on the west-facing slopes at Zürs, which have many flat/uphill sections.

Anton-St Christoph-Stuben and
Sonnenkopf. Piste marking is OK, but
there is a confusing system that in
places gives the same number to
several pistes. Piste classification
understates difficulty in places.

EXTENT OF THE SLOPES ★★★★
One-way traffic

The main slopes centre on **Oberlech**,
250m/820ft above Lech (just below the
treeline), and can be reached by cable
car or chairlifts. The wide, open pistes
above here are perfect intermediate
terrain and there is also lots of off-
piste. Zuger Hochlicht, the high point
in the sector, gives stunning views.

The **Rüfikopf** cable car takes Lech
residents to the west-facing slopes of
Zürs. This mountainside, with its high
point at **Trittkopf**, is a mix of quite
challenging intermediate slopes and
flat/uphill bits. On the other side of
Zürs the east-facing mountainside is of
a more uniform gradient. Chairs go up
to **Seekopf** with intermediate runs
back down. There's a chair (to be
upgraded to a six-pack for 2009/10)
from Zürsersee up to **Muggengrat** (the
highest point of the Zürs area). This
has a good blue run back under it and
accesses the long, scenic, lift-free and
quiet (till now – the new fast chair
may change that) Muggengrat Täli; it

starts with a choice between a cat track and a mogul field, but develops into a fine, varied red with lots of nearby off-piste options on the way down to Zürs; at the bottom you can take lifts up the other side or walk through the village to the Zürsersee chair. From the top of that you can ski down to the Madloch chair – slow and vulnerable to closure by wind – which leads to the long, scenic ski route ('full of beginners and quite risky' said one 2009 reporter) back to the fringes of Lech, completing a clockwise circuit. You can peel off part-way down and head for Zug and the slow chairlift up to the Kriegerhorn above Oberlech.

FAST LIFTS ★★★★
Hotting up
A high proportion of lifts are now fast chairs – many with the luxury bonus of heated seats. But there are still a few slow, old lifts.

QUEUES ★★★★
Still a few bottlenecks
The resort proudly boasts that it limits numbers on the slopes to 14,000 for a more enjoyable experience. Most reporters also stress how much quieter Lech's slopes are than St Anton's. There have been significant lift improvements and feedback is generally positive, but there are still

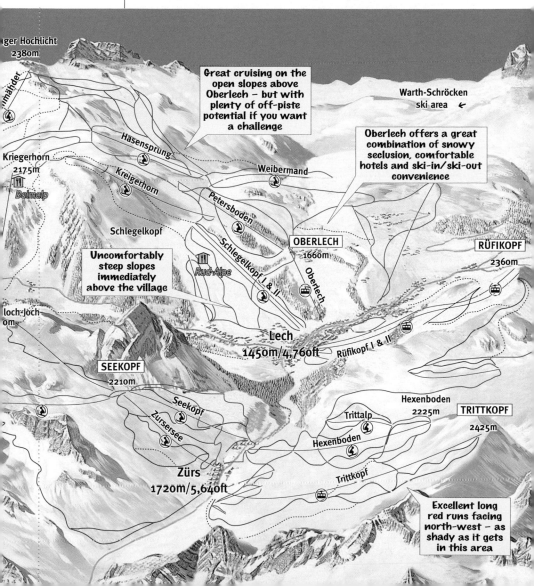

ger Hochlicht
2238m

Kriegerhorn
2175m
Balmalp

Great cruising on the open slopes above Oberlech – but with plenty of off-piste potential if you want a challenge

Hasensprung

Kriegerhorn

Weibermand

Warth-Schröcken
ski area ←

Oberlech offers a great combination of snowy seclusion, comfortable hotels and ski-in/ski-out convenience

Petersboden

Schlegelkopf

Schlegelkopf I & II

Rud-Alpe

OBERLECH
1660m

Oberlech

RÜFIKOPF
2360m

Uncomfortably steep slopes immediately above the village

loch-Joch
om

Lech
1450m/4,760ft

Rüfikopf I & II

SEEKOPF
2210m

Seekopf

Zürsersee

Hexenboden
2225m

Trittalp

Hexenboden

TRITTKOPF
2425m

Zürs
1720m/5,640ft

Trittkopf

Excellent long red runs facing north-west – as shady as it gets in this area

A lot of Lech's key runs are 'ski routes'; these are treated like pistes in many ways and some even have signs like this to tell you which are open or closed ↗

DAVE WATTS

LIFT PASSES

Arlberg Ski Pass

Prices in €

Age	1-day	6-day
under 16	26	122
16 to 19	39	177
20 to 64	43	204
over 65	39	177

Free no one, but season pass only €10 if under 8 or over 75
Senior min. age for senior women is 60
Beginner points ticket
Notes
Covers all St Anton, St Christoph, Lech, Zürs and Stuben lifts, and linking bus between Rauz and Zürs; also covers Sonnenkopf (10 lifts) at Klösterle, 7km/4 miles west of Stuben (bus link from Stuben); single ascent, half-day and pedestrian options

one or two bottlenecks – the Schlegelkopf fast quad out of Lech gets very busy first thing ('20 minutes at Easter') and the crucial ('slow and cold') Madloch double chair at the top of the Zürs area generates peak-time queues on the Lech-Zürs-Lech circuit – 'up to 30 minutes', says a reporter. Some readers mention the Rüfikopf cable car to Zürs as generating queues, particularly at peak times.

TERRAIN PARKS ★★★★
In Lech only

Just above the Schlegelkopf and visible from town lies what has become one of the best snow-parks in Austria. There are two main kicker lines, separated into medium and pro categories, which will suit good riders as well as seasoned pros. The kickers are outstanding, and are followed by two kinked boxes and a wall ride. The rails are also set in lines so you can hit several in a row. A fun box, 8m/26ft down rail, rainbow and a C-box, lie next to an easy rail and kicker line for beginners. There is also a designated area made up of little banks and jumps, great for getting used to air time. Check www.mellowparks.com for the latest news.

SNOW RELIABILITY ★★★★
One of Austria's best

Lech and Zürs both get a lot of snow. Lech gets an average of almost 8m/26ft of snow between December and March, almost twice as much as St Anton and three times as much as Kitzbühel; but Zürs gets 50% more than Lech. The altitude is high by Austrian resort standards, and there is excellent snowmaking, helping to counter the sunny exposure.

This combination, together with excellent grooming, means that the Lech-Zürs area normally has good coverage until late April.

FOR EXPERTS ★★★★
Off-piste is main attraction

There is only one (very short) black piste on the map, and there is no denying that for the competent skier who prefers to stick to patrolled runs the area is very limited. But the two types of off-piste route explained earlier offer lots to enjoy. Experts will get a lot more out of the area if they have a guide, as there is plenty of excellent off-piste other than the marked ski routes, much of it accessed by long traverses – and the ski routes get heavily skied, not surprisingly. By comparison with St Anton, fresh powder lasts well here.

Many of the best runs start from the top of the fast Steinmähder chair, which finishes just below Zuger Hochlicht. Some routes involve a short climb to access bowls of untracked powder. From the Kriegerhorn there are shorter off-piste runs down towards Lech and a very scenic long ski route down to Zug (followed by a slow chair and a rope tow to pull you along a flat area). Most runs, however, are south- or west-facing and can suffer from sun. At the end of the season, when the snow is deep and settled, the off-piste off the shoulder of the Wöstertäli from the top of the Rüfikopf cable car down to Lech can be superb. And a reporter enjoyed great April powder at Zuger Hochlicht. There are also good runs from the Trittkopf cable car in the Zürs sector, including a tricky one down to Stuben.

The steeper red runs (notably on Zuger Hochlicht and both sides of Zürs) are well worth a try, as is the lovely away-from-the-lifts Langerzug ski route back to Lech on the Rüfikopf side (steep start, then a gentle cruise, flattish run-out). And you'll want to visit St Anton during your stay, where there are more challenging pistes as well as more off-piste.

Heli-lifts are available to a couple of remote spots, at least on weekdays.

FOR INTERMEDIATES ★★★★
Flattering variety for all
The pistes in the Oberlech area are nearly all immaculately groomed blue runs, the upper ones above the trees, the lower ones in wide swathes cut through them. It is ideal territory for cruisers not wanting surprises.

Strong intermediates will want to do the circuit to Zürs and back. Whether it's wise for less confident intermediates to tackle the beautiful red ski route from Madloch depends, simply, on the conditions. It is not steep, and part or all of it may be groomed despite its non-piste status, but parts can be heavily mogulled and congested, and lots of people find the run a struggle.

It's worth noting that the final blue-run descents to Lech (as opposed to Oberlech) are uncomfortably steep for nervous novices.

More adventurous intermediates will want to spend time on the fast Steinmähder chair on Zuger Hochlicht – a choice of satisfying pistes and ski routes, and from there take the scenic red run all the way to Zug (the latter part on a ski route rather than a piste). They may even want to give the Langerzug ski route (see For Experts) a go. Lech is an excellent place to try skiing deep snow for the first time.

Zürs has many more interesting red runs, on both sides of the village. We like the north-west-facing reds from Trittkopf and the excellent Muggengrat Täli (see 'Extent of the Slopes').

FOR BEGINNERS ★★★★
Easy slopes in all areas
The main nursery slopes are in Oberlech, but there is also a nice dedicated area in Lech. There are good, easy runs to progress to, both above and below Oberlech. You can buy a points card rather than a full lift pass.

FOR CROSS-COUNTRY ★★★
Picturesque valley trail
A 19km/12 mile trail starts from the centre of Lech and leads through the beautiful but shady valley, along the Lech river to Zug and back. A reporter recommends the Älpele for lunch en route. In Zürs there is a 4km/2.5 mile track to the Flexen Pass and back.

MOUNTAIN RESTAURANTS ★★★★★
Improving but pricey
The lunch scene is dominated by the many big places in Oberlech and the hotels in Zürs. But more remote options have improved in recent years (though overcrowding is still a problem and prices are high, especially when compared to other Austrian resorts, including St Anton).

Editors' choice Rud-Alpe (418250), on the lower slopes above Lech, just counts as a mountain restaurant – a welcoming rustic place, lovingly rebuilt using timbers from other old huts. On each of our visits, we only had a drink on the terrace, but happily we have reports of 'very good food' and 'friendly staff'. In 2009 we ate at the smartly revamped, modern, woody Balmalp, above Zug; cool music (loud on the terrace, quieter inside); simple food (pasta, pizza, ribs, salad). It is very popular with reporters too – 'our favourite', 'an absolute beauty', 'stunning views', 'huge portions'.

Worth knowing about Kriegeralpe is rustic and charming, with 'jolly music and delicious food'. Above Zürs, Seekopf now offers table service, does 'quality food at decent prices' and has a lovely big terrace.

At Oberlech there are several big sunny terraces set prettily around the piste. Quite often you'll find a live band playing outside one. Reader recommendations include the Ilga Stüble, the lovely old Alter Goldener Berg, the Mohnenfluh and Burgwald.

A reporter praises the restaurants down in Zug, especially the Klösterle – 'lovely restored farmhouse'.

SCHOOLS AND GUIDES ★★★★★
Excellent in parts
The ski schools of Lech, Oberlech and Zürs all have good reputations and the instructors speak good English. Group lessons are divided into no fewer than 10 ability levels. A regular visitor writes: 'I've used the same instructor for three seasons; probably the best I have ever had – friendly, helpful, knowledgeable.' 'Outstanding – could find no fault' and 'world-class', say others. A few years ago the mountain guides office started the Omeshorn Alpincenter school. In peak periods, you should book instructors and guides well in advance, as many are booked every year by regular visitors.

FOR FAMILIES ★★★★★
Oberlech's fine, but expensive
Oberlech makes an excellent choice for families who can afford it, particularly as its hotels are so convenient for the slopes. Reporters have praised the family-friendly approach and attention paid to children using the lifts: 'Mountain staff were really polite and helpful.' Goldener Berg has an in-house kindergarten. Children of visitors staying in Oberlech have free access to the kindergarten there, Kinderland. The Oberlech school is normally well-regarded (small groups, good English spoken), but two recent reporters have criticised it for poor organisation. Private lessons were more successful – 'my older children improved immediately.'

STAYING THERE
Hotels and guest houses dominate, though there are alternatives.
Chalets There are a couple run by British operators, including two chalet hotels by Ski Total, one with pool.
Hotels There are four 5-stars, over 30 4-stars and countless modest places.
LECH
★★★★★Arlberg (21340) Elegantly rustic central chalet. Pool. 'Probably the best in Lech.'
★★★★★Post (22060) Lovely old Relais & Châteaux place on the main street; pool, sauna. 'Remains fantastic. Very good bar and food, perfect service,' a regular visitor told us this year.
★★★★Gotthard (35600) – 'Warm service, spacious room, great breakfast spread, large spa with pool – a real find.'
★★★★Haldenhof (24440) Friendly and well run, with antiques and fine paintings. 'Highly recommended.'
★★★★Kristiania (25610) 'Outstanding decor, ambience and service – feels very homely,' says a reporter.
★★★★Krone (2551) One of the originals, by the river. 'Food, service faultless', but 'small rooms and some noise', 'superb' wellness centre with pool.
★★★★Monzabon (2104) 'Characterful, friendly staff.' Pool, indoor ice rink.
★★★★Schwarzwand (2469) Perfectly positioned for beginners, by the separate nursery slope. Sauna, steam room, solarium. 'Food and service very high standard and excellent value'.
★★★★Sursilva (29700) Good value, small place. Sauna. 'Good food; beautifully cooked and presented.' Recommended by two recent visitors.

UK PACKAGES

Alpine Answers, Alpine Weekends, Crystal, Crystal Finest, Elegant Resorts, Erna Low, Flexiski, Independent Ski Links, Inghams, Interactive Resorts, Jeffersons, Kaluma, Made to Measure, Momentum, Oxford Ski Co, Powder Byrne, Scott Dunn, Simply Alpine, Ski Activity, Ski Expectations, Ski Freshtracks, Ski Independence, Skiing Austria, Ski Solutions, Ski Total, Skitracer, Skiworld, Snow Finders, STC, Supertravel, White Roc **Oberlech** Kaluma **Zürs** Alpine Answers, Alpine Weekends, Crystal, Crystal Finest, Inghams, Made to Measure, Oxford Ski Co, Powder Byrne, Scott Dunn, Skiing Austria, STC

****Tannbergerhof (22020) Splendidly atmospheric inn on the main street, with outdoor bar and popular disco (tea time as well as later). Pool.

***Pension Angerhof (2418) Beautiful ancient pension, with wood panels and quaint little windows.

***Garni Lärchenhof (2300) 'Very nice, reasonably priced B&B – excellent breakfast, wellness area, nice modern rooms and friendly family owners.'

OBERLECH

****Bergkristall (2678) Smart, on slopes, hot tub, steam, solarium, massages. Own in-house nanny.

****Burg Vital (3140) 'Excellent – no criticism,' said a reporter.

****Burg (22910) Sister hotel of Burg Vital – same facilities and with famous outdoor umbrella bar.

****Montana (2460) Welcoming chalet run by the family of Patrick Ortlieb. Consistently praised by reporters. 'Best hotel food ever, friendly and efficient service,' says a repeat visitor. Pool, smart wellness centre.

****Sonnenburg (2147) Family-run chalet with a relaxed, traditional atmosphere. Good children's facilities. Pool, impressive wellness centre.

****Pension Sabine (2718) 'Charming and comfortable with spa facilities.' 'Excellent food, very friendly and welcoming.'

Apartments There are lots available to independent bookers.

EATING OUT ★★★
Mainly hotel-based

There are over 50 restaurants in Lech, but nearly all of them are in hotels. Reporter recommendations include the Krone ('amazingly courteous service'), Post ('modern Austrian food'), Almhof Schneider ('traditional'), Lecher Stube in hotel Gotthard ('very good value'), Don Enzo Due ('good pizzas'), Rudi's Stamperl ('top-notch and reasonably priced') and Fux ('modern/Asian food, utterly un-Austrian', 'good sashimi and sushi'). Hûs Nr 8 is one of the best non-hotel restaurants for traditional Austrian food. The Olympia has been suggested for cakes, coffee and 'excellent pork medallions', while the apple strudel at Backstüble is 'to die for'. Café Fritz is 'cosy and quite cheap for local standards'.

In Oberlech, hotel Montana is consistently praised, a recent visitor had 'the perfect' Wiener schnitzel in the hotel Sonnenburg, Schlössle is

ACTIVITIES

Indoor Tennis, hotel swimming pools, saunas and fitness centre, squash, museum, galleries, library, ice rink (in hotel Monzabon)

Outdoor Cleared walking paths, ice rink, curling, toboggan run (from Oberlech), snowshoeing, horse-drawn sleigh rides

Phone numbers
From elsewhere in Austria add the prefix 05583; from abroad use the prefix +43 5583

TOURIST OFFICES

info@lech-zuers.at
www.lech-zuers.at
Lech
t 2161
Zürs
t 2245

'enjoyable for light meals' and Ilga Stüble has 'delicious venison'.

In Zug, the Rote Wand is excellent for traditional Austrian food, but is 'frighteningly expensive'. Reporters recommend the 'simple and charming' Alphorn and Klösterle ('tops all as far as food and charm is concerned').

APRES-SKI ★★★★
Good but expensive

At Oberlech, the umbrella bar of the Burg hotel is popular immediately after the slopes close, as is the champagne bar in hotel Montana.

Down in Lech the outdoor bars of hotels Krone (in a lovely, sunny setting by the river) and Tannbergerhof (where there's an afternoon as well as a late-night disco) are popular. Later on, discos in the hotels Almhof-Schneider and Krone liven up too. The Ilga is a good place for a drink, as is S'Pfefferkörndl. Two 'smart' choices are Schneggarei's for funky house music early and late and Fux jazz bar/restaurant, which has live music and a huge wine list. Archiv is good for cocktails and attracts a younger crowd.

Zug makes a good night out: you can take a sleigh ride for a meal at the Rote Wand, Klösterle or Auerhahn, and have drinks at the Vinothek wine bar at the s'Achtele restaurant.

After 7.30pm the free resort bus becomes a pay-for bus called James, which runs until 3am.

OFF THE SLOPES ★★★
At ease

Many visitors to Lech don't indulge in sports, and the main street often presents a parade of fur-clad strollers. The range of shopping is surprisingly limited – Strolz's plush emporium (including a champagne bar) right in the centre is the main attraction.

It's easy for pedestrians to get to Oberlech or Zug for lunch. The village outdoor bars make ideal posing positions. There are various sporting activities and 29km/18 miles of walking paths ('superb'; 'great map from the Tourist Office') – the one along the river to Zug is 'outstandingly' beautiful, and recommended by several readers.

There is a floodlit sledging run from Oberlech to town: 'loved by kids and not to be missed', say reporters.

Zürs 1720m/5,640ft

Some 10 minutes' drive towards St Anton from Lech, Zürs is almost on the Flexen Pass, with good snow virtually guaranteed. Austria's first recognisable ski lift was built here in 1937. Along with snow, Zürs offers some excellent hotels, and once inside them, all is well with the world. But the village as a whole doesn't have much appeal – it has nothing resembling a centre, few shops and intrusive traffic to/from Lech on the central through-road.

The village is a fraction of the size of Lech, but still has three 5-star hotels. We stayed at the 5-star Zürserhof (25130) and found it excellent – great service, food and spa facilities. There are nine 4-stars.

If you want to eat out in the evening, it will probably be in another hotel. Toni's Einkehr (a rustic hut at the foot of the Trittkopf slopes) is an exception and has been recommended. Nightlife is quiet. Vernissage is said to be the best nightspot. There's a disco in the Edelweiss hotel, a piano bar in the Alpenhof and the bar at the Hirlanda is 'pleasant'.

Many of the local Zürs instructors are booked up for private lessons for the entire season by regular clients.

Mayrhofen

Large, lively resort with relatively reliable snow on local slopes and access to other good areas nearby, including a glacier

£90
RESORT PRICE INDEX

RATINGS

The mountains
Extent	★★★
Fast lifts	★★★★
Queues	★
Terrain p'ks	★★★★★
Snow	★★★
Expert	★★
Intermediate	★★★
Beginner	★★
X-country	★★
Restaurants	★★★
Schools	★★★★
Families	★★

The resort
Charm	★★★
Convenience	★
Scenery	★★★
Eating out	★★★
Après-ski	★★★★
Off-slope	★★★★

NEWS

For 2008/09 snowmaking was improved on the Ahorn valley run. Coverage is now 100% on Ahorn and Penken. A new beginner zone and more features were built in the Vans terrain park on Penken.

At Gerlos, two new red runs opened, a children's restaurant opened in the Arena Centre at the bottom station, and snowmaking was increased.

At Zell am Ziller a new gondola from the valley opened.

➕ Good for confident intermediates

➕ Snow more reliable than usual in the Tirol, plus the snow guarantee of the Hintertux glacier nearby

➕ Several worthwhile nearby areas on the same pass and reached by free bus or train

➕ Lively après-ski – though it's easily avoided if you prefer peace

➕ Excellent children's amenities

➖ Often long queues for the gondola to Penken – the main slopes

➖ Slopes can be crowded

➖ Many lodgings a bus ride from lifts

➖ Runs mostly short, though linked Lanersbach slopes are longer

➖ Few steep pistes – though they do include Austria's steepest

➖ No pistes to the valley from Penken

Mayrhofen has long been a British favourite. Like so many popular Tirolean resorts, it manages to meet the needs of young people bent on partying and families looking for a quieter time. What makes it different from the Tirolean norm is its relatively high, relatively snow-sure slopes.

If it's the skiing that mainly attracts you, be sure to check out the Hintertux chapter, which also covers quieter villages between Mayrhofen and Hintertux that offer quick access to the slopes they share with Mayrhofen. And don't forget that the valley lift pass is valid in lots of other places that are well worth exploring – it covers over 170 lifts and more than 640km/400 miles of pistes.

THE RESORT

Mayrhofen is a fairly large resort sitting in the flat-bottomed, steep-sided Zillertal. Most shops, bars and restaurants are on one long street, with hotels and pensions spread over a wider area. The valley road bypasses the village, but it is not traffic-free.

Free buses and trains linking the Zillertal resorts mean you can easily have an enjoyably varied week visiting different areas on the Ziller valley lift pass including the excellent glacier at Hintertux (which has its own chapter). At the end of this chapter we cover the Zillertal Arena area, which starts at Zell am Ziller. The other major Zillertal area is Hochzillertal/Hochfugen above Kaltenbach, dealt with in the Directory at the back of the book. There's a good train service to Salzburg, Innsbruck and Munich.

VILLAGE CHARM ★★★
Traditional and lively
As the village has grown, architecture has been kept traditional. The resort has a well-deserved reputation for lively après-ski, but the central hotels are mainly slightly upmarket and overall the place feels pleasantly civilised.

CONVENIENCE ★
Stay near the Penken gondola
The main lift to the major Penken sector of slopes is set towards one end of the main street, and the newish cable car to the much smaller Ahorn

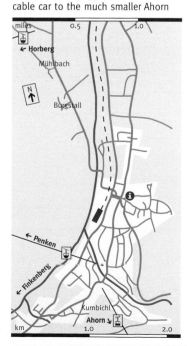

KEY FACTS

Resort	630m
	2,070ft

Ski and Glacier World Zillertal 3000	
Slopes	630-3250m
	2,070-10,660ft
Lifts	59
Pistes	227km
	141 miles
Blue	26%
Red	58%
Black	16%
Snowmaking	66%

Mayrhofen-Lanersbach only (ie excluding Hintertux glacier)	
Slopes	630-2500m
	2,070-8,200ft
Lifts	48
Pistes	157km
	98 miles

For Ziller valley	
Slopes	630-3250m
	2,070-10,660ft
Lifts	174
Pistes	646km
	401 miles

LIFT PASSES

Zillertaler Superskipass

Prices in €

Age	1-day	6-day
under 15	18	88
15 to 18	31	149
over 19	38	186

Free under 6
Senior no deals
Beginner no deals

Notes
1-, 2- or 3-day passes cover Mayrhofen areas only; 4-day and over passes include all Ziller valley lifts; part-day and pedestrian passes available

sector starts 200m/66oft further along the road. The free bus service can be crowded, and it finishes early (5pm), so location is important. The original centre, around the market, tourist office and bus/railway stations, is now on the edge of things. The most convenient area is on the main street, close to the Penken gondola station.

SCENERY ★★★
Views to the glacier
Mayrhofen is set between its two steep-sided mountains. From the top of each there are good views to the Hintertux glacier.

THE MOUNTAINS

Practically all Mayrhofen's slopes are above the treeline, and many are challenging reds.

EXTENT OF THE SLOPES ★★★
Fair-sized but inconvenient
The larger of Mayrhofen's two areas of slopes is **Penken-Horberg**, accessed by the main gondola from one end of town. It is also accessible via gondolas at Hippach and Finkenberg, both a bus ride away. You cannot get back to Mayrhofen on snow – you can catch the main gondola down or, if snow cover is good enough (it rarely is), you can descend to either Finkenberg or Hippach on unpisted ski routes. The buses back from Finkenberg run at only hourly intervals.

A big cable car links the Penken area with the **Rastkogel** slopes above Vorderlanersbach, which is in turn linked to **Egggalm** above Lanersbach – see the Hintertux chapter. These links are a great asset, and the run to Egggalm has been more reliable since snowmaking was installed. Getting back from Rastkogel on skis means braving a red run that can be heavily mogulled, but you can avoid it by taking the linking cable car down.

The smaller, gentler **Ahorn** area is

good for beginners. It tends to be neglected, but has some impressive lifts: access is by a 160-person cable car and the main lift at altitude is a newish eight-seat chairlift. There is a lovely, long red run (over 1300m/ 4,260ft vertical) to the valley.

FAST LIFTS ★★★★
Not enough to cope
Look at the map and a good proportion of the lifts are fast – gondolas and high-speed chairs. But given the queues (see below), more are needed to cope with the crowds.

QUEUES ★
Still a real problem
The Penken gondola is very oversubscribed at peak times. Reports of queues of 45 or 60 minutes at the morning peak are still common. An alternative is to take the bus to one of the other gondolas (those at Lanersbach and Vorderlanersbach are quieter than those at Finkenberg and Hippach). There can be queues for some lifts once you get up the mountain and to get down at the end of the day, too. No queues have been reported for the Ahorn cable car, and a reader recommends using it to do the long red run down while waiting for the Penken queue to subside.

TERRAIN PARKS ★★★★★
Something for everyone
One of the finest parks in the Alps (sponsored by Vans – www.vans-penken-park.com) is built beneath the Sun-Jet chairlift on Penken – but it can get crowded. There's an easy line (with a great mini wall ride), an intermediate line and a pro line of tabletops ranging in length between 3m/1oft and 19m/62ft, as well as a big hip jump. Every year there are more combinations of kinked, curved and flat boxes and rails in the jib line. This great park can be intimidating, as it is home to a lot of local pros. However,

boarding

Mayrhofen has long been popular with snowboarders. There is a large British contingent who make this their winter home because of the extensive off-piste available. But beginners may have a hard time getting around, as the terrain tends to be relatively steep, the nursery slopes are inconvenient, and the area still has quite a few draglifts. Intermediates and upwards, however, will relish the abundance of good red runs and easily accessible off-piste. The terrain park is one of the best in Europe. Snowbombing, a music festival and snowboard contest, is held here each year as well as the 5-star TTR event, Ästhetiker Wängl Tängl.

Die Roten Profis
(Manfred Gager)
t 6380

Total (Max Rahm)
t 63939

Mount Everest
(Peter Habeler)
t 62829

Mayrhofen 3000
(Michael Thanner)
t 64015

Classes
(Roten Profis prices)
6 days (2½hr am or
pm) €119

Private lessons
1 day: €119 for 1
person

new for 2008/09 was a full beginner zone with over nine obstacles and jumps. The half-pipe is now always maintained to a high spec; but pipe jocks should head to the 360m/1,180ft long super-pipe in Hintertux.

SNOW RELIABILITY ★★★
Good by Tirolean standards
Although the lifts go no higher than 2500m/8,200ft, the area is better than most Tirolean resorts for snow because the slopes are mostly above 1500m/4,920ft. Snowmaking covers the whole Ahorn area, all the main slopes on Penken-Horberg and some on Rastkogel and Eggalm. Hintertux is probably the best glacier in the world.

FOR EXPERTS ★★
Commit Harakiri
Austria's steepest piste, called Harakiri and under the Knorren chair, has a gradient of 78% (or 38°). It is certainly steep for a European piste; when we tried it, the run was mogul-free but rock hard except near the edges; not surprisingly, it was delightfully deserted. A reporter described it as 'one hell of a ride'. It does offer a worthwhile challenge for the brave but is quite short. The black run under the Schneekar chair on Horberg is a good, fast cruise when groomed, but there

are few other steepish pistes. The long unpisted trail to Hippach is quite challenging but rarely has good snow because of its low altitude. There is, however, some decent off-piste to be found, such as from the top of the Horbergjoch at the top of Rastkogel – we had a great time there in fresh powder – and under the cable car linking to Lanersbach. You can also try the other resorts covered by the valley lift pass.

FOR INTERMEDIATES ★★★
On the tough side
Most of Mayrhofen's slopes are on the steep side of the usual intermediate range – great for confident or competent intermediates. And the Lanersbach expansion has made the area much more interesting for avid piste-bashers, with some good long runs on Rastkogel and delightfully quiet runs on Eggalm. But many of the runs in the main Penken area are quite short. And (except on Ahorn) there are few really gentle blue runs, making the area less than ideal for nervous intermediates or near-beginners. The overcrowding on many runs can add to the intimidation factor.

Each of the main areas covered by the Ziller valley pass is large enough for an interesting day out.

Mayrhofen

169

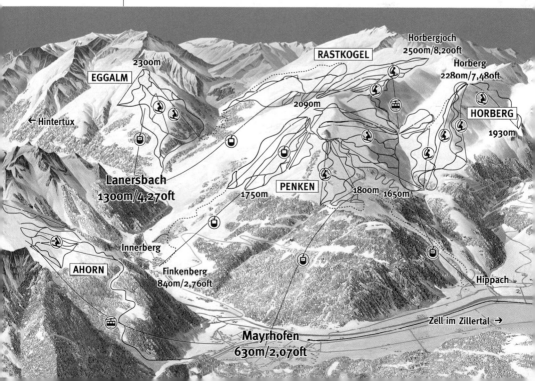

CHILDCARE

Wuppy's Kinderland
t 63612
Ages 3mnth to 7yr;
9am to 5pm, Mon-Fri

Die Roten Profis
t 6380
From age 3; 10am-3.30

Total
t 63939
Ages 2 to 4, 9.30-3.30

Ski school
All run classes for children aged 4 or 5 to 14. Lunch can be provided (6 days including lunch €141)

GETTING THERE

Air Salzburg 175km/110 miles (2hr15); Munich 195km/120 miles (2hr45); Innsbruck 70km/45 miles (1hr15)

Rail Local line through to resort; regular buses from station

FOR BEGINNERS ★★★★★
Overrated: big drawbacks
Despite its reputation for teaching, Mayrhofen is not ideal for beginners. The Ahorn nursery slopes are excellent – high, extensive and sunny – and an Easter reporter found them 'very quiet' too. But intermediate mates will want to be on Penken. The Penken nursery area is less satisfactory and there are very few easy blues to progress to.

FOR CROSS-COUNTRY ★★★★★
Go to Lanersbach
There are 30km/18 miles of trails in the area. Snow in the valley is not reliable but higher Vorderlanersbach has a much more snow-sure trail.

MOUNTAIN RESTAURANTS ★★★★★
Plenty of them
Most of Penken's many mountain restaurants are attractive but they can get crowded. The Schneekar restaurant at the top of the Horberg section has been highly recommended ('table-service, traditional food, open fire, wooden beams, leather sofa, but expensive', say reporters). Almstüberl at the mid-station of the Finkenberg gondola 'was usually quiet when others were packed'. Kressbrunnalm, Schiestl's Sunnalm and Grillhofalm ('cheapest we found and a great place to watch the terrain park action') have also been recommended.

SCHOOLS AND GUIDES ★★★★★
Excellent reputation
Mayrhofen's ski schools have good reputations, and we have received many positive reports over the years, but a few negative ones too – including a shortage of English-speaking instructors. Reports welcome.

FOR FAMILIES ★★★★★
Good but inconvenient
Mayrhofen majors on childcare and the facilities are excellent. But children have to be bussed around and ferried up and down the mountain.

STAYING THERE

There is a wide choice of hotel holidays available from UK tour operators, but few catered chalets.
Hotels Most of the hotels packaged by UK tour operators are centrally located, a walk from the Penken gondola. You can stay at the White Lounge ice-hotel too (see 'Après-ski').
★★★★★Elisabeth (6767) The only 5-star. 'Superb, excellent food and service.'
★★★★Manni's (633010) Well placed, smartly done out; pool, sauna, steam.
★★★★Kramerwirt (6700) Lovely hotel, oozing character. 'Friendly and helpful staff, good rooms.'
★★★★Strass (6705) By the gondola. Lively bars, disco, wellness centre, pool; but very big, with a downmarket feel and rooms that lack style.
★★★★Neuhaus (6703) 'First-class facilities,' says a reporter. Good food, but rooms above the bar are not ideal.
★★★★Rose (62229) Near centre. Good food. Sauna, steam, hot tub.
★★★★Neue Post (62131) Convenient, family-run, on the main street – 'nice big rooms'. Pool, sauna, steam.
Apartments A recent visitor recommends the Sonnenhof apartments (62520), near the gondola. 'Delightful, clean, spacious.'

EATING OUT ★★★★★
Wide choice
Mayrhofen has a wide range of restaurants, from local specialities to

SNOWPIX.COM / CHRIS GILL

Mayrhofen's local slopes are linked via Rastkogel to Eggalm, where you get good views towards the Hintertux glacier →

Crystal, Crystal Finest, Directski.com, First Choice, Independent Ski Links, Inghams, Interhome, Kuoni, Neilson, Rocketski, Simply Alpine, Ski Expectations, Skiing Austria, Ski Line, Ski McNeill, Skitracer, Skiworld, Snowcoach, STC, Thomson
Gerlos Interhome, Skiing Austria
Königsleiten Skiing Austria
Zell im Zillertal Crystal, Skiing Austria

Indoor Adventure pool, two hotel pools open to the public, massage, sauna, squash, fitness centre, bowling, casino

Outdoor Ice rink, curling, 40km/25 miles of paths, snowshoeing, sleigh rides, paragliding, tobogganing

Phone numbers
From elsewhere in Austria add the prefix 05285 (Mayrhofen), 05282 (Zell), 05284 (Gerlos), 06564 (Königsleiten); from abroad use the prefix +43 and omit the initial '0'

Mayrhofen
t 6760
info@mayrhofen.at
www.mayrhofen.at

Zillertal Arena
Zell im Zillertal
t 22810
www.zell.at

Gerlos
t 52440
www.gerlos.at

Königsleiten
t 82430
www.wald-koenigsleiten.info

Chinese. Manni's has been rated as 'expensive' for wine but does good pizzas. Wirthaus zum Griena is a 'wonderful old wooden building with traditional cuisine'. The Kramerwirt has 'excellent food with large portions'. We had good lamb and pepper steak at Tiroler Stuben.

APRES-SKI ★★★★
Lively

Après-ski is a great selling point. At close of play, the umbrella bar at the top of the Penken gondola, the Ice Bar at the hotel Strass and Nicki's Schirmbar in the Brücke hotel get packed out. Some of the other bars in the Strass are rocking places later on, including the Speak Easy Arena, with live music and dancing until 4am. Reporters have preferred the Apropos ('great music'), Brücke's Schlüssel Alm ('still the best all-round late-night venue') and Coup & More ('a lively atmosphere without the rowdiness of some other places'). Mo's American theme bar has an international clientele and Scotland Yard is popular with Brits (and has 'a new conservatory/extension making it more roomy and less dingy'. The Neue Post bar and the Passage are good for a quiet drink. You can also party (or stay overnight) at the White Lounge ice-hotel at the top of the Ahorn gondola.

OFF THE SLOPES ★★★★
Good for all

Innsbruck and other resorts are easily reached by train or bus. There are also good walks and sports amenities, including the swimming pool complex – with saunas, solariums and lots of other fun features. Pedestrians have no trouble getting up the mountain to meet friends for lunch. 'Once again we had a non-skier in our party and they found plenty to do,' says a reporter.

Zillertal Arena

The Zillertal Arena was created in 2000 by linking the slopes of Zell am Ziller, a short drive down the valley from Mayrhofen, to those above the villages of Gerlos and Königsleiten. They now share 51 lifts and 160km/99 miles of pistes (as much as the Mayrhofen-Lanersbach area). The slopes reach as high as 2400m/7,870ft, and most of them are above the 1500m/4,900ft mark, but they also get a lot of sun, so the snow message is a mixed one.

The slopes suit intermediates best. You can really get a sense of travelling around: the trip from one end to the other is 17km/11 miles and takes you over several peaks and ridges. Our attempt to explore it two seasons ago was spoilt by thick fog, but a more fortunate reporter said: 'Starting from Zell am Ziller, a return trip is a full day's skiing. We did the tour over two days to fit in all the other runs.' Most runs are fairly short, the longest being down to Gerlos (4km/2.5 miles).

Zell am Ziller, the main town in the area, is a real working town rather than just a resort – it is a sprawling place, and has the oldest working brewery in the Tirol. There are some good hotels, including the 4-star Zapfenhof (2349) on the outskirts (with pool) and the Brau (2313) in the centre. The town is a bus ride from the two gondolas into the ski area. You have to ride these down as well as up – there is no piste. Après-ski centres around a few bars near the base of the gondola.

Gerlos has the advantage of being centrally situated in the ski area, allowing you to explore in either direction each day. It is a bustling resort that straddles the road up to the Gerlos pass and is a bus ride from the gondola that takes you into the slopes. The home slope benefits from top-to-bottom snowmaking; there's a good local terrain park and half-pipe, and a toboggan run. A 2009 visitor reports 'no queues and good signposting'. Après-ski is lively and there are several good local hotels, including the 4-star Gaspingerhof (52160) with a very smart spa.

Königsleiten is an unusual resort – very spread-out, in a scenic wooded setting above a dam; mostly small chalets, but half a dozen hotels including the 4-star Königsleiten (82160). It has more extensive local slopes than Gerlos, on either side of the Gerlospass road, but less vertical. On the north side, the runs are mostly genuine reds, radiating from the peak of Königsleitenspitze (2315m/7,595ft). The lower southern sector has a row of quad chairs serving easier slopes. The Obermoser ski school was praised by a 2009 reporter who also warned 'the draglift on the village nursery slope is not covered by the regional lift pass and cost 13 euros a day'.

Both Gerlos and Königsleiten attract a lot of Dutch visitors.

Obergurgl

A combination of high altitude and traditional Alpine atmosphere keeps the regulars going back, despite the drawbacks

£90
RESORT PRICE INDEX

RATINGS

The mountains

Extent	★★
Fast lifts	★★★★★
Queues	★★★★★
Terrain p'ks	★★★★
Snow	★★★★★
Expert	★★
Intermediate	★★★
Beginner	★★★★
X-country	★★
Restaurants	★★★
Schools	★★★★
Families	★★★★

The resort

Charm	★★★★
Convenience	★★★★
Scenery	★★★
Eating out	★★★
Après-ski	★★★★
Off-slope	★★

172

NEWS

For 2008/09 the first UK-operated catered chalets opened in the resort – run by Esprit Ski and Ski Total. And a new children's area was built behind the hotel Hochfirst.

For 2009/10 a new 3km/2 mile long toboggan route is planned.

+ Glaciers apart, one of the Alps' most snow-sure resorts – especially good for a late-season holiday

+ Excellent area for beginners, timid intermediates and families

+ Mainly queue- and crowd-free

+ Traditional-style village with comfortable hotels and little traffic

+ Jolly teatime après-ski

− Limited area of slopes, with no tough pistes and no terrain park

− Exposed setting, with very few sheltered slopes for bad weather

− Few off-slope leisure amenities except in hotels

− Village is basically one long street

− For a small Austrian resort, hotels are rather expensive

A loyal band of visitors go back every year to Obergurgl or its higher satellite Hochgurgl, booking a year in advance in recognition of the limited supply of beds. We understand the appeal of high, snow-sure, uncrowded, easy-intermediate slopes. But if we're going to a bleak, remote resort where there is not much to do but ski or board, we'd rather go somewhere with more skiing or boarding to do. Of course, most such places aren't in Austria – and perhaps that is the key to Obergurgl's appeal. It's snow-sure, and it's in Austria.

THE RESORT

Obergurgl is based on a traditional old village, set in a remote spot, the dead end of a long road up past Sölden. It is the highest parish in Austria and is usually under a blanket of snow from November until May.

At the northern entrance to the resort is a cluster of hotels near the Festkogl gondola. The road then passes another group of hotels set on a little hill to the east, around the ice rink (beware steep, sometimes treacherous walks here). The village proper starts with an attractive little square with church, fountain, and the focal village hotel (Edelweiss und Gurgl) next to the Rosskar chairlift and Gaisberg gondola stations. There is an underground car park in the centre.

Hochgurgl, a mid-mountain

gondola-ride away, is little more than a handful of hotels at the foot of its own slopes. It looks like it might be a convenient ski-in/ski-out resort, but it isn't: from nearly all the hotels you have to negotiate roads and/or stairs to get to or from the snow.

It's a short bus trip to Sölden (hourly buses, covered by the lift pass), and a long car trip to Kühtai (a high area near Innsbruck). Much closer is the tiny touring launch pad of Vent.

VILLAGE CHARM ★★★★
On the quiet side

Obergurgl has no through traffic and few day visitors. The village centre is mainly traffic-free, and entirely so at night. Village atmosphere is relaxed during the day, jolly immediately after the slopes close, but rather subdued later at night; there are nightspots, but most people stay in their hotels.

CONVENIENCE ★★★★
Lifts at both ends

Obergurgl is a small place and there are lifts at both ends. Nowhere is a long walk from a lift.

SCENERY ★★★
High and bleak

Obergurgl's altitude and position mean the surrounding slopes are bleak. But it also means good panoramic views from the top of the lifts.

---

miles 0.5   1.0

Untergurgl ↑   Hochgurgl   N ↑

Festkogl →

Gaisberg →

km   1.0   2.0

↑ A mid-mountain gondola links the Obergurgl and Hochgurgl ski areas but you have to ride it both ways; they aren't linked by pistes

ÖTZTAL TOURISMUS / PHOTO LOHMANN

KEY FACTS

Resort	1930m
	6,330ft
Slopes	1795-3080m
	5,890-10,100ft
Lifts	24
Pistes	110km
	68 miles
Blue	32%
Red	50%
Black	18%
Snowmaking	100%

THE MOUNTAINS

A gondola links the Obergurgl and Hochgurgl ski areas at mid-mountain level. But you have to ride it both ways – there are no pistes between them. And the gondola closes absurdly early at 4pm. The total area of slopes is quite limited and most of them are very exposed – with few woodland runs to head to in poor conditions. Wind and white-outs can shut the lifts and, especially in early season, severe cold can curtail enthusiasm.

The lift pass is quite expensive for the relatively small area, but the 10 euro upgrade to cover a day in Sölden is good value and any keen intermediate should pay the supplement (note that this must be bought at the same time as the full pass). While piste grooming is very good, signposting and, especially, piste edge marking is continually criticised by reporters : 'amazingly awful', 'non-existent in places – we found ourselves inadvertently off-piste on two occasions', 'one of our group plunged 15 metres off the edge of a blue run in a white-out and took 30 minutes climbing back up'. We checked these complaints out on our 2009 visit and totally agree – there are huge drop-offs that are not marked and slopes seem to be marked either on one side only (often the uphill side) or in the middle only. Crazy.

EXTENT OF THE SLOPES ★★
Limited cruising
Obergurgl is the smaller of the two linked areas. It is in two sections, with a link at altitude in only one direction.

The gondola from the village entrance and the Rosskar fast quad chair go to the higher **Festkogl** section. This is served by a short drag and a longer chair up to 3035m/9,960ft. From here you can head down to the gondola base or over to the **Gaisberg** sector, now also reached from the village via a gondola, which goes on to the sector high point at Hohe Mut. A blue run links across from the mid-station of the gondola to slopes served by a slow quad and a six-pack, and a red run links across from the top.

There are two ski routes which were ungroomed on our 2009 visit but their status is not explained on the piste map. On Tuesdays 8km/5 miles of slopes are floodlit for night skiing.

The slopes of **Hochgurgl** consist of high, gentle bowls, with fast lifts – chairs and two gondolas – serving the main slopes above the village, but drags serve the more testing outlying slopes. From the top stations there are spectacular views to the Dolomites. A single run leads down through the woods from Hochgurgl to Untergurgl.

FAST LIFTS ★★★★★
Among the best
Most lifts are now high-capacity gondolas or fast chairs.

QUEUES ★★★★★
Few problems
Major lift queues are rare.

TERRAIN PARKS ★★★★★
There isn't one
There used to be a terrain park and pipe but these were scrapped a few years ago.

Interactive resort shortlist builder at **www.wtss.co.uk**

AUSTRIA

174

boarding

Beginners can access most of the slopes without having to ride draglifts. There's some good off-piste potential for more advanced riders but the lack of any terrain features or park is a major drawback for most.

SNOW RELIABILITY ★★★★★
Excellent
Obergurgl has high slopes and is arguably the most snow-sure of Europe's non-glacier resorts – even without its snowmaking, which the resort claims covers all the pistes. It has a long season by Austrian standards.

FOR EXPERTS ★★★★★
Not generally recommendable
There are few challenges on-piste – most of the blacks could easily be red, and where they deserve the classification it's only for short stretches (for example, at the very top of Wurmkogl). There is a lot of easy off-piste to be found with a guide – the top school groups often go off-piste when conditions are right. This is a well-known area for ski touring, and we have reports of very challenging expeditions on the glaciers at the head of the valley.

FOR INTERMEDIATES ★★★★★
Good but limited
There is some perfect intermediate terrain here, made even better by the normally flattering snow conditions. The problem is, there's not much of it. Keen piste-bashers will quickly tire of skiing the same runs and be itching to catch the free bus to Sölden, down the valley – you can upgrade a week's lift

pass for 10 euros at the time of purchase to include a day on Sölden's slopes – well worth it.

Hochgurgl has the bigger area of easy runs, and these make good cruising. For more challenging intermediate runs, head to the Vorderer Wurmkogllift, on the right as you look at the mountain.

The Obergurgl area has more red than blue runs but most offer no great challenge to a confident intermediate. There is some easy cruising around mid-mountain on the Festkogl. The blue run from the top of the Festkogl gondola down to the village, via the Gaisberg sector, is one of the longest cruises in the area. And there's another long enjoyable run down the length of the gondola, with a scenic black run and ski route variant (neither of them very steep) in the adjoining valley.

On Gaisberg, there are very easy runs in front of the Nederhütte and back towards the village. The red run from Hohe Mut is narrow and in places winding – not recommended for timid intermediates.

FOR BEGINNERS ★★★★★
Fine for first-timers
The inconveniently situated Mahdstuhl nursery slope above Obergurgl is adequate for complete beginners. And the gentle Gaisberg run – under the gondola out of the village – is ideal to

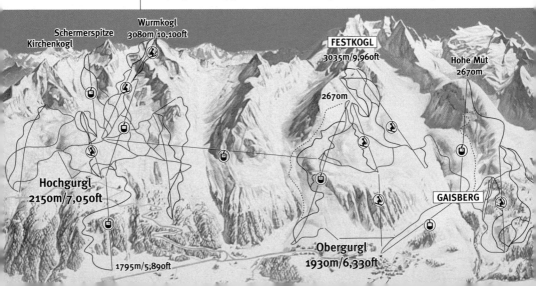

Schermerspitze
Kirchenkogl

Wurmkogl
3080m/10,100ft

FESTKOGL
3035m/9,960ft

Hohe Mut
2670m

2670m

Hochgurgl
2150m/7,050ft

GAISBERG

1795m/5,890ft

Obergurgl
1930m/6,330ft

SCHOOLS

Obergurgl
t 6305

Hochgurgl
t 626599

Classes
(Obergurgl prices)
6 days (2hr am and
pm) €207

Private lessons
From €120 for 2hr;
€9 for additional
person

CHILDCARE

Alpina and Hochfirst hotels
Kindergartens in these hotels

Kindergarten (ski school)
t 6305
From age 3; can include some skiing

Ski schools
From age 4 (6 days €207)

GETTING THERE

Air Innsbruck 95km/ 60 miles (2hr); Salzburg 285km/ 175 miles (4hr15); Munich 245km/ 150 miles (4hr30)

Rail Train to Ötz; regular buses from station

move on to as soon as a modicum of control has been achieved. The easy slopes that are served by the Bruggenboden chair are also suitable.

The Hochgurgl nursery slopes are an awkward walk from the hotels, but otherwise satisfactory. And there are good blue slopes to move on to.

The quality of the snow and piste preparation make learning here easier than in most lower Austrian resorts.

CROSS-COUNTRY ★★★★★
Limited but snow-sure
Three small loops, two at Obergurgl and one at Hochgurgl, give just 12km/7 miles of trail. At Hochgurgl 1km/0.5 miles are floodlit. All are relatively snow-sure and pleasantly situated. Lessons are available.

MOUNTAIN RESTAURANTS ★★★★★
Improving choice
Things have looked up in the last couple of years.
Editors' choice The newish Hohe Mut Alm (639632) has fabulous views from the huge terrace and a woody interior. We had a good Tirolergöstl there in 2009. But a reporter found it a 'nightmare on a sunny lunchtime; staff overworked'. The jolly Nederhütte (6425) at Gaisberg is lively and serves good food.
Worth knowing about David's Skihütte has 'traditional Austrian food and good service'. The Top Mountain Star at Wurmkogl looks like an air traffic control tower, has great 360° views, a varied menu but more of a modern bar than a restaurant ambience – small round tables and high bar stool-type chairs. Kirchenkarhütte could not be more of a contrast – a basic old hut that serves basic food ('good goulaschsuppe').

SCHOOLS AND GUIDES ★★★★★
Positive reports
We continue to receive positive reports of the Obergurgl school and guides, with good English spoken, a maximum of nine per group except at busy times and excellent lessons and organisation. Reporters find the instructors 'friendly, supportive and professional', and classes 'a very positive and pleasant experience' with 'excellent' English spoken. Demand for private instruction appears to be increasing and it is advisable to book ahead during all peak periods.

FOR FAMILIES ★★★★★
Check out your lodgings
Children's ski classes start at four years and children from age three can join Bobo's ski-kindergarten. There's lunchtime supervision for ski school and kindergarten children alike. Many hotels offer childcare of one sort or another (the Alpina has particularly recommended) and Ski Esprit is a family-specialist UK chalet operator here.

STAYING THERE

Most tour operators feature hotels and pensions. Demand exceeds supply, and for once it is true that you should book early to avoid disappointment. Family specialist Esprit has a couple of large chalets; all its guests have access to its usual comprehensive childcare facilities. Ski Total opened a chalet last season.
Hotels Accommodation is of high quality: most hotels are 4-stars, and none is less than a 3-star.
OBERGURGL
★★★★Edelweiss und Gurgl (6223) The focal point; on the central square, near the main lifts. Pool and outdoor hot tub. 'Good marks for food, service, comfort and location.'
★★★★Josl (6205) Uber-modern, convenient – close to the gondola. Big rooms, lots of storage, glass walls to bathrooms. Top floor has suite of saunas, steam rooms etc. We stayed here in 2009 and loved it.
★★★★Alpina de Luxe (6000) Big, smart, excellent children's facilities. Pool.
★★★★Bergwelt (6274) Recommended as 'very smart'. Beauty and spa facilities, including indoor and outdoor pool.
★★★★Hochfirst (63250) 'Superb' spa facilities, comfortable, 'very good food', five minutes from gondola. Ski-bus stop outside. Casino sometimes.
★★★★Crystal (6454) Refurbished. Near the Festkogl lift. Ocean-liner appearance, but one of the best.
★★★★Gamper (6545) 'Excellent,' says a reporter. 'Good food, friendly staff.' Far end of town, past the square.
★★★★Gotthard-Zeit (6292) 'Elegant', comfortable, good food. Spa facilities. Small pool. Convenient for skiing, but a 'steep walk from the village'.
★★★★Jenewein (6203) 'Convenient with attractive spa facilities.'
★★★★Wiesental (6263) Comfortable, well situated, good value. Terrace popular for lunch and après-ski. 'Good

UK PACKAGES

Alpine Answers, Crystal, Crystal Finest, Directski.com, Esprit, First Choice, Independent Ski Links, Inghams, Interactive Resorts, Made to Measure, Momentum, Neilson, Simply Alpine, Ski Expectations, Ski Freshtracks, Ski Independence, Ski McNeill, Ski Solutions, Ski Total, Skiing Austria, Skitracer, Snow Finders, Thomson
Hochgurgl *Crystal Finest, First Choice, Inghams, Neilson, Ski Expectations, Skiing Austria, Skitracer, Snow Finders, Thomson*

ACTIVITIES

Indoor Pools, saunas, whirlpools, steam baths and massage in hotels; bowling, indoor golf, library

Outdoor Natural ice rink, curling, snowshoeing, winter hiking paths

Phone numbers
From elsewhere in Austria add the prefix 05256; from abroad use the prefix +43 5256

TOURIST OFFICE

t 05720 0100
obergurgl@oetztal.com
www.obergurgl.com

food, very friendly staff.'
***Granat-Schlössl (6363) Amusing pseudo-castle, surprisingly affordable.
***Pension Gurgl (6533) Friendly B&B near Festkogl lift; pizzeria; same owners as Edelweiss und Gurgl.
***Garni Schönblick (6251) B&B with downhill walk to main lifts. 'Big rooms, hearty breakfast, friendly.'
HOCHGURGL
*****Top Hotel Hochgurgl (6265) Relais & Chateaux – the only 5-star in the area. Luxurious, with pool.
****Angerer Alm (6241) 'Staff really friendly and helpful.' Pool.
****Riml (6261) Ski-in/ski-out location. A 2009 reporter says, 'Excellent pool, amazing wellness area, friendly staff, the most stunning hotel I've stayed in.'
****Sporthotel Olymp (6591) Near the Grosse Karbahn chair. 'Excellent food and service.'
***Sporthotel Ideal (6290) Well situated for access to the slopes. Pool and spa facilities.
***Laurin (6227) Well-equipped, traditional rooms, excellent food.
Apartments The Lohmann (6201) is modern and well placed for the slopes, less so for the village centre below. The 3-star Pirchhütt (6390) has apartments close to the Festkogl gondola, and the Wiesental hotel has more central ones.

EATING OUT ★★★☆☆
Wide choice, limited range

Hotel à la carte dining rooms dominate almost completely. A reporter recommends the independent and rustic Krumpn's Stadl (where staff dress in traditional clothing). The Hexenkuchl in the Jenewein receives favourable reports, serving 'good quality Austrian food'. The Romantika at the hotel Madeleine and the Belmonte are popular pizzerias. Hotels Alpina, Hochfirst ('food excellent, good wine selection') and Gotthard-Zeit have

been recommended. The Angerer Alm does 'good meals in relaxing surroundings'. The two restaurants in the Edelweiss und Gurgl are reportedly 'superb', and food at the Josl 'excellent'. The 5-star Top Hotel Hochgurgl was recommended for a 'delicious' treat. Some evenings you can eat on the hill, at Nederhütte (a fondue and live music evening, which 'rocks') and David's Skihütte – both popular snowmobile destinations.

APRES-SKI ★★★★☆
Lively early, quiet later

Obergurgl is more animated than you might expect, at least in the early evening. Nederhütte at Gaisberg is the place to be when the lifts close ('get there at 2pm if you want a table inside'). It has live music most days and 'even 70-year-olds were dancing on the tables', says a recent reporter. You ski home afterwards though (or ride down on a snowmobile). All the bars at the base of the Rosskar and Gaisberg lifts are also popular at close of play – the Pic-Nic is said to be lively and friendly. The Hexenkuchl at the Jenewein is also popular and a reporter enjoyed the 'excellent' and 'popular sun terrace' at the Wiesental.

Later on, the crowded Krumpn's Stadl barn is the liveliest place in town with live music on alternate nights. The Josl Keller is popular with all ages and gets busy with 'a western-style saloon downstairs and a posh wine bar upstairs'. The Jenewein and Edelweiss und Gurgl ('terrible live music but good service and comfy sofas') hotels have atmospheric bars. Reporters enjoy the Tuesday night ski school display/mountain party/night ski on Festkogl ('great night out').

Hochgurgl is very quiet at night except for Toni's Almhütte bar with live music in the Sporthotel Olymp.

OFF THE SLOPES ★★☆☆☆
Very limited

There isn't much to do during the day – few shops, limited public facilities – though a 2009 visitor recommends the ice rink. Innsbruck is over two hours away by post bus. Sölden (20 minutes away) has a leisure centre and shopping facilities. Pedestrians can ride gondolas to restaurants for lunch, or walk to the Gaisberg area; there are 12km/7 miles of hiking paths. The health suite at the Hochfirst is said to be open to non-residents.

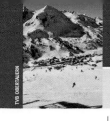

Obertauern

French-style convenience and high altitude married to traditional architecture and Austrian après-ski – what could be better?

➕ Excellent snow record

➕ Efficient modern lifts

➕ Slopes for all abilities

➕ Good mountain restaurants

➕ Lively but not intrusive après-ski

➕ Compact resort core, but ...

➖ Village lacks traditional charm and spreads along the pass a long way

➖ Peaks are not high, so slopes are of limited vertical and extent is too small for keen piste-bashers

➖ Lifts and snow can suffer from exposure to high winds

TOP 10 RATINGS

Extent	★★
Fast lifts	★★★★★
Queues	★★★★
Snow	★★★★
Expert	★★★
Intermediate	★★★★
Beginner	★★★★
Charm	★★
Convenience	★★★★
Scenery	★★★

KEY FACTS

Resort	1740m
	5,710ft
Slopes	1630-2315m
	5,350-7,600ft
Lifts	26
Pistes	95km
	59 miles
Blue	59%
Red	37%
Black	4%
Snowmaking	90%

Obertauern's attractions are unique. If you're looking for a change from the slush and ice of lower Austrian resorts, moving up in the world by 1000m/ 3,300ft or so could be just the ticket – French-style snow without losing that inimitable Austrian après-ski jollity.

THE RESORT

In the land of picture-postcard resorts grown out of rustic valley villages, Obertauern is different – a mainly modern development at the top of the Tauern pass road.

Village charm Built in (high-rise) chalet style, the resort is not unattractive – though it's a linear affair, lacking a central focus of shops and bars.

Convenience Although the core is compact, accommodation is spread widely along the road, with lifts going up either way of the road at various points.

Scenery The setting is satisfyingly rugged, with some long views from the high points of the area.

THE MOUNTAINS

IAIN HOOLEY

The sunny side of the bowl is broad and spacious – on the far side, just the opposite applies ↓

The slopes and lifts form a circuit around the village that can be travelled either way in a couple of hours. Visitors used to big areas will soon start to feel they have seen it all. Runs are short and vertical is limited –

most major lifts are in the 200m to 400m (660ft to 1,310ft) range. The piste map and signposting are slowly improving. The pistes are now numbered on both the map and the mountain, though reports are mixed on their effectiveness – 'the colours don't always agree', says one visitor.

Slopes Most pistes are on the sunny slopes to the north of the road and village: a wide basin of mostly gentle runs, some combining steepish pitches with long schusses. The slopes on the other side of the road – beneath Gamsleitenspitze – are quieter and have some of the steeper runs. There is floodlit skiing twice a week.

Fast lifts There are fast chairs all over. The lift system is impressively efficient and lifties reportedly fill the chairs.

Queues Crowded pistes can be more of a problem than queues. But the Grünwaldkopfbahn quad may generate queues in the mornings – huge when we visited. The Sonnenlift double chair can have problems at ski school time. The six-pack at Hundskogel should have relieved congestion there.

Terrain parks The small Longplay Park is above the Almrausche hut, on the far left on our piste map.

Snow reliability The resort has exceptional snow reliability because of its altitude. But lifts can be closed by wind (which may blow snow away too). Snowmaking is efficient, but grooming needs improvement.

Experts There are genuinely steep black pistes from the top Gamsleiten chair, but it is prone to closure. The icy race course under the Schaidberg-bahn is also a challenge. And try the black run from Seekarspitze and the

NEWS

For 2009/10 the 4-star Manggei designer hotel and spa is due to open.

Two chalet-style apartment buildings opened for 2008/009: the Cabana-Alm and the Primus Lodge.

The Snowgolf World Championships were held here from 29 to 31 January 2009.

UK PACKAGES

Alpine Answers, Crystal Finest, Inghams, Simply Alpine, Skiing Austria, Snow Finders, Snowscape, STC, Thomson

Phone numbers
From elsewhere in Austria add the prefix 06456; from abroad use the prefix +43 6456

TOURIST OFFICE

t 7252
info@obertauern.com
www.obertauern.com

ski route from Hundskogel (flat to start, steep moguls later). Reporters recommend joining an off-piste guided group to explore the area.

Intermediates Most of the circuit is of intermediate difficulty. Stay low for easier pistes, or try the tougher runs higher up; you can't do the whole circuit without skiing reds.

Beginners The nursery slopes are very good, but they are spread around and may involve long walks to and from accommodation. The Schaidberg chair leads to a high-altitude beginners' slope and there is an easy run down.

Snowboarding Draglifts are optional except for beginners. Blue Tomato is a specialist school.

Cross-country There is a 10km/6 mile loop in the centre and more locally.

Mountain restaurants Mountain restaurants are numerous but often crowded. Readers approve of most, but particular favourites are: Hochalm for its lively terrace; the village-level Heustadl ('superb gulaschsuppe'; the tiny Achenrainhütte for its 'jolly atmosphere'. Other tips: Treff 2000 ('excellent, good value dishes'), the 'cosy' Mankeialm and the Sonnhof ('best gröstl of the week', 'fast table-service').

Schools and guides Of the seven schools, we have had good reports on Frau Holle, Willi Grillitsch, Krallinger and Koch.

Families The resort isn't particularly family-oriented and the nursery slopes can be inconvenient, but most of the schools take children.

STAYING THERE

A handful of tour operators offer packages here.

Hotels Practically all accommodation is in hotels (mostly 3-star and 4-star) and guest houses. The cool Manggei 'designhotel' (7236) is new for 2009/10; B&B only; pool and spa. Past reader tips: Steiner (7306) 'smart and comfortable'; D'Glöcknerin (7805) 'lovely bar and spa facilities'; Marietta (72620) 'couldn't fault it'; Appparthotel Hubertus (20084) 'spacious and comfortable'.

Eating out The choices are mostly hotels and the busy après-ski bars at the foot of the lifts. The Almrausch, north of the town, is 'fantastic'.

Après-ski It's lively and varied. Hochalm's terrace is crowded from mid-afternoon. The Latsch'n Alm, with terrace and dancing, is good at tea time, as is the Lürzer Alm – 'full of character, lively, one of the best'. The Gruber Stadl is 'built to charm' and equally popular. The Tauernkönig hotel has 'a cosy outdoor après area hidden away off the 8a home run'. Monkey's Heaven and the People bar have dancing. The Taverne, Römerbar and the 'quaint' Nanu Irish bar have been recommended too.

Off the slopes There's an excellent, large sports centre – no pool, though. There are marked walks up to Kringsalm. Salzburg is an easy trip.

Saalbach-Hinterglemm

Lively, noisy, traditional-style villages and extensive, varied, prettily wooded slopes; pity they are mostly so sunny

£90
RESORT PRICE INDEX

RATINGS

The mountains

Extent	★★★
Fast lifts	★★★★★
Queues	★★★
Terrain p'ks	★★★★
Snow	★★
Expert	★★
Intermediate	★★★★
Beginner	★★★
X-country	★★
Restaurants	★★★★
Schools	★★★★
Families	★★★

The resort

Charm	★★★★
Convenience	★★★★
Scenery	★★★
Eating out	★★★
Après-ski	★★★★★
Off-slope	★★

KEY FACTS

Resort	1000m
	3,280ft
Slopes	930-2095m
	3,050-6,870ft
Lifts	55
Pistes	200km
	124 miles
Blue	45%
Red	48%
Black	7%
Snowmaking	90%

- + Large, well-linked, intermediate circuit, good for mixed groups
- + Impressive lift system – world's highest proportion of fast lifts
- + Saalbach is a big but pleasant, affluent village, lively at night
- + Main streets are largely traffic-free
- + Lifts and pistes are conveniently close to centres of both villages
- + Dozens of good mountain huts
- + Large snowmaking installation
- + Sunny slopes, but ...

- – Most slopes are low as well as sunny, and the snow suffers
- – Limited steep terrain
- – Nursery slopes in Saalbach are not ideal – sunny, and crowded in parts
- – Saalbach spreads along the valley – some lodgings are far from central
- – Hinterglemm sprawls along a long street with no clearly defined centre
- – Both are noisy from 4pm and Saalbach can get rowdy at night

A recent Austrian tour confirmed that the 'Skicircus' is in most respects the best of the major ski areas east of Innsbruck – it has more challenging intermediate terrain and better mountain restaurants than the SkiWelt (Söll, Ellmau etc), slicker lifts than Kitzbühel, and has the edge on both in terms of village altitude and ski convenience, provided you pick your spot.

The snowmaking is now good enough to make a midwinter holiday a fairly safe bet, but there is a limit to what snowmaking can achieve on low, sunny slopes as spring approaches. Like the other areas we mention, this is really a place to book at short notice, when conditions are good.

THE RESORT

Saalbach and Hinterglemm are separate villages, their centres 4km/ 2.5 miles apart, which have expanded along the floor of their dead-end valley. They haven't quite merged, but some years back they adopted a single marketing identity.

Saalbach has a justified reputation as a party town – but those doing the partying seem to be a strangely mixed bunch. Big-spending BMW and Mercedes drivers staying in the smart, expensive hotels that line the main street share the bars with teenagers (including British school kids) spending more on alcohol than on their cheap and cheerful pensions strung along the valley road.

Hinterglemm is a more diffuse collection of hotels and holiday homes, where prices are lower and less cash is flashed.

There is a good valley bus service, but it isn't perfect: it finishes early, gets very busy at peak times and doesn't get you back to hotels in central Hinterglemm, or to hotels set away from the main road – and one reporter complains of poorly marked stops. Taxis are plentiful. The Nightliner bus runs intermittently from 7.30pm to 12am (2am at weekends) between Saalbach and Hinterglemm.

Several resorts in Salzburg province are reachable by road – including Bad Hofgastein, Kaprun and Zell am See, the last a short bus ride away.

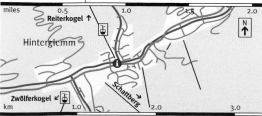

↑ Excellent long runs to the valley on the south side – from Schattberg to Hinterglemm

VILLAGE CHARM ★★★★
Very appealing
Saalbach is an attractive, typically Tirolean village, with traditional-style (although mostly modern) buildings huddled together around a classic onion-domed church. Hinterglemm is less cute, but its main street lined with bars and hotels is much better now that it is relieved of through traffic (though it is not quite car-free).

Both villages are lively and noisy from mid-afternoon until the early hours. Saalbach in particular can get rowdy, with drunken revellers still in their ski boots long after dark. If you are not among them, you might find this a problem.

CONVENIENCE ★★★★
Lifts near the centre
Saalbach is more convenient than most Austrian villages, with lifts into three sectors of the slopes starting close to the traffic-free village centre; the result is near to an ideal blend of Austrian charm with French convenience. Hinterglemm also has lifts and runs close to the centre, and offers quick access to some of the most interesting slopes – and, importantly, to most of the north-facing runs. In both villages, the amount of walking depends heavily on where you stay.

SCENERY ★★★
Pleasant rather than dramatic
The villages are flanked by modest, broad mountain ridges. The high points give more dramatic views of the mountains to the north.

THE MOUNTAINS

The slopes form a 'circus' almost entirely composed of broad slopes between swathes of forest.

EXTENT OF THE SLOPES ★★★
User-friendly circuit
Travelling anticlockwise, you can make a complete circuit of the valley on skis, crossing from one side to the other at Vorderglemm and Lengau – if you wish you can stick to blues almost the whole way. Going clockwise, you have to truncate the circuit – there is no lift at Vorderglemm – and there is more red-run skiing to do (and a black if you want to do the full circuit).

On the south-facing side, five sectors can be identified, each served by a lift from the valley – from west to east, **Hochalm**, **Reiterkogel**, **Bernkogel**, **Kohlmaiskopf** and **Wildenkarkogel**. The links across these south-facing slopes work well: when traversing the whole hillside you need to descend to the valley floor only once – at Saalbach, where the main street separates Bernkogel from Kohlmaiskopf. The Wildenkarkogel sector connects via Seidl-Alm to the slopes of **Leogang**; a small, high, open area served by four fast lifts (including an eight-pack and new quad) leads to a long, north-facing slope down to the base of an eight-seat gondola near Hütten, 3km/2 miles from Leogang village.

Back in the main valley, the north-facing slopes are different in character: two widely separated and steeper mountains, one split into twin peaks. An eight-seat gondola rises from Saalbach to **Schattberg Ost**, where the high, open, sunny slopes behind the

For 2009/10 a six-pack with covers and heated seats is planned to replace the Turm draglift, on the lower slopes of Kohlmaiskopf at Saalbach. Above Hinterglemm, an eight-seat chair is expected to replace the quad to Hasenauer Köpfl.

At Leogang, a fast quad is due to replace the Almlift T-bar below the gondola mid-station.

For 2008/09 an eight-pack with heated seats and covers replaced the Asitz quad up to Kl. Asitz on the return from Leogang.

Skicircus Saalbach Hinterglemm Leogang

Prices in €

Age	1-day	6-day
under 16	20	98
16 to 18	31	152
over 19	41	196

Free under 6
Senior no deals
Beginner points card

Notes
Covers Saalbach, Hinterglemm and Leogang, and the ski-bus; also Reiterkogel toboggan run at night; part-day passes available; supplement for swimming pool

Alternative passes
Salzburg Super Ski Card covers 22 ski areas in the Salzburg province; Kitzbüheler Alpen All Star Card covers seven ski areas – Kitzbühel, Schneewinkel (St Johann), Ski Welt, Alpbach, Wildschönau, Skicircus Saalbach, Zell-Kaprun

peak are served by a fast quad. The slightly higher peak of **Schattberg West** is reached by gondola from Hinterglemm. Another gondola makes the link from Schattberg Ost to Schattberg West. The second north-facing hill is **Zwölferkogel**, served by a two-stage eight-seat gondola from Hinterglemm. A six-pack and draglift serve open slopes on the sunny side of the peak, and a second gondola from the valley provides a link from the south-facing Hochalm slopes.

The Hinterglemm nursery slopes are well used, and floodlit every evening.

FAST LIFTS ★★★★★
A new world champion
The already impressive lift system gained another fast chair last season, and with three more planned for 2009/10 ('see 'News') Saalbach-Hinterglemm now has the highest proportion of fast lifts of any major resort in the world. Bizarrely, Bernkogel remains free of fast lifts.

QUEUES ★★★
A problem in high season
In high season, the lifts from Saalbach up the south-facing slopes can have waits of up to 15 minutes at peak times, at the end as well as the start of the day. A mid-February visitor found 30-minute queues for the Schönleiten gondola up from Vorderglemm. High-season queues for the chair to Hasenauer Köpfl should be relieved by the new eight-pack planned for 2009/10. Generally, March visitors have found few queues, but the slow and unreliable Bernkogel chairlift out of Saalbach can be a problem – see 'Fast lifts', above.

TERRAIN PARKS ★★★★
Excellent
There's a floodlit terrain park with Big Air, waves and kickers, a half-pipe and boardercross course near the nursery slopes just above Hinterglemm ('loved' by one reporter's teenagers), and another below Kl. Asitz on the way to Leogang. Several dedicated 'carving' and 'mogul' zones are dotted around.

SNOW RELIABILITY ★★
A tale of two sides
Most slopes are low (below 1900m/6,235ft) and the south-facing slopes are in the majority; they can suffer when the sun comes out (on an early March 2007 visit, the south-facing side just had strips of machine-made snow amid green and brown fields). The north-facing slopes keep their snow better but can get icy. The long north-facing run down to Leogang often has the best snow in the area. Piste maintenance is good and snowmaking now covers 90% of the area, including many top-to-bottom runs; but the fundamental problems won't go away.

FOR EXPERTS ★★
Little steep stuff
There are a few challenging slopes on the north-facing side. The long (4km/2.5 mile) Nordabfahrt run beneath the Schattberg Ost gondola is a genuine black – a fine fast bash first thing in the morning if it has been groomed and not icy. The Zwölferkogel Nordabfahrt at Hinterglemm is less consistent, but its classification is justified by a few short, steeper pitches. The World Cup downhill run from Zwölferkogel is interesting, as is the 5km/3 mile Schattberg West–Hinterglemm red (and its scenic 'ski route' variant). Off-piste guides are available, but snow conditions and forest tend to limit the potential. Given decent snow, however, you can have a good time (a lucky reporter 'had two days of powder and saw no more than 20 other skiers off-piste – excellent').

FOR INTERMEDIATES ★★★★
Paradise for most
The sunny side of the area is ideal for both the mileage-hungry piste-basher and the more leisurely cruiser, although more than one early-intermediate reporter has judged the majority of the blues quite testing. For those looking for more of a challenge, the long red runs to the valley ranged along the north side are good fun. The otherwise delightful blue run from Bernkogel to Saalbach gets really

boarding

Saalbach is great for boarding. Slopes are extensive, lifts are mainly chairs and gondolas (though there are some connecting drags), and there are pistes to appeal to beginners, intermediates and experts alike – with few flats to negotiate. For experienced boarders, there's plenty of off-piste terrain between the lifts.

crowded at busy times of day.

The north-facing area has some more challenging runs, with excellent relentless reds from both Schattberg West and Zwölferkogel, and a section of relatively high, open slopes around Zwölferkogel – good for mixed-ability groups wishing to ski together, a happy reporter points out. None of the black runs is beyond an adventurous intermediate. The long, pretty run to Vorderglemm gets you right away from lifts – but it gets a bit steep and tricky towards the end, and probably should be red not blue.

Our favourite intermediate run is the long, off-the-main-circuit cruise (on relatively good snow) to Leogang.

FOR BEGINNERS ★★★☆☆
Head for Hinterglemm
Saalbach's two sunny nursery slopes are right next to the village centre. But the upper one gets a lot of through-traffic. A new six-pack should help progression at Kohlmais. Alternatives are trips to the short, easy runs at Bernkogel and Schattberg.

Hinterglemm's spacious nursery area is separate from the main slopes and preferred by reporters. It faces north, so lacks sun in midwinter but is more reliable for snow later on.

There are lots of easy blue runs to move on to, especially on the south-facing side of the valley, but it pays to take advice on which are easiest.

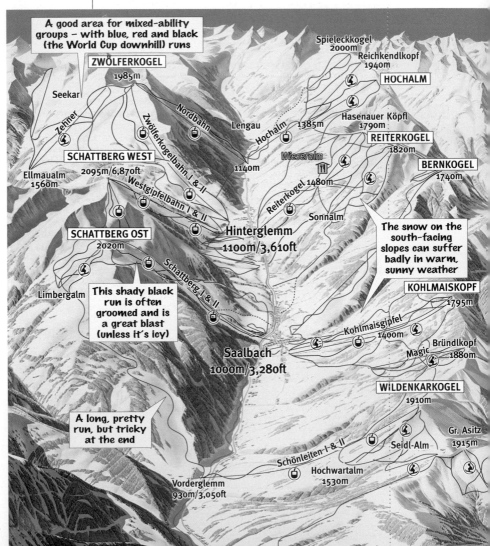

SCHOOLS

Saalbach

Fürstauer
t 8444

Snow Academy
t 668256

Hinterholzer
t 7607

Zink
t 0664 162 3655

Snowboard
t 20047

easySki
t 0699 111 80010

Hinterglemm

Hinterglemmer
t 634640

Activ
t 0676 517 1325

Classes
(Fürstauer prices)
5 days (4hr) from
€148

Private lessons
From €139 for 3hr,
for 1 or 2 people;
extra person €15

FOR CROSS-COUNTRY ★★☆☆☆
Go to Zell am See

Some 10km/6 miles of trails run beside the road along the valley floor from Saalbach to Vorderglemm, between Hinterglemm and the valley end at Lindlingalm, and there is a high trail on the Reiterkogel. In mid-winter the valley trails get very little sun, and are not very exciting. The area beyond nearby Zell am See offers considerably more scope.

MOUNTAIN RESTAURANTS ★★★★
Excellent quality and quantity

The area is liberally scattered with around 40 attractive huts, most serving good food. Many have warm, rustic interiors and a lively ambience. All are marked and named on the piste map. Why isn't this simple thing done everywhere?

Editors' choice The Wieseralm (6939), at the heart of the Hinterglemm south-facing slopes, is a welcoming woody chalet doing table service of satisfying dishes; fine views from the terrace.

Worth knowing about This year's reader recommendations are Alte Schmiede towards Leogang ('excellent food, huge portions') and Westernstadl on Bernkogel ('good food and service, cosy, beautifully decorated'). On Bründlkopf, Thurneralm is an enduring reader favourite. Other reader tips in recent years include Walleggalm ('brilliant – they have a DJ at lunchtime'), Bäckstättstall, Bergstadl, Bärnalm, Grabenhütte, Rosswaldhütte, Simalalm and Breitfussalm.

SCHOOLS AND GUIDES ★★★★
Plenty of choice

There's plenty of choice. We've had good reports on the Snow Academy recently – a beginner had a week of group morning and afternoon lessons which 'brought him on a treat'. A boarder had 'worthwhile' lessons with Hinterglemmer. One 2008 reporter enjoyed two 'excellent' days with the Fürstauer school.

FOR FAMILIES ★★★
Hinterglemm tries harder

Saalbach doesn't go out of its way to sell itself to families, although it does have a ski kindergarten. Hinterglemm has some good hotel-based nursery facilities – the one at the Theresia is reportedly excellent –and probably makes a better family base.

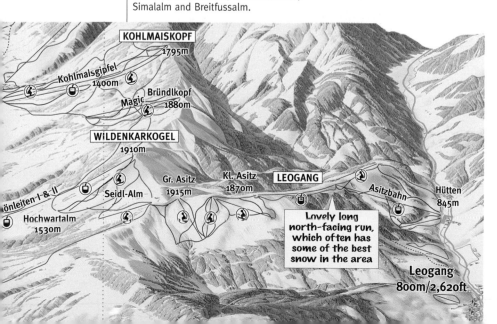

Lovely long north-facing run, which often has some of the best snow in the area

Leogang
800m/2,620ft

CHILDCARE

Several hotels have
nurseries

Ski schools
Some take children in
mini-clubs from about
age 3 and can provide
lunchtime care; from
about age 4, children
can join ski school
(€208 for 6 days,
including lunch –
Fürstauer prices)

STAYING THERE

Chalets We are aware of a few 'club
hotels', but Saalbach isn't really a
chalet resort.

Hotels There are a large number of
hotels in both villages, mainly 3-star
and above. Be aware that some
central hotels are affected by disco
noise and front rooms by street noise
into the early hours.

SAALBACH

****Alpenhotel** (6666) Luxurious, with
open-fire lounge, disco, small pool.
Various bars, restaurants, Arena club.
****Berger's Sporthotel** (6577) Lively,
with a daily tea dance, disco and lap-
dancing club. Small pool.
****Gartenhotel Eva** (7144) Small hotel
and spa, recommended by a reporter.
****Kendler** (62250) Position second
to none, right next to the Bernkogel
chair. Classy, expensive, good food.

****Kristiana** (6253) Near enough to
lifts but away from night-time noise.
Sauna, steam bath.
****Panther** (6227) 'Excellent,
practically ski-in/ski-out, good food.'
****Saalbacher Hof** (71110) Retains a
friendly feel despite its large size;
'excellent wellness centre'; apparently
being revamped for 2009/10.
***Haider** (6228) Best-positioned of
the 3-stars, right next to the main lifts.
***Peter** (6236) 'Excellent value for
main street location. Food OK.'

HINTERGLEMM

****Egger** (63220) 'I'll stay here next
time, on the slopes,' says a reader.
****Theresia** (74140) Hinterglemm's
top hotel (Michelin recommended),
one of the best for families and a
reader favourite. Out towards
Saalbach, but nursery slopes nearby.
Pool and spa. 'Superb food and
friendly staff.'
***Sonnblick** (6408) Convenient 3-star
in a quiet location.
Haus Ameshofer (8119) 'Great value
ski-in/ski-out B&B.' At Reiterkogel lift.
Apartments There's a big choice for
independent travellers.
At altitude It is possible to stay up the
mountain in several hotels and
gasthofs. A 2007 reporter highly
recommends the 3-star Sonnhof
(6295) at the top of the Hochalmbahn:
'Large rooms, friendly staff, good
value.' The upper lifts start early, so
you get the slopes to yourself for half
an hour.

EATING OUT ★★★
Wide choice of hotel restaurants
This is essentially a half-board resort,
with strikingly few restaurants other
than those in hotels. A welcome
alternative in Saalbach is the Kohlmais
Stub'n at the foot of the Kohlmaiskopf
slopes – excellent steaks, good
friendly service, warm woody
ambience. The hotel Peter's restaurant,
at the top of Saalbach's main street, is
atmospheric and serves excellent meat
dishes cooked on hot stones. The
Alpenhotel's Trattoria is a good place
for a casual meal. The Auwirt hotel on
the outskirts of Saalbach has a good à
la carte restaurant. Berger Hochalm
part way up the toboggan track has
great views and serves 'the best pasta
ever and excellent pizzas'.

APRES-SKI ★★★★★
It rocks from early on
Après-ski is very lively from mid-

GETTING THERE

Air Salzburg 90km/ 55 miles (2hr); Munich 225km/140 miles (3hr30)

Rail Zell am See 19km/12 miles; hourly buses

UK PACKAGES

Alpine Answers, BoardnLodge, Chalet Group, Crystal, Crystal Finest, Directski.com, First Choice, Inghams, Interactive Resorts, Interhome, Neilson, Rocketski, Simply Alpine, Ski Expectations, Ski Independence, Skiing Austria, Ski McNeill, Ski Miquel, Skitracer, Snow Finders, Snowscape, STC, Thomson **Leogang** *Inntravel, Skiing Austria*

ACTIVITIES

Indoor Swimming pools, sauna, massage, solarium, tennis, museum, gallery

Outdoor Ice rink, curling, tobogganing, sleigh rides, snowshoeing, snowmobiling, quad bikes, ice karts, 40km/25 miles of cleared paths, archery

Phone numbers From elsewhere in Austria add the prefix 06541 (Saalbach), 06583 (Leogang); from abroad use the prefix +43 and omit the initial '0'

TOURIST OFFICES

Saalbach
t 680068
contact@saalbach.com
www.saalbach.com

Leogang
t 8234
info@saalfelden-leogang.at
www.leogang-saalfelden.at

afternoon until the early hours, and can get positively wild. Most places are packed by 4pm. On the hill above Saalbach, the rustic Hinterhagalm has live bands and rock music; when it closes around 6pm, the crowds slide down to the already packed Bauer's Schi-alm – an old cow shed and 'one of the liveliest and most atmospheric après-ski bars in Austria'. The Bäckstättstall is recommended for tea dancing. The main bar of Berger's Sporthotel also has dancing when the lifts close. The tiny Zum Turm (next door to the church) is a medieval jail that also offers 'unusual bar games'. The Neuhaus Taverne has live music and attracts a mature clientele. Alibi plays 'great tunes'. Jack-in has wi-fi and big screen TVs so attracts the sports fans. Bobby's Pub is cheap, has bowling and serves Guinness. King's, Arena and Castello's are clubs that liven up later on and have lap dancing adjuncts. For a civilised drink, a reader recommends the bar of the central Alpenhotel.

Several readers have enjoyed the lively and rustic goat-themed Goasstall just above Hinterglemm. There are a number of ice bars, popular at close of play, including the central Gute Stube of hotel Dorfschmiede, with loud music blasting out and people spilling into the street. A wider age group enjoys the live music later on at the smart, friendly Tanzhimmel – an open, glass-fronted bar with a dance floor. The Hexenhäusl gets packed. The Almbar has good music and dancing.

OFF THE SLOPES ★★ ☆☆☆
Surprisingly little to do

Saalbach is not very entertaining if you're not into winter sports. There are few shops other than supermarkets and ski shops. There are some cleared paths and a walkers' lift pass (65 euros) gives access to two lifts per day – which also means a mixed group of skiers and non-skiers could easily meet for lunch. Hinterglemm's toboggan run is said to be great fun and great value. There are excursions to Salzburg.

Leogang 800m/2,620ft

THE RESORT

Leogang is a much less expensive alternative to Saalbach-Hinterglemm.
Village charm The village is quiet, attractive but rather scattered.

Convenience If you're concerned about convenience, it's best to stay in the hamlet of Hütten, near the gondola into the main ski area.
Scenery The village sits in a pretty valley beneath the impressive Birnhorn.

THE MOUNTAIN

The village is linked to the eastern end of the main ski circuit.
Slopes A gondola from Hütten takes you into the ski area. The local slopes tend to be delightfully quiet.
Fast lifts Nursery slopes aside, all the lifts are fast.
Queues No local problems.
Snow reliability The local slopes have some of the best snow in the region, being north- and east-facing, with snowmaking on the run home.
Experts Not much challenge locally.
Intermediates Great long blue/red run cruise home from the top of the gondola. Plus the circuit to explore.
Beginners Good nursery slopes by the village, and short runs to progress to.
Snowboarding The whole area is great for boarding and there's a terrain park.
Cross-country The best in the area. There are 20km/12 miles of trails, plus a panoramic high altitude trail.
Mountain restaurants A couple of good local huts.
Schools and guides Leogang Altenberger school has a good reputation.
Families There is a non-ski nursery, and children can start school at four years old.

STAYING THERE

Hotels The luxury Krallerhof (8246) has its own nursery lift, which can be used to get across to the main lift station. The 4-star Salzburger Hof (7310) is well placed, a two-minute walk from the gondola; sauna and steam.
Apartments There are quiet apartments available.
Eating out Restaurants are hotel-based. The 'flawless' Kirchenwirt, upscale Krallerhof and much cheaper Hüttwirt have high reputations.
Après-ski The rustic old chalet Kraller Alm is very much the focal tea-time and evening rendezvous.
Off the slopes Excursions to Salzburg are possible.

Schladming

Old valley town with pleasant main square and extensive intermediate slopes on four linked mountains

£80
RESORT PRICE INDEX

RATINGS

The mountains

Extent	★★★
Fast lifts	★★★★
Queues	★★★★
Terrain p'ks	★★★
Snow	★★★★
Expert	★★
Intermediate	★★★★
Beginner	★★★
X-country	★★★★
Restaurants	★★★★
Schools	★★★
Families	★★★★

The resort

Charm	★★★
Convenience	★★★
Scenery	★★★
Eating out	★★★
Après-ski	★★★
Off-slope	★★★★

NEWS

For 2009/10 an eight-pack is planned to replace a T-bar near the top of Planai.

For 2008/09 access to Hochwurzen was improved by a chondola from a new departure point above Rohrmoos, and two new pistes were created. And a terrain park was built on Planai for the first time.

KEY FACTS

Resort	745m
	2,440ft
Schladming Ramsau/ Dachstein area	
Slopes	745-2015m
	2,440-6,610ft
Lifts	81
Pistes	175km
	109 miles
Blue	29%
Red	61%
Black	10%
Snowmaking	99%

+ Extensive intermediate slopes in four main sectors

+ Very sheltered slopes, among trees

+ Lots of good mountain restaurants

+ Appealing town with friendly people

+ Extensive snowmaking, good grooming and shady slopes mean good piste conditions, but ...

− The mainly north-facing runs can be cold in early season

− Slopes lack variety

− Very little to entertain experts

− Nursery slopes not central and may involve a bus ride

− Runs to valley level are not easy

− Limited but improving nightlife

With its four distinct mountains all linked by lifts (and to varying degrees by pistes), Schladming offers the keen intermediate a real sense of travelling around on the snow. But you may find one slope rather like another.

The resort does not offer one of Austria's wildest après-ski scenes, but most of our reporters don't mind that – they find its solid, valley-town ambience a pleasant change from the Austrian norm.

THE RESORT

The old town of Schladming has a long skiing tradition and has hosted World Cup races for many years. It sits at the foot of Planai, one of four linked mountains. A gondola a few minutes' walk from the centre goes most of the way up this hill, from a recently redeveloped base area.

From the western suburbs, chairlifts serve the next peak to the west, Hochwurzen. The chairlifts access Rohrmoos, a quiet, scattered village set on an elevated slope that forms a giant nursery area – an excellent base for beginners. From Hochwurzen you can progress to Reiteralm.

To the east of Schladming is the small, attractively rustic village of Haus, where a cable car and gondola go up to the highest of the four linked mountains, Hauser Kaibling.

Timetabled buses link the villages and lift bases, but they are not as frequent as reporters wish. A night bus runs until 1am (5 euros).

There are several other separate mountains nearby covered by the local lift pass – including Fageralm, Galsterbergalm, the Dachstein glacier and Stoderzinken. The Ski Alliance Amadé lift pass also covers many other resorts. A car is useful for getting the most out of it: trips are feasible to Bad Gastein, Wagrain/Flachau, Zauchensee and Hochkönig (and to Obertauern – not on the Amadé pass). The station is served by direct trains from Salzburg, so Schladming makes an excellent short break destination.

VILLAGE CHARM ★★★
Cute and car-free centre
Schladming has a pleasant, traffic-free main square, prettily lit at night, around which you'll find most of the shops, restaurants and bars (and some appealing hotels). The busy main road bypasses the town.

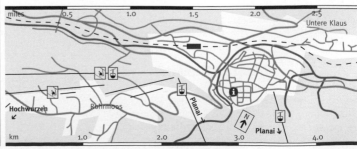

LIFT PASSES

Ski Alliance Amadé Ski Pass

Prices in €

Age	1-day	6-day
under 17	21	98
17 to 19	34	159
over 20	40	189

Free under 6
Senior no deals
Beginner no deals

Notes
Day-pass price is for Schladming Ramsau Dachstein only; part-day tickets available; 2-day-plus passes cover the 865km/ 538 miles of pistes and 270 lifts in five regions: Dachstein Tauern; Gastein; Salzburger Sportwelt; Grossarl; Hochkönig Winterreich

Alternative pass
Salzburg Super Ski Card: all lifts in Salzburgerland including Zell am See, Kaprun and Saalbach-Hinterglemm

CONVENIENCE ★★★
Pleasantly compact
Much of the accommodation is close to the town centre; the sports centre and tennis halls are five minutes' walk away, as is the gondola to Planai.

SCENERY ★★★
Four points of view
All four mountains are broadly similar, pleasantly wooded and share decent views along the valley and to the Dachstein glacier.

THE MOUNTAINS

Most pistes are on the wooded north-facing slopes above the main valley, with some going into the side valleys higher up; there are a few open slopes above the trees.

Piste maps (you can get separate ones for each mountain) are generally clear, though oddly no longer show the mountain restaurants. Signposting could be better. At the Skiline terminals at the Planai base you can get a printout showing lifts you used, height gained and distance covered in the day – a neat free souvenir.

EXTENT OF THE SLOPES ★★★
Four linked sectors – and more
Each of the sectors is quite a serious mountain, with a variety of lifts and runs to play on. **Planai** and **Hauser Kaibling** are linked at altitude via the high, wooded bowl between them. But the links to **Hochwurzen** and **Reiteralm** are at valley level (and the first involves riding a gondola both ways). Several lower runs go across roads

that aren't well signposted – care is needed, particularly with children. There are handy ski lockers to rent at the Planai base station.

FAST LIFTS ★★★★
Some swanky new ones
Each sector has gondola access and there are lots of fast chairs, including an eight-pack for 2009/10. But some slow old lifts remain.

QUEUES ★★★★
Avoid peaks at Planai
Generally there are few problems. Readers still complain of 'serious' queues for the Planai gondola at peak times. A New Year visitor experienced long waits for lifts on Hochwurzen and crowded pistes are also criticised there. The outlying Fageralm area is a quieter alternative on busy days.

TERRAIN PARKS ★★★
New one on Planai
Planai has a new park above Larchkogel, with medium and pro lines of kickers, jumps, boxes and rails. Hochwurzen has the Playground park by the Gipfelbahn, with similar features – floodlit until 10pm. Reiteralm has a half-pipe and Dachstein another park.

SNOW RELIABILITY ★★★★
Excellent in cold weather
The northerly orientation of the slopes and good maintenance help keep the pistes in better shape than in some neighbouring resorts. The serious snowmaking operation makes it a particularly good choice for early

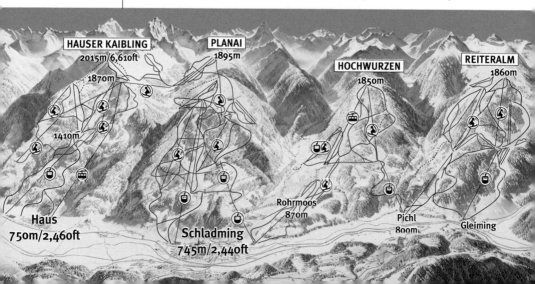

HAUSER KAIBLING
2015m/6,610ft
1870m
1410m
Haus
750m/2,460ft

PLANAI
1895m

HOCHWURZEN
1850m

REITERALM
1860m

Rohrmoos
870m

Schladming
745m/2,440ft

Pichl
800m

Gleiming

↑ The traffic-free main square is prettily lit at night

SCHOOLS
Tritscher
t 2264710
Hopl (Hochwurzen-Planai)
t 23582
Blue Tomato (snowboard)
t 2422316

Classes
(Tritscher prices)
5 days €158
Private lessons
Half day €98; each additional person €20

CHILDCARE
Mini club
t 22647
For ages 3 and 4
Nannies
Details at tourist office

Ski school
From age 4 (€208 for 5 days including lunch – Tritscher price)

holidays; coverage is comprehensive (99%), and the system is put to good use. But reporters regularly complain of poor conditions on the lower slopes, notably on the steep bottom part of the World Cup downhill run back to town. Piste grooming is fine.

FOR EXPERTS ★★
Strictly intermediate stuff
Schladming's status as a World Cup downhill venue doesn't make it macho. The steep black finish to the Men's Downhill course and the moderate mogul runs at the top of Planai and Hauser Kaibling are the only really challenging slopes. Hauser Kaibling's off-piste is good, but limited. The area around run 5 on Reiteralm has been recommended.

FOR INTERMEDIATES ★★★★
Red runs rule
The area is ideal for intermediate cruising. The majority of runs are red but it's often difficult to distinguish them from some of the blues. One notable exception is the final very red section of the run below Rohrmoos, which makes it awkward for near-beginners to get to the Planai link.

The open sections at the top of Planai and Hauser Kaibling have some more challenging slopes. And the two World Cup pistes, and the red that runs parallel to the Haus downhill course to the village, are ideal for fast intermediates in good snow conditions but can get very icy and tricky.

Hauser Kaibling has a lovely meandering blue running from top to bottom, and Reiteralm has some gentle blues with good snow. Runs are well groomed, so intermediates will find the slopes generally flattering.

FOR BEGINNERS ★★★
Good slopes but poorly sited
The ski schools generally take beginners to the extensive but low-altitude Rohrmoos nursery area – fine if you are based there, a discouraging bus ride away if you are not. Another novice area near the top of Planai is more convenient for residents of central Schladming and has better snow, but the runs are less gentle.

FOR CROSS-COUNTRY ★★★★
Extensive network of trails
Given sufficient snow-cover, there are 400km/250 miles of trails in the region, and the World Championships have been held at nearby Ramsau. There are local loops along the main valley floor and between Planai and Hochwurzen.

MOUNTAIN RESTAURANTS ★★★★
A real highlight
There are plenty of attractive rustic huts, and most get enthusiastic reports from readers.

On Planai the Schladminger Hütte, at the top of the gondola has 'friendly and efficient service'. Onkel Willy's Hütte is as popular as ever, often with live music. We enjoyed good home-cooked food at the pleasant Weitmoosalm – tucked away in the gentle Larchkogel area. The Zum Holzhacher and the Schafalm have also been mentioned.

On Hochwurzen try the 'cosy' Hochwurzenalm and the 'excellent meals and cakes' at Hochwurzenhütte. On Reiteralm the Gasslhöh-Hütte has 'awesome' spare ribs. On Hauser Kaibling the tiny Kulmhoferhütte has a real mountain hut atmosphere, with fur-lined walls. Higher up, the hut off the Almlift feels wonderfully isolated, with great views. The Knapplhof is full of ski-racing mementos and Harry's Lärchenpavillion is good for 'snacks and valley views'.

SCHOOLS AND GUIDES ★★★
Generally okay reports
We have generally had good reports: 'In five visits I have never had a bad instructor or a wasted lesson,' says a recent visitor. 'Excellent' is the verdict on private lessons with the Hopl school and another reader had a 'nice instructor who tried his best' despite poor January conditions. But the Tritscher school has been rated 'poor' for both adults' and children's classes.

boarding

Schladming is popular with boarders. Most lifts on the spread-out mountains are gondolas or chairs, with some short drags around. The area is ideal for beginners and intermediates, except when the lower slopes are icy, though there are few exciting challenges for expert boarders bar the off-piste tree runs. The Blue Tomato snowboard shop runs the 'impressive' specialist snowboard school.

GETTING THERE

Air Salzburg 95km/ 60 miles (1hr15); Munich 255km/160 miles (3hr30)

Rail Main line station in resort

UK PACKAGES

Alpine Answers, Crystal, Crystal Finest, Interhome, Rocketski, Simply Alpine, Skiing Austria, Skitracer, Snowscape

ACTIVITIES

Indoor Swimming pool, fitness club, tennis, sauna

Outdoor Ice skating, curling, tobogganing, snowshoeing, sleigh rides, 50km/31 miles of cleared paths

Phone numbers From elsewhere in Austria add the prefix 03687; from abroad use the prefix +43 and omit the initial '0'

TOURIST OFFICES

Schladming t 22777 office@schladming.at www.schladming.at www.skiamade.com

Haus t 23310 info@schladming-dachstein.at www.haus.at

FOR FAMILIES ★★★★
Rohrmoos is the place
The extensive gentle slopes of Rohrmoos are ideal for building up youngsters' confidence. There are Kinderlands on Planai and Hochwurzen. The Top school at Pichl has 'excellent' children's classes.

STAYING THERE

Packaged accommodation is in hotels and pensions, but there are plenty of apartments for independent travellers.
Hotels Most of the accommodation is in modestly priced pensions but there are also a few more upmarket hotels.
★★★★Sporthotel Royer (200) Big and comfortable, a few minutes' walk from the main Planai lift. Pool, sauna.
★★★★Stadttor (24525) 'Quiet, spacious and comfortable, with excellent food.'
★★★★Almdorf-Reiteralm (72444) Ski-in/ ski-out village at Hochalm, above Pichl. Individual chalets and a hotel; restaurant, shop and spa facilities.
★★★★Raunerhof (7356) In Pichl. 'Superb position, friendly, good food.' No pool.
★★★Kirchenwirt (22435) Just off the main square. 'Wonderful food', 'great value for money', 'very atmospheric'.
★★★Neue Post (22105) Large rooms, friendly, good food, central.
★★★Zum Kaiserweg (22038) Family run. Very near the Planai West gondola. 'Quiet, good rooms but lacks charm.'
★★★Rohrmooser Schlössl (61237) Near Planai West gondola. 'Really friendly', with 'excellent food and views'.
Apartments Schütter (23230) at Planai West is 'spacious and comfortable'.

EATING OUT ★★★
Some good places
Recommendations include the Kirchenwirt hotel ('fine home cooking'), Giovanni's (pizza), Charly's Treff, the Alte Post ('good food, first class service') and Neue Post hotel ('good but expensive'). The Friesacher Lanstuberl steakhouse near the church is 'well worth a visit'. Mäk's is a pizzeria at the Hohenhaus Tenne (see 'Après-ski'). Maria's Mexican has

'fabulous food and service'. Biochi specialises in organic and vegan food. We liked the Lasser Cafe and the Stadttor for coffee and cakes, and the Schwalbenbräu brewery.

APRES-SKI ★★★
Hohenhaus gets lively
Schladming's après-ski is unusually low-key, but there are lively places. On the mountain, the Schladminger Hütte has live music on Wednesdays and the gondola stays open to bring you down. In town, the focus is the Hohenhaus Tenne by the Planai gondola station. This smart woody building has a fabulous main bar, dance floor and regular live music – great when the lifts close. Later on there's a disco and various other bars to entertain. Charly's Treff (with umbrella bar) opposite also gets busy. A reporter preferred the Tauernalm on Hochwurzen. Many of the central bars stay open until dawn, but they lack the 'buzz' of other Austrian resorts. Choices include the 'small and friendly' Neider and Szenario, the Neue Post ('lively without being raucous') and the Hanglbar for 'good music and a friendly atmosphere'. Cult and Angels are new nightclubs.

OFF THE SLOPES ★★★★
Good for all but walkers
Non-skiers are fairly well catered for. There's a floodlit 7km/4 mile toboggan run at Hochwurzen, 'excellent' pool and an ice rink. Some mountain restaurants are accessible to pedestrians. The town shops and museum are worth a look. Trips to Salzburg or Radstadt are easy.

Haus 750m/2,460ft

Haus is a real village with its own ski schools and kindergartens. The user-friendly nursery slopes are between the village and the gondola. There's a railway station, so excursions are easy, but off-slope activities and nightlife are very limited. Hotel prices are generally lower here.

Sölden

A valley town dominated by traffic and throbbing après-ski/ nightlife – but with excellent slopes reaching glacial heights

£90
RESORT PRICE INDEX

TOP 10 RATINGS

Extent	★★★
Fast lifts	★★★★
Queues	★★★
Snow	★★★★★
Expert	★★★
Intermediate	★★★★
Beginner	★★
Charm	★★
Convenience	★★
Scenery	★★★

KEY FACTS

Resort	1380m
	4,530ft
Slopes	1380-3250m
	4,530-10,660ft
Lifts	34
Pistes	151km
	91 miles
Blue	38%
Red	40%
Black	22%
Snowmaking	80%

190

+ Excellent snow reliability, with access to two high glaciers

+ Fairly extensive network of slopes suited to adventurous intermediates

+ Impressive lift system

+ Very lively après-ski/nightlife, but ...

– It's a bit raunchy, and can be rowdy

– Busy road through sprawling village

– Some central hotels are distant from the two main access lifts

– Inconvenient beginners' slopes

– English not universally spoken

Sölden deserves a close look from intermediates keen on Austrian après-ski – as long as you are prepared to deploy your German occasionally (British visitors are still few, although several tour ops go there). The resort has invested massively in lifts to link its extensive glaciers to the lower slopes, and there are some seriously long runs to be done. Good for a late-season holiday.

THE RESORT

Despite its traditional Tirolean-style buildings, Sölden is no beauty: it is a large, traffic-filled place that sprawls along both sides of a busy main road and across the valley floor. For 10 euros extra on the 6-day lift pass price (you need to pay when you buy the pass) you can ski for a day in nearby Obergurgl (hourly buses included in the lift pass).

Village charm The resort attracts a young, lively crowd – mostly Dutch

and German – bent on partying. Ads for strip clubs are prominent.

Convenience Gondolas from opposite ends of town go up to the peak of Gaislachkogl and the lift junction of Giggijoch. An efficient and frequent free shuttle-bus serves both lift stations. High above the town is the satellite resort of Hochsölden – a group of 4-star hotels, and little else.

Scenery Some of Austria's highest mountains overlook Sölden; above its wooded valley setting is craggy and glacial terrain.

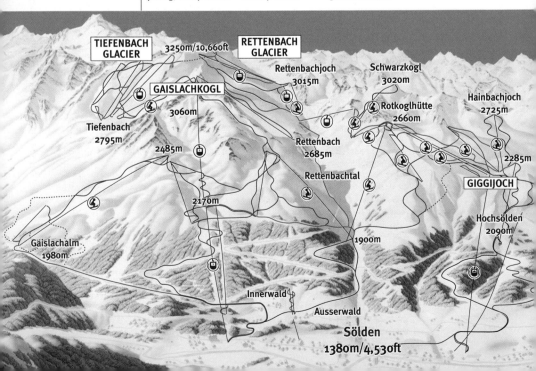

↑ The Rettenbach glacier and the Tiefenbach glacier (behind it) make Sölden great for a late-season holiday

DAVE WATTS

NEWS

For 2008/09 the ski route back from the glacier was made into a blue piste and equipped with snow-guns – a huge improvement. And an eight-seat chairlift replaced an old triple chair at Giggijoch. The Giggijoch restaurant in the same sector was revamped and a new table-service option added.

THE MOUNTAINS

Practically all the slopes you spend your days on are above the trees, though there are red and black runs through trees to the village. All sectors offer serious vertical and some long runs (it's 1880m/6,170ft and 12km/ 7 miles from the top of the glacier to the village, almost 1700m/5,580ft vertical from Gaislachkogl and almost 1400m/4,590ft from Hainbachjoch and all these runs are doable top to bottom with no need for lifts). The resort also promotes a Big 3 Rally to three viewing platforms at over 3000m/9,840ft (two spectacularly built out over the valleys below) – the full circuit entails skiing 50km/31 miles and 10,000m/32,810ft vertical and can be done in four hours by a good skier. Reporters have complained of poor piste marking, notably around the Gaislachkogl.

Slopes The two similar-sized home sectors are linked by fast six-seater chairlifts out of the Rettenbachtal that separates them. Fast lifts from the Giggijoch sector lead to the Rettenbach glacier, and on to the Tiefenbach. It may be a long journey (at least five lifts to reach the top) but we found the glacier slopes

delightfully quiet and with excellent powdery winter snow on our April 2009 visit, in contrast to the slushy, crowded slopes lower down.

Fast lifts Most of the area is very well served by fast chairs and gondolas, but there are still some slow lifts around – including (avoidable) T-bars on the glaciers.

Queues Like many reporters we met a huge queue for the Giggijoch gondola out of town in the morning peak on our April 2009 visit. Get there early or, as we did, take the nearby antique single chair to Hochsölden. The chairs to Rotkogljoch get busy too but shift crowds quickly. We also have reports of queues for the Einzeiger chair on the way to the glacier; and the Seiterkar chair gets busy from mid-afternoon (it's the only way back from the Tiefenbach glacier).

Terrain parks There is a park above Giggijoch, with beginner and pro kickers, waves, rails, boxes and a chill-out zone.

Snow reliability The slopes are high and mainly north-east- or south-east-facing; and there are two extensive glaciers. Snowmaking now covers 80% of the area, including all slopes on Giggijoch. Grooming is generally good.

Experts None of the black pistes

dotted around Sölden's map is serious, and some are silly; but you won't lack vertical or long runs. There are quite a few non-trivial reds. And there are extensive off-piste possibilities with a guide. At the top of the valley is one of the Alps' premier touring areas.

Intermediates Most of Sölden's main slopes are genuine red runs ideal for adventurous intermediates and there are several easy blacks. Keen piste-bashers will love the serious verticals and long runs to be done. The blue run that has replaced the ski route down from the glacier is easy but narrow (it's the summer glacier access road) and can get very busy at the end of the day. The long, quiet red to Gaislachalm is relatively easy, and ideal for high-speed cruising. Giggijoch offers gentler gradients, but the blues here get extremely crowded. Less confident intermediates should beware the tricky red runs to town from Giggijoch and Rettenbachtal.

Beginners The beginners' slopes are situated inconveniently, just above the village at Innerwald. They are prone to poor snow and not ideal as the busier home runs converge there. Near-beginners can use the blues at Giggijoch. Stay away from Hochsölden.

Snowboarding Sölden is not ideal for beginners but there's great freeriding for experienced boarders. And all draglifts can be avoided.

Cross-country There are a couple of uninspiring loops by the river, plus small areas at Zwieselstein and Vent.

Mountain restaurants There are nearly 30 to choose between. Our favourite is the rustic Gampe Thaya just above Rettenbachtal on the way down from Giggijoch – simple food, table service, lovely terrace with views to Obergurgl, cosy interior. Just below here in the valley Hühnersteign is popular and famous for its chicken. The newly renovated self-service at Giggijoch is

huge – but the Wirthaus table-service option is smaller scale and looked nice. Eugens Obstlerhütte below Hochsölden has been recommended – 'cosy, efficient; good food'.

Schools and guides The four schools all restrict class sizes. The Sölden school has 'patient' instructors, though spoken English can be limited.

Families The Sölden school is praised. There are kindergartens at three schools. Yellow Power takes children from three years.

STAYING THERE

There are a few UK packages.

Hotels The warmly welcoming Central Spa (22600) is not only central but also the biggest and best in town – the only 5-star; beautiful pool. We were very happy in the 4-star Stefan (2237), right next to the Giggijoch gondola; good food. Reporters recommend Gasthof Grauer Bär (2564) – 'large rooms, excellent food', the 4-star Bergland (22400) and the Grüner-Hof B&B (2477) above town on run 7. The 'lavishly beautiful' 4-star Valentin (2267) at Gaislachkogl is also mentioned.

Eating out We usually end up in the Tavola in the hotel Rosengarten, because it doesn't take reservations, and haven't been disappointed. Recommendations from readers: Dominic, Cafe Hubertus, Nudeltopf and Corso for pizza; and s'Pfandl, above the town at Ausserwald, for traditional Tirolean food.

Après-ski Sölden's après-ski is justly famous. It starts up the mountain, notably at Giggijoch, and progresses (possibly via the 'crowded' Philipp's Eisbar at Innerwald) to packed bars in and around the main street, and later to countless places with live bands and throbbing discos, often with table dancing and/or striptease. Readers also mention: Snow Rock Cafe ('best atmosphere'), Otzi's, BlaBla, Fire & Ice and Alibi's ('smartest bar, good live music'). Try Grizzly's for a quieter time. The Rodelhütte has 'go-go' girls. There are nightly toboggan evenings – starting at Gaislachalm.

Off the slopes There's a sports centre, a swimming pool and an ice rink. Ice climbing and sleigh rides can be arranged. Trips to Innsbruck are possible. Aqua Dome is a thermal spa centre at Längenfeld.

Söll

The ski area is big, but the attractive village is surprisingly small and intimate; shame it is not set right by the lifts

£80
RESORT PRICE INDEX

RATINGS

The mountains

Extent	★★★★
Fast lifts	★★★
Queues	★★★
Terrain p'ks	★★★
Snow	★★
Expert	★
Intermediate	★★★★
Beginner	★★
X-country	★★★
Restaurants	★★
Schools	★★★
Families	★★★

The resort

Charm	★★★
Convenience	★★
Scenery	★★★
Eating out	★★
Après-ski	★★★★
Off-slope	★★

NEWS

For 2008/09 the Siller-Keat six-pack replaced a slow chair, improving access to Zinsberg. Above Hopfgarten a gondola was built from the mid-station to Hohe Salve. A new terrain park was built below Hochsöll. Westendorf was at last connected to the rest of the SkiWelt via Brixen. And a new Skiline system to track your progress around the SkiWelt was introduced. See Westendorf chapter.

- ➕ Part of the SkiWelt, Austria's largest linked ski and snowboard area
- ➕ Local slopes are north-facing, so they keep their snow relatively well
- ➕ Pretty village with lively après-ski
- ➕ Cheap, even by Austrian standards
- ➕ Snowmaking is now more extensive and well used; even so ...

- ➖ Low altitude can mean poor snow
- ➖ Long walk or inadequate bus service from the village to the lifts
- ➖ Little to challenge decent riders; mostly short runs in the local sector
- ➖ Not ideal for beginners either
- ➖ The SkiWelt slopes can get crowded
- ➖ Appallingly inadequate piste map

Söll has long been popular with British beginners and intermediates, attracting both singles looking for a fun week and families looking for a quiet time. The resort is in fact far from ideal for beginners, but when the snow is good- it can be a great place for intermediates – cruising the attractive, friendly pistes of Austria's largest linked area. Many visitors are surprised by the small size of the village (there aren't many shops) and the long trek out to the slopes. You may prefer to stay near the lifts and trek into the village in the evening. Or you may prefer, like us, to stay in Westendorf now that it is properly connected to the SkiWelt (and has good access to Kitzbühel too).

THE RESORT

Söll is a pleasant, friendly village, bypassed by the main valley road; although its chalets spread quite widely, the core is compact – you can explore it thoroughly in a few minutes.

The SkiWelt pass also covers Westendorf, linked by a new gondola from Brixen; from there you can also progress to the Kitzbühel slopes – see the Westendorf chapter. These, along with Waidring, Fieberbrunn and St Johann, are possible day trips covered by the Kitzbuheler Alpen All Star pass.

VILLAGE CHARM ★★★
Follows tradition
Söll is quite attractive, with chalet-style buildings and a huge church near the centre (its graveyard prettily lit by candles at night).

CONVENIENCE ★★
Not for the slopes
The slopes are well outside the village, on the other side of a busy road crossed by a pedestrian tunnel. You can leave your equipment at the bottom of the gondola for a small charge. There is some accommodation out near the lifts, but most is in or around the village centre. From there, it's a 15-minute walk or a crowded ski-bus, heavily criticised as inadequate by reporters. A base on the far side of the village may mean that you can board the bus before it gets too crowded. But the bus does not serve every corner of the community.

SCENERY ★★★
Head for Hohe Salve
Söll sits in a woody valley, below the distinctive dome-shaped peak of Hohe Salve. From the top, there are stunning views to the whole SkiWelt and craggy Wilder Kaiser ridges.

THE MOUNTAINS

The SkiWelt is the largest piste network in Austria, linking eight resorts. It will easily keep an early or average intermediate amused for a week. Our 2009 visit confirmed our view that the piste map is hopelessly over-ambitious in trying to show the

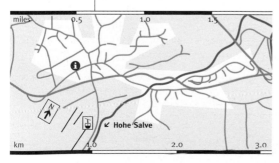

miles | 0.5 | 1.0 | 1.5

N

↙ Hohe Salve

km | 1.0 | 2.0 | 3.0

KEY FACTS	
Resort	700m 2,300ft
Entire SkiWelt	
Slopes	620-1890m 2,030-6,200ft
Lifts	91
Pistes	279km 173 miles
Blue	44%
Red	46%
Black	10%
Snowmaking	75%

whole area in a single view; the result is a map that is appallingly inadequate, especially on the Zinsberg side of Hohe Salve and between Eiberg and Brandstadl. Not surprisingly, it generates a lot of complaints from reporters; a solution would be to have a series of smaller maps with a smaller overview map on each – or a big booklet-style map with separate details for each sector. Signposting is also criticised, but we found it OK once you realise that the signs point out the direction to the next lift you want and that the signs use the number of the lift to indicate the colour of the run.

EXTENT OF THE SLOPES ★★★★☆
Short run network

The SkiWelt is a big area but except for runs right down to the valleys, most runs are very short (runs of less than 300m/980ft vertical are not unusual). A gondola takes all but complete beginners up to the mid-mountain shelf of Hochsöll, where there are a couple of short lifts and connections in several directions.

These include an eight-seat gondola to the high point of Hohe Salve. From here there are runs down to Kälbersalve, Rigi and Hopfgarten. Rigi can also be reached by chairs and runs without going to Hohe Salve – to which it is itself linked by chairs. Rigi is also the start of runs down to Itter. From Kälbersalve you can head down south-facing runs to Brixen or up to Zinsberg and towards Ellmau.

FAST LIFTS ★★★☆☆
Improving but not fast enough

Lifts from the valley are mainly gondolas, with a growing number of fast chairs on the upper slopes. But

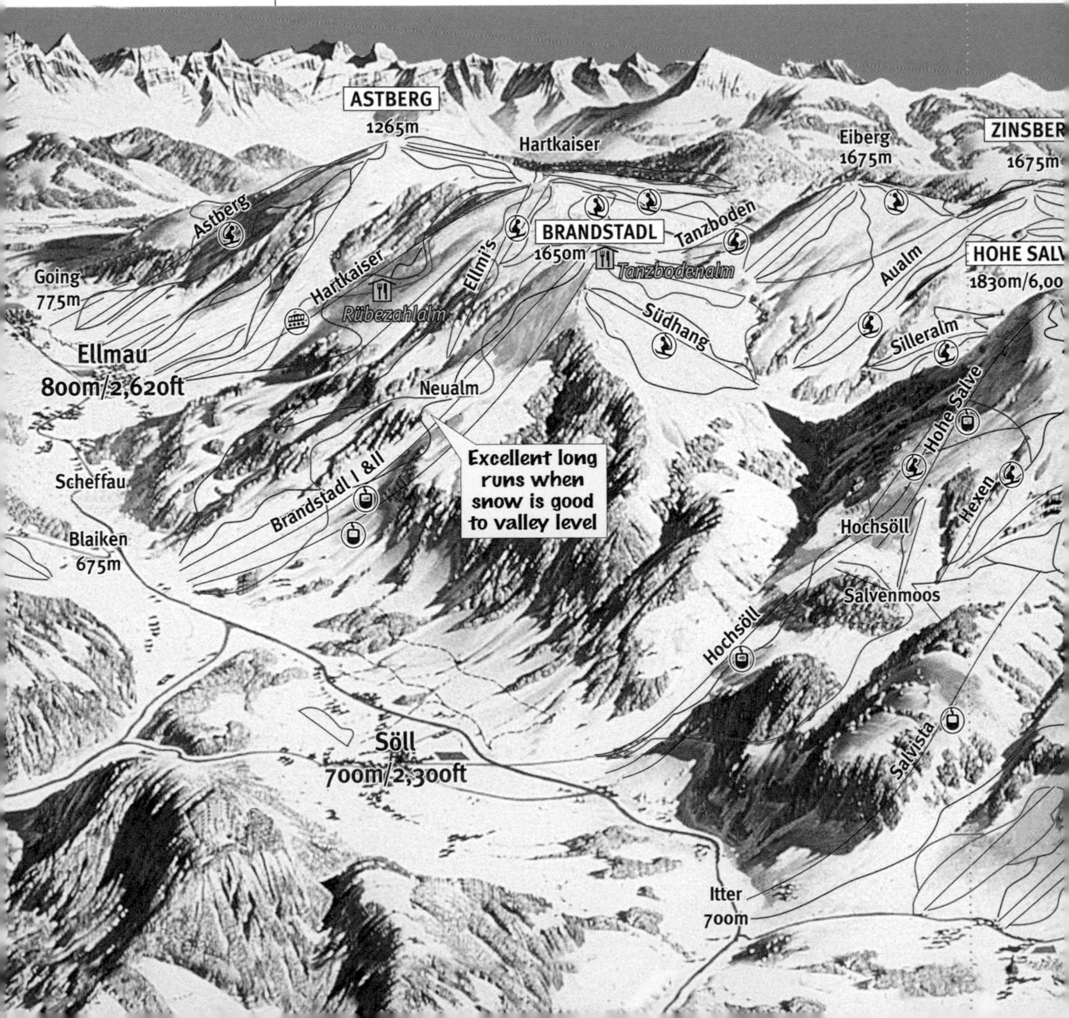

ASTBERG
1265m
Hartkaiser
Eiberg
1675m
ZINSBER
1675m
Astberg
BRANDSTADL
1650m
Tanzboden
Tanzbodenalm
HOHE SALV
1830m/6,00
Going
775m
Hartkaiser
Ellmi's
Aualm
Rübezahlalm
Südhang
Silleralm
Ellmau
800m/2,620ft
Neualm
Hohe Salve
Excellent long runs when snow is good to valley level
Scheffau
Brandstadl I & II
Hexen
Hochsöll
Blaiken
675m
Salvenmoos
Hochsöll
Söll
700m/2,300ft
Salvista
Itter
700m

there are still a lot of slow lifts around and moving around the ski area can be tediously slow.

QUEUES ★★★
Some high-season waits

Lift upgrades have greatly improved this once queue-prone area and 2009 reporters found few queues. But the nursery drag up to the gondola at Söll remains a serious obstacle, particularly at ski-school time in the mornings, and there are several bottlenecks at slow chairs around the mountain. When snow is poor, the links between Zinsberg and Eiberg get crowded.

TERRAIN PARKS ★★★
There is one at last

Söll has now got its own park below Hochsöll with beginner and expert lines; features include boxes, frames and rails. It's floodlit for night riding.

SNOW RELIABILITY ★★
Erratic – but has artificial help

The SkiWelt has had some good seasons of late, with several reporters experiencing good fresh powder for much of their holidays. But it is not always like that, and with a low average height, and important links that get a lot of sun, the snow can suffer badly in warm weather; and precipitation can fall as rain. So the snowmaking that the SkiWelt has installed is essential. At 210km/130 miles and covering about 75% of the area's pistes, it is Austria's biggest snowmaking installation. Reporters are regularly impressed by its use and efforts to maintain the pistes in times of drought. We were there one January before any major snowfalls, and snowmaking was keeping the links open well. It did not, however, stop slush and ice forming.

LIFT PASSES

SkiWelt Wilder Kaiser-Brixental

Prices in €

Age	1-day	6-day
under 16	19	91
16 to 17	30	146
over 18	36	182

Free under 7

Senior no deals

Beginner points cards

Notes
Covers Wilder Kaiser-Brixental area from Going to Westendorf, and the ski-bus; single ascent and part-day options; family discounts

Alternative passes
Kitzbüheler Alpen All Star card covers seven ski areas: Schneewinkel (St Johann), Kitzbühel, SkiWelt, Wildschönau, Alpbachtal, Skicircus Saalbach-Hinterglemm and Zell am See-Kaprun

SCHOOLS

Söll-Hochsöll
t 5454

Black Sheep Ski
t 6649 338 527

Classes
5 4-hr days: €140

Private lessons
€55 for 1hr; each additional person €25

CHILDCARE

Mini-club Hexenstube
t 0664 441 2773
9am–4.30; ages 6mnth to 4yr

Monti's Kinder-welt (bambinis)
t 5454
10am–4pm; for ages 3 to 5

Ski school
Takes children from 5 to 14 for 4hr daily (5 days €140)

boarding

Söll is a good place to try out boarding: slopes are gentle and there are plenty of gondolas and chairs. And now it has its own terrain park. For competent boarders it's more limited – the slopes of the SkiWelt are tame.

FOR EXPERTS ★☆☆☆☆
Not a lot
The two black runs from Hohe Salve towards Hochsöll and Kälbersalve and the black run alongside the Brixen gondola are the only challenging pistes. There are further blacks in Scheffau and Ellmau, but the main challenges are off-piste – from Brandstadl down to Söll, for example.

FOR INTERMEDIATES ★★★★☆
Mainly easy runs
When blessed with good snow – not something to bank on – the SkiWelt is a paradise for early intermediates and those who love easy cruising and don't mind short runs. It is a big area and you really get a feeling of travelling around. There are lots of blue runs and many of the reds could be blue. In general the most difficult slopes are those from the mid-stations to the valleys – to Blaiken, Brixen and Söll, for example. For more challenging reds head for Westendorf (and don't miss the excellent red back down from there to Brixen).

FOR BEGINNERS ★★☆☆☆
Not ideal
The big area of nursery slopes between the main road and the gondola station is fine when snow is good – gentle, spacious, uncrowded and free from good skiers whizzing past. But it can get icy or slushy. In poor snow the Hochsöll area may be used. Progression to longer runs is likely to be awkward – there aren't many blue runs in this part of the SkiWelt. One is the narrow blue from Hochsöll, on which fast learners can get home when the run is not too icy.

FOR CROSS-COUNTRY ★★★☆☆
Neighbouring villages are better
Söll has 30km/19 miles of local trails but they are less interesting than those between Hopfgarten and Kelchsau and around and beyond Ellmau. There is a total of 170km/106 miles in the SkiWelt area. Lack of snow-cover can be a problem.

MOUNTAIN RESTAURANTS ★★☆☆☆
Good, but crowded
There are quite a few jolly little chalets scattered about, but we have had a few complaints of insufficient seating and long queues.

Editors' choice On our 2009 visit, we enjoyed lunch at Tanzbodenalm near Brandstadl – newish but pleasantly woody, delicious deer stew. We also really enjoy Rübezahlalm (see Ellmau).

Worth knowing about Just below Hochsöll the atmospheric converted cow shed Stöckalm is frequently recommended by reporters ('superb spit-roasted chicken'). Hochsöll itself is also reportedly 'excellent'. The highly rated Hohe Salve (top of the gondola) offers a large revolving terrace and 'stunning views' (from the loos as well, says a female reporter). The Stoagrub'nhütte above Hopfgarten serves 'generous and reasonably priced spaghetti'. Above Brixen the Filzalm is a good place for a quick drink on the way back from the circuit. Below Zinsberg, the Aualm has been recommended, especially for its cakes and glühwein. Above Scheffau, Neualm has been praised and a bit lower down, Bavaria is a 'lovely comfy bar on the home run' to Scheffau.

SCHOOLS AND GUIDES ★★★☆☆
A good reputation
The Söll-Hochsöll school has a fairly good reputation. A recent reporter and her family enjoyed 'very good' lessons; the children 'were confidently doing red runs by the end of the week', but groups were large ('up to 12'). A 2009 visitor had a 'very good' carving clinic with Black Sheep Ski.

FOR FAMILIES ★★★☆☆
A range of options
Söll has fairly wide-ranging facilities – the focus is the Söll-Hochsöll school's Kinder-welt at the gondola mid-station, which takes children from age five to 14 years and has a well-equipped snow garden. Bambini's caters for children aged three to five. There's a special kids-only drag and slope on the opposite side of the village to the main lifts. Reports welcome.

The nursery slope is fine when the snow is good. But it's a long walk (or crowded bus ride) from the village to the gondola up to the main slopes →
JILL COOK

Söll

Interactive resort shortlist builder at **www.wtss.co.uk**

GETTING THERE

Air Salzburg 90km/ 55 miles (1hr30); Innsbruck 80km/ 50 miles (1hr15); Munich 260km/160 miles (3hr45)

Rail Wörgl (13km/ 8 miles) or Kufstein (15km/9 miles); bus to resort

STAYING THERE

The major mainstream tour operators offer packages here.

Hotels There is a wide choice of simple gasthofs, pensions and B&Bs, plus better-quality hotel accommodation – mainly 3-star.
****Greil (5289) Attractive, but out of the centre and far from the lifts.
****Postwirt (5081) Attractive, central, traditional, with stube; outdoor pool.
****Alpenpanorama (5309) Far from lifts but with own bus stop; wonderful views; pleasant rooms.
***Bergland (5454) Well placed between the village and lifts. Recently refurbished.
***Tulpe (5223) Next to the lifts.
***Feldwebel (5224) Central.
***Hexenalm (5544) Next to the lifts.
***Eggerwirt (5236) 'Modern and comfortable.' Between centre and main road, bus stop outside.
***Gasthof Tenne (5282) B&B gasthof between centre and main road.
Chalets There are surprisingly few catered chalets or 'club hotels' run by British tour operators.
Apartments The central Aparthotel Schindlhaus has nice accommodation. Some of the best apartments in town are attached to the Bergland hotel, but a recent reporter recommends the 'ideally located' Alpin apartments ('fabulous', 'outstanding in terms of cleanliness and space').

EATING OUT ★★
A fair choice
Some of the best restaurants are in hotels. The Greil and Postwirt ('extensive and delicious New Year buffet') are good. The Schindlhaus is said to be the best, at least if you enjoy 'rich meat' dishes. Giovanni does excellent, large pizzas, while other places worth a visit include the Dorfstub'n ('varied menu, extremely good steaks') and the Venezia.

APRES-SKI ★★★★
Still some very loud bars
Söll is not as raucous as it used to be, but it's still very lively and a lot of places have live music. The Salvenstadl (Cow Shed) bar is regularly recommended by reporters ('the best live music'). Moonlight at the gondola base is 'less Brit-dominated and has dancing on the tables even low-season'. The Whisky-Mühle is a large disco that can get 'wild', especially after the bars close. Buffalo's is popular and the hotel Austria bar has 'cool music and pool tables' and quiz evenings. Rossini is a 'lovely, modern bar', good for cocktails and live music.

OFF THE SLOPES ★★
Not bad for a small village
You could spend a happy day in the wonderfully equipped Panoramabad: taking a sauna, swimming, lounging about. There's 'fantastic' tobogganing from the top of the gondola. The large baroque church would be the pride of many tourist towns. There are numerous coach excursions, including trips to Salzburg, Innsbruck and even Vipiteno over in Italy.

Scheffau 745m/2,440ft

THE RESORT
Scheffau is one of the most attractive of the SkiWelt villages. It is a rustic little place with pretty white church.

ACTIVITIES

Indoor Swimming, sauna, solarium, massage, bowling, squash

Outdoor Natural ice rink (skating, curling), sleigh rides, 3km/ 2 miles of floodlit ski and toboggan runs, walks, snowshoeing, snow tubing

UK PACKAGES

Crystal, Directski.com, First Choice, Independent Ski Links, Inghams, Interactive Resorts, Neilson, Simply Alpine, Skiing Austria, Ski Line, Ski McNeill, Skitracer, STC, Thomson
Brixen *Skiing Austria*
Scheffau *Crystal, First Choice, Neilson, Simply Alpine, Skiing Austria, STC, Thomson*
Hopfgarten *Contiki, First Choice, Skiing Austria*
Itter *Skiing Austria*

Village charm It is spacious yet not sprawling, and has a definite centre 1km/0.5 miles off the busy main road (away from the slopes), which increases its charm at the cost of convenience.

Convenience The slopes and lifts at Blaiken (where there are several hotels) are a bus ride away.

Scenery Much like Söll and Ellmau.

THE MOUNTAIN

Scheffau is well placed for the most central section of pistes in the SkiWelt.

Slopes Two gondolas (including an eight-seater) give rapid access directly to Brandstadl from Blaiken.

Fast lifts See Söll and Ellmau.

Queues The two gondolas shift weekend queues well at Blaiken.

Snow reliability Eiberg is the place to go when snow is poor.

Experts The pistes above Blaiken are some of the longest and steepest in the SkiWelt.

Intermediates This is as good a base as any except Westendorf in the area.

Beginners The nursery slope is in the village, nowhere near other slopes, making Scheffau a poor choice for mixed-ability parties; but a reporter rates the easy blues at Brandstadl as 'excellent' for beginner snowboarders.

Cross-country See Söll and Ellmau.

Mountain restaurants See Söll, Ellmau.

Schools and guides There are two, but groups can be large. A reporter's private snowboarding lesson was 'the best I've ever had'.

Families The non-ski nursery has a good reputation. There's a children's ski area and both schools have a 'Kinder-Kaiserland'. And excellent progress was made by a four-year-old at Ski Esprit's nursery.

STAYING THERE

Several major tour operators offer packages here.

Hotels Reporters recommend the 3-star Alpin (8556) – 'excellent food, lots of choice, spacious rooms'; pool, sauna and steam room. The Zum Wilden Kaiser (8118) has 'a sauna and good fish dishes'. The central Gasthof Weberbauer (8115) is said to be 'good value' and 'efficient'. At the Blaiken gondolas, the Blaiken (8126) and Waldhof (8122) are good-value gasthofs (the latter 'worth a visit for the loos alone – done up like a cow shed with wooden stalls and rough hewn granite sinks').

Eating out There aren't many village restaurants. Donatello has been recommended for pizza and Gastof Weberbauer for good varied food.

Après-ski 'Non-existent,' says one happy reporter, but there are a couple of bars. The Sternbar is nearest to the gondolas and lively after the lifts close. Bowling and tobogganing are available.

Off the slopes Walking apart, there is little to do. Tour operators organise trips to Innsbruck and Salzburg.

Hopfgarten 620m/2,030ft

THE RESORT

Hopfgarten is an unspoiled, friendly, traditional resort off the main road.

Village charm The village is a good size: small enough to be intimate, large enough to have plenty of off-slope amenities.

Convenience Most hotels are within five minutes' walk of the gondola.

Scenery You get a different perspective of Hohe Salve from here.

THE MOUNTAIN

Hopfgarten is at the western extremity of the SkiWelt.

Slopes Two successive gondolas take you to Hohe Salve – the high point of the main SkiWelt circuit.

Fast lifts See Söll.

Queues We've had no reports of queues to leave the village since the eight-seat gondola was installed.

Terrain parks Söll has a new one.

Snow reliability The resort's great weakness is the poor snow quality on the south-west-facing home slope – especially vulnerable in late season.

Experts Experts should venture off-piste for excitement.

Intermediates When snow is good, the runs down to Hopfgarten and the nearby villages of Brixen and Itter are some of the best in the SkiWelt.

Beginners There is a beginners' slope in the village, but it is sunny as well as low; lack of snow-cover means paying for a lift pass to higher slopes. There are few easy longer runs to progress to in this part of the SkiWelt.

Snowboarding See Söll.

Cross-country Hopfgarten is one of the best cross-country bases in the area. There are fine trails to Kelchsau (7km/4 miles) and the Itter-Bocking loop (15km/9 miles) starts nearby. Westendorf's trails are close. But all of these are at valley level.

Mountain restaurants See Söll.

Schools and guides Partly because Hopfgarten seems to attract large numbers of Australians, English is widely spoken in the two schools.

Families Hopfgarten is a family resort, with a nursery and ski kindergarten.

STAYING THERE

How to go Cheap and cheerful gasthofs, pensions and little private B&Bs are the norm here.

Hotels The comfortable hotels Hopfgarten (3920) and Sporthotel Fuchs (2420) are both well placed for the main lift.

Eating out Most of the restaurants are hotel-based, but there are exceptions, including a Chinese and a pizzeria.

Après-ski Après-ski is generally quiet, though a lively holiday can usually be ensured if you go with Aussie-dominated tour operator Contiki.

Off the slopes Activities include swimming, riding, bowling, skating, tobogganing, paragliding and sleigh rides. You can go by train to Salzburg, Innsbruck and Kitzbühel.

Itter 700m/2,300ft

Itter is a tiny village half-way around the mountain between Söll and Hopfgarten, with a gondola just outside the village that goes up to Hochsöll above Söll. There's a hotel and half a dozen gasthofs and B&Bs. The school has a rental shop, and there are nursery slopes close to hand but few easy longer runs to progress to in this part of the SkiWelt.

Brixen 800m/2,620ft

THE RESORT

Brixen im Thale is a very scattered roadside village at the south-east edge of the main SkiWelt area. It may not be pretty, but with its new gondola Brixen now makes a very efficient base for exploration of the SkiWelt circuit on one side, and the slopes of Westendorf (and thus Kitzbühel) on the other.

Village charm The village is not particularly cute, but it is now bypassed by the main road and for keen skiers it is worth considering.

Convenience The main hotels are near the railway station, a bus ride from the lifts.

Scenery Low, partly-wooded hills flank both sides of the village.

THE MOUNTAIN

Brixen is on the south side of the main SkiWelt circuit, and on the north side of the Westendorf slopes.

Extent of the slopes One gondola takes you to Hochbrixen, where lifts diverge for Hohe Salve and Söll, or Astberg and Ellmau. There's a small area of north-facing runs, including nursery slopes, on the other side of the village, and a new gondola up to Choralpe on Westendorf's slopes with a lovely red run back down.

Fast lifts Gondolas go to both sectors.

Queues Lift upgrades have improved the once queue-prone area.

Terrain parks None locally but there's a good park nearby at Westendorf and others at Söll and Ellmau.

Snow reliability A chain of snow-guns on the main south-facing piste helps to preserve the snow as long as possible and the area as a whole now has effective snowmaking.

Experts The black run alongside the Brixen gondola is one of the few challenging pistes in the area.

Intermediates When snow is good, Brixen has some of the best slopes in the SkiWelt – including some challenging ones.

Beginners The nursery slopes are secluded and shady, but meeting up with friends for lunch is a hassle – the area is a bus ride from the village.

Snowboarding See Söll and Westendorf.

Cross-country In addition to valley-floor trails, a 3km/2 mile loop up the mountain at Hochbrixen provides fine views and fairly reliable snow.

Mountain restaurants See Söll, Ellmau and Westendorf.

Schools and guides The ski schools run the usual group classes, and mini-groups for up to six people.

Families There is a baby-sitting service.

STAYING THERE

There are plenty of hotels and pensions.

Hotels The Alpenhof (88320) and Sporthotel (8191) are 4-stars with pool.

Eating out Mainly hotel-based, but the Talhof restaurant has been highly recommended.

Après-ski Après-ski is quiet, but livelier Westendorf is a short taxi ride away.

Off the slopes Activities include tennis, hotel-based spa facilities and days out to Salzburg, Innsbruck and Kitzbühel.

Phone numbers
From elsewhere in Austria add the prefix 05358 (Wilder Kaiser, Scheffau), 05333 (Söll), 05332 (Hohe Salve), 05335 (Hopfgarten, Itter), 05334 (Brixen); from abroad use the prefix +43 and omit the initial '0'

TOURIST OFFICES

WILDER KAISER
(Söll, Scheffau, Going, Ellmau)
t 050509
www.wilderkaiser.info

Söll
t 050509 210
soell@wilderkaiser.info

Scheffau
t 050509 310
scheffau@wilderkaiser.info

HOHE SALVE
(Hopfgarten, Itter)
www.hohe-salve.com

Hopfgarten
t 2322
hopfgarten@hohe-salve.com

Itter
t 2670
itter@hohe-salve.com

BRIXEN
t 05357 2000 200
brixen@kitzbuehel-alpen.com
www.kitzbuehel-alpen.com

SKIWELT
www.skiwelt.at

Söll

199

Interactive resort shortlist builder at **www.wtss.co.uk**

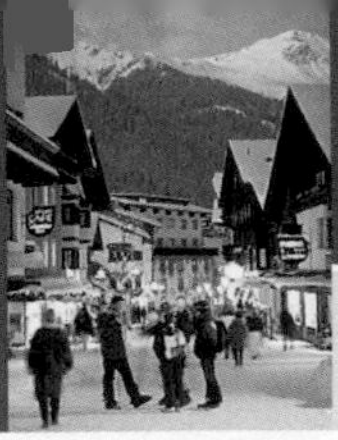

TVB ST ANTON AM ARLBERG

St Anton

If what you seek is dumps, bumps, boozing and bopping, there's nowhere quite like it – and with a neat Tirolean town as a bonus

£95
Resort Price Index

RATINGS

The mountains	
Extent	****
Fast lifts	***
Queues	***
Terrain p'ks	***
Snow	****
Expert	*****
Intermediate	***
Beginner	*
X-country	**
Restaurants	***
Schools	***
Families	****

The resort	
Charm	****
Convenience	***
Scenery	***
Eating out	****
Après-ski	*****
Off-slope	**

KEY FACTS

Resort	1305m 4,280ft
Arlberg region	
Slopes	1305-2650m 4,280-8,690ft
Lifts	85
Pistes	276km 172 miles
Blue	39%
Red	50%
Black	11%
Snowmaking	59%
St Anton, St Christoph and Stuben	
Slopes	1305-2650m 4,280-8,690ft
Lifts	39
Pistes	127km 79 miles
Snowmaking	94%

+ Varied terrain for experts and adventurous intermediates – and a lot of it, once you include Lech-Zürs, a bus ride away
+ Heavy snowfalls, lots of snow-guns
+ Car-free village centre retains solid traditional charm
+ Very lively après-ski
+ Improved lift system has cut queues from the base areas, but ...

– Pistes can get very crowded – some of them dangerously so
– Slopes really don't suit beginners or timid intermediates
– Most of the tough stuff is off-piste – including many popular runs
– Snow quality can suffer from sun
– Resort sprawls, with long treks from some lodgings to key lifts and bars
– Centre can get rowdy at night

St Anton is one of the world's best resorts for competent skiers and riders, with great steep slopes on both its local mountains. And the village centre is lively and attractive too. If you want to, you can party from 3pm to 3am. We don't, of course, because we want to be up bright and early to catch the first lift up.

But the place doesn't suit everyone, as our list of – points makes clear. If you are thinking of trying an Austrian change from a major French resort, or of taking a step up from Kitzbühel or Söll, take full account of this list, especially if you get thrown by blues that should be red, and reds that might be black.

The resort is making major improvements to its access lifts. In 2006/07 the impressive new Galzig gondola opened. For 2009/10 there will be a new gondola to Rendl from near the village centre. What the resort needs to do next is deal with the dangerously busy piste down the Steissbachtal by constructing a new piste from Galzig to share the traffic. There is already a red ski route; they should get the diggers in, and carve out a blue piste. Now!

THE RESORT

St Anton is at the foot of the road up to the Arlberg pass, at the eastern end of a lift network that spreads across to St Christoph and over the pass to Stuben. These two tiny villages are described at the end of the chapter.

The resort is a long, sprawling mixture of traditional and modern buildings crammed into a narrow valley. It used to be sandwiched between the busy bypass road and the mainline railway; but since the railway was moved in 2000, a little area of parkland has taken its place.

St Anton spreads down the valley, thinning out before broadening again to form the suburb of Nasserein.

Development spreads up the hill to the west, towards the Arlberg pass – first to Oberdorf, then Gastig, 10 minutes' walk from the centre. Further up the hill are the suburbs of Stadle, Dengert and Moos – a long way out, but the latter two next to the slopes.

Regular free ski-buses go to Stuben, Zürs and Lech (the latter two described in the Lech chapter) and the less well-known Sonnenkopf area above Klösterle. These buses can get crowded early and late in the day and

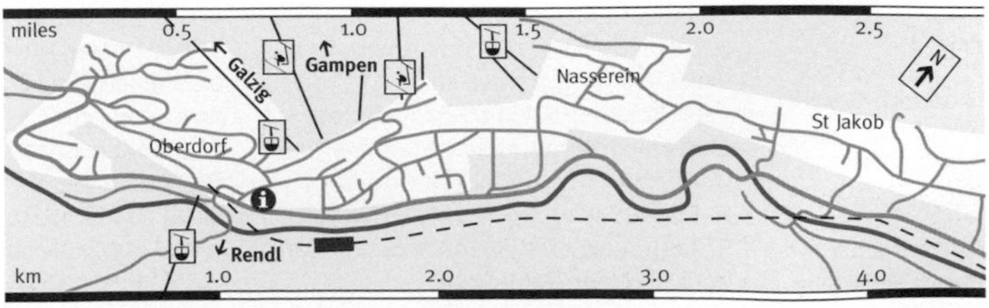

↑ A view of Kapall and Gampen from Rendl with one of the Valluga's famous bowls in the centre

IAN STRATFORD

St Anton

201

Interactive resort shortlist builder at **www.wtss.co.uk**

NEWS

The old Rendl gondola is to be replaced by a new eight-seater for 2009/10. And it will start near the centre of town, so you will no longer have to catch a shuttle-bus.

For 2008/09, the Kandahar Haus ski museum was fully revamped. And a new sports centre opened.

LIFT PASSES

Arlberg Ski Pass

Prices in €

Age	1-day	6-day
under 16	26	122
16 to 19	39	177
20 to 64	43	204
over 65	39	177

Free season pass €10 if under 8 or over /5

Senior min. age for senior women is 60

Beginner points ticket

Notes
Covers all St Anton, St Christoph, Lech, Zürs and Stuben lifts, and linking bus between Rauz and Zürs; also covers Sonnenkopf (10 lifts) at Klösterle, 7km/ 4 miles west of Stuben (bus link from Stuben); single ascent, half-day and pedestrian options

often provoke complaints from reporters. The post bus offers a less crowded alternative, but is not free. Taxis can be economic if shared.

Serfaus, Ischgl and Sölden are feasible outings by car.

VILLAGE CHARM ★★★★
Traditional but lively
Although it is crowded and commercialised, St Anton is full of character, its traffic-free main street lined by traditional-style buildings. It is an attractively bustling place, day and night. Its shops offer little in the way of entertainment, but meet everyday needs well – self-catering reporters have observed that it has a 'wonderful' Spar, for example.

CONVENIENCE ★★★
Not bad for a large resort
The hub of the resort is at the western end of the main street, between the base stations of the lifts to Gampen (a fast quad chair) and to Galzig (a fancy jumbo gondola that opened in 2006) and the new gondola that will access Rendl from 2009/10 (see 'News'). For most purposes a location on or close to this main street is ideal.

Nasserein has an eight-person gondola up to Gampen, and makes an appealing base for a quiet time. The nightlife action is a short bus ride or 15-minute walk away ('quite a hike'). Staying between the centre and Nasserein is fairly convenient too as the Fang chairlift gives access to the Nasserein gondola.

SCENERY ★★★
Head for the Valluga
St Anton squeezes into a narrow, partly wooded valley. But its highlight is the splendid view from the summit of the Valluga – eye-catching itself when viewed from Rendl.

THE MOUNTAINS

The main slopes are essentially open: only the lower Gampen runs and the run from Rendl to the valley offer much shelter from bad weather.

St Anton vies with Val d'Isère for the title of 'resort with most underclassified slopes'. During our last couple of visits in 2008 and 2009 we paid particular attention to this; we didn't ski every blue, but all those we did would have been better classified as red; there are also plenty of reds that could be black; but paradoxically, none of the blacks is seriously steep.

Many of the most popular steep runs marked on the piste map are classified as 'ski routes'. The piste map says these are marked and avalanche controlled but not groomed or patrolled. If you believe that, then clearly these routes should not be tackled alone. But hundreds of people ski them every day and treat them like pistes. And what the piste map says is nonsense; on our 2009 visit lots of ski routes were groomed, including the Schindlerkar in the Valluga bowl and all of the ski routes at Stuben and on Rendl. So in practice, assuming they are patrolled (which they should be), they are treated like pistes and should be classified thus. The introduction to the Austrian section of the book has more on this ludicrous state of affairs.

The piste map also shows (at Stuben and Lech) lots of 'high-alpine touring runs', and says that these are not marked or avalanche controlled and that an 'authorized guide' is recommended. We have no problem with this category – in other resorts these off-piste runs would simply not appear on the piste map at all.

The Arlberg lift companies seem determined to present all their widely spread terrain in a single view. The result is a map that is inadequate and misleading in places. Smaller, separate maps would be much better. Piste marking is adequate. The local cable TV shows the state of the pistes and queues – very useful.

EXTENT OF THE SLOPES ★★★★
Large linked area
St Anton's slopes fall into three main sectors, two of them linked. The major sector is that beneath the local high-spot, the **Valluga**, accessed by the jumbo gondola to Galzig, then a cable car. The tiny top stage of the cable car

to the Valluga itself is mainly for sightseeing – you can take skis or a board up only if you have a guide to lead you down the tricky off-piste run to Zürs. The slightly lower station of Valluga Grat gives access to St Anton's famous high, sunny bowls, and to the long, beautiful red/blue run to Alpe Rauz, at the western end of St Anton's own slopes. From here there's a six-pack, the Valfagehr, to return, or you can go on to explore the rather neglected slopes of **Stuben**, described at the end of the chapter. The high Valluga runs can also be accessed by riding the Schindlergrat triple chair, though some also involve a hike.

Other runs from **Galzig** go south-west to St Christoph and east into the Steissbachtal. Beyond this valley, with lift and piste links in both directions, is the **Kapall-Gampen** sector, reachable by chairlift from central St Anton or gondola from Nasserein. From Gampen at mid-mountain, pistes lead back to St Anton and Nasserein. Or you can ride a six-pack on up to Kapall to ski the treeless upper mountain.

The third main sector is **Rendl**, reached by a new gondola for 2009/10 (see 'News'). A handful of lifts (including a six-pack to Gampberg) serve the west-facing runs above the gondola, with a single north-facing piste returning to the valley. Until now Rendl has usually been delightfully quiet, but the new gondola may change all that.

FAST LIFTS ★★★☆☆
Better access on both sides
Access to St Anton's mountains is improving: Gampen and Galzig are served by a fast chair and a jumbo gondola, and a new gondola will serve Rendl for 2009/10. But while the

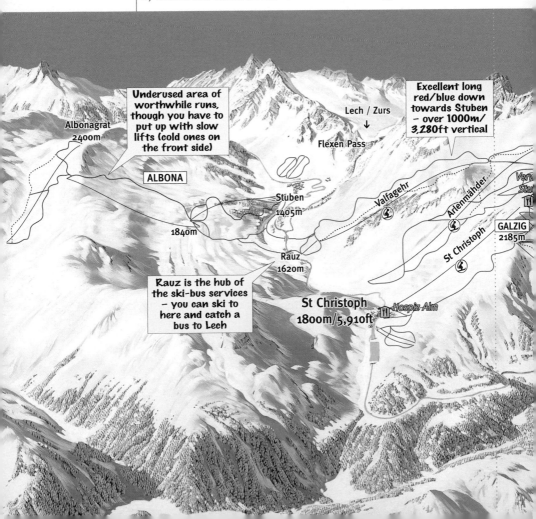

Underused area of worthwhile runs, though you have to put up with slow lifts (cold ones on the front side)

Albonagrat
2400m

Lech / Zurs
↓

Flexen Pass

Excellent long red/blue down towards Stuben – over 1000m/ 3,280ft vertical

ALBONA

Stuben
1405m

1840m

Valfagehr

Arlenmähder

Veri Stu

GALZIG
2185m

St Christoph

Rauz
1620m

Rauz is the hub of the ski-bus services – you can ski to here and catch a bus to Lech

St Christoph
1800m/5,910ft

Hospiz Alm

The Steissbachtal:
one of the world's
most crowded pistes
→

IAN STRATFORD

Gampen and Galzig sector have a lot
of fast chairs higher up, Rendl and
Stuben still have a lot of slow ones.

QUEUES ★★★ ☆☆
Much improved, but ...

Queues are not the problem they once
were. The replacement of the cable car
to Galzig by the gondola has reduced
queueing at the base significantly.
There can still be problems up the
mountain, notably the Valluga I cable
car from Galzig, the alternative
Schindlergrat chair to Schindler Spitze
and the Zammermoos chair out of the
Steissbachtal (a reporter found it as
quick to ski down to the Galzig
gondola as to wait in the long queues
at the weekend). But 2009 visitors
didn't find many problems; even over
New Year queues were 'reasonable'.

Perhaps more of a worry than the
lift queues are the crowded pistes.

Clearly the worst is the Steissbachtal
(aka 'Happy Valley') and the home run
below it, which can be uncomfortably
crowded even in January – and a
nightmare on a peak weekend. So
acute is this problem that several
reporters have preferred to catch a bus
home from Rauz or St Christoph. Other
alternatives are to use the ski route

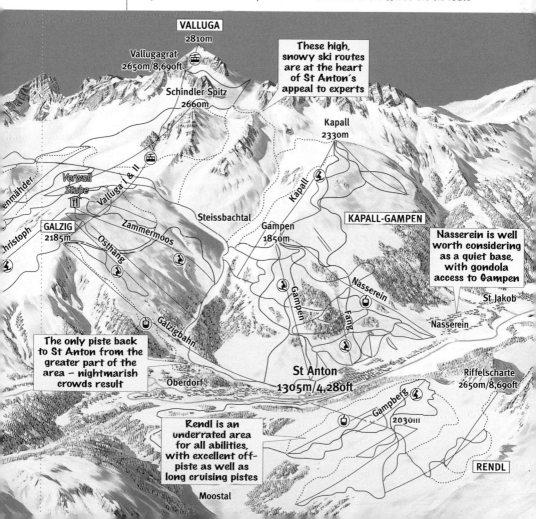

VALLUGA 2810m

Vallugagrat 2650m/8,690ft

Schindler Spitz 2660m

Kapall 2330m

These high, snowy ski routes are at the heart of St Anton's appeal to experts

Verwall Stube

Valluga I & II

Steissbachtal

Zammermoos

GALZIG 2185m

Osthang

Gampen 1850m

KAPALL-GAMPEN

Kapall

Nasserein

Nasserein is well worth considering as a quiet base, with gondola access to Gampen

St Jakob

Nasserein

Fang

Galzigbahn

Gampen

The only piste back to St Anton from the greater part of the area – nightmarish crowds result

Oberdorf

St Anton 1305m/4,28oft

Gampberg

2030m

Riffelscharte 2650m/8,690ft

Rendl is an underrated area for all abilities, with excellent off-piste as well as long cruising pistes

Moostal

RENDL

boarding

Many consider St Anton the Mecca of Austrian freeriding. Countless steep gullies and backcountry powder fields with challenging terrain form a big draw for advanced riders. The Arlberg Snowboard academy has a reputation for showing all levels where best to apply their respective skills – whether a beginner on the wide-open pistes or a more advanced rider wanting guidance through trees or steeps and deep off-piste. Rendl is an excellent mountain for freeriders and freestylers alike.

under the gondola (but it can be quite testing) or to ride the gondola down. The run to Rauz can get very busy too. When heavy snow closes the top runs on the Valluga, the crowds shift to Rendl, where the home run again gets unpleasantly busy.

TERRAIN PARKS ★★★
Head for Rendl
The 200m/660ft-long park on Rendl, just below the top of the gondola, is narrow and doesn't touch the park over in Lech for maintenance or size – but it will easily keep beginners and intermediates entertained. It has only a single kicker line, with various-sized tabletops and a corner jump. Around the jumps are four to six rails. There's a large A-frame, flat slidebox and a small rainbow rail.

SNOW RELIABILITY ★★★★
Generally very good cover
If the weather is coming from the west or north-west (as it often is), the Arlberg gets it first, and as a result St Anton and its neighbours get heavy falls of snow. They often have much better conditions than other resorts of a similar height, and we've had great fresh powder here as late as mid-April. But many of the slopes face south or south-east, causing icy or heavy conditions at times. It's vital to time

descents of the steeper runs off the Valluga to get decent conditions, or you can find yourself in trouble.

The lower runs are well equipped with snowmaking, which generally ensures the home runs remain open.

FOR EXPERTS ★★★★★
One of the world's great areas
St Anton vies with Chamonix, Val d'Isère and a handful of other resorts for the affections of experts. There are countless opportunities for going off-piste, and guidance is very desirable. Read the feature panels on the Valluga runs and off-piste routes.

Lower down, there are challenging runs in many directions from both Galzig and Kapall-Gampen. These lower runs can be doubly tricky if the snow has been hit by the sun.

Don't overlook the Rendl area, which has plenty of open space served by the top lifts, and several quite challenging runs. This is a great area for a mixed group and is generally quieter than the main sector (though that may change with the new gondola – see 'News'). One of our reporters really liked the quieter Sonnenkopf area, down-valley from Stuben, for its excellent off-piste route to Langen. See also the Stuben section.

Each of the main sectors has its toughest piste classified as black; a

THE VALLUGA RUNS

The runs in the huge bowl beneath the summit of the Valluga, reached by either the Schindlergrat chair or the Valluga I cable car, are justifiably world-famous. In good snow, this whole area is an off-piste delight for experts. Except immediately after a fresh snowfall, you can see tracks going all over the mountain. There are two main ski routes marked on the piste map – now sometimes groomed (see 'The Mountains'). Both are long, steep descents that quickly get mogulled if ungroomed. The Schindlerkar is the first you come to, and it divides into two – the Schindlerkar gully being the steeper option. For the second, wider and somewhat easier Mattun run, you traverse further at the top. Both these feed down into the Steissbachtal where there are lifts back up to Galzig and Gampen.

There are, of course, more adventurous ways down than the ski routes. The Schweinströge starts off in the same direction as the red run to Rauz, but you traverse the shoulder of the Schindler Spitze and descend a narrow gully. Perhaps the ultimate challenge is to ski off the back of the Valluga – a great adventure (see the off-piste panel opposite for more on this).

The Arlberg region is an off-piste skier's dream – renowned for its consistently high snowfall record, incredible deep powder and enormous diversity of terrain. We invited Piste to Powder Mountain Guides to give us an introduction to the possibilities. Remember you should never explore far off-piste without a guide.

Piste to Powder Mountain Guides

All day guiding 9am to 5pm. Choose from four skill levels. All safety equipment provided.

t 01434 676837
00 43 664 174 6282
info@pistetopowder.com
www.pistetopowder.com

Runs from Rendl

After initial practice close to the pistes, the natural progression is to go beyond the furthest lift to access the wide rolling bowls of powder of Rossfall.

More serious routes from Rendl take you well away from all lifts. The North Face, accessed from the Gampberg six-seat chair, offers challenging terrain to the intermediate/confident off-piste skier. The Riffel chairlifts access the imposing Hinter Rendl – a gigantic high-mountain bowl offering a huge descent down to St Anton, often in deep powder. A variant involves a climb to Rendl Scharte and a demanding descent with sections of 35° down the remote Malfontal to the village of Pettneu and a taxi back to St Anton.

Runs from Albona, above Stuben

Stuben's outstanding terrain, reached from the Albonagrat chair, is suited to the more experienced off-piste skier, as the descents are long. The open treelines of the Langen forest, where the powder is regularly knee to waist deep, form some of the world's finest tree skiing. A 30-minute climb from Albonagrat, with skis on your shoulder, opens up further outstanding terrain from Maroikopfe – either west, down undulating open slopes to Langen, or east, down steep 40° slopes to Verwalltal, where this glorious run ends with a glass of wine at an old hunting lodge.

Runs from the Valluga

The legendary runs from the summit cable car of the Valluga must be on the tick list of all keen and experienced off-piste skiers – the North Face, Bridge Couloir or East Couloir. Your pulse will race as you trace a steep ski line between cliff bands in the breathtaking scenery of the Pazieltal, leading down to Zürs. Here, at the top of the Madloch chairlift and after a short hidden climb, you will be roped down into the steep Valhalla Couloir, accessing 1200m/3,940ft vertical of open slopes ending in the hamlet of Zug, close to Lech.

St Anton

205

Interactive resort shortlist builder at **www.wtss.co.uk**

couple deserve their classification, but most don't – the Fang race course from Gampen used to be red, in fact. The distinction between reds and blacks is in general a fine one.

FOR INTERMEDIATES ★★★
Some real challenges

St Anton is well suited to good, adventurous intermediates. As well as lots of testing pistes, they will be able to try the Mattun ski route and the easier of the Schindlerkar routes from Valluga Grat (see 'The Valluga runs' feature panel). The run from Schindler Spitze to Rauz is very long (over 1000m/3,280ft vertical), varied and ideal for good (and fit) intermediates. Alternatively, turn off from this part-way down and take the Steissbachtal to the lifts back to Galzig or Gampen. The Kapall-Gampen section is also interesting, with sporty bumps among trees on the lower half. Good intermediates may enjoy the men's downhill run from the top to the town.

Timid intermediates will find St Anton less to their taste – 'too steep to even think of bringing nervous skiers', says a 2009 reporter. There are few easy cruising pistes; most blues would be red elsewhere and get bumpy, especially just after a snowfall (on our April 2009 visit blue run 1 back to the village had huge slushy moguls all the way at the end of the day – worthy of a black run). The most obvious cruisers are the short blues on Galzig and the Steissbachtal. These are quite gentle but get extremely crowded (see 'Queues'). The blue from Kapall to Gampen is wide and cruisy.

The underrated Rendl area has a variety of trails suitable for good and moderate intermediates, including the long and genuinely blue Salzböden. The long treelined run to the valley (over 1000m/3,280ft vertical from the top) is the best run in the area when visibility is poor, but it has some quite awkward sections and can get very busy at the end of the day – early intermediates beware. Intermediates of all standards should take the bus to Lech-Zürs (see separate chapter) at least once during a week's stay.

SCHOOLS

Arlberg
t 3411

St Anton
t 3563

Classes
(Arlberg prices)
6 days (2hr am and
2hr pm) €226
Private lessons
€156 for 2hr; each
additional person €20

GUIDES

Piste to Powder
t 0664 174 6282
UK 01434 676837

CHILDCARE

**Kindergartens (run by
ski schools)**
t 3411 / 3563
From age 30mnth;
must be toilet trained

Ski schools
Both Austrian schools
take children aged
from 5 (6 days
including lunch €310)

FOR BEGINNERS ★☆☆☆☆
Far from ideal

The best bet for beginners is to start at Nasserein, where the nursery slope is less steep than the one close to the main lifts. There are further slopes up at Gampen and a short, gentle blue run at Rendl, served by an easy draglift. But there are no other easy, uncrowded runs for beginners to progress to. A mixed party including novices would be better off staying in Lech or Zürs; those who want to explore St Anton can get on the bus.

FOR CROSS-COUNTRY ★★☆☆☆
Limited interest

St Anton is not great for cross-country, but trails total around 40km/25 miles and snow conditions are usually good.

MOUNTAIN RESTAURANTS ★★★☆☆
Lots of options

Editors' choice The Verwallstube at Galzig (2352501) is in a class of its own – an expensive table-service place with all the trimmings and splendid views through big windows. We've had seriously good lunches in both the last two seasons – but wouldn't want to do it every day! The noodles with truffle sauce are delicious (you pay for the truffle itself by the amount the waiter shaves onto your plate – stop him soon unless you want a huge bill). We often lunch in St Christoph at the atmospheric, buzzing Hospiz Alm (3625), famed for its slide down to the toilets as well as its satisfying table-service food and amazing wine cellar. Service gets stretched at times and it can be expensive.

Worth knowing about The Arlberg Taja is a 'jolly and welcoming' alternative to the Hospiz Alm in St Christoph. Reader recommendations on Galzig include the Ulmer Hütte near the top of the Arlenmähder chair, and the big, smart self-service restaurant at Galzig itself. Lower down, the Sennhütte is 'best for value, food and situation'. Just above the village, the Mooserwirt serves typical Austrian food; Griabli right opposite has been praised; Heustadl is popular; the Krazy Kanguruh does burgers, pizzas and snacks; and Taps Bar next door is a 'firm favourite'. The Rodelalm on Gampen is regularly praised ('a real hut, good food, low prices, a lovely fire'). On Rendl, the self-service Rendl restaurant is surprisingly good (in 2009 we had an excellent spicy oriental dish cooked to order in a wok), but it gets very busy; in good weather you can sit outside on what locals call Rendl Beach and watch the antics in the terrain park below. Or you can head down the valley run to the Bifang-Alm for regional specialities and excellent service.

SCHOOLS AND GUIDES ★★★☆☆
Mixed reports

The St Anton school and the Arlberg school are under the same ownership but continue to operate separately. Past reports on the Arlberg school are mixed. One reporter commented, 'Not enough attention was paid to putting equal standards together, and groups were big.' But other reporters were very happy: an adult beginner made 'good progress' during five days of group lessons. One reader joined a top-level guided group and was impressed with the 'superb value'. A 2009 visitor enrolled with the St Anton school and wouldn't recommend it: 'The groups were too large, and the ability of the pupils was far too wide.'

We have had good reports in 2008 and 2009 on Piste to Powder, a specialist off-piste outfit run by British guide Graham Austick. Comments in 2009 include: 'one of the best days ever on a mountain'; 'a great operation'. Earlier comments include: 'absolutely corking day with a great guide'; 'wonderful week'; 'exactly the right balance of instruction and guiding'. If you have particular ambitions, make sure your group is all of the required standard, though. We've had mixed reports of beginners to off-piste: some have been known to give up halfway through the day; others have had the 'best day ever'.

FOR FAMILIES ★★★★☆
Nasserein 'ideal'

The youth centre attached to the Arlberg school is excellent, and the special slopes both for toddlers (at the bottom) and bigger children (at Gampen) are well done. Children's instruction is reportedly 'very good'. At Nasserein there is a moving carpet lift on the baby slope, and a reporter rates Nasserein an 'absolutely ideal' place to stay with young kids. There's also a good children's area by the Gampen fast quad. Family specialists Esprit Ski and Mark Warner both have their own childcare facilities in chalets or chalet hotels in the Nasserein area.

↑ There are plenty of steep slopes, bumps and bowls to keep experts happy – most of them off-piste

IAN STRATFORD

GETTING THERE

Air Innsbruck 95km/ 60 miles (1hr15); Zürich 210km/ 130 miles (2hr45); Friedrichshafen 135km/85 miles (1hr45); Munich 210km/130 miles (3hr)

Rail Mainline station in resort

ACTIVITIES

Indoor Swimming pool (also hotel pools open to the public, with sauna and massage), fitness centre, tennis, squash, museum, library

Outdoor Cleared walking paths, natural ice rink (skating, curling), sleigh rides, snowshoeing, tobogganing, paragliding

STAYING THERE

There's a wide range of places to stay, from quality hotels to cheap and cheerful pensions and apartments.
Chalets Plenty of catered chalets are offered by UK operators, and they now include some seriously smart ones.
Hotels There are two 5-star hotels and lots of 4- and 3-stars and B&Bs.
*****Raffl's St Antoner Hof (2910) Best in town, but its position on the bypass is less than ideal. Pool.
****Alte Post (2553) Atmospheric central place with lively après-ski bar.
****Banyan (30361) Newish upmarket B&B with a fitness centre and pool.
****Brunnenhof (2293) 'Romantic and cosy; fantastic five-course dinners.' In St Jakob – hotel minibus to lifts.
****Post (2213) Comfortable if uninspiring; close to lifts and nightlife.
****Schwarzer Adler (22440) Centuries-old inn on main street. Varying bedrooms. 'Lovely pool.'
****Sporthotel (3111) Central position, varied bedrooms, good food. Pool.
****Galzig (42770) Smart, central. Recommended by a regular visitor.
****Kertess (2005) in Oberdorf. 'Very comfortable, good food, friendly staff and a large pool.'
***Edelweiss (2249) Centrally located but 'small rooms'.
***Goldenes Kreuz (22110) Halfway to Nasserein; comfortable B&B hotel.

***Grischuna (2304) Welcoming and family-run in peaceful position up the hill west of town; close to the slopes.
***Parseierblick (3374) 'Stayed in the apartment; fantastic for a family.'
***Nassereinerhof (3366) Close to the Nasserein gondola. Family-run with sauna, steam room. Recommended; 'very pleasant with good food'.
***Montfort (2310) On main street. Good value B&B with rooms and apartments, sauna, steam; friendly, family-run. We stayed here in 2009.
Pepi's skihotel (2830) Stylish, modern, central B&B; 'huge rooms'.
Almjur (2728) Convenient B&B near the Museum. 'Good breakfasts.'
Pension Alpenheim (3389) 'Basic but good breakfast, ski-in/ski-out to Nasserein lifts.'
Apartments There are plenty available, but few package deals. Reporters like the Bachmann apartments ('spacious and comfortable') and the H Strolz ('well equipped'), both in Nasserein, and Haus Rali at the western end of St Anton ('very friendly, family-owned, a bargain for New Year').

EATING OUT ★★★★
Some excellent spots

There's a lot of half board in St Anton, so the restaurant scene is not huge. Our standard port of call for a drink or two and a relaxed meal is the cool Hazienda – a basement place in the main street, with a wide-ranging menu (steaks, seafood, pasta); you can eat at the bar. For more of a blowout, it's up the hill to the village museum's restaurant – excellent, sophisticated food served in elegant panelled rooms. The Fuhrmannstube and Trödlerstube serve big portions of traditional Austrian food. Readers recommend Underground on the Piste ('great food, especially steaks'), Pomodoro for pizzas, the Sporthotel Steakhouse, Bodega ('a delicious and

UK PACKAGES

Albus, Alpine Answers, Alpine Weekends, Crystal, Crystal Finest, Directski.com, Elegant Resorts, Erna Low, Esprit, First Choice, Flexiski, Friendship Travel, Independent Ski Links, Inghams, Interactive Resorts, Kaluma, Kuoni, Made to Measure, Mark Warner, Momentum, Neilson, Oxford Ski Co, Powder White, Scott Dunn, Simply Alpine, Ski Activity, Ski Expectations, Ski Freshtracks, Ski Independence, Skiing Austria, Ski Line, Ski McNeill, Ski Solutions, Ski Total, Ski-Val, Skitracer, Skiworld, Snow Finders, Snoworks, Snowscape, STC, Supertravel, Thomson, White Roc
Stuben *Alpine Answers, Kaluma, Skiing Austria*
St Christoph *Alpine Answers, Crystal Finest, Flexiski, Jeffersons, Kaluma, Made to Measure, Neilson, Powder Byrne, Scott Dunn, Skiing Austria, Thomson*

busy tapas bar') and the Dolce Vita. The Funky Chicken offers 'good food at reasonable prices', including 'top-notch curry'. The cosy Sonnbichl has been mentioned. In Nasserein, the Tenne is noted for game and fish dishes. Robi's Rodel-Stall at the end of the toboggan run has a cosy log fire.

APRES-SKI ★★★★★
Throbbing till late
St Anton's bars rock from mid-afternoon until the early hours. Après-ski starts in a collection of bars on the slopes above the village. The Krazy Kanguruh is probably the most famous, but the Mooserwirt is the favourite with many reporters – 'still great and a must-visit'. It fills up as soon as the lunch trade finishes – reputedly dispensing more beer than any other bar in Austria. Griabli, opposite, is quieter, and the terrace gives you a good view of the goings-on at the Mooserwirt; we enjoyed a live band there in 2009. The Heustadl is 'the best place to boogie Tirolean-style'. The Sennhütte also has 'a fantastic atmosphere'. All this is followed by a slide down the (usually mogulled) piste in the dark. The bars in town are in full swing by 4pm, too. Most are lively, with loud music; sophisticates looking for a quieter time are less well provided for. The Anton bar is 'a great place to watch the world go by' and has comfy sheepskin on the chairs outside. The Hazienda and the Piccadilly (live bands, singing and late-night dancing) are popular choices. Underground on the Piste has 'a great party atmosphere, super staff and live music'. Reporters also recommend Scotty's (in Mark Warner's chalet hotel Rosanna), Bar Cuba ('a good party'), Jacksy's ('good for a quiet drink'), Kandahar ('best for watching sport') and Funky Chicken. The St Antoner Hof

is suggested for pre-dinner 'canapés and champagne'. In Nasserein, the Fang House and 'jolly' Sonnegg are recommended.

OFF THE SLOPES ★★★★★
Some improvement
St Anton is a resort for keen skiers and riders. We loved the ludicrously named but excellent Arlberg-well.com, a leisure centre with great indoor and outdoor pools – including one with jets that propel you around at lightning speed – plus three types of sauna and a huge steam room. A new sports centre with indoor climbing and outdoor ice climbing walls opened last year. The village is lively during the day, but has few diverting shops. Getting to the other Arlberg resorts by bus is easy, as is visiting Innsbruck by train. Some of the better mountain huts are accessible by lift or bus. A reporter suggests using the winter walking trails to visit Pettneu, and another enjoyed the walk to Verwall; it's worth considering Lech for 'more interesting walks'. The ski museum was revamped for 2008/09 and is 'well worth the 4 euros entry'.

St Jakob 1295m/4,250ft

Beyond Nasserein is St Jakob. It can be reached on snow, but is dependent on the free shuttle-bus in the morning.

Stuben 1405m/4,610ft

Stuben (in Vorarlberg) is linked by lifts and pistes over the Arlberg pass to St Anton (in Tirol). There are infrequent buses from the village to Lech/Zürs, and more frequent ones from Rauz, the roadside lift station for St Anton.

Dating back to the 13th century, Stuben is a small, unspoiled village, with an old church, a few unobtrusive hotels, a school, two or three bars, a

Phone numbers
From elsewhere in Austria add the prefix 05446 (St Anton and St Christoph), 05582 (Stuben); from abroad use the prefix +43 and omit the initial '0'

TOURIST OFFICES

St Anton
t 22690
info@stantonam
arlberg.com
www.
stantonamarlberg.com

St Christoph
www.tiscover.com/
st.christoph

Stuben
info@stuben.at
www.stuben.com

couple of banks and a few little shops. Heavy snowfalls add to the charm.

The Albona above Stuben makes a refreshingly quiet change from the busy slopes of St Anton. It has old, very slow chairlifts and the shady chair from the village can be a cold ride, but blankets are available. The reward is north-facing slopes that hold powder well and some wonderful, deserted off-piste descents, including beautiful long runs down to Langen and to St Anton ('lovely sense of travel and isolation'). A regular visitor recommends the small Rasthaus Verwall for lunch at the end of the latter. Staying within the lift network, the Albonagratstube at the very top is a simple hut serving simple food. Lower down, the Albona self-service place gets packed, even on a quiet day. A 2009 reporter recommends heading back to the village for lunch at Willys ('outstanding').

Reporters continue to recommend the school ('hard to fault, really good teacher' said a 2009 visitor who put his three children in the school). A quicker and warmer way to get to St Anton in the morning, if you have a car, is to drive up the road to Rauz.

Stuben has sunny nursery slopes separate from the main slopes, but lack of easy runs to progress to makes it unsuitable for beginners.

Evenings are quiet, but several places have a pleasant atmosphere. The charming old Post (761) and Albona (712) are very comfortable. The Hubertushof (7710) is continually recommended by reporters: 'a real little gem', 'gourmet food, kids' menu and great wellness centre'.

St Christoph 1800m/5,910ft

St Christoph is small collection of smart and expensive hotels, restaurants and bars just down from the summit of the Arlberg pass. There are decent beginner slopes served by draglifts and a fast quad chairlift to the heart of St Anton's slopes at Galzig, but the blue back down is not an easy run to progress to. St Christoph is quiet at night. You can't miss the huge 5-star Arlberg-Hospiz (2611). A more affordable but still excellent place is the 4-star Maiensee (21610), right on the slopes by the chair up to Galzig, with health and spa facilities and treatments.

Stubai valley

A choice of pretty little villages with their own wooded slopes, and one of the best glaciers in the world at the head of the valley

➕	High, snow-sure glacier slopes plus lower bad-weather options	➖	Beginners are better off sticking to the lower slopes
➕	Quiet, pretty Tirolean villages	➖	Not much to challenge experts

TOP 10 RATINGS

Extent	★★★
Fast lifts	★★
Queues	★★★
Snow	★★★★★
Expert	★★★
Intermediate	★★★
Beginner	★★
Charm	★★★★
Convenience	★★
Scenery	★★★★

KEY FACTS

Resort	935-1000m
	3,070-3,280ft
Slopes	935-3210m
	3,070-10,530ft
Lifts	45
Pistes	147km
	91 miles
Blue	40%
Red	31%
Black	29%
Snowmaking	some

210

Think Austrian glaciers, and the Stubaier Gletscher should feature near the top of your list. It is the country's largest glacier ski area, and among the world's best. For a winter holiday you need non-glacial slopes as well, for the bad-weather days – and the Stubai valley has adequate supplies at Schlick 2000 (above Fulpmes), Elfer (above Neustift) and Serles (above Mieders).

The Stubai valley lies a short drive south of Innsbruck. It is a long valley (about 30km/19 miles) with countless hamlets dotted along it – and a handful of bigger villages, three of which have their own wooded ski slopes and lift systems and are described in this chapter. Altogether the valley offers a sizeable area of mostly intermediate terrain, all of which is covered by the Stubai-Superski lift pass (which also covers the shuttle-bus). All the villages have impressive toboggan runs.

The Stubaier Gletscher offers an extensive area of runs between 3200m/10,500ft and 2300m/7,550ft accessed by two alternative two-stage gondolas from the huge car park at Mutterberg to the two mid-mountain stations of Eisgrat and Gamsgarten. A third gondola from Eisgrat takes you right to the top of the slopes.

The slopes are broken up by rocky peaks giving more sense of variety than is normal on a glacier. Chairs (including three six-packs) and draglifts serve fabulous blue and red cruising runs, all of which normally have excellent snow, naturally. There is also a lovely 10km/6 mile ungroomed ski route (Wilde Grub'n) down to the valley – a run of 1450m/4,760ft vertical from the top of the glacier. And some good off-piste can be found with a guide.

There aren't the challenges here that there are on the Hintertux glacier. But there are some good long runs, and some excellent ski routes – notably the short ones near the Rotadl chair and the 4km/2.5 mile Fernau-Mauer at the eastern extremity of the area. For intermediates it is splendid territory, with lots of fabulous cruising. Novices are better off learning lower down, but there is a short beginner slope at Gamsgarten.

The area is popular with snowboarders. There are lots of natural hits and kickers across the mountain, and the newly expanded terrain park has rails, boxes, triple kicker line and a wall ride.

Queues are not a serious problem. The gondola and Eisjoch six-pack can get busy at weekends.

There are two huge self-service restaurants at Eisgrat – due to be renovated for 2010/11 – and Gamsgarten. The Zur Goldenen Gams has table service. At Jochdohle, Austria's highest restaurant gives stunning views but can get crowded.

STUBAIER GLETSCHER
3210m/10,530ft

1720m

ELFER
2080m

SERLES
1680m

Sennjoch
2225m

SCHLICK 2000

Neustift
1000m/3,280ft

Schlickalm

Fulpmes
935m/3,070ft

Froneben

Telfes

Mieders
980m

The ski routes in the middle of the slopes are short but entertaining – and there are longer ones out on the fringes of the area ➜

SNOWPIX.COM / CHRIS GILL

UK PACKAGES

Neustift Crystal, Crystal Finest, Interactive Resorts, Interhome, Made to Measure, Simply Alpine, Skiing Austria
Fulpmes Crystal, Skiing Austria

Phone numbers
From elsewhere in Austria add the prefix 05226; from abroad use the prefix +43 5226

TOURIST OFFICE

t 05018 810
info@stubai.at
www.stubai.at

The Dresdner Hütte near the gondola mid-station is a proper climbing refuge – no frills, but 'a pleasant alternative'.

There is a ski school at the glacier. There is a comprehensive family area at Gamsgarten, incorporating new kids' camps, childcare and school facilities. Children under ten get a free lift pass when with an adult.

Après-ski starts up the mountain in the lively Gamsgarten bar and new Ice Cube bar at Fernau.

Neustift 1000m/3,280ft

The major village closest to the glacier, 20km/12 miles away, and served by regular buses. It's an attractive, traditional Tirolean village, with limited local slopes at Elfer.
The slopes at Elfer consist of a narrow chain of runs and lifts from Elferhütte at 2080m/6,820ft down to the village. The pistes are all red and there's not much to entice experts, but it is a quiet place for intermediates to practise. This area is north-east-facing; there is a sunny nursery slope at village level, on the other side. There are some 45km/28 miles of cross-country trails.

There are lots of 3- and 4-star hotels. The 4-star Tirolerhof (3278) is excellent – comfortable and relaxed with good food. It has a hire shop, and the owner is a qualified instructor and guide. Three 4-stars have been recommended – the central Sonnhof (2224); the Gasteigerhof in Gasteig (2746) is good for families with a pool and a children's fun area; and the Almhof-Danler (2626) has sauna, steam and hot tub.

Nightlife is focused on the Dorf and Bierfassl bars and the Nachtkastl and Rumpl discos. Most restaurants are hotel-based. Neustift has quite a lot to offer off the slopes: a leisure centre with two pools, saunas and bowling.

Fulpmes 935m/3,070ft

Fulpmes (with its satellite village of Telfes) sits at the foot of Schlick 2000, the most extensive of the lower ski areas. The pleasant, sizeable village is said to be the sunniest in the valley.
A two-stage gondola takes you to Kreuzjoch (2135m/7,000ft), opening up excellent views across the Stubaital and across the Schlick slopes to the dramatic Kalkkogel range. Most of the skiing is below the top station – essentially a single open slope centred on a quad chair rising 580m/1,900ft, with three draglifts serving the outermost runs. There are about five different pistes down, mostly of red difficulty with some easier blue options. There is also a ski-route which is challenging at the best of times, very much so if snow is poor. Below the main slopes is a long easy run-out to the gondola mid-station at Froneben (1365m/4,480ft). This is the location of the nursery slope, including Ronny's Kinderland, with moving carpets and fun features, and a couple of thumping après-ski bars. The blue run winding through woods to the village from here is good fun or tricky, depending on conditions and your competence. There is a terrain park.

There's a good choice of 3- and 4-star hotels, most with pools and spa facilities. The 4-star Stubaierhof (62266) is central, with a pool and a children's play room. Café Dorfkrug has been recommended for food.

The nearest leisure centre is in Neustift, but Fulpmes has ice skating, snowshoeing and tobogganing.

Mieders 980m/3,220ft

Mieders is near the entrance to the Stubai valley, 15 minutes' drive from Innsbruck. It's an unspoiled village with its own tiny area of slopes.
The slopes of Serles are limited to four blues and two short reds. A gondola takes you to Kopponeck at 1680m/5,510ft, where a couple of T-bars serve the upper runs. There are a couple of mountain restaurants and 45km/28 miles of cross-country tracks above 1600m/5,250ft. The village has a small selection of hotels and guest houses.

Vorarlberg

*Lech and Zürs are not the only resorts west of the Arlberg pass,
above St Anton – the others include Europe's snowiest*

**Ski from St Anton to Stuben, and you cross over the Arlberg pass, moving from
the Tirol to the province of Vorarlberg. Here, the melting snow drains into the
Rhine, not the Inn and the Danube. It's a famously snowy area, catching the full
force of storms sweeping in across the Bodensee. Fashionable and expensive
Lech and Zürs are the resorts that are well known internationally, but there are
small family resorts elsewhere that deserve attention.**

Vorarlberg is small – the smallest
'land' in the Austrian federation
(unless you count the city of Vienna).
Its capital is Bregenz, down on the
shores of the Bodensee.

Lech, Vorarlberg's best-known
resort internationally, gets full
coverage in its own chapter a few
pages back, which also covers its
linked close neighbour **Zürs**.

Those resorts aside, there are two
main skiing regions, each of which is
covered in its own chapter following
this introductory one. Although very
different in character, both areas have
a handful of small resorts. Few UK tour
operators go to these areas.

Bregenzerwald, to the north-west of
the Arlberg, is a delightfully unspoiled

area, very proud of its cheeses – and
it's here that two small resorts, Damüls
and Warth, vie for the title of snowiest
resort in the Alps. Warth is linked to
Schröcken, and Damüls is about to be
linked to Mellau. Au and next-door
Schoppernau share the third-biggest
ski area, Diedamskopf.

The **Montafon** valley, to the south-
west of the Arlberg, is rather more
developed, and attracts many visitors
from Germany. They go particularly to
the biggest ski area, shared by
Gaschurn and St Gallenkirch. The
Hochjoch area above Schruns and
Golm above Vandans are less well
known, and Gargellen is a bit of a
backwater. At the top of the valley is
famously good ski touring terrain.

Then there are three other areas
with some skiing to offer.

The **Alpenregion Bludenz**, west of
the Arlberg, embraces Sonnenkopf
above Klösterle – a popular outing
from the Arlberg resorts – and the
Brandnertal area shared between
Brand (1035m/3,400ft) and Bürserberg
(890m/2,920ft). This offers 55km/
34 miles of pistes with a top height of
2000m/6,560ft served by 14 lifts. Most
of the skiing is easy, with open slopes
above Brand and more woodland runs
above Bürserberg. But all three runs to
valley level are classified red.

In the north-east corner of the
province is a real curiosity.
Kleinwalsertal is cut off from the rest
of Austria, at the head of a German
valley. It is close to one of the main
German resorts, Oberstdorf, and is
described briefly in the introduction to
our new section on Germany.

Finally, the **Bodensee-Vorarlberg**
area in the north-west corner of
Vorarlberg has some small areas – the
largest, Laterns, has six lifts and
27km/17 miles of runs, and a top
height of 1780m/5,840ft.

Vorarlberg – Bregenzerwald

An unspoiled region that is hardly heard of on the British market, with a lot of relatively small ski areas covered on one big pass

Bregenzerwald is tucked away between Germany and Switzerland at the westernmost end of Austria in the Vorarlberg. Skirted by all the major road and rail links, it has remained remarkably unspoiled and is still primarily a farming community famous for its cheeses. But it is the snowiest region in the Alps and has mountains rising up to over 2400m/7,870ft, with almost 260km/162 miles of slopes served by around 100 lifts in 22 villages. There is some seriously good skiing here, especially for intermediates, and Bregenzerwald is well worth considering for a quiet holiday exploring several different ski areas or for a family holiday. And prices for accommodation and eating and drinking are lower than many better-known, more fashionable resorts.

Skiing began in Bregenzerwald in 1894 when the parish priest, Father Johann Müller – garbed in his flowing robes – careered down the slopes on two wooden planks, amazing the local farmers. Until then, if you absolutely had to get around in winter, you wore a type of snowshoe. The priest had sent away to Norway for his newfangled 'Hickoryski', and in doing so he established a trend that has transformed the region's economy.

There is now a ski lift in almost every village. But few of the ski areas are large. They are all covered by the 3-Valley ski pass, which also covers two areas outside Bregenzerwald. The pass is valid in 34 ski areas and covers around 340km/211 miles of slopes served by around 140 lifts.

There's a ski-bus service between different resorts in Bregenzerwald that is included in the pass, and there's a special offer for families who stay for a week on certain dates in December 2009 and January and March 2010: children between the ages of three and six get a six-day lift pass and four days of lessons free.

Nearly all the resorts offer activities other than skiing, including walking (there are lots of cleared paths), tobogganing and cross-country skiing.

213

THE BIGGEST SKI AREAS

Warth and **Schröcken** are at opposite ends of their shared 60km/37 miles of slopes, mainly between 1500m and 2000m (4,920ft and 6,560ft) served by

Widderstein 2535m
Lechtal
↙ Innsbruck
Warth 1500m
Schröcken 1260m
Schoppernau 860m
Au 800m
Damüls 1430m
Niedere 1710m
Mellau 700m
Hochhäderich 1565m
Bezau 620m
Hochälpelekopf 1465m
Schetteregg 1065m
Andelsbuch 615m
Schwarzenberg 700m
Egg 565m
Hittisau
Riefensberg 780m
Müselbach 585m
Bödele 1140m
Alberschwende 720m
Dornbirn 475m
Friedrichshafen
München
Stuttgart ↙
BREGENZ 400m/1,310ft
Feldkirch
Zürich →

NEWS

For 2009/10 Damüls (already the biggest ski area in Bregenzerwald) will be linked to Mellau, forming an area that will have 92km/57 miles of piste; that's almost as much as such well-known names as Obergurgl, Courmayeur and Livigno. A new red piste (including a 100m/330ft long ski-through tunnel) is being built from the Damüls area into the Mellau area, and an eight-seat gondola will take you back to Damüls from Mellau.

In Mellau, the Sonne Lifestyle Resort opened in December 2008, with uber-modern minimalist decor, spacious rooms and a spa.

Bregenzerwald is the snowiest region in the Alps; there was certainly more than enough when we skied the Warth-Schröcken area (pictured) last season ↓

15 lifts, including five high-speed chairs. The ski area is the snowiest in the Alps and gets on average between 10m and 11m of snow each winter. That compares, for example, with a mere 2m to 3m for Kitzbühel, 3m to 4m for Chamonix and 5m to 6m for St Anton and Val d'Isère. So the pistes are almost always in excellent condition (and the off-piste powder gets tracked out much less quickly than in the better-known resorts). The runs include several easy blacks and ski routes as well as reds and blues, and there's a terrain park. Most of the pistes are ideal for high-speed cruising and were very quiet on our January 2009 visit.

Warth is only a few kilometres up the valley from Lech (see separate chapter). The road is closed in winter because of avalanche danger, but you get good views of the Lech ski area from the top of the slopes and you can ski there and back off-piste (the schools organise weekly excursions).

There are 17km/11 miles of cross-country loops and 20km/12 miles of walking trails.

The villages are small, pretty and unspoiled. There are six 4-star hotels, three 3-star hotels and one 2-star, plus inns and gasthofs. The 4-stars include the Walserberg (5583 3502) – with smartly renovated rooms and themed suites, saunas, steam room and fitness room – and the Sporthotel Steffisalp (5583 3699) with rooms in four different categories, a formal restaurant, après-ski hut and umbrella

bar – and a spa area. Both these are in Warth and right by the pistes and lifts (a fast quad followed by a six-pack). Schröcken can be reached on skis only by a ski route, and there are no lifts there – you have to drive or catch a bus to the Hochtannberg pass, where a six-pack whisks you into the centre of the ski area.

Damüls and **Mellau** will share a ski area from 2009/10 (see 'News'). This will be by far the biggest single ski area in Bregenzerwald, with 92km/57 miles of runs between 700m and 2000m (2,300ft and 6,560ft). Just over half of these are red runs, around 35% are blue and the rest are blacks and ski routes. And there's a good terrain park in both sectors. Altogether there are 19 lifts – including two gondolas and 11 chairs (with five six-packs and a fast quad).

Damüls was recently named as the most snow-sure village in the world. It is high (the base area is at 1430m/4,690ft), and the sunny south-facing but snow-sure slopes go up to 2000m/6,560ft. Most runs are quite short, above the treeline and of genuine red steepness, and some of the blues are quite narrow; so it's best for adventurous rather than timid intermediates. On our 2009 visit, all of the ski routes we tried had been groomed and were of red run steepness – and some were busier than the pistes. Damüls also has 16km/10 miles of sunny cross-country tracks and over 22km/14 miles of winter walking trails.

Mellau's ski area is reached by an old gondola from the edge of the village and is on the more shady side of the mountain (most of the slopes are north-facing).

There's a steep black run that deserves its grading, as do the reds, and a ski route that is short but enjoyable (beware the drop on the right near the top, though). Most of the blues have fairly steep sections at the top – not good for timid intermediates. There's a long red through the trees right back to the village – enjoyable but narrow (it's a summer road for much of the way).

There's no real village centre to Damüls: it's more a series of small collections of hotels – six 4-stars, five 3-stars – inns and gasthofs, scattered in groups at the edge of the slopes; most of the accommodation is ski-in/ ski-out.

SKI Bregenzerwald

bregenzerwald

SKI Bregenzerwald Package:
4 nights' accommodation,
Sunday to Thursday or 3 nights'
accommodation, Thursday to
Sunday in the accommodation
category of your choice, plus
three-valley ski pass for three
days' varied skiing in all skiing
areas in the Bregenzerwald.

PRICE PER PERSON:
from € 275,00
in ****Hotels with half-board
from € 245,00
in ***Hotels with half-board

BOOKING:
10 January–18 April 2010
(excl. 11 February–21 February)

INFORMATION AND BOOKING:
Bregenzerwald Tourismus
T +43(0)5512-2365
info@bregenzerwald.at
www.bregenzerwald.at/uk

Further info on Vorarlberg
www.vorarlberg.travel

VOR
ARL
BERG

Weekly news updates and resort links at www.wtss.co.uk

Mellau, on the other hand, is a proper little village, quiet and peaceful and bypassed by the main road. There's little more to it than a few hotels – two 4-stars, three 3-stars – some gasthofs and a couple of bars. We enjoyed our 2009 stay at the new 4-star Sonne Lifestyle (5518 2010) – modern, minimalist, wooden floors, spacious rooms, friendly staff, good food and spa facilities.

Au and **Schoppernau** are neighbouring villages sharing the **Diedamskopf** ski area, which boasts Bregenzerwald's highest lift station at 2,060m/6,760ft and fabulous 360° views from the top. The sunny slopes (most are south or south-west facing) also have good views of the surrounding peaks and are popular with families. The eight lifts serve 44km/27 miles of slopes, of which around 30% are red or black ski routes, 33% are blue pistes, 20% are red pistes and the rest are black pistes. The lifts include a two-stage gondola that takes you to the Panorama restaurant at the top.

The slopes suit good intermediates best; the blacks are of serious black steepness, and some of the blues should be classified red, especially the blue from the top chair (which had moguls on it the afternoon we skied it in January 2009). On the other hand, the reds in the Breitenalpe sector were easy and should really be classified blue. The runs are short, except for the 10km/6 mile runs back to the valley station at 820m/2,690m, which have a vertical of over 1200m/3,940ft. The lower section of this is served only by one red run and a ski route (the route was closed on our visit and the lowest section of the red run was stony; many people take the gondola down from mid-station). The rest of the pistes are above 1470m/4,820ft. The resort claims that its Sajas terrain park – with around 20 varied features including rails, boxes and kickers – is the best in Bregenzerwald, and it attracts snowboarders and freestyle skiers from across Europe. There's night skiing twice a week.

At the top of the mountain, the Kids Adventure Land takes children aged three to eight years old.

Cross-country enthusiasts will find over 60km/37 miles of trails. There are 40km/25 miles of cleared walks and a natural ice rink.

The villages of Au and Schoppernau

between them have eleven 4-star and five 3-star hotels plus gasthofs and plenty of dining options. Both are a ski-bus ride or drive from the ski area and are rather spread out. We preferred Schoppernau, off the main road on the slopes as the slopes, and with nice snowy lanes and snow-covered chalets.

SMALLER SKI AREAS

Andelsbuch and **Bezau** share the local **Niedere** ski area with eight lifts serving three short blue runs, a 7km/4 mile long red, a short black and several ski routes – 20km/12 miles in total. It's a family ski area, and, given good snow, the ski routes offer more experienced skiers a challenge too. The top height is 1715m/5,630ft. Andelsbuch has just one 3-star hotel plus a few gasthofs, and Bezau has three 4-star hotels.

Alberschwende has 18km/11 miles of runs, which are served by a chairlift and seven T-bars, and it is popular with beginners. There's a 10km/6 mile cross-country track and an ice rink. It has two 4-star hotels and a 3-star, plus a few gasthofs.

Riefensberg has the tiny **Hochlitten** ski area, with just 5km/3 miles of easy blue and red runs and four T-bars. It also shares the **Hochhäderich** ski area with neighbouring **Hittisau**. This has 11km/7 miles of runs (mainly blue and red but with a couple of blacks) served by four T-bars and a quad chair specially designed to be appropriate for children. It also has 12km/7 miles of cross-country tracks at altitude and 12km/7 miles of walking paths. Hittisau has a 4-star hotel and three 3-star hotels, while Riefensberg has a 2-star inn.

Egg is the biggest village in Bregenzerwald with around 3,500 inhabitants and a small ski area at **Schetteregg**, which has six lifts serving 10km/6 miles of easy blue and red runs between 1100m and 1400m (3,610ft and 4,590ft). There are also 9km/6 miles of cleared walks. There's just one 3-star hotel, and there are a couple of inns.

Schwarzenberg's local **Bödele** mountain has 16km/10 miles of runs (mainly easy blues and reds) served by nine lifts (eight of them draglifts). There are also 6km/4 miles of cross-country tracks and 30km/19 miles of walking trails. Schwarzenberg has a 4-star and two 2-star hotels.

UK PACKAGES

Damüls, Au, Schröcken, Warth Skiing Austria

Phone numbers
From abroad use the prefix +43 and omit the initial '0'

TOURIST OFFICE

t 05512 2365
info@bregenzerwald.at
www.bregenzerwald.at/uk

ALPENSZENE MONTAFON

Vorarlberg – Montafon

Extensive slopes in several areas covered by a single lift pass – and attractive places to stay, well off the beaten package path

The 40km/25 mile long Montafon valley contains no fewer than 11 resorts and four main lift systems. Packages from the UK are few, but for the independent traveller the valley is well worth a look – especially the biggest area (linking Gaschurn and St Gallenkirch) and high, tiny, isolated Gargellen.

NEWS

The Silvretta Nova and Hochjoch areas now share the same ownership and new name of Silvretta Montafon. There are plans for a new lift to connect the two ski areas eventually. But the tiny ski area above Tschagguns, Grabs, has closed.

For 2009/10 above St Gallenkirch, an eight-pack with covers and heated seats is due to replace the Gampabing T-bars at Valisera.

For 2008/09 on Golm, an Alpine Coaster ride opened.

ARCHIV MONTAFON TOURISMUS

The valley at the heart of the slopes shared by St Gallenkirch and Gaschurn has great off-piste potential ↓

The Montafon is neglected by the UK travel trade. The valley is said to lack the large hotels that big operators apparently need. But it is being discovered by more independent travellers from the UK, and resort literature is available in English. The valley runs south-east from the medieval city of Bludenz – parallel with the nearby Swiss border.

The ski areas in the valley have had a bit of a shake-up recently. One area – tiny Grabs, above Tschagguns – has closed. Two major areas have been sold to a single owner and are now jointly branded as Silvretta Montafon. This will make more sense if and when the plan to link them comes off, but doesn't help at present.

The biggest area, formerly Silvretta Nova, is between St Gallenkirch and Gaschurn, well up the valley on the south-west side. This is being married to Hochjoch, on the opposite side of the valley and currently accessed from Schruns, nearer the entrance to the valley. Slightly nearer that entrance is Vandans, where a gondola goes up into the Golm area. Up a side valley near St Gallenkirch is tiny Gargellen, close to the Swiss border.

The valley road goes on up to Partenen. You can take a cable car from Partenen to Trominier, and then a minibus (covered by the area pass) on up to Bielerhöhe and the Silvrettasee dam, at the foot of glaciers and Piz Buin (of sunscreen fame) – the highest peak in the Vorarlberg. Bielerhöhe is a great launch pad for ski tours, and there are high, snow-sure cross-country trails totalling 22km/14 miles on and around the lake. From here you can ski down to Galtür, near Ischgl. Some ski schools organise ski trips, with the return to Bielerhöhe by snowcat; you end the day with a long run back down to Partenen.

There are more ordinary cross-country trails along the valley, and an 11km/7 mile woodland trail at Kristberg, above Silbertal – up a side valley east of Schruns. One trail near Gaschurn is floodlit each evening. Trails total over 100km/62 miles.

The shared valley lift pass covers the post bus service and the Bludenz-Schruns trains, as well as all the lifts. But the valley is best explored by car.

The top heights hereabouts are no match for the nearby Arlberg resorts; but there is plenty of skiing above the mid-mountain lift stations at around 1500m/4,920ft, and most of the slopes are not excessively sunny, so snow reliability (aided by snowmaking on

217

KEY FACTS

Resorts	655-1425m
	2,150-4,680ft
Slopes	655-2395m
	2,150-7,860ft
Lifts	61
Pistes	219km
	136 miles
Blue	50%
Red	36%
Black	14%
Snowmaking	47%

quite a big scale) is reasonable. Practically all of the slopes are above the trees, so exposed in bad weather. Nearly all the pistes are accurately classified blue or red, but there is plentiful off-piste (and quite a few 'ski routes') to amuse experts. There are terrain parks in most sectors, including the NovaPark above St Gallenkirch. Reports suggest few lift queues.

All the areas are covered by one giant, misconceived map: most of the space is given to marketing drivel, leaving no room to name or even number the lifts and runs.

There are 10 ski schools in the valley, operating in each of the different ski areas. And the eight ski kindergartens take kids from age two.

Tobogganing is popular, with several runs – the 6km/4 mile floodlit run down to St Gallenkirch being the most impressive.

For those with a car, there is accommodation in various smaller villages in addition to those dealt with below. Reporters suggest the Zum Guten Tropfen (8322) and Partenerhof (8319) in Partenen, and the Adler (67118) in St Anton im Montafon.

Gargellen 1425m/4,680ft

Gargellen is a bit of a backwater – a tiny, friendly village tucked up a side valley near the Swiss border, with a small but varied and blissfully quiet piste network on Schafberg.
The eight-person gondola from the village up to the Schafberg slopes seems rather out of place in this tiny collection of hotels and guest houses, huddled in a steep-sided, narrow valley. The runs it takes you to are gentle, with not much to choose between the blues and reds; but there is lots of off-piste terrain, including five ski routes. A special feature is the day tour around the Madrisa – a small-scale off-piste adventure taking you over to Klosters in Switzerland. It involves a 300m/980ft climb, but is otherwise easy.

The altitude of the village (the highest in the Montafon) and north-east facing slopes make for reasonable snow reliability. And there is snowmaking on one of the several pistes to the valley, which include a couple of excellent, scenic away-from-the-lifts runs at the extremities of the area. With care you can ski to the door of some hotels, including the highly

rated hotel Madrisa (6331) – 'Superb staff, excellent facilities – it made the holiday,' enthuses a visitor. Behind the hotel is a rather steep nursery slope. There are pleasant mountain huts: Schafberghüsli at the top of the gondola and two rustic huts at the treeline – the Obwaldhütte and the Kesslhütte. The Barga pizzeria at the foot of the Vergalden drag can also be reached by walkers.

Schruns 700m/2,300ft

Schruns is a towny little place, with shops in its car-free centre catering for locals and summer tourists.
A cable car and gondola go up from points outside the village into the Hochjoch slopes. Above the trees is a fair-sized area of easy blue runs, with the occasional red alternative, served by slow chairs and drags and the fast eight-seat Seebliga chair. A reporter enjoyed 'excellent' guided off-piste there. There are restaurants at strategic points – the Wormser Hütte is a climbing refuge with 'stunning' views, the Grasjoch Hütte is 'pleasant' and the Kapell has 'good choices'. Parents can leave their kids under supervision at the huge Dreamland children's facility at the top of the cable car, by the skier services building. The blue run from Kreuzjoch back to Schruns is exceptional: about 12km/7 miles long and over 1600m/5,250ft vertical. Snowmaking covers the lower half of this, plus the Seebliga area.

Easily accessible across the valley is the more extensive area of Golm, where a gondola goes from Vandans up to a handful of chairs and drags serving easy slopes above the trees – offering a vertical descent of over 1400m/4,590ft. A six-pack goes to the top of the area, linked via a ski tunnel to a quad on the Aussergolm slopes on the back of the hill. This serves the Diabolo black run, reputedly the steepest in the Montafon. Snow-guns cover much of the upper slopes, and the run to the valley.

As you are reminded frequently, Ernest Hemingway ensconced himself in Schruns in 1925/26, and his favourite drinking table in the hotel Taube (72384) can be admired. The Löwen (7141) and the Alpenhof Messmer (726640) ('great meals') are elegant, well-equipped 4-stars with big pools, the former a hub of the 'quite

UK PACKAGES

Gargellen *Interhome, Skiing Austria*
Schruns *Interhome, Skiing Austria*
Gaschurn *Made to Measure*

TOURIST OFFICE

Montafon
t 722530
info@montafon.at
www.montafon.at

The tourist office is in Schruns, so from elsewhere in Austria add the prefix 05556, from abroad use the prefix +43 5556

lively' après-ski scene. The 3-star Both (726568) is 'very hospitable'. And the 4-star Montafoner Hof (71000) in Tschagguns, near the station, is 'delightful; great food, top wellness/pool', says a 2009 visitor.

Gaschurn / St Gallenkirch

1000m/3,28oft / 900m/2,95oft

These villages share the biggest lift and piste network in the valley. As a result, German cars fill to overflowing the huge car parks at the valley lift stations. Gaschurn is an attractive place to stay.

The two main resorts here are quite different. Whereas St Gallenkirch is strung along the main road and spoiled by traffic, Gaschurn is a pleasant village, bypassed by the valley traffic, with the wood-shingled Posthotel Rössle (8333) in the centre.

The lift network covers two parallel ridges running north-south, with most of the runs on their east- and west-facing flanks. The slopes are accessed from three points along the valley. A gondola from Gaschurn (prone to peak-season queues) takes you up to the east ridge, while another gondola from St Gallenkirch goes up to Valisera on the west ridge. A chairlift to Garfrescha from a roadside station at

Gortipohl, between the resorts, serves its own slopes and gives access to the central valley. Snowmaking covers almost half the area, including runs down to two valley stations.

This is generally the most challenging area in the valley, with as many red as blue runs, and some nominal blacks. Most of the slopes are above the treeline, typically offering a modest 300m/98oft vertical. There is lots of off-piste potential, including steep (and quite dangerous) slopes down into the central valley. The map shows seven 'ski tour' routes – completely unexplained, of course.

The NovaPark terrain park features a half-pipe and boardercross course.

There are lots of mountain restaurants, many impressive in different ways. At the top of the east ridge, the state-of-the-art Nova Stoba can seat over 1,500 people in various spaces, including splendid panelled rooms with table service. The big terrace bar gets seriously boisterous in the afternoons. At the top of the other ridge is the splendidly woody Valisera Hüsli ('great food'). The Zur Brez'n and the Lammhütta on run 1a down to Gaschurn are also worth trying.

In the evening, Fischer's Fritz (at Gortipohl) is a quiet restaurant and the Heuboda disco bar 'lively'. And the Brunellawirt has live music at 6pm on Saturdays.

Phone numbers
From elsewhere in Austria, add the prefix 05557 (Gargellen), 05556 (Schruns), 05558 (Gaschurn); from abroad, use the prefix +43 and omit the initial '0'

TOURIST OFFICES

Gargellen
t 6303
info@gargellen.at
www.gargellen.at

Schruns
t 721660
info@schruns-tschagguns.at
www.schruns-tschagguns.at

Gaschurn
t 82010
info@gaschurn-partenen.com
www.gaschurn-partenen.com

Interactive resort shortlist builder at www.wtss.co.uk

Westendorf

This cute little village has access to a vast amount of terrain and should start attracting a lot more keen intermediates

➕ Charming traditional village, with jolly if rather limited après-ski

➕ Now a proper part of the extensive SkiWelt circuit, also with access to Kitzbühel's slopes

➕ Slopes highest in the SkiWelt area

➕ Good local beginners' slopes, but ...

➖ Local slopes are mainly of genuine red gradient, with easier runs for novices to progress to confined to the lower mountain

➖ Access to Kitzbühel depends on a (short) valley bus ride

➖ Appallingly inadequate piste map

Cute little Westendorf must be a contender for the 'most improved resort in the world' award. Four years ago the resort was effectively linked to Kitzbühel; last season a new gondola from Brixen completed the link to the SkiWelt – the mega area between Söll and Brixen with which it has long shared a lift pass. If you overlook a short bus ride on the Kitzbühel side, you could say Westendorf is now at the heart of one of the biggest lift-linked ski areas in the Alps. It's undoubtedly the best place to stay for exploring both areas in a week.

THE RESORT

Westendorf is a small, pretty village near Brixen im Thale. It is now linked by a piste down to Brixen and a gondola back up, providing direct connections with the SkiWelt. Getting to Kitzbühel (covered by the regional Kitzbüheler Alpen All Star pass) still involves a short bus ride.

Village charm Westendorf was once declared 'Europe's most beautiful village' in a floral competition. The main street is charming, with an attractive onion-domed church.

Convenience The centre is close to the nursery slopes and a five minute walk or free ski-bus ride from the main gondola.

Scenery A wide sunny valley contrasts with gentle, quite shady mountains.

THE MOUNTAINS

The local slopes are separated by valleys from the main SkiWelt circuit to the north and from the Kitzbühel slopes to the east.

The piste map is the general SkiWelt one, which is awful – see Söll chapter for more on this.

Slopes A two-stage gondola takes you to Talkaser, from which you can progress to the further peaks of Fleiding and Gampenkogel. The latter is the start of the lovely long blue run (about 800m/2,625ft vertical) down to the valley for the bus to Skirast and the Kitzbühel lifts. Or you can ski from either the gondola mid- or top stations down to the mid- or bottom stations of the new Choralmbahn and take it up to Choralpe for the splendid 5.5km/3.5 miles long red run to Brixen (over 1000m/3,280ft vertical). All the local peaks have other short runs, mostly facing east or west. One main north-west-facing red run goes back to the resort (with blue options on the lower half). There's weekly floodlit skiing. The free Skiline system (see 'News') allows you to track the lifts you take and the vertical you do – and estimates the distance you ski.

Fast lifts Two new gondolas have vastly improved access.

Queues Until now queues have been rare. But if the new gondola from Brixen attracts more people that may change – reports welcome.

Terrain parks There's an excellent

For 2008/09 Westendorf was properly linked to the SkiWelt by a new gondola from Brixen to Choralpe. A new red run from there down to Brixen opened the previous season. At the end of it, a moving carpet followed by a solar-powered rope tow take you to the gondola up to Hochbrixen. The link to Choralpe has been improved, with another new gondola (the Choralmbahn), which starts at the bottom of a new run.

Also for 2008/09 a new Skiline system was introduced. It tracks your progress around the SkiWelt, measures the vertical and estimates the distance you do – you can see it by entering your ski pass number on the SkiWelt website.

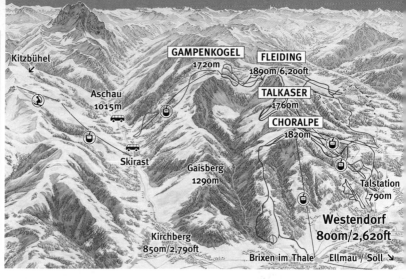

Kitzbühel
GAMPENKOGEL 1720m
FLEIDING 1890m/6,200ft
Aschau 1015m
TALKASER 1760m
CHORALPE 1820m
Skirast
Gaisberg 1290m
Talstation 790m
Westendorf 800m/2,620ft
Kirchberg 850m/2,790ft
Brixen im Thale **Ellmau / Söll ↘**

UK PACKAGES

Inghams, Simply Alpine, Skiing Austria, Snowscape, Thomson

Phone numbers
From elsewhere in Austria add the prefix 05334; from abroad use the prefix +43 5334

TOURIST OFFICES

Westendorf
t 6230
westendorf@
kitzbuehel-alpen.com
www.kitzbuehel-alpen.com

SkiWelt
www.skiwelt.at

terrain park with something for all levels – jumps, boxes, kickers, rails and a half-pipe (www.boardplay.com).
Snow reliability Westendorf's snow reliability is a bit better than some other SkiWelt resorts and nearly all of its pistes now have snowmaking. Grooming is excellent, says one visitor.
Experts The slopes are among the most testing in the SkiWelt area, and we guess it's possible to have a lot of fun off-piste with a guide.
Intermediates Nearly all the local terrain is genuinely red in gradient, though some former reds have been reclassified blue. There is no blue option on the top half of the run down to town from the top of the gondola. The rest of the SkiWelt area has lots of easier intermediate runs. And it's easy to access Kitzbühel-Kirchberg.
Beginners The village nursery slopes are extensive and excellent. There are a couple of genuine blues to progress to, but they are on the lower mountain where snow isn't so good.
Snowboarding There are some tedious flat areas at altitude (especially from Choralpe to Talkaser) but most lifts are chairs and gondolas and the park is great.
Cross-country There is a total of 170km/106 miles in the SkiWelt area but snow-cover is erratic.
Mountain restaurants Alpenrosenhütte is woody and warm, with 'good cheese and ham toastie'. The quiet, pleasant Brechhornhaus and the Choralpe are popular. The Gassnerwirt is good.
Schools and guides Both the Westendorf and the Top schools have been praised by reporters.

Families Westendorf sells itself as a family resort. The ski kindergarten takes children from age three.

STAYING THERE

Hotels Of the 4-star hotels the Jakobwirt (6245) and the 'excellent' Schermer (6268) are central; in 2009 we stayed at the small Glockenstuhl (6175) a short walk to the centre with a good wellness centre. Of the dozen 3-stars the Post (6202) is central and 'traditional and charming'. Among more modest guest houses, Haus Wetti (6348) is popular, and away from the church bells. Pension Ingeborg (6577) has been recommended – next to the gondola.
Apartments The Schermerhof apartments (6979) are of good quality.
Eating out Most of the best places are in hotels – the Schermer and Jakobwirt are good. The Wastlhof and Klingler have also been recommended, as has Berggasthof Stimlach (a taxi ride out).
Après-ski Nightlife is quite lively, but it's a small place with limited options. The Liftstüberl, at the bottom of the gondola, and Gerry's Inn on the nursery slope are packed at the end of the day. Bruchtall 'caters for kids too'. The Moskito Cafe Bar has a funky design, live music and theme nights. The Village Pub is very popular, with 'good Irish craic' and Guinness. In's Moment has been recommended for live music. Karat is a smart lounge bar.
Off the slopes There are excursions by rail or bus to Innsbruck and Salzburg. Walks and sleigh rides are very pretty.

Interactive resort shortlist builder at **www.wtss.co.uk**

Zell am See

A real one-off, this: a charming lakeside town, with varied local slopes and a very worthwhile glacier option nearby at Kaprun

£85
RESORT PRICE INDEX

RATINGS

The mountains

Extent	★★
Fast lifts	★★★★
Queues	★★★
Terrain p'ks	★★★
Snow	★★
Expert	★★
Intermediate	★★★
Beginner	★★★
X-country	★★★★
Restaurants	★★★
Schools	★★★
Families	★★

The resort

Charm	★★★★
Convenience	★★★
Scenery	★★★
Eating out	★★★★
Après-ski	★★★★
Off-slope	★★★★

222

NEWS

For 2009/10 a six-pack is to replace the Gipfelbahn triple chair on the back of Schmittenhöhe; the Kettinglift draglift will also be removed. The resort plans to increase snowmaking to 100% cover.

A new children's area is planned at the bottom of the Schüttdorf gondola.

For 2008/09 at the glacier, a 150m/490ft super-pipe opened in the main terrain park.

➕ Pretty, wooded slopes with fine views down to the lake

➕ Lively, but not rowdy, nightlife

➕ Charming old town centre with pretty lakeside setting

➕ Lots to do off the slopes

➕ Huge range of cross-country trails

➕ Kaprun glacier nearby

➕ Varied terrain including a couple of genuine black runs

➖ Sunny, low slopes often have poor conditions, despite snowmaking

➖ Very limited area, especially when lower slopes are in poor shape

➖ Many hotels are distant from the lifts; buses can be crowded

➖ Less suitable for beginners than most small Austrian resorts

➖ The Kaprun glacier gets lengthy queues when it is most needed

Zell am See is not a rustic village like most of its Austrian rivals, but a lakeside summer resort town with a characterful old centre. Its prominence on the UK market probably has more to do with availability of hotel rooms than with the merits of its ski area; it is very limited in extent – it just scrapes into our ★★ category – and shrinks even further when snow low down is poor.

Kaprun is good for a day out or three, though – not only for its Kitzsteinhorn glacier but also for its little local hill, Maiskogel.

THE RESORT

Zell am See is a long-established, year-round resort town set between a large lake and the mountain. About 3km/2 miles south of Zell is Schüttdorf, also with lift access to the hill.

Kaprun's snow-sure glacier slopes are only a few minutes away, but the buses to get there are often crowded; getting on in Schüttdorf can be a particular problem.

There are other resorts nearby. Saalbach is easily reached by bus, Hochkönig less so. Rauris is worth a look. Bad Hofgastein is not far, and you can get trains to Kitzbühel.

VILLAGE CHARM ★★★★
Attractive old centre
Zell has a charming, traffic-free medieval centre occupying a flat promontory. The narrow cobbled streets are lined with traditional buildings, including an attractive old church, shops, cafes and restaurants. Schüttdorf is a characterless and lifeless dormitory, which may outweigh its practical advantages.

CONVENIENCE ★★★
Practical or central
A gondola from the edge of town goes up the southern arm of the horseshoe-shaped Schmittenhöhe mountain; so

far, so good. But two lifts further up, you often face a queue to join the busy gondola up from Schüttdorf. You can avoid this problem by starting from Schüttdorf; or, having ridden the Zell gondola, by descending a black run to the queue-free lifts in Schmittental (in the centre of the horseshoe, 2km/1 mile west of Zell); or

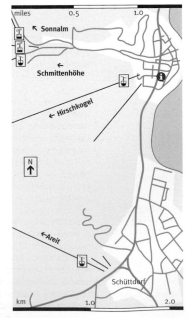

miles   0.5   1.0

↖ Sonnalm

Schmittenhöhe →

← Hirschkogel

N ↑

← Areit

Schüttdorf

km   1.0   2.0

↑ Schmittenhöhe is at the heart of the area (and the top)

EUROPASPORTREGION ZELL AM SEE-KAPRUN

KEY FACTS

Resort	755m
	2,480ft

Zell and Kaprun

Slopes	755-3030m
	2,480-9,940ft
Lifts	54
Pistes	138km
	86 miles
Blue	41%
Red	36%
Black	23%
Snowmaking	70%

Zell (Schmittenhöhe) only

Slopes	755-2000m
	2,480-6,560ft
Lifts	27
Pistes	77km
	48 miles
Snowmaking	88%

Kaprun only

Slopes	785-3030m
	2,580-9,940ft
Lifts	28
Pistes	61km
	38 miles
Snowmaking	46%

you can have a perfectly convenient holiday by choosing one of the few hotels near those lifts. Riding up from Schüttdorf has another advantage: direct access to the Areitalm nursery area and half-pipe.

SCENERY ★★★
Lakes and mountains
Zell am See enjoys a pretty lakeside setting and Schmittenhöhe offers good views down across the lake, with more drama to the south – Kaprun's distinctive Kitzsteinhorn and the much higher Grossglockner beyond that.

THE MOUNTAINS

Zell's horseshoe-shaped mountain is open at the top, mostly densely wooded lower down.

EXTENT OF THE SLOPES ★★
Varied but limited
Gondolas from Zell and Schüttdorf go up along the southern arm of the horseshoe to Schmittenhöhe, meeting the gondola from Schmittental. The several lifts on the back of the hill and on the sunny slopes of the northern arm are accessed via Schmittenhöhe or by riding another cable car from Schmittental to Sonnalm.

Black runs descend from various points to Schmittental; intermediate runs go down the southern arm to Zell and Schüttdorf. The slopes steepen as they descend – it's a red run to Schüttdorf, a black to Zell but with a winding blue alternative.

FAST LIFTS ★★★★
Only one weak area
With the planned upgrade of the Gipfelbahn on the back of the hill for the coming season, Zell has covered nearly all the bases. Only the sunny Sonnkogel sector now relies on slow chairs and draglifts.

QUEUES ★★★
Valley problems easing
Despite the fast lifts, queues to get out of Zell and Schüttdorf have long been a problem. But recent investment has helped, and all our 2009 reports are more positive. The newish gondola from Schmittental has relieved pressure there ('no queuing even in half term'), and the old parallel cable car is due a revamp for 2009/10. Once you are on the mountain, there aren't many problems. When snow is poor there are few daytime queues at Zell – many people are away queueing at Kaprun. And crowded slopes can be a problem there too; one reporter 'gave up and went back to Zell'.

TERRAIN PARKS ★★★
When in Rome ...
Schmittenhöhe has a newly revamped park, Rome Rodeo, by the Glocknerbahn chairlift, with jumps, boxes, rails and various kickers.

SNOW RELIABILITY ★★
Good snowmaking, but sunny
Many of Zell am See's slopes get a lot of sun, and at these altitudes that is bad news. Over 70% of pistes are now

LIFT PASSES

Kaprun–Zell am See

Prices in €

Age	1-day	6-day
under 16	20	96
16 to 18	32	154
over 19	40	192

Free under 6
Senior no deals
Beginner limited pass

Notes
Covers Zell and Kaprun; one-day price is for Schmittenhöhe (Zell) only

Alternative passes
Kitzsteinhorn only and Maiskogel only; Salzburg Super Ski Card covers 22 ski areas in the Salzburg province; Kitzbüheler Alpen All Star Card covers seven ski areas – Kitzbühel, Schneewinkel (St Johann), Ski Welt, Alpbach, Wildschönau, Skicircus Saalbach, Zell-Kaprun

boarding

Zell is well suited to boarders and most lifts are chairs, gondolas or cable cars. You'll also find plenty of life in the evenings. The Kaprun glacier has powder in its wide, open bowl. But it also has a fair proportion of draglifts (though they are gradually being replaced) – a day of this and the 'small walk' to enter the main terrain park exhausted some reporters. Snowboard Academy is a specialist school.

covered by snow-guns, and the resort predicts 100% cover for 2009/10. But holidays can still be marred by slush, ice and bare patches. The Kaprun glacier is oversubscribed when snow is short in the region. Grooming is good.

FOR EXPERTS ★★
Several blacks, but still limited
Zell has more black runs than most resorts this size, but they are not seriously steep and are usually groomed. The winding, shady runs down to Schmittental are great fun if the snow is good, quite challenging if it's hard. Off-piste opportunities are limited, but there is a nice 'glade' area on the back of the hill, under the Gipfelbahn chairlift.

FOR INTERMEDIATES ★★★
Bits and pieces for most grades
Good intermediates have a couple of fine, long runs, but this is not a place for high mileage. The blacks are within a confident intermediate's capability

unless icy. The red home run to Schüttdorf is great when conditions are good, but a struggle for many at the end of a warm day. The wide Sonnkogel runs are relatively quiet – great for carving. The timid can cruise the southern ridge blues.

Kaprun's high, snow-sure glacier runs are also ideal for intermediates.

FOR BEGINNERS ★★★
Two low nursery areas
There are small, sometimes crowded, nursery slopes at Schmittental and at Schüttdorf – both covered by snow-guns. There are short, easy runs at Schmittenhöhe, Areitalm and Breiteckalm (some used by complete beginners when snow conditions are poor, but it means buying a lift pass).

FOR CROSS-COUNTRY ★★★★
Excellent if snow allows
The valley floor has extensive areas and at altitude there are short loops, above Zell and on the Kitzsteinhorn,

SCHOOLS

Zell am See
t 56020
Sport Alpin
t 0664 453 1417
Snowboard Academy
t 0664 253 0381
Outdo
t 70165
AllMountain
t 0664 787 5713

Classes
(Zell prices)
5 days (2hr am and
pm) €159
Private lessons
€58 for 1hr; €10 for
each additional
person

GUIDES

Ski Safari
t 0664 336 1487

CHILDCARE

Kinderskiwelt Areit
t 56020
From age 2; with ski
lessons for over 3s
Babysitter list
At the tourist office

Ski schools
From age 4 (5 days
€159 – Zell price)

GETTING THERE

Air Salzburg 80km/
50 miles (1hr30);
Munich 215km/
135 miles (3hr30)

Rail Station in resort

making a total of 33km/20 miles, with 18km/11 miles on the Kaprun golf course. There are specialist centres at Schüttdorf and at Kaprun.

MOUNTAIN RESTAURANTS ★★★
Plenty of little refuges
Zell has plenty of cosy, atmospheric huts, helpfully named on the piste map. But some of them can get crowded – notably restaurants around Areitalm. Among the best is the Breiteckalm, on the Panorama run from Schmittenhöhe – 'excellent, varied food', says a 2009 visitor. Blaickner's Sonnalm has a log fire and 'good service'. The Ebenbergalm and the Berghotel are worth a visit.

SCHOOLS AND GUIDES ★★★
A wide choice
There is a choice of schools. Groups may be quite large, but reports are generally positive. A 2009 visitor says, 'My daughter went from "zero to hero" in five days thanks to a wonderful young instructor.' The Outdo school gets a rave review in 2009 for both group and private lessons: 'the best school I have dealt with over the years; very attentive, good instruction'. And the Sport Alpin is similarly praised.

FOR FAMILIES ★★
Schüttdorf's the place
There isn't a great deal of particular interest to families. But staying in Schüttdorf has the advantage of direct gondola access to the Areitalm snow-kindergarten. And a new children's area is due to open at the bottom of that gondola for 2009/10. We have no recent reports on childcare.

STAYING THERE

Lots of hotels, pensions and apartments.
Hotels A broad range of hotels (more 4- than 3-stars) and guest houses.
★★★★★Salzburgerhof (7650) Best in town; pool. It's nearer the lake than the gondola, but has a courtesy bus.
★★★★Feinschmeck (725490) Fine traditional hotel in the pedestrian core of Zell. Newly renovated.
★★★★Freiberg (72643) 'Fantastic – great views, excellent food, service and spa,' says a 2008 visitor. Lakeside setting, with minibus to the lifts.
★★★★Lebzelter (7760) In pedestrian area. 'Good sports bar, but basic

rooms for a 4-star,' says a 2009 visitor.
★★★★Romantik (72520) Good location. 'Comfortable, good food and service.'
★★★★Schloss Prielau (72911) Converted castle on the outskirts of town, but with a shuttle-bus service. Highly rated by a 2008 visitor.
★★★★Tirolerhof (7720) In the old town. New spa centre. Pool. 'Wonderful, friendly,' says a 2009 report.
★★★★Zum Hirschen (7740) Comfortable. Easy walk to Zell gondola. Sauna, steam room, splash pool, popular bar.
★★★Margarete (72724) B&B at Schmittental, by the cable cars.
★★Haus Wilhelmina (72607) B&B, convenient for the town gondola.
Apartments Lots of options. Lederer is close to the Ebenberg lift.
At altitude As well as the Berghotel (72489) at Schmittenhöhe, the Breiteckalm (73419), Blaikner's Sonnalm (73262) and Pinzgauer Hütte (53472) restaurants have rooms.

EATING OUT ★★★★
Plenty of choice
Zell has more non-hotel options than is usual in a small Austrian resort. Mayer's beside the Schloss Prielau hotel is 'amazing but pricey', which is what you expect with two Michelin stars. Kupferkessel and Traubenstüberl have good regional dishes. There are Italian and Chinese restaurants in Zell, and Schüttdorf has a Chinese.

APRES-SKI ★★★★
Plenty for all tastes
There are plenty of cafes, bars and discos. Start at the top of the slopes at the Berghotel – where the ice bar has a good vibe, live music and dancing. The Lounge Bar at Schüttdorf has 'comfy sofas, good beers'. In town, Pinzgauer Diele club rocks too – 'younger crowd but fun'. Flannigan's Irish bar was a good choice for a 2009 reporter's 20ish kids. Villa Crazy Daisy is popular. The B17 Hangar bar has 'cracking cocktails and a party buzz'. Two 2008 visitors enjoyed the 'trendy' Insider bar. The Ginhouse and cave-like Lebzelter Keller sports bar are quieter venues.

OFF THE SLOPES ★★★★
Lots of choices
There is plenty to do in this year-round resort. The train trip to Salzburg is a must, and Kitzbühel is also well worth a visit. You can often walk across the frozen lake to

UK PACKAGES

BoardnLodge, Crystal, Crystal Finest, Directski.com, Erna Low, First Choice, Independent Ski Links, Inghams, Interactive Resorts, Interhome, Neilson, Simply Alpine, Ski Freshtracks, Skiing Austria, Ski Line, Ski McNeill, Skitracer, Snow Finders, STC, Thomson **Kaprun** *Crystal, Crystal Finest, Directski.com, Esprit, First Choice, Interactive Resorts, Interhome, Neilson, Simply Alpine, Skiing Austria, Ski Line, Ski McNeill, Skitracer, Snow Finders, STC, Thomson*

ACTIVITIES

Indoor Swimming, sauna, solarium, massage, fitness centre, tennis, squash, museums, cinema, gallery, library

Outdoor Ice rink, curling, walking, tobogganing, horse riding, plane flights, sleigh rides, snow kiting, paragliding

Phone numbers
From elsewhere in Austria add the prefix 06542 (Zell), 06547 (Kaprun); from abroad use the prefix +43 and omit the initial '0'

TOURIST OFFICE

Zell am See/Kaprun
t 770
welcome@zellamsee-kaprun.com
www.zellamsee-kaprun.com

Thumersbach; there are marked paths up at Schmittenhöhe, too. Plus there are good sports facilities, a motor museum, sleigh rides, Alpine flights and you can watch ice hockey.

Kaprun 785m/2,580ft

THE RESORT
Apart from providing Zell's snow guarantee, Kaprun is a worthwhile destination in its own right.
Village charm The village centre is a pleasant and quite lively place, with a pretty church and bypassed by the road up to the glacier.
Convenience The village sprawls over a considerable area, so it's worth picking your spot with care.
Scenery The high glacier slopes give great views down the valley to Zell.

THE MOUNTAIN
There is a small area of easy intermediate slopes on the outskirts of the village at Maiskogel. Most of the slopes – blue, red and black runs – are served by a six-pack from mid-mountain, reached by a fast quad. There is also a separate nursery area. You can pass a quiet day here when weather affects the glacier. But most people will want to spend their time on the glacier, which is what the remarks that follow relate to. The local lift pass covers only one ascent of the Kitzsteinhorn access gondola per day.
Slopes A 15-person, two-stage gondola goes up to the Alpincenter at the base of the Kitzsteinhorn's main slopes. The first stage runs parallel to an older eight-seat gondola and the second stage parallel to a fast quad chair. The main slopes are in a big bowl above the Alpincenter, served by a cable car, lots of T-bars and four chairs (including a six-pack). The area above the top of the Alpincenter is open in summer and is particularly good for an early pre-Christmas or late post-Easter break.
Fast lifts There is fast lift access from the valley to the top of the glacier, but there are still lots of T-bars.
Queues There are more likely to be queues here than not, though one lucky visitor reports few problems on his March 2008 visit. High winds may shut the top lifts, increasing crowds lower down the slopes – when it may be worth trying Maiskogel's quieter slopes.
Terrain parks There are three parks

and a new super-pipe. The main Gletscher Park is open all year round.
Snow reliability Snow is nearly always good because of the glacier. And there's snowmaking too.
Mountain restaurants There's a decent choice. One of the best is the Gletschermühle near the Alpincenter, which has a 'good selection'. The Krefelder Hütte below it is a genuine mountain refuge. For fine views, try Bella Vista at the top of the glacier.
Experts There's little to challenge experts on-piste – the blacks are not steep, and groomed when we last visited – but some good off-piste possibilities.
Intermediates Pistes are mainly gentle blues and reds, and make for great easy cruising. From Alpincenter there is an entertaining red run down to the gondola mid-station, away from the lifts. There's a good unpisted ski route.
Beginners There are two nursery slopes in the village and some gentle blues on the glacier to progress to.
Snowboarding Intermediates and better will love the wide open powder bowl. Beginners may find there are too many T-bars for their liking.
Cross-country The 18km/11 miles of trails on the Kaprun golf course are good, but at altitude there is just one short loop – at the top of the glacier.
Schools and guides There are several.
Families Nothing special, but all the schools offer children's classes and there's a kindergarten in the village.

STAYING THERE
There are some catered chalets and chalet hotels. The Dorfkrug apartments are recommended ('cosy, traditional').
Hotels The 4-star Sonnblick (8301) has 'spacious rooms, good pool' and 'crucially the best food ever', says a 2009 reporter. The Tauernhof (8235) and 3-star Mitteregger (8207) are other tips. There are igloos to stay in at the Volvo Ice Camp on the glacier.
Eating out Good restaurants include the Dorfstadl, Hilberger's Beisl and Schlemmerstube.
Après-ski There are a few good bars, often with music. Try the Baum bar or Kitsch & Bitter. A reporter recommends the Volvo Ice bar by the terrain parks – an outdoor music camp and cafe.
Off the slopes There's a sports centre with outdoor rapids, bowling at the Sportsbar, and the adventure park on the Nagelkopfel at Piesendorf is 'worth an evening out'.

Zugspitz Arena

Half a dozen family-friendly little resorts sharing a lift pass and (to a degree) proximity to the spectacular Zugspitze

Zugspitz Arena is the name adopted by a group of small villages in the Tirol just to the west of Zugspitze, peak of the mighty Wetterstein massif which forms the border with Germany (Garmisch-Partenkirchen lies on the other side). They appeal particularly to families, who will be happy with limited and mainly gentle ski areas. There is the bonus of genuinely spectacular scenery.

NEWS

There are plans to install a new lift, Gamsalmbahn, in Ehrwald's Wetterstein sector for 2009/10. A new blue piste was created there for 2008/09. The Schnee Express is a new free rail service between the Zugspitz Arena and Garmisch.

The view of the Wetterstein massif from Lermoos is quite something. At its foot is Ehrwald, with its Wetterstein slopes in clear view and Ehrwalder Alm tucked up the valley on the right ↓

Three of the Zugspitz Arena villages – Ehrwald, Lermoos and Biberwier – sit around the edge of a little plain, the Lermooser Moos, from which the Wetterstein massif rises dramatically 2000m/6,560ft to the peak of the Zugspitze. There is skiing on the Zugspitze itself (on glacier slopes on the German side of the border, and accessible via a spectacular cable car from the Austrian side), and each of the villages has its local slopes too. The other villages operating under the Zugspitz Arena banner – Berwang and Bichlbach – are a few miles to the west of the Moos.

The Zugspitz Arena lift pass covers 52 lifts and 147km/91 miles of pistes. There is also a more extensive pass – the Happy Ski Card – which also covers Garmisch (on the German side of the Zugspitze) and Seefeld. Garmisch has its own lifts up to the Zugspitze (including a cog railway), and challenging slopes lower down on the shady side of the Wetterstein massif. See our new Garmisch chapter.

There are also over 100km/62 miles of cross-country trails in the Zugspitz Arena area, with the potential to string together some long days. And 60km/37 miles of cleared footpaths.

Ehrwald 1000m/3,280ft

Ehrwald is a pleasant village set right under the towering western wall of the Wetterstein massif, with easy access to three small ski areas.

There are two separate ski areas starting at valley level – Wetterstein and Ehrwalder Alm.

The mainly gentle **Wetterstein** slopes are accessed by draglifts from the village fringes, linking to the main Wetterstein triple chairlift, slightly further out. The runs total only 22km/14 miles, with a top height of 1530m/5,020ft and a longest run of under 500m/1,640ft vertical. There's a 120m/390ft half-pipe. Although it's a tiny area, there are three restaurants, all with some après-ski animation.

The more rewarding **Ehrwalder Alm** slopes on the sunny side of the Wetterstein massif are accessed by an eight-seat gondola starting just outside the village. At the heart of the area is a broad, gentle nursery slope with several drags. From here a slow chair crosses a steep rocky mountainside to access good open red and blue slopes, one of which goes on into the woods to the Gaistal six-pack. The longer Ganghofer six-pack starts lower down the mountain and serves two genuine red runs and some winding blue variants. There's a blue run back down the gondola. The lifts and runs are quite short – typically 300m to 400m vertical – but from the top there's a run of 7km/4 miles (and over 800m/2,620ft vertical) to the base. The runs total 26km/16 miles, mostly blue. Half the area has snowmaking, including the valley run.

The terrain park in the centre of the slopes has easy, medium and pro lines of rails, boxes and kickers.

A couple of miles outside the village in the opposite direction, a spectacular cable car climbs an impressive 1725m/5,660ft up to the

KEY FACTS

Resorts	990-1340m
	3,250-4,400ft
Slopes	990-2960m
	3,250-9,710ft
Lifts	52
Pistes	147km
	91 miles
Blue	55%
Red	40%
Black	5%
Snowmaking	51%

peak of the **Zugspitze**, on the border with Germany. The Zugspitze is not remarkably high by Austrian standards, but it is the highest mountain in Germany and a major tourist attraction, with a museum at the peak as well as a restaurant. At the top, take an internal lift up, walk across into Germany, take another lift down and finally another cable car down to the glacial slopes of the Zugspitzplatt. This is a good area, and much better than the Ehrwald piste map suggests (get hold of the much more useful Garmisch map). There's more detail on the slopes in our Garmisch chapter.

There are two ski schools, Ehrwald Total and Intersport Tiroler.

The village spreads over a wide area but does have a pleasant central core around the church and a little open park nearby. Accommodation is dominated by 4-star hotels, but there are plenty of cheaper alternatives.

Twice a week the 3.6km/2 mile home run from Ehrwalder Alm is floodlit for evening tobogganing, and the restaurants at the top and halfway down are kept open.

The Zugspitz Arena FamilienBad is a big, bright leisure centre with multiple pools, gym and massage.

Lermoos 1005m/3,300ft

Directly across the Moos from the Zugspitze, Lermoos and its slopes – arguably the best in the Zugspitz Arena area – offer great views of the dramatic Zugspitze.
Lermoos has lifts on the north-east-facing slopes of Grubigstein, a mainly wooded peak rising about 1000m/3,280ft above the village. The top

height of 2060m/6,760ft, shady orientation and snowmaking on about two-thirds of the slopes means that (apart from the glacial Zugspitze) this is the most snow-sure of the local areas. The slopes total 33km/21 miles.

Fast lifts from both ends of the village converge at mid-mountain. From here a single chairlift goes almost to the top. The more popular alternative is a fast quad leading to the main lift, a six-pack. This goes up over an extraordinary area of gigantic ready-made moguls – great fun for kids, given good snow – and serves a short but good red run and a winding blue as well as accessing further runs on a double chair and a long run back to the mid-station. This is an excellent descent, with a decent black variant part-way down. The runs below mid-mountain are worthwhile, given good snow; you can descend the whole mountain, top to bottom, on red or blue runs. There are nursery slopes just above the village and at mid-mountain. Bizarrely, Lermoos relies on the sketchy Zugspitz Arena piste map.

Lermoos is a slightly more compact, towny place than Ehrwald, more tightly focused on the main street running through it. This was an important thoroughfare until Fernpass traffic was banished to a tunnel in the 1980s, and is still far from traffic-free

There are several 3-star hotels, but notably two 'superior' 4-star hotels, which are quite different in style but equally impressive, and each a short walk from an access lift. The hotel Post (22810) is an ancient inn, greatly expanded over the years and entirely revamped in opulent fashion a few years back. It now offers 76 suites,

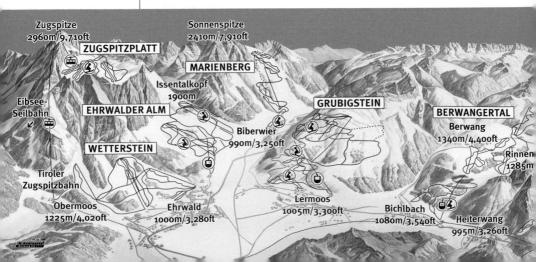

and the facilities include a swanky 2,000m² spa, rated highly by our spa specialist. The terrace has the perfect view across the Moos to the Zugspitze. We found the food and service excellent. The Leading Family Hotel & Resort Alpenrose (2424) is an amazing place for families, but its facilities also include a cool, stylish wine bar, the Wine Lounge. There are traditional alternatives in the village, and a very non-traditional one – the American-style, youth-oriented Bar Wetterloch.

At Grubigalm (1710m/5,610ft) there's a fun park (called NTC) with tubing, snow scooters and various other diversions. A 3km/2 mile toboggan run goes from Brettalm (1330m/4,360ft) to the valley. There's skating and curling on a natural open-air rink.

Biberwier 990m/3,250ft

The third of the villages around the Moos, Biberwier is set in the valley leading up to the Fernpass, with its own small area of slopes.
The mainly shady Marienberg slopes total 14km/9 miles, more or less equally split into blue and red, with over a third protected by snowmaking. A six-pack serves a long blue slope at the bottom; a double chair up to 1675m/5,500ft serves red runs and a ski route above that; and on the back of the hill a drag serves a sunny slope from the top height of 1880m/6,170ft. Back at the base, the beginner lifts include an exceptionally long magic carpet. There's a boardercross course, half-pipe, and an NTC fun park as at Lermoos. At altitude there are a couple of pleasant restaurants, and an umbrella bar next to the nursery slopes.

Like Lermoos, the village benefits from the tunnel keeping Fernpass traffic out of the centre. The best base is the solid old gasthof Goldenen-Löwen (2293). There's a curling rink.

Bichlbach 1080m/3,540ft

Bichlbach is a quiet valley village with fast lift access to the slopes of higher Berwang (described next).
On the fringes of Bichlbach, the Tirol's first hybrid chair/gondola lift goes up to Hochalm (1610m/5,280ft), for access to Berwang. You can ski to it from the top of the village nursery slope. There's a short, easy toboggan run, and a natural open air ice rink.

Berwang 1340m/4,400ft

Berwang is a quiet village tucked away in a slightly elevated valley, about 350m/1,150ft higher than the other villages in the region. It claims the most skiing, but most of the runs are short as well as easy.
The slopes total 40km/25 miles, making this the most extensive network in the area on paper.

The village enjoys a splendid winter-wonderland setting, with lifts rising on two sides, and slopes running down the very gentle valley. It looks an attractive place for a quiet family holiday, although some of the accommodation is quite a walk from the lifts. On the sunny side, the Sonnalmbahn quad chair goes up to Hochalm where it meets the chondola up from Bichlbach; the shady runs to Bichlbach are about the best in the local area, giving over 500m/1,640ft vertical to the lift base station. All the runs from Hochalm have snowmaking. Across the village, drags go up the shady side. Runs down the valley dropping only about 50m/164ft in 1.5km/1 mile bring you to further lifts, including the Panoramabahn double chairlift to the area high-point at 1740m/5,710ft. From here there are runs of 450m/1,480ft vertical to Rinnen, and ski routes to Brand. There are plenty of huts on the slopes.

The cross-country loops up here (totalling 25km/16 miles) are separate from those down in the main valley, and look a bit more challenging.

There are three 4-star hotels, four 3-stars and lots of guest houses. The 4-star Kaiserhof (8285) is a giant family-oriented chalet-style place with pools and spa. There's a 1.5km/1 mile toboggan run dropping 120m/390ft from Jägerhaus to Berwang, open most evenings; and skating and curling on a natural open-air rink. There are lots of local footpaths.

Heiterwang 995m/3,260ft

Another valley-level base for access to the Berwang slopes.
Heiterwang is a little way down the valley from Bichlbach, a short drive or bus ride from the chondola up to the Berwang slopes. It's near a sizeable lake and is a major cross-country centre (venue for the 2006 Austrian championships). There are a couple of short local downhill slopes, too.

France

Over one-third of British skiers and snowboarders choose France for their holidays each year, almost double the number who go to Austria, the next most popular country. It's not difficult to see what attracts us to France. The country has the biggest lift and piste networks in the world; for those who like to cover as many miles in a day as possible, these are unrivalled. Most of these big areas are also at high altitude, ensuring high-quality snow for a long season. The best of them have state-of-the-art lift systems, too – but it's a myth that all French lift systems are wonderfully efficient. In quite a few areas, the draglift and the slow chairlift still dominate.

On the other hand, French resort villages don't all conform to the standard image of soulless, purpose-built service stations, thrown up without concern for appearance during the boom of the 1960s and 1970s. We come back to this theme below. Many French resorts are now distinctly lively in the evening – a great change over the last 20 years. But there is no real sign of French resorts developing the on-mountain afternoon party scene that is so common in Austria, and for some people that counts for a lot.

Many people who visited major French resorts last season, when the pound reached parity with the euro, were shocked by on-the-spot prices – and our Resort Price Index survey confirmed that the big-name French resorts were the most expensive in the Alps. For next season we must hope that restaurants in these resorts will moderate their prices – aided by the hefty VAT cut in July 2009 – and that the current slight recovery in the value of the pound is maintained. Bear in mind that lots of British tour operators run chalets in France: staying in a chalet means that at least you don't have to worry about the cost of wine with dinner.

ANY STYLE OF RESORT YOU LIKE

The main drawback to France, hinted at above, is the monstrous architecture of some of the purpose-built resorts. But not all French resorts are hideous. Certainly, France has its fair share of Alpine eyesores, chief among them central Les Menuires, central La Plagne, Flaine, Tignes, Isola 2000 and Les Arcs. But all these places have learned from past mistakes, and newer developments there are being built in a much more attractive, traditional chalet style. In Les Menuires, they have even knocked down a couple of the original hideous buildings (as we advised them to do over a decade ago) and replaced them with tasteful wood and stone structures. The later generation of purpose-built resorts, such as Valmorel, La Rosière, La Tania and Arc 1950 have been built in much more sympathetic style.

If you prefer, there are genuinely old mountain villages to stay in, linked directly to the big lift networks. These are not usually as convenient for the slopes, but they give you a feel of being in France rather than in a winter-holiday factory. Examples include Montchavin or Champagny for La Plagne, Vaujany for Alpe-d'Huez, St-Martin-de-Belleville for the Trois Vallées, and Morillon or Samoëns for Flaine. There are also old villages with their own slopes that have developed as resorts while retaining at least some of their

← Woodland skiing isn't exactly typical of France, but it's well worth having some on hand for bad weather days. This is Les Houches, which acts as the main bad-weather option for the Chamonix valley

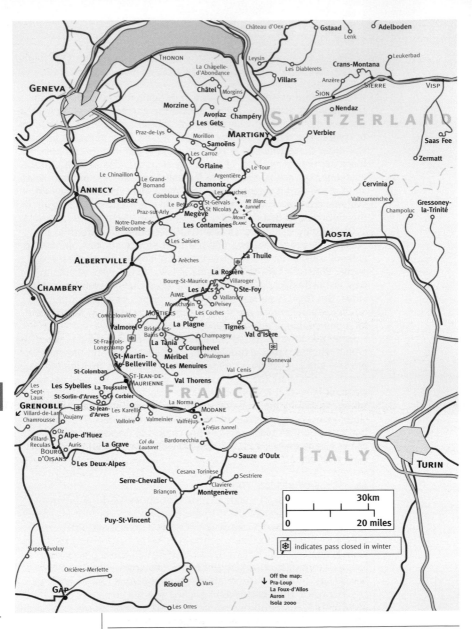

Getting around the French Alps

Pick the right gateway as your initial target – Geneva, Chambéry or Grenoble – and you can hardly go wrong. The only high pass is on the approach to Serre-Chevalier and Montgenèvre – the 2060m/6,760ft Col du Lauteret; but the road is a major one and kept clear of snow or reopened quickly after a fall (or you can fly to Turin and avoid that pass). Crossing the French-Swiss border between Chamonix and Verbier involves two closure-prone passes – the Montets and the Forclaz. When necessary, one-way traffic runs beside the tracks through the rail tunnel beneath the passes.

rustic ambience – such as Serre-Chevalier and La Clusaz.

Two other resorts – neighbours with a shared regional lift pass, as it happens – deserve a special mention. Megève is an exceptionally charming little town combining rustic style with sophistication; when weather bounces off nearby Mont Blanc and dumps on the low-altitude wooded slopes here, there is nowhere to beat it. And then there is Chamonix, a big, bustling town sitting literally in the shadow of Mont Blanc, Europe's highest peak, and the centre of the most radical off-piste terrain in the Alps.

PLAT DU JOUR

France has advantages over some rival destinations in the gastronomic stakes. Table service in mountain restaurants is common, and most places do at least a plat du jour that is in a different league from what you'll find in Austria or North America. In the evening, most resorts have restaurants serving good traditional French food as well as regional specialities.

IMPROVING APARTMENTS

One of the most welcome developments on the French resort scene in recent years has been the availability of genuinely comfortable and stylish apartments, in contrast to the cramped and, frankly, primitive places that have dominated the market since the 1960s. Our luxury apartments chapter is largely about this new generation of French apartments, which have opened up self-catering holidays to people who previously would not have contemplated them.

STELLAR HOTELS

The French, of course, like doing things their own way, and up to now have rated hotels using a system unlike any other, with only four stars. But no more: with very little fuss, the body responsible announced in June that they would henceforth use a five-star scale. At the same time, they announced a list of a dozen hotels that were the first to ascend to the new category – and no less than half of them are in Courchevel 1850.

PERFECT PISTES

France remains unusual among European countries in rating pistes on a four-point scale. The very easiest runs are classified green; except in Val d'Isère, they are reliably gentle. This is a genuinely helpful system, which ought to be used more widely. Some French resorts, sadly, make little use of it – notably Les Arcs and La Plagne.

DRIVING AMBITION?

The French Alps are easy to get to by car. In our features section there is a chapter on driving to the French Alps – still very popular, despite the growth of the budget airlines, especially with people going self-catering. As smart apartments become more common, the self-catering by car formula becomes more attractive.

AVOID THE CROWDS

French school holidays mean crowded slopes, so they are worth avoiding. The country is divided into three zones, with fortnight holidays staggered between 6 February and 7 March 2010. Avoid particularly the week beginning 13 February (both Marseille and Lyon on holiday) and the following week (Lyon and Paris).

Introduction

Interactive resort shortlist builder at **www.wtss.co.uk**

Alpe-d'Huez

Impressive and sunny slopes above a hotchpotch of a purpose-built village, but with attractive alternative bases

£105
RESORT PRICE INDEX

RATINGS

The mountains

Extent	★★★★
Fast lifts	★★
Queues	★★★★
Terrain p'ks	★★★
Snow	★★★★
Expert	★★★★
Intermediate	★★★★
Beginner	★★★★★
X-country	★★★
Restaurants	★★★★
Schools	★★★★
Families	★★★

The resort

Charm	★★
Convenience	★★★★
Scenery	★★★★
Eating out	★★★★
Après-ski	★★★★
Off-slope	★★★★

NEWS

For 2009/10 a six-pack with covers is planned to replace the first stage of the Marmottes gondola. A new blue slope from the arrival point will run to the mid-station of the DMC. More snowmaking is planned.

For 2008/09 two new runs were created, including a red alternative to the black runs from Clocher de Macle.

+ Extensive, high, sunny slopes, split interestingly into different sectors

+ Huge snowmaking installation

+ Vast, gentle, sunny nursery slopes

+ Efficient access lifts from villages

+ Some good mountain restaurants

+ Livelier than many French resorts

+ Pleasant alternative bases in outlying villages and satellites

− Some main intermediate runs get badly overcrowded in high season

− Many of the tough runs are very high, and closed in bad weather

− Practically no woodland runs to retreat to in bad weather

− Lots of south-facing runs that can be icy early and slushy later

− Sprawling resort

There are few places to rival Alpe-d'Huez and its Massif des Grandes Rousses for extent and variety of terrain – in good wintery conditions it's one of our favourites. But as the season progresses the effects of the strong southern sun become more and more of a problem. You can stay in the sprawling village of Alpe-d'Huez or in the smaller alternative bases of Vaujany, Villard-Reculas, Oz-en-Oisans or Auris-en-Oisans, which are described at the end of this chapter.

THE RESORT

Alpe-d'Huez is a large, modern resort on a high, open, sunny mountainside east of Grenoble. Although developed for skiing, it has grown in a seemingly unplanned, sprawling fashion.

The resort spreads down a gentle slope in a triangular shape from the main lift station at the top corner. Access roads enter the village at the two lower corners, west and east.

The 'reliable' bus service around the resort is free with the lift pass, and during the day there's a bucket-lift (with a piste beneath it) running through the resort to the main lifts. This is handy but slow, and some people don't like jumping on and off.

Outings by road are feasible to other resorts covered on a week's lift pass, including Serre-Chevalier and Les Deux-Alpes. A helicopter does day trips to Les Deux-Alpes (only 65 euros) and a bus goes twice a week (must book).

VILLAGE CHARM ★★
Bit of a hotchpotch

The nearest thing to a central focus is the main Avenue des Jeux in the middle, with an ice rink, indoor-outdoor swimming pool, shops, bars and restaurants. The buildings come in all shapes, sizes and designs but most new development is now in a pleasant chalet-style. Reporters have remarked on the warm welcome from the locals.

CONVENIENCE ★★★★
Good in clusters

Two satellite 'quarters' are a bit of a trek from the centre but with their own lifts, bars and restaurants. Les Bergers is at the eastern entrance to the resort; a chalet suburb is expanding this quarter uphill – convenient for skiing but even more remote from the village centre. L'Eclose is to the south of the main village. You can also stay down the hill in the old village of Huez, linked by lift to the resort.

SCENERY ★★★★
Glorious gorge, splendid views

The resort has a fabulous high setting on a sunny plateau. There are splendid views to the southern Alps and pretty Sarenne Gorge from Pic Blanc.

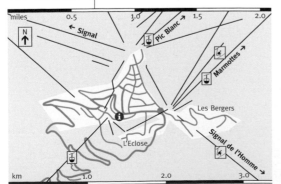

↑ Almost all the slopes are above the treeline, with easy slopes near the bottom and steeper stuff higher up

OT ALPE-D'HUEZ / FRANCOIS MAIRE

LIFT PASSES

Visalp

Prices in €

Age	1-day	6-day
under 13	29	145
13 to 59	39	203
over 60	33	173

Free under 5, over 72
Beginner four free lifts

Notes
Covers all lifts in Alpe-d'Huez, Auris, Oz, Vaujany and Villard-Reculas; half-day passes; discounts for families and regular visitors; 2-day-plus passes cover sports centre, ice rink, swimming pools, concerts, two museums; 6-day-plus passes allow one day's skiing at each of Serre-Chevalier, Puy-St-Vincent and the Milky Way in Italy, and two days in Les Deux-Alpes

Alternative passes
Auris only, Oz-Vaujany only, Villard-Reculas only

THE MOUNTAINS

Alpe-d'Huez is a big-league resort, ranking alongside giants such as Val d'Isère or La Plagne for the extent and variety of its slopes. Practically all the slopes are above the treeline, and so there may be little to do when a storm socks in. Because of the weather, no lifts above 2100m/6,890ft were working on our two-day visit in 2008.

Reporters find the piste grading very unreliable and we received another tirade of complaints in 2009: 'a lot of the reds should be marked black', 'some reds should be blue and some blacks red'. The inconsistency can make life scary for timid intermediates.

EXTENT OF THE SLOPES ★★★★
Several well-linked areas
The slopes divide into four sectors, with good connections between them, though one reporter complained of having to pole or walk between lifts.

The biggest sector is directly above the village, on the slopes of **Pic Blanc**. The huge Grandes Rousses gondola, otherwise known as the DMC (a reference to its clever technology), goes up in two stages from the top of the village. Above it, a cable car goes up to 3330m/10,930ft on Pic Blanc itself – the top of the small Sarenne glacier and start of the longest piste in the Alps (see the feature panel). The glacier is also reached via the Marmottes gondola, which also serves lower runs from Clocher de Macle.

The Sarenne gorge separates the main resort area from **Signal de l'Homme**. It is crossed by a down-and-

up fast chairlift from the Bergers part of the village. From the top you can take excellent north-facing slopes towards the gorge, or head south to Auris or west to tiny Chatelard.

On the other side of town from Signal de l'Homme is the small **Signal** sector, reached by draglifts next to the main gondola or by a couple of chairs lower down. Runs go down the other side of the hill to the old village of Villard-Reculas. One blue run back to Alpe-d'Huez is floodlit twice a week.

The generally quieter **Vaujany-Oz** sector consists largely of north-west-facing slopes, accessible from Alpe-d'Huez via red runs. At the heart of this sector is Alpette, the mid-station of the cable car from Vaujany. From here a disastrously sunny blue/red goes down to Oz, a much more reliable blue (which boarders will find a bit flat in places) goes north to the Vaujany home slopes around Montfrais, and a shady black plunges down to L'Enversin, just below Vaujany. Using different black, red and blue pistes and ending up at L'Enversin gives an on-piste descent of 2230m/7,320ft from Pic Blanc – one of the biggest verticals in the world (just 30m/100ft short of nearby Les Deux-Alpes). The links back to Alpe-d'Huez are by the top cable car from Alpette, or a gondola from Oz.

FAST LIFTS ★★
Efficient from the base
Gondolas and fast chairs are the main access lifts and serve most areas adequately, but there are lots of old chairs and draglifts scattered around.

KEY FACTS

Resort	1860m
	6,100ft
Slopes	1100-3330m
	3,610-10,920ft
Lifts	84
Pistes	237km
	147 miles
Green	32%
Blue	26%
Red	28%
Black	14%
Snowmaking	30%

QUEUES ★★★★☆
Generally few problems

Even in French holiday periods, there are few long hold-ups. The village bucket-lift is said to generate lengthy queues first thing. Queues can build up for the lifts out of the village, but the DMC shifts its queue quickly and the bottom section can be avoided by taking alternative lifts.

Over much of the area a greater problem than lift queues is that the main pistes can be unbearably crowded. We and many reporters rate the Chamois and Couloir runs from the top of the DMC among the most crowded we've seen. The reds to Vaujany and Oz can also be too busy for comfort – 'carnage all the way', said one reporter of the Oz run.

TERRAIN PARKS ★★★☆☆
A choice

There are two parks: one for novices near the bottom of the slopes, with various jumps and rollers ('excellent, the jumps were beautifully graded'); and a 1.5km/1 mile advanced park near the Babars drag, with half-pipe, jumps, hips, big air and a boardercross course ('good; fast and aggressive'). There's also a beginners' park above Vaujany. The ESF runs some freestyle courses for teenagers.

THE LONGEST PISTE IN THE ALPS – AND IT'S BLACK?

It's no surprise that most ski runs that are seriously steep are also seriously short. The really long runs in the Alps tend to be classified blue, or red at the most. The Parsenn runs above Klosters, for example – typically 12km to 15km (7 to 9 miles) long – are manageable in your first week on skis.

So you could be forgiven for being sceptical about the 'black' Sarenne run from the Pic Blanc: even with an impressive vertical of 2000m/6,560ft, a run 16km/10 miles in length means an average gradient of only 11% – typical of a blue run. But the Sarenne is a run of two halves. The bottom half is virtually flat (boarders beware), but the top half is a genuine black if you take the direct route – a demanding and highly satisfying run (with stunning views) that any keen, competent skier will enjoy. The steep mogul field near the top can be avoided by taking an easier option (or by using the Marmottes III gondola); and the whole run can be tackled by an adventurous intermediate. It gets a lot of sun, so pick your time with care – there's nothing worse than a sunny run with no sun. You can ski the Sarenne by 'moonlight' or wearing a head torch occasionally during the season. Take the last lift up, have a gourmet dinner, then ski back down with guides. The cost is 65 euros per person.

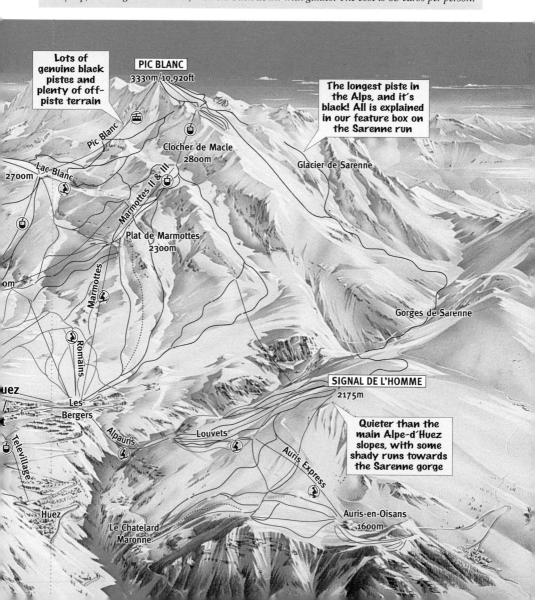

boarding

The resort suits experienced boarders well – the extent and variety of the mountains mean that there's a lot of good freeriding to be had; the off-piste is vast and varied and well worth checking out with a guide. There are quite a few flat areas to beware of though. The nursery slopes are excellent for learning but accessed mainly by draglifts (which can be avoided once a modicum of control has been achieved). Planète Surf is the main snowboard shop.

SNOW RELIABILITY ★★★★
Affected by the sun
Alpe-d'Huez is unique among major purpose-built resorts in the Alps in having mainly south- or south-west-facing slopes. The strong southern sun means that late-season conditions may alternate between slush and ice on most runs, with some lower runs closed altogether. There are shady slopes above Vaujany and at Signal de l'Homme. The glacier area is small.

In midwinter the runs are relatively snow-sure, thanks to extensive snowmaking on the main runs above Alpe-d'Huez, Vaujany and Oz. But reports suggest that neither the grooming nor the snowmaking is as enthusiastic as we would wish; several January 2009 visitors commented that snow conditions were poor and snow-guns lay idle.

FOR EXPERTS ★★★★
Plenty of blacks and off-piste
There are long and challenging pistes as well as more serious off-piste routes (see feature box).

The slope beneath the Pic Blanc cable car, usually an impressive mogul field, is reached by a 300m/980ft tunnel from the back side of the mountain. Despite improvements to the tunnel exit, the start of the actual slope is often awkward. The slope is of ordinary black steepness, but can be very hard in the mornings because it gets a lot of sun. Get advice.

The long Sarenne run on the back of the Pic Blanc is described in a special feature panel. Thanks to snowmaking, we've been able to ski the black Fare piste to L'Enversin on each of our last two visits – a highly enjoyable and varied long run, away from the lifts but not steep (really of red gradient with some blue sections, we thought). The Marmottes II gondola serves genuine black runs and a new red from Clocher de Macle; Balcons is steep and quiet, often with good snow; Clocher de Macle is easier but busier; don't miss the beautiful, long,

lonely Combe Charbonnière (but there's a fairly long traverse on moderately steep ground at the start). The Lièvre Blanc chairlift serves further testing slopes – Balme, looping away from the lifts, is a black, and one or two reds would be classified black in many resorts, especially when grooming is poor or non-existent.

FOR INTERMEDIATES ★★★★
Fine selection of runs
Good intermediates have a fine selection of runs all over the area. In good snow conditions the variety of runs is difficult to beat. Every section has some challenging red runs to test the adventurous intermediate. The Canyon run is one of the most challenging. There are lovely long runs down to Oz – the Champclotury blue from the mid-station of the gondola above Oz is a lovely, gentle run and usually quiet – and to Vaujany, with space for some serious carving. The Villard-Reculas and Signal de l'Homme sectors also have long challenging reds. Those at Signal de L'Homme are quieter, which keeps their snow better.

The Chamois red from the top of the gondola down to the mid-station is quite narrow, and miserable when busy and icy and/or heavily mogulled. Fearless intermediates should enjoy the super-long Sarenne black run. For less ambitious intermediates, there are usually blue alternatives, except on the upper part of the mountain. The main Couloir blue from the top of the big gondola is a lovely run, well served by snowmaking, but it does get scarily crowded at times.

There are some great cruising runs above Vaujany; but the red runs between Vaujany and Alpe-d'Huez can be too much for early intermediates. You can travel via Oz on gondolas, if you are that keen to get around.

Early intermediates will also enjoy the gentle slopes leading back to Alpe-d'Huez from the main mountain, and the Signal sector. But the unreliable piste grading (see remarks

There are vast amounts of off-piste terrain in Alpe-d'Huez, from fairly tame to seriously adventurous. Here we pick out just a few of the many runs to be explored – always with guidance, of course.

*There are lots of off-piste variants on both sides of the Sarenne run that are good for making your first turns off-piste. The **Combe du Loup**, a beautiful south-facing bowl with views over the Meije, has a black-run gradient at the top, and you end up on long, gentle slopes leading back to the Sarenne gorge. **La Chapelle Saint Giraud**, which starts at Signal de l'Homme, includes a series of small confidence-boosting bowls, interspersed with gentle rolling terrain.*

*For more experienced and adventurous off-piste skiers, the **Grand Sablat** is a classic that runs through a magnificently wild setting on the eastern face of the Massif des Grandes Rousses. This descent of 2000m/6,560ft vertical includes glacial terrain and some steep couloirs. You can either ski down to the village of Clavans, where you can take a pre-booked helicopter or taxi back, or traverse above Clavans back to the Sarenne gorge. In the **Signal** sector, there are various classic routes down towards the village of Huez or to Villard-Reculas.*

*The north-facing Vaujany sector is particularly interesting for experienced off-piste enthusiasts. Route finding can be very tricky, and huge cliffs and rock bands mean this is not a place to get lost. From the top of Pic Blanc, a 40-minute hike takes you to Col de la Pyramide at 3250m/10,660ft, the starting point for the classic itinerary **La Pyramide** with a vertical of over 2000m/6,560ft. Once at the bottom of the long and wide Pyramide snowfield, you can link into the Vaujany pistes.*

CHILDCARE

Les Crapouilloux
t 0476 113923
From age 4; 9.30-5.30

Les Intrépides
t 0476 112161
Ages 6mnth to 4yr;
8am-6.30

Les Eterlous (ESF)
t 0476 806785
Ages 2½ to 5

Tonton Mayonnaise
(International school)
Ages 2½ to 3½;
10am-12 noon

Ski schools
Take children from 4
to 13 (ESF 6 days
€185)

under 'The Mountains') can make life scary for early intermediates, never knowing what to expect.

FOR BEGINNERS ★★★★★
Good facilities
The large network of green runs immediately above the village is as good a nursery area as you will find anywhere. The six-pack installed at Les Bergers a few seasons ago has made that part much easier for novices. Sadly, these slopes get very crowded and carry a lot of fast through-traffic. A large area embracing half a dozen runs has been declared a low-speed zone, but the restriction is not policed and so achieves very little. All in all, with a special lift pass covering 11 lifts, Alpe-d'Huez makes a good choice.

FOR CROSS-COUNTRY ★★★
High-level and convenient
There are 50km/31 miles of trails, with three loops of varying degrees of difficulty, all at around 2000m/6,560ft and consequently relatively snow-sure.

MOUNTAIN RESTAURANTS ★★★★
Some excellent rustic huts
Mountain restaurants are generally good – even self-service places are welcoming, and there are more rustic places with table service than is usual in high French resorts. But the restaurants in the more obvious positions get over-busy.
Editors' choice Compared with some of the places on the main pistes, the

cosy little Chalet du Lac Besson (0476 806537) is an oasis of calm – tucked away on the cross-country loops north of the DMC gondola mid-station (and now with an official access piste, the Boulevard des Lacs, which some reporters say is 'difficult to spot'). Food and service are excellent. It's repeatedly endorsed by enthusiastic reporters – 'fabulous place', 'fantastic setting', 'worth every cent'.
Worth knowing about There are a couple of good spots low down – not mountain restaurants as such, but very popular targets nonetheless. The pretty Forêt de Maronne hotel at Chatelard, below Signal de l'Homme, is 'a delightfully quiet suntrap', enthuses a reporter, and has a good choice of traditional French and international cuisine: 'The chicken satay kept us raving about the place all week.' The Bergerie at Villard-Reculas has 'outstanding' views and is 'highly recommended'.

The Combe Haute, at the foot of the Chalvet chair in the gorge towards the end of the Sarenne run, is welcoming but gets very busy ('excellent profiteroles'). The Signal is quieter and has 'postcard views'. The 'cosy' Perce Neige, just below the Oz-Poutran gondola, 'made a great lunch' for a recent visitor. The Plage des Neiges at the top of the nursery slopes is one of the best places available to beginners. The Cabane du Poutat, halfway down from Plat de Marmottes, does 'excellent food'.

Air Lyon 155km/
95 miles (2hr30);
Geneva 210km/
130 miles (3hr30);
Grenoble, 105km/
65 miles (2hr15)

Rail Grenoble (63km/
39 miles); daily buses
from station

ACTIVITIES

Indoor Sports centre
(tennis, gym, squash,
aerobics, swimming,
shooting range,
climbing wall), sauna,
cinemas, concerts,
theatre, library,
museum

Outdoor Ice rink,
curling, cleared
walking paths, dog
sledding,
snowshoeing,
snowmobiling,
microlight flights,
sightseeing flights, ice
cave, off-road vehicle
tours, hang-gliding,
paragliding, ice
driving school

The restaurants in the Oz and Vaujany sectors tend to be cheaper, but no less satisfactory. At Montfrais, the Airelles is a rustic hut, built into the rock, with a roaring log fire, atmospheric music and excellent, good-value food (the plat du jour is consistently recommended: 'best ever', 'top-notch duck à l'orange'; 'great vin chaud'). The Auberge de l'Alpette also gets enthusiastic reviews emphasising that it is 'really good value'. The Grange at Alpette does a 'good warm chèvre salad and huge pizzas'. The P'Oz is also worth a visit.

SCHOOLS AND GUIDES ★★★★
Plenty of choice
Stance is run by two experienced instructors and specialises in teaching British clients. We've received rave reviews: 'absolutely terrific', 'my technique moved forward several notches in the two hours', 'very impressed'. A 2009 visitor found Masterclass, an independent school made up of British instructors and run by Stuart Adamson, 'outstanding' for the seven in her party aged 11-21 – 'interesting techniques; he made it fun and relaxed and gave them plenty of skiing'. We've had mixed reports of the ESF in the past and a 2009 visitor confirms that. He found the instructor at his wife's ESF beginner class 'patient', but his strong intermediate daughter was 'not challenged enough'. A recent reporter said of the International school that the two snowboarders in their party 'were given all kinds of things to practise and learn' and that the three skiers thought their lessons 'great', 'quite good' and 'alright'. The Bureau des Guides has a good reputation.

FOR FAMILIES ★★★
Positive reports
Les Crapouilloux day care centre (for children aged four plus) is reported to be 'very well organised'. The children's garden and nursery at Vaujany have been recommended.

STAYING THERE

Chalets UK tour operators run a few chalets and chalet hotels, many in the area above Les Bergers. Snowline has five very smart new chalets in Le Village at the top of the resort; all have hot tub, sauna and pistes running past two sides.

Hotels There are more hotels than is usual in a high French resort.
★★★★Royal Ours Blanc (0479 650765) Central, but public areas lack atmosphere. Fitness centre.
★★★★Au Chamois d'Or (0476 803132) Good facilities, modern rooms, one of the best restaurants in town and well placed for the main gondola.
★★★Grandes Rousses (0476 803311) A visitor says, 'Great atmosphere, charming Madame, goodish food and a good guitarist.' Close to the lifts.
★★★Alpages (0476 110799) B&B with modern rooms with lots of wood. Small bar. Close to lifts.
★★★Pic Blanc (0476 114242) Across the car park from Les Bergers lifts. Comfortable; in 2008 we stayed in a big ('superior') room.
★★Gentianes (0476 803576) Close to the Sarenne gondola in Les Bergers; a range of rooms, the best comfortable.
★★Ancolie (0476 111313) Good-value chalet down the hill in Huez.
Apartments There is an enormous choice available. Pierre et Vacances Les Bergers near the Marmottes chair has an outdoor pool and 'very friendly staff, superb food – the seven-night evening meal option is a bargain'. Ski Collection has smart looking chalets as well as apartment options. Leisure Direction has properties here. Privately owned Chalet Gothix is 'comfortable and spacious'.

EATING OUT ★★★★
Good value
Alpe-d'Huez has dozens of restaurants, some of high quality; many offer good value by resort standards. We've had a fabulous meal (four types of foie gras, carré d'agneau, mango tatin) at Au P'tit Creux, which also gets rave reviews from reporters. The Crémaillère is recommended by a frequent visitor. The Pomme de Pin is repeatedly approved of. A recent visitor liked the 'good selection of steaks' at Lounge 21. Of the pizzerias, the Origan serves 'fabulous pizza and pasta', and we enjoyed a calzone there. The Farmer in Les Bergers has 'excellent food and ambience'; Pinocchio 'gets very busy early', says a reporter, who also liked the 'enormous helpings' at Smithy's Tavern (Tex-Mex). The 'spruced up' Edelweiss is recommended for its 'excellent value set menus and grills'. A recent reporter was very impressed by the helpful staff at both the Fondue en Folie and the Crêperie des Jeux.

↑ Downtown Alpe-d'Huez, with the Avenue des Jeux behind the ice rink

OT ALPE-D'HUEZ / FRANCOIS MAIRE

Phone numbers
From abroad use the prefix +33 and omit the initial '0' of the phone number

TOURIST OFFICE

t 0476 114444
info@alpedhuez.com
www.alpedhuez.com

SMART LODGINGS

Check out our feature chapters at the front of the book.

APRES-SKI ★★★★
Plenty going on

There's a wide range of bars, some of which get fairly lively later on. There are several British-run bars in chalet hotels, mostly pretty basic and appealing mainly to a young crowd. The small but 'lively' Sphere bar is popular after the lifts close. O'Sharkey's (with 'comfortable leather sofas') and the Pacific (sister bar to the one in Val d'Isère) are also popular. Smithy's has 'plenty of atmosphere' but can get pretty rowdy late on. The live bands at the Grotte du Yéti make for 'some great nights', but a reporter said it had 'all the atmosphere of a youth club'.

The Etalon, Underground ('fun') and Free Ride cafes ('relaxed, cheery atmosphere with great sports videos') have been recommended. The Zoo is great for a relaxed drink. The Sporting is 'a great bar with class bands' but has 'the highest prices in town'; this and the Igloo club ('head there if you're on your 29th vodka!') liven up in peak season.

OFF THE SLOPES ★★★★
Good by high-resort standards

There is a wide range of facilities, including an indoor pool, a big indoor-outdoor pool (boxer-style cozzies not allowed), an Olympic-size ice rink and a splendid sports centre – all covered by the lift pass. There's also an ice driving school and a toboggan run. You can try airboarding and snow biking on Fridays, beside the Poutran lift. Visits to the Ice Cave are highly recommended by reporters. Shops are numerous but limited in range. The helicopter excursion to Les Deux-Alpes is amusing. There are well-marked walkers' trails (map available), and there's a pedestrian lift pass. The better mountain restaurants are widely spread though – and some are too remote for pedestrians.

Villard-Reculas
1500m/4,920ft

Villard-Reculas is a secluded village just over the hill (Signal) from Alpe-d'Huez, complete with an old church and set on a small shelf wedged

Alpe-d'Huez

241

Interactive resort shortlist builder at **www.wtss.co.uk**

between an expanse of open snowfields above and tree-filled hillsides below. A fast quad up to Signal has increased the village's popularity as a base. Its visitor beds are mainly in self-catering apartments and chalets, booked either through the tourist office or La Source – an English-run agency that also runs a comfortable catered chalet in a carefully converted stone barn (highly recommended by a 2009 reporter: 'great location, fantastic views, very comfortable and good value'). There is one 2-star hotel (the newly-extended Beaux Monts – 0476 804314), an 'outstanding' restaurant (Bonsoir Clara, which is Michelin-listed) and a couple of bars. The village is very quiet in the evenings.

The local slopes have something for everyone, including a nursery slope at village level. But a reporter warns that beginners 'will be stuck here because the runs that link to the rest of the skiing are undergraded'. A 2009 visitor found the ESF 'excellent'.

Oz-en-Oisans Station

1350m/4,430ft

The purpose-built ski station above the old village of the same name is a 'thriving small resort', says a reporter who has an apartment there. It has been built in an attractive style, with much use of wood and stone, and has a ski school, sports shops, nursery slopes, bars, restaurants, supermarket, skating rink, large underground car park and now two mid-range hotels. The pool in the hotel Les Cristaux is open to all. But another reporter complains that there is still no nightlife. Two gondolas whisk you out of the resort – one goes to Alpette above Vaujany and the other goes in two stages to the mid-station of the DMC above Alpe-d'Huez. The main run home is liberally endowed with snow-guns, but it needs to be – and a 2009 visitor saw no evidence of them working. One clear advantage of staying here is that the slopes above Oz are about the best in the area when heavy snow is falling – and those based elsewhere may not be able to reach them.

The smart Chalet des Neiges apartments are in chalet-style buildings with pool, sauna, fitness area, bar and restaurant. Available through Peak Retreats.

Auris-en-Oisans 1600

1600m/5,250ft

Auris-en-Oisans 1600 is another tiny, purpose-built ski station – a series of wood-clad, chalet-style apartment blocks with a few shops, bars and restaurants set just above the treeline. It's a compact family resort, with a ski school, a nursery and a ski kindergarten. Beneath it is the original old village of Auris, complete with attractive traditional buildings, a church and all but one of the resort's hotels. Staying here with a car you can drive up to the lift base or make excursions to other resorts.

Unsurprisingly, evenings are quiet, with a handful of bar-restaurants to choose from. The Beau Site (0476

Phone numbers
From abroad use the
prefix +33 and omit
the initial '0' of the
phone number

TOURIST OFFICES

Villard-Reculas
t 0476 804569
info@villard-reculas.
com
www.villard-reculas.
com

Oz-en-Oisans
t 0476 807801
info@oz-en-oisans.
com
www.oz-en-oisans.
com

Auris-en-Oisans
t 0476 801352
info@auris.en.oisans.
fr
www.auris-en-oisans.
com

Vaujany
t 0476 807237
info@vaujany.com
www.vaujany.com

800639), which looks like an apartment block, is the only hotel in the upper village. A couple of miles down the hill, the traditional Auberge de la Forêt (0476 800601) gives you a feel of 'real' rural France.

Access to the slopes of Alpe-d'Huez is no problem (but returning to Auris may prove difficult for novices – the top of Signal de L'Homme is a bit steep). There are plenty of local slopes to explore, for which there is a special lift pass. Most runs are intermediate, though Auris is also the best of the local hamlets for beginners.

Vaujany 1250m/4,100ft

Vaujany is a quiet, rapidly growing village, perched on a sunny hillside opposite its own sector of the domain. Hydroelectric riches have financed huge continuing investment in lifts and other infrastructure. A giant 160-person cable car whisks you into the heart of the Alpe-d'Huez lift system, and a two-stage gondola takes you to the local slopes at Montfrais via a mid-station below the tiny, rustic hamlet of La Villette. Accommodation is mainly in apartments, and Peak Retreats has a good selection available.

As you enter the village, you come to a couple of small, simple hotels. The Rissiou is well run by British tour operator Ski Peak: delicious food and helpful staff. Ski Peak also has comfortable catered chalets in Vaujany and La Villette; a minibus service for guests is available.

You then come to a recently built complex around a small pedestrian square, Place Centre Village, with spacious, mid-range apartments built in traditional style. There's a good ski shop, a restaurant, food shops, a cafe/bar and a cavernous underground car park – and an escalator down to the nearby cable car and gondola stations. An elevator takes you further down the hill to the superb sports centre.

An impressive enclosed escalator goes up the hillside past chalets and farm buildings to the top of the village, where sizeable apartment buildings are grouped around the Galerie Marchande – a small car-free zone with a small supermarket, a food shop, a couple of bars and a couple of restaurants. Since most of the visitor beds are up here, it is naturally the focus of evening activity.

There are no slopes leading directly to the village. But there is a 'pulse' gondola up from L'Enversin where the Fare black run finishes (a great run and not steep – see 'For experts' earlier in chapter), or you can take a blue to the mid-station of the Montfrais gondola and ride down. Beginner children are taken to a gentle roped-off area at the top of the gondola and adult beginners to the nursery slope at the cable car mid-station. There's a good self-service restaurant with sunny terrace right by the children's learning area. The ski school (adults' and children's) and the nursery have been praised.

Alpe-d'Huez

243

Interactive resort shortlist builder at **www.wtss.co.uk**

Les Arcs

Three first-generation purpose-built resorts plus a cute modern alternative – with an exceptional variety and extent of slopes

£105
RESORT PRICE INDEX

RATINGS

The mountains

Extent	★★★
Fast lifts	★★★
Queues	★★★★
Terrain p'ks	★★★★
Snow	★★★★
Expert	★★★★★
Intermediate	★★★★
Beginner	★★★
X-country	★★
Restaurants	★★
Schools	★★★★
Families	★★★★

The resort

Charm	★
Convenience	★★★★
Scenery	★★★
Eating out	★★★
Après-ski	★★
Off-slope	★

244

NEWS

For 2009/10 a six-pack is planned to replace the Arpette and Col des Frettes chairs above Arc 1800, doubling capacity and speed.

Runs from the top of the Aiguille Rouge are to be widened.

In Arc 1600, the Roc Belle Face 4-star apartments, with pool and spa, are due to open.

Snowmaking was increased above Arc 1800 for 2008/09, and the Cimes des Arcs apartments opened in Arc 2000, complete with bar; a pool and spa are to follow.

The cable car linking Les Arcs and La Plagne reopened in December 2008 after a year-long closure for repairs.

+ A wide variety of pistes and easily accessed off-piste terrain; great for mixed-ability groups

+ Huge amounts of genuinely challenging skiing above Arc 2000

+ Some excellent woodland runs

+ Car-free, mainly convenient villages

+ Some quiet alternative bases

+ Fast cable car link to La Plagne

+ Funicular to Bourg for town amenities and trains to UK

+ Arc 1950 offers a rare blend of convenience and ambience, but ...

− Original village centres lack charm, and aren't the most convenient

− Few off-slope diversions

− Still many slow old chairlifts

− Fairly quiet nightlife, though bar/restaurant choice improving

− No long green runs – a helpful feature of other French resorts – and not all blues are easy

− Lots of flat linking runs to annoy snowboarders

− Accommodation in high villages is nearly all in apartments

We've always liked Les Arcs' slopes: they offer impressive variety, including some of the longest descents in the Alps, and plenty of steep stuff. And the link with La Plagne puts these resorts in the same league as the Three Valleys; it makes a good day out for strong skiers, though Les Arcs has enough terrain to keep most mixed-ability groups happy.

We've never been keen on the functional main villages, with their depressing mall-style centres. But newer development is appearing in more tasteful style. And the Arc 1950 mini-village is something else: a resort that's even more conveniently arranged than the others, and a lot more pleasant to inhabit.

THE RESORT

Les Arcs is made up of four modern resort units, all purpose-built, traffic-free and apartment-dominated.

Arc 1600 and 1800 stand a couple of km apart, roughly at the treeline on a broad, steepish mountainside overlooking the town of Bourg-St-Maurice. Both consist mainly of large apartment blocks sitting below their slopes, with some development beside the slopes. 1600 was the first Arc, built at the top of a funicular railway up from Bourg. 1800 is much the largest of the villages; three main sections can be identified: Charvet, Villards and Charmettoger.

Arc 2000 is quite separate – on the far side of the mountain ridge, at the bottom of a high, treeless bowl. It consists mainly of half a dozen huge, linked apartment buildings. Just below Arc 2000 and linked to it by a short gondola, the mini-village of Arc 1950 is the newest resort but is built in traditional style – see feature panel.

The numbers in the village names relate only loosely to their altitudes.

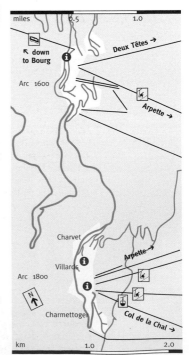

KEY FACTS

Resort	1600-2120m
	5,250-6,960ft
Slopes	1200-3225m
	3,940-10,580ft
Lifts	54
Pistes	200km
	124 miles
Green	1%
Blue	51%
Red	30%
Black	18%
Snowmaking	
	267 guns

Paradiski area	
Slopes	1200-3250m
	3,940-10,660ft
Lifts	144
Pistes	425km
	264 miles
Green	5%
Blue	56%
Red	27%
Black	12%
Snowmaking	
	626 guns

'Arc 2000' was meant to evoke the millennium – the future; its altitude is actually over 2100m.

At the southern end of the area is Peisey-Vallandry, from where a cable car links with La Plagne, covered by the Paradiski passes. Even from Arc 1950 you can be at the cable car in 20 minutes, ready for a long day at La Plagne. At the northern end of the ski area, at much lower altitude, is the rustic hamlet of Villaroger. These outlying villages are described at the end of the chapter, as is Bourg.

Day trips by car to Val d'Isère-Tignes are possible. La Rosière and Ste-Foy-Tarentaise are closer. We understand there is no longer any free parking at any of the Arcs.

VILLAGE CHARM ★
Head for 1950

Les Arcs was conceived to be functional, but the charm factor varies. Reporters repeatedly comment on the friendliness of the locals.

The apartment blocks of Arc 1600 and 1800 are low-rise, and not hugely intrusive seen from the slopes – they are much more conspicuous from below than from above. Arc 1600 is set in the trees and has a friendly, small-scale atmosphere, but doesn't amount to much. In bigger Arc 1800, Charvet and Villards are focused on small shopping centres, mostly open-air but still managing to seem claustrophobic. More easy on the eye is Charmettoger, with smaller, wood-clad buildings.

Arc 2000 consists of little more than large blocks with swooping roof lines, plus surrounding snow. 1950 has been designed to be cute, its smaller apartment buildings have been finished in traditional styles, and are clustered around a pleasant traffic-free square and street, which can be quite lively at close of play.

CONVENIENCE ★★★★
Generally very good

The villages of 1600 and 1800 offer some very convenient lodgings, a few yards from the lifts, but you can also walk miles within the apartment buildings to get to the snow. The central area in Arc 1600 is good for families: uncrowded, compact, and set on even ground. Arc 1800 is more spread-out, and some lodging is further up the hill. The lifts depart from Villards. Arc 2000 and Arc 1950 are compact, ski-in/ski-out places, with lifts starting below them as well as above. At Arc 1950 you park directly under the apartment buildings.

SCENERY ★★★
Attractively varied

Arcs 1600 and 1800, and the slopes, enjoy wide views across the valley to Mont Blanc. The lower villages enjoy good views along the Nancroix valley and to La Plagne's splendid north face of Bellecôte. Higher up, Arc 2000 and Arc 1950 sit beneath the Aiguille Rouge – great views from the top.

THE MOUNTAINS

Les Arcs' terrain is notably varied; it has a good mixture of high, snow-sure slopes and low-level woodland runs.

EXTENT OF THE SLOPES ★★★
Well planned and varied

Our rating relates to just the Les Arcs area; the whole Paradiski area easily scores 5 stars.

Arc 1600 and Arc 1800 share a west-facing mountainside laced with runs down to one or other village. At the southern end is an area of woodland runs above Peisey-Vallandry.

From various points on the ridge above 1600 and 1800 you can head down into the wide Arc 2000 bowl. Across this bowl, lifts take you to the highest runs of the area, from the Aiguille Rouge and the Grand Col. As well as a variety of steep north-west-facing runs back to Arc 2000, the Aiguille Rouge is the start of an epic run (over 2000m/6,560ft vertical and 7km/4 miles long) down to Villaroger.

The resort now identifies eight black runs and one red as 'natural' pistes, which means never groomed.

On the lower half of the Aiguille Rouge is a speed-skiing run, which is sometimes open to the public; the fee includes helmet, goggles and skis.

FAST LIFTS ★★★
Still a way to go
Each of the four main villages has fast chair or gondola access to the slopes, but there are lots of old chairs – some of them very long and cold (one reader claims to have suffered frostbite in his glutei). The new Arpette six-pack for 2009/10 will replace two more old lifts, but even so Les Arcs' system needs further investment.

QUEUES ★★★★
Not without problems
Queues aren't generally an issue in low season and peak-time queues are improving – a 2009 visitor says 'the busiest half term for years had queues of no more than 10 minutes'.

The lifts above Arc 2000 are a particular bottleneck, especially on sunny days. The Varet gondola to the shoulder of the Aiguille Rouge is always busy, but shifts its queue quickly because it has lifties filling the cabins – excellent. Queues for the cable car to the top can be serious; go at lunchtime, or late in the day, to avoid them. At 1800 the Transarc gondola is queue prone, especially late in the day. At 1600 the Cachette chair gets queues when crowds arrive on the funicular from the valley. At Plan Peisey, morning queues for the chair are not unknown.

At peak periods crowded pistes can be more of a problem.

TERRAIN PARKS ★★★★
One excellent park
The Apocalypse Parc is above Arc 1600 and served by the Clair Blanc chairlift. For years, this has been one of the most advanced parks in the Alps – on a par with the main park at Avoriaz. Snow-guns have been installed due to recent poor snowfall, which means there will always be something built. Three kicker lines are in place for all levels. There is a good rail and box line, and a big wall ride – varied and fun for all ('the kids loved it'). Two

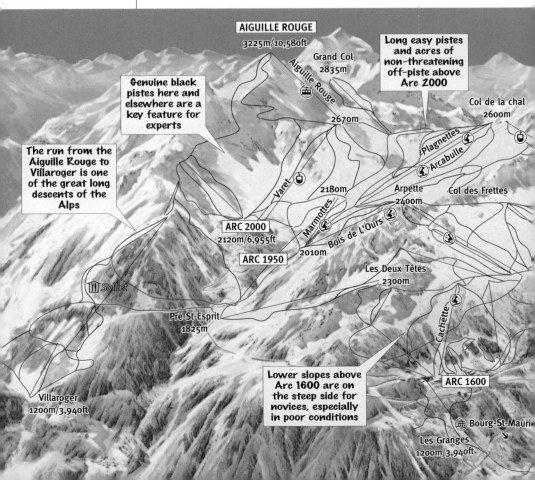

AIGUILLE ROUGE
3225m/10,58oft

Grand Col
2835m

Aiguille Rouge

Long easy pistes and acres of non-threatening off-piste above Arc 2000

Genuine black pistes here and elsewhere are a key feature for experts

2670m

Col de la chal
2600m

Plagnettes

Arcabulle

The run from the Aiguille Rouge to Villaroger is one of the great long descents of the Alps

Varet

2180m

Marmottes

Arpette
2400m

Col des Frettes

Bois de L'Ours

ARC 2000
2120m/6,955ft

ARC 1950

2010m

Les Deux Têtes
2300m

Solliet

Pré-St-Esprit
1825m

Cachette

Villaroger
1200m/3,940ft

Lower slopes above Arc 1600 are on the steep side for novices, especially in poor conditions

ARC 1600

Bourg-St-Mauri

Les Granges
1200m/3,940ft

beginner and intermediate lines, with tables and rails were added for 2008/09. On the far side of the park is a 500m/1,640ft long boardercross course. Queues form at peak times. There is also a good-sized half-pipe at Arc 2000, floodlit until late, plus a boardercross below Col de la Chal. And a small park above Plan-Peisey.

SNOW RELIABILITY ★★★★
Good – plenty of high runs

A high percentage of the runs are above 2000m/6,560ft and when necessary you can stay high by using lifts that start around that altitude. Most of the slopes face roughly west, which is not ideal. Those from the Col de la Chal and the long runs down to Villaroger are north-facing, and the blacks on the Aiguille Rouge are shady enough to keep their snow well. The limited snowmaking is being gradually extended, including full coverage for the terrain park at 1600 and above 1800 last season. Grooming is good.

FOR EXPERTS ★★★★★
Challenges on- and off-piste

Les Arcs has a lot to offer experts – at least when the high lifts are open (the Aiguille Rouge cable car, in particular, is often shut in bad weather).

There are a number of truly black pistes above Arc 2000 (though one was removed in 2007), and a couple in other areas. After a narrow shelf near the top (which can be awkward), the epic Aiguille Rouge-Villaroger run is superb, with remarkably varying terrain. There is also a great deal of off-piste potential. There are steep pitches on the front face of the Aiguille Rouge and secluded runs on the back side, towards Villaroger. A short climb to the Grand Col accesses several routes, including a quite serious couloir and an easier option. From Col de la Chal there is an easy route down towards Nancroix. The wooded slopes above 1600 are another attractive possibility and there are open slopes beside the pistes all over the place.

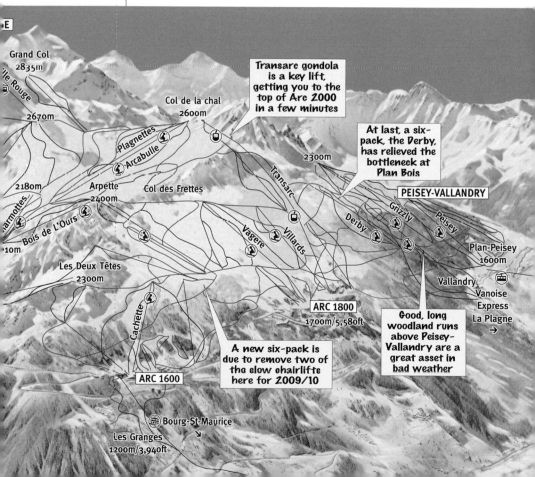

LIFT PASSES

Massif Les Arcs / Peisey-Vallandry

Prices in €

Age	1-day	6-day
under 14	32	153
14 to 64	43	203
over 65	32	153
Free under 6, over 72		

Beginner pass covering specific lifts

Senior Pass for 1-15 days for €5 if over 72

Notes
Covers Les Arcs lifts; half-day pass; family reductions; one-day Paradiski extension

Paradiski Découverte

Prices in €

Age	6-day
under 14	162
14 to 64	216
over 65	162
Free under 6, over 72	

Beginner no deals

Notes
Covers all lifts in Les Arcs areas with one day in Paradiski

Paradiski

Prices in €

Age	1-day	6-day
under 14	36	183
14 to 64	47	243
over 65	36	183
Free under 6; over 72 €9		

Beginner no deals

Notes
Covers all lifts in Les Arcs area and La Plagne area and a day in Val d'Isère-Tignes or the Three Valleys; family reductions

Les Arcs has always been a hot spot for snowboarders. Les Arcs offers incredible off-piste terrain, mainly in the back bowls of Arcs 2000. Gullies, trees, natural jibs and hits, steep terrain – this place has it all (enthusiastically endorsed by a 2008 visitor). The good mix of terrain also means that there are plenty of wide-open rolling slopes for beginners, especially at Vallandry and 1800. Be careful of long near-flat cat-tracks and some of the blues at Arc 2000. Fast chairlifts and gondolas serve much of the area. There is a good terrain park at 1600.

FOR INTERMEDIATES ★★★★
Plenty for all abilities

One strength of the area is that most main routes have easy and more difficult alternatives, making it good for mixed-ability groups. An exception is the solitary Comborcière black from Les Deux Têtes down to Pré-St-Esprit, which has no nearby alternatives. This long mogul-field justifies its classification and can be great fun for strong intermediates. Malgovert, from the same point towards Arc 1600, is now classified a 'natural' piste and is tricky – it is narrow, as well as mogulled.

The woodland runs at either end of the domain, above Peisey-Vallandry and Villaroger, and the bumpy Cachette red down to 1600, are also challenging. We especially like the Peisey-Vallandry area: its well groomed, treelined runs have a very friendly feel and are remarkably uncrowded much of the time, allowing great fast cruising – readers agree; notably for the isolated Combe run (though it is often closed and snow conditions can be challenging). Good intermediates can enjoy the Aiguille Rouge-Villaroger run. The lower half of the mountainside above 1600/1800 is great for mixed-ability groups, with a choice of routes through the trees. The red runs down from Arpette and Col des Frettes towards 1800 are quite steep but usually well groomed (except Clair Blanc). Cautious intermediates have plenty of blue cruising terrain. Many of the runs around 2000 are rather bland and prone to overcrowding. Edelweiss is more interesting, with a short red alternative, and takes you to Arc 1950 from Col des Frettes. The blues above 1800 are attractive but also crowded. A favourite blue of ours is Renard, high above Vallandry, usually with excellent snow.

And, of course, you have the whole of La Plagne's slopes to explore if you get bored locally.

FOR BEGINNERS ★★★
No long greens, but lots of blues

There are 'ski tranquille' nursery-slope zones above each of the three main Arcs, and at mid-mountain above Peisey-Vallandry; we and readers haven't found them always tranquil though we've had reports of some efforts to define and police them. Three of their serving lifts (at 1600, 1800 and 2000) are free to use at the weekends – 'good for a warm-up on arrival day'. There are also a few enclosed learning areas with draglifts, used by the schools. In all sectors there are long, wide blue runs to move on to, and some are gentle. The problem is you don't know which ones; which is why the green-run classification widely used in other French resorts is so valuable.

FOR CROSS-COUNTRY ★★
Very boring locally

Short trails, mostly on roads, is all you can expect, but the pretty Nancroix valley's 43km/26 miles of pleasant trails are easily accessible by free bus.

MOUNTAIN RESTAURANTS ★★
Not much choice high-up

The proper mountain restaurants – as opposed to resort restaurants – are mainly unremarkable.

Editors' choice The Solliet (0612 533627) above Villaroger is a charming woody chalet with a warm ambience delivering excellent food. There's table- or self-service, and great views from the terrace.

Worth knowing about The Chalets de l'Arc, just above Arc 2000, is a rustic place built in wood and stone and noted for its good home-baked bread. We're regular visitors, and although the food remains good we've lately found the service pressed and the welcome nominal. 'Go early' is one reporter's solution. The Arpette, above 1800, is a self-service that hits its target. The little Blanche Murée is a pleasant, simple table-service place

GETTING THERE

Air Geneva 160km/100 miles (3hr); Lyon 215km/135 miles (3hr); Chambéry 130km/80 miles (2hr)

Rail Bourg-St-Maurice; frequent buses and direct funicular to resort

SMART LODGINGS

Check out our feature chapters at the front of the book.

doing a good job. The Cordée above Plan-Peisey serves 'good tasty food' but gets crowded. The slightly off-piste Ferme is 'well worth seeking out'.

The other good options are not very mountainous. At Pré-St-Esprit below Arc 2000, the 500-year-old Belliou la Fumée is set beside a car park; but it is charmingly rustic, and we've had good meals here. Nearby is Au Pré Gourmand, which two 2009 reporters recommend ('lovely sun terrace'). The Ferme and the Aiguille Rouge down at rustic Villaroger are also worth a try. If you are tempted to resort to a real resort, go to Chalet d'Arcelle at 1600 (see 'Eating out').

SCHOOL AND GUIDES ★★★★
Several, including a Brit school

The ESF here is renowned for being the first in Europe to teach ski évolutif, where you start by learning parallel turns on short skis, gradually moving on to longer skis. Progress can be spectacular, but classes can be large. One reader's son 'progressed quickly', despite being 'the only British child in a class of French'. The 2000 branch has had glowing comments though from reporters: 'our daughters

had an excellent instructor who really moved them on', 'top guy; lots of fun'. Kids' classes were 'very highly praised by a 14-year-old boy and 10-year-old girl'. British school New Generation are consistently praised, this year and in past years. Two of this year's reports are typical: 'superb – we improved considerably'; 'used them for the last three seasons, as have two sets of friends; emphatically good reports from all'. Arc Adventures (International school) has impressed reporters. Private lessons with Snow Escape, also in Vallandry have been recommended. The Spirit school in 1950 gets mixed reviews – may be

NORTH AMERICA MEETS EUROPE: ARC 1950

Arc 1950, just below Arc 2000, is a fully functioning mini-resort with powerful attractions. It is high and relatively snow-sure; absolutely traffic-free (you park beneath your apartment building); very conveniently laid out, with genuinely ski-in/ski-out lodgings; and it is built in a traditional, easy-on-the-eye style, with the buildings grouped around a central square and street. Although entirely new – the first phase opened in 2003 – it feels well established.

All the accommodation is in apartments, furnished to a high standard. The living rooms are spacious, at least by French standards, but some incorporate tiny kitchens – and the bedrooms are mostly compact. The outdoor hot tubs and pools, saunas and steam rooms are added attractions – as are the 'animations' planned for the village every evening, such as fireworks and live music.

There are just enough restaurants to allow you to eat out in a different place each night for a week, there is a reasonable choice of après-ski bars, a tiny but well stocked supermarket, a bakery, a gift shop, a crêperie, ski and board equipment shops.

SCHOOLS

ESF Arc 1600
t 0479 074309

ESF Arc 1800
t 0479 074031

ESF Arc 2000
t 0479 074752

Arc Aventures (ESI)
t 0479 076002

Darentasia
t 0479 041681

New Generation
t 0479 010318
0844 484 3663 (UK)
www.skinewgen.com

Initial-Snow
t 0673 514419

Privilege
t 0479 072338

Spirit 1950
t 0479 042572

Classes (ESF prices)
6 days (3hr am or
pm) €140

Private lessons
€38 for 1hr, for 1 or 2
people

GUIDES

Bureau des Guides
t 0479 077119

ACTIVITIES

Indoor Squash (1800),
saunas, solaria, multi-
gym (1800), cinemas,
bowling (1800),
billiards

Outdoor Natural
skating rinks (1800/
2000), tobogganing,
snowshoeing, dog
sledding, cleared
paths, paragliding,
horse riding, skijoring,
ice grotto

better for private lessons than classes.
Off-piste discovery days are
recommended, though.

FOR FAMILIES ★★★★
Convenient choices

Les Arcs is a good choice for families
wanting convenience. There is a
children's area at 1800, complete with
moving carpet lifts, a sledging track
and a climbing wall. There are also a
couple of discovery pistes, at 1800
and 1600, for children to find out
about flora and fauna of the Alps. The
Pommes de Pin facilities in Arc 1800
have received favourable reports. Arc
1950 is particularly family friendly too.
Spirit 1950 there reportedly provides
good care facilities for smaller
children, returning them well fed and
rested. Comments on children's ski
classes have been positive.

STAYING THERE

Most resort beds are in apartments.
There is a long-established Club Med
presence in Arc 2000 and there's a
smarter 'village' at Peisey-Vallandry.
Chalets There are lots of catered
chalets in the Peisey-Vallandry area,
and Villaroger has a couple (see end
of this chapter), but there are few in
the high villages. Family specialist
Esprit has chalet apartments in Arc
2000, sharing a pool.
Hotels The choice of hotels in Les Arcs
is gradually widening.
★★★Grand Paradiso (1800) (0479
076500) Locally judged to be worth
four stars rather than its actual three
('very comfortable, good food').
★★★Golf (1800) (0479 414343) An
expensive but good 3-star, with
'friendly' jazz bar, sauna, gym, covered
parking, kindergarten. Spa and heated
pool. Accepts weekend bookings.
★★★Cachette (1600) (0479 077050)
Recommended, but expect lots of kids
– 1600's childcare facilities are here.
★★Aiguille Rouge (2000) (0479
075707) 'Stylish' lounge bar. Free ski
guiding.
★★Mélèzes (2000) (0479 075050)
'Fantastic value for a mixed family
group. Good food, great choices for
vegetarians.' Spa.
Apartments Beware – there are still
plenty of apartments in the older
resort units that are unbearably
cramped. But there are now lots of
good, modern developments. The
various parts of Arc 1950 vary in style

and space, but the general level of
comfort is very high by French
standards. (Some of these places have
a reception desk and a lounge,
blurring the distinction between
apartments and hotels; some people
are shocked to find that cleaning
incurs a hefty charge, and that you are
expected to strip the beds on
departure.) In Arc 2000 the Chalet des
Neiges, Chalet Altitude and new Cimes
des Arcs offer 'luxury' apartments. The
Alpages de Chantel above Arc 1800 is
typical of MGM apartments – attractive
and comfortable, with pools, saunas
and gyms. It is very convenient for
skiing, but a bit isolated. The Roc
Belle Face is due to open in Arc 1600
for 2009/10. Most of these better
developments are featured by Erna
Low, Lagrange, Ski Collection and Ski
Independence. The Ruitor apartments,
set among trees between
Charmettoger and Villards (in 1800),
are 'excellent in all respects'.

EATING OUT ★★★
Fair choice in Arc 1800

Arc 1800 has the best choice – about
15 restaurants; an ad-based (so not
comprehensive) guide is given away
locally. Reporters favour the Mountain
Cafe, which has a varied menu and
caters well for groups ('consistently
good food, great buzz'), Chez les
Filles, and San Diego. The Jungle Cafe
has 'great kebabs, and violet vodka!'
and the Laurus does a 'superb goat-
cheese tartiflette'. Beware the wine
prices at next-door Casa Mia.

Arc 1600's handful of restaurants
include a couple of excellent ones.
Chalet de L'Arcelle on the fringe of the
village is a clear reporter favourite; it
has a warm, quirky wood-and-stone
interior and a mouth-watering carte. La
Malouine ('excellent pierrade') is also
praised. Arc 2000 has even fewer
places, on which we lack reports.

Arc 1950 has a wide choice for a
small place. They get very busy, and
we have some sympathy with the view
of a 2009 visitor that they are
generally 'uninspiring'. But most
receive positive reports. A 2008
reporter rated La Table des Lys 'by far
the best', and we had an excellent
meal there in 2009. Chalet de Luigi
has a 'great ambience', and
Hemingway's is popular; Valentino's
('good pizza') and East (Asian dishes)
are other choices. A reporter praised
Meli's snack bar as 'great for the kids'.

APRES-SKI ★★
Arc 1800 is the place to be

Nightlife mainly revolves around the bars. 1800 is the liveliest centre; some places have regular live music. The JO bar is open until the early hours and has a friendly atmosphere. Reporters like the friendly Red Hot Saloon for bar games, Chez Boubou at Charvet, the Jungle Cafe for cocktails, the Jazz Bar in the hotel Golf ('great band, big sofas') and the cosy Etranger.

Although quieter, there are several options in 1600. The Abreuvoir, with live music and pool, is one reporter's 'favourite ski resort bar'. In 2000 the Red Rock has 'lots of seasonaires, but lots of atmosphere'. The Whistler's Dream, in the Chalet des Neiges, could be worth a try. At 1950, there are bars at Chalet de Luigi and Hemingway's. The Belles Pintes serves a 'great Guinness'. O'Chaud is 'the best' – open late, with live music or a DJ.

OFF THE SLOPES ★
Very limited

Les Arcs is not the place for an off-the-slopes holiday. There is very little to do, though several of the newer apartment blocks have pools; there are spa facilities at Arc 1950. There's bowling at 1800 and skating at 1800 and 2000. The cinemas have English films weekly. You can visit the Beaufort dairy and go shopping in Bourg-St-Maurice and there are a few walks – nice ones up the Nancroix valley. There's also an ice grotto at the top of the Transarc, which pedestrians can reach.

Peisey-Vallandry
1600m/5,250ft

Plan-Peisey and Vallandry are small, still-developing ski stations above the old village of Peisey, which has a bucket-lift up to Plan-Peisey. They market themselves as Peisey-Vallandry, and the cluster of villages hereabouts is known collectively as Peisey-Nancroix. Clear as mud, eh?

The cable car to La Plagne leaves from Plan-Peisey, which has one hotel, a few shops, bars and restaurants but no real focus other than the lift station. A fast six-seat chair takes you into the slopes. The hotel Vanoise (0479 079219) has a good location, new pool and fitness room.

UK operator Ski Beat has 10 specially built chalets here, with 8 to 15 beds: 'Comfortable, very good food and excellent childcare,' said a 2008 reporter. Family specialist operator Esprit has six neat chalets, each with hot tub.

For eating out, the Ancolie at Nancroix (a short bus ride from Peisey) is not to be missed. This fabulous traditional auberge has welcoming hosts, lots of character and great views. We had a splendid set menu here of pork stew and raspberry brulé. Reporters recommend Brasserie Maxima ('great little place'), the Vache ('excellent food, relaxed friendly bar') and rustic Solan. The Flying Squirrel is a British-run bar.

There is lodging down the hill in the characterful old village of Peisey which dates back 1,000 years and has a fine baroque church. The other, mostly old, buildings include a few shops and a couple of bars and restaurants – a reader enjoyed the Ormelune. There are several chalets run by UK operators.

Vallandry is a few hundred metres away from Plan-Peisey and linked by shuttle-bus. A fast quad takes you into the slopes. There are lots of chalets and a small pedestrian-only square at the foot of the slopes with a small supermarket and a ski shop.

Ski Olympic's big piste-side chalet hotel La Forêt has 'outstanding food,

Phone numbers
From abroad use the prefix +33 and omit the initial '0' of the phone number

TOURIST OFFICES

Les Arcs
1600: 0479 077070
1800: 0479 076111
1950: 0479 071257
2000: 0479 071378
lesarcs@lesarcs.com
www.lesarcs.com

Bourg-St-Maurice
t 0479 070492

Peisey-Vallandry
t 0479 079428
info@peisey-vallandry.com
www.peisey-vallandry.com

SNOWPIX.COM / CHRIS GILL

Sadly this ungroomed black run above 2000 has been abolished, but there are still five others – an excellent area for experts, with good snow ⬎

good rooms, fabulous views, friendly and helpful staff'. Among the other developments are some notable self-catering properties. The Orée des Cimes is a comfortable, traditional-style CGH development with a pool and great views.

There are several locally owned restaurants. The Refuge is good for pizza. Jimmy's and the Mont Blanc are cool bars.

Villaroger 1200m/3,940ft

Villaroger is a charming, quiet, rustic little hamlet with three successive chairlifts (the first two quite slow) going up to a point above Arc 2000. It has a couple of small bar-restaurants and a couple of British-run chalets, including chalet Tarentaise – a lovingly renovated old farmhouse run by Optimum Ski. All bedrooms are en-suite and there's a sauna and massage room (complete with qualified masseuse). The chalet also has Wi-Fi internet access. And the chef is said to be a bit of a star. Note that Villaroger is not suitable for beginners.

Les Granges 1200m/3,940ft

This hamlet at the mid-station of the funicular makes an interestingly rustic alternative to the bigger resorts if you want a quiet time. It's reached from 1600 by two red runs and a winding blue following a minor road. There is a good (but low and sunny) free nursery slope and kids' snow garden. No restaurants or bars, last train from Arc 1600 at 8pm (9pm weekends).

Bourg-St-Maurice
850m/2,790ft

Bourg-St-Maurice is a real French town, with cheaper hotels and restaurants and easy access to other resorts for day trips. The funicular starts next to the TGV station and goes straight to Arc 1600 in seven minutes – but beware, the last one down is at 8pm. The convenient Coeur d'Or apartments open for 2009/10. The Hostellerie du Petit-St-Bernard (0479 070432) – 'looks run-down, but is friendly with super food', and there's the cheap and cheerful Savoyard (0479 070403).

Avoriaz 1800

The 'ski to and from the door' purpose-built resort option on the French side of the big Portes du Soleil circuit

RATINGS

The mountains

Extent	★★★★★
Fast lifts	★★★★
Queues	★★★
Terrain p'ks	★★★★★
Snow	★★★
Expert	★★★
Intermediate	★★★★
Beginner	★★★★
X-country	★★★
Restaurants	★★★★
Schools	★★★
Families	★★★★

The resort

Charm	★★
Convenience	★★★★★
Scenery	★★★
Eating out	★★★
Après-ski	★★★
Off-slope	★

KEY FACTS

Resort	1800m
	5,910ft

Portes du Soleil

Slopes	950-2300m
	3,120-7,550ft
Lifts	194
Pistes	650km
	404 miles
Green	13%
Blue	40%
Red	37%
Black	10%
Snowmaking	
	694 guns

Avoriaz only

Slopes	1100-2275m
	3,610-7,460ft
Lifts	38
Pistes	150km
	93 miles

Fine views of the Swiss Dents du Midi from Pointe de Mossettes. Looks like making space for the pistes and restaurant was hard work →

+ Good position on the main Portes du Soleil circuit, giving access to very extensive, quite varied runs

+ Very successful design – car-free, with ski-in/ski-out lodgings

+ Good children's facilities

+ Local slopes are among the best in the Portes du Soleil and generally have the best snow, but ...

– Linked resorts you visit present the risk of poor snow low down

– Architecture doesn't suit everyone

– Needs a slick bag delivery system

– Can get very crowded at weekends

– Limited range of restaurants, very limited range of other amenities

– Practically all lodgings are simple 'compact' apartments

Of the purpose-built resorts thrown up in the 1960s, Avoriaz is one of the better designed – genuinely convenient in most respects, completely car-free and visually striking rather than offensive. If there were a fleet of flunkies on hand to shift your bags to your apartment while you downed a welcome glass of fizz, it would be the perfect base for skiing the Portes du Soleil. Well, if the apartment you were heading for were a bit smarter, too. Oh, and if they had ...

THE RESORT

Avoriaz 1800 is a purpose-built resort perched on a sloping shelf above a dramatic, sheer rock face.

It is entirely free of wheeled traffic; cars are left in paid-for parks at the edge of the village – book a space underground to avoid a chaotic departure if it snows. You drag your luggage to your apartment on a borrowed sled, or fork out for a ride on a snowcat or horse-drawn sleigh. (The problem of horse mess has been cut since horses now wear 'nappies'.)

Avoriaz is on the main lift circuit of the Portes du Soleil – for an overview, look at our separate chapter. It has links to Châtel in one direction and to Champéry in Switzerland in the other – both covered in separate chapters. It is above the valley resort of Morzine, to which it is linked by gondola (but not by piste). The slopes of Morzine and Les Gets, on the far side of Morzine, are not on the core circuit but are covered by the Portes du Soleil lift pass; both get their own chapters. There are two hamlets on the fringes of the Avoriaz ski area with a lift into it – Ardent and Les Prodains. Both have some accommodation and are briefly described at the end of this chapter. Car trips to Flaine and Chamonix are possible.

NEWS

For 2008/09 two new freestyle areas opened for beginners, including the 'Little Stash' – a mini variant of the main Stash park. A bar, Chapka, opened. And a beginner package, 'Soft Ski' – including a lift pass, ski hire and lessons – was introduced.

LIFT PASSES

Portes du Soleil

Prices in €

Age	1-day	6-day
under 16	26	134
16 to 60	39	200
over 61	31	160

Free under 5
Beginner Half-day €17 (Avoriaz only)

Notes
Covers lifts in all Portes du Soleil resorts; half-day pass available

Alternative passes
Avoriaz only; limited pass for boarders

VILLAGE CHARM ★★
One of the best modern places

The village is all angular, dark, wood-clad, high-rise buildings – almost all apartments. It's not what you would call charming, but it is at least designed coherently. The snow-covered paths and pistes give the place quite a friendly Alpine feel, and both we and reporters have enjoyed the ambience, both day and night. Family-friendly events are laid on all season. A floodlit cliff behind the resort adds to its nocturnal charm.

CONVENIENCE ★★★★★
It doesn't get much better

As our scale plan suggests, it's a compact place, with everything close to hand (turn to the Chamonix chapter for a striking comparison). Wherever you stay, you should be able to ski from the door. The village is set on quite a slope; but elevators inside the buildings (and chairlifts outside, during the day) mean moving around is no problem except when paths are icy. Even so, if you plan to go out much in the evening, it's worth staying near the central focus.

SCENERY ★★★
Clifftop panorama

The village is high and its position on a sunny balcony gives long views. From the top of the lifts the mighty Dents Blanches range is clearly visible.

THE MOUNTAINS

The slopes closest to Avoriaz are bleak and treeless, but snow-sure. For notes on the main Portes du Soleil circuit see our special chapter on it.

The Avoriaz piste map attempts to show the whole of the circuit in detail and is therefore useful for circuit navigation – but it omits the whole of the (admittedly complex) Super-Châtel sector. More seriously, it fails to show the local Avoriaz slopes clearly, which ought to be the main objective. Daft.

Four runs – a blue, a red and two blacks – are now called 'snowcross' runs. The piste map offers no explanation; the resort's special 'terrain' website appears to say that they are ungroomed pistes, monitored by the ski patrol. But a 2009 reporter found at least one – a black at the edge of the ski area – was 'completely unmarked'. So how do you avoid straying off into unsafe territory?

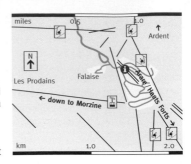

EXTENT OF THE SLOPES ★★★★★
360° choice

The village has lifts and pistes fanning out in all directions. Facing the village are the slopes of **Arare-Hauts Forts** and, when snow conditions allow, there are long, steep runs down to Les Prodains, way below the resort. The lifts off to the left go to the **Chavanette** sector on the Swiss border – a broad, undulating bowl. Beyond the border is the infamous Swiss Wall – a long, mogul slope with a tricky start, but not the terror it is cracked up to be unless it's icy or you're on a snowboard. It's no disgrace to ride the chair down – lots of people do. At the bottom of the Wall is the open, gentle terrain of Planachaux, above Champéry, with links to the even bigger open area around Les Crosets and Champoussin.

Taking a lift up through the village of Avoriaz to the ridge behind it is the way to the prettily wooded **Lindarets-Brocheaux** valley, from where lifts go over to Châtel's Linga sector.

FAST LIFTS ★★★★
Good system here and at Linga

In the Avoriaz sector the lifts are impressively modern – hence our rating. On the Linga slopes, on the way to Châtel, you'll again be mainly riding fast lifts. But be warned: beyond Châtel, and in the opposite direction towards Champéry, it's like stepping back 20 years.

QUEUES ★★★
Main problems now gone

Most of the bad queues have been eliminated by newish fast lifts. The main long-standing problem is the queue for the cable car at Prodains, when snow attracts visitors from Morzine. Visitors report few other problems. But peak-time crowds on the pistes (especially around the village) can be hazardous.

SCHOOLS
ESF
t 0450 740565
International (L'Ecole de Glisse)
t 0450 740218
Alpine (AASS)
t 0450 383491

Classes
(ESF prices)
6 days (2½hr am and pm) €165
Private lessons
€38 for 1hr, for 1 or 2 people

CHILDCARE
Les P'tits Loups
t 0450 740038
8.45 to 5.15; ages 3mnth to 5yr; 6 days €222 inc. lunch
Annie Famose Children's Village
t 0450 740446
From age 3; 9.30 to 5.30; 6 days with meal €240

Ski schools
Take children from 4 to 12 (6 days €150)

boarding

Avoriaz is great for expert riders. As well as state of the art 'conventional' parks, there's The Stash, combining natural and pseudo-natural obstacles (see 'Terrain parks'). For safe freeriding after a dump, head for the ungroomed snowcross pistes. Check www.snowparkavoriaz.com for details. It is well worth hiring a guide here to exploit the vast quantity of serious off-piste riding too. There are also plenty of wide, easy pistes (though some flat sections), and very few draglifts, making this a good choice for beginners and intermediates too.

TERRAIN PARKS ★★★★★
Still leading the way
Avoriaz was one of the pioneers of snowboarding in France, and the first terrain park to be built in the country was here in 1993. Avoriaz is still leading the way, and there are now four permanent parks and a super-pipe, all superbly maintained. The main park is Arare; it has its own draglift and is a pro-park, often used for high-profile contests. Four big kickers with red and black take-offs, big rails, a C-box, wall ride and corner jump are the order of the day.

Beginners and intermediates should head to La Chapelle. This is littered with jumps of all sizes and fun little boxes. Trashers is strictly for kids. It has several mini-jumps and ride-on boxes.

The fourth park, The Stash in the Lindarets valley, is a great innovation imported from California – a wooded mountainside, with narrow winding runs cut through the forest, and wooden and natural elements bringing all-mountain skiing/riding and freestyle together. Great fun for anyone who likes larking about, whether on skis or a board, especially adventurous teenagers – and a special mini version for younger kids opened in 2008/09. The Kids Parkway is also new, with lots of interactive features and trick tips. Just above the village is a good super-pipe. Terrain park lift passes are available.

SNOW RELIABILITY ★★★
High resort, low slopes
Although Avoriaz itself is high, its slopes don't go much higher – and some parts of the Portes du Soleil circuit are much lower. Considering their altitude, the north-facing slopes below Hauts Forts hold snow well and the snow in Avoriaz is usually much better than over the border on the south-facing Swiss slopes. But when snow was sparse on one of our visits we found the smooth, grassy, lower slopes of Morzine-Les Gets much better than the rocky ones around Avoriaz, which need more snow-cover. We've had reports of poor piste maintenance.

FOR EXPERTS ★★★
Several challenging runs
Tough terrain is scattered about. The challenging runs down from Hauts Forts to Prodains (including a World Cup downhill) are excellent. There is a tough red and several long, truly black runs including one of the 'snowcross' runs we've talked about. Two chairlifts serve the lower runs, which snow-guns help to keep open. The Swiss Wall at Chavanette will naturally be on your agenda, and Châtel's Linga sector is well worth a trip. The black runs off the Swiss side of Mossettes and Pointe de l'Au are worth trying, and one reporter had a 'very good day' here exploring off-piste with a guide.

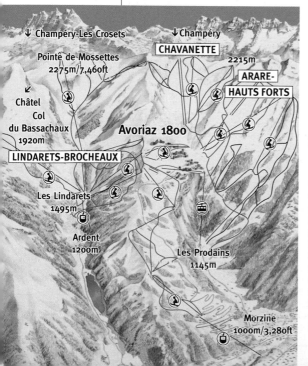

Champéry-Les Crosets
Pointe de Mossettes 2275m/7,460ft
Châtel
Col du Bassachaux 1920m
LINDARETS-BROCHEAUX
Les Lindarets 1495m
Ardent 1200m
Avoriaz 1800
Champéry
CHAVANETTE
2215m
ARARE-HAUTS FORTS
Les Prodains 1145m
Morzine 1000m/3,280ft

GETTING THERE

Air Geneva 90km/ 55 miles (2hr); Lyon 215km/135 miles (3hr30)

Rail Cluses (42km/ 26 miles) or Thonon (45km/28 miles); bus and cable car to resort

UK PACKAGES

Alpine Answers, Club Med, Crystal, Directski. com, Erna Low, First Choice, Independent Ski Links, Interactive Resorts, Lagrange, Leisure Direction, Neilson, PV-Holidays. com, Rude Chalets, Simply Alpine, Ski Collection, Ski France, Skiholidayextras.com, Ski Independence, Ski McNeill, Ski Total, Skitracer, Thomson, White Roc **Ardent** *Family Ski Company*

FOR INTERMEDIATES ★★★★
Virtually the whole area

Although some sections lack variety, the Portes du Soleil circuit through Châtel, Morgins and Champéry is excellent for all grades of intermediates, provided snow is in good supply on the lower slopes. Timid types not worried about pretty surroundings need not leave the Avoriaz sector. There are quiet and scenic blues to Prodains. Arare and Chavanette are gentle, spacious and above-the-treeline bowls. The Lindarets area is also easy, with pretty runs through the trees, but several reporters complain about long flat sections. Further afield, Champoussin has a lot of easy runs, reached without too much difficulty via Les Crosets and Pointe de l'Au. Better intermediates have virtually the whole area at their disposal. The runs down to Pré-la-Joux and L'Essert on the way to Châtel, and those either side of Morgins, are particularly attractive – as are the long runs down to Grand-Paradis near Champéry when snow conditions allow. Brave intermediates may want to take on the Swiss Wall at Chavanette, but Pointe de Mossettes offers a less challenging route to Switzerland.

FOR BEGINNERS ★★★★
Convenient and good for snow

The nursery slopes seem small in relation to the size of the resort, but seem to cope. The slopes are sunny, yet good for snow, and link well to longer, easy runs. The main problem can be the crowded pistes.

FOR CROSS-COUNTRY ★★★
Varied, with some blacks

There are 45km/28 miles of trails, mainly between Avoriaz and Super-Morzine, with others around Lindarets and Montriond.

MOUNTAIN RESTAURANTS ★★★★
Good choice over the hill

Editors' choice The hamlet of Les Lindarets in the next valley consists of countless rustic restaurants – it is a popular tourist spot in summer. The jolly Crémaillière (0450 741168) has wonderful chanterelle mushrooms and great atmosphere, but on a good day it's difficult to beat the terrace of the, er, Terrasse (0450 741617).

Worth knowing about The rustic Grenouille du Marais has good food and views. The table-service Abricotine, Refuge des Brocheaux, Marmottes and Pas de Chavanette (good views) have also been tipped.

SCHOOLS AND GUIDES ★★★
Try AASS

We lack new reports, but the ESF has generated good reports in recent years. One visitor had 'inspirational' snowboard lessons with former pro Angelique Corez-Hubert through the International school. The Avoriaz Alpine Ski School has British instructors and has been highly recommended, especially for 'quite excellent children's lessons'.

FOR FAMILIES ★★★★
'Annie Famose delivers'

With snow everywhere and not a wheeled vehicle to be seen, Avoriaz has obvious appeal. Then there's the Village des Enfants, which takes children from age three and is run by ex-downhill champ Annie Famose. Its facilities are excellent – a chalet full of activities and special slopes with Disney characters.

STAYING THERE

Alternatives to apartments are very few indeed.

Chalets There are several available – comfortable and attractive but mainly designed for small family groups.

Hotels There is one good hotel. *****Dromonts** (0450 740811) Renovated by a celebrity French chef and in the Hip Hotels guidebook. 'Bit expensive but very nice, with excellent food.'

Apartments Reporters say that some apartments need refurbishing, and others are typically 'cramped and basic'. But the Falaise apart-hotel, the Balcons du Soleil, Sepia and Datcha ('very basic') residences have all been recommended. The Shopi supermarket is 'far superior to the Sherpa'.

↑ Snow everywhere, and not a car to be seen – it's one of the most successfully designed modern French resorts

OT AVORIAZ 1800 / STEPHANE LERENDU

ACTIVITIES

Indoor Health centre 'Altiform' (sauna, gym, hot tub), squash, cinema, bowling
Outdoor Ice rink, dog sledding, ballooning, mountain biking on snow, ice diving, walking, sleigh rides, snowshoeing, paragliding, snowmobiling, helicopter flights

Phone numbers
From abroad use the prefix +33 and omit the initial '0' of the phone number

TOURIST OFFICE

t 0450 740211
info@avoriaz.com
www.avoriaz.com

EATING OUT ★★★☆☆
Some interesting options
There are supposedly 20 restaurants in the resorts, but there isn't much variety and the number is barely adequate – they get very busy. The hotel Dromonts' Table du Marché (sister to a similarly cool place in St Tropez) is best in town, but of course pricey. We had an excellent meal last season in the cosy new wood-panelled Salle à Manger at the Garde-Manger deli, serving three-course fixed-price menus changing daily. Chapka (see below) does appetising snacks. Earlier reporter tips include: the Bistro, the Cabane, the Fontaines Blanches for Savoyard food, Douchka for its 'excellent Moroccan lamb shank', Intrêts for pizza, pasta and Savoyard fare, Au Briska for a cosy night out and Falaise (pizza).

APRES-SKI ★★★☆☆
The bars are fun
A few bars have a good atmosphere, particularly in happy hour. Chapka is a hip new bar with TV, live music and pool which seemed to satisfy a broad market when we visited. Fantastique is a popular, simple bar. The Yeti and the Tavaillon are past reader tips. For late-night dancing, we're told the Place has bands.

OFF THE SLOPES ★☆☆☆☆
Not much at the resort
Those not interested in the slopes are better off in Morzine – though Avoriaz does have the Altiform Fitness Centre, with saunas and hot tubs. Pedestrians are not allowed to ride the chairlifts.

Ardent 1200m/3,940ft

Ardent is a very quiet little place at the foot of the gondola up to Les Lindarets. It has the basics of life, including a restaurant (La Chalande) that is better than you would expect to find in a place this size, a bar and a ski shop. The Family Ski Company has seven chalets here, the most remote 150m from the gondola, the nearest only 30m from it.

Les Prodains
1145m/3,760ft
Les Prodains, at the foot of the cliffs on which Avoriaz sits, has a cable car that is principally a quick way in and out of the resort, for Morzine-based people to get to the Portes du Soleil circuit, and for Avoriaz-based people to sample the bright lights of Morzine in the evening. But there are also some chalets and small hotels, and there are runs from Haut Forts.

Interactive resort shortlist builder at www.wtss.co.uk

Chamonix

Traditional tourist/mountaineering town with great atmosphere and towering mountains, offering stunning views and off-piste

£115
RESORT PRICE INDEX

RATINGS

The mountains

Extent	★★★
Fast lifts	★★★
Queues	★★
Terrain p'ks	★★★
Snow	★★★★
Expert	★★★★★
Intermediate	★★
Beginner	★★
X-country	★★★
Restaurants	★★
Schools	★★★★★
Families	★★

The resort

Charm	★★★★
Convenience	★
Scenery	★★★★★
Eating out	★★★★★
Après-ski	★★★★★
Off-slope	★★★★★

258

NEWS

For 2008/09 a 10-person gondola replaced the old access lift to Le Brévent, doubling the capacity and easing queues to return to the valley as much as queues to go up. Snowmaking was increased at Flégère and Les Houches. And Les Aiglons resort and spa hotel reopened following renovation.

For 2009/10 the Mont Blanc Unlimited lift pass will again cover Les Houches and, for the first time, Verbier as well. A new quad will be in place at the Planards beginner area. And the new Aiguille de Midi valley station should be ready after redevelopment to provide skier services, shops and accommodation.

➕ A lot of very tough terrain, especially off-piste

➕ Stunning views

➕ Amazing cable car to the Aiguille du Midi, for the famous Vallée Blanche (or just the views)

➕ Lots of different resorts and areas covered on Mont Blanc lift pass

➕ Town steeped in Alpine traditions

➕ Easy access by road, rail and air – excellent short break destination

➖ Several separate mountains: mixed ability groups are likely to have to split up, and the bus service gets mixed reviews

➖ Pistes in each area are quite limited

➖ Bad weather can shut the best runs

➖ Still some old lifts and queues in key spots

➖ Few good mountain restaurants

➖ It's a busy town, with lots of road traffic – not a relaxing place

Chamonix could not be more different from the archetypal high-altitude, purpose-built French resort. Unless you are based next to one of the half-dozen separate mountains and stick to it, you have to drive or take a bus each day. There is all sorts of terrain, but the place really makes sense as a destination only for the expert and the adventurous would-be expert. Chamonix is neither convenient nor conventional.

But it is special. The Chamonix valley cuts deeply through Europe's highest mountains and glaciers. The runs it offers are everything really tough runs should be – not only steep, but high and long. If you like your snow and scenery on the wild side, give Chamonix a try. But be warned: there are those who try it and never go home – including lots of Brits.

THE RESORT

Chamonix is a long-established, year-round tourist town that spreads for miles along the valley in the shadow of Mont Blanc. It's a bustling place with scores of hotels and restaurants and has shops dealing in everything from tacky souvenirs to high-tech climbing and skiing gear.

On either side of the centre, just within walking distance, are base stations of the cable car to the Aiguille du Midi, starting point of the famous Vallée Blanche glacier run, and a new gondola to Le Brévent. The third high-altitude area close to the town, La Flégère, is reached by cable car from the nearby village of Les Praz. The three other major ski areas are more widely spread along the valley.

At the top of the valley are the villages of Le Tour, at the foot of the Balme slopes, and Argentière, at the foot of the Grands Montets – for many visitors, the core of Chamonix's appeal. These villages are described at the end of the chapter, but their slopes are taken in to the main part of

the chapter. In the opposite direction, down the valley, is Les Houches. This is entirely described at the end of the chapter, because its lifts are separately owned and not covered by the basic Chamonix pass. Regular buses, free with a guest card, link all these points but can get very crowded and aren't always reliable. The evening service finishes early. Like many reporters, we rate a car essential. A car also means you can get easily to other resorts covered by the regional Mont Blanc Unlimited ski pass, such as Megève and Les Contamines, Courmayeur in Italy and now Verbier in Switzerland.

VILLAGE CHARM ★★★★
Lots of atmosphere
The car-free centre of town is full of atmosphere, with cobbled streets and squares, beautiful old buildings, a fast-running river and pavement cafes. But not everything is rosy: there are lots of obtrusive apartment blocks, some of the old buildings have fallen into disrepair, and traffic clogs the streets around the centre at times.

↑ Development spreads for miles along the narrow Chamonix valley; this photo is taken from the lower slopes of Les Houches

SNOWPIX.COM / CHRIS GILL

KEY FACTS

Resort	1035m	
	3,400ft	
Slopes	1035-3840m	
	3,400-12,600ft	
Lifts	44	
Pistes	155km	
	96 miles	
Green	16%	
Blue	36%	
Red	32%	
Black	16%	
Snowmaking		
	125 guns	

CONVENIENCE ★☆☆☆☆
You don't come here for that
The obvious place to stay for the full experience is in downtown Chamonix, unless you plan to spend your time mainly on one mountain, such as the Grands Montets.

SCENERY ★★★★★
As dramatic as it gets
Some of the most famous mountains in the Alps tower above Chamonix – the mighty Mont Blanc massif is the highest in Western Europe. The views from the Aiguille du Midi to the rocky spires and ridges are breathtaking.

THE MOUNTAINS

Each of the different areas is worth exploring. Practically all the slopes – with the notable exception of Les Houches – are above the treeline; there are some runs through woods to the valley, but the ones to Chamonix, in particular, are often tricky or closed.

There is a valley piste map and individual area maps. Reporters repeatedly complain of poor signing and marking of runs – 'virtually non-existent', and 'several of our party went off the edge of a long cat-track at Balme in near white-out conditions'.

EXTENT OF THE SLOPES ★★★☆☆
Very fragmented
There are several low beginner areas dotted along the Chamonix valley but there are five main areas.

The gondola for **Le Brévent** departs a short, steep walk or bus ride from the centre of town. There are runs on open slopes below the arrival point and a cable car above takes you to the summit. There is lift link to **La Flégère**, also accessible via an inadequate old cable car from the village of Les Praz. Both of these sunny areas give stunning views of Mont Blanc.

Up the valley at Argentière a cable car or chairlift take you up to **Les Grands Montets**. Chairs and a gondola serve excellent steep terrain above mid-mountain, but much of the best terrain is accessed by a further cable car of relatively low capacity, not covered by the basic valley pass (Chamonix Le Pass). This shady area can be very cold in early season.

A little way further up the valley, the secluded village of Le Tour sits at the foot of the **Balme** area of mainly easy pistes. A gondola goes up to mid-mountain, with a mix of drags and chairs above. The slopes are also accessible from Vallorcine. It is also the starting point for good off-piste runs, some ending in Switzerland.

Les Houches is the only major area down-valley of Chamonix. This low, wooded area is accessed by a gondola or cable car from the village. The lifts are not covered by the standard pass, and we describe the skiing separately at the end of the chapter.

FAST LIFTS ★★★☆☆
Brévent gets a new one
Cable cars and gondolas serve each sector, but many need upgrading to be fully efficient. The handful of fast chairs are widely scattered.

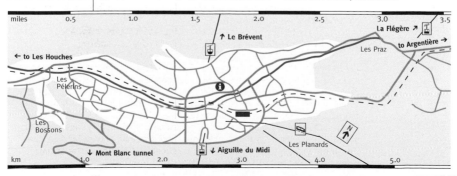

QUEUES ★★☆☆☆
Ancient lifts, serious queues

The overdue replacement of the Brévent gondola for 2008/09 is very welcome, and reporters find it a huge improvement. But this was only one of the valley's problem lifts. The ancient Flégère cable car can generate queues of an hour or more – to go down as well as up. The lifts out of Argentière build queues, and the chairlift appears to be on its last legs – it no longer operates from the main station, but starts a short way up the slope. At mid-mountain, the top cable car is a famous bottleneck. You can book slots in advance (at the ticket office or online) and it's 'best to do this the day before as places tend to sell out

early', says a reporter. Instead you can join the 'stand by' queue, which we've found to be an effective alternative. At Les Houches the two access lifts are widely separated, and it's worth going for the modern gondola rather than the inadequate Bellevue cable car. Both lifts build queues in poor weather when woody Les Houches gets crowded. Expect queues on the hill, too – all the chairs here are slow.

Crowded pistes are also reported to be a problem in places – most notably at Lognan on Grands Montets.

TERRAIN PARKS ★★★☆☆
Head for the Grands Montets

The experienced HO5 crew, responsible for parks in several other resorts and

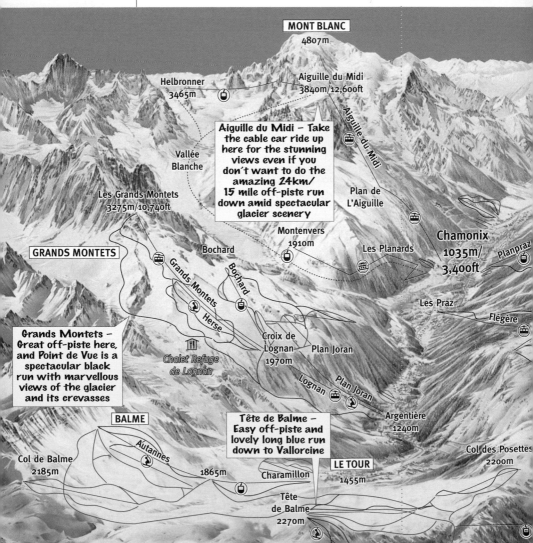

MONT BLANC
4807m

Helbronner
3465m

Aiguille du Midi
3840m/12,600ft

Aiguille du Midi

Vallée
Blanche

Plan de
L'Aiguille

Aiguille du Midi – Take the cable car ride up here for the stunning views even if you don't want to do the amazing 24km/ 15 mile off-piste run down amid spectacular glacier scenery

Les Grands Montets
3275m/10,740ft

Montenvers
1910m

Chamonix
1035m/
3,400ft

GRANDS MONTETS

Bochard

Les Planards

Planpraz

Grands Montets

Bochard

Les Praz

Grands Montets – Great off-piste here, and Point de Vue is a spectacular black run with marvellous views of the glacier and its crevasses

Herse

Chalet Refuge
de Lognan

Croix de
Lognan
1970m

Plan Joran

Flégère

Lognan

Plan Joran

BALME

Autannes

Argentière
1240m

Tête de Balme – Easy off-piste and lovely long blue run down to Vallorcine

Col de Balme
2185m

1865m

Charamillon

LE TOUR
1455m

Col des Posettes
2200m

Tête
de Balme
2270m

headed by ex-international pro Nico Watier, has been working hard to fine-tune the 800m/2,620ft long Snow Bowl park on the Grands Montets. It features over 16 obstacles including jumps, rails and a wall ride. You can check the latest details at www.ho5park.com. A snow bowl gap jump was new in 2008/09 and is very similar to a skate bowl feature. The fun zone is designed for beginners wanting their first taste of air time.

SNOW RELIABILITY ★★★★
Good high up; poor low down

The top runs on the north-facing Grands Montets slopes above Argentière generally have good snow, and the season normally lasts well into May. The risk of finding the top lift shut because of bad weather is more of a worry. There's snowmaking on the busy Bochard piste and the run to the valley, which can now be kept open late in the season. Balme has a snowy location, a good late-season record and snowmaking on the run down to the valley at Le Tour. The largely south-facing slopes of Brévent and Flégère suffer in warm weather, and the steep black runs to the resort are often closed. Don't be tempted to try these unless you know they are in good condition – they can be very tricky. Some of the low beginners' areas have snowmaking. Most of our reporters have been surprised by the respectable piste grooming.

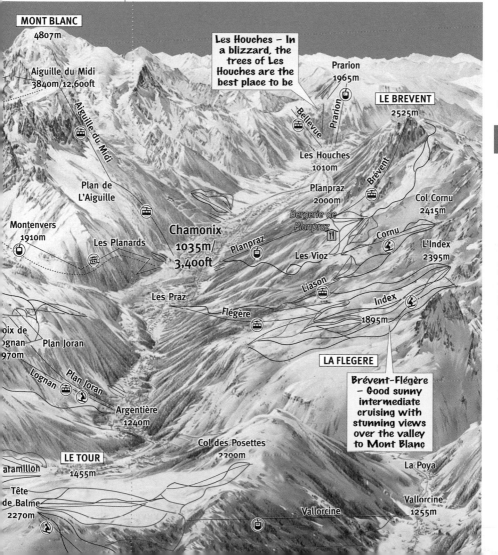

MONT BLANC
4807m

Aiguille du Midi
3840m/12,600ft

Aiguille du Midi

Les Houches – In a blizzard, the trees of Les Houches are the best place to be

Prarion
1965m

Prarion

LE BREVENT
2525m

Bellevue

Les Houches
1010m

Brévent

Plan de L'Aiguille

Planpraz
2000m

Col Cornu
2415m

Montenvers
1910m

Bergerie de Planpraz

Cornu

Chamonix
1035m/
3,400ft

Planpraz

L'Index
2395m

Les Planards

Les Vioz

Liason

Index
1895m

Les Praz

Flégère

LA FLEGERE

oix de ognan 970m

Plan Joran

Brévent-Flégère – Good sunny intermediate cruising with stunning views over the valley to Mont Blanc

Lognan

Plan Joran

Argentière
1240m

Col des Posettes
2200m

La Poya

aramilloh

LE TOUR
1455m

Tête de Balme
2270m

Vallorcine

Vallorcine
1255m

LIFT PASSES

Chamonix Le Pass

Prices in €

Age	1-day	6-day
under 16	31	154
16 to 64	39	192
over 65	31	154

Free under 4; over 75
Beginner no deals
Senior Over 65 50%
of adult price

Notes
Covers Brévent,
Flégère, Balme,
Grands Montets
except top cable car
plus four small
beginner areas; family
reductions

Alternative passes
Mont Blanc Unlimited
pass covers all the
above plus Les
Houches, Aiguille du
Midi and Helbronner
cable cars,
Montenvers train,
Lognan-Grands
Montets cable car,
and the Verbier
(Switzerland) and
Courmayeur (Italy) ski
areas; Skipass Mont
Blanc covers all the
lifts in the 13 resorts
of the Mont Blanc
area and Courmayeur
(Italy)

boarding

The undisputed king of freeride resorts, Chamonix is a haven for advanced snowboarders who relish the steep and wild terrain. This means, however, that in peak season it's crowded and fresh snow gets tracked out very quickly. The rough and rugged nature of the slopes means it is not best suited for beginners, but for more experienced adventurous riders, willing to try true all-mountain riding. If you do the Vallée Blanche, be warned: the usual route is flat in places. Check out former British champ Neil McNab's excellent extreme backcountry camps at www.mcnabsnowboarding.com. Most areas are equipped mainly with cable cars, gondolas and chairs. However, there are quite a few difficult drags at Balme that cause inexperienced boarders problems – though you can avoid these if you can hack the cat tracks to take you to other lifts, says a reporter. There are terrain parks on Grands Montets and at Les Houches.

FOR EXPERTS ★★★★★
One of the great resorts
Chamonix is renowned for its extensive steep terrain and deep snow. To get the best out of the area you really need to have a local guide. There is also lots of excellent terrain for ski-touring on skins. See the feature panel for more on off-piste possibilities.

The Grands Montets cable car offers stunning views from the observation platform above the top station – if you've got the legs and lungs to climb the 121 steep metal steps. (But beware: it's 200 more slippery steel steps down from the cable car before you hit the snow.) The ungroomed black pistes from here – Point de Vue and Pylones – are long and exhilarating. The former sails right by some dramatic sections of glacier, with marvellous views of the crevasses.

The Bochard gondola serves a challenging red back to Lognan and a black to either Plan Joran or the chairlift below. Shortly after you have made a start down the black, you can head off-piste down the Combe de la Pendant bowl ('excellent, so much space, always great snow').

At Le Brévent there's more to test experts than the piste map suggests – there are a number of variations on the runs down from the summit. Some are very steep and prone to ice. The runs in Combe de la Charlanon are quiet and include one red piste and excellent off-piste if the snow is good.

At La Flégère there are further challenging slopes – in the Combe Lachenal, crossed by the linking cable car, say – and a tough run back to the village when the snow permits. The short draglift above L'Index opens up a couple of good steep runs (a red and a black) plus a good area of off-piste.

Balme boasts little tough terrain on-piste but there are off-piste routes from the high points to Le Tour, towards Vallorcine or into Switzerland.

FOR INTERMEDIATES ★★
It's worth trying it all
For less confident intermediates, the Balme area above Le Tour is good for cruising and usually free from crowds (a recent reporter enjoyed 'untracked powder here well into the afternoon'). There are excellent shady, steeper runs, wooded lower down, on the north side of Tête de Balme, served by a fast quad. A lovely blue run goes on down to Vallorcine but it is prone to closure.

Don't be put off by the other, apparently macho areas, all of which actually provide a good mix of genuine blue and red runs as well as the seriously steep unpisted terrain that attracts the experts. Even the Grands Montets has an excellent area of blue runs at mid-mountain, served by several chairs (all slow, sadly). The step up to the red terrain higher up is quite pronounced, however.

If the snow and weather are good, confident intermediates can join a guided group and do the Vallée Blanche (see feature panel).

A day trip to Courmayeur makes an interesting change of scene, especially when the weather is bad (it can be sunny there when Chamonix's high lifts are closed by blizzards or high winds).

FOR BEGINNERS ★★
Head for Le Tour
There are nursery slopes either side of Chamonix itself, but they are limited, low and (in the case of Les Planards) dark and cold in mid-winter. They are separated from the other sectors of slopes, so moving on to longer runs is a major upheaval. La Vormaine, at Le

Tour, is a much better bet: extensive, relatively high, sunny, and connected to the slopes of the Balme sector, where there are easy long runs to progress to.

FOR CROSS-COUNTRY ★★★
A decent network of trails
Most of the 40km/25 miles of prepared trails lie at valley level in and between Chamonix and Argentière. All the trails are shady and cold in midwinter, and they fade fast in the spring sun. Catch the bus rather than ski between the Chamonix and Argentière areas, suggests a reporter, as the link is by 'steep and difficult trails'.

MOUNTAIN RESTAURANTS ★★
Mainly dull
Editors' choice On Le Brévent the Bergerie de Planpraz (0450 530542) is the most attractive option: a wood and stone building with self- and table-service and good food; but it gets very busy. On the Grands Montets the tiny, rustic Chalet-Refuge de Lognan (06 8856 0354), off the Variante Hôtel run to the valley, has marvellous views and simple but satisfying food.
Worth knowing about On Le Brévent the little Panoramic at the top enjoys amazing views over to Mont Blanc and the food is fine. There's a self-service place at La Flégère with a large terrace and excellent views. On the Grands Montets the Plan Joran has table- and self-service ('excellent pizzas'), but gets busy. There's also an indoor picnic area and 'good sunny terrace'. Tucked away in the woods to skier's right of the home run, the Crémerie du Glacier is a cosy spot for a croûte. At

THE BEST OFF-PISTE SKIING IN THE WORLD?

Chamonix is renowned as an extreme sports Mecca, with arguably some of the best off-piste skiing in the world. And while thrill seekers and off-piste specialists are spoiled for choice, there is plenty for those looking for their first powder experience, too.

Les Houches and *Balme*, at opposite ends of the Chamonix Valley, are ideal for a first taste off the beaten track. The forested slopes of Les Houches are easy to navigate on bad-weather days, with gentle blue runs bringing you back to the valley. Balme's open slopes are perfect for a foray into deep snow in between the pistes, with firmer ground just a few reassuring metres away.

Snowboarders flock to **La Flégère** *after a snowfall, its array of boulders and drop-offs turning it into a massive terrain park. The open bowl of Combe Lachenal is easily accessed from the top of the Index lift, and the south-facing slopes of this ski area provide excellent spring skiing.*

From the top of **Les Grands Montets** *(3275m/10,740ft) skiing is mostly off-piste and on glacial terrain. The vast north-facing slope of the main face offers countless ways down, satisfyingly steep without being at all intimidating, with snow conditions that are often among the best in the valley. Off the back, there are several rewarding ways down to the Glacier d'Argentière. In the opposite direction you have access to the steep Pas de Chèvre run. Skiing under the colossal granite spire of Le Dru, with views of the Vallée Blanche, is an unforgettable experience. The Couloir du Dru and the Rectiligne are also on this face, reserved for the adventurous – with some slopes of 40/45°.*

These are just some of the off-piste options in the Chamonix valley, but the possibilities are endless. Together with ski-touring itineraries like the Haute Route (Chamonix to Zermatt), and heli-skiing on the Italian side of Mont Blanc and in neighbouring Switzerland, the wealth of off-piste on offer could keep you skiing for a lifetime. The Vallée Blanche is covered in a feature panel later in this chapter.

Stay from just £6.00 per person, per night only with P&V.

pv-holidays.com/ski

CHILDCARE

Panda Club (Argentière)
t 0450 540476
From age 3

Piou Piou
0450 532257
Run by ESF; ages from 3

Babysitter list
Available from the tourist office

Ski schools
Take children aged 3 to 12 (6 half days from €110 – ESF price)

Balme at the top of the gondola from Le Tour, there's an adequate self-service, Chalet de Charamillon, and also a picnic area. The charming Refuge du Col de Balme – a short hike beyond the lifts – used to be famed for its grumpy reception, but we're told that visitors are now 'welcomed rather than treated as a nuisance'. Reports are welcome on the inviting little chalet at the foot of the Aiguillette draglift.

SCHOOLS AND GUIDES ★★★★★
The place to try something new
The schools here are particularly strong in specialist fields – off-piste, glacier and couloir skiing, ski touring, snowboarding and cross-country. English-speaking instructors and mountain guides are plentiful, and specialist Chamonix tour operators can arrange them in advance for guests. At the Maison de la Montagne is the main ESF office and the HQ of the Compagnie des Guides, which has taken visitors to the mountains for 150 years. Both offer ready-made week-long 'tours' taking clients to a different mountain or resort each day. We have a good report of the ESF Ski Fun Tour, where they ski a different Mont Blanc

region resort each day, transport included: 'Fantastic – we cannot speak highly enough of the guides.'
Reporters have also praised the ESF instructors provided by Club Med: 'a witty, friendly instructor who spoke excellent English'; 'our instructor found good off-piste for us'; but 'some class sizes were large – up to 14'. Competition is provided by a number of smaller, independent guiding and teaching outfits. Evolution 2 has been recommended. Mark Gear, who runs All Mountain Performance, has been highly praised by a recent reporter. Chamonix Experience offers a full range of options, from classic itinéraires and Italian heli-skiing to hidden off-piste routes and avalanche courses.

FOR FAMILIES ★★★★★
Couple of choices
Evolution 2's Panda Club is used by quite a few British visitors and reports have been enthusiastic. The Argentière base can be inconvenient for meeting up with children for the afternoons. Specialist family tour operator Esprit Ski has a nursery in its Sapinière chalet hotel, which is situated near the Savoy nursery slope.

FRANCE

264

Weekly news updates and resort links at **www.wtss.co.uk**

THE VALLEE BLANCHE

This is a trip you do for the stunning scenery. The views of the ice, the crevasses and seracs – and the spectacular rock spires beyond – are simply mind-blowing. The standard run, although exceptionally long, is not steep – mostly effortless gliding down gentle slopes with only the occasional steeper, choppy section to deal with. In the right conditions, it is well within the capability of a confident, fit intermediate (but the usual route is rather flat for snowboarders). If snow is sparse, as it can be in early season especially, the run can be very tricky – there can be patches of sheet ice, exposed stones and rocks, and narrow snow bridges over gaping crevasses. And if fresh snow is abundant, different challenges may arise. Go in a guided group – dangerous crevasses lurk to swallow those not in the know – and check conditions before signing up. The trip is popular – on a busy day 2,500 people do it; book in advance at the Maison de la Montagne or other ski school offices. To miss the crowds go very early on a weekday, or in the afternoon if you are a good skier and can get down quickly.

The Aiguille du Midi cable car takes you to 3840m/12,600ft and the 3842 cafeteria (claimed to be Europe's highest restaurant) – the view of Mont Blanc from here should not be missed, and it gives you the opportunity to adjust to the dizzying altitude. Be prepared for extreme cold up here, too. A tunnel delivers you to the infamous ridge-walk down to the start of the run. Except at the start of the season, the walk is well prepared, with regular steps cut in the snow and fixed guide-ropes for you to hang on to. If you have a backpack capable of carrying your skis, and crampons to give your heels some grip, it's no problem; ask when you book for your guide to provide them. Without those accessories, it can be tiring and worrying. Many parties rope up to their guides.

There are variants on the classic route, of varying difficulty and danger; on our last descent we did a mixture of the Petit Envers du Plan and the Vrai Vallée Blanche in 20cm of fresh snow under a bluebird sky and with few other people around – it was absolutely magical, with hundreds of fresh-track turns among all that stunning scenery. Lack of snow often rules out the full 24km/15 mile run down to Chamonix; a steep stairway (be warned: 311 steps) leading to a slow gondola links the glacier to the station at Montenvers, for the half-hour mountain railway ride down to the town.

IAN STRATFORD

The infamous ridge-walk down to the start of the Vallée Blanche is OK if you have a guide, crampons and a backpack to carry your skis ↓

STAYING THERE

There is all sorts of accommodation, and lots of it.

Chalets Many are run by small specialist operators. Quality tends to be high and value for money good.

Hotels A wide choice, many modestly priced, the majority with no more than 30 rooms or so. Bookings for short stays are no problem – the peak season is summer. Ski Weekends specialise in, er, weekends and offer Le Vert (see below) and other 2- and 3-stars. Club Med has three linked buildings near the centre; 2009 reporters rate it highly ('absolutely excellent; varied and plentiful food').

****Hameau Albert 1er** (0450 530509) Smart, 100-year-old chalet-style Relais et Châteaux hotel with 'truly excellent' food (two Michelin stars) but expensive rooms (especially in the farmhouse annexe). Pool.

****Auberge du Bois Prin** (0450 533351) A small modern chalet with a big reputation; great views; bit of a hike into town (closer to Le Brévent).

****Mont-Blanc** (0450 530564) Grand 19th-century place in a central location, with gastro restaurant.

****Jeu de Paume** (Lavancher) (0450 540376) Alpine satellite of a chic Parisian hotel: a beautifully furnished modern chalet halfway to Argentière: 'Tasteful... friendly staff... lovely.'

****Grand Hotel des Alpes** (0450 553780) Elegant, central; with pool, sauna, hot tub. Friendly Italian staff.

****Morgane** (0450 535715) Cool modern style; excellent restaurant; convenient location near Aiguille de Midi cable car; pool, sauna.

***Alpina** (0450 534777) Much the biggest in town: modernist-functional place just north of centre.

***Croix-Blanche** (0450 530011) Central, dates from 1793. Reportedly traditional, simply-furnished rooms.

***Gourmets et Italy** (0450 530138) Spot-on central mid-price B&B hotel.

***Labrador** (Les Praz) (0450 559009) Scandinavian-style chalet close to the Flégère lift. Good restaurant.

***Prieuré** (0450 532072) Mega-chalet on northern ring-road – handy for drivers, quite close to centre.

***Vallée Blanche** (0450 530450) Small, low-priced 3-star B&B hotel, handy for centre and Aiguille du Midi.

***Gustavia** (0450 530031) Central. 'Spacious, clean and modern rooms.'

Chamonix

Interactive resort shortlist builder at **www.wtss.co.uk**

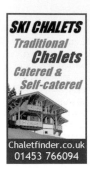
ACTIVITIES

Indoor Sports complex (swimming pool, sauna, steam room, tennis, squash, ice rink, fitness room, climbing wall), Alpine museum, library, cinemas, bowling

Outdoor Ice rink, snowshoeing, walking paths, tobogganing, dog sledding, paragliding, paintballing

UK PACKAGES

Alpine Answers, Alpine Ski and Golf Company, Alpine Weekends, Barrelli, Bigfoot, BoardnLodge, Chalet Group, Chalet la Forêt, Chamonix.uk.com, Club Med, Collineige, Crystal, Crystal Finest, Directski.com, Elegant Resorts, Erna Low, Esprit, Flexiski, High Mountain, Huski, Independent Ski Links, Inghams, Inspired to Ski, Interactive Resorts, Interhome, Jeffersons, Kuoni, Lagrange, Leisure Direction, Made to Measure, Marmotte Mountain, McNab Snowsports, Momentum, Mountain Tracks, Neilson, Oxford Ski Co, Peak Retreats, PV-Holidays.com, Rude Chalets, Simply Alpine, Ski Activity, Ski Collection, Ski Expectations, Ski France, Ski Freshtracks, Ski Independence, Ski Line, Ski McNeill, Ski Solutions, Skitracer, Ski Weekend, Skiweekends.com, Snow Finders, Thomson, White Roc

***Hermitage** (0450 531387) Central, very close to sports centre and cross-country tracks. Said to be 'modern and Savoyard-style smart'.
***Savoyarde** (0450 530077) Handy for the Brévent lifts. Recommended by a reporter.
****Arve** (0450 530231) Central, by the river; small rooms. Praised for good service and modest prices.
****Faucigny** (0450 530117) Cottage-style; in centre.
****Les Lanchers** (0450 534719) Near La Flégère, British owner, 11 rooms, recommended by 2009 reporter.
Clubhouse (0450 909656) Boutique hotel with a wide choice of rooms.
Le Vert (0450 531358) In Le Gailland 1.5km/1 mile from Chamonix, with en suite rooms for one to six people. 'Good bar, pool table, Sunday roast.'
Apartments Many properties in UK package brochures are in convenient but cramped blocks in Chamonix Sud. The Balcons du Savoy and Ginabelle are a cut above the rest: spacious, pool, gym, steam room etc. Both are featured by Erna Low, and Pierre et Vacances offers the Ginabelle.

EATING OUT ★★★★★
Plenty of quality places
The top hotels all have excellent restaurants and there are many other good places. One or two local guides give useful information about a selection of places.

The Impossible is a favourite with us and with readers – a rustic chalet a bit out of the centre with a varied menu ('superb, one of the best meals we've had in the Alps').

We always enjoy the intimate Atmosphère, by the river, despite its two-sitting system ('excellent', 'completely renovated'). The Panier des Quatre Saisons is a lot better than its shopping-gallery setting would suggest. Alan Peru is an excellent Asian-fusion place that makes a great change from the French norm.

Other reader recommendations include Maison Carrier in the Albert 1er hotel ('Bustling, rustic, traditional food'), Monchu (Savoyard specialities), Bergerie ('traditional'), Casa Valerio (pasta and pizza), Pitz ('decent, not too expensive meal'), Caleche ('adventurous dishes'), Tigre Tigre ('English-run curry house'), Munchies (fusion food; 'small, friendly, good atmosphere'), Sahara cafe (Asian) and Petite Kitchen (traditional French).

APRES-SKI ★★★★★
Lots of bars and music
Many of the bars around the pedestrianised centre of Chamonix get crowded at sundown – none more so than the Choucas video bar. At the bottom of La Flégère, the bar of the Rhododendrons hotel has 'live music, great atmosphere'. Back in town, during the evening, The Pub ('friendly staff and good British/Irish beer') and Bar'd Up are busy. The Chambre Neuf at the Gustavia hotel has live music and dancing ('crowded, noisy, but great fun'). The Micro Brasserie is 'very good', with live bands and DJs. No Escape is a 'funky, upmarket' lounge bar/restaurant. Along with Privilege, it's aimed 'at a more discerning clientele who like their après-ski at a less frantic pace'. Elevation 1904 is also 'quieter'. The Brit-run Dérapage is 'small but cosy'.

There's a lively variety of nightclubs and discos. The Choucas (again) and Garage ('lap dancing') are popular. The Mix has DJs into the night. The Cantina sometimes has live music. Bar Terrasse has 'live rock' every night and serves 'a good snack menu till 10pm'.

OFF THE SLOPES ★★★★★
An excellent choice
There's more off-slope activity here than in many resorts. Excursion possibilities include Annecy, Geneva, Martigny, Courmayeur and Turin. The Alpine Museum is 'very interesting but all in French', the library has some English language books and there's a good sports centre with a pool, ice skating and ice hockey matches.

Argentière 1240m/4,070ft

The old village is in a lovely setting towards the head of the valley – the Glacier d'Argentière pokes down towards it and the Aiguille du Midi and Mont Blanc still dominate the scene down the valley. There's a fair bit of modern development, but it still has a rustic appeal.

A number of the hotels are simple, inexpensive and handy for the village centre – but it's a fair hike (uphill on the way back) or a bus ride to and from the slopes. The 3-star Grands-Montets (0450 540666) is handy for the slopes but a hike to the village. It's a large chalet-style building and 'offers the comfort and service of a 4-star', says a visitor; 'luxurious rooms

UK PACKAGES

Argentière *Action
Outdoors, Alpine
Answers, AmeriCan Ski,
BoardnLodge,
Collineige, Crystal,
Crystal Finest, Erna
Low, Independent Ski
Links, Interactive
Resorts, Interhome,
Lagrange, Leisure
Direction, Peak
Retreats, Simply Alpine,
Ski France, Ski
Freshtracks, Skiholiday
extras.com, Ski
Independence, Ski
Weekend, TheWhite
Chalet.com, White Roc*
Les Houches *Alpine
Answers, Alpine Ski
and Golf Company,
AmeriCan Ski, Barrelli,
Bigfoot, Erna Low,
Inghams, Lagrange,
Peak Retreats,
PV-Holidays.com, Ski
Expectations, Ski
France, Skiholiday
extras.com,
Skiweekends.com*
Les Praz *Bigfoot,
Chalet la Forêt*
Vallorcine *Erna Low,
Peak Retreats*

Phone numbers
From abroad use the
prefix +33 and omit
the initial '0' of the
phone number

TOURIST OFFICES

Chamonix
t 0450 530024
info@chamonix.com
www.chamonix.com
Argentière
t 0450 540214
argentiere.info
@chamonix.com
Les Houches
t 0450 555062
info@leshouches.
com
www.leshouches.com

and a superb pool', says another. The
3-star Montana (0450 541499) has
'lovely rooms, excellent food', the
2-star Couronne (0450 540002) is
basic but 'a great value, old-fashioned
French hotel', the 2-star Dahu (0450
540155) is 'excellent value'.

Restaurants and bars are informal
and inexpensive. The Dahu is
recommended by a recent reporter for
'great food, good value set menus',
has a 'lovely terrace' and is 'busy with
locals and residents'. The Stone serves
'authentic pizzas and a few pasta
dishes' and 'is the place for a game of
darts or table football'. The Office is
always packed with Brits and
Scandinavians and has live bands and
'terrific cooked breakfasts'. The Savoy
bar is another traditional favourite –
'lively, friendly, well priced'. The
'friendly' Rencard plays reggae music
and 'is a great place to relax with fine
pizzas, omelettes and beer'. The
Rusticana is 'laid back' with 'friendly
staff, good selection of beers and
decent food', says a recent visitor.

Le Tour 1455m/4,770ft

Le Tour is a charming, unspoiled
hamlet at the head of the Chamonix
valley, handy for Argentière.
A gondola from here serves the
Domaine de Balme slopes, an area of
mainly easy runs that it shares with
Vallorcine in the next valley. The
valley's best nursery slopes are next to
the village, at La Vormaine.

Vallorcine 1255m/4,120ft

Vallorcine is a small, but developing,
traditional mountain village over the
Col des Montets, near the Swiss
border and 16km/10 miles from
Chamonix. The village shares with Le
Tour the main valley's Balme area.

A gondola and chairlift take you to
Tête de Balme. A gentle blue run leads
back to the village, but it is prone to
closure. There's a separate small area
of local slopes at La Poya.

Accommodation is mainly
apartment-based. The 4-star L'Ours
Bleu, with pool and spa facilities,
opened near the gondola for 2008/09
(featured by Erna Low and Peak
Retreats). There's a limited choice of
restaurants and bars. The Buvette at
the station is recommended for drinks
while waiting for the train back to
Chamonix (it takes 20 minutes).

Les Houches 1010m/3,310ft

Les Houches is 6km/4 miles down the
valley from Chamonix. The wooded
slopes – popular when bad weather
closes other areas – are the biggest
single area of pistes in the valley. But
the lifts are owned separately, and are
not covered by the standard Chamonix
pass – you need the Mont Blanc
Unlimited or the resort's own pass.

Les Houches is a pleasant village,
sitting in the shade of the looming
Mont Blanc massif. There is an old
core with a pretty church, but modern
developments in chalet style have
spread widely along the road at the
foot of the slopes, with the result that
some of them are quite a way from
the lifts. These are widely separated –
a queue-prone cable car and a
gondola, going to opposite ends of
the slopes. Up the mountain, all the
lifts are drags or slow chairs. There are
some awkward links in the network,
and signing is poor.

There are nursery slopes and open,
gentle runs at the top of the main lifts
and long, worthwhile runs back
towards the village – blue, red and
black. The last is Chamonix's World
Cup Downhill race course: an excellent
intermediate run, scarcely deserving its
black status. The terrain park is geared
to beginners and intermediates with
blue and red kicker lines and a few
rails at the bottom. But there are lots
of draglifts and flat areas in Les
Houches for boarders to beware of.

Beyond the summit ridge is a very
gentle area with cross-country loops
and then some pleasant, sunny
woodland runs on the back of the
mountain with views across to the
slopes of Megève.

In good weather the slopes are
quiet, and the views superb from the
several attractive restaurants, which
are cheaper than others in the valley.
Recommendations include the Terrain,
Vieilles Luges and the Ferme des
Agapes ('excellent'). Snow cover on
the lower slopes is not reliable, but
there is a fair amount of snowmaking.

The village is quiet, but there are
some pleasant bars and restaurants.
Reporters have recommended the
3-star Hotel du Bois (0450 545035).
There are some good apartments
available, including the Hameau de
Pierre Blanche with pool, sauna,
steam, hot tub (available through Peak
Retreats and Erna Low).

Interactive resort shortlist builder at **www.wtss.co.uk**

Châtel

A distinctively French base in an ideal position for exploring the huge Portes du Soleil circuit which spans the French-Swiss border

£105
RESORT PRICE INDEX

RATINGS

The mountains

Extent	★★★★★
Fast lifts	★★
Queues	★★★
Terrain p'ks	★★★
Snow	★★
Expert	★★★
Intermediate	★★★★
Beginner	★★★
X-country	★★★
Restaurants	★★★
Schools	★★★
Families	★★★

The resort

Charm	★★★
Convenience	★★
Scenery	★★★
Eating out	★★★
Après-ski	★★★
Off-slope	★★

NEWS

For 2009/10 a new six-pack is due to replace the Linga double chair to Tête du Linga, starting from a lower point. Snowmaking will also be expanded at Linga.

For 2008/09 the resort introduced a lift pass for six non-consecutive half-days.

The hotel Macchi gained a new spa and there's a new children's themed trail at Pré-la-Joux.

➕ Very extensive, pretty, intermediate terrain – the Portes du Soleil

➕ Wide range of cheap and cheerful, good-value accommodation

➕ Pleasant, lively, French-dominated village, still quite rustic in parts

➕ Local slopes are among the best in the Portes du Soleil and relatively queue-free

➕ Easily reached – one of the shortest drives from the Channel, and close to Geneva

➖ Traffic congestion can be a problem at weekends and in peak season

➖ Both the resort and the slopes are low for a French resort, with the resulting risk of rain and poor snow – though snowmaking is now extensive

➖ Some main lifts are a bus ride from the village centre

➖ Best nursery slopes are reached by bus or gondola

Châtel offers an attractive blend of qualities much like that of Morzine – another established valley village in the Portes du Soleil. Morzine is a bit more polished, Châtel (with a claimed 40 working farms) more rustic. But its key advantage is that it is part of the main Portes du Soleil circuit. There is a gap in the circuit at Châtel, filled by buses; but this is more of an irritant to those passing through than for Châtel residents, for whom the excellent local bus services are part of the daily routine. At weekends it's worth trying the slopes of nearby La Chapelle-d'Abondance, which are pleasantly uncrowded.

THE RESORT

Châtel is a much expanded village near the head of the wooded Dranse valley, at the north-eastern limit of the huge French-Swiss Portes du Soleil ski circuit. It has two separate sectors of slopes, one linked to its French neighbour – high, purpose-built Avoriaz – and the other to two resorts in Switzerland: Morgins (on the Portes du Soleil circuit) and Torgon (not on the circuit).

A few kilometres down the valley is the rustic village of La Chapelle-d'Abondance, with lifts into the Torgon slopes; it is covered at the end of this chapter.

VILLAGE CHARM ★★★
Rustic style, urban traffic
Châtel is still an attractive village, despite the inevitable expansion. Modern, unpretentious chalet-style hotels and apartments rub shoulders with old farms where cattle still live in winter. But it is no rustic idyll: life revolves around two streets that are far from traffic-free: lots of visitors take cars, and the centre can get clogged with traffic – especially at weekends.

CONVENIENCE ★★
No perfect position
Although there is a definite centre, the village sprawls along the road in from lake Geneva and the diverging roads up the hillside towards Morgins and along the valley towards the Linga and Pré-la-Joux lifts. There is an excellent, frequent though sometimes crowded

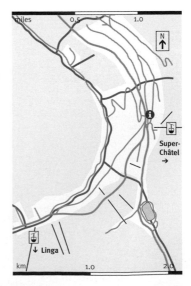

KEY FACTS

Resort	1200m
	3,940ft

Portes du Soleil	
Slopes	950-2300m
	3,120-7,550ft
Lifts	194
Pistes	650km
	404 miles
Green	13%
Blue	40%
Red	37%
Black	10%
Snowmaking	
	694 guns

Châtel only	
Slopes	1100-2205m
	3,610-7,230ft
Lifts	47
Pistes	83km
	52 miles
Green	23%
Blue	34%
Red	33%
Black	10%
Snowmaking	
	98 guns

free bus service linking the sectors. Staying centrally helps with catching the ski-bus to the outlying lifts before it gets very crowded, and simplifies après-ski outings – the night bus finishes at 9.30pm. But there is accommodation near the Linga lift, if first tracks are the priority.

SCENERY ★★★
Lots of variety
Châtel's broad valley setting is very scenic, with Linga providing a splendid backdrop and pleasantly woody slopes curving away in both directions. The lifts above Torgon give great views over Lake Geneva, and around the PdS circuit the dramatic Dents du Midi are constantly popping up.

THE MOUNTAINS

Châtel sits between two sectors of the main Portes du Soleil circuit, each offering a mix of open and wooded slopes. For notes on the circuit see our special chapter on it. The Châtel piste map deals adequately with the local slopes but covers the rest of the Portes du Soleil in one hopelessly ambitious map on the back.

EXTENT OF THE SLOPES ★★★★★
Two sectors to choose between
Directly above the village is **Super-Châtel** – an area of easy, open and lightly wooded slopes, accessed by a gondola or two-stage chair; the lifts in this sector are rather antiquated. From here you can embark on a clockwise Portes du Soleil circuit by heading to the Swiss resort of Morgins. Or you

can head north for the slopes straddling a different bit of the Swiss border, above **Torgon** (which has great views over Lake Geneva).

An anticlockwise circuit starts outside the village with a lift into the **Linga** sector – a gondola and new six-pack from Villapeyron to Tête du Linga or a choice of fast chairs from Pré-la-Joux. The faster way to Avoriaz is via Pré-la-Joux, but the new chair means you can take the enjoyable Tête route without enduring a slow, cold chair ride. There is night skiing on the Stade de Slalom run on Linga once a week.

FAST LIFTS ★★
Luxurious Linga
Linga and the slopes running across to Avoriaz are well served now that a new six-pack serves Tête du Linga itself – but in the Super-Châtel sector the lifts beyond the access gondola are almost entirely slow chairs and drags, whether you head for Morgins or for Torgon. Hence our rating.

QUEUES ★★★
Bottlenecks have been eased
Queues have been eased throughout the Portes du Soleil circuit in recent years by the introduction of several fast chairlifts. But queues form for the gondola to Super-Châtel when school parties gather and you can face queues to get down again if the sunny home slope is shut by poor snow. The slow Morclan chair at Super-Châtel has queues too, if the gondola is coming up full. Reporters have also found lengthy queues at the Tour de Don and Chermeu draglifts at certain times

↑ When you get near
the high points of the
area, the dramatic
Dents du Midi start to
come into view
OT CHATEL / JF VUARAND

Weekly news updates and resort links at **www.wtss.co.uk**

LIFT PASSES

Portes du Soleil

Prices in €

Age	1-day	6-day
under 16	26	134
16 to 60	39	200
over 61	31	160

Free under 5

Beginner points
tickets for private
village ski tows

Notes
Covers lifts in all
Portes du Soleil
resorts; half-day pass
available

Alternative pass
Châtel only (free for
over-75s)

of day, causing difficulties for skiers
rushing back to Super-Châtel to pick
up children from ski school.

TERRAIN PARKS ★★★
One at either end
Châtel has two parks: the Happy Park
built in the Cornebois sector is for
intermediates and experts. The main
Smooth Park at Super-Châtel was
redesigned recently to suit beginner
and intermediate freestylers, including
a half-pipe and boardercross.

SNOW RELIABILITY ★★
The main drawback
The main drawback of the Portes du
Soleil as a whole is that it is low, so
snow quality can suffer when it's
warm. But a lot of snowmaking has
been installed at Super-Châtel and on
runs down to resort level. Linga and
Pré-la-Joux are mainly north-facing and
generally have the best local snow.
The pistes to Morgins and Lindarets
get full sun.

FOR EXPERTS ★★★
Some challenges
The best steep runs – on- and off-piste
– are in the Linga and Pré-la-Joux area.
Beneath the Linga gondola and chair
there's a pleasant mix of open and
wooded ground, which follows the fall
line fairly directly. And there's a serious
mogul-field between Cornebois and
Plaine Dranse. Two pistes from the
Rochassons ridge are steep and kept

well groomed. On the way to Torgon
from Super-Châtel, the Barbossine
black run is long, steep and quite
narrow and tricky at the top. There's
plenty of good lift-served off-piste to
be explored with a guide: on a recent
visit we did a great run from Tête du
Linga over into the next (deserted)
valley of La Leiche.

FOR INTERMEDIATES ★★★★
Some great local terrain
When conditions are right the Portes
du Soleil is an intermediates' paradise.
Good intermediates need not go far
from Châtel to find amusement; Linga
and Plaine Dranse have some of the
best red runs on the circuit. The
moderately skilled can do the Portes
du Soleil circuit without problem, and
will particularly enjoy runs around Les
Lindarets and Morgins. Even timid
types can do the circuit, provided they
take one or two short cuts and ride
chairs down trickier bits. But some
blues are difficult when conditions are
poor – in particular, one reporter
witnessed skiers 'in tears' on the way
down to Morgins from Châtel.

Visits to the Hauts Forts runs above
Avoriaz are worthwhile. And note that
the runs back to Plaine Dranse are real
reds, and the Rochassons piste
especially can get extremely busy at
the end of the day.

Don't overlook the Torgon sector,
which has some excellent slopes,
including challenging ones.

ESF
t 0450 732264

International (ESI)
t 0450 733192

Henri Gonon
t 0450 732304

Francis Sports
t 0450 813251

Snow Ride (Ecole de Glisse)
t 0608 337651

Classes
(ESF prices)
6 half-days (2½hr am or pm) €119

Private lessons
€36 for 1hr, for 1 or 2 people

CHILDCARE

Mouflets Garderie
t 0450 813819
Ages 3mnth to 6yr;
8am to 7pm; full day with lunch €40

Club Piou Piou (Village des Marmottons)
t 0450 733379
Ages 3 to 6; 6 days
€352 (with lunch)

Le Jardin des Pitchounes
t 0450 813251
Ages 3 and 4

Ski schools
Generally take children from age 4 or 5 (International 6 half-days from €135)

GETTING THERE

Air Geneva 80km/ 50 miles (2hr)

Rail Thonon les Bains (40km/25 miles)

boarding

Avoriaz is the hard-core destination in the Portes du Soleil. Châtel is not a bad place to learn or to go to as a budget option. But many lifts in the Super-Châtel sector are drags and reporters warn they can be a 'painful experience'. The Linga area has good, varied slopes and off-piste possibilities as well as more boarder-friendly chairlifts.

FOR BEGINNERS ★★★
Three possible options
There are good beginners' areas at Pré-la-Joux (a bus ride away) and at Super-Châtel (a gondola ride above the village). And there are nursery slopes at village level if there is snow there. Reporters have praised the Super-Châtel slopes and lifts, which 'allow the beginner to progress' and 'safely practise' on gentle gradients away from the main runs. Getting up to them is a bit of an effort, though. The home run from Super-Châtel can be tricky – narrow, busy, steep at the end and often icy. The Pré-la-Joux slopes are less varied, with some steeper draglifts.

FOR CROSS-COUNTRY ★★★
Pretty, if low, trails
There are pretty trails (12km/8 miles) along the river and through the woods on the lower slopes of Linga, but snow-cover can be a problem. When combined with La Chapelle-d'Abondance's trails, the total is 60km/37 miles. The tourist office produces good maps with suggested routes and trail times.

MOUNTAIN RESTAURANTS ★★★
Some quite good local huts
Atmospheric chalets can be found both around the Portes du Soleil circuit and locally, notably in a cluster at Plaine Dranse – the Bois Prin, Tan ô Marmottes, Vieux Chalet ('fabulous meal, low ceilinged, laden with teddies, run by a mad woman'), Chaux des Rosées and Chez Denis have been recommended. In the Linga area the Ferme des Pistes is a cosy alpine barn, complete with stable-door and said to do 'simply the best tarte aux pommes'. At Super-Châtel the Portes du Soleil at the foot of the Coqs drags is much better than the big place at the top of the gondola. The Escale Blanche is worth a visit. The 'reasonable-priced' Panoramique at Torgon has 'views to die for' across Lac Leman. The chapter on Avoriaz has recommendations in the Lindarets valley, close by.

SCHOOLS AND GUIDES ★★★
Plenty of choice
There are five ski and snowboard schools in Châtel. The International school has been recommended by reporters, including visitors who had a private lesson that was 'one of our best ever' and a 2008 visitor's grandson who had 'so much more fun' than in previous lessons with the ESF. But the ESF has also been praised, with comments such as 'very helpful and customer-focused'.

FOR FAMILIES ★★★
Some good facilities
The Marmottons nursery has good facilities, including toboggans, painting, music and videos, and children are reportedly happy there. Francis Sports ski school has its own nursery area with a drag lift and chalet at Linga, all approved by a past reporter.

STAYING THERE

Although this is emphatically a French resort, packages from Britain are plentiful.

Chalets A fair number of UK operators have places here, including some Châtel specialists.

Hotels Practically all the hotels are 2-stars, mostly friendly chalets, wooden or at least partly wood-clad. But there are some smarter places.

★★★Macchi (0450 732412) Smart, modern chalet, with spacious, comfortable rooms, 'excellent food'; small pool, newish spa; most central of the 3-stars.

★★★Fleur de Neige (0450 732010) Welcoming chalet on edge of centre; Grive Gourmande restaurant is one of the best in town.

★★Belalp (0450 732439) Simple chalet with small rooms, but offering 'very good food'.

★★Choucas (0450 732257) Central location. 'Friendly owner.'

★★Kandahar (0450 733060) One for peace lovers: a Logis by the river, a walkable distance from the centre.

UK PACKAGES

Chalet Group, Connick, Interactive Resorts, Interhome, Lagrange, Simply Alpine, Ski Addiction, Skialot, Ski France, Skiholiday extras.com, Ski Independence, Ski Line, Ski Rosie, Skitracer, Snow Finders, Snowfocus, Susie Ward **La Chapelle-d'Abondance** *Ski Addiction, Ski La Cote*

ACTIVITIES

Indoor Spas in hotels, cinemas, library, bowling, drawing and painting lessons

Outdoor Ice rink, walks, tobogganing, cheese factory visits, ice diving, ice fishing, skijoring, snowshoeing (special route map for Châtel and Morgins)

Phone numbers
From abroad use the prefix +33 and omit the initial '0' of the phone number

TOURIST OFFICES

Châtel
t 0450 732244
touristoffice@chatel.
com
www.chatel.com

La Chapelle-d'Abondance
t 0450 735141
ot.lachapelle@
valdabondance.com
www.lachapelle74.
com

**Lion d'Or (0450 813440) In centre, is fairly basic with a 'good atmosphere'.
**Rhododendrons (0450 732404) 'Great service, friendly, comfortable.'
**Tremplin (0450 732306) 'Excellent, good value. Owner cooks well but speaks no English.'
Apartments Many of the better places are available through agencies specialising in Châtel or in self-drive holidays. The Gelinotte (out of town but near the Linga lifts and children's village) and the Erines (five minutes from the centre; can also be provided catered) look good. The Avenières is right by the Linga gondola. Châtel's supermarkets are reported to be small and overcrowded, so you'll be relieved to hear that there is a large supermarket out in the direction of Chapelle-d'Abondance.

EATING OUT ★★★
Fair selection
There is an adequate number and range of restaurants. The Macchi and Fleur de Neige hotels both have ambitious restaurants – and a reader points out that the Macchi's set menus are reasonably priced. We've also enjoyed the Table d'Antoine restaurant of the hotel Chalet d'Alizée, though it's a year or two since we were there. The excessively rustic Vieux Four does ambitious dishes alongside Savoyard specialities and is approved by readers ('good value and the best food we had all week'). The Pierrier and the Fiacre are more modest, everyday restaurants, good for families.

Out of town, the Ripaille, almost opposite the Linga gondola, is popular with locals and praised by reporters, especially for its fish. The hotel Cornettes in La Chapelle-d'Abondance is worth a trip.

APRES-SKI ★★★
All down to bars
The Tunnel bar is very popular with the British and has a DJ or live music every night (the caramel vodka has been recommended). The Avalanche is a very popular English-style pub with a 'good atmosphere and live music'. The Godille – close to the Super-Châtel gondola and crowded when everyone descends at close of play – has a more French feel. The 'small and cosy' Isba is the locals' choice, and shows extreme-sports videos. The bowling alley, the Vieille Grange, also has a good bar.

OFF THE SLOPES ★★
Less than ideal
Those with a car can easily visit places such as Geneva, Thonon and Evian. There are some pleasant walks, you can visit the cheese factory or the two cinemas, or join in daily events organised by the tourist office.

The Portes du Soleil as a whole is less than ideal for non-skiers who like to meet their more active friends for lunch: they are likely to be at some distant resort at lunch time and very few lifts are accessible to pedestrians.

La Chapelle-d'Abondance
1010m/3,310ft
This unspoiled, rustic farming community, complete with old church and friendly locals, is 5km/3 miles down the valley from Châtel. 'A car and a bit of French are virtually essential,' says a reporter. It has its own quiet little north-facing area of easy wooded runs and a gondola a bus ride away links it to slopes between Torgon in Switzerland and Super-Châtel, and so the Portes du Soleil circuit. The Mousseron hut, near the Braitaz chairlift, is 'well worth a visit', says a visitor.

Nightlife is virtually non-existent – just a few quiet bars, a cinema and torchlit descents. The Fer Rouge is a popular microbrewery, with live music.

The hotel Cornettes (0450 735024) is an amazing 2-star that has been run by the Trincaz family since 1894, with renovated rooms and 4-star facilities, including an indoor pool, a sauna, a steam room and hot tubs. It has an atmospheric bar and an excellent restaurant with good-value menus. Look out for the showcases displaying puppets and dolls and for eccentric touches, such as ancient doors that unexpectedly open automatically.

La Clusaz

*Attractive, scenic, distinctively French all-rounder; we like it a lot –
but we'd like it a lot more if it was 500 metres higher*

+ Traditional village in scenic setting with very French atmosphere

+ Interesting, varied slopes

+ Very short transfer from Geneva

+ Good, rustic mountain restaurants

− Snow conditions unreliable because of low altitude, but increased snowmaking has helped

− Some slow old chairs and drags

− May be crowds at peak times

TOP 10 RATINGS

Extent	★★★
Fast lifts	★★
Queues	★★★
Snow	★★
Expert	★★★
Intermediate	★★★★
Beginner	★★★★
Charm	★★★★
Convenience	★★★
Scenery	★★★

Few other major French resorts are based around what is still, essentially, a genuine mountain village that exudes rustic charm and Gallic atmosphere. Combine that with more than 200km/124 miles of largely intermediate slopes (if you add in nearby Le Grand-Bornand), above and below the treeline, and there's a good basis for an enjoyable, relaxed week. Snowmaking is continually increased, but of course it makes no difference if the temperatures are too high.

NEWS

For 2008/09 a hands-free lift pass system was introduced. The terrain park was revamped with new features, and a park-only lift pass was made available.

La Croix-Fry has been reinstated on the lift pass – good news as the slopes there link Beauregard and Manigod.

KEY FACTS

Resort	1100m
	3,610ft

La Clusaz only	
Slopes	1100-2470m
	3,610-8,100ft
Lifts	55
Pistes	132km
	82 miles
Green	28%
Blue	36%
Red	28%
Black	8%
Snowmaking	
	107 guns

THE RESORT

La Clusaz is built beside a fast-flowing stream at the junction of a number of narrow wooded valleys.

The resort is close to Geneva and Annecy, so is good for short transfers, but it does get crowded at peak times, and there can be weekend traffic jams. Buses (two euros) link with Le Grand-Bornand's 100km/62 miles or so of largely intermediate pistes (covered by the area lift pass).

Village charm La Clusaz has retained the Gallic charm of a genuine and friendly French mountain village quite unlike so many French resorts; the newer buildings have been built in chalet style and blend in well.

Convenience The resort's valley position has meant that it has grown in a rather rambling way, with roads running in a confusing mixture of directions. You can hire a locker next to the slopes to leave kit.

Scenery The scenery is attractively varied. Beauregard, as the name implies, has splendid views of the village and woody valleys.

THE MOUNTAINS

Like the village, the slopes are rather sprawling. There are five main areas.

Slopes Several points in La Clusaz have lifts giving access to the predominantly west- and north-west-facing slopes of L'Aiguille. From here you can reach the slightly higher and shadier slopes of the La Balme area, and a gondola returns you to Côte 2000 on L'Aiguille. La Balme is a splendid, varied area with good lifts. Going the other way from L'Aiguille leads you to L'Etale via the Transval cable car, which shuttles people between the two areas. L'Etale is now served by a chondola and quad chair. From there you can make your way over to Merdassier and the Manigod area; or from the bottom of L'Etale, you can take a piste to the village and the gondola up to Beauregard. From the top you can link via an easy piste and a two-way chair with La Croix-Fry, which has some good, gentle slopes. There is night skiing once a week.

Fast lifts Access is fine but there are still some old slow chairs and drags.

Queues Not a major problem except on peak weekends.

Terrain parks The newly revamped park on the L'Aiguille has 18 features, and a half-pipe. A park-only pass is now available (17 euros.)

Snow reliability Most of the ski area is low by French standards (below 2000m/6,560ft) so the snow can deteriorate if it's warm. The best snow is on the north-west-facing slopes at La Balme (the highest area, reaching 2470m/8,100ft). There is a lot of snowmaking on the lower mountain, and the home runs can depend on it. A 2008 visitor found the run from L'Aiguille to L'Etale closed in January.

Experts The best terrain is at La Balme – the black Vraille run is seriously steep. On the opposite side of the sector, the entirely off-piste Combe de Bellachat can be reached. The Noire run down the face of Beauregard can be tricky in poor snow and is often closed. The Tétras on L'Etale is steep

peak retreats

Quality self-
catering chalets
& apartments and
handpicked hotels

0844 576 0173
peakretreats.co.uk
ABTA W5537

Phone numbers
From abroad use the
prefix +33 and omit
the initial '0' of the
phone number

TOURIST OFFICE

t 0450 326500
infos@laclusaz.com
www.laclusaz.com

Weekly news updates and resort links at www.wtss.co.uk

only at the top. The Mur Edgar bumps run on L'Aiguille is steep but short. L'Aiguille has a good off-piste run down the Combe de Borderan and the long Lapiaz black piste runs down the Combe de Fernuy from Côte 2000.
Intermediates Early intermediates will delight in the gentle slopes at the top of Beauregard (plus the blue Guy Périllat run, with lovely views, back down to the bottom) and the slopes at Manigod. L'Etale and L'Aiguille have more challenging but wide blue runs. More adventurous intermediates will prefer the steeper slopes of La Balme.
Beginners There are nursery slopes at village level, and better ones up on Beauregard and at Crêt du Merle. Beauregard has lovely gentle blue runs to progress to; those from Crêt du Merle are steeper, but there is a green.
Snowboarding There are some good nursery slopes, served by chairlifts, and cruising runs to progress to. La Balme is great for good freeriders.
Cross-country The region has much better cross-country facilities than many resorts, with around 70km/ 43 miles of loops of varying difficulty.
Mountain restaurants A highlight: there are lots of them, and most are rustic and charming, serving good food at reasonable prices. Readers repeatedly recommend the Télémark ('fine food') above the chairlift to L'Etale and the Relais de L'Aiguille at Crêt du Loup ('superb food and wine', 'fabulous views'). The 'good value' Chez Arthur at Crêt du Merle has table- and self-service. The Bercail ('good but very

crowded'), Vieille Ferme at Merdassier ('excellent menu du jour') and U'Freddy at the base of the chondola ('Savoyard specialities') have also been recommended.
Schools and guides The ESF has received consistently good reports.
Families We have no recent reports on the kindergarten.

STAYING THERE

Hotels Small, friendly 2- and 3-star family hotels are the mainstay here; luxury is not an option. Reporters recommend the 3-star Alp'Hotel (0450 024006) ('brilliant') and Carlina (0450 024348) ('excellent food') and the 2-star ski in/ski out Les Sapins (0450 633333) ('good food, superb views').
Apartments There's quite a good choice, but some are out of town. Peak Retreats has a couple of options.
Eating out There's a wide choice of restaurants, some a short drive away. The St Joseph at the Alp'Hotel is regarded as the best in the village. Reporters recommend the Ecuelle ('fine food, great ambience') and Scierie ('lovely alpine feel').
Après-ski The 'olde-worlde' Caves du Paccaly has live music, the 'quaint' Le Salto draught Guinness, and L'Ecluse nightclub an 'excellent atmosphere'. The Bar au Vin, Grolle and lively Yeti have also been recommended.
Off the slopes There's tobogganing, an excellent aquatic centre, an ice rink and good walks. Some of the lifts and huts are accessible to non-skiers.

Les Contamines

A traditional French village with its own area of reliably snowy slopes and easy road access to nearby big-name resorts

- ✚ Largely unspoiled French village
- ✚ Fair-sized intermediate area
- ✚ Good snow record for its height
- ✚ Lift pass covers nearby resorts

- ▬ Lifts a bus ride from main village
- ▬ Can be some lengthy queues
- ▬ Lack of smart lodgings
- ▬ Quiet nightlife

TOP 10 RATINGS

Extent	★★★
Fast lifts	★★
Queues	★★★
Snow	★★★★
Expert	★★★
Intermediate	★★★★
Beginner	★★
Charm	★★★
Convenience	★★
Scenery	★★★★

NEWS

Snowmaking was increased for 2008/09. And a new guest house, Home Saint Roch, opened at Le Lay, beside the gondola.

Only a few miles from the fur coats of Megève and the ice axes of Chamonix, Les Contamines is quite a contrast to both, with pretty wooden chalets, an impressive old church, a weekly market in the village square and prices more typical of rural France than of international resorts. Its position at the shoulder of Mont Blanc gives it an enviable snow record.

THE RESORT

Les Contamines is a sprawling resort, with chalets scattered over a 3km/2 mile stretch of the valley. But it has a compact core. Bizarrely, the local pass does not cover the buses (8.50 euros per week). The weekly Mont Blanc pass covers Chamonix, Megève and other resorts too. A car is useful.

Village charm The centre is largely unspoiled with attractive old buildings.

Convenience The main access lift is 1km/0.5 miles from the centre at the expanding development of Le Lay. You can stay there or in the village centre, a shuttle-bus ride away.

Scenery There are magnificent views of Mont Blanc from the slopes.

THE MOUNTAINS

Most of the slopes are above the treeline, though the runs down from Signal are bordered by trees (as is the run from La Ruelle down to Belleville).

Slopes From Le Lay a two-stage gondola climbs up to the slopes at Signal. Another gondola leads to the Etape mid-station from a car park a little further up the valley, with a fast quad above it. Above these, a sizeable network of open, largely north-east-facing pistes fans out, with lifts approaching 2500m/8,200ft in two places. You can drop over the ridge at Col du Joly to south-west-facing runs down to La Ruelle, with a single red run going on down to Belleville. From Belleville, a 16-person gondola runs back up to La Ruelle, followed by a fast chair to Col du Joly.

Fast lifts Access is fine, but the upper mountain is poorly served.

Queues There can be 15- to 20-minute peak-period queues for the gondolas, especially if people are bussed in from other resorts with less snow. More irritating on our recent visit was a long wait for the old Grevettaz draglift when it kept breaking down.

Terrain parks They call these X Zones.

275

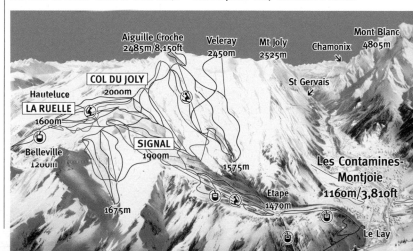

Aiguille Croche 2485m/8,150ft — Veleray 2450m — Mt Joly 2525m — Chamonix — Mont Blanc 4805m

COL DU JOLY 2000m

Hauteluce — St Gervais

LA RUELLE 1600m

Belleville 1200m — SIGNAL 1900m — 1575m

1675m — Etape 1470m

Les Contamines-Montjoie 1160m/3,810ft

Le Lay

KEY FACTS

Resort	1160m
	3,810ft

Les Contamines-
Montjoie/Hauteluce

Slopes	1160-2485m
	3,810-8,150ft
Lifts	24
Pistes	120km
	75 miles
Green	19%
Blue	21%
Red	36%
Black	24%
Snowmaking	
	162 guns

UK PACKAGES

Action Outdoors, Alpine
Answers, Chalet Kiana,
Interhome, Lagrange,
Simply Alpine, Ski
Expectations, Ski
France,
Skiholidayextras.com,
Skitracer

Phone numbers
From abroad use the
prefix +33 and omit
the initial '0' of the
phone number

TOURIST OFFICE

t 0450 470158
info@lescontamines.
com
www.lescontamines.
com

AGENCE NUTS / OT LES
CONTAMINES-MONTJOIE

The village centre is
largely unspoiled and
has pretty wooden
chalets and an old
church ↓

The main ski area has one (on Aiguille Croche), with a boardercross. There is another in the tiny Loyers area by the village, with a 120m/390ft super-pipe.

Snow reliability Many of the shady runs on the Contamines side are above 1700m/5,580ft, and the resort has a justifiable reputation for good snow late into the season, said to be the result of proximity to Mont Blanc. Snowmaking covers runs from Col du Joly down to the valley and some runs towards La Ruelle/Belleville. We have several reports of snow being better here when poor elsewhere; and a regular visitor tells of the combination of natural and man-made snow and careful piste management giving 'good conditions from December to April'.

Experts The steep western section has black runs, which are enjoyable but not terribly challenging. But there is substantial and varied off-piste terrain within the lift system and outside it – including a 'seriously steep and challenging' descent to Megève.

Intermediates Virtually all the runs are ideal for good intermediates, with a mix of fairly similar blues and reds. Some of the best go from the gondola's top station to its mid-station, and others are served by the Roselette and Bûche Croisée lifts. Given good snow, the south-facing runs down to La Ruelle are a delight. And the black runs are enjoyable for good intermediates. Timid intermediates might find sections of many blue runs too steep for comfort.

Beginners In good snow, the village nursery area is adequate for beginners. There are other areas at the mid-station and the top of the gondola. And there's a long green run from Col du Joly to La Ruelle. Novices should take the gondola down to the

village at the end of the day – the narrow red run can be icy.

Snowboarding There are quite a few draglifts, including four marked on the piste map as difficult, so inexperienced boarders beware. But there is excellent off-piste boarding on offer.

Cross-country There are 26km/16 miles of trails of varying difficulty. One of the loops is floodlit once a week.

Mountain restaurants There are quite a few lovely woody huts – not all marked on the piste map. Ferme de la Ruelle is a jolly barn, and the Grange just above it has been praised. Roselette ('classic Savoyard cooking') and Bûche Croisée (aka R'mize à Louis) are cosy chalets consistently recommended by reporters. Chez Gaston has great views. Signal is not rustic, but does 'tasty food'.

Schools and guides In the past we have had mixed reports on the ESF. But a 2009 reporter's 3-year-old got 'very good instruction and she still asks after the instructress'. There's an alternative International school, and mountain guides. One visitor enjoyed the 'challenging off-piste' found for him by Miage Aventure. Excursions are offered, including the Vallée Blanche.

Families Galipette's next to the central nursery slopes takes children from age one. Children can join ski school from age two and a half.

STAYING THERE

Hotels The 'comfortable' 3-star Chemenaz (0450 470244) at Le Lay has been praised. The Ferme de Bon Papa is a lovingly restored old farmhouse offering B&B.

Apartments A 2009 reporter found Chalet Kiana 'perfect for a large group'; hot tub and sauna.

Eating out Recommendations include the Husky, Op Traken and, for Savoie specialities, the Savoisien and Auberge du Chalézan. The O-à-la-Bouche has stylish gourmet dining (including the Marmot fondue restaurant).

Après-ski Après-ski is quiet, but there are several bars. The Saxo and the Ty Breiz with live music are rated the liveliest venues and O-à-la-Bouche has a smart wine bar. There's a varied programme of weekly events, including floodlit skiing twice a week.

Off the slopes There are good walks, tobogganing, snowmobiling, dog sledding, snowshoeing and a natural ice rink, but the village is limited.

Courchevel

Arguably the best of the half-dozen resorts that make up the famous Three Valleys – with a choice of four different villages

£145
RESORT PRICE INDEX

RATINGS

The mountains

Extent	★★★★★
Fast lifts	★★★★
Queues	★★★★
Terrain p'ks	★★
Snow	★★★★
Expert	★★★★
Intermediate	★★★★★
Beginner	★★★★
X-country	★★★★
Restaurants	★★★★
Schools	★★★★
Families	★★★★

The resort

Charm	★★
Convenience	★★★★
Scenery	★★★
Eating out	★★★★★
Après-ski	★★★★
Off-slope	★★★

NEWS

For 2009/10 a six-pack will replace the Roc Mugnier and Prameruel double chairs from Prameruel to the slopes above 1650 – speeding up access from 1850.

The beginner's lift pass will cover some lifts at Courchevel 1650. And a new three-hour lift pass will be available for the Courchevel valley.

Yet another 4-star luxe hotel, Le Strato, is due to open in 1850, with 25 rooms and spa. Six hotels have been elevated to the new 5-star classification.

For 2008/09 a blue run was created between the Pralong and Suisses chairs; snowmaking was increased and more lifts were fitted with the child safety 'Magnestick' system.

➕ Extensive, varied local terrain to suit everyone from beginners to experts – plus the rest of the Three Valleys easily accessible

➕ Lots of slope-side accommodation

➕ Impressive snowmaking and piste grooming, and a decent lift system

➕ Wooded setting is pretty, and useful in bad weather

➕ Choice of four very different villages

➕ Some great restaurants, and good après-ski by French standards

➖ Some pistes get crowded (though they can usually be avoided)

➖ Unremarkable villages – central 1850, in particular, is not the lovely spot you might hope it to be

➖ 1850 has the highest prices in the Alps (though in the lower parts prices are no higher than in other big French resorts)

➖ The French feel has been lost, with half the visitors now from abroad

➖ Not a great place for the indolent non-skier

Courchevel is the most extensive and varied sector of the famous Three Valleys, the biggest linked ski area in the world; it has slopes to satisfy everyone, from broad green motorways to narrow black couloirs. The snow over here is reliably better than in chief rival Méribel, over the hill – and they look after it better, too. Although links via Méribel-Mottaret to Val Thorens (at the head of the third valley) are good, a high proportion of visitors stray over the ridge rarely, or not at all. If we're heading for the 3V, more often than not we'll head for Courchevel.

But it's not one destination: the four villages making up the resort vary widely. It's high, swanky 1850 that catches the headlines, with its airstrip, ritzy hotels, grand chalets and Michelin-starred restaurants. The other villages – 1650, 1550 and 1300 – have none of 1850's pretensions. They also have few of 1850's high prices. Our RPI figure of 145 – the highest in the book – simply reflects the 115 prices we and readers recorded when in the area last season. They include pizza and pasta costing up to €20, and pints costing €10. But if you were careful you could pay half these amounts. If you caught happy hour at the Bubble bar in 1650, you could slake your thirst for only €4.

THE RESORT

Courchevel 1850 was one of the first French resorts to be purpose-built in the years immediately after World War Two. The other resort units were developed later, although they already existed as villages or hamlets. A road winds up from 1300 (still more often referred to as Le Praz) past 1550 (the original Courchevel), through 1650 (formerly Moriond) to 1850. The numbers are very loosely related to the resorts' altitudes; 1850 ought to be 1750, strictly speaking.

1850 is big enough to have several distinguishable quarters. The main lift base and the central area around it is La Croisette; the resort spreads widely across the hillside to the left through the chalet-filled suburbs of Cospillot and Nogentil to the Altiport, the

resort's famously hazardous little airport. Above these suburbs is a forested area with some of the swankiest hotels (and more modest chalets and apartments), the Jardin Alpin, served by its own gondola from La Croisette. On the opposite, right-hand side of La Croisette is another little 'downtown' area of shops and restaurants, with the suburbs of Chenus above it and Plantret below.

The other resort villages are smaller and simpler. The main part of 1650 has grown up along the road up to 1850: on one side, at the foot of the slopes, is a series of apartment blocks, plus an area of newer, more stylish development around the lift base area; and on the other side, individual chalets spreading down the hill. Then there is an area of more modern chalet development beside the

KEY FACTS

Resort	1260-1850m
	4,130-6,070ft

The Three Valleys	
Slopes	1260-3230m
	4,130-10,600ft
Lifts	180
Pistes	600km
	373 miles
Green	15%
Blue	38%
Red	37%
Black	10%
Snowmaking	33%

Courchevel/ La Tania only	
Slopes	1260-2740m
	4,130-8,990ft
Lifts	62
Pistes	150km
	93 miles
Green	23%
Blue	37%
Red	32%
Black	8%
Snowmaking	
	563 guns

slopes, the upper part known as Belvedère. 1650 has its own distinct sector of slopes, increasingly well connected to 1850. 1550 is a bit of a backwater with a mix of a few blocks and many more individual properties, directly below 1850 and sharing essentially the same position within the ski area. Le Praz is an old village set amid woodland, at the bottom of wooded slopes from 1850.

La Tania, built for the 1992 Olympics and a short drive from Le Praz, has managed to retain its own identity and gets its own chapter. The other resorts in the famous Three Valleys network are summarised in our short Three Valleys chapter, and of course get their own individual chapters. Given a car, Champagny is an easy outing, for access to La Plagne, and even Les Arcs.

VILLAGE CHARM ★★
Not a strong point
Courchevel 1850 has most of the smart hotels, nightlife and shops, and you would expect it to be a pretty smooth place in general. The reality is disappointing, particularly on arrival – although improvements are in train, the approach is dreary, and at La Croisette you are confronted by the backside of the main lift station building, complete with garage entrances. Past this point, things

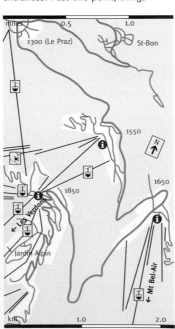

improve: the streets are lined by smart shops and jolly restaurants. But these streets are not a particularly attractive place to spend time, and the nearest thing to a central focus is where a hairpin bend on the road through touches the slopes; the contrast with old-money Megève, to make an obvious comparison, is sharp. The areas above the centre are more pleasant – in places, peacefully rustic.

These days, central 1650 is arguably more pleasant than central 1850. Most visitors don't find traffic intrudes, there is a quiet square off the main road with buildings that are smaller in scale than the apartment blocks along the road, and newer buildings are in a traditional style. There are plenty of quietly situated chalets. 1550 is a quiet, spacious dormitory, bypassed by the road to 1850. Le Praz suffers from through-traffic in parts, but away from the road is a low-key rustic place, with quiet streets and a friendly atmosphere, relatively unspoilt despite expansion for the 1992 Olympics – the ski jump is a prominent legacy.

CONVENIENCE ★★★★
Largely ski-in, partly ski-out
The villages all have lifts into the slopes, with much of the lodging close by, but in all cases you need to be careful about location if you want to avoid walks. 1850 has several pistes running through it, and a high proportion of ski-in/ski-out lodgings in all parts except the very centre, where you just plod to the lift base. 1550 and 1650 have a lot in common: they are essentially arranged along the bottom of the slopes, with lifts immediately above most of the lodgings – so they may be ski-in, but are more likely to be plod-out. But both villages have some lodgings beside the home slope as well. Le Praz is in general the least convenient place: the lifts start a short walk outside the village. And novice skiers based here face rides down from ski school as well as up to it. Efficient free buses run between the villages.

SCENERY ★★★
Go high for the best of it
Most of the villages enjoy a pretty woodland setting but the broad, open slopes above them have the best views to Mont Blanc and over the valley to Champagny and Bellecôte.

↑ First thing is a great time to ride the Saulire cable car to carve down the Combe Saulire red run before anyone else gets on to it
COURCHEVEL TOURISME / SEMAPHORE – PASCAL LEROY

LIFT PASSES

Three Valleys

Prices in €

Age	1-day	6-day
under 13	34	169
13 to 64	44	225
over 65	39	212

Free under 5, over 75
Beginner limited pass €16

Notes
Covers Courchevel, La Tania, Méribel, Val Thorens, Les Menuires and St-Martin; family reductions; pedestrian and half-day passes

Alternative passes
Courchevel/La Tania only with one-day Three Valleys extension; Courchevel 1650 only

THE MOUNTAINS

Although there are plenty of trees around the villages, most of the slopes are essentially open, with the notable exception of the runs down to 1550 and to 1300, and the valley between 1850 and 1650. These are great areas for experts when the weather closes in. Many reporters recommend buying only a Courchevel pass and then one-day extensions for the Three Valleys as necessary.

EXTENT OF THE SLOPES ★★★★★
Huge variety to suit everyone
A network of lifts and pistes spreads out from 1850. The main axis is the **Verdons** gondola, leading to a second gondola to La Vizelle and a nearly parallel cable car up to La Saulire. These high points of the **Saulire-Creux** sector give access to a wide range of terrain above Courchevel (including a number of couloirs), to Méribel and thus the whole of the Three Valleys. Next to the Verdons gondola is the Jardin Alpin gondola, which leads to runs back to 1850, and serves the higher hotels until 8pm. It also gives access via higher chairs to the valley of Prameruel and so to 1650 (now reached by a new fast chairlift).

To the right looking up, the Chenus gondola goes towards the **Loze-Praz** sector, a second link with Méribel. Runs go back to 1850, and through the woods to La Tania and 1300.

There are various ways up from 1650 to the minor high-points of Bel Air and Signal, and on into the **Chanrossa** sector. From here you can link across via the valley of Prameruel to Saulire-Creux, or head for the far end of the sector, where there is another link to Saulire-Creux via the col of Chanrossa.

FAST LIFTS ★★★★
Plenty of them
Courchevel has a generally impressive lift system, with pretty good links between all the village stations – the new six-pack due for 2009/10 will enhance the link from 1850 to the distinct 1650 sector. But slow old lifts are still in the majority – perhaps surprisingly, Courchevel scores less well than the other Three Valleys resorts in this respect.

QUEUES ★★★★
Not a problem
Even at New Year and in mid-February, when 1850 in particular positively teems with people, queues are minimal, thanks to the generally excellent lift system. However, there can be a build-up at 1850 for the gondolas and chairs as the ski school gets going. The Biollay chair is very popular with the ski school (which gets priority) and can be worth avoiding. Queues for the huge Saulire cable car are rare. At 1650, the main gondola may have peak time queues.

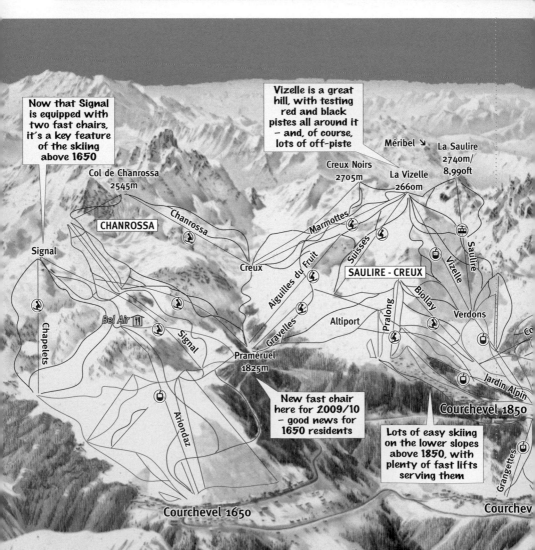

↙ Méribel

Col de la Loze
2275m

Chenus
2245m

Dou des Lanches

LOZE - PRAZ

Excellent, testing runs in the woods, which really come into their own in bad weather

A long green run has made La Tania a much better place for beginners than it used to be

aulire
.om/
9oft

Saulire

'erdons

Coqs

Chenus

Plantrey

Jardin Alpin

rchevel 1850

Grangettes

Touvets

Praz-Juget

Foret

La Tania

Praz

Courchevel 1550

La Tania
135om/4,43oft

Courchevel 1300 (Le Praz)
1260m/4,13oft

The Courchevel **ESF** is the largest ski school in Europe with over 700 instructors. They can help you find the best off-piste and explore it safely. For phone numbers see the schools list. The websites of the three different branches (1550, 1650, 1850) are given on the facing page.

ONE OF THE BEST FOR OFF-PISTE SKIING

Courchevel's image is of upmarket luxury and pampered piste skiing. But it is a great resort for off-piste too. Manu Gaidet is a Courchevel mountain guide and a ski instructor with the Courchevel ESF. He is also one of the world's top freeriders, and won the Freeride World Championship three years running. We asked him to pick out a few of the best runs.

These suggested routes are limited to the Courchevel valley. There is great off-piste in the rest of the Three Valleys, too. And you can heli-ski in Italy and Switzerland (it is banned in France). But never venture off-piste without a qualified ski instructor or mountain guide and safety equipment.

For a first experience off-piste, the Tour du Rocher de l'Ombre is great. Access is easy from the left of the Combe de la Saulire piste, and you are never far from the piste. It is very quiet, the slope is very broad and easy and you get a real sense of adventure as you plan your way between the rocks. And the view of the Croix des Verdons is impressive. Keep to the left for the best snow.

Les Avals is one of my favourite routes. The easiest way to get to it is to take the Roc Merlet piste from the top of the Chanrossa chairlift. Leave the piste on the right as soon as you can, then climb up and cross the ridge. Once you've arrived at a group of rocks (in the form of towers) descend the south side. This run is not technically difficult and is particularly beautiful in spring conditions. Another possibility from the Chanrossa chair is to traverse towards the Aiguille du Fruit. Almost anywhere along this very wide slope, you can choose your spot to start skiing down to rejoin the end of the Chanrossa black piste at the bottom. A technically more difficult run, for experienced off-piste skiers only, is Plan Mugnier. This starts with a 20-minute walk from the top of the Chanrossa chair but you are normally rewarded by very good snow because the slope you ski down faces north. Le Curé is in the Saulire area: this narrow gully starts under a towering rock and offers a steady 35° slope; it is only for expert skiers who don't mind climbing to the Doigt du Curé starting point.

TERRAIN PARKS ★★☆☆☆
Smaller than it used to be
Courchevel has undergone a bit of a change. It used to have four freestyle areas, but it now has only two, both in the 1850 sector. Along the Loze piste you'll find a decent boardercross. Last season the main terrain park was at Plantret, just below 1850. It had become a rail park only, with good boxes and rails along with a wall ride and rainbow box. The park may move to a new location for 2009/10, accessed from the Verdons gondola. Two shapers are on constant duty keeping the park in great shape and offering help if you need it.

SNOW RELIABILITY ★★★★☆
Very good
The combination of Courchevel's orientation (its slopes are north- or north-east-facing), its height, an abundance of snowmaking and excellent piste maintenance usually guarantees good snow down to at least 1850 and 1650. The snow is usually much better than in neighbouring Méribel, where the slopes get more sun – and one side

gets the afternoon sun, in particular. The runs to 1300 are still prone to closure in warm weather. Daily maps showing which runs have been groomed overnight are now only available at the tourist office or online.

FOR EXPERTS ★★★★☆
Some black gems
There is plenty to interest experts, even without considering the rest of the Three Valleys. The most obvious expert runs are the shady couloirs you can see on the right near the top of the Saulire cable car. All three main couloirs were once black pistes (some of the steepest in Europe), but now only the Grand Couloir remains a piste – the widest and easiest of the three, but reached by a narrow, bumpy, precipitous access ridge.

There is a lot of steep terrain, on- and off-piste, on the shady slopes of La Vizelle, both towards Verdons and towards the link with 1650. Some of the reds on La Vizelle verge on black and the black M piste is surprisingly little used. If you love moguls, try the black Suisses and Chanrossa runs – and the off-piste moguls under the

Les Ecoles du Ski Français de Courchevel

Conception graphique Pierre de Lune • © photos: S. Cunningham-Fotolia.com / C. Arnal

1550
www.esf-courchevel.com
+33 (0)4 79 08 21 07

1650
www.esfcourchevel1650.com
+33 (0)4 79 08 26 08

1850
www.esfcourchevel.com
+33 (0)4 79 08 07 72

SCHOOLS

ESF in 1850
t 0479 080772

ESF in 1650
t 0479 082608

ESF in 1550
t 0479 082107

ESF Centre Pralong
t 0479 011581

Supreme
t 0479 082787
(UK: 01479 810800)

New Generation
t 0479 010318
0844 484 3663 (UK)
www.skinewgen.com

Magic Snowsports Academy
t 0479 010181

Oxygène
t 0479 551745

Classes
(ESF 1850 prices)
6 days (2½hr am and pm): €288

Private lessons
€95 for 1½hr

GUIDES

Guides de Courchevel
t 0623 924612

boarding

Despite being an upmarket resort, Courchevel has always been popular with snowboarders. There are miles of well-groomed pistes, and the lifts are in general very modern and quick, with few drags. As it is very expensive, Courchevel best suits intermediates and advanced riders who can fully take advantage of this resort's resources. The big snowboard hangout in 1850 is Prends ta luge et tire toi, a combined shop/bar/internet cafe.

Chanrossa chair. For a change of scene and a test of stamina, a couple of long (700m/2,300ft vertical) blacks cut through the trees down to 1300 – though Jockeys, at least, barely deserves the black classification.

In good snow conditions you can ski all the way down (around 2000m/6,560ft vertical) from La Saulire to Bozel, way below 1300, over meadows and through trees on the final section.

There is plenty of other off-piste terrain in this valley to try with a guide – see the feature panel.

FOR INTERMEDIATES ★★★★★
Paradise for all levels
The Three Valleys is the greatest intermediate playground in the world, but all grades of intermediates will love Courchevel's local slopes too.

Early intermediates will enjoy the gentle Pyramides and Grandes Bosses blues above 1650, and the Biollay and Pralong blues above 1850. Those of average ability can handle most of the red runs without difficulty. Our favourite is the long, sweeping Combe de la Saulire from top to bottom of the cable car first thing in the morning, when it's well groomed and free of crowds; but it's a different story at the end of the day – cut up snow and crowds. Creux, behind La Vizelle, is another splendid, long red that gets bumpy and unpleasantly crowded later on. Marmottes from the top of Vizelle is quieter and more challenging.

The Loze-Praz sector has excellent blues and reds down towards 1850 and 1550 and through the trees towards La Tania – long, rolling cruises. Over at 1650, the Chapelets and Rochers reds right at the edge of the area are great fun for fast cruising, although with a six-pack serving them they are not as quiet as they were.

FOR BEGINNERS ★★★★
Great graduation runs
There are excellent nursery slopes above both 1650 and 1850. At the former, lessons are likely to begin on the short drags close to the village, but quick learners will soon be able to go up the gondola. The best nursery area at 1850 is at Pralong, above the village, near the airstrip. A reporter points out that getting to it from the village isn't easy, unless you go by road, which absolute beginners would. A blue path links this area with chairs to 1650, so keen novices can soon move further afield. The Bellecôte green run down into 1850 is an excellent, long, gentle slope – but it is used by other skiers and does get unpleasantly crowded. It is served by the Jardin Alpin gondola, and a drag that is one of eight free beginner lifts. 1550 and 1300 have small nursery areas, but most people go up to 1850 for its more reliable snow.

FOR CROSS-COUNTRY ★★★★
Long wooded trails
Courchevel has a total of 66km/41 miles of trails, the most in the Three Valleys. 1300 is the most suitable village, with trails through the woods towards 1550, 1850 and Méribel. Given enough snow, there are also loops around the village.

MOUNTAIN RESTAURANTS ★★★★
Good but can be very expensive
Mountain restaurants are plentiful and pleasant, but before you install yourselves at a table it is sensible to check the prices, which are generally high (and can be sky-high).
Editors' choice The Bel Air (0479 080093), above 1650, stands out. It is unfailingly welcoming, with good food at prices that are reasonable by local standards (and house wine that our comprehensive survey has shown to be about the cheapest in the Alps), friendly and efficient service and the bonus of a splendid tiered terrace. Our readers agree: 'superb food', 'stunning views', 'outstanding value' and 'excellent service'.
Worth knowing about The Soucoupe, near the top of the Chenus gondola, has good food and views; we tried the

Ski schools
Most offer lessons from age 3 or 4 (ESF 1850 prices €290 for 6 days)

Phone numbers
From abroad use the prefix +33 and omit the initial '0' of the phone number

SMART LODGINGS
Check out our feature chapters at the front of the book.

---

cosy, atmospheric table-service section upstairs and found the steaks OK, but the prices for both food and wine were a bit steep. The Chenus itself is 'OK for a quick lunch'. The Bergerie on the Bellecôte piste has 'a splendid terrace and lively music'. Chalet de Pierres, close to 1850, is famously pricey, but we confess to calling in for an occasional treat, and a reporter confirms it is 'as good as ever'.

SCHOOLS AND GUIDES ★★★★
Plenty of choice
Courchevel's branches of the ESF add up to the largest ski school in Europe, with over 700 instructors. It is conscientiously managed, and operates an impressive system of assessing and improving the foreign language skills of its instructors. Recent reports have been positive.

A 2009 reporter praises RTM Snowboarding, 'Excellent. My wife rated her private lesson as the best she has had.'

New Generation is a school run by top British instructors. We continue to receive rave reviews about this outfit: 'really great lesson – we both got a lot out of it', 'the highlight of the trip',

'head and shoulders above any other ski school I've come across'.

Supreme in 1850 is also British-run and has received good past reports.

Magic Snowsports Academy now incorporates Ski Academy and Magic in Motion – reports please.

The Bureau des Guides runs all-day off-piste excursions. There's also an area at the foot of Les Suisses piste with at least weekly transceiver practice and avalanche rescue sessions with dogs and pisteurs (free).

FOR FAMILIES ★★★★
Lots of suitable options
Courchevel is a good choice for families; there is lots of convenient lodging and gentle slopes. The resort was one of the first to use the magnetic system, 'Magnestick', to hold children securely on chairlifts; it is now Installed on six lifts. ESF at 1850 offers a Kids 'Up' programme for English-speaking children between six and 12 years with a maximum of eight children per group. Their Club des Piou-Piou at 1650 is reportedly 'very well run and a good introduction to skiing for children'. Several UK chalet operators run nurseries.

GETTING THERE

Air Geneva 195km/
120 miles (2hr45);
Lyon 195km/
120 miles (2hr30);
Chambéry 110km/
70 miles (1hr30);
direct flights to
Courchevel altiport
from London on
request only (contact
tourist office for
details)

Rail Moûtiers (24km/
15 miles); transfer by
bus or tax

STAYING THERE

Chalets Take your pick; there are lots
available – specialist travel agents list
dozens of them. And the resort
literature lists a score or more of
swanky places to rent.

In 1850 several operators offer
notably comfortable chalets, and a few
genuinely luxurious ones. Kaluma,
Descent, Scott Dunn and Supertravel
would be the first to look at. Ski Total,
Mark Warner and Skiworld all have
central chalet hotels in 1850.

Le Ski has specialised in 1650 for
27 years and has 12 chalets there,
from comfortable to classy – over half
with sauna or steam room. Ski
Olympic has the central Les Avals
chalet hotel in 1650 (complete with
Rocky's bar) plus a couple of large
chalets – Mors was praised in 2009
('beautiful lounge, fantastic staff,
superb food') and Monique has been
newly revamped to become one of the
company's two Gold Collection chalets.
Finlays has six chalets in 1550, and
one up in 1850. Family specialist Esprit
Ski has several chalets and chalet
apartments down in 1300.

Hotels There are more than 40 hotels
in Courchevel, mostly at 1850 and
many of them very swanky. Half a
dozen are in the newly created 5-star
category, and a further half dozen in
the 4-star luxe category – the top of
the French scale until now. The prices
of the top places give new meaning to
the word 'exorbitant' – it is possible to
pay £1,000 per person per night
without too much difficulty, though
you can of course pay a lot less. In
our listings we try to concentrate
mainly on more affordable places.

COURCHEVEL 1850

*****Sivolière** (0479 080833) Chalet
set among pines on the western edge
of the village, with a reputation for
friendly service despite the stars.

****Bellecôte** (0479 081019) A bit of
Alpine atmosphere as well as luxury.
Close to the Bellecôte piste.

****Chabichou** (0479 080055)
Distinctive white building, right on the
slopes; family-run, friendly and rustic,
with very good food plus the option of
a restaurant with two Michelin stars.

***Ducs de Savoie** (0479 080300)
'Comfortable, friendly' ski-in/ski-out
hotel in the Jardin Alpin area.

***Courcheneige** (0479 080259)
Welcoming spot well out of town on
Bellecôte piste with a pleasant rustic
restaurant (popular for lunch).

COURCHEVEL 1650

*****Manali** (0479 080707) Opened
two seasons ago; slope-side, just
above the gondola, with terrace; spa
and pool (open to the public).

***Portetta** (0479 080147) Very smart
new place next to the Manali, with a
good restaurant, a pool – and the
most civilised ski/boot room this side
of the Atlantic.

***Seizena** (0479 082636) Stylish and
central (over road from the gondola).

Alpine Answers, Alpine Weekends, Chalet Group, Crystal, Crystal Finest, Descent International, Elegant Resorts, Erna Low, Family Friendly Skiing, Finlays, First Choice, Flexiski, Friendship Travel, Independent Ski Links, Inghams, Inspired to Ski, Interactive Resorts, Jeffersons, Kaluma, Kuoni, Lagrange, Leisure Direction, Le Ski, Made to Measure, Mark Warner, Momentum, Neilson, Oxford Ski Co, Powder White, PV-Holidays. com, Richmond Holidays, Scott Dunn, Silver Ski, Simply Alpine, Ski Activity, Ski Amis, Ski Collection, Ski Deep, Ski Expectations, Ski France, Skiholiday extras.com, Ski Independence, Ski Line, Ski Link, Ski Olympic, Ski Power, Ski Solutions, Ski Total, Skitracer, Ski-Val, Ski Weekend, Skiworld, Snow Finders, Snowworks, Supertravel, Thomson, White Roc

ACTIVITIES

Indoor Ice rink, bowling, exhibitions, concerts, cinemas, language and computer courses, cookery courses, library; in hotels: health and fitness centres (swimming pools, saunas, steam room, hot tub, water therapy, weight training, massage)

Outdoor Hang-gliding, helicopter flights, paragliding, flying lessons, dog sledding, ice driving, go-karts on ice, snowshoeing, snowmobile rides, climbing, ice karting, ballooning, walking on cleared paths, tobogganing

TOURIST OFFICE

t 0479 080029
info@courchevel.com
www.courchevel.com

COURCHEVEL 1550
***Flocons** (0479 080270) Handsome chalet just yards from the Tovets six-pack and the piste from 1850.
COURCHEVEL 1300 (LE PRAZ)
***Peupliers** (0479 084147) Traditional, smartly renovated and expanded, good restaurant.
Apartments Excluding the swanky private chalets, the best bets are the Montagnettes at the top end of 1650 (apartments and semi-detached chalets) and the Chalets du Forum in the heart of 1850.

EATING OUT ★★★★★
Pick your price
There are a lot of good, very expensive restaurants in Courchevel, and some that are more affordable. A non-comprehensive pocket guide is distributed locally.

In 1850, among the best and priciest, with two Michelin stars, are the Chabichou and the Bateau Ivre. The restaurant at the new four-star hotel Kilimandjaro has a Michelin star too. We and reporters have enjoyed the Saulire (aka Chez Jacques), though the prices are said to have risen hugely – and one 2009 visitor was bugged by the excessively noisy clientele. Alternatives include the Chapelle for meat cooked on an open fire, the Italian Cendrée ('excellent food, quiet – strongly recommended'), the Anerie ('nice meal but a little pricey'), the 'charming' Refuge, the Fromagerie and Genepy ('delightful French food'). If you fancy Tex-Mex or pizza, try Kalico. The Mangeoire is mainly popular for its party atmosphere, but does straightforward food (at high prices).

In 1650 the new hotel Manali is 'good but pricey' and the cosy Eterlou has an 'excellent array of local dishes, with plenty of local speciality meat and cheese dishes'. The Petit Savoyard is recommended for 'excellent' pizzas.

In 1300, Bistrot du Praz is expensive but excellent; two separate reports this year speak of 'one of the finest meals I have ever eaten' and worth the high prices. We've had excellent meals at the hotel Peupliers.

APRES-SKI ★★★★
1850 has most variety
1850 is the focus for après-ski and lively nightlife, though residents of the other villages with a more limited range of options have the considerable

compensation of much more tolerable prices. The Cap Horn on the lower slopes is a 'good place to relax and listen to the DJ spin some tunes', but you pay for the privilege. The Jump at the foot of the main slope has for years been very popular as the lifts close, but whether it will remain so now that it is in French hands remains to be seen. We're told the Brit-run hotel Olympic has 'possibly the cheapest pint in Courchevel'. Or maybe in Courchevel 1850.

But it's later on when things really get going. There are some exclusive nightclubs, such as the Caves. The Grange, a Moroccan-style place, and the Kalico are pumping until the early hours. The Mangeoire piano bar gets going late and is 'great fun' for live music, says a 2009 reporter. The Bergerie has entertaining themed evenings and the Tremplin has karaoke. The Petit Drink specialises in wine and tapas. And Oxygen is a cool new lounge bar.

In 1650, the Brit-run and Brit-filled Bubble bar is said to be even more pivotal following 'a big makeover' – a favourite among reporters, with satellite TV, Wi-Fi, live music, quiz nights and 'very friendly' atmosphere. Views differ on the attractions of the rival Rocky's bar (Brit-run, again). The Funky Fox has pool, games and live music or DJs and the Club disco stays open till 4am.

In 1550 try the Chanrossa bar or the Taverne. And in 1300 the Escorchevel bar is said to be lively.

OFF THE SLOPES ★★★
Not ideal
There is quite a bit to do, as our margin panel spells out, but the emphasis is very much on physical activities. A non-skiers' guide is distributed by the tourist office. Cinemas in 1850 and 1650 show English-speaking films. Snowshoeing among the trees is growing in popularity. A pedestrian lift pass for the gondolas and buses in Courchevel and Méribel makes it easy for non-skiers to get up the mountain to meet others for lunch. A 2008 visitor recommends the toboggan run from 1850 to 1550 ('great fun ... very fast'). And you can take joyrides from the altiport. There is a pocket shopping guide listing about a dozen fashion and jewellery shops in 1850, and a couple of galleries.

Courchevel

Interactive resort shortlist builder at **www.wtss.co.uk**

Les Deux-Alpes

Sprawling resort with a high, narrow ski area that will disappoint many intermediates; popular for summer skiing and boarding

£105
RESORT PRICE INDEX

RATINGS

The mountains

Extent	★★★
Fast lifts	★★
Queues	★★
Terrain p'ks	★★★★★
Snow	★★★★
Expert	★★★★
Intermediate	★★
Beginner	★★★
X-country	★★
Restaurants	★★★
Schools	★★★
Families	★★★★

The resort

Charm	★★
Convenience	★★★
Scenery	★★★★
Eating out	★★★★
Après-ski	★★★★
Off-slope	★★

288

NEWS

For 2009 the summer terrain park's super-pipe walls were increased to 6.7m/22ft high and the park got its own dedicated drag. A new 'shred zone' was also created. For 2008/09, the winter park gained new, beginner-friendly fun features.

- ➕ High, snow-sure, varied slopes, including an extensive glacier area
- ➕ Lots of good off-piste terrain
- ➕ Stunning views of the Ecrins peaks
- ➕ Lively resort with varied nightlife
- ➕ Wide choice of affordable hotels

- ➖ Piste network modest by big resort standards and congested in places
- ➖ Home runs are either steep and icy or dangerously overcrowded – so people queue for a lift down
- ➖ Virtually no woodland runs
- ➖ Spread-out resort

We have a love-hate relationship with Les Deux-Alpes. We quite like the buzz of the village and we understand the appeal of its vibrant nightlife. We love the high-Alpine feel of its main mountain, and the good snow to be found on the north-facing slopes at mid-mountain. But we're unimpressed by the limited extent of the pistes and we hate the congestion that results in peak season when most of the town's 35,000 visitors are crammed on to them.

THE RESORT

Les Deux-Alpes is a narrow village sitting on a high, remote col. Access is from the Grenoble-Briançon road to the north. The resort has grown haphazardly over the years, and there is a wide range of building styles, from old chalets through 1960s blocks to more sympathetic recent buildings. It looks better as you leave than as you arrive, because all the balconies face the southern end of the resort.

The six-day pass covers two days in Alpe-d'Huez and one in Serre-Chevalier (an hour away over the Col du Lautaret) and a day in several other resorts. Helicopter trips to Alpe-d'Huez are good value at 65 euros return and a shuttle-bus goes on Wednesdays and Thursdays (must book for both).

VILLAGE CHARM ★★
Lively, but that's all

The village is a long, sprawling collection of apartments, hotels, bars and shops, most lining the busy main street and the parallel street that completes the one-way traffic system. It has a lively ambience and a 2009 visitor particularly liked the 'many, varied shops strung out through the village'.

CONVENIENCE ★★★
Three main parts

Lifts are spread fairly evenly along the village and there is no clear centre. But three sectors can be identified. As you enter the village from the north, roads go off on the left to wind up the hill to Les 2 Alpes 1800 – inconvenient for shopping and nightlife, though not necessarily for skiing. Carry on and you come to the geographical centre of the resort, with the major gondola stations, popular outdoor ice rink and lots of shops and restaurants. At the end of the resort is Alpe de Venosc, with many of the nightspots and hotels, the most character, the fewest cars, the best shops and the Diable gondola. The free shuttle-bus service saves some long walks.

SCENERY ★★★★
High, southern peaks

The resort sits high among the southern Alps, with great views from the glacier to the rugged Ecrins mountains and over the Briançon valley.

↑ The village sprawls along the valley floor and most runs back to it are quite steep

KERRY LEWIS

KEY FACTS

Resort	1650m
	5,410ft
Slopes	1300-3570m
	4,270-11,710ft
Lifts	51
Pistes	225km
	140 miles
Green	20%
Blue	40%
Red	21%
Black	19%
Snowmaking	
	214 guns

THE MOUNTAINS

The slopes are fragmented and the main ones are very high but narrow. Virtually all are above the treeline. The western **Pied Moutet** side of Les Deux-Alpes is served by lifts from various parts of town. It is relatively low (the top is 2100m/6,890ft) and now that the lift from Bons has be closed, it has only short pistes back to town, which get the morning sun (though you can still go off-piste down to the Mont de Lans chairlift).

On the broad, gentle slope east of the resort are about a dozen beginner lifts, and above them a steep slope down from the ridge of **Les Crêtes**. To get back to the village you have a choice of one winding green run, often very crowded, or four short black runs. These are usually mogulled (two are

ungroomed), and often icy at the end of the day. Many visitors ride down.

The ridge has lifts and gentle runs along it, and behind it lies the deep, steep Combe de Thuit. Lifts span the combe to the mid-mountain station at **Toura** at the heart of the slopes. We seem to spend a lot of time on three key fast lifts. Above Toura, the Glaciers chair takes you up 600m/1,970ft for blue and red runs back down. Below it, the Bellecombes chair serves a range of good, high slopes. And off to the north, the Fée chair serves its own (relatively quiet) sector. The chairs going up to La Toura serve short runs and various terrain features. The middle section of the mountain, around Toura, is very narrow, and prone to crowding (you can avoid the narrow section below Toura by going down to La Fée and taking the gentle

boarding

Les Deux-Alpes has become a snowboard Mecca over the past few years. Its cheap and cheerful atmosphere counts for a lot – while the limited pisted slopes aren't as off-putting to boarders as to skiers. The kick-off to the French winter season begins here with a huge Rock On Snowboard Tour, with snowboard competitions and free snowboard tests (24-25 October in 2009, with the glacier staying open till 1 November). In town there are good trampoline facilities and a huge airbag to get a feeling of what air-time is all about. Although the focus is on the terrain park, the freeriding is not to be underestimated, with plenty of steep challenging terrain. Beginners will find the narrow, flat crowded areas mid-mountain and the routes down to the village intimidating. Most of the lifts on the higher slopes are chairs, and there are the specialist Primitive and Bliss snowboard schools.

piste to the Truite and Voûte chairs).

The top **Glacier du Mont de Lans** section has fine, easy runs with great views, served by an underground funicular and draglifts. You can go from the top all the way down to Mont-de-Lans – a descent of 2270m/7,450ft vertical that we believe is the world's biggest on-piste vertical. A walk (or snowcat tow) takes you to the slopes of La Grave (covered by the lift pass). There are more slopes off to the north, served by chairs.

The piste map is inadequate, especially for the area around Toura and Crêtes. A few blue runs have short steep sections and some runs are different colours on the map and on the mountain.

EXTENT OF THE SLOPES ★★★☆☆
Surprisingly small
Despite the long description above (necessary because of the fragmented nature of the slopes), for a big resort Les Deux-Alpes has a disappointingly small piste area (especially if the snow on the Pied Moutet side is poor and rules it out – as has been the case on each of our visits). A recent reporter confirms our view: 'A real lack of mileage; we skied pretty much everything in a day.'

FAST LIFTS ★★☆☆☆
Main lifts OK but ...
Les Deux-Alpes has some impressive lifts, with fast chair alternatives to the gondolas. But there are still lots of draglifts and a few slow chairs around.

QUEUES ★★☆☆☆
Can be a problem
The village is large and queues at the morning peak can be 'diabolically' long for the Jandri Express and Diable gondolas. The top lifts are prone to closure if it's windy, putting pressure on the lower lifts. We have repeated reports of queues for the gondolas back to the village when snow is poor low down.

TERRAIN PARKS ★★★★★
A real highlight
The heavyweight terrain park is located on the Toura run in the winter, then shifts up to the glacier in the summer and reopens mid-June (www.2alpes-snowpark.com). Easily one of the top parks in Europe, this has something for everyone (including beginners). All sizes of kickers, hips, rails and boxes will keep all levels challenged throughout the day. The highlights of this 800m/2,620ft-long park are an impeccable super-pipe in the winter and two of them in the

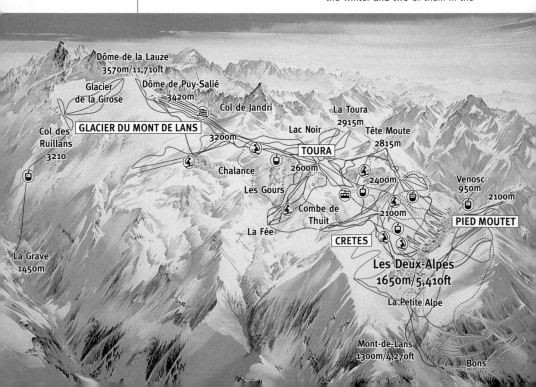

The off-piste routes in Les Deux-Alpes are numerous and varied in difficulty. But never try them without the right equipment and a qualified guide.

Both sides off the **Bellecombes** *piste offer a wide range of varying terrain; it's important to take care here – there are several small cliff faces. For those keen to tackle couloirs this descent offers small ones that are ideal for your first attempts; they can be avoided, though.*

Traversing across the top of the black Grand Couloir piste leads to the **North Rachas** *area, with off-piste faces that normally offer good snow conditions all winter. The first large valley leads to three couloirs – one fairly broad and easy, the others much narrower and steeper. Traversing further leads to a much wider descent that avoids the three couloirs.*

Strong skiers will enjoy the famous **Chalance** *run (our favourite), which starts just below the glacier and descends 1000m/3,280ft vertical to the Gours run; there are several variations, mixing wide open slopes and rocky pitches. These faces are at times subject to quite a high avalanche risk.*

Traversing above the north face of the Chalance leads to the couloir **Pylone Electrique** *– a steep, narrow 200m/660ft-long couloir with the reward below it of an excellent wide powder field of moderate gradient. A rest on the Thuit chairlift is a must after this adrenalin-charged descent.*

As well as these routes within the local lift network, there is a renowned descent to **St-Christophe** *(you get a taxi back) and the famous* **La Grave** *terrain (see separate chapter) is easily accessed.*

Les Deux-Alpes

Interactive resort shortlist builder at **www.wtss.co.uk**

SCHOOLS

ESF
t 0476 792121

International St-Christophe
t 0476 790421

European
t 0476 797455

Primitive Snowboard
t 0607 907135

Ski Privilege
t 0476 792344

Easiski
t 0476 795884

Bliss
t 0476 795676

Damien Albert
t 0476 795038

Classes
(ESF prices)
6 half days (2¼hr am or pm) €147

Private lessons
€37 for 1hr

GUIDES

Bureau des guides
t 0476 113629

glacier park for the summer. In 2009 the big summer super-pipe increased in size yet again – to walls of 6.7m/22ft. It now also has its own dedicated draglift. Also new for 2009 was the 'shred zone' with a focus on street obstacles. The boardercross course has been completely redesigned and sits in its own area next to the park. DJs regularly play music, and a BBQ area and chill-out zone complete the mix.

SNOW RELIABILITY ★★★★
Excellent on higher slopes
The snow on the higher slopes is normally very good, even in a poor winter. Above 2200m/7,220ft most of the runs are north-facing, and the top glacier section guarantees good snow. More of a concern is bad weather shutting the lifts, or extremely low temperatures at the top. But the runs just above the village from Les Crêtes face west, so they get a lot of afternoon sun and can be slushy or icy. Snowmaking has been improved on the lower slopes – but a January visitor skiing on rocky pistes saw it used 'not once'. We have never found the snow on the relatively low Pied Moutet sector good enough to ski.

FOR EXPERTS ★★★★
Off piste is the main attraction
The area offers wonderful off-piste – see above. We especially loved the long, deserted Chalance run which is easier than it looks from the bottom.

A free weekly Free Respect event promotes off-piste safety (see 'Schools and guides').

But there are few on-piste challenges. The black runs down to the resort are steep, but they often have poor snow conditions. Elsewhere, don't miss the black Grand Couloir and its off-piste variant (which often has better snow) from Tête Moute; the black and red runs down from the top of the Fée chair are enjoyable, and so is the red run served by the Super Diable chairlift.

FOR INTERMEDIATES ★★
Limited cruising
Les Deux-Alpes can disappoint keen intermediates because of the limited extent of the pistes. Avid piste-bashers will cover the pistes in a couple of days, especially if the snow in the Pied Moutet sector is not good enough to be enjoyable. A lot of the runs are either rather tough – some of the blues could be reds – or boringly bland. The runs higher up generally have good snow, and there is some great fast cruising, especially from the glacier to Toura and on the mainly north-facing pistes served by the chairlifts off to the sides. You can often pick gentle or steeper terrain in these bowls as you wish. The chairlifts at the glacier serve great carving pistes. Many visitors do day trips to Alpe-d'Huez (by helicopter).

Less confident intermediates will love the quality of the snow and the

CHILDCARE

Crèche 2 Alpes 1800
t 0476 790262
Ages 6mnth to 2yr;
8.30-5.30
Bonhomme de Neige
t 0476 790677
Ages 2 to 6; 8.30-5.15
(also activity centre
for ages 6 to 12)

Ski schools
Classes for ages 6 to
12 (6 mornings €122
with ESF)

GETTING THERE

Air Lyon 160km/
100 miles (2hr45);
Grenoble 110km/
70 miles (2hr15);
Chambéry 135km/
85 miles (2hr15);
Geneva 220km/
135 miles (3hr30)

Rail Grenoble
(70km/43 miles); four
daily buses from
station

gentleness of most of the runs on the upper mountain. Their problem might lie in finding the pistes too crowded.

FOR BEGINNERS ★★★
Good slopes
The nursery slopes beside the village are spacious and gentle – excellent for kids. The run along the ridge above them is excellent, too, except when it's crowded at the end of the day. The glacier also has a fine array of very easy slopes.

FOR CROSS-COUNTRY ★★
Needs very low-altitude snow
There are small, widely dispersed areas. Given good snow, Venosc, reached by a gondola down, has the only worthwhile picturesque ones. Total trail distance is 20km/12 miles.

MOUNTAIN RESTAURANTS ★★★
A few good places
There are mountain restaurants at all the major lift junctions, but they are generally unremarkable.
Editors' choice Diable au Coeur (0476 799950) at the top of the Diable gondola has excellent food (we had delicious confit de canard on our last visit), service and views. On the terrace, get as far as you can from the noisy adjacent chairlift machinery. The bigger but similarly excellent Chalet la Toura (0476 792096), in the middle of the domain, is pleasantly woody and serves good food.
Worth knowing about The table-service half of the Panoramic at Toura has been recommended for its 'mouth-watering cuisine' – but 'it gets very crowded'. There is a small table-service restaurant attached to the big self-service Les Glaciers at 3200m/10,500ft and the Bergerie on the Pied Moutet slopes has been recommended for 'good local dishes and atmosphere'.

SCHOOLS AND GUIDES ★★★
Fair selection to choose from
A recent reporter 'highly recommends' Easiski who were 'very helpful and friendly'. We have a positive report on the tuition and organisation of the European school, composed of instructors of various nationalities, all speaking good English. Class sizes are small – as few as four pupils if you go for their advanced classes. Bliss is a snowboard school, featuring two-hour beginner courses. There's a free Free Respect off-piste safety course (held weekly between mid-January and early-April with both evening and daytime sessions) run by guides and patrollers who provide transceivers, shovels, probes etc and teach you how to use them.

FOR FAMILIES ★★★★
Fine facilities
The village nursery takes kids from six months to two years, the kindergarten from three to six years, and there are chalet-based alternatives run by UK tour operators. There are also four free T-bars for children at the village level and a kids' freestyle area. A 2009 reporter says 'a lot going on for kids at the foot of the slopes (kids quad bikes, ice rink, pool) and good tobogganing terrain too'.

STAYING THERE

Les Deux-Alpes has plenty of that rarity in high-altitude French resorts, reasonably priced hotels.
Chalets Several UK tour operators run catered chalets. Mark Warner runs an excellent chalet hotel with pool, sauna – the Bérangère in a slope-side position on the road up to Les 2 Alpes 1800.
Hotels There are about 30 hotels, of which the majority are 2-star or below.
★★★★Farandole (0476 805045) The one 4-star. At the Venosc end of the resort.
★★★Mariande (0476 805060) Highly recommended, especially for its 'excellent' five-course dinners. At the Venosc end of the resort.
★★★Chalet Mounier (0476 805690) Smartly modernised. Good reputation for food. Swimming pool and fitness room. At the Venosc end of the resort.
★★★Souleil'or (0476 792469) Looks like a lift station, but pleasant and comfortable. Rooms and food reported to be 'fantastic'. Central.
★★Lutins (0476 792152) Central,

The middle section of the mountain is narrow and gets crowded →

Les Deux-Alpes

Interactive resort shortlist builder at **www.wtss.co.uk**

UK PACKAGES

Alpine Answers, AmeriCan Ski, Chalet Group, Club Med, Crystal, Erna Low, First Choice, Independent Ski Links, Interactive Resorts, Interhome, Lagrange, Leisure Direction, Made to Measure, Mark Warner, Neilson, Peak Retreats, PV-Holidays.com, Rocketski, Simply Alpine, Ski Activity, Ski France, Skiholiday extras.com, Ski Independence, Ski Line, Ski Solutions, Ski Supreme, Skitracer, Skiworld, Snoworks, Thomson, UCPA

ACTIVITIES

Indoor Swimming pool, hot tub, sauna, sports centres (Club Forme, Acqua Center), squash, cinemas, games rooms, bowling, museum, library

Outdoor Ice rink, snowmobiling, paragliding, quad bikes, snowshoeing, ice climbing, helicopter rides, Kanata (Inuit) village visit

SMART LODGINGS

Check out our feature chapters at the front of the book.

Phone numbers
From abroad use the prefix +33 and omit the initial '0' of the phone number

TOURIST OFFICE

t 0476 792200
info@les2alpes.com
www.les2alpes.com

'basic, dated décor but very convenient, clean and friendly'.
**Côte Brune (0476 805489) Slope-side, near Jandri Express. Large, basic, modern rooms.
Apartments Erna Low and Peak Retreats have several apartments, and the latter has self-catered chalets too (including two with pools and saunas down in Venosc). Cortina apartments at the south end are spacious, with sauna, steam room and hot tubs. Alpina Lodge is central and right by the slopes. Goleon and Val Ecrin, at the entrance to the resort, are smart, with sauna and steam room. Alba is a smart place, new for 2009/10, at the foot of the Pied Moutet slopes.
Out of resort Close to the foot of the final ascent to Les Deux-Alpes are two small hotels, near-ideal for anyone thinking of visiting Alpe-d'Huez, La Grave and Serre-Chevalier – the cheerful Cassini (0476 800410) at Le Freney and the even more appealing Panoramique (0476 800625) at Mizoën – approved of by a recent reporter for 'hearty food, informative Dutch hosts' and the 'wondrous' panorama.

An alternative is to stay in one of the hamlets close to the bottom of the gondola up from Venosc.

EATING OUT ★★★★
Plenty of choice
Chalet Mounier's P'tit Polyte restaurant has a high reputation. Petite Marmite has good food and atmosphere at reasonable prices. Bel'Auberge does classic French and is 'quite superb'. The Patate, Cloche and Crêpes à Gogo ('great food') and Etable ('best pizza ever') are reader recommendations.

You can get a relatively cheap meal at Bleuets bar, the Vetrata or the Spaghetteria. One regular visitor says that Smokey Joe Tex-Mex is the best value in the resort.

APRES-SKI ★★★★
Unsophisticated fun
Les Deux-Alpes is one of the liveliest of French resorts, with plenty of bars, several of which stay open until the early hours. Smithy's Tavern is a 'massive party venue' that pulls in a young crowd and serves 'amazing fajitas'. Pub le Windsor is a smaller, quieter place popular with locals. Smokey Joe's is a popular central sports bar and the Secret has live music, big-screen TV, and a wide choice of beers. Other places mentioned by reporters include Bar Brésilien and Bleuets. The main bar at 1800 is O'Brian's; the Tribeca has 'a lovely ambience for grown-ups'. The Avalanche is the main nightclub, at the Venosc end of town; up at 1800, the Opéra is recommended by locals.

OFF THE SLOPES ★★
Limited options
The pretty valley village of Venosc is worth a visit by gondola, and you can take a scenic helicopter flight to Alpe-d'Huez. There are lots of walks and the Acqua Center has a pool, sauna, steam room and hot tub. Several mountain restaurants are accessible to pedestrians. The White Cruise in a snowcat takes you across the glacier and provides wonderful views. You can visit an exhibition on avalanches (which includes a simulator showing you what it's like to be caught in one).

Flaine

Uncompromisingly modern, high-altitude resort sharing a big, broad area of varied slopes with more rustic alternatives

£110
RESORT PRICE INDEX

RATINGS

The mountains

Extent	★★★★
Fast lifts	★★
Queues	★★★
Terrain p'ks	★★★
Snow	★★★★
Expert	★★★★
Intermediate	★★★★★
Beginner	★★★★★
X-country	★★
Restaurants	★★
Schools	★★★
Families	★★★★

The resort

Charm	★
Convenience	★★★★★
Scenery	★★★★
Eating out	★★
Après-ski	★
Off-slope	★

294

NEWS

For 2009/10 a new six-pack is due to replace the quad above Les Molliets, improving the links from the Les Carroz sector. Another six-pack (Chariande Express) is replacing two old chairs and a drag between Samoëns 1600 and Tête des Saix – cutting the journey time by two-thirds.

In Flaine, the new Refuge de Golf development is due to open above the Hameau de Flaine.

For 2008/09 the new 4-star Terrasses d'Eos opened at Flaine Montsoleil – Intrawest's second major development in the Alps. A quad chair and blue run were built to make it ski-in/ski-out. There's also a smart new piste map.

- ＋ Big, varied area, with plenty of terrain to suit most levels
- ＋ Reliable snow in the main bowl
- ＋ Compact, convenient, mainly car-free village, plus traditional villages on the lower fringes of the area
- ＋ Excellent facilities for children
- ＋ Scenic setting, and glorious views
- ＋ Very close to Geneva but ...

- － Weekends can be busy as a result
- － Many slow old chairlifts, though things are improving
- － Austere 1960s buildings
- － In bad weather, main Flaine bowl offers little to do, and links to outer sectors of the area may be closed
- － Nightlife not a highlight
- － Little to do off the slopes (in Flaine)

Flaine is best known as a convenient resort catering particularly well for families, but it has a much broader appeal than that. The Grand Massif is almost a match for Val d'Isère/Tignes in terms of extent, at least.

Flaine's family orientation is underlined by the domination of self-catering accommodation. But you open up more lodging options by considering the outlying villages – Samoëns (which has its own chapter) and Les Carroz and Morillon (covered at the end of this chapter). Not only are they more attractive places to stay but they also offer some woodland slopes for bad-weather days.

THE RESORT

The concrete Bauhaus-style blocks that form the core of Flaine were conceived in the sixties as 'an example of the application of the principle of shadow and light'. They look shocking from the approach road – a mass of blocks at the foot of a big snowy bowl. From the slopes they are less obtrusive, blending into the rocky grey hillside.

There are two parts to the main resort: a lower one – Forum – and Forêt up the hillside. Hameau-de-Flaine is an inconvenient 1km/0.5 miles from the slopes and main village, and has only one shop/bar/restaurant; the new Refuge de Golf is in the same area. Much nearer to Flaine (a few hundred metres walk) is Intrawest's Montsoleil mini-resort. The bus service to/from these areas is good but stops early.

A car gives you the option of visiting the Portes du Soleil, Chamonix, Megève or Courmayeur in Italy.

VILLAGE CHARM ★
Not to our taste

Flaine has an austere ambience and some of the buildings are now looking tatty. For us, the outdoor sculptures by Picasso, Vasarely and Dubuffet do little to improve things. In contrast, the Hameau-de-Flaine is built in a much more attractive chalet style, as is Intrawest's new Montsoleil mini-resort.

CONVENIENCE ★★★★★
A fine example

In Flaine proper, everything is close by: supermarket, ski shops, ski schools, main lifts out etc. Forum is centred on a snow-covered square with buildings on three sides, the open fourth side blending with the slopes. Flaine Forêt, linked by lift, has its own bars and shops, and most of the apartments. There are children all over the place; they are catered for with play areas, and the resort is supposed to be traffic-free. In fact, roads penetrate the village and you don't have to go far to encounter traffic; but the Forum, leading to the pistes, is pretty safe.

Montsoleil is linked to Flaine proper by a new lift and run. Hameau is a bus ride away. A 2009 reporter feels these areas 'introduce an element of sprawl that was avoided in the original resort'.

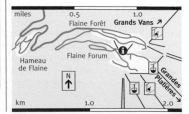

↑ Flaine has a great combination of easy intermediate cruising and fabulous off-piste in its high bowls
DSF / CYRIL FERRAND

KEY FACTS

Resort	1600m
	5,250ft

Grand Massif (Flaine, Les Carroz, Morillon, Samoëns, Sixt)

Slopes	700-2480m
	2,300-8,140ft
Lifts	77
Pistes	265km
	165 miles
Green	12%
Blue	43%
Red	34%
Black	11%
Snowmaking	
	218 guns

For Flaine only

Slopes	1600-2480m
	5,250-8,140ft
Lifts	29
Pistes	140km
	87 miles
Green	12%
Blue	40%
Red	40%
Black	8%

LIFT PASSES

Grand Massif

Prices in €

Age	1-day	6-day
under 15	31	150
16 to 59	39	192
over 60	35	171
Free under 5, over 75		
Beginner four free lifts		

Notes
Covers all lifts in Flaine, Les Carroz, Morillon, Samoëns and Sixt

Alternative passes
Flaine area only

SCENERY ★★★★
Good all around the Massif
The scenery is quite varied, with rocky ridges, partly wooded hillsides and splendid views of the region's great mountains from Les Grandes Platières, including Mont Blanc.

THE MOUNTAINS

The Grand Massif is an impressive area; but the greater part of the domain lies outside the main Flaine bowl and the links can be closed by excessive wind or snow.

Signing is generally fine. The new piste map is a vast improvement: much clearer, with a better attempt to define the individual bowls.

EXTENT OF THE SLOPES ★★★★
A big white playground
The day begins for most people at the **Grandes Platières** jumbo gondola, which speeds you in a single stage up the north face of the Flaine bowl to the high-point of the Grand Massif. A six-pack offers an alternative, going part-way up.

Most of the runs are reds (though there are some blues curling away to skier's right, and one direct black). There are essentially four or five main ways down the barren, treeless, rolling terrain back to Flaine, or to chairs in the middle of the wilderness.

On the far right, the Cascades blue run leads away from the lift system behind the Tête Pelouse down to the outskirts of Sixt, dropping over 1700m/5,580ft vertical in its exceptional 14km/9 mile length. The gentle/flat top half is hard work, especially for boarders, and the run is scenic rather than exciting – so we're not greatly concerned that it isn't reliably open; readers seem more impressed than we are. At the end you can get buses (often crowded) to the lifts at Samoëns. Or spend some time exploring the slopes of Sixt – very quiet, with a non-trivial vertical.

On the other side of the Tête Pelouse, a broad catwalk leads to the experts-only **Gers** bowl. At the bottom, a flat trail links with the lower (more interesting) half of the Cascades run.

Back at Platières, an alternative is to head left down the long red Méphisto to the **Aujon** area – again mostly red runs but with some blues further down. The lower slopes here are used as slalom courses. This sector is also reachable by gondola or draglifts from below the resort.

The eight-seat Grands Vans chair, reached from Forum by means of a slow bucket-lift (or from Montsoleil via a new short quad that you don't need a lift pass to use), gives access to the extensive slopes of **Les Carroz**, **Morillon** and **Samoëns** via the wide Vernant bowl, which is equipped with two fast chairlifts.

FAST LIFTS ★★
More being installed
Five fast lifts serve the main bowl and two more much-needed fast chairs are planned outside the bowl for 2009/10 (see 'News'). But there are still lots of slow old chairs and draglifts throughout the Grand Massif area.

QUEUES ★★★
A few problems
Many of the trouble spots have now been eliminated and several reporters have had queue-free weeks, even in high season. But there can be problems when the resorts are full and at weekends (the area is very close to

boarding

Flaine suits boarders quite well – there's lots of varied terrain and plenty of off-piste with interesting nooks and crannies, including woods outside the main bowl. The key lifts are now chairs or gondolas (but beware the absurdly vicious Aujon draglift, which serves the terrain park). There's a big terrain park in Flaine and a couple of smaller kids' areas further afield. Black Side is the local specialist shop, with a cafe and bar in the central Forum.

Geneva). Towards the end of the day expect delays at the Vernant chair to get back to the Flaine bowl (an alternative is to descend to one of the lift-bases along the access road, and catch a bus). There have been queues at Les Molliets too, though these should be relieved by the new-six-pack planned for 2009/10.

Back in the Flaine bowl, the Aup de Veran gondola still has queues, notably in the mornings. The nearby six-pack that goes part way up the slopes has eased queues for the Grand Platières gondola. Queues elsewhere in the bowl can build up at weekends and when the lifts out are shut due to high winds or when it is warm and the lower resorts have poor snow.

TERRAIN PARKS ★★★☆☆
Cater for kids to experts
The main terrain park (called the JamPark Pro – standing for Jib and Air Maniacs) is in Flaine's Aujon area. It has a quarter-pipe, tables, rails, a boardercross and a chill-out zone. Watch out for the Aujon draglift, though, which is as much of a challenge as the park. There are kids' parks in Samoëns and Morillon if snow permits.

SNOW RELIABILITY ★★★★☆
Usually keeps its whiteness
The main part of Flaine's slopes lie on the wide north- and north-west-facing flank of the Grandes Platières, and keep snow well. There is snowmaking

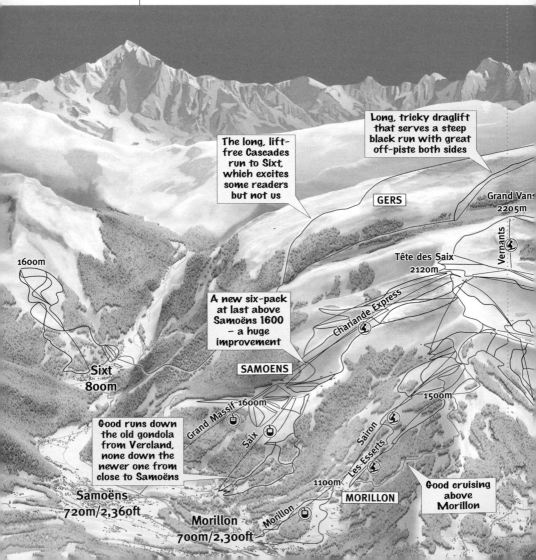

The long, lift-free Cascades run to Sixt, which excites some readers but not us

Long, tricky draglift that serves a steep black run with great off-piste both sides

GERS

Grand Vans 2205m

Vernants

Tête des Saix 2120m

1600m

A new six-pack at last above Samoëns 1600 – a huge improvement

Charlande Express

SAMOENS

Sixt 800m

Grand Massif 1600m

Saix

1500m

Sairon

Les Esserts

Good runs down the old gondola from Vercland, none down the newer one from close to Samoëns

Samoëns 720m/2,36oft

Morillon 700m/2,30oft

Morillon

1100m

MORILLON

Good cruising above Morillon

on the greater part of the Aujon sector and on the nursery slopes. The runs towards Samoëns 1600 and Morillon 1100 are north-facing too, and some lower parts have snowmaking, but below these mid-stations the runs can be tricky or closed. The Les Carroz runs are south-west-facing and low, and can suffer from strong afternoon sun as a result, but a few runs have snowmaking. Grooming is excellent.

FOR EXPERTS ★★★★
Great fun with guidance
Flaine has some seriously challenging terrain, despite its family orientation. But much of it is off-piste and, although some of it looks like it can safely be explored without guidance,

this impression is mistaken. The Flaine bowl is riddled with rock crevasses and potholes, and should be treated with the same caution that you would use on a glacier. We are told that these hazards cause deaths most years.

All the black pistes on the map deserve their classification. The Diamant Noir, down the line of the main gondola, is tricky because of moguls, narrowness and other people, rather than great steepness; the first pitch is the steepest, with spectators applauding from the chairlift.

To skier's left of the Diamant Noir are several short but steep off-piste routes through the crags.

The Lindars Nord chair serves a

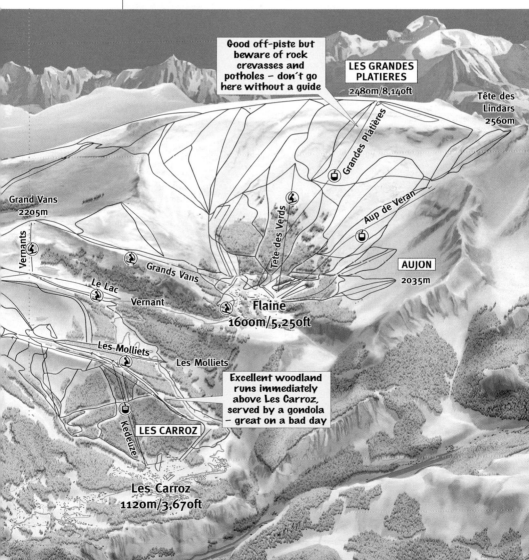

Good off-piste but beware of rock crevasses and potholes – don't go here without a guide

LES GRANDES PLATIERES
2480m/8,140ft

Tête des Lindars
2560m

Grandes Platières

Grand Vans
2205m

Tête des Verds

Aup de Veran

Vernants

Grands Vans

Le Lac

Vernant

Flaine
1600m/5,250ft

AUJON
2035m

Les Molliets

Les Molliets

Excellent woodland runs immediately above Les Carroz, served by a gondola – great on a bad day

LES CARROZ

Kedeuze

Les Carroz
1120m/3,670ft

SCHOOLS

ESF
t 0450 908100

International
t 0450 908441

**Moniteurs
indépendants**
t 0450 937978

Flaine Super Ski
t 0450 778690

Flaine Ski Clinic
t 0666 139281

Freecimes
t 0664 118329

François Simond
t 0450 908097

Skiyourbest
t 0610 183082

Hameau Master Class
t 0450 908716

Classes (ESF prices)
6 (3hr) days €138

Private lessons
From €32 for 1hr

GETTING THERE

Air Geneva 80km/
50 miles (1hr30)

Rail Cluses (30km/
19 miles); regular bus
service

shorter slope that often has the best snow in the area, and some seriously steep gradients. Mind the chair doesn't whack you as you exit.

The Gers draglift, outside the main bowl, serves great on- and off-piste expert terrain in a north-facing bowl (of about 550m/1,800ft vertical) that normally has good snow and powder or moguls top to bottom. The Styx piste is a proper black, but nearby off-piste slopes reach 45°. There are more adventurous ways in from the Grands Vans and Véret lifts.

There are further serious pistes on the top lifts above Samoëns 1600.

There are some scenic off-piste routes from which you can be retrieved by helicopter – such as the Combe des Foges, next to Gers.

FOR INTERMEDIATES ★★★★★
Something for everyone

Flaine is ideal for confident intermediates, with a great variety of pistes (and usually the bonus of good snow conditions, at least above Flaine itself). As a reporter puts it, 'There may not be many challenging runs, but there are very few dull ones.' The diabolically named reds that dominate the Flaine bowl tend to gain their status from short steep sections rather than overall difficulty. The relatively direct Faust is great carving territory, at least in January when it isn't cluttered. There are gentler cruises from the top of the mountain – Cristal, taking you to the Perdrix chair, or Serpentine, all the way home. The blues at Aujon are excellent for confidence building, but the drag serving them is not.

The connections with the slopes outside the main bowl are classified blue and can be tricky because of narrowness, crowds or poor snow. Once the connection has been made, however, all intermediates will enjoy the long tree-lined runs down to Les Carroz, as long as the snow is good. The Morillon slopes are also excellent intermediate terrain – the long green Marvel run to Morillon 1100 is an easy cruise with excellent signs along the way explaining the local wildlife (in English as well as French).

Crowds on the lower slopes returning to Flaine are a problem – a prime example is the lower Tourmaline run from Grand Vans, the only way back into Flaine.

FOR BEGINNERS ★★★★★
Fairly good

There are excellent nursery slopes right by the village, served by free lifts which make a pass unnecessary until you are ready to go higher up the mountain. The area is roped off, but it is still used as a short cut back to the village by other skiers. There are some gentle blues to progress to over on skier's right, beneath Tête Pelouse. Progress to the 'interesting and gentle blues' in the Aujon sector is not easy due to several steep draglifts. If you have a really nervous intermediate to deal with, it's worth driving or bussing down the access road to a gentle, quiet green at Vernant.

CROSS-COUNTRY ★★★★★
Very fragmented

The Grand Massif claims 64km/40 miles of cross-country tracks but only about 17km/11 miles of that is around Flaine itself. The majority is on the valley floor and dependent on low snow. There are extensive tracks between Morillon and Les Carroz, with some tough uphill sections.

MOUNTAIN RESTAURANTS ★★★★★
Back to base, or quit the bowl

In the Flaine bowl, there are few restaurants above the resort's upper outskirts. Reports suggest most are overcrowded – notably the Grandes Platières self-service, which gets mixed reviews from reporters. The rustic Blanchot, at the bottom of the Serpentine run has a restaurant and a snack bar – both recommended. At Forum level, across the piste from the gondola, is the welcoming Michet ('definitely worth a visit'), with very good Savoyard food and table service, and the 'rustic' Eloge. Up the slope a bit, the Cascade is self-service but with a good terrace. Epicéa is 'high quality', but we've received a report of 'poor service'.

Outside the Flaine bowl, we still love the remote Gîte du Lac de Gers (book in advance and ring for a snowcat to tow you up from the Cascades run) – simple hearty food but splendid isolation. We had a huge Savoyard omelette there in 2009. The cosy and rustic Igloo above Morillon is 'friendly, with good food and service'. We had an excellent plat du jour there. Chalet d'Clair is a good self-service. The woody Chalet les Molliets is repeatedly praised – 'top food',

↑ Flaine Forum at the lift base, Forêt above it and the new Intrawest Montsoleil development on the left

DSF / CYRIL FERRAND

CHILDCARE

Les P'tits Loups
t 0450 908782
Ages 6mnth to 3yr
Rabbit Club
t 0450 908100
From 3yr; 9am-5pm
La Souris Verte
t 0450 908441
Ages from 3
Hotels Flaine / Aujon
t 0492 126212
Ages 18mnth to 14yr

Ski school
For ages 3 to 11:
€118 for 6 (3hr) days (ESF prices); English-speaking tuition:
Catherine Pouppeville (0609 266008)

UK PACKAGES

Action Outdoors, Alpine Answers, Altitude, Crystal, Crystal Finest, Erna Low, First Choice, Independent Ski Links, Inghams, Lagrange, Leisure Direction, Neilson, PV-Holidays. com, Ski Collection, Ski France, Ski Freshtracks, Skiholidayextras.com, Ski Independence, Skitracer, Ski Weekend, Thomson

SMART LODGINGS

Check out our feature chapters at the front of the book.

'excellent plats du jour'. Cupress above Les Carroz has 'friendly table service'.

SCHOOLS AND GUIDES ★★★
Getting better
We've received good reports for ESF in Flaine and Les Carroz: 'We advanced more than in any other resort we have been to.' However, one reader found that classes were 'far too big – twenty in a couple of cases'. A beginner boarder enjoyed an 'excellent' week with the International school recently. The competition-oriented Super Ski has 'small classes, good instruction'.

FOR FAMILIES ★★★★
Parents' paradise?
Flaine prides itself on being a family resort, and the number of English-speaking children around is a bonus. There are some free children's lift passes available in low season weeks. The International school offers classes for three to five year olds. The P'tits Loups nursery takes children from six months. Crystal's 'well-organised and popular' hotel Le Totem has good childcare facilities for residents only.

STAYING THERE

Accommodation is overwhelmingly in self-catering apartments.
Chalets There are few catered chalet options, but they include a couple of Scandinavian-style huts in Hameau. The 'good food, friendly staff' and childcare facilities of Crystal's Totem club hotel continue to receive favourable reports.
Hotels The other hotels now seem to be called 'club' hotels, marketed by big French agencies – but also bookable through UK operator Erna Low. B&B is available at the Cascade restaurant, above the village.
Apartments Those out at Hameau are 'fabulous', says one visitor. We had an

enjoyable stay at the new ski-in/ski-out Montsoleil apartments: comfortable, good outdoor pool, sauna, steam, hot tub – but no restaurant or bar. Its own evening shuttle stops around 11pm, so after that it's an uphill walk of a few hundred metres. In Flaine Forêt, the Forêt (Pierre et Vacances) and Grand Massif apartment buildings are attractively woody. The Pleiades are 'very smart and spacious'. Most of these are featured by Erna Low, Ski Independence and Ski Collection; and the Forêt by Leisure Direction.

EATING OUT ★★
Limited choice
The choice is adequate, no more. Reporters have enjoyed the small Chez Pierrot pizzeria for 'lovely local specialities', the 'pricey' Perdrix Noire (seafood and grills) for 'friendly and pleasant service' and the family-friendly Chez Daniel – which also serves a good range of Savoyard specialities. The 'lively' Brasserie les Cîmes has 'very good food, prices, very friendly service'. The Sucré Salé is an arty place serving pitta and grills specials. The West Mountain is a new Tex-Mex. A couple of places close to the village and described under 'Mountain restaurants' are open in the evening – the Michet and the Bissac. The Ancolie in Hameau is said to be worth the trip for its 'first class food' and 'beautiful wooden chalet interior'.

APRES-SKI ★
Signs of life
You can eat and drink into the early hours here if you move around a bit – but you don't have much choice of venue. The White pub has a big screen TV, rock music and punters trying to get pints in before the end of happy hour. The Flying Dutchman is lively early on, with karaoke and themed

Hôtel Le Bois de la Char

Your stay right on the pistes

Les Carroz-d'Arâches
40 minutes from Geneva Airport
10 minutes from highway A40

Tel: 00 33 (0) 4 50 90 06 18
E-mail: contact@hotel-boisdelachar.com
Website: www.hotel-boisdelachar.com

Photo credit: PHOTOTEM – Claude Monvoisin

UK PACKAGES

Les Carroz *360 Sun and Ski, Alps Accommodation, Altitude, AmeriCan Ski, Crystal Finest, Erna Low, Holiday in Alps, Lagrange, Leisure Direction, Peak Retreats, PV-Holidays.com, Simply Alpine, Ski France, Skiholiday extras.com, Ski Independence, Skiology.co.uk*
Sixt *AmeriCan Ski, Chalet Group, Peak Retreats*

Phone numbers
From abroad use the prefix +33 and omit the initial '0' of the phone number

TOURIST OFFICES

Flaine
t 0450 908001
welcome@flaine.com
www.flaine.com

Les Carroz
t 0450 900004
carroz@lescarroz.com
www.lescarroz.com

evenings, but 'tends to wind down around 11pm'. The Perdrix Noire is also a bar. The bar at the bowling alley is popular with families, and stays open late – 'the only place still serving food until 3am'. There's one nightclub, but drinks are reportedly 'very expensive' and the music 'not up to much'.

OFF THE SLOPES ★✰✰✰✰
Curse of the purpose-built

Flaine is not recommended for people who don't want to hit the slopes. But there is a great ice driving circuit where you can take a spin (literally) in your car or in theirs. Snowmobiling and dog sledding are popular, and there's a cinema and a gym. Shopping is limited.

Les Carroz 1120m/3,670ft

This is a sprawling, sunny, traditional, family resort where life revolves around the village square with its pavement cafes and restaurants. It is a sizeable place – much bigger than Flaine, in fact – that has the lived-in feel of a real French village. Traffic can be busy at peak times though. There is more après-ski animation than Flaine. But a thorough report tells us that things are much quieter later on: the Marlow pub is popular at close of play but soon becomes quiet; Pointe Noire, next door, is cheaper and more animated; Carpe Diem is devoid of customers until the other places close. The Servages d'Armelle is praised for its 'truly outstanding dinner' and has a Michelin listing.

The Bois de la Char (0450 900618) hotel is 'well managed, perfectly situated, excellent value'. The hotel Arbaron (0450 900267) has been commended for food and views.

Les Fermes du Soleil and (new for 2009/10) Les Chalets de Jouvance are both very comfortable apartment complexes with pools, hot tubs and saunas. Holiday in Alps feature various apartments, as do Peak Retreats, Erna Low, Leisure Direction and Ski Independence.

The gondola starts a steep 300m/980ft walk up from the centre – the nursery drag is a help or you can catch the free ski-bus (though we're told it finishes too early). It serves some excellent slopes in the woods above the village, so this is a great place on a bad-weather day. It's a good place for novices, as it has a wide green to progress to. Reporters have praised ESF for its 'excellent group lessons'.

The ski school's torchlit descent is 'not to be missed' – ending with vin chaud and live jazz in the square.

Morillon 700m/2,300ft

Morillon is a small, quiet, traditional old village, with a few cafes and shops clustered around an old church. Newer buildings are in chalet style and quite attractive. A gondola goes up to the mid-mountain mini-resort of Morillon 1100, with slope-side apartments at the foot of wide, gentle and tree-lined slopes – popular with families and novices. A long, pretty blue run (or a red alternative) takes you back down to the valley – though these runs are low and good snow is unreliable.

Les Gets

Traditional-style village with a very French feel, providing serious competition for its more established linked neighbour, Morzine

£105
RESORT PRICE INDEX

TOP 10 RATINGS

Extent	*****
Fast lifts	**
Queues	***
Snow	**
Expert	***
Intermediate	****
Beginner	****
Charm	****
Convenience	***
Scenery	***

Extent rating
This relates to the whole Portes du Soleil area.

Piste map
The whole local area is covered by the map in the Morzine chapter.

KEY FACTS

Resort	1170m
	3,840ft

Portes du Soleil	
Slopes	950-2300m
	3,120-7,550ft
Lifts	194
Pistes	650km
	404 miles
Green	13%
Blue	40%
Red	37%
Black	10%
Snowmaking	
	694 guns

Morzine-Les Gets only	
Slopes	1000-2010m
	3,280-6,590ft
Lifts	50
Pistes	110km
	68 miles
Snowmaking	
	295 guns

SNOWPIX.COM / CHRIS GILL

Fine views across to the major slope area from Mont Chéry ➔

- ✚ Good-sized, varied and treelined slopes shared with Morzine
- ✚ Attractive chalet-style village
- ✚ Relatively short drive from the UK
- ✚ Few queues or crowds locally
- ✚ Part of the vast Portes du Soleil ski pass region, but ...

- ▬ It's quite a long way to the main Portes du Soleil circuit at Avoriaz
- ▬ Modest altitude means there is always a risk of poor snow
- ▬ Few challenging pistes
- ▬ Slow, old chairs in some sectors
- ▬ Weekend crowds

Les Gets is an attractive, small, family-friendly resort with a very French feel to it, partly because of appetising food and wine shops lining the main street. The area of slopes that it shares with Morzine offers the most extensive local network in the Portes du Soleil, and in some respects Les Gets is the better base for that area. But if you intend to visit the main Portes du Soleil circuit repeatedly, it makes sense to stay closer to it in Morzine.

THE RESORT

Les Gets is an attractive, sunny village of traditional chalet-style buildings, on the low pass leading to Morzine. The main road bypasses the village centre.

The local pass saves a fair bit on a Portes du Soleil pass, and makes a lot of sense for many visitors.

Village charm The village has a quiet ambiance that appeals to families, though it does liven-up at weekends. The centre is gradually becoming more pedestrian-friendly too, and a popular outdoor ice rink adds to the charm.

Convenience Although the village has a scattered appearance, most facilities are close to the main lift station – and the free 'petit train' road-train shuttle is a cute way of travelling around. You can store skis and boots at the Perrières ski shop. The main street is lined with plenty of attractive food and other shops and restaurants. And

there are two adequate supermarkets. There are also free conventional buses around the village and to Morzine.

Scenery Good views from the high points – from Mont Chéry you get a great panorama of the village and the prettily wooded slopes, with Mont Blanc beyond.

THE MOUNTAINS

Les Gets is not an ideal base for the Portes du Soleil, but its local slopes are extensive.

Slopes The main local slopes – accessed by a gondola and fast chair-lift from the nursery slopes beside the village – are shared with Morzine, and are mainly described in that chapter. On the opposite side of Les Gets is Mont Chéry, accessed by a gondola and parallel chair. The slopes include some of the most challenging in the area, and are usually very quiet. Both

301

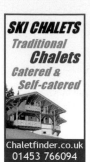
Weekly news updates and resort links at **www.wtss.co.uk**

NEWS

Work has focused on improving the beginner area at Chavannes – set back from the main slopes and now with four free lifts.

For 2008/09 snowmaking was increased around the Folliets chairlift.

Phone numbers
From abroad use the prefix +33 and omit the initial '0' of the phone number

TOURIST OFFICE

t 0450 758080
lesgets@lesgets.com
www.lesgets.com

sectors offer wooded and open slopes.
Fast lifts The village lifts are gondolas, but there are a lot of slow, old chairs both on Mont Chéry and in some sectors of the Morzine slopes.
Queues See the Morzine chapter. Mont Chéry is crowd-free.
Snow reliability The nursery slopes benefit from a slightly higher elevation than Morzine, but otherwise our general reservations about the lack of altitude apply. You may get rain. The runs to the resort have snowmaking. The front slopes of Mont Chéry face south-east – bad news at this altitude; grooming is good though, and the other two flanks are shadier. But: grassy slopes don't need much snow-cover and in a sparse snow year you may do better here than in higher, rockier resorts such as Avoriaz.
Terrain parks There's a park on the upper slopes of Mont Chéry with airbag, hips, handrails, tables and a wall; plus a Jib park with a table and handrail. And there's a boardercross near the top of Chavannes.
Experts Black runs on the flank and back of Mont Chéry are quite steep and often bumped. In good snow there's plenty to do off-piste, including some excellent wooded areas.
Intermediates High-mileage piste-bashers might prefer direct access to the main Portes du Soleil circuit, but the local slopes have a lot to offer, with excellent reds on Mont Chéry.
Beginners The village nursery slopes are convenient. A bigger and more snow-sure area has been created at Chavannes, with four free lifts. There are lots of easy runs to progress to.
Snowboarding The local slopes are good for beginners and intermediates.
Cross-country There are 18km/11 miles of good, varied loops on Mont Chéry and Les Chavannes.
Mountain restaurants See Morzine for places on the shared slopes. On Mont Chéry, reporters enthuse about the Grande Ourse, run since 2006 by an English family and offering both snacks and 'very special' table-service lunches. Fab view of Mont Blanc.

Schools and guides You're spoilt for choice. British-run Les Gets Snowsports is 'excellent'. The British Alpine Ski & Snowboard School (see Morzine) operates here, too. And a reporter says the instructors at Ecole de Ski 360 'spoke very good English' and her six-year-old daughter was 'cruising down the main slopes on day two'.
Families This is a good resort for families. As well as comprehensive resort facilities, including a cowboy-themed trail area, family-specialist tour operators Esprit Ski and Ski Famille offer holidays here.

STAYING THERE

There is a good selection of chalets and mid-range hotels. A 2009 reporter had a 'jolly nice' stay at Ski Famille's Le Marjorie chalet.
Hotels We loved the Ferme de Montagne (0450 753679) and so have reporters. It's a kind of cross between a small hotel and a chalet – a beautifully renovated farmhouse with eight luxury bedrooms, gourmet food, ski guiding, sauna, outdoor hot tub, massage therapist; right on the edge of town at La Turche. Of the 3-stars, the Crychar (0450 758050), 100m/330ft from central Les Gets at the foot of the slopes, is one of the best. Other reader tips are the Nagano (0450 797146), the Marmotte (0450 758033) and the Alpages (0450 758088) – with a pool.
Apartments The central Sabaudia apartments have a pool and hot tub. Peak Retreats offers several self-catered chalets (some luxurious) as well as apartments.
Eating out The Tourbillon and Choucas ('fabulous house red') are recommended this year. Try the Tyrol and the Schuss for pizza, the rustic Vieux Chêne for Savoyard specialities.
Après-ski Après-ski is quiet, especially on weekdays. But there are half a dozen bars; the obvious first target is the Irish Pub and the Black Bear above it. The Igloo disco is popular.
Off the slopes There's a well-equipped fitness centre with a pool, an outdoor ice rink and bowling. There good shops, a cinema and an intriguing Mechanical Music Museum; husky sleigh rides, snowshoeing and parapenting are possible. Visits to Geneva, Lausanne and Montreux are feasible.

SNOWPIX.COM / CHRIS GILL

La Grave

A world apart: an unspoiled mountain village beneath high, untamed off-piste slopes, some of them extreme and hazardous

+ Legendary off-piste mountain
+ Usually crowd-free
+ Usually good snow conditions
+ Link to Les Deux-Alpes
+ Easy access by car to other nearby resorts

− Village spoiled by through-traffic
− Poor weather means lift closures – on average, two days per week
− Suitable for experts only, despite some easy slopes at altitude
− Nothing to do off the slopes

TOP 10 RATINGS

Extent	★★★★★
Fast lifts	★★★★★
Queues	★★★★
Snow	★★★
Expert	★★★★★
Intermediate	★★★★★
Beginner	★★★★★
Charm	★★★
Convenience	★★★
Scenery	★★★★

La Grave enjoys cult status among experts. It's a quiet old village with around 500 visitor beds and just one serious lift – a small stop-start gondola serving a high, wild and almost entirely off-piste mountainside. The result: an exciting, usually crowd-free area. Strictly, you ought to have a guide, but in good weather many people go it alone.

NEWS

La Grave does not change much, and that is half the charm of the place.

THE RESORT

La Grave is a small, unspoiled mountaineering village. It's rather drab, and the busy road through to Briançon doesn't help. Storms close the slopes on average two days a week – so a car is useful for access to nearby resorts.

Village charm The centre has a rustic feel, some welcoming hotels and friendly inhabitants. But the through-road rather undermines all that.
Convenience The single serious lift starts just below the centre.
Scenery La Grave is set on a steep hillside facing the impressive glaciers of the majestic La Meije. Great views.

303

THE MOUNTAIN

A slow two-stage 'pulse' gondola (with an extra station at a pylon halfway up the lower stage) ascends into the slopes and finishes at 3200m/10,500ft. Above that, a short walk and a draglift give access to a second drag serving twin blue runs on a glacier slope of about 350m/1,150ft vertical – from here (after another walk) you can ski to Les Deux-Alpes. But the reason that people come here is to explore the legendary slopes back towards La Grave. These slopes offer no defined, patrolled, avalanche-protected pistes – but there are two marked itinéraires (with several variations usefully marked on the 'piste' map) of 1400m/4,590ft vertical down to the pylon lift station, or all the way down to the valley – a vertical of 2150m/7,050ft.
Slopes The Chancel route is mostly of red-run gradient; the Vallons de la Meije is more challenging but not too steep. People do take these routes without a guide or avalanche protection equipment, but we couldn't possibly recommend it.

OT LA GRAVE-LA-MEIJE

← This is what you are going there for – deep snow, steep slopes, very few people

KEY FACTS

Resort	1450m
	4,760ft
Slopes	1450-3550m
	4,760-11,650ft
Lifts	4
Pistes	5km
	3 miles
Green/Blue	100%

The figures relate only to pistes; practically all the skiing – at least 90% – is off-piste

Snowmaking	none

UK PACKAGES

Alpine Answers, AmeriCan Ski, Interhome, Lagrange, Meije Tours, Mountain Tracks, Peak Retreats, Ski Freshtracks, Ski Weekend

Phone numbers
From abroad use the prefix +33 and omit the initial '0' of the phone number

FRANCE

304

TOURIST OFFICE

t 0476 799005
ot@lagrave-lameije.com
www.lagrave-lameije.com

There are many more demanding runs away from the itinéraires, including couloirs that range from the straightforward to the seriously hazardous, and long descents from the glacier to the valley road below the village, with return by taxi, bus, or strategically parked car. The dangers are considerable (people die here every year), and good guidance is essential. You can also descend a 'spectacular valley' southwards to St-Christophe, returning by bus and the lifts of Les Deux-Alpes.

Fast lifts There aren't any, and there's no need for any.

Queues Normally, there are queues only at weekends. March is reportedly the busiest month, when queues can be serious. If snow conditions back to the valley are poor, queues can build up for the gondola down from the mid- and lower stations.

Terrain parks There aren't any.

Snow reliability The chances of powder snow on the high, north-facing slopes are good, but if conditions are tricky, there are no pistes to fall back on apart from the three short blue runs at the top of the gondola.

Experts La Grave's uncrowded off-piste slopes have earned it cult status among hard-core skiers. Only experts should contemplate a stay here – and then only if prepared to deal with bad weather by sitting tight or struggling

over the Col du Lautaret to the woods of Serre-Chevalier.

Intermediates The itinéraires get tracked into a piste-like state, and adventurous intermediates could tackle the Chancel. Most folk will soon tire of the three blue runs at the top of the gondola. The valley stations of Villar d'Arène and Lautaret, around 3km/2 miles and 8km/5 miles to the east respectively, and Chazelet, 3km/2 miles to the north-west, offer very limited slopes with a handful of runs.

Beginners Novices tricked into coming here can go up the valley to the beginner slopes at Villar d'Arène, or to Le Chazelet, which has a new fast quad and two snow-guns.

Snowboarding There are no special facilities for boarders, but advanced freeriders will be in their element on the open off-piste powder.

Cross-country There is a total of 22km/13 miles of loops in the area.

Mountain restaurants Surprisingly, there are three; the Refuge Chancel, where supplies are backpacked in, is the pucka La Grave experience.

Schools and guides There are claimed to be 30 or so guides, offering a wide range of services through their bureau. 'Excellent' is the usual verdict. See also 'Hotels' below.

Families Not really a family resort, but babysitting can be arranged through the tourist office.

STAYING THERE

There are very few options.

Hotels There are several simple options. The comfortable 2-star Edelweiss (0476 799093) has been strongly recommended for its 'excellent' food and wines. The Skiers Lodge/Hotel des Alpes (0476 110318) offers all-inclusive week-long packages including guiding. A visitor had an 'excellent' week, advising that 'you need to get really fit beforehand'.

Apartments Bookable through the tourist office.

Eating out Most people eat in their hotels, though there are alternatives.

Après-ski The central Cafe des Glaciers, and the Castillan are the standard teatime venues. The bars of both the Edelweiss and the Skiers Lodge have live music. The Vieux Guide gets crowded later.

Off the slopes Anyone not using the slopes will find La Grave much too small and quiet.

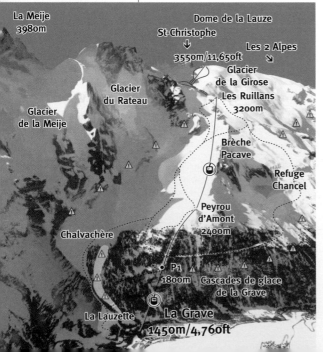

La Meije 3980m
Dome de la Lauze
St-Christophe
Les 2 Alpes
3550m/11,650ft
Glacier de la Girose
Glacier du Rateau
Les Ruillans 3200m
Glacier de la Meije
Brèche Pacave
Refuge Chancel
Peyrou d'Amont 2400m
Chalvachère
P1 1800m
Cascades de glace de la Grave
La Lauzette
La Grave 1450m/4,760ft

Megève

One of the traditional old winter holiday towns; best for those who enjoy relaxed cruising among splendid scenery

£125
RESORT PRICE INDEX

RATINGS

The mountains

Extent	★★★★★
Fast lifts	★
Queues	★★★★
Terrain p'ks	★★★
Snow	★★
Expert	★★
Intermediate	★★★★
Beginner	★★★
X-country	★★★★
Restaurants	★★★★
Schools	★★★
Families	★★★

The resort

Charm	★★★★
Convenience	★★
Scenery	★★★★★
Eating out	★★★★
Après-ski	★★
Off-slope	★★★★

NEWS

For 2008/09 a new terrain park was built in the Rochebrune area, and a mini-pipe and boardercross were added to the park on Mont-Joux.

➕ Extensive easy slopes

➕ Scenic setting, with splendid views

➕ Charming old village centre

➕ Some very smart hotels and shops

➕ Both gourmet and simple mountain lunches in attractive surroundings

➕ Excellent cross-country trails

➕ Great for weekends

➕ Great when it snows – woodland runs with no one on them

➕ Plenty to do off the slopes

➖ Low altitude of slopes means a risk of poor snow – but the grassy terrain does not need much cover, and snowmaking has improved

➖ Lots of slow, old lifts remain

➖ Three separate mountains, only two linked (and by lift but not by piste)

➖ Not many challenging pistes – though there is good off-piste

➖ Very muted après-ski scene

➖ Meals and drinks pricey

Megève is the essence of rustic chic. It has a medieval heart but it was, in a way, the original purpose-built French ski resort – developed in the 1920s as an alternative to St Moritz. Although Courchevel took over as France's swankiest resort ages ago, Megève's smart hotels still attract 'beautiful people' with fur coats and fat wallets. Happily, you don't need either to enjoy the place. And it is enjoyable – the list of plus points above is as long as they come.

The risk of poor snow still makes us wary of low resorts like this. But it is true that a few inches of snow is enough to give skiable cover on the grassy slopes, and when there's fresh snow falling this is a great place to be.

The resort's managers can't do much about the altitude. What they could do, though, is buy some more modern lifts: the area still ranks close to the bottom of our fast lifts league table. Of course, clocking up piste mileage is not the top priority for Megève's main clientele.

THE RESORT

Megève is in a lovely sunny setting and has a beautifully preserved, traditional, partly medieval centre.

The main Albertville-Chamonix road bypasses the centre, and there are expensive underground car parks. But the resort's clientele arrives mainly by car and the resulting traffic jams and fumes are a major problem. It's worst at weekends, but can be serious every afternoon in high season. Visitors are mainly well-heeled French couples and families, who come here for an all-round winter holiday. What they don't come for is après-ski action. The tea-time atmosphere is muted, and later on the nightlife is smart rather than lively.

The Chamois gondola, within walking distance of central Megève, gives direct access to one of the three mountains, Rochebrune. This sector can also be reached by a cable car from the southern edge of town. The main lifts for the bigger Mont d'Arbois sector start from an elevated suburb of the resort – though there is also a cable car link from Rochebrune. The third sector, Le Jaillet, starts out on the north-west fringes of the town.

There are several alternative bases (which offer some good-value lodging)

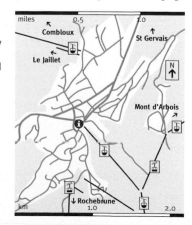

↑ Gentle, well-groomed slopes cut through the woods: that's what Megève's regulars love

KEY FACTS

Megève	
Resort	1100m
	3,610ft
Slopes	850-2355m
	2,790-7,730ft
Lifts	83
Pistes	325km
	202 miles
Green	17%
Blue	30%
Red	40%
Black	13%
Snowmaking	
	673 guns

on the fringes of the area. St-Gervais and Le Bettex above it have gondola access (St-Gervais is described at the end of this chapter). But beware slow access lifts from otherwise attractive spots such as St-Nicolas and Combloux. The most recently linked village, La Giettaz, is out on a limb but offers interesting local terrain. The Evasion Mont Blanc lift pass also covers Les Contamines and the Mont Blanc weekly pass covers all the Chamonix valley plus Courmayeur in Italy. A car is handy for visiting these resorts.

VILLAGE CHARM ★★★★
Old France at its best
Megève's charming centre is pedestrianised and comes complete with open-air ice rink, horse-drawn sleighs, cobbled streets and a fine church. Lots of smart clothing, jewellery, antique, gift and food shops add to the chic atmosphere.

CONVENIENCE ★★
Stay close to a lift
Unless you have a car, staying close to one of the main lifts makes a lot of sense. Some accommodation is a long walk from the lifts, and the free bus services are a source of complaints.

SCENERY ★★★★★
Beautiful town, beautiful views
The resort enjoys a splendid position between its three attractive mountains, with wonderful views of Mont Blanc from much of the ski area.

THE MOUNTAINS

The three different mountains provide predominantly easy intermediate cruising, much of it prettily set in the woods and with some spectacular views. The wooded slopes make it a great resort in poor weather. Pistes tend to be overclassified – so many reds would be blue elsewhere. Signposting needs improvement. Given the lack of fast lifts, it's not surprising that the piste map doesn't mark them, but it is regrettable.

EXTENT OF THE SLOPES ★★★★★
More than enough for a week
Each of the three mountains has a worthwhile amount of terrain. The biggest, highest and most varied sector is **Mont d'Arbois**, accessible not only from the town but also by a gondola from La Princesse, way out to the north-east of town, with extensive free car parking. It offers some wooded slopes but is mainly open.

The slopes above the resort are sunny, but there are north-east-facing slopes to Le Bettex and on down to St-Gervais. A two-stage gondola returns you to the top. You can work your way over to Mont Joux and up to the small Mont Joly area – Megève's highest slopes. And from there you can go to the backwater village of St-Nicolas-de-Véroce (there's a splendid red run along the ridge with wonderful views of Mont Blanc); the return to Mont Joux is now faster with a six-pack in place.

From the Mont d'Arbois lift base, the Rocharbois cable car goes across the valley to **Rochebrune** (also reached by a gondola from the centre of town and a cable car a little way out of the centre). Alpette is the starting point for Megève's historic downhill course, now revived as an off-piste route, and narrow enough to be quite tricky. A network of gentle, wooded, north-east-facing slopes, served by drags and mainly slow chair lifts, leads to the high point of Côte 2000, which often has the best snow in Megève.

The third area is **Le Jaillet**, accessed by gondola from just outside the north-west edge of town, or from Combloux, linked by a series of long, gentle treelined runs. In the other direction is the high point of Le Christomet, which is linked to the slopes of Le Torraz, above **La Giettaz**, a tiny resort halfway to La Clusaz. The

Evasion Mont Blanc

Prices in €		
Age	1-day	6-day
under 15	29	137
15 to 59	36	171
over 60	33	154
Free under 5, over 80		
Beginner no deals		

Notes
Covers lifts at Les Contamines as well as those of the Megève pass (see list below); family reductions

Alternative passes
Megève pass (covers Megève, La Giettaz, Combloux, St-Gervais and St-Nicolas); Jaillet-Combloux-Giettaz only pass; pedestrian pass; weekly Mont Blanc pass (all resorts in the Mont Blanc area plus Courmayeur in Italy)

Alpine Answers, AmeriCan Ski, Erna Low, Flexiski, Interhome, Lagrange, Leisure Direction, Made to Measure, Momentum, Oxford Ski Co, Peak Retreats, PV-Holidays.com, Simon Butler Skiing, Simply Alpine, Ski Collection, Ski Expectations, Ski France, Skiholiday extras.com, Ski Independence, Ski Solutions, Skitracer, Ski Weekend, Snow Finders, Stanford Skiing, White Roc
St Gervais AmeriCan Ski, Chalet Group, Erna Low, Holiday in Alps, Interhome, Lagrange, Mountain Tracks, Peak Retreats, Ski France, Skiholidayextras.com, Snowcoach
Combloux Erna Low, Peak Retreats

slopes of Le Torraz are worth visiting, not least for the spectacular views from the summit.

FAST LIFTS ★
Still too many slow ones
Megève doesn't have enough fast lifts for a resort of its size. Gondolas and cable cars provide the main access, and fast chairs are dotted around – but three out of four lifts are slow.

QUEUES ★★★★
Few weekday problems
Megève is relatively queue-free during the week, except at peak holiday time. But school holidays and sunny Sunday crowds can mean some delays. The long, steep Lanchettes and Roche fort drags between Cote 2000 and the rest of the Rochebrune slopes get busy ('ridiculously long waits') – as does the cable car linking the two mountains. Crowded pistes at Mont Joux and Mont d'Arbois can also be a problem. But out of peak season, slow lifts and breakdowns (eg of the gondola from St Gervais) provoke more complaints than queues or crowds. And on a snowy day the slopes can be delightfully quiet as the pampered clientele stay in bed, leaving the fresh snow to you and us.

TERRAIN PARKS ★★★
Four, surprisingly
You wouldn't have thought there was much call for terrain parks from Megève's clientele – but the place has four. For 2008/09 the new Waidzai park was located by the Grands Champs chairlift in the Rochebrune area. However, it is small with a few medium jumps and rails. There is a 500m/1,640ft long boardercross course as well. Six snow-guns mean the snow

coverage is there until the resort closes for the season. There is also a park on Mont d'Arbois by the Mont Joux chair, with a good double line of intermediate and beginner jumps as well as an expert line. These are flanked by a host of rails and boxes. New this year is a mini-pipe and boardercross as well. Combloux also has a park and La Giettaz a smaller park, albeit with a real multitude of jump sizes and a few rails.

SNOW RELIABILITY ★★
The area's main weakness
The problem is that the slopes are low, with very few runs above 2000m/ 6,560ft, and partly sunny – the Megève side of Mont d'Arbois gets the afternoon sun. So in a poor snow year, or in a warm spell, snow on the lower slopes can suffer badly. Fortunately, the grassy slopes don't need much depth of snow. A 2008 visitor found conditions much better at Combloux when patchy elsewhere. And the resort has an extensive snowmaking network but that can't work in warm weather. Piste grooming is of a high standard.

FOR EXPERTS ★★
Off-piste is the main attraction
One of Megève's great advantages for expert skiers is that there is not much competition for the powder – you can often make first tracks on challenging slopes many days after a fresh dump.
The Mont Joly and Mont Joux sections offer the steepest slopes. The top chair here serves a genuinely black run, with some serious off-piste off the back of the hill, and the slightly lower Epaule chair has some steep runs back down and also accesses some good off-piste, as well as pistes, down to St-Nicolas. The

Megève

307

Inte-active resort shortlist builder at www.wtss.co.uk

boarding

Boarding doesn't really fit with Megève's traditional, rather staid, upmarket image. But freeriders will find lots of untracked off-piste powder for days after new snowfalls. It's a good place to try snowboarding for the first time, with plenty of fairly wide, quiet, gentle runs and a lot of chairlifts and gondolas. The draglifts around are generally avoidable. There are no specialist schools, but all the ski schools offer boarding lessons. There are four terrain parks.

steep area beneath the second stage of the Princesse gondola can be a play area of powder runs among the trees. Cote 2000 has a small section of steep runs, including good off-piste.

The terrain under the Christomet chair can be a good spot to practise off-piste technique, given decent snow.

FOR INTERMEDIATES ★★★★
Superb if the snow is good

Good intermediates will enjoy the whole area – there is so much choice it's difficult to single out any particular sectors. Keen skiers are likely to want to focus on the fast lifts, and happily several of these serve excellent terrain – the Princesse and Bettex gondolas on Mont d'Arbois, the Fontaine and Alpette chairs on Rochebrune and the Christomet chair in the Le Jaillet sector.

But don't confine yourself to those – there are lots of other interesting areas, including the shady north-east-facing slopes on the back of Mont d'Arbois and Mont Joux and the front of Rochebrune, and the genuinely red/black slopes of La Giettaz. The slopes above Combloux are well worth exploring, particularly the quiet reds and black served by the Jouty chairlift.

Megève is also a great area for the less confident. There are long, easy blue runs in all sectors. A number of gentle runs lead down to Le Bettex and La Princesse from Mont d'Arbois, while nearby Mont Joux accesses long, problem-free runs to St-Nicolas. Alpette and Cote 2000 are also suitable. As is most of Le Jaillet, especially the long easy runs down to Combloux.

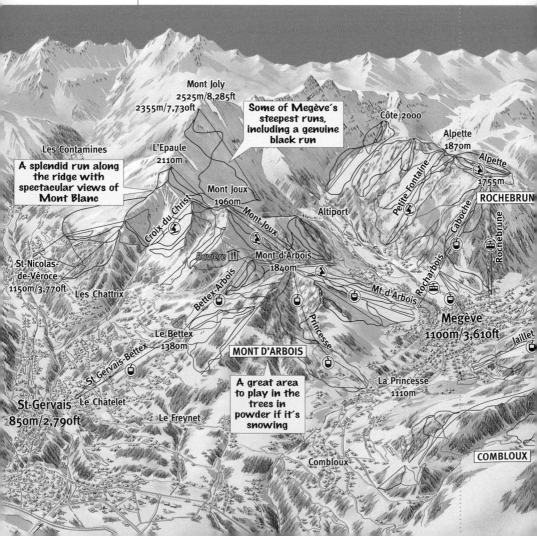

CHILDCARE

Meg'Accueil
t 0450 587784
Ages 1 to 12

Club des Piou-Piou
t 0450 589765
Ages 3 and 4

Ski schools
From age 3 or 4 (ESF
prices: 5 mornings
€110 for ages 3 and
4, €128 for ages 5 to
12)

FOR BEGINNERS ★★★☆☆
Good choice of nursery areas
There are beginner slopes at valley
level, and more snow-sure ones at
altitude on each of the main
mountains. There are also plenty of
very easy green runs to progress to.

FOR CROSS-COUNTRY ★★★★☆
An excellent area
There are 43km/27 miles of varied
trails spread throughout the area.
Some are at altitude, making meeting
with Alpine skiers for lunch simple.

MOUNTAIN RESTAURANTS ★★★★☆
Something for all budgets
Megève has some chic, expensive,
gourmet mountain huts but plenty of
cheaper options too. Booking ahead is
advisable for table-service places.
Editors' choice On Mont d'Arbois, the
Ravière (0450 931571), tucked away in
the woods near the La Croix chair, is a
tiny rustic hut that does a set three-
course meal and where booking is
essential. On Le Jaillet, Auberge du
Christomet (0450 211134) at the foot
of the fast Christomet chair has a

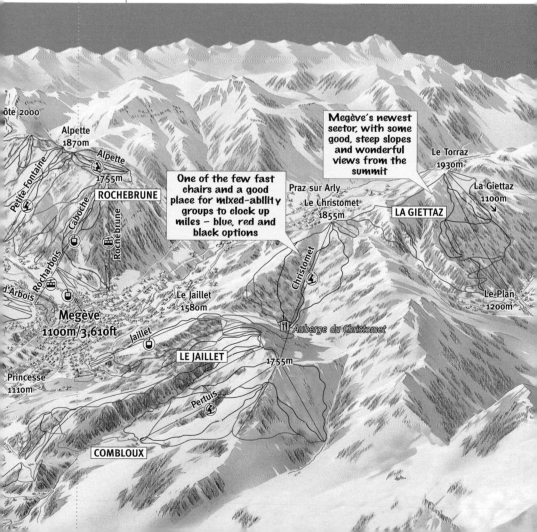

↑ The pretty, traffic-free centre is charming and a lovely place to stroll around

OT MEGEVE / BIONNASSAY

SCHOOLS

ESF
t 0450 210097
International
t 0450 587888
Freeride
t 0680 306898
Summits
t 0450 933521
Agence de Ski
t 0450 891273
Ski Pros
t 0681 610615

Classes (ESF prices)
5 mornings (2½hr)
€147
Private lessons
€40 for 1hr

GUIDES

Compagnie des Guides
t 0450 215511

GETTING THERE

Air Geneva 90km/
55 miles (1hr15);
Lyon 180km/
110 miles (2hr30)

Rail Sallanches
(12km/7 miles);
regular buses from
station

lovely terrace with fabulous views and a cosy rustic interior; it is highly rated for its plats du jour. It is accessible by car, and gets booked out.
Worth knowing about The Mont d'Arbois area is very well endowed with restaurants. Idéal 1850 is a suave place popular with poseurs with small dogs and fur coats. The Mont d'Arbois self-service has a varied menu. The Igloo, 'quiet but expensive', with wonderful views of Mont Blanc, has both self- and table-service sections and, we hear, charge a euro to use the loo. Espace Mont Joux ('friendly, great views') and Chez Marie du Rosay self-service have been recommended. Prices are lower on the back side of the hill. A regular visitor says that the Refuge de Porcherey there and the little family-run Gouet on the way back are the best places on the mountain. In the Communailles bowl, as well as the Ravière (see above), Alpage and Relais de Communailles are good. The hut at the bottom of the Mont Rosset chair is worth a visit, say reporters.

On Rochebrune, on the Cote 2000 slopes Radaz has been recommended; so have the 'cosy' Chalet Forestier ('good plats du jour') and the Super Megève. On Le Jaillet we hear the Face au Mont Blanc at the top of the gondola does a great fixed-price buffet. Auberge Bonjournal on the ridge on the way to/from La Giettaz has fantastic views from the terrace, a cosy, rustic interior and 'good food and friendly staff'. The places down at Le Plan, the lift station for La Giettaz, are said to offer 'great value'.

SCHOOLS AND GUIDES ★★★
Good private lessons
The International school has been more popular with readers than the ESF, but we have several reports of successful private lessons with the ESF. A 2009 reporter had an 'excellent

private lesson' with Ski Pros; the instructor 'spoke good English and successfully dealt with our differing needs'. Expeditions to the Vallée Blanche (in Chamonix) and to heli-skiing (in Italy) can be arranged, and mountain guides are available (we had a great morning powder skiing in the trees with Alex Périnet: 0685 428339).

FOR FAMILIES ★★★
Language problems
The kindergartens offer a wide range of activities. But lack of English-speaking staff could be a drawback. The slopes are family-friendly and the schools rated by reporters. There are snow gardens in the main sectors.

STAYING THERE

Relatively few British tour operators go to Megève, but there is an impressive range of accommodation in the area.
Chalets A few UK tour operators offer catered chalets. Stanford is a Megève specialist and has three; for a cheap and very cheerful base, you won't do better than its Sylvana – a creaky, unpretentious old hotel, run along chalet lines, close to the Rochebrune cable car and to the centre of town.
Hotels Megève offers a range of exceptionally stylish and welcoming hotels, and more modest places, too.
★★★★Mont Blanc (0450 212002) Megève's traditional leading hotel – elegant, fashionable, central.
★★★★Chalet du Mont d'Arbois (0450 212503) Prettily decorated Relais et Châteaux hotel secluded near the Mont d'Arbois gondola.
★★★★Chalet St Georges (0450 930715) Central, very close to the gondola. Only 24 rooms, so intimate for a 4-star. 'Two very good restaurants.'
★★★★Fer à Cheval (0450 213039) Rustic-chic at its best, with a warmly welcoming wood-and-stone interior and excellent food. Close to the centre. Spa and pool. 'A memorable stay,' writes a reporter.
★★★Prairie (0450 214855) Opposite Fer à Cheval. 'Reasonably priced' B&B.
★★★Coin du Feu (0450 210494) 'Very well managed' chalet midway between Rochebrune and Chamois lifts.
★★★Coeur de Megève (0450 212530) Central, very close to the gondola. Restaurant has been highly rated.
★★Sévigné (0450 212309) Ten minutes from the centre, but 'very quaint'.
Apartments Château & Résidence

ACTIVITIES

Indoor Sports centre (tennis, ice rink, climbing wall, swimming pool, sauna, solarium, gym), beauty treatments, health and fitness centres, bowling, museum, library, cinemas, casino, language courses, concerts and exhibitions, bridge, painting courses

Outdoor Cleared paths, snowshoeing, ice rink, sleigh rides, dog sledding, paintballing, ice climbing, adventure park, tobogganing, sightseeing flights, hot air ballooning, paragliding

Phone numbers
From abroad use the prefix +33 and omit the initial '0' of the phone number

TOURIST OFFICES

Megève
t 0450 212728
megeve@megeve.com
www.megeve.com

St-Gervais
t 0450 477608
welcome@st-gervais.
net
www.st-gervais.net

L'Arboise, set on the Mont d'Arbois road overlooking the village, has sauna, steam, indoor/outdoor pool, restaurant/bar – bookable via Erna Low. Stanford also has apartments.

EATING OUT ★★★★
Very French
Lots of upmarket restaurants – many recommended in the gastro guides. Flocons de Sel (two Michelin stars) and the restaurants in all the best hotels are excellent but very pricey. The fashionable Cintra, also expensive, is 'great for fresh seafood'.

The Brasserie Centrale 'serves almost anything you ask for', says an impressed reporter. The Prieuré has been highly rated for atmosphere, food and good value, while the Bistrot does 'good' salads and pizzas. The Delicium is also popular. The Crystobald and Bouddha Moor (Asian) are newish places.

APRES-SKI ★★
Strolling and jazz
Megève is a pleasant place to stroll around after the lifts close, but exciting it isn't. If there are atmospheric bars for a post-piste beer, they have eluded us. And those looking for loud disco-bars later may be disappointed. We liked the Club de Jazz (aka the 5 Rues) – a very popular, if rather expensive, jazz club-cum-cocktail bar, that gets some big-name musicians and opens from tea-time to late. But one reporter reckons 'it's cold, impersonal, and the pure jazz seems to have given way to more rock and roll.' The Kitschen bar is lively, Brit-run, 'serves tapas with a French twist'. The Cocoon is popular with Brits, and the Wake-Up look. The casino is more slot machines than blackjack tables. Palo Alto has two discos.

OFF THE SLOPES ★★★★
Lots to do
There is a 'fantastic' sports centre with a pool (which a reporter says is 'sometimes out of commission in the low season'), an outdoor ice rink, cinemas and a weekly market. Trips to

Annecy and Chamonix are possible. Walks are excellent, with 50km/30 miles of marked paths classified for difficulty on a special map. Meeting friends on the slopes for lunch is easy.

St-Gervais 850m/2,790ft

St-Gervais is a handsome 19th-century spa town set in a narrow river gorge, on the far side of Mont d'Arbois, with access to the slopes via a 20-person gondola from just outside the town. A 2009 reporter praises the ESF for their four-year-old's first ski lessons. St-Gervais is an urban but pleasant place, with interesting food shops and cosy bars, thermal baths and an Olympic ice rink. Prices are noticeably lower than in Megève. Buses are reported to be regular and convenient. Two hotels convenient for the gondola are the Liberty Mont Blanc (0450 934521), a pleasantly traditional 2-star, and the 'quite charming' 3-star Carlina (0450 934110), with a small pool and sauna. The 2-star Val d'Este (0450 936591) and its restaurant (the Serac) have been praised. Holiday in Alps has a large selection of apartments and self-catered chalets to rent. And the smart new Fermes de St Gervais with pool etc will open for 2009/10; inconveniently situated out of town but OK if you have a car; bookable through Peak Retreats and Erna Low.

On the opposite side of St-Gervais is a rack-and-pinion railway, which in 1904 was intended to go to the top of Mont Blanc but actually takes you to the slopes of Les Houches.

Interactive resort shortlist builder at **www.wtss.co.uk**

Les Menuires

The bargain base for the Three Valleys – with increasing amounts of stylish accommodation as well as the original dreary blocks

£100
RESORT PRICE INDEX

TOP 10 RATINGS

Extent	★★★★★
Fast lifts	★★★★
Queues	★★★★
Snow	★★★★
Expert	★★★★
Intermediate	★★★★★
Beginner	★★★
Charm	★
Convenience	★★★★★
Scenery	★★★

NEWS

For 2009/10 a six-pack is due to replace three chairs (Arcosses, Sapinière and Etelè) and a draglift at Reberty.

For 2008/09 more snowmaking was installed on the Pelozet piste to improve connections with St-Martin and several pistes reworked to better suit their grading.

The child safety system 'Magnestick' was fitted to several chairlifts. And the chalet-style MGM apartment complex, Les Clarines, opened.

- **+** Speedy access to wide range of slopes, via impressive lift system
- **+** Lots of slope-side accommodation
- **+** Many attractive new developments
- **+** French atmosphere, with few Brits (and no Russians)

- **–** Big, dreary blocks and gloomy indoor shopping malls in centre
- **–** Main intermediate and beginner slopes get a lot of sun
- **–** Some lower slopes get crowded

Les Menuires has always had a great position in the Three Valleys, and we've warmed to it as better (and better-looking) lodgings have been added over recent years. With our RPI confirming it as the most affordable major resort in the area, we expect more interest from readers in those better lodgings – which is why we've added a special Belles-Menuires section to highlight them.

THE RESORT

Les Menuires is in the same valley as Val Thorens and has excellent links to the Méribel valley. In contrast to the other Three Valleys resorts, it is heavily apartment-dominated, and about 60% of the visitors are French.

Recent development has added various suburbs to the original core. The most attractive of these are covered in our Belles-Menuires feature, over the page.

Village charm The original buildings that surround the main lift base, La Croisette, are among the most brutal examples of the low-budget building of the 1960s/70s. But the resort is trying hard to smarten up. A couple of the original buildings have been demolished (as we advised over a decade ago) and replaced by traditional-style chalets. All the more recent developments are in stone-and-wood chalet style.

Convenience The resort is one of the most convenient you'll find anywhere, with lifts, pistes and lodgings all thoroughly integrated. The newer outposts have their own shops and bars, but most are a bus-ride from the resort centre if you want more choice. Les Bruyères is now a more-or-less self-contained resort, and readers find it a satisfactory base.

Scenery The scenery can be rather bleak, but there are grand views from the peaks of the ski area.

THE MOUNTAINS

Les Menuires is set at about the treeline, with almost all open slopes. The latest piste map meets with reader approval. Signing is good.

Slopes The major part of the network spreads across the broad, west-facing mountainside between Les Menuires and St-Martin, with links to the Méribel valley at four points and to Val

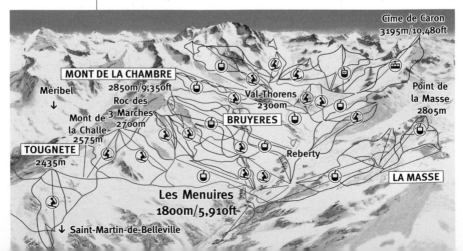

↑ You get an appetising view of La Masse from Tougnète, one of the links with Méribel

KEY FACTS

Resort	1800m
	5,910ft

Three Valleys	
Slopes	1260-3230m
	4,130-10,600ft
Lifts	180
Pistes	600km
	373 miles
Green	15%
Blue	38%
Red	37%
Black	10%
Snowmaking	33%

Les Menuires / St-Martin only	
Slopes	1400-2850m
	4,590-9,350ft
Lifts	36
Pistes	160km
	99 miles
Green	8%
Blue	42%
Red	40%
Black	10%
Snowmaking	45%

Thorens. A gondola and a fast chair go up from La Croisette, and a gondola from Les Bruyères (also accessible from much of Reberty). A chair and gondola to the separate sector of La Masse start below the village.

Fast lifts Fast chairs or gondolas are the norm, and a new six-pack for 2009/10 will replace four slow lifts, lifting Les Menuires to 4 stars.

Queues Not usually a problem; most of our 2009 reporters comment on few queues. But the Bruyères gondola and Mont de la Chambre chair may get busy at peak times – and the latter was reportedly unreliable in 2009. Overcrowding on the slopes down to the resort centre is more of a problem.

Terrain parks The Becca park above Reberty (confusingly called 'snowcross' – which means a ski route in some resorts) has rails, slides and big air, two boardercrosses and a learner area.

Snow reliability La Masse's height and orientation ensure good snow for a long season. The west-facing slopes have lots of snowmaking but the snow lower down is often icy or slushy. The lift company is continuing to expand the snowmaking facilities.

Experts The upper slopes of La Masse are virtually all of stiff red/soft black steepness – great fast cruises when groomed. There is also a huge amount of off-piste, including Vallon du Lou – a broad valley towards Val Thorens.

Intermediates With good snow, you may be content with the local slopes, which are virtually all blue and red. In poor snow you can head up to Val Thorens on blue runs. Don't miss La Masse – the blacks are not super-steep – but beware the steep Masse draglift.

Beginners There is now a dedicated nursery area with free moving carpets and a special lift pass for beginners, but the snow quality on the nursery slopes is a worry, and the progression slopes can be crowded.

Snowboarding There are few drags but some flattish sections of piste.

Cross-country The 28km/17 miles of prepared trails are along the valley between St-Martin and Les Menuires.

Mountain restaurants Readers' current favourite is the Grand Lac, a big chalet in a fine spot half-way to St-Martin – 'huge portions, great value, friendly'. Higher up, the Alpage offers 'really good food and excellent value'. The busy Sonnailles is a 'great little restaurant' – 'service with a smile'. Many people head down to the resort for lunch; you can retain some sense of being on the mountain by using the piste-side places on the upper fringes of the village. Favourites in this department are the 'great' Ferme, at Reberty 2000 and the Etoile at La Sapinière. Check out the slope-side hotel terraces up here, too.

Schools and guides ESF gets mixed reviews: A 2009 reporter praises 'excellent' private lessons, but we've had reports of disappointing group lessons – large groups, mainly French, changes of instructor. A 2008 reporter used SnowBow and said: 'We had one of the scariest instructors I have met but, boy, did she teach us technique.'

Families Good facilities. There are kids' 'villages' with indoor and outdoor facilities at both Croisette and Les Bruyères. The chalet operators in Reberty operate their own nurseries. There are fun parks, tubing, and kids' snow scooters and quad bikes.

STAYING THERE

Reberty has most of the hotels and chalets, and Club Med.

Chalets There's a growing range of options in the more appealing suburbs – see our Belles-Menuires feature.

Hotels The two best are on the slopes at Reberty: the Kaya (0479 414200) is the resort's only 4-star – attractively smart and modern; the top 3-star is the Ours Blanc (0479 006166). A 'chalet hotel', Isatis (0479 004545), opened in Les Bruyères in 2008 – basically, chalet-style apartments with an attached restaurant.

Apartments In contrast to the blocks of the main resort, there are lots of new developments in chalet style on the slopes – see our Belles-Menuires feature. The pick of these is probably Les Clarines, opened in 2008/09 – 'very comfortable, well equipped, excellent facilities'.

UK PACKAGES

Chalet Group, Club Med, Crystal, Directski. com, Erna Low, Family Ski Company, First Choice, Independent Ski Links, Interhome, Lagrange, Leisure Direction, Neilson, PV-Holidays.com, Simply Alpine, Ski Amis, Ski Collection, Ski Famille, Ski France, Skiholidayextras.com, Ski Independence, Ski McNeill, Ski Olympic, Ski Supreme, Skitopia, Skitracer

Phone numbers

From abroad use the prefix +33 and omit the initial '0' of the phone number

TOURIST OFFICE

t 0479 007300
lesmenuires@
lesmenuires.com
www.lesmenuires.com

OT LES MENUIRES / GILLES LANSARD

The chalets of Reberty-Village, a major part of Reberty 2000, are largely run by UK operators ↓

Eating out In Reberty, the Ferme is very popular for its food, atmosphere and good-value menus. The hotel Kaya is a good gourmet option. Other tips include: the 'reasonable' Trattoria, the Perdrix Blanche ('excellent food, friendly service'); and the 'friendly' Chouette ('good chilli') and hugely popular Vieux Grenier in Les Bruyères.
Après-ski The Chouette at Les Bruyères gets this year's readers' vote for close-of-play beers, sometimes with live music. There is no shortage of bars in La Croisette, but many are in the dreadfully claustrophobic mall.

The Medz'é-ry at Preyerand is 'unusually friendly' and later on does an after-dinner cabaret – 'excellent entertainment.' There are discos in both La Croisette and Les Bruyères – the latter said to get 'really lively'.
Off the slopes The resort does make an effort on this front. There is a big, impressive sports/spa/fitness centre. The various outdoor activities include a new toboggan run down the Roc des 3 Marches gondola this year. Engine-driven options include microlight flights. But this is basically a destination for skiers and boarders.

La Plagne has its Belle-Plagne – why shouldn't Les Menuires have its Belles-Menuires? Or should it be Beaux-Menuires? Whatever ... We've made up this name to represent the attractive, chalet-style suburbs of Les Menuires – places where Méribel habitués might be happy.

Reberty 2000, in a convenient ski-in/ski-out location pictured below left, has it all – a cluster of comfortable chalets, the resort's two best hotels – the Ours Blanc and the 4-star Kaya – the smart MGM Alpages apartment development (and the Chalets du Soleil further up) and an excellent slope-side restaurant, the Ferme. Practically all the chalets are operated by British firms – notably Family Ski Company, Ski Olympic and (new this year) Ski Famille. Lower down the hill are Reberty 1850 and La Sapinière, with the smart Montagnettes apartments. At the bottom of the slope is the mini-resort of Les Bruyères (complete with ice rink and swimming pool, as well as shops). There are luxury apartments here (Les Chalets de l'Adonis and the new Chalet La Dame Blanche). Right next to the base of the Bruyères gondola for Mont de la Chambre and Méribel, Ski Amis has half a dozen neat chalet units.

On the opposite, down-valley side of the resort centre are further traditional-style, small-scale, relatively upmarket developments. In Preyerand, just below the main valley road, the new chalet-style MGM apartment complex Les Clarines opened last season, with spa. A short piste further down the valley (with return chairlift to the top of Preyerand) is the hamlet of Le Bettex (or Le Bettaix), where Ski Amis has a cluster of smart, newly built, independent chalets with outdoor hot tubs.

Selected chalets in Les Menuires

SKI AMIS *www.skiamis.com*   T **0207 692 0850** F **0207 692 0851**

↑ CHALETS DE BRUYERES   CHALET DE BRUYERES' LOUNGE →

↑ CHALETS DE BETTAIX

Chalets de Bruyeres
Superb on-piste location at the foot of the gondola lift for ski-in/ski-out – fully catered chalets with en-suite facilities and hot-tubs

Chalet Hayley – sleeps 12

Chalets Estelle, Flora and Gabrielle – each sleep 12 adults and 4 kids

Chalet Delfina – sleeps 14

Chalets de Bettaix
Located in the village of Le Bettaix, just below the centre of Les Menuires on one side and La Masse on the other with lift and piste access 150m away. Each fully catered chalet has its own sauna and outside hot-tub

Chalets Irene, Jasmine, Katerina and Lorraine – each sleeps 8-10 people

Chalets Miranda and Nicolette – each sleeps 12-14 people

Méribel

The enduring British favourite: a comfortable, upmarket chalet-style resort in the centre of the incomparable Three Valleys

£125
RESORT PRICE INDEX

RATINGS

The mountains

Extent	★★★★★
Fast lifts	★★★★★
Queues	★★★★
Terrain p'ks	★★★★
Snow	★★★
Expert	★★★★
Intermediate	★★★★★
Beginner	★★★★
X-country	★★★
Restaurants	★★★
Schools	★★★★
Families	★★★

The resort

Charm	★★★
Convenience	★★★
Scenery	★★★
Eating out	★★★★
Après-ski	★★★★★
Off-slope	★★★

NEWS

For 2009/10 a fast quad is to replace the old Golf chairlift from Méribel-Village up to the Altiport area. Snowmaking is planned for the Hulotte blue run in the same area.

Also, a three-hour lift pass will be available for the local area. And the new 4-star hotel Hélios is due to open beside the Doron piste at Chaudanne.

For 2008/09 the capacity of the Tougnète gondola was increased. Two more lifts were fitted with the child safety system, 'Magnestick'.

The Olympic Centre opened new fitness facilities. The terrain park moved to a new location, and half-day (mornings) and beginner lift passes were introduced.

+ In the centre of the biggest linked lift network in the world – ideal for intermediates, great for experts, too

+ Pleasant chalet-style architecture – much less brutal than other purpose-built resorts

+ Impressive lift system

+ Very lively après-ski scene

+ Excellent piste maintenance and snowmaking; nevertheless ...

− Not the best snow in the Three Valleys especially on the afternoon-sun side

− Sprawling main village, with lots of accommodation far from the slopes

− Expensive

− Full of Brits

− Some pistes can get crowded

− Méribel-Mottaret and Méribel-Village satellites are rather lifeless

A loyal band of regular visitors just love Méribel, and it's not difficult to see why. For keen piste-bashers who like to rack up the miles but dislike tacky purpose-built resorts, it's difficult to beat; and experts can find more to amuse them than is popularly supposed. The Three Valleys can keep anyone amused for a fortnight – and Méribel-Mottaret, in particular, has quick access to every part. And then you have the clincher for we Brits: unlike other purpose-built resorts, Méribel has always insisted on chalet-style architecture. What more could you ask? Well, our − points are mostly non-trivial, and other 3V resorts have the edge in some respects. For better snow opt for Courchevel or Val Thorens. For lower prices, Les Menuires. For a more compact village and a lower concentration of Brits, go virtually anywhere. But the other resorts have their drawbacks, too. So why not love Méribel?

THE RESORT

Méribel was founded in 1938 by a Brit, Peter Lindsay, and has retained a strong British presence and influence ever since. It occupies the central valley of the Three Valleys system and consists of two main resort villages.

The original resort is built on a steepish west-facing hillside with the home piste running down beside it to the main lift stations in the valley bottom, slightly below the village centre. The resort now spreads widely away from the centre and the piste; various quarters can be identified – among them Mussillon, beside the road in, where many individual chalets are located. A road winds up from the centre to the top of the main village. From there, one road goes on through woods to the outpost of the altiport (a snow-covered airstrip) while another goes under the home piste to a more recently developed area, Belvedere.

The satellite resort of Méribel-Mottaret, a mile or two up the valley, is centrally placed in the Three Valleys ski area, offering swift access to Courchevel, Val Thorens and Les

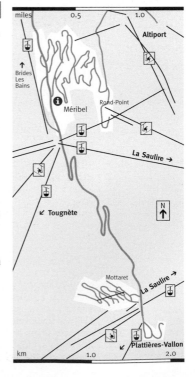

↑ Sweeping pistes and fabulous off-piste terrain at the head of the valley, between the Plattières gondola on the right and the Côte Brune chair on the left

SNOWPIX.COM / CHRIS GILL

KEY FACTS

Resort	1400-1700m
	4,590-5,580ft

Three Valleys

Slopes	1260 3230m
	4,130-10,600ft
Lifts	180
Pistes	600km
	373 miles
Green	15%
Blue	38%
Red	37%
Black	10%
Snowmaking	33%

Méribel only

Slopes	1400-2950m
	4,590-9,680ft
Lifts	53
Pistes	150km
	93 miles
Green	11%
Blue	47%
Red	30%
Black	12%
Snowmaking	42%

Menuires. The hamlet of Méribel-Village, at the bottom of a blue run on the road from Méribel to Courchevel, has developed into a pleasant although quiet mini-resort. Upgrading of its access chairlift to a fast quad will make it a more attractive base.

You can stay in the valley below Méribel, in the spa town of Brides-les-Bains – see the end of this chapter – or in the village of Les Allues at a mid-station of the gondola up from Brides.

A car is mainly of use for outings to other resorts in the Tarentaise; you can access La Plagne via Champagny. But it can be useful around the village too (see remarks on buses, below).

VILLAGE CHARM ★★★
Built with style

Méribel is one of the most tastefully designed of French purpose-built resorts. The buildings are wood-clad, chalet-style and mainly low-rise, and they include a lot of individual chalets as opposed to chalet-shaped apartment blocks. Mottaret lacks these chalets, and looks more block-like as a result, despite wood cladding on its apartment buildings. Even so, it's more attractive than many other resorts built for slope-side convenience. It has far fewer shops and bars and much less après-ski than Méribel, and nothing like the feel of a village.

CONVENIENCE ★★★
Shuttle to the slopes, usually

Although some lodgings are right on the piste beside the village, many depend on using public buses (free, but inadequate) or private minibuses to and from the slopes. There are collections of shops and restaurants at a couple of points on the road through the resort – Altitude 1600 and Plateau de Morel – so you are not obliged to descend to the centre every evening.

Méribel-Village is a small place; it has some luxury chalets and apartments, but has very limited amenities – a bread shop, a small supermarket, fitness centre, bar, pizzeria and a couple of restaurants.

Mottaret has spread up both steep sides of the valley, though most of the blocks are on the west side. Many lodgings are ski-in/ski-out, but not all. Both sides are served by lifts for pedestrians – but the gondola up the western slope stops at 7.30pm and it's a long, tiring walk up.

SCENERY ★★★
Head for Vallon

The village is attractively set among woodland, below long craggy ridges – a satisfying although unspectacular scene. But there are wonderful glacial views from Mont du Vallon at the head of the valley.

Interactive resort shortlist builder at **www.wtss.co.uk**

THE MOUNTAINS

Most of the slopes are above the treeline, but there are some sheltered runs for bad-weather days. Piste classification is not always reliable – a problem compounded by exposure of many slopes to a lot of sun. Signposting has been improved and our 2009 reporters seemed happy.

EXTENT OF THE SLOPES ★★★★★
Centre of a huge area
The Méribel valley runs roughly north-south, and in late season you soon get into the habit of avoiding the afternoon-sun side in the morning, when it is still rock-hard having frozen overnight. There are two entry points to the Courchevel valley, but no less than six entry points to the Belleville valley shared by St-Martin, Les Menuires and Val Thorens.

On the morning-sun side, chairs go up to the first two links with St-Martin, and some relatively quiet slopes back towards Méribel. To the left, a gondola and then a six-pack go from Méribel to **Tougnète**, for both Les Menuires or St-Martin. You can also head down to **Mottaret** from here. From there, a fast chair then a drag take you to Belleville entry point number four.

South of Mottaret are some of the best slopes in the valley, in the **Plattières-Vallon** sector at the head of the valley. The Plattières gondola ends at the fifth entry point to the Belleville valley. To the east of this is the big stand-up gondola to the top of Mont

Mont du Vallon
2950m/9,680ft

Mont Vallon

PLATTIÈRES - VALLON

Plan des Mains

Mures Rouge

Great hill, both on- and off-piste: high, steep but not too steep, 750m/2,460ft vertical

↙ Courchevel ↘

SAULIRE
2740m

Excessive afternoon sun means the run down to Mottaret is often more difficult than you might wish

Plattières

Better snow here than on most of the afternoon-sun side of the valley

Pas du Lac I & II

1700m

BURGIN

↙ Courchevel

Dent du Burgin

MOTTARET

Col de la Loze
2275m

Ardret

Saulire

Rhodos I & II

Chaudanne

Altiport

Méribel
1450m/4,76oft

A great area for beginners and near-beginners, with long green runs and a fast slow-loading chairlift

Altiport

Méribel-Village
1400m/4,590ft

Olympic

Brides-les-Bains
↓

du Vallon. The Côte Brune fast quad from near this area goes up to Mont de la Chambre, the sixth link with the next valley, and the only one giving direct access to Val Thorens.

On the afternoon-sun side, gondolas leave both Méribel and Mottaret for **Saulire**. From here you can head back down towards either village, or over the ridge towards Courchevel 1850. There is also a gondola from Méribel up to the slopes above Altiport, were there is another link to Courchevel via Col de la Loze.

FAST LIFTS ★★★★★
Highly efficient system
Modern chairs and gondolas serve either side of the valley, with good links into the rest of the Three Valleys.

QUEUES ★★★★
3V traffic a persistent problem
The area is generally queue-free most of the time, but as more and more visitor beds are added to the Three Valleys resorts, new bottlenecks emerge. The lift company is doubtless planning bigger lifts, but they could achieve a lot by employing lifties to usher people into half-empty cabins. If Les Arcs can do it …

The Plattières gondola and the Côte Brune chair, serving great terrain and accessing Val Thorens, both attract crowds – though the fast Combes and Chatelet chairs are a viable alternative to the former. Capacity on the Tougnète gondola was increased for 2008/09, but the six-pack above it can't cope with the combination of

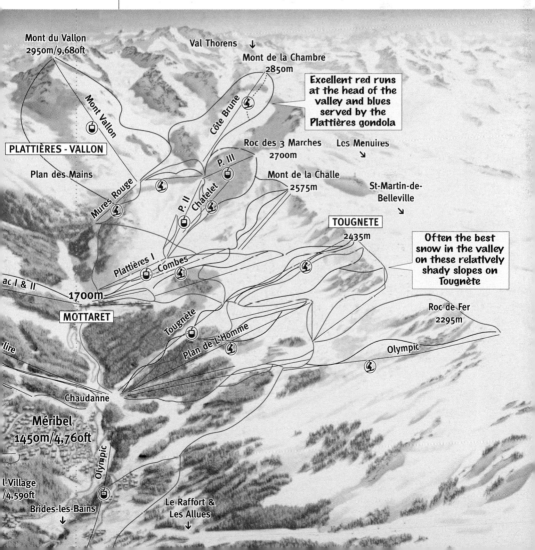

Mont du Vallon
2950m/9,680ft

Val Thorens ↓

Mont de la Chambre
2850m

Excellent red runs at the head of the valley and blues served by the Plattières gondola

Mont Vallon

Côte Brune

PLATTIÈRES - VALLON

Plan des Mains

Roc des 3 Marches
2700m

Les Menuires ↘

P. III

Mont de la Challe
2575m

St-Martin-de-Belleville ↘

Mures Rouge

P. II Chatelet

TOUGNETE
2435m

Often the best snow in the valley on these relatively shady slopes on Tougnète

Plattières I Combes

ac I & II

1700m

Roc de Fer
2295m

MOTTARET

Tougnète

Plan de l'Homme

Olympic

Chaudanne

Méribel
1450m/4,760ft

Olympic

l-Village
/4,590ft

Le Raffort & Les Allues ↓

Brides-les-Bains ↓

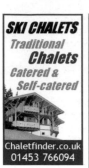
LIFT PASSES

Three Valleys

Prices in €

Age	1-day	6-day
under 13	34	169
13 to 64	44	225
over 65	39	212
Free under 5, over 75		
Beginner pass for five lifts €19 per day		

Notes
Covers Courchevel, La Tania, Méribel, Val Thorens, Les Menuires and St-Martin; family reductions; pedestrian and half-day passes

Alternative passes
Méribel and Méribel-Mottaret only with one-day Three Valleys extension available

Weekly news updates and resort links at www.wtss.co.uk

people coming up the gondola and people descending the handful of pistes above. Both of the main gondolas for Courchevel from Méribel and Mottaret can build queues.

In this central valley the most serious problems result from the tidal flows of people passing through in the morning (when the tide coincides with the start of ski school) and in the late afternoon, when crowds on the runs to Mottaret can also be a problem.

Most people returning from Val Thorens form a queue for the Plan des Mains chair so as to avoid the flat start of the 'blue' Ours valley run. Confident skiers should use our trick instead: by-pass Plan des Mains by traversing above it, off-piste.

TERRAIN PARKS ★★★★
There's a choice

The main Moonpark is accessed by the Arpasson draglift (www.moonpark.net), but has grown and now spills over onto the Grive slope. It includes a triple kicker line for all levels with smooth take-offs; the rails here are quite advanced, as is the big spine jump. There is a new step-up to step-down obstacle, and S-box. A wooden goal post feature and a 'chill and grill' BBQ zone, were new for 2008/09. The Magic ski school gives free lessons in the Moonpark between 2pm and 5pm. There is also a new beginner area called the P'tit Moon (small moon), including some mini jumps, boxes and even a small boardercross.

SNOW RELIABILITY ★★★
Not the best in the Three Valleys

Méribel's slopes aren't the highest in the Three Valleys, and they mainly face east or west; the latter (the runs down from Courchevel) get the full force of the afternoon sun. So snow conditions are often better elsewhere. And grooming seems to be rather better in neighbouring Courchevel.

Snowmaking has been increased and the lower runs have substantial cover. Lack of snow is rarely a problem, but ice at the start of the day or slush at the end can be. The run down from Saulire to Mottaret is famously prone to concrete-like conditions; we're not sure we can remember good snow on it ever, in our countless visits. The north-west-facing slopes above Altiport generally have decent snow.

At the southern end of the valley, towards Les Menuires and Val Thorens, a lot of runs are north-facing and keep their snow well, as do the runs on Mont du Vallon. A daily map is available at the tourist office showing which runs were groomed overnight.

FOR EXPERTS ★★★★
Exciting choices

The size of the Three Valleys means experts are well catered for. In the Méribel valley, Mont du Vallon has lots to interest. The long, steep Combe Vallon run here is classified red; it's a wonderful, long, fast cruise when groomed (which it normally is), but presents plenty of challenge when mogulled. And there's a beautiful off-piste run in the next valley to the main pistes, leading back to the bottom of the gondola.

A good mogul run is down the side of the double Roc de Tougne draglift which leads up to Mont de la Challe. And there are steep, unrelenting runs from Tougnète back to Méribel – the upper Ecureuil piste is now a black while the adjacent Combe Tougnète has been reclassified red. At the north end of the valley the Face run was created for the women's downhill race in the 1992 Olympics. Served by a fast quad, it's a splendid cruise when freshly groomed (with good views over the village), and you can terrify yourself just by imagining what it must be like to go straight down.

boarding

Méribel is a favourite for British snowboarders. The terrain is good and varied, with a lot more tree runs than in neighbouring Val Thorens. Mont du Vallon has some very good steep freeriding that stays relatively untracked, as well as two new designated off-piste areas, 'zone des cretes' and 'zone du chevreuilles'. There are lots of red runs here for intermediates and gentle blues and greens for beginners. Most lifts are chairs or gondolas but beware of flat sections on the main routes to and from Val Thorens – avoid the Ours blue run down to Mottaret from Mont du Vallon, which is very hard work. Specialist shops include Board Brains (in Méribel) and Quiksilver Gotcha Surf (in Mottaret).

Méribel has a lot of very good off-piste to discover, as well as the pistes that the Three Valleys is famous for. We asked Pierre-François Papet, head of Méribel's Snow Systems ski school, to pick out some of the best off-piste runs for skiers with at least some off-piste experience. Don't tackle them without guidance.

Some of the best snow is to be found on the north-facing run accessed from the 3 Vallées 2 chairlift at Val Thorens. Ducking the rope at the top takes you into varied terrain mixing couloirs and gentle slopes, with exposures from north-east to north-west. Eventually you join the red Lac de la Chambre piste.

The run from near Roc de Fer to Le Raffort, a mid-station on the gondola from Brides-les-Bains, is an adventure with exceptional views. You ride the Olympic chairlift, go along the ridge, then ski a gentle bowl to finish among the trees.

The wide, west-facing slope above Altiport is enjoyable when the snow is fresh – varied terrain, from average to steep, some open some wooded, reached from the Tétras black run.

There are lots of runs suitable for more accomplished off-piste skiers. One is a descent known as The Cairn from the Mouflon piste at the top of the Plattières gondola; it starts in a fairly steep couloir and becomes wider, with a consistent pitch, until you reach the Sittelle piste.

The Roc de Tougne draglift accesses some challenging runs. To the right of the Lagopéde red piste is an area we call the Spot – a rather technical and steep descent to the Sittelle piste. Alternatively, a 15-minute hike brings you to the Couloir du Serail, leading to the Mouflon red piste – one of my favourites because of the vertical, the constant pitch and the quality of snow.

The Col du Fruit is a classic, far away from the lifts and resorts. You ride the Creux Noirs chairlift in Courchevel, then walk along the ridge for 15 minutes before descending through the national park to Lac de Tueda and the cross-country tracks ... 800m/half a mile of flat ground from the Mottaret lifts.

All of these routes require experience and training to ski them safely, and within the rules – only certain routes are allowed in the national park and Tueda reserve. Go with the pros.

Snow Systems is a ski school that operates from both Méribel and Mottaret. As well as group and private on- and off-piste lessons, they run children's lessons, snowboard lessons and instructor training.
t 00 33 479 004 022
www.snow-systems.com

Méribel

321

Interactive resort shortlist builder at **www.wtss.co.uk**

SCHOOLS

ESF Méribel
t 0479 086031

ESF Méribel-Mottaret
t 0479 004949

Magic Snowsports
t 0479 085336

New Generation
t 0479 010318
www.skinewgen.com

Parallel Lines
t 01702 589580 (UK)

Snow Systems
t 0479 004022

Eskilibre
t 0609 154987

Snow D'Light
t 0664 816010

Classes
(ESF prices)
5 half-days (2½hr per
day): from €122

Private lessons
From €127 for a half-
day

GUIDES

Mountain guide office
t 0479 003038

Nothing on the Saulire side is as steep as on the other side of the valley. The Mauduit red run is quite challenging, though – it used to be classified black. Ice can of course add an extra dimension of challenge.

Throughout the area there are good off-piste opportunities – see the special feature panel.

FOR INTERMEDIATES ★★★★★
Paradise found
Méribel and the rest of the Three Valleys form something close to paradise for intermediate skiers and riders; there are few other resorts where a keen piste-basher can cover so many miles so easily and with such satisfaction. Virtually every slope in the region has a good intermediate run down it, and to describe them all would take a book in itself.

For less adventurous intermediates, the run from the second station of the Plattières gondola above Mottaret back to the first station is ideal, and used a lot by the ski school. It is a gentle, north-facing, cruising run and is generally in good condition. But below that the run can get tricky, bumpy and very crowded later in the day. The red run into Mottaret on the other side of the valley, which used to be a blue, also gets dangerously icy and crowded. Nothing has been done yet to tackle these two problems, which spoil an otherwise ideal intermediate area.

Even early intermediates should find the runs over into the other valleys well within their capabilities, opening up further vast amounts of intermediate runs. In Courchevel or Val Thorens you also get the bonus of better snow.

Virtually all the pistes on both sides of the Méribel valley will suit more advanced intermediates. Few of the reds are easy.

FOR BEGINNERS ★★★★
Strengths and weaknesses
Méribel has its attractions for beginners, with a special lift pass covering three lifts and an excellent slope (where one of the editors of this book learned to ski, [cough] years ago). But it's out of the resort up at Altiport, which is a bit of a nuisance. There is a small nursery slope at Rond-Point, at the top of the village, which is mainly used by the children's ski school, and there are three enclosed beginner areas ('zen zones') at Plattières, above Mottaret.

The Altiport area is accessible from the village by the Morel chairlift, or by free bus. Once you have found your feet, a free draglift takes you halfway up a long, gentle, wide, treelined green run – ideal except that it can get crowded and have good skiers speeding through. Next, a longer drag takes you to the top of this run, then a chair a bit higher, then another chair higher still, on to an excellent blue usually blessed with good snow.

FOR CROSS-COUNTRY ★★★
Scenic routes
There are about 33km/21 miles in total. The main area is in the forest near Altiport and great for trying cross-country for the first time. There's also a loop around Lake Tueda, in the nature reserve at Mottaret, and for the more experienced an itinéraire from Altiport to Courchevel.

MOUNTAIN RESTAURANTS ★★★
Leave the valley
A real disappointment, this: nowhere here is worth singling out as 'Editors' choice'. What's more, there aren't enough places to meet the demand, so many places get very crowded. You're better off lunching above Les Menuires. We had a good lunch last season in the table-service part of

GETTING THERE

Air Geneva 190km/
120 miles (2hr45);
Lyon 190km/120
miles (2hr30);
Chambéry 100km/
60 miles (1hr30)

Rail Moûtiers
(18km/11 miles);
regular buses

SNOWPIX.COM / CHRIS GILL

The British connection
personified – David
Lindsay, ESF moniteur,
above the resort his
father Peter founded
in 1936 ↓

Plan des Mains, but would welcome more reports from readers. The newish Coeur de Cristal, low down beside the Adret chair, does 'very nice, well presented food and sweet display worthy of a 5-star hotel'. We continue to get good reports on the 'small and cosy' Arpasson at the mid-mountain station of the Tougnète gondola ('a variety of good-value choices'). The 'delightfully quaint' Crêtes, near the top of Tougnète, is well liked generally too, though a 2008 reporter found 'average food and poor service'. Lower down, the Togniat and the expensive Chardonnet have table- and self-service choices. The Rhododendrons, at the top of the Altiport drag, is a popular spot for its large terrace but gets mixed reviews. Some visitors have preferred the views, food and service from the Darbollées. Two self-service places notable for their views are the Pierres Plates, at the top of Saulire, and the Sittelle above the first section of the Plattières gondola.

This is one of the few resorts where we can be persuaded to descend to resort level for lunch on one of three slope-side hotel terraces – the Adray Telebar, the Allodis or the Altiport.

SCHOOLS AND GUIDES ★★★★
Some excellent options

The ESF is by far the biggest school, with over 450 instructors. It has a special international section with instructors speaking good English. Past reports have been mixed. It offers useful options, such as off-piste groups, heli-skiing on the Italian border and Three Valleys tours. But these days readers are much more likely to go with one of the smaller schools appealing mainly to Brits.

Snow Systems is enthusiastically praised by reporters for private instruction and personal service – 'a perfect combination of professionalism and fun. The confidence and technique that our tutor gave us allowed us all to successfully attempt challenging red runs after only five days,' says a 2009 visitor. Others comment: 'My wife had no confidence, but by the last day was skiing from the top to the bottom of the mountain'; 'Within 30 minutes we were skiing with confidence and style.'

New Generation, a British school which operates in Courchevel, La Tania and Méribel, continues to receive excellent reports. The latest is from a beginner teenager: 'The perfect

Méribel

323

Interactive resort shortlist builder at **www.wtss.co.uk**

CHILDCARE

Les Saturnins
t 0479 086690
Ages 18mnth to 3yr

Kids Etc
t 0479 007139
From 18mnth to 10yr

Les Piou Piou
t 0479 086031 (Mér)
t 0479 004949 (Mot)
Ages 3 to 5; 9am-5pm

Childminder list
Available from the tourist office

Ski school
The ESF runs classes for ages 5 to 13: 6 half-days (2½hr) from €118

ACTIVITIES

Indoor Parc Olympique (ice rink, swimming pool, climbing wall, karting on ice), fitness centres in hotels, bowling, library, cinemas, museum, heritage tours

Outdoor Flying lessons and excursions, snowmobiles, snowshoeing, cleared paths, paragliding

amount of jokes, drills, talks and brilliant skiing. After only two weeks skiing in my life, I was able to complete black runs.' Other testimonials: 'I cannot recommend them highly enough, they were patient and kept groups small.' 'I progressed quickly in a group of only three; the instructor explained and demonstrated techniques clearly.' Magic Snowsports Academy, the second largest school, also offers special sessions as well as normal lessons. A 2008 reporter had used them twice and rated them 'superb – significant progress while having a fantastic time'.

FOR FAMILIES ★★★☆☆
A popular chalet choice
Méribel is a sensible choice for families wanting a chalet holiday. What it lacks in convenience it gains in an impressive area, with gentle beginner slopes. 'Magnestick' child safety systems are now fitted to several chairlifts. Some of the children's classes have received good reports (see 'Schools'). But we rarely get reports on childcare facilities – no doubt many readers use the facilities of chalet operators who run their own nurseries.

STAYING THERE

Chalets Méribel has more chalets dedicated to the British market than any other resort, and over 50 operators offering them – many, as you may have noticed, advertising their properties in these pages. The specialist agents list scores of options. What really distinguishes Méribel is the range of recently built luxury chalets. Some are perfectly positioned for the slopes, but many rely on minibus services. Many have saunas, hot tubs or both.
Méribel chalet specialists include

Purple Ski, with places in different parts of the resort, including the lovely lamato in Village and the swanky Lapin Blanc, in a great on-piste location in Méribel itself; and Meriski, with nine small, smart chalets.
Snowline's seven chalets include some lovely places, the very attractive Mira Belum now among them – though they are overshadowed by the exceptionally swanky properties offered by sister company VIP. Alpine Action has four smart-looking chalets, most with saunas and hot tubs.
Ski Beat has half a dozen properties, mostly in Mussillon but including one apartment in a central location. Ski Olympic has the smooth Parc Alpin at 1600 with 12 luxurious rooms (all with plasma screen TVs), dinky swimming pool and sauna.
Descent has some very desirable properties here. Total has 11 chalets. Family specialist Esprit has a chalet-hotel in a good slope-side position, up at Rond Point.
Hotels Méribel has some excellent hotels, but they're not cheap.
****Grand Coeur** (0479 086003) Our favourite almost-affordable hotel in Méribel. Just above the village centre. Welcoming, mature building with plush lounge. Huge hot tub, sauna etc.
****Mont-Vallon** (0479 004400) The best hotel at Mottaret; good food, and excellently situated for the Three Valleys' pistes. Pool, sauna, squash, fitness room etc.
***Altiport** (0479 005232) Smart and luxurious hotel, isolated at the foot of the Altiport lifts. Convenient for Courchevel, not for Val Thorens.
***Allodis** (0479 005600) Out of town at Belvedere, but ski-in/ski-out and excellent in every other way. Seriously good restaurant, superb service, nice terrace and valley views.
***Arolles** (0479 004040) Right on the slopes at Mottaret. Pool and sauna.
***Eterlou** (0479 088900) One of three sister hotels in 'fantastic' location near main lifts that share a health club.
Adray Télébar (0479 086026) Welcoming piste-side chalet with pretty, rustic rooms, good food and popular sun terrace.
Roc (0479 003618) A good-value B&B hotel, in the centre, with a lively bar-restaurant and crêperie below.
Apartments Les Fermes de Méribel (in Méribel-Village) is a classic tasteful MGM development of six large chalets with the usual impressive pool.

Phone numbers
From abroad use the prefix +33 and omit the initial '0' of the phone number

EATING OUT ★★★★
Fair choice

There is a reasonable selection of restaurants, from ambitious French cuisine to pizza and pasta. For the best food in town, in plush surroundings, you won't beat the top hotels – try Grand Coeur and Allodis, where we've had excellent food. We also enjoyed the Kouisena on our 2009 visit, with its very rustic, intimate interior and open-fire cooking of good meat. The Tremplin is recommended for its varied menu. Tucked away near the Plattières lift, Zig Zag is a good cheaper option. Up the hill in Morel the Galette, the Fromagerie and Cro-Magnon are popular for raclette and fondue. The Blanchot just below Altiport offers the choice of two dining areas, one dedicated to dishes of the region, and Scott's does good American-style food.

In Méribel-Village the unpretentious Brit-run Lodge du Village serves 'some of the tastiest food in the Three Valleys', and at prices that are modest by local standards. The Arbé (formerly Chemina) and Martagon at Le Raffort, between Méribel and Les Allues, are worth a try.

APRES-SKI ★★★★★
Méribel rocks – loudly

Méribel's après-ski revolves around British-run places, and is far more animated than is usual in most French resorts. Piste-side, the 'legendary' Rond Point is as lively as they come, packed from happy hour 4pm–5pm – live music and toffee vodka are the norm. Or you could try Jack's, not far from the main lift stations. The ring of bars around the main square do good business at teatime. The Pub has videos, pool and 'good live bands' both at tea-time and later on, attracting a younger crowd. For a quieter drink, try the Taverne, 50/50 or the Barometer, which has lots of leather seating. La Poste injects a bit of French cool into the scene. Central to the late-night scene is Dick's Tea Bar – well established, but away from the centre and slopes. Scott's (next to the Pub) is also 'good later on'.

In Mottaret the bars at the foot of the pistes get packed at tea time – Rastro has been a regular favourite and it also has a lively disco later on.

In Méribel-Village, the bar at Lodge du Village has live music at teatime a couple of nights a week.

OFF THE SLOPES ★★★
Quite a bit to do

A non-skier's guide to Courchevel, Méribel and La Tania is distributed free by the tourist offices. The Olympic Centre has the ice rink where the Olympic events were held in 1992 and where you can watch regular ice hockey matches. It also has a good public swimming pool, a climbing wall and a spa. A fitness area was added for 2008/09. You can take joyrides in the little planes that operate from the altiport. There are pleasant marked walks in the altiport area and a signposted trail through some of the hamlets down to Les Allues (you can return from there or Le Raffort in the Brides gondola). The pedestrian's lift pass covers all the gondolas, cable cars and buses in the Méribel and Courchevel valleys, and makes it very easy for pedestrians to meet friends for lunch. Both villages have a cinema. There are very few shops other than sports equipment places, even in Méribel itself.

Brides-les-Bains

600m/1,970ft

Brides-les-Bains is an old spa town way down in the valley. For the 1992 Olympics the competitors were accommodated here and a gondola was built linking it to Méribel. It offers a quieter, cheaper alternative to the higher resorts and has some simple hotels, adequate shops and a decent choice of bars and restaurants. Ski Weekends runs a chalet hotel here. The 3-star hotel Amelie (0479 553015) is near the spa and gondola ('delicious food, great atmosphere'). There is a casino, but evenings are distinctly quiet. The gondola ride to and from Méribel takes a tedious 25 minutes or so, can be cold and arrives at a point irritatingly short of the main lifts up the mountain. It also closes rather early, at 5pm. But in good conditions you can ski off-piste to one or other of the mid-stations at the end of the day (or in exceptional conditions down to Brides itself). Given a car, Brides makes a good base for visiting other resorts.

Montgenèvre

The snowiest part of the Milky Way circuit reaching across to Sauze d'Oulx in Italy – now with through-traffic buried in a tunnel

£95
RESORT PRICE INDEX

RATINGS

The mountains

Extent	**
Fast lifts	**
Queues	***
Terrain p'ks	***
Snow	****
Expert	**
Intermediate	****
Beginner	*****
X-country	***
Restaurants	**
Schools	***
Families	****

The resort

Charm	***
Convenience	***
Scenery	***
Eating out	**
Après-ski	***
Off-slope	*

NEWS

For 2009/10 work is expected to focus on improving the beginner area.

For 2008/09 a hybrid chondola replaced the Chalmettes gondola to Les Gondrans. Another new chondola provides a second way into the Chalvet sector, also opening up new slopes – a black, a red and a blue – all equipped with snowmaking. There are also plans for another new lift on the local high point of Mont Chaberton, currently lift-free.

The long blue run from Col de l'Alpet towards Claviere gained snowmaking too. And the 4-star Hameau des Airelles apartments opened in the developing Hameau de l'Obélisque quarter.

+ Good snow record, and local slopes largely north-facing – often the best snow in the Milky Way area

+ Plenty of intermediate cruising and good, convenient nursery slopes

+ A lot of accommodation close to the slopes, and some right on them

+ Great potential for car drivers to explore other nearby resorts, but ...

− Italian Milky Way resorts are difficult to explore without the use of a car

− Lots of slow lifts and mainly short runs in local area

− Local mountain restaurants poor

− Little to challenge experts on-piste

− Limited, mostly unsophisticated restaurants and après-ski places

Montgenèvre is set on a minor pass between France and Italy, at one end of the big cross-border Milky Way network. On snow, it's a time-consuming trek from here to Sestriere and Sauze d'Oulx at the far end (you may have to ride some slow lifts down as well as up). So unless you have a car it's best to focus on the local slopes shared with Claviere (in Italy, but very close). Thanks to the setting on a high pass, they often have the best snow in the region.

The village is pleasant – much more so since the traffic between France and Italy was consigned to a 400m/1,300ft tunnel in 2005. It is edging out of the cheap-and-cheerful category with the development of the Hameau de l'Obélisque quarter, containing smart apartments and one very smart hotel.

THE RESORT

Montgenèvre is a small roadside village set on a high pass only 2km/ 1 mile from the Italian border – this is an area where the euro has really simplified things.

On the village side of the col are the south-facing slopes of Le Chalvet. The more extensive north-facing slopes of Les Gondrans are across the main road, with nursery slopes at the bottom. Both sectors have piste links with Claviere, gateway to the other Italian resorts of the Milky Way – Sansicario, Sestriere and Sauze d'Oulx. But it takes ages to get to those resorts on skis.

Serre-Chevalier and Puy-St-Vincent, with lift pass sharing arrangements, are easily reached by car, and well worth an outing each. Different lift pass options cater for most needs.

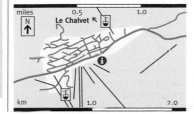

miles 0.5 1.0

N Le Chalvet

km 1.0 2.0

VILLAGE CHARM ★★★
Vibrant cafe life

Cheap and cheerful cafes, bars and restaurants line the road running along the bottom of the nursery slopes, now happily free of through-traffic. And tucked away off the main road is a quite pleasant old village, complete with quaint church and friendly natives. The generally good snow adds to the charm factor.

CONVENIENCE ★★★
Not as good as it looks

Most of the accommodation is less than five minutes from a lift, but it may not be the right lift, and getting to the one you want can be a pain. The main gondolas are at opposite ends of the village. Some of the newer accommodation is uphill, away from the slopes – but there is a free shuttle-bus. The smarter accommodation is in a newly developed area at the east side of the village, Hameau de l'Obélisque.

SCENERY ★★★
Look north or south

The area around the border is broken up by rocky outcrops and woods, and there are good views from both sides of the valley.

The restaurant at the top of the Chalvet gondola is no beauty, is it? But its sunny terrace gives a fine view of the slopes across the valley →
OT MONTGENEVRE / A BENE

KEY FACTS

Resort	1850m
	6,070ft

Montgenèvre-Monts de la Lune (Claviere)

Slopes	1760-2630m
	5,770-8,630ft
Lifts	31
Pistes	110km
	68 miles
Green	11%
Blue	27%
Red	42%
Black	20%
Snowmaking	35km
	22 miles

For the whole Milky Way area

Slopes	1390-2825m
	4,560-9,270ft
Lifts	82
Pistes	400km
	249 miles
Blue	24%
Red	56%
Black	20%
Snowmaking	33%

LIFT PASSES

Montgenèvre + Monts de la Lune

Prices in €

Age	1-day	6-day
under 12	26	135
12 to 59	33	169
over 60	26	135

Free under 6, over 75
Beginner no deals
Notes
Covers Montgenèvre and Claviere; 6-day and over pass allows one day in the Milky Way; family reductions
Alternative passes
Montgenèvre only and Voie Lactée (Milky Way) area passes

THE MOUNTAINS

The slopes of Montgenèvre and Claviere offer lots of variety – some high and open, some wooded lower down. Run classification on the local map and Milky Way map have differed in the past, which can be confusing – however, none of the blacks is much more than a tough red.

EXTENT OF THE SLOPES ★★☆☆☆
Nicely varied
Our stars are based on the local slopes of Montgenèvre and Claviere.

The north-facing slopes above Montgenèvre divide into two sectors. The high, open slopes of **Les Gondrans** are reached by the newly upgraded Chalmettes hybrid chondola from the west end of the village; a green run brings you back. The lower, steeper wooded slopes of **Le Prarial** are reached by chairlifts – the Prarial from the slopes directly in front of the village, or the Tremplin from a point well to the east of the village.

From both of these sectors you can descend into a valley separating them from the peak of l'Aigle. This has no skiing, but there are links below it and behind it into Italy and the **Monti della Luna** slopes of Claviere.

The sunny sector behind the village of Montgenèvre – **Le Chalvet** – has long been accessed by a gondola from the east end of the village. Now, access is also possible via the new Serre Thibaud chondola starting at the same point as the aforementioned Tremplin chair to Prarial. This new lift also opens up new runs into the main Chalvet bowl and into the valley beyond the Col de l'Alpet. The Chalvet runs are mainly on open slopes above the gondola; there are blue and green runs back to Montgenèvre, and a blue run to Claviere, for access to Italy.

FAST LIFTS ★★☆☆☆
Still a way to go
Recent investment has added more fast lifts, but lots of slow chairs and some vicious drags remain.

QUEUES ★★★☆☆
Mixed reports
Our 2009 reporters found the resort queue-free, even at New Year. But queues can be a problem at weekends or when snow in Italy is poor, so people come here instead. In high season there may be serious queues for the main lifts out of the village first thing but the new Serre Thibaud chondola should ease the problems.

TERRAIN PARKS ★★★☆☆
High and low
There's a half-pipe on the lower slopes near the Prarial chair, and a natural one at Chalvet. At the top of the Gondrans sector there is a safe freeride zone ('good fun'), and just across the hill a boardercross course.

SNOW RELIABILITY ★★★★☆
Excellent locally
Montgenèvre has a generally excellent snow record, receiving dumps from westerly storms funnelling up the valley to the col. The high north-facing slopes naturally keep their snow better than the south-facing area. Snowmaking covers several higher pistes as well as most lower slopes – 'intensive and very effective'.

FOR EXPERTS ★★☆☆☆
Limited, except for off-piste
There are very few challenging pistes locally. Many of the runs are overclassified. There is, however, ample off-piste terrain. The remote north-east-facing bowl beyond the Col de l'Alpet on the Chalvet side is superb in good snow and has black pistes, too. The open section between

SCHOOLS

ESF
t 0492 219046

A-Peak
t 0492 244997

Classes (ESF prices)
6 half days (2½hr)
€106

Private lessons
€34 for 1hr

CHILDCARE

Les Sourires
t 0492 215250
Ages 6mnth to 6yr;
€24 per day

Les Marmottes and Piou Piou (ESF)
t 0492 219046
Ages 2 to 5

Ski school
For ages 5 to 12
(6 half days €102)

UK PACKAGES

AmeriCan Ski, Crystal, Crystal Finest, Erna Low, Independent Ski Links, Lagrange, Leisure Direction, Neilson, Peak Retreats, Rocketski, Simply Alpine, Ski Etoile, Ski France, Skiholidayextras.com, Skitopia, Skitracer, Thomson
Claviere *Crystal, First Choice, Rocketski, Skitracer*

boarding

There's plenty to attract boarders to Montgenèvre. There are good local beginner slopes and long runs on varied terrain for intermediates. The only real drawback is that a fair number of the lifts are drags and there are some flat sections (especially getting to and from Sestriere). There are some excellent off-piste areas with a few natural hits for more advanced boarders and a dedicated freeride area at Les Gondrans (shown on the piste map). Snow Box is a specialist shop.

La Montanina and Sagnalonga on the Italian side is another good powder area. A 2008 visitor was taken on long off-piste runs off the back of Les Gondrans by ESF instructors. Heli-skiing can be arranged in Italy.

FOR INTERMEDIATES ★★★★
Plenty of cruising terrain
The overclassified blacks are just right for adventurous intermediates, though none holds the interest for very long. The pleasantly narrow treelined runs to Claviere from Pian del Sole, the steepest of the routes down in the Chalvet sector and the runs off the back of Col de l'Alpet are all fine in small doses. Average intermediates will enjoy the red runs, though most are short. On the major sector, both the runs from Colletto Verde can be great fun. Getting to Cesana via the lovely sweeping run starting at Colle Bercia, and heading home from Pian del Sole, are both easier than the classifications suggest, and can be tackled by less adventurous intermediates, who also have a wealth of cruising terrain high up at the top of Les Gondrans. The runs down to the village are easy cruises.

FOR BEGINNERS ★★★★★
Fine and gentle progress
There is a fine selection of convenient nursery slopes with reliable snow at the foot of the north-facing area. Progression to longer runs could not be easier, with a very gentle blue starting at Les Gondrans, leading on to a green and finishing at the village. And there is now a green run down from the Chalvet gondola, too.

FOR CROSS-COUNTRY ★★★
Travel to the best of it
The two local trails, totalling 23km/14 miles, offer quite a bit of variety, but the best trails are a drive away – a further 60km/37 miles of trails in the unspoiled Clarée valley starts in Les Alberts, 8km/5 miles away at the bottom of the pass road's winding ascent from Briançon.

MOUNTAIN RESTAURANTS ★★
Head for Italy
The options on Montgenèvre's local slopes are few, and unremarkable; but reporters have enjoyed the Bergerie in the Chalvet sector ('good food, no crowds', 'marvellous views'). In the Claviere sector there is a slightly wider

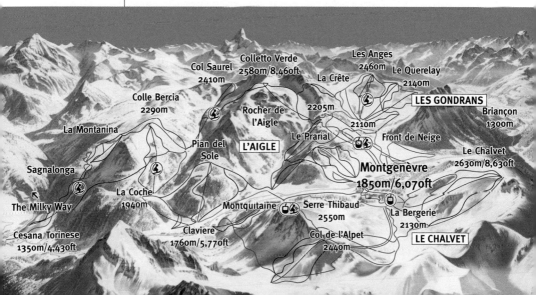

GETTING THERE

Air Turin 100km/ 60 miles (1hr30); Grenoble 170km/ 105 miles (3hr); Lyon 235km/145 miles (3hr)

Rail Briançon (12km/ 7 miles) or Oulx (15km/9 miles); buses available from both five times a day

ACTIVITIES

Indoor Cinema, exhibition hall

Outdoor Natural ice rink, snowshoeing, snowmobiling, walking, tobogganing

Phone numbers From abroad use the prefix +33 and omit the initial '0' of the phone number

TOURIST OFFICE

Montgenèvre t 0492 215252 info@montgenevre. com www.montgenevre. com

Claviere t 0122 878856 info.claviere@ turismotorino.org www.claviere.it

---

choice of atmospheric little huts; the two places at La Coche are 'very friendly' with 'great food'.

SCHOOLS AND GUIDES ★★★
Encouraging reports

Reports are few. Those on the ESF are usually positive: 'friendly, helpful, with good English' says a reporter this year. A beginner reporter last year joined the A-Peak school and thought they were 'very good'.

FOR FAMILIES ★★★★
Hugely improved

With the intrusive main road traffic removed, Montgenèvre would now seem a fine family resort. A past reporter praised the ski school's 'secure area with indoor and outdoor facilities' for younger children. Sledging on the nursery slopes is assisted by a free moving carpet.

STAYING THERE

The options are widening with the development of the Hameau de l'Obélisque, at the east end.
Hotels There is a handful of places.
★★★★Chalet Blanc (0492 442702) Recently opened, and we've had to guess the stars – but with 24-hour room service etc four seems safe. Very successful blend of modern and trad styles. Some family suites and luxury suites as well as plain rooms. Spa.
★★★Napoléon (0492 219204) Facing the snow near the Chalvet lift; restaurant and bar popular with readers.
Apartments Résidences La Ferme d'Augustin are simple, ski-to-the-door apartments on the fringes of the main north-facing slopes. The Hameau de l'Obélisque apparently includes the new 4-star Hameau de l'Airelles residences, with pool and spa.
At altitude The Sporthotel Sagnalonga is halfway down the piste to Cesana,

---

reached by chairlift or snowmobile. Even in peak weeks you get the surrounding slopes to yourself until skiers based elsewhere arrive, mid-morning. We lack recent reports.

EATING OUT ★★
Smart new place to try

With about ten no-frills places in the village, the choice is no more than adequate. For gourmets the big news is the arrival of the Table Blanche at the smart new hotel Chalet Blanc; reports, please. The Graal does 'out-of-this-world' burgers. Past reader tips include the Napoléon ('fantastic Italian food') the Italian-run Capitaine ('magnificent calzone') and the Refuge. The Estable is reportedly 'a great find, full of locals'.

APRES-SKI ★★★
Mainly bars, but fun

The range is limited. The Refuge and the Jamy are the focal cafe-bars at tea time. The Crepouse is now the Cloche. The Graal is a friendly, unsophisticated place with big TVs; the Ca del Sol bar is a cosy place with open fire. The Chaberton has pool tables. Blue Night is a popular disco.

OFF THE SLOPES ★
Very limited

There is a weekly market and various low-key outdoor activities. A bus trip down to the beautiful old town of Briançon is possible.

Claviere 1760m/5,770ft

Claviere is a small, traditional village, barely a mile to the east of Montgenèvre and just over the border in Italy. It's no great beauty, and the main road to Montgenèvre and Briançon that divides it in two has an obvious impact, but despite this visitors seem to like its quiet, relaxed ambience, and are ready to go again. The hotel Roma (01228 78914) is a 'simple but friendly' and convenient place to stay. Montgenèvre's slopes are now as easily reached as those on the Italian side of the border, thanks to recent lift additions.

Claviere's nursery slope is small and steep but usually uncrowded and snow-reliable. We have had mixed reports of its ski school. The Kilt restaurant gets good reviews, especially for pizza and a 'hugely warm welcome'.

Morzine

A large, lively, year-round resort with its own attractive slopes and linked by lift to the main Portes du Soleil circuit

£105
RESORT PRICE INDEX

RATINGS

The mountains

Extent	*****
Fast lifts	**
Queues	***
Terrain p'ks	**
Snow	**
Expert	***
Intermediate	****
Beginner	***
X-country	****
Restaurants	***
Schools	***
Families	****

The resort

Charm	***
Convenience	**
Scenery	***
Eating out	***
Après-ski	****
Off-slope	***

NEWS

Last season more snow-guns were added at Nyon, with more planned at Le Pléney in 2009/10.

A boardercross was built at Nyon.

KEY FACTS

Resort	1000m
	3,280ft

Portes du Soleil	
Slopes	950-2300m
	3,120-7,550ft
Lifts	194
Pistes	650km
	404 miles
Green	13%
Blue	40%
Red	37%
Black	10%
Snowmaking	
	694 guns

Morzine-Les Gets only	
Slopes	1000-2010m
	3,280-6,590ft
Lifts	48
Pistes	120km
	75 miles
Snowmaking	
	295 guns

- ➕ Larger local piste area (shared with Les Gets) than other resorts in the vast Portes du Soleil area
- ➕ Good nightlife by French standards
- ➕ Quite attractive summer-resort town
- ➕ Few queues locally, in general
- ➕ Lots of treelined runs

- ➖ Just off the Portes du Soleil circuit
- ➖ Bus ride or long walk to lifts from much of the accommodation
- ➖ Low altitude means there is an enduring risk of rain and poor snow
- ➖ Few tough pistes for experts
- ➖ Weekend crowds

Morzine is a long-established year-round resort, popular for its easy road access, traditional atmosphere and gentle wooded slopes; bad weather rarely causes problems (except that it rains here not infrequently). For keen piste-bashers wanting to ski the Portes du Soleil circuit regularly, the main drawback is that you're slightly off the main circuit.

Such problems can be avoided by taking a car or using a tour operator who will drive you around. The little-used Ardent gondola, a short drive from Morzine, is a particularly neat option, giving the alternative of a shorter circuit that misses out Avoriaz, where the worst crowds tend to be found.

THE RESORT

Morzine is a well established mountain resort, as popular in summer as in winter, sprawling along both sides of a river gorge – though with the centre emphatically on the west side, at the foot of the local ski slopes. These slopes are shared with slightly higher Les Gets (covered in a separate chapter). Across town is a gondola forming the link with a chain of lifts leading to Avoriaz on the Portes du Soleil circuit.

Our view that the resort suits car drivers is widely shared. But the roads are busy and the one-way system takes some getting used to. Car trips to Flaine and Chamonix are feasible.

VILLAGE CHARM ***
Quietly attractive
The resort consists of chalet-style buildings large and small; they look cute under snow, and as that snow disappears towards spring the village quickly takes on a spruce appearance. Morzine is a family resort, and village ambience tends to be fairly subdued – but there is plenty of après-ski action.

CONVENIENCE **
It's a big resort ...
Morzine is a town where getting from A to B can be tricky, as the extensive network of bus routes and a growing number of hotel mini-buses imply. The best plan is to stay in or near the centre of town, a short walk from one or both of the gondolas.

Restaurants and bars line the streets up to the lifts to Le Pléney, where a busy one-way street runs along the foot of the slopes. Accommodation is widely scattered, but a very good multi-route bus service (including two electric buses) links all parts of the town to the lifts, including those for Avoriaz. There's a bus to Les Gets too.

SCENERY ★★★☆☆
Quite good from the tops
Despite their modest top heights, the local peaks of Pointe de Nyon and Chamossière are not without drama (or impressive views), and the slopes below them are attractively wooded.

THE MOUNTAINS

The local slopes are mainly wooded, with some open areas higher up. The piste map is fine, but a couple of 2009 visitors criticise signposting and links between pistes.

EXTENT OF THE SLOPES ★★★★★
Good local area, plus the PdS
Our rating is for the whole Portes du Soleil linked area, the bulk of which is reached via Avoriaz. Morzine is not an ideal base for the main circuit, but its local area of slopes shared with Les Gets is very satisfactory.

A gondola rises from the edge of central Morzine to **Le Pléney**. (The parallel cable car is apparently for the hotel up there and ski school kids only, unless the gondola breaks down.) Numerous routes return to the valley, including a run down to Les Fys – a quiet lift junction at the foot of the **Nyon-Chamossière** sector where the area's most challenging slopes are served entirely by slow chairs only. This sector can also be accessed by a cable car starting a bus ride from Morzine. A slow chair from Les Fys and a fast one from Le Grand Pré, further up the valley, connect with the sector of **Les Chavannes**, above Les Gets. At the far end of this sector, the bowl beneath Le Ranfoilly forms a sub-sector, where no fewer than five

Good, challenging runs both on- and off-piste

Chamossière
2000m

Le Ranfoilly
1850m

Pointe de Nyon
2010m/6,590ft

La Ros
1665

NYON-CHAMOSSIERE

Ranfoilly

Chez
Nannon

Des Têtes

Charniaz

Nauchets

Grains d'Or

Pointe
de Nyon

Nyon
1420m

Le Grand Pré

LES CHAVANNES

Nyon

L
Tu

Les Fys

Belvédère

1510m

LE PLENEY

Les Gets
1170m/3,8

The gondola is a link to Avoriaz from the centre of town. But you have to catch it down too – there's no piste back

← Avoriaz

Pléney

Super Morzine

Morzine
1000m/3,280ft

Lovely easy blue run away from all the lifts

LIFT PASSES

Portes du Soleil

Prices in €

Age	1-day	6-day
under 16	26	134
16 to 59	39	200
over 60	31	160

Free under 5

Beginner no deals

Notes
Covers lifts in all Portes du Soleil resorts; half-day pass available

Alternative passes
Morzine-Les Gets only

chairlifts have their base stations clustered together.

Beyond Les Gets, **Mont Chéry** is notably quiet, and well worth a visit.

Across town from the Le Pléney sector – a handy 'petit train' shuttle service runs between the two – is a gondola leading (via another couple of lifts and runs) to Avoriaz and the main Portes du Soleil circuit. You take the gondola down at the end of the day to get back to Morzine (there's no piste back). Alternatives are a bus ride or short drive to either Les Prodains, from where you can get a (queue-prone) cable car to Avoriaz or a chairlift into the **Hauts Forts** slopes above it, or to Ardent, where a gondola accesses Les Lindarets for lifts towards Châtel, Avoriaz or Champéry. There's floodlit skiing and torchlit descent on Thursdays.

FAST LIFTS ★★☆☆☆
An area of parts

The main access lifts are either gondolas, cable cars or fast chairs, but higher up things are not so good: the only area with a decent supply of fast lifts is Le Ranfoilly/La Rosta. Elsewhere, slow chairs dominate, supplemented by drags.

QUEUES ★★★☆☆
Resort-level problems

Queues can be a problem during peak holidays and at weekends, especially for both the gondolas out of the resort – and for the cable car from Les Prodains to Avoriaz. Later on, bottlenecks may form when everyone returns from Les Gets – notably at Le Grand Pré, says a reporter. Once you are up the mountain, queues are not usually a problem in the local area.

La Rosta
1665m

Grains-d'Or

Pointe de la Turche

Perrières

LES CHAVANNES

If you're driving, park here and take the fast chair into the slopes

Underused, quiet sector with some of the steepest runs in the area and great red run cruising

MONT CHERY
1850m

La Turche

Les Perrières

Col de l'Encrenaz
1435m

Les Gets
1170m/3,840ft

Mont Chéry

boarding

Morzine is very popular with boarding seasonaires because of the extensive slopes, the splendid terrain parks in Avoriaz and the lower prices here. Former British champ Becci Malthouse is one of the people running the British Alpine Ski & Snowboard School. Specialist boarding shops include The Park and Misty Fly. The slopes in Morzine are great for all abilities of rider, with very few draglifts. But a 2009 reporter complains of irritating flat areas locally. Plenty of tree-lined runs make for scenic and interesting snowboarding and the more adventurous should hire a guide to explore off-piste.

TERRAIN PARKS ★★★★★
Nyon has one now
There is now a freestyle area and boardercross below Pointe de Nyon, or you can try one of the four terrain parks in Avoriaz. Les Gets has a park at Mont Chéry and boardercross areas (see Les Gets chapter).

SNOW RELIABILITY ★★★★★
A weakness at resort level
Morzine has a very low average height, and it can rain here when it is snowing higher up (almost every year some reporters mention days of rain). But because you ski on grassy pastures you need relatively little depth of snow to be able to ski. Snowmaking is being increased, most noticeably on runs at Nyon, Le Pléney and the home runs. Grooming is good.

FOR EXPERTS ★★★★★
A few possibilities
The runs down from Pointe de Nyon and Chamossière are quite challenging, as are the black runs down the back of Mont Chéry and the excellent Hauts Forts blacks at Avoriaz. There is plenty of lift-served off-piste scope – see feature panel.

FOR INTERMEDIATES ★★★★★
Something for everyone
Good intermediates will enjoy the challenging red and black down from Chamossière. Mont Chéry, on the other side of Les Gets, has some fine steepish runs which are usually very quiet, as everyone heads from Les Gets towards Morzine. Those looking for something less steep have a great choice. Le Pléney has a compact network of pistes that are ideal for groups with mixed abilities: there are blue and red options from every lift. One of the easiest cruises on Le Pléney is a great away-from-it-all, snow-gun-covered blue from the top to the valley lift station. Heading from Le Ranfoilly to Le Grand Pré on the blue is also a nice cruise. And the

OFF-PISTE RUNS IN THE PORTES DU SOLEIL AREA

The Portes du Soleil offers a lot of great lift-served off-piste. Here is a small selection. Like all serious off-piste runs, these should only be done with a guide.

Morzine – Nyon/Chamossière area
From the Chamossière chairlift, heading north brings you to two runs – one on the same north-west slope as the pistes, the other via a col down the north-east slope to the Nyon cable car in the Vallée de La Manche – a wild area, with a great view of Mont Blanc at first.

Avoriaz area – two suggestions
From the Fornet chairlift on the Swiss border, you head west to descend a beautiful, unspoiled bowl leading down to the village of L'Erigné. In powder snow you descend the west-facing slopes of the bowl; when there is spring snow, you traverse right to descend the south-facing slopes. Medium-pitch slopes, for skiers and snowboarders.

From the top of the Machon chairlift you traverse west, beneath the peaks of Les Hauts Forts, across Les Crozats de la Chaux – a steep, north-facing slope. You then turn north to descend through the forest to the cable car station at Les Prodains. Testing terrain, for very good skiers. And beware that the traverse can be dangerous following a snowfall.

Châtel area
From the top of the Linga chair, head north-west to cross the ridge on your right at a col and then head down the La Leiche slope to the draglift of the same name. It's a north-facing slope, starting in a white wilderness, taking you through trees back to civilisation. Steep slopes – for good skiers only.

CHILDCARE

L'Outa nursery
t 0450 792600
Ages 3mnth to 5yr

Club des Piou-Piou
t 0450 791313
From age 3; with ESF instruction and lunch

Cheeky Monkeys
t 0450 750548
Ages from 3mnth

Jack Frosts
t 07817 138678
Ages 3mnth to 13yr

Ski school
ESF takes children from age 5: 6 half days €113

GETTING THERE

Air Geneva 95km/ 60 miles (1hr30); Lyon 215km/ 135 miles (3hr)

Rail Cluses or Thonon (30km/19 miles); regular bus connections to resort

ACTIVITIES

Indoor Ice rink, fitness centre, sauna, hot tub, yoga, library, cinemas

Outdoor Snowshoeing, helicopter flights, snowmobiles, ice diving, ballooning, tobogganing, paintballing, paragliding, sleigh rides, cheese factory and slate workshop visits

Phone numbers
From abroad use the prefix +33 and omit the initial '0' of the phone number

SMART LODGINGS

Check out our feature chapters at the front of the book.

slopes down to Les Gets from Le Pléney are easy when conditions are right (the slopes face south). The Ranfoilly and Rosta sectors have easy blacks and cruisey reds served by fast chairs. And, of course, there is the whole of the extensive Portes du Soleil circuit to explore by going up the opposite side of the valley.

FOR BEGINNERS ★★★
Good for novices and improvers
The wide village nursery slopes are convenient, and benefit from snow-guns, though crowds are reported to be a problem ('insanely busy in French holiday weeks – 10 minute queues for the magic carpet'). There are excellent progression runs on Le Pléney, at Nyon, and at Super-Morzine.

FOR CROSS-COUNTRY ★★★★
Good variety
There are 95km/59 miles of varied cross-country trails, not all at valley level. The best section is in the pretty Vallée de la Manche beside the Nyon mountain up to the Lac de Mines d'Or, where there is a good restaurant. The Pléney-Chavannes loop is pleasant and relatively snow-sure.

MOUNTAIN RESTAURANTS ★★★
Some excellent huts
Editors' choice We have had several very enjoyable Savoyard lunches at the rustic Chez Nannon (0450 792115), near the top of the Troncs chair between Nyon and Chamossière – cosy inside and a nice terrace. A reader endorses our choice this year – 'the grilled meats were a delight'. We are still looking forward to trying the Pointe de Nyon (0450 791174), which has impressed several reporters.
Worth knowing about The nice little Atray des Neiges at the foot of the d'Atray chair is good. The 'good value' Raverettes crêperie at Nyon is newly refurbished and has a 'warm, friendly atmosphere', says a 2009 visitor. The Vaffieu above the Folliets chair has several recommendations for its 'good food, large portions'. And the Mouflon at the top of Rosta has 'great pizzas'.

SCHOOLS AND GUIDES ★★★
Good reports
Recent reports have been positive. ESF gets a good review this year – a reporter remarked that his group were 'full of praise for their instructor and doing well by the end of the week'.

The British Alpine Ski & Snowboard School (BASS) is a pricey alternative, but has been praised for its children's classes. And there's E2SA (International) to try.

FOR FAMILIES ★★★★
A fine family choice
Morzine, like Les Gets, caters well for families. On the mountain there are gentle, sheltered slopes and play areas. And there are plenty of other activities. Club des Piou-Piou is run by the ESF school and takes children from three to 14 years old. Above Les Gets, at Chavannes there is a big children's area, the Zone Enfant. Day care is provided by several organisations: Cheeky Monkeys got a good report last year, after a bit of a glitch the year before.

STAYING THERE

The tour operator market concentrates on hotels and chalets.
Chalets There's a wide choice, but position varies enormously and you need to check this carefully before booking. Snowline has an impressive portfolio of smart places.
Hotels The handful of 3-star hotels includes some quite smart ones; and there are dozens of 2-stars and 1-stars.
***Airelles (0450 747121) Central 3-star close to Pléney lifts and bus routes. Good pool.
***Champs Fleuris (0450 791444) Comfy 3-star next to Pléney lifts. Pool.

UK PACKAGES

Alpine Answers, Alpine Weekends, AmeriCan Ski, Chalet Chocolat, Chalet Company, Chalet Entre Deux Eaux, Chalet Famille, Chalet Group, Chalet Gueret, Chalet Snowboard, Challenge Activ, Crystal, Directski.com, Erna Low, First Choice, Haig, Independent Ski Links, Inghams, Inspired to Ski, Interactive Resorts, Lagrange, Momentum, Mountain Tracks, Oxford Ski Co, Peak Retreats, Reach4theAlps, Ride & Slide, Rude Chalets, Simply Alpine, Ski Activity, Ski Chamois, Ski Expectations, Ski France, Skiholidayextras.com, Ski Independence, Ski Line, Ski McNeill, Ski Morzine, Skitracer, Ski Weekend, Snow Finders, Snowline, Starski Chalets, Sugar Mountain, Thomson, Trail Alpine, White Roc

TOURIST OFFICE

t 0450 747272
info@
morzine-avoriaz.com
www.morzine-avoriaz.
com

***Dahu** (0450 759292) 3-star linked to centre by footbridge over river; good restaurant; pool. Shuttle to lifts.
***Tremplin** (0450 791231) Small rooms but next to the lifts.
***Bergerie** (0450 791369) Rustic B&B chalet, in centre. Friendly staff. Outdoor pool, sauna, massage.
***Chalet Philibert** (0450 792518) Traditional, small chalet-style hotel, with 18 rooms. Fairly central.
****Côtes** (0450 790996) Simple 2-star on the edge of town. Pool.
****Equipe** (0450 791143) One of the best 2-stars; next to the Pléney lift.
****Soly** (0450 790945) 'Great value, loads of car parking, fabulous and generous portions of food.'
Apartments. There's a good choice from companies such as Peak Retreats and Erna Low – their new Aiglon de Morzine offers 12 luxury units.

EATING OUT ★★★☆☆
A reasonable choice
There is a fair choice, including some fine hotel restaurants but also traditional and Italian fare. The best place in town is probably the Atelier in the hotel Samoyède, which offers traditional and modern cuisine – we enjoyed lobster ravioli, truffle risotto and scallops. The hotel Rhodos has a 'child-friendly restaurant, with a good choice of meals' and the Airelles and Dahu are other hotel-based options. The Flamme is very highly rated in 2009 ('amazing duck and salads; one of our group was made speechless by his dish'). The unpretentious Etale is popular with visitors and does 'very good pizzas'. The Tyrolien has been praised for steaks and grilled meats and the 'traditional' Kinkerne is 'friendly and does excellent salads'.

APRES-SKI ★★★★☆
One of the livelier French resorts
Nightlife is good by French resort standards, and several places around the base area get busy as the slopes empty. The Crépu is pleasantly quiet early on but livens up late and has a 'very good atmosphere'. Other options include Bar Robinson and the Dixie, with sport on TV, MTV, a cellar bar and some live music. Between the slopes and the centre, and all in the same building are: the Cavern, which is popular with seasonaire's; the Coyote for arcade games and DJ; and the Boudha, with Asian decor and recommended by a reporter. Roger's is a new wine bar. The Opéra and Laury's are late-night haunts.

OFF THE SLOPES ★★★☆☆
Quite good; excursions possible
There are two cinemas, an excellent ice rink and lots of pretty walks, and a visit to the cheese factory is recommended by a 2008 visitor. Some hotels have pools open to non-residents. Morzine has a good range of shops. Buses run to Thonon for more shopping, and car owners can drive to Geneva, Annecy or Montreux.

SNOWPIX.COM / CHRIS GILL

Le Pléney is a busy lift/piste junction at the top of the gondola from Morzine ↓

Paradiski

Les Arcs and La Plagne are pretty impressive resorts in their own right; the ability to explore both is just the icing on the cake

KEY FACTS

Paradiski area

Slopes	1200-3250m
	3,940-10,660ft
Lifts	144
Pistes	425km
	264 miles
Green	5%
Blue	56%
Red	27%
Black	12%

December 2003 saw the opening of the world's largest cable car – a double-decker holding 200 people – crossing a wooded valley to link **Les Arcs** and **La Plagne** and form Paradiski, one of the biggest joint ski areas in the Alps. When it opened, we were a bit sceptical about its value, particularly in view of the sheer width of the La Plagne area. But we're now quite used to staying in Arc 1950 and having lunch above Champagny, or staying in Belle-Plagne and having lunch above Arc 2000.

The cable car, called the Vanoise Express, spans the 2km/1 mile-wide valley between Plan-Peisey (in the Les Arcs area) and a point 300m/980ft above Montchavin (in La Plagne).

The linking of these two major resorts is good news for the great British piste-basher who likes to cover as much ground as possible. For those who like a bit of a challenge, getting from your home base to both far-flung outposts of the area – Villaroger in Les Arcs and Champagny in La Plagne – would make quite a full day.

The link is also good for experts. Those based in either resort can more easily tackle the north face of La Plagne's Bellecôte, finishing the run in Nancroix. Those based in La Plagne who are finding the piste skiing a bit

tame can easily get across to Les Arcs' excellent Aiguille Rouge.

If you want to make the most of the link it's sensible to stay near one of the cable car stations. But once you start to study the piste maps you realise that it's easily accessible from many other bases.

On the Les Arcs side, **Plan-Peisey** and nearby **Vallandry** are in pole position. They are basically small, low-rise, modern developments, but built in a much more sympathetic style than the original Les Arcs resorts. They are quiet places to stay, but are expanding rapidly and a few UK operators have chalets there. You can also stay in the unspoiled old village of **Peisey**, 300m/980ft below and linked by bucket-lift to Plan-Peisey.

337

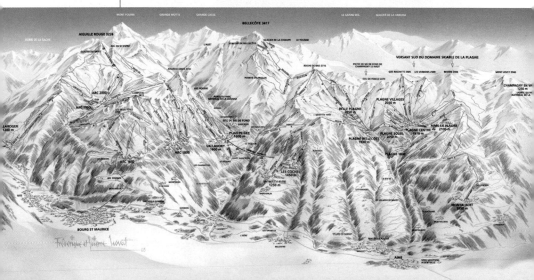

LIFT PASSES

Paradiski
Covers lifts in whole Paradiski area.
6-day pass €243 (over 65 and under 14 €183).

Paradiski Découverte
Covers lifts in Les Arcs area or La Plagne area plus one day Paradiski extension.
6-day pass €216 (over 65 and under 14 €162)

It's easy to get to the cable car station at Plan-Peisey from the main resort parts of Les Arcs. One lift and a blue run is all it takes to get there from **Arc 1800**, which is the biggest of the main resort units. From quieter **Arc 1600**, along the mountainside from 1800, it takes two lifts. **Arc 2000** and the stylish **Arc 1950** development seem further away, over the ridge that separates them from 1600 and 1800; but all it takes is one fast chair to the ridge and one long blue run down the other side. Beyond Arc 2000, Villaroger is not an ideal starting point.

On the La Plagne side, the obvious place to stay is **Montchavin**, which is below the Vanoise Express station. Montchavin is a well-restored traditional old village with modern additions built in traditional style. **Les Coches**, across the mountain from the station, is most easily reached with the help of a lift. It is entirely modern, but built in a traditional style. From either, one lift brings you to the Vanoise Express cable car.

The other parts of La Plagne are some way from the cable car. But one long lift is all it takes to get from monolithic **Plagne-Bellecôte** up to L'Arpette, from which point it's a single long blue descent. The most attractive of the resort villages, **Belle-Plagne**, is only a short run above Plagne-Bellecôte. From the villages further across the bowl – **Plagne-Villages**, **Plagne-Soleil**, dreary **Plagne-Centre**, futuristic **Aime-la-Plagne** – you have to ride a lift to get to Plagne-Bellecôte. From **Plagne 1800**, below the bowl, add another lift. From the villages beyond the bowl – rustic, sunny **Champagny-en-Vanoise** and expanding **Montalbert** – it's going to be pretty hard work, but it's certainly possible.

RIDING THE VANOISE EXPRESS

The cable car ride from one resort to the other takes less than four minutes. The system is designed to be able to operate in high winds, so the risk of getting stranded miles from home is low. It can shift 2,000 people an hour, and end of the day crowds don't seem to be a problem.

The lift company offers a six-day pass covering the whole Paradiski region, perhaps most likely to appeal to people based in the villages close to the lift. But it also offers a pass (Paradiski Découverte) that includes just one day in the other resort. Alternatively, you can buy one-day extensions to a Les Arcs or La Plagne six-day lift pass.

La Plagne

Villages from the rustic to the futuristic, spread over a vast area of intermediate terrain – mainly high and snow-sure

£115
RESORT PRICE INDEX

RATINGS

The mountains

Extent	★★★★
Fast lifts	★★
Queues	★★★
Terrain p'ks	★★★★
Snow	★★★★
Expert	★★★★
Intermediate	★★★★★
Beginner	★★★★
X-country	★★★★
Restaurants	★★★★
Schools	★★★
Families	★★★★

The resort

Charm	★★
Convenience	★★★★★
Scenery	★★★
Eating out	★★★
Après-ski	★★★
Off-slope	★

NEWS

For 2009/10 a six-pack is planned at Plagne Soleil, replacing the Saint-Esprit drag at Plagne Villages and the Mélèzes chair below it. This chair will be moved to Plagne 1800, near the beginner area, so that you'll be able to travel from 1800 towards Bellecôte without passing through Plagne Centre. The old Vega chairlift above Plagne Centre will also be removed.

Plagne 1800 is due to receive its first snowmaking.

For 2008/09 a bucket-lift was installed at Les Coches. Snowmaking was increased

➕ Extensive and varied intermediate slopes, plus plentiful, excellent off-piste terrain

➕ Good nursery slopes

➕ High and fairly snow-sure – and with some wide views

➕ Choice of convenient purpose-built resorts at altitude and attractive, traditional-style villages lower down

➕ Wooded runs of lower satellite resorts are useful in poor weather

➕ Cable car link to Les Arcs from one of those satellite villages

➖ Challenging pistes are few, and confined to a couple of sectors, of which one is not reliably open

➖ Pistes get very crowded in places

➖ Still lots of slow old chairlifts

➖ Lower villages can have poor snow – sunny Champagny especially

➖ Unattractive architecture in some of the higher resort units

➖ No long green runs – though some blues are very easy

➖ Upscale accommodation still rare, though things are improving

With 225km/140 miles of its own slopes, of which 85% are blue or red, La Plagne is an intermediate's paradise, even if you don't use the link to Les Arcs. It also has some splendid off-piste terrain – vast areas of slopes within the piste network and some long descents outside it – that doesn't get skied out too quickly. But for many visitors the limited on-piste challenge can be a disappointment. And the lift system needs investment: by comparison with the best mega-resorts, it is not at all impressive.

The choice of bases here is unparalleled, from the monolithic blocks of bleak Aime-la-Plagne to the chalets and orchards of Montchavin. La Plagne remains the least fashionable of French mega-resorts, but there are now some genuinely good hotels, chalets and apartments, and they are increasing every year.

THE RESORT

La Plagne consists of no fewer than ten separate 'villages'. Each is a self-sufficient mini-resort, though they vary widely in what they have to offer. They divide basically into two groups: six units purpose-built at altitude in a broad bowl, on or above the treeline; and four real villages, adapted and expanded for skiing, at lower altitude on the fringes of the area.

At the heart of the high-altitude area, Plagne-Centre is aptly named: it

is the focal point for shops and après-ski. Directly below Centre is the chalet-filled suburb of Plagne 1800, spread across a steep hillside. A short lift ride away from Centre are the slightly higher units of Aime-la-Plagne, Plagne-Soleil and Plagne-Villages. Over a low ridge, beyond the last two, are Plagne-Bellecôte and Belle-Plagne above it.

Outside the main bowl, at the northern edge of the area, are Les Coches and Montchavin. At the southern edge is rustic Champagny. Beyond Aime-la-Plagne, at the western

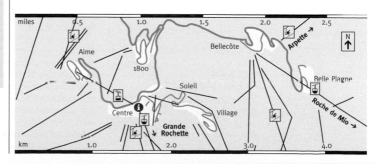

LIFT PASSES

La Plagne

Prices in €

Age	1-day	6-day
under 14	32	153
14 to 64	42	203
over 65	32	153

Free under 6
Beginner 17 free lifts
Senior pass for 1-15 days for €6 if over 72

Notes
Covers all lifts in La Plagne areas; individual village-area and half-day passes; Paradiski extension

Paradiski Découverte

Prices in €

Age	6-day
under 14	162
14 to 64	216
over 65	162

Free under 6, over 72
Beginner no deals

Notes
Covers all lifts in La Plagne areas with one day in Paradiski

Paradiski

Prices in €

Age	1-day	6-day
under 14	36	183
14 to 64	47	243
over 65	36	183

Free under 6; over 72 €9
Beginner no deals

Notes
Covers all lifts in Les Arcs area and La Plagne area and a day in Val d'Isère-Tignes or the Three Valleys; family reductions

---

edge, is growing Montalbert. These are described later in the chapter.

A free bus system between the core villages within the bowl runs until after midnight. Lifts between some resort units run until 1am.

A cable car from Montchavin links to Les Arcs via Peisey-Vallandry. Day trips by car to Val d'Isère-Tignes or the Three Valleys resorts are possible.

VILLAGE CHARM ★★★★★
Take your pick

The high-altitude villages vary quite a lot in character; our rating relates to Belle-Plagne and Plagne 1800, where most Brits go. The first unit to be built, in the 1960s, was Plagne-Centre. Typical of its time, it has ugly square blocks and dreary indoor 'malls' that house a reasonable selection of shops, bars and restaurants. More recent developments are more stylish, though none of the other high-altitude resort units can compete with Centre in terms of facilities. Plagne 1800 is all in chalet style, so is visually inoffensive. Aime-la-Plagne, in stark contrast, is a group of monolithic blocks given a nominal chalet-roof shape. Plagne-Soleil and Plagne-Villages mainly consist of small-scale apartment buildings finished in chalet style; Soleil is developing something like a resort centre. The apartment buildings of Plagne-Bellecôte form a gigantic wall at the foot of the slopes leading down to it. By contrast, Belle-Plagne just above is built in a pleasant chalet style, and has a mini-resort centre, though few shops.

CONVENIENCE ★★★★★
No worries at altitude

The high-altitude villages are mostly ski-in/ski-out – but much of Plagne 1800 presents challenges because of its steep setting, which has to be negotiated on foot. At Plagne Bellecôte you'll walk further inside your apartment building than outside. Belle-Plagne is now quite large, and spread over a steepish hillside that provokes complaints from readers who find its multiple levels exhausting.

SCENERY ★★★★★
Look to the horizon

The scenery makes an attractive and varied backdrop to the less attractive core villages. And Mont Blanc looms big on the horizon, especially from Montchavin and Les Coches.

The majority of the slopes in the main bowl are above the treeline, though there are trees scattered around most of the resort centres. The slopes outside the bowl are open at the top but descend into woodland.

Some runs are more difficult than their classification suggests, while others are easier – note our warning in 'For intermediates'. Piste names and classification seem to alter regularly, too. Signposting and the piste map are fine, though marking can be a bit vague in places.

EXTENT OF THE SLOPES ★★★★★
Multi-centred; can be confusing

Our rating relates to just the La Plagne area; the whole Paradiski area easily scores five stars.

La Plagne's pistes spread over a wide area that can be broken down into seven distinct but interlinked sectors. From Plagne-Centre you can take a lift up to **Le Biolley**, from where you can head back to Centre, to Aime-la-Plagne or progress to **Montalbert**, from where you ride several successive lifts back up. But the main lift out of Plagne-Centre leads up to **La Grande Rochette**. From here there are good sweeping runs back down and an easier one over to Plagne-Bellecôte, or you can drop over the back into the mainly south-facing **Champagny** sector, for excellent long runs and great views over to Courchevel.

From Plagne-Bellecôte and Belle-Plagne, you can head up to **Roche de Mio**, and have the choice of a gondola or two successive fast chairs (the first of which also accesses Champagny). From Roche de Mio, runs spread out in all directions – towards La Plagne, Champagny or **Montchavin/Les Coches**. This sector can also be reached by taking an eight-seat chair from Plagne-Bellecôte to L'Arpette.

From Roche de Mio you can also take a gondola and then up to the **Bellecôte glacier**. It is prone to closure by high winds or poor weather. The top chair is normally shut in winter – but if open, it offers excellent snow and stunning views. You can descend 2000m/6,560ft vertical to Montchavin, with a not-difficult off-piste stretch in the middle of the run. The piste map marks three draglifts as 'difficult', and they are. Plagne-Centre has night skiing on the slalom slope.

KEY FACTS

Resort	1800-2100m
	5,900-6,890ft
La Plagne only	
Slopes	1250-3250m
	4,100-10,660ft
Lifts	104
Pistes	225km
	140 miles
Green	7%
Blue	60%
Red	22%
Black	11%
Snowmaking	
	359 guns
Paradiski area	
Slopes	1200-3250m
	3,940-10,660ft
Lifts	144
Pistes	425km
	264 miles
Green	5%
Blue	56%
Red	27%
Black	12%
Snowmaking	
	626 guns

FAST LIFTS ★★☆☆☆
Slipping behind again?
Years ago La Plagne fell behind its French mega-resort rivals in lift investment; there have been spurts of improvements, but now we get the sensation that the area is again slipping behind. Happily, many key lifts are fast, and the Montchavin/Les Coches sector is pretty much sorted, but once you start to really explore other sectors of the slopes you find lots of old chairs and draglifts – above Les Bauches, all around Centre and above Montalbert, for example.

QUEUES ★★★☆☆
Main problems being sorted
La Plagne's lift and piste network has some fundamental flaws – in particular, moving between sectors often involves descending to Plagne-Bellecôte – where long queues can build in high season. The Roche de Mio gondola is a persistent cause of complaint, but the chairs towards Centre and Montchavin are also not queue-free. What's needed is some lifts from Belle-Plagne, higher up.

There are other queue-prone lifts that you can't avoid, once you've descended to them – at Les Bauches for example, and in the Champagny sector (especially Verdons Sud). The gondola to the glacier is queue-prone when snow is poor lower down.

Crowds on the pistes are now as much of a problem as lift queues. The worst-affected area is from Roche de Mio down to Belle-Plagne and Plagne-Bellecôte. The slopes outside the main bowl are quieter, except runs to Montchavin late in the day.

TERRAIN PARKS ★★★★☆
Lots of choices
Belle-Plagne, Montchavin/Les Coches and Champagny all have decent parks and there's another one at Montalbert. The 7cube park above Plagne-Centre, served by the Colorado chairlift, is one of the better parks in France. There are three lines: the expert line has three big kickers, several standard rails and an S-rail; the intermediate line features only boxes and rails, though still good fun for advanced riders and the easy line has three small rollers and several ride-on rails and boxes for first timers. There is a separate 'initiation park' at Montalbert. Plagne-Bellecôte has two half-pipes; go to Belle-Plagne to ride the boardercross.

SNOW RELIABILITY ★★★★☆
Generally good except low down
Most of La Plagne's runs are snow-sure, being at altitudes between 2000m and 2700m (6,560ft and 8,860ft) on the largely north-facing open slopes above the purpose-built centres. The two sunny runs to Champagny are often closed. The plan to increase snowmaking on the main runs to all the villages means that Plagne 1800 is to get its first cover for 2009/10, on the Mines and Loup-Garou pistes. Grooming could be better.

boarding

With such a huge amount of terrain, there is something for everyone in La Plagne. Expert freeriders, however, are advised to hire a guide as there is so much hidden terrain to be had off the mainly motorway-style pistes. When light gets flat hit the lower tree runs, as the open nature of the higher slopes will be a nightmare. Although this is a great place for beginners, with huge wide-open rolling pistes, be careful as there is also a lot of flat land, especially above Belle-Plagne, in the middle of the Tunnel run and the blue run linking Montchavin with Les Bauches. Make sure to get enough speed, or to avoid such areas, or you'll be doing a lot of walking. Most draglifts have been replaced, and others can be avoided; the more difficult ones are marked on the resort piste map.

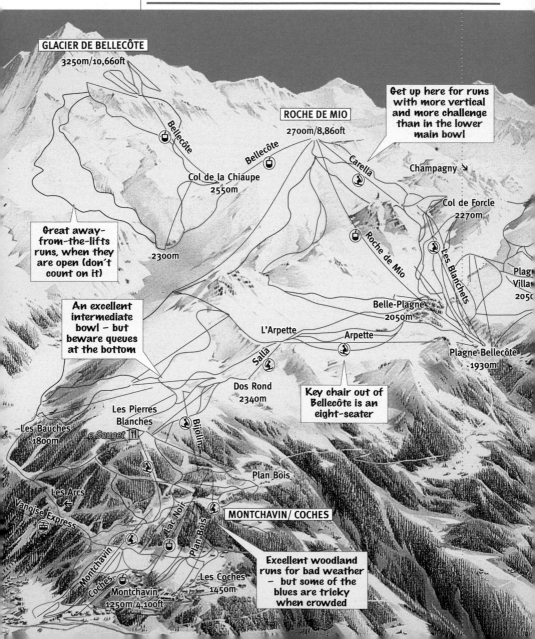

GLACIER DE BELLECÔTE
3250m/10,66oft

Bellecôte

Bellecôte

ROCHE DE MIO
2700m/8,86oft

Get up here for runs
with more vertical
and more challenge
than in the lower
main bowl

Carella

Champagny ↘

Col de la Chiáupe
2550m

Col de Forcle
2270m

Great away-
from-the-lifts
runs, when they
are open (don't
count on it)

2300m

Roche de Mio

Les Blanchets

Plag
Villa
205o

An excellent
intermediate
bowl – but
beware queues
at the bottom

Belle-Plagne
2050m

L'Arpette

Arpette

Plagne-Bellecôte
1930m

Salla

Dos Rond
2340m

Key chair out of
Bellecôte is an
eight-seater

Les Pierres
Blanches

Bijolin

Les Bauches
1800m

Le Sauget

Plan Bois

Les Arcs ←

Vanoise Express

Lac Noir

Plan Bois

MONTCHAVIN/ COCHES

Montchavin

Coches

Montchavin
1250m/4,10oft

Les Coches
1450m

Excellent woodland
runs for bad weather
– but some of the
blues are tricky
when crowded

If the thrills of a day on the slopes aren't enough, you can round it off by having a go on the bobsleigh run built for the 1992 Winter Olympics. The floodlit 1.5km/1 mile run has 19 bends, generating forces as high as 3g.

You can go in a driverless bob-raft (37 euros) reaching 80kph/50mph, which most people find quite exciting enough. Then there's the faster solo mono-bob (102 euros); we found this a great thrill – we had to close our eyes on the sharper bends. Fastest of all is the 'taxi-bob' (107 euros), where three of you are wedged in a real four-man bob behind the driver – advertised speed 110kph/68mph. Be sure your physical state is up to the ride; there are minimum age limits. The run is open on certain days only – book ahead. Additional insurance is available. A 2008 visitor loved the ride, but found the staff rude and impatient: 'They rushed us through, despite the fact that we were early.'

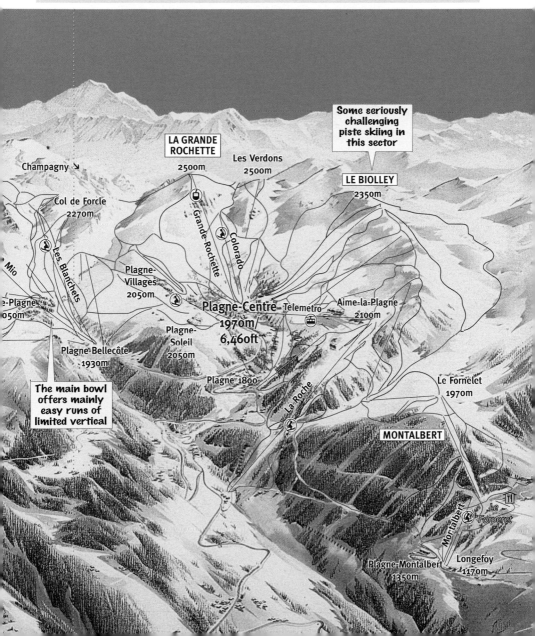

Belle-Plagne is, predictably, the British favourite for an apartment holiday →

B KOUMANOV / OT LA PLAGNE

CHILDCARE

Les P'tits Bonnets
(Plagne-Centre)
t 0479 090083
Ages from 10wk

Marie Christine
(Plagne-Centre)
t 0479 091181
Ages 2 to 6

ESF nurseries (ages from 18 mnth or 2yr):
Aime 0479 090475
Belle 0479 090668
Bellecôte 0479 090133
1800 0479 090133
Snow gardens run by ESF: ages from 3 to 5

Ski schools
Children's classes are available up to 12 or 16 depending on the village: 6 days from €213 (ESF prices)

Phone numbers
From abroad use the prefix +33 and omit the initial '0' of the phone number

FOR EXPERTS ★★★★
A few good blacks; good off-piste

There is challenging piste skiing in two widely separated sectors. There are two beautiful, long, steep and bumpy black runs from Bellecôte to a lift below Col de la Chiaupe – almost 1000m/3,280ft vertical. But don't count on skiing them: in countless visits over the years, we have found these open only once. The other pistes from the glacier – to the gondola station – are more reliable and certainly worthwhile; Chiaupe merits its black status for a short stretch.

The other tough sector is Biolley. The long Emile Allais red run down to La Roche, on the road up from the valley, is little used, north-facing and very enjoyable in good snow. On the back of the hill, the Coqs and Morbleu blacks are seriously steep, Palsembleu less so. From the very top of this sector, Etroits (as its name suggests) owes its black status to a quite short pitch that is both steep and narrow, but is otherwise harmless.

But experts will get the best out of La Plagne if they hire a guide and explore the vast off-piste potential – which takes longer to get tracked out than in more 'macho' resorts. The two sectors discussed above have some excellent off-piste terrain. More serious undertakings include numerous runs from Bellecôte to Les Bauches (a drop of over 1400m/4,590ft). For the more experienced, the north face of Bellecôte presents a splendid challenge with usually excellent snow at the top. You can descend to Peisey-Nancroix (a drop of 2000m/6,560ft), enjoy a splendid lunch at the charming, rustic Ancolie (a real favourite of ours) and then catch a taxi or free bus to the Vanoise Express cable car. Another beautiful and out-of-the-way run starts with a climb and goes over the Cul du Nant glacier to Champagny-le-Haut.

FOR INTERMEDIATES ★★★★★
Great variety

Virtually the whole of La Plagne's area is a paradise for intermediates, with blue and red runs wherever you look.

For early intermediates there are plenty of gentle blue motorway pistes in the main La Plagne bowl, and a long, interesting run from Roche de Mio back to Belle Plagne, the Tunnel (going through, er, a tunnel). The blue runs either side of Arpette, on the Montchavin side of the main bowl, are glorious cruises – but beware, the blues further down towards Montchavin are quite challenging. The easiest way to and from Champagny is from the Roche de Mio-Col de Forcle area. Warning: the Mira piste from Grande Rochette back towards Plagne Centre is the steepest blue run we have ever encountered – it should without question be red; lower down it turns into an excellent cruise. Verdons, nearby, is a great cruise too.

Better intermediates have lots of delightful long red runs to try. There are challenging red mogul pitches down from Roche de Mio to Les Bauches (a drop of 900m/2,950ft) – the first half is a fabulous varied run with lots of off-piste diversions possible; the second half, Les Crozats, is classified black, and can be tricky if snow is less than ideal. The Sources red to Belle Plagne is a good run, too.

The Champagny sector has a couple of tough reds – Kamikaze and Hara-Kiri – leading from Grande Rochette. And the long blue cruise Bozelet has one surprisingly steep section. The long Mont de la Guerre red, with 1250m/4,100ft vertical from Les Verdons to Champagny, is a fine away-from-all-lifts run with a decent red-gradient stretch half-way down, but long flattish tracks at the start and finish. There are further excellent red slopes in the other outlying areas – including the winding, treelined Les Coches, above ... Les Coches.

FOR BEGINNERS ★★★★
Comprehensive facilities

La Plagne is a good place to learn, with generally good snow and good facilities for beginners, provided you go to the right bits. There are beginner areas in Centre, 1800, Aime and Bellecôte; and in Montchavin, Les Coches and Montalbert. There's at least one free draglift in each resort as well. But there are no long green runs to progress to from the nursery slopes. Although a lot of the blue slopes are easy, you can't count on that; some, as we note above, are quite testing.

CROSS-COUNTRY ★★★★
Open and wooded trails

There are 80km/50 miles of prepared cross-country trails scattered around. The most beautiful of these are the 22km/14 miles of winding track set out in the sunny valley around

Champagny-le-Haut. The north-facing areas have more wooded trails that link the various centres. A car will help you make the most of it all.

MOUNTAIN RESTAURANTS ★★★★
An enormous choice

Mountain restaurants are an attraction of the area: numerous and varied – and crowded only in peak periods. **Editors' choice** We've had excellent meals at Chalet des Verdons Sud (0621 543924) above Champagny – appetising food and good service on a big terrace with a fine view, or in the warmly woody interior. Once a week they open in the evening, taking you up there by snowcat; we enjoyed a seven-course feast and wonderful Gamay wines. The Rossa (0479 082803), in the same sector, has friendly staff, and good, basic cooking. Above Montalbert, the Forperet (0479 555127) is an old farm, doing super home-made dishes. We had an excellent tartiflette there in 2009. The rustic Sauget (0479 078351), above Montchavin, is a great place to hole up in poor weather for some highly traditional dishes. **Worth knowing about** Plein Soleil at Plan Bois is a bit cramped but does excellent food. Readers' tips include the 'terrific' Roc des Blanchets, and the Borseliers ('great atmosphere and food'); the Inversens ('good quality food', 'great views and roaring log fire'); the 'cosy' Ferme de Cesar above Montchavin ('varied menu').

Many people have lunch in one of the resorts – particularly Champagny or Montchavin/Les Coches.

SCHOOLS AND GUIDES ★★★
Better alternatives to ESF

Each centre has its own ESF school; recent reports are not encouraging. But there are some very worthwhile alternatives. The Oxygène school in Plagne-Centre continues to receive the most positive reports: 'Superb private lessons.' 'Brought us on simply by stretching us over more and more difficult terrain.' 'Excellent. My three-year-old son got on fine.' We hear that the El Pro school in Belle-Plagne is 'not allowed to do group classes outside the main school holidays'. Reflex based in 1800 and Evolution 2 (based in Montchavin) have had good past reviews. Antenne Handicap offers private lessons for skiers with any kind of disability.

FOR FAMILIES ★★★★
Good choice

Children are well catered for with facilities in each of the villages. The nursery at Belle-Plagne is 'excellent, with good English spoken'. The one in Les Coches is not apparently (see 'Les Coches'). Several UK chalet operators run childcare services.

STAYING THERE

The resort is apartment-dominated, but alternatives are increasing. There are two Club Meds.
Chalets Snowline now has seven catered apartments with three to six rooms in the suave Summit Hill development, right on the 'front de neige' in Centre – five with a cool 'boutique hotel vibe', the others more traditional. There's a large number of proper little chalets available in 1800. Mountain Heaven has two mid-sized, all en suite places, one in a prime spot at the foot of the slopes. Ski Beat has 15 chalets here, ranging from 6 beds to 18, dotted around the hillside, some of them ski-to-the-door. Family specialist Esprit has the exceptionally cool chalet hotel Deux Domaines, in an excellent position at Belle-Plagne, with good pool and spa. In Centre, there are ski-in chalet hotels run by Mark Warner and Ski Olympic (Graciosa has been highly praised: 'great team, service and food'). See also our descriptions of lower villages.

Weekly news updates and resort links at **www.wtss.co.uk**

SCHOOLS

ESF (Belle Plagne)
t 0479 090668
Schools in all centres.
Oxygène (Plagne-Centre)
t 0479 090399
El Pro (Belle-Plagne)
t 0479 091162
Reflex (Plagne 1800)
t 0613 808056
Evolution 2
(Montchavin)
t 0479 078185

Classes (ESF prices)
6 days from €213
Private lessons
From €57 for 1hr
15min for 1-2 people

GETTING THERE

Air Geneva 200km/
125 miles (3hr); Lyon
195km/120 miles
(2hr45); Chambéry
120km/75 miles
(1hr45)

Rail Aime (18km/
11 miles) and Bourg-
St-Maurice (35km/
22 miles) (Eurostar
service available);
frequent buses from
stations

Hotels There are very few, and most are of 2-star or 3-star grading. The new 3-star hotel Vancouver is due to open at Plagne Soleil for 2009/10.
***Carlina (0479 097846) We've enjoyed our recent stays at this newly extended 3-star beside the piste below Belle-Plagne. Pleasant rooms, good restaurant, pool and spa centre. Family-friendly.
***Araucaria (0479 092020) Very modern 3-star at Plagne-Centre.
***Balcons (0479 557655) 3-star at Belle-Plagne. Pool.
***Terra Nova (0479 557900) Big, 120-room 3-star in Plagne-Centre.
Apartments There is a wide choice, including luxury places available through UK operators such as Erna Low, Peak Retreats and Ski Amis. Chalets les Montagnettes in Belle-Plagne are spacious with good views. The MGM/CGH Aubois Bois in Aime-la-Plagne is 'excellent, with a decent pool'. There's the newly extended MGM/CGH Les Granges du Soleil (Plagne-Soleil). Lagrange has lots of its own properties here, including the new luxury 4-star residence, Chalet Edelweiss, in Plagne 1800 – handy for the new chairlift.

EATING OUT ★★★☆☆
A reasonable choice
There is a decent range of casual restaurants including pizzerias and traditional Savoyard places. In Belle-Plagne, the Matafan served up a hearty meal of grilled meats, followed by very good desserts on our 2009 visit. And we thoroughly enjoyed a very tasty three course meal of scallops, steak and lemon parfait at the hotel Carlina's new restaurant 'C'.
    Reader recommendations in Plagne-Centre include the Maison ('worth a trip, great steaks') and Scotty's for 'friendly service and good food'. The Refuge is charmingly rustic and Legend

Cafe a trendy place with a terrace.
    Plagne-Villages has a couple of decent places; the Casa de l'Ours does pizzas and steaks and the Grizzli has been recommended.
    In Plagne 1800, the Loup Blanc is popular for 'fine steaks and local specialities' and Petit Chaperon Rouge has a 'great atmosphere, excellent home cooking and reasonable prices'.
    At Aime-la-Plagne, the rustic Au Bon Vieux Temps on the slopes is open in the evening and there's the smart, family-friendly Arlequin.

APRES-SKI ★★★☆☆
Bars, bars, bars
Though fairly quiet during low season, La Plagne has plenty of bars, catering particularly for the younger crowd.
    In Belle-Plagne, the Tête Inn, the Cheyenne and Maître Kanter are the main bars. The No Bl'm Café is a saloon-style place and the liveliest bar in Plagne-Centre. The PlanJA is popular and has English cider, apparently. The Mine is the focal point in Plagne 1800 – complete with old train and mining artefacts: 'good beer and live music'. Mama Mia's is a fun spot. Plagne-Bellecôte only has one real bar – Show Time Café, with regular karaoke. But there is bowling, and tubing. Plagne Soleil has Monica's pub. Aime-la-Plagne is quiet. There are discos at Plagne Centre and at Belle-Plagne.

OFF THE SLOPES ★☆☆☆☆
OK for the active
As well as the sports and fitness facilities, there are plenty of winter walks along marked trails. It's also easy to get up the mountain on the gondolas, which both have restaurants at the top. There's an ice grotto on the glacier (special pass available). The Olympic bobsleigh run is a popular evening activity (see feature box). There are cinemas at Aime, Bellecôte and Plagne-Centre. Excursions are limited.

Montchavin 1250m/4,100ft

Montchavin is based on an old farming hamlet and has an attractive traffic-free centre. There are adequate shops, a kindergarten and a ski school. The local slopes have quite a bit to offer – pretty, sheltered runs, well endowed with snowmaking, with nursery slopes at village level. The blue home runs can be quite tricky. Après-ski is quiet,

La Plagne

347

Interactive resort shortlist builder at **www.wtss.co.uk**

but the village doesn't lack atmosphere and has a couple of nice bars, a nightclub, cinema and night skiing. The Bellecôte hotel (0479 078330) is convenient for the slopes.

Les Coches 1450m/4,760ft

Les Coches is a little way above Montchavin, across the hillside, and shares the same slopes. It is a sympathetically designed, quiet, modern mini-resort with a traffic-free centre. There are nursery slopes across the mountainside, linked by bucket lift. It has its own school and kindergarten. But we've received a scathing report on the nursery from a 2008 visitor.

Dining out options approved by readers include the Poze (pizza), the Lauzes, the Savoy'art ('stunning interior'), and Taverne du Monchu. There's a shuttle to the cinema in Montchavin. Finlays has six chalets here, mostly with en suite bathrooms.

Montalbert 1350m/4,430ft

Montalbert is a traditional but much expanded village – now with a proper little front de neige area with a choice of restaurant terraces. The lift out of the village is a fast one, but your progress to the main bowl depends on two further slow ones, and at that point you are still a long way from Roche de Mio or the Les Arcs link. The local slopes are easy and wooded – a useful insurance against bad weather. Restaurant choice is adequate and the Tourmente pub is a popular drinking spot. The Aigle Rouge (0479 555105) is a simple hotel. Ski Amis has a

central all-en-suite 7-room chalet with all the trimmings here, and various self-catering options. Mountain Heaven has a duplex apartment run as a catered chalet, and self-catering apartments in four modern developments. The Chalets de Montalbert units are 'simply furnished but pleasantly spacious'.

Champagny 1250m/4,100ft

Champagny is a charming village in a pretty, wooded, sunny setting, with its modern expansion done sensitively. It is at the opposite end of the slopes from the link to Les Arcs, but the tricky red runs to the village will be a bigger drawback for many potential visitors. Even in good snow, they are rather steep and narrow for nervous intermediates – and the snow is often far from good, despite artificial help. The village is well placed for an outing by taxi or car to Courchevel.

There are several hotels, of which the two best are both Logis de France. The Glières (0479 550552) is a rustic old hotel with varied rooms, a friendly welcome and good food. The Ancolie (0479 550500) is smarter, with modern facilities.

The Alpages de Champagny is an impressive-looking chalet-style development, with a pool and sauna.

The village is quiet in the evenings, but the Poya ('superb atmosphere, friendliness and food') and Rochers, near the church ('lovely food, by far the best value') are recommended.

Portes du Soleil

Low altitude, largely intermediate circuit of slopes straddling the French-Swiss border, with a variety of contrasting resorts

The Portes du Soleil vies with the Trois Vallées for the title 'World's Largest Ski Area', but its slopes are very different from those of Méribel, Courchevel, Val Thorens and neighbours. The central attraction is an extensive circular tour, straddling the French-Swiss border, taking you through two French resorts and several small Swiss ones – great for keen intermediates who like a sensation of travel while skiing. You can travel the circuit in either direction.

We have separate chapters on all the major Portes du Soleil resorts. On the French side, purpose-built **Avoriaz** and the traditional village of **Châtel** are on the main circuit. The circuit breaks down at Châtel – you have to take a bus between the resort's two sectors of slopes. **Morzine** and **Les Gets** are another two traditional-style villages but are set off the main circuit.

On the Swiss side, **Champéry** is a classic, charming mountain village with slopes that form a large part of the main circuit, above the tiny, purpose-built satellite stations of **Champoussin** and **Les Crosets**. Then there is the larger, traditional village of **Morgins**.

There's a short walk across the village here – less of an effort if you are travelling the circuit clockwise.

The lifts you ride doing the circuit vary widely. In the Avoriaz sector and in the Linga sector of Châtel the lifts are mainly modern and fast. On the far side of Châtel and on the Swiss side of the network, drags and old chairlifts dominate, and progress is slow.

The slopes are low by French standards, with top heights in the range 2000m to 2300m (6,560ft to 7,550ft) and low points where snow may be particularly poor in Morgins and Châtel (1200m/ 3,940ft), despite improving snowmaking.

Puy-St-Vincent

*Underrated small modern resort with limited but varied slopes –
good for young families who haven't been spoilt by mega-resorts*

TOP 10 RATINGS

Extent	★★
Fast lifts	★★
Queues	★★★
Snow	★★★
Expert	★★★
Intermediate	★★★
Beginner	★★★
Charm	★★
Convenience	★★★★★
Scenery	★★★★

NEWS

For 2008/09 the terrain park was moved to a new location on the upper slopes, and the children's nursery at 1600 was extended.

Five more snow-guns improved artificial snow-cover.

SMART LODGINGS

Check out our feature chapters at the front of the book.

- ➕ Mostly convenient, friendly, not too hideous purpose-built resort
- ➕ Splendid scenery
- ➕ Fairly reliable snow
- ➕ Some great cross-country routes
- ➕ Good variety of pleasantly uncrowded slopes with challenges for all abilities, but ...

- ➖ Slopes very limited in extent
- ➖ Upper village has only apartment-based accommodation
- ➖ Queues in French holidays
- ➖ Still lots of draglifts
- ➖ Limited après-ski/restaurants
- ➖ Limited village diversions

Puy-St-Vincent's ski area may be limited, but it offers a decent vertical and a lot of variety, including a bit of steep stuff. Provided you pick your spot with care, it makes an attractive choice for a family not hungry for piste miles. Beware long, winding airport transfers with sickness-prone kids, though.

THE RESORT

Puy-St-Vincent proper is an old mountain village, but you're more likely to be staying in one of the two ski-stations that make up the modern resort. Station 1400 is a small development just along the mountainside from Puy-St-Vincent proper; the major part, Station 1600, with long, low apartment blocks arranged across the hill, is a few hairpins further up.

The six-day Galaxie pass covers a series of major resorts beyond Briançon. More to the point, it also covers a day's skiing above the hamlet of Pelvoux, 10 minutes' drive away. This area has quiet, very rewarding blue, red and black runs, and a

vertical of over 1000m/3,28oft.

Village charm The modern resort is functional rather than charming, though newer buildings have a more traditional style. We and our reporters have found PSV a friendly, welcoming resort.

Convenience Station 1600 is compact, with its few shops, bars and restaurants ranged along the foot of the slopes. Much of the lodging is ski-in/ski-out, but not all; one main lift starts just below the village, which helps. Spreading up the hillside from 1600 are newer developments – sometimes referred to as Station 1800.

Scenery The resort has a lovely woody position above the valley, with great views from La Pendine over the Ecrins mountains.

KEY FACTS

Resort	1400-1600m
	4,590-5,250ft
Slopes	1250-2700m
	4,100-8,860ft
Lifts	12
Pistes	75km
	47 miles
Green	18%
Blue	41%
Red	35%
Black	6%
Snowmaking	10km
	6 miles

OT PUY-ST-VINCENT

There are pleasant views even low down; higher up, you get grand views of the 4000m peaks of the Ecrins massif to the north-west ⭦

UK PACKAGES

Erna Low, Interhome, Lagrange, Ski Collection, Ski France, Skiholidayextras.com, Skitracer, Snowbizz

Phone numbers
From abroad use the prefix +33 and omit the initial '0' of the phone number

TOURIST OFFICE

t 0492 230531
infos@
paysdesecrins.com
www.paysdesecrins.
com

THE MOUNTAINS

Within its small area, PSV packs in a lot of variety, with runs from green to black that justify their classification. It doesn't get crowded, which adds considerably to the attraction.

Slopes There are gentle slopes between the two villages, but most of the runs are above 1600. A fast quad goes up to the treeline at around 2000m/6,560ft. The main higher lift is a long chair to 2700m/8,860ft, serving open slopes. Drags and another quad either side serve further open runs here, and access splendid cruising runs that curl around the edges of the area into the woods – one linking to a blue, La Balme, all the way down to 1400. 1400 has a six-pack up into the main slopes.

Fast lifts Three fast chairs give access from the main stations, but there are many old chairs and drags higher up.

Queues There may be problems during French school holiday periods.

Terrain parks There is a new terrain park near the top of the Pendine chair, with jumps, rails and boardercross.

Snow reliability The slopes face north-east and are reasonably reliable for snow. Snowmaking covers much of the slopes at 1600 and on runs to 1400.

Experts The black runs are short but genuinely black, some with moguls. There are off-piste routes to be tackled with guidance.

Intermediates Size apart, it's a good area for those who like a challenge – but there aren't many very easy runs.

Beginners Beginners should be happy on either of the nursery slopes, and on the long green from 2000m/6,560ft.

Snowboarding There are slopes to suit all levels, but still some draglifts.

Cross-country There are 30km/19 miles of cross-country trails, including some varied routes between 1400m and 1700m (4,590ft and 5,580ft).

Mountain restaurants There is a modern but pleasantly woody place at mid-mountain, but the sunny terraces of 1600 get most of the business.

Schools and guides You have a choice of ESF and International schools. Tour operator Snowbizz works with the latter to operate (they claim) the largest English-speaking children's school in the French Alps.

Families The resort is favoured by families for its quieter slopes and friendly nurseries. The nurseries at 1400 and 1600 take children from 18

months, and both schools run ski kindergartens. 'A great resort for my five-year-old daughter to start her skiing career,' sums up a reporter.

STAYING THERE

Most accommodation is in self-catering apartments at the foot of the slopes.

Hotels There are two cheap hotels in 1400, but none in 1600.

Apartments The Gentianes apartments at 1800 are spacious, with the use of an indoor pool. They are handy for the slopes but not for shops.

Eating out There's a fair choice in 1600. Petit Chamois serves 'generous portions' and caters well for kids.

Après-ski Après-ski amounts to a few bar-restaurants in each village. There's a nightclub in 1600.

Off the slopes Village diversions are very limited, but there are outdoor pursuits – 20km/12 miles of walks, snowshoeing, parapenting, dog sled rides, tobogganing and skating. The cinema shows English-speaking films. With a car you can visit Vallouise.

Risoul / Vars

Two high, purpose-built resorts in an attractive setting, with a traditional French atmosphere and a big linked area of slopes

+ Attractive purpose-built resorts

+ Fair-sized, uncrowded area of slopes good for novices and intermediates

+ High resorts, reasonably snow-sure, but with lots of tree-lined runs

+ Family-friendly

+ Novel approach to off-piste safety

− Still mainly draglifts and slow old chairs, though a few fast ones

− Not too much to challenge expert skiers and boarders

− Little to do off the slopes

− Fairly remote location

− English less widely spoken in Vars

TOP 10 RATINGS

Extent	★★★
Fast lifts	★
Queues	★★★★
Snow	★★★
Expert	★★
Intermediate	★★★★
Beginner	★★★★
Charm	★★
Convenience	★★★★
Scenery	★★★

NEWS

At Vars, the new 4-star Hameau des Rennes residence in Le Fournet, which partly opened in 2008, is due to open more apartments for 2009/10. A new short chairlift is planned to link them to the slopes at Peynier. A connecting run may be built from the other side of town to link the two sectors.

Several pistes were improved for 2008/09 and a couple of old draglifts removed.

KEY FACTS

Resort	1850m
	6,070ft

The entire Forêt Blanche ski area

Slopes	1660-2750m
	5,450-9,020ft
Lifts	48
Pistes	180km
	112 miles
Green	18%
Blue	38%
Red	34%
Black	10%
Snowmaking	
	116 guns

Slowly but surely the international market is waking up to the merits of the southern French Alps. Were they nearer Geneva, Risoul and its linked neighbour Vars would be as well known as Les Arcs and Flaine – and the villages are more attractive than either. Reporters like it, and would consider going again. Brush up your school French before you go, especially for Vars.

THE RESORT

Risoul, purpose-built in the late 1970s, is a quiet, apartment-based resort south of Briançon and popular with families – but not exclusively so. The resort is quite a distance from most major airports, but flights into Grenoble have improved access.
Village charm Many of the resort buildings are bulky, but wood-clad with some traditional style. The busy little main street, with a small range of shops, bars and restaurants, is far from traffic-free. But the locals offer a friendly and welcoming atmosphere.
Convenience The village meets the mountain in classic French purpose-built style, with sunny restaurant terraces facing the slopes and a compact centre. But some lodgings are a short but 'knackering' uphill walk away, if you miss the last lift.
Scenery Risoul has a pleasantly woody setting beneath its slopes.

THE MOUNTAINS

The upper slopes are open, but those back to Risoul are prettily wooded, and good for bad-weather days. The piste map is adequate.
Slopes Together with Vars, the area amounts to one of the biggest domains in the southern French Alps – marketed as the Forêt Blanche. The slopes, mainly north-facing, spread over several minor peaks and bowls, and connect with the sunnier slopes of neighbouring Vars via the Pointe de Razis and the lower Col des Saluces.

Fast lifts There are three fast chairs accessing a good number of runs, but still lots of tricky 'difficile' draglifts.
Queues Queues are rare and the slopes generally uncrowded. In January you get pistes to yourself at times.
Terrain parks There's a decent park under the Melezet chair, revamped with jumps and rail lines for all levels, big air and boardercross ('good fun').
Snow reliability Snow reliability is reasonably good; the slopes are all above 1850m/6,070ft and mostly north-facing. Snowmaking is fairly extensive. Grooming is fine.
Experts Risoul's main top stations access a couple of steepish descents. And there is some good off-piste terrain – some of it made more accessible by an unusual system of dividing the terrain within the lift network into different categories, including controlled areas accessed through gates that are closed when there is a risk of avalanche.
Intermediates There are decent reds and blues in all sectors. Almost all Risoul's runs return to the village, making it difficult to get lost.
Beginners Risoul's local area includes good, convenient, nursery slopes with a free lift, and a lot of easy longer pistes to move on to.
Snowboarding There is a lot of good freeriding to be done throughout the area, although beginners might not like the large proportion of draglifts.
Cross-country There are 35km/22 miles of cross-country trails in the whole domain. A trail through the Peyrol forest links the two resorts together.

↑ The slopes of Peynier, and Vars-les-Claux: the large apartment blocks are at the original centre of the village; Point Show is out of the shot to the right, up the hill

SNOWPIX.COM / CHRIS GILL

Mountain restaurants. Choice is limited. But the self-service Tetras is a small, attractive hut, with 'good food, friendly staff,' says a 2009 visitor who went there every day of his trip.
Schools and guides Past reports on the ESF have been very positive.
Families Risoul is very much a family resort. Both ski schools operate ski kindergartens, slightly above the village, reached by a child-friendly lift.

STAYING THERE

Most visitors stay in apartments, but there are a few hotels and chalets.
Hotels The Chardon Bleu (0492 460727) is right on the slopes. You can also stay overnight up at the Tetras mountain refuge (0492 460983).
Apartments The Constellation Forêt Blanche apartments are small but convenient; Balcons de Sirius is less so, but with a good pool and sauna.

Eating out There's a decent choice offering fairly good value. Readers recommend the Marmite for 'superb steaks and friendly staff' and Entre Pot – 'very friendly, fantastic food'. There is reportedly 'a conspiracy to not offer pizza,' which families should note.
Après-ski Nightlife is livelier than most people expect. There are several bars and two clubs. Try the Caribbean-themed Babao and the Chalet or Eterlou for a quieter drink.
Off the slopes There's not much. A reporter tells us the snowmobiling is of the off-piste variety, which is good. A toboggan run is planned; excursions to Briançon are possible.

Vars 1850m/6,070ft

THE RESORT
Vars includes several small, old villages on or near the road running southwards towards the Col de Vars, chief among them Vars-Ste-Marie. There are lifts into both sectors of the slopes starting on the fringe of this village, but the focus for winter visitors is purpose-built Vars-les-Claux, higher up the road. The resort is bigger than Risoul, with more amenities; but less English is spoken.
Village charm Vars-les-Claux has a lot of block-like apartments, but it is not a complete eyesore, thanks to a wooded setting and newer chalet-style developments. Reporters like its pleasant, relaxed atmosphere.
Convenience It's a small place, but spread along a winding, quite steep road, with two main clusters of shops and lodgings; each has nursery slopes

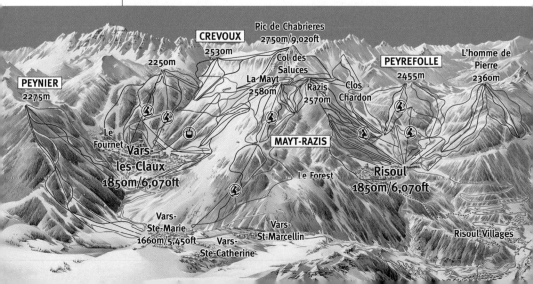

PEYNIER 2275m

Le Fournet

Vars-les-Claux 1850m/6,070ft

Vars-Ste-Marie 1660m/5,450ft

Vars-Ste-Catherine

Vars-St-Marcellin

CREVOUX

2530m

2250m

Pic de Chabrieres 2750m/9,020ft

Col des Saluces

La-Mayt 2580m

Razis 2570m

Clos Chardon

MAYT-RAZIS

Le Forest

PEYREFOLLE 2455m

L'homme de Pierre 2360m

Risoul 1850m/6,070ft

Risoul-Villages

Vars
Close to Ste-Marie fast chairs (150m)
Chalet-Hotel
Alpage
Cosy lounge with open fireplace
Standard to DeLuxe bedrooms
Sauna & Fitness
Excellent cuisine
www.hotel-alpage.com

Phone numbers
From abroad use the
prefix +33 and omit
the initial '0' of the
phone number

TOURIST OFFICES

www.foretblanche.com
Risoul
t 0492 460260
info@risoul.com
www.risoul.com

Vars
t 0492 465131
info@otvars.com
www.vars-ski.com

and fast lifts into the major sector of slopes. The original focus is at the base of the main gondola; Point Show is 10 minutes' walk up the hill. Apartments and chalets spread beyond these points, varying in convenience.

Scenery Pretty wooded slopes surround the village, and Pic de Chabrières has fine views.

THE MOUNTAINS

There are slopes on both sides of the village, linked by pistes and by chairlift at the lower end of Les Claux.

Some reporters have found piste classification variable, and the map unclear on the links between resorts.

Slopes The wooded, west-facing Peynier area is the smaller sector, and reaches only 2275m/7,460ft. The main slopes are in an east-facing bowl with direct links to the Risoul slopes at the top, Col du Vallon (via a tunnel) and at the Col des Saluces. There's also a speed-skiing course. Beneath it are easy runs, open at the top but descending into trees. A six-pack has improved the connection towards Crevoux, above Les Claux.

Fast lifts With three fast lifts out of the village, the day starts well. But that's your lot – after that it's draglifts and slow chairs. The 'glacial' Mayt chair for Risoul attracts regular complaints.

Queues Queues are rare outside the French holidays, and even then Vars is not as busy as most family resorts.

Terrain parks There's a terrain park at Crevoux, with a new chill-out zone. There's also a jib park at resort level.

Snow reliability Snow reliability is not as good here as in Risoul: the main slopes are around 2000m/6,560ft and east-facing, so get the morning sun. But snowmaking is widespread.

Experts There is little to challenge experts, though the Crête de Chabrières top section accesses some off-piste and a tricky couloir at Col de

Crevoux. The Olympic red run from the top of La Mayt down to Ste-Marie delights most reporters and is a very respectable 920m/3,020ft vertical.

Intermediates Vars has fine intermediate slopes, with a good mix of comfortable reds and easy blues; Jas de Boeuf from La Mayt is a quiet cruise first thing. If you can face the slow chairlift, there are good treelined runs in the separate Peynier sector.

Beginners There is are good nursery areas in central Vars, with lots of 'graduation' runs throughout the area. Quick learners will be able to get over to Risoul by the end of the week.

Snowboarding There is good freeriding to be done throughout the area, although beginners might find the number of draglifts a problem.

Cross-country There are 25km/16 miles of trails in Vars itself. Some start at the edge of town, but those above Ste-Marie are more extensive.

Mountain restaurants There are several in both sectors, but many people head back to the villages for lunch.

Schools and guides We've had good past reports on ESF, but a lack of English speaking may be a problem.

Families Vars makes a quiet family choice. The ski school runs a nursery for children from two years old and there is a ski kindergarten.

STAYING THERE

There are a few small hotels, but Les Claux is dominated by apartments.

Hotels The Ecureuil (0492 465072) is an attractive, modern B&B chalet. Ste-Marie has two typically attractive members of the Logis de France 'chain' – the 3-cheminée Alpage (0492 465052), with sauna and fitness room, and the simpler Vallon (0492 465472).

Apartments P&V's 3-star Albane is recommended in 2009, and the new 4-star Hameau des Rennes chalet-style residences should have 60 apartments open for 2009/10 (but no pool yet).

Eating out There is a choice of simple, good-value places. The Après Ski at Point Show is worth a look, as it the Chaudron in Ste-Marie.

Après-ski Après-ski is animated at tea time. Later on, nightlife revolves around one or two bars.

Off the slopes There isn't a great deal to do, but there are 35km/22 miles of walking paths, a cinema, leisure centre, tobogganing, snowmobiling and an ice rink. There's dog sledding at Ste-Marie.

La Rosière

The sunniest slopes in the Tarentaise, but also about the snowiest; the link to La Thuile in Italy adds an extra dimension

+ Attractive, friendly, purpose-built resort with panoramic views

+ Fair-sized area of slopes shared with La Thuile in Italy

+ Sunny home slopes

+ Heli-skiing over the border in Italy

+ Good nursery slope

+ Big dumps of snow when storms sock in from the west, but ...

− Wind can close link with Italy, which involves a red run and long drag.

− Snow affected by sun in late season

− Lots of slow old lifts

− Few on-piste challenges

− Pistes lack variety – though La Thuile is better

− Limited après-ski

− Few off-slope diversions

La Rosière is much smaller and quieter than the nearby mega-resorts such as Val d'Isère-Tignes, Les Arcs and La Plagne; and many reporters stress the friendliness of the locals. The ski area is very sunny, but gets a lot of snow; and the link with the north-facing slopes of La Thuile in Italy adds variety. All in all, the resort best suits families and groups of skiers with mixed abilities looking for a relaxed time.

THE RESORT

La Rosière has been built in traditional chalet style beside the road that zigzags its way up from Bourg-St-Maurice towards the Petit-St-Bernard pass to Italy (closed to traffic in winter – on the Italian side the road itself becomes a piste). Several parts can be distinguished, but the obvious distinction is between the main village and the developing satellite of Les Eucherts, a short bus ride – or 'great woodland walk' – to the east. This is more or less self-sufficient, but offers less choice of everything than the main village.

Village charm The resort is attractive and quiet, with a few shops and friendly locals; don't expect much lively nightlife.

Convenience It's a small place, but big enough to require use of a free shuttle bus if you pick a location not handy for one of the lifts. Les Eucherts has its own fast chair into the slopes.

Scenery La Rosière's home slopes are south-facing with great views over the Isère valley to Les Arcs and La Plagne.

THE MOUNTAINS

La Rosière and La Thuile in Italy share a big area of slopes called Espace San Bernardo. The link with Italy's slopes is prone to closure because of high winds or heavy snow and early intermediates may find it tricky.

Slopes Two fast chairs, one in La Rosière and one at Les Eucherts, take you into the heart of the slopes, from where a series of lifts, spread across the mountain, takes you up to Col de la Traversette. From there, you can get over the ridge and to the lifts which link with Italy at Belvédère.

Fast lifts There are just two fast chairs; slow lifts cause regular complaints.

Queues Not usually a problem.

Terrain parks There's a terrain park served by the Poletta draglift, just above the village centre and a boardercross course by the Fort chair below Col de la Traversette.

355

Snow reliability The slopes get a lot of snow from storms pushing up the valley, but in late season the sunny orientation takes its toll and winds on the link to Italy may blow.

Experts There's little to keep experts amused. The steepest terrain is on the lowest slopes, down the Marcassin black run below Les Eucherts and down the Ecudets black to the west of Le Gollet. There's also a freeride area just above the latter and some enjoyable off-piste between the pistes. And there's excellent heli-skiing from just over the Italian border (you descend into France, arriving just a few miles from La Rosière).

Intermediates There's a fair amount to explore if you take into account La Thuile. The main part of La Rosière's area is a broad open mountainside offering straightforward red and blue pistes. More interesting is the excellent Fontaine Froide red, dropping 750m/ 2,460ft vertical through woods to the Ecudets chair, far below the village at the western end. The red beyond Col de la Traversette has good snow and views, but is narrow at the top.

Beginners There are good nursery slopes and short lifts near the main village and near Les Eucherts.

Snowboarding Most of the lifts are chairs, making the place good for learner and early intermediate boarders. And the sunny slopes are good for gentle freeriding when the snow is soft.

Cross-country There are 14km/9 miles of trails.

Mountain restaurants There are half a dozen, but none has impressed us and we get few reports. Friendly service is the main feature, it seems.

Schools and guides We have had consistently good reports over recent years of the ESF – 'excellent beginner instruction' this year, 'great private lesson' last year. Brit Simon Atkinson, former technical director at the ESF, has opened the Elite ski school – reports please. Evolution 2, with a class limit of 8 pupils, disappointed our one reporter this year.

Families Club des Galopins has a 'very good' snow garden, and British tour operators Esprit, Crystal and Ski Beat (see 'Chalets') all have their own childcare facilities here. In general it is a good family resort.

← Great views from the village across to the slopes of Les Arcs

SNOWPIX.COM / CHRIS GILL

UK PACKAGES

A Mountain Chalet, Alpine Answers, BoardnLodge, Chalet Group, Crystal, Erna Low, Esprit, Independent Ski Links, Interactive Resorts, Interhome, Leisure Direction, Mountain Heaven, Neilson, Richmond Holidays, Simply Alpine, Ski Activity, Ski Amis, Ski Beat, Ski Collection, Ski Expectations, Ski France, Skiholiday extras.com, Ski Olympic, Skitracer, Skiworld, SnowCrazy, Vanilla Ski

SMART LODGINGS

Check out our feature chapters at the front of the book.

Phone numbers
From abroad use the prefix +33 and omit the initial '0' of the phone number

TOURIST OFFICE

t 0479 068051
info@larosiere.net
www.larosiere.net

STAYING THERE

A number of British tour operators now offer packages here.

Chalets There is an increasing number of companies with chalets here. Ski Olympic has operated here for years and has a chalet hotel and four chalets (including two with access to a pool, sauna, steam and hot tub). Ski Beat has nine places purpose-built for themselves in Les Eucherts, with childcare facilities and two shared saunas. Mountain Heaven has a splendid-looking penthouse there too with a huge top-floor living room, six en-suite rooms and an outdoor hot tub. And Skiworld has five smart chalets there. Family-specialist Esprit Ski has over a dozen chalets in the resorts, plus its usual comprehensive childcare facilities.

Hotels There are a few 2-star hotels in the village, and more in the valley.

Apartments The best places are newly built at Les Eucherts. Cîmes Blanches is smart, with a 'lovely' pool, hot tub, sauna and steam room. A reporter who doesn't take self-catering too literally recommends highly Montagne Saveurs, an outfit delivering 'fantastic food at a third of restaurant prices'.

At altitude The hotel San Bernardo (0165 841444), at the top of the pass on the border with Italy, and reachable only on skis, provided a memorable two-night stay for an adventurous reporter – 'comfortable and peaceful'.

Eating out There is an adequate choice – about a dozen restaurants. Readers' current top tips are the central Génépi – 'superb food and service' – and the 'charming' and 'excellent' Ancolie in Les Eucherts. The Grange offers 'good variety, pleasant service'.

Après-ski Just a couple of bars in the village. Last we heard, the 'relaxed' Petit Danois had a 'good live band'.

Off the slopes Not a huge amount to amuse the non-skier – walks, paragliding, dog sledding and snowshoeing. There is a cinema. Pedestrian access to mountain restaurants is scarcely an issue: your skiing friends should be happy to descend to meet.

La Rosière

357

Interactive resort shortlist builder at **www.wtss.co.uk**

Selected chalet in La Rosière

Samoëns

Characterful but inconvenient base for the extensive and varied Grand Massif, shared with Flaine, Morillon and Les Carroz

NEWS

For 2009/10 a six-pack (the Chariande Express) is due to replace two old chairs and a drag from Samoëns 1600 to Tête des Saix – cutting the journey time by two-thirds.

For 2008/09 the Marmotte red run was improved.

+ Lovely historic village, with traffic-free centre and weekly market

+ Lift into big, varied area shared with Flaine and Les Carroz

+ Glorious views from top heights

+ Very close to Geneva, but ...

− Weekends can be busy as a result

− Main access lift is way outside the village – and has no return piste

− Not the best base for beginners

− Surprisingly intrusive traffic

The impressive Grand Massif area is chiefly associated in Britain with high, purpose-built, apartment-dominated Flaine; but the network can also be accessed from much more attractive traditional villages – Les Carroz, Morillon and Samoëns. And the cutest of these, if not the most convenient, is Samoëns.

THE RESORT

Samoëns is an attractive 'Monument Historique' – once a thriving centre for stonemasons, with their work much in evidence.

Village charm The resort has a small traffic-free centre of narrow streets lined by appealing food shops, and nearby a pretty square (sadly not traffic-free) with a stone fountain, an ancient linden tree, a fine church and other medieval buildings. Also nearby is a nominally car-free area of modern development. The place as a whole retains the feel of 'real' rural France and makes a compelling base for families. There is a good weekly market.

Convenience Slope access is by one of two gondolas, both a drive or bus ride from the village: an old one (furthest from the village) that you can ski back to on red or black pistes if conditions permit, and a newer one (nearer to the village) which you can't ski back to. So it's a bus ride and maybe a gondola ride at the end of the day. Not a problem, but not convenient.

Scenery The village has a pretty valley setting, with attractively woody ridges and glorious views from the tops.

THE MOUNTAINS

Most of the skiing directly above Samoëns is on open slopes beneath the peak of Tête des Saix, from which point there are links to the next-door Morillon sector and the slightly more distant sectors of Les Carroz and Flaine (both of these are covered in the Flaine chapter).

Slopes The two gondolas from the valley arrive at separate points on the 'hilly plateau' of Samoëns 1600. This mini-resort is also reachable by road. Tête des Saix will be served by a new six-pack from 1600 for 2009/10. From the Tête you can reach Flaine via a narrow, crowded piste followed by a fast chair in the Vernant bowl. Or you can descend to Morillon or Les Carroz.

Fast lifts Locally, only the gondolas up from the valley and the new fast chair.

Queues We have a report of 'up to 20 minute' waits for the gondola at the busy Easter period. Queues at 1600 for access to Tête des Saix should be greatly relieved by the new six-pack; but the narrow piste towards Vernant is likely to become even more crowded.

Terrain parks A tiny park for kids is built if snow conditions permit. The main park is in Flaine.

Snow reliability The slopes above Samoëns face due north, so above 1600 snow is fairly reliable. There is snowmaking around 1600.

Experts The upper pistes on Tête des Saix are among the most testing in the

The upper pistes
above Samoëns are
among the most
challenging in the
Grand Massif →

SNOWPIX.COM / CHRIS GILL

Phone numbers
From abroad use the
prefix +33 and omit
the initial '0' of the
phone number

Grand Massif, and there is lots of good off-piste in the valleys and bowls between Samoëns and Flaine.

Intermediates Samoëns makes a perfectly satisfactory base for all but the most timid intermediates, who might be better off in Morillon. From Tête des Saix you have a choice of good long runs in various directions. In good snow the valley runs to Vercland are highly enjoyable – the black is little steeper than the red, and used less.

Beginners Beginners buy a special pass and go up to 1600, where they will find gentle, snow-sure slopes – excellent when not crowded – but no long green runs to progress to. Morillon is a better bet; and the nursery slopes at Sixt are quiet.

Snowboarding Beware draglifts on the nursery slopes.

Cross-country There are trails on the flat valley floor around Samoëns, and more challenging ones up the valley beyond Sixt and up at Col de Joux Plane (1700m/5,580ft).

Mountain restaurants There are more captivating places at Morillon and Les Carroz (see Flaine chapter). But we enjoyed excellent service and pork provençale at the new Lou Caboëns (table-service), a small, woody place at Samoëns 1600.

Schools and guides A 2009 visitor praises his private instructor from the ZigZag school for 'great attitude, patience and encouragement'. Another reader had a 'much better' lesson with 360 International than with ESF. And yet another found the ESF's private boarding instruction 'very good'.

Families The kindergarten takes kids from three years old, and ski lessons are available. The ZigZag school offers multi-activity courses.

STAYING THERE

A few specialist UK operators now go to Samoëns.

Hotels We and readers have enjoyed the Neige et Roc (0450 344072), a walk from the centre – 'friendly staff, excellent food, big spa area'. Avoid the annexe, though. The central Glaciers (0450 344006) is recommended.

Chalets Samoëns doesn't seem to figure in the programmes of major operators, but we have glowing reports of owner-run chalets Marie Stuart ('superb food, very welcoming') and Moccand. And Chalet Bezière

continues to be highly endorsed too: 'wonderful hospitality', 'great food', 'outstanding'.

Apartments Self-catering is mostly in small-scale developments, and quite a lot of it in individual chalets. Appealing places available through UK firms include the Fermes de Samoëns (with pool), and Ferme de Fontany. The 4-star Reine des Prés is new for 2009/10, with pool and spa. Peak Retreats features these and lots more options, Lagrange and Erna Low have smaller selections.

Eating out The Table de Fifine is a short drive from the centre, but a fine spot for a proper dinner – beautiful wooden interior and 'good quality, imaginative menu'. The Muscade et Basilic is 'excellent, with an extensive wine list'. The Bois de Lune and Savoie are also praised. The Louisiane has 'great' pizzas but when busy the staff will rudely turn you away.

Après-ski Nightlife is quiet. Of the few bars, Irish pub Covey's is 'the only place worth a visit'.

Off the slopes Samoëns offers quite a range of activities. Snowmobiling up at Samoëns 1600 is wilder than is usual in the Alps. A reader recommends the snowshoeing. There is an outdoor, covered ice rink, hosting regular hockey matches, and a sports and cultural centre.

Interactive resort shortlist builder at **www.wtss.co.uk**

Serre-Chevalier

*Odd mixture of ancient and modern villages sit beneath an
extensive and varied mountain with lots of woodland runs*

£105
RESORT PRICE INDEX

RATINGS

The mountains

Extent	★★★★
Fast lifts	★★
Queues	★★★
Terrain p'ks	★★★
Snow	★★★
Expert	★★★
Intermediate	★★★★
Beginner	★★★★
X-country	★★★
Restaurants	★★★★
Schools	★★★★
Families	★★★

The resort

Charm	★★★
Convenience	★★★
Scenery	★★★
Eating out	★★★★
Après-ski	★★
Off-slope	★★★

360

NEWS

For 2008/09 a smart thermal spa with pools and saunas opened in Le Monêtier. And Serre-Chevalier's first 4-star hotel, the Best Western Premier, opened in Chantemerle, with 51 rooms and suites. The main terrain park was improved and a draglift installed to serve it. The Mélèzone is a new family area in the woods with picnic tables.

+	Big, varied mountain	−	Crowds/queues in French holidays
+	Lots of good woodland runs	−	Still too many slow, old lifts
+	One of the few big French areas based on old villages with character	−	Busy road runs through the villages
+	Good-value and atmospheric old hotels, restaurants and chalets	−	A lot of indiscriminate new building took place in the 1960s and 70s
+	Very friendly and welcoming locals	−	Limited nightlife

Serre-Chevalier is one of the few French resorts offering the ambience you might look for on a summer holiday – a sort of Provence in the snow, with lots of small, family-run hotels and restaurants in old stone buildings (though the immediate impression is of insensitive development along the main road).

The excellent, varied slopes are split into different segments, so you get a sensation of travel. What really sets the area apart from the French norm is the quantity of sheltered woodland runs – though there are open bowls, too. Great strides were made by installing fast lifts a few years ago. But progress seems to have halted, which is a shame; there are still lots of slow, old lifts around.

THE RESORT

Serre Chevalier is made up of a string of 13 villages set on a valley floor. These run roughly north-west to south-east, below the north-east-facing slopes of the mountain range that gives the resort its name. From the north-west – coming over the Col du Lautaret from Grenoble – the three main villages are Le Monêtier (or Serre-Che 1500), Villeneuve (1400) and Chantemerle (1350), spread over a distance of 8km/5 miles. Finally, at the extreme south-eastern end, is Briançon (1200) – not a village but a town (the highest in France). Some of the nine smaller villages give their names to the communes: Villeneuve is in the commune of La Salle les Alpes, for example. Confusing.

There are few luxury hotels or notably swanky restaurants, though the resort's first 4-star, Best Western Premier hotel in Chantemerle, opened last year. On the other hand, there are more hotels in the modestly priced Logis de France 'club' here than in any other ski resort. This is a family resort, which fills up (even more than most others) with French children in the February/March school holidays. Be warned (see introduction to France chapter for 2010 dates).

Ski-buses are covered on the free guest card and all lift passes. These circulate around and between each village, with links to and from the lift bases along the valley. But they finish quite early (the local navettes stop soon after the lifts close, and the valley buses at approximately 7pm); taxis aren't cheap.

A six-day area pass (or rather your receipt) covers a day in each of Les Deux-Alpes, Alpe-d'Huez, Puy-St-Vincent and the Milky Way. All of these outings are possible by bus, but are easier by car. The road from Grenoble and Lyon goes over the Col du Lautaret, which may require chains and is very occasionally closed.

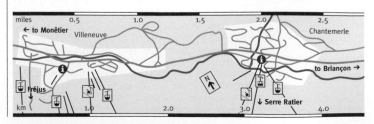

↑ There are still a lot
of slow old lifts
around, especially in
and on the way to the
Le Monêtier sector

SNOWPIX.COM / CHRIS GILL

VILLAGE CHARM ★★★
Some quaint old parts

Serre-Chevalier is not a smart resort,
in any sense and even the older parts
are roughly rustic rather than
chocolate-box pretty. (A ban on
corrugated iron roofs would help.)
Each of its parts is based on a simple
old village, around which there is a lot
more modern development ranging
from brash to brutal.

In the older sectors, there are
narrow cobbled streets lined by small
shops, cosy bars, hotels and
traditional restaurants that give each
village a very French feel – Le Monêtier
is the smallest, quietest and most
unspoiled of the main villages, with
new building which is mostly in
sympathetic style. Briançon's 17th-
century fortified upper quarter is a
delight, with its traditional auberges
and pâtisseries; it is now a UNESCO
World Heritage Site. By contrast, the
wide selection of modern facilities,
including hotels and a casino, at its
lift station has no character.

Because the resort is so spread
out, the impact of cars and buses is
difficult to escape too, even if you're
able to manage without them yourself.
Sadly, the road to Grenoble, which
skirts the other villages, bisects Le
Monêtier; pedestrians stroll about
hoping the cars will avoid them. But
when blanketed by snow the older
villages and hamlets do have an
unpretentious charm, and we find the
place as a whole easy to like. Every
year reporters stress how friendly and
welcoming the locals are (and we were
struck by this on our 2009 visit too) –
hardly the norm in France.

CONVENIENCE ★★★
Good access but expect a walk

All of the main villages have lift
access, either by gondola, cable car or
fast chairs to different parts of the ski
area; Briançon has a gondola from the
bottom of town. From Villeneuve, two
gondolas and a fast chair give a wide
choice at the mid-mountain area. The
old village is across the valley from
the lifts, but the nearby hamlet of Le
Bex makes a peaceful and more
convenient alternative – with its own
gondola. Chantemerle's old sector is
closer to the lifts – a cable car,
gondola and chairlift – but a lot of
accommodation is further away across
the main road and can be quite a long
walk from the lifts. Le Monêtier has
one main access lift – a fast quad
chair to mid-mountain, reached from
the village by bus or a 10-minute walk
(downhill in the morning, uphill at the
end of the day and tricky when ice is
around, though you can leave your
skis and boots at the lift base).

SCENERY ★★★
Six good viewpoints

The Serre-Chevalier range is not
notably dramatic seen from the valley,
though there are great views from
Briançon's old town. And there are fine
views of the rugged Ecrins massif from
each of its six main summits.

THE MOUNTAINS

Trees cover almost two-thirds of the
mountain, providing some of France's
best bad-weather terrain (we once had
a great day here when all the upper
lifts were closed by high winds).

Several 2009 reporters speak

FRANCE

favourably of the new piste signposting. Piste classification is unreliable – many reds, in particular, could be classified blue, but there are occasional stiff blues, too.

EXTENT OF THE SLOPES ★★★★
Interestingly varied and pretty
Serre-Chevalier's 250km/155 miles of pistes are spread across four main sectors above the four main villages and you get a real feeling of travel as you move from one to another. The sector above **Villeneuve** is the most extensive, reaching back a good way into the mountains and spreading over four or five identifiable bowls. The main mid-station is Fréjus. This sector is linked to the slightly smaller **Chantemerle** sector. The link from Chantemerle to **Briançon** is over a high, exposed col via a six-pack. The link between Villeneuve and **Le Monêtier** is liable to closure by high winds or avalanche danger. Travelling from here towards Villeneuve is a slow business – and it involves a red run, so timid intermediates may prefer to use the bus.

FAST LIFTS ★★
Investment has slowed down
A range of big lifts gets you out of the valley and investment a few years ago added four new six-packs above them. But progress seems to have stopped: nothing new last season or this. There are still many old, slow lifts at altitude that hinder the whole process of exploration and that need updating.

QUEUES ★★★
Still some bottlenecks
There are few problems getting up the mountain now, but there can be queues high up. Bottlenecks include the slow and unreliable Balme chair on the way to Le Monêtier, the Fréjus chair above the Pontillas gondola and the Crêtes draglift it links with.

More than most resorts, Serre-Chevalier fills up with French families in the February holidays, producing serious mid-mountain queues, especially in the central sectors. The lower slopes above Chantemerle, in particular, can get very crowded – head for the Aiguillette chair at these times (see 'For intermediates').

LIFT PASSES

Grand Serre-Che

Prices in €

Age	1-day	6-day
under 12	31	150
12 to 64	39	187
over 65	31	150

Free under 6, over 75
Beginner limited pass in each area: eg Villeneuve €15

Notes
Covers all lifts in Briançon, Chantemerle, Villeneuve and Le Monêtier; 6 days or more passes give one day in each of Les Deux-Alpes, Alpe-d'Huez, Puy-St-Vincent and Voie Lactée (Milky Way); reductions for families

Alternative passes
Individual areas of Serre-Chevalier

TERRAIN PARKS ★★★☆☆
Fully featured

Legendary French ripper Guillaume Chastagnol and the Serre Che Brigade have been building the freestyle infrastructure here for several years, trying to improve the terrain park. The snowpark is a situated under the Forêt chair above Villeneuve. It incorporates over 25 different features and a new drag dedicated solely to the park. The park is clearly marked out in three zones for all levels, including ramps, step-ups, rails, kickers and log-jibs. A major focus has been placed on the beginner area, which makes it a great learning park. A boardercross accessible by the Grande Serre or Combe lifts is 'good, fast and flowing' says a reporter (and we enjoyed it on skis in 2009 too). There's also a half-pipe at the bottom of the Aravet gondola in Villeneuve.

SNOW RELIABILITY ★★★☆☆
Good – especially upper slopes

Most slopes face north or north-east and so hold snow well, especially high up (there are lots of lifts starting above 2000m/6,56oft). The weather pattern is different from that of the northern Alps and even that of Les Deux-Alpes or Alpe-d'Huez, only a few miles to the west. Serre-Che can get good snow when there is a shortage elsewhere, and vice versa.

Snowmaking covers over 30% of the pistes, including long runs down to each village. Piste grooming is generally excellent.

FOR EXPERTS ★★★☆☆
Deep, not notably steep

There is plenty to amuse experts – except those wanting extreme steeps.

The broad black runs down to Villeneuve (Casse du boeuf – our favourite) and Chantemerle (Luc Alphand) are only just black in steepness. But they are regularly groomed and great for high-speed cruising with their gradient sustained over an impressive vertical of around 800m/2,620ft. One or the other may be closed for days on end for racing or training. The rather neglected Tabuc run, sweeping around the mountain away from the lifts to Le Monêtier, has

Serre-Chevalier

Excellent off-piste from here, including Voie Jackson, where you climb up between rocks part-way down

L'Eychauda 2660m/8,730ft

Clot Gauthier

Clot G

Tête de la Balme

Col de la Cucumelle 2500m/8,200ft

Pic de L'Yret 2735m/8,970ft

Tabuc black run is mainly easy but with a couple of seriously steep sections that can be mogulled

VILLENEUVE

Fréjus 2100m

Aravet 2000m

Casse de Boeuf

Aravet

Fréjus

Pi Maï

Pontillas

Cucumelle is a beautiful long red run away from all the lifts

LE MONETIER

Bachas 2180m

Bachas

Charvet

Le Bez
Villeneuve 1400m/4,590ft

Le Freyssinet

Le Monêtier 1500m/4,920ft

vouac de la Casse

boarding

The term 'natural playground' could have quite easily been coined in Serre-Chevalier. The slopes are littered with natural obstacles that seem made for confident snowboarders. Try the Cucumelle slope and the areas around the Rocher Blanc lift at Prorel for such terrain. For beginners and intermediates the many draglifts can be a problem, as can the flat areas. There's a good terrain park for all abilities and Generation Snow in Chantemerle is a school that offers all sorts of courses from beginners' lessons to advanced freestyle courses.

SCHOOLS

ESF In all centres
t 0492 241741
Génération Snow
(Chantemerle)
t 0492 242151
Evasion (Chantemerle)
t 0492 240241
Buissonnière
(Villeneuve)
t 0492 247866
EurekaSki
t 0492 245647
0679 462484
Axesse (Villeneuve)
t 0662 765354
Ski Connections
(Villeneuve)
t 0492 462832
Internationale
(Le Monêtier)
t 0683 670642

Classes (ESF prices)
6 half days from €138
Private lessons
From €45 for 1hr

GUIDES

Montagne Aventure
(Chantemerle)
t 0492 247440
Office des Guides
t 0492 247320
Montagne à la carte
(Villeneuve)
t 0492 247320
Montagne et Ski
(Le Monêtier)
t 0492 244681

a couple of genuinely steep pitches (which may be heavily mogulled) but is mainly a cruise. For other steepish runs, look higher up the mountain to slopes served by the two top lifts above Le Monêtier and the three above Villeneuve. The runs beside these lifts – on and off-piste – form a great playground in good snow. The piste map says there are marked, ungroomed 'brut de neige' runs but they aren't marked on the map – you have to get location details from the information points. Weird.

There are huge amounts of off-piste terrain throughout the area – both high-up and in the trees above Villeneuve and Chantemerle. In each of the last two seasons, we've enjoyed the La Voie Jackson run accessed from the Yret chair above Le Monêtier, which includes a short climb between rocks to a deserted open bowl. There are plenty of more serious off-piste expeditions, including: Tête de Grand Pré to Villeneuve (a climb from Cucumelle); off the back of L'Eychauda to Puy-St-André (isolated, beautiful, taxi ride home); L'Yret to Le Monêtier via Vallons de la Montagnolle; Tabuc also to Le Monêtier (steep at the start in a big bowl, very beautiful). The experts' Mecca of La Grave is nearby.

FOR INTERMEDIATES ★★★★
Ski wherever you like

Serre-Chevalier's slopes ideally suit intermediates, who can buzz around without worrying about nasty surprises on the way. On the trail map red runs far outnumber blues – but most reds are at the easy end of the scale and the grooming is usually good, so even nervous intermediates shouldn't have problems with them. The broad, open bowls above Grande Alpe and Fréjus offer lots of options. And the runs on skier's right on the lower slopes above Le Monêtier are gentle, quiet and wind prettily through the woods.

There's plenty for more adventurous intermediates, though. Many runs are wide enough for a fast pace. Cucumelle on the edge of the Villeneuve sector is a beautiful long red, away from the lifts. The red runs off the little-used slow Aiguillette chair in the Chantemerle sector are worth seeking out – quiet, enjoyable fast cruises. Other favourites include Aya and Clos Galliard at Le Monêtier, and the wonderful long run from the top to the bottom of the gondola at Briançon (with great views of the town).

If the reds are starting to seem a bit tame, there is plenty more to progress to. Unless ice towards the bottom is a problem, the usually well-groomed blacks on the lower mountain should be first on the agenda; try them early in the day when they are uncrowded.

FOR BEGINNERS ★★★★
All four areas OK

All four sectors have nursery areas (at Chantemerle the area is small, and you generally go up to Serre Ratier or Grand Alpe – both rated as good by a beginner reporter) and there are some easy high runs to progress to. Villeneuve has excellent green runs above Fréjus.

Both Chantemerle and Villeneuve have green paths down from mid-mountain that are narrow, and not enjoyable when the runs become hard and others are speeding past. Le Monêtier's easy runs are at resort level, next to excellent nursery slopes, which beginners have recommended for 'better snow and fewer people'. But progression to long runs here isn't so easy, and the link to Villeneuve involves the red Cucumelle run.

FOR CROSS-COUNTRY ★★★
Excellent if the snow is good

There are 35km/22 miles of tracks along the valley floor, mainly following the gurgling river between Le Monêtier and Villeneuve and going on up towards the Col du Lautaret.

CHILDCARE

Les Schtroumpfs
t 0492 247095
Ages 6mnth upwards;
9am-5pm

Les Poussins
t 0492 240343
Ages 8mnth upwards;
9am-5pm

Les Eterlous
t 0492 244266
Ages 9mnth to 6yr;
9am-5pm

Ski school
Snow gardens for
ages 3 to 5; from age
5 children can join ski
school classes (ESF 6
half-days €138)

MOUNTAIN RESTAURANTS ★★★★
Some good places

Mountain restaurants are quite well distributed (and, usefully, marked clearly on the piste map).

Editors' choice At the top of the cable car and chair from Chantemerle, Chalet Hotel Serre Ratier (0492 205288) has a delightful large terrace and pretty indoor dining room, good service and delicious food – we had lunch there twice in 2009. Just above the Casse du Boeuf quad from Villeneuve, the Bivouac de la Casse (0492 248772) is an attractive chalet with both self- and table-service (inside and out). We were mightily impressed by both the food and service and several 2009 reporters endorse our view. Shame about the plastic chairs on the terrace though. Pi Maï (0492 248363) in the hamlet of Fréjus is cosy on a bad day and charming on a sunny day, with excellent food such as 'steaks cooked over a log fire'. But both Bivouac and Pi Maï are relatively expensive.

Worth knowing about The Echaillon, just below the Bivouac, is a lofty chalet with open fire and a table-service section doing 'excellent confit de canard'. The Bercail, near the top of the Aravet lift, is an unusual mixture – table-service except that you go and order your food and pay self-service style, then it's cooked fresh and delivered to your table. In the Chantemerle sector, the busy Soleil self-service pleases reporters – 'sun trap', 'excellent food for good prices'. We loved the small table-service Troll just beneath here – great good-value food and very jolly service. The Grand Alpe self-service is spacious, and a bit cheaper than most places.

In the Briançon sector, the 'attractive' Pra Long chalet at the gondola mid-station has good views and food in both table- and self-service sections. The little Chalet de

Serre Blanc, just down from the top of Prorel, has superb views and is basic ('good hot chocolate').

Above Le Monêtier the choice is between the self-service Bachas at mid-mountain ('good choice but not cheap anymore') and the tiny Peyra Juana ('surprisingly good wholesome food') on a blue run near the bottom. Both get packed on bad-weather days.

SCHOOLS AND GUIDES ★★★★
Nearly all good

EurekaSki, British-run by BASI Alpine Trainer Gavin Crosby, gets consistently good reports every year. A 2009 visitor found him 'fantastic, well worth it'. Classes with a maximum size of six (for adults and children) range from beginner to off-piste adventure. Gavin also offers 'Explore Serre-Chevalier' days, which take in as much terrain as possible with instructional tips and lift priority, for £50 per person per day. We've skied with him on one of these and for a morning off-piste and both were fantastic. Book up well in advance of your holiday – we get reports from lots of disappointed would-be customers who find the school fully booked.

Another British-run school, Ski Connections, is also praised by a 2009 reporter: 'We all took lessons ranging from beginner to advanced intermediate. I had the perfect combination of fun, challenge and learning, a great leap forward.'

We have received a number of reports on the Ecole de Ski Buissonnière over the years – most of them full of praise ('I learnt 10 times more because of the personal service,' says a recent reporter), but some not, including a distressing report of early-intermediate boarders being put with a couple of experts. Two absolute beginners in a recent visitor's group were 'satisfied' with their snowboard lessons with Generation Snow.

A 2009 reporter booked on a course with the ESF at Le Monêtier that was cancelled; she had to drop to a lower level and 'was not stretched'. But local chalet-operator Hannibals says their Chantemerle clients are very happy with the ESF there. A recent reporter on the Internationale school says, 'My 6- and 14-year-old nephews made a huge amount of progress, and my parents (both beginners, aged 68 and 70) were reasonably confident by the end of the week and had been

Air Turin 120km/ 75 miles (1hr45); Grenoble 150km/ 95 miles (2hr45); Lyon 200km/125 miles (3hr15)

Rail Briançon (6km/ 4 miles); regular buses from station

There's a lot of great off-piste to be explored with a guide ↓

challenged without being too scared!'

We have had great off-piste trips with Bertrand Collet of Axesse school and with the ESF.

FOR FAMILIES ★★★★★
Facilities at each village

The Ecole de Ski Buissonnière has been praised in the past, and Les Schtroumpfs in Villeneuve was 'brilliant, and the baby loved it'.

STAYING THERE

There's a wide choice of packages from UK tour operators. Resort based EurekaSkiplus (www.eurekaski.com/ plus.htm) can arrange accommodation, childcare, transfers etc.

Chalets Several operators offer catered chalets. Hannibals' Marmottes is a well renovated old farmhouse in old Chantemerle, all en suite. Ski-In has a four-bed newly renovated chalet three minutes' walk from the slopes in Villeneuve which they normally rent self-catered but can arrange for catering (or cooked food to be delivered for you to heat up).

Hotels One of the features of this string of little villages is the range of

attractive family-run hotels – many of them members of Logis de France.

LE MONETIER

***Auberge de Choucas** (0492 244273) Smart but small wood-clad rooms. 'Excellent, seven-course dinners in stone-vaulted restaurant.' We enjoyed staying there in 2008.

**Europe (0492 244003) Simple well-run Logis in heart of old village, with pleasant bar and 'very good' food.

**Alliey (0492 244002) 'Excellent rooms with an indoor/outdoor pool and spa.' Good restaurant.

Rif Blanc (0492 244135) Good value, friendly, refurbished hotel. Popular bar.

VILLENEUVE

***Christiania** (0492 247633) Civilised, family-run hotel on main road, crammed with ornaments.

**Vieille Ferme (0492 247644) Stylish conversion on the edge of the village.

*Chatelas (0492 247474) Prettily decorated simple chalet by river in old part of town.

CHANTEMERLE

****Best Western Premier** (0492 222090) 300m/980ft from the lifts, spacious apartments, helpful staff, small indoor-outdoor pool, sauna. We enjoyed staying here in 2009; book a

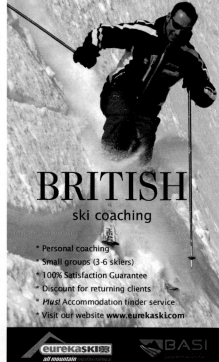

UK PACKAGES

Action Outdoors, Alpine Answers, Alpsholiday, AmeriCan Ski, Chalet Group, Club Med, Crystal, Erna Low, First Choice, Hannibals, Independent Ski Links, Interactive Resorts, Interhome, Lagrange, Leisure Direction, Neilson, Peak Retreats, PV-Holidays.com, Rocketski, Simply Alpine, Ski Activity, Ski Expectations, Ski France, Skiholiday extras.com, Ski Independence, Ski Miquel, Ski Solutions, Ski-in.co.uk, Skitopia, Skitracer, Snow Finders, Thomson **Briançon** *BoardnLodge, Leisure Direction*

ACTIVITIES

Indoor Swimming pools, sauna, fitness centres, thermal baths, cinemas, libraries

Outdoor Ice rinks, paragliding, cleared paths, snowshoeing, snowmobiling, ice driving, snowkites, horse riding

SMART LODGINGS

Check out our feature chapters at the front of the book.

Phone numbers
From abroad use the prefix +33 and omit the initial '0' of the phone number

TOURIST OFFICE

t 0492 249898
contact@
ot-serrechevalier.fr
www.serre-chevalier.
com

room well away from the main road.
***Plein Sud (0492 241701) Modern; pool, steam; 'superbly run by a Brit'.
**Grand (0492 241516) Right by the lifts; 85 varied rooms.
**Boule de Neige (0492 240016) In the old centre. 'Good food, comfortable and friendly.'
*Ricelle (0492 240019) Charming, but across the valley from the slopes in Villard-Laté. Good food.
Maison du Bez (0492 248696) Ski-in/ski-out, traditional, 'quirky with cosy lounge'. Outdoor hot tub.
Apartments The Hameau du Rocher Blanc, by the slopes in Chantemerle (pool, gym, sauna, steam), is a cut above what was on offer before. The 4-star Arts et Vie with 40 apartments and 10 chalets opened in Le Monêtier last year ('impressed, right on slopes, great value'). The Best Western hotel (see above) is really apartments with hotel facilities. These are bookable through Peak Retreats and Erna Low and the Rocher Blanc is through Lagrange. The hotel Alliey in Le Monêtier has apartments too.
At altitude Pi Maï (0492 248363) above Villeneuve and the Chalet Hotel Serre Ratier (0492 205288) above Chantemerle have rooms (see also 'Mountain restaurants').

EATING OUT ★★★★☆
Unpretentious and traditional
In Le Monêtier, there are several good hotel-based options. At the upper end, the Maison Alliey (hotel Alliey) has a good reputation and we had an excellent dinner at the Auberge du Choucas a couple of seasons ago. The Europe has reliable cooking at more modest prices. The Boîte à Fromages has been recommended and Brasera is a 'good' pizzeria. The Kawa and the Belote have been recommended for 'cosy atmosphere, good staff and excellent value'.
In Villeneuve the Swedish-run Vieille Ferme is a 'great, stylish eating place'. The Frog is 'better than its name suggests'. The Marotte, a tiny stone building with classic French cuisine in the old part of Villeneuve, 'offers a wide choice of very good food at very reasonable prices'. The Refuge specialises in fondue and raclette. And there are good crêperies – try the Manouille. Over in Le Bez, the Bidule is said to have 'first-class food and service, at good value' and is recommended by locals. The Passé

Simple ('terrific pizzeria') has been recommended.
In Chantemerle, we had delicious dinner at the unpretentious Loup Blanc. Arbre à Pain ('cheap and cheerful'), Petit Chalet ('charming and friendly'), Cabassa (pizzas), Triptyque ('delicious buffalo burgers'), and Batchi have been recommended by reporters.
In Briançon the Club, Origan, Péché Gourmand ('excellent value'), Esperance ('great pizzas') have been recommended.

APRES-SKI ★★☆☆☆
Quiet streets and few bars
Nightlife seems to revolve around bars, scattered through the various villages, and several reporters complain that the resort is too quiet.
In Le Monêtier the British-run Alpen has a happy hour, free nibbles and welcoming staff; the bar at the hotel Rif Blanc is popular, and the Que Tal warms up later on. In Villeneuve, Loco Loco in the old village gets lively. So does the Grotte du Yeti by the slopes (and with live music). The Frog has 'good local beer' and the Cocoon is a 'friendly little bar in the modern part, patronised by the ESF'. In Chantemerle the Kitz shows sporting events on TV and 'does good pizzas'. The other Chantemerle bars to look out for are the Taverne de la Bière, the Extreme bar and the 'cool' Triptyque.

OFF THE SLOPES ★★★☆☆
Try the hot baths
The old town of Briançon is well worth a visit. There is a leisure complex with pools, sauna, hot tub and steam room. Briançon also has an ice hockey team – their games make 'a good night out', says one reporter. In Le Monêtier there's a large, new thermal spa complex, Les Grands Bains ('superb tonic for tired limbs'), with indoor and outdoor pools, saunas, steam rooms and a waterfall (some areas only for the over-18s, no boxer shorts for men only tight speedo type trunks – we had to buy some on the spot). The hotel Alliey has a pool and spa. There is a public swimming pool and health spa near the hotel Sporting in Villeneuve. Each of the villages has a cinema. Chantemerle, Villeneuve and Briançon have ice rinks, and there is good walking on 'well-prepared trails'. You can also learn to drive a piste grooming machine.

Ste-Foy-Tarentaise

Tasteful, modern mini-resort appealing to families and experts – and to motorists as a base for expeditions to nearby mega-resorts

➕	Safe untracked powder within the lift system, and epic runs outside it	➖	Too quiet for many other visitors
➕	Cheap lift pass and good quality and good-value lodging	➖	Very limited piste network
		➖	Mainly slow chairlifts
➕	Quiet, good for families, but …	➖	Lack of good long green runs on the higher slopes

Ste-Foy is a small, attractive, unpretentious resort built in the last few years, at the foot of what started life as a cult off-piste mountain. It remains excellent for experts but is now very attractive for families too. But the extent of the pistes is tiny and keen piste-bashers will want to travel to big resorts nearby.

TOP 10 RATINGS

Extent	★☆☆☆☆
Fast lifts	★★☆☆☆
Queues	★★★★★
Snow	★★★☆☆
Expert	★★★★☆
Intermediate	★★★☆☆
Beginner	★★☆☆☆
Charm	★★★☆☆
Convenience	★★★☆☆
Scenery	★★★☆☆

NEWS

For 2009/10 the Ruitor apartments with spa and seven new luxury chalets are due to open.

KEY FACTS

Resort	1550m
	5,090ft
Slopes	1550-2620m
	5,090-8,600ft
Lifts	7
Pistes	32km
	20 miles
Green	6%
Blue	24%
Red	47%
Black	23%
Snowmaking	Some

THE RESORT

Ste-Foy itself is a village straddling the busy road up from Bourg-St-Maurice to Val d'Isère. Its slopes start at Ste-Foy-Station (aka Bonconseil), set 4km/2.5 miles off the main road. With a car you can visit some excellent restaurants close by and explore nearby resorts – Val d'Isère, Tignes, Les Arcs, La Plagne and La Rosière. You can have a day at each for around 23 euros a time with a Ste-Foy five-day pass (109 euros).

Village charm Ste-Foy-Station is a complete resort in miniature, with a limited choice of bars and restaurants, a small supermarket and a newsagent; these are surrounded by a growing cluster of chalets and chalet-style apartment blocks, all in the traditional Savoyard style of wood and stone.

Convenience No accommodation is far from the lifts or nursery slope.

Scenery The Tarentaise mountains give a dramatic backdrop to Ste-Foy's pleasant setting among the trees.

THE MOUNTAIN

There is an attractive mix of wooded slopes above the village and open slopes higher up.

Slopes The slow quad from the village takes you up to a tiny mid-mountain station at Plan Bois. A second goes on to the treeline, and a third to Col de l'Aiguille accesses almost 600m/1,970ft of vertical above the treeline. The two black runs from this chair form the basis of two special off-piste zones; the piste map shows these but does not explain them – we're told they are avalanche controlled and that the Crystal Dark/Off Tracks one is rarely officially open. Slightly further down the hill is another such zone, less steep. The two lower chairs serve a few pleasant runs through trees and back to the base station. A six-pack opened to the east of the main area a few seasons ago, along with a new blue run. A new red run is also planned. Most reporters have been amazed by the off-piste terrain the few lifts access (in addition to the official zones mentioned above). But don't expect miles of groomed pistes.

Fast lifts Just one fast chair.

Queues Except in peak season and on fresh powder days, despite all the new building and slow lifts, reporters have still failed to find queues at Ste-Foy.

Terrain parks There isn't one. But in the lower off-piste zone mentioned above you are encouraged to build your own features.

Snow reliability The slopes face north or west. Snow reliability is good on the former but can suffer on the latter, especially as there is snowmaking only on the run down to the resort.

Experts Experts can have great fun on

Pointe de la Foglietta 2930m — Col de l'Aiguille 2620m/8,600ft — Rocher d'Arbine 2645m — 2040m — 1710m — Bonconseil dessus — La Bataillettaz — ↓ Ste-Foy — Ste-Foy-Station 1550m/5,090ft

The two small huts at Plan Bois get packed and many people head back to base for lunch ↗

OT STE-FOY-TARENTAISE

TOURIST OFFICE

t 0479 069519
info@saintefoy.net
www.saintefoy.net

and between Ste-Foy's black and red runs, exploring lots of easily accessible off-piste and trees, including the special zones mentioned above. The lack of crowds means you can still make fresh tracks days after a storm. There's more serious off-piste on offer too, for which you need a guide. There are wonderful runs from the top of the lifts down through deserted old villages, either to the road up to Val d'Isère or back to the base, and a splendid route which takes you through trees and over a stream down to the tiny village of Le Crot. The ESF runs group off-piste trips, with transport back to base from the village of Le Miroir, where the route ends. There's also a Bureau des Guides, which can arrange heli-skiing in Italy, including a route which also brings you back to Le Miroir.

Intermediates Intermediates can enjoy 900m/2,950ft vertical of uncrowded reds and blues on the upper slopes, and worthwhile descents to the village when conditions are good. The red from the Col de l'Aiguille is a superb test for confident intermediates, who would also be up to the off-piste routes, especially the Monal route back to base. Anyone not wanting to try off-piste will tire of the limited runs in a day or two and be itching to get to Val d'Isère or Les Arcs.

Beginners Not the best place. But there are nursery slopes with moving carpets near the ski school. You can progress to a long green run off the first chair and then blues higher up.

Snowboarding Great freeriding terrain, with lots of trees and powder between the pistes to play in, plus a dedicated freestyle area for building kickers.

Cross-country No prepared trails.

Mountain restaurants There are two rustic restaurants at Plan Bois, Les Brevettes and Chez Léon; both are tiny and get over busy. Many people head

back to the base, where the Maison à Colonnes gets good reports.

Schools and guides We've had good reports of the ESF, especially for children (from age four). K Spirit opened here two seasons ago.

Families Les P'tits Trappeurs takes children from age three to 11. UK tour operator Première Neige also runs a nursery ('the nannies were so lovely our kids didn't want to leave').

STAYING THERE

Hotels Auberge sur la Montagne (0479 069583), just above the turn-off at La Thuile, Ferme du Baptieu (0479 069752) and the smartly refurbished Monal (0479 069007) in Ste-Foy village have good reputations.

Chalets and apartments Première Neige has lots of chalets and apartments here, with catered and self-catered options. Peak Retreats offers Les Fermes de Ste-Foy, with pool, hot tub, sauna, steam, fitness.

Eating out In Ste-Foy-Station the Bergerie does excellent food and Maison à Colonnes is 'simple and good', especially for Savoyard dishes. In the village of Le Miroir, Chez Mérie is excellent (for lunch as well as dinner). So are two hotels mentioned above: the Monal ('the best restaurant this Francophile has ever eaten in', says a regular reporter) and Auberge sur la Montagne.

Après-ski Pretty quiet. Reporters enjoyed the Iceberg piano bar. The Pitchouli is the place to go for a drink later on. The bar of the hotel Monal can get busy, too, and tastings are held in the wine bar there.

Off the slopes There's not a lot to do off the slopes, but paragliding, dog sledding and snowshoeing are available. The excellent pool and spa at the Balcons de Ste-Foy apartments are open to non-residents for a fee.

SNOWPIX.COM / CHRIS GILL

St-Martin-de-Belleville

Explore the Three Valleys from a traditional old village – and so avoid the Méribel crowds who descend on it for lunch

TOP 10 RATINGS

Extent	★★★★★
Fast lifts	★★★★
Queues	★★★★
Snow	★★★
Expert	★★★★
Intermediate	★★★★★
Beginner	★★
Charm	★★★★
Convenience	★★★
Scenery	★★★

NEWS

A new lift is planned at Les Menuires for 2009/10 (see separate chapter).

For 2008/09 snowmaking was installed on the Pelozet piste.

KEY FACTS

Resort	1400m
	4,590ft

Three Valleys	
Slopes	1260-3230m
	4,130-10,600ft
Lifts	180
Pistes	600km
	373 miles
Green	15%
Blue	38%
Red	37%
Black	10%
Snowmaking	
	33%

Les Menuires / St-Martin only	
Slopes	1400-2850m
	4,590-9,350ft
Lifts	36
Pistes	160km
	99 miles
Green	8%
Blue	42%
Red	40%
Black	10%
Snowmaking	45%

PISTE MAP

St-Martin is covered on the Les Menuires map

+ Attractively developed traditional village with pretty church

+ Access to the whole of the extensive Three Valleys network

+ Long, easy intermediate runs on rolling local slopes

+ Extensive snowmaking keeps runs open in poor conditions, but ...

− Snow on runs to the resort suffers from afternoon sun, and altitude

− No green runs for novices

− Taxing climb up from the lower part of the village to the lifts

− Limited après-ski

− Few off-slope diversions

St-Martin is a lived-in, unspoiled village with an old church (prettily lit at night), small square and buildings of wood and stone, a few miles down the valley from Les Menuires. As a quiet, inexpensive, attractive base for exploration of the Three Valleys as a whole, it's unbeatable.

THE RESORT

St-Martin was a backwater until the 1980s, when chairlifts were built linking it to the slopes of Méribel and Les Menuires.

Village charm The name – 'beautiful town' – exaggerates both pulchritude and town, but St Martin is a pleasant old village, set on a steep slope, with its extensive modern developments all in traditional style. The main feature remains the lovely 16th-century church – prettily floodlit at night.

Convenience The village is small – you can walk around it in a few minutes – but the main lift is above the centre and we get regular complaints about the hike up from those based lower down. There are some good local shops and a few 'touristy' ones.

Scenery St Martin has one of the more attractive locations in the valley, set among quiet, lightly wooded slopes.

THE MOUNTAINS

The whole of the Three Valleys can easily be explored from here. The piste map for Les Menuires covers this area.

Slopes A gondola followed by a fast quad take you to a ridge from which you can access Méribel on one side and Les Menuires on the other.

Fast lifts Fast lifts get you into the slopes of Les Menuires or Méribel.

Queues The second stage of the lifts above the village – the chair to Tougnète, is now inadequate. It might not be if the chairs were filled.

Terrain parks There isn't a terrain park

in the St-Martin sector, but you can get to those above Les Menuires and Méribel relatively easily.

Snow reliability The local slopes get the full force of the afternoon sun, and the village is quite low. The home run is kept open by snowmaking to the bottom, but the conditions are often poor. You can ride the gondola down if snow is poor.

Experts Locally there are large areas of gentle and often deserted off-piste. A reader recommends the descent from Roc de Fer to the village of Béranger. Head to La Masse for steep slopes.

Intermediates The local slopes are pleasant blues and reds, mainly of interest to intermediates. It's a pity that the main blue home run includes an awkward section above the mid-station – steep, narrow, often icy and congested. The alternative is to use the Méribel lifts to access the Verdet blue – an easy cruise, usually very quiet. One of our favourite runs is the rolling, wide Jerusalem red.

Beginners St-Martin is far from ideal – there's a small nursery slope but no long green runs to progress to. Note that the lift pass included in the beginners' package covers only the two lifts above St-Martin.

Snowboarding There is some great local off-piste freeriding available.

Cross-country There are 28km/17 miles of trails in the Belleville valley.

Mountain restaurants Reporters love the Grand Lac (see Les Menuires). There are three atmospheric old places lower on the home run: Chardon Bleu ('lovely food' but erratic service), the

UK PACKAGES

*Alpine Club, Chalet
Group, Crystal, Erna
Low, First Choice,
Independent Ski Links,
Kaluma, Leisure
Direction, Mountain
Action, Oxford Ski Co,
Peak Retreats, Simply
Alpine, Ski France,
Skiholidayextras.com,
Ski Independence, Ski
l'Alpage, Skitracer,
Snow Finders*

SMART LODGINGS

**Check out our feature
chapters at the front
of the book.**

Phone numbers
From abroad use the
prefix +33 and omit
the initial '0' of the
phone number

TOURIST OFFICE

t 0479 002000
stmartin@st-martin-
belleville.com
www.st-martin-
belleville.com

small, woody Corbeleys ('good for
catching the last rays') and the Loy
('the best steak and chips').
Schools and guides Reports on ESF
lessons are generally positive: a
regular visitor finds the group lessons
'very helpful', and friends who had
several private lessons found them
'excellent'.
Families It's all a bit steep for families,
but the Piou Piou club at the ESF
takes children from three months to
five years old. A list of babysitters is
available.

STAYING THERE

For a small village there's a good
variety of accommodation.
Chalets The Brit-run Alpine Club – not
really a club – now has three chalets
with good food and service ('chalet as
nice as ever, hosts great, lovely food –
our 2nd visit'). Ferme de Belleville is a
nicely renovated 400-year-old
farmhouse in the heart of the old
village; Maison de Belleville,
overlooking the village, is spacious,
light and airy ('excellent all round,
food fantastic'). Abode enjoys a lovely
location near the church, sleeps 10
and combines original farmhouse
features with a contemporary interior.
The company runs a minibus to and
from the gondola.
Hotels The Alp Hôtel (0479 089282) is
at the foot of the slope by the main
lift. The Saint-Martin (0479 008800) is
right on the slope, and the Edelweiss
(0479 089667) is in the village itself.
All are 3-stars. Options elsewhere in
the valley include the cute restaurant
with rooms La Bouitte (0479 089677)

in St-Marcel (see 'Eating out') –
spacious, woody rooms with antiques,
and two suites.
Apartments The stylish CGH/MGM
Chalets du Gypse is well placed beside
the piste, with a smart pool.
Eating out For such a small village
there is a good choice. Readers still
enjoy the Montagnard: 'good food'
with a 'more exotic range than it used
to offer'. Next door is the Petit Creux,
for 'enormous, fine pizzas, steaks and
kebabs at good prices'. The popular
Voûte has 'consistently good food and
prices' – 'fabulous pasta with a rich
veal sauce'. The Etoile des Neiges is a
smart, traditionally French restaurant,
recommended by a reporter. The Ferme
de la Choumette, slightly out of the
village, is a working farm and cheesery
– 'a little gem'. Two readers suggest
the Ferme du Dahu in Villarbon, 2km/1
mile down the valley (the owners will
ferry you at no charge): 'extremely
atmospheric', 'one of the best meals in
years', 'grossly underpriced'. La
Bouitte, up the road in St-Marcel, now
has two Michelin stars, which is rarely
good news – 'eye-watering prices' and
'fashionably fussy food'.
Après-ski The Dahlia, at the bottom of
the gondola, is 'popular for après-ski
drinks'. The Pourquoi Pas?, with a log
fire and comfortable sofas, is well
patronised by British visitors; it has
live music and is cosy. Brewski's has
nightly entertainment and stays open
till 2am, as does the Joker.
Off the slopes Off-slope is limited. The
village has a sports hall, a new
museum and musical events in the
church. And there's dog sledding,
snowshoe trips, and pleasant walks.

Les Sybelles

Chalk-and-cheese resorts linked rather tenuously by slow lifts to form an area that's one of the biggest in the Alps

➕ Extensive area of largely easy intermediate slopes and gentle, uncrowded off-piste

➕ Inexpensive by French standards

➕ Unusual mixture of stark, purpose-built resorts and old villages

➖ Lift network painfully slow

➖ Few pistes steep enough to interest adventurous intermediates

➖ Après-ski limited and quiet

➖ Mainly simple accommodation

➖ Few off-slope diversions

NEWS

For 2009/10 two additional draglifts are planned to reduce the peak season queues for the existing drags at Pte de L'Ouillon, the hub of the Les Sybelles ski area.

For 2008/09 in Le Corbier, phase two of the 4-star Résidence Odalys Les Alpages du Corbier was completed. In La Toussuire a toboggan run was built and a new residence opened. In Les Bottières, 60 new apartments opened.

Les Sybelles is not a resort but a lift network linking a handful of little-known resorts in the Maurienne massif in the French Alps. When formed in 2003, Les Sybelles' 310km/193 miles of pistes put it straight into the big league, alongside such giants as Val d'Isère-Tignes.

Our first visit to the newly launched Les Sybelles gave us a bit of a shock; we had forgotten just how slow progress can be on a mountain with 70 slow lifts and just one fast one. Matters have since improved – there are now seven fast chairs. But Les Sybelles still languishes at the bottom of our fast-lift league table, with less than one lift in ten being fast. And installation of fast lifts out of the big resorts without similar improvements at altitude has created queue problems in peak season for the draglifts that form the links; their solution is to install two new drags for 2009/10. Crazy: what they need is more six-packs.

The resorts are sharply contrasting in character. La Toussuire and Le Corbier are most politely described as modern, functional and downmarket, while St-Sorlin-d'Arves and St-Jean-d'Arves are largely unspoiled, traditional villages that are expanding tastefully and have attracted some major UK tour operators.

The links between the resorts are high – mostly over 2000m/6,560ft – so they are relatively snow-sure – though some slopes get a lot of sun and can suffer in late season. All the slopes are easily negotiated by competent intermediates, consisting of easy reds and tough blues (one or two of which might be better classified red). But getting from one resort to another can be slow going, because of slow lifts.

Le Corbier 1550m/5,090ft

Le Corbier is centrally placed in the ski area, with direct links to St-Jean-d'Arves in one direction and La Toussuire in the other, as well as a high link to St-Sorlin.

THE RESORT

Designed in the 1960s, Le Corbier is a no-compromise functional resort. Most of its accommodation is in eight inner-city-style tower blocks – one as high as 19 storeys – with subterranean shops beneath. They are all right at the foot of the slopes. The resort sells itself firmly as a family resort and runs

a French Family Championship with teams of mother, father and one child.

Village charm To our eye, Le Corbier is a blot on the landscape. But new building is in traditional style. And it does accommodate its 9,000 visitors efficiently in the minimum space, so in functional terms it is hard to criticise.

Convenience The resort is traffic-free, compact and entirely ski-in/ski-out.

Scenery Le Corbier's balcony setting gives good views over the valley.

THE MOUNTAIN

The local ski area has 90km/56 miles of gentle pistes, almost entirely on open slopes above the treeline.

Slopes The Sybelles Express, a six-pack, rises over 700m/2,300ft vertical to Pte du Corbier, from where pistes and lifts go along the ridge to the hub of Les Sybelles at Pte de L'Ouillon. Runs spread across a wide, north-east-facing mountainside return to the resort, and there are links at the extremities to La Toussuire and St-Jean-d'Arves.

Fast lifts Just one bottom-to-top chair.

Queues We have no reports of

KEY FACTS

Slopes	1100-2620m
	3,610-8,600ft
Lifts	85
Pistes	310km
	193 miles
Green	21%
Blue	39%
Red	35%
Black	5%
Snowmaking	
	293 guns

problems, but see introduction.

Terrain parks There's a park on the lower slopes just above the resort.

Snow reliability The mix of reasonable altitude and lack of crowds means the snow tends to stay in fairly good condition high up. There is snowmaking on all the main pistes back to the resort. The low connection from La Toussuire is a problem spot.

Experts The area lacks challenges – the one short black piste scarcely deserves a red classification. There are off-piste options in the valley between Le Corbier and La Toussuire.

Intermediates Le Corbier's gentle slopes are ideal cruising terrain, though the runs aren't very long and they rather lack variety.

Beginners There is an extensive nursery area with a moving carpet right in front of the resort, with gentle progression runs directly above.

Snowboarding The wide, open terrain is ideal for riders, as long as they don't want anything too challenging.

Cross-country There are loops either side of the resort, one of which leads to La Toussuire and back. The two villages have 25km/15miles but it's all a bit bleak.

Mountain restaurants Table-service La Picoraille, next to Le Yeti, has 'large portions at reasonable prices'. Le Charmun, at the foot of the Vadrouille area has 'delicious crozets with wild

mushrooms and lardons' and Chalet 2000 near the top has been praised.

Schools One past reporter judged the ESF 'disdainful, uncaring, very disorganised; bad tuition'.

Families The Nursery takes children from three months. A reporter praised the ski kindergarten (for age three up): 'Nice, well-equipped ski-park; good instructors.' Its location up on the pistes means a bit of a hike.

STAYING THERE

Chalets Equity Ski runs its own chalet hotel, described by one reporter as 'clean, comfortable and very good value' and approved by others, too.

Hotels None in resort.

Apartments Nearly all the accommodation here is in apartments. There's a central reservations system.

Eating out The Grillon, 3km/2 miles away in Villarembert, makes a pleasant, rustic change from Le Corbier's tower blocks – and serves traditional French food.

Après ski Very quiet. The Equity Ski chalet-hotel bar is popular. Roches Blanches restaurant in the centre includes a cosy bar area with an open fire. For dancing, the Président gets busy only at peak holiday periods.

Off the slopes There's a natural ice rink, outdoor pool, fitness centre, dog sledding, snowmobiling, paragliding and snowshoeing.

Les Perrons 2620m/8,600ft
Petit Perran
L'Ouillon 2430m/7,970ft
La Balme 2240m
Mt Cuinat 2080m
Pte du Corbier 2265m/7430ft
Tête de Bellard 2225m
St-Sorlin-d'Arves 1600m/5,250ft
Grande Verdette
Le Grand Truc 2210m
St-Jean-d'Arves 1550m/5,090ft
St-Colomban-des-Villards 1100m/3,610ft
Le Corbier 1550m/5,090ft
La Toussuire 1750m/5,740ft
Les Bottières 1300m/4,270ft

La Toussuire 1750m/5,740ft

La Toussuire, along with Le Corbier, is one of the central resorts of the piste network. It makes a convenient base with good local intermediate slopes and three fast lifts which give reasonably quick access to the hub of Les Sybelles at Pte de L'Ouillon.

THE RESORT

La Toussuire has grown up over many years but most buildings date from the 1960s and later.

Village charm The car-free and snow-covered main street is lined by dreary-looking buildings and was plagued by piped music from loudspeakers when we were there.

Convenience The resort has now spread widely from here, with wooden chalets as well as older hotels and small apartment blocks scattered across the mountainside.

Scenery Much like Le Corbier, but in a higher gentle bowl.

THE MOUNTAIN

The local slopes amount to 45km/ 28 miles of pistes and were judged by a recent reporter to be the best in the area for variety and snow conditions. All the slopes are above the treeline.

Slopes The resort sits in the pit of a wide bowl. Drags and chairlifts rise just over 500m/1,640ft vertical to the high point of Tête de Ballard and the link to L'Ouillon. At one end of the bowl is the low-level link to Le Corbier and at the other the start of a long red run of 900m/2,950ft vertical to the hamlet of Les Bottières.

Fast lifts There are three six-packs in the local area, more than in any other sector of Les Sybelles.

Queues We have no reports of problems, but see introduction.

Terrain park There's a boardercross.

Snow reliability With every run above 1800m/5,910ft snow-cover is fairly assured, but some of the slopes are rather too sunny – particularly the low-level connection to Le Corbier.

Experts There are few challenges here, and not much space between the pistes. The main interest is the ungroomed black Vallée Perdue run, which descends the valley separating La Toussuire from Le Corbier, away from the lifts. But it gets a lot of sun, and snow conditions can suffer. The link lifts towards L'Ouillon open up off-piste routes down this valley.

Intermediates This is ideal terrain for cruisers who don't mind mainly short runs. The longer run that goes down to Les Bottières is one of the most appealing in the whole area – but you face a long drag ride back, too.

Beginners There are nice, gentle nursery slopes immediately above the centre of the village, and good, easy progression slopes.

Snowboarding There are quite a few draglifts in the area.

Cross-country A narrow loop goes to Le Corbier, but it is in bleak surroundings and close to the road. There are also loops on the lower slopes of Le Grand Truc. There's 25km/16 miles in total.

Mountain restaurants Reporters like the Foehn at Le Marolay for its 'stunning views' and interesting interior of old photos and carvings, and the Cigales, near the foot of the bowl. The refuge on the Bouyans blue run down to St-Colomban has a 'fantastic setting'. The Carlines self-service at Tête de Bellard has a 'huge' sun terrace and does 'nice local sausages'. The Chamois features lots of ski racing memorabilia.

Schools A lack of English-speaking tuition can be a problem, as confirmed by a visitor with children. However, he also 'had a fantastic time in the ESF with a great bilingual teacher'.

Families The nursery accepts children from one to three years. The kindergarten takes children from three to 14. Language may be a problem.

STAYING THERE

Hotels There are several small 3-star and 2-star places. The 3-star Ruade (0479 830179) and Soldanelles (0479 567529) both have pools and saunas.

Apartments The Hauts de Comborcière and Balcons des Aiguilles are both at the foot of the slopes and Ecrin des

↑ The Bergerie on St-Sorlin's La Balme area, with great views of the Aiguilles d'Arves

SNOWPIX.COM / CHRIS GILL

UK PACKAGES

Le Corbier *Erna Low, Interhome, Lagrange, Leisure Direction, PV-Holidays.com, Rocketski, Ski France, Skiholidayextras.com, Ski Independence* **La Toussuire** *Erna Low, Interhome, Lagrange, Leisure Direction, Ski Collection, Ski France, Skiholidayextras.com* **St-Sorlin-d'Arves** *AmeriCan Ski, Crystal, Erna Low, Lagrange, Leisure Direction, Peak Retreats, Ski France, Skiholidayextras.com, Ski Independence, Thomson* **St-Jean-d'Arves** *Leisure Direction, Peak Retreats, Ski France, Skiholidayextras.com, Thomson*

Sybelles is 400m away (served by a ski-bus); all have pool, sauna, steam, hot tub and are bookable through Ski Collection. Most other apartments are cheap and not so cheerful.
Eating out Most places are inexpensive pizzerias and bar-restaurants.
Après-ski Fairly dire. There are a few bars, including the Tonneau. The Pop Club nightclub can get busy at peak French holiday time.
Off the slopes There's a reasonable amount to do, including snowshoeing, snowmobiling, dog sledding, skating on a 'very seedy' rink on the roof of a building in the main street, bowling and hang-gliding.

St-Sorlin-d'Arves

1600m/5,250ft

St-Sorlin is based on a traditional village and has the most interesting slopes in the area for good intermediates – the slopes on Les Perrons, reached by two fast quads.

THE RESORT
St-Sorlin-d'Arves is a real, medium-sized village with a year-round life outside skiing.
Village charm It's a picturesque mixture of well-preserved traditional farmhouses, a baroque church and long-established shops – fromagerie, boulangerie, crafts etc – alongside more modern resort development.
Convenience There isn't much room for expansion, so the village has grown in a ribbon-like fashion along the main road – not ideal for strolling around. There is a frequent bus service, but some visitors have complained that it is 'crowded and disorganised'.
Scenery St-Sorlin's position on a narrow shelf gives fine views.

THE MOUNTAIN
St-Sorlin's local slopes form the biggest single sector of the linked network, with 120km/75 miles of piste. Although very much an intermediate mountain, it does offer much more variety, including some steeper options, than the rest of the area.
Slopes There are two distinct sections. The lower, gentler left side on La Balme, reached by a choice of slow chairs from the village, is crammed with lots of short, easy runs. The higher, right side on Les Perrons, reached by two successive fast six-packs, has long, sweeping, generally steeper pistes. The Vallons run off the back of Les Perrons (which forms the first part of the link to L'Ouillon and onwards to the other resorts) and the runs from Petit Perron add a lot of interest to the local skiing.
Fast lifts Les Perrons has two; there's another towards L'Ouillon.
Queues There may be queues out of the village first thing and when moving between sectors.
Terrain park There is one on La Balme, accessed by a chairlift.
Snow reliability Not bad. Les Perrons' slopes are the highest in the area and the main runs back to the village are covered by snowmaking. Grooming seems to be erratic.
Experts There isn't much on-piste challenge, but Les Perrons has the best off-piste in the whole area; the slopes beneath the Petit Perron chair offer more interest.
Intermediates There is only one run on the back of Les Perrons and a couple on the front; but they go from top-to-bottom and have the whole mountainside to themselves, giving a great away-from-it-all feel. And the reds here are quite challenging – the best in the area for good intermediates. The Perrons red run to the village is challenging too – expect major moguls unless recently groomed. La Balme has shorter, more leisurely runs. Timid intermediates may find the rather narrow Combe Balme blue to the village tricky and crowded at the end of the day.
Beginners The nursery slope is right by the village, and there are plenty of slopes to progress to on La Balme.
Snowboarding The terrain suits beginners and intermediates but there are a lot of draglifts. Freeriders will enjoy the quiet off-piste slopes.
Cross-country There's a 16km/10 mile

Phone numbers
From abroad use the
prefix +33 and omit
the initial '0' of the
phone number

TOURIST OFFICES

t 0479 598800
info@les-sybelles.com
www.les-sybelles.com
La Toussuire
t 0479 830606
info@la-toussuire.com
www.la-toussuire.com
Le Corbier
t 0479 830404
info@le-corbier.com
www.le-corbier.com
St-Sorlin-d'Arves
t 0479 597177
info@saintsorlin
darves.com
www.saintsorlin
darves.com
St-Jean-d'Arves
t 0479 597330
info@saintjeandarves.
com
www.saintjeandarves.
com
**St-Colomban-des-
Villards**
t 0479 562453
villards@wanadoo.fr
www.saint-colomban.
com
Les Bottières
t 0479 832709
info@bottieres-jarrier.
com
www.bottieres-jarrier.
com

loop along a side valley past the foot of La Balme's Alpine area.

Mountain restaurants We enjoyed lunch on and stunning views of the Aiguilles d'Arves from the sunny terrace of the rustic Bergerie at La Balme – endorsed by a reporter.

Schools ESF children's classes have been criticised: 'Almost no feedback from their teacher, classes a bit too big and poor English.'

Families The Petits Diables nursery accepts children from three months; a reporter said, 'It was poor; no effort to be welcoming. We left after two days.' The ski kindergarten accepts kids from three-and-a-half years. Language can be a problem.

STAYING THERE

Hotels Only two (both 2-star attractive chalets): the Beausoleil (0479 597142) and Balme (0479 597021).

Apartments L'Orée des Pistes is at the bottom of the slopes and 1km/0.5 miles from the village centre. Chalet de l'Arvan is a ski-bus ride from the slopes. Both are smart with pool, sauna, steam and are featured by Peak Retreats. There are scores of small properties – and the Grignotte bakery sells 'the best bread ever'.

Eating out The choice is limited to cheap and cheerful pizzerias and raclette/fondue places. The Table de Marie, Gargoulette, Petit Ferme ('hearty portions of lasagne') and the place above the Avalanche cafe have been recommended. A recent visitor enjoyed the 'quiet' Regal Savoyard ('best choice, best prices').

Après-ski St-Sorlin-d'Arves is even quieter than the other major resorts, but has the lively Yeti bar and D'sybell nightclub. The Avalanche reportedly attracts more of a 'student-age' group.

Off the slopes There is not much to do. Dog sledding, snowmobiling and snowshoeing are options and there's a museum of the village's history.

St-Jean-d'Arves

1550m/5,090ft

St-Jean-d'Arves is a small, yet quite scattered community. Reporters generally find it very friendly. The original old village, with the usual ancient church, is set across the valley from the slopes, which are at the mid-mountain hamlet of La Chal. Here, where a tasteful development of chalet-style buildings is still

expanding, there are nursery slopes, small terrain park and the lift link to and piste back from Le Corbier.

St-Jean/La Chal is not a good base for anyone wanting to exploit the larger area – and that will include most energetic beginners as well as intermediates. The chairlift towards Le Corbier is painfully slow – 'enough to make you cry', say reporters. The return slopes are excessively sunny – bare and rocky when we visited; there is snowmaking, but a cure is unlikely. Usually it will be better to take the shuttle-bus to St-Sorlin to use its fast lifts. There are several cross-country trails ranging from 3km/2 miles to 17km/10 miles.

Off-slope diversions are few – dog sledding, snowshoeing, snowmobiling, paragliding and cheese farm visits. Après-ski is basic, with a few bars, an Irish pub, night-tobogganing with music, and a cinema. The best apartment options include Marmottes (with access, at a cost, to an outdoor hot tub), Fontaine du Roi and Hameau de St Jean; Marmottes is featured by Peak Retreats.

St-Colomban-des-Villards 1100m/3,610ft

St-Colomban-des-Villards is a tiny old village in the next valley to La Toussuire, only a few miles up from the Maurienne valley with 30km/18 miles of slopes.

There is a chain of drags and chairlifts on north- and east-facing slopes to the south of the village, with a high point at Mt Cuinat, and a link to L'Ouillon, at the hub of Les Sybelles. The run down is reportedly 'interesting and attractive', but the return lifts take an hour. A battery of snow-guns keeps the home slope open. The Auberge du Coin at Ormet has 'lovely views', table- and self-service choices.

Les Bottières

1300m/4,270ft

Down the mountain from La Toussuire, this tiny hamlet offers little infrastructure and extremely indirect access to the main network – it takes three long lifts to get over to La Toussuire, before setting off for L'Ouillon. The restaurant at the bottom of the Marmottes draglift has 'good food and excellent service'.

Les Sybelles

Interactive resort shortlist builder at **www.wtss.co.uk**

La Tania

A very attractive budget base for the vast slopes of Courchevel and Méribel – and not bad looking, for a purpose-built resort

378

TOP 10 RATINGS

Extent	★★★★★
Fast lifts	★★★★
Queues	★★★★
Snow	★★★
Expert	★★★★
Intermediate	★★★★★
Beginner	★★★
Charm	★★★
Convenience	★★★★
Scenery	★★★

NEWS

For 2009/10 a three-hour lift pass will be available, covering the Courchevel valley.

A new nursery is due to open close to the gondola – taking children from three years old.

For 2008/09 the Arolles and Bouc Blanc runs were widened and more snow-guns installed. And the Dou des Lanches quad was fitted with the child safety device, Magnestick.

+ Part of the Three Valleys – the world's biggest linked ski area, with good access to the slopes of Courchevel and Méribel

+ Long, rolling intermediate runs through woods back to the village

+ Good green run to the village means it's now more attractive for beginners and timid intermediates

+ Greatly improved snowmaking

+ Attractive, small, traffic-free village

− Small development: limited après-ski, no doctor, no pharmacy

− Main nursery slope is part of the blue run to the village, and gets a lot of through-traffic

− Some accommodation is a hike from the centre and the gondola

− Access to the highest and most rewarding slopes of the Three Valleys is some distance, with some slow lifts on the way

La Tania has carved out its own niche as a good-value, quiet, family-friendly base from which to explore the slopes of its swanky neighbours, Courchevel and Méribel. Trips to the furthest corners of the immense Three Valleys take a little more time than from better-placed starting points, but they are certainly possible. It is a second-generation purpose-built resort, and at 1350m/4,430ft about the lowest you'll find; its wood-clad buildings sit comfortably in a pretty woodland setting – quite a contrast to the bleak slopes and bleak buildings of classic French ski stations such as Les Menuires.

THE RESORT

La Tania is set just off the minor road linking Le Praz (Courchevel 1300) to Méribel. Free buses go to Courchevel. For those with a car, Méribel is probably a bigger draw – and a lot nearer than Courchevel 1850.
Village charm The village has grown into a quiet, attractive, car-free collection of mainly ski-in/ski-out chalets and apartments. It does now have a few lively bars and restaurants, but nightlife is still relatively low-key.
Convenience It's a small place – you can walk around the village in a couple of minutes – but big enough to have all the basic amenities (except a pharmacy). A gondola from the heart of the village leads up into the slopes. And the nursery slope is on your doorstep. There is an easy slope back to the village, but the return from Courchevel involves a blue.

There's not much more to the village than this – apart from lots of chalets up in the woods →

Scenery The resort is prettily set among the trees. But Col de la Loze makes a better viewpoint, overlooking Courchevel's slopes.

THE MOUNTAINS

The slopes immediately above La Tania and nearby Le Praz are wooded, and about the best place in the whole Three Valleys to spend your time in bad weather. Above mid-mountain, the slopes are open.

Slopes The gondola out of the village goes to Praz-Juget. From here draglifts go on up to Chenus or to Loze and the slopes above Courchevel 1850, and a fast quad goes to the link with Méribel via Col de la Loze. From all these points, varied, interesting intermediate runs take you back into the La Tania sector.

Fast lifts Our rating is for the whole Courchevel area lift system. The lifts above La Tania are not great – the gondola is not super-quick, and the alternative is long draglifts that are labelled 'difficile'.

Queues There may be peak-time queues for the village gondola, but one of the attractions of La Tania in general is the lack of crowds. However, we have received reports of frequent stoppages last season.

Terrain parks There is no local terrain park or half-pipe, but you can get to Courchevel's parks easily.

Snow reliability Good snow-cover down to Praz-Juget is usual all season. Snowmaking covers the whole of the blue run back to the village; if, despite this, the run is icy in the afternoon, you have the option of riding the gondola down.

Col de Chanrossa 2545m

Méribel
La Vizelle 2705m 2660m
La Saulire 2740m/8,99oft

↙ Méribel
Col de la Loze 2275m

Signal

CHANROSSA
Creux

Chenus 2245m

SAULIRE - CREUX

LOZE - PRAZ

Mt. Bel Air
Altiport
Verdons

Praméruel 1825m

Praz Juget

Courchevel 1850

Courchevel 1650

Courchevel 1550

Courchevel 1300 (Le Praz) 1260m/4,130ft

La Tania 1350m/4,430ft

KEY FACTS

Resort	1350m
	4,430ft

The Three Valleys	
Slopes	1260-3230m
	4,130-10,600ft
Lifts	180
Pistes	600km
	373 miles
Green	15%
Blue	38%
Red	37%
Black	10%
Snowmaking	33%

Courchevel/ La Tania only	
Slopes	1260-2740m
	4,130-8,990ft
Lifts	62
Pistes	150km
	93 miles
Green	23%
Blue	37%
Red	32%
Black	8%
Snowmaking	
	563 guns

UK PACKAGES

Alpine Action, Alpine Answers, Chalet Group, Crystal, Directski.com, Erna Low, Family Friendly Skiing, Independent Ski Links, Interactive Resorts, Lagrange, Leisure Direction, Le Ski, Neilson, Nick Ski, Oxford Ski Co, PV-Holidays.com, Silver Ski, Simply Alpine, Ski Activity, Ski Amis, Ski Beat, Ski-Dazzle, Ski Deep, Ski Expectations, Ski France, Ski Hame, Skiholidayextras.com, Ski Independence, Ski Line, Ski Magic, Ski McNeill, Ski Power, Ski Solutions, Skitopia, Skitracer, Skiweekends. com, Snowline, Thomson

Experts There are no particularly testing runs directly above La Tania – the Jean Blanc and Jockeys blacks from Loze to Le Praz are challenging more because of length than gradient. But there is good off-piste terrain beneath the Col de la Loze ridge, with more close by above Courchevel.

Intermediates There are two lovely, long, undulating intermediate runs back through the trees to La Tania – though there's little difference in gradient between the blue and the red, and timid intermediates may want to use the Plan Fontaine green. On the higher slopes you have a choice of three or four pistes. Both the red Lanches and the black Dou des Lanches are excellent and challenging.

Beginners There is a good beginner area and lift right in the village, and children are well catered for. But there's a lot of through traffic on the main slope. The steepness of the longer runs above the village used to be a key weakness, but the Plan Fontaine green run from Praz-Juget to the village gives novices a long easy slope to progress to.

Snowboarding It's easy to get around on gondolas/chairs, avoiding drags.

Cross-country There are 39km/24 miles of trails with links through the woods to Méribel and Courchevel – which has an extensive 66km/41 miles of trails.

Mountain restaurants Bouc Blanc (0479 088026), near the top of the gondola out of La Tania, is our favourite in this sector of the slopes: it has friendly table service in a wood-clad dining room, good food (reliable plat du jour) and a big terrace. Reporters regularly agree with us about the food ('fantastic value'), but complaints surface occasionally about the service. The tiny Roc Tania, higher up at Col de la Loze, is very pretty inside, and the terrace is 'great for sun and views'.

Schools and guides Reports of the ESF vary and groups can be large. A 2009 visitor complains of 'not enough consistency' among the children's groups, but another says that her son was 'skiing with absolute confidence' by the end of his week, despite some frustrations. Magic Snowsports Academy has been recommended. Highly regarded British school New Generation, well established in Courchevel, is expanding into La Tania for 2009/10.

Families La Tania is popular with families looking for a quiet and convenient base, and child-friendly atmosphere. Chez Nounours is a new kindergarten for non-skiing children from three years old; the Jardin des Neiges takes skiing children from the age of four. UK tour operators Le Ski and Ski Beat both operate nurseries. A list of babysitters (for children over six months old) is available from the tourist office.

STAYING THERE

Hotels The Montana (0479 088008) is a slope-side 3-star next to the gondola with a sauna and fitness club. The Télémark (0479 089349) is recommended by a reader: 'Compact but very comfortable; friendly staff and good value.' It is also a hub of the après-ski scene, which may be a plus?

Chalets There are dozens of catered chalets here. Major Courchevel operator Le Ski has three chalets here ('great food, capable and friendly staff, lived up to expectations'); two are particularly child-friendly, with family rooms. And they run a large crèche. Ski Amis has three chalets – one aimed at families, one budget and one premium (with sauna) – plus some self-catering places. Alpine Action has four smart chalets near the centre, all with outdoor hot tubs, one with spa-

Phone numbers
From abroad use the prefix +33 and omit the initial '0' of the phone number.

baths in the bathrooms. Ski Beat has six chalets, two split into two units; most offer skiing from the door if not to the door. Snowline has five chalets, including the central Folyeres with outdoor hot tub.

Apartments There are lots of apartments – and most are more spacious and better equipped than usual in France. There is a deli, a bakery, and small supermarket.

Eating out There's a very limited choice. Three 2009 reporters praise the Taïga for 'good food, excellent service' and fewer crowds. And the Ski Lodge does 'great value, excellent food – the chèvre chaud was delicious'. The Marmottons has a traditional feel and makes a 'popular and pleasant evening; the pizzas and the tiramisu were fab'. Another visitor rated the restaurant of the Télémark

hotel 'completely fantastic: exemplary pork ... chips worthy of Heston Blumenthal'. We get few reports on the Michelin-starred Farçon.

Après-ski It's quite lively at close of play, but again the choice is limited. The Ski Lodge has long been the focal après-ski place and has live bands – one visitor comments: 'It is always good, but it can get quite busy.' The hotel Télémark is reported to be 'welcoming and reasonably priced, with charming staff'. The newish Chrome bar has regular live music. For a quieter time, the hotel Montana bar is worth trying.

Off the slopes The place is very small and limited. However, snowmobile trips, snowshoeing, tobogganing and paragliding are possibilities, and the hotel Montana has a fitness club with a swimming pool.

Selected chalets in La Tania

The Three Valleys

With the swankiest resort in the Alps at one end, and the highest at the other: the biggest lift-linked ski area in the world

Despite competing claims, notably from the Portes du Soleil, in practical terms the Three Valleys cannot be beaten for sheer quantity of lift-served terrain. There is nowhere like it for a keen skier or boarder who wants to cover as much mileage as possible while rarely taking the same run repeatedly. It has a lot to offer everyone, from beginner to expert. And its resorts offer a wide range of alternatives – not only the widely known attractions of the big-name mega-resorts but also the low-key appeal of the smaller villages.

What's more, the area undersells itself. It should actually be known as the Four Valleys, since its expansion south into the Maurienne. But when you've spent millions on building a brand name why change? Three valleys or four – whatever, the place is huge.

The runs of the Three Valleys and their resorts are dealt with in six chapters. The four major resorts are Courchevel, Méribel, Les Menuires and Val Thorens, but we also give chapters to St-Martin-de-Belleville, a village down the valley from Les Menuires, and La Tania, a modern development between Courchevel and Méribel.

None of the resorts is cheap, but of the major resorts **Les Menuires** is clearly the cheapest. The centre of the resort is an eyesore, but new developments have been built in a much more acceptable style, and two of the original buildings have been demolished to make way for new ones in a much more sympathetic style – something we suggested over a decade ago. Across the valley are some of the best (and quietest) challenging pistes in the Three Valleys on the north-facing La Masse. Down the valley from Les Menuires is **St-Martin-de-Belleville**, a charming traditional village that has been

expanded sympathetically. It has good-value accommodation and lift links towards Les Menuires and Méribel.

Up rather than down the Belleville valley from Les Menuires, at 2300m/ 7,550ft, **Val Thorens** is the highest resort in the Alps, and at 3230m/ 10,600ft the top of its slopes is the high point of the Three Valleys. The snow in this area is almost always good, and it includes two glaciers where good snow is guaranteed. But the setting is bleak and the lifts are vulnerable to closure in bad weather. The purpose-built resort is very convenient. Visually it is not comparable to Les Menuires, thanks to the smaller-scale buildings and more traditional styles.

Méribel is a multi-part resort. The highest component, **Méribel-Mottaret**, is the best placed of all the resorts for getting to any part of the Three Valleys system in the shortest possible time. It's now quite a spread-out place, with some of the accommodation a long way up the hillsides – great for access to the slopes, less so for access to nightlife. **Méribel** itself is 200m/660ft lower and has long been a British favourite, especially for chalet holidays. It is the most attractive of

the main Three Valleys resorts, built in chalet style beside a long winding road up the hillside. Parts of the resort are very convenient for the slopes and the village centre; parts are very far from either. The growing hamlet of **Méribel-Village** has its own chairlift into the system but is very isolated and quiet. You can also stay below Méribel in the valley town of **Brides-les-Bains**, or in hamlets along the route of the gondola to Méribel.

Courchevel has four parts. 1850 is the most fashionable resort in France, and can be the most expensive resort in the Alps (though it doesn't have to cost a fortune to stay there). The less expensive parts – 1300 (Le Praz), 1550 and 1650 – don't have the same choice of nightlife and restaurants. Many people rate the slopes around Courchevel the best in the Three Valleys, with runs to suit all standards.

La Tania was built for the 1992 Olympics, just off the minor road linking Le Praz to Méribel. It has now grown into an attractive, car-free collection of chalets and chalet-style apartments set among the trees, and is popular with families. It has a good nursery slope and good intermediate runs in the woods above.

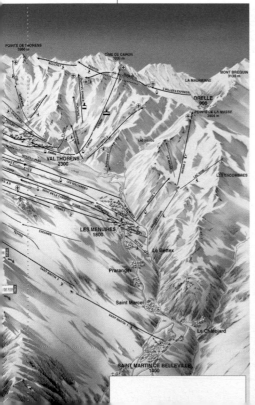

Tignes

Stark apartment blocks and a bleak, treeless setting are the prices you pay for the high, snow-sure slopes and varied terrain

£115
RESORT PRICE INDEX

RATINGS

The mountains
Extent	★★★★★
Fast lifts	★★★
Queues	★★★★
Terrain p'ks	★★★
Snow	★★★★★
Expert	★★★★★
Intermediate	★★★★★
Beginner	★★
X-country	★★★
Restaurants	★★★
Schools	★★★★
Families	★★★

The resort
Charm	★
Convenience	★★★★
Scenery	★★★
Eating out	★★★★
Après-ski	★★★
Off-slope	★

384

NEWS

For 2008/09 a six-pack replaced the Tufs chairlift from Val Claret to Tovière. Also in Val Claret, the Nevada 4-star hotel and spa resort opened. The terrain park was redesigned and a 'Shoot my Ride' scheme started where your run is filmed.

+ Good snow guaranteed for a long season – about the best Alpine bet

+ One of the best areas in the world for lift-served off-piste runs

+ Huge amount of varied terrain, with swift access to Val d'Isère

+ Lots of accommodation close to the slopes

+ Efforts to make the resort villages more welcoming are paying off

− Resort architecture not to everyone's taste (including ours)

− Bleak, treeless setting – many lifts prone to closure by storms

− Still a few long, slow chairlifts – though progress is being made

− You need an area pass to find long green runs

− Limited, but improving, après-ski

The appeal of Tignes is simple: good snow, spread over a wide area of varied terrain, shared with Val d'Isère. The altitude of Tignes is crucial: a forecast of 'rain up to 2000m' means 'fresh snow down to village level in Tignes'.

We prefer to stay in Val, which is a more human place. But in many ways Tignes makes the better base: appreciably higher, more convenient, surrounded by intermediate terrain, with quick access to the Grande Motte glacier. And the case gets stronger as results flow from Tignes' campaign to reinvent itself in a more cuddly form. The place is a lot less hostile to the visitor than it once was.

In the past few seasons the resort has also, at last, got around to installing some fast chairs on the western side of the Tignes bowl. But there are still a few key links that need upgrading.

THE RESORT

Tignes was created before the French discovered the benefits of making purpose-built resorts look acceptable. But things are improving, and the villages are gradually acquiring a more traditional look and feel.

Tignes-le-Lac is the hub of the resort, split into two sub resorts, Le Rosset and Le Bec-Rouge. It's at the point where these two meet – a snowy pedestrian area, with valley traffic now passing through a tunnel beneath – that the lifts are concentrated: a powerful gondola towards Tovière and Val d'Isère and a fast six-pack up the western slopes. There is also a suburb built on the lower slopes known as Les Almes. A nursery slope separates Le Rosset from the fourth component part, the group of apartment blocks called Le Lavachet, below which there are good fast lifts up both sides.

Val Claret is 2km/1 mile up the valley, beyond the lake. From there, fast chairs head up to the western slopes, towards Val d'Isère and to the Grande Motte. An underground funicular also accesses Grande Motte.

Beside the road along the valley to the lifts is a ribbon of development in traditional style, named Grande Motte (after the peak). Val Claret is built on two levels, which are linked by a couple of (unreliable) indoor elevators, stairs and by hazardous paths.

Down the valley from the main resort villages are two smaller places. Tignes-les-Boisses, quietly set in the

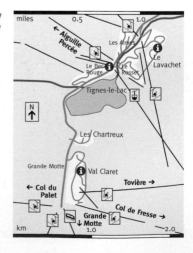

↑ Tignes-le-Lac in the valley on the left, Val Claret to the right. Great view of le-Lac's nursery slope and the steep black Trolles run coming down from Val d'Isère too

KEY FACTS

Resort	2100m
	6,890ft

Espace Killy	
Slopes	1550-3455m
	5,090-11,340ft
Lifts	89
Pistes	300km
	186 miles
Green	15%
Blue	40%
Red	28%
Black	17%
Snowmaking	
	692 guns

Tignes only	
Slopes	1550-3455m
	5,090-11,340ft
Lifts	47
Pistes	150km
	93 miles

trees beside the road up, consists of a barracks and a couple of simple hotels. Tignes-les-Brévières is a renovated old village at the lowest point of the slopes – a favourite lunch spot, and a friendly place to stay.

VILLAGE CHARM ★
Functional, not fancy
Some of Tignes-le-Lac's smaller buildings in the central part are being successfully revamped in chalet style. But the place as a whole is dreary, and the blocks overlooking the lake from Le Bec-Rouge will remain monstrous until the day they are demolished. But some attractive new buildings are being added both in the centre and on the fringes. The main part of Val Claret, Centre, is an uncompromisingly 1960s-style development on a shelf above the valley floor. So, if it's more charm you seek, try the lower villages.

CONVENIENCE ★★★★
Good all rounder
Location isn't crucial, as a regular free bus service connects all the villages until midnight – though in the daytime the route runs along the bottom of Val Claret, leaving residents of Val Claret Centre with a climb.

SCENERY ★★★
Great from the glacier
Tignes is in a high, bleak, treeless bowl; when the sun shines the rugged mountain terrain is splendid, especially from the glacial heights of the Grande Motte.

THE MOUNTAINS

The area's great weakness is that it can become unusable in bad weather. There are no woodland runs except immediately above Tignes-les-Boisses and Tignes-les-Brévières. Heavy snow produces widespread avalanche risk and wind closes the higher chairs.

Piste classification here is more reliable than in Val d'Isère ('excellent' says a 2009 visitor) and signposting is 'very clear'. But we've had complaints that lift and piste opening information is unreliable.

EXTENT OF THE SLOPES ★★★★★
High, snow-sure and varied
Tignes and Val d'Isère share a huge area of slopes known as L'Espace Killy. Locally, Tignes' biggest asset is the **Grande Motte** – and the runs from, as well as on, the glacier. The underground funicular from Val Claret whizzes you up to over 3000m/9,840ft in seven minutes. There are blue, red and black runs to play on up here, as well as beautiful long runs back to the resort.

The main lifts towards Val d'Isère are efficient: a high-capacity gondola from Le Lac to **Tovière**, and a fast chair with covers from Val Claret to **Col de Fresse**. You can head back to Tignes from either: the return from Tovière to Tignes-le-Lac is via a steep black run but there are easier blue runs to Val Claret.

Going up the opposite side of the valley takes you to a quieter area of

Interactive resort shortlist builder at **www.wtss.co.uk**

predominantly east-facing slopes split into two main sectors, linked in both directions – **Col du Palet** and **l'Aiguille Percée**. This whole mountainside has at last been given some of the fast lifts it has needed for years – there are five so far.

The Col des Ves chairlift, at the south end of the Col du Palet sector, serves one of the six 'naturides' (see 'For experts'). You can descend from l'Aiguille Percée to Tignes-les-Brévières on blue, red or black runs. There's an efficient gondola back, but the chairs above it are old and slow and need upgrading ('a quicker route back is the bus', says a reporter).

FAST LIFTS ★★★☆☆
Improved but not good enough
Fast chairs and gondolas get you up the mountain from most parts of the resort. Recent investment has added more fast chairs higher up too, but a few key slow ones remain that could do with being upgraded.

At the top, the best snow in Espace Killy. Lower down, the lovely red back to Val Claret can be very crowded – try the scenic Génépy blue alternative

The only run from Tovière to Tignes-le-Lac is a black, and the blue run to Val Claret gets very busy. Accessing Tignes from Col de Fresse is more relaxing

QUEUES ★★★★☆
Very few

The queues here depend on snow conditions. If snow low down is poor, the Grande Motte funicular generates queues; the fast chairs in parallel with it are often quicker, despite the longer ride time. These lifts jointly shift a lot of people, with the result that the red run down to Val Claret can be unpleasantly crowded (the roundabout Génépy blue is a much quieter option). The worst queues now are for the cable car on the glacier – half-hour waits are common. Of course, if higher lifts are closed by heavy snow or high winds, the lifts on the lower slopes have big queues. Otherwise there are usually few problems; crowded pistes are more of an issue.

TERRAIN PARKS ★★★☆☆
Vastly improved

Tignes was one of the first French resorts to build a terrain park but we've had some criticism of the park

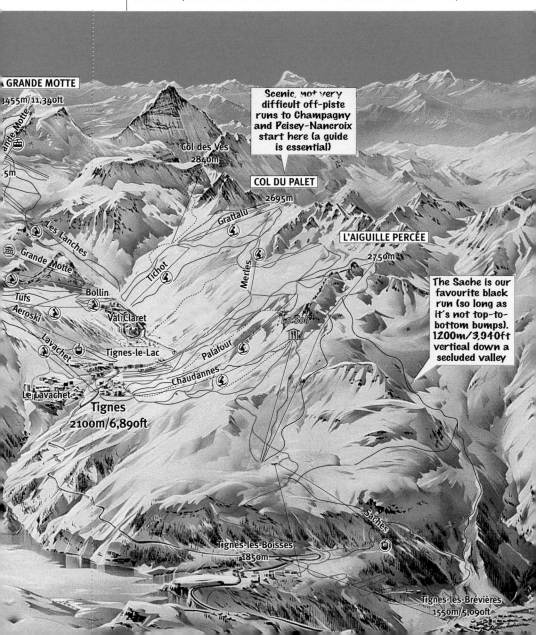

GRANDE MOTTE
3455m/11,340ft

Grande Motte

Les Lanches

Grande Motte

Tufs
Aeroski

Bollin

Lavachet

Tignes-le-Lac

Le Lavachet

Tignes
2100m/6,890ft

Col des Vés
2840m

COL DU PALET
2695m

Scenic, not very difficult off-piste runs to Champagny and Peisey-Nancroix start here (a guide is essential)

Grattalu

Tichot

Merles

Val Claret

Palafour

Chaudannes

L'AIGUILLE PERCÉE
2750m

Lo Soli

The Sache is our favourite black run (so long as it's not top-to-bottom bumps). 1200m/3,940ft vertical down a secluded valley

Saches

Tignes-les-Boisses
1850m

Tignes-les-Brévières
1550m/5,090ft

LIFT PASSES

Espace Killy

Prices in €

Age	1-day	6-day
under 14	35	167
14 to 64	44	209
over 65	35	167

Free under 5, over 75
Beginner five free lifts
Notes
Covers Tignes and Val d'Isère; half-day and pedestrian passes; family discounts; 5-day plus passes valid for one day in the Three Valleys, one day in Paradiski (La Plagne-Les Arcs)

Alternative passes
Tignes-only pass available

boarding

Tignes has always been a popular destination for snowboarders. Lots of easily accessible off-piste and the fact that it's cheaper than Val d'Isère are the main attractions, and quite a few top UK snowboarders make this their winter home. For those who buy the Espace Killy lift ticket, the backside of Col de Fresse in Val d'Isère is a natural playground. There are a few flat areas (avoid Génépy and Myrtilles), but the lift system relies more on chairs and gondolas than drags (though a long drag serves the boardercross area). There are long, wide pistes to blast down, such as Grattalu, Carline and Piste H, with acres of powder between them to play in. There are three specialist snowboard schools (Snocool, Surf Feeling and Alliance) and a snowboarder chalet (www.dragonlodge.com). Go to Snowpark-shop in Tignes-le-Lac for all your freestyle needs.

in the past. However, for 2008/09 Swatch started sponsoring it and the park (on Col du Palet above Val Claret) was completely redesigned with all levels in mind. A new 'Shoot my Ride' scheme was also started; your run is filmed and then played back on a giant screen at the bottom of the park. You can watch it later online. There's a boardercross too. Tignes also has a 120m/390ft long half-pipe, which is well shaped and a good size for those not comfortable with a super-pipe. It is right at the bottom of the mountain, which means if you have the energy to hike, you can ride it for free. In the summer the park doubles in size and moves up to the Grande Motte for freestyle camps. There's also a children's park in Le Lac.

SNOW RELIABILITY ★★★★★
Difficult to beat
Tignes has all-year-round runs (barring brief closures in spring or autumn) on its Grande Motte glacier. And the resort height of 2100m/6,890ft generally means good snow-cover right back to base for most of the long winter season – November to May. The west-facing runs down from Col de Fresse and Tovière to Val Claret suffer from the afternoon sun, although they now have serious snowmaking. Some of the lower east-facing and south-east-facing slopes on the other side of the valley can suffer late in the season, too. Grooming is 'excellent'.

FOR EXPERTS ★★★★★
An excellent choice
Tignes has converted six of its black runs into 'naturides', which means they are never groomed (a neat way of saving money!) but they are marked, patrolled and avalanche protected. Many of them are not especially steep (eg the Ves run – promoted from red

status and renamed after the local freeride hero Guerlain Chicherit). Perhaps the most serious challenge is the long black run from Tovière to Tignes-le-Lac, with steep, usually heavily mogulled sections (the top part, Pâquerettes, is now a naturide, but the bottom part, Trolles, is a normal black). Parts of this run get a lot of afternoon sun. Our favourite black run (still a 'normal' black) is the Sache, from l'Aiguille Percée down a secluded valley to Tignes-les-Brévières. It can become very heavily mogulled, especially at the bottom – you can avoid this section by taking the red (used to be blue) Arcosses piste option part-way down.

But it is the off-piste possibilities that make Tignes such a draw for experts. Go with one of the off-piste groups that the schools organise and you'll have a great time. See the feature box for a few of the options.

And the bizarre French form of heli-skiing is available: mountaintop drops are forbidden, but from Tovière you can ski down towards the Lac du Chevril to be retrieved by chopper.

FOR INTERMEDIATES ★★★★★
One of the best
For keen intermediate piste-bashers the Espace Killy is one of the top three or four areas in the world.

Tignes' local slopes are ideal intermediate terrain. The runs on the Grande Motte glacier nearly always have superb snow. The runs from the top of the cable car are bizarrely classified red and black, but they are wide and mostly easy on usually fabulous snow and could easily be blues. The Leisse run down to the chairlift is classified black and can get very mogulled but has good snow. The long red run all the way back to town is a delightful long cruise – though

SCHOOLS

ESF
t 0479 063028

Evolution 2
t 0479 063576

Snocool
t 0479 243094

333
t 0479 062088

Surf Feeling
t 0608 486430

Alliance
t 0645 120824
0844 484 9390 (UK)

New Generation
t 0479 01 03 18
www.skinewgen.com

Ali Ross Skiing Clinics
t 0479 400440

Classes (ESF prices)
6 half days: €140

Private lessons
From €42 for 1hr

GUIDES

Bureau des Guides
t 0479 064276

Tetra
t 0631 499275

often crowded. The roundabout blue (Génépy) is much gentler and quieter.

From Tovière, the blue 'H' run to Val Claret is an enjoyable cruise and generally well groomed. But again, it can get very crowded. There is lots to do on the other side of the valley and the runs down from l'Aiguille Percée to Tignes-les-Boisses and Tignes-les-Brévières are also scenic and fun. There are red and blue options as well as the beautiful Sache black run – adventurous intermediates shouldn't miss it. The runs from l'Aiguille Percée to Le Lac are gentle, wide blues.

FOR BEGINNERS ★★
Good nursery slopes, but...
The nursery slopes of Tignes-le-Lac and Le Lavachet (which meet at the top) are excellent – convenient, snow-sure, gentle, free of through-traffic and served by a slow chair and a drag. The ones at Val Claret are less appealing: an unpleasantly steep slope within the village served by a drag, and a less convenient slope served by the fast Bollin chair. All of these lifts are free.

Although there are some fairly easy blues on the west side of Tignes, for long green runs you have to go over to the Val d'Isère sector. You need an Espace Killy pass to use them, and to get back to Tignes you have a choice

between the blue run from Col de Fresse (which has a tricky start) or riding the gondola down from Tovière. And in poor weather, the high Tignes valley is an intimidatingly bleak place – enough to make any wavering beginner retreat to a bar with a book.

FOR CROSS-COUNTRY ★★★
Interesting variety
The Espace Killy has 44km/27miles of cross-country trails, including 20km/12 miles of tracks on the frozen Lac de Tignes, along the valley between Val Claret and Tignes-le-Lac, at Les Boisses and Les Brévières and up on the Grande Motte.

MOUNTAIN RESTAURANTS ★★★
A couple of good places
The mountain restaurants are not a highlight – a regular hazard of high, purpose-built resorts, where it's easy to go back to the village for lunch. **Editors' choice** Lo Soli (0479 060742) at the top of the Chaudannes chair is a clear favourite. The terrace shares with the adjacent self-service Alpage a superb view of the Grande Motte; a reporter endorses our opinion: 'excellent food, ambience and service; excellent gâteau d'agneau, Caesar salad and melt-in-the-mouth pot-au-feu'. The table-service bit of the

A MECCA FOR OFF-PISTE SKIERS

Tignes is renowned for offering some of the best lift-served off-piste skiing in the world. There is a tremendous choice, with runs to suit all levels, from intermediate skiers to fearless freeriders and off-piste experts. Here's just a small selection. Don't go without a guide.

*For a first experience of off-piste, **Lognan** is ideal. These slopes – down the mountainside between the pistes to Le Lac and the pistes to Val Claret – are broad and not very difficult.*

*One of our favourite routes is the **Tour de Pramecou**. After a few minutes' walking at the bottom of the Grande Motte glacier, you pass around a big rock called Pramecou. There is then a multitude of possibilities, varying in difficulty – so routes can be found for skiers of different abilities.*

***Petite Balme** is a run for good skiers only – access is easy but leads to quite challenging north-facing slopes in real high-mountain terrain, far from the pistes.*

*To ski **Oreilles de Mickey** (Mickey's Ears) you start from Tovière and walk north along the ridge to the peak of Lavachet, where you get a great view of Tignes. The descent involves three long couloirs, narrow and pretty steep, which bring you back to Le Lavachet.*

*The best place to find good snow is the **Chardonnet** couloirs – they never get the sun. The route involves a 20-minute walk from the top of the Merle Blanc chairlift.*

*The **Vallons de la Sache** is one of the most famous routes – a descent of 1200m/3,940ft vertical down a breathtaking valley in the heart of the National Park, overlooked by the magnificent Sache glacier. Starting from l'Aiguille Percée you enter a different world, high up in the mountains, far away from the ski lifts. You arrive down in Les Brévières, below the Tignes dam.*

*One of the big adventures is to go away from the Tignes ski area and all signs of civilisation, starting from the Col du Palet. From there you can head for **Champagny** (linked to La Plagne's area) or **Peisey-Nancroix** (linked to Les Arcs' area) – both very beautiful runs, and not too difficult.*

Weekly news updates and resort links at **www.wtss.co.uk**

Panoramic (0479 064721) at the top of the funicular competes; one regular reporter gives it the edge: 'a veritable joy – excellent rack of lamb, tiramisu'. **Worth knowing about** The atmospheric chalet at the top of Tovière is 'fairly basic' but does 'very good portions'. A reporter found the 'service just OK'. At the top of the Tichot chair from Val Claret, the Palet 'serves good food at good prices'. On the nursery slope above Val Claret, the 'expensive' Chalet du Bollin has been recommended for its 'casserole served from the pot and the portion is huge! Excellent'. The big Panoramic self-service at the top of the funicular gets crowded, but has great views from its huge terrace and 'good portions at reasonable prices'.

There are lots of easily accessible places for lunch in the resorts. One ski-to-the-door favourite of ours in Le Lac is the hotel Montana, on the left as you descend from l'Aiguille Percée. Another is La Ferme des 3 Capucines (see 'Eating out') a short walk down from the bottom of the Chaudannes and Paquis chairs. In Val Claret the Taverne des Neiges has 'good food and service' and Pignatta serves 'quality and value succulent pizzas'. In

Le Lac, the Arbina offers 'consistent high quality'.

At the extremity of the lift system, Les Brévières makes an obvious lunch stop. A short walk round the corner into the village brings you to places much cheaper than the two by the piste. Sachette, for example, is crammed with artefacts from mountain life and offers 'lots of good cheese dishes'. The Etoile des Neiges 'serves great, typical Savoyard food'.

SCHOOLS AND GUIDES ★★★★
Plenty of choice
There are over half-a-dozen schools, including three specialist snowboard schools, plus various independent instructors. A recent reporter recommends Ali Ross Skiing Clinics (pre-booking required) – 'a great character who achieved results'. Reporters advise that at busy times pre-booking is 'essential' for normal schools as well. ESF gets mixed reviews: one 2008 reporter tells of an instructor losing a pupil, who then had to find and fund his own way home from Val d'Isère, and all of those in this reporter's group who tried the ESF had 'bad experiences'. But one child was 'admirably looked after' and the instructor showed 'great professionalism and understanding'.

New Generation, a British-run school with branches in five other resorts, opened in Tignes last season. See the Courchevel, Méribel, Les Arcs and Val d'Isère chapters for glowing reports of their instruction.

Reports on Evolution 2 are generally positive for adult tuition. Members of a recent reporter's group were pleased with their progress and one took private lessons with an 'encouraging and very patient instructor'. The off-piste 'Tarentaise Tour' has also been praised ('a superb long day, with an enthusiastic guide'). But one visitor was 'very unhappy' with the children's lessons: 'The children changed level every class. At the end of one lesson, the class arrived back without our child – when asked where she was, the instructor said he simply didn't know. She returned later with another group.' The same reporter moved his children to the 333 school where 'the difference was dramatic – I would highly recommend them'.

BASS has 'excellent, small group clinics', and we have a glowing report

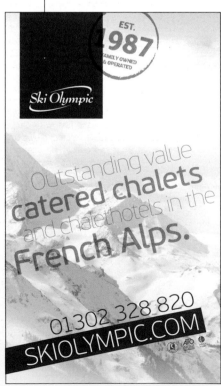

Tignes-le-Lac is a bit of an eyesore, especially when it's not covered in snow. But you come here for the great snow-sure slopes not the village charm →

OT TIGNES / MONICA DALMASSO

CHILDCARE

Les Marmottons
t 0479 065167
Ages 30mnth to 6yr

Ski schools
Evolution 2 takes children from age 5 and ESF takes children from age 4 (6 days €210)

GETTING THERE

Air Geneva 225km/140 miles (3hr30); Lyon 230km/145 miles (3hr15); Chambéry 145km/90 miles (2hr15)

Rail Bourg-St-Maurice (30km/19 miles); regular buses or taxi from station

ACTIVITIES

Indoor Wellness and fitness centres (pools, saunas, Turkish baths, hot tub, spa and beauty treatments, weight training), multi-sports hall, yoga, squash, climbing wall, library, bowling, heritage centre

Outdoor Dog sledding, mountaineering, ice climbing, ice driving, ice diving, ice rink, tobogganing, paragliding, skijoring, snowmobiling, snowshoeing, biking on snow, horse riding, helicopter flights

SMART LODGINGS

Check out our feature chapters at the front of the book.

of a British-run snowboarding outfit, Alliance: 'They teach with passion and enthusiasm; by far the best week's instruction I have received.'

FOR FAMILIES ★★★★★
Mixed reports
We have had good reports on the Marmottons kindergartens – 'brilliant' said a father of a four year old – and the Spritelets ski classes arranged by Esprit Ski and Evolution 2: 'She loved her class and could snowplough by the end of the week.' But we've also received a poor report for Evolution 2 (see 'Schools').

STAYING THERE

All three main styles of accommodation are available through tour operators. More luxury options are appearing.

Chalets The choice of catered chalets is increasing. Ski Total have several smart chalets, including some with pool, hot tub and sauna. Total's Chalet Arctik is 'excellent, comfortable', with pool and sauna. Family specialist Esprit has a chalet hotel and several chalets here, including the smart new Corniche with sauna, steam and hot tub for this season. Ski Olympic's chalet hotel Rosset and chalet Madeleine have been recommended by reporters; their other chalets look good too. Mark Warner has two chalet hotels, one with an outdoor pool.

Hotels The few hotels are small and concentrated in Le Lac.

***Campanules** (0479 063436) Smartly rustic chalet in upper Le Lac, with good restaurant. One reporter was impressed enough to suggest that it deserved a 4-star rating.

***Village Montana** (0479 400144) Stylishly woody, on the east-facing slopes above Le Lac, with a 4-star suites section. Outdoor pool, sauna, steam, hot tub.

***Lévanna** (0479 063294) Central in Le Lac – comfortable, with a 'generous hot tub'; a reporter found 'friendly staff but a woeful lack of them'.

***Diva** (0479 067000) Biggest in town (121 rooms). On lower level of Val Claret, a short walk from lifts. 'Very comfy rooms, excellent meals.' Recommended again in 2008. Sauna.

Arbina (0479 063478) Well-run place close to the lifts in Le Lac, with lunchtime terrace, crowded après-ski bar and one of the best restaurants.

Marais (0479 064006) Prettily furnished, simple hotel in Les Boisses.

Génépy (0479 065711) Simple Dutch-run chalet in Les Brévières.

Apartments There are lots of apartments in all price ranges. Erna Low and Ski Collection have some good-looking options and Leisure Direction and Ski Amis do self-catered places here too. The growing number of smart places include the Ecrin des Neiges, Ferme du Val Claret and Nevada in Val Claret and Telemark and Residence Village Montana in Le Lac. In Les Brévières, the Belvedere has very smart large apartments and chalets with three to six bedrooms. All the above have access to pool, sauna etc, but at extra cost in some cases.

UK PACKAGES

Action Outdoors, Alpine Answers, Chalet Group, Club Med, Crystal, Crystal Finest, Directski.com, Erna Low, Esprit, First Choice, Friendship Travel, Independent Ski Links, Inghams, Inspired to Ski, Interactive Resorts, Interhome, Kuoni, Lagrange, Leisure Direction, Made to Measure, Mark Warner, Mountainsun, Neilson, Oxford Ski Co, Peak Retreats, PV-Hollidays. com, Simply Alpine, Ski Activity, Ski Amis, Ski Collection, Ski Expectations, Ski France, Ski Freshtracks, Skiholidayextras.com, Ski Independence, Ski Line, Ski McNeill, Ski Olympic, Ski Solutions, Ski Supreme, Ski Total, Skitracer, Skiworld, Snow Finders, Snoworks, Snowpod, Snowstar, Thomson, UCPA

Phone numbers
From abroad use the prefix +33 and omit the initial '0' of the phone number

TOURIST OFFICE

t 0479 400440
information@tignes.
net
www.tignes.net

The Chalet Club in Val Claret is a collection of simple studios, but it has a free indoor pool, sauna and in-house restaurant and bar.

Alpservice specialises in cheap accommodation for young people who want to spend the season – or at least several weeks – in a resort.

The supermarket at Le Lac is reported to be 'comprehensive but very expensive'.

EATING OUT ★★★★
Good places scattered about

The options in Le Lavachet are rather limited, though a recent reporter enjoyed the Grenier with its 'excellent cold meats and tartiflette' and another the 'novel experience' of eating with over-wintering farm animals on display through a viewing window at the 'atmospheric' Ferme des 3 Capucines (we had a good lunch here in 2009 too). And we have very positive reports of the British-run Brasero: 'This restaurant is establishing a good reputation in Tignes; the food was quite simply excellent. We were made to feel very welcome.' Finding anywhere with some atmosphere is difficult in Le Lac, though the food in some of the better hotels is good. The Campanules has 'exemplary service', but the food 'wasn't as memorable as on other occasions', says a regular visitor. The Arbina continues to provide 'outstanding food, very good value and first-class service'. The Escale Blanche is almost as popular. Two visitors recommend the 'delicious food' at the 'quirky' Clin d'Oeil. Bagus Cafe's 'eclectic cuisine' is also praised. One visitor particularly highlights the Monday champagne nights at the Alpaka Lodge – 'a relaxed restaurant with duck breast the star attraction'. A recent visitor enjoyed 'traditional food' at the Eterlou.

In Val Claret the Caveau is

recommended for a special treat – 'superbly presented food and good service in an intimate cellar setting'. The Petit Savoyard 'is friendly with efficient service'. The buffet at the Indochine has been strongly recommended by several reporters. Pepe 2000 has 'reasonable prices and helpful staff', but a reporter says the Pignatta 'slightly trumps it' and is enjoyable at lunchtime too – one reporter's group 'savoured really tasty meals'. The Auberge des 3 Oursons was recommended for 'massive portions, friendly service'.

The Cordée in Les Boisses offers unpretentious surroundings, good traditional French food, modest prices.

APRES-SKI ★★★
Hidden away

Reporters agree that there is plenty going on if you know where to find it. Val Claret has some early-evening atmosphere, and happy hours are popular. Reporters differ on the merits of the Crowded House (popular with Brits). Grizzly's is 'cosy and atmospheric, but you pay for the ambience'. The 'whisky lounge' in the Couloir is a 'great place to relax'.

Le Lac is a natural focus for immediate après-ski drinks. The 'lively' Loop, with pool table, has a 'two for one' happy hour from 4 to 6pm. The bar of the hotel Arbina is our kind of spot – adequately cosy, friendly service. It's a great place to sit outside and people-watch. The Alpaka Cocktail Bar is 'hard to leave', 'a real gem later on'. TC's bar is 'very friendly, with good music'. Jack's is a popular late haunt.

OFF THE SLOPES ★
Forget it

Despite the range of alternative activities, Tignes is a resort for those who want to use the slopes, where anyone who doesn't is liable to feel like a fish out of water. Some activities do get booked up quickly as well – a reporter said it was impossible to find a free dog sledding slot in April. The ice skating on the lake includes a 500m/1,640ft circuit as well as a conventional rink. There's ice driving at Les Brévières. The Lagon leisure centre, with various pools, slides, wellness and fitness facilities, meets with readers' approval and a 2009 visitor's kids 'really enjoyed the bowling alley' at Tignes le Lac.

Val d'Isère

One of the great high mega-resorts, particularly (though not only) for experts – with a very attractive town at the base

£125
RESORT PRICE INDEX

RATINGS

The mountains

Extent	★★★★★
Fast lifts	★★★★
Queues	★★★★
Terrain p'ks	★★★
Snow	★★★★★
Expert	★★★★★
Intermediate	★★★★★
Beginner	★★★
X-country	★
Restaurants	★★★
Schools	★★★★★
Families	★★★★

The resort

Charm	★★★
Convenience	★★★
Scenery	★★★
Eating out	★★★★★
Après-ski	★★★★
Off-slope	★★

NEWS

For 2009/10 a big new sports centre is due to open with a pool, kids' pool, climbing area, sports hall, squash courts, sauna, steam, hot tub etc.

For 2008/09, a six-pack replaced the triple Marmottes chair up to Bellevarde from above La Daille. This ends near the top of the Olympique gondola (so it's now easy to ride the gondola down at the end of the day).

- ➕ Huge area shared with Tignes, with lots of runs for all abilities
- ➕ One of the great resorts for lift-served off-piste runs
- ➕ Once the snow has fallen, high altitude of slopes keeps it good
- ➕ Wide choice of schools, especially for off-piste lessons and guiding
- ➕ For a high Alpine resort, the town is attractive, very lively at night, and offers a good range of restaurants
- ➕ Wide range of package holidays – including very swanky chalets

- ➖ Some green and blue runs are too challenging, and all runs back to the village are tricky
- ➖ You're quite likely to need the bus at the start and end of the day
- ➖ Most lifts and slopes are liable to close when the weather is bad
- ➖ At times seems more British than French – especially in low season
- ➖ Increasingly pricey – among the most expensive in our eating and drinking price survey

Val d'Isère is one of the world's best resorts for experts – attracted by the extent of lift-served off-piste – and for confident, mileage-hungry intermediates. You don't have to be particularly adventurous to enjoy the resort; but it would be much better for novices if the piste classifications were more reliable.

The drawbacks listed above are mainly not serious complaints, whereas most of the plus-points weigh heavily in the balance. For a combination of seriously impressive skiing and captivating village ambience, there aren't many places we'd rather go – especially if we're looking for a luxurious chalet.

THE RESORT

Val d'Isère spreads along a remote valley, which is a dead end in winter. The road in from Bourg-St-Maurice brings you dramatically through a rocky defile to La Daille – a convenient but hideous slope-side apartment complex and the base of lifts into the major Bellevarde sector of the slopes.

Turn right at the centre and you drive under the nursery slopes and chairlifts and a jumbo gondola up the mountains to a lot of new development. Continue up the main valley instead, and you come to Le Laisinant, a peaceful little outpost with a fast lift out of the valley, and then to Le Fornet, the fourth major lift station.

The developments up the side valley beyond the main lift station – in Le Châtelard and La Legettaz – are mainly attractive, and some offer ski-in/ski-out convenience. La Daille and Le Fornet have their (quite different) attractions for those less concerned about nightlife. A car is of no great value around the resort. The supermarkets have been praised for 'enticing pre-cooked food'.

VILLAGE CHARM ★★★
Developing nicely

The outskirts of Val proper are dreary, but as you approach the centre the improvements put in place over the last 15 years become evident: wood- and stone-cladding, culminating in the tasteful pedestrian-only Val Village complex. Many first-time visitors find the resort much more pleasant than they expect a high French resort to be.

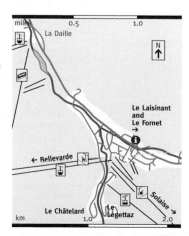

↑ Val d'Isère-Tignes is one of the best ski areas in the world for lift-served off-piste

Weekly news updates and resort links at **www.wtss.co.uk**

CONVENIENCE ★★★
Mostly fine

There is a lot of traffic around, but the resort has worked hard to get cars under control and has made the centre more pedestrian-friendly. The location of your accommodation isn't crucial, unless you want to ski from the door or be close to a nursery slope. The main lift stations are served by very efficient free shuttle-buses; in peak periods you never have to wait more than a few minutes. But in the evening frequency plummets and dedicated après-skiers will want to be within walking distance of the centre.

SCENERY ★★★
Valley deep, mountain high

The resort sprawls along a steep-sided river valley, beneath a series of high and partly-wooded mountain ridges. There are splendid views from the Pissaillas glacier.

THE MOUNTAIN

Although there are wooded slopes above the village on all sectors, in practice most of the runs here are on open slopes above the treeline, and a lot of lifts can close in bad weather. Several 2009 visitors confirm that piste grooming is good, but we still get complaints about poor signing (especially at piste junctions). And Val d'Isère vies with St Anton for the title of 'resort with most underclassified slopes'. Many blue and some green runs (including runs to the valley) are

simply too steep, narrow and even bumpy; in other resorts they would be reds, or even blacks. We are pleased to see that some pistes have recently been reclassified but more need to be.

The local radio carries weather reports in English as well as in French.

EXTENT OF THE SLOPES ★★★★★
Vast and varied

Val d'Isère's slopes divide into three main sectors, two reachable from the village. **Bellevarde** is the mountain that is home to Val d'Isère's two famous downhill courses: the OK piste that is used for the World Cup every December and the Face piste that was used for the 1992 Winter Olympics and the 2009 World Championships. You can reach Bellevarde quickly by underground funicular from La Daille or the powerful Olympique gondola from near the centre of town. From the top you can descend to the valley, play on a variety of drags and chairs at altitude or take a choice of lifts to Tignes's slopes (see separate chapter).

Solaise is the other mountain accessible directly from the village. The Solaise fast quad takes you a few metres higher than the parallel cable car. Once up, a short drag or rope tow takes you over a plateau and down to a variety of chairs that serve this very sunny area of predominantly gentle pistes. From near the top of this area you can catch the fast Leissières chair (which climbs over a ridge and down the other side) to the third main area, in the valley running up to the **Col de**

l'Iseran. This area can also be reached by the fast chair from Le Laisinant or by cable car from Le Fornet. At the top here is the **Glacier de Pissaillas**.

FAST LIFTS ★★★★
Access all areas
High capacity lifts provide good access from the valley and there are lots of fast chairs higher up. But there are still a few slow chairs and draglifts around.

QUEUES ★★★★
Few problems
Queues to get out of the resort have been kept in check by lift upgrades and additions. At Solaise the slow Lac chair up to the Tête Solaise can generate queues, but a recent reporter praises 'the good queueing systems with each chair filled to capacity'. Crowded pistes in high season is a more common complaint than queues.

TERRAIN PARKS ★★★
Beginners and experts welcome
Above the La Daille gondola and served by the Mont Blanc chairlift lies the very good DC terrain park (www.valdiserevalpark.com). Maintenance can be a bit hit or miss, but on a good day this park has a bit of everything. There are four kicker lines, with jumps ranging from 3m/10ft in the blue line to 20m/66ft in the pro line.

With more and more earth-work being done during the summer to pre-shape jumps, there are now up to five jumps in a row on some of the lines. The large hip is a main attraction of the park and 18 new rails and a 3m/10ft wall ride appeared for 2008/09, encasing a somewhat cramped park in a shroud of metal. Head over to Tignes for a nice half-pipe.

SNOW RELIABILITY ★★★★★
One of the best
In years when lower resorts have suffered, Val d'Isère has rarely been short of snow. Once a big dump of snow has fallen, the resort's height means you can almost always get back to the village. But even more important is that in each sector there are lots of lifts and runs above mid-mountain, between about 2300m and 2900m (7,550ft and 9,510ft). Many of the slopes face roughly north. And there is access to glaciers at Pissaillas or over in Tignes, although both take a while to get to.

FOR EXPERTS ★★★★★
One of the world's best
Val d'Isère is one of the top resorts in the world for experts. The main attraction is the huge range of beautiful off-piste possibilities – see the feature panel below.

THE BEST LIFT-SERVED OFF-PISTE IN THE WORLD?

Few resorts can rival the extent of lift-served off-piste skiing in Val d'Isère. Here is a selection of what's on offer. But don't try any of it without a guide and essential safety equipment.

Some runs are ideal for adventurous intermediates looking to try off-piste for the first time. The **Tour du Charvet** *goes through glorious scenery from the top of the Grand Pré chairlift on the back of Bellevarde. For most of the way it is very gentle, with only a few steeper pitches. It ends up at the bottom of the Manchet chair up to the Solaise area. The* **Pays Désert** *is an easy run with superb views on the Pissaillas glacier, high above Le Fornet and reached by traversing away from the pistes above cliffs from the top of the lift system. You end up at the Pays Désert T-bar.*

For more experienced off-piste skiers, **Col Pers** *is one of our favourite runs. Again, it starts a traverse from the Pissaillas glacier. You go over a pass into a big, fairly gentle bowl with glorious views and endless ways down. If there is enough snow, you drop down into the Gorges de Malpasset and ski over the frozen Isère river back to the Fornet cable car. If not, you can take a higher route.*

Cugnai *is a wide, secluded bowl reached from the chair of the same name at the top of the Solaise sector. A steep (37 degree) slope at the far end descends beneath a sheer black rock wall and then narrows into a gulley to the valley floor, leading to the Manchet chair.*

Banane *is reached via the Face de Bellevarde piste and is a long and impressive run (37 to 40 degrees) with spectacular views over the Manchet valley. For a real challenge intrepid experts should try the* **Couloir des Pisteurs,** *which requires a 20-minute climb from the Tour de Charvet. The view from the top is simply stunning. A very narrow steep couloir (44 degrees) bounded by rock faces brings you out on to a wide open slope above Le Grand Pré, right opposite Bellevarde.*

Then there's the whole of Tignes' extensive off-piste to explore of course.

Col Pers – one of our favourite off-piste runs, from the glacier down to Le Fornet

Worth getting up here for the snow and the views

3300m/10,830ft

GLACIER DE PISSAILLAS

Cascade

COL DE L'ISERAN
2765m

2900m

2950m

Cugnai

Leissières

Vallon de l'Iseran

Pyramides

Glacier

Madeleine

Manche

2325m

Fornet

Edelweiss

Laisinant

SOLAISE
2560m

Le Fornet
1930m

Good shady red run served by the Laisinant fast chair

No easy way back to the village from Solaise

Solaise

Le Châtelard

Le Laisinant

Bel

Val d'Isère
1850m/6,070ft

E PISSAILLAS

COL DE
'ISERAN
2765m

Good area of varied intermediate runs at altitude, with a couple of fast chairs

2900m

Cugnai

Leisseres

Glacier

Madeleine

Manchet

Excellent runs down to the Manchet chair – though affected by sun later in the season

Le Manchet
1940m

Grand Pte

BELLEVARDE
2705m

Marmottes

Lots of long, high easy runs – but also lots of slow old lifts

The blue from here is the easiest and least crowded intermediate route to Tignes

COL DE FRESSE
2770m

Borsat

Glacier de la Grande Motte

Tignes
Fresse

TOVIERE
2705m

Tommeuses

LAISE
6om

Le Châtelard

Loyes

L'Olympique

Solaise

Bellevarde

Fruitière

The world's trickiest green run – narrow in parts and crowded and mogulled at the end of the day

Val d'Isère
85om/6,07oft

Funival

Daille

The 1992 Winter Olympic men's downhill course is now a genuine black run and often mogulled from top to bottom

La Daille
1785m/5,86oft

SCHOOLS

Alpine Expérience
t 0479 062881

BASS
t 0679 512405

DC
t 0479 220263

Development Centre (TDC)
t 0615 553156

ESF
t 0479 060234

Evolution 2
t 0479 411672

Misty Fly Snocool
t 0479 243094

Mountain Masters
t 0479 060514

New Generation
t 0479 010318
www.skinewgen.com

Ogier
t 0479 061893

Oxygène
t 0479 419958

Progression
t 0621 939380

Ski Concept
t 0479 401919

Ski-lesson.com
t 0621 652944

Snow Fun
t 0479 061979

Top Ski
t 0479 061480

Val Gliss
t 0479 060072

Classes (ESF prices)
6 days (3hr am, 2½hr pm) €378

Private lessons
From €42 for 1hr

GUIDES

Mountain guides
t 0687 528503

Tetra
t 0479 499275

boarding

Val d'Isère's more upmarket profile attracts a different kind of holiday boarder from Tignes; the resort is, perhaps, seen as Tignes' less hard core cousin. But the terrain here is phenomenal and still draws a fair few boarders. The easier slopes are suitable for beginners, and there are now very few draglifts. But there are quite a few flat areas where you'll end up scooting or walking. There is a very good terrain park and a boardercross is on the cards for 2009/10. Specialist snowboard shops are Misty Fly and Quiksilver Boardriders. Check your email and have a coffee at the snowboarder-run Powder Monkey internet cafe.

There may be better resorts for really steep pistes – there are certainly lots in North America – but there is plenty of on-piste action to amuse most experts, despite the small number of blacks on the piste map. Many reds and blues are steep enough to get mogulled.

On Bellevarde the famous Face run is the main attraction – often mogulled from top to bottom, but not worryingly steep. Epaule is the sector's other black run – where the moguls are hit by long exposure to sun and can be slushy or rock hard (it is prone to closure for these reasons too). There are several challenging ways down from Solaise to the village: all steep, though none fearsomely so (Piste S is now classified a 'Naturide' – which means it is never groomed).

Wayne Watson of off-piste school Alpine Expérience puts a daily diary of off-piste snow conditions and runs on the web at www.alpineexperience.com.

FOR INTERMEDIATES ★★★★★
Quantity and quality

Val d'Isère has just as much to offer intermediates as experts. There's enough here to keep you interested for several visits – though pistes can be crowded in high-season, and the less experienced should be aware that many runs are under-classified.

In the Solaise sector is a network of gentle blue runs, ideal for building confidence. And there are a couple of beautiful runs from here through the woods to Le Laisinant – ideal in bad weather, though prone to closure in times of avalanche danger.

Most of the runs in the Col de l'Iseran sector are even easier – ideal for early and hesitant intermediates. Those marked blue at the top of the glacier could really be classified green.

Bellevarde has a huge variety of runs ideally suited to intermediates of all levels. From Bellevarde itself there is a choice of green, blue and red runs

of varying pitch. The World Cup Downhill OK piste is a wonderful rolling cruise when groomed. The wide runs from Tovière normally offer the choice of groomed piste or moguls.

A snag for early intermediates is that runs back to the valley can be challenging. The easiest way is down to La Daille on a green run which would be classified blue or red in most resorts. It gets very crowded and mogulled by the end of the day. None of the runs from Bellevarde and Solaise back to Val itself is easy. Many early intermediates ride the lifts down.

FOR BEGINNERS ★★★
OK if you know where to go

The nursery slope right by the centre of town is 95% perfect; it's just a pity that the very top is unpleasantly steep. The lifts serving it are free.

Once off the nursery slopes, you have to know where to find easy runs; many of the greens should be blue, or even red. One local instructor admits: 'We have to have green runs on the map, even if we don't have so many green slopes – otherwise beginners wouldn't come to Val d'Isère.'

A good place for your first real runs off the nursery slopes is the Madeleine green run on Solaise – served by a six-pack. The Col de l'Iseran runs are also gentle and wide, and not overcrowded. There is good progression terrain on Bellevarde, too – though getting to it can be tricky. From all sectors, it's best to take a lift back down to the valley.

FOR CROSS-COUNTRY ★
Limited

There are a couple of loops in each of three areas – towards La Daille, on Solaise and out past Le Laisinant. More picturesque is the one going from Le Châtelard (on the road past the main cable car station) to the Manchet chair. But keen cross-country enthusiasts should go elsewhere.

MOUNTAIN RESTAURANTS ★★★★★
Acceptable – at long last

It's been a long, slow business, but three editions ago Val eventually managed a three-star rating for mountain restaurants, which mainly consist of big self-service places at the top of major lifts. There are now more exceptions – but they are too few, so they are too busy, so high-season service can be poor. And many are pricey, as you can see by Val d'Isère's position near the top of our resort price index – only Courchevel is pricier.

Editors' choice The wood-and-stone Edelweiss (0610 287064), above Le Fornet, is our current favourite for the best food. We've had delicious lamb, duck and fish there; reporters also send us rave reviews. The Fruitière (0479 060717) at the top of La Daille gondola, kitted out with stuff rescued from a dairy in the valley, crams in way too many people but handles them well. We had a good lunch here, and a 2009 visitor found it 'one of the best mountain restaurants we've eaten in – big portions, I recommend their duck shepherd's pie and beef stew'.

Worth knowing about The busy table-service Trifollet halfway down the OK run 'always has a good plat du jour'. On the lower slopes at La Daille, and reachable by pedestrians, Tufs serves good food. The Marmottes, in the middle of the Bellevarde bowl, is one of the cheapest places to eat – an efficient self-service with a big sunny terrace and good food ('decent goulash and spag bol without requiring a second mortgage'). And the Tanière (popular with locals) set between the two chairs going up Face de Bellevarde has been recommended.

On Solaise, the small and friendly Bar de L'Ouillette, at the base of the Madeleine chairlift, does good food at reasonable prices. La Datcha at the bottom of the Glacier Express has a small table-service section ('succulent slow-cooked lamb'). The Clochetons, in the Manchet valley, has excellent food and is a good place to meet up with walkers or cross-country skiers.

The Signal at the top of the cable car from Le Fornet has self- and table-service sections ('nice atmosphere, sensational food, free genepis'.

Val d'Isère

399

Interactive resort shortlist builder at **www.wtss.co.uk**

Of course there are lots of places in the resort villages. Arolay at Le Fornet is 'excellent for both lunch and dinner, with a lovely terrace'. The terrace of hotel Brussel's in Val d'Isère, right by the nursery slopes, has 'good food and excellent service' and the Grand Paradis, next door, is 'an enjoyable lunch venue, very well run and efficient'. The Gourmandine serves 'very good lunches and is popular with locals'. The Sun Bar at the base of the Olympique cable car is 'surprisingly good value'. Apart from prices, reporters' main gripe has been having to pay to use the loos in many mountain restaurants, regardless of being a patron or not.

SCHOOLS AND GUIDES ★★★★★
A very wide choice
There is a huge choice of schools, guides and private instructors. But as they all get busy, at peak periods it's best to book in advance. Practically all the schools run off-piste groups at various levels of competence, as well as on-piste lessons. A 2009 visitor had 'a great time' with her off-piste ESF group: 'our instructor spoke good English, was safety conscious, found

lots of interesting and challenging skiing and provided useful coaching tips'.

New Generation, a British-run school, has a branch here. Reports are very positive: 'the morning we had was one of the highlights of our holiday – lots of fun and we learned a lot too'; 'worth every euro; they managed to find fresh powder wherever we went'. The Development Centre, based in the Precision Ski shop in the heart of the village, is a group of British instructors who offer intensive clinics for all levels of skier, and have been highly praised: 'simply excellent, small classes of three or four and really good value'.

Mountain Masters is a group of British and French instructors and guides, and a reporter said: 'They knew exactly how to take me over that seventh-week plateau.' Progression is a newish British-run school with a maximum group size of 6 or 8: 'great progress in the space of one lesson'.

We've heard from lots of satisfied pupils of Snow Fun ('good value and good instructors', 'coped well with a range of abilities') and Evolution 2 ('turned the corner from beginner to

AGENCE NUTS / JP NOISILLIER / OT VAL D'ISERE

The village sprawls along the valley beneath its three impressive linked sectors of slopes ↘

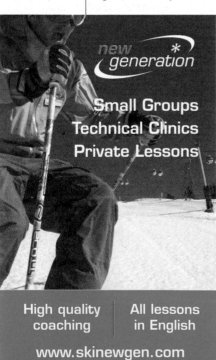

CHILDCARE

Le Village des Enfants
t 0479 400981
Ages 3 to 13

Le Petit Poucet
t 0479 061397
Ages from 3; 9am-
3.30

Babysitter list
Contact tourist office

Ski schools
Most offer classes for
ages 5 up (ESF prices
€378 for 6 days)

GETTING THERE

Air Geneva 230km/
145 miles (3hr30);
Lyon 240km/
150 miles (3hr15);
Chambéry 145km/
90 miles (2hr15)

Rail Bourg-St-Maurice
(30km/19 miles);
regular buses from
station

intermediate in 90 minutes'). Reporters consistently praise Bernard Chesneau of Ski Mastery. Misty Fly is a specialist snowboard school. Private lessons with BASS were 'the best any of us have ever had'.

Alpine Expérience and Top Ski specialise in guided off-piste groups – an excellent way to get off-piste safely without the cost of hiring a guide as an individual. We have had great mornings out with both. A reporter says of Alpine Expérience: 'We had great days with them, including our first experience of putting on skins to make some fresh tracks.' And a 2009 visitor 'highly recommends Top Ski and had 'a great tour with a fun and very attentive guide'. Heli-skiing trips can be arranged from over the border in Italy – heli-drops are banned in France. Henry's Avalanche Talk at Dick's Tea Bar (every Tuesday and Thursday evening) was 'very engaging and interesting', says a reporter.

FOR FAMILIES ★★★★
Good tour op possibilities
Many people prefer to use the facilities of UK tour operators such as Esprit, Ski Beat or Mark Warner. But there's a 'children's village' for three to eight year olds, with supervised indoor and outdoor activities on the village nursery slopes. A reporter was 'very pleased' with the childcare there: 'The staff speak English and are very organised, in particular about safety.'

STAYING THERE

More British tour operators go to Val (and Méribel) than anywhere else. Val d'Isère à la Carte specialises in arranging tailor-made holidays there.
Chalets This is Planet Chalet, with properties at every level of the market. Many of the most impressive are in the side valley running south from the

village – some in the elevated enclave of Les Carats. YSE is a Val d'Isère specialist, with 21 varied chalets – from swanky apartments for four or six to proper big chalets. VIP has 14 very smart chalets including the beautiful old Farmhouse, plus 12 chalet-apartments in Aspen Lodge in the centre of town with its own hotel-style reception. Le Ski has nine chalets, including six splendid all-en-suite places grouped together just up from the main street (with a big outdoor hot tub) and two swanky chalets for eight nearby (which share another outdoor hot tub). Snowline has half a dozen good-looking chalets. Ski Total has several very smart places, including a couple with sauna, steam room or pool. Ski Beat has five en-suite apartments in one grand chalet at La Daille. Finlays has nine chalets plus a self-catered apartment. There are several chalet hotels. Mark Warner has three: the family-friendly Cygnaski, the nightlife hot spot Moris and the central Val d'Isère with outdoor swimming pool. Total has the modern Champs Avalins at La Daille. Esprit, the family specialist, has the Ducs de Savoie and another large chalet André near the centre.
Hotels There are over 30 to choose from and they have moved distinctly up-market in the past few years; there are now two luxury 4-stars and six plush 4-stars (but there are plenty of 2- and 3 stars too).
★★★★**Barmes de L'Ours** (0479 413700) The best in town. Good position, close to slopes and centre. The fabulous rooms are in a different style on each floor. Three restaurants, Excellent indoor pool, and sauna.
★★★★**Savoie** (0479 000115) Luxury. Completely rebuilt. Central. Smart spa.
★★★★**Christiania** (0479 060825) Big chalet. Chic but friendly. Pool, sauna.
★★★★**Blizzard** (0479 060207)

ACTIVITIES

Indoor New sports centre (see 'News'), cinema, fitness and health clubs, yoga, bridge, chess

Outdoor Ice rink, walking, snowshoeing, snowmobiles, ice climbing, dog sledding, ice driving, paragliding, microlight flights, helicopter flights, igloo evenings

SMART LODGINGS

Check out our feature chapters at the front of the book.

Comfortable. Convenient. Indoor-outdoor pool and sauna. Good food.
****Aigle des Neiges (0479 061888) Highly rated refurbished version of former Latitudes. Cool and central. Sauna.
****Brussel's (0479 060539) Excellent location, right on nursery slope, with big terrace. Sauna, steam, hot tub.
****Tsanteleina (0479 061213) On the main road. 'Courteous staff, welcoming bar area, but not outstanding food.'
***Savoyarde (0479 060155) Rustic decor. Leisure centre. Good food (except for vegetarians). Small rooms.
***Grand Paradis (0479 061173) Next to Brussel's. Good food.
***Kandahar (0479 060239) Smart, newish building above Taverne d'Alsace on main street.
***Mercure (0479 061293) 'The food and wine list are excellent.' 'Convenient and pleasant.'
***Sorbiers (0479 062377) Modern but cosy chalet hotel, not far out. 'Clean, comfortable, good-sized rooms.'
***Samovar (0479 061351) In La Daille. Traditional, with good food.

'Very friendly and helpful staff.'
**Danival (0479 060065) B&B, piste-side location. 'Very reasonable.'
**Galise (0479 060504) Central, family-run. 'Comfortable, clean and quiet rooms.'
Apartments There are thousands of apartments available. Among the best are Chalets de Solaise (with outdoor pool) and Alpina Lodge close to the centre, Chalets du Jardin Alpin at the foot of Solaise and Chalets du Laisinant (at Laisinant). Erna Low, Ski Amis, Ski Independence, Ski Collection and local agency Val d'Isère Agence (0479 067350) have good selections. Alpservice specialise in cheap accommodation for young people who want to spend the season – or at least several weeks – in a resort.

EATING OUT ★★★★★
Plenty of good places
The 70-odd restaurants offer a wide variety of cuisines; there's a free *Guide des Tables* booklet covering 23, but many worthwhile places are missing.

The Grande Ourse, by the nursery slope, is one place to head for a top-

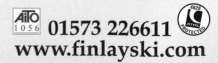

UK PACKAGES

Action Outdoors, Alpine Answers, Alpine Weekends, Chardon Mountain Lodges, Club Med, Crystal, Crystal Finest, Descent International, Directski. com, Elegant Resorts, Erna Low, Esprit, Finlays, First Choice, Flexiski, Friendship Travel, Independent Ski Links, Inghams, Inspired to Ski, Interactive Resorts, Interhome, Jeffersons, Kuoni, Lagrange, Le Ski, Leisure Direction, Made to Measure, Mark Warner, Momentum, Neilson, Oxford Ski Co, Powder White, PV-Holidays.com, Scott Dunn, Silver Ski, Simply Alpine, Ski Activity, Ski Amis, Ski Beat, Ski Collection, Ski Expectations, Ski France, Ski Freshtracks, Skiholidayextras.com, Ski Independence, Ski Line, Ski McNeill, Ski Power, Ski Solutions, Ski Supreme, Ski Total, Skitracer, Ski-Val, Ski Weekend, Skiworld, Snow Finders, Snowline, Snoworks, Supertravel, Thomson, Val d'Isère A La Carte, VIP, White Roc, YSE

Phone numbers
From abroad use the prefix +33 and omit the initial '0' of the phone number

TOURIST OFFICE

t 0479 060660
info@valdisere.com
www.valdisere.com

of-the-range meal. Another is the Clochetons, out in the Manchet valley (they run a free minibus service). The Table de l'Ours, in the Barmes de l'Ours hotel, has a Michelin star. The hotel Aigle des Neiges restaurants are rated highly by locals.

There are plenty of pleasant mid-priced places. We always enjoy the unchanging Taverne d'Alsace and it was a 'highlight' for a 2009 visitor. The Perdrix Blanche went through a bad spell but has now improved again. Tufs, on the snow at La Daille, is open in the evenings (see 'Mountain restaurants'). The 'impressive' Austrian-influenced menu of the Schuss restaurant in the Grand Paradis hotel has been recommended. The Barillon de la Rosée Blanche is 'completely splendid, with great steaks and home-made ice-creams'. Bar Jacques is 'small but very welcoming with excellent food'. Chez Paolo has been praised for 'excellent' pizza and pasta; the Corniche for being 'traditional French, very enjoyable'; Casa Scara does 'good food'; the Canyon 'caters to all pockets'; but service at these last two has been criticised. The Grand Cocor has 'excellent food and choice', plus a 'very accommodating manager who'd show Champions League matches if asked'. The Belle Etoile is popular with locals for 'excellent French/Asian cuisine'. 1789 has 'great service, excellent meals and value for money', plus 'outstanding' côte de boeuf that kept a group of 30-year-old lads coming back for more. The Petit Danois and Spatule are recommended.

APRES-SKI ★★★★
Very lively
Nightlife is surprisingly energetic, given that most people have spent a hard day on the slopes. There are lots of bars, many with happy hours and then music and dancing later on.

The Folie Douce, at the top of the La Daille gondola, has become an Austrian-style tea-time rave, with music and dancing on tables; you can ride the gondola down. At La Daille the bar at the Samovar hotel is 'a good spot for a beer after skiing'. In downtown Val, Bananas is a cosy wooden chalet with a nice terrace (but a 2009 reporter complains of 'stained seating and filthy toilets'). At Café Face the 'early beer prices start at 2 euros and increase hourly until they reach 5 euros – great'. The Moris pub (live music at tea time and later, special nights such as Beach Party and 'Chav it up') and Saloon (underneath hotel Brussel's) fill up as the slopes close; the 'friendly' Boubou, Bar Jacques and the Perdrix Blanche are popular with locals. The Petit Danois is said to be better than Victor's bar. The Pacific Bar has sport on big-screen TVs. The basement Taverne d'Alsace is quiet and relaxing, as is Bar XV. For a civilised drink in welcoming surroundings head for the first-floor bar of the hotel Blizzard.

Later on, the famous Dick's Tea Bar is the main disco, but it gets mixed reviews. Graal is 'usually good'. Doudoune is a 'very expensive' new nightclub.

OFF THE SLOPES ★★
A reasonable amount to do
Val is primarily a resort for those keen to get on to the slopes. But there's a new sports centre (see 'News'), an outdoor ice rink, ice driving and the range of shops is better than in most high French resorts. Lunchtime meetings present problems for non-skiers: the easily accessible mountain restaurants are few, and your friends may prefer lunching miles away. A reporter suggests the 'fascinating' nature walk from Le Fornet to Pont St Charles in late season.

Val d'Isère

403

Interactive resort shortlist builder at www.wtss.co.uk

Valmorel

The purpose-built resort the French got mainly right: easy on the eye, as well as convenient; sadly, they didn't pick the ideal site

- ➕ A sympathetically designed purpose-built, car-free resort
- ➕ Largely slope-side accommodation
- ➕ Extensive easy slopes linked to St-François-Longchamp give even the timid a chance to travel around
- ➕ Beginners and children particularly well catered for

- ➖ Most pistes are easy, and of limited vertical
- ➖ Fairly low, so snow can suffer
- ➖ Still lots of slow lifts and drags, and peak-season lift queues
- ➖ Steep site, and outlying parts are very separate from the main street
- ➖ Few alternatives to self-catering

TOP 10 RATINGS

Extent	★★★
Fast lifts	★★
Queues	★★★
Snow	★★
Expert	★★
Intermediate	★★★★
Beginner	★★★★★
Charm	★★★★
Convenience	★★★★★
Scenery	★★★

NEWS

Snowmaking is planned for the Valette blue run for 2009/10.

For 2008/09 an eight-seat gondola was built from the isolated hamlet of Celliers in the next valley up to the slopes above Combelouvière. It serves no pistes.

Built from scratch in the mid-1970s, Valmorel was intended to look and feel like a mountain village – or perhaps a tiny mountain town; shops and restaurants line the cute, narrow, traffic-free main street. Compared with its illustrious neighbours in the Three Valleys, the mountain feels a bit second-rate; but it really competes for French family business with cheaper resorts to the south.

THE RESORT

Valmorel is the main resort in 'Le Grand Domaine' – a ski area shared with St-François and Longchamp, across the Madeleine pass. All the mega-resorts of the Tarentaise are within driving distance.

Village charm Bourg-Morel is the heart of the resort – an intimate, traffic-free street where you'll find most of the shops and restaurants. It is a pleasant and relaxing place to visit, with a lively cafe scene and a family feel.

Convenience Scattered here and there on the hillside are the six 'hameaux' with most of the lodgings. Hameau-du-Mottet is convenient – it is at the top of the Télébourg (the cross-village lift) with good access to the main lifts and from the return runs.

Scenery The resort sits among lightly wooded, hilly slopes. Although modest in height, there are good views to the Maurienne valley from the main peaks.

THE MOUNTAINS

Variety is not lacking, and the extent is enough to provide interesting day trips. The new gondola from Celliers forms a link with ski-touring terrain on the Chaîne de la Lauzière, but may be more to do with the hamlet's survival.

Slopes The pistes are spread over a number of minor valleys and ridges either side of the Col de la Madeleine. The most heavily used route out of the village is the fast Altispace quad chair. From the top, a network of lifts and pistes takes you to the Col de la Madeleine and beyond that to Lauzière or the slopes of Longchamp and St-François. The Pierrafort sector has its own runs back towards the village, or you can work your way round to the Beaudin and Madeleine sectors.

Fast lifts There are fast chairs on the main links, but still a lot of draglifts and slow chairs.

Queues The Altispace chair may be busy in the morning rush. Both village lifts can build big queues at peak times; depending on your location, you may be able to avoid these.

Terrain parks The Snowzone at the top of the Crève Coeur chair has a park with jumps, rails and tables, half-pipe and boardercross. There is a chill zone and boardercross at the Biollène chair, St François has boardercross too.

OT VALMOREL

The village spreads up both sides of the home piste, with the towny bit at the bottom ↓

JEANNE CATTINI

Col du Mottet 2405m
Col du Gollet 1980m
PIERRAFORT
BEAUDIN 2020m
2185m
ST FRANCOIS LONGCHAMP
Crey
Lauzière 2550m/ 8,370ft
Longchamp 1650m
Les Avanchers Valmorel
MADELEINE
St François 1400m
Doucy Combelouvière 1400m/ 4,590ft
COMBELOUVIERE

KEY FACTS

Resort	1400m
	4,590ft

Le Grand Domaine

Slopes	1250-2550m
	4,100-8,370ft
Lifts	50
Pistes	152km
	94 miles
Green	33%
Blue	39%
Red	19%
Black	9%
Snowmaking	
	342 guns

Valmorel only

Slopes	1250-2405m
	4,100-7,890ft
Lifts	39
Pistes	95km
	59 miles

UK PACKAGES

Alpine Answers, Crystal, Erna Low, Independent Ski Links, Interactive Resorts, Lagrange, Leisure Direction, Neilson, PV-Holidays.com, Simply Alpine, Ski France, Skiholiday extras.com, Ski Independence, Ski Supreme, Skitracer
Doucy-Combelouvière *Lagrange*
St-François *Erna Low, Lagrange, Ski Independence, Ski Leisure Direction*

Phone numbers
From abroad use the prefix +33 and omit the initial '0' of the phone number

TOURIST OFFICE

t 0479 098555
info@valmorel.com
www.valmorel.com

Snow reliability The area is low by local standards, and quite sunny – not good news. There's snowmaking on the nursery slopes and the main runs back to base, but when we last visited it wasn't used sufficiently and slopes were bare and icy. But some new snowmaking is planned in the Madeleine sector for 2009/10. A 2009 visitor found grooming to be poor.
Experts There are a few challenging pistes; the steepest are in the Pierrafort sector; but there is good off-piste that doesn't get skied out.
Intermediates The whole area – except for the steepest black runs – is ideal, though the main home run can be quite daunting at the end of the day.
Beginners Valmorel is a good place for first-timers. Beginners have a dedicated nursery area right by the village and local passes are available. There are lots of gentle green runs for progression.
Snowboarding There are decent intermediate runs; but new boarders will find some of the draglifts tricky.
Cross-country Trails adding up to 20km/12 miles can be reached by bus.
Mountain restaurants There are half a dozen or so. Recommended are the Prariond (Pierrafort sector) for its 'excellent, lovely terrace' and 'delicious raspberry flan' and Banquise 2000, with a great location at Col de la Madeleine. The Altipiano and Alpage have also been suggested. The Arbet self-service does 'good omelettes'.
Schools and guides Past reports for both adult and children's classes have been positive, notably for the children's private lessons. Teaching for first-timers is a speciality of the resort.
Families Valmorel goes out of its way to cater for children; there are good, gentle nursery slopes and play areas.

Piou-Piou club is a comprehensive childcare facility run by the ski school, taking children from 18 months to six years. Children taking ski lessons can have lunch there, too. Advance booking is essential.

STAYING THERE

Self-catering packages are the norm.
Hotels The Village Club du Soleil (0479 098777), on the slopes, offers all-inclusive weekly family holidays. The 2-star Hotel du Bourg (0479 098666) is a simple, central hotel.
Apartments The Athamante et Valeriane apartments have been praised. Interchalet offer a range of 'excellent, well equipped' apartments.
Eating out There are a handful of places, offering mostly traditional fare. Petit Prince, Marmite, Table du Berger and Ski Roc have won approval from past reporters.
Après-ski Immediate après-ski centres on the lively cafe-bars with terraces at the foot of the slopes; it's pretty quiet later on.
Off the slopes It's not a great place to hang around but there are various activities, such as snowshoeing and horse sleigh rides. There's a fitness centre, a cinema and a toboggan run.

Doucy-Combelouvière

1260m/4,130ft

This is a small place at the end of a long, gentle green run from the Valmorel slopes, with a fast chair out of the village and a series of three draglifts to get up to the top of the Beadin sector. There are chalets and apartments grouped around the lift base, and a two-star hotel a short drive away.

Val Thorens

Europe's highest resort, with guaranteed good snow – and other attractions: stylish lodgings and good restaurants among them

£120
RESORT PRICE INDEX

RATINGS

The mountains

Extent	★★★★★
Fast lifts	★★★★
Queues	★★★
Terrain p'ks	★★★
Snow	★★★★★
Expert	★★★★
Intermediate	★★★★★
Beginner	★★★★
X-country	★
Restaurants	★★★★
Schools	★★★
Families	★★★

The resort

Charm	★★
Convenience	★★★★★
Scenery	★★★
Eating out	★★★★
Après-ski	★★★★
Off-slope	★★

NEWS

For 2009/10 moving carpets are to replace the two free Retour beginner draglifts. More are to be added lower down, creating another nursery area. There are plans for a new gondola to Col du Bouchet, opening up new high slopes – but the timing is not yet clear.

For 2008/09 The terrain park was extended and a boardercross built.

➕ Extensive slopes for all abilities, locally and in the vast Three Valleys

➕ The highest resort in the Alps, and one of the most snow-sure

➕ Compact, with ski-in/out lodgings

➕ Convenient, gentle nursery slopes

➕ Not as much of an eyesore as most high, purpose-built resorts

➕ Unusual range of hotels for a purpose-built resort, plus more and more smart apartments

➖ Not a tree in sight – in bad weather it can be bleak, and in seriously bad weather entirely closed

➖ Away from the 'front de neige', not an attractive place to walk around

➖ Not much to do off the slopes, though there are worse places

➖ Some very crowded pistes and dangerous intersections

➖ Still some queues – and really serious ones for the justifiably popular Cîme de Caron

For the enthusiast looking for the best snow available, it's difficult to beat Val Thorens. That wonderful snow lies on some pretty wonderful slopes suitable for everyone from beginner to expert. And the village – always one of the better-designed high-altitude stations – gets more attractive as it continues to develop, and gain more smart accommodation and restaurants.

But we still prefer a cosier base elsewhere in the Three Valleys. That way, if a storm socks in, we can play in the woods; if the sun is scorching, we have the option of setting off for Val Thorens. The formula simply doesn't work the other way round. For a pre-Christmas or an April trip, though, it's the best base.

THE RESORT

Val Thorens is a classic purpose-built resort, high above the treeline at the head of the valley it shares with Les Menuires and St-Martin-de-Belleville. The slopes at the top of the Méribel valley are two lift-rides away

VILLAGE CHARM ★★
Functional but pleasantly so

Seen from the slopes, the resort is not as ugly as many of its rivals, and it has more of a lively ski-resort buzz than most people expect. The buildings are mainly medium-rise and wood-clad; some are distinctly stylish. But many are designed with their smart 'fronts' facing the slopes, and look very dreary from the streets. And the place lacks a focus. The streets are

supposedly traffic-free; most visitors' cars are banished, except on Saturday. Workers' cars still generate a fair amount of traffic, though, and Saturdays can be mayhem. Book parking in advance to get a handy spot and a good rate.

CONVENIENCE ★★★★★
Ski through the centre

It's a compact village – our scale plan is one of the smallest in these pages – but also quite complex. There is lots of convenient slope-side lodging, though some newer buildings above the centre are less convenient.

At its heart is the snowy Place de Caron, on the slope side rather than the street side of the central buildings, where pedestrians mix with skiers and boarders. Many of the shops and restaurants are clustered here, along with the best hotels; the sports and leisure centres are nearby. The resort is basically divided in two by a little slope (with a moving carpet lift) that leads down from here to the broad main nursery slope running the length of the village. The upper half of the village is centred on the Place de Péclet, where there is one of two

KEY FACTS

Resort	2300m
	7,550ft

Three Valleys

Slopes	1260-3230m
	4,130-10,600ft
Lifts	180
Pistes	600km
	373 miles
Green	15%
Blue	38%
Red	37%
Black	10%
Snowmaking	33%

Val Thorens only

Slopes	1800-3230m
	5,900-10,600ft
Lifts	29
Pistes	140km
	87 miles
Green	12%
Blue	37%
Red	40%
Black	11%

shopping malls. A road runs across the hillside from here to the chalet-style Plein Sud area, where many of the most attractive new apartments have been built. The highest of these can be reached and left on snow only by awkward icy or off-piste sections, or by road. There's a frequent free ski-bus or it's a short walk. The lower half of the village is more diffuse, with the Rue du Soleil winding down from the revamped bus station.

SCENERY ★★★
Panoramas on high
The resort sits on a sunny, west facing slope surrounded by peaks, slopes and lifts. It can be bleak, but there are fabulous views from the high point at Cîme de Caron.

THE MOUNTAINS

The main disadvantage of Val Thorens is the lack of trees. Heavy snowfalls or high wind can shut practically all the lifts and slopes, and even if they don't close, poor visibility can be a problem. Piste marking and signposting are adequate. Piste classification is generally accurate (but see 'For intermediates', below).

EXTENT OF THE SLOPES ★★★★★
High and snow-sure
The resort has a wide piste going right down the front of it, leading down to a number of different lifts. The big **Péclet** gondola, with 30-person cabins, rises 700m/2,300ft to the Péclet glacier, with a choice of red runs down. One links across to a wide area of intermediate runs served by lifts to cols either side of the **Pointe de Thorens**. You can take red or blue runs into the 'fourth valley', the Maurienne, from one of these – the **Col de Rosaël**, served by the Grand Fond 30-person gondola.

Above **Orelle** in the Maurienne valley two successive slow chairs go up to 3230m/10,600ft on the flanks of Pointe du Bouchet – the highest lift-served point in the Three Valleys, with stunning views. The former black run off the back of here is now off-piste because of crevasse and avalanche danger, and often poor snow.

The 150-person cable car to **Cîme de Caron** is one of the great lifts of the Alps, rising 900m/2,950ft in no time at all. It can be reached by skiing across from mid-mountain, or by coming up on the Caron gondola that starts below the village. From the top

boarding

Val Thorens has always been popular with snowboarders as it is the highest and most snow-sure of the Three Valleys resorts, as well as having a younger and more affordable feel in comparison with Courchevel and Méribel. The slopes are rather bleak; however, there are great steep runs, gullies and groomed pistes for all levels. The terrain park is worth a visit. The lifts are mainly chairs and gondolas.

there is a choice of red and black pistes down the front, or a black into the Maurienne.

The relatively low **Boismint** sector is overlooked by many visitors, but is actually a very respectable hill with a total vertical of 860m/2,820ft.

Chairlifts heading north from the resort serve sunny slopes above the village and also lead to the link to the Méribel valley. Les Menuires can be reached via these lifts; the alternative Boulevard Cumin along the valley floor is nearly flat, and can be hard work.

FAST LIFTS ★★★★
Very few slow ones
Recent investment means the lift system is impressive, with jumbo gondolas and fast chairs in most of the key places. It's quite surprising that none of the chairs have bubbles. Moving carpets are gradually replacing old draglifts on the nursery slopes.

QUEUES ★★★
Persistent at the Cîme de Caron
Serious peak-time queues for the Cîme de Caron cable car are just a fact of life. You can plug in your iPod and accept the wait, or get there early to avoid it. We think it's time a ticket system was operated here, so that you could ski while you wait. When the village lifts are busy, queues build for the Deux Lacs chair further down the slope. In good weather the Rosaël chair back from the fourth valley is a serious bottleneck. And a 2009 visitor noted frequent breakdowns on the

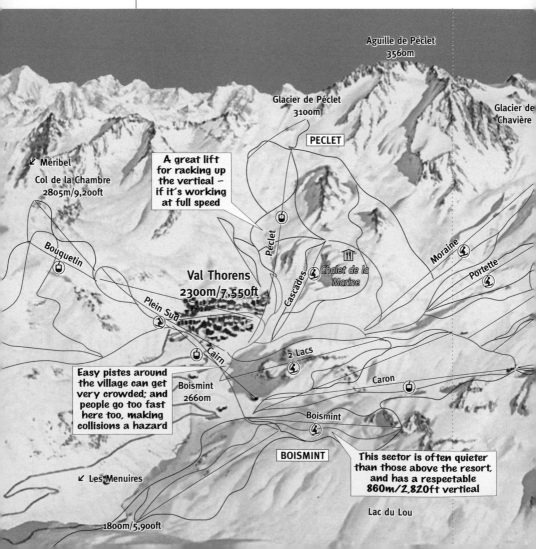

Aguille de Péclet
3560m

Glacier de Péclet
3100m

Glacier de Chavière

PECLET

↙ Méribel
Col de la Chambre
2805m/9,200ft

A great lift for racking up the vertical – if it's working at full speed

Péclet

Moraine

Bouquetin

Cascades

Chalet de la Marine

Portette

Val Thorens
2300m/7,550ft

Plein Sud

Cairn

2 Lacs

Caron

Easy pistes around the village can get very crowded; and people go too fast here too, making collisions a hazard

Boismint
2660m

Boismint

↙ Les Menuires

BOISMINT

This sector is often quieter than those above the resort, and has a respectable 860m/2,820ft vertical

Lac du Lou

1800m/5,900ft

LIFT PASSES

Three Valleys

Prices in €

Age	1-day	6-day
under 13	34	169
13 to 64	44	225
over 65	39	212

Free under 5, over 75

Beginner Four lifts for 50% of Val Thorens day rate

Notes
Covers Courchevel, La Tania, Méribel, Val Thorens, Les Menuires and St-Martin; family reductions; pedestrian and half-day passes

Alternative pass
Val Thorens-Orelle only

Peclet gondola. These problems apart, the system works well – though when snow is in short supply elsewhere, the pressure on the Val Thorens lifts can increase markedly.

But crowded pistes, especially around the village, are a bigger problem than queues – compounded by people going too quickly. We noticed this on our recent visit and lots of reporters have commented on it too; an April 2009 visitor, having experienced Easter week in other French resorts, says: 'I have never witnessed slopes as crowded as these – frightening for a beginner.'

TERRAIN PARKS ★★★☆☆
More than adequate
The terrain park is on the 'Plateau'

and has been improved a lot recently. It is accessible via various chairlifts, and has a nice open layout (www.snowparkvalthorens.com). There are four different areas that range from beginner to pro, with all sorts of kickers, rails and box combinations. New this year were a log jib and a huge pro kicker dubbed the 'perfect jump'. There is also a boardercross, which has some great banked turns, and 2008/09 saw the beginner lines grow in size. The whole park is well maintained, and new obstacles are often built for local competitions. The park also has a giant airbag jump, to test your aerials before you put them to proper use on the snow. Neighbouring Les Menuires has a good park, at Reberty.

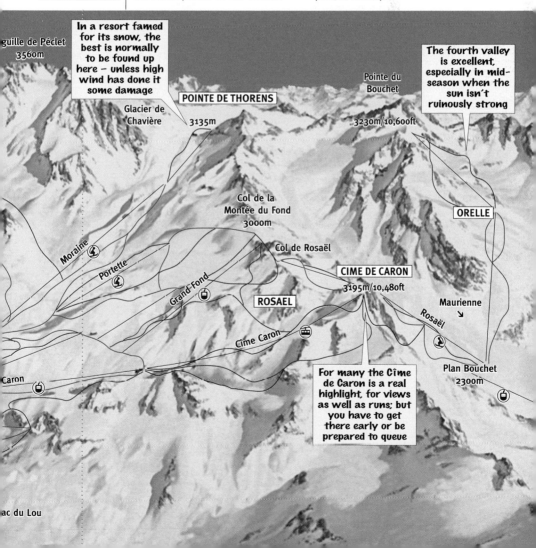

SNOW RELIABILITY ★★★★★
One of the best
Few resorts can rival Val Thorens for reliably good snow-cover, thanks to its altitude and generally north-facing slopes. Snowmaking covers a lot of the key pistes, including the crowded south- and west-facing runs on the way back from the Méribel valley and in the Orelle sector. But the terrain is rocky and needs a lot of snow for good coverage – we have found the higher runs patchy in recent early season visits when snow throughout the Alps has been slow to arrive, and at times like that the off-piste terrain is obviously hazardous. The resort offers a 'snow guarantee' that at least 70% of the area's lifts will be open, with free skiing days on a future visit if this guarantee is not met.

FOR EXPERTS ★★★★☆
Lots to do off-piste
Val Thorens' local pistes are primarily intermediate terrain; many of the blacks could easily be classified red instead. The fast Cascades chair serves a short but steep black run that quickly gets mogulled. The pistes down from the Cîme de Caron cable car are challenging, but not seriously steep, and there's a good, sunny black run off the back into the fourth valley.

The red Chamois, Falaise and Variante runs from Col de Rosaël can get heavily mogulled and challenging.

The sunny Marielle run, one of the routes from the Méribel valley, is one of the easiest blacks we've come across, but it can get crowded and be icy in the morning.

There is a huge amount of very good off-piste terrain to explore with a guide – see the off-piste feature panel. But bear in mind that it does need good snow cover.

FOR INTERMEDIATES ★★★★★
Great in good weather
The scope for intermediates throughout the Three Valleys is enormous. It will take a keen intermediate only 90 minutes or so to get to Courchevel 1650 at the far end, if not distracted by the endless runs on the way.

The local slopes in Val Thorens are some of the best intermediate terrain in the region. Most of the pistes are easy reds and blues (the runs on the top half of the mountain are steeper than those back into the resort) and made even more enjoyable by the excellent snow.

The snow on the red Col run is normally some of the best around. The blue Moraine below it is gentle and popular with the schools. The Grand Fond gondola serves a good variety of red runs. The red and blue runs from the Péclet gondola are excellent. The Pluviomètre from the Trois Vallées chair is a glorious varied run, away

FABULOUS OFF-PISTE IN VAL THORENS

Val Thorens offers a huge choice of off-piste. And because of the high altitude, the snow stays powdery longer here than in lower parts of the Three Valleys.

For those with little off-piste experience, the Pierre Lory Pass run is ideal. It is a very large and gentle slope, and you access the pass by doing an easy traverse on the Chavière glacier from the top of the Col chairlift. When you arrive at Pierre Lory Pass there are breathtaking views of the Aiguilles d'Arves in the Maurienne valley, and you will be just above the glacier du Bouchet, which you then ski down, rejoining the lift system at Plan Bouchet.

For those with more off-piste under their belt already, the Lac du Lou is a famous off-piste run of 1400m/4,590ft vertical. It is easily accessible from the Cîme de Caron. The many ways into this long, wide valley allow plenty of variety and opportunities for making first tracks; because many of the slopes face north or north-west it is not unusual to find good powder most of the ski season, even in late April. The views are stunning and you'll notice the quietness and vastness of the whole valley.

La Combe sans Nom in the fourth valley, also accessible from the Cîme de Caron cable car, usually offers superb skiing and snowboard conditions. There's a choice of south-, west- and, on the far side, some east-facing slopes, which makes for excellent spring skiing conditions.

For the more adventurous there are many options, including hiking up from the Col chairlift to a long run over the Gébroulaz glacier down to Méribel-Mottaret.

But don't even think about doing any off-piste runs without a fully qualified guide or instructor. Route finding can be difficult, there can be avalanche danger, and hidden hazards such as cliffs and crevasses lurk.

SCHOOLS

ESF
t 0479 000286

Ski Cool
t 0479 000492

Prosneige
t 0479 010700

Attitude
t 0479 065772

Classes (ESF prices)
6 half-days (2hr
45min am) €142

Private lessons
from €40 for 1hr

CHILDCARE

**Nursery/mini-club
(ESF)**
t 0479 000286
Ages from 3mnth

Ski school
The schools offer
classes for children
aged 4 and over (ESF:
6 mornings from
€133)

GETTING THERE

Air Geneva 205km/
125 miles (3hr30);
Lyon 205km/
125 miles (3hr15);
Chambéry 120km/
75 miles (2hr15)

Rail Moûtiers
(37km/23 miles);
regular buses from
station

SMART LODGINGS

Check out our feature
chapters at the front
of the book.

from the lifts. Adventurous intermediates shouldn't miss the Cîme de Caron runs. The black run is not intimidating – it's very wide, usually has good snow, and is a wonderful fast cruise when freshly groomed (though reports suggest this is less likely than it was). Don't neglect the excellent, quiet Boismint area next door to Caron, either.

FOR BEGINNERS ★★★★
Good late-season choice
The slopes at the foot of the resort are very gentle and provide convenient, snow-sure nursery slopes, now with moving carpet lifts. These are free, and there is a cheap pass for four serious lifts on the lower slopes – and excellent package. There are no long green runs to progress to, but the blues immediately above the village are easy. The resort's height and bleakness make it cold in midwinter, and intimidating in bad weather.

FOR CROSS-COUNTRY ★
Go to Les Menuires
There are no cross-country trails in Val Thorens. Your best bet is the 28km/17 mile link between Les Menuires and St Martin-de-Belleville.

MOUNTAIN RESTAURANTS ★★★★
Lots of choice
For a high modern resort, the choice of restaurants is good, though a couple of 2009 reporters complain of poor service in several huts.
Editors' choice We've had several good lunches in the rustic table-service section of the Chalet de la Marine (0479 000186), on the Dalles piste, repeatedly endorsed by readers. It has a big terrace with 'funky' music after 3pm. The self-service section below does 'fantastic quality pizzas'.
Worth knowing about The Marine has two clear challengers among reader reports. The Chalet des 2 Ours on the Blanchot run in the Boismint sector gets repeated recommendations – 'one of the best we've experienced: tasty, well-portioned fare and great views', 'good food and price'. But the Chalet des 2 Lacs has the edge for 'good food, prices and service' (despite popularity); lovely sunny terrace.
There are of course plenty of options in the village, including some upscale slope-side terraces. The set lunch at the Oxalys is not cheap but gives 'superb value'.

SCHOOLS AND GUIDES ★★★
Good reports
The ESF offers a wide choice of private and group classes, including freestyle and 3Vallées explorer sessions once a week. Prosneige is a smaller school that limits class sizes to 10. All recent reports on both schools are positive. A 2008 visitor was pleased to tell us that there is now an English instructor on the ESF staff. Ski Cool class sizes are also guaranteed not to exceed 10. There are several specialist guiding outfits.

FOR FAMILIES ★★★
Coolly efficient
There is a children's area, Espace Junior, beside the 2 Lacs chairlift and a good family toboggan run. The Prosneige school takes children from age five, and a 2008 reporter was 'very happy' with the standard of instruction and care provided. We lack recent reports on the ESF nursery.

STAYING THERE

Accommodation is of a higher standard than in many purpose-built resorts – more comfortable as well as more stylish.
Chalets There are apartments operated as catered chalets. Ski Total offers several, including new ones last season, as well as an actual chalet sold as two units sharing a sauna.
Hotels Unusually for a high, purpose-built resort, there are plenty of hotels, and there's a Club Med, too.
★★★★Fitz Roy (0479 000478) The sole 4-star is smart, with good service and lovely rooms. Good restaurant with flexible half-board menu. Pool. Well placed at the heart of things.
★★★Val Thorens (0479 000433) Next door to Fitz Roy.
★★★Sherpa (0479 000070) Highly recommended for 'interested staff and good food'. Location is ski-in/ski-out, but a hike up from the centre.
★★★Val Chavière (0479 000033) Friendly, convenient.
★★★Bel Horizon (0479 000477) Friendly, family-run.
Apartments Val Thorens now has an exceptional range of smart chalet style developments – the special 'chalet residence' section of the resort brochure contains over a dozen. Many are offered by UK operators Erna Low and Ski Collection. In the Plein Sud area above the main village, Balcons

Interactive resort shortlist builder at **www.wtss.co.uk**

Weekly news updates and resort links at **www.wtss.co.uk**

↑ Settings for ski resorts don't come any more bleak than this, Europe's highest

ALAN SHEPHERD

Monthly Accommodation

VAL THORENS
VAL D'ISERE
TIGNES
AVORIAZ
LES 2 ALPES

ALPSERVICE

HOUSING SINCE 1994

www.alpservice.co.uk

Call - 020 7193 2577

ACTIVITIES

Indoor Sports centre (spa, sauna, fitness room, hot tub, tennis, squash, swimming pool, volleyball, table tennis, badminton, football), cinema, bowling, concerts

Outdoor Paragliding, sightseeing microlight flights, snowmobiles, snowshoeing, walks, tobogganing

Phone numbers
From abroad use the prefix +33 and omit the initial '0' of the phone number

TOURIST OFFICE

t 0479 000808
valtho@valthorens.com
www.valthorens.com

de Val Thorens, Chalet Altitude, Chalets du Soleil, Chalet Val 2400 have all been recommended; some have a pool. On its own just above the village is the Chalet des Neiges, with pool. At the very bottom of the resort, the Residence Oxalys has its own wonderful restaurant (see 'Eating out') as well as a large lounge, pool and sauna. There are three Montagnettes developments in different locations. A very smart new residence, the Sabot de Venus, opened near the centre for last season.

EATING OUT ★★★★
Star quality

Val Thorens has something for most tastes and pockets. The resort's excellent 'Practical Booklet' includes a very helpful guide, with photos and some idea of the cuisine.

Top of the range is the Michelin-starred restaurant in the Residence Oxalys ('the highest star in Europe', the resort claims). We had a delicious and very inventive meal here; expensive, but worth it. The Fitz Roy and Val Thorens hotels also have serious restaurants.

There are plenty of more modest places. This year's reports are a bit thin on recommendations, but good bets include the 'good value, rustic' Chaumière and the 'friendly, authentically French' Cabane; and for pizzas, the Scapin and Chamois d'Or. And there are plenty of other alternatives; past recommendations include the Vieux Chalet and the Galoubet, and the Auberge des Balcons ('nice food, attentive staff'). The Blanchot is a stylish wine bar with a simple but varied carte.

APRES-SKI ★★★★
Livelier than you'd imagine

Val Thorens is more lively at night than most high-altitude ski-stations. The Red Fox up at Balcons is crowded at close of play, with karaoke. At the opposite extreme there's the Moo Bar in the Temples du Soleil. The Frog and Roastbeef at the top of the village claims to be the highest pub in Europe and is a cheerful British ghetto – now under new management but still lively and welcoming according to this year's reports. The Saloon and the Viking are lively bars on the same block. Dick's Tea Bar (formerly the Underground) in Place de Péclet has a lively disco. For live bands and dancing, the Malaysia cellar bar rocks until late. Quieter bars include O'Connells and the cosy Rhum Box Cafe (aka Mitch's).

OFF THE SLOPES ★★
Forget it

There's a good sports centre with big pool, saunas, steam room, hot tubs, gym etc and a leisure centre with bowling lanes and pool tables. Free weekly concerts are held in the church, there's a small cinema and twice-weekly street markets. There's a good toboggan run (longest in France), and an ice-driving course. You can get to some mountain restaurants by lift, and the 360° panorama from the top of the Cîme de Caron cable car is not to be missed. But it is not a good place to choose if you're not going to hit the slopes.

The French Pyrenees

An underrated region with decent skiing and boarding at half the price of the Alps and villages that remain distinctly French

It took us a long time to get round to visiting the resorts of the French Pyrenees – mainly because we had the idea that they were second-rate compared with the Alps. Well, it is certainly true that they can't compete in terms of size of ski area with the mega-resorts of the Three Valleys and Paradiski. But don't dismiss them: they have considerable attractions, including price – hotels cost half as much as in the Alps, and meals and drinks are cheap.

The Pyrenees are serious mountains, with dramatic, picturesque scenery. The resorts are attractively French and many have a rustic, rural Gallic charm.

One of the biggest ski areas – shared by **Barèges** and **La Mongie** – is called **Domaine Tourmalet**. It has 100km/62 miles of runs, and 39 lifts. Most are drags and slow chairs but there are three fast chairs. The area suits intermediates best, with tree-lined runs above Barèges and open bowl skiing above La Mongie. The best bet for an expert is to try off-piste with a guide. Rustic mountain huts are scattered around the slopes; Chez Louisette is one of the best. There are 20km/12 miles of cross-country.

Barèges is a spa village set in a narrow, steep-sided valley, which gets little sun in midwinter; there's one main street with rather drab buildings and little to do in the evenings other than visit the thermal spa. The lift base is at Tournaboup, 4km/2.5 miles up the valley and served by ski-bus. It's the second oldest ski resort in France and the pioneer of skiing in the Pyrenees. Accommodation is mainly in 2-star hotels such as the Montagne Fleurie ('good room and food') and Europe ('good food, friendly'). The 300-year-old chalet Les Caillaux (www.mountainbug.com) is of a 'very high standard', and the owners offer free ski guiding. One reporter stayed in nearby Luz in the Chimes hotel, describing the food as 'divine'. La Mongie is a modern, purpose-built resort: 'small, friendly, great restaurants but not cheap'.

Cauterets is another spa town but a contrast to Barèges – it's much bigger, set in a wide, sunny valley and is a popular summer resort. A gondola takes you from town to slopes and you have to ride it down as well as up. There are only 36km/22 miles of usually quiet slopes (mainly beginner and intermediate), set in a bowl that can be cold and windy. But Cauterets' jewel is its cross-country, a long drive or bus ride from town at Pont d'Espagne and served by a gondola. It is the start of the Pyrenees National Park and the old smugglers' route over the mountains to Spain. The 36km/22 miles of snow-sure tracks run up this beautiful deserted valley, beside a rushing stream and waterfall.

Font-Romeu has 23 lifts, serving 58km/36 miles of mainly easy and intermediate pistes; it is popular with families. The slopes get a lot of sun, but it has the biggest snowmaking set-up in the Pyrenees. When weekend crowds arrive, lifts and pistes can get crowded. It has 111km/69 miles of cross-country skiing. The village is a bus ride from the slopes, and hotels are mainly 2- and 3-star.

The other major resort is **St-Lary-Soulan**, a traditional village with stone houses and a cable car going up to the slopes, of which there are 100km/62 miles, mainly suiting intermediates. There's a satellite called **St-Lary-Espiaube**, which is purpose-built and right at the heart of the slopes.

A reporter also visited other small resorts such as **Formiguères**, **Eyne** and **Les Angles**, and suggests staying down in a small valley town and visiting different resorts daily.

413

Germany

We don't get many requests for coverage of Germany, but we get a few, and here it is, at last. Over the page is a chapter on Garmisch-Partenkirchen, by far the most important downhill resort in Germany – famously the venue for the 1936 Olympics (when downhill racing was introduced, and A Hitler got the facilities built on time), and now the venue for the 2011 world championships. On this page, a non-comprehensive tour of the country's main skiing regions.

THE ALPS

Allgäu This region claims 300km/186 miles of downhill runs and an amazing 700km/430 miles of cross-country trails. The main lift systems operate under the regional name Das Hoechste. Highest of all is Nebelhorn (2225m/7,300ft) reached from **Oberstdorf** by a two-stage cable car to the main slopes (served by two chairs), with a third stage to the top for Germany's longest piste (7.5km/5 miles). South of Oberstdorf you enter **Kleinwalsertal**, which belongs to Austria, strangely. The Kanzelwand slopes link with Fellhorn to form Germany's 'biggest and most modern' area, with three six-packs, two gondolas and nine other lifts. Two smaller areas are Walmendingerhorn, a little further up the valley, and Ifen. The Allgäu has lots of other resorts, such as Oberjoch and Pfronten.

Bavarian Alps Garmisch-Partenkirchen is covered over the page. **Mittenwald** (915m/3,000ft) is a cute town in a spectacular setting. The cable car to Karwendel accesses an epic ski route dropping 1300m/4,270ft in 6km/4 miles. Across the valley seven lifts serve modest slopes up to 1350m/4,430ft. The other resorts are on the fringes of the Alps, with less dramatic scenery. In other ways, **Oberammergau** (835m/2,740ft) resembles Mittenwald:

a gondola to Laber (1685m/5,530ft) accesses a long ski route and a direct black piste; across town a chairlift serves Kolbensattel (1270m/4,170ft). There are more extensive slopes on Brauneck above **Lenggries** (680m/2,230ft) – 35km/22 miles of pistes with a top height of 1710m/5,610ft, and about 20 lifts including a gondola.

There are other small resorts, some near the infamous Berchtesgaden.

THE REST

Black Forest In the south-west corner: a lot of cross-country, but good amounts of downhill. Feldberg goes up to 1500m/4,920ft with 28 lifts and 50km/31 miles of pistes.
Harz A low mountain range, south of Hanover. A handful of small resorts, the biggest being Braunlage.
Sauerland Low mountains east of Düsseldorf, big on snowmaking. Some 300km/186 miles of cross-country in the region. Winterberg has 18 lifts and Willingen a gondola and 15 drags.
Saxony On the border with the Czech Republic: a handful of low, small resorts, the most compelling at Fichtelberg above Oberwiesenthal.
Thüringer Wald In the middle of Germany, north-east of Frankfurt: extensive cross-country, and a bit of easy downhill. The best-known resort is Oberhof.

← The Bavarian Alps are right on the northern fringe of the whole range. On a clear day, from above Garmisch, you can probably see downtown Munich

WEBSITES

Allgäu
www.english.allgaeu.info
www.das-hoechste.de
Bavarian Alps
www.karwendelbahn.de
www.laber-bergbahn.de
www.brauneck-bergbahn.de
Black Forest
www.blackforest-tourism.com
Harz
www.harzinfo.de
Sauerland
www.wintersport-arena.de
Saxony
www.oberwiesenthal.com
www.fichtelberg-ski.de
Thüringer Wald
www.oberhof.de

Garmisch-Partenkirchen

Twin resort towns sprawling at the foot of Germany's highest mountain, reaching glacial heights on the Austrian border

TOP 10 RATINGS

Extent	★☆☆☆☆
Fast lifts	★★☆☆☆
Queues	★★★
Snow	★★★
Expert	★★★★
Intermediate	★★★
Beginner	★☆☆☆☆
Charm	★★★
Convenience	★★
Scenery	★★★★

NEWS

In the middle of the 'Classic' area, the Kreuzjoch double chair and the drag below it are to be replaced by a fast quad for 2009/10.

The gondola to Hausberg was new for 2008/09.

MOMENTUM SKI

Weekend & a la carte ski holiday specialists

100% Tailor-Made

Individuals or Corporate Groups

No. 1 specialists in Garmisch

020 7371 9111
www.momentumski.com

- ✚ Weather-proof combo of fair-sized glacier and woods lower down
- ✚ Some spectacular views
- ✚ Some excellent, challenging runs
- ✚ Good-value hotels

- ▬ Very few long easy runs – beginners and timid intermediates beware
- ▬ Many of the best runs descend to low altitude, where conditions are rarely good
- ▬ Glacier access takes time

With Garmisch hosting the World Championships in 2011, the time seems right to introduce Germany's major resort to these pages. Its small ski area, complete with glacier, has plenty to amuse confident skiers for a couple of days, and with short transfers from Munich it makes a good short-break destination.

THE RESORT

Garmisch and Partenkirchen are separate towns that have merged as they have spread to fill the broad, flat valley bottom beneath the Zugspitze, while keeping their centres distinct.

There are smaller resorts on the Austrian side of the Zugspitze (dealt with in our Zugspitz Arena chapter). These and other resorts nearby – Mittenwald in Germany and Seefeld in Austria – are covered by the Happy Ski card (the only weekly pass available). **Village charm** Each half of the resort is a sizeable town – spacious and pleasant but not notably captivating. **Convenience** You'll probably need to use trains, buses or cars at both ends of the day. The Zugspitze railway starts next to the main station, more or less between the two town centres; it goes to the glacier via the other lift bases. **Scenery** The Wetterstein massif, of which the Zugspitze is the peak, is impressive, and there are great panoramic views from the top – plus some dramatic scenery lower down.

THE MOUNTAINS

The glacier is quite separate from the lower slopes, which the resort calls the 'Classic' area. In fact, that area also divides into two parts, awkwardly linked – a higher, almost treeless part (Alpspitz) and a lower, heavily wooded part (Hausberg-Kreuzeck). **Slopes** The **Hausberg-Kreuzeck** sector directly below the resort is accessed by two gondolas; these start out of town, but you can reach them by the railway to the glacier. These lower lifts have decent verticals and serve long

runs; the lifts higher up are all much shorter. An inconspicuous narrow path and a rope tow form the link between this sector and the base of the higher **Alpspitz** sector, more directly reached via the Alpspitz cable car. Although the altitude is modest, this sector feels like high-mountain terrain, with dramatic scenery – Dolomite-like on the isolated Ostfelder and Bernadein runs, on skier's right.

There are two routes to the glacier: a railway that skirts the lower mountain, climbs above Eibsee and tunnels slowly through the mountain, emerging in the middle of the glacier; or a much quicker cable car from Eibsee that climbs 1950m/6,400ft to the Zugspitze – but from there you have to ride another cable car down to the slopes. Although the Zugspitze is not notably high (2960m/9,710ft), its isolated position gives great views.

Above the main lift junction are typical blue glacier slopes served by multiple drags. Below it and spreading across the bowl are a range of good red runs and some good off-piste terrain served by three drags and one six-seater chairlift. None of these lifts rises more than 350m/1,150ft vertical, but in other respects it's a good area. **Fast lifts** Access lifts are fast, but up the hill drags and slow chairs still dominate, despite the new fast chair for 2009/10. On the glacier drags also dominate, as they usually do. **Queues** Fine weekends are bound to attract crowds from Munich, but at other times we don't expect problems. **Terrain parks** On the glacier there is a long park with expert and novice lines, with a kicker and a rail area in each. **Snow reliability** The glacier area is

Map labels:
ZUGSPITZPLATT 2720m/8,920ft
Zugspitze 2960m/9,710ft
ALPSPITZ
Osterfelderkopf 2050m
Ehrwald ↓
1720m
Kreuzeck 1650m
HAUSBERG-KREUZECK
Kandahar
Alpspitzbahn
Elbsee
Hausberg 1310m
Kreuzeckbahn
Grainau 750m
Hausbergbahn
Garmisch-Partenkirchen 710m/2,330ft
Wank 1780m

KEY FACTS

Resort	710m
	2,330ft
Slopes	720-2720m
	2,360-8,920ft
Lifts	30
Pistes	48km
	30 miles
Blue	16%
Red	71%
Black	13%
Snowmaking	47%

UK PACKAGES

Momentum

Phone numbers
From elsewhere in
Germany add the
prefix 08821. From
abroad use the prefix
+49 and delete the
initial '0'

TOURIST OFFICE

t 180700
tourist-info@gapa.de
www.gapa.de

small and remote, so conditions lower down are important. The lower main area is shady, but some of the best runs descend to valley level – ie 700m/2,300ft. Despite comprehensive snowmaking, conditions at these altitudes are often poor even when there's great snow higher up, as we confirmed last January.

Experts The long runs to the valley are challenging enough to amuse most experts, particularly the excellent Kandahar downhill race course. The final pitch of this takes real bottle when icy at the end of the day. Higher up, there are off-piste opportunities in the Alpspitz sector and the glacier area. (We're told a 'safe' area is marked out, which sounds ideal.)

Intermediates For confident skiers it's fine, but this is not a hill where timid intermediates can build confidence.

Beginners One of the few resorts you should try to avoid. The nursery slopes are fine if you don't mind the cost (there is no special beginner pass) and inconvenience of getting up to them, but the only easy runs to move on to are busy links between Kreuzeck and Hausberg.

Snowboarding There are quite a few drags in all sectors. Getting up to the park on the glacier is another drag.

Cross-country There are several trails along the valleys, of varying difficulty.

Mountain restaurants The glass-sided Gletschergarten (yes, on the glacier) does remarkable Punjabi-Arabic-Mediterranean fusion dishes.

Schools and guides We lack reports.

Families The Kinderland centre at Hausberg looks good, with magic carpet and snow sculptures.

STAYING THERE

Hotels There is one 5-star – Reindl's Partenkirchnerhof (943870), well placed for the rail stations – two dozen 4-stars and 3-stars. Tips are the 3-star Garmischer Hof (9110) and Atlas Post (7090), and the 4-star Zugspitze (9010). Rates are low in Alpine terms.

Apartments Can be booked via the tourist office.

Eating out Towns this big offer plenty of choice. The Gasthof Fraundorfer is 'awesome'. Other tips are the upscale Alpenhof and 'superb' Spago (Italian).

Après-ski There are bars at the lift bases where you can enjoy waiting for the next train home, and in town there are lots of cosy bars such as Zirbel Stube. Peaches is a lively bar.

Off the slopes There's lots to do, both outdoors and indoors. Walks include one through the Partnachklamm gorge – 'very easy and spectacular' – and paths on the lift-served hill across town from the slopes, called Wank.

Interactive resort shortlist builder at **www.wtss.co.uk**

Italy

Italy has a lot going for it as a destination: it remains generally the cheapest of the four major Alpine countries, despite strong competition from Austria; the atmosphere is jolly; it has good food and wine; the scenery, especially in the Dolomites and Courmayeur, is simply stunning; the lift systems include some of the most modern in Europe; the snowmaking is state-of-the-art (and they use it well); the grooming is top-notch; and most of the slopes are ideal for intermediates.

Italian resorts vary as widely in their characteristics as they do in location – and they are spread along the full length of the Italian border, from Sauze d'Oulx to the Dolomites.

A lot of Italian runs, particularly in the north-west, seem flatteringly easy. This is partly because grooming is immaculate and partly because piste classification seems to overstate difficulty. Nowhere is this clearer than in the linked slopes of La Rosière – in France – and La Thuile – in Italy, despite the French-sounding name. Venturing from the Italian motorways to the French moguls is like moving from the shelter of the harbour to the open sea.

Many Italians based in the northern cities ski at weekends, and it's very noticeable that many resorts are busy only then, and become peaceful once the weekend invaders retreat. It's a great advantage for those of us who are there for the whole week. This pattern is especially noticeable at the chic resorts, such as Cortina, Courmayeur and Madonna, and resorts that have not yet found international fame such as the Monterosa region. On the other hand, it doesn't really happen in parts of the Dolomites favoured by German visitors – like Brits, they tend to go for a week.

In general, Italians don't take their skiing or boarding too seriously. A late start, long lunch and early finish are the norm – leaving the slopes delightfully quiet for the rest of us. Mountain restaurants are welcoming places almost everywhere, encouraging leisurely lunching. Mountain restaurant prices are reasonable (check out our feature chapter on prices). Our reporters' standard complaint about the primitive hole-in-the-ground loos in mountain restaurants (and sometimes in resorts, too) is becoming less common. A persistent drag, though, is the ludicrous system in many self-service places where you have to queue to pay and then queue again to acquire your food or drink.

One thing that Italian resorts do have to contend with is erratic snowfall. While the snow in the northern Alps tends to come from the west, Italy's snow tends to come from storms arriving from the south. So it can have great conditions when other countries are suffering; or vice versa. Italian resorts have extensive snowmaking, and our observation is that they tend to use it more effectively than other Alpine countries. We have skied in Courmayeur and in the Dolomites when little natural snow has fallen, and in each case there has been excellent cruising on man-made snow.

Italy seems to be in the grip of 'legislation fever' at present, with mixed results. Italian bars and restaurants are now smoke-free, a huge improvement. And it is now compulsory for children (under 14, we understand) to wear helmets on the slopes.

← Fabulous scenery is part of the deal in the Dolomites – this is above San Cassiano, in Alta Badia (part of the Sella Ronda area)

But many areas have also made it illegal to go off-piste near their pistes; or to go off-piste at all; or to go off-piste outside defined routes. We've tried to get to the bottom of this development; but prompt, clear, accurate response to a slightly technical question like this is not a speciality of Italian tourist bodies. Some resorts tell us there are national laws; others, that it's a regional matter; others, that it's a local matter. Of course, there is then the matter of whether the law is applied, and how it is policed. Where we have a clear view of the situation in a given resort, we've included that in the relevant chapter. We'll continue to investigate, and post the results on our website. Perhaps the main thing to report at present is that we have no evidence of any interference in off-piste skiing in the Aosta valley, which is Italy's off-piste/heli-skiing HQ.

DRIVING IN THE ITALIAN ALPS

There are four main geographical groupings of Italian resorts, widely separated. Getting to some of these resorts is a very long haul, and moving from one area to another can involve very long drives (though the extensive motorway network is a great help).

The handful of resorts to the west of Turin – Bardonecchia, Sauze d'Oulx, Sestriere and neighbours in the Milky Way region – are easily reached from France via the Fréjus tunnel, or via the good road over the pass that the resort of Montgenèvre sits on.

Further north, and somewhat nearer to Turin than Milan, are the resorts of the Aosta valley – Courmayeur, Cervinia, La Thuile and the Monterosa area are the best known. These (especially

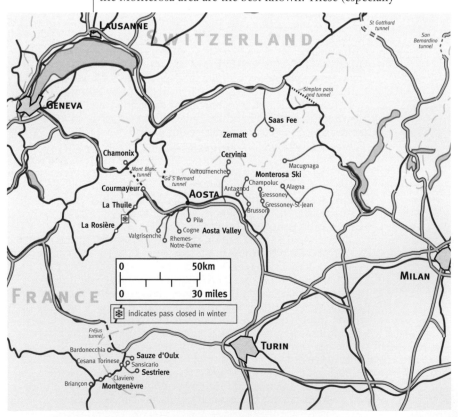

Courmayeur) are the easiest of all Italian resorts to reach from Britain (via the Mont Blanc tunnel from Chamonix in France). The Aosta valley can also be reached from Switzerland via the Grand St Bernard tunnel. The approach is high and may require chains. The road down the Aosta valley is a major thoroughfare, but the roads up to some of the other resorts are quite long, winding and (in the case of Cervinia) high.

To the east is a string of scattered resorts, most close to the Swiss border, many in isolated and remote valleys involving long drives up from the nearest Italian cities, or high-altitude drives from Switzerland. The links between Switzerland and Italy are more clearly shown on our larger-scale Switzerland map at the beginning of that section than on the map of the Italian Alps included here. The major routes are the St Gotthard tunnel between Göschenen (near Andermatt) and Airolo – the main route between Basel and Milan – and the San Bernardino tunnel reached via Chur.

Finally, further east still are the resorts of the Dolomites. Getting there from Austria is easy, over the Brenner motorway pass from Innsbruck. But getting there from Britain is a very long drive indeed – allow at least a day and a half. We wouldn't lightly choose to drive there and back for a week's skiing, except as part of a longer tour including some Austrian resorts. It's also worth bearing in mind that once you arrive in the Dolomites, getting around the intricate network of valleys linked by narrow, winding roads can be a slow business – it's often quicker to get from village to village on skis. Impatient Italian driving can make it a bit stressful, too.

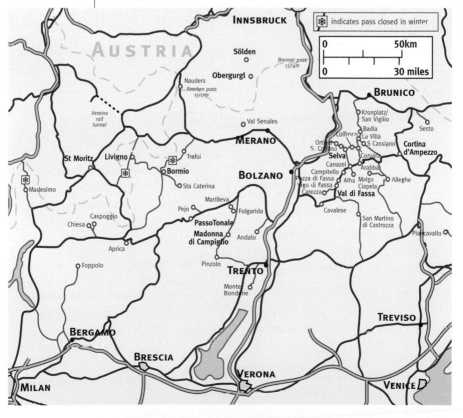

l'amore

Ski Italy. And fall in love

Fall in love with the prices too:
you'll find that hearty bowl of soup
or plate of delicious pasta will still
be at prices you can afford – and
not outrageously expensive as they
can be in some resorts across the
border. The wine too – as well as the
accommodation. Yet of course the
quality will still be outstanding!

Make the Aosta Valley your next winter
holiday destination – great skiing,
boarding and a whole lot more...

Champoluc & Gressoney –
links with the spectacular Monte
Rosa and Alagna ski areas - Italy's
cheaper answer to the Three Valleys.
It's one of Europe's best-kept ski
secrets... idyllic Alpine villages,
exciting slopes and exceptional
off-piste opportunities too.

Courmayeur – fabulous slopes
and gastronomy give a characteristic
village atmosphere beneath the
towering Mont Blanc massif. Ski the
Vallée Blanche from the Italian side.

with Italy's Aosta Valley.

Cervinia – the majestic Matterhorn, glacier skiing, linked with glamorous Zermatt and 350km of fantastic, snow-sure pistes.

Pila – well-groomed slopes and an informal atmosphere… just a gondola ride away from the historic Roman town of Aosta.

La Thuile – a wide range of exhilarating ski slopes linking Italy and La Rosière in France - superb for winter sports enthusiasts of all levels.

Valle d'Aosta
Vallée d'Aoste

www.lovevda.it

Aosta valley

The Aosta valley can reasonably claim to contain the best skiing that Italy has to offer – it certainly includes the highest

Aosta is a mid-sized city that is the capital of an autonomous (ie largely independent) region north of Turin called Valle d'Aosta. The valley has high mountains on both sides, and comes to an abrupt stop at Monte Bianco. Courmayeur – the resort at the foot of Europe's highest mountain – is well known in the UK, as is Cervinia, up a long side valley on the Swiss border. But the valley has many more resorts worth knowing about.

It's perhaps not surprising that the valley has managed to retain a degree of independence. It shares a long border with France, and French was the dominant language for centuries until Italian was imposed in the Fascist period in the early 20th century. The region was even French territory for a time. Almost all place names and local surnames are French in origin. These days, street signs are bilingual.

A Valle d'Aosta lift pass is available covering all the resorts in the region, and the related website (www.skivallee.it) is a useful starting point.

MAJOR RESORTS

We devote separate chapters in the book to three individual resorts.

Courmayeur is one of the Italian resorts best known in Britain – a charming, lively old village with a big cable car into a small but quite challenging ski area – and access to the famous Vallée Blanche glacier.

Not far down the valley, a road branches off south-west for the Petit St Bernard pass leading to Bourg St Maurice, in France. In winter the road is closed – and in fact becomes a piste leading down to the small resort of **La Thuile**. Its lifts and pistes link with those of La Rosière, in France.

Much further down the valley, beyond Aosta, a long side valley leads northwards towards the Swiss border, and climbs through Valtournenche to the other well-known resort, **Cervinia**. This exceptionally high resort was developed in the Fascist era around the small old climbing village of Breuil, at the foot of Monte Cervino – better known to us as the Matterhorn. Its glacial ski area is linked to that of Zermatt in Switzerland.

MONTEROSA SKI

We have a fourth full chapter devoted to Aosta valley skiing: it covers not a single resort but the ski area called

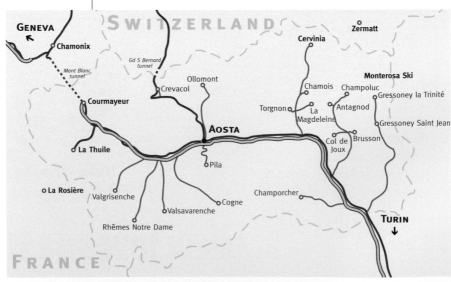

Monterosa Ski. This is a three-valley system to the east of the Cervinia valley, linking the village of Champoluc in the Val d'Ayas to Gressoney la Trinité and Alagna, which is outside the Aosta region and reached by a quite different route from the east. The main Monterosa Ski area combines a network of pistes covering a huge area of mountain with an exceptional range of off-piste and heli-skiing terrain.

A short way down the Val d'Ayas from Champoluc is **Antagnod** (1710m/5,610ft). It's a family-oriented resort with a great view of Monte Rosa itself. As well as good nursery slopes with moving carpets it has two chairlifts, the major one rising 575m/1,890ft and serving blue and red runs to the village. Further down the valley is **Brusson** (1330m/4,360ft). This is a major venue for international cross-country races along the valley, back towards Antagnod. There is sunny downhill skiing up a side valley at Estoul – easy red slopes served by two chairlifts, the major one rising 500m/1,640ft vertical.

In the central valley of the Monterosa Ski area, **Gressoney Saint Jean** is an old village with a rich heritage. It's equally good for cross-country and downhill skiing; as well as a well-equipped nursery slope it has a chairlift rising 675m/2,210ft serving not only blue and red slopes but also a single black.

All of these resorts offer 100% snowmaking on their pistes.

GRAN PARADISO/RUITOR AREA

Gran Paradiso, less often called by its French name Grand Paradis, is a glacier-draped 4000m peak south of Aosta – the only such peak entirely in Italy. Surrounding it is a national park of the same name, and on the fringes of the park are two small resorts. Ice climbing and ski touring are popular activities in and around the park.

Cogne (1535m/5,040ft) is the main resort for exploration of the park in summer, and has a privileged position only a few km from the peak itself, with the slightly lower peak of La Grivola even closer. It is a major centre for cross-country skiing, with 70km/43 miles of trails along the valley; international races include the Marcia Gran Paradiso. The downhill slopes above the village offer 9km/6 miles of runs; a pulse gondola takes you up to 2060m/6,760ft, and a chairlift then to 2250m/7,380ft. At the base is another chairlift and a moving carpet. There are three 4-star hotels, and over 20 3-star and 2-star ones.

Rhêmes Notre Dame (1725m/5,660ft) is a small village with a handful of 2-star and 3-star hotels in a quiet valley with a fine view up to the peaks on the French border. It has a tiny amount of lift-served downhill skiing. Skin up to the head of the valley and descend into France, and you'll end up near Val d'Isère.

The next valley to the west of Val di Rhêmes is **Valgrisenche**, also the name of a small village immediately below the glacial slopes of Tête du Ruitor. There are cross-country loops around the village and short, mainly red downhill runs served by two draglifts. But the area is best known for heli-skiing from a base at Bonne, just above the village of Valgrisenche. The head of the valley is reputed to have a particularly snowy micro-climate, and there are about 20 established heli-drop points on the surrounding peaks, with runs into France as well as Italy.

AOSTA/PILA

Aosta – rich in Roman and medieval remains – is a very unusual valley city in also being a ski resort. No, there are no pistes to the city, but a gondola from quite close to the centre takes you in 20 minutes to the very worthwhile slopes of Pila.

Pila (1800m/5,910ft) is a modern ski station, looking much like a French purpose-built resort, with 2,000 beds in hotels and apartments. Chairlifts (some fast, most slow) fan out from the resort serving an interesting mix of slopes totalling 70km/43 miles, mostly classified red with some blue. The treeline is high, at about 2300m/7,550ft, and most runs are below it. From the top heights there are grand views to Mont Blanc in the west and the Matterhorn in the east.

SMALLER RESORTS

There are lots of other, smaller resorts in the Aosta valley region that are worth considering for a quiet skiing holiday: Chamois, Champorcher, Col de Joux, Crevacol, La Magdeleine, Ollomont, Torgnon and Valsavarenche. Go to: www.regione.vda.it/turismo.

For contact details of relevant tourist offices and lift companies go to www.wtss.co.uk

Bormio

One on its own, this: a tall, narrow mountain above a very unusual, historic town – a spa as well as a ski resort

£75
RESORT PRICE INDEX

TOP 10 RATINGS

Extent	★★
Fast lifts	★★★★
Queues	★★★
Snow	★★★
Expert	★
Intermediate	★★★
Beginner	★★
Charm	★★★★
Convenience	★★★
Scenery	★★★

+ Good mix of high, open pistes and woodland runs adding up to some good long descents
+ Worthwhile neighbouring resorts
+ Attractive ancient town centre
+ Good mountain restaurants
+ Cheap, even by Italian standards

− Slopes all of medium steepness
− Rather confined main mountain, with other areas some way distant
− Off-piste is officially banned
− Town centre hotels inconvenient
− Long airport transfers

If you like historic Italian towns and don't insist on a traditional Alpine resort atmosphere, you'll find the town of Bormio very appealing – though you're unlikely to be staying right in the old centre. Given the limited slopes of Bormio's own mountain, plan on taking the free bus out to the Oga-Valdidentro area and perhaps on making longer outings – to Santa Caterina or Livigno.

THE RESORT

Bormio is in a remote spot close to the Swiss border; the airport transfer can exceed three hours. The Oga-Valdidentro area, a short bus ride out of Bormio, shouldn't be overlooked. The open and woodland runs are very pleasant and usually empty. Day trips to Santa Caterina (20 minutes by bus) and Livigno (around an hour) are possible. All these areas are covered by the Alta Valtellina lift pass. A pass of three days or more entitles you to half price on a one-day pass in St Moritz (three hours away).
Village charm The town has been a spa since Roman times and has a splendid 17th-century centre, with narrow, cobbled streets and grand stone facades – very atmospheric.
Convenience The centre is a 15-minute

walk from the gondola station across the river to the south. There are reliable free shuttle-buses, but many people walk. Closer to the lifts is a suburban sprawl of hotels for skiers. Several major hotels are on Via Milano, leading out of town, which is neither convenient (unless the hotel has a shuttle-bus) nor atmospheric.
Scenery The top of Cima Bianca exceeds 3000m/10,000ft and gives extensive views along the pretty wooded valleys.

THE MOUNTAINS

There's a nice mix of high, snow-sure pistes and lower wooded slopes. Both the piste map and the piste marking need substantial improvement.
Slopes The main area of slopes is tall (vertical drop 1800m/5,900ft), narrow and not extensive.
Fast lifts Access is by an eight-seat gondola to the mid-mountain mini-resort of Bormio 2000, with successive fast chairs or a cable car taking you on up to the top at 3010m/9,880ft.
Queues There should be few problems outside real peak weeks.
Terrain parks The resort has a terrain park and super-pipe on the slopes at Bormio 2000. As well as the usual jumps and rails, there's also a separate beginner area.
Snow reliability Runs above Bormio 2000 are usually snow-sure; most pistes face north-west, and snowmaking now covers 90% of them, though this doesn't necessarily help in late March. The Valdidentro area is

ALTA VALTELLINA

The town is very spread out but the 17th-century centre is charming and atmospheric ↓

Cima Bianca
3010m/9,880ft

Val di Sotto

OGA-VALDIDENTRO
2200m   2500m

BORMIO 2000

Ciuk
1640m

Oga
1475m

Bormio
1225m/4,020ft

Le Motte   Isolaccia
1430m   1345m

Bormio

427

Interactive resort shortlist builder at www.wtss.co.uk

KEY FACTS

| Resort | 1225m |
| | 4,020ft |

Bormio, S Caterina and Valdidentro

Slopes	1225-3010m
	4,020-9,880ft
Lifts	31
Pistes	100km
	62 miles
Blue	27%
Red	60%
Black	13%
Snowmaking	50%

Bormio only

Slopes	1225-3010m
	4,020-9,880ft
Lifts	14
Pistes	50km
	31 miles

UK PACKAGES

Directski.com, Interhome, Simply Alpine, Ski McNeill

Phone numbers
From abroad use the prefix +39 (and do **not** omit the initial '0' of the phone number)

TOURIST OFFICE

t 0342 902769
info@bormio.to
www.bormio.to
www.alta-valtellina.it

more reliable, and the high, shaded, north-facing slopes of Santa Caterina usually have good snow.

Experts There are a couple of short black runs in the main area, and off-piste is officially banned.

Intermediates The men's downhill race course starts with a steep plunge, but otherwise is just a tough red, ideal for strong intermediates. Stella Alpina, down to Bormio 2000, is also fairly steep. Many runs are less tough – ideal for most intermediates. The longest is a superb top-to-bottom cruise. The outlying mountains are also suitable for early intermediates.

Beginners The nursery slopes at Bormio 2000 offer good snow, but there are no very easy pistes to move on to. Novices are better off at nearby Santa Caterina.

Snowboarding The terrain park is the main attraction. The slopes are too steep for novices, and there's little to attract experienced boarders either. Hang Five (Bormio 2000) is a specialist school.

Cross-country There are 10km/6 miles of trails either side of Bormio, towards Piatta and beneath Le Motte and Valdidentro, but cross-country skiers are better off at snow-sure Santa Caterina.

Mountain restaurants The mountain restaurants are generally good – 'wonderful', says a recent visitor – and many have table- and self-service sections. Bormio 2000 has a big building with lots of eating options. Above Ciuk, the Rocca is a smart, woody chalet with table- or self-service and a large terrace. The place

at Cima Bianca is welcoming and good value. Past reporters have recommended the Baita de Mario as a great place for a long lunch.

Schools and guides There is a choice. The Nazionale school reportedly offers 'satisfactory lessons in English'.

Families The ski schools take children from the age of three from 10am to 4pm. The Contea di Bormio school at Bormio 2000 has its own snow garden and kindergarten.

STAYING THERE

There are plenty of apartments, but hotels dominate the package market.

Hotels There are 40-plus hotels, mostly 2- and 3-star. Of the 4-stars the Palace (0342 903131) is the most luxurious. We stayed at the Sant Anton (0342 901906), on the road out towards Livigno comfortable and with its own minibus shuttle to and from the lifts. Other 4-stars are the Posta (0342 904753) in the centre of the old town – rooms vary widely – and the Baita dei Pini (0342 904346) – the best placed of the top hotels – on the river, between the lifts and centre. Of the 3-stars, the Alu (0342 904504) and the Ambassador (0342 904625) are both close to the gondola and heartily recommended by recent visitors.

Apartments Try the modern Cristallo apartments (0342 902700).

At altitude The modern Girasole 2000 (0342 904652), at Bormio 2000, is simple but comfortable, and offers lots of evening events.

Eating out There's a wide choice. We had an excellent set menu of traditional local food (including pizzoccheri – noodles with melted cheese, potatoes and cabbage) at Rasiga – an atmospheric old barn near the centre of town. The Kuerc, Vecchia Combo, Al Filo and Rododendri have been recommended, as has Al Taula at San Antonio. There are some excellent pizzerias.

Après-ski The action starts on the mountain at the Rocca, and at bars near the foot of the piste. The Clem Pub, Cafe Mozart and the Aurora are popular. The Sunrise is a nightclub and restaurant, with live music.

Off the slopes Diversions include thermal baths, riding and walks in the Stelvio National Park. Excellent sports centre, ice rink and 'superb' swimming pool. St Moritz and Livigno are popular excursions.

SNOWPIX.COM / CHRIS GILL

Cervinia

One of a kind, this: for extensive, sunny, easy skiing, there is nowhere to match Cervinia. But that's about all there is to it.

£90
RESORT PRICE INDEX

RATINGS

The mountains

Extent	★★★☆☆
Fast lifts	★★★★☆
Queues	★★★★☆
Terrain p'ks	★★★★☆
Snow	★★★★★
Expert	★☆☆☆☆
Intermediate	★★★★☆
Beginner	★★★★★
X-country	★☆☆☆☆
Restaurants	★★★☆☆
Schools	★★★★☆
Families	★★☆☆☆

The resort

Charm	★★☆☆☆
Convenience	★★★☆☆
Scenery	★★★★☆
Eating out	★★★★☆
Après-ski	★★☆☆☆
Off-slope	★☆☆☆☆

NEWS

For 2009/10 the slow chairlifts above Plan Torrette are to be replaced by one fast chair, removing the one remaining weakness in the lift system.

For 2008/09 more snowmaking was added in the Valtournenche sector, particularly on the home run to the village. A children's area opened at Plan Maison. The gondola up to Laghi Cime Bianche was revamped, though without increasing its capacity.

➕ Miles of long, consistently gentle runs – ideal for intermediates wary of steep slopes or bumps

➕ Slopes are sunny, but high and snow-sure

➕ Impressive scenery

➕ Excellent village nursery slope

➕ Link with Zermatt in Switzerland provides even more spectacular views and good lunches

➖ Very little to interest good or aggressive intermediates and above

➖ Little to do in bad weather – almost entirely treeless, and lifts prone to closure by wind

➖ Not particularly attractive village

➖ Few off-slope amenities

➖ Steep climb to main gondola – though there is a chairlift alternative

If there is a better resort than Cervinia for those who like cruising motorways in spring sunshine, we have yet to find it. And then there's the easiest of Zermatt's slopes just over the Swiss border, and linked by lift and piste.

And for the rest of us? Well, to be frank, the rest of us are better off elsewhere. In particular, those with an eye on bumps or powder over in Zermatt should probably think about staying there, not here. The link is prone to closure by bad weather (especially in early season) and, despite major lift improvements in Zermatt, access to its best slopes is still a time-consuming business.

The village was branded Cervinia when it was developed for skiing, but these days harks back to its roots by prefixing that with its original name, Breuil.

THE RESORT

Cervinia is on the Italian side of the Matterhorn, at the head of a long valley. At weekends and public holidays, the resort can fill up with visitors from Milan and Turin.

The slopes link to Valtournenche further down the valley (covered by the lift pass) and at high altitude to Zermatt in Switzerland (covered by a daily supplement, or a more expensive weekly pass – take your passport as random checks are made).

Day trips by car are possible to Courmayeur, La Thuile and the Monterosa Ski resorts of Champoluc and Gressoney. A six-day pass covers two days in these other resorts.

VILLAGE CHARM ★★☆☆☆
Somewhat lacking

The old climbing village grew into a ski resort (in the years before and after WW2) in a haphazard way, and the result is a bit of a mess – neither pleasing to the eye nor as offensive as the worst of the French purpose-built resorts. The centre is compact and traffic-free, and a pleasant enough place to walk around. But ugly apartment blocks and hotels spoil the views from the slopes.

CONVENIENCE ★★★☆☆
Up or down

As our plan makes clear, this is not a big place, so choice of location isn't crucial; but it is certainly worth considering. The main lift, a gondola to Plan Maison, starts a hike up from the south end of the village – irritating for some, 'truly awful' for others. But there is now an alternative six-pack from the nursery slopes, next to the village centre, making this the obvious place to stay – especially now that it leads to another six-pack. Footpaths can be 'lethally slippery'.

There are also developments above the main village, closer to the gondola. Some hotels run their own

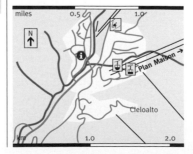

↑ Gentle slopes stretch away to the Swiss border from Plan Maison, the main mid-mountain focus

AIAT MONTE CERVINO / STEFANO VENTURINO

KEY FACTS

Resort	2050m
	6,730ft

Cervinia/ Valt'nenche	
Slopes	1525-3480m
	5,000-11,420ft
Lifts	24
Pistes	150km
	93 miles
Blue	30%
Red	59%
Black	11%
Snowmaking	38%

Cervinia/ Valt'nenche/ Zermatt combined	
Slopes	1525-3820m
	5,000-12,530ft
Lifts	57
Pistes	350km
	217 miles
Blue	22%
Red	60%
Black	18%
Snowmaking	33%

UK PACKAGES

Alpine Answers, Club Med, Crystal, Crystal Finest, Elegant Resorts, First Choice, Independent Ski Links, Inghams, Interhome, Italian Safaris, Jeffersons, Just Skiing, Kuoni, Momentum, Simply Alpine, Ski Line, Ski Solutions, Skitracer, Ski Weekend, STC, Thomson

shuttle-bus and there's an efficient public bus from the Cieloalto complex, well to the south of the main village.

SCENERY ★★★★
Monte Cervino rules

The Matterhorn is less special from the Italian than from the Swiss side, but Cervinia's setting is impressive by normal standards, with the peak towering above the village, and fine views from the slopes.

THE MOUNTAINS

Cervinia's main slopes are high, open, sunny and mostly west-facing. If the weather is bad, the top lifts often close because of high winds – and even the lower slopes may suffer poor visibility because of the lack of trees. Old decommissioned lifts left on the slopes give 'an atmosphere of shabby neglect', in the view of one reporter.

There is now a handy quick-folding piste map that covers both Cervinia and Zermatt fairly clearly.

EXTENT OF THE SLOPES ★★★
High, wide and easy

Cervinia has the biggest, highest, most snow-sure area of easy, well-groomed pistes we've come across. The area has Italy's highest pistes and some of its longest. Nearly all the runs are accessible to average intermediates. The high number of red runs on the

piste map is misleading: most of them would be classified blue elsewhere.

A deep gorge splits the slopes into two main sectors. Looking up the hill, the lifts from the village take you into the left-hand sector at first.

A gondola takes you to the mid-mountain base of **Plan Maison**. We've rarely seen the parallel cable car working, but a regular visitor assures us it does move occasionally. An attractive alternative route now is the six-pack from the village nursery slopes to Plan Torrette, where another six-pack, new for this season, will now serve the good slopes under the Matterhorn – and give pretty quick access to Plan Maison.

Above Plan Maison, a chain of three fast quads goes on up to Theodulpass, slightly the lower of two links with the slopes of Zermatt. From Plan Maison you can instead take a gondola across to **Laghi Cime Bianche**, and the right-hand sector. From there a giant cable car goes up to Plateau Rosa, the other link with Zermatt. This is the start of the splendid, wide Ventina run back to the cable car station (or on down to the village).

Part-way down you can branch off left for **Valtournenche**. The slopes here are served by three fast chairlifts, above a modern gondola from the village – but the final lift back to Cervinia is still a long draglift. From top to bottom the run down is not far short of 2000m/6,560ft vertical and a claimed 13km/8 miles in length, interrupted only by a newish quad part-way.

There is also the very small, little-used **Cieloalto** area at the bottom of the Ventina run, served by a slow old chair to the south of the village. This has some of Cervinia's steeper pistes, and the only trees in the area.

FAST LIFTS ★★★★
Farewell to slow chairs

Cervinia's long process of transition to a modern lift system should be completed for the coming season with

boarding

The wide, gentle and always groomed slopes, generally good snow and lack of many draglifts make Cervinia pretty much ideal for beginner and early intermediate boarders. But there are some long, flat parts to beware (notably around Plan Maison). Serious boarders will enjoy the terrain park, and there's an exclusive terrain park pass that costs 27 euros a day; they could also try heli-boarding.

the replacement at long last of the two old chairs above Plan Torrette by a six-pack.

QUEUES ★★★★
Very few problems
Readers do not normally find queues a big problem. We experienced few delays on our March 2008 visit, and favourable 2009 reports have encouraged us to up the rating this year. An upgrade to the Cervinia-Plan Maison gondola and a fast six-pack from the nursery slopes have eased pressure out of the resort at peak times, but the chair above Plan Maison – the route to Zermatt – does still get busy. There may, of course, be queues for lower lifts when upper lifts are shut by wind.

TERRAIN PARKS ★★★★
One of Italy's best
The 'Indian' terrain park (www.indianpark.it; in Italian only) by the Fomet run is one of the best parks in Italy and is serviced by a quick quad. Run by *Snowboard Italy*'s former editor, it gains new creative obstacles every year. The park has been shaped so that riders can hit an easy line or an intermediate line. There are also expert jumps that culminate in a 20m/66ft monster. The Italian flag box is still a fun feature for all levels and advanced riders can test their skills on the 6m/20ft and 10m/33ft tube rails. For a half-pipe head to Zermatt, which has an equally impressive freestyle area (and a park on the glacier, open in the summer for freestyle camps).

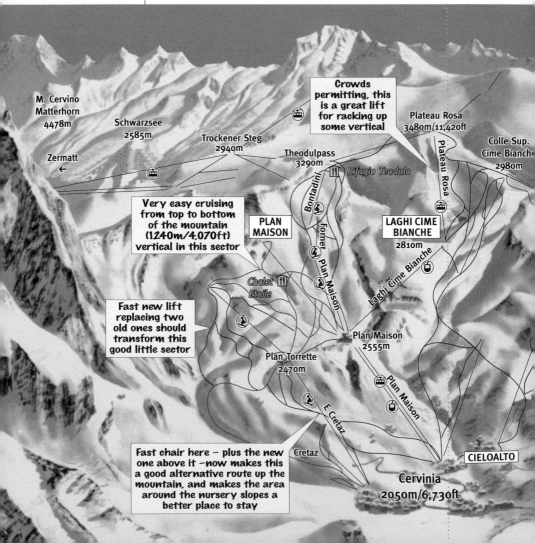

SCHOOLS

Cervino
t 0166 949034
Breuil
t 0166 940960
Matterhorn-Cervinia
t 0166 949523

Classes
(Cervino prices)
6 days (2hr 45min per
day) €180
Private lessons
€37 for 1hr for 1
person

GUIDES

Guide del Cervino
t 0166 948169

SNOW RELIABILITY ★★★★★
Superb

The slopes are among the highest in Europe and, despite getting a lot of afternoon sun, can usually be relied on to have good snow conditions from early to late season. Grooming is generally very good too.

Snowfall is not super-abundant though, so there is snowmaking almost from top to bottom, both on the Plateau Rosa/Laghi Cime Bianche side and the Theodulpass/Plan Maison sectors of the Cervinia slopes. The last two years have brought additional snowmaking above Valtournenche – now, at last, it covers the home run from Salette down to Valtournenche – this long run was often closed or in poor condition in the past.

FOR EXPERTS ★★★★★
Forget it

This is not a resort for experts. There are a few black runs scattered here and there, but most of them would be classified red elsewhere. Accessible off-piste terrain is limited, and even there high winds can play havoc with the snow. But of course there is some off-piste potential – in particular, around Plan Torrette and Rocce Bianche – and of course conditions are sometimes brilliant, and you then have the advantage that the snow can remain untracked for ages. Heli-drops with guides can be arranged (see Zermatt chapter for routes).

Many reporters head over to Zermatt for more challenging slopes and find it easier to reach them now

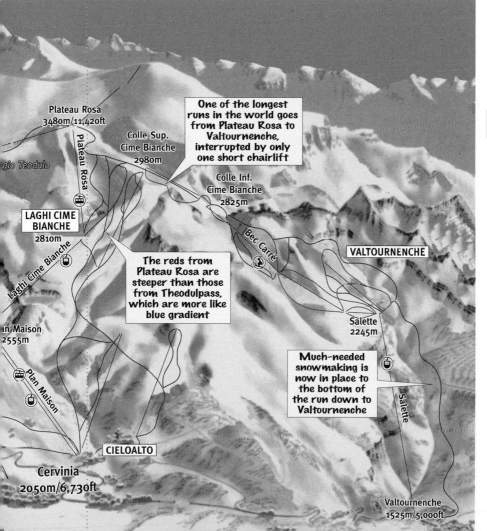

THE ZERMATT CONNECTION

Getting to Zermatt's classic terrain on the Rothorn/Stockhorn sectors is much quicker than it once was, thanks to the Furi to Riffelberg gondola, built in 2006. Getting there and back by mid-afternoon is now no problem.

But don't expect to spend very long on those Triftji moguls. On the way back there may be long queues for the Klein Matterhorn cable car and for the alternative long, slow T-bars.

LIFT PASSES

Breuil-Cervinia

Prices in €

Age	1-day	6-day
under 13	18	95
13 to 64	36	190
over 65	29	152
Free under 6		
Beginner limited day pass		

Notes
Covers all lifts on the Italian side, including Valtournenche; half-day passes; daily Zermatt extension

Alternative passes
International (covers Italian side and Zermatt); Aosta Valley pass

that new lifts have improved the links – see the 'Zermatt connection' box in the margin.

FOR INTERMEDIATES ★★★★
Miles of long, flattering runs
Virtually the whole area can be covered comfortably by average intermediates. From top to bottom there are gentle blue runs, and almost equally gentle reds in the beautiful scenery beneath the Matterhorn.

But strong intermediates will get bored quickly. The area on the right as you look at the mountain is best for more adventurous intermediates. The Ventina red is a particularly good fast cruise. You can use the cable car to do the top part repeatedly.

The runs towards Valtournenche are great cruises and very popular with reporters; many of the reds are more like blue gradient. The 13km/8 mile run all the way down is very satisfying, through splendid rocky scenery (and snowmaking has at last being installed on the lower part).

FOR BEGINNERS ★★★★★
Gentle progress
Complete beginners start on the good village nursery slope, with its long moving carpet. They should graduate quickly to the fine flat area around Plan Maison and the gentle blue runs above. Fast learners will be going all the way from top to bottom of the mountain in a few days.

FOR CROSS-COUNTRY ★☆☆☆☆
Hardly any
There are two short trails – 3km/2 miles and 5km/3 miles – but this is not a cross-country resort.

MOUNTAIN RESTAURANTS ★★★☆☆
OK if you know where to go
There are some good places if you know where to go. Toilet facilities are a traditional cause of complaints from reporters, but several have now been improved. You can, of course, head over to Zermatt for lunch.

Editors' choice Chalet Etoile (0166 940220), on a blue run above Plan Maison is an old favourite, happily supported by a continuing flood of reader reports – 'great food, lovely setting'. There's a self-service section too, which of course we haven't tried. The more basic Rifugio Teodulo (0166 949400) at Theodulpass is another good option – excellent pasta.

Worth knowing about Several readers recommend the Bontadini at the top of the Fornet chair ('good food and superb view'). Other reporter tips include the 'bright and cheerful' Ventina self-service. The British-run Igloo, near the top of the Bardoney chair, has its supporters.

The restaurants are cheaper and less crowded in the Valtournenche sector. There is growing support for Lo Baracon dou Tene above Salette (Becca d'Aran chair) – 'excellent location, service and food'. The Motta does 'basic but good pasta' and 'wonderful' gulaschsuppe.

SCHOOLS AND GUIDES ★★★★☆
Generally positive reports
Cervinia has three main schools, Cervino, Breuil and Matterhorn-Cervinia. Curiously, we lack new reports, but the Cervino school got generally good reports in 2008: 'excellent off-piste week', said one who was with Club Med (they use Cervino instructors); 'well organised, learnt a lot', said another. The Breuil school has been praised in the past.

FOR FAMILIES ★★☆☆☆
No recent reports
The Cervino ski school runs a ski kindergarten that looks very appealing. And there's a babysitting and kindergarten area at Plan Maison.

STAYING THERE

Most of the big operators come here, offering a wide selection of hotels, though other types of accommodation are rather thin on the ground. Crystal's club hotel Petit Palais is reportedly 'excellent'. Club Med is 'comfortable, excellent food, huge pool'.

Hotels There are almost 50 hotels, mostly 2- or 3-stars. Unless they run their own minibus to the slopes, choose your location with care.
★★★★Hermitage (0166 948998) Small, luxurious Relais et Château just out of the village on the road up to Cieloalto. Pool. Minibus to the lifts. Great views.
★★★★Excelsior Planet (0166 949426) Comfortable, near the nursery slopes. Pool, spa and minibus to the lifts. Regularly recommended by reporters.
★★★★Sertorelli Sport Hotel (0166 949797) At south end of village. Sauna and hot tub.
★★★★Europa (0166 948660) Well placed near nursery slope. Pool. Repeated

CHILDCARE

Mini Club Bianca Neve
t 0166 940201
Ages from 0 to 10;
9am-5pm daily

Mini Club (Cervino school)
t 0166 949034
Up to 12yr; 5 days inc ski lessons and lunch
€330

Ski school
Classes for children over 5

GETTING THERE

Air Turin 120km/ 75 miles (2hr); Geneva 185km/ 115 miles (2hr45)

Rail Châtillon (27km/17 miles); regular buses from station

ACTIVITIES

Indoor Swimming pools and saunas in hotels, fitness centre, squash

Outdoor Natural ice rink, paragliding, hiking, snowmobiles, mountaineering, snowshoeing, air boarding, snow biking, snow dinghies, ice climbing, ice cave visit

Phone numbers
From abroad use the prefix +39 (and do **not** omit the initial '0' of the phone number)

TOURIST OFFICE

t 0166 949136
breuil-cervinia@ montecervino.it
www.montecervino.it
www.cervinia.lt

recommendations for 'exceptionally friendly and helpful staff, very good room, good food'.

***Edelweiss (0166 949078) At south end of village. 'Cosy rooms, good bar and spa'.

***Furggen (0166 948928) Above the village (reached by Campetto chair or shuttle). 'Cosy, with pleasant staff.'

***Mignon (0166 949344) Central – 50 yards from the lifts. Good reports over the years – one reader goes annually.

***Serenella (0166 949041) 'Very Italian feel (and food), brilliant location, friendly, excellent value.'

**Marmore (0166 949057) Friendly, family run, on main street – an easy walk to the lifts.

**Meynet (0166 948696) Central, family hotel, slightly dated but repeatedly recommended.

Apartments There are many apartments, but few are available via UK tour ops. The Escargot ones in Cieloalto are 'very spacious'.

At altitude Up at Plan Maison, Lo Stambecco (0166 949053) is a 50-room 3-star hotel ideally placed for early nights and early starts.

EATING OUT ★★★★
Plenty to choose from
Cervinia's 50 or so restaurants allow plenty of choice, but one reader notes that prices climb steeply once you leave pizza territory. Current readers' favourite is the Matterhorn – 'friendly, good value', 'lively – children welcome'. Jour et Nuit is recommended particularly for its steaks – 'We went back a second night,' says one reporter. The Copa Pan, beneath the bar of that name, is an established recommendation, although 'a bit formal and subdued this year', says a regular. The lively Vieux Grenier at the hotel Grivola has 'excellent pizza', as does the 'great' Falcone. Other recommended pasta/pizza-oriented spots include Capanna Alpina and Al Solito Posto. Dinner at Baita Cretaz, above the village, makes a change.

APRES-SKI ★★★★★
Disappoints many Brits
Plenty of Brits come here looking for action but find there isn't much to do except tour the bars. 'Take a good book,' said one reporter. At tea time you can do worse than to hit the 'great cakes' at the Samovar. The hotel Grivola's bar, next to the Vieux Grenier restaurant, is attractively woody,

friendly and lively. The Copa Pan is lively, with great music ('Really liked it, difficult to leave,' said a 2008 visitor). The Dragon Bar is popular with Brits and Scandinavians and has satellite TV and videos, but a 2008 visitor preferred the 'friendly' Yeti for its 'dark ale and grolla' (and its happy hour). The Ymeletrob, next to the Punta Maquignaz hotel, is 'cosy, has live music and great canapés'. Other recommendations include Gran Beca for traditional Italian atmosphere and Hostellerie des Guides (with mementos of the owner's Himalayan trips). Discos liven up at weekends; Bianconiglio can be 'a bit cheesy, but it's great on Friday night', said a 2008 reporter.

OFF THE SLOPES ★★★★★
Little attraction
There is little to do for those who don't plan to hit the slopes. Amenities include hotel pools, a fitness centre and a natural ice rink. There are few shops. The walks are disappointing. The mountain restaurants reachable by gondola or cable car are not special.

Valtournenche 1525m

500m lower than Cervinia and 9km/5.5 miles down the road, Valtournenche offers lower prices and a rather more traditional style, and is well worth considering as a base. The village spreads along the busy, steep road up to Cervinia; it is reported to be 'not so much quiet as dead' in the evening.

A gondola leaves from the edge of the village, and fast lifts predominate above that. The epic run back from Plateau Rosa on the Swiss border is a great way to end the day – and now has snowmaking. There's a fair selection of simple hotels; some have shuttles to the lift. The 3-star Bijou (0166 92109) is 'friendly'. The 3-star Les Rochers (0166 92119) has 'excellent food; very good value'.

Cervinia

433

Interactive resort shortlist builder at www.wtss.co.uk

Cortina d'Ampezzo

The scenery will take your breath away even if the slopes don't; take your posh frocks to feel part of the high-season scene

£95
RESORT PRICE INDEX

RATINGS

The mountains

Extent	★★★
Fast lifts	★★★
Queues	★★★★
Terrain p'ks	★★
Snow	★★★
Expert	★★
Intermediate	★★★
Beginner	★★★★★
X-country	★★★★★
Restaurants	★★★★
Schools	★★★
Families	★★

The resort

Charm	★★★★
Convenience	★
Scenery	★★★★★
Eating out	★★★★★
Après-ski	★★★
Off-slope	★★★★★

NEWS

In early April 2010 Cortina will host the men's curling world championship.

For 2008/09 a new link (a chair followed by a piste) allowed access from Fedare on the back side of the Cinque Torri area to the Col Gallina area (and the cable car from Passo Falzarego to Lagazuoi).

➕ Magnificent Dolomite scenery – a quite exceptional setting

➕ Marvellous nursery slopes and good long cruising runs

➕ Access to the vast area covered by the Dolomiti Superski pass

➕ Attractive, although rather towny, resort, with lots of upmarket shops

➕ Good off-slope facilities

➕ No crowds or queues

➖ Several separate areas of slopes – though well linked by buses

➖ Erratic snow record

➖ Expensive by Italian standards

➖ Still quite a few slow lifts

➖ Gets very crowded in town and in restaurants during Italian holidays

➖ Few tough runs – though experts can have a fine time off-piste in a season like 2009

If you like lazy days centred around indulgent lunches on sunny terraces, gazing at scenery that is just jaw-droppingly wonderful, this is the place. The town is ringed by dramatic, pink-tinged cliffs and peaks soaring above the slopes, giving picture-postcard views wherever you look. Every time we go back, the memory has faded and our jaws drop again.

Cortina is Italy's most fashionable resort, with all that entails – in high season, when the money is in town, a lot of strolling, people-watching, serious shopping and lengthy lunching goes on. The majority of Italian visitors don't go near the slopes except to drive up to a 'mountain restaurant' for lunch.

Like most such swanky resorts, Cortina mainly caters for skiers driving Fords, not Ferraris – so it is not literally exclusive. But is it a 'proper' ski resort? Well, yes – up to a point. Those who went last winter and enjoyed fresh tracks for weeks on end would certainly say so. In an ordinary year, its limitations become more conspicuous.

THE RESORT

Cortina is a sizeable town spread across a wide, impossibly scenic bowl. Although it runs World Cup races, and leapt to international prominence as host of the 1956 Winter Olympics, it relies for its appeal on other things – 70% of all Italian visitors don't step on to the slopes. People leave the slopes early, and by 5pm hardly anyone is still in ski gear. In season the streets are packed with people parading up and down in their furs and baubles, shouting into their mobile phones. It's all pretty flat, so it's easy to get around in Gucci loafers.

Unlike most of the Dolomites, Cortina is pure Italy. The Veneto region has none of the Germanic traditions of the Südtirol, only a few miles away. And everyone is 'friendly and welcoming', say reporters.

San Cassiano is a short drive to the west, with links from there to Corvara and the other Sella Ronda resorts.

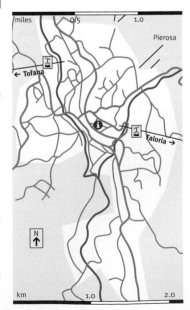

↑ Nice shot of Tofana from Faloria (thanks, Michael); but even the best pics don't convey just how impressive the scenery is
MICHAEL MARLAIS

KEY FACTS

Resort	1225m
	4,020ft
Slopes	1225-2930m
	4,020-9,610ft
Lifts	51
Pistes	120km
	75 miles
Blue	33%
Red	62%
Black	5%
Snowmaking	90%

VILLAGE CHARM ★★★★☆
Bella Italia
The centre is the traffic-free Corso Italia, full of chic designer clothes, jewellery and antique shops, art galleries and furriers – finding a ski shop can be tricky. The picturesque church tower adds to the atmosphere.

Surrounding the centre is a busy one-way system, reportedly less traffic-clogged now than it was last time we tackled it on a weekend.

CONVENIENCE ★☆☆☆☆
Widely scattered
Staying centrally is best: the lifts to the two main areas of slopes are a fair way from the centre, and at opposite sides of town. Other lifts are bus rides away. There are plenty of hotels in the centre but some are scattered around the outskirts. The top ones have their own shuttles, of course. But the town bus service is good ('very efficient and punctual'), and free to ski pass holders. A car can be useful, especially for getting to the outlying areas and to make the most of other areas on the Dolomiti Superski pass.

Visitors last season found snow removal from footways 'terrible'.

SCENERY ★★★★★
Stand and admire
Cortina is surrounded by some of the most stunning mountain scenery in Europe – the Dolomite mountains are magnificent, with their cliffs and peaks rising up from pretty wooded valleys.

THE MOUNTAINS

There is a good mixture of slopes above and below the treeline and new lifts are slowly replacing old ones.

Reporters consistently praise quiet slopes, at least in the areas close to the town, but regularly complain about signs, piste classification and marking, and the piste map.

EXTENT OF THE SLOPES ★★★☆☆
They add up ...
All Cortina's smallish separate areas are a fair trek from the town centre. The largest is **Pomedes**, accessed by chair and draglifts a bus ride away from the centre. You can reach it by tricky black piste from **Tofana**, Cortina's highest area, accessed by cable car from near the ice rink. There is no link in the opposite direction.

On the opposite side of the valley is the tiny **Mietres** area. Another two-stage cable car from the east side of town leads to the **Faloria** area, from where you can head down to chairs that lead up into the limited but dramatic runs beneath **Cristallo**.

Other areas are reachable by road – in particular the road west over Passo Falzarego towards San Cassiano and the Sella Ronda area. (Taxis are an affordable means of access if shared.)

First, there's the small but scenic **Cinque Torri** area. Excellent north-facing cruising runs are accessed by a fast quad, followed by an ancient one-person chair; beyond that, a rope tow

LIFT PASSES

Dolomiti Superski

Prices in €

Age	1-day	6-day
under 16	31	154
16 to 59	44	220
over 60	40	198

Free under 8

Beginner no deals

Notes
Covers 450 lifts and
1220km/758 miles of
piste in the
Dolomites, including
all Cortina areas

Alternative passes
Cortina d'Ampezzo
(Cortina, San Vito di
Cadore, Auronzo and
Misurina)

boarding

*Despite its upmarket chic, Cortina is a good resort for learning to board. The
Socrepes nursery slopes are wide, gentle and served by a fast chairlift. And
progress on to other easy slopes is simple because you can get around in all areas
using just chairs and cable cars – although there are drags, they can be avoided.
Boarderline is a specialist snowboard shop that organises instruction as well as
equipment hire. In a normal snow year there is little off-piste, but there are some
nice trees and hits under the one-person chair at Cinque Torri.*

leads to a sunny, panoramic red run
on the back of the hill to Fedare.

From Fedare the new Croda Negra
chairlift links to the tiny **Col Gallina**
area – north-facing, again – from
where you can take a green back to
Cinque Torri. The cable car from nearby
Passo Falzarego up to Lagazuoi serves
an excellent red run back down to the
base station and accesses the
famously beautiful 'hidden valley' run
to the fringe of the Alta Badia area.
(For more on this run see the Sella
Ronda chapter.)

Two other tiny out-of-town areas
are San Vito di Cadore (11km/7 miles
away) and Auronzo di Cadore
(33km/20 miles).

One way to tour the area is to use
special ski itineraries (maps are
available at the tourist and ski pass
offices). 'Skitour Olympia' takes you on
the 1956 Olympic courses and the
bobsleigh run. 'Skitour Romantik View'
covers the Lagazuoi-Cinque Torri area.

FAST LIFTS ★★★☆☆
Some in each sector
The main access lifts are cable cars
and there are fast chairs scattered
throughout each sector, but a lot of
slow old lifts remain too.

QUEUES ★★★★☆
No problem
Most Italian visitors rise late, lunch
lengthily and leave the slopes early to
get scrubbed up. That means few lift
queues and generally uncrowded
pistes – in the afternoon especially. A
2009 visitor, however, reports crowded
runs at Cinque Torri, even in low
season. He speculates that the crowds
came from the Sella Ronda resorts,
encouraged by the new link with the
Col Gallina area to take in Cinque Torri
before riding the cable car to Lagazuoi
for the famous 'hidden valley' run.
Queues can form for this cable car, not
surprisingly.

TERRAIN PARKS ★★☆☆☆
Not a bad one
There is a terrain park at Faloria that
has some decent kickers and rails, and
a half-pipe. It's not open to skiers.

SNOW RELIABILITY ★★★☆☆
Lots of artificial help
The snowfall record is erratic – it can
be good here when it's poor on the
north side of the Alps, and vice versa.
But 95% of the pistes are now covered
by snowmaking, so cover is good if it
is cold enough to make snow. As so

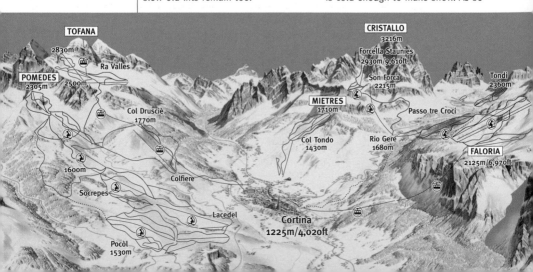

Cortina d'Ampezzo

Interactive resort shortlist builder at **www.wtss.co.uk**

SCHOOLS

Cortina
t 0436 2911

Azzurra Cortina
t 0436 2694

Cristallo
t 0436 870073

Dolomiti
t 0436 862264

Classes (Cortina prices)
6 mornings (2½hr)
€240

Private lessons
€47 for 1hr; each additional person €16

GUIDES

Guide Alpine
t 0436 868505

CHILDCARE

Gulliver Park
at the Pocòl ski area
t 0340 055 8399
Play area with babysitting available by the hour

Ski school
The schools offer classes for ages 4 to 14

GETTING THERE

Air Venice 160km/100 miles (2hr15). Treviso 130km/80 miles (2hr). Sat and Sun transfers for hotel guests (advance booking required); 35-minute heli-transfers from Venice

Rail Calalzo (35km/22 miles) or Dobbiaco (32km/20 miles); frequent buses from station

often, it's the black runs that are most vulnerable when natural snow is short – several are south-facing, and liable to closure. Grooming is excellent.

FOR EXPERTS ★★★★★
Normally rather limited
Decent amounts of natural snow are the key factor – not only to provide plentiful off-piste (which will offer fresh tracks for days on end) but to ensure adequate snow cover on the sunny black runs. These include the excellent Forcella from Tofana to Pomedes: deservedly graded black, it goes through a gap in the rocks, and gives wonderful views of Cortina way down in the valley below. And Cortina's most serious challenge, the Staunies run at the top of the Cristallo area – a south-facing couloir that we have never found open (tougher than it looks from below, warns a reporter). There are short but genuinely black runs below Pomedes and Duc d'Aosta.

There are some excellent red runs too, notably at Pomedes and Faloria. Heli-skiing is available.

FOR INTERMEDIATES ★★★★★
Fragmented and not extensive
To enjoy Cortina you must like cruising in beautiful scenery, and not mind doing runs repeatedly.

The runs at the top of Tofana are short but normally have the best snow. The highest are at over 2800m/9,190ft and mainly face north. But be warned: the only way back down is by the tricky black run described above or by cable car. The reds in the linked Pomedes area offer good cruising and some challenges.

Faloria has a string of fairly short north-facing runs – we loved the Vitelli red run, round the back away from the lifts. And the Cristallo area has a long, easy red run served by a fast quad.

It is well worth making the trip to Cinque Torri for fast cruising on usually excellent north-facing snow. And do not miss the wonderful 'hidden valley' red run from the Passo Falzarego cable car (see the Sella Ronda chapter).

FOR BEGINNERS ★★★★★
Wonderful nursery slopes
The Socrepes area has some of the biggest nursery slopes and best progression runs we have seen. You'll find ideal gentle terrain on the main pistes but some of the blue forest paths can be icy and intimidating.

FOR CROSS-COUNTRY ★★★★★
One of the best
Cortina has around 75km/47 miles of trails suitable for all standards, mainly in the Fiames area, where there's a cross-country centre and a school – and night skiing on a Wednesday. Trails include a 25km/16 mile itinerary following an old railway from Fiames to Cortina, and there is a beginner area equipped with snowmaking. Passo Tre Croci offers more challenging trails, covering 10km/6 miles. A Nordic area pass is available.

MOUNTAIN RESTAURANTS ★★★★★
Good, but get in early
Many restaurants can be reached by road or lift, and fur coats arrive as early as 10am to sunbathe, admire the views and idle the time away on their mobile phones. In some places, skiers are decidedly in the minority. Although prices are high in the swishest establishments, we've found plenty of reasonably priced places, serving generally excellent food (our price index is not high). Reporters stress the consistently high standard.

In the Socrepes area, the Rifugio Col Taron is highly recommended and the Rifugio Pomedes is endorsed by a recent visitor. The Piè de Tofana and El Faral are also good.

The restaurants at Cinque Torri – the Scoiattoli ('magnificent home-made pastas' and 'excellent service') and the Rifugio Averau ('marvellous pasta and great wine') – offer fantastic views. The Rifugio Fedare, over the back of Cinque Torri, is also recommended – 'great pasta with hare sauce'. Rifugio Lagazuoi, a short hike up from the top of the Passo Falzarego cable car, also has great views.

SCHOOLS AND GUIDES ★★★★★
Mixed reports
Of the four ski schools, we've had mixed reports of the Cortina school over the years – though we lack recent reports. The Guide Alpine offers off-piste and touring.

FOR FAMILIES ★★★★★
Better than average
By Italian standards childcare options at Gulliver Park are comprehensive, with all-day care arrangements for children of practically any age. But don't count on good spoken English. And the fragmented slopes can make for stressful days with children.

↑ Keeping the terraces free of snow must have been a full-time job last season. This is Faloria

MICHAEL MARLAIS

UK PACKAGES

Alpine Answers, Italian Safaris, Kuoni, Momentum, Simply Alpine, Ski Freshtracks, Ski Solutions, Ski Weekend, Ski Yogi, Snow Finders, White Roc

ACTIVITIES

Indoor Swimming pool, saunas, health spa, fitness centre, ice stadium, curling, museums, art gallery, cinema

Outdoor Olympic bobsleigh run, snow rafting down Olympic ski jump, snowshoe tours, sleigh rides, 6km/4 miles of walking paths, tobogganing

Phone numbers
From abroad use the prefix +39 (and do **not** omit the initial '0' of the phone number)

TOURIST OFFICE

t 0436 866252
cortina@dolomiti.org
www.cortina.dolomiti.org

STAYING THERE

Hotels dominate the market but there are some apartments and chalets.
Hotels There's a big choice, from 5-star luxury to 1-star and 2-star pensions.
*****Cristallo (0436 881111) Top of the market. A hike from the town centre and Faloria lift, but there's a shuttle, of course. Pool etc.
*****Miramonti Majestic (0436 4201) Spectacularly grand hotel, 2km/1 mile south of town. Pool etc.
****Poste (0436 4271) At the heart of the town, on the car-free Corso Italia. Large rooms, some with spa baths. An established reader favourite, though we lack recent reports.
****Ancora (0436 3261) Elegant public rooms. On the traffic-free Corso Italia.
****Parc Victoria (0436 3246) Rustic and family-run with small rooms but good food, at the Faloria end of town.
****Park Faloria (0436 2959) Near ski jump, splendid pool, good food.
***Columbia (0436 3607) B&B hotel a short walk from Tofana lift, a bit of a hike from town. Recommended by a reader this year – 'very helpful staff'.
***Menardi (0436 2400) Welcoming roadside inn, a long walk from the town centre.
***Olimpia (0436 3256) Comfortable B&B hotel in centre, near Faloria lift.
***Villa Resy (0436 3303) Small and welcoming, just outside centre, with British owner.
***Alpes (0436 862021) On the edge of town. 'Excellent food and service and friendly staff.' Hot tub.
**Montana (0436 862126) Central B&B. 'Excellent – amazing value.'
Apartments There are some chalets and apartments – usually well outside the town centre – available for independent travellers.

EATING OUT ★★★★★
Huge choice
There's an enormous selection of restaurants, both in town and a little way out, doing mainly Italian food. The very smart and expensive El Toulà is in a beautiful old barn, just on the edge of town. Many of the best restaurants are further out: the Michelin-starred Tivoli, the Meloncino al Camineto, the Leone e Anna, the Rio Gere and the Baita Fraina. Similarly outside town but handy for the slopes is a new reader recommendation this year: Baita Son del Prade – 'never too crowded, wonderful lasagne'.

APRES-SKI ★★★★★
Lively in high season
Cortina is a lively social whirl in high season, with lots of well-heeled Italians staying up very late.
The Lovat is one of several high-calorie teatime spots. There are many good wine bars: Enoteca has 700 wines and good cheese and meats; Osteria has good wines and local ham; and Villa Sandi and LP26 have been recommended. Reporters have enjoyed the hospitality of the hotel Poste. The liveliest bar is the Clipper, with a bobsleigh by the door. Discos liven up after 11pm.

OFF THE SLOPES ★★★★★
A classic resort
Cortina attracts lots of people who don't use the slopes, unless you count strolling across them – despite a lack of published information, a reporter tells us there are good and popular walks to be done in several sectors, particularly Pocol and Socrepes. The shopping is 'fabulous'; as well as high fashion 'you can get anything and everything at the Co-operativa di Cortina'. Mountain restaurants are accessible by road. And there's plenty more to do, such as swimming and skating. There is an observatory at Col Drusciè that has star-gazing tours. You can take a taxi-bob down the Olympic bobsleigh run (unless closed by heavy snow, as it was for long periods last season). There's horse jumping and polo on the snow occasionally. Excursions to Venice are easy. You can visit the First World War tunnels at Lagazuoi or the memorial at Pocòl.

Courmayeur

Stunning scenery and seductive, charming village, on the opposite side of the valley from its small area of slopes

£95
RESORT PRICE INDEX

RATINGS

The mountains

Extent	**
Fast lifts	****
Queues	****
Terrain p'ks	*****
Snow	****
Expert	***
Intermediate	****
Beginner	**
X-country	***
Restaurants	****
Schools	****
Families	**

The resort

Charm	****
Convenience	*
Scenery	****
Eating out	****
Après-ski	****
Off-slope	***

NEWS

For 2008/09 the draglift serving the high-altitude Tzaly beginner slope was replaced. More snowmaking was added.

The City Ski Championships, in association with Momentum Ski, will be held here from 18 to 21 March 2010.

- Charming old village, with car-free centre and stylish shops and bars
- Stunning views of Mont Blanc
- Access to the famous Vallée Blanche run to Chamonix (day trips there are possible by road, too)
- Heli-skiing available
- Comprehensive snowmaking
- Some good mountain restaurants

- Relatively small area, with mainly short runs; high-mileage piste-bashers should stay away
- Lack of nursery slopes and easy runs for confidence-building
- No tough pistes
- No pistes back to the village, only to Dolonne (where you catch a bus)
- Crowded at weekends

Courmayeur is a great place for a weekend away (or a day trip to escape bad weather in Chamonix), and we always look forward to a quick visit here. (Excellent restaurants both on and off the mountain plus village bars among the most civilised in the skiing world are factors, we admit.) Whether it makes sense for a week's holiday is another matter. Its pistes are best suited to competent intermediates, who are likely to have an appetite for mileage that Courmayeur will arouse but not satisfy. Off-piste, there is more to do; experts who hire a guide (and the odd helicopter) can have a fine time. And with a car you can explore several other worthwhile resorts nearby.

THE RESORT

Courmayeur is a traditional old Italian mountaineering village that has retained much of its character. Pila, La Thuile and Chamonix are an easy drive or bus ride and Cervinia is reachable.

VILLAGE CHARM ****
Attractive and sophisticated
The village has a charming traffic-free centre of attractive shops, cobbled streets and well-preserved buildings. An Alpine museum and a statue of a long-dead mountain rescue hero add to the historical feel.

The centre has a great evening atmosphere, focused around the Via Roma. As the lifts close, people pile into the many bars, some of which are very civilised. Others wander in and out of the many small shops, which include lots of smart clothes shops, nice delis and a good bookshop. At weekends people-watching is part of the scene, when the fur coats of the Milanese and Torinese take over.

CONVENIENCE *
Buses to the lifts
You cannot ski back to the village itself. But a huge cable car on the southern edge will take you to and from Plan Checrouit, at the heart of the slopes. A gondola from Dolonne (a few minutes' bus ride away) offers a popular alternative way up and you can ski back there. Both the cable car and the gondola are bus-served, and while parking at the cable car is very limited, there's a big car park at Dolonne. Many hotels run shuttles to and from Dolonne. Drivers can also go

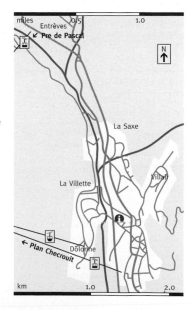

KEY FACTS

Resort	1225m
	4,020ft
Slopes	1210-2755m
	3,970-9,040ft
Lifts	21
Pistes	100km
	62 miles
Blue	27%
Red	62%
Black	11%
Snowmaking	22%

Weekly news updates and resort links at www.wtss.co.uk

LIFT PASSES

Courmayeur

Prices in €

Age	1-day	6-day
under 12	21	98
12 to 64	41	195
over 65	31	156

Free under 6

Beginner two free nursery lifts

Notes
Covers Courmayeur and the Mont Blanc cable cars; half-day passes; some single ascent passes; 3+ day passes allow at least one day in the Aosta valley

Alternative passes
Non-skier; Mont Blanc Unlimited (includes Chamonix valley); Valle d'Aosta (covers Valle d'Aosta ski areas)

---

to Entrèves, up the valley, where there is a large car park at the cable car. Most people leave skis or boards and boots in lockers up the mountain or at the lift base.

Buses, infrequent but timetabled (though a 2009 visitor could not get a timetable to take away), go to La Palud, just beyond Entrèves, for the Monte Bianco cable car to Punta Helbronner (for Vallée Blanche). Taxis are easily arranged for evening excursions to valley restaurants.

SCENERY ★★★★☆
Mont Blanc rules
The high glacial slopes of Mont Blanc's massif overlook Courmayeur's slopes. The views from the high points at Cresta d'Arp and Cresta Youla are stunning.

THE MOUNTAINS

The pistes suit intermediates, but are surprisingly limited for such a well-known, large resort. They are varied in character, if not gradient. Signposting of pistes has recently been improved, and a new piste map now shows lift names and direction.

EXTENT OF THE SLOPES ★★☆☆☆
Small but interestingly varied
There are two distinct sections, both almost entirely intermediate. The east-facing **Checrouit** area, accessed by the Checrouit gondola, catches morning sun and has open, above-the-treeline pistes. The 25-person, infrequently running Youla cable car goes to the top of Courmayeur's pistes. A further tiny cable car to Cresta d'Arp serves only long off-piste runs (a guide is recommended but no longer compulsory to ride this cable car).

Most people follow the sun over to the north-west-facing slopes towards **Val Veny** in the afternoon. These are interesting, varied and treelined, with great views of Mont Blanc and its glaciers. There are a few alternative routes between the Checrouit and Val Veny areas; it's not always easy to figure them out. The Val Veny slopes are also accessible by cable car from Entrèves, a few miles outside Courmayeur.

A little way beyond Entrèves is La Palud, where a cable car goes up in three stages to Punta Helbronner, at the shoulder of **Mont Blanc**. There are no pistes from the top, but you can do

SCHOOLS

Monte Bianco
t 0165 842477

Courmayeur
t 0165 848254

Classes
(Monte Bianco prices)
5 days (3hr per day)
€175

Private lessons
From €36 for 1hr;
additional person €11

GUIDES

Guides Courmayeur
t 0165 842064

the famous Vallée Blanche run to Chamonix from here without the scary ridge walk that forms the start on the Chamonix side (for some of the more interesting and steeper variants of the Vallée Blanche you need start on the Chamonix side, though). Or you can tackle the tougher off-piste runs on the Italian side of Mont Blanc. For obvious reasons, none of these glacier runs should be done without a guide. There are buses to and from Chamonix through the Mont Blanc tunnel.

FAST LIFTS ★★★★☆
Adequately serviced
The main access lifts are cable cars or a gondola, with fast lifts above them. There are still a few old, slow chairs, although these can be largely avoided.

QUEUES ★★★★☆
Much improved
The introduction of the Dolonne gondola a few seasons ago seems to have reduced the weekend and peak period queues for the Checrouit and Val Veny cable cars, offering a 'quick and efficient' way up and down the mountain. The infrequent Youla cable car may require patience – it's worth it only for those heading off-piste. Overcrowded slopes on weekends, particularly down to Zerotta, can be a problem.

TERRAIN PARKS ★★★★★
There isn't one
Courmayeur has no terrain park or half-pipe. And now it has scrapped its boardercross.

SNOW RELIABILITY ★★★★☆
Good for most of the season
Courmayeur's slopes are not high – mostly between 1700m and 2250m (5,600ft and 7,400ft). Those above Val Veny face north or north-west, so they keep their snow well, but the Plan Checrouit side is too sunny for comfort in late season. There is snowmaking on most main runs, including the red run to Dolonne in the valley. So good coverage in early and mid-season is virtually assured – we've been there in a snow drought and enjoyed decent skiing entirely on man-made snow.

FOR EXPERTS ★★★☆☆
Off-piste is the only challenge
Courmayeur has few challenging pistes. The black runs on the Val Veny side are not severe, and few moguls form elsewhere. But if you're lucky enough to find fresh powder – as we have been several times – you can have fantastic fun among the trees.

Classic off-piste runs go from Cresta d'Arp, at the top of the lift network, in three directions: a clockwise loop via Arp Vieille to Val Veny, with close-up views of the Miage glacier; east down a deserted valley to Dolonne or Pré-St-Didier; or south through the Youla gorge to La Balme, near La Thuile.

On Mont Blanc, the Vallée Blanche is not a challenge (though there are more difficult variations), but the Toula glacier route on the Italian side from Punta Helbronner to Pavillon most certainly is, often to the point of being dangerous. There are also heli-drops available, including a wonderful 20km/12 mile run from the Ruitor glacier down into France – you ride the lifts back up from La Rosière and descend to La Thuile (a taxi ride from

boarding

Courmayeur's pistes suit intermediates well, and most areas are easily accessible by novices as the main lifts are cable cars, chairs and gondolas. Although it's a bit steep for absolute beginners, a recent reporter says, 'I'd bring beginner friends to Courmayeur with a clean conscience. And for intermediates and experts it's lots of fun – there seemed to be an above-average number of lumps and bumps to the side of the piste for playful frolics.' For the more adventurous, there are good off-piste routes. But there's no park or pipe and the boardercross course is no longer being built.

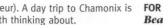
CHILDCARE

Fun park Dolonne
9am-4.30

Mini club Plan Chécrouit (Monte Bianco school)
Ages 0 to 10; 9am to 4.30

Ski schools
Take children from age 5

AIAT MONTE BIANCO

The magnificent Monte Bianco massif dominates the view from most of the slopes ↓

Courmayeur). A day trip to Chamonix is well worth thinking about.

FOR INTERMEDIATES ★★★★☆
Good reds, but limited extent

The whole area is suitable for most intermediates, but it is small. The avid piste-basher will ski it in a day but enjoy the very long (1400m/4,590ft vertical) red run from Cresta Youla all the way to Dolonne. The area lacks long, easy runs to suit the more timid.

The open Checrouit section is pretty much go-anywhere territory, but it is basically just one wide red slope. Timid skiers should take the fast six-seater Pra Neyron chair for access to the area's few blues. The Val Veny side of the mountain is basically steeper, with manageable blacks going close to the fall line and good reds and the occasional blue taking less direct routes. These runs link in with pretty, wooded slopes heading to Zerotta. The fast Zerotta chair serves runs of varying difficulty including a long blue.

Adventurous, fit intermediates can try the off-piste Vallée Blanche and the local heli-skiing.

FOR BEGINNERS ★★☆☆☆
Consistently too steep

Courmayeur is not well suited to beginners. There are several nursery slopes, none ideal. The area at Plan Checrouit gets crowded, and there are few easy runs for the near-beginner to progress to. The small area just above the Entrèves cable car top station, has decent beginner terrain, and it tends to have good snow. And there are easy blues at Dzeleuna (top of the Pra Neyron chair). The Maison Vieille chair can be ridden both ways, for access to the Tzaly blue slope.

FOR CROSS-COUNTRY ★★★☆☆
Beautiful trails

There are 35km/22 miles of trails. The best are the five covering 20km/12 miles at Val Ferret, served by bus. Dolonne has a couple of short trails.

MOUNTAIN RESTAURANTS ★★★★☆
Lots – some of them very good

The area is lavishly endowed with 27 establishments ranging from rustic little huts to a large self-service place. Most huts do table service of delicious pizza, pasta and other dishes and it is best to reserve tables in advance. But there are also snack bars selling more basic fare and relying on views and sun to fill their terraces.

Several restaurants are excellent. At Plan Checrouit, Chiecco serves the best and most refined food, with friendly service: 'the owner is passionate about her food'; 'wonderful pasta and amazing meat courses – expensive but worth it'. Bar du Soleil now has a 'really nice' restaurant with 'stunning' views from the terrace. Reporters also enjoy the 'convenient' Christiania (book a table downstairs) – 'great pizzas'. Etoile Ski – just above here – was new for 2008/09 and serves 'excellent pizzas and roasts'. Further up the hill, Maison Vieille is a welcoming rustic place with traditional Italian food including good home-made pastas. At Col Checrouit, Chez Croux serves 'the best cakes and hot drinks on the mountain'. There is another clutch of worthwhile places in Val Veny, all with excellent views: the Grolla, Zerotta and Baita da Geremia (with sandwiches served from an old gondola outside) have lovely sunny terraces, though one reporter preferred the food at the nearby Petit Mont Blanc. Courba Dzeleuna just below the top of the Dzeleuna chair serves snacks, but is best known for its delicious home-made myrtle grappa (but beware of the alcohol-soaked berries left in the glass).

SCHOOLS AND GUIDES ★★★★☆
Good reports

The Monte Bianco ski school gets good reviews: 'the best instructor for ages – possibly ever'. There is a thriving guides' association ready to help you explore the area's off-piste; it has produced a helpful booklet showing the main possibilities. The Courmayeur school has 'a more snowboardy and young funky image'.

Air Geneva 100km/ 60 miles (1hr30); Turin 150km/95 miles (2hr)

Rail Pré-St-Didier (5km/3 miles); regular buses from station

Indoor Hotel swimming pools, Alpine museum, cinema, library, art gallery, sports centre with climbing wall, ice rink, curling, fitness centre, indoor golf, squash, tennis

Outdoor Walking paths in Val Ferret, snowshoeing, paragliding, hang-gliding, golf on snow, snow biking, dog sledding

Alpine Answers, Alpine Weekends, Crystal, Crystal Finest, First Choice, Friendship Travel, Independent Ski Links, Inghams, Interactive Resorts, Interhome, Interski, Just Skiing, Kuoni, Mark Warner, Momentum, Simply Alpine, Ski Activity, Ski Expectations, Ski Freshtracks, Ski Line, Ski Solutions, Skitracer, Ski Weekend, Skiweekends.com, Ski Yogi, STC, Thomson, White Roc

Check out our feature chapters at the front of the book.

Phone numbers From abroad use the prefix +39 (and do **not** omit the initial '0' of the phone number)

t 0165 842060 info@aiat-monte-bianco.com www.aiat-monte-bianco.com

FOR FAMILIES ★★☆☆☆
Some facilities
There are children's playgrounds at Dolonne and Val Veny and a nursery at Plan Checrouit.

STAYING THERE

Courmayeur's long-standing popularity ensures a wide range of packages (including some excellent weekend deals), mainly in hotels. Tour op Momentum is a Courmayeur specialist and can advise about and fix pretty much whatever you want here. Some UK operators have catered chalets.

Hotels There are nearly 50 hotels, spanning the star ratings.

★★★★Royal e Golf (0165 831611) Large, grand place in centre just off Via Roma. Outdoor pool, sauna, piano bar.

★★★★Gran Baita (0165 844040) Luxury place with antiques. Panoramic views. Pool. Shuttle-bus to cable car.

★★★★Pavillon (0165 846120) Comfortable hotel near cable car, with a pool. Friendly staff.

★★★★Auberge de la Maison (0165 869811) Small, atmospheric hotel in Entrèves; owned by the same family as Maison de Filippo (see 'Eating out').

★★★★Cresta e Duc (0165 842585) Just renovated. In centre off Via Roma. 'Great management and service.'

★★★Walser (0165 844824) Near main road. 'Good value hotel with exemplary service.'

★★★Bouton d'Or (0165 846729) Small, friendly B&B near main square. 'Very welcoming; owner ferries you to/from lifts if you wish,' says a reporter.

★★★Berthod (0165 842835) Friendly, family-run hotel near centre.

★★★Grange (0165 869733) Rustic farmhouse in Entrèves.

★★★Triolet (0165 846822) Comfortable, with excellent location near the lifts.

★★★Maison Saint Jean (0165 842880) Central, family-run, pool.

★★Edelweiss (0165 841590) Friendly, cosy, good value; close to the centre.

★★Scoiattolo (0165 846/16) Good rooms, good food; shame it's at the opposite end of town to the cable car.

Apartments The Grand Chalet (0165 841448) is central with spacious apartments, hot tub, steam, sauna.

At altitude Visiting Courmayeur and not staying in the charming village seems perverse – if you're that keen to get going in the morning, this is probably the wrong resort. But at Plan Checrouit, the 1-star Christiania (0165

843572 – see 'Mountain restaurants') has simple rooms; the 3-star Baita (0165 841611) is smarter; book early.

EATING OUT ★★★★☆
Jolly Italian evenings
There is a great choice; there's a handy promotional booklet describing many of them (in English as well as Italian). In downtown Courmayeur, we've been impressed by the traditional Italian cuisine of both Pierre Alexis and Cadran Solaire. But the popular Terrazza is reportedly the 'best in town', with wonderful local food and great service'. The 'good value' Mont-Fréty, the Tunnel pizzeria, the Piazzetta ('excellent seafood pastas'), Al Camin ('meat lover's paradise') and the Vieux Pommier (for fondue and raclette) have also been recommended. And the Aria has 'an amazing wine list'. Within taxi range, the touristy but very jolly Maison de Filippo in Entrèves is rightly famous for its fixed-price, 36-dish feast. A local recommends the restaurant in the hotel Dente del Gigante at La Palud and the Clotze in Val Ferret ('expensive but modern, refined Italian cuisine').

APRES-SKI ★★★★☆
Stylish bar-hopping
Courmayeur has a lively evening scene – at weekends, at least – centred on stylish bars with comfy armchairs or sofas to collapse into, often serving free canapés in the early evening. Our favourites are the Roma, the back room of the Caffè della Posta and the Bar delle Guide. The Cadran Solaire is where the big money from Milan and Turin hangs out. The Privé serves great cocktails. Poppy's is popular for drinks and pizza, and the American Bar has good music and wines.

OFF THE SLOPES ★★★☆☆
Lots on for non-slope users
If you're not interested in hitting the snow, you'll find the village pleasant – parading up and down is a favourite pastime for the many non-skiers the resort attracts. You can go by cable car up to Punta Helbronner, by bus to Aosta, or up the main cable car to Plan Checrouit to meet friends for lunch. The huge sports centre is good (but no pool). Don't miss a visit to the thermal baths at Pré-St-Didier – with over 30 spa 'experiences' including saunas, waterfall and outdoor thermal pools.

Livigno

*Lowish prices and highish altitude – a tempting combination,
especially when you add in a quite pleasant Alpine ambience*

£80
RESORT PRICE INDEX

RATINGS

The mountains

Extent	★★
Fast lifts	★★★★
Queues	★★★★
Terrain p'ks	★★★★
Snow	★★★★
Expert	★
Intermediate	★★★
Beginner	★★★★
X-country	★★★★
Restaurants	★★★
Schools	★★★
Families	★★

The resort

Charm	★★★
Convenience	★★
Scenery	★★★
Eating out	★★★
Après-ski	★★★
Off-slope	★★

444

NEWS

For 2007/08 an eight-seat gondola replaced the Tagliede double chair at the north end of the village, below Costaccia. A second stage to the top is planned, but no firm date has been given.

For 2009/10 a new thermal spa and wellness centre is expected to open.

+ High altitude plus snowmaking means reliable snow

+ Large choice of beginners' slopes

+ Impressive modern lift system

+ Cheap by the standards of high resorts, with the bonus of duty-free shopping (eg for new equipment)

+ Lively, friendly, quite smart village with some Alpine atmosphere

+ Long, snow-sure cross-country trails

– No challenging pistes and off-piste without a guide officially banned

– Bleak setting, susceptible to wind

– Very long transfers – over five hours for some 2009 reporters

– Village is very long and straggling – with no buses later in the evening

– Few off-slope amenities

– Nightlife can disappoint

Livigno's recipe of a fair-sized mountain, high altitude and fairly low prices is uncommon, and obviously attractive. Despite its duty-free status, the hotels, bars and restaurants are not much cheaper than in other Italian resorts, but shopping is – there are countless camera and clothes shops. As a relatively snow-sure alternative to the Pyrenees or to the smallest, cheapest resorts in Austria, Livigno may make your shortlist. But don't overlook the drawbacks.

THE RESORT

Livigno is an amalgam of three villages in a wide, remote valley near the Swiss border; the airport transfers are long and winding – not great for kids. The Alta Valtellina lift pass covers Bormio and Santa Caterina, about an hour's bus ride (free with the lift pass). A pass of three days or more entitles you to half-price on a day in St Moritz – an excursion not easily done from any other major resort.

VILLAGE CHARM ★★★
Pleasant enough
Hotels, bars, specialist shops and supermarkets line a single long, pedestrian-friendly street. The buildings are small in scale and mainly traditional in style, giving the village a pleasant atmosphere.

CONVENIENCE ★★
Stay near the centre
The original hamlet of San Antonio is the nearest thing Livigno has to a centre, and the best all-round location. Here, the main street and those at right angles, linking it to the busy bypass road, are nominally traffic-free, but actually are just through-traffic-free. The road that skirts the centre is constantly busy, and becomes intrusive in the hamlets of Santa Maria, 1km/0.5 miles to the north, and

San Rocco, a bit further away to the south (and a bit uphill).

Lifts along the length of the village access the western slopes of the valley (Costaccia and Carosello). The main lift to the eastern (Mottolino) slopes is across the flat valley floor from the centre – an inconvenient walk away.

Depending on where you are based, you may make heavy use of the free bus services. They are fairly frequent, but get overcrowded at peak times and stop mid-evening. One 2009 visitor found the service 'excellent,

Livigno

Prices in €

Age	1-day	6-day
under 13	30	123
13 to 59	36	177
over 60	30	123

Free under 8

Beginner points card

Notes

Covers Livigno only; half-day passes and reduced Saturday passes; family reductions

Alternative passes

Alta Valtellina pass covers Livigno, Bormio and Santa Caterina

boarding

Livigno offers a refreshing sense of space, but it is a shame that off-piste without a guide is now officially banned. So you are technically confined to the pistes, which are in general big, wide, open and rolling motorways. But you do see a lot of people riding between the pistes, despite the prominent signs telling you not to. The terrain park infrastructure is very good, and has a long history of hosting world-class events. Beginners be warned: practically all the smaller lower slopes are serviced by drags. But the resort still attracts good numbers of beginners, and Madness snowboard school (see www.madnessnow.com) gets good reports (see 'Schools') and now offers mountain bike courses in the summer too.

every 15 minutes, never unable to get on', but another says the three bus routes are not easy to understand at first and it can take a long time to get from San Antonio to the Mottolino slopes. Taxis (including minibuses for groups) are an affordable alternative.

SCENERY ★★★☆☆
Bleakness a feature

Livigno's high position and long ridges provide attractive views from both sides of the valley – but it can feel bleak and isolated.

THE MOUNTAINS

The slopes are on either side of the valley and are mainly above the treeline. Signposting is patchy and the piste map does not identify runs. Night skiing is available on Thursdays.

EXTENT OF THE SLOPES ★★☆☆☆
Widely spread

The slopes are more extensive than in many other budget destinations but it's not a huge area and lots of the runs are very similar to each other.

There are three sectors, two of them linked high-up and low-down.

The first stage of a new two-stage gondola (we don't have a definite date for the second stage, see 'News') at the north end of the village followed by a slow chair takes you up to **Costaccia**, where a long fast quad chairlift goes along the ridge towards the **Carosello** sector. The blue linking run back from Carosello to the top of Costaccia is flat in places and may involve energetic poling if the snow conditions and the wind are against you. Carosello is more usually accessed by the optimistically named Carosello 3000 gondola at San Rocco, which goes up, in two stages, to 2750m/9,020ft. Most runs return towards the village, but there are a couple on the back of the mountain, on the west-facing slopes of Val Federia, served by a six-pack.

The ridge of **Mottolino** is reached by an efficient gondola from Teola, a tiresome walk or a bus ride across the valley from San Antonio. From the top, you can descend to fast quads on either side of the ridge; you can take

KEY FACTS

Resort	1815m
	5,950ft
Slopes	1815-2795m
	5,950-9,170ft
Lifts	31
Pistes	115km
	71 miles
Blue	25%
Red	58%
Black	17%
Snowmaking	70%

Livigno

445

Interactive resort shortlist builder at **www.wtss.co.uk**

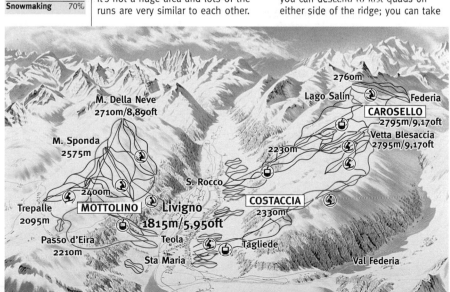

↑ The village is a classic ribbon development, but the centre is pleasant and largely traffic-free
APT LIVIGNO

SCHOOLS

Centrale
t 0342 996276

Azzurra Livigno
t 0342 997683

Livigno Italy
t 0342 996767

Livigno Galli Fedele
t 0342 970300

Madness Snowboard
t 0342 997792

New
t 0342 997801

Classes
(Centrale prices)
6 days (2hr per day)
€103

Private lessons
€34 for 1hr; each
additional person €8

CHILDCARE

Kinder Club Dau di Livigno
t 0342 996276
Ages 3 and over; Sun
to Fri; 8.30 to 3.30

Mini Club and Baby Club
t 0342 970822

M'eating Point
t 0342 970025

Spazio gioco Per i bimbi
t 0342 970711
Ages 18mnth to 3yr;
8.30-1pm

Ski school
Takes children from
age 4 (6 2hr days
€100)

a slow antique chair up the ridge to Monte della Neve, but it's better to descend to faster lifts to the top.

We don't show on our map a low-level link from the nursery drags at the bottom of Carosello to those below Costaccia; it's more of a walk than a run – not recommended for boarders.

FAST LIFTS ★★★★
A positive attraction
The lift system is impressively modern, with fast chairs and gondolas covering both sectors – though draglifts still serve the valley nursery slopes.

QUEUES ★★★★
Few problems these days
Queues are generally not a problem. Delays can occur at the main gondolas at peak times, such as the Carosello 3000. A bigger problem is that winds can close the upper lifts, causing crowds lower down. And the top of the mountain can be very cold and bleak on a bad weather day.

TERRAIN PARKS ★★★★
Serious facilities
The main Fun Mountain park behind Mottolino is an awesome freestyle zone for all levels. It also plays host to the World Rookie fest and River Jump contest – both on the Ticket to Ride calendar. It has three kicker lines for all levels and a hip. This is bordered by a big super-pipe, often used as a training ground by pros. There are advanced rails in and around the jumps as well. Beyond lies the smaller Snow-park Medio with nice lines of small to intermediate kickers, good entry-level rails of varying difficulty, a mini spine and a small boardercross. In 2008 the Carosello 3000 park was built with a focus on beginner obstacles. The area is littered with ride-on boxes and rails as well as good intermediate jumps.

SNOW RELIABILITY ★★★★
Very good, despite no glacier
Livigno's slopes are high (you can spend most of your time around 2500m/8,200ft), and with snow-guns on the lower slopes of Mottolino and Costaccia, the season is long.

FOR EXPERTS ★
Not recommended
The piste map shows a few black runs, but these are really no more than stiff red in gradient. And going off-piste without a guide is now officially banned, though you see a lot of tracks between the pistes.

FOR INTERMEDIATES ★★★
Flattering slopes
Good intermediates will be able to tackle all the blacks without worry. The woodland black run from Carosello past Tea da Borch is narrow in places and can get moguled and icy in the afternoon. Moderate intermediates have virtually the whole area at their disposal. The long run beneath the Mottolino gondola is one of the best, and there is also a long, varied, under-used blue going less directly to the valley. Leisurely types have several long cruises available; the run beneath the fast chair at the top of Costaccia is a splendid slope.

FOR BEGINNERS ★★★★
Excellent but scattered slopes
A vast array of nursery slopes including those along the sunny lower flanks of Costaccia, are excellent for novices – although some of the slopes at the northern end are steep enough to cause difficulties. There are lots of longer runs to progress to.

CROSS-COUNTRY ★★★★
Good snow, bleak setting
Long snow-sure trails (40km/25 miles in total) follow the valley floor, making

GETTING THERE

Air Bergamo 190km/120 miles (3hr45); Brescia 225km/140 miles (4hr45); Innsbruck 180km/110 miles (3hr15); Zürich 190km/120 miles (3hr30)

Rail Tirano (48km/ 30 miles), Zernez (Switzerland, 28km/ 17 miles); regular buses from station, weekends only

UK PACKAGES

Directski.com, Independent Ski Links, Inghams, Interhome, Italian Safaris, Neilson, Simply Alpine, Ski McNeill, Skitracer

ACTIVITIES

Indoor Saunas, fitness rooms and swimming pools (in hotels), badminton, billiards, bowling, basketball, cinema

Outdoor Cleared paths, ice rink, snowshoeing, horse riding, dog sledding, go-karts on ice, snowmobiling, paragliding

Phone numbers
From abroad use the prefix +39 (and do **not** omit the initial '0' of the phone number)

TOURIST OFFICE

t 0342 052200
info@livigno.eu
www.livigno.eu

Livigno a good choice, provided you don't mind the bleak scenery. There is a specialist school, Livigno 2000.

MOUNTAIN RESTAURANTS ★★★☆☆
Adequate
On Mottolino, the M'eating Point refuge at the top of the gondola has a self-service section which can be 'slow, resulting in cold food'. The small table-service section has 'little variety or imagination'. There are better places lower down. The rustic restaurants at Passo d'Eira and Trepalle are quieter options – the Trela has been recommended. And the welcoming Tea is at the base of the same sector. Costaccia's Berghütte is pleasantly rustic and sunny, with good food and a great atmosphere. Carosello has a popular but acceptable self-service place and a table-service wine bar and restaurant below. Tea da Borch, in the trees lower down, has a Tirolean-style atmosphere.

SCHOOLS AND GUIDES ★★★☆☆
Watch out for short classes
There are several schools. Reports are generally good, praising instruction and English. Classes are short at only two hours, but are rated great value for money. The Madness snowboard school offers 'relatively small' groups.

FOR FAMILIES ★★☆☆☆
Not bad for Italy
The schools run children's classes. The Centrale school offers all-day care; the staff speak English.

STAYING THERE

Livigno has an enormous range of hotels and a number of apartments. There are some attractively priced catered chalets from UK operators and the Park Village at Teola offers smart chalet accommodation.
Hotels There is a wide choice of 2-, 3- and 4-star places.
****Intermonti** (0342 972100) Modern with pool and other mod cons; on the Mottolino side of the valley.
****Touring** (0342 996131) 'Very comfortable and competitively priced.'
****Bivio** (0342 996137) In central Livigno; with pool.
****Camana Veglia** (0342 996310) Charming old wooden chalet. Popular restaurant, well placed in Santa Maria.
***Steinbock** (0342 970520) Nice little place, far from major lifts.

***Loredana** (0342 996330) Modern chalet on the Mottolino side.
***Montanina** (0342 996060) Central.
***Alpi** (0342 996408) In San Rocco, not far from Carosello gondola.
***Larice** (0342 996184) Stylish little B&B well placed for Costaccia lifts.
***Champagne** (0342 996437) 'In lovely condition and close to centre.'
Silvestri (0342 996255) Comfortable place in the San Rocco area.
Apartments Some tour operators that come here offer apartments.

EATING OUT ★★★☆☆
Still value for money
Livigno's restaurants are mainly traditional, unpretentious places, many hotel-based. Hotel Concordia is considered one of the best. Mario's impressed a recent visitor with its 'great food and service'. Similarly praised are the 'good value' Helvetia, Mirage and Astoria. The Bellavista has a 'bustling bistro style', with 'simple tasty food', while the Garden was praised by a 2009 visitor: 'excellent dinner – T-bone steaks a winner and staff brilliant'. Readers also recommend Galli's, the Grolla ('popular pizzas'), Pastorella and Echo. The Rusticana is a good-value pizzeria and Pesce d'Oro specialises in seafood.

APRES-SKI ★★★☆☆
Lively, but disappoints some
The scene in Livigno is quieter than some people expect in a duty-free resort. And the best places are scattered about, so the village lacks evening buzz. At tea time Tea del Vidal, at the bottom of Mottolino, gets lively, as does the 'friendly' Stalet bar at the base of the Carosello gondola and the central umbrella bar. Nightlife gets going only after 10pm. The Kuhstall under the Bivio hotel is an excellent cellar bar with live music, as is the Helvetia, over the road. The San Rocco end is quietest, but Daphne's has a 'great party atmosphere', Miky's gets packed, and Marco's is popular. Kokodi is the main disco.

OFF THE SLOPES ★★☆☆☆
New spa promised
A recent visitor 'thoroughly enjoyed' the dog sledding. Tobogganing is also popular. Walks are uninspiring. A new thermal spa/wellness centre is due to open for 2009/10. There's always duty free shopping, of course – and trips to Bormio and St Moritz.

Madonna di Campiglio

Chic, very Italian but rather spread-out resort with mainly easy intermediate local slopes amid stunning scenery

✚	Pleasant, friendly town in a pretty valley with splendid views	▬	Spread-out village and infrequent shuttle-bus service
✚	Generally easy slopes, best for beginners and early intermediates	▬	Lacking in challenge
		▬	Quiet in the evenings

Campiglio is a pleasant Dolomite town with an affluent, almost exclusively Italian clientele – a bit like Cortina, though the scenery isn't in quite the same league. Folgarida and Marilleva (to which the slopes are linked) are quite different and worth exploring by adventurous intermediates and better.

TOP 10 RATINGS

Extent	★★★
Fast lifts	★★★
Queues	★★★
Snow	★★★
Expert	★★
Intermediate	★★★★
Beginner	★★★★
Charm	★★★
Convenience	★★★
Scenery	★★★★

 TRENTINO

VISITTRENTINO.IT

NEWS

Long-standing plans to link Campiglio's Cinque Laghi sector to one extremity of Pinzolo's slopes are moving along. The link – a three-stage, 5km/3 mile gondola – is planned to open in late 2010. Also planned for opening then are two new pistes at Pinzolo.

For 2008/09 two new 4-star hotels opened – the Cristal Palace and the 'boutique' hotel Chalet Dolce Vita.

BEWARE THE BEGINNER DRAGS

Several reporters point out that the beginner draglifts at Campo Carlo Magno are separately owned to the main lifts and not covered by the resort pass.

THE RESORT

Campiglio is a towny, fashionable resort, set in a broad valley that includes a pretty frozen lake.
Village charm Campiglio has a traditional style with a pleasant core where there are lots of smart shops. The place is busy all day, and promenading is an early evening ritual.
Convenience The centre is fairly compact: the lifts to Cinque Laghi (to the west) and to Pradalago (to the north) bracket most of the central hotels, and are about a five-minute walk apart. Five minutes outside the centre is a gondola to Monte Spinale, for the Grostè sector. A short bus ride outside the town is a roadside station with lifts to Grostè and Pradalago. Beyond this are the main nursery slopes at Campo Carlo Magno. There is a lot of modern development stretching along the valley roads. The free ski-bus is infrequent, but some hotels run their own shuttles.
Scenery The resort has a splendid setting, with the dramatic cliffs of the Brenta Dolomites towering above attractively wooded lower slopes.

↑ Monte Spinale has some serious runs through the woods; higher Grostè is all gentle

MICHAEL MARLAIS

KEY FACTS

Resort	1520m
	4,990ft
Madonna, Folgarida, and Marilleva combined area	
Slopes	1300-2505m
	4,270-8,220ft
Lifts	46
Pistes	120km
	75 miles
Blue	35%
Red	50%
Black	15%
Snowmaking	64%

UK PACKAGES

Alpine Answers, Crystal, Crystal Finest, Interhome, Italian Safaris, Kuoni, Momentum, Powder Byrne, Rocketski, Simply Alpine, Ski Expectations, Ski Yogi, Solo's, STC

Phone numbers
From abroad use the prefix +39 (and do **not** omit the initial '0' of the phone number)

TOURIST OFFICE

t 0465 447501
info@campiglio.to
www.campiglio.to

THE MOUNTAINS

The Pradalago sector is linked via Monte Vigo to the slopes of Folgarida and Marilleva (covered in the Trentino chapter). Run classification generally overstates difficulty.

Slopes The terrain is mainly easy intermediate, both above and below the treeline. Reporters have been very impressed with the 'immaculate' grooming.

Fast lifts Most of the key lifts are fast chairs and gondolas.

Queues Rarely a problem except at ski school time. Access to Cinque Laghi was transformed by the gondola to the top, built in 2007.

Terrain parks The Ursus park, at Grostè, includes boardercross, half- and quarter-pipes and, new for last season, rails, a fun box and a kicker.

Snow reliability Although many of the runs are sunny, they are at a fair altitude, and there has been hefty investment in snowmaking. As a result, snow reliability is reasonable.

Experts Experts should hope for good snow off-piste. The trees under the Genziana chair are 'a good spot for untracked snow'. The short Canalone on Cinque Laghi and the Spinale Direttissima are proper blacks. Few of the reds present much challenge – the 3 Tre race course is one. For more challenging runs, head to Folgarida and, particularly, Marilleva.

Intermediates Grostè and Pradalago have long, easy runs and timid intermediates will love them. Cinque Laghi, Campiglio's racing mountain, is a bit tougher, as are the runs at Folgarida, Marilleva and Pinzolo, which keen intermediates should explore.

Beginners The nursery slopes at Campo Carlo Magno are excellent, but do involve a bus ride. The draglift here is not covered by the main lift pass and you have to buy a separate day ticket when you get there. Progression to longer runs is easy.

Snowboarding The resort is popular with boarders and some major events have been held here.

Cross-country There are 22km/14 miles of pretty trails through the woods.

Mountain restaurants There are lots, and reports are all positive. Some of the best are mountaineering/walking huts. Recommendations on Grostè: Boch, Stoppani, Dosson Chalet Fiat ('modern, stylish, excellent food') and Malga Montagnoli; on Pradalago: Pradalago ('best pasta'), Cascina Zeledria ('great lunch') and Viviani.

Schools and guides Language can be a problem. One reporter found the Nazionale school 'very good', but admits he speaks a little Italian.

Families Very limited.

STAYING THERE

There is a wide choice of hotels and some self-catering.

Hotels Of the 4-stars, we enjoyed the Zeledria (0465 441010) out at Campo Carlo Magno on our 2006 visit. Spinale (0465 441116), Bertelli (0465 441013) – 'excellent food' – and Alpen Suite (0465 440100) – 'clean, welcoming, good food' – are well positioned. The Savoia Palace (0465 441004) is 'comfortable and friendly', but the location can be noisy. Of the 3-stars, the central St Hubertus (0465 441144) was rated 'charming' by a 2008 visitor. The central Arnica B&B (0465 442227) is again recommended, chiefly for its helpful English-speaking owner.

Eating out There are around 20 restaurants. Our chief reporter this year recommends Antico Focolare ('spectacular ravioli in creamy nut sauce') and Le Roi ('a joy – great pizza and pasta, without spending a fortune'). He reckons the Stube Rosengarten is overpriced, but it was one of last year's recommendations, along with Da Alfiero and La Tana dell Orso. Locanda degli Artisti ('worth the expense for a special night out') has also been recommended.

Après-ski It's a quiet spot. Stube di Franz-Joseph, Bar Suisse, Bacchus Enotica (a 'classy wine bar') and Cantina del Suisse have been recommended. The Alpes is perhaps the smartest club.

Off the slopes There's not a huge amount to do. Skating on the lake and walking are popular.

Monterosa Ski

One of Europe's best-kept secrets: three unspoiled villages, long easy pistes and excellent, uncrowded off-piste terrain

£85
RESORT PRICE INDEX

TOP 10 RATINGS

Extent	★★★
Fast lifts	★★★★★
Queues	★★★★
Snow	★★★★
Expert	★★★★
Intermediate	★★★★
Beginner	★★
Charm	★★★
Convenience	★★★
Scenery	★★★★

KEY FACTS

Slopes	1200-2970m
	3,940-9,740ft
Lifts	21
Pistes	135km
	84 miles
Blue	26%
Red	64%
Black	10%
Snowmaking	94%

➕ Fabulous off-piste and heli-skiing, for both intermediates and experts

➕ Slopes usually very quiet weekdays

➕ Panoramic views

➕ Good snow reliability and grooming

➕ Quiet, unspoiled villages

➕ Lovely long runs and a sensation of travel from place to place, but ...

➖ Virtually no choice of route when touring the three valleys on-piste

➖ Few challenges (or moguls) on-piste

➖ High winds can close links

➖ Few off-slope diversions

➖ Can be surprisingly busy at weekends

➖ Limited après-ski

Monterosa Ski's three resorts – Champoluc, Gressoney la Trinité and Alagna – are popular with weekenders from Milan and Turin, but are little-known internationally. As a result, they retain a friendly, small-scale, unspoiled Italian ambience that we (and a growing band of readers) like a lot.

The three-valley network of lifts and pistes is anything but small-scale: Alagna and Champoluc are an impressive 17km/11 miles apart – slightly further apart than Courchevel and Val Thorens in the Trois Vallées. But a glance at the piste map reveals that the Italian network is skeletal compared with the full-bodied French one. The figure of 135km that we give for the total length of pistes is lower than it was – we have cut out the separate smaller ski areas down-valley from Champoluc and Gressoney, dealt with in our new Aosta Valley chapter – but several readers have expressed scepticism about even this lower figure. They have a point; more about this later in the chapter.

Outside the piste network is a lot of great off-piste terrain that has long attracted experts. For two seasons, aficionados have been denied lift access to some of the best routes because of the closure in 2007 of the antique Punta Indren cable car; the word from the lift company is that the replacement will be opening for the coming season. Given good snow, we'll be in the queue.

THE RESORT

There is one main village in each of the area's three valleys. Champoluc in the western Val d'Ayas and Gressoney in the central valley are both about an hour's drive up from the Aosta valley, to the south. Alagna is even more remote, and approached by a quite different route from the east. Like most Italian resorts, the villages really come to life at weekends – not always a welcome change for some reporters.

Down-valley from Gressoney la Trinité is Gressoney St Jean. Down-valley from Champoluc are Antagnod and Brusson. All have small slope areas covered by the Monterosa Ski lift pass. Go to the Aosta Valley chapter for more information.

Trips to Cervinia, La Thuile, Courmayeur and Pila are possible by car. An Aosta Valley pass covering all of them is available.

Village charm All three villages are small-scale and pleasantly rustic, without being picture-postcard pretty. None has much ski-resort buzz (not necessarily a bad thing).

Champoluc is strung out along the road running up the valley from the centre, which is more or less devoid of bars and inviting shops.

Gressoney la Trinité is a quiet, neat little village, with cobbled streets, wooden buildings and an old church – but also many buildings that appear to be disused.

Alagna is a secluded village with a solid church and some lovely old wooden farmhouses built in the distinctive Walser style.

Convenience Champoluc's village gondola starts from a kind of micro-resort several minutes' walk up the road. You can store boots and skis/boards there overnight. The valley road continues past several hotels

NEWS

For 2008/09 snowmaking was increased, particularly improving the links between Gressoney and Alagna.

Good progress is reported on the construction of a new cable car to replace the ancient Punta Indren lift (removed in 2007). The lift company now thinks it will be ready for 2009/10. The lift restores access to some excellent off-piste routes back towards Gabiet and Stafal. It starts at Passo Salati, so facilitating circuits via Gabiet in conjunction with the gondola from there. But sadly the new set-up does not restore the ability to do laps in the splendid 1000m vertical Balme bowl on the Alagna side.

Permission has been given for a funicular railway to replace the chairlift out of Frachey, up the valley from Champoluc; but this seems unlikely to be ready for the 2009/10 season.

towards Frachey, where there is a chairlift into the slopes.

Gressoney la Trinité is about 800m/0.5 miles from the base station of a slow chairlift into the local slopes, where there are a few convenient hotels. The lifts for the other valleys go from the mini-resort of Stafal at the head of the Gressoney valley. But its hotels and guest houses are quite widely spread away from the lifts.

Alagna is streets ahead of its neighbours in this respect: the gondola starts from the village square.
Scenery Some of the highest peaks in the Alps surround Monterosa Ski – a string of peaks over 4000m, and some over 4500m; the panoramic views from restaurant terraces are fabulous.

THE MOUNTAINS

The slopes offer an attractive mix of woodland runs low-down, particularly at Gressoney, and open slopes higher up; but the latter dominate, and reporters visiting at various times have found the top lifts closed by wind, severely limiting the available terrain. Many runs are satisfyingly long. Run classification generally exaggerates difficulty – with some notable exceptions. Signposting is excellent.
Slopes The slopes span vast distances, but don't add up to a huge amount of piste skiing. The claimed total of 135km for the linked area is based on figures that look suspicious – the Pistone Betta down to Stafal, for example, is a lovely long cruise, but is

it really 10.5km long for a drop of only 550m? We're not convinced.

The main three-valley network is very simple. Starting from Frachey, up the valley from Champoluc, or from Alagna at the opposite end, you ride two or three lifts up to the first ridge, ski down to Stafal, ride two or three lifts up to the second ridge, ski down. All the descents are gloriously long (even if not 10.5km long); the descent from Passo Salati to Alagna is a notable 1760m/5,770ft vertical. But there is little choice of route along the way. Added to this core are the local slopes of Champoluc and Gressoney. (Alagna has no such gloriously additional area of slopes, which is a real drawback.)

A gondola on the edge of Champoluc goes up to Crest, a mid-mountain nursery area with a further gondola and chairlift above it climbing a further 700m/2,300ft to Colle Sarezza. This area is linked to the runs above Frachey (and the link to Stafal) via a steep, narrow, bumpy red run – very difficult for timid intermediates, who are better off starting at Frachey.

At Gressoney, a pair of chairlifts go up from two points serving wooded runs of 400m/500m (1,300ft/1,650ft) vertical, with piste links across the mountainside to Gabiet where you can join the three-valley link towards Alagna, or descend to Stafal to go towards Champoluc.
Fast lifts The lifts are virtually all chairs and gondolas; most of the important chairs are fast.
Queues Problems occur only at

weekends and peak periods, in general. But the second chairlift above Frachey can have serious queues morning and afternoon. We presume the new funicular, when it arrives, will remove this bottleneck. The double chair to Belvedere, on the way from Frachey to Champoluc, can have long afternoon queues. The gondola out of Alagna builds queues at weekends, as does the cable car above it. Pistes can get crowded at weekends.

Terrain parks Gressoney has a boardercross but there's no park. Big air jumps are sometimes built near the top of the gondola from Champoluc.

Snow reliability Generally good, thanks to altitude and extensive snowmaking, which impresses reporters. Grooming is very thorough – one or two reporters have complained that 'to find bumps you have to go off-piste'.

Experts The attraction is the off-piste, with great runs from the high points of the lift system and some excellent heli-drops. Among the adventures we've enjoyed here was a heli-drop on Monte Rosa, skiing down to Zermatt and returning via the Cervinia lifts. The opening of the new lift to Punta Indren (see 'News') will restore some sorely

SNOWPIX.COM / CHRIS GILL

One of the routes that will be lift-served again when the new Punta Indren cable car opens next season ↘

missed off-piste opportunities, but guides can take you to plenty of places lower down, including an excellent area of forest above Frachey. There is good, shady, easily accessible off-piste beside the long, lovely run from Passo Salati towards Alagna.

Intermediates There are excellent, long cruising runs from the ridges down into the valleys ('wonderful, carefree carving'). Down towards Alagna, the black Olen piste (which is more like a tough red and was classified red originally) is a great blast. There isn't much on-piste challenge for more demanding intermediates – take a guide and explore the gentler off-piste.

Beginners The high nursery slopes at Crest above Champoluc, served by two moving carpets, are better than the lower ones at Gressoney. But neither has ideal gentle runs to progress to.

Snowboarding There's a boardercross at Gressoney and great freeriding.

Cross-country There are long trails: 24km/15 miles around Gressoney St Jean, 17km/11 miles in Champoluc; Brusson, in the Champoluc valley, has the best trails in the area.

Mountain restaurants The mountain restaurants are generally simple, but

453

UK PACKAGES

Champoluc Alpine Answers, Crystal, Interactive Resorts, Italian Safaris, Kuoni, Momentum, Ski 2, Ski Expectations, Skitracer, Ski Yogi, Snow Finders, White Roc
Gressoney la Trinité Alpine Answers, Crystal, Crystal Finest, Inghams, Italian Safaris, Momentum, Mountain Tracks, Ski Freshtracks, Skitracer, Ski Yogi, Snoworks
Alagna Alpine Answers, Italian Safaris, Mountain Tracks, Ski Freshtracks, Ski-Monterosa, Ski Weekend

Phone numbers
From abroad use the prefix +39 (and do **not** omit the initial '0' of the phone number)

TOURIST OFFICE

t 0125 303111
info@monterosa-ski.com
www.monterosa-ski.com

---

there are plenty of them (sadly, not all named on the piste map), and readers enthuse about most, prompting us to up our star rating this year.

In the Val d'Ayas, recent reader tips include: above Champoluc the 'lively' Belvedere, the Ostafa ('great food – staggeringly large sausage') and Tana del Lupo; above Frachey the modern Campo Base ('eccentric owner, great food'), Stadel Soutzun ('charming, excellent menu') and Lo Retsignon ('friendly staff, great view'). In the Gressoney valley tips include the Sitten ('excellent specials and stunning view') and Gabiet ('friendly, good value'), both above Stafal, also the good-value Bedemie and 'classy' Morgenrot above Orsia, the Mandria ('excellent and friendly') and the Chamois ('small but charming') at Punta Jolanda. Over in the Alagna valley the Alpen Stop at Pianalunga, the Baita just below and the Shoppf Vittine on the home run have been recommended. A diversion to the right at the top of the run from Passo Salati brings you to the Rifugio Guglielmina ('fab place, great food and views').

Schools and guides We have had mixed reports on the Italian ski schools but universally good reports on the Monterosa mountain guides and the ski school run by tour op Ski 2 ('good, friendly instructors').

Families Facilities are limited. Talk to your tour operator.

STAYING THERE

Surprisingly few tour operators feature the area. We've had good reports of Monterosa specialists Ski 2 ('great from pick-up to drop-off').

Hotels For a small place, Champoluc has a striking range of attractive hotels. We have a minor flood of favourable reports this year on the 3-star Champoluc (0125 308088) –'friendly, comfortable' – despite complaints that the spa facilities cost extra. There is continued support for the central Relais des Glaciers (0125 308182) – a welcoming 4-star with 'lovely' spa and shuttle to the gondola ('food excellent'). And for the central, 3-star, creaky old Castor (0125 307117), managed by a British guy who married into the family; desserts repeatedly commended. Our favourite luxury option is the 4-star Breithorn (0125 308734), just up the road, with beautifully furnished public areas,

beamed bedrooms and good spa facilities. But this year one reporter reckons the service is a weak point.

At Gressoney la Trinité you have a choice of locations. Staying right by the Punta Jolanda lift is one option. Choose between the 'very cosy and friendly' 4-star Jolanda Sport (0125 366140), with gym, saunas, pool, and the 3-star Dufour (0125 366139) ('amazing plentiful food and welcoming staff'). In the village of Gressoney, Lo Scoiattolo (0125 366313) is run by 'lovely cheerful people, trying hard' (who will ferry you to the lift). In a peaceful setting mid-way between Gressoney and Stafal is the Anderbätt (0125 366600), newly recommended this year – a 'really lovely, friendly' restaurant with six rooms. At Stafal is a 'fabulous' little B&B run by a 'super-friendly family' – the Rédélnäscht (+39 347 797360). Up the mountain the Guglielmina refuge (01631 91444) at the top of Col d'Olen was praised in 2008 ('better than some hotels I've stayed in!').

In Alagna, try the 3-star Monterosa (0163 922993), 4-star Cristallo (0163 922822) or the Residence Mirella (0163 922965) – 50m from the lifts and right over the village bakery ('superb' breakfasts, not surprisingly).

Eating out Most restaurants are in hotels, but there are a few stand-alone places. Reader recommendations include: in Champoluc, the Bistrot and Atelier Gourmand ('fantastic wines') – and the Grange up at Frachey; in Stafal, the Capanna Carla ('a rustic gem'); in Alagna, the Unione and Dir und Don pizzeria/grill.

Après-ski The evenings are generally quiet, at least during the week. In Champoluc, the bar of the hotel Castor is cosy and popular with resort workers; the Golosone is a small, atmospheric, distinctly Italian wine bar; the Galion opposite the gondola is busy as the lifts close; the West Road pub in the hotel California has karaoke some nights. At weekends, the Gram Parsons disco beneath the California gets going. Gressoney is even quieter; the bar-restaurant Da Giovanni underneath the Nordend hotel in Stafal has 'cool decor and music'. In Alagna, the An Bacher Wi wine bar gets good reports; there are several cafe-bars, where reportedly there are free antipasti at weekends.

Off the slopes There is an outdoor ice rink at Champoluc, but little else.

ADAMELLO SKI

Passo Tonale

An excellent place to learn or to build confidence at moderate cost, with its appeal broadened by the link with Ponte di Legno

VISITTRENTINO.IT

NEWS

A new mountain restaurant is planned for the 2010/11 season.

454

PETER GILLETT

The main slopes conveniently run down to the village ↓

➕ Good-value, plain accommodation

➕ Sunny, easy, snow-sure slopes

➕ Good for beginners and early or timid intermediates

➕ Link to Ponte di Legno adds attractive, steeper, treelined runs

➖ Not much locally for experts or keen intermediates

➖ Main slopes are above the treeline and unpleasant in bad weather

➖ Linear village strung along the pass road lacks charm

Passo Tonale offers that rare combination of a fair-sized, uncrowded, snow-sure ski area and slope-side hotels at a bargain price. Who cares if it lacks charm? It's a great place for beginners and, now that it is linked to the slopes above Ponte di Legno, a more interesting destination for intermediates than it was.

THE RESORT

Passo Tonale sits on a wide, treeless pass; it is in Trentino but right on the border with Lombardia.

Village charm The village was developed mainly for skiing, along the road over the pass; many of the buildings are in chalet style, but it lacks a focus, and traffic intrudes.

Convenience Tonale is fairly compact, with its hotels, shops, bars and restaurants spread along the bottom of the main slope area – so the nearest lift is generally not far away.

Scenery The setting can feel rather bleak, but Ponte di Legno's woods offer an attractive contrast – and there are some wide views.

THE MOUNTAINS

The home slopes are entirely above the treeline, and bad weather can mean white-outs and closures. The Tonale slopes are linked to those of Ponte di Legno, below the pass in Lombardia; these slopes are generally steeper and quieter than Passo Tonale's main area. The regional pass covers Marilleva, down the valley (free daily buses), which is linked to Madonna di Campiglio.

Slopes Tonale's slopes are spread over two main sectors on opposite sides of the valley. The broad, south-facing area is much the larger, starts right at the village and is served by a well-laid-out mix of chairs and drags. Most runs are short, with limited vertical. The north-facing Presena area is steeper, narrower and taller. First, there is an eight-seat gondola; above that is a double chairlift; and at the top, on the Presena glacier, there are two draglifts.

Ponte di Legno is reached by a blue/red run through the trees (mostly wide and easy but including a short much steeper section) followed by an (easy) black run that you can't avoid on the Ponte di Legno side. A gondola takes you back to Tonale.

Fast lifts The lift system is impressive, with seven fast chairs in the main local areas of slopes.

Queues We have no reports of queues.

Terrain parks There's a park with kickers, boxes and a half-pipe served by the fast Valena chair at Passo Tonale.

Snow reliability The Presena slopes are high and shady, so they are fairly snow-sure even below the glacier. But

KEY FACTS

Resort	1885m
	6,180ft

Passo Tonale and Ponte di Legno combined area

Slopes	1120-3015m
	3,670-9,890ft
Lifts	30
Pistes	100km
	62 miles
Blue	17%
Red	66%
Black	17%
Snowmaking	100%

UK PACKAGES

Crystal, First Choice, Independent Ski Links, Inghams, Neilson, Rocketski, Simply Alpine, Skitracer, STC, Thomson

Phone numbers
From abroad use the prefix +39 (and do **not** omit the initial '0' of the phone number)

TOURIST OFFICE

t 0364 903838
tonale@valdisole.net
www.adamelloski.com
www.valdisole.net

the main slope area gets a lot of sun, and there can be slush or ice in March and April. Ponte di Legno's slopes are lower and more dependent on snowmaking, which is claimed to cover all the joint area's pistes.

Experts This isn't a resort for experts. The black piste down the gondola on the Presena sector deserves its grading but is not a serious challenge. In the right conditions there are epic off-piste runs from the glacier, including the impressive 16km/10 mile Pisgana run towards Ponte di Legno (a vertical of 1650m/5,410ft) – you should take a guide.

Intermediates The south-facing slopes offer gentle terrain ideal for cruising; many of these runs are graded red but are really no more than gentle blue gradient. We particularly enjoyed the 4.5km/3 mile Alpino piste down a deserted valley to the village. The runs at the top of the glacier are short and easy, and again there is little difference between the reds and the black. Below that the run beneath the chair is no more than a cat-track, but the black beneath the gondola will be too much for timid intermediates, who should ride down. The runs at Ponte di Legno are much more serious reds and deserve their classification.

Beginners It's an excellent resort for novices. The sunny lifts on gentle slopes right by the village are ideal, and there are plenty of easy, wide blue runs to move on to (usually with good snow) in order to gain confidence.

Snowboarding The gentle slopes and ability to get around mainly on chairlifts mean the area is good for beginner and intermediate boarders.

Cross-country There are 44km/27 miles of trails, with loops at Passo Tonale, in the valley and at altitude at Ponte di Legno.

Mountain restaurants Readers have generally been unimpressed with the mountain restaurants, and it's easy to return to the resort for lunch. But past recommendations include Scorpion Bay and the Nigritella in the main area of slopes and the 'rustic' Cappanna Valbione at Ponte di Legno.

Schools and guides You may get an instructor with excellent English, or you may not. Our most recent report speaks of disappointingly slow progress.

Families There's a kindergarten at hotel Miramonti for ages four to 12; the ski school takes kids from four.

STAYING THERE

Passo Tonale has long been popular with tour operators.

Hotels There are around 30, most of them 3-stars. This year we have a glowing report on the location, rooms, owners and 'amazing' food of the Edelweiss (0364 903789). The 4-star Miramonti (0364 900501) has a pool and spa, and a good location.

Apartments There are 1,400 beds in apartments, a few on the UK market.

Eating out Mainly hotel restaurants.

Après-ski There are quite a few spots to try. Reader recommendations include the Magic Pub, El Bait, Nico's Bar, Heaven and the Miramonti disco.

Off the slopes If you don't intend to hit the slopes, forget Tonale. There's snowmobiling, snowshoeing, etc.

SAUZE D'OULX TOURIST OFFICE

Sauze d'Oulx

'Suzy does it' still, up to a point – a lively village beneath an attractive area of slopes; but non-trivial drawbacks persist

£85
RESORT PRICE INDEX

RATINGS

The mountains

Extent	★★★★
Fast lifts	★★★
Queues	★★★
Terrain p'ks	★
Snow	★★
Expert	★★
Intermediate	★★★★
Beginner	★
X-country	★
Restaurants	★★★
Schools	★★
Families	★★

The resort

Charm	★★
Convenience	★★
Scenery	★★★
Eating out	★★★
Après-ski	★★★★
Off-slope	★

KEY FACTS

Resort	1510m
	4,950ft

Milky Way	
Slopes	1390-2825m
	4,560-9,270ft
Lifts	82
Pistes	400km
	249 miles
Blue	24%
Red	56%
Black	20%
Snowmaking	33%

Sauze d'Oulx-Sestriere-Sansicario	
Slopes	1390-2825m
	4,560-9,270ft
Lifts	42
Pistes	250km
	155 miles
Snowmaking	38%

➕ Extensive and uncrowded slopes – great intermediate cruising

➕ Mix of open and tree-lined runs is good for all weather conditions

➕ Entertaining nightlife

➕ Some scope for off-piste adventures

➕ Part of the Milky Way network spreading across the border into France, but ...

➖ Full exploration of the Milky Way area really requires a car or taxis

➖ Erratic snow record – and far from comprehensive snowmaking

➖ Still lots of ancient slow lifts

➖ Several drawbacks for beginners

➖ Steep walks around the village, and an inadequate shuttle-bus service

➖ Crowds at weekends in season

➖ Few challenging pistes

➖ Still very British-dominated

In the days when Britain had lager louts rather than binge drinkers, Sauze was their Alpine HQ, and they dominated the place. It still seems British-dominated, with lots of lively bars and shops festooned in English signs, and lots of young Brits working in them, but it is a much more civilised place. The resort's Italian clientele is more in evidence, especially at weekends (Sauze is the closest decent-sized ski area to Turin) and in most respects it now seems much like any other mass-market resort. When we visit, we find ourselves liking Sauze more than we expect to – as do many reporters.

But Sauze still has a problem: investment, lack of. With its acutely unreliable natural snow, it needs the kind of comprehensive snowmaking that many other major Italian resorts now enjoy. And the rate of progress in upgrading lifts needs a serious boost, as well.

THE RESORT

Sauze d'Oulx sits on a sloping mountain shelf facing north-west across the Valle di Susa to the mountains bordering France.

It is a mid-sized resort – a big village rather than a town – but it spreads quite widely. Out of the bustle of the centre, there are secluded apartment blocks in quiet, wooded areas and a number of good restaurants also tucked away.

VILLAGE CHARM ★★
Falling behind?
The village has an attractive old core, with narrow, twisting streets and houses roofed with huge stone slabs. But most of the resort is modern and undistinguished, made up of block-like hotels relieved by the occasional chalet, spreading down the steep hillside from the slopes. It rather gives the impression of falling behind the times, with none of the investment in smart, woody hotels and apartments

that goes on in more dynamic resorts.

There is a central car-free zone, but at both ends of the day the rest of the village can be congested. The roads have few pavements and can be icy.

Despite the decline in lager sales, the centre is still lively at night; the late bars are usually quite full, and the handful of discos do brisk business – at the weekend, at least. Noise can be a problem in the early hours.

CONVENIENCE ★★
Uphill struggles
The Clotes chair, for the left-hand side of the network, is at the top of the village, up a short but steep hill. Some

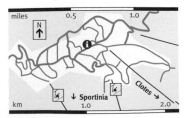

Lovely, long runs in the woods around Sansicario; spot any piste markers? →

PAUL CARTER

NEWS

For 2009/10 major changes are planned for the lifts in the area of M Fraiteve, which is to become the central link between Sauze, Sestriere and Sansicario. The main lifts to Col Basset (from Sestriere as well as Sauze) will be removed. The two parallel drags below the Col will be removed, too, and the Basset slow quad chair which ran from the bottom of the Rio Nero bowl to the Col will be rebuilt on the line of those drags. A new double chair will go from the bowl to M Fraiteve. As a result, you will not need to use the tricky bent drag that currently gives access to Sansicario; but that too is to be replaced – bizarrely, by a new drag. The black run beside this drag is no longer the only way back from Sansicario: a new red piste runs from M Fraiteve to Col Basset. And lifts are no longer the only way out of the bowl: a black piste now links the bottom of the bowl to the main lift network.

Elsewhere, a blue run now links the top of the Clotes chairlift to the start of the Sportinia chairlift, improving access to Sportinia. And the resort has quietly removed from its map the little-used lifts – a chair and two drags – on the far left of the system, beneath M Genevris.

hotels are above this lift, and in good snow offer ski-in/ski-out convenience – but most are not. There is now a magic carpet that cuts out part of the climb. The Sportinia chair, for the heart of the slopes, is a strenuous and hazardous walk (often on slippery roads) further out. But you can now ride the Clotes chair and ski across to the Sportinia one. The ski-bus service (not covered by the lift pass) is frankly a bit of a joke.

The smaller, lower village of Jouvenceaux is worth considering as a base, with a fast lift into the slopes and good red run back down.

SCENERY ★★★☆☆
Plenty of trees
The scenery is attractively woody, especially low down and along Valle di Susa. The sunny, open slopes higher up give wide panoramic views of the mountains bordering France.

THE MOUNTAINS

Sauze's mountains provide excellent intermediate terrain. The higher slopes are open, the lower ones pleasantly wooded. The piste classification changes from year to year, so not surprisingly the signs on the ground don't always match the piste map. Piste marking is often absent. Many runs classified red should really be blue. As in so many Italian resorts, signposting isn't great; if there are any large-scale maps at the top of lifts, neither we nor our reporters have seen them. Despite a redesign, the piste map is very difficult to follow.

The Via Lattea (Milky Way) lift pass covers not only next-door Sestriere and Sansicario, easily reached by lift and piste, but also the more remote area of slopes around the French border, above Claviere and Montgenèvre. These resorts are much more easily reached by car, or by taxi, though it is possible by bus.

EXTENT OF THE SLOPES ★★★★☆
Big and varied enough for most
Sauze's local slopes are spread across a broad wooded bowl above the resort, ranging from west- to north-facing. The main lifts are chairs, slow from the top of the village and fast from the western fringes to **Sportinia** – a sunny mid-mountain clearing in the woods, with a ring of restaurants and hotels and a small nursery area. In the past, movement from Clotes to Sportinia depended on the high Triplex chairlift, which is prone to closure by high winds. Now there is an easy blue piste link just above village level.

The high point of the system is **Monte Fraiteve**. From here you can travel west on splendid broad, long runs to **Sansicario** – and on to a two-stage gondola near **Cesana Torinese** that links with **Claviere** and then **Montgenèvre**, in France, at the far end of the Milky Way (both are reached more quickly by car).

M Fraiteve is now also the way to **Sestriere**. There is supposed to be a piste all the way down, but the slope faces south; we've never known the bottom section to be open – expect to ride the gondola down.

LIFT PASSES

La Via Lattea

Prices in €

Age	1-day	6-day
over 8	31	180

Free under 8; over 75
Beginner Restricted day passes (€20)
Notes
Covers lifts in Sauze d'Oulx, Sestriere, Sansicario, Cesana and Claviere; half-day passes
Alternative passes
Sauze only, Sestriere only, Cesana only

ITALY

458

boarding

Sauze has good local tree-lined slopes (with space in the trees, too), high, open terrain, and links to other Milky Way resorts. But a 2008 reporter found little to interest adventurous boarders and 'far too many drags'. And there are a lot of drags – a serious drawback for novice riders, despite a fair number of chairs. Don't count on finding a terrain park.

FAST LIFTS ★★★☆☆
Few and far between
Fast lifts are in a minority. The number of drags is dwindling (see 'News') but there are still some very old and very slow chairlifts in a poor state of repair.

QUEUES ★★★☆☆
Slow lifts the biggest problem
There can be irritating waits at Sportinia, especially when school classes set off, or just after lunch. The quad that replaced the old double chair out of the village to Clotes can still generate queues. Breakdowns of elderly lifts has caused queues for some reporters. We hope they've got their sums right in planning the changes around M Fraiteve, or some serious queues could result there.

TERRAIN PARKS ★☆☆☆☆
Will they, won't they?
The location of the park changes from year to year – last year's piste map shows it by the Triplex chairlift – but more importantly it is rarely in operation. Too much snow was the excuse last season. There are parks at Sansicario and Sestriere.

SNOW RELIABILITY ★★☆☆☆
Can be poor, affecting the links
The area is notorious for erratic snowfalls, suffering droughts with worrying frequency. Snowmaking has been increased throughout the area (including the Sportinia nursery slopes) but coverage is still far from complete. Of course, there was plenty of snow last season. In thin years, reporters have been impressed by the efforts to keep runs open in poor conditions ('they worked miracles'), and grooming is in general 'superb'.

FOR EXPERTS ★★☆☆☆
Head off-piste
There are five black runs, some of which deserve the classification. Two of the steeper slopes are shown on the piste map as bump runs – a short, high, north-facing run from the M Fraiteve, and a sunnier slope down the

SCHOOLS

Sauze Sportinia
t 0122 850218

Sauze d'Oulx
t 0122 858084

Sauze Project
t 0122 850654

Classes
(Sauze Sportinia prices)
6 3hr days: €180

Private lessons
€35 for 1hr

GUIDES

Marco Deganl
t 0335 398984

CHILDCARE

Ludoteca Sauze In
t 0122 858009
Mon-Sat; 9am-5pm

Ski school
6 half days €180
(Sportinia prices)

Moncrons draglift. The new run out of the bottom of the Rio Nero bowl is classified black, too. We're told it is not fiercely steep, but it is narrow and very isolated. There are plenty of off-piste opportunities within the lift network – between the pistes and down lift lines – and of course last season there was great fun to be had.

FOR INTERMEDIATES ★★★★☆
Splendid cruising terrain
The whole area is ideal for confident intermediates who want to clock up the kilometres. For the less confident, the piste map doesn't help because it picks out only the very easiest runs in blue – when actually there are many others that are manageable.

The Moncrons sector at the east of the area is served only by drags but offers some wonderful, uncrowded cruising, some of it above the treeline. In the central part of the slopes there are some good long descents – red 11 is about 1000m vertical.

At the higher levels, where the slopes are above the treeline, the terrain often allows a choice of route. Lower down are pretty runs through the woods, where the main complication can be route-finding. The mountainside is broken up by gullies, limiting the links between pistes that appear to be quite close together.

The long runs down to Jouvenceaux are splendid, flattering intermediate terrain, as are those below Sportinia.

The slopes above Sansicario are also excellent, including the amiable Olympic Women's Downhill and the particularly fine red run, away from the lifts, down to Pariol, the mid-station on the Cesana-Sansicario gondola. These runs are affected by the afternoon sun, though. You can now get to and from the Sansicario sector without using the tricky bent drag out of the Rio Nero bowl, or the black run beside it.

FOR BEGINNERS ★☆☆☆☆
Not a good choice
You might think a resort like this, with cheap accommodation and gentle terrain, would cater well for beginners, but you would be wrong. The main nursery area up at Sportinia has only a short magic carpet lift, and is reached by a chairlift – how is that supposed to work? There is no suitable longer lift-served slope to progress to from there. There is a slope at village level

SKI-DIRECT

Lowest Prices
Expert Advice
All Ski Resorts
Open 7 Days

www.ski-direct.co.uk
0844 553 3501
ABTA D9779. Agents for ATOL Protected Operators

with a free moving carpet, but the slope is too steep for complete beginners. Equally importantly, the mornings-only classes don't suit everyone. Once off the nursery slopes, the main problem is that virtually all of the runs are classified red, whether they deserve it or not.

FOR CROSS-COUNTRY ★☆☆☆☆
You're on your own
We understand that there are now no prepared loops.

MOUNTAIN RESTAURANTS ★★★☆☆
Some pleasant possibilities
Restaurants are numerous and generally pleasant, though few are particularly special. Stupidly, only some are marked on the piste map. There are several places at Sportinia; the Rocce Nere is repeatedly praised for 'good food and service'; the Capanna Kind is a bit pricier, and views differ on whether it delivers. The hotel Capricorno, at Clotes, is the place for a serious table-service lunch. It is not cheap, and midweek in low season it can be deserted. Clot Bourget is recommended for 'fast service, best pizzas on the slopes and good value'. The rustic Bar Clotes is 'a great end-of-day-bar'.

SCHOOLS AND GUIDES ★★☆☆☆
More reports, please
Our only report this year is of a disappointing private lesson.

FOR FAMILIES ★★☆☆☆
Tour operator alternatives
You might want to look at the nursery facilities offered by major UK tour operators in the chalets and chalet-hotels that they run here. All the schools take children from four years, and spoken English should be OK. The magic carpet on the village nursery slope is a great aid to sledging.

GETTING THERE

Air Turin 90km/
55 miles (1hr30)

Rail Oulx (5km/
3 miles); frequent
buses

UK PACKAGES

*Crystal, First Choice,
Independent Ski Links,
Inghams, Interhome,
Neilson, Simply Alpine,
Ski Line, Skitracer,
Thomson*
Sansicario *Crystal,
Solo's, Thomson*

ACTIVITIES

Indoor Sauna,
solarium, massage

Outdoor Ice rink,
snowmobiling

Phone numbers
From abroad use the
prefix +39 (and do **not**
omit the initial '0' of
the phone number)

TOURIST OFFICES

Sauze d'Oulx
t 0122 858009
from UK: 0871 222
0604
info.sauze@
turismotorino.org
www.turismotorino.it
www.vialattea.it

**Cesana Torinese
(Sansicario)**
t 0122 89202
from UK: 0871 226
7709
info.cesana@
turismotorino.org

STAYING THERE

All the major mainstream operators
offer hotel packages here, but there
are also a few chalets.
Hotels Simple 2-star and 3-star hotels
form the core, with a couple of 4-stars
and some more basic places.
****Torre (0122 859812) Cylindrical
landmark 200m/650ft below the
centre. Excellent rooms, mini-buses to
lifts. Newish pool and health suite.
***Gran Baita (0122 850183)
Comfortable place in quiet, central
backstreet, with excellent food and
good rooms, some with sunset views.
***Stella Alpina (0122 858731)
Between main lifts. Well run by very
helpful Anglo-Italian family; food 'good
and plentiful'.
***Terrazza (0122 850173) In a quiet
part of town, near the Clotes chair.
***Des Amis (0122 858488) Down in
Jouvenceaux, near bus stop; simple
hotel run by Anglo-Italian couple.
**Bianceneve (0122 850160) Pleasant,
with smallish rooms. Near the centre.
**Hermitage (0122 850385) Neat
chalet-style hotel beside the piste.
**Villa Cary (0122 850191)
Comfortable 2-star, repeatedly
recommended by readers for 'excellent
food and service'.
Apartments Apartments/chalets are
available, some through UK operators.
At altitude The 4-star Capricorno (0122
850273), up at Clotes, is the most
attractive and expensive hotel in
Sauze – a charming little chalet beside
the piste, with only eight bedrooms.
Not quite in the same league are the
places up at Sportinia – though
reporters have enjoyed them.

EATING OUT ★★★✩✩
Caters for all tastes and pockets
Typical Italian banquets of five or six
courses can be had in the places such
as the Cantun. But a 2008 reporter
pronounces the Falco 'the best in town
– terrific'. In the old town there are
several cutely rustic places. Paddy
McGinty's does Mexican and steaks.
Pizzeria Albertino is 'a bit cafe-like but
the food was great'. Sugo's Spaghetti
House has 'a good atmosphere'.

APRES-SKI ★★★★✩
Suzy does it with more dignity
Sauze's bars now impress most
reporters young and old – though one
reporter used to Austrian resorts rates
the early evening scene disappointing.

Choice is wide, with multiple happy
hours, and lots of entertainments later
on. One reporter regrets the lack of
open air bars at the foot of the slopes,
but at least there are terraces at the
popular Assietta and Forgia.

The Scotch bar in the hotel Stella
Alpina is popular for English beer with
a 'friendly welcome'. Reporters are
also keen on the 'big, friendly, fun'
Village Cafè in a basement at the foot
of the slopes. But Miravallino got more
reports than anywhere else this year –
a smart, lively bar where free antipasti
are served in the early evening, and
every night there is a different
entertainment (karaoke, bar games
etc). Try the Derby (below the hotel)
for a quiet, civilised drink – log fire,
sofas, but also video screens. Osteria
dei Vagabondi is the only live music
venue – but it starts late in the
evening; prices are not surprisingly a
bit higher here.

Of the discos, Banditos
(ex-Clarabella) is a walk away, and
popular with Italians as well as Brits.

Other reader recommendations: the
intimate, atmospheric bar Moncrons,
which holds regular quiz nights; the
Cotton Club, 'an attractively woody
late-night bar' which sounds like it is
spoilt by video screens; the Lounge
(formerly Crowded House), a 'modern
and comfortable' bar; Max's and Scatto
Matto – both popular for 'excellent
food, service and ski videos'.

No reports this year on the trendy
Ghost Bar or the Gran Trun, a
converted barn.

OFF THE SLOPES ★✩✩✩✩
Go elsewhere
Shopping is limited, there are no
gondolas or cable cars for pedestrians
and there are few off-slope activities.
Turin and Briançon are worth visiting.

Sansicario 1700m/5,580ft

Sansicario is ideally placed for
exploration of the whole Milky Way. It
is a modern, purpose-built, self-
contained but rather soulless little
resort, mainly consisting of apartments
grouped around the small shopping
precinct. The 45-room Rio Envers
(0122 811333) is a comfortable,
expensive hotel. There are now taxi-
bob rides on the Olympic bobsleigh
run, between Sansicario and Cesana.
One reporter enjoyed it so much he
did it twice.

Sella Ronda

*Endless intermediate slopes amid spectacular Dolomite scenery,
with a choice of attractive valley villages, mainly German-speaking*

TOP 10 RATINGS

Extent	★★★★★
Fast lifts	★★★★
Queues	★★★
Snow	★★★★
Expert	★★
Intermediate	★★★★★
Beginner	★★★★
Charm	★★★
Convenience	★★★
Scenery	★★★★★

➕ Vast network of connected slopes – suits intermediates particularly well

➕ Stunning, unique Dolomite scenery

➕ Lots of mountain huts with good food as well as fab views

➕ Excellent value for money

➕ Extensive snowmaking – one of Europe's best systems, but ...

➖ They need it: natural snowfall is erratic in this southerly region

➖ Few challenges, and off-piste limited – possibly banned in places

➖ Mostly short runs with limited vertical (with notable exceptions)

➖ Crowds on the Sella Ronda circuit

➖ Still some old draglifts

➖ Après-ski is not a highlight

The Sella Ronda is an amazing circular network of lifts and pistes taking you around the Gruppo Sella – a mighty limestone massif with villages scattered around it. Among the main attractions is the simply spectacular Dolomite scenery – like something Disney might have conjured up for a theme park. But the geology that provides the visual drama also dictates the nature of the slopes. Sheer limestone cliffs rise out of gentle pasture land, which is where you spend your time. Individual runs are short; verticals of more than 500m/1,600ft are rare, while runs of under 300m/1000ft vertical are not. And they are predominantly easy: there's scarcely a black run to be seen.

The distances you can cover on skis are huge. In overall dimensions, the network exceeds even the famed Three Valleys in France. In addition to the main Sella Ronda circuit, major lift systems lead off it at three main points along the way: Selva (covered in the chapter after this), Corvara and Arabba, dealt with here. These three should obviously be on your shortlist. But there are other villages worth considering. Santa Cristina and Ortisei, next to Selva, are covered in that chapter. San Cassiano and La Villa, which share the friendly and scenic Alta Badia area, linked to Corvara, are dealt with here. Canazei and Campitello, at the south-west corner of the Sella Ronda circuit, are now covered in our new Val di Fassa chapter.

This is one of the few areas where we unreservedly welcome continuous sunny weather; the snowmaking is fantastic and we really don't want clouds and snow to interfere with our lunches gazing at the views.

461

ALAN LIPTROT

The views from Alta Badia are just stunning. Hidden among those peaks is the famous, er, hidden valley run ↓

For 2008/09 a quad chairlift was installed in the centre of La Villa, linking the slopes of Piz La Villa with the slopes above Badia (no more carrying skis across the street). And the queue-prone Masarei double chair at Pralongia was replaced by a six-pack.

For 2009/10 the Ciampai double chairlift to Piz Sorega above San Cassiano is to be replaced by a six-pack.

CHOOSING A BASE

It's important to pick the right resort. For good skiers, the best bases are Selva (covered in a separate chapter) and Arabba, a small village where classic Dolomite terrain gives way to steeper slopes with bigger verticals. Corvara is well placed for all the options – the Sella Ronda circuit, the Alta Badia area, excursions to Cortina. San Cassiano is off the Sella Ronda circuit, but otherwise attractive.

Your choice might be influenced by how you are going to get to your resort. There are countless possible arrival airports, and various possible transfer routes – some can take four or five hours, including interminable stretches of winding mountain roads.

The vast network of slopes seems to require a vast selection of piste maps – 12 in all, plus variations. There are individual ones for each resort.

Some cover the main circuit – others do not – and it's worth picking up detailed local maps of each area as you pass through. Reporters generally find the system confusing. To add to the confusion, the main resorts now promote additional tours, away from the main circuit. A First World War circuit of 78-100km/ 48-62 miles is one ('A macho day out for mileage-hungry intermediates,' said a recent reporter).

The Dolomiti Superski pass covers not only the Sella Ronda resorts but dozens of others, amounting to an impressive 1220km/758 miles. We'd recommend anyone based in Corvara or San Cassiano, in particular, to make a day trip to Cortina, taking in the famous 'hidden valley' run – see feature panel later in this chapter. The lift system logs your lift rides, and you can check your lift rides, skiing distance and vertical online.

THE SELLA RONDA CIRCUIT

The Sella Ronda is a unique circular tour around the Sella massif, easily managed in a day by even an early intermediate. The slopes you descend are almost all easy and take you through Selva, Colfosco, Corvara, Arabba and Canazei (or at least the slopes above it). You can do the circuit in either direction by following very clear coloured signs. The clockwise route is slightly quicker and offers more interesting slopes, but the downside is that it is much busier. Many reporters prefer the anticlockwise route because of that. Some resort piste maps incorporate a Sella Ronda map of the usual panoramic kind; map-literate people will want the proper topographical one with contour lines, available from the tourist offices (not lift stations).

The runs total around 23km/14 miles and the lifts around 14km/9 miles. The lifts take a total of about two hours (plus any queuing). We've done the circuit in just three and a half hours excluding diversions and hut stops; five or six hours is a realistic time in busy periods, when there are crowds both on the pistes and on the lifts. If possible, choose low season or a Saturday, and start early.

Not everyone likes it. Reporters' comments include: 'it's a bit of a slog', 'too busy and crowded', 'over-hyped, over-sold and over-regimented' and 'not a relaxing business when it's busy'. And boarders should be aware that there are quite a few flat bits.

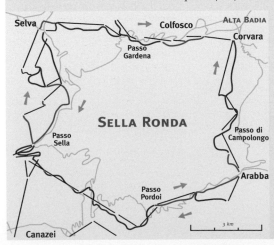

If you set out early, you can make more of the day by taking some diversions from the circuit. Among the most entertaining runs are the long ones down from Ciampinoi to Santa Cristina and Selva, from Dantercëpies to Selva, from the top of the Boé gondola back down to Corvara, and from the top of the Arabba gondola. Take in all those in a day doing the circuit and you'll have had a good day.

Intermediates could explore the Alta Badia area towards San Cassiano and La Villa from Corvara. Groups of different abilities can do the circuit and arrange to meet along the way at some of the many welcoming rifugios.

LIFT PASSES

Dolomiti Superski

Prices in €

Age	1-day	6-day
under 16	31	154
16 to 59	44	220
over 60	40	198

Free under 8
Beginner no deals

Notes
Covers 1220km/758 miles of piste and 450 lifts in the Dolomites, including all Sella Ronda resorts

KEY FACTS

Sella Ronda
The linked lift network of Val Gardena, Alta Badia, Arabba, and the Canazei and Campitello slopes of Val di Fassa

Slopes	1005-3250m
	3,300-10,660ft
Lifts	207
Pistes	460km
	286 miles
Blue	38%
Red	53%
Black	9%
Snowmaking	90%

Arabba 1600m/5,250ft

Arabba, diagonally opposite Selva on the Sella Ronda circuit, is a small, quiet village appealing particularly to good skiers because of its relatively steep, shady local slopes. Off the circuit there is good skiing to be done on the Marmolada glacier.

THE RESORT

Arabba is growing fast, and we are receiving more reports on it.

Village charm The village is small and traditional in style. There are some shops, bars and restaurants, but this is not a place for lively nightlife.

Convenience It's a small place, but staying in the older part involves an uphill walk to reach the ski area, which provokes a few complaints from reporters. A new area of hotels and chalets has opened higher up, better placed for the lifts and slopes.

Scenery Arabba is beautifully positioned between the stunning Gruppo Sella and the Marmolada glacier, with great views at altitude.

THE MOUNTAIN

Arabba's local slopes cover 62km/ 39 miles and have some of the best natural snow and steepest pistes in the Dolomites. In various places around Arabba, reporters reckon the runs are at the steep end of their classification, and in one or two cases blues might be better classed as reds. Runs from the high point of Porta Vescovo are north-facing, with more vertical than most in the region. The Marmolada glacier, beyond Arabba, is open most of the winter and is included on the main lift pass. It is a trip to do as much for its spectacular views as for skiing, though the red run from top to bottom is a notable 1490m/4,900ft vertical.

Slopes The two-stage double-cable gondola and the cable car beside it rise almost 900m/2,950ft vertical to the high point at Porta Vescovo (2475m/8,120ft). From here a choice of runs return to the village or you can head off around the Sella Ronda circuit, following a busy red run to Pont de Vauz. From the mid-station of the DMC, a series of chairs take you to Passo Padon and onwards to the Marmolada glacier – a highly recommended outing, despite the queues described later.

On the opposite side of the village,

a fast quad gets you on the way to Burz and Passo Campolongo. You can then head down to Corvara and the rest of the Sella Ronda or divert right on to the quieter, gentle slopes of the Alta Badia, and San Cassiano.

Fast lifts New lifts have improved access to and from the village.

Queues This year's reporters seem to have met few problems. There are always delays somewhere on the Sella Ronda circuit, though. The outing to Marmolada can be troublesome on a busy day. The Sass de la Vegla double chair you have to take from the mid-station of the gondola is a serious bottleneck. And, despite upgrading of the Marmolada cable cars, there are long waits at the bottom station – a 2008 reporter had a 40-minute wait at lunchtime (he advises going early morning before people based further away have time to get there).

Terrain park None in Arabba. There's a half-pipe at Belvedere above Canazei.

Snow reliability Arabba offers some of the most snow-sure slopes in the Sella Ronda region. Good snow is far from assured, but snowmaking is extensive and the main runs are north-facing.

Experts Arabba has the best steep slopes of all the Sella Ronda resorts. The north-facing blacks and reds from Porta Vescovo offer genuine challenges and are great fun. Off-piste is limited – see feature panel.

Intermediates The local slopes suit adventurous intermediates best. Most are quite challenging and those on the main circuit suffer from crowds.

Beginners It is not a good choice for beginners. There is a small nursery slope near the Burz chair, but access to longer easy runs is tricky.

Snowboarding Porta Vescovo offers some decent challenges. Most of the lifts are fast chairs or gondolas.

Cross-country There is one loop at village level.

Off-piste skiing close to pistes is discouraged or even prohibited in parts of this area – but this doesn't rule out some spectacular routes.

The cable car from Passo Pordoi gets you up on to the Sella massif. There are fairly direct descents from here back to the pass (the very sunny Forcella) or down the Val Lasties towards Canazei. But the classic run is the Val Mesdì, a long, shady couloir on the northern side of the Gruppo Sella down to Colfosco, reached by skiing and hiking across the massif.

Marmolada, the highest peak of the Dolomites, now reached by reasonably efficient lifts from Malga Ciapela, is the other obvious launching point. It offers a range of big descents on and off the glacier. Proguide in Arabba offers guidance on these and other routes – see www.proguide.it.

Mountain restaurants There's lots of choice, from rustic huts to larger places. Most are lively and many have great views – in this respect, Luigi Gorze at the top of the Porta Vescovo lifts takes some beating – but this year we don't have any recommendations in this sector of the Sella Ronda for notably good food.

Schools The local Arabba school offers group and private classes. Proguide guides off-piste – see feature panel.

Families The kindergarten at the ski school takes children from two years.

STAYING THERE

Several UK tour operators offer packages. New accommodation has been built at the top end of town, closer to the lifts.

Chalets There are several, including a good selection from Neilson.

Hotels There are about a dozen hotels. The 3-star Portavescovo (0436 79139) is repeatedly recommended by readers ('great – very well cooked food'), as is the 4-star Sporthotel (0436 79321) – 'very convenient, excellent service, outstanding dinners, comfortable bar and lounge'. Other recent reader tips include the 'friendly' Garnì Astor (0436 79326); Garnì Laura (0436 780055) near the Burz lift – 'the wellness suite is pure 5-star luxury'; and the Grifone (0436 780034) out at Passo Campolongo – 'remote, but food and service were superb; excellent bar and health club/pool'.

Apartments Self-catering accommodation is available.

Eating out Restaurant choice is limited. The central hotels all have busy restaurants (see above). Past reporters have heartily approved Micky's Grill in the hotel Mesdì ('best steaks in the Alps'; 'best restaurant in Arabba'). The Alpenrose hotel will send its horse-drawn sleigh to pick you up if you book a table in its Stube Ladina ('good food and surroundings'). The 7 Sass does 'delicious pizzas'. You can go up to Rifugio Plan Boé by snowmobile on Thursdays for a 'special' three-course dinner and dancing – 'the best meal we had'.

Après-ski The après-ski is cheap but very limited. 'There are still only three bars, but at last there are signs of life,' says one regular. According to recent reports, the central Bar Peter seems to be the focus – 'very friendly, good value', with a DJ some nights. But earlier reports favour the Stube and the Treina. Cosy hotel bars are other options in the village. The atmospheric Rifugio Plan Boé up the mountain is good for a last drink on the pistes before heading back to the village – 'loud 70s, 80s and Europop music'. It is possible to take a taxi to nearby Corvara (6km/4 miles away) for a more animated choice.

Off the slopes Off-slope diversions are few. There's a small selection of shops, and cafes, and there's an ice rink. Snowmobile excursions are available.

Corvara 1570m/5,150ft

Gentle slopes at the heart of the Sella Ronda circuit. There are plenty of hotels, restaurants, bars and sports facilities, making Corvara one of the better bases for families and novices.

THE RESORT

Corvara is the most animated village east of Selva and well connected to the Alta Badia slopes as well as the Sella Ronda circuit.

Village charm The place is lively and family-friendly, with a pleasant centre.

Convenience The main shops and some hotels cluster around a small piazza, but the rest of Corvara sprawls along the valley floor.

Scenery The impressive rock faces of the Gruppo Sella overlook the village.

THE MOUNTAIN

Corvara is well positioned with village lifts heading off to reasonably equidistant Selva, Arabba and San Cassiano. The local slopes are gentle and confidence-boosting.

Slopes A long gondola heads out of the village towards Boé and the clockwise Sella Ronda circuit. Two successive fast quads head in the opposite direction towards Colfosco and the anticlockwise route. The area around both lifts can get congested at peak times. A slow chair and a couple of drags take you towards the quieter area of slopes shared with San Cassiano and La Villa. A faster alternative from the other side of town is a gondola to Col Alto.

Fast lifts As elsewhere on the circuit, new fast lifts are gradually improving the area.

Queues We still get reports about long waits for the Borest chair between Corvara and Colfosco (on the anticlockwise Sella Ronda circuit), but otherwise there are few problems.

Terrain park There is a terrain park on the Ciampai run above San Cassiano.

Snow reliability As in the rest of the Sella Ronda area, natural snowfall is erratic, but snowmaking is excellent.

Experts Very few of Corvara's slopes offer any real challenges, and those that do are short. There are very few black runs – the one above Boé 'was red 28 years ago and is no harder now', a reporter points out. There's the long World Cup run at La Villa. See feature panel for off-piste runs.

Intermediates The slopes are superb for cruising and confidence-boosting and there's a vast network of interconnected slopes to explore; don't miss the Val Stella Alpina area (see Colfosco, below) and the easy runs of the Alta Badia, between Corvara and San Cassiano. The red underneath the Boé cable car in Corvara is usually uncrowded and retains good snow. The adventurous can head for the steeper, wooded pistes going down to La Villa.

Beginners There's a nursery area and lots of easy runs to progress to.

Snowboarding Novices can make rapid progress on gentle slopes. A few awkward draglifts remain, but most can be avoided.

Cross-country The Alta Badia area offers 38km/24 miles of trails, including a 16km/10 mile valley loop on the way to Colfosco.

Mountain restaurants Lots of choice. Reader tips include the Marmotta ('lovely – old skis and photos'), rifugio Col Alto ('excellent venison') and the Brancia ('brill hunter's platter').

Schools There's a local branch of the Alta Badia school – reports welcome.

Families Kinderland takes children from the age of three.

STAYING THERE

There is a wide choice of accommodation, but some can be a longish walk from the lifts.

Hotels There are some deeply comfortable 4-stars. The reader who rated the Col Alto (0471 831100) 'top class and cosy with beautifully prepared five-course meals and a free minibus service' has been back to confirm that verdict. Another reader favourite is the Posta Zirm (0471 836175) which has a large spa: 'very good food, ski-in/ski-out, comfortable rooms'. Also recommended are the pensione Villa Tony (0471 836193) – 'very reasonably priced half board'.

Eating out A reasonable choice. Most of the hotels have restaurants – the Stüa de Michil in the Perla has a Michelin star. See also San Cassiano.

Après-ski The Posta Zirm in Corvara does a ski-boot tea dance, but support may depend on tour ops organising group transport back to other villages. 'I can't recommend this bar enough,' said a 2008 visitor. The hotel Tablè is recommended by reporters for its piano bar and good cakes. Other suggestions from reporters are the smart bar in the Perla hotel and the 'trendy' cocktail bar at the Marmolada.

Off the slopes There's a covered ice rink, indoor tennis courts and an outdoor artificial climbing wall.

Colfosco 1645m/5,400ft

Colfosco is a smaller, quieter satellite of Corvara, 2km/1 mile away. It has a fairly compact centre with a sprawl of large hotels along the road towards Passo Gardena. It's connected to Corvara by a horizontal chairlift. In the opposite direction, a gondola goes to Passo Gardena. There are a couple of short nursery slopes and the runs back from Passo Gardena are easy, long cruises. Immediately above the village, the Val Stella Alpina (aka Edelweisstal), off the Sella Ronda circuit, offers gentle, normally quiet pistes ideal for fast cruising. The three pleasant

SIMON MEDLEY

Spot the difference? South of Arabba, the geology changes: 'normal' mountains, with less contrast between upper and lower slopes ... ➘

restaurants can get very busy. A 2007 visitor recommends the slope-side hotel Sport (0471 836074) with 'spacious rooms, excellent food'.

San Cassiano

1530m/5,020ft

A quiet village with some good hotels, easy slopes away from the main Sella Ronda circuit and with easy access to the famous 'hidden valley' run.

THE RESORT
San Cassiano is a pleasant little village, bypassed by the road to Cortina, and is working towards becoming car-free.
Village charm It's a quiet, civilised resort, without much animation.
Convenience A drawback: hotels are close to the centre, but the main lift is a short bus ride away.
Scenery The village is set in an attractive, tree-filled valley. The views from the slopes are superb.

THE MOUNTAIN
The local slopes, shared with Corvara and La Villa, form a spur off the main Sella Ronda circuit.

Slopes The gondola, a drive from the centre (many hotels run buses), rises to Piz Sorega. From the top, fast chairs form the links with Corvara and La Villa, or you can head for Pralongia and the long runs home. Most of the area has very gentle slopes, ideal for easy cruising.
Fast lifts Essentially well-connected, but old chairs and draglifts remain.
Queues Few problems, thanks to continual lift upgrades.
Terrain park It's at Ciampai, with boardercross, jumps, rails and humps.
Snow reliability The Dolomites have an erratic snowfall record, but snowmaking is excellent.
Experts Experts would be wise to stay elsewhere. There are a few steeper runs at La Villa, but not much else.
Intermediates Pretty much ideal if you love easy cruising on flattering, well-groomed runs. The red option back to town is a serious red though.
Beginners There are nursery slopes a short bus ride away at Armentarola and at the top of the gondola – not ideal. But there are plenty of long, easy slopes to progress to.
Snowboarding Endless carving on quiet pistes and there's a terrain park.

If you like runs surrounded by spectacular scenery well away from all signs of civilisation, don't miss the easy red run from Lagazuoi, reached by cable car from Passo Falzarego. The pass is easily accessible from Armentarola, close to San Cassiano – shared taxis run an affordable shuttle service (5 euros each) to the pass from here. There's also a bus from San Cassiano, but a recent reporter says that it is 'very crowded and slow'. And buses go to the pass from Cortina – or at least to the Cinque Torri lift network, which is now linked to the Col Gallina slopes next to Passo Falzarego.

The run is one of the most beautiful we've come across, and delights most reporters. Views from the top of the cable car are splendid, and the run offers isolation amid sheer, pink-tinged Dolomite peaks and frozen waterfalls. Because the cable car has low capacity, the run is never crowded. Make time to stop at the atmospheric Rifugio Scotoni near the end ('nice kaiserschmarren').

At the bottom, it's a long skate to a horse-drawn sled with ropes attached, which tows you back to Armentarola (for a couple of euros). This is more of a challenge than the run, and the risk of a pile-up if someone falls has concerned some reporters. We're told there is a bus alternative. At Armentarola there is a draglift up to a run back to San Cassiano.

Cross-country There's a branch of the Dolomiti Nordicski in Armentarola. It offers tuition and equipment hire, as well as 23km/14 miles of trails.

Mountain restaurants There are countless options. Most are woody and cosy in traditional style, but Las Vegas is a wild exception – cool, minimalist, with huge windows to make the most of the views, and 'irresistible dishes and wines'. Pralongia is 'a great place for a last drink before descending'. Other reader tips include Punta Trieste.

Schools We have no reports.

Families The school offers the usual arrangements for children and there are several kids' parks.

STAYING THERE
Tour operator Ski 2 offers a wide range of options.

Hotels The Rosa Alpina (0471 849500) is a splendid place, coupling genuine comfort, great food and a good spa with a relaxed atmosphere. Its three restaurants include the St Hubertus, which has two Michelin stars. The Fanes (0471 849470) is a smart chalet-style place with indoor-outdoor pool and a spa. You can stay up the mountain at the modern, trendy Las Vegas restaurant (0471 840138).

Eating out As well as the Rosa Alpina's St Hubertus, two restaurants in the area have one Michelin star; one, the Siriola in the hotel Ciasa Salares, is in Armentarola, just up the road; for the other see Corvara.

Après-ski It starts up the mountain with loud music at Las Vegas. A reporter recommends the Utia on the home run and skiing down after dark. Nightlife is very limited.

Off the slopes There are some lovely walks amid the stunning scenery.

La Villa 1435m/4,710ft

La Villa is similar to neighbouring San Cassiano in most ways – small, quiet, pretty, unspoiled. But the home pistes (served by a gondola) are challenging – a genuine red and a just-about-genuine black dropping 600m/1,970ft through woods to the village. There's a kids' snow garden at the top. Across the village, a fast chair serves a blue and a red slope and a link to Badia. A well travelled reporter this year sends a glowing report on the Antines (0471 844234) – 'one of the nicest hotels I have visited, with an outstanding restaurant'.

Badia 1325m/4,350ft

This small roadside village (formerly known as Pedraces) has become more important to skiers since a free bus link started between here and Piccolino (20 mins) where you can take a gondola into the Plan de Corones/Kronplatz ski area – well worth a day trip, and covered of course by the Dolomiti Superski lift pass. At the end of the village a new quad takes you to the link with La Villa (and hence the rest of the Alta Badia and Sella Ronda area). The village also has its own small ski area on the other side of the valley with a fast quad (with a red run underneath) and a slow double chair (with a blue underneath) to Santa Croce (2045m/6,710ft). A reporter recommends Ospizió di S Croce ('fabulous views, good omelette').

Phone numbers
From abroad use the prefix +39 (and do **not** omit the initial '0' of the phone number)

TOURIST OFFICES

ALTA BADIA:
Corvara, Colfosco, San Cassiano, La Villa
t 0471 836176
www.altabadia.org

ARABBA
t 0436 780019
info@arabba.it
www.arabba.it

VAL DI FASSA:
Canazei, Campitello
t 0462 609500
www.fassa.com

Sella Ronda

467

Interactive resort shortlist builder at **www.wtss.co.uk**

Selva / Val Gardena

Pleasant village amid spectacular Dolomite scenery, with the vast Sella Ronda lift network on its doorstep

£85
RESORT PRICE INDEX

RATINGS

The mountains

Extent	★★★★★
Fast lifts	★★★
Queues	★★★
Terrain p'ks	★★★
Snow	★★★★
Expert	★★★
Intermediate	★★★★★
Beginner	★★★
X-country	★★★★★
Restaurants	★★★★★
Schools	★★★
Families	★★

The resort

Charm	★★★
Convenience	★★★
Scenery	★★★★★
Eating out	★★★
Après-ski	★★★
Off-slope	★★★

468

NEWS

For 2008/09 a six-pack replaced the Panorama quad at Alpe di Siusi and the gondola to Col Raiser was upgraded with smart eight-person cabins.

For 2009/10 one of the most radical lift upgrades of all time is planned: the old Bullaccia single chairlift on Alpe di Siusi will be replaced by a hybrid chairlift/gondola. We guess the key factor is that it serves a toboggan run and a restaurant, as well as a piste.

➕ Part of the Sella Ronda region, with all the plus points we list in that chapter (immediately before this one): vast intermediate area, extensive snowmaking, stunning scenery, good mountain huts

➕ Attractive but strung-out village in an impressive wooded setting

➕ Excellent local slopes, with big verticals by Sella Ronda standards

➕ Mix of open and wooded slopes

➕ Excellent nursery slopes

➖ Some of the minus points of the Sella Ronda region too: erratic natural snowfall, many short runs with limited vertical in some sectors, crowds on the main Sella Ronda circuit

➖ No easy long runs immediately above Selva – buses or taxis are needed for access to them

➖ Bus services are frequently criticised by reporters

➖ Busy road through the village

Selva (known to 'Ski Sunday' viewers as Val Gardena – the name of the valley) is one of the main bases to consider for a visit to the unique Sella Ronda region. (The Sella Ronda as a whole, and the other villages that make it up, are covered in a separate chapter, immediately before this one.) Selva remains one of our favourite bases in the area, essentially because of the local slopes, including two race courses through woods to the village that are among the most satisfying runs in the area – not least because they offer decent verticals. Beginners, near-beginners and timid intermediates, though, are probably better off staying in the Alta Badia area – in Corvara, Colfosco or San Cassiano. And places such as San Cassiano and Arabba have much more of a small village feel than sprawling Selva.

THE RESORT

Selva is a long roadside village at the head of the Val Gardena, almost merging with the next village down-valley, Santa Cristina.

For many years this area was part of Austria, and it retains a Tirolean charm. German is the main language, not Italian, and many visitors are German, too. Most places have two names: Selva is also known as Wolkenstein and the Gardena valley as Gröden. We do our bit for Italian unity by using the Italian place names. The local language, Ladin, also survives –

giving a third name to some places. Not surprisingly, visitors find all this confusing, 'especially on the buses'. The valley is famed for wood carvings, which are on display (and sale) wherever you look.

VILLAGE CHARM ★★★
Pity about the traffic

The village has traditional Tirolean-style architecture and an attractive church, but is a sprawling place and suffers from through-traffic (and a lack of parking facilities).

Despite the World Cup fame of Val Gardena, Selva is neither upmarket nor

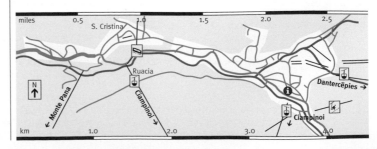

↑ Start of the runs
from Dantercëpies to
Selva, with the
plateau of Alpe di
Siusi directly ahead
VAL GARDENA TOURIST OFFICE

KEY FACTS

Resort	1565m
	5,130ft

The linked lift
network of Val
Gardena, Alta Badia,
Arabba, and the
Canazei and
Campitello slopes of
Val di Fassa

Slopes	1005-2520m
	3,300-8,270ft
Lifts	207
Pistes	460km
	286 miles
Blue	38%
Red	53%
Black	9%
Snowmaking	90%

Val Gardena-
Alpe di Siusi only

Slopes	1005-2520m
	3,300-8,270ft
Lifts	83
Pistes	175km
	109 miles
Blue	30%
Red	60%
Black	10%
Snowmaking	90%

brash. It's a good-value, civilised, low-key resort – relaxed and family-friendly in many respects, once you get away from the intrusive through-road.

CONVENIENCE ★★★☆☆
Choose your spot with care

From the village, gondolas rise in two directions. The Ciampinoi gondola goes south from near the centre of the village to start the anticlockwise Sella Ronda route. The Dantercëpies gondola, for the clockwise Sella Ronda route, starts above the village at the top of the nursery slopes (but accessible via a central chairlift and a short run down). The most convenient position to stay is near this chair or one of the gondolas.

There are local buses until early evening – five euros for a weekly card – but they generate numerous complaints from reporters about infrequency, unreliability, inadequate capacity (especially at the end of the day), poorly sited stops and lack of services to Corvara and Plan de Gralba. The latest complaint is that there is no service on Saturday. There's a night bus between Selva and Ortisei. Many reporters use taxis, although they are expensive unless you share. All the 4-star hotels run their own free transport.

Ortisei, the main town of Val Gardena, is described at the end of the chapter; it is not so convenient for the Sella Ronda slopes.

SCENERY ★★★★★
Pretty in pink

The village enjoys a lovely setting under the impressive pink-tinged walls of Sassolungo and the Gruppo Sella – a fortress-like massif 6km/4 miles across that lies at the hub of the Sella Ronda circuit (see separate chapter).

THE MOUNTAINS

Selva's own slopes cover both sides of the valley. The lower slopes are wooded, with open slopes higher up. Most of the lifts stay open until around 5pm in high season.

The local piste map exists in several variations, which reporters find confusing. The maps show neither names nor numbers for the runs. Piste marking and signing also provoke complaints.

The Dolomiti Superski pass covers not only Selva and the Sella Ronda resorts but dozens of others. It's an easy road trip to Cortina. You can check your lift rides, skiing distance and vertical descended online.

EXTENT OF THE SLOPES ★★★★★
High-mileage excursions

The **Ciampinoi** gondola accesses several shady pistes, including the famous World Cup Downhill run, leading back down to Selva and Santa Cristina. In the opposite direction, runs go on to **Plan de Gralba** – and to the anticlockwise Sella Ronda circuit.

469

Interactive resort shortlist builder at www.wtss.co.uk

In the opposite direction, the **Dantercëpies** gondola serves lovely red runs back to Selva and accesses the clockwise Sella Ronda circuit.

The sunny **Seceda** area is accessed by a gondola on the outskirts of Santa Cristina. This is also accessible by descending from Ciampinoi to ride a slick underground train across the valley. Runs descend to Santa Cristina or to Ortisei – a red run of about 7km/4 miles. And from Ortisei a cable car on the other side of the valley takes you to and from **Alpe di Siusi** – a gentle elevated area of quiet, easy runs, cross-country tracks and walks. This area can also be accessed via the big gondola from the village of Siusi, way off to the west.

FAST LIFTS ★★★★★
Getting better
The main access lifts are gondolas, and there are lots of fast chairs above them – in particular at Alpe di Siusi and a Plan de Gralba. But there are still plenty of slow chairs and drags – hence our middling rating.

QUEUES ★★★★★
Still some problems
New lifts have vastly improved the area as a whole, but at most stages of the season the gondolas out of the village regularly build 'morale-sapping morning queues'; the draglifts up to the Dantercëpies gondola may hold you up, too. There are bottlenecks on the main Sella Ronda circuit.

Good, long blue runs for beginners to progress to – but you have to catch a bus from Selva to avoid a tricky red from Ciampinoi

Lovely long reds; the one on skier's right of the gondola used to be the Women's Downhill run

Efficient underground train links the gondolas for the Ciampinoi and Seceda sectors

TERRAIN PARKS ★★★☆☆
Facilities spread around

There are boardercross runs at Passo Sella by the Cavazes Grohmann chair and at Piz Sella by the Comici chair. And there's a half-pipe and a natural pipe at Plan de Gralba. Alpe di Siusi has a terrain park and a half-pipe by the Laurin chair.

SNOW RELIABILITY ★★★★☆
Excellent when it's cold

The slopes are not high – there are few above 2200m/7,200ft and most are between 1500m and 2000m (4,900ft and 6,500ft). Natural snowfalls are erratic, but Selva's slopes are well covered by snowmaking. During severe droughts we have enjoyed excellent pistes here, and our reporters are regularly impressed – 'a revelation', 'wonderful', 'stunning', 'unbelievable coverage and quality'. Problems arise only if it is too warm to make snow.

FOR EXPERTS ★★★☆☆
A few good runs

There are few challenges, essentially no moguls (the blacks all get groomed) and a low likelihood of powder. There are few major off-piste routes because of the nature of the terrain; see the off-piste panel in the Sella Ronda chapter. But Selva is one of the better spots in this region, all the same. The Val Gardena World Cup piste, the Saslong, is one of several

Sassolungo/ Langkofel 3180m

Punta d'Oro/Goldknopf 2210m

ALPE DI SIUSI

Paradiso

1940m

Ideal area for early intermediates – very gentle pistes (almost flat in places), quiet and set amid superb scenery

Fiè/ Vòls 88om

Mont de Seura 2115m

Alpe di Siusi Seiser Alm 2000m

Siusi/ Seis 1005m

5m

Sothers

Mont Seura

2100m

Castel Rotto/ Kastel Ruth 1060m

Saslong

1665m

MONTE PANA

Alpe di Siusi

S Cristina/ St Christina 1430m

Beautiful long run with a vertical drop of 1300m/4,270ft: not steep but quite narrow in places; wonderful views over the valley and through a very picturesque canyon

Ortisei/ St Ulrich 1235m/4,05oft

The Saslong World Cup Downhill piste is a wonderful, fast, rolling cruise that's especially good in January when it's not too crowded

l Raiser

Furnes

2280m

SECEDA

Seceda 2520m

↑ A lot of boot faffing rightly goes on here, at the top of the steep runs from Ciampinoi to the villages. In the distance on the left, the gentler open slopes of Seceda

steepish runs between Ciampinoi and both Selva and Santa Cristina. Unlike many World Cup pistes it is kept in racing condition for Italian team practices, but it is open to the public much of the time and makes a wonderful fast cruise – it's one of our favourite runs. The long red runs from Dantercëpies are entertaining, too.

FOR INTERMEDIATES ★★★★★
Fast cruising on easy slopes
There is a huge amount of skiing to do, in several areas.

Competent intermediates will love the red and black descents from Dantercëpies and Ciampinoi to Selva.

The blue runs in the Plan de Gralba area are gentle; the red run to get there from Ciampinoi is a real obstacle – steep and crowded – but reporters find it worth the struggle. You can return to Selva at low level or at altitude – and the high-road option no longer needs to involve the short black run from Piz Sella. The quiet runs at Mont de Seura, above Monte Pana, are worth exploring.

The Alpe di Siusi above Ortisei is ideal for confidence-building – very

gentle (almost flat in places), quiet, set in superb scenery with no crowds. Runs are mostly short, the main exception being the red down to Saltria from Punta d'Oro, offering 500m/1,640ft vertical.

The Seceda sector has good red and blue runs at altitude, and splendid runs to the valley – an easy blue/red to Santa Cristina and the beautiful red Cucasattel, passing through a natural gorge to Ortisei.

FOR BEGINNERS ★★★★★
Great slopes, but ...
The village nursery slopes below the Dantercëpies gondola are excellent – spacious, convenient, and kept in good condition. There are lots of gentle, long runs to progress to, but they are not immediately above Selva. Plan de Gralba has easy blues, but you need to take a taxi to get there. Near-beginners would be better off taking the bus to Alpe di Siusi.

FOR CROSS-COUNTRY ★★★★★
Beautiful trails
There are 98km/61 miles of trails, all enjoying wonderful scenery. The 12km/

boarding

Selva attracts few boarders. There's little to challenge experts, and off-piste opportunities are limited, but the nursery slopes are good and there are lots of gentle runs to progress to. The main lifts out of the village are all gondolas or chairs. There's a terrain park at Alpe di Siusi and a couple of half-pipes.

SCHOOLS

Selva Gardena - Ski Academy Peter Runggaldier (Ski Factory)
t 0471 795156

2000
t 0471 773125

Top School Val Gardena
t 0471 794099

Classes
(Selva prices)
6 days €176

Private lessons
€38 for 1hr

GUIDES

Val Gardena Mountain Guide Association
t 0471 794133

CHILDCARE

Selvi mini club
0471 795156
Ages 0 to 4; 9am to 4pm, Sun to Fri

Casa Bimbo (at S Cristina)
0471 793013
From 4mnth to 7yr

Ski school
For age 4 to 12:
6 days (10am to 4pm)
€305, lunch included
(Selva school price)

GETTING THERE

Air Verona 215km/ 135 miles (2hr45); Bolzano 55km/ 35 miles (1hr); Treviso 200km/ 125 miles (3hr30); Brescia 240km/150 miles (3hr30); Milan 340km/210 miles (4hr30); Innsbruck 120km/75 miles (1hr45)

Rail Chiusa (27km/ 17 miles); Bressanone (35km/22 miles); Bolzano (40km/ 25 miles); frequent buses from station

---

7 mile trail up the Vallunga-Langental valley is particularly attractive, with neck-craning views all around. Almost half the trails have the advantage of being at altitude (so better snow as well as better views), running between Monte Pana and across Alpe di Siusi.

MOUNTAIN RESTAURANTS ★★★★★
A real highlight
There are lots of huts all over the area, and virtually all of them are lively, with helpful staff, good food, lots of character and modest prices. 'Not a bad one all week' is a typical reporter's comment, leading us to bestow a rare 5-star rating. What follows is not a complete guide.

In the Dantercëpies sector, the Panorama is a small, cosy, rustic suntrap at the foot of the drag near the top, tipped for its coffee, chocolate and cakes as well as views. Not far away at the bottom of the Val double chair, the Ciampac is 'brilliant for coffee or lunch in the sun'. While at the top of the Costabella chair, Rif Pastura is a great place for lunch or 'chocolate to die for' at the end of the day.

In the Plan de Gralba area the Rif Enrico Comici is atmospheric, with a big terrace. Piz Seteur has 'superb lasagne' and is also recommended late in the day (see 'Après-ski').

In the Seceda sector there are countless options. Baita Gamsblut is a 'super rustic hut with a good menu and a warm, friendly atmosphere'. Daniel's Hütte is 'very cosy in a storm, with excellent food and good service'. Curona is a favourite of one repeat visitor. On the long Cucasattel run, Val d'Anna is another reader favourite.

On Alpe di Siusi there are again plenty of attractive possibilities, but we get fewer reports on this sector.

SCHOOLS AND GUIDES ★★★★★
No worries
The setup seems to have changed in the last year or two: 90s racing star Peter Runggaldier seems to have merged his Ski Academy with the resort's main Selva Gardena school, which has been recommended by several readers – most recently for children's classes. Reports on the 2000 school are less consistent – two women last year were put in a class well below their proper standard – but this year's one report is positive, as were earlier ones.

FOR FAMILIES ★★★★★
It's all down to the detail
We get reports from people who have very successful family holidays here – and if your childcare arrangements or ski school classes work out well, and you pick your location with care, your whole holiday may work out well, too. Some UK tour operators have their own nursery facilities, which is an excellent start. But in general the village is not ideal. It's a sprawling place requiring use of inadequate buses, with a busy through-road. If your kids are beginners, they face the same problem as other beginners.

STAYING THERE

Selva now features in most major tour op brochures, and some minor ones.
Chalets There is a fair choice of catered chalets, including some good ones with en suite bathrooms, and some with childcare on hand.
Hotels There are about 20 4-star hotels in Selva, about 40 3-stars and numerous lesser hotels. It is not a small place. Few of the best are well positioned – though they generally operate shuttle buses.
★★★★Aaritz (0471 795011) Best-placed 4-star, opposite the Ciampinoi gondola, and with an open fire.
★★★★Gran Baita (0471 795210) Large, luxurious sporthotel, with lots of mod cons including indoor pool. A few minutes' walk from centre and lifts.
★★★★Granvara (0471 795250) Just out of town but free hotel bus, great views, pool and a spa.
★★★★Migon (0471 795092) Good-value discovery this year, close to lifts and main street – 'comfortable, with fantastic dinners, friendly staff'.
★★★★Oswald (0471 771111) Near a ski bus stop and with its own free bus. 'Good rooms and fantastic food,' said a 2007 reporter.

Selva / Val Gardena

UK PACKAGES

Selva *Alpine Answers, Crystal, Crystal Finest, Esprit, First Choice, Independent Ski Links, Inghams, Interactive Resorts, Italian Safaris, Kuoni, Momentum, Neilson, Simply Alpine, Ski Activity, Ski Total, Ski Yogi, Skitracer, Snow Finders, Thomson* **Ortisei** *Inghams, Interhome, Neilson, Ski Expectations* **S Cristina** *Neilson*

ACTIVITIES

In Val Gardena:

Indoor Swimming pool, sauna, bowling, squash, ice rink, museum, library, chess, tennis, climbing wall, fitness centre

Outdoor Sleigh rides, snowshoeing, tobogganing, ice climbing, ice rink, horse riding, paragliding, extensive cleared paths, climbing

Phone numbers
From abroad use the prefix +39 (and do **not** omit the initial '0' of the phone number)

TOURIST OFFICES

VAL GARDENA
t 0471 777777
info@valgardena.it
www.valgardena.it

Selva
t 0471 777900
selva@valgardena.it

Ortisei
t 0471 777600
ortisei@valgardena.it

***Des Alpes** (0471 772700) Recommended last year and this – good location at a bus stop, 'warm, friendly staff and amply portioned four-course meals'.
***Linder** (0471 795242) An established reader favourite in an excellent central location, endorsed again this year. 'Cosy, comfortable, very welcoming family, fantastic breakfast and dinner and excellent free guiding service.' Pool.
***Pralong** (0471 795370) Uphill walk from the centre, but 'one of the best we've visited', said a 2007 reporter.
***Rodella** (0471 794553) Friendly pensione just outside Selva but with free taxi, spa.
***Solaia** (0471 795104) Superbly positioned for lifts and slopes.
***Stella** (0471 795162) Tipped this year for great location right at the Sella Ronda lifts and 'very good food'.
***Wolkenstein** (0471 772200) Reader favourite in S Cristina, endorsed again this year – 'very friendly', 'superb service and food', 'spacious rooms', 'three very lively bars'.
Villa Seceda (0471 795297) A 'friendly' B&B near the nursery slopes, recommended again this year.
Apartments We have had excellent reports of the Villa Gardena and Isabell apartments.

EATING OUT ★★★☆☆
Adequate choice
The better restaurants are mainly based in hotels or, ironically, B&B guest houses – this year's top tip is the Sal Fëur in the Garni Broi ('best meal we had all week; very Tyrolean, pleasant room, excellent service and super food'). The hotel Des Alpes gets mixed reviews – the trick seems to be to avoid the budget menu. Other reader tips include La Bula, the Rino and the Bellavista for pizza, and the Costabella for Tirolean specialities.

APRES-SKI ★★★☆☆
Not without action
At close of play some of the mountain restaurants offer distractions before descent to the village. Piz Seteur is one place where you can expect a bit of a buzz. At the base, La Stua is a popular last stop (and if you settle in for the evening, live music may arrive mid-evening). Café Mozart on the main street 'serves the best hot chocolate in the world and the cakes to match'. The hotel Sochers is said to be good for a

quiet drink. Later on the village streets are fairly quiet, but there are places to go. Goalie's Irish bar, with its hockey memorabilia, gets renewed support this year – 'very friendly owner and staff, good range of music from 60s to 80s'. There are several places with DJs open until about 1am – notably the Laurinkeller and the 'very German' Luislkeller – 'bonkers', according to this year's report, with 'a DJ so bad he's good'. The serious disco dancing spot is the Dali.

OFF THE SLOPES ★★★☆☆
Good variety
There's a sports centre, snowshoeing, lovely walks (buy a map at the tourist office) tobogganing and sleigh rides on Alpe di Siusi. One reporter enjoyed an organised bowling night.

Pedestrians can reach numerous good restaurants by gondola or cable car. There are buses to nearby Ortisei and more distant Bolzano.

Ortisei 1235m/4,050ft

Ortisei is an attractive, prosperous market town with a life of its own apart from tourism. It's full of lovely buildings, pretty churches and pleasant shops and has an interesting museum, a large hot-spring swimming pool and an ice rink. The local slopes aren't on the main Sella Ronda circuit. The lift to the Seceda slopes is easily reached from the centre by a 300m/980ft-long series of underground moving walkways and escalators. The Alpe di Siusi lifts are a similar distance out, and the cable car is now accessed via a long pedestrian footbridge, an improvement over the previous steep, icy, uphill walk. The nursery area, school and kindergarten are at the foot of these slopes, and there's a fair range of family accommodation on the piste side of the road. The fine public indoor pool and ice rink are also here.

There are hotels and self-catering accommodation to suit all tastes and pockets and many good restaurants, mainly specialising in local dishes. A 2008 visitor recommended the hotel Tablick (0471 796051) for its 'great food, efficient staff and the ski bus to the door'. Other past reader tips include the Alpenheim (0471 796515) and the 5-star Adler (0471 775000), which has a very impressive spa. Après-ski is quite jolly, and many bars keep going till late.

Sestriere

Altitude is the main attraction of this, Europe's first purpose-built resort; some would say it's the only attraction

➕ Local slopes suitable for most levels, with some tougher runs than in most neighbouring resorts

➕ Part of the extensive Milky Way area, with Sauze d'Oulx and Sansicario only one lift away

➕ Snowmaking covers all but one or two marginal slopes, but ...

➖ It needs to, given the very erratic local snowfall record

➖ The village is a bit of an eyesore

➖ For a purpose-built resort, not conveniently arranged

➖ Weekend and peak-period queues

➖ Little après-ski during the week

Sestriere was built for snow – high, with north-west-facing slopes – and it has very extensive snowmaking, too. So even if you are let down by the notoriously erratic snowfalls in this corner of Italy, you should be fairly safe here – certainly safer than in Sauze d'Oulx, over the hill. All of which makes Sestriere a great weekend away for the residents of Turin. As a holiday destination for residents of Tunbridge Wells, it doesn't have such a strong case.

TOP 10 RATINGS

Extent	★★★★
Fast lifts	★★★
Queues	★★★
Snow	★★★★
Expert	★★★
Intermediate	★★★★
Beginner	★★★
Charm	★
Convenience	★★★
Scenery	★★★

NEWS

The gondola to Col Basset, the original link with Sauze, is to be removed during 2009. Access to and from Sauze will in future be via the top of M Fraiteve.

KEY FACTS

Resort	2000m
	6,560ft

Milky Way	
Slopes	1390-2825m
	4,560-9,270ft
Lifts	82
Pistes	400km
	249 miles
Blue	24%
Red	56%
Black	20%
Snowmaking	60%

Sestriere-Sauze d'Oulx-Sansicario

Slopes	1390-2825m
	4,560-9,270ft
Lifts	42
Pistes	250km
	155 miles
Snowmaking	38%

THE RESORT

Sestriere was the Alps' first purpose-built resort, developed by Fiat's Giovanni Agnelli in the 1930s, though now run by a local consortium.
Village charm The resort sits on a broad, sunny and windy col, and neither the site nor the village, with its rows of square apartment blocks, looks very hospitable – though some of the buildings benefited from investment for the 2006 Olympics.
Convenience The village is not huge, and some accommodation is close to the snow – it depends where you stay; but basically the buildings are on one side of the col and the skiing is on the other, and some of the walks between the two are non-trivial. The satellite of Borgata, 200m/660ft lower, is less convenient for nightlife and shops. The valley town of Pragelato is a viable base now that it has a cable car link up to Borgata.
Scenery The Motta slopes are high and rolling, with extensive views across the Milky Way and its part-wooded slopes to the mountains on the French border.

THE MOUNTAINS

The local skiing is on shady slopes, mainly open with some woodland, facing the village. Sestriere is at one extreme of the big Franco-Italian Milky Way area – though the slopes around the border are best reached by road.

Slopes The local slopes, served by drags and chairs, are in two main sectors: Sises, directly in front of the village, and Motta, above Borgata; Motta is more varied and bigger, with almost twice the vertical. Across the valley, a gondola goes up from a car park west of the village to M Fraiteve, for access to Sauze d'Oulx, Sansicario and the rest of the Milky Way. (The original gondola to Col Basset at the shoulder of M Fraiteve has been retired.) For the return to Sestriere there is a red run, but it is sunny and the lower half, in particular, is rarely open. Signposting is poor, piste marking is 'appalling' and the piste map is inadequate. There's night skiing twice a week.
Fast lifts The lifts are mainly modern, though there are still some inadequate, 'painfully slow', old ones, both here and over in Sauze.
Queues The main lifts have queues on sunny weekends when people flock up from Turin; there can be lengthy delays for the Cit Roc chair up M Sises. The impact of the removal of the Col Basset gondola remains to be seen.
Terrain parks There is a park but it is low, limited and not lift-served.
Snow reliability The Italian part of the Milky Way gets notoriously unreliable snowfalls, but Sestriere has comprehensive snowmaking. When combined with its altitude and orientation, this means you can count on good cover on the pistes. Don't expect powder, though.

PISTE MAP

Sestriere is covered on the Sauze d'Oulx map a few pages back

UK PACKAGES

Alpine Answers, Club Med, Crystal, First Choice, Independent Ski Links, Inghams, Interhome, Kuoni, Momentum, Neilson, Rocketski, Simply Alpine, Ski Line, Skitracer, Thomson

Phone numbers
From abroad use the prefix +39 (and do **not** omit the initial '0' of the phone number)

TOURIST OFFICE

t 0122 755444
from UK: 0871 226 7876
sestriere@
turismotorino.org
www.turismotorino.
org
www.sestriere.it
www.vialattea.it

PAUL CARTER

Snow-sure slopes directly above the village ↓

Experts There is a fair amount to amuse – steep pistes served by the drags at the top of both sectors. Given snow, there is some decent off-piste. Don't count on it – or on moguls, which are erased religiously.

Intermediates Both sectors also offer plenty for confident intermediates, who can also explore practically all of the Milky Way areas, conditions permitting. The runs in the Motta sector offer more of a challenge.

Beginners The terrain is good for beginners, with several nursery areas and the gentlest of easy blue runs down to Borgata. But there is a lack of easy intermediate runs to progress to.

Snowboarding Sestriere has a reasonable number of chairs, but there are also lots of draglifts.

Cross-country There are three loops covering a total of 10km/6 miles.

Mountain restaurants The woody Raggio di Sole at Anfiteatro offers 'good local food, and good music'. Despite its valley-bottom location, Il Capret at Borgata is popular with readers – 'very friendly staff, reasonable prices, clean toilets'.

Schools and guides Lack of spoken English can be a problem. We lack recent reports.

Families There are no special facilities for children.

STAYING THERE

Most accommodation is in apartments. The complex of apartments built for the 2006 Olympics are an option well worth considering – 'good value,

spacious rooms, with good facilities in the complex'.

Hotels There are a dozen hotels, mostly 3-star or 4-star (and a repeated criticism from reporters is that some of those with 4 stars only deserve 3). The central hotel du Col (0122 76990) offers an 'ideal location, friendly staff and excellent breakfast'. The Cristallo (0122 750190) is also recommended for its position and food. The Shackleton Mountain Resort (0122 750773) is a smart, modern complex with pool and wellness centre. Just out of the village is the luxurious Principi di Piemonte (0122 7941).

Eating out There are plenty of options. The rustic Antica Spelonca in Borgata is recommended again for 'great local dishes'. Other reader tips include Pinky ('steak to die for'), Last Tango, Ritrovo and Lo Sciatolo for pizza.

Après-ski The quietness of the place during the week, when the Italians are absent, disappoints some visitors. Some bars come to life when there is an organised attraction – quizzes and karaoke at the Sestriere, live music at the Cavern. Pinky is a popular bar and restaurant, with low sofas in the classic Italian casual-chic style. Other reader tips for a good atmosphere include Brahms, Pub Black Pepper and the Tabata disco.

Off the slopes There's more to do than most visitors realise. There are some smart shops and there's a fitness centre, an ice rink, a sports centre and pool, and various other diversions. Outings are possible to nearby Pragelato and to Turin.

La Thuile

A revitalised mining town and a modern lift-base complex, with extensive, easy slopes linked with La Rosière in France

➕ Fair-sized area linked to La Rosière in France

➕ Free of crowds and queues

➕ Excellent beginner and easy intermediate slopes

➖ The tough runs are low down, and most low, woodland runs are tough

➖ The link with France relies on slow lifts, and is vulnerable to wind

➖ Not the place for lively après-ski

La Thuile deserves to be better known internationally. The slopes best suit beginners and intermediates looking for smooth cruises, but are not devoid of interest for experts, particularly if the snow conditions are good – and expeditions to La Rosière add interest. Those who try it seem to appreciate the quiet village as much as the quiet slopes.

NEWS

For 2008/09 the Maison Blanche 'micro ski area' was created above the base, in a spot sheltered from wind – with a new fast quad chair, rising just 180m/590ft, serving new blue and red pistes. A black will open for 2009/10, plus a terrain park.

THE RESORT

La Thuile is a bit like a French purpose-built resort, with a modern 'complex' at the base, but with an old, distinctly Italian quarter nearby.

Village charm Many people find the main complex rather soulless and prefer to stay in the old village. Much of it has been restored and new buildings tastefully added. There are a few restaurants and bars.

Convenience At the foot of the lifts is the modern Planibel complex, with places to stay, a leisure centre, bars, shops and restaurants. There are also a few other hotels around the base area. The main part of the old village spreads over a wide area across the river (served by a regular free bus).

Scenery There scenery is varied, with open bowls and lower wooded slopes overlooked by the nearby Mont Blanc Massif. Good views into France from the top of the ski area.

THE MOUNTAINS

La Thuile has quite extensive slopes that share a link with La Rosière, over the border in France. The great attraction is that they are normally very uncrowded. Many runs are marked red, but deserve no more than a blue rating. A 2008 visitor found the grading 'variable' while another found the 'signposting not always as good as it should be'. The link with La Rosière adds adventure; the runs there are steeper, sunnier and bumpier – and the start of the route back is a fairly tricky red. Reporters have found that strong winds can close the high lifts, including the link. Courmayeur is easily reached by car, and Cervinia is about an hour away.

Slopes The lifts out of the village (a gondola and a fast chair) take you to Les Suches, with shady black runs going back down directly to the village through the trees, and reds taking a more roundabout route. From here chairs take you to Chaz Dura for access to a variety of gentle bowls facing east. You can go off westwards from here to the Petit St Bernard road or across to a quad up to Belvedere, the launch pad for excursions to La Rosière. Below Belvedere are the slopes of Gran Testa, served by a fast and a slow chair and a drag.

Fast lifts The key lifts are fast chairs and a gondola.

Queues Short queues may form at the gondola first thing, but not at the chair. There are no problems once you are up the hill.

Terrain parks They are building one for next season in the new Maison Blanche area (see 'News').

Col de Fourclaz
2610m/8,560ft

Chaz Dura
2580m

La Rosière

Arnouvaz

Les Suches
2200m

La Thuile
1440m/4,720ft

↑ There are genuine red runs on the back of the hill, going down to the pass

CONSORZIO OPERATORI TURISTICI LA THUILE

KEY FACTS

Resort	1440m
	4,720ft

Espace San Bernardo (La Rosière and La Thuile)	
Slopes	1175-2610m
	3,850-8,560ft
Lifts	37
Pistes	150km
	93 miles
Green	9%
Blue	36%
Red	40%
Black	15%
Snowmaking	17%

UK PACKAGES

Alpine Answers, Crystal, First Choice, Independent Ski Links, Inghams, Interski, Just Skiing, Neilson, Simply Alpine, Skitracer, Thomson

Phone numbers
From abroad use the prefix +39 (and do **not** omit the initial '0' of the phone number)

TOURIST OFFICE

t 0165 883049
info@lathuile.it
www.lathuile.it

Snow reliability Most of La Thuile's slopes are north- or east-facing and above 2000m/6,560ft, so the snow generally keeps well. There's also a decent amount of snowmaking and 'grooming is immaculate'.

Experts The steep pistes down through the trees from Les Suches – the Diretta, Berthod and Muret – are serious stuff. The Fourclaz area has some genuinely black terrain and plenty of off-piste – the fast quad means you can do quick circuits in this area. A past reporter was still making fresh tracks there three days after snowfall. The short black Maisonettes, by the Arnouvaz chair, is usually quiet.

Heli-lifts are available. The Ruitor glacier offers a 20km/12 mile run to Ste-Foy in France, a short taxi ride from La Rosière and lifts for La Thuile.

Intermediates The bowls above Les Suches have many gentle blue and red runs, ideal for cruising. There are also long reds through the trees back to the resort. One reporter enjoyed runs around the Argillien Express for 'fast turns and empty pistes'. The red runs on the other side of the top ridge, in the Fourclaz area, down towards the Petit St Bernard road, offer more challenge. The road forms the roundabout San Bernardo red to the village, taking 11km/7 miles to drop 1100m/3,610ft; 'bleak' is one view, 'boring' probably nearer the mark; avoid in fresh snow.

Beginners There are nursery slopes at village level and up at Les Suches, and long easy blues above there, including Promenade, which is served by draglifts. You ride the gondola down.

Snowboarding These are great slopes for learning. You need ride only chairlifts and the gondola, and most of the slopes are easy. For the more experienced there are great tree runs, good freeriding and some good carving runs. But there are some

frustratingly flat sections too.

Cross-country La Thuile has four loops of varying difficulty on the valley floor, adding up to 17km/11 miles of track.

Mountain restaurants There is a reasonable choice – 13 places dotted around the slopes. This year's reporters evidently didn't do lunch, unless it was in France, but we have some strong recommendations from last year. Maison Carrel on the top part of run 6 is a good-value table-service place with floor to ceiling windows and 'excellent food'. The Foyer does 'good-value meal deals'. The self-service Mélèze, near the top of the gondola, serves 'tasty and generous portions'. The Off Shore, above Arnouvaz, has an 'eclectic African decor with very friendly staff and good lasagne'. The Roxi does 'nice hot rolls and good chips'.

Schools and guides In the past we've had good reports, but a 2008 reporter found the school 'horrendously obstructive when trying to book in advance'. More reports, please.

Families There's a mini-club and snow garden for ages four to 12. Children over five can join adult ski classes.

STAYING THERE

The number of tour operators going there is increasing.

Hotels The 4-star Planibel (0165 884541) is large and characterless, and its food has few fans, but it has an ideal location right at the foot of the slopes, a pool, gym, sauna and steam room. The 'quiet, friendly' hotel du Glacier (0165 884137), a short walk above the lifts, is 'the best hotel I have stayed in', says a repeat visitor, thanks to its energetic owner Susanna.

Apartments A 2008 reporter was 'very pleased' with the Planibel apartments (in the same building as the hotel); they are spacious and good value.

Eating out Reader tips include the Bricole ('a very decent eatery – try the lamb'), and this year the Grotta ('very friendly, great pizza and steak').

Après-ski Nightlife is 'even quieter' than one reporter expected. The Bricolette bar and the neighbouring Bricole 'videodiscopub' are the liveliest bars. The Fantasia disco at the Planibel warms up well after midnight.

Off the slopes There are few shops; the Planibel complex has a pool and there are marked walks. Pedestrians can ride up the gondola for lunch.

Trentino

Not a resort, but a region with a few big resorts and a lot of smaller ones that deserve to be better known on the UK market

Trentino is a fabulously scenic region that is rather neglected by the British. The resorts best known in the UK, Madonna di Campiglio and Passo Tonale, are covered in detail in their own chapters. Canazei and Campitello, linked to the huge and increasingly well known Sella Ronda network, are covered in a new chapter on Val di Fassa. That leaves a lot of small ski areas that you may not have heard of, most of which are covered here.

NEWS

After a period of hectic activity, not much is happening on the lift front. The newish gondola from Daolasa into the Folgarida/Marilleva slopes can now be reached by train from Trento direct to the gondola station – about 12 services a day.

Long-standing plans to link Campiglio's Cinque Laghi sector to one extremity of Pinzolo's slopes are moving along. The link – a three-stage, 5km gondola – is planned to open in late 2010. Also planned for opening then are two new pistes at Pinzolo.

This year nine groups of Dolomite mountains – spread across Trentino and four other provinces – were declared a UNESCO World Heritage Site.

WESTERN TRENTINO

Madonna di Campiglio is Trentino's biggest and best-known resort – a chic place with mainly easy slopes that attracts an affluent, almost exclusively Italian clientele. It has its own chapter. Its ski area is linked to those of much smaller Marilleva and Folgarida, and in a couple of years will be linked in the opposite direction to Pinzolo.

The slopes above **Marilleva** are excellent, steep, north-facing reds (with a few blues higher up the mountain), much better for adventurous intermediates than Campiglio's main Pradalago slopes. And the snow is usually the best in the area because of the largely north-facing orientation. There's also a serious black run served by a two-stage chair to Doss della Pesa (2230m/7,320ft). And there's a gondola that connects with a six-pack to Monte Vigo (2180m/7,150ft) and the links to Campiglio and Folgarida.

Marilleva itself is a modern resort consisting of several 1960s-style, ugly but functional, low-rise concrete buildings (most of them well screened by trees, thankfully) built on a mid-mountain shelf at 1400m/4,590ft and reached by road or gondola from the lower part of the resort at 900m/2,950ft, on the valley floor.

The slopes down to **Folgarida** are gentler than those above Marilleva. The main part of Folgarida itself is clustered around the gondola station at 1400m/4,590ft – and purpose-built in a much more traditional style than Marilleva. It feels much more upmarket, with smart hotels, a few shops and some fur-clad patrons – though in mid-January 2009 it was full of Polish families, says a reporter who judged the 4-star hotel Caminetto 'almost perfect'. There's another base area at 1300m/4,270ft by another gondola station.

Midway between Marilleva and Folgarida, an eight-seat gondola runs

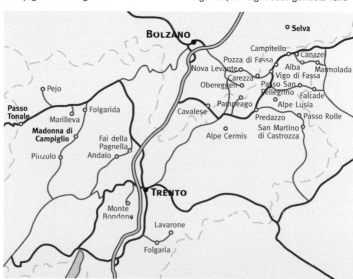

TRENTINO

Tread into Temptation

Promise to enjoy yourself and we promise to entice you. Sun, snow, fast pistes, slow food - stray no further for your winter thrills. The Dolomites promise you the passion of Italy on seductive slopes. Trentino - for those who can resist everything except temptation. **visittrentino.it**

TRENTINO

ITALIA

from the village of Daolasa up to Val Mastellina with a beginner area at mid-mountain.

Pinzolo (780m/ 2,560ft) is the main town of the Val Rendena, south-east of Madonna di Campiglio, and currently a 20-minute drive away. But a long and long-planned link with the Cinque Laghi slopes of Campiglio is now expected to be complete by late 2010.

From Pinzolo, a gondola followed by a fast chair take you to the area's high point of Doss del Sabion (2100m/ 6,890ft), where there are great views of the Brenta massif. The area has mainly genuinely challenging red runs and an excellent groomed black (the Competition piste), and the snow keeps in condition because most of the runs are northish-facing. The Cioca and Patagonia reds are lovely steep cruises (though Cioca is steep enough to be a black in parts).

Passo Tonale is a short drive west of Marilleva and Folgarida – a high, snow-sure resort on the border of Lombardia. It has its own chapter.

Just down the Val di Sole is **Pejo** (1400m/ 4,590ft), a spa village with a narrow but tall slope area rising to 2340m/ 7,680ft, served by a gondola, three chairlifts and a couple of drags.

All these areas (and the resorts described in the 'Around Trento' section below) are covered by the Superskirama Adamello-Brenta ski pass. With a car, it is perfectly possible to explore all these areas in a week.

AROUND TRENTO

Trento is the main town of Trentino, and its local hill is **Monte Bondone**. Five roadside chairlifts serve partly wooded slopes here on Palon (2090m/ 6,860ft), with a longest run of 4km/2.5 miles dropping 800m/2,620ft and served by a fast quad. The whole area is covered by snowmaking. There's a terrain park – and great views to the Brenta Dolomites around Madonna.

To the south-east of Trento are the small resorts of **Folgaria** (1165m/ 3,820ft – not to be confused with Folgarida) and **Lavarone**. Lavarone has a handful of lifts, but Folgaria has more than 20, serving 60km/37 miles of runs with 100% snowmaking.

To the north-west are the slopes on Paganella (2125m/6,970ft) shared by **Fai della Paganella** (1000m/3,280ft) and **Andalo** (1050m/3,440ft). Andalo is a sizeable resort and a pleasant

enough place with a small local town feel. One eight-seat gondola goes up from near the centre of Andalo, and another leaves from a big car park nearby. Five of the other 16 lifts are fast chairs. The runs are mainly genuinely challenging reds and can be long (a maximum vertical of almost 1100m/3,610ft); most are northish-facing and so keep their snow in good condition. We especially enjoyed the Dosa Larici and La Rocca reds down to Santel (the nearest lift base to Fai). There's a beginner area near the Andalo base but only a few short blue runs (all at the top), so we don't recommend it for novices or timid intermediates.

OTHER TRENTINO RESORTS

The biggest linked ski area in the world, the Sella Ronda circuit plus offshoots, is partly in Trentino. The resorts of **Canazei** and **Campitello**, at the south-west corner of the Sella Ronda circuit, were previously covered in this chapter but are now covered in our new chapter on Val di Fassa.

At the bottom of the Val di Fassa is the small town of Moena. About 2km east of the town is the lift system of **Alpe Lusia**. Further east are more extensive slopes at **Passo San Pellegrino**, linked with **Falcade** in Veneto. To the west is another lift network at **Carezza**, linked with **Nova Levante** in Alto Adige.

Continuing downstream from the Val di Fassa, you are now in the Val di Fiemme. Near **Predazzo** there is a lift up to the slopes shared with **Pampeago** and **Obereggen**, across the border in Alto Adige. Finally, the town of **Cavalese** has lifts up to the Alpe Cermis slopes.

To the south of the Val di Fassa/Val di Fiemme axis, a steep road over the high **Passo Rolle** – where there is a small network of drags and chairs serving easy slopes on either side of the road – leads down to the resort of **San Martino di Castrozza** (1470m/ 4,820ft). San Martino has a fabulous setting beneath a soaring wall of Dolomite cliffs and peaks – the Pale di San Martino. The village is not notably cute – there are some large, block-like buildings – but it is pleasant enough. The slopes – which are entirely intermediate in difficulty – are split into three sectors, only two of them linked (at altitude).

Val di Fassa

Two resorts linked in to the Sella Ronda circuit, and several much smaller separate areas well worth exploring for a day or two

VISITTRENTINO.IT

NEWS

In the last two years there has been major investment in new lifts at Carezza.

The Val di Fassa runs from the town of **Moena** to an abrupt end at the massive twin obstacles of the Gruppo Sella and glacial Marmolada. The valley's biggest resort, Canazei, is at the south-west corner of the famous Sella Ronda circuit (see separate chapter). Campitello, 2km/1 mile down the valley, also has a lift into the circuit. A separate network links Alba (up the valley) to Pozza di Fassa (down the valley). And there are separate areas at Vigo di Fassa and Carezza.

Canazei is a sizeable, bustling, pretty, roadside village of narrow streets, rustic old buildings, traditional-style hotels and nice little shops, set at 1465m/4,810ft beneath a heavily wooded mountainside.

The village itself is slightly off the main Sella Ronda circuit, but its main slopes form part of it. A 12-person gondola (powerful, but queue-prone) rises 470m/1,540ft to Pecol, at the foot of the slopes of Belvedere. These are linked in one direction to the slopes of Passo Pordoi and Arabba, and in the other direction to Passo Sella and Col Rodella (above Campitello), and then on to Selva. A red run returns to Canazei, but it gets the afternoon sun and is often closed.

The Belvedere slopes are open and sunny, with modest verticals of about 450m/1,480ft. Almost all are graded red; this exaggerates their difficulty, but rules the resort out for nervous intermediates and beginners – the nursery slope, across the valley from the village, is inconvenient, too.

The grand 3-star hotel Dolomiti (0462 601106) in the centre is one of the original resort hotels. 'Spacious room with private hot tub and superb service,' said a 2008 reporter. The charming, chalet-style Diana (0462 601477) is five minutes outside.

There are numerous restaurants, and the après-ski is surprisingly animated. The Rose Garden and Osteria, at the bottom of the home run, are naturally popular at close of play. La Stua di Ladins serves local wines and the Husky (sometimes with live music) and Roxi bars are tipped.

Off-slope entertainment consists of beautiful walks and shopping. There's also a pool, sauna and Turkish baths.

Campitello (1445m/4,740ft) is a pleasant, unremarkable village, smaller and quieter than next-door Canazei, and still unspoiled. It's quiet during the day, having no pistes on the rocky mountainside above the village.

A cable car rising 1000m/3,280ft takes you up to Col Rodella and the slopes above Passo Sella. At the start of the day this lift can build queues even in January, and in high season they can be 'massive' – it's quicker to get the bus up to Canazei's gondola.

A 2008 visitor recommended the 3-star Gran Paradis (0462 750135) – 'good food and amazing wine list'. Campitello has quite lively après-ski – the Da Giulio bar gets packed.

About 2km/1 mile up the valley from Canazei, a cable car just beyond **Alba** goes up to a small area of slopes (6 lifts, 15km/9 miles of runs) above Ciampac, which is linked around the back of the low peak of Crepa Negra to another small area of slopes (7 lifts, 17km/11 miles of runs) above **Pozza di Fassa**, which is down-valley from Canazei and Campitello.

Over the road from Pozza another small area of slopes (6 lifts, 16km/10 miles of runs) links Pera to **Vigo di Fassa**. A road from there leads west to **Carezza** (aka Passo Costalunga) where yet another area of slopes (16 lifts, 30km/19 miles of runs, 20 huts!) links with Nova Levante, in Alto Adige.

Switzerland

Switzerland is home to some of our favourite resorts. Only three resorts in this book are awarded ★★★★★ for both resort charm and spectacular scenery – the essentially traffic-free Swiss villages of Wengen, Mürren and Zermatt. Many other Swiss resorts are not far behind. Many resorts have impressive slopes, too – including some of the biggest, highest and toughest runs in the Alps – as well as a lot of good intermediate terrain. For fast, queue-free lift networks, Swiss resorts are not known for setting the standards – too many historic cable cars and mountain railways for that. But the real bottlenecks are steadily disappearing. And there are compensations – the world's best mountain restaurants, for one, and pretty reliable accommodation too.

Until recently, one of the drawbacks of Switzerland was that smoking was allowed in public areas. But now nearly every canton containing major ski resorts has banned smoking except in dedicated smoking rooms, and all hotels, restaurants and bars will have smoke-free areas.

A perceived drawback is that many people think Switzerland is expensive. But Swiss hotel prices are generally lower than French ones. And although swanky resorts such as St Moritz and Verbier came out as pricey in our food and drink price survey, many others came out about average, which makes them cheaper than most major French places. And what you get for your Swiss francs is generally first class.

Many Swiss resorts have a special relationship with the British, who invented downhill skiing in its modern form in Wengen and Mürren by persuading the locals to run their mountain railways in winter and so act as ski lifts, and by organising the first downhill races. An indication of the continuing strength of the British presence in these resorts is that Wengen has an English church.

While France is the home of the purpose-built resort, Switzerland is the home of the mountain village that has transformed itself from traditional farming community (or health retreat) into year-round holiday resort. Many of Switzerland's most famous mountain resorts are as popular in the summer as in the winter, or more so. This creates places with a more lived-in feel to them and a much more stable local community.

Many villages are still dominated by a handful of families lucky or shrewd enough to get involved in the early development of the area. This has its downside as well as advantages. The ruling families have been able to stifle competition and bar newcomers from taking a slice of their action. Alternative ski schools – to compete with the traditional, nationally organised school and thus push up standards – are still less common than in other Alpine countries, for example. But this grip has at last started to weaken.

The quality of service throughout Switzerland is generally high. The trains run like clockwork to the advertised timetable (and often they run to the top of the mountain, doubling as ski lifts). The food is almost universally of good quality and much less stodgy than in neighbouring Austria. Even the standard rustic dish of rösti is haute cuisine compared to Austrian sausages. And in Switzerland you get what you pay for: the cheapest wine, for example, is not cheap, but it is reliable.

CHANDOLIN

GRIMENTZ

ST-LUC

SIERRE

VERCORIN

ZINAL

sierre anniviers

CŒUR DU VALAIS SWITZERLAND

DE

AU

SWITZERLAND

FR

IT

Valais/Wallis

Switzerland.
get natural

Valais

Avoid the crowds...
enjoy pure skiing

220 km of slopes, 1 skipass, 7 nights + 6 days skipass

From £ 498.– /person*

+41 (0)848 848 027
www.sierre-anniviers.ch

* Indicative price – depending on exchange rate

↑ Switzerland has an
unfair share of the
best scenery. This is
the Dents du Midi,
above Champéry
(probably shot from a
few metres inside
France, in fact)

SNOWPIX.COM / CHRIS GILL

Perhaps surprisingly for such a traditional, rather staid skiing nation, Switzerland has gone out of its way to attract snowboarders. Davos may hit the headlines mainly when it hosts huge economic conferences, but yards from the conference hall there are dudes getting big air on the Bolgen slope's training kickers. Little-known Laax claims one of Europe's best terrain parks.

GETTING AROUND THE SWISS ALPS

Access to practically all Swiss resorts is fairly straightforward when approaching from the north – just pick your motorway. But many of the high passes that are perfectly sensible ways to get around the country in summer are closed in winter, which can be inconvenient if you are moving around from one area to another.

There are very useful car-carrying trains in various places; they can cut out huge amounts of driving. One key link is between the Valais (Crans-Montana, Zermatt etc) and Andermatt via the Furka tunnel, and another is from Andermatt to the Grisons (Laax, Davos etc) via the Oberalp pass – closed to road traffic in winter but open to trains except after very heavy snowfalls. Another rail tunnel that's very handy is the Lötschberg, linking Kandersteg in the Bernese Oberland with Brig in the Valais. A couple of years ago a new tunnel opened in parallel – the lower, longer, faster Lötschberg Base Tunnel. But it takes only passenger and freight trains – car-carrying trains continue to use the old tunnel.

St Moritz is more awkward to get to than other resorts. The main road route is over the Julier pass. This is normally kept open, but at 2285m/7,500ft it is naturally prone to heavy snowfalls that can shut it for a time. Fallbacks are car-carrying rail tunnels under the Albula pass and the Vereina tunnel from near Klosters – a relatively new option, opened in 1999.

These car-carrying rail services are generally painless. Often you can just turn up and drive on. But carrying capacities are obviously limited. Some services (eg Oberalp) carry only a handful of cars, and booking is vital. Others (eg Furka, Lötschberg, Vereina) are

much bigger operations with much greater capacity – but that's a reflection of demand, and at peak times there may be long queues – particularly for the Furka tunnel from Andermatt, which Zürich residents use to get to the big Valais resorts. There is a car-carrying rail tunnel linking Switzerland with Italy – the Simplon. But most routes to Italy are kept open by means of road tunnels. See the Italy introduction for more information.

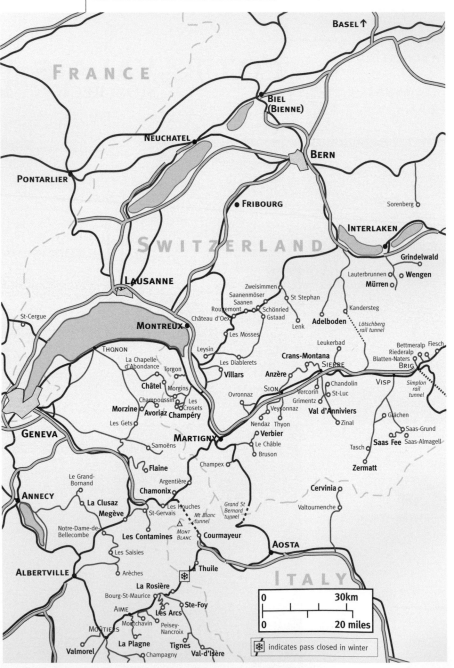

To use Swiss motorways (and it's difficult to avoid doing so if you're driving serious distances within the country) you have to buy an annual permit to stick on your windscreen. Permits cost SF40 and are valid for 14 months – from December to the end of January. They are sold at the border, and are, for all practical purposes, compulsory.

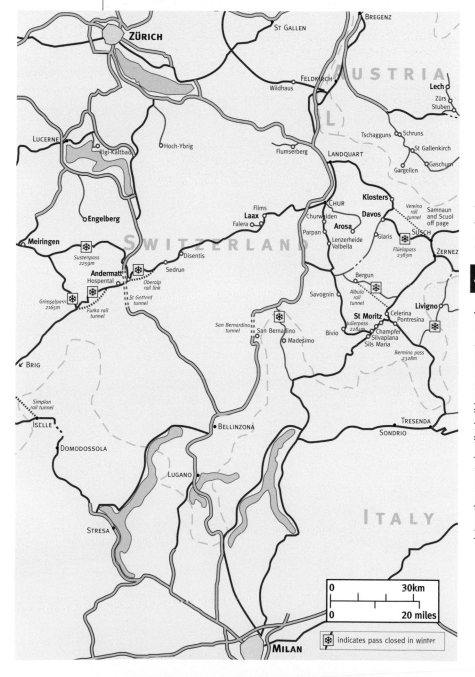

Introduction

Interactive resort shortlist builder at **www.wtss.co.uk**

Adelboden

Chocolate-box village with plenty to do off the snow – but also with extensive slopes including an area shared with Lenk

NEWS

There are plans to build a large spa and wellness complex, which will include a new 5-star luxury hotel. It is now expected to open in 2012.

- ➕ Traditional, pretty mountain village in a splendid setting
- ➕ Good off-slope facilities
- ➕ Some pleasantly uncrowded slopes linked to Lenk, but ...

- ➖ The slopes are fragmented and widely spread – access can be slow
- ➖ Few challenges on-piste – though plenty of off-piste opportunities
- ➖ Quiet, limited nightlife

Adelboden is unjustly neglected by the international market: for intermediates looking for a relaxing holiday in pretty surroundings – and perhaps spending some time doing things off the slopes – it has a lot of appeal. Surprisingly, the resort literature includes English translations.

THE RESORT

Adelboden fits the traditional image of a Swiss mountain village: characterful and attractive. It shares slopes with the village of Lenk and there are infrequent buses to the outlying areas (most covered on the lift pass). The Jungfrau resorts (Wengen, Mürren etc) are within day-trip range, as is Gstaad.
Village charm Lots of old chalets with overhanging roofs line the quiet main street; cars are discouraged.
Convenience The village is fairly compact. The best location for most people is close to the main street – but you'll probably make a lot of use of buses, wherever you stay.
Scenery The 3000-metre peaks of the Bernese Oberland make an impressive backdrop.

THE MOUNTAINS

Adelboden's slopes are split into five varied sectors, spread over a wide area. One sector stretches across to Lenk, with a sixth area of slopes a bus ride across the valley from there.
Slopes Village lifts access three of the sectors. A small cable car/gondola hybrid goes up to Tschentenalp, just above the village. An even smaller one goes down to Oey (where there is a car park). From here, a proper gondola goes up to the Chuenisbärgli sector and then on (in two further stages) to more remote Silleren-Hahnenmoos. This is much the biggest sector, with long, gentle runs (and some short, sharp ones) back towards the village and over to Lenk.
Engstligenalp, a flat-bottomed high-altitude bowl, is reached by a cable car 4km/2.5 miles south of the resort;

Elsigenalp (with another cable car) is more extensive, but remote.
Fast lifts The main lifts are gondolas and fast chairs, but there are still a fair few slow lifts.
Queues The main access gondolas get busy at peak times, but the minibus service to the main sector is an alternative. The fast quad from Geils to Lavey has greatly improved the return to Adelboden from that sector, and from Lenk. If snow is poor, queues build up at Engstligenalp.
Terrain parks The Gran Masta Park at Hahnenmoos has jumps, big air, rails, snack bar and chill-out zone. There's a boardercross run at Silleren.
Snow reliability Despite unremarkable top heights, most slopes are above 1500m/4,920ft, so snow reliability is reasonable. North-facing Tschentenalp often has the best snow. Snowmaking covers over half the main pistes. Grooming is reportedly good.
Experts The few genuine black pistes don't add up to much. But off-piste possibilities are good and don't get tracked out quickly; the Lavey and Luegli chairs in the Geils bowl access routes to Adelboden and Lenk. Engstligenalp has off-piste potential – and is a launching point for tours.
Intermediates All five areas deserve exploration by intermediates. There is a lot of ground to be covered in the main sector. Tschentenalp is quieter, and worth a visit. Various timed runs are dotted around the area.
Beginners There are good nursery slopes in the village and at the foot of nearby sectors. At Geils there are glorious long, easy runs to progress to. Engstligenalp is 'superb'.
Snowboarding Two specialist schools offer lessons. There's a freeride zone

ENGSTLIGENALP 2360m/7,740ft

2290m Elsigenalp

Luegli 2140m
Metschstand 2105m
BETELBERG
Leiter 2000m

1905m

ELSIGEN
Unter Birg CHUENISBÄRGLI
Geils 1710m
1960m
Stoss 1645m

Elsigbach 1250m
Adelboden 1355m/4,450ft
Oey 1260m
Boden
Sillerenbühl 1975m
Rothenbach 1070m
Lenk 1070m/3,510ft

Lavey 2200m
Bühlberg 1665m

1950m
SILLEREN-HAHNENMOOS
1540m
1135m

TSCHENTENALP
1645m

KEY FACTS

Resort	1355m
	4,450ft
Slopes	1070-2360m
	3,510-7,740ft
Lifts	56
Pistes	185km
	115 miles
Blue	41%
Red	52%
Black	7%
Snowmaking	60%

SWITZERLAND

492

Weekly news updates and resort links at **www.wtss.co.uk**

at Engstligenalp. The many draglifts are gradually being replaced.
Cross-country There are extensive trails along the valley towards Engstligenalp where there is a high altitude, snow-sure circuit.
Mountain restaurants There are plenty of pleasant spots. Past reporters say Tschenten Alp is 'the best' with 'excellent meals'.
Schools and guides The main Adelboden school has received mixed reviews and we have no new reports.
Families The resort sets out to cater for families (there is a special leaflet summarising all relevant info), and seems to succeed, with lots of facilities including several toboggan runs. Several hotels offer childcare.

STAYING THERE

Several UK operators go here. There is locally bookable self-catering, and some 30 pensions and hotels (mainly 3- and 4-star).
Hotels The central 4-star Solis Cambrian (673 8383) opened last season – the old Regina, given a super-cool makeover. 'Brilliant: excellent quality and value for money, and friendly staff,' says a 2009 reporter. Pool and smart new spa. The little Bären (673 2151) is a simple but captivating wooden chalet. The Beau-Site (673 2222) has a good, central location, as does the Viktoria-Eden (673 8888) – 'decent rooms; good breakfast'.
Eating out The choice is not enormous. The Bären is 'good value'. Guests on half board can 'dine around' at affiliated hotels twice a week – an excellent arrangement.
Après-ski There are several bars and tea rooms. The Time Out bar has a

'good atmosphere' at close of play. The Arte Bar offers a bit of artistic flair. Scott's bar (Cambrian hotel) is smart, modern and 'absolutely the best'. The Berna-Bar nightclub is 'surprisingly good'.
Off the slopes There are quite a few activities – indoor and outdoor curling and skating, sleigh rides, toboggan runs, hiking paths, hotel pools open to the public. Some mountain huts are reachable on foot. Special lift passes are available for walkers.

Lenk 1070m/3,510ft

Lenk is a traditional village linked to Adelboden by cable car at Rothenbach, or six-pack from Bühlberg, further up the mountain. Both lifts are a bus ride from the centre and 'infrequently timetabled', says a 2008 reporter. Closer to the village are the gondola and fast chair serving the two arms of the Betelberg slopes on the opposite side of the valley (covered on the area lift pass) – a series of gentle reds and blues. There are a couple of 'delightfully quiet', wooded runs back to the valley.

Andermatt

A slow-paced, old-fashioned resort with some great steep, high terrain on- and off-piste (and the snowfall to go with it)

493

TOP 10 RATINGS

Extent	★
Fast lifts	★
Queues	★★
Snow	★★★★
Expert	★★★★
Intermediate	★★
Beginner	★
Charm	★★★★
Convenience	★★★
Scenery	★★★

+ Attractive, traditional village

+ Excellent snow record

+ Some excellent steep pistes and great off-piste terrain – plus ski-touring opportunities

+ Easy access from Zürich

− Slopes split into separate, rather limited sectors

− Unsuitable for beginners

− Limited off-slope diversions

− Little English spoken

− Busy at weekends

Little old Andermatt was rather left behind in the mega-resort boom of the 1960s and 1970s. If current plans come to fruition (see 'News'), it may soon start to catch up. Meanwhile, its attractions have not faded for those who like their mountains tall, steep and covered in powder. Strangely, we have had no reports from readers this year, in sharp contrast to last year. Do report!

NEWS

Plans for a huge luxury development largely based on redundant army property appear to be going ahead – six upscale hotels, 750 homes, an 18-hole golf course and a spa/leisure complex. Go now, before it changes.

KEY FACTS

Resort	1445m
	4,740ft
Slopes	1445-2965m
	4,740-9,730ft
Lifts	20
Pistes	125km
	78 miles
Blue	22%
Red	46%
Black	32%
Snowmaking	36%

UK PACKAGES

Alpine Answers, Mountain Tracks, Simply Alpine, Ski Freshtracks, Ski Weekend, Switzerland Travel Centre

THE RESORT

Andermatt is quite busy in summer and gets weekend winter business, but at other times seems deserted apart from residents of the local barracks. In winter, east-west links with the Grisons and the Valais rely on car-carrying trains. The lift pass also covers Sedrun's slopes – 20 minutes away and a popular excursion. The lift pass covers linking trains. The small Winterhorn area at Hospental is out of action at present, and is being sold.

Village charm The town is quietly attractive, with wooden houses lining the main street that runs from the central river bridge to the cable car, and some grand churches.

Convenience The centre is compact, but the lifts are on opposite sides of the town; take your choice.

Scenery The local Gemsstock peak is well defined and higher than its neighbours, with rugged steep terrain.

THE MOUNTAINS

Andermatt's local skiing is split over two unlinked mountains, both limited in extent. Most slopes are above the trees and piste marking is slack, which is bad news in a white-out.

Slopes A two-stage cable car from the edge of the village serves the open, steep, north-facing and usually empty slopes of Gemsstock. Across town is the gentler, sunny Nätschen area.

Fast lifts Apart from the Gemsstock cable car, there are none.

Queues The Gemsstock cable car can generate queues on fine weekends.

Terrain parks Gemsstock has one.

Snow reliability The area has a justified reputation for reliable snow. Nätschen gets a lot of sun. Piste grooming is generally good.

Experts It is most definitely a resort for experts. The north-facing bowl beneath the top Gemsstock cable car is a glorious, long, steep slope (about 900m/2,950ft vertical), usually with excellent snow, down which there are countless off-piste routes, an itinerary and a piste. Outside the bowl, the Sonnenpiste is a fine open red run curling away from the lifts to the mid-station, with more off-piste opportunities. From Gurschen to the village there is a black run, not steep but often tricky. Routes outside the bowl go down the Felsental or Guspis valleys towards Hospental, or steeply into the deserted Untertal, to the east (ending in a bit of a walk). Nätschen and Winterhorn both have black pistes and off-piste opportunities, including worthwhile itinerary routes.

Intermediates Intermediates needn't be put off Gemsstock: the Sonnenpiste can be tackled and there is a pleasant red run and some short blues at mid-mountain. Nätschen's sunny mountain is well worth a visit.

Beginners Not ideal; but the lower half of Nätschen has a long, easy blue run.

Snowboarding The cable car accesses some great freeride terrain.

Cross-country There are 40km/25 miles of loops along the valley.

Mountain restaurants The Gadäbar (Gemsstock) is a simple, quiet hut serving 'delicious rösti and strudel'.

Schools and guides Bergschule Uri/

↑ It's a compact village, set right against the foot of the Gemsstock

ANDERMATT-GOTTHARD TOURISMUS

Phone numbers
From elsewhere in Switzerland add the prefix 041; from abroad use the prefix +41 41

TOURIST OFFICE

t 888 7100
info@andermatt.ch
www.andermatt.ch

Mountain Reality, a guiding outfit run by local big wheel Alex Clapasson, is very pricey. The Swiss ski school has cheaper options. Snowlimit is a specialist snowboard school.
Families There are slopes kids can handle at Nätschen, and the Swiss school does classes.

STAYING THERE

Andermatt's accommodation is in cosy 2- and 3-star hotels (for the moment – see 'News').
Hotels Our 2008 reporters were all greatly impressed by River House (887 0025), a stylish, upmarket B&B in a 250-year-old building – 'comfortable rooms; charming, helpful staff'. And see 'Eating out'. Gasthaus Sternen (887 1130) is an attractive central chalet with a cosy restaurant and bar. The lovely old 3-star Sonne

(887 1226), between the centre and the lift, is welcoming and comfortable. Alpenhotel Schlüssel (888 7088) is 'good value', with spacious rooms.
Apartments Those at hotel Monopol (887 1575) are central and 'very good'.
Eating out We can't wait to try the tiny Alte Apotheke at the River House B&B – 'best food of the trip: wonderful home-made ravioli'. Gasthaus Tell and the Sonne do 'good schnitzel' and Stefano 'very good pizzas'.
Après-ski The bar at River House is 'excellent, with live music later'; the Spycher and Piccadilly are also popular. The Curva at the hotel Monopol is 'very pleasant'. Dancing at Gotthard livens up at weekends.
Off the slopes There's a toboggan run at Nätschen. The fitness centre at the hotel Drei König is open to the public. There are maintained footpaths.

Sedrun 1450m/4,760ft

Sedrun is a sizeable roadside village east of the Oberalp Pass, with the most extensive piste skiing in the area. From a tiny train station at the pass, lifts take you over two ridges to the main slopes around Milez, which go on down to Dieni on the outskirts of Sedrun. There's a good choice of red runs, a rewarding black and a 'freeride' route, plus plenty of scope for off-piste. At Milez there's a terrain park. Sedrun has several hotels and a popular spa centre.

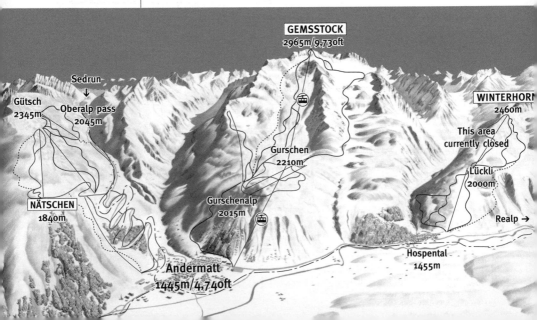

Anzère

Attractive, purpose-built resort set in a sunny position, with spectacular views and a small area of intermediate slopes

➕ Attractive and family-friendly with traffic-free central square

➕ Sunny intermediate slopes good for leisurely cruising

➖ Small area of slopes

➖ Little to interest experts

This small resort set on a sunny shelf with great views over the Rhône valley is little known on the UK market. Its position and small area of local slopes makes it good for a quiet, relaxing time and for families. It will be of more interest to keen piste-bashers when the planned link to Crans-Montana happens.

THE RESORT

Anzère is an attractive, purpose-built resort dating from 1965.
Village charm The buildings are mainly in chalet style if not chalet scale, and the heart is a traffic-free square with shops, restaurants, terraces, a children's area and an ice rink.
Convenience Most amenities are close enough to the gondola.
Scenery Anzère is set on a sunny plateau with spectacular views over the Rhône valley to the peaks beyond.

THE MOUNTAINS

The village sits at the western end of the ski area, which spreads eastwards to Les Rousses, from where a link to Crans-Montana is planned.
Slopes From the western end of the village a gondola takes you up to Pas de Maimbre at 2360m/7,740ft. From there a series of lifts (mostly drags) serves mainly red runs leading to the high point of Le Bâte and a lovely long red run down to Les Rousses.
Fast lifts Lots of drags and slow chairs.
Queues No problems reported.
Terrain parks There is a park, and from this season a boardercross course.
Snow reliability The slopes are not especially high and face south, so the snow can suffer in warm weather.
Experts There's a 5km/3 mile black run from Pas de Maimbre back to the village served top-to-bottom by snowmaking and a marked ungroomed itinerary. Plus lots of gentle off-piste.
Intermediates This is primarily an intermediate resort, with 75% of the runs being red. But keen piste-bashers will find the extent limited.
Beginners There's a village nursery slope and short, easy blue slopes at the top of the gondola.

Snowboarding The snow soon softens in the sun – good for boarding. But there are a lot of draglifts for beginner boarders to cope with.
Cross-country The 5km/3 mile Go cross-country trail heads off west from the village and is ideal for beginners.
Mountain restaurants We enjoyed the table-service section of the Pas de Maimbre at the top of the gondola. A reporter recommends Les Rousses at the end of the slope there.
Schools and guides We have no reports on either the Swiss School or the rival Glycérine Sliding School.
Families This is very much a family resort, with a playground in the village square, a toboggan run, and a nursery open from 9am to 4pm Monday to Friday. The ski school takes children from age four.

STAYING THERE

Lodging A few small operators run packages here. There are three 3-star hotels and lots of apartments.
Eating out For a small place there's a reasonable choice – from gastronomic to pizzerias.
Après-ski As well as seven bars there are three discos, amazingly. And activities are arranged – such as a vin chaud welcome evening in the village square.
Off the slopes There are 166km/100 miles of marked walks, three snowshoe trails, a parapenting school, an ice rink and a 3km/2 mile toboggan run. Down in the valley, the old town of Sion is at the heart of the Coeur du Valais region of which Anzère is part, and is worth exploring. Attractions include Europe's largest navigable underground lake and walking in the Val d'Hérens, as well as trying the local Valais wines.

Arosa

A classic all-round winter resort, where walking is as much part of the scene as skiing; choose your spot with care

- ➕ Classic winter resort ambience
- ➕ Excellent cross-country loops
- ➕ Few queues
- ➕ Choice of good nursery slopes
- ➕ Relatively good snow reliability
- ➕ Prettily wooded setting, but ...

- ➖ Block-like buildings in main village
- ➖ Spread-out village lacks a heart
- ➖ Slopes too limited for mileage-hungry intermediates
- ➖ Few challenging pistes for experts – though there is good off-piste

TOP 10 RATINGS

Extent	★
Fast lifts	★★★
Queues	★★★★
Snow	★★★
Expert	★★
Intermediate	★★★
Beginner	★★★★
Charm	★★
Convenience	★★
Scenery	★★★

NEWS

Plans for a link with Lenzerheide have been shelved, after Lenzerheide voted against. Shame.

There are plans to renew the restaurant at the Weisshorn summit.

KEY FACTS

Resort	1740-1830m
	5,710-6,005ft
Slopes	1800-2655m
	5,910-8,710ft
Lifts	13
Pistes	60km
	37 miles
Blue	27%
Red	60%
Black	13%
Snowmaking	50%

Picture it: an isolated, snowy Swiss village, with skating on a frozen lake, horse-drawn sleighs jingling along and people strolling around in fur coats. Arosa offers exactly that. It's just a pity that many of its comfortable hotels date from an era when wood and pitched roofs were out of fashion.

THE RESORT

Arosa is in a high, remote valley – a long, winding drive or splendid rail journey from Chur (both take just under an hour). The village spreads for 2km/1 mile or more along the road that rises quite steeply from the lower lift base at Obersee towards the slightly separate, rustic satellite of Inner-Arosa.

The resort attracts a mixed clientele, but with a high proportion of older people who come for the cross-country, the sleigh rides and the walking – the slopes are criss-crossed by prepared paths, creating an unusual collision hazard. Very few visitors are British, but the key literature exists in English versions.

Village charm The village is not unpleasant, but the boxy style of many buildings and the central layout along a pedestrian-unfriendly road detract. You can escape both, of course, notably at Inner-Arosa. There are quite a few everyday shops and a couple of galleries, but nothing fancy.

Convenience Lifts go up from Obersee into the Weisshorn sector of the slopes. Up at Inner-Arosa, widely separated lifts go up towards Hörnli and the Weisshorn/Brüggerhorn sectors. Some accommodation is a long walk from the lifts; there are frequent, scheduled free ski-buses, but they get crowded.

Scenery Arosa's sheltered position at the head of a beautiful wooded valley, is in sharp contrast to the open slopes above it. There are excellent panoramic views from the top lift stations.

THE MOUNTAINS

Arosa's slopes form a wide, open bowl, facing north-east to south-east, with all the runs returning eventually to the village at the bottom. All the slopes are above the treeline, except those just above Obersee. Various night-skiing events are held once a week at Tschuggen.

Slopes The slopes are spread widely over two main sectors. The major lift junction in the Weisshorn/ Brüggerhorn sector is Tschuggen (strangely not named on the resort piste map), 500m/1,640ft away from the Mittelstation of the Weisshorn cable car, and reachable from both Obersee and Inner-Arosa. From Mittelstation, you can take a chair to the lower peak of Brüggerhorn. The main access to the Hörnli sector is a slow gondola from Inner-Arosa.

Fast lifts Access to the slopes is by gondola or cable car. A couple of fast chairs serve the upper slopes.

Queues Arosa does not suffer from serious queues. The Weisshorn cable car may generate short delays, though.

Terrain parks At Tschuggen there is a park with jumps, rails and a 150m/490ft half-pipe.

Snow reliability The slopes are quite high, but the Weisshorn sector gets a lot of sun; the shadier Hörnli slopes hold their snow better. Grooming is good, and snowmaking on the home runs is often used.

Experts Arosa isn't an obvious target for experts, but there is plenty of gentle off-piste terrain. The Brüggerhorn is generally considered the freeride mountain, and used to be

UK PACKAGES

Alpine Answers, Crystal, Crystal Finest, Interhome, Kuoni, Made to Measure, Momentum, Neilson, Powder Byrne, Simply Alpine, Ski Freshtracks, Ski Safari, Ski Weekend, Snow Finders, Snowy Pockets, Switzerland Travel Centre, White Roc

Phone numbers
From elsewhere in Switzerland add the prefix 081; from abroad use the prefix +41 81

TOURIST OFFICE

t 378 7020
arosa@arosa.ch
www.arosa.ch

promoted as such; but It no longer features any marked ski routes.

Intermediates This is a good area for intermediates who aren't looking for high mileage or huge challenges. The runs from Hörnli are enjoyable cruises, the black including a short steeper pitch. The Weisshorn runs are generally steeper, with some rewarding reds. The long blue to Obersee from Brüggerhorn via Prätschli is a great way to end the day, with fab views of sunlit peaks from the shady piste – though finding the start can be tricky.

Beginners The easy slopes up at Tschuggen are excellent and usually have good snow, but they get a lot of through traffic. Inner-Arosa has a quieter, 'gentle' area for kids.

Snowboarding Bananas is the specialist school and Mountain Surf Club offers two-day freeride camps.

Cross-country Arosa's modest 26km/ 16 miles of loops include some of the best and most varied in the Alps.

Mountain restaurants There's a fair choice, several with sunbeds where you can lunch while lounging; Carmennahütte has row upon row of them – and does 'fine rösti and delicious soup' too. Alpenblick is the current reader favourite – 'cosy, friendly', with 'great food'. Hörnli-Hütte offers a fabulous high position.

Schools and guides Swiss and ABC are the main schools. We have a positive report on the Swiss school this year.

Families Despite the rather family-hostile layout, the resort has attractions, with plenty to do off the slopes, and family reports are positive. As well as baby slopes at Obersee and Inner-Arosa, there is a kids' fun park up at Tschuggen.

STAYING THERE

Arosa is a hotel resort, with a high proportion of 3- and 4-stars. But Snowy Pockets' catered chalet Runca is a welcome departure.

Hotels We have an enthusiastic report this year on the 4-star Blatter's Bellavista (378 6666) – 'exceptionally friendly, with good food and a pleasant pool'. The 5-star Tschuggen Grand (378 9999) has a spectacular wellness centre (designed by a famous architect) with a dozen treatment rooms, two pools and so on.

Apartments The Paradies apartments have been recommended – quiet, spacious, with pool and sauna.

Eating out Most restaurants are hotel-based, some with a very high reputation – but we have few recent reports. The 'charmingly rustic' Burestübli at the hotel Arlenwald, up at Prätschli, satisfied one reporter this year – cheesy specialities.

Après-ski Après-ski is quite lively, but we get few reports on this angle.

Off the slopes There's an indoor pool. You can get a pedestrian's lift pass, and many mountain restaurants are reachable via 60km/37 miles of cleared, marked paths shown on a special map. Sleigh rides are popular, and there are indoor and outdoor ice rinks. Shopping is limited.

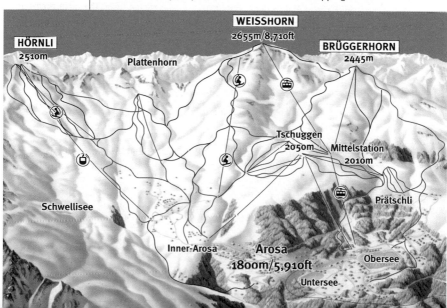

WEISSHORN
2655m/8,710ft

HÖRNLI
2510m

Plattenhorn

BRÜGGERHORN
2445m

Tschuggen
2050m   Mittelstation
2010m

Prätschli

Schwellisee

Inner-Arosa   Arosa
1800m/5,910ft   Obersee

Untersee

Champéry

Picture-postcard village that few UK tour operators feature these days, with access to the Portes du Soleil circuit

- ➕ Charmingly rustic mountain village
- ➕ Quick access to the Franco-Swiss Portes du Soleil piste circuit
- ➕ Quiet, relaxed – yet plenty to do off the slopes

- ➖ Local slopes suffer from the sun
- ➖ No runs back to the village
- ➖ Lift system is antiquated, and breaking down in places
- ➖ Not good for beginners

Champéry is great for intermediate skiers looking for a quiet time in a lovely place. Access to the Portes du Soleil circuit is not bad: Avoriaz is fairly easy to get to – and there may be good snow there when Champéry is suffering.

TOP 10 RATINGS

Extent	★★★★★
Fast lifts	★
Queues	★★★★
Snow	★★
Expert	★★★
Intermediate	★★★★
Beginner	★★
Charm	★★★★
Convenience	★
Scenery	★★★★

NEWS

For 2008/09 a fast eight-person chair replaced a quad and a drag from Les Crosets towards Champéry. A key lift above Champoussin was out of action all season; we are assured it will be in action in 2009/10.

For 2009/10, the Grande Conche chairlift from Les Crosets is to be upgraded to a six-pack.

THE RESORT

Champéry is on the Swiss side of the Portes du Soleil region, with fairly quick links to Avoriaz in France, and to the Lindarets valley separating Avoriaz from Châtel.

Village charm The village is friendly and relaxed, with classic old wooden chalets and a charming atmosphere.

Convenience Champéry's slopes are mainly high above the village, reached by a cable car which starts at the railway station, down a steepish hill, away from the main street. The village spreads over quite an area, but there is a free shuttle-bus.

Scenery The resort sits beneath the dramatic Dents du Midi – impressive both from the village and the slopes.

THE MOUNTAINS

Once you get up to them, the local slopes are open, friendly and relaxing.

Slopes Champéry's sunny slopes are part of the big Portes du Soleil circuit, which links resorts in Switzerland and France. See our special chapter on the

Portes du Soleil in the France section. The village cable car or a fast six-seat chairlift from Grand Paradis, a short free bus ride from Champéry, go up to the edge of the bowl of Planachaux. If snow is good, there are a couple of pistes back to Grand Paradis – one curling well away from the lift system – with an efficient bus service back to the village, but no pistes back to Champéry. With a couple of lift rides you can end up at the French border.

Fast lifts With a new one due this season, fast chairs are common at Les Crosets, less so at Planachaux. But the real problem is above Champoussin, where there are many ancient, slow lifts. Last season, one key chairlift was out of action, making progress across that area painful. The lift company says it will be in action for 2009/10.

Queues If snow is poor, expect end-of-day queues for the cable car down to the village. Few other problems.

Terrain parks The Superpark is a good terrain park at Les Crosets. The 25 features include gaps, kickers, rails, hips, spines and boxes. The Micropark is for beginners and schools.

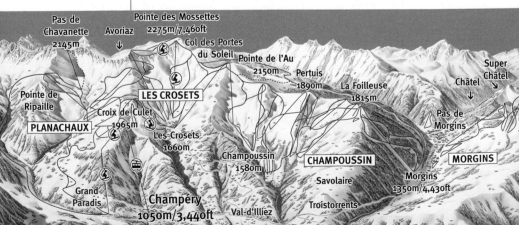

↑ It looks pretty stiff from the gentle slopes of Planachaux, but the 'Swiss Wall' isn't actually all that steep
CHAMPÉRY TOURISME

KEY FACTS

Resort	1050m
	3,440ft

Portes du Soleil	
Slopes	950-2300m
	3,120-7,550ft
Lifts	194
Pistes	650km
	404 miles
Green	13%
Blue	40%
Red	37%
Black	10%
Snowmaking	
	694 guns

Swiss side only	
Slopes	1050-2275m
	3,440-7,460ft
Lifts	35
Pistes	100km
	62 miles

Snow reliability The snow on the north-facing French side of the link with Avoriaz is usually better than on the Swiss side, which basically faces east but includes some south-facing slopes. The Champéry area would benefit from more snowmaking.

Experts Few local challenges and badly placed for most of the tough Portes du Soleil runs. The Swiss Wall, on the Champéry side of Pas de Chavanette, is long and bumpy, and provides great amusement when riding the chairlift that rises above it, but is not terrifyingly steep. There's scope for off-piste on the broad slopes of Les Crosets and Champoussin, and good terrain across the border at Pas de Chavanette where the slopes are less sunny and snow is often better.

Intermediates Confident intermediates have the whole Portes du Soleil at their disposal. Locally, the runs home to Grand Paradis are good when the snow conditions allow. Les Crosets is a junction of several fine runs. There are slightly tougher pistes from Mossettes and Pointe de l'Au, leisurely cruising above Champoussin, and delightful tree-lined meanders from La Foilleuse to Morgins. From Col des Portes du Soleil a long blue run goes down a quiet, wooded valley to Morgins; but after a good descent to the rustic Tovassière restaurant the run is a path dropping only 200m in 4km.

Beginners Not an ideal spot. The Planachaux runs, where lessons are held, are steepish and small (as well as remote from the village) and some of the local blue runs are verging on red steepness.

Snowboarding Not ideal for beginners (see above) and there are several draglifts (some quite steep). Good terrain parks in Les Crosets and Avoriaz for experts though, and some good powder areas between pistes.

Cross-country It's advertised as 10km/ 6 miles – not a lot – with 4km/2 miles floodlit every night, but it's very unreliable snow.

Mountain restaurants There are about 15 in this sector of the Portes du Soleil, between Champéry and Morgins, marked but not named on the piste map. Chez Coquoz near the Planachaux chair offers a warm welcome and lovingly prepared food (try the lamb shank), and a knockout Valais wine list (we loved the Cornalin). The tiny Lapisa on the way to Grand Paradis is delightfully rustic – they make cheese and smoke meat on the spot.

Schools and guides We get few reports. At least the Swiss school faces healthy competition from the Freeride Co and Redcarpet Snowsport School.

Families Champéry wouldn't be high on our shortlist for a family trip, given the lack of slopes at village level.

UK PACKAGES

Alpine Answers, Chalet Group, Erna Low, Scott Dunn, Ski Freedom, Ski Independence, Skitracer, Ski Weekend, White Roc
Les Crosets Mountain Lodge
Morgins Chalet Group, Ski Morgins, Ski Rosie

Phone numbers
From elsewhere in Switzerland add the prefix 024; from abroad use the prefix +41 24

TOURIST OFFICES

Champéry
t 479 2020
info@champery.ch
www.champery.ch
Les Crosets / Champoussin / Val-d'Illiez
t 477 2077
info@valdilliez.ch
www.valdilliez.ch
Morgins
t 477 2361
touristoffice@morgins.ch
www.morgins.ch

STAYING THERE

A few UK tour operators offer packages here.
Hotels There's a handful of 3-star and 2-star hotels, and more than the usual number outside the star system. According to past reports the friendly 3-star Beau Séjour (479 5858) has 'large rooms'; the 3-star National (479 1130) has 'excellent food, very friendly and helpful staff'; and the Auberge Le Paradis (479 1167) is 'charmingly rustic but noisy'.
Apartments The Lodge has very smart, spacious apartments with good views and contemporary decor.
Eating out Mitchell's is stylish and modern and we had a good meal there on our last visit a couple of years back. Local culinary star Denis Martin has added to his gloriously woody bistro Centre an emphatically modern place called C21, with expensive fixed-price menus of innovative dishes. Other reader tips are the bistro in the hotel National, the Farinet and Le Pub.
Après-ski Mitchell's is popular at tea time – big sofas and a fireplace. The Café du Centre has a micro brewery. Below Le Pub, the Crevasse disco is one of the liveliest places. The Farinet and the Mine are alternatives, apparently.
Off the slopes Walks are pleasant and the railway allows lots of excursions. A key feature is the Palladium at the bottom of the village, incorporating the Swiss national ice sports centre with various other facilities including pool and tennis; plus ice climbing and snowshoeing.

Les Crosets 1660m/5,450ft

A good base for a quiet time and slopes on the doorstep. The 3-star Télécabine hotel (479 0300) has 'basic rooms but extremely helpful staff, and the five-course dinner is delicious'.

Champoussin 1580m/5,180ft

A good family choice – no through traffic, on the slopes, with the 3-star Royal Alpage Club hotel (pool, gym, disco, two restaurants – 476 8300).

Val-d'Illiez 950m/3,120ft

About 4km/2.5 miles down the valley from Champéry, and in a similar position facing the Dents du Midi, Val-d'Illiez has no lifts or slopes, but makes a viable base – there are buses and trains up to Champéry. The road up to Les Crosets and Champoussin branches off here. Down in the valley bottom is the Thermes Parc thermal spa. The hotel du Repos (477 1414) is a British-run chalet-style place in the centre, opposite the station, with a piano bar, a bistro and a pizzeria as well as a dining room.

Morgins 1350m/4,430ft

Over the hill from the other resorts covered here and close to Châtel in France, Morgins is a fairly scattered, but attractive, quiet resort with a gentle nursery slope right in the village. The hotel Reine des Alpes (477 1143) is well thought of, and there are catered chalets. There's not much to do off the slopes.

Crans-Montana

A big-town base with a fabulous panoramic view and sun-soaked slopes – hit it straight after a January dump if you can

- ➕ Large, varied piste area
- ➕ Splendid setting and views
- ➕ Excellent, gentle nursery slopes
- ➕ Excellent cross-country trails
- ➕ Very sunny slopes, but ...

- ➖ Snow badly affected by sun
- ➖ Large town (rather than village), devoid of Alpine atmosphere
- ➖ Bus or car rides to lifts from much of the accommodation
- ➖ Few challenges except off-piste

When conditions are right – clear skies above fresh, deep snow – Crans-Montana takes some beating: the mountains you bounce down are charmingly scenic, the mountains you gaze at are mind-blowing, and Crans-Montana's flaws can be forgiven. Sadly, the midday sun ensures that conditions are more often wrong. If, despite this warning, you give it a try, do send us a report.

TOP 10 RATINGS

Extent	★★★
Fast lifts	★★★★
Queues	★★★
Snow	★★
Expert	★★
Intermediate	★★★★
Beginner	★★★
Charm	★★
Convenience	★★
Scenery	★★★★

NEWS

For 2009/10 a stylish mountain restaurant and hotel, including a lounge bar and three terraces, will replace the former Chetzeron building.

A 5-star hotel, the Guarda Golf, with 25 rooms, spa and two restaurants, is due to open in Crans.

For 2008/09 a 5-star chalet-style hotel and spa, Le Crans, opened at Plan Mayens above Crans. The Violettes mountain restaurant was revamped.

THE RESORT

Set on a broad shelf facing south across the Rhône valley, Crans-Montana is really two towns, their centres a mile apart and their fringes merging. The resort is reached by road or by a fast funicular railway from Sierre. It has a big summer conference trade; hotels tend to be formal, and visitors dignified. There are also places to stay at the other base stations, Les Barzettes and Aminona. Anzère is nearby, and you can get to Zermatt, Saas-Fee and Verbier by road or rail.

Village charm Strung along a busy road, the resort's many hotels, villas, apartments and smart shops are mainly dull blocks with little traditional Alpine character. Crans is the more upmarket part, with fancy shops, an increasing number of 5-star hotels and improved pedestrian-friendly centre.

Convenience The towns spread widely away from their respective gondola stations and many visitors need to use the free half-hourly shuttle-bus; it can get crowded.

Scenery The panoramic views over the Rhône valley to the peaks bordering Italy are breathtaking.

THE MOUNTAINS

Crans-Montana has slopes with few challenges and no nasty surprises, and there is a pleasant mix of open and wooded slopes, but we find signing still ridiculously slack – pistes are rarely named or numbered.

KEY FACTS

Resort	1500m
	4,920ft
Slopes	1500-3000m
	4,920-9,840ft
Lifts	28
Pistes	140km
	87 miles
Blue	38%
Red	50%
Black	12%
Snowmaking	35%

Plaine Morte
3000m/9,840ft

GLACIER

Bella-Lui
2545m

La Toula

Petit Bonvin
2400m

CRY D'ER
2265m

LES VIOLETTES
2250m

La Barmaz   La Tza

AMINONA

Chetzeron
2100m

Mt Lachaux
2140m

Merbé

Plumachit

Aminona
1500m

Verdets

Les Marolires

Plans Mayens

Vermala

Crans-Montana Montana
Crans 1500m/4,920ft

Les Barzettes

There are some very
pretty runs, and
always that fabulous
vista to the south →

WENDY-JANE KING

Phone numbers
From elsewhere in
Switzerland add the
prefix 027; from
abroad use the prefix
+41 27

Slopes The slopes are spread over a broad mountainside, with lifts from four valley bases. Gondolas from Crans and Montana meet at Cry d'Er – an open bowl descending into patchy forest. The next sector, focused on Les Violettes, can be accessed from Les Barzettes. A six-pack from the mid-station here goes up to Cry d'Er; it can also be joined mid-way. Above Les Violettes, a jumbo gondola goes up to the Plaine Morte glacier. The fourth sector is served by a gondola up from Aminona. Some of the runs down to the valley are narrow woodland paths.

Fast lifts Quite a few lifts are fast, but many are not; the slow chair up from La Barmaz to Les Violettes is a particularly weak point.

Queues Our late-January visit last season was queue-free, but we lack reports on high season.

Terrain parks Aminona has a good park with features for all levels and a boardercross course. Features are sometimes built at Cry d'Er.

Snow reliability The runs on the Plaine Morte glacier are limited, and nearly all the other slopes get a lot of direct sun. There is snowmaking on the main runs, but we have rarely found good snow on the runs to the valley – our 2009 visit was exceptional, of course.

Experts There are few steep pistes and the only decent moguls are on the short slopes at La Toula. There's plenty of off-piste, particularly beneath Chetzeron and La Tza.

Intermediates Pistes are mostly wide, and many of the red runs don't justify the grading. They tend to be uniform in difficulty from top to bottom, with few surprises. Avid piste-bashers enjoy the length of many runs that allow a lot of mileage. The 12km/8 mile run from Plaine Morte to Les Barzettes starts with top-of-the-world views and powder, and finishes among pretty woods. The Piste Nationale downhill course is a good fast cruise.

Beginners There are three excellent nursery areas, including the golf course fairways which are near-ideal.

Snowboarding Despite the resort's staid image, boarding is very popular. The Avalanche Pro is a specialist shop and school. There are few draglifts.

Cross-country The 35km/22 miles of trails include a glacier area.

Mountain restaurants Over 20 huts are usefully marked on the piste map (although some are just bars). Above Crans, Merbé is one of the most

attractive places. We can't wait to try the new table- and self-service restaurants at Chetzeron, opening for 2009/10 (see 'News'). Cabane des Violettes has been smartly revamped, with table service. We had good food at the cute Cabane CAS, with a great position overlooking the valley. Chez Erwin, Bella-Lui and Petit Mont-Bonvin are also worth a look.

Schools and guides The Swiss schools have attracted mainly favourable comments over the years.

Families This doesn't strike us as a natural family resort.

STAYING THERE

There is a wide choice of hotels and apartments.

Hotels This conference resort has over 50 mainly large, comfortable, pricey hotels. Pas de l'Ours (485 9333) is our favourite – chic but welcoming. Aïda Castel (485 4111) is also well-furnished in rustic style. Art de Vivre (481 3312) has a newish spa. The new 5-star Crans hotel (486 6060) has 13 chalet-style suites, pool and spa facilities.

Eating out There is a good variety of places, from French to Lebanese. Among the best is the Bistrot in the Pas de l'Ours hotel. Other choices include the Chalet, Plaza, Rafaele's, Padrino and the Nouvelle Rötisserie.

Après-ski There are tents on the hill for late-afternoon drinks, but nightlife and evening atmosphere may disappoint. The George & Dragon in Crans is lively, and we liked Monki's for a beer. Bar 1900, the Grange, the Baiser de la Rose and Harry's Club have been recommended.

Off the slopes There are swimming pools (in hotels), two ice rinks, dog sledding, snow tubing, a cinema and a casino. There are also 60km/37 miles of walking. Sierre and Sion are close.

Davos

A grey urban sprawl at the centre of a glorious Alpine playground
(for skaters and langlaufers as well as downhillers)

£110
RESORT PRICE INDEX

RATINGS

The mountains

Extent	★★★★★
Fast lifts	★★★
Queues	★★★
Terrain p'ks	★★★★
Snow	★★★★
Expert	★★★★
Intermediate	★★★★★
Beginner	★★
X-country	★★★★★
Restaurants	★★★
Schools	★★★
Families	★★

The resort

Charm	★★
Convenience	★★
Scenery	★★★★
Eating out	★★★
Après-ski	★★★
Off-slope	★★★★★

+ Very extensive slopes

+ Some superb, long, and mostly easy pistes away from the lifts, with trains to bring you back to base

+ Lots of accessible off-piste terrain, with several marked itineraries

+ Good cross-country trails

+ Plenty to do off the slopes – from skating to shopping

− Davos is a huge, city-like place with dreary block-style buildings, plagued by traffic, lacking Alpine and après-ski atmosphere

− Five separate areas of slopes

− Lots of T-bars, and some other inadequate lifts

− The only piste back to town from the main Parsenn area is a black

One of your editors learned to ski in Davos, so it has a special place in our affections. Many return visits have confirmed the appeal of its slopes, which are both distinctive and extensive – you could say it was the original mega-resort – and have revealed its considerable off-piste potential. But the town/city (it could never be called a village) does not get any easier to like. Davos may be the more convenient base for access to most of the mountains it shares with Klosters, but when choosing a place to stay, for us there is no contest: Klosters has the welcoming, intimate feel of a ski resort, and Davos does not.

THE RESORT

Davos is set in a high, broad, flat-bottomed valley, with its lifts and slopes either side. Arguably it was the very first place in the Alps to develop its slopes. The railway up the Parsenn was one of the first built for skiers (in 1931), and the first draglift was built on the Bolgen nursery slopes in 1934. You can reach the resort by train, but the trip from Zürich airport involves two changes. The Davos Express coach transfer service is a recommended alternative. Or you can take the Graubünden Express service from Friedrichshafen airport.

Trips are possible by car or rail to St Moritz (via the Vereina rail tunnel) and Arosa, and by road to Laax-Flims and Lenzerheide – but none of them is quick enough to have wide appeal.

VILLAGE CHARM ★★
City in the mountains

The resort is more like a city than a village. It started life as a health resort and many of its massive luxury hotels were built as sanatoriums. Sadly, that's just what they look like and the place lacks a ski resort ambience. It is now well-known for its conference and sporting facilities too. Readers suggest arming yourself with train and bus timetables to get around.

CONVENIENCE ★★
Take the train

The resort has two main centres, Dorf and Platz, about 2km/1 mile apart. Transport is good, with buses around the town as well as the railway linking Dorf and Platz to Klosters and other villages. Easiest access to the slopes is from Dorf to the main Parsenn area, via the funicular railway; Platz is better placed for the Jakobshorn area, the big sports facilities, the smarter shopping and the evening action.

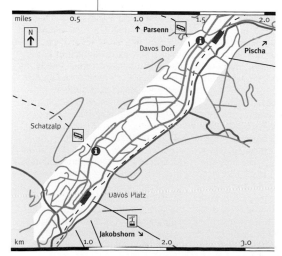

↑ Davos is a big town surrounded by glorious scenery. We prefer to stay in more rustic Klosters

SIMON MEDLEY

NEWS

As we went to press, we heard that the Schatzalp/Strela ski area will reopen for 2009/10 after being closed since 2002/03. It will be served by a funicular from Davos Platz, followed by a chair and a draglift and have two easy pistes, a link from the Parsenn area and a run down to the valley.

For 2008/09 snowmaking in the Davos/Klosters area was increased by 15km/9 miles.

Major hotel development is under way and should be complete for the 2010/11 season: a new 5-star and two new 4-stars.

There are plans to connect Rinerhorn and Jakobshorn with a gondola. The link is expected to be ready for either the 2011/12 or 2012/13 season.

SCENERY ★★★★
Pick your viewpoint
With five different sectors there is plenty of interest visually high up. And all the lower slopes are attractively wooded, with deep valleys.

THE MOUNTAINS

Davos shares its slopes with the famously royal resort of Klosters, which gets its own chapter. They have something for everyone, though experts and nervous intermediates need to choose their territory with care. Piste classification is questionable; many blue and red runs are of similar pitch. The piste map generally looks clear, but tries to cover too much ground in a small space – at some points, it is simply misleading. Signposting is generally good, but a lack of edge marking has been criticised by reporters.

EXTENT OF THE SLOPES ★★★★★
Vast and varied
You could hit a different mountain around Davos nearly every day for a week. The out-of-town areas tend to be much quieter than the ones directly accessible from the resort.

The Parsennbahn funicular from Davos Dorf ends at mid-mountain, where a choice of a fast six-pack or old funicular take you on up to the major lift junction of Weissfluhjoch, at one end of the **Parsenn**. The only run back to the valley is a black that used to end on the outskirts of Dorf, but now finishes in the centre, close to the bottom station. At the other end of the wide, open Parsenn bowl is Gotschnagrat, reached by cable car from the centre of Klosters. There are exceptionally long intermediate runs down to Klosters and other villages (see feature panel).

Across the valley, **Jakobshorn** is reached by cable car or chairlift from Davos Platz; this is popular with snowboarders but good for skiers too. **Rinerhorn** and **Pischa** are reached by bus or (in the case of Rinerhorn) train.

Pischa is now a designated freeride area, with half the runs left ungroomed and just three main lifts. Several of the runs here are now marked as unpatrolled as well as ungroomed – a very unusual arrangement for runs going down beside a lift, and one we don't like. But reporters tell us that some of these runs are sometimes groomed and have piste markers which can be turned round – yellow if the piste is ungroomed and blue if groomed.

Beyond the main part of Klosters, a gondola goes up from Klosters Dorf to the sunny, scenic **Madrisa** area.

There are too many T-bars for the comfort of some reporters – Rinerhorn and Pischa have little else. It's time Davos invested in more chairs.

FAST LIFTS ★★★
Key ones are fine but ...
The main lifts are mostly gondolas or cable cars, but there are fewer fast chairs than one might expect – the Jakobshorn is best served – and too many T-bars for an area its size.

QUEUES ★★★
Few problems
Davos has improved its key lifts and now generates relatively few complaints ('no queues longer than three minutes', says a March visitor). But there can still be long queues at the cable car out of Klosters and the Totalp chair on the mountain at Parsenn at peak times and weekends. Crowded pistes have raised concern – in the Parsenn sector around Weissfluhjoch especially. In contrast, the Jakobshorn is said to be quiet.

TERRAIN PARKS ★★★★
Lots of choice
All four of the surrounding mountains have terrain parks; the main one is the Sunrise park on Jakobshorn – home to the O'Neill Evolution contest. It is open as early as November, weather permitting, and is by far the best in the area. There is a good variety of jumps and rails, and a large number of

THE PARSENN'S SUPER-RUNS

The runs from Weissfluhjoch that head north, on the back of the mountain, make this area special for many visitors. The pistes that go down to Schifer and then to Küblis, Saas and Serneus, and the one that curls around the mountain to Klosters, are a fabulous way to end the day, given good conditions. If you are based in Davos, the return journey is by train (included in the lift pass).

The runs are classified red but are not steep. The latter parts can be challenging – they are not reliably groomed, and you need to remember that you are at low altitudes by the end (1190m/3,900ft at Klosters, 810m/2,660ft at Küblis). Signposting is not always good, either.

What marks these runs out is their sheer length (10-12km/6-7 miles) and the resulting sensation of travel they offer – plus a choice of huts in the woods at Schifer and lower down on the way to Klosters (see 'Mountain restaurants'). You can descend the 1100m/ 3,610ft vertical to Schifer and take the gondola back. Once past there, you're committed to finishing the descent.

KEY FACTS

Resort	1550m
	5,090ft
Slopes	810-2845m
	2,660-9,330ft
Lifts	59
Pistes	305km
	190 miles
Blue	20%
Red	44%
Black	36%
Snowmaking	16%

LIFT PASSES

Davos/Klosters

Prices in SF

Age	1-day	6-day
under 13	27	118
13-17	47	207
over 18	67	295

Free under 6
Senior no deals
Beginner no deals

Notes
Covers all Davos and Klosters areas

Alternative passes
Individual and combined areas (eg Parsenn/Gotschna, Jakobshorn, Pischa/ Rinerhorn/ Madrisa); pedestrian single tickets

boxes including a nice C-box. But the park is quite narrow and can feel cramped when busy. Two floodlit pipes are the training grounds for a host of Swiss professionals and evening sessions until 9.30pm are popular with locals. For smaller crowds though a less well-maintained park, head to Pischa – next to the Mitteltäli lift you'll find an array of rails and kickers. There are two boardercross courses, one at Parsenn; the other on Madrisa, 200m/660ft below the top of the Schaffürggli lift. There is also a mini park for beginners next to the Trainer lift in Rinerhorn.

SNOW RELIABILITY ★★★★
Good, but not the best
Davos is high by Swiss standards. Its mountains go respectably high, too – though not to glacial heights. Not many of the slopes face directly south, but Pischa does suffer from excessive sun. Snow reliability is generally good higher up. It can be poor lower down, but in 2007 (considered a poor snow

year) the lower runs were reportedly functional into late March. Snow-guns cover a few of the upper runs on the Parsenn, several on the Jakobshorn, and the home runs from the Parsenn to Davos Dorf and Klosters. Piste grooming is generally good; but some runs on Parsenn are said to be 'poorly maintained' – in particular, the super-long runs to the valley.

FOR EXPERTS ★★★★
Plenty to do, given snow
The appeal of this area for experts depends to a degree on the snow conditions. Although there are challenges to be found at altitude, most of the rewarding runs descend through the woods to valley level, and are not reliable for snow.

The black pistes include some distinctive, satisfying descents. The Meierhofer Tälli run to Wolfgang is a favourite – quite steep, narrow and 'exciting'. The run from Parsennhütte to Wolfgang is less challenging; it probably owes its black status due to

boarding

Davos is now part of the 'top snowboard resort' alliance. In conjunction with Val d'Isère, Ischgl and Madonna di Campiglio, the resort is working toward providing top-quality facilities for sideways sliders. The mountain has a lot to offer confident riders in terms of powder, tree runs, natural hits, cliffs and gullies. The established boarder mountain is the Jakobshorn with its 'monster-pipes', park and boardercross as well as night-riding on Fridays and its funky Jatzhutte bar. The terrain is vast and will keep any boarder entertained for a long time. The Pischa has a freeride area with a large chunk of terrain left ungroomed and a park by the Mitteltäli lift. One reporter says, 'There are no problems with crowds. The powder is amazing, and there are endless kicker-building spots with loads of windlips and cliff drops.' There are wide, mellow slopes for beginners on Parsenn but watch out for the flats on the runs down to the Schifer gondola. Top Secret (www.topsecretdavos.ch) is a specialist snowboard shop and school. There are several cheap hotels geared to boarders, notably the 180-bed Bolgenhof near the Jakobshorn, the Snowboardhotel Bolgenschanze and the Snowboarders Palace.

one short 'tricky' section.

There are also some off-piste itineraries – runs that are supposedly marked but not patrolled. At one time, these runs were a key attraction for adventurous skiers not wanting to pay for guidance, but over the decade to 2005 no fewer than 10 of them disappeared from the map, including the infamous Gotschnawang run down the top stage of the Klosters cable car and its less fearsome neighbours, Drostobel and Chalbersäss. Many of these abandoned runs have had piste status at some time in the past, and are not difficult to follow if you know what you are doing. Two of the most satisfying itineraries that remain are the long ones from the top of Jakobshorn, both with restaurants at

the end where a good lunch can be had. The start of the run to Mühle is not obvious, which has led more than one reporter into difficulty; once found, the run is 'nowhere steeper than a tough red'. The run to Teufi is more often closed: it goes first down a steep 200m/66oft gully, but thereafter is 'not difficult'.

There is also excellent 'proper' off-piste terrain, for which guidance is more clearly needed. Reporters have enjoyed heading away from the pistes above Serneus and Küblis. The long descent from Madrisa to St Antönien, north of Küblis, is popular, not least for the 'spectacular views' along the way. And there are some short tours to be done. Arosa can be reached with a bit of help from a train or taxi, and

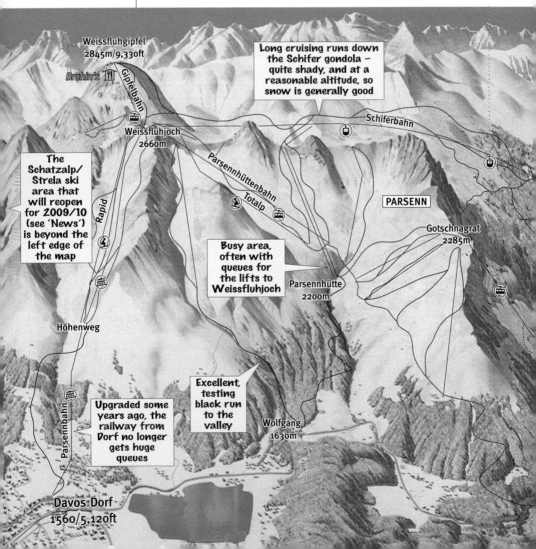

Weissfluhgipfel
2845m/9,33oft

Brühin's

Gipfelbahn

Long cruising runs down
the Schifer gondola –
quite shady, and at a
reasonable altitude, so
snow is generally good

Schiferbahn

Weissfluhjoch
2660m

Parsennhüttenbahn

The
Schatzalp/
Strela ski
area that
will reopen
for 2009/10
(see 'News')
is beyond the
left edge of
the map

Rapid

Totalp

PARSENN

Gotschnagrat
2285m

Busy area,
often with
queues for
the lifts to
Weissfluhjoch

Parsennhütte
2200m

Höhenweg

Parsennbahn

Excellent,
testing
black run
to the
valley

Wolfgang
1630m

Upgraded some
years ago, the
railway from
Dorf no longer
gets huge
queues

Davos Dorf
1560/5,120ft

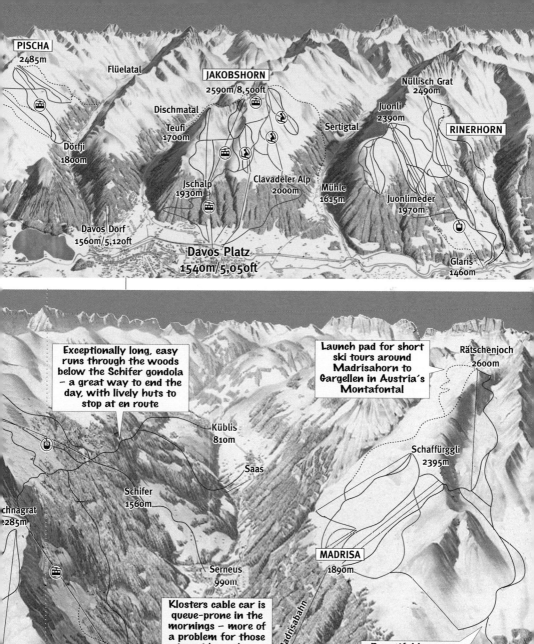

SCHOOLS

Swiss Davos
t 416 2454

Top Secret
t 413 4043

Planetskier
t 079 776 4655

Fullmoons
t 420 1477

Pat. Skilehrer Rageth
t 416 3901

Snow & You
t 079 636 7030

Classes
(Swiss prices)
6 4hr days SF340

Private lessons
Half day SF220 for
1-2 persons

CHILDCARE

Kinderland Pischa
t 416 1313
Ages from 3; 11am to
4pm

Bobo Club
t 416 2454
Ages 4 to 10;
10am-noon, 2pm-4pm

Babysitter list
At tourist office

Ski school
Takes ages 5 to 14 (6
days SF340)

from there you can go on to Lenzerheide, but you'll need a train back. From Madrisa you can make circular tours to Gargellen in Austria.

FOR INTERMEDIATES ★★★★★
A splendid variety of runs
For intermediates this is a great area. There are good cruising runs on all five mountains, so you would never get bored in a week. This variety of different slopes, taken together with the wonderful long runs to the Klosters valley, makes it a compelling area with a unique character.

As well as the epic runs described in the feature panel there is a beautiful away-from-the-lifts run to the valley from the top of Madrisa back to Klosters Dorf via the Schlappin valley (it's an easy black – classified red until the mid-1990s).

The Jakobshorn has some genuine challenges, notably by the Brämabüel drag. Rinerhorn is more of a cruise. Pischa is the gentlest of the Davos mountains but now branded as freeride territory; in good snow it should be a decent spot for first attempts at skiing ungroomed stuff.

FOR BEGINNERS ★★
Platz is the more convenient
The Bolgen nursery slope beneath the Jakobshorn is adequately spacious and gentle, and a bearable walk from the centre of Platz. But Dorf-based beginners face more of a trek out to Bünda – unless staying at the hotel of the same name. There is no shortage of easy runs to progress to, spread around all the sectors. The Parsenn sector probably has the edge, with long, easy intermediate runs in the main Parsenn bowl, as well as in the valleys down from Weissfluhjoch.

FOR CROSS-COUNTRY ★★★★★
Long, scenic valley trails
Davos is a popular spot for langlauf. It has a total of 75km/47 miles of trails running along the main valley and reaching well up into the side valleys of Sertigtal, Dischmatal and Flüelatal. There is a cross-country ski centre and special ski school on the outskirts. Trails are free.

MOUNTAIN RESTAURANTS ★★★
Stay high or go low
Most high-altitude restaurants are dreary self-service affairs – but there are exceptions. Overall, reports are

mixed – slow service is a regular comment.

Editors' choice The best is the highest of all: Bruhin's at Weissfluhgipfel (417 6644) – a great place for a hang-the-cost blow-out, with table service of excellent rustic as well as gourmet dishes, and some knockout desserts.
Worth knowing about The Gruobenalp at Gotschnagrat is 'outstanding' with 'excellent service from pleasant staff'. There are other compelling places lower down in the Parsenn sector. Readers enjoy the Höhenweg at the Parsennbahn mid-station for 'excellent pizzas' and 'quick service, even when busy'. There are several rustic 'schwendis' in the woods on the way down to the Klosters valley: the cosy Chesetta gets good reviews, with its 'super sun terrace'. These are fun places to end up as darkness falls – some sell wax torches for your final descent.

On Jakobshorn the Jatzhütte near the terrain park is wild – with changing scenery such as mock palm trees, parrots and pirates. One recent visitor enjoyed the 'small and cosy' Chalet Güggel on Jakobshorn: 'fast service and tasty portion of cured meat with asparagus'.

On Pischa, the Mäderbeiz at Flüelamäder is an 'extremely pleasant' and spacious woody hut, cheering on a cold day. On Rinerhorn, the Hubelhütte is the best bet.

There are several handy valley restaurants; the Kulm at Wolfgang is rated 'one of the best' and the Gotschnastübli at Serneus has 'brilliant food and service'.

SCHOOLS AND GUIDES ★★★
Decent choice
There are several options. Reporters have praised friendly, English-speaking instructors at the main Swiss school – 'both my kids had a terrific time'. Top Secret offers small groups (maximum of six). Swissfreeride is a guiding company offering all-inclusive off-piste weeks.

FOR FAMILIES ★★
Not ideal
Davos is a rather spread-out place in which to handle a family. The kids' ski school operates a special Disney-themed slope at Bolgen. We're told the nursery is 'well organised, but even the best instructors may slip into German'.

No we haven't made a mistake. This is downtown Davos not Zürich city centre ➔

GETTING THERE

Air Zürich 165km/ 105 miles (2hr30); Friedrichshafen 150km/95 miles (2hr30)

Rail Stations in Davos Dorf and Platz

ACTIVITIES

Indoor Fitness centres, tennis, squash, swimming pools, climbing wall, sauna, solarium, massage, wellness centres, ice rink, cinema, casino, galleries, museums, libraries, badminton, golf driving range

Outdoor Over 110km/ 68 miles of cleared paths, ice climbing, snowshoeing, tobogganing, ice rink, curling, sleigh rides, hang-gliding, paragliding

Phone numbers
From elsewhere in Switzerland add the prefix 081; from abroad use the prefix +41 81

TOURIST OFFICE

t 415 2121
info@davos.ch
www.davos.ch

STAYING THERE

Although most beds are in apartments, hotels dominate the UK market.
Hotels A dozen 4-stars and about 30 3-stars form the core. The tourist office runs a central booking service.
*****Flüela (410 1717) The more atmospheric of the 5-star hotels, in central Dorf. Pool.
****Waldhuus (417 9333) Convenient for langlaufers. Quiet, modern, tasteful. Pool and spa facility.
****Sunstar Park (413 1414) At far end of Davos Platz. Pool, sauna, spa. Recommended by reporters.
****Meierhof (416 8285) Close to the Parsenn funicular. 'Large rooms and good food.' Pool, sauna.
****National (415 1010) Five minutes from centre of Davos Platz. 'Good service and five-course dinners.'
***Davoserhof (417 6777) Our favourite. Small, old, beautifully furnished, with excellent food; well placed in Platz.
***Panorama (413 2373) In central Platz. Recommended by a reporter for 'excellent, good value' food. Piano bar.
***Ochsen (417 6777) Good-value; with triple- and four-bedded rooms as well as doubles and singles.
**Alte Post (414 9020) In central Platz. Traditional; popular with boarders.

EATING OUT ★★★☆☆
Wide choice, mostly in hotels
In a town this size, you need to know where to go. For a start, get the tourist office's pocket guidebook. The more ambitious restaurants are mostly in hotels. There are two good Chinese places – the lavish Zauberberg in the Europe and the Goldener Drachen in the Bahnhof Terminus. Good-value places include the jolly Al Ponte (pizza and steak both approved of), the Carretta (good for home-made pasta), the small and cosy Gentiana (with an upstairs stübli), and the hotel Dischma's Röstizzeria. Excursions out of town are popular. The Höhenweg is open in the evenings, but you have to pay to ride the funicular. Schatzalp (also reached by a funicular), the Schneider and the Landhaus in Frauenkirch have been recommended.

APRES-SKI ★★★☆☆
Lots on offer, but quiet clientele
There are plenty of bars, discos and nightclubs, and a large casino in the hotel Europe. But we're not sure how

some of them make a living – Davos guests tend to want the quiet life. At tea time, mega-calories are consumed at the Weber, and Schneider's might be worth a look. The Scala (hotel Europe) has a popular outside terrace. The liveliest place in town is the rustic little Chämi bar; popular with locals. The smart Ex-Bar attracts a mixed age group. Nightclubs tend to be sophisticated, expensive and lacking atmosphere during the week. The pick are the Cabanna, Cava Davos (both in the hotel Europe), Rotliechtli, and Paulaner's. Bolgenschanze and Bolgen-Plaza attract lots of boarders.

OFF THE SLOPES ★★★★★
Great, apart from the buildings
Looks aside, Davos has lots to offer the non-skier/rider. The towny resort has shops and other diversions, and transport along the valley and up on to the slopes is good – though the best of the mountain restaurants are well out of range. The sports facilities are excellent; Europe's biggest natural ice rink is supplemented by artificial rinks, both indoor and outdoor. Spectator events include speed skating as well as 'hugely popular' ice hockey. And there are lots of walks on the slopes, around the lake and along the valleys (special map available). There's a toboggan run on Rinerhorn, floodlit twice weekly, but the best in the area is the longer run on Madrisa, at Klosters. The Eau-là-là leisure centre incorporates pools and wellness facilities. A reader recommends the local museums and galleries. Day trips to St Moritz and Chur are possible.

Engelberg

One of the biggest verticals in the Alps with some snow-sure slopes and epic off-piste runs

- ➕ Close to Zürich airport
- ➕ Predominantly north-facing slopes keep their snow well
- ➕ Some classic off-piste runs

- ➖ Fragmented slopes
- ➖ Town is spread out and it's a long walk or bus ride from town to lifts
- ➖ Limited piste area

TOP 10 RATINGS

Extent	**
Fast lifts	***
Queues	**
Snow	***
Expert	****
Intermediate	***
Beginner	**
Charm	**
Convenience	*
Scenery	****

The short transfer from Zürich airport and the large number of hotels and apartments makes Engelberg great for short breaks. It has one of the biggest verticals in the Alps, awesome off-piste and some good intermediate slopes.

510

MOMENTUM SKI

**Weekend &
a la carte ski
holiday specialists**

100% Tailor-Made

**Individuals or
Corporate Groups**

**No. 1 specialists
in Engelberg**

020 7371 9111
www.momentumski.com

THE RESORT

The resort was named after the 12th-century Benedictine monastery (Engelberg means the mountain of the angel) that dominates the town as you look down from the lifts. It was very popular with Brits in the early 1900s.
Village charm The place is more of a town than a village. Its grand Victorian hotels, some recently renovated, have been joined by chalet-style buildings and concrete blocks. There is one traffic-free cobbled street, and lots of locals cycle to and from the lifts.
Convenience It's a free shuttle-bus or long walk to the lifts from most hotels.
Scenery There's lots of visual drama from the high, glacial slopes.

THE MOUNTAINS

The main slopes rise almost 2000m/ 6,560ft above the town by three successive lifts: a gondola and two cable cars, the top one rising above glacial crevasses and rotating 360° on the way to Klein Titlis at 3030m/

9,940ft. A much smaller second area of slopes, Brunni, is largely intermediate and reached by a new cable car from the other side of town. There's also a small kids'/nursery area behind the monastery, and a mountain (Fürenalp) just for walking and tobogganing, served by a gondola up the valley.
Slopes The pistes in the main area are limited and fragmented by the glaciers and rugged terrain. There are two main sectors, both above the treeline: Titlis-Stand and Jochpass. Titlis-Stand is served by the two successive cable cars that are accessed from Trübsee at the top of the gondola out of town; there are three chairs and a drag here too. This area gives access to the two epic off-piste runs mentioned under 'Experts'. From Trübsee, you can also head for Jochpass via a two-way chairlift to Alpstübli. At Jochpass the top is served by a fast six-pack, with another couple of chairs lower down. Brunni's slopes are sunnier and gently wooded, and served by a chair and a T-bar above the cable car.
Fast lifts High-capacity cable cars and

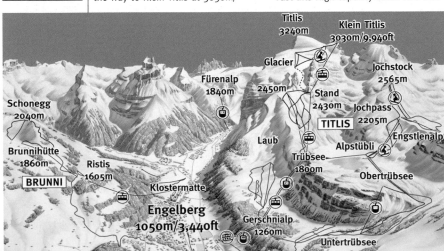

For 2008/09 the cable car to Brunni was upgraded to carry more passengers – it can now take 65. The base station was moved from the centre of town to the nursery slope at Klostermatte behind the monastery. An ice rink was created at Trübsee for skating and curling. And a speed slope opened on Jochpass.

KEY FACTS

Resort	1050m
	3,440ft
Slopes	1050-3030m
	3,440-9,940ft
Lifts	25
Pistes	82km
	51 miles
Blue	28%
Red	56%
Black	16%
Snowmaking	40%

UK PACKAGES

Alpine Answers, Chalet Espen, Crystal, Independent Ski Links, Inntravel, Interhome, Kuoni, Made to Measure, Momentum, Mountain Tracks, Neilson, Simply Alpine, Ski Freshtracks, Ski Independence, Ski Safari, Ski Solutions, Skitracer, Ski Weekend, Switzerland Travel Centre, White Roc

Phone numbers
From elsewhere in Switzerland add the prefix 041; from abroad use the prefix +41 41

TOURIST OFFICE

t 639 7777
welcome@
engelberg.ch
www.engelberg.ch

gondolas provide the main access.
Queues Weekend queues can be long, especially for the gondola out of town. Sometimes an old funicular followed by a cable car that run parallel to the gondola operate to alleviate queues.
Terrain parks The park is at Jochpass, with jumps, kickers and rails.
Snow reliability The high, north-facing slopes of Titlis and Jochpass keep their snow well and have a longer season than Brunni's sunnier slopes. The resort says 50% of the resort is snow-sure, including glacial runs and those with snowmaking.
Experts There is superb off-piste for experts who hire a guide. The classic Laub run is 1000m/3,28oft vertical down an immensely wide face with a consistent pitch and magnificent views of town. We enjoyed even more the 2000m/6,56oft vertical Galtiberg run, which starts over glaciers and ends among mountain streams and trees: we saw only three other people on it. You catch a bus back to town from the end of it. There's plenty more off-piste, too. There are few black pistes but lots of easily accessed off-piste at the top of Titlis, and the itinerary route from there to Stand is seriously steep and usually mogulled.
Intermediates Most runs are steep reds and there are few easy cruises. The good snow on the reds at the top of the rotating cable car, along with the views, make it worth the trip to the top (catch the cable car down to avoid the itinerary mentioned above). The Jochpass area is often quieter than Titlis, with enjoyable red and blue runs, including long ones to town.
Beginners There's a good isolated beginner area, Gerschnialp, near the mid-station of the gondola, served by draglifts, and others at Trübsee and Untertrübsee. But you have to catch lifts up and down to use them and there are no ideal runs to progress to.
Snowboarding The beginner area is served by draglifts, so it's not ideal. But there is excellent freeriding if you hire a guide. Beware of the flat start to the runs down from Jochpass.
Cross-country There are 44km/27 miles in total with valley trails and loops at altitude. The 1.5km/1 mile World Cup route near the sports centre in town is floodlit two nights a week.
Mountain restaurants The Ritz (at the Gerschnialp beginner area and the bottom of the Laub run) and Jochpass are rustic table-service places.

Schools and guides As well as the Swiss ski and snowboard school there are three others, Prime, Boardlocal and Active Snow Team. The local guiding outfit is Outventure (611 1441).
Families The ski school takes children from age three, and the kindergarten from two. Some hotels offer childcare, and the tourist office has details of babysitters.

STAYING THERE

There are lots of hotels, B&Bs and apartments. Chalet Espen (637 2220) is a catered chalet owned by Brits ('very comfortable, excellent food, a relatively short walk from the lift').
Hotels The 3-star Europe (639 7575) and Schweizerhof (637 1105) are centrally located (the latter with 'very comfortable rooms, pleasant public areas, tasty food'). Also 3-starred, the 'very grand' art nouveau Terrace (639 6666) is above the centre, reached by a free funicular. The Alpenclub (637 1243) is a friendly, central guest house with popular restaurant.
Eating out There is a huge variety of restaurants – more than 50 – from traditional Swiss to Tex-Mex (at the Yucatan), Chinese (Moonrise) and Indian (Chandra at the Terrace hotel). Try the modernised Schweizerhaus for a Swiss/French gourmet blow out and the Alpenclub – 'great for pizza and traditional cheesy fare'. Once a month there is a dining trip to Titlis and there are also sleigh and fondue evenings.
Après-ski At the bottom of the gondola, the Chalet has a big terrace and a popular happy hour, while in the main square the Yucatan happy hour is 'really something'. The party at the Yucatan continues till late, and the CC bar and Eden are popular for dancing, along with the Spindle nightclub. Recent visitors 'enjoyed a trip up to the Terrace Hotel for a preprandial G&T – perfect for a relaxed drink'.
Off the slopes The 12th-century monastery and its cheese-making shop are worth a visit, and as Engelberg is a real town, there's quite a range of shops. It's worth taking a trip up the rotating cable car to the top for the views and a tour around the ice grotto. There are also many winter walking and snowshoeing trails, an igloo building at Trübsee (you can stay the night there), tubing, sledging and a good sports centre.

Grindelwald

Traditional mountain town set beneath the towering Eiger and with an old cog railway still the main way up to the slopes

£90
RESORT PRICE INDEX

RATINGS

The mountains

Extent	★★★
Fast lifts	★★★
Queues	★★
Terrain p'ks	★★★
Snow	★★
Expert	★★
Intermediate	★★★★
Beginner	★★★
X-country	★★
Restaurants	★★★
Schools	★★★
Families	★★

The resort

Charm	★★★★
Convenience	★★
Scenery	★★★★★
Eating out	★★★
Après-ski	★★★
Off-slope	★★★★

512

KEY FACTS

Resort	1035m
	3,400ft

Jungfrau region	
Slopes	945-2970m
	3,100-9,740ft
Lifts	44
Pistes	213km
	132 miles
Blue	33%
Red	49%
Black	18%
Snowmaking	38%

First-Männlichen-Kleine-Scheidegg	
Slopes	945-2485m
	3,100-8,150ft
Lifts	30
Pistes	160km
	99 miles

- ✚ Dramatically set in magnificent scenery, directly beneath the towering north face of the Eiger
- ✚ Lots of long, gentle runs, ideal for intermediates, with links to Wengen
- ✚ Pleasant old village with long mountaineering history
- ✚ Fair amount to do off the slopes, including splendid walks

- ▬ Main slopes accessed by slow trains or by a painfully slow, queue-prone gondola
- ▬ Few challenging pistes for experts
- ▬ Inconvenient for visiting Mürren
- ▬ Natural snow-cover unreliable (but snowmaking has been increased)
- ▬ Village gets little midwinter sun

For stunning views from the town and the slopes, there are few places to rival Grindelwald. The village is nowhere near as special as Mürren or Wengen, just over the hill, but staying here does give you direct access to Grindelwald's own First slopes. But you can spend ages queueing for, waiting for or sitting in the gondola or trains up into the slopes (and back down if snow is poor). The gondola ride – the longest in Europe according to Grindelwald's literature – takes half an hour. The train to Kleine Scheidegg from Grindelwald takes about the same. Grindelwald regulars accept all this as part of the scene.

THE RESORT

Grindelwald is set either side of a road along a narrow valley. Towering mountains rise steeply from the valley, which means that the resort and main slopes get very little sun in January.

Getting to the tougher, higher slopes of Mürren is a lengthy business unless you go to Lauterbrunnen by car. (It took us three hours to get from Grindelwald to the top of Mürren's Schilthorn on skis.) Trips to other resorts are not very easy, but you can drive to Adelboden and Meiringen.

VILLAGE CHARM ★★★★
A mountaineer's haven
The central village buildings are mainly old traditional chalet style, in keeping with its long mountaineering history. And the station and cog railway add to the olde-worlde charm. The village

can feel very jolly at times (eg during the ice carving festival in January, when huge ice sculptures are created).

CONVENIENCE ★★
Depends where you ski
The most convenient places to stay are in the centre near the main station or at Grund. But Grund is right at the bottom of the sloping village and rather charmless; you can ski right back to it from the main slopes shared with Wengen, though, and you can choose between the train and the gondola to take you up. If you stay in the centre, you can also take the train up, but you need to catch it back up from Grund on the way home too. Near the opposite end of the village to Grund (walkable from the centre) a gondola goes to the separate First area. At the foot of the First area are nursery slopes, ski school and kindergarten. Buses link the lift stations – but these get congested at times, and reporters say that they are too infrequent. There's a wide range of hotels in the heart of the village.

SCENERY ★★★★★
History all round
The mountains in these parts are legendary among climbers – from all over the slopes there are superb views, not only of the Eiger but also of the Wetterhorn and other peaks.

miles 0.5   1.0   1.5   2.0

↑ First

N ↑

← Männlichen

Grund ⓘ

↓ Kleine Scheidegg

km   1.0   2.0   3.0

NEWS

For 2009/10 there are plans to replace the Salzegg drag to Eigergletscher with a six-pack, starting lower down on the other side of the railway by the Arven chair. And snowmaking on the slopes around Fallboden and Wixi is being upgraded.

For 2008/09 snowmaking was increased in the Kleine Scheidegg/ Männlichen area and now covers 50% of the slopes. On First, the First Flyer – zip wires you can fly down at up to 90kph/56mph – was built.

UK PACKAGES

Alpine Answers, Crystal, Elegant Resorts, Independent Ski Links, Inghams, Interhome, Kuoni, Made to Measure, Momentum, Neilson, Powder Byrne, Simply Alpine, Ski Freshtracks, Skitracer, Switzerland Travel Centre, Thomson, White Roc

THE MOUNTAINS

The major area of slopes is shared with Wengen and offers a mix of wooded runs and open slopes higher up. The smaller First area is mainly open; at the top on skier's left is a protected area for chamois and you can spot lots of them there.

EXTENT OF THE SLOPES ★★★
Broad and mainly gentle
From Grund, near the western end of town, you can get to **Männlichen** by an appallingly slow two-stage gondola or to **Kleine Scheidegg** by an equally slow cog railway (with some trains starting in the centre of town). The slopes of the separate south-facing **First** area are reached by a long, slow gondola starting a walk or short bus ride east of the centre.

Piste marking is poor; several reporters found the Männlichen slopes, in particular, confusing. The new piste map is much smaller than the old one (a good thing) but more schematic in style (bad).

FAST LIFTS ★★★
Better high up
Getting up from the village is a slow process, but new fast chairlifts have improved the area higher up.

QUEUES ★★
Can be dreadful at the bottom
We still receive mixed reports on queues. Waiting times for the gondola

and train at Grund can be very bad in high season, especially at weekends. Some reporters have told of half-hour waits for the gondola, which then takes a further half-hour to get to the top – one reporter also found 'big queues to download at the end of the day' when the lower runs were closed. Despite queues to get up in the morning, reporters find few problems once on the mountain.

TERRAIN PARKS ★★★
First things first
There is a terrain park on First with rails, boxes and jumps; plus a separate super-pipe.

SNOW RELIABILITY ★★
Improved snowmaking helps
Grindelwald's low altitude means that natural snow is often in short supply or in poor condition. First is sunny, and so even less snow-sure than the main area. But a lot of snowmaking has been added recently, and by last season 50% of the slopes in the Kleine Scheidegg-Männlichen area were covered by snowmaking. When we were there in 2009 it had not snowed for a few weeks and a warm Foehn wind had melted a lot of snow, but most slopes were in good condition. More reports please.

FOR EXPERTS ★★
Few on-piste challenges
The area is quite limited for experts, but there is some fine off-piste if the

LIFT PASSES

Jungfrau

Prices in SF

Age	1-day	6-day
under 16	30	151
16 to 19	47	242
20 to 61	59	302
over 62	53	272

Free under 6 (if with parent)

Beginner points card

Notes
Covers Wengen, Mürren and Grindelwald, trains between them and Grindelwald ski-bus; day pass price is for First-Kleine Scheidegg-Männlichen area only

Alternative passes
Grindelwald and Wengen only; Mürren only; non-skier pass

SCHOOLS

Grindelwald Sports
t 854 1290

Buri Sport
t 853 3353

Snowsports Kleine Scheidegg
t 855 1545

Felix Ski Paradies
t 853 1288

Privat
t 853 0473

Classes (Sports prices) 5 (4hr) days SF395

Private lessons
SF80 for 1hr for 1 or 2 persons

---

snow is good. Heli-trips are organised. We enjoyed the splendid Bort Direct black run on First that was built a couple of years ago. This turns into a downhill route between Bort and town and is quite tough, especially when the snow has suffered from the sun.

FOR INTERMEDIATES ★★★★
Ideal intermediate terrain
In good snow, First makes a splendid intermediate playground, though the general lack of trees makes the area less friendly than the larger Kleine Scheidegg-Männlichen area. The runs to the valley are great fun. Nearly all the runs from Kleine Scheidegg are long blues or gentle reds. On the Männlichen there's a choice of gentle runs down to the mid-station of the gondola – and in good snow, down to the bottom. For tougher pistes, head for the top of the Lauberhorn lift and the runs to Kleine Scheidegg, or to Wixi (following the World Cup downhill course). The north-facing run from Eigergletscher to Salzegg often has the best snow late in the season.

FOR BEGINNERS ★★★
Depends where you go
The Bodmi nursery slope at the bottom of First is scenic but not particularly convenient ('the chore of getting to and from it with small children was too much,' said one reporter). Snow quality can also suffer from the sun and the low altitude, and fast skiers and tobogganers racing through are off-putting. Kleine Scheidegg has a better, higher beginner area and splendid, long runs to progress to, served by the railway.

FOR CROSS-COUNTRY ★★
Okay but shady
There are 17km/10 miles of prepared tracks. Almost all of this is on the valley floor, so it's shady in midwinter and may have poor snow later on.

MOUNTAIN RESTAURANTS ★★★
Wide choice
See the Wengen chapter for options around Kleine Scheidegg and down towards Wengen. We enjoyed a good lunch at Bort on First, where the old building houses a restaurant built in contemporary style. Brandegg, on the railway, is recommended for 'wonderful' apple fritters and its sunny terrace. The table-service restaurant at the top of Männlichen has splendid views, and a reporter says, 'The fillet of beef on toast was a highlight; and the self-service section does good home-made hamburgers.' Other reader recommendations are the Jägerstubli, off the Rennstrecke piste, and the Berghaus Aspen ('huge portions'), above Grund. The Spycher has a cosy indoor bar plus deckchairs and an ice-bar, which also serves sandwiches. At First, Café Genepi, at the bottom of the Oberjoch chair, is 'a must' for Flammenkuchen (thin pizza) and 'a good place to begin your après-ski'.

SCHOOLS AND GUIDES ★★★
Mixed views
Historically, reporters have generally praised the main school, Grindelwald Sports, but there has been some criticism. However, we lack recent reports – more welcome. The Privat school offers off-piste guiding.

FOR FAMILIES ★★
Decent choice
The First mountain restaurant runs a day nursery, which is a neat idea, and the Kinderhort Sunshine is a nursery at the top of Männlichen.

STAYING THERE

The hotels UK tour operators offer are mainly at the upper end of the market.
Hotels There's a 5-star, seven 4-stars and plenty of more modest places.
★★★★★Grand Regina (854 8600) Big and imposing; right next to the station. Nightly music in the piano bar. 'Expensive but friendly, with good food, service, pool and amazing spa.'
★★★★Belvedere (854 5757) Over 100 years old, family-run, close to the

← The train from Grindelwald to Kleine Scheidegg takes around half an hour. But at least you get to admire magnificent scenery on the way

GRINDELWALD TOURISMUS

CHILDCARE

Kinderhort Sunshine
t 854 8080
Ages from 1mnth to 8yr; 8.30-5pm

Snowli Kinderclub
t 854 1290
From age 3; 9.30-4pm

Felix Ski Paradies
t 853 1288
From age 4;
10pm-3pm

Ski schools
Take children from age 3 or 4 (5 half days SF180)

GETTING THERE

Air Zürich 160km/ 100 miles (2hr45); Bern 70km/45 miles (1hr30); Basel 165km/105 miles (2hr30)

Rail Station in resort

ACTIVITIES

Indoor Sports centre (pool, sauna, steam, fitness), ice rink, curling, museum, cinema

Outdoor 80km/ 50 miles of cleared paths, ice rink, tobogganing, snowshoeing, climbing, tubing, glacier tours, sleigh rides

Phone numbers
From elsewhere in Switzerland add 033. From abroad use the prefix +41 33.

TOURIST OFFICE

t 854 1212
touristcenter@
grindelwald.ch
www.grindelwald.com

boarding

Intermediates will enjoy the area most, while experts will hanker for Mürren's steep, off-piste slopes. First is the main boarders' mountain, not only because of the terrain park and big pipe but also because of the open freeride terrain accessed via the top lifts. There are quite a few drags.

station. We stayed here in 2009 and found it very comfortable, well-run and friendly; pool, steam, sauna, outdoor salt water hot tub; choice of seven types of pillows. Great views of Eiger from south-facing rooms.

****Schweizerhof (854 5858) Close to the station. Pool. Due to be refurbished for 2009/10.

****Spinne (854 8888) Central. A reporter 'cannot praise it enough: friendly, superb food, good rooms'.

***Hirschen (854 8484) Family-run; by nursery slopes. Good food.

***Derby (854 5461) Popular, modern, next to station, with 'first class' service, good food and great views.

***Eigerblick (854 1020) A bit away from the station but 'great service, including free taxi'. Huge bedrooms.

*Wetterhorn (853 1218) Cosy, simple chalet way beyond the village, with great views of the glacier.

Apartments Readers recommend those in the Hirschen and Eiger hotels.

At altitude The Berghaus Bort (8535 1762), at the gondola station in the middle of the First area, has everything from single rooms to dormitories.

EATING OUT ★★★
Hotel based

There's a wide choice of good hotel restaurants such as Bistro-Bar Memory in the Eiger; Chalti-Stübli in the Kreuz; Schmitte in the Schweizerhof; and the Alte Post. The Kirchbühl and Oberland are good for vegetarians. Hotel Spinne has an Italian option and the candlelit Rôtisserie. The C&M Café und Mehr is 'well priced and friendly'. Onkle Tom's Hütte was recommended for pizza. The Latino does Italian home cooking.

APRES-SKI ★★★
Getting livelier

Tipirama (a wigwam at Kleine Scheidegg) is a fun place immediately after skiing, sometimes with DJs and live bands. There are various (mainly open air) bars to stop in on the way down to Grund. Holzerbar (on run 21) was lively when we called in, and the tiny Holdrio (relatively cheap beer) and the outdoor bar of the Aspen hotel (just below) usually are, too. The Rancher bar (on run 22) does good alcoholic coffees. In town, the terrace of the C&M Café und Mehr is good for coffee and cake. Later on, there's live music in several bars and hotels, but it isn't a place for bopping until dawn. The Espresso bar in the Spinne hotel seems to be the liveliest and the Hotel Eiger has the Gepsi. Later on, people head for the Mescalero (in the Spinne) and Plaza (in the Sunstar) clubs.

OFF THE SLOPES ★★★★
Plenty to do, easy to get around

There are many cleared paths with magnificent views and a special (though pricey) pedestrian bus/lift pass. First also has the First Flyer (see 'News'). Many of the mountain huts are accessible to pedestrians. A trip to Jungfraujoch is spectacular (see the feature panel), and excursions by train are easy to Interlaken. There are 70km/43 miles of toboggan runs, including the world's longest (15km/ 9 miles) – but it's an uphill walk of 2hr30 from the top of the First gondola. There's a cinema, ice hockey and curling to watch, and an excellent sports centre with pool. Helicopter flights from Männlichen are popular.

THE JOURNEY TO THE TOP OF EUROPE

From Kleine Scheidegg you can take a train through the Eiger to the highest railway station in Europe – Jungfraujoch at 3450m/11,320ft. The journey is a bit tedious – you're in a tunnel except when you stop to look out of two galleries carved into the sheer north face of the Eiger – magnificent views over to Männlichen, and then over the glacier. At the top is a big restaurant complex. There's an 'ice palace' carved out of the glacier and a viewing tower with fabulous views of the Aletsch glacier (a UNESCO World Heritage Site). The cost for 2008/09 was SF53.50 with a Jungfrau lift pass for three days or more.

Klosters

Ski the extensive slopes of Davos from a traditional village base –
with Davos traffic at last banished to a bypass

£110
RESORT PRICE INDEX

TOP 10 RATINGS

Extent	★★★★★
Fast lifts	★★★
Queues	★★
Snow	★★★★
Expert	★★★★
Intermediate	★★★★★
Beginner	★★★
Charm	★★★★
Convenience	★★
Scenery	★★★★

NEWS

Snowmaking is
increased each year
but there have been
no major new lifts
recently and none are
planned for 2009/10.

KEY FACTS

Resort	1190m
	3,900ft
Slopes	810-2845m
	2,660-9,330ft
Lifts	59
Pistes	305km
	190 miles
Blue	20%
Red	44%
Black	36%
Snowmaking	16%

+ Extensive slopes shared with Davos

+ Splendid long intermediate runs to the village from the Parsenn

+ Lots of accessible off-piste terrain

+ Some cute mountain restaurants

+ Pleasant traditional village, now bypassed by the valley traffic

− The slopes are spread over five widely separated areas

− Preponderance of T-bars is a problem for some visitors

− Queue-prone cable car into the main Parsenn area

In a word association game, 'Klosters' might trigger 'Prince of Wales'. The resort has even named its queue-prone cable car after him. Don't be put off: Klosters is not particularly exclusive, and it does have a lot going for it. The relaxed, chalet-style village has always been an attractive alternative to staying in towny Davos, with which it shares its slopes; more so since 2005, when a bypass road removed the intrusive Davos and Vereina tunnel traffic from the village. It is far from traffic-free, but pedestrians no longer go in fear of their lives.

THE RESORT

Klosters is a comfortable, quiet village with a much more appealing Alpine flavour than Davos.
Village charm Klosters Platz is the main focus – a collection of upmarket, traditional-style hotels around the railway station, at the foot of the steep, wooded slopes of Gotschna. Traffic bound for Davos and the Vereina rail tunnel, once an acute problem, now takes a bypass.
Convenience The village spreads along the valley road, fading into the countryside; then you come to the even quieter village of Klosters Dorf, at the base of the gondola to Madrisa.

Local train and bus services are good.
Scenery The contrast between steeply wooded valleys and high, craggy peaks is impressive.

THE MOUNTAINS

Most of the runs are on open slopes above steeper woodland.
Slopes A cable car from the railway station in Platz takes you to the Gotschnagrat end of the Parsenn area shared with Davos, and a gondola from Dorf takes you up to the scenic Madrisa area. There's also a little slope at Selfranga (floodlit some evenings), a suburb of Platz. Davos's other three separate ski areas are further afield.

↑ One of the Parsenn super-runs that you can take all the way down to the valley, a distance of six to seven miles

ALAN SHEPHERD

UK PACKAGES

Alpine Answers, Crystal Finest, Descent International, Flexiski, Inghams, Kuoni, Made to Measure, Momentum, Neilson, Oxford Ski Co, Powder Byrne, Simply Alpine, Ski Expectations, Ski Freshtracks, Ski Independence, Ski Safari, Ski Solutions, Ski Weekend, Skitracer, Snow Finders, Switzerland Travel Centre, White Roc

Phone numbers
From elsewhere in Switzerland add 081; from abroad use the prefix +41 81

TOURIST OFFICE

t 410 2020
info@klosters.ch
www.klosters.ch

Fast lifts Apart from the gondola, Madrisa is poorly served – mostly by draglifts (too many, says a 2009 visitor). All the Davos ski areas could do with more fast chairs instead of T-bars.

Queues Queues for the Gotschna cable car can be a problem at weekends and peak times.

Terrain parks The Madrisa area has a boardercross course, and there are more options on the other mountains.

Snow reliability It's usually good higher up. The home runs are quite low, but are now equipped with snowmaking.

Experts The lift-served off-piste possibilities are the main appeal of the area – see Davos.

Intermediates There are excellent cruising runs in all five ski areas. For details, see the Davos chapter.

Beginners There is a slope between Dorf and Platz, plus Selfranga; but the slopes of Madrisa are more appealing.

Snowboarding Local slopes are good, but more boarders stay in Davos.

Cross-country There are 35km/22 miles of trails and lots more up at Davos; a Nordic ski school offers lessons. Trails are now free to use.

Mountain restaurants There are a number of atmospheric huts in the woods above the village – see Davos chapter. The main Madrisa restaurant is adequate, but a better option is to take the black run to the valley for lunch at the woody Erika at Schlappin – 'excellent atmosphere and food'.

Schools and guides There is a choice. Saas is well regarded for good, English-speaking instructors and 'fun' private lessons, though one group got two instructors during their week. Adventure-Skiing was praised last year for private guiding.

Families The ski schools offer 'excellent' classes for children, and the Madrisa Kids' Land takes two to six year olds.

STAYING THERE

There is a wide choice of packages offered by UK tour operators.

Hotels There are some particularly attractive hotels. For most people, central Platz is the best location. Here, the smart Chesa Grischuna (422 2222) combines traditional atmosphere and modern comfort. In 2009 we stayed at the comfortable and welcoming 3-star Rustico (see 'Eating out'). The readers' favourite is the 'wonderful' 4-star Alpina (410 2424) – 'friendly and helpful staff', excellent spa facilities. The 2-star Bündnerhof (422 1450), 400m/1,300ft from the train/lift station is good value. Next door, the cosy old Wynegg (422 1340) is a perennial British favourite. In Dorf, the Sunstar Albeina (423 2100) is convenient for Madrisa and cheaper than the other 4-stars, has a good spa and is 'very comfortable, friendly', with 'excellent food'. The Sport (423 3030) is 'pleasant with good facilities'.

Apartments Apartments are available through local agencies.

Eating out Good restaurants abound, but there are few cheap and cheerful places. Top of the range is the Walserhof, with a Michelin star – 'one of the best meals we've had', says a recent visitor. We enjoyed an Asian fusion dinner at the Rustico hotel (the owner's wife is Asian). Al Berto's serves 'wonderful' pizza. The Casanna at Platz serves 'excellent steaks', and the Chesa Grischuna is recommended for 'fabulous venison' and good wines. Fellini's pizzeria is 'child-friendly'.

Après-ski In the village, the Chesa Grischuna is a focus from teatime onwards, with its live music. Gaudy's at the foot of the slopes is a popular stop after skiing 'if you're happy to drink in a tent', as is the lively bar at the Alpina and the warmly panelled Wynegg. The Rossli bar is the place to watch sport on TV. The It's Bar was new last year (opposite hotel Rustico). The Casa Antica is a small disco that livens up on Saturday night.

Off the slopes Klosters is an attractive base for walking (there's a special map available) and cross-country skiing – hiking to Schifer is 'a nice adventure'. Tobogganing is popular – there is an exceptional 8.5km/5 mile run from Madrisa to Saas. There is a leisure centre with an ice rink, and some hotel pools are open. Train outings can include the old town of Chur.

Laax

Pleasant, unremarkable villages – but with high, wide, sunny slopes that are slowly attracting more international attention

£100
RESORT PRICE INDEX

TOP 10 RATINGS

Extent	★★★★
Fast lifts	★★★★
Queues	★★★★
Snow	★★★
Expert	★★★
Intermediate	★★★★★
Beginner	★★★★
Charm	★★★
Convenience	★★★
Scenery	★★★

NEWS

The first phase of the huge Rocksresort lodging/restaurant/ shops complex opened at Laax in 2008. By the end of 2009, most of the complex's 11 'cubes' will be open.

KEY FACTS

Resort	1100m
	3,610ft
Altitude	1100-3020m
	3,610-9,910ft
Lifts	27
Pistes	220km
	137 miles
Blue	29%
Red	32%
Black	39%
Snowmaking	11%

MOMENTUM SKI

Weekend &
a la carte ski
holiday specialists

100% Tailor-Made

Premier hotels &
apartments

Flexible travel
arrangements

020 7371 9111

+ Extensive, varied slopes ideal for intermediates, shared with Flims

+ Impressive lift system with few queues most of the time

− Sunny orientation can cause icy or slushy pistes and bare lower runs

− Long walks or bus rides from some lodgings

− Quiet in the evenings

Laax, marketed in the past (and still in the summer) as Flims, is in terms of area and piste km one of Switzerland's biggest resorts. It is now managed in a very dynamic, focused way, and is finding an international market as a result – we now get a substantial flow of reports from readers, all enthusiastic.

THE RESORT

Laax itself – now called Laax Dorf – is a quiet rustic village. Just outside it is a big, busy lift base/hotel/parking complex, formerly Murschetg but now called Laax, where the new 1,000-bed Rocksresort is taking shape. The slopes spread across to the second major lift base of Flims Dorf and the minor one of Falera. Trips are possible to Lenzerheide, Klosters and Arosa.

Village charm Laax Dorf is pleasantly traditional, with quiet suburbs spreading around a lake. In contrast, the new Laax is uncompromisingly modern. Flims Dorf is a normal resort – traditional, but not picture-postcard material; it benefits hugely from a bypass tunnel. Nearby Flims Waldhaus is a leafy suburb with smart, secluded hotels. Falera was once a quiet backwater but has now expanded considerably, all in traditional style.

Convenience You can find lodgings near any of the main lift bases. The smart hotels in Waldhaus run courtesy buses. The free public ski-buses are supposed to run ever 10 minutes.

Scenery There are grand panoramic views to the peaks on the Italian border from the upper slopes.

THE MOUNTAINS

The villages share extensive, varied slopes. There are some treelined runs. The resort piste map shows a dozen unexplained 'freeride runs' (dotted on our map) – probably avalanche-protected and patrolled. Many readers judge the few blacks to be reds, really.

Slopes There are big gondolas into the slopes from both Flims Dorf and Laax (alongside a cable car of exceptional length). Above mid-mountain, there is a complex web of lifts and runs. The glacier offers limited vertical, but also accesses superb long runs, away from the lifts, to Alp Ruschein. There is night skiing at Laax.

Fast lifts A high proportion of lifts are gondolas or fast chairs.

Queues Few problems, except on peak weekends. There may be queues for the isolated chair at Alp Ruschein, and for the glacier drags at times. High winds can close the upper lifts.

Terrain parks The park at Crap Sogn Gion is claimed to be Europe's best, and certainly impresses readers. There are three areas plus, they say, Europe's largest pipe. Regular high-profile competitions are held here. The glacier sometimes has a park, too.

Snow reliability Upper runs are fairly snow-sure. The lower ones can suffer from sun, but key ones have snowmaking. The runs from Cassons and the glacier are prone to closure. Grooming is 'outstanding'.

Experts The black pistes present few challenges, but the 'freeride runs' add a lot of excellent terrain – timing your descents can be crucial, though, to avoid rock-hard moguls. There is abundant off-piste terrain too, particularly on Cassons and La Siala.

Intermediates A superb area. Reporters are often surprised by the extent and length of the slopes. The bowl below La Siala is huge and gentle. For the more confident, there are plenty of reds and some easy blacks. The sheltered Grauberg valley is a favourite – long and fast. The long black run from the glacier is steep only at the top. The Downhill piste from Crap Sogn Gion is excellent. Some of the freeride runs are great for experiments off-piste, but some are steep.

Beginners OK in midwinter; later on the village slopes suffer from the sun. There are nursery lifts up the mountain at Crap Sogn Gion and Nagens, but apparently no special lift pass. The Foppa and Curnius areas have good, easy runs to move on to.

Snowboarding Hugely popular. Apart from the top terrain park, there's good freeriding. Many linking pistes have flat/uphill stretches – plan carefully.

Cross-country There are 60km/37 miles of trails scattered around.

Mountain restaurants We are told all 17 huts are now described on the piste map. The Startgels (aka Alpenrose) remains a firm favourite ('glorious views', 'top-notch grills'). There are some stylish modern table-service places at altitude – Das Elephant and Capalari. Other reader tips include Tegia Curnius, Nagens, Tegia Larnags, Plaun and SegnesHütte.

Schools and guides Unusually, the school appears to be run by the lift company, US-style. Reports please.

Families Flims is family-friendly; We thought the children's area at Flims base very impressive; now there are new 'Wonderlands' at all three bases. Last year we had rave reviews of both the childcare and kids' ski classes.

STAYING THERE

Only a handful of UK tour operators feature Laax or Flims.

Hotels At Laax lift-base the Laaxerhof (920 8200) is 'almost ski-out/in', has 'good rooms' and 'great food and staff' in its stubli. Laax Dorf offers the charming little Posta Veglia (921 4466). In Flims Dorf the cheap and cheerful Arena (920 9393), with 'great location, terrace and bar' suits boys' trips (see 'Après-ski'). In Waldhaus the Adula (928 2828) has a 'great spa' and 'surprisingly good' food. The swanky, 'superb' Park (928 4848) is popular with families. The Sunstar Survelva (928 1800) does 'wonderful food'. The Waldeck (928 1414) has 'great food' and pizzeria and brewery attached.

Apartments The tourist office has a long list of available apartments.

Eating out In Laax Dorf the Posta Veglia does excellent food in a lovely old stube, and a plainer room behind. In Flims, readers tip the two à la carte restaurants of the hotel Adula, Cavi Gilli (an old farmhouse) and the hotel Bellevue's Keller.

Après-ski There are busy bars at the lift bases at close of play. Reader tips include the Crap Bar at Laax, and in Flims the Legna, the Iglu and the bar of the hotel Arena. The Livingruhm is a bit more smooth, with sofas and log fire. Later on, Flims seems quiet, but there are places to go. Residents of the hotel Arena are issued with earplugs, and need them when its club closes at 2am. The Riders Palace at Laax throbs into the early hours.

Off the slopes There's an enormous sports centre on the edge of Flims, with ice rink, and 60km/37 miles of marked walks. Shopping is limited. Outings to historic Chur are possible.

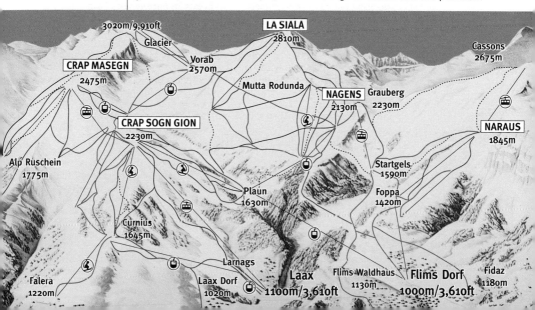

CRAP MASEGN 2475m

3020m/9,910ft

Glacier

Vorab 2570m

LA SIALA 2810m

Cassons 2675m

Mutta Rodunda

NAGENS 2130m

Grauberg 2230m

CRAP SOGN GION 2230m

NARAUS 1845m

Alp Ruschein 1775m

Startgels 1590m

Plaun 1630m

Foppa 1420m

Curnius 1645m

Larnags

Falera 1220m

Laax Dorf 1020m

Laax 1100m/3,610ft

Flims Waldhaus 1130m

Flims Dorf 1000m/3,610ft

Fidaz 1180m

Meiringen

Small area of varied slopes above a traditional resort, ideal for families, Sherlock Holmes fans and those with a sweet tooth

+ Good for short breaks

+ Unspoiled, traditional resort with access to quiet, crowd-free slopes

+ Good for families and intermediates

+ Plenty to do off the slopes

− Slopes are limited in extent, with a bus ride to the lifts

− No runs back to the valley

− Little to interest experts, at least on-piste

− Sunny slopes may suffer poor snow

NEWS

For 2008/09 a special kids' terrain park was built at Käserstatt, with lots of boxes, rollers and jumps – the first family-only park of its kind in the Bernese Oberland.

FIS World Cup Ski Cross races are held in Meiringen-Hasliberg every March.

Meiringen's claims to fame include Sherlock Holmes – the fictional detective whose creator Conan Doyle was a regular visitor and a keen skier – and the meringue – the oh-so-sweet dessert that was created here and named after the town. Its ski area, on the other hand, is rather less well known in the UK these days. Yet this pleasant resort and its varied slopes at Hasliberg make it a sensible choice for families and intermediates who are content with limited slopes, and for those wanting to spend time on other activities. It is also good for short breaks and a worthwhile outing from the nearby Jungfrau resorts. For a good-value, relaxing break away from the crowds Meiringen is worth a look.

THE RESORT

Meiringen is an old town in the Hasli valley in the scenic Bernese Oberland, between Interlaken and Lucerne. It is about 90 minutes' drive from Zürich or Bern, and is also on the railway line from Interlaken.

As well as Meiringen's association with Sherlock Holmes (the falls where he and his arch enemy Moriarty died in the final Holmes novel – the Reichenbach Falls – are on the outskirts of town), in the 18th century an Italian chef created the meringue and named it after the town, his adopted home. Local bakeries produce huge quantities of the sugary treat for the town's restaurants and cafes.

The ski area is at Hasliberg, the collective name for a few small villages on the sunny, south-facing hillside above the town and reached by bus or cable car. It used to be popular with the British when winter sports began in the region. World Cup downhill races were held here in the 1970s.

As well as the local downhill ski area, the six-day Haslital lift pass covers Axalp – a limited but varied ski area above lake Brienz – and the nordic trails at Gadmen. Outings to the Jungfrau resorts of Wengen, Mürren and Grindelwald are possible.

Village charm The centre is not chocolate-box pretty, and many of the buildings are block-like. But there is a charming little church with a 14th century tower and wooden spire, and much of the area is pleasantly woody.

Convenience Most of the lodgings are close to the railway station and along the main street. There are free ski-buses to the cable car station at Alpbach and up to the slopes at Hasliberg, where you can also stay.

Scenery Meiringen enjoys a splendid setting in the heart of the Bernese Oberland, at the foot of three stunning Alpine passes and overlooking beautiful lakeland region. From Planplatten (the second highest peak in the ski area) there are fabulous views to the Jungfrau peaks and Mount Titlis at Engelberg.

THE MOUNTAINS

Meiringen-Hasliberg's 60km/37 miles of slopes are on a broad, sunny mountainside beneath the Glogghüs and Rothorn mountains. They are reached by cable car from the eastern end of town or by bus up to one of the two main gondola stations. Most of the slopes face west to south-west and are partly wooded below 1800m/5,910ft. But there are no runs down to Meiringen itself.

Slopes The slopes are spread across two main sectors, Reuti and Twing. The cable car up from Meiringen arrives at Reuti, from where two successive eight-seat gondolas serve stations at Bidmi and then Mägisalp.

From Mägisalp, another gondola goes to Planplatten for more challenging slopes, or two successive quads (the lower one is fast) take you to the highest point in the ski area and runs leading to Käserstatt, above Twing. Twing has a six-seat gondola to Käserstatt, where a six-pack serves wide cruising red runs below Hochsträss. There are several draglifts in this area. A slow double chair up from Bidmi also connects the two sectors. There is night skiing at Käserstatt on Fridays.

Fast lifts For an area its size there is a good proportion of fast lifts – mainly gondolas.

Queues The area is generally crowd-free and the gondolas make light work of any peak-time queues.

Terrain parks The terrain park at Mägisalp is well regarded, with big jumps, rails, kickers and a quarter pipe. There's also a boardercross and children's park (see 'Families').

Snow reliability The slopes are quite high and enjoy a good snow record, but they mostly face south to south-west, so the snow can suffer in warm weather. Snowmaking covers the main slope from Häägen to Bidmi and the nursery slopes there. The run from Käserstatt to Bidmi is also covered.

Experts This isn't really a resort for experts; apart from the former World Cup downhill black run from Planplatten, there are few on-piste challenges. But there are some good off-piste opportunities to be explored with a guide, notably long routes towards the Grimsel and Sustens passes and on north-facing slopes between Titlis and Tällistock.

Intermediates It is a good area for intermediates who don't want long runs or high mileage. Most of the pistes are classified red, and Planplatten's slopes offer a fair choice of different descents. In good conditions, it's possible to ski down to Hasliberg Hohfluh on a run leading away from all the lifts. Buses take you back to the gondolas.

Beginners The nursery slopes at Bidmi are gentle and sheltered. There are some good progression runs served by gondolas and by a chair and a draglift – the blue from Mägisalp back to Bidmi is among the trees and has snowmaking.

Snowboarding The area is quite a boarding and new school mecca: the resort has regularly hosted World Cup freestyle and ski cross events. There are good beginner slopes at Bidmi and lots of natural gullies and bowls to be explored with a guide.

Cross-country There are 38km/24 miles of trails in the Haslital. The Gadmen circuit is 15km/9 miles, along a pretty river valley. Part of the loop is floodlit several nights a week.

Mountain restaurants There is a good choice of table- and self-service huts, plus several snack bars. At Planplatten, the Alpentower has spectacular panoramic views (of over 400 peaks, it is claimed) and opens early for a breakfast buffet. There's a splendid terrace and indoor dining, with a wide choice on the menu. The chalet-style Mägisalp has a central

Meiringen

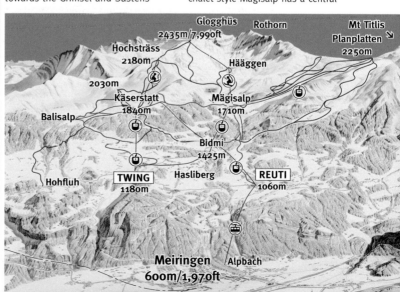

↑ The lift system includes four gondolas, so it's easy for pedestrians to get around the mountain and use the extensive walking trails

BERGBAHNEN MEIRINGEN-HASLIBERG AG

Phone numbers From elsewhere in Switzerland add the prefix 033; from abroad use the prefix +41 33

t 972 5050
info@haslital.ch
www.haslital.ch

location, and the restaurant at Bidmi is a large family-friendly place. Higher up, the cosy Hääggenstubli has traditional home-made dishes and cakes.

Schools and guides As well as private and group lessons, the Swiss school offers heli-skiing and touring specials. Castor mountain guides operate off-piste tours.

Families Meiringen is a good place for families, with comprehensive children's facilities. Ski häsliland at Bidmi is a large area with kids' snow gardens, carousel, special family restaurants and fun areas. The ski school has a kindergarten. And a new children's terrain park has recently opened at Käserstatt, with lots of fun features. The Swiss school takes children from five years old.

STAYING THERE

At present no UK tour operators feature Meiringen. There is a choice of hotels, including one 4-star and several 3-stars; most are central.

Hotels The 3-star Park Hotel du Sauvage (972 1880) is one of the oldest and most elegant in the resort, with pool and sauna. By contrast the 3-star Victoria (972 1040) is a smart, modern place in an art deco style, with a wellness centre. The Sporthotel Sherlock Holmes (972 9889) has a quiet location near the cable car, with a pool, sauna and restaurant. Nearby, the Alpbach (971 1831) is a good-value family choice.

Apartments There are plenty of apartments available in Meiringen.

At altitude You can also stay up the mountain at Hasliberg. There are several hotels at Wasserwendi/Twing and Reuti. The Reuti (917 1832) has simple lodging, with family rooms. And the 3-star Viktoria (972 3072) is handy for the lifts to Bidmi.

Eating out Most of the restaurants are hotel based, but offer a wide range of cuisine. Among the best in town is the restaurant at the hotel Victoria, specialising in French and Asian dishes and with a Michelin entry. There are a couple of pizzerias.

Après-ski Après-ski is quite lively up the mountain. The Aquarium at Käserstatt has a big terrace and regular live music. The Kuhstall at Mägisalp is popular and is home to the 'Muh' spring snow party. In town, nightlife is quiet and relaxed, mostly confined to hotel bars. The Lyon's pub is a sports bar.

Off the slopes Meiringen has plenty of attractions. Pedestrians can get around the ski area easily by riding gondolas, and there are more than 40km/ 25 miles of walking tracks on the Hasliberg plateau and marked on the piste map. You can ride the gondola to the Alpentower, which also has a museum and bar. The snowshoeing is good, as are the two 3km/2 mile toboggan runs. There's a fitness centre, ice rink and indoor pool – and, of course, the Sherlock Holmes museum. Excursions to Interlaken or Lucerne are possible by train.

Mürren

The dinky, car-free mountain village where the British invented downhill ski racing; stupendous views from one epic run

£90
RESORT PRICE INDEX

RATINGS

The mountains

Extent	★
Fast lifts	★★★★
Queues	★★★
Terrain p'ks	★★
Snow	★★★
Expert	★★★
Intermediate	★★★
Beginner	★★
X-country	★
Restaurants	★★
Schools	★★★
Families	★★★

The resort

Charm	★★★★★
Convenience	★★★
Scenery	★★★★★
Eating out	★★
Après-ski	★★
Off-slope	★★★

+ Tiny, charming, traditional village, with 'traffic-free' snowy paths

+ Stupendous scenery, best enjoyed descending from the Schilthorn

+ Good sports centre

+ Good snow high up, even when the rest of the region is suffering

− Extent of local pistes very limited, no matter what your level of expertise

− Lower slopes can be in poor condition

− Quiet, limited nightlife

Mürren is one of our favourite resorts. There may be other mountain villages that are equally pretty, but none of them enjoys views like those from Mürren across the deep valley to the rock faces and glaciers of the Eiger, Mönch and Jungfrau: simply breathtaking. Then there's the Schilthorn run – 1300m/4,270ft vertical with an unrivalled combination of varied terrain and glorious views.

But our visits are normally one-day affairs; holidaymakers, we concede, are likely to want to explore the extensive intermediate slopes of Wengen and Grindelwald, across the valley. And that takes time.

It was in Mürren that the British more or less invented modern skiing. Sir Arnold Lunn organised the first ever slalom race here in 1922. Some 12 years earlier his father, Sir Henry, had persuaded the locals to open the railway in winter so that he could bring the first winter package tour here. Sir Arnold's son Peter has been a regular visitor since he first skied here in November 1916.

THE RESORT

Mürren is set on a shelf high above the valley floor, across from Wengen, and can be reached only by cable car from Stechelberg (via Gimmelwald) or from Lauterbrunnen (via Grütschalp where you change to catch a train). Day visitors can get off the train at Winteregg and access the slopes from there (by new faster lifts for 2009/10 – see 'News') or take the train to the village and walk through it.

Mürren is not the place to go for nightlife, shopping or showing off your latest gear to admiring hordes. It is the place to go if you want tranquillity and stunning views.

To get to Wengen, you go down to Lauterbrunnen and catch the cog railway up. It's a long trek to get to Grindelwald.

VILLAGE CHARM ★★★★★
Picturesque and peaceful
You can't fail to be struck by Mürren's beauty and tranquillity. Paths and narrow lanes weave between little wooden chalets and a handful of bigger hotel buildings – all normally blanketed by snow.

Mürren's traffic-free status is being

somewhat eroded; there are now a few delivery vehicles. But it still isn't plagued by electric carts and taxis in the way that many other traditional 'traffic-free' resorts are.

The views over the valley from Mürren and its slopes are stunning →

KEY FACTS

Resort	1650m
	5,410ft

Jungfrau region	
Altitude	945-2970m
	3,100-9,740ft
Lifts	44
Pistes	213km
	132 miles
Blue	33%
Red	49%
Black	16%
Snowmaking	38%

Mürren-Schilthorn only	
Slopes	1650-2970m
	5,410-9,740ft
Lifts	12
Pistes	53km
	33 miles

CONVENIENCE ★★★
Small enough not to matter
The village is so small that location is not a concern. Nothing is more than a few minutes' walk.

SCENERY ★★★★★
Glorious panorama
The views from the village and from the Schilthorn are magnificent. The grandeur of the Eiger, Mönch and Jungfrau across the valley as you descend the slopes is outstanding.

THE MOUNTAINS

Mürren's slopes aren't extensive (53km/33 miles in total). But it has something for everyone, including a vertical of some 1300m/4,270ft to the village. And those happy to take the time to cross the valley to Wengen-Grindelwald will find plenty of options.

EXTENT OF THE SLOPES ★
Small but interesting
There are three connected areas around the village, reaching no higher than 2145m/7,040ft. The biggest is **Schiltgrat**, served by a fast quad chair behind the cable car station. A funicular goes from the middle of the village to the nursery slope at **Allmendhubel** – from where a run and a fast double chair take you to the slightly higher **Maulerhubel**. Runs go down from here to Winteregg.

Much more interesting are the higher slopes reached by cable car to **Birg**. Below Birg, the Engetal area has the Riggli quad, serving short, shady slopes including a black mogul run. Two chairlifts below this serve some snow-sure intermediate slopes. The final stage of the cable car takes you up to the Schilthorn and its revolving restaurant, made famous by the James Bond film *On Her Majesty's Secret Service*. In good snow you can ski down to Lauterbrunnen – almost 16km/10 miles and 2175m/7,140ft vertical. The Inferno race (see separate box) takes place over this course, snow permitting. Below Winteregg, it's all boring paths.

FAST LIFTS ★★★★
Cable cars galore
Big cable cars are the main access to Mürren's slopes, and chairlifts are gradually being updated – two more high-speed chairs are planned for 2009/10 (see 'News').

QUEUES ★★★
Generally not a problem
Mürren doesn't get as crowded as Wengen and Grindelwald, except on sunny Sundays. There can be queues for the cable cars to Birg and Schilthorn; the top stage has only one cabin, so capacity is limited. And a recent visitor was not impressed with the lift staff's attitude when under pressure.

TERRAIN PARKS ★★
Affirmative
There is a terrain park on the lower slopes of Schiltgrat.

SNOW RELIABILITY ★★★
Good on the upper slopes
The Jungfrau region does not have a good snow record – but Mürren always has the best snow in the area. When Wengen-Grindelwald (and Mürren's lower slopes) have problems, the Schilthorn and Engetal often have packed powder snow because of their height and orientation – north-east to east. The runs from below Engetal to Allmendhubel and parts of the lower slopes have snowmaking.

FOR EXPERTS ★★★
One wonderful piste
The run from the top of the Schilthorn starts with a steep but not terrifying slope, in the past generally mogulled but now more often groomed. It flattens into a schuss to Engetal, below Birg. Then there's a wonderful, wide run with stunning views over the valley to the Eiger, Mönch and Jungfrau. Since the chairlifts were built here, you can play on these upper runs for as long as you like before resuming your descent. Below the lifts you hit the Kanonenrohr (gun barrel). This is a very narrow shelf with solid rock on one side and a steep drop on the other – protected by nets. After an open slope and scrappy zigzag path, you arrive at the 'hog's back' and can descend towards the village on either side of Allmendhubel.

From Schiltgrat a short, serious mogul run – the Kandahar – descends towards the village, but experts are more likely to be interested in the off-piste runs into the Blumental – from here (the north-facing Blumenlucke) and from Birg (the sunnier Tschingelchrachen) – or the more adventurous runs from the Schilthorn.

LIFT PASSES

Jungfrau

Prices in SF

Age	1-day	6-day
under 16	30	151
16 to 19	47	242
20 to 61	59	302
over 62	53	272

Free under 6 (if with parent)

Beginner points card

Notes
Covers Wengen, Mürren and Grindelwald, trains between them and Grindelwald ski-bus; day pass price is for Mürren-Schilthorn area only

Alternative passes
Grindelwald and Wengen only; Mürren only; non-skier pass

SCHOOLS

Swiss
t 855 1247

Classes
5 half-days SF170

Private lessons
SF130 for 2hr for 1-2 persons

Like many Swiss resorts, Mürren has a traditional image, but it is trying to move with the times and offer a more snowboard-friendly attitude – and the major lifts are cable cars and chairlifts. The terrain above Mürren is suitable mainly for good freeriders – it's steep, with a lot of off-piste. Intermediates will find the area tough and limited; nearby Wengen is ideal, and much better for beginners.

FOR INTERMEDIATES ★★★
Limited, but Wengen nearby
Keen piste-bashers will want to make a few trips to the long cruising runs of Wengen-Grindelwald. The best easy cruising run in Mürren is the north-facing blue down to Winteregg. The reds on the other low slopes can get mogulled, and snow conditions can be poor. The runs served by the Riggli chair to Birg normally have good snow, and you can choose your gradient.

Competent, confident intermediates should consider tackling the Schilthorn run if snow conditions are good.

FOR BEGINNERS ★★
Not ideal, but adequate
The nursery slopes at Allmendhubel, at the top of the funicular, are on the steep side. And there are only two or three easy runs to graduate to.

FOR CROSS-COUNTRY ★
Forget it
There's a 12km/7 mile loop along the valley, between Stechelberg and Lauterbrunnen. But snow is unreliable at valley height.

MOUNTAIN RESTAURANTS ★★
Nothing outstanding
Piz Gloria revolves once an hour, displaying a fabulous 360° panorama of peaks and lakes. We don't like the ambience here, but a recent reporter had 'four different meals there – all were amazingly tasty and good value'. Another reporter says, 'It is incredible value for money just for the view,' The Schilthornhütte, by the Engetal chairlifts, is small and rustic and has 'good food and friendly service'. Lower down, the rustic Suppenalp in the Blumental is quietly set, gets no sun in January but is 'cosy with excellent food'. Sonnenberg is sunnier and

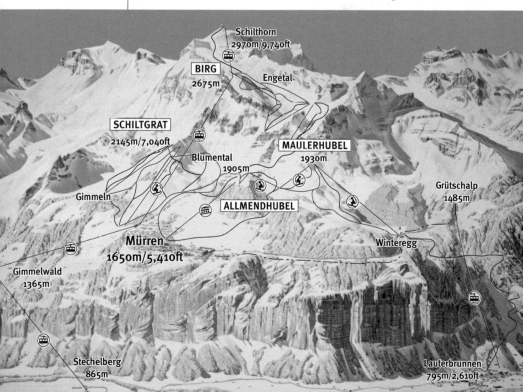

CHILDCARE

Kinder Paradis
t 856 8686
Ages 2 to 8yr; 9.30-
12noon; 1.30-4.30;
SF78 for one day inc.
lunch

Babysitter list
Available from tourist
office

Ski school
Takes age 5 and over
(5 2hr days SF170)

GETTING THERE

Air Zürich 155km/
95 miles (3hr); Bern
65km/40 miles (2hr);
Basel 160km/100
miles (2hr45)

Rail Lauterbrunnen;
transfer by mountain
railway and cable car

UK PACKAGES

Inghams, Kuoni, Made
to Measure, Simply
Alpine, Ski Freshtracks,
Ski Line, Ski Solutions,
Switzerland Travel
Centre
Lauterbrunnen Ski
Miquel

ACTIVITIES

Indoor Alpine Sports
Centre: swimming
pool, sauna, solarium,
steam bath, massage,
fitness room; tennis,
gymnasium, squash,
library, museum

Outdoor Ice rink,
curling, tobogganing,
cleared paths,
snowshoeing

Phone numbers
From elsewhere in
Switzerland add the
prefix 033; from
abroad use the prefix
+41 33

TOURIST OFFICE

t 856 8686
info@muerren.ch
www.wengen-
muerren.ch

readers have enjoyed the food and
speciality coffees. Gimmeln is self-
service with a large terrace, famous for
its apple cake. Winteregg does 'superb
rösti and burgers'. Both have little
playgrounds for kids.

SCHOOLS AND GUIDES ★★★
No recent reports
We lack recent reports. But the school
has a long tradition of teaching Brits.

FOR FAMILIES ★★★
Adequate
There is a nursery slope with a rope
tow. The Kinder Paradis nursery takes
children from two years old and the
ski school from the age of five.

STAYING THERE

A handful of operators offer packages.
Hotels There are fewer than a dozen
hotels, ranging widely in style.
★★★★Eiger (856 5454) Plain-looking
'chalet' blocks next to the station;
widely recommended; good blend of
efficiency and charm; good food; pool.
★★★Alpenruh (856 8800) Attractively
renovated chalet next to the cable car.
'Cuisine is second to none'. Sauna.
★★★Alpin Palace (856 9999) Victorian
pile near the station.
★★★Edelweiss (856 5600) Block-like
but friendly. 'Good wholesome food
and excellent views.'
★★★Jungfrau (856 6464) Perfectly
placed for families, in front of the
baby slope and close to the funicular.
★★Alpenblick (855 1327) Simple, small,
modern chalet near the station.
Apartments There are plenty of chalets
and apartments in the village for
independent travellers to rent.

EATING OUT ★★
Mainly in hotels
The main alternative to hotels is the
rustic Stägerstübli – a bar as well as a

restaurant and popular with locals.
The food at the Eiger hotel is good,
and the Bellevue and Alpenruh have
both received good reports too.

APRES-SKI ★★
Not devoid of life
The tiny Stägerstübli is cosy, and the
place to meet locals. The Alpin
Palace's Ballon bar is an attempt at a
trendy cocktail bar; it also has a
weekend disco, the Inferno. The
Bliemlichäller disco in the Blumental
hotel caters for kids, the Tächi disco in
the Eiger for a more mixed crowd.

OFF THE SLOPES ★★★
Tranquillity but not much else
There isn't a lot to amuse people who
don't hit the slopes apart from the
scenery and a very good sports centre
with an outdoor ice rink. There are
12km/7 miles of prepared winter
walking trails, which a reporter
thoroughly enjoyed. Excursions to Bern
and Interlaken are easy, and you can
readily return to the village to meet
non-skiers for lunch. The only problem
with meeting non-skiers at the top of
the cable car is the expense of it.

Lauterbrunnen
795m/2,610ft
This is a good budget base, with a
resort atmosphere and access to both
Wengen (until late) and Mürren. We've
happily stayed at the 3-star Schützen
(855 3026) and 2-star Oberland (855
1241); rooms at the 3-star Silberhorn
(856 2210) have been renovated, and
it is highly recommended by a regular
visitor ('great five-course dinners'). For
more of a pub atmosphere, he
recommends the bar in the 'popular'
Horner hotel but it 'only has a telly
and plastic dartboard'. A 2009 visitor
found Ski Miquel's chalet hotel Rosa
to be of an 'excellent standard'.

THE INFERNO RACE

*Every January 1,800 amateurs compete in Mürren's spectacular Inferno race.
Conditions permitting, and they usually don't, the race goes from the top of the
Schilthorn right down to Lauterbrunnen – a vertical drop of 2175m/7,140ft and
a distance of almost 16km/10 miles, including a short climb at Maulerhubel.
The racers start individually at 12-second intervals; the fastest finish the course
in around 15 minutes, but anything under half an hour is very respectable. The
race was started by Sir Arnold Lunn in 1928, when he and his friends climbed
up to spend the night in a mountain hut and then raced down in the morning.
For many years the race was organised by the British-run Kandahar Club, and
there is still a strong British presence among the competitors.*

Saas-Fee

Charming, car-free old village set amid spectacular scenery and snow-sure but rather less captivating slopes

£100
RESORT PRICE INDEX

RATINGS

The mountains

Extent	★★
Fast lifts	★★★★
Queues	★★★
Terrain p'ks	★★★★★
Snow	★★★★★
Expert	★★
Intermediate	★★★★
Beginner	★★★★★
X-country	★★★
Restaurants	★★
Schools	★★★★
Families	★★★★

The resort

Charm	★★★★★
Convenience	★★
Scenery	★★★★
Eating out	★★★★
Après-ski	★★★★
Off-slope	★★★★

NEWS

For 2008/09 snowmaking was increased around Spielboden. New rails were installed at the terrain park and a new terrain park was built at Saas Grund.

SAAS-FEE TOURISMUS

The magnificent glacier makes a fine backdrop, but it limits both the piste and the off-piste skiing ↓

+ Spectacular setting amid high peaks and glaciers

+ Traditional, 'traffic-free' village

+ Most of the runs are at exceptionally high altitude and are snow-sure

+ Good off-slope facilities – even a mountain for non-skiing activities

− Disappointingly small area of slopes, with mainly easy runs

− Lot of walking needed in village and on mountain, and few chairlifts

− Not much to amuse experts – glacier limits off-piste exploration

− Shady and cold in midwinter

− Bad weather can shut the slopes

Saas-Fee is one of our favourite places – a sort of miniature Zermatt without the conspicuous consumption. And it's not just looks that attract us: good snow is guaranteed, even late in the season. The altitude you spend your day at – between 2500m and 3500m (8,200ft and 11,480ft) – is unrivalled in the Alps.

But we tend to drop in here for a couple of days at a time, so the limited extent of the slopes never becomes a problem; for a week's holiday, it would. Top to bottom there is an impressive 1700m/5,580ft vertical – but there aren't many alternative ways down. Keen, mileage-hungry intermediates should look elsewhere, as should experts (except those prepared to go touring). For the rest, it's a question of priorities and expectations. Over to you.

THE RESORT

Like nearby Zermatt, Saas-Fee is a high-altitude mountain village centred on narrow streets lined by attractive old chalets, and it's free of cars (there are car parks at the resort entrance). But it's not free of electric taxis and delivery vehicles, which several 2009 reporters complained about – 'taxis passing every 30 seconds'; 'some have considerate drivers, but some do not!'; 'my wife was very nearly run over'. And some streets can be treacherous if they are not cleared of snow and ice. In other respects, the two resorts are a long way apart in style.

The worthwhile slopes of Saas-Almagell and Saas-Grund are not far away, and you can buy a lift pass that covers all three resorts and linking buses. Day trips by car/train to Zermatt are also possible (it takes over two hours by public transport), and if you have a six-day lift pass, a day pass for Zermatt costs just SF20.

VILLAGE CHARM ★★★★★
Unpretentious rural idyll

Saas-Fee still feels like a village – with cow sheds still obviously containing cows. It may be chilly in January, but when the spring sun is beating down, it is a beautiful place just to stroll

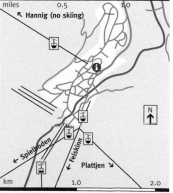

miles 0.5 1.0
↖ Hannig (no skiing)

← Spielboden

Felskinn

Plattjen ↘

km 1.0 2.0

N ↑

around and relax in. The centre has the school and guides office, the church and a few more shops than elsewhere, but it doesn't add up to much. There are some very smart hotels (plus many more modest ones) and good bars and restaurants.

CONVENIENCE ★★☆☆☆
A hike maybe
Depending on where you're staying and which way you want to go up the mountain, you may do more marching through the village than strolling. It's a long walk from one end to the other. Three major lifts start from the southern end of the village, at the foot of the slopes, and lots of the hotels and apartments (particularly cheaper ones) are 1km/0.5 miles or more away. The biggest lift, though – the Alpin Express gondola – starts from a more central location. Your hotel may run a courtesy taxi; regular taxis are not cheap – but the little public buses and the electric road-train are free. You can store kit near the lifts, which helps.

SCENERY ★★★★☆
The Pearl of the Alps
Saas-Fee has stunning views up to a ring of 4000-metre peaks – on a sunny

day the restaurant terraces by the nursery slopes at the south end of the village are a magnet. Sitting here, you can begin to see why the village is called 'The Pearl of the Alps'.

THE MOUNTAINS

The upper slopes are largely gentle, while the lower mountain, below the glacier, is steeper and rockier, needing good snow-cover. There is very little shelter in bad weather: during and after heavy snowfalls you may find yourself limited to the nursery area.

Readers have complained about the walks and climbs at high altitude involved in getting between certain lifts. Take it easy when climbing out of the top lift station: some people feel faint because of the thin air.

Readers also complain of a poor piste map and slope classification.

Saas-Fee is one of the leading resorts for mountaineering and ski touring, and the extended Haute Route from Chamonix via Zermatt ends here.

EXTENT OF THE SLOPES ★★☆☆☆
A glacier runs through it
There are two routes up to the main **Felskinn** area. The 30-person Alpin

SWITZERLAND

528

KEY FACTS		
Resort		1800m
		5,910ft
Slopes	1800-3500m	
		5,910-11,480ft
Lifts		22
Pistes		100km
		62 miles
Blue		25%
Red		50%
Black		25%
Snowmaking		18%

ALLALIN
3500m/11,480ft

GLACIER

Egginerjoch
3100m

FELSKINN
3000m

Britanniahütte
3030m

LÄNGFLUH
2870m

Spielboden
2450m

Morenia
2550m/8,370ft

PLATTJEN
2570m

HANNIG
2340m

Saas-Almagell
1675m

Saas-Fee
1800m/5,910ft

Saas-Grund
1560m

Saas-Fee has backed snowboarding from its inception and provides year-round riding at more affordable prices than neighbouring Zermatt. The terrain suits intermediates and beginners best; there's little to satisfy experts and the glacier limits freeriding. The main access lifts are gondolas, cable cars and a funicular, but nearly all the rest are T-bars. The high altitude and the glacier mean the resort is a favourite for early-season and summer riding (the British Olympic half-pipe team uses Saas-Fee for off-season training). Carvers will find wide, well-groomed pistes to shred down. Half-pipe enthusiasts will love the perfect pipe next to the good terrain park at Morenia. The Popcorn bar and shop is the favourite spot for après-snowboard beers.

Saas-Fee

Prices in SF

Age	1-day	6-day
under 16	36	182
17 to 18	55	280
19 to 64	65	329
over 65	59	299

Free under 10

Beginner pass for village lifts only

Notes

Covers lifts in Saas-Fee only; single and return tickets available on most main lifts; also afternoon passes and family reductions

Alternative passes

Whole valley pass; separate passes for each of the other Saastal ski areas (Saas-Grund, Saas-Almagell, Saas-Balen); non-skier single fares

Express gondola, starting across the river from the main village, takes you to Felskinn via a mid-station at Morenia. The alternative is a short drag across the nursery slope at the south end of the village, and then the recently upgraded Felskinn cable car. From Felskinn, the Metro Alpin underground funicular hurtles up to **Allalin**. From below here, two draglifts access the high point of the area.

Also from the south end of the village, a gondola leaves for Spielboden. This is met by a cable car that takes you up to **Längfluh**.

Between Felskinn and Längfluh is an off-limits glacier area. A very long draglift from Längfluh takes you to a point where you can get down to the Felskinn area. These two sectors are served mainly by draglifts, and you can get down to the village from both.

Another gondola from the south end of the village goes up to Saas-Fee's smallest area, **Plattjen**.

FAST LIFTS ★★★★
Too many T-bars
The area is a strange mixture of powerful fast lifts (which explain the 4-star rating) and a lot of old-fashioned T-bars; there are only two chairlifts, and a 2009 reporter complains of having to stand a lot ('we felt knackered by the time we got to the top'). Blame the glaciers, on which it's tricky to build chairlifts.

QUEUES ★★★
Gradual improvement?
There are signs that Saas-Fee is at last getting on top of its queuing problems. The Felskinn cable car, which regularly produced long queues, has been upgraded and Morenia has a six-pack at mid-mountain. Even so, there may be irritating queues up at Längfluh and for the draglifts at the top of the mountain. Crowded pistes

can be a problem below Morenia at the end of the day, and when bad weather closes lifts higher up.

TERRAIN PARKS ★★★★★
Well developed
The 42 Crew (www.42crew.ch) are renowned for building great parks and maintaining them all year round. While the slopes may not provide the biggest challenge for advanced riders, the big Morenia park has a plethora of kickers, rails and boxes, and a truly world-class half-pipe that will challenge anyone on a board. In 2008/09 the park gained some nice new wide rails, as well as a new shaping machine to increase the size of the half-pipe walls. Shapers are constantly changing the rail and box lines to keep the park creative as well as adding interesting obstacles like a gondola roof jib. There is now also a dedicated female kicker line. Beginners may be best off starting out in the snow-skate park in Stafelwald, near the nursery slopes. You'll find plenty of entry level jumps and rails here. In summer, a park is built on the glacier and you will often see pro riders honing their skills. The park gets good snow coverage even throughout July and August.

SNOW RELIABILITY ★★★★★
Good at the highest altitudes
Most of Saas-Fee's slopes face north and many are above 2500m/8,200ft, making this one of the most reliable resorts for snow in the Alps. The glacier is open most of the year. Lower down, on the runs back to the resort, snow quality and cover can be much more patchy. There has been a big investment in snow-guns, and more were installed up to the Spielboden cable car for last season; but reports say they aren't used enough. Grooming has been criticised too.

Saas-Fee

529

Interactive resort shortlist builder at **www.wtss.co.uk**

↑ The cute village still has a rustic feel in places, with lots of little barns and cow sheds around

SAAS-FEE TOURISMUS

SCHOOLS

Swiss
t 957 2348

Eskimos
t 957 4904

Classes
5 3hr days SF188

Private lessons
SF70 for 1hr

CHILDCARE

Kindergarten Ferien-Kinderparadies
t 957 4057
Ages 18mnth to 6yr;
9am to 5pm

Swiss
t 957 2348
From age 3; 9.45 to
3.30 (half skiing, half
activities)

Ski school
From age 5 (5 days
SF188)

FOR EXPERTS ★★☆☆☆
Not a lot to keep your interest
There is not much steep stuff, except on the bottom half of the mountain where the snow is less likely to be good (a short black run from Felskinn is the high-altitude exception). The slopes around the top of Längfluh often provide good powder, there are usually moguls above Spielboden and the trees on Plattjen are worth exploring. The glacier puts limits on the local off-piste even with a guide – crevasse danger is extreme. But there are extensive touring possibilities.

FOR INTERMEDIATES ★★★★☆
Great for gentle cruising
For early intermediates and those not looking for much of a challenge, Saas-Fee is ideal. For long cruises, head for Allalin. The top of the mountain, down as far as Längfluh in one direction and Morenia in the other, is ideal, with gentle blues, slightly steeper reds and usually excellent snow. For more of a challenge, head across to Längfluh. The 1700m/5,580ft vertical descents from Allalin to the village are great tests of stamina – or, if you choose, an enjoyable long cruise with plenty of view stops. The lower runs have steepish, tricky sections and can have poor snow – timid intermediates might prefer to take a lift down from mid-mountain. Plattjen has a variety of runs, all of them fine for ambitious intermediates, and often under-used.

FOR BEGINNERS ★★☆★★
A great place to start
There's a good, large, out-of-the-way nursery area at the edge of the village, as snow-sure as any you will find. Those ready to progress can head for the gentle blues on Felskinn just above Morenia – it's best to return by the Alpin Express (the blue runs below here are narrow and often crowded). There are also gentle blues right at the top of the mountain, from where you can head down without difficulty to Längfluh. Again, use the lifts to return to base. A useful beginners' pass covers all the short village lifts.

FOR CROSS-COUNTRY ★★★☆☆
Good local trail and lots nearby
There is a nice short (6km/4 mile) trail at the edge of the village and 26km/16 miles down in the Saas valley.

MOUNTAIN RESTAURANTS ★★☆☆☆
Disappointing
The restaurants at the main lift stations are functional; at least the table-service place at Allalin gives changing views – see separate box. **Editors' choice** If you're up for a trek (about 15 minutes each way) the Britanniahütte (957 2288) is special, not because of the food, which is understandably simple, but because of the setting: it's a real climbing refuge, with atmosphere and great views. **Worth knowing about** The best places are slightly off the beaten track: the Berghaus Plattjen (just down from Plattjen) and the 'fabulous', cosy Gletschergrotte, halfway down from Spielboden (watch for the arrow and sign on the left of the piste). The Gletscherwelt at Längfluh has a great view of the glacier and its crevasses from its large terrace.

SCHOOLS AND GUIDES ★★★★☆
Good reports
It's a choice between the Swiss school and Eskimos. Recent visitors said of

WORLD'S HIGHEST REVOLVING LUNCH?

If you fancy 360° views during lunch, head up to the world's highest revolving restaurant at Allalin, where you can get a different vista with starters, mains and pud. Only the bit of floor with the tables on it revolves; the stairs stay put (along with the windows – watch your gloves). The other two revolving cafes in the Alps are also in Switzerland – at Mürren and Leysin – and we rate the views there better. But it's an amusing novelty that most visitors enjoy; lunch is OK too, but a 2009 reporter said that service was 'slow' by 'staff who didn't seem to care'. To reserve a table next to the windows phone 957 1771.

GETTING THERE

Air Sion 75km/
45 miles (1hr45);
Geneva 225km/
140 miles (3hr30);
Zürich 250km/
155 miles (4hr);
Milan 200km/
125 miles (3hr30)

Rail Brig (38km/
24 miles) or Visp;
regular buses from
station

UK PACKAGES

Alpine Answers, Alpine Life, Crystal, Crystal Finest, Erna Low, Esprit, Family Ski Company, Independent Ski Links, Inghams, Interactive Resorts, Interhome, Kuoni, Made to Measure, Momentum, Neilson, Oxford Ski Co, Ski Activity, Ski Expectations, Ski Independence, Ski Line, Ski Safari, Ski Solutions, Ski Total, Skitracer, Snow Finders, Switzerland Travel Centre, Thomson

ACTIVITIES

Indoor Bielen leisure centre (swimming, hot tub, steam bath, whirlpool, solarium, sauna, aerobics, massage, tennis, badminton, gym, bodyforming, aquafitness), museums

Outdoor 30km/
19 miles of cleared paths, ice rink (skating, curling, snow bowling), tobogganing, ice climbing, snowshoeing

Phone numbers
From elsewhere in Switzerland add the prefix 027; from abroad use the prefix +41 27

TOURIST OFFICE

t 958 1858
to@saas-fee.ch
www.saas-fee.ch

the Swiss school: 'a great success for our seven year old' and 'one instructor offered to help me when I looked intimidated on a steep piste, even though I wasn't in a lesson'. Eskimos gets rave reviews: 'well organised' and 'the best instructor ever'.

FOR FAMILIES ★★★★
Seems adequate
The kids' fun park proved a 'great introduction' for one toddler. Several hotels have an in-house kindergarten. There's a day care centre for children from six months to six years and there's also a babysitting service.

STAYING THERE

Quite a few UK tour operators sell holidays to Saas-Fee. But there are surprisingly few chalet holidays, though a 2009 visitor sings the praises of Alpine Life's luxury chalet.
Hotels There are over 50.
★★★★Schweizerhof (958 7575) Stylish, in quiet position above the centre. 'Fantastic food, friendly, excellent kindergarten, wonderful service.' Extensive spa facilities.
★★★★Beau-Site (958 1560) Central position. Good food. Pool. Recommended by a reporter.
★★★★Flaire & Golfhotel Saaserhof (958 9898) Good location near lifts. 'Outstanding – excellent service and food,' says a 2009 reporter.
★★★Bristol (958 1212) 'A quiet, quality hotel; beside the nursery slopes,' says a recent visitor. Highly recommended.
★★★Christiania (957 3166) Good value, central hotel, approved by readers in the past.
★★★Alphubel (958 6363) At the wrong end of town. Family-friendly, with a recommended nursery.
★★★Waldesruh (958 6464) Recommended for its location close to the Alpin Express.
★★★Astoria (958 5500) Very handy for the Alpin Express. Hot tub and sauna.
★★★Jägerhof (957 1310) At foot of slopes. 'Service simply phenomenal.'
★★★Europa (958 9600) Near the Hannig gondola. Recommended for 'exemplary' food. Wellness facilities.
★★Belmont (958 1640) The most appealing of the hotels looking directly on to the nursery slopes.
Fletschhorn (957 2131) Not part of the Swiss star rating system, but distinctly upmarket, elegant chalet in the woods. Original art and individual rooms, a

trek from the village and lifts, but fabulous food (Michelin star).
Hohnegg (957 2268) Small rustic alternative to the Fletschhorn, in a similarly remote spot.
Apartments Most apartments featured by UK operators are a long way from the slopes. A recent reporter recommends the 'great and convenient' Perla apartments, near the main gondola.

EATING OUT ★★★★
Good variety
Gastronomes will want to head for the Michelin-starred and expensive Fletschhorn – 'the best meal I've ever had', says a reporter. We like the woody Bodmen, which has great food from a varied menu. We have also enjoyed meals at the hotel Ferienart's Mandarin (Thai restaurant). Don Ciccio's is 'child-friendly' and does 'great pizzas and veal'. Boccalino is also good for pizzas. The rustic Alp-Hitta is worth a try. The Ferme, Arvu Stuba, Zur Mühle, Gorge, Feeloch and the Sport-Hotel's Rôtisserie have all been recommended.

APRES-SKI ★★★★
Excellent and varied
Late afternoon, Nesti's Ski-Bar, Zur Mühle, the Black Bull (with outdoor seating only) and the little snow-bars near the lifts are all pretty lively, especially if the sun's shining. Later on, Nesti's and the Alpen-Pub keep going till 1am. Popcorn is a long-time favourite for many visitors. The Metro-Bar is said to feel like a 19th-century mine shaft. Why-Not is the place for a Guinness and the Happy bar's happy hours are popular. The Living Room in the hotel Dom has 'modern sofas, a giant fountain and is relaxing'. Poison is the place to drink shots and party the night away, while Night-Life disco 'livens up late'.

OFF THE SLOPES ★★★★
A mountain for pedestrians
The whole of the Hannig mountain is dedicated to walking, paragliding and tobogganing. The splendid Bielen leisure centre boasts a 25m/82ft pool, indoor tennis courts and a sunbed area. The museums are interesting – kids can make bread at the bakery one. The Feeblitz toboggan ride beside the Alpin Express is popular. If you like ice caves, don't miss the world's largest at the top of the funicular.

St Moritz

Ignore the stuffy 5-star hotels: you don't need to be rolling in it to enjoy this panoramic high-altitude playground

£125
RESORT PRICE INDEX

RATINGS

The mountains

Extent	★★★★★
Fast lifts	★★★★
Queues	★★★
Terrain p'ks	★★★★
Snow	★★★★
Expert	★★★★
Intermediate	★★★★
Beginner	★★
X-country	★★★★★
Restaurants	★★★
Schools	★★★
Families	★★

The resort

Charm	★★
Convenience	★
Scenery	★★★★
Eating out	★★★★
Après-ski	★★★
Off-slope	★★★★★

532

NEWS

For 2008/09 a new double chair was installed from Rabgiusa to Curtinella on Corvatsch and the top cable car from Murtèl to Corvatsch was upgraded with bigger cabins. Plans to install a fast quad and create new pistes at Diavolezza to improve the link with Lagalb have been delayed.

- ➕ Wonderful panoramic scenery
- ➕ Extensive, mainly intermediate slopes
- ➕ High, and fairly snow-sure
- ➕ Off-slope activities second to none
- ➕ Good mountain restaurants, some with magnificent views

- ➖ A sizeable town, with little traditional Alpine character and some hideous block buildings
- ➖ Several unlinked mountains, and inadequate valley bus service
- ➖ Runs on home mountain all fairly easy and most lacking variety
- ➖ Expensive

St Moritz is Switzerland's definitive 'exclusive' winter resort: glitzy, expensive, fashionable and, above all, the place to be seen – a place for an all-round winter holiday, with an unrivalled array of wacky diversions such as polo, golf and cricket on snow, and countless festivals. It has long been popular with upper-crust Brits, who stay in the top hotels in order to go sledging. Well, OK: in order to descend the world-famous Cresta Run. But, like all such self-consciously smart resorts, it makes a perfectly good destination for anyone.

The town of St Moritz is undeniably an eyesore. But you may find, as we do, that you can ignore the scar, and appreciate the beauty of St Moritz's spectacular setting regardless. This is one of those areas where our progress on the mountain is regularly interrupted by the need to stand and gaze.

THE RESORT

St Moritz is at the heart of the upper Engadin – the remote, high valley of the En, which flows on into the Austrian Tirol as the Inn (as in Innsbruck). The valley bottom is filled by a chain of lakes, one of which separates the two parts of St Moritz. On a steep hillside above the lake, St Moritz Dorf is the fashionable main town. Beside the lake is the more ordinary spa resort, St Moritz Bad. The skiing is in several separate sectors; only one, Corviglia, is reachable directly from the resort; the higher, wider Corvatsch is a bus ride away.

In winter the lake is used for eccentric activities including horse and greyhound racing, show jumping, polo, 'ice golf' and even cricket. The town's clientele is typified by the results of a Cresta Run race we saw on one of our visits. In the top 30 were three lords, a count, an archduke and a baronet. The upper Engadin also makes a superb setting for walking and cross-country skiing, which is very big here; the Engadin Ski Marathon is held every March – over 12,000 take part.

The home slopes are shared with Celerina, down the valley – an attractively rustic alternative base (see the end of this chapter). And there are other options – 'chocolate-box-pretty' Sils Maria, for example, has good access to the big Corvatsch sector of the slopes via Furtschellas.

There are good rail links from Zürich, but it's quicker to drive. A car

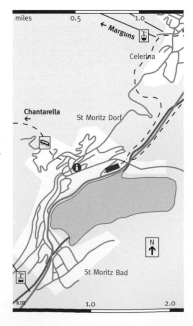

↑ The view from the 'terrace' of Fuorcla Surlej is one of our top three in the world

KEY FACTS

Resort	1770m
	5,810ft
Slopes	1730-3305m
	5,680-10,840ft
Lifts	56
Pistes	350km
	217 miles
Blue	20%
Red	70%
Black	10%
Snowmaking	20%

For Corviglia only

Slopes	1730-3055m
	5,680-10,020ft
Lifts	23
Pistes	100km
	62 miles

is handy, too: the valley bus service (needed for access to the outlying slopes) is free with the lift pass but extremely crowded at peak times. And a car greatly speeds up visits to the more distant mountains. Trips are possible to Davos and other resorts, including Austrian and Italian ones.

The proximity of Italy results in a clear influence – lots of Italian visitors and workers, food and wine

VILLAGE CHARM ★★
Urban glitz instead
In the main resort towns there is little traditional Alpine character; St Moritz is very much a glitzy town rather than a cute village. Dorf has two main streets – lined with boutiques selling Rolex, Cartier, Hermes – a few side lanes and a small main square. Bad is less urban, and less prestigious. Many of the buildings are block-like, and spoil otherwise superb views until you train yourself to look past them.

CONVENIENCE ★
Bad is good – or best, at least
It's a perfectly convenient resort if you are content to ski Corviglia, stay in central Dorf and ride the funicular, or stay on the edge of Bad and use the Signal cable car. But both parts of the resort spread widely away from these lifts, and you will probably want to ski other mountains, for which transport is needed. For keen skiers, Bad is the better base – you can ski back to it from the big Corvatsch sector. If this is all too much for you, the local heli-skiing outfits will drop you at the top of the lifts. It's that kind of place.

SCENERY ★★★★
Fabulous panoramas
The lake-filled valley, with 4000-metre peaks forming the Italian border to the south, provides mesmerising views from Corviglia, and the close-up views of Piz Bernina from Corvatsch are stunning. Should we award 5 stars?

THE MOUNTAINS

There are lots of long, wide, well-groomed runs with varied terrain – practically all on open slopes above the trees. The 350km/217 miles of pistes are in three separate areas, covered on three very clear piste maps; our maps show only the two main areas close to St Moritz. Pistes are numbered on the map, but not on the ground. Ingenious, eh?

EXTENT OF THE SLOPES ★★★★★
Big but broken up
From St Moritz Dorf a two-stage railway goes up to **Corviglia**, a lift junction at the eastern end of a sunny and rather monotonous area of slopes facing east and south over the main valley. The peak of Piz Nair, reached from here by cable car, separates these slopes from the less sunny and more varied ones in the wide bowl above **Marguns** – and gives fabulous views across the valley to Piz Bernina. From Corviglia you can (snow permitting) head down easy paths to Dorf and Bad; you'll probably pass through Salastrains – just above Dorf, with nursery slopes, restaurants and two hotels. There is a red run from Marguns to Celerina.

Interactive resort shortlist builder at **www.wtss.co.uk**

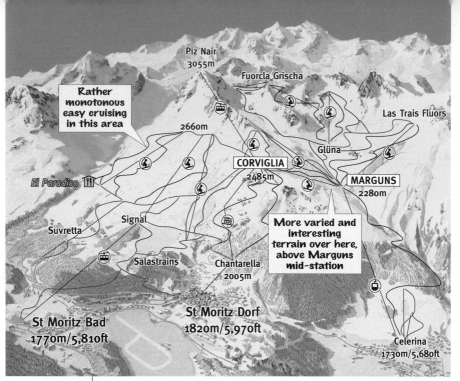

Rather monotonous easy cruising in this area

Piz Nair
3055m

Fuorcla Grischa

Las Trais Fluors

2660m

Glüna

El Paradiso

CORVIGLIA
2485m

MARGUNS
2280m

Suvretta

Signal

More varied and interesting terrain over here, above Marguns mid-station

Salastrains

Chantarella
2005m

St Moritz Dorf
1820m/5,970ft

St Moritz Bad
1770m/5,810ft

Celerina
1730m/5,680ft

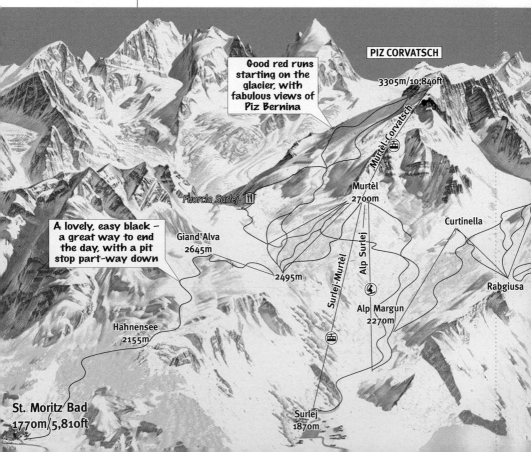

PIZ CORVATSCH

Good red runs starting on the glacier, with fabulous views of Piz Bernina

3305m/10,840ft

Murtèl-Corvatsch

Fuorcla Surlej

Murtèl
2700m

Curtinella

A lovely, easy black – a great way to end the day, with a pit stop part-way down

Giand'Alva
2645m

Surlej-Murtèl

Alp Surlej

Rabgiusa

2495m

Hahnensee
2155m

Alp Margun
2270m

St. Moritz Bad
1770m/5,810ft

Surlej
1870m

Upper Engadine

Prices in SF

Age	1-day	6-day
under 13	23	118
13 to 17	46	233
Over 18	69	348

Free under 6
Senior no deals
Beginner no deals

Notes
Covers all lifts in Corviglia, Corvatsch, Diavolezza-Lagalb and Zuoz, and includes the Engadine bus services and certain stretches of the Rhätische Bahn railway; 1-day price is for Corviglia only

Alternative passes
Half-day and day passes for individual areas within Upper Engadine

boarding

The terrain in St Moritz is boarder-friendly and there's a special boarder's booklet with a lot of good information. Freeride tours are available through the ski schools and the best freeride terrain is on Diavolezza and Corvatsch, but there are several draglifts on Corvatsch. Apart from those, most of St Moritz's lifts are chairs, gondolas, cable cars and trains; beginners will enjoy the rolling blue runs, and intermediates will relish the red runs. The great thing for freeriders is that most people tend to stay on-piste in this resort, leaving terrain untracked for days after a snowfall. There's a very good and varied park on Corviglia that is open late for great sunset sessions. Playground in Paradise is a specialist board shop.

From Surlej, a few miles from St Moritz, a two-stage cable car takes you to the north-facing slopes of **Corvatsch**, which reach glacial heights. From the mid-station at Murtèl you have a choice of reds to Stüvetta Giand'Alva and Alp Margun. From the latter you can work your way to **Furtschellas**, also reached by cable car from Sils Maria. If you're lucky with the snow, you can end the day with the splendid Hahnensee run, from the northern limit of the Corvatsch lift system at Giand'Alva down to St Moritz Bad – a black-classified run that

is of red difficulty for 95% of its 6km/ 4 mile length. It often opens around noon, when the snow softens. It's a five-minute walk from the end of the run to the cable car to Corviglia.

The third area consists of two peaks on opposite sides of the road to the Bernina pass and Italy, about 20km/12 miles away (a 50-minute bus ride). **Diavolezza** (2980m/9,780ft) has excellent north-facing pistes of 900m/ 2,950ft vertical, down its big 125-person cable car. **Lagalb** (2960m/ 9,710ft) is a smaller area with quite challenging slopes – west-facing, 850m/2,790ft vertical – served by a smaller cable car. From late February these cable cars run until 5pm.

FAST LIFTS ★★★★
Plenty of options
St Moritz has invested heavily in new lifts, especially on Corviglia and Marguns, where there are fast chairs all over the place. The area as a whole has a lot of modest-sized cable cars – both for getting out of the resort and for access to peaks.

QUEUES ★★★
Not much of a problem
Queues for the cable cars are not unknown, and this year we have a high-season report of a one-hour queue to get out of Bad. But reporters have generally had good experiences lately and say that the slopes tend to be quiet early and late in the day.

TERRAIN PARKS ★★★★
Four-year-old playground
The Mellow park on Corviglia is easily reached from Celerina as well as St Moritz. The park was actually designed with female pro skiers and snowboarders and advanced riders in mind and is home to some of the biggest contests for women. There are three lines, the hardest comprising a big 12m/39ft table jump, plus a

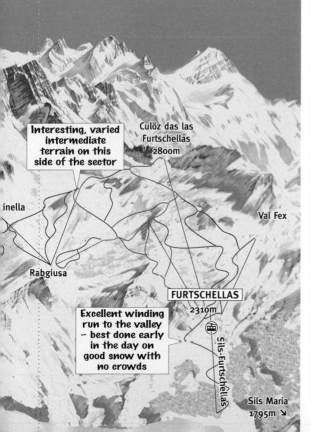

Interesting, varied intermediate terrain on this side of the sector

Culöz das las Furtschellas 2800m

Val Fex

Rabgiusa

inella

Excellent winding run to the valley – best done early in the day on good snow with no crowds

FURTSCHELLAS 2310m

Sils-Furtschellas

Sils Maria 1795m ↘

St Moritz

Interactive resort shortlist builder at www.wtss.co.uk

↑ Just one of the sporting activities they get up to on the frozen lake – most seem to involve horses

brilliant 400m easy line. There are straight, kinked and rainbow rails and boxes of all sizes, and the park has a great relaxed atmosphere to learn in. 2009 saw a roller coaster ramp with three humps built. There are now an impressive 30 obstacles.

SNOW RELIABILITY ★★★★
Improved by good snowmaking
This corner of the Alps has a rather dry climate, but the altitude means that any precipitation is likely to be snowy. The top runs at Corvatsch are glacial and require good snow depths to be safe. There is snowmaking in each sector, and grooming is excellent.

FOR EXPERTS ★★★★
Dispersed challenges
There are few challenges on-piste. The few black runs are scattered about in different sectors, and few are genuine blacks; those at Lagalb and Diavolezza are the most challenging, and include one of the few sizeable mogul-fields – the Minor run down the Lagalb cable car (though it's seriously steep only at the start). But there is good off-piste terrain, and it doesn't get tracked out. There is an excellent north-facing slope immediately above Marguns, for example. There are tough routes from Piz Nair or the Corvatsch summit. More serious expeditions can be undertaken – eg the Roseg valley from Corvatsch.

Out at Diavolezza, a very popular and spectacular off-piste glacier route goes off the back beneath Piz Bernina to Morteratsch. There's a 30-minute plod at first, then it's downhill, with splendid views. It is not difficult, but may take you close to crevasses; we wouldn't do it without a guide – and we are told you can join guided groups on the spot at 1pm. On the

front of the mountain, the Gletscher chair accesses an excellent shady run down Val d'Arlas. And across at Lagalb, a route goes steeply off the back down towards La Rosa.

There are a couple of firms offering heli-drops on Fuorcla Chamuotsch, for runs back to the Engadine valley down Val Suvretta or Valletta dal Guglia.

FOR INTERMEDIATES ★★★★
Good but flattering
St Moritz is great for intermediates. Most pistes on Corviglia are very well groomed, easyish reds that could well have been classified blue – ideal cruising terrain, or monotonous, depending on your requirements. The Marguns bowl is more interesting, including some easy blacks and the pleasant Val Schattain run away from the lifts. The Corvatsch-Furtschellas area is altogether more varied, interesting and challenging, as well as higher and wider. There are excellent red runs in both parts of the area, including descents to the two valley stations – particularly the Furtschellas one; do these in the morning, and return to St Moritz Bad via the lovely Hahnensee run – an easy black. The runs from the Corvatsch top station are genuinely red in parts, with fabulous views of Piz Bernina.

Diavolezza is mostly intermediate stuff, too. There is an easy open slope at the top, served by a fast quad, and a splendid long intermediate run back down under the lift. The link to Lagalb requires use of parts of a black run, but it is of red gradient. There are plans to improve this link. Lagalb has more challenging pistes – basically two good reds and a genuine black.

FOR BEGINNERS ★★
Not ideal
Beginners start up at Salastrains or Corviglia, or slightly out of town at Suvretta. Celerina has good, broad nursery slopes at village level and a child-friendly lift. Ironically, in a resort full of easy red runs, progression from the nursery slopes to longer runs is rather awkward – there are few blue runs without a difficult section.

FOR CROSS-COUNTRY ★★★★★
Excellent
The Engadine is one of the premier regions in the Alps for cross-country, with 180km/112 miles of trails, including floodlit loops, amid splendid

Air Zürich 220km/
135 miles (3hr15);
Friedrichshafen
210km/130 miles
(2hr45); Upper
Engadine airport
5km/3 miles

Rail Mainline station
in resort

SCHOOLS

Swiss
t 830 0101
Suvretta
t 836 6161
Privat
t 852 1885

Classes
(Swiss prices)
6 days SF290
Private lessons
SF100 for 1hr

CHILDCARE

Salastrains
t 830 0101
Run by Swiss school
Schweizerhof hotel
t 837 0707
From age 3; 9.30-
6pm; Mon-Sat; SF45
per day for non-
residents
**Palazzino – in
Badrutt's Palace Hotel**
t 837 1000
Ages 3 to 12; 9am to
7pm; SF50 per day for
non-residents
**Kempi Kids Club – in
Kempinski Hotel**
t 838 3838

Ski school
Ages from 5; 6 days
SF290

SMART LODGINGS

Check out our feature
chapters at the front
of the book.

scenery and with fairly reliable snow.
A reporter recommends the lessons at
the Langlauf Centre near the Hotel
Kempinski. For cross-country, the best
bases are outside St Moritz – Sils or
Silvaplana, suggests one reporter.

MOUNTAIN RESTAURANTS ★★★
Some special places
Mountain restaurants are plentiful, and
include some of the most glamorous
in Europe. Prices can be high, but
standards can be disappointing. We
had the worst rösti in a skiing lifetime
at the otherwise attractive Chamanna.
The piste maps have pictures of the
restaurants, and phone numbers.
Editors' choice El Paradiso (833 4002),
secluded at the extreme southern end
of Corviglia, has it all: breathtaking
views, a tastefully renovated, slightly
trendy interior, great service and top-
notch food. Fuorcla Surlej (842 6303,
though we doubt they'll take a
reservation), on the Fuorcla run from
the Corvatsch glacier, could not be
more different: a remote refuge serving
basic food very slowly. But the view
from the ramshackle terrace is among
our top three in the world.
Worth knowing about On Corviglia, the
top lift station houses several
restaurants run under the umbrella
title of Mathis Food Affairs, including
the famously swanky Marmite. The
Salastrains continues to serve
'magnificent' food. The Chasellas is
also recommended, particularly for
strudel. Lej de la Pêsch, behind Piz
Nair, is a cosy spot, better for a snowy
day than a sunny one. On the
Corvatsch side, the rustic Alpetta has
been recommended. Hahnensee, on
the run of that name to Bad, is a
splendid place to pause in the sun.

SCHOOLS AND GUIDES ★★★
Internal competition
There are two main schools, the St
Moritz and the Suvretta (see 'Hotels').
A reporter received 'excellent'
instruction from the latter. The St
Moritz Experience runs heli-trips, and
some hotels have their own instructors
for private lessons.

FOR FAMILIES ★★
Choose a hotel with a nursery
There's a kindergarten and children's
restaurant at Salastrains, and we'd be
inclined to stay up there if you can
afford it. Some hotel nurseries are
open to non-residents.

STAYING THERE

Packages are available. There is a Club
Med. The tourist office can provide a
list of apartments.
Hotels Over half the hotels are 4-stars
and 5-stars – Switzerland's highest
concentration. We are persuaded by a
reader to list one of the 5-stars; the
others – the all-suite Carlton, the staid
but revamped Kulm, the Gothic
Badrutt's Palace and the newish
Kempinski – leave us cold.
*****Suvretta House (818 363636) The
5-star for skiers, in a secluded location
with its own branch of the lift system.
'Splendid views, magnificent fitness
centre and pool – difficult to fault,
except that jackets and ties required
after 6pm.' That's us ruled out, then.
****Bären (830 8400) Heartily
recommended in 2008. 'More
welcoming than the glitzier places,
top-notch staff and very good food.'
****Schweizerhof (837 0707) 'Relaxed'
hotel in central Dorf, five minutes from
the Corviglia lift. Après-ski hub.
****Monopol (837 0404) Good value
(for St Moritz); in centre of Dorf.
Repeatedly approved by readers. Good
new spa facilities.
***Sonne (833 0363) 'Very
comfortable and generous rooms' In
Bad, not far from the lake.
***Laudinella (836 0000) Innovative
place in Bad, with austere decor; you
can dine enjoyably in any of five
different restaurants. But fitness
facilities are 'disappointing' and the
spa is not free.
***Nolda (833 0575) One of the few
chalet-style buildings, close to the
cable car in Bad.
At altitude Next door to each other at
Salastrains are two chalet-style hotels,
the 3-star Salastrains (833 3867), with
60 comfy beds, and the slightly
simpler and much smaller Chesa
Chantarella (833 3355). Great views,
and no queues.

EATING OUT ★★★★
Mostly chic and expensive
It's easy to spend £50 a head eating
out in St Moritz – without wine. Of
course you can eat more cheaply, and
that often means eating Italian; we
liked the excellent Italian food at the
down-to-earth Cascade in Dorf. The
hotels Laudinella and Sonne, in Bad,
both have wood-fired pizza ovens,
approved of by a reader. We liked the
three smooth, expensive restaurants in

UK PACKAGES

Alpine Answers, Alpine
Weekends, Club Med,
Crystal, Crystal Finest,
Descent International,
Elegant Resorts,
Flexiski, Independent
Ski Links, Inghams,
Interhome, Jeffersons,
Kuoni, Made to
Measure, Momentum,
Oxford Ski Co, Scott
Dunn, Simply Alpine,
Ski Independence, Ski
Line, Ski Safari, Ski
Solutions, Skitracer,
Switzerland Travel
Centre
Celerina Switzerland
Travel Centre
Sils Maria Interhome
Silvaplana Interhome,
Switzerland Travel
Centre

ACTIVITIES

Indoor Swimming
pool, sauna, solarium,
golf range, tennis,
squash, fitness centre,
health spa, casino,
cinema, museums

Outdoor Ice rink,
curling, snowshoeing,
sleigh rides,
tobogganing, sky
diving, hang-gliding,
bobsleigh rides,
Cresta Run,
180km/112 miles
cleared paths, horse
riding, snow kiting

Phone numbers
From elsewhere in
Switzerland add the
prefix 081; from
abroad use the prefix
+41 81

TOURIST OFFICES

St Moritz
t 837 3333
stmoritz
@estm.ch
www.stmoritz.ch

Celerina
t 830 0011
celerina@estm.ch
www.celerina.ch

the Chesa Veglia (an ancient 'rustic'
outpost of Badrutt's hotel) – 'excellent
food, service and ambience', confirms
a 2008 reporter. The two top, world-
class restaurants are fine old houses
out of town: Jöhri's Talvo at Champfèr
and Bumanns Chesa Pirani in La Punt.
We also liked the rustic Landhotel
Meierei, by the lake.

An evening up at Muottas Muragl,
between Celerina and Pontresina,
offers spectacular views, a splendid
sunset and an unpretentious dinner.

APRES-SKI ★★★☆☆
Caters for all ages
There's a big variety of après-skiing
age groups here. The fur coat count is
high – people come to St Moritz to be
seen. At tea time, Hanselmann's offers
'fabulous tea and strudels' though 'the
place is a bit dull'. The Roo bar
outside the hotel Hauser hotel is 'a
comfortable après-ski spot' with a
terrace (blankets for those in need).

Bobby's Pub attracts a young
crowd, as does the loud music of the
Stübli, one of three bars in the 'great'
hotel Schweizerhof ('excellent
cocktails'): the others are the Mulibar,
with a country and western theme and
live music, and the chic Piano Bar. The
Enoteca is said to be the place to
sample 'wonderful wines'. The Cresta,
at the Steffani, is popular with the
British, while the Cava below it is
louder, livelier and younger. We don't
get many reports on the late-night
scene, but the Diamond bar and disco
have been mentioned. The two most
popular discos are Vivai (expensive) at
the Steffani, and King's at Badrutt's
Palace (even more expensive; jackets
and ties required). And if they don't
part you from enough of your cash, try
the casino.

OFF THE SLOPES ★★★★★
Excellent variety of pastimes
Even if you lack the bravado for the
Cresta Run, there is lots to do – a
recent visitor found the only problem
with the resort is there is 'too much to
do'. In midwinter the snow-covered
lake provides a playground for bizarre
events, but in March the lake starts to
thaw. There's an annual 'gourmet
festival', with chefs from all over the
world. The Engadin museum is said to
be 'very interesting'. And the shopping
is simply 'incredible'.

There are extensive well-marked
walking trails which a 2008 reporter
loved (a map is available).

Some hotels run special activities,
such as a curling week. Other options
are hang-gliding and indoor tennis.
Several reporters rave about the views
from the Bernina Express train to Italy,
with 'amazing bends and scenery'. And
a 2008 reporter highly recommends a
trip (90 minutes on the train) to Scual
for the 'fabulous spa with lots of great
facilities; buy the combi pass covering
the train, bus and spa entrance'.
There's a public pool in Pontresina.

Celerina 1730m/5,680ft

At the bottom end of the Cresta Run,
Celerina is an appealing base if you
want a quiet time – it is unpretentious
and villagey, but lacks a central focus
(and has very few shops). It has good
access to Corviglia – a gondola to
Marguns. It is sizeable, with a lot of
second homes, many owned by
Italians (the upper part is known as
Piccolo Milano). There are some
appealing small hotels – reporters like
Chesa Rosatsch (837 0101) – and a
couple of bigger 4-stars. The Inn
Lodge (834 4795) is newish, with
rooms and dormitories for the budget-
conscious. The food at the Chesa
Rosatsch attracts non-resident diners
and is recommended.

THE CRESTA RUN

*No trip to St Moritz is really complete without a visit to the Cresta Run. It's the
last bastion of Britishness (until recently, payment had to be made in sterling)
and male chauvinism (women who want to do the run need an invitation from
a club member).*

*Any adult male can pay around £200 for five rides (helmet and lunch at the
Kulm hotel included). You lie on a toboggan (aptly called a 'skeleton') and
hurtle head-first down a sheet ice gully from St Moritz to Celerina. Watch out
for Shuttlecock corner – that's where most of the accidents happen and the
ambulances ply their trade.*

Val d'Anniviers

Europe's best-kept secret: five charming unspoiled villages beneath high, snow-sure slopes with spectacular scenery

- ➕ Charming unspoiled villages
- ➕ Four contrasting ski areas with good uncrowded intermediate cruising and few queues
- ➕ Excellent extensive off-piste
- ➕ Reliable snow-cover

- ➖ Resorts might be too quiet for some; few shops, limited nightlife
- ➖ Each area has very limited pistes and lots of draglifts
- ➖ Treeless exposed slopes
- ➖ To make the most of all the areas you really need a car

TOP 10 RATINGS

Extent	★★
Fast lifts	★
Queues	★★★★
Snow	★★★★
Expert	★★★★
Intermediate	★★★
Beginner	★★★
Charm	★★★★★
Convenience	★★
Scenery	★★★★

NEWS

For 2009/10 in Zinal the cable car out of the village is due to be upgraded with smart new cabins, increasing capacity and reducing ride time.

At St Luc-Chandolin eight new snow-guns are planned above Chandolin.

Work to improve the lower part of the Piste du Chamois run from Zinal to Grimentz is due to start in 2010. And they plan to start work on a new gondola from the centre of Grimentz into the Zinal slopes in 2011.

Val d'Anniviers is one of Europe's rare 'hidden gems'. If you want to experience resorts as they used to be – ancient, quiet, totally unspoiled mountain villages with small varied ski areas attached – get to Val d'Anniviers now. Keen piste-bashers will find the slopes limited, but they are delightfully uncrowded and have a good snow record. And there is great off-piste to explore with a guide.

When you turn off the Rhône valley road at Sierre and head up the Val d'Anniviers (opposite Crans-Montana) you head into a time warp. It is incredible that the ski resorts in this valley can have remained so amazingly unspoiled when they are so close to big-name resorts such as Verbier, Crans-Montana and Zermatt. The villages all have lots of old wooden houses and barns, narrow paths and lanes and few shops except ski shops and those catering for locals' needs. The whole place has a charming, old-world atmosphere – reporters agree, and most beg us not to publicise it for fear that it will be ruined by an influx of Brits. Our advice is to get there quickly before it has time to catch up with the 21st century. There are signs of that, with a lot of (tasteful and low-rise) new building going on – mainly aimed at providing apartments and chalets for sale as second homes. And more (small) UK tour operators are beginning to move in.

There are four main areas of slopes, only two of which are linked (and then only in one direction, by a long black/itinéraire). If you plan to explore them all, it's best to have a car as the bus links are not that great.

Nearly all the slopes are above the treeline and there's a lot of skiing above 2400m/7,870ft, which usually means good snow conditions. None of the areas is huge in terms of piste mileage. Good skiers will probably cover all Zinal's pistes in a half-day, St Luc-Chandolin's and Grimentz's in a day each. But there is some very good off-piste (especially in Grimentz).

Grimentz has a good beginner area at the top of the gondola and easy runs to progress to ➜

KEY FACTS

Resorts	1340-2000m
	4,400-6,560ft
Slopes	1340-3000m
	4,400-9,840ft
Lifts	45
Pistes	220km
	137 miles
Blue	36%
Red	52%
Black	12%
Snowmaking	11%

UK PACKAGES

St Luc Inntravel, Made to Measure, Ski Safari **Zinal** Interhome, Mountain Tracks, Ski Freedom **Grimentz** Alpine Answers, Erna Low, Mountain Heaven, Mountain Tracks, Simply Alpine, Ski Freshtracks, Ski Safari

St Luc / Chandolin

1650m/5,410ft / 2000m/6,560ft
These are the sunniest of the main ski resort villages and share the biggest ski area. St Luc also has the attraction of a fabulous hotel.

A funicular goes up from the edge of St Luc and a high-speed chair from the edge of Chandolin. Both are served by free ski-buses. The 75km/47 miles of slopes face south and west so get a lot of sun, and we had classic spring skiing on a recent March visit – hard in the morning, softening up by noon. Apart from the one fast quad from Chandolin, there is only one other chair – the other 11 lifts are all drags.

The pistes suit beginners and intermediates best; there are no black runs though there are three short itinéraires and a gnarly freeride area where competitions are held. Most of the reds and blues have a fairly similar pitch whatever the colour – best for those who like easy cruising in the sun. We loved the long red run from the high point of Bella Tola at 3000m/9,840ft away from all the lifts down to the Tipi bar in the valley, where you catch the navette back to

town or the funicular – a great way to end the day. There's a good beginner area and a terrain park near the top of the St Luc funicular. Two good mountain restaurants are the tiny Illhorn above Chandolin and the Bella Tola above St Luc – both with terraces with stunning views.

Both Chandolin and St Luc are fairly spread out. But St Luc has a charming compact centre with a small outdoor après-ski bar. The delightful, well-run, friendly 4-star hotel Bella Tola (475 1444) is just a few strides from here and loved by reporters. We managed to get in for one night only, but loved it too – built in 1859, it has been beautifully renovated by its current owners with a fine spa, great sunny terrace and excellent restaurant.

Zinal 1670m/5,480ft

This small village near the head of the valley has a small area of slopes with stunning views over to a series of high peaks including the Matterhorn.

A cable car (being upgraded for 2009/10) takes you up to Sorebois at 2440m/8,010ft, the hub of the small ski area. Most of the slopes face north or east and keep their snow well, but it can be bleak in poor weather. Zinal is popular with families and there's a good beginner area and children's garden near the top of the cable car.

The runs are mainly short (some only 200m/660ft or 300m/980ft vertical) but include some good reds – our favourites are those from Combe Durand at the edge of the ski area and served by a steepish draglift (there's a freeride area served by this drag too).

The one fast chairlift serves wide and gentle blue runs, ideal for novices. The two short black runs in the main ski area are really of red steepness, but the long black run back to town can be tricky and many people ride the cable car back down. Piste du Chamois is a long black run/itinéraire leading to Grimentz, which reporters rave about ('fabulous, lots of fresh tracks', 'one of the best runs in the Alps'); the lower part is due to be improved (see 'News'). And there's great off-piste in bowls between the pistes in the main ski area. There are only two huts; the Sorebois self-service gets crowded but is good value. Zinal has a handful of hotels, including the central, modern 3-star Europe (475 4404).

Grimentz Location

Beautiful 15th Century village
High varied skiing
Luxury chalets and apartments
Catered option available

+41 27 475 3131
info@grimentz-location.ch
www.grimentz-location.ch

Phone numbers
From elsewhere in Switzerland add the prefix 0848 (for Coeur du Valais) and 027 (for everywhere else); from abroad use the prefix +41 and omit the initial '0'

TOURIST OFFICES

Val d'Anniviers
www.sierre-anniviers.ch

Grimentz
t 475 1493
grimentz@sierre-anniviers.ch
www.grimentz.ch

St Luc
t 475 1412
saint-luc@sierre-anniviers.ch
www.saint-luc.ch

Vercorin
t 455 5855
vercorin@sierre-anniviers.ch
www.vercorin.ch

Zinal
t 475 1370
zinal@sierre-anniviers.ch
www.zinal.ch

Chandolin
t 475 1838
chandolin@sierre-anniviers.ch
www.chandolin.ch

Coeur du Valais
www.coeurduvalais.ch

Grimentz 1570m/5,150ft

Grimentz has a richly deserved reputation for its extensive off-piste. And it has a small area of varied pistes above its very cute old village.
The village is spread out on quite a steep slope and a lot of new building is going on. But the centre is charming – lots of tiny old barns and narrow paths. It's best to stay near there, close to the gondola, which takes you up to Bendolla at 2130m/6,990ft.

There's a good, roped-off beginner area there, and above it are two main sectors. On the right as you look up are easy blue and red runs. On the left are steeper and quieter runs, including two blacks, one of which goes from the top to almost the bottom of the mountain (1300m/4,270ft vertical) and is interestingly varied. The main run to the village is quite steep, but you can ride the gondola down instead.

The real attraction for experts is the extensive off-piste. We did a great run with a guide off the back of Roc d'Orzival: a huge, ski-anywhere bowl that goes on for hundreds of turns before dropping into an area of widely spaced trees and a long run-out.

The International ski school has been 'highly recommended' by a reporter and his three beginner children who have used it more than once. The functional main restaurant near the top of the gondola is mainly self-service, with a small table-service section that serves good food. We enjoyed good pasta at the Orzival by the terrain park, and the rustic Etable

du Marais does 'really good food'.

As the lifts close, Chez Florioz on the piste just above the village is the place for après-ski. We enjoyed an excellent meal at Arlequin (a pizzeria) on our 2009 visit and a recent reporter praised Claire Fontaine (a crêperie) for family eating at reasonable prices. Bar le Country is a lively sports bar.

We stayed at the comfortable 3-star Alpina (476 1616) almost opposite the gondola. A reporter recommended the 2-star Moiry (475 1144).

UK tour operator Mountain Heaven has a catered chalet on the slopes with an outdoor hot tub, sauna and stunning views from the huge lounge. It also has a smart, central self-catered chalet-apartment (Les Vieux Chalets). Grimentz Location has apartments and chalets to rent and for sale.

Vercorin 1340m/4,400ft

The smallest area of slopes and not as easy to get to from the other resorts.
The pretty village of Vercorin, perched on a shelf overlooking the Rhône valley, is reached by a winding road or by a cable car from just outside Sierre. The slopes suit intermediates best.

Sierre 560m/1840ft

Not a ski resort but the hub of the Coeur du Valais region of which the Val d'Anniviers is a part.
This small town is known as the 'city of sunshine' and is the centre of the Valais vineyards; there's a wine-growing marked walk and a museum.

Verbier

Big, chalet-style resort that attracts powder hounds from all over the world – and big-spending night owls from Geneva

£125
RESORT PRICE INDEX

RATINGS

The mountains

Extent	★★★★★
Fast lifts	★★★★
Queues	★★★
Terrain p'ks	★★★
Snow	★★★
Expert	★★★★★
Intermediate	★★★
Beginner	★★
X-country	★
Restaurants	★★★
Schools	★★★★★
Families	★★★

The resort

Charm	★★★
Convenience	★★
Scenery	★★★★
Eating out	★★★★
Après-ski	★★★★★
Off-slope	★★★

KEY FACTS

Resort	1500m
	4,920ft

4 Valleys area

Slopes	1500-3330m
	4,920-10,930ft
Lifts	92
Pistes	412km
	256 miles
Blue	33%
Red	41%
Black	26%
Snowmaking	12%

Verbier, Bruson and Tzoumaz/Savoleyres sectors only (covered by Verbier pass)

Slopes	1500-3025m
	4,920-9,920ft
Lifts	35
Pistes	210km
	130 miles
Blue	44%
Red	23%
Black	33%
Snowmaking	13%

Pros
- Extensive, challenging slopes with a lot of off-piste and long bump runs
- Upper slopes offer a real high-mountain feel plus great views
- Pleasant, animated village in a sunny, panoramic setting
- Lively, varied nightlife
- Much improved lift system, piste grooming and signposting, but...

Cons
- Piste map and piste naming still have a long way to go
- Some overcrowded pistes and areas
- The 4 Valleys network is much less wonderful than it looks on paper
- Sunny lower slopes will always be a problem, even with snowmaking
- Some long walks/rides to lifts
- Expensive bars and restaurants

For serious off-piste routes and for mogul fields, Verbier is one of the world's cult resorts. For vibrant nightlife, too, it is difficult to beat. At first, with its claimed 410km/255 miles of pistes, Verbier also seems to rank alongside the French mega-networks as a dream resort for keen piste skiers who like to ski for a week without doing the same run twice. But if the French 3 Vallées are what floats your boat, you may be sorely disappointed by the Swiss 4 Vallées. The network is an inconveniently sprawling affair, with lots of tedious links.

Verbier's local pistes leave a lot to be desired, too: in comparison with the slopes of somewhere like Courchevel, they are crowded and limited. A good intermediate skier could cover them in a day. (And they are still, we record wearily, unnecessarily difficult to navigate, for reasons explained later.)

This year, for reasons we can't guess, we've had few reports from readers on Verbier. You can put that right after your next visit by going to www.wtss.co.uk.

THE RESORT

Verbier is in an impressive setting on a wide, sunny balcony facing spectacular peaks. It's a fashionable, informal, very lively place that teems with cosmopolitan visitors. Most are younger than visitors to other big Swiss resorts.

The resort is at one end of a long, strung-out series of interconnected slopes, optimistically branded the 4 Valleys and linking Verbier to Nendaz, Veysonnaz, Thyon and other resorts. These other resorts have their own pros and cons. All are much less lively in the evening than Verbier, appreciably cheaper places to stay, and some are more sensible bases for those who plan to stick to pistes rather than venture off-piste – the Veysonnaz-Thyon sector, in particular, is much more intermediate friendly than Verbier. As bases for exploration of the whole 4 Valleys, only tiny Siviez is much of an advance on Verbier. You can also stay down in the valley village of Le Châble, which has a

gondola up to Verbier and on into the slopes. Across the valley, Bruson is more attractive as a place to visit for a day than to stay in. For more on these alternatives, see end of the chapter.

Chamonix and Champéry are within reach by car. But a car can be a bit of a nuisance in Verbier itself. Parking is tightly controlled; your chalet or hotel may not have enough space for all guests' cars, which means a hike from the free parking at the sports centre or paying for garage space.

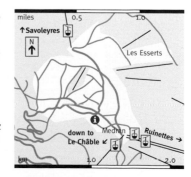

544

VILLAGE CHARM ★★★
Busy upmarket chalet town
The resort is an amorphous sprawl of chalet-style buildings. Most of the shops and hotels (but not chalets) are set around the Place Centrale and along the sloping streets stretching both down the hill and up it to the main lift station at Médran 500m/ 1,640ft away. Much of the nightlife is here, too. These central areas get unpleasantly packed with cars at busy times, especially weekends.

CONVENIENCE ★★
Pick your spot
The Médran lift station is a walkable distance from the Place Centrale, so staying near there has attractions. If nightlife is not a priority, staying somewhere near the upper (north-east) fringes of the village may mean that you can almost ski to your door – and there is a piste linking the upper nursery slopes to the one in the middle of the village. More chalets and apartments are built each year, with many newer properties inconveniently situated along the road to the lift base for the secondary Savoleyres area, about 1.5km/1 mile from Médran. But most people just get used to using the free buses, which run efficiently on several routes until 8pm. Some areas have quite an infrequent service.

SCENERY ★★★★
A circle of Alpine peaks
Verbier is surrounded by stunning Alpine scenery; from the top of Mont Fort there are impressive views to the Mont Blanc massif to the west and the Matterhorn to the east.

THE MOUNTAINS

Essentially this is high-mountain terrain. There are wooded slopes directly above the village, but the runs here are basically just a way home at the end of the day. There is more sheltered skiing in other sectors – particularly above Veysonnaz. The piste signposting has been improved, and the piste map now has some (but not all) runs named – but in type too small to read. What's more, the piste names are still not posted on the mountain. So it's less of a shambles than it was, but still a shambles.

EXTENT OF THE SLOPES ★★★★★
Very spread out
Savoleyres is a small area effectively isolated from the major network, reached by a gondola from the north-west end of the village. This area is underrated and generally underused, and plans to encourage its use by building a new access gondola from the central nursery slopes have now

For 2009/10 the Tortin-Gentianes cable car above Siviez is to get new jumbo cabins, increasing its carrying capacity. More snowmaking is expected for the Médran home runs. And the Vanessa hotel is being refurbished.

But the chondola planned to access Savoleyres from the nursery slopes won't now be built before 2010.

For 2008/09 a short red run was created from the top station of the Chaux chondola to Les Ruinettes, as an easier alternative to the busy Attelas piste. A restaurant opened at Croix-de-Coeur on Savoleyres and an umbrella bar above La Tzoumaz. A tiny bar opened at the Mont Fort top station. The Ruinettes restaurants received a revamp and a new bar, the Rocks. Several new clubs and bars opened in the resort centre.

LIFT PASSES

4 Valleys/Mont-Fort

Prices in SF

Age	1-day	6-day
under 14	33	169
14 to 19	52	270
20 to 64	65	337
over 65	52	270

Free under 6; over 77

Beginner no deals

Notes

Covers all lifts and ski-buses in Verbier, Mont-Fort, Bruson, La Tzoumaz, Nendaz, Veysonnaz and Thyon; part-day passes; family reductions

Alternative passes

Verbier only; La Tzoumaz/Savoleyres only; Bruson only

been delayed, at least until 2010/11. It has open, sunny slopes on the front side, and long, pleasantly wooded, shadier runs on the back. You can take a catwalk across from Savoleyres to the foot of Verbier's main slopes.

These are served by lifts from Médran, at the opposite end of the village. Two gondolas rise to **Les Ruinettes** and then a gondola and chairlift continue on to **Les Attelas**. From Les Attelas a small cable car goes up to Mont-Gelé, for steep off-piste runs only. Heading down instead, you can go back westwards to Les Ruinettes, south to La Chaux or north to Lac des Vaux. From Lac des Vaux chairs go to Les Attelas and to Chassoure, the top of a wide, steep and shady off-piste mogul field going down to **Tortin**, with a gondola back.

You can ski from Les Attelas or ride a chondola from Les Ruinettes to the sunny, easy slopes of La Chaux. At the bottom of these slopes a jumbo cable car goes up to **Col des Gentianes** and the glacier area. The lovely, often quiet, red run back down to La Chaux is one of our favourites. A second, much smaller cable car goes up from Gentianes to the **Mont-Fort** glacier, the high point of the 4 Valleys. From the top, there's only a long, steep black run back down. From Gentianes you can head down on another off-piste route to Tortin; the whole north-facing run from the top to Tortin is almost 1300m/4,270ft vertical. A cable car returns to Col des Gentianes.

Below Tortin is the gateway to the rest of the 4 Valleys, **Siviez**. From here, a ridiculously outdated chair (due for replacement in 2010) goes off into the long, thin **Nendaz** sector (described later in this chapter). A fast quad heads the other way towards **Thyon-Veysonnaz**, via a couple of lifts and a lot of catwalks.

Allow plenty of time to get to and from these remote corners – the taxi-rides home are expensive.

The slopes of **Bruson** are described briefly at the end of this chapter.

FAST LIFTS ★★★★
Locally fine
The main access lifts are gondolas and chairs. Further afield, more upgrades are needed to improve links throughout the 4 Valleys.

QUEUES ★★★
Not the problem they were
Queues have been greatly eased by recent investment in powerful new lifts. The cable cars can still generate delays, but an upgrade to the Tortin-Col des Gentianes lift for 2009/10 should help. Some queues at the main village lift station at Médran can arise if Sunday visitors fill the gondola down at Le Châble, but the crowds shift quickly.

Queues can occur for outdated double chairs and inadequate draglifts in the outlying 4 Valleys resorts. Savoleyres is generally queue-free.

TERRAIN PARKS ★★★
Expert and beginner options
The 1936 Neipark, Verbier's main freestyle area, is at La Chaux. The park has four separate lines they call soft, medium, hard and rail. Maintenance has been questioned, but when in condition there are kickers, gap jumps, step-ups and hips and rails. The rails are varied with boxes and rails of all types and a skate-style pyramid, which is the outstanding feature and gives the park its identity. A giant airbag was set up for 2008/09, with a video screen for watching your performance. There is a chill-out zone with deckchairs, DJs and permanent BBQ – great for avoiding crowded

boarding

Verbier has become synonymous with extreme snowboarding and is generally seen as a freeriders' resort, with powder, cliffs, natural hits and trees all easily accessible. Not surprisingly, this is the best resort on the Freeride world tour (see www.freerideworldtour.com). For years the Bec des Rosses has been home to the most high-profile events of the sort on the calendar. There is a lot of steep and challenging terrain to be explored with a guide, but the pistes and itinéraires will provide most riders with plenty to think about. Chairlifts and gondolas serve the main area, with no drags. Beginners should stick to the lower blue runs and the Savoleyres area, but there are several draglifts there. There is a good terrain park at La Chaux, which improves every year. Advanced riders can find heli-boarding offers at www.lafantastique.com.

restaurants. A day terrain park pass (40 euros) and freestyle coaching (check www.snowschool.ch) are both available. Note that helmets are mandatory. Savoleyres has a smaller park better suited to beginner freestylers. There are two boardercross courses (Le Taillay and La Chaux).

SNOW RELIABILITY ★★★☆☆
Improved snowmaking
The slopes of the Mont-Fort glacier always have good snow. The runs to

Tortin are normally snow-sure, too. But nearly all of this is steep, and much of it is formally off-piste. Most of Verbier's main local slopes face south or west and are below 2500m/8,200ft – so they can be in poor condition at times. Snowmaking covers the whole main run down from Les Attelas to Médran, with more planned above Médran for 2009/10. La Chaux, the nursery slopes and some of the Savoleyres sector are also well-served. At Veysonnaz-Thyon snowmaking now

It's slow work getting to Thyon and Veysonnaz, with a lot of traversing, but there are good cruising runs when you get there

Greppon Blanc
2700m

Classic off-piste run off back of Mont-Fort comes down this deserted valley

TORTIN
2050m

SIVIEZ

Novelli

Tortin

Siviez
1730m

Thyon 2000
2100m

Les Collons

THYON-VEYSONNAZ

Veysonnaz

Piste de l'Ours

Plan-du-Fou
2430m

Plan-du-Fou

Tracouet
2200m

Mayens-de-L'Ours
1470m

Veysonnaz
1300m/4,270ft

Tracouet

NENDAZ

Nendaz has great views over the Rhône valley and short airport transfer times

Nendaz
1365m/4,480ft

1

covers 80% of the area. On our last visit we were very impressed with its use on the runs down to Mayens-de-L'Ours and to Veysonnaz. Piste grooming is good throughout the 4 Valleys, particularly at La Chaux.

FOR EXPERTS ★★★★★
The main attraction
Verbier has some superb tough slopes, many of them off-piste and needing a guide – see separate feature panel. There are few conventional black

pistes; most of the runs that might have this designation are now defined as itinéraires – which means they are 'marked, not maintained, not controlled'. But they are closed if unsafe or if snow-cover is insufficient. We'd like to see them given official black piste status, so you know clearly where you stand. The blacks that do exist are mostly indistinguishable from nearby reds. The front face of Mont-Fort is an exception: a long mogul field, with a choice of gradient from

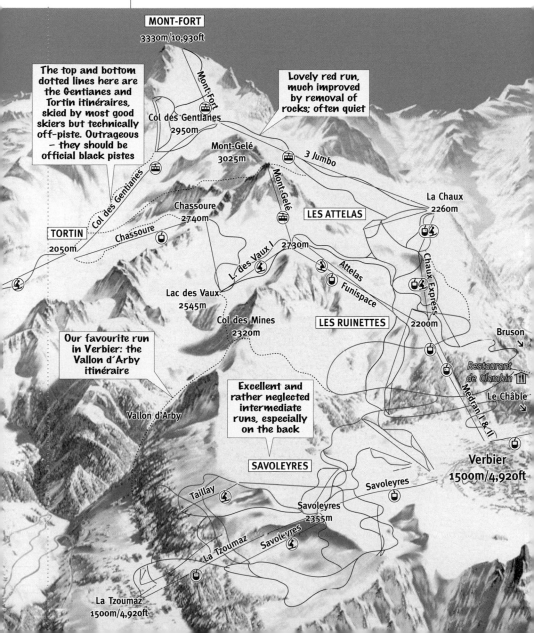

MONT-FORT
3330m/10,930ft

The top and bottom dotted lines here are the Gentianes and Tortin itinéraires, skied by most good skiers but technically off-piste. Outrageous – they should be official black pistes

Col des Gentianes
2950m

Lovely red run, much improved by removal of rocks; often quiet

Mont-Gelé
3025m

3 Jumbo

La Chaux
2260m

Chassoure
2740m

LES ATTELAS

TORTIN
2050m

Chassoure

Col des Gentianes

Mont-Gelé

L. des Vaux I   2730m

Attelas

Funispace

Chaux Express

Lac des Vaux
2545m

Col des Mines
2320m

LES RUINETTES   2200m

Bruson

Our favourite run in Verbier: the Vallon d'Arby itinéraire

Restaurant de Clambin

Le Châble

Excellent and rather neglected intermediate runs, especially on the back

Medran I & II

Vallon d'Arby

Verbier
1500m/4,920ft

SAVOLEYRES

Savoleyres

Taillay

Savoleyres
2355m

La Tzoumaz   Savoleyres

La Tzoumaz
1500m/4,920ft

SCHOOLS

Swiss
t 775 3363

Fantastique
t 771 4141

Adrenaline
t 771 7459

Altitude
t 771 6006

New Generation
t 771 1181 /
+33 479 010318

European Snowsport
t 771 6222

Powder Extreme
t 020 8123 9483 (UK)

Warren Smith Ski Academy
t 01525 374757 (UK)

Classes
(Swiss prices)
5 2½hr days SF240

Private lessons
From SF155 for 2hr
for 1 or 2 people

GUIDES

Bureau des guides
t 775 3363

Olivier Roduit
t 771 5317

steep to intimidatingly steep. The World Cup run (Piste de l'Ours) at Veysonnaz is a steepish, often icy red, ideal for really speeding down when in good nick. The two itinéraires to Tortin are both excellent in their different ways. The one from Chassoure starts with a rocky traverse at the top and is then normally one huge, steep, wide mogul field. The north-facing itinéraire from Gentianes is longer, less steep, but feels much more of an adventure (keep left for quieter and shallower slopes and better snow).

FOR INTERMEDIATES ★★★☆☆
Hit Savoleyres – or Veysonnaz
Many mileage-hungry intermediates find Verbier disappointing. The intermediate slopes in the main area are concentrated between Les Attelas and the village, above and below Les Ruinettes, plus the little bowl at Lac des Vaux and the sunny slopes at La Chaux. This is all excellent and varied intermediate territory, but there isn't much of it – to put it in perspective, this whole area is no bigger than the tiny slopes of Alpbach – and it is used by the bulk of the visitors staying in one of Switzerland's largest resorts. So it is often very crowded, especially the otherwise wonderful sweeping red from Les Attelas to Les Ruinettes and on down to the village. There is excellent easy blue-run skiing at La Chaux, including a 'slow skiing' piste. Getting back from La Chaux to Les Ruinettes is now a lot easier: as well as the chondola, there is a short new piste from the top of the lift avoiding the steepest section down.

Intermediates should exploit the under-used Savoleyres area. This has good intermediate pistes, usually better snow and fewer people (especially on Sundays). It is also a good hill for mixed abilities, with variations of many runs. There is a

blue run linking this sector to Médran but the way down to that link from the top of Savoleyres is not easy.

The Veysonnaz-Thyon and Nendaz sectors are worth exploring (those not willing to take on the itinéraires can ride the lifts down). Some of the reds here might be blacks elsewhere – the one at Combatzeline for example.

FOR BEGINNERS ★★☆☆☆
OK but not ideal
There are sunny nursery slopes close to the middle of the village and at Les Esserts, at the top of it. These are fine provided they have snow, and they are well-equipped with snowmaking. For progression, there are easy blues at La Chaux and the back side of Savoleyres – from both areas you can ride the lifts down. Siviez has a really gentle, wide blue.

FOR CROSS-COUNTRY ★☆☆☆☆
Little on offer
There's a 4km/2.5 mile loop in Verbier, 6km/4 miles at Les Ruinettes-La Chaux and 12km/7 miles down the valley in Champsec and Lourtier.

MOUNTAIN RESTAURANTS ★★★☆☆
Some improvement
The number of huts is gradually increasing, but it remains inadequate for the demand, and overcrowding remains a problem. The standard of food and service is improving.
Editors' choice In the main area, the rustic Restaurant de Clambin (771 2524), on the itinéraire on the southern fringe of the area, is a classic cosy old chalet. It used to be Chez Dany but now has new management.
Worth knowing about For a choice of good spots, Savoleyres is the place to go. Reporters favour the rustic Marmotte and the Namasté. The Sonalon, on the fringe of the village, is 'excellent, with great views', but reached off-piste, as is the nearby Marlenaz ('what a great find, hearty and well recommended').

The self-service at the top of Savoleyres has 'good value' Italian and traditional dishes. A new restaurant/bar opened at Croix de Coeur for 2008/09; the attractive 15-sided building has great views from the terrace but a limited menu. The Poste hotel by the Tzoumaz chair takes some beating for value and lack of crowds.

Back in the main sector, the restaurants at Les Ruinettes have been

Schtroumpfs
t 771 6585
Ages 3mnth to 4yr;
8.30 to 5.30

Kids Club
t 775 3363
From age 3; 8.30-
5pm; 6 days SF495
including lunch

Ski school
Takes children aged 4
to 12 (5 half days
SF225)

smartened up with new terraces and menus – the Cristal table-service upstairs offers fine dining under the former chef of Chalet d'Adrien. The Olympique at Les Attelas is a good table-service restaurant. Au Mayen has 'interesting seafood choices'. Everyone loves the Cabane Mont-Fort – a proper mountain refuge off the run to La Chaux from Col des Gentianes – so it gets packed. Chalet Carlsberg has a good position at La Combe and impressed us with fast and efficient service. The Carrefour by the road near the top of the nursery slopes is 'very, very good' says a reporter who lives locally in winter; further afield, he recommends the Chottes beneath Greppon Blanc ('not cheap but excellent food') and the Cambeuse at Les Collons. A tiny bar has opened at the Mont Fort top station – just for refreshments.

SCHOOLS AND GUIDES ★★★★★
Good reports
There's no shortage of schools to choose between. We were very impressed with our mountain guide from Adrenaline and it has had good reviews for its private lessons. Altitude

was started by top British instructors in 2001 and a 2008 reporter found it 'excellent for children. English instructors guaranteed and only two in their class.' The Swiss school has received a good report for private snowboard lessons. A reporter praised his Swiss instructor with European Snowsport. British instructor Warren Smith runs his Ski Academy here. Powder Extreme specialises in off-piste. We have skied with both Warren Smith and Powder Extreme and thought them both good. New Generation, well established and a reader favourite in several top French resorts, have their first Swiss branch in Verbier.

FOR FAMILIES ★★★☆☆
Wide range of options
The nursery slopes are central, and the Swiss school's facilities are good. The possibility of leaving very young babies at the Schtroumpfs nursery is valuable. A 2008 visitor recommends the nanny services provided by Chalet Services Verbier. There are considerable reductions on the lift pass price for families.

STAYING THERE

Given the size of the place there are surprisingly few apartments and B&Bs available, though those on a budget have inexpensive B&B options in Le Châble. Hotels are expensive for their gradings. If you take a sleeping bag, you can bed down cheaply at the sports centre (The Bunker), with use of the pool.

Chalets Verbier is the chalet-party capital of Switzerland. Lots of companies have properties here. Ski Verbier repeatedly gets good reports from readers and has an extensive and impressive portfolio at the top of the market, including the superb Septième Ciel. Descent now offers the Pierre Avoi, but no longer Chalet Goodwood. Virgin has The Lodge. One of the top hotels, the Rosalp, will be offered as a chalet-hotel by Total this season.

Hotels There is a 5-star, five 4-stars, 10 3-stars and a few simpler places.

*****Chalet d'Adrien (771 6200) Relais & Chateaux. A beautifully furnished low-rise 29-room chalet, with top-notch cooking. In a peaceful setting next to the Savoleyres lift, with great views. Neat spa/gym/pool.

****Nevaï (775 4000) Modern, minimalist, trendy, next to Farm Club (same ownership). New après-ski bar.

****Montpelier (771 6131) Very comfortable, but out of town (free courtesy bus). Pool.

****Vanessa (775 2800) Central, with spacious apartments as well as rooms; being refurbished for 2009/10.

***Rotonde (771 6525) Much cheaper; well positioned between centre and Médran; some budget rooms.

***Poste (771 6681) Midway between centre and Médran; pool. Some rooms small. 'Friendly staff and great food.'

***Farinet (771 6626) Central, British-owned, with a focal après-ski bar.

***Au Vieux Valais (775 3520) Charming old chalet with friendly service at entrance to resort. We stayed there in 2008 and enjoyed it.

Apartments Ski Verbier has some nice looking self-catered places.

EATING OUT ****
Plenty of choice

There is a wide range of restaurants; many are listed in a free pocket guide, which would be much more useful if it gave some clues about price.

The 5-star Chalet d'Adrien is one of the best gourmet places in town (one Michelin star). We had an excellent meal in the Nevaï hotel. King's (under the same ownership) is another of our favourites – innovative food in a stylish, club-like setting. We've also had good meals in the stylish Millénium. The traditional, small Ecurie does 'excellent steaks'. The new Rouge Restaurant and Club has replaced the Mignon as a smart dinner and après-ski venue.

OFF-PISTE FOR ALL

Verbier has some of the best, most extensive and most varied off-piste in the world, and major freeride competitions are held there every year. Here, we pick out just a few of the off-piste runs on offer. See 'For experts' for the status of itinéraires; for the other runs here you should hire a guide.

The Col de Mines and Vallon d'Arby itinéraires, accessible from Lac des Vaux, are relatively easy, though there may be some unnerving moments on the traverse to the point where they split. The first is a long, open slope back to Verbier and the latter a very beautiful run in a steep-sided valley down to La Tzoumaz and the Savoleyres lifts. Further afield, the long Eteygeon itinéraire from Greppon Blanc above Siviez is 'heavenly, and way better than Vallon d'Arby' says a reporter who lives locally; it ends up on the road and you catch a bus back to Les Masses (see end of chapter).

Stairway to Heaven is usually quiet (we were the only people on it on a recent March visit) and its snow is kept in good condition by the lack of crowds and its shady orientation. It starts a short ski, pole and steep climb from Col des Gentianes. Then you drop over the ridge into a deserted valley, and it's a long, relatively easy ski down to Tortin, pretty much parallel to the Gentianes itinéraire.

The Mont-Gelé cable car offers some of the most amazing terrain accessible anywhere by lift, with long runs down to Siviez on steep but open slopes, before a scenic traverse and schuss along the valley. Or go down the opposite side of the mountain through the steep rock face towards Lac de Vaux (not a route for the faint hearted). The many couloirs accessible from Attelas can also be fantastic. There are serious adventures to be had off the back of Mont-Fort – we loved it (except for the long walk out past Lac de Cleuson); it's a vast bowl and we found fresh powder, even though it hadn't snowed for days and there were lots of people dotted around; you end up at Siviez.

For Swiss specialities, try the Relais des Neiges, the Caveau, Au Vieux Verbier by the Médran lifts or Esserts by the nursery slopes. The ever-popular Fer à Cheval does reasonably priced pizza and other simple dishes. Downstairs in the Pub Mont-Fort you can get good value gastropub food. The 'hanging meat' has to be tried at Al Capone's, out near the Savoleyres gondola – also known for its pizzas; we had excellent pizzas at Borsalino, near the centre of town. Harold's Snack internet cafe is a 'reasonable burger joint', and Chez Martin does good pasta.

You can be ferried by snowmobile up to Clambin or the Marmotte for a meal, followed by a torchlit descent.

APRES-SKI ★★★★★
Throbbing but expensive
On the slopes, popular stops include the new Rocks bar at Ruinettes, either of the tents of 1936 or the Chalet Carlsberg (with a pay-as-you-soak hot tub). In town, the Offshore Cafe at Médran is ever-popular for people-watching, milk shakes and cakes. The

Big Ben pub is lively. The Nevaï hotel now has live music on its terraces and the Rouge (formerly Mignon) at the bottom of the golf course has a popular sun deck.

Then if you're young, loud and British, it's on to the Pub Mont-Fort – there's a widescreen TV for live sport. The Nelson and Fer à Cheval are popular with locals. The Farinet has won awards for its après-ski and regularly rocks to live bands ('beer, band and bop were great'). Or you can sip sophisticated cocktails in its lounge bar next door.

After dinner the Pub Mont-Fort is again popular (the shots bar in the cellar is worth a visit). Crok No Name is a cool bar with good live bands or a DJ. King's is a quiet candlelit cellar bar with 60s decor – 'hip crowd, good music'. New Club is a sophisticated piano bar, with comfortable seating and a more discerning clientele. The Farm Club is seriously expensive – on Friday and Saturday packed with rich Swiss paying SF220 for bottles of spirits. You'll find us having a quiet nightcap in the basement Bar'Jo,

ACTIVITIES

Indoor Sports centre (swimming pools, ice rink, curling, squash, sauna, solarium, steam bath, hot tub), cinema, museums, galleries

Outdoor 25km/ 16 miles of cleared walking paths, paragliding, snowshoeing, horse riding, dog sledding, tobogganing, airboarding

across the road.

The Casbah, in the basement of the Farinet hotel, and the Coup d'Etat (formerly Icebox) are nightclubs.

OFF THE SLOPES ★★★
No great attraction
Verbier has an excellent sports centre (with pool, saunas and hot tubs), some nice walks and a big Alpine museum, but otherwise not much to offer if you don't want to hit the slopes. Montreux is an enjoyable train excursion from Le Châble, and Martigny is worth a visit for the Roman remains and art gallery. Reporters have recommended the spa complex at Lavey-les-Bains. Various mountain restaurants are accessible to pedestrians – a walker's pass covers most of the local lifts. Swiss Mountain Spirit offer dog sledding trips. There are well-prepared toboggan runs on Savoleyres – improved for 2008/09.

Nendaz 1365m/4,480ft

THE RESORT
Nendaz is a big, expanding resort with over 17,000 beds, but relatively little known in Britain. It is of course appreciably cheaper than Verbier. Airport transfers are quick, especially from Sion (20 minutes away).
Village charm Most of the resort is modern but built in traditional chalet style, and the original old village of Haute-Nendaz is still there, with its narrow streets, old houses and barns, and baroque chapel dating from 1499. The centre is being revamped to make it more pedestrian-friendly.
Convenience It's a sizeable and

sprawling resort, where life revolves around buses and cars. Although it appears to be centrally set in the 4 Valleys, getting to and from the other sectors is a slow business unless you drive/take a bus to Siviez ('To get into the Verbier skiing takes a decent skier up to an hour,' said a reporter).
Scenery Nendaz enjoys great views across the Rhône valley.

THE MOUNTAIN
Nendaz has its own area of slopes and a link to the rest of the 4 Valleys via Siviez.
Slopes There's a 12-person gondola straight to the top of the local north-facing slopes at Tracouet. Here there are good, snow-sure nursery slopes plus blue and red intermediate runs.

Intermediates can head off down the back of Tracouet to a cable car that takes you to Plan du Fou at 2430m/7,970ft (but this area has no snowmaking and the runs can be closed – as they were on our March 2008 visit). From there you can go down to Siviez, on to a couple of sunny, steeper runs and the links to Verbier one way and Veysonnaz-Thyon the other. To return to Nendaz you have to negotiate an itinéraire from Plan du Fou (or you can take the cable car down), followed by a black run. When poor snow closes the runs mentioned above, you need to drive or catch the regular bus between Nendaz and Siviez.
Fast lifts Access to the local slopes is by gondola, but thereafter you're mainly using draglifts.
Queues There may be queues during peak periods, especially for some old

Alpine Answers, Alpine Weekends, Belvedere Properties, Bramble Ski, Chalet Group, Crystal, Crystal Finest, Descent International, Elegant Resorts, Erna Low, First Choice, Flexiski, Independent Ski Links, Inghams, Interactive Resorts, Interhome, Jeffersons, Made to Measure, Momentum, Mountain Beds, Mountain Tracks, Oxford Ski Co, Peak Ski, Powder White, Simply Alpine, Ski Activity, Ski Expectations, Ski Freedom, Ski Freshtracks, Ski Independence, Ski Line, Ski Solutions, Ski Total, Skitracer, Ski Verbier, Ski Weekend, Skiweekends.com, Ski with Julia, Skiworld, Snoworks, Supertravel, White Roc
Nendaz Alpine Answers, Crystal, First Choice, Interhome, Lagrange, Ski Freshtracks, Ski Independence, Ted Bentley
Siviez Interhome
Veysonnaz Crystal

lifts either side of Plan du Fou
Terrain parks The beginner and advanced terrain parks have kickers, slides and a box.
Snow reliability Nendaz sits on a north-facing shelf so its local slopes don't get the sun that affects Verbier. The main run back to town has snowmaking, as does another blue. But see above for the link with Plan du Fou.
Experts Access to the tough stuff above Tortin is a bit slower from here than from Verbier.
Intermediates The local slopes are quite varied, but not very extensive.
Beginners There are good nursery slopes at Tracouet.
Snowboarding The terrain is fine but there are quite a few draglifts.
Cross-country There are 12km/7.5 miles of cross-country tracks.
Mountain restaurants The Cabane de Balavaux under the Prarion chair is rustic; views on its food are mixed.
Schools and guides There are four ski schools plus mountain guides.
Families The schools have a nursery area at Tracouet and there are two kindergartens.

STAYING THERE
UK chalet company Ted Bentley has four chalets; all have outdoor hot tubs. We loved the chalets Merri (great views over the Rhône valley) and Alice (modern and sleek), especially.
Hotels There are four small hotels. The 3-star Mont-Fort (288 2616) is 150m from the lifts. A new 4-star hotel/spa Mer de Glace is planned for 2010/11.
Apartments There is no shortage of apartments and chalets to rent.
Eating out The Mont Rouge hotel restaurant is said to be 'the best in town, but not cheap'. The Cabane is 'very atmospheric, and serves fondue, raclette etc' (pity!); Au Petit Valais and the Raccard also do local mountain food. Chez Edith, out of town on the way to Siviez is recommended by a local.
Après-ski The Cantina gets packed (outside and in) when the lifts close and is popular with ski instructors, the Malabar is 'a funky wine bar'. Later on 'head for the Canadian, which has a disco and opens till 4am or the Tchin Tchin piano bar for a quieter time'. A 17-year-old reporter recommended the Cactus Saloon as one of the livelier spots.
Off the slopes Nendaz has 100km/

62 miles of walks, an ice rink, fitness centre, climbing wall, squash courts.

Siviez 1730m/5,680ft

Siviez is a small huddle of buildings in an isolated spot, where the slopes of Verbier, Nendaz and Veysonnaz-Thyon meet. One of these buildings is the 3-star hotel de Siviez (288 1623). It is an ideal base from which to explore the whole 4 Valleys lift network. The long and gentle blue run through the sheltered valley from Tortin is ideal beginner territory. Being set a little way down the valley from Tortin, at the foot of the steep itinerary runs from Chassoure and Mont-Fort, means it is also an excellent base for doing the tough skiing of Verbier – you can end the day with a descent of 1600m/5,250ft vertical from Mont-Fort; no noise in the evenings; perfect.

Veysonnaz 1300m/4,270ft

Veysonnaz is a small, quiet, family resort, sunny in the afternoon, at the foot of an excellent, long red slope from the ridge above Thyon. A second excellent (though often icy) red regularly used for international races descends to the isolated lift base of Mayens de l'Ours.

The resort is spread widely across and down the hillside, with wide views across the Rhone valley. Taking a car means you can drive to Siviez for quick access to the Verbier or Nendaz slopes, and the resort is only 15km/9 miles from the old town of Sion, at the heart of the Coeur du Valais region of which Veysonnaz is a part and well worth exploring. The link up to Thyon is an eight-seat gondola, but progress towards Verbier is a slow business.

The original attractive old village, complete with church, is two hairpin bends below Veysonnaz Station, the lift base and the main focus of the place for the visitor. This has the essential facilities – half a dozen bars and cafes, four restaurants, a disco or two and a 'good' wellness centre with swimming pool and spa facilities. There are adequate shops.

Accommodation is mainly in apartments – substantial chalet-style buildings dotted along the road across the hillside from the lift base. There are plenty of smaller chalets, too. There are two 3-star hotels, the 'very comfortable' Chalet Royal (208 5644)

Interactive resort shortlist builder at **www.wtss.co.uk**

NEWS

At Thyon-Les Collons, a fast quad replaced the ancient Etherolla double chair.

Phone numbers
From elsewhere in Switzerland add the prefix 027; from abroad use the prefix +41 27

TOURIST OFFICES

Verbier
t 775 3888
info@verbier.ch
www.verbier.ch

Nendaz
t 289 5589
info@nendaz.ch
www.nendaz.ch

Siviez
www.siviez-nendaz.ch

Veysonnaz
t 207 1053
tourism
@veysonnaz.ch
www.veysonnaz.ch

Thyon 2000 /
Les Collons
t 281 2727
thyon-region
@coeurduvalais.ch
www.thyon-region.ch

Le Châble and Bruson
bagnestourisme
@verbier.ch

and the Magrappé, which is the focus of lively après-ski. There are some B&Bs.

The Swiss ski school has a branch, and its literature is in English as well as French and German. There is a 5km/3 mile cross-country trail along the mountainside, with grand views.

Thyon 2000 2100m/6,890ft

Thyon 2000 – also part of the Coeur du Valais region – is a functional, purpose-built collection of plain, medium-rise apartment blocks just above the treeline at the hub of the Thyon-Veysonnaz sector of the 4 Valleys. It has the basics of resort life – supermarket, newsagent, a couple of bar-restaurants, an indoor pool, a disco. A free shuttle-bus runs to Les Collons. There's a fair-sized terrain park with snowmaking – reputedly one of Switzerland's first – and boardercross, 'good' children's snow-garden and a kindergarten as well as a ski school. The slopes are ideal for families and beginners, with two nursery lifts close to the accommodation. The lift network shared with Les Collons and Les Masses is elderly and slow, so the fast quad that replaced the Etherolla chair for 2008/09 was a welcome addition. Snowmaking is extensive.

Les Collons 1800m/5,910ft

Some 300m/980ft below Thyon, at the foot of a broad, east-facing slope, Les Collons is a couple of strings of chalet-style buildings spread along two roads following the hillside, 50m/160ft vertical apart; a lot of building has been going on here recently. Most accommodation is in apartments, but there are also a couple of modest hotels – including the 3-star Cambuse (281 1883) just below one of the lift bases. There's a wider range of bars, restaurants and other diversions than in Thyon. There is a 1km/0.5 mile toboggan run through the woods above the village. Prepared walking trails add up to a modest 7km/4 miles. Three draglifts go up towards Thyon from the upper level of the resort, and a chairlift from the lower level takes you above Thyon. There's 6km/4 miles of cross-country. A free shuttle-bus runs to Thyon.

Les Masses 1515m/4,970ft

Half-a-dozen hairpins down the mountainside from Les Collons, Les Masses is no more than a hamlet at the base of the double chairlifts that form the southern limit of the Thyon-Veysonnaz slopes. The home run is a red. Accommodation is in apartments. There is a grocery and a restaurant.

Le Châble 820m/2,690ft

Le Châble is a busy roadside village in the valley, at the bottom of the hairpin road up to Verbier. It is linked to Verbier by a queue-free gondola that goes on (without changing cabins) to Les Ruinettes, which means access to the slopes can be just as quick as from Verbier. Buses run late too. Le Châble is on the rail network, and is also convenient for drivers who want to visit other resorts in the Valais or further afield. And it is handy for Bruson. There are several modest hotels, of which the 2-star Giétroz (776 1184) is the pick. The Tzana restaurant is 'well presented; good meat, very good wines'.

Bruson 1000m/3,280ft

Bruson is a small village on a shelf just above Le Châble, across the valley from Verbier, and reached by a short free bus ride. Its lifts are covered by the Verbier pass. From the village a slow chair goes up over gentle east-facing slopes dotted with chalets to Bruson les Forêts (1600m/5,250ft).

The open slopes above Bruson les Forêts are served by a quad chair up to the ridge, on the far side of which is a short draglift serving a tight little bowl. In addition to the intermediate pistes served by these lifts there are large areas of underused off-piste terrain, notably through woods on the front side accessed by the drag on the back. The off-piste down the back towards Orsières is good; you return by train. For years there have been plans to develop Bruson – building lifts from Le Châble and Orsières, and extending the lift network. For now, it remains a great place to escape Verbier crowds: 'worth going for a day out – we had excellent powder', says a recent visitor.

Villars

Traditional year-round resort with local low-altitude slopes, a cog railway and a much needed but far-flung glacier

£95
RESORT PRICE INDEX

- ➕ Pleasant, year-round resort
- ➕ Fairly extensive intermediate slopes
- ➕ Good nursery slopes
- ➕ Close to Geneva airport

- ➖ Unreliable snow-cover
- ➖ Short runs on the upper slopes
- ➖ Access lifts from village not ideal
- ➖ Not much to amuse experts

TOP 10 RATINGS

Extent	★★★
Fast lifts	★★
Queues	★★★
Snow	★★
Expert	★★
Intermediate	★★★
Beginner	★★★★
Charm	★★★
Convenience	★★
Scenery	★★★

NEWS

There are plans for a fast lift to replace the Petit Chamossaire double chair and for a new family fun zone – hopefully this will be for 2009/10.

The 5-star hotel Chalet Royalp opened in December 2008.

Villars is popular with second-home owners because of its closeness to Geneva airport. For many keen skiers, its low altitude and far from snow-sure slopes will rule it out. But for a varied family holiday it is worth considering.

THE RESORT

Villars sits on a sunny shelf, looking across the Rhône valley to the Portes du Soleil. Its home slopes link to those of Les Chaux, above the delightfully rustic village of Gryon. You can get a whole area pass covering Les Diablerets (linked by lifts and pistes) and Glacier 3000, plus Leysin and Les Mosses, both of which are easy outings by rail or road. Getting to and from the glacier is a long, slow business though – buses between it and Les Diablerets are infrequent (and it's a 10-minute walk across Les Diablerets to the Isenau area, from which you can ski to the glacier lift). Outings to Verbier are easily possible.

Village charm Villars is more like a town than a village, with sprawling suburbs of smart chalets and several international schools. The focus is a longish, traffic-filled but pleasant high street lined with a variety of shops.

Convenience A slow cog railway goes from the main street up to the slopes around Bretaye. A gondola at the other end of town is quicker. It's best to stay near to one of these or at a hotel with its own shuttle-bus, since ski-buses can be infrequent and crowded.

Scenery The scenery is more dramatic than you might expect.

555

(Map of the ski area showing:)

- Floriettez 2120m/6,96oft
- Gstaad Reusch
- Cabane 2525m
- Sex Rouge 2970m/9,740ft
- Iseneau 1760m
- GLACIER 3000
- Col du Pillon 1545m
- Vers L'Eglise
- MEILLERET 1950m
- Croix des Chaux 2020m/6,63oft
- Petit Chamossaire
- Laouissalet
- Les Diablerets 1200m/3,940ft
- LES CHAUX 1750m
- Grand Chamossaire 2035m/6,68oft
- Chaux de Conches
- Alpe des Chaux 1515m
- Grand Chamossaire 2120m
- Chaux Ronde 1985m
- Roc d'Orsay 2000m
- BRETAYE 1810m
- Sodoleuvre
- Col de Soud 1525m
- La Rasse 1350m
- Villars 1300m/4,270ft
- Barboleuse 1200m/3,940ft
- Gryon 1115m/3,66oft

Bretaye is the hub of the local slopes, with lifts from here going in all directions ➔

WENDY-JANE KING

KEY FACTS

| Resort | 1300m |
| | 4,270ft |

Villars, Gryon and Les Diablerets, but excluding Glacier 3000

Slopes	1115-2120m
	3,660-6,960ft
Lifts	35
Pistes	100km
	62 miles
Blue	40%
Red	50%
Black	10%
Snowmaking	10%

Phone numbers
From elsewhere in Switzerland add the prefix 024; from abroad use the prefix +41 24

TOURIST OFFICE

t 495 3232
information@villars.ch
www.villars.ch

THE MOUNTAINS

There's a good mix of wooded and open slopes throughout the area, but the piste map and signing are poor.

Slopes The cog train goes up to the col of Bretaye, which has intermediate slopes on either side. To the east, open slopes (often spoilt by sun) go to La Rasse and the link to Les Chaux – the run from Chaux Ronde is shown as red on the 2008/09 piste map, but has a tricky section at the top that gets a lot of sun (so often has poor snow and is sometimes closed). It should be marked black (and has been in the past). There's an alternative blue run to La Rasse. From Les Chaux there are runs to the valley station at Barboleuse (above Gryon); a gondola brings you back up. The gondola from town takes you to Roc d'Orsay, from where you can head for Bretaye or back to Villars. A long, slow, two-way chairlift links to Les Diablerets. The slopes on the glacier are limited and very gentle at the top, but there is a splendid red run down the Combe d'Audon with a dramatic cliff face rising up on the right. You can go all the way down to the valley or catch a fast chair part way down (that serves another splendid red run).

Fast lifts Fast lifts exist, but so do old chairs and drags.

Queues Queues appear for the lifts at Bretaye mainly at peak times, and the buses and train can get overcrowded.

Terrain parks The park is at Chaux Ronde and a half-pipe at Diablerets.

Snow reliability Low altitude and sunny slopes mean snow reliability isn't good – though a modest snowfall produces good conditions on such gentle, grassy terrain. More snowmaking is badly needed. On the glacier the snow is normally excellent.

Experts The main interest for experts

is off-piste. Heli-skiing is available.

Intermediates The local slopes offer a good variety. Les Chaux has some steeper slopes and a lovely long cruisy blue to Barboleuse. The run from Meilleret to Les Diablerets is a delightful long cruise and was deserted when we did it first thing on the way to the glacier.

Beginners Beginners will enjoy the village nursery slopes and riding the train to Bretaye. There are gentle runs here, too, but it's also very crowded.

Snowboarding There are quite a few draglifts.

Cross-country The trails up the valley past La Rasse are long and pretty, and there are more in the depression beyond Bretaye (44km/27 miles in all).

Mountain restaurants They are often oversubscribed – best to book. The Golf Club restaurant is very civilised. We also enjoyed the relatively quiet Des Chaux at Les Chaux and Refuge Frience at the edge of the ski area below here (it's a walk back to the T-bar though). On the glacier don't miss the stunning views from the bar on a 1000m cliff (top of lift 8G).

Schools and guides We've had good reports of both the Swiss and the Villars schools.

Families There is a non-ski nursery for children up to six.

STAYING THERE

Several tour operators offer packages.

Hotels We enjoyed staying at the 5-star Chalet Royalp (495 9090) near the railway, with good spa facilities. The Golf (496 3838) is popular, with 'spacious rooms' and 'excellent restaurant'. The Eurotel Victoria (495 3131) lacks style but is near the gondola. The Bristol (496 3636) is not, but is comfortable and recommended. All are 4-star. The 3-star Alpe Fleurie (496 3070) near the railway station is 'spacious and comfortable'.

Eating out Many restaurants are hotel-based. Apart from these, the Sporting is recommended for pizza, the Vieux-Villars for local specialities and the Rôtisserie des Alpes for 'great service'.

Après-ski Popular bars include Charlie's, the Sporting, the Mini Pub and the Bowling bar. El Gringo is the only nightclub and is popular.

Off the slopes Paragliding is available, plus tennis, skating, snowshoeing, swimming, 'excellent' walks and trips on the train – to Lausanne, say.

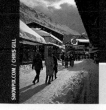

Wengen

A charming old village amid stunning scenery, where life revolves around the mountain railway; the slopes, somehow, are secondary

£90
RESORT PRICE INDEX

RATINGS

The mountains

Extent	★★★
Fast lifts	★★★
Queues	★★★
Terrain p'ks	★
Snow	★★
Expert	★★
Intermediate	★★★★
Beginner	★★★
X-country	★
Restaurants	★★★★
Schools	★★★
Families	★★★★

The resort

Charm	★★★★★
Convenience	★★★
Scenery	★★★★★
Eating out	★★
Après-ski	★★
Off-slope	★★★★

NEWS

For 2009/10 there are plans to replace the Salzegg drag to Eigergletscher with a fast six-pack, the Eigernordwand, starting lower down on the other side of the railway.

For 2008/09 snowmaking was increased in the Kleine Scheidegg/ Männlichen area, and now covers 50% of the slopes including all the runs into Wengen.

Snowmaking on the slopes around Fallboden and Wixi is due to be upgraded for this season.

➕ Some of the most spectacular scenery in the Alps	➖ Limited terrain for experts and adventurous intermediates
➕ Tiny, traditional, nearly traffic-free Alpine village	➖ Natural snow unreliable (but snowmaking has been increased)
➕ Lots of long, gentle runs, ideal for intermediates	➖ Trains to slopes are slow – and there are quite a few drags and slow chairs
➕ Nursery slopes in heart of village	
➕ Calm, unhurried atmosphere	➖ Getting to Grindelwald's First area can take hours
➕ Good resort for families and groups that include non-skiers – easy to get around on mountain railways	➖ Subdued in the evening, with little variety of nightlife

Given the charm of the village, the friendliness of the locals and the drama of the scenery, it's easy to see why many people love Wengen – including large numbers of Brits who have been going for decades. It's great for a relaxing time, for those who don't take their skiing too seriously, for families and for mixed groups of intermediates and non-skiers.

But keen piste-bashers should beware of the drawbacks: the only ways up from the village are a slow, infrequent cog railway and a queue-prone cable car; there's a lack of challenging pistes; and there's poor natural snow reliability (though the snowmaking network is a lot better than it was a few years ago). If you're used to the modern village ambience and snow-sure networks of slopes of the Trois Vallées resorts or Val d'Isère, you'll find Wengen a huge contrast. Come here for the relaxed ambience, not for piste-bashing.

THE RESORT

Wengen is set on a shelf high above the Lauterbrunnen valley, opposite Mürren, and reached only by a cog railway, which carries on up the mountain as the main lift. You can get to Mürren by taking the train to Lauterbrunnen, then a cable car and train to Winteregg (where you get a chairlift up) or to Mürren itself, where you have to walk through the village to the other lifts. Getting to the First area of Grindelwald is a long trek: a ski down to Grund, a train up to Grindelwald and then a walk or bus to the First gondola. The Jungfrau lift pass covers all of this. Outings further afield aren't really worth the effort.

VILLAGE CHARM ★★★★★
Small and almost traffic-free
The village was a farming community long before skiing arrived; it is still tiny, but dominated by sizeable hotels, mostly of Victorian origin. So it is not exactly chocolate-box pretty, but it is charming and relaxed, and almost

traffic-free. There are electric hotel taxi-trucks and a few ordinary, engine-driven taxis. (Why, we wonder?)

The short main street is the hub. Lined with chalet-style shops and hotels, it also has the ice rink and village nursery slopes right next to it. The nursery slopes double as the venue for floodlit ski jumping and parallel slalom races.

CONVENIENCE ★★★
Fine, but hilly
Wengen is small, so location isn't as crucial as in many resorts. The main way up the mountain is to take the train from the station at the southern end of the main street to Kleine Scheidegg (about a half-hour journey), where the slopes of Wengen meet those of Grindelwald. The cable car is a much quicker way to the Grindelwald slopes, and starts conveniently close to the main street. There are hotels on the home piste, convenient for the slopes. Those who don't fancy a steepish morning climb should avoid places down the hill below the station.

SCENERY ★★★★★
Three of the best are here
The views across the valley are stunning. They get even better higher up, when the famous trio of peaks comes fully into view – the Mönch (Monk) in the centre protecting the Jungfrau (Maiden) on the right from the Eiger (Ogre) on the left.

THE MOUNTAINS

Although Wengen is famous for the fearsome Lauberhorn Downhill course – the longest and one of the toughest on the World Cup circuit – its slopes are best suited to early intermediates. Most of the Downhill course is now open to the public and the steepest section (the Hundschopf jump) can be avoided by an alternative red route. Most of Wengen's runs are gentle blues and reds, ideal for cruising.

EXTENT OF THE SLOPES ★★★
Picturesque playground
Most of the slopes are on the Grindelwald side of the mountain. From the railway station at Kleine Scheidegg you can head straight down to Grindelwald or work your way across the mountain with the help of a couple of lifts to the top of the Männlichen. This area is served by a drag and several chairlifts, and can be reached directly from Wengen by the cable car. There are a few runs back down towards Wengen from the top of the Lauberhorn, but there's really only one below Wengernalp. Following heavy snowfalls in 2009, one visitor found piste markers had disappeared under the deep snow – 'a potentially dangerous, not to mention avoidable, problem' – and a couple more had some trouble finding their way around.

FAST LIFTS ★★★
OK except for the train
The fast cable car and slow train are the main access lifts; new fast chairs replacing old lifts have improved things higher up.

QUEUES ★★★
Village crowds, better higher up
Both the train and the cable car can be crowded at peak periods. It is best to avoid travelling up at the same time as the ski school. Queues up the mountain have been alleviated a lot in the last few years by the installation of fast chairs, and recent reporters

have experienced few problems in midweek. But weekend invasions can increase the crowds, especially on the Grindelwald side and especially on a Saturday, when children up to 15 can ski free if a parent buys a day pass.

TERRAIN PARKS ★
Try the Bumps
There has been a small park by the Bumps draglift below Wengernalp for the last couple of seasons, and we are told it's to be extended for 2009/10; but it's privately run so it isn't certain. Otherwise, the nearest parks are at First and Mürren – each a fair trek.

SNOW RELIABILITY ★★
Improved snowmaking helps
Most slopes are below 2000m/6,560ft, and at Grindelwald they go down to less than 1000m/3,280ft. Very few slopes face north, and the long blue run back to the village suffers from sun and lack of altitude. So good natural snow is far from certain. But a lot of snowmaking has been added recently, and by last season 50% of the slopes in the Kleine Scheidegg-Männlichen area were covered by snowmaking. When we were there in 2009, it had not snowed for a few weeks and a warm Foehn wind had melted a lot of snow, but most slopes were in good condition. More reports please. A reporter found 'piste maintenance awful'.

FOR EXPERTS ★★
Few challenges
Wengen is quite limited for experts. The only genuine black runs in the area are parts of the Lauberhorn World Cup Downhill and a couple of pistes from Eigergletscher towards Wixi including Oh God (which used to be off-piste). There are some decent off-piste runs such as White Hare from under the north face of the Eiger and more adventurous runs from the Jungfraujoch late in the season (see the Grindelwald chapter for more about going to the Jungfraujoch).

For more serious challenges it's well worth going to nearby Mürren, around an hour away. Heli-trips are organised if there are enough takers.

FOR INTERMEDIATES ★★★★
Wonderful if the snow is good
Wengen and Grindelwald share superb intermediate slopes. Nearly all are long blue or gentle red runs – see the

Wengen is not a bad place for gentle boarding – the nursery area is not ideal, but beginners have plenty of slopes to progress to, with lots of long blue and red runs served by the train and chairlifts. Getting from Kleine Scheidegg to Männlichen means an unavoidable draglift, though. And the slope back to Wengen is narrow and almost flat in places, so you may have to scoot. For the steepest slopes and best freeriding, experts will want to head for Mürren.

Grindelwald chapter. The run back to Wengen is a relaxing end to the day, as long as it's not too crowded.

For tougher pistes, head for the top of the Lauberhorn chair and then the runs to Kleine Scheidegg, or to Wixi (following the start of the Downhill course). You could also try the north-facing run from Eigergletscher to Salzegg, which often has the best snow late in the season and should have improved access for 2009/10 with a new six-pack (see 'News').

FOR BEGINNERS ★★★
Not ideal
There's a nursery slope in the centre of the village – convenient and gentle, but the snow is unreliable. There's a beginners' area at Wengernalp and another on the Grindelwald side of Kleine Scheidegg, but to get back to Wengen you either have to take the train or tackle the run down, which can be tricky, with some flat sections. There are plenty of good, long, gentle runs to progress to above Grindelwald.

FOR CROSS-COUNTRY ★
There is none
There's no cross-country in Wengen itself. There are 12km/7 miles of tracks down in the Lauterbrunnen valley, where the snow is unreliable.

MOUNTAIN RESTAURANTS ★★★★
Plenty of variety
Editors' choice The Jungfrau hotel at Wengernalp (855 1622) – where the views of the Jungfrau from the sunny terrace are superb – is expensive but worth it; note that you need to book. 'The best lunch on the mountain bar none' and 'the best rösti of the week', said two 2009 visitors. You also get magnificent views from the narrow outside balcony of Wengen's highest restaurant Eigergletscher – get there early to grab a table. A recent reporter recommends the 'fresh half pineapple with curry filling'.
Worth knowing about The station buffet at Kleine Scheidegg gets repeated rave reviews, so it's not surprising it also gets packed –

Wengen

559

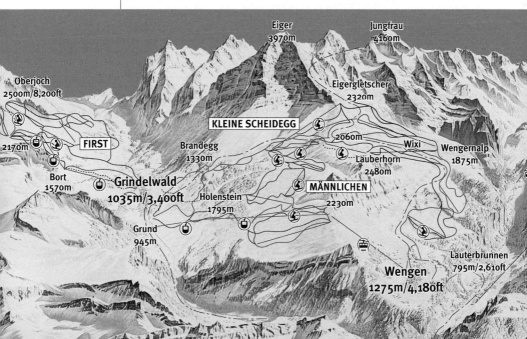

SCHOOLS

Swiss
t 855 2022

Privat
t 855 5005

Classes
(Swiss prices)
6 3hr days SF268

Private lessons
SF148 for 2hr

CHILDCARE

Playhouse
t 855 1414
From 18mnth;
9am-5pm; Sun-Fri

Kinderhort Sunshine
t 854 8080
Ages from 1mnth to
8yr; 8.30-5pm

Babysitters
List available from
tourist office

Ski school
The Swiss school
takes ages 4 up
(6 3hr days SF268)

The backdrop is
simply stunning: from
left to right, the Eiger,
Mönch and Jungfrau.
Kleine Scheidegg is in
the foreground ↓

'Wonderful food at reasonable prices,' says a 2009 visitor. A recent reporter recommends the nearby Bellevue hotel for 'good food and excellent service'. The Grindelwaldblick is a worthwhile trudge uphill from Kleine Scheidegg, for 'a tasty and good value lunch with generous portions and attentive service' and views of the Eiger.

The Allmend, near the top of the Innerwengen chair and the train stop, is a 'great place to meet towards the end of the day' with 'friendly service' and wonderful views of the valley from the terrace. Reports on Mary's Cafe (situated at the end of the World Cup runs) are mixed. For restaurants on the Grindelwald slopes, see that chapter.

SCHOOLS AND GUIDES ★★★
Healthy competition
Reports on the Swiss school are generally good. One recent visitor found the lessons 'excellent, well organised and friendly with the school prepared to change people from one class to another'. Another 'had private lessons with the Privat school and would recommend it'. Guides are available for heli-trips and off-piste.

FOR FAMILIES ★★★★
Conveniently placed
It is an attractive and reassuring village for families. The nursery slope is in the centre and there are two kindergartens. There is a list of babysitters available at the tourist office. A recent reporter praised the children's ski school classes – 'The best so far by a mile. My four year old really enjoyed all the activities.'

The train gives easy access to higher slopes.

STAYING THERE

Most accommodation is in hotels. There is only a handful of catered chalets (none especially luxurious). Self-catering apartments are few, too.

Staying down in Lauterbrunnen will halve your accommodation costs and give faster access to Mürren (see Mürren chapter).

Hotels There are about two dozen hotels, mostly 4-star and 3-star, with a handful of simpler places.
★★★★Beausite Park (856 5161) Reputedly the best in town. Good pool, steam and massage. But poorly situated at top of nursery slopes – a schlep up from the main street.
★★★★Wengener Hof (856 6969) No prizes for style or convenience, but recommended for peace, helpful staff, spacious rooms with good views.
★★★★Sunstar (856 5200) Family-friendly, modern hotel on main street right opposite the cable car. Comfortable rooms. Pool with views. Recommended by reporters.
★★★★Silberhorn (856 5131) Comfortable, modern and central. Frequently praised by reporters.
★★★★Caprice (856 0606) Small, smartly furnished, chalet-style, just above the railway. Sauna and steam room. 'Comfortable and friendly'; 'fabulous views, excellent food'. Kindergarten.
★★★Belvédère (856 6868) Some way out, buffet-style meals ('good for families'), spacious rooms and grand art nouveau public rooms. Endorsed by a recent reporter ('excellent').
★★★Alpenrose (855 3216) Long-standing British favourite; eight minutes' climb to the station. Small, simple rooms, but good views; 'first-class' food; friendly staff.

There's a very strong British presence in Wengen. Many Brits have been returning for years to the same rooms in the same hotels in the same week, and treat the resort as a sort of second home. There is an English church with weekly services, and a British-run ski club, the DHO (Downhill Only) – so named when the Brits who colonised the resort persuaded the locals to keep the summer railway running up the mountain in winter, so that they would no longer have to climb up in order to ski down again. That greatly amused the locals, who until then had regarded skiing in winter as a way to get around on snow rather than a pastime to be done for fun. The DHO is still going strong.

GETTING THERE

Air Zürich 155km/ 95 miles (3hr); Bern 65km/40 miles (2hr); Basel 160km/100 miles (2hr45)

Rail Station in resort

UK PACKAGES

Alpine Answers, Club Med, Crystal, First Choice, Independent Ski Links, Inghams, Kuoni, Made to Measure, Neilson, Simply Alpine, Ski Freshtracks, Ski Line, Ski Solutions, Skitracer, Switzerland Travel Centre, Thomson

ACTIVITIES

Indoor Swimming pools (in hotels), sauna, solarium, whirlpool, massage (in hotels), art gallery, museum

Outdoor Ice rink, curling, 50km/ 31 miles of cleared paths, tobogganing, snowshoeing, hang-gliding, helicopter flights

Phone numbers From elsewhere in Switzerland add the prefix 033; from abroad use the prefix +41 33

TOURIST OFFICE

t 855 1414
info@wengen.ch
www.wengen-muerren.ch

***Falken** (856 5121) Further up the hill. Another British favourite, 'the service was first class and the live jazz pianist had the place rocking'.

Apartments The hotel Bernerhof's decent Résidence apartments are well positioned just off the main street, and the hotel facilities are available for guests to use.

At altitude You can stay at two points up the mountain reached by the railway: the expensive Jungfrau hotel (855 1622) at Wengernalp – with fabulous views – and at Kleine Scheidegg, where there are rooms in the big Scheidegg Hotels (855 1212) and dormitory space above the Grindelwaldblick restaurant (855 1374) and the station buffet.

EATING OUT ★★☆☆☆
Mainly hotel-based
Most restaurants are in hotels. They offer good food and service. The Eiger has a traditional restaurant and a stube with Swiss and French cuisine. The Bernerhof has good-value traditional dishes. The little hotel Hirschen has good steaks. The hotel Brunner servers 'sumptuous four course meals and delicious home-made soups'. There's no shortage of fondues in the village, and several bars do casual food. Da Sina does 'succulent and ample sirloin steaks' and is recommended by a couple of recent visitors. Cafe Gruebi has been recommended for 'the most wonderful cakes'. The Jungfrau at Wengernalp has an excellent restaurant – but you have to get back on skis or on a toboggan.

APRES-SKI ★★☆☆☆
It depends on what you want
People's reactions to the après-ski scene vary widely, according to their expectations and their appetites.
If you're used to raving in Kitzbühel or Les Deux-Alpes, you'll rate Wengen dead, especially for young people. If you've heard it's dead, you may be pleasantly surprised to find that there

is a handful of bars that do good business both early and late in the evening. But it is only a handful of small places. On the mountain, Tipirama (a wigwam at Kleine Scheidegg) is a fun place immediately after skiing ('vibrant and welcoming'), sometimes with DJs and live bands. Reporters have enjoyed the 'fun' Start Bar on the Lauberhorn ('fantastic views and live music at weekends'). The bar at the Bumps section of the home run is a popular final-run stop-off. Further down, the snow bar at the hotel Brunner was 'enjoyable', and in the village the tiny, 'always welcoming' Eiger Bar is popular at the end of the day. The small, traditional Tanne is 'relaxed, friendly, and cocktails and champagne are popular' – but it can get crowded. The 'animated' Sina's, a little way out by Club Med, has big-screen TV, a live DJ and special evenings such as karaoke and quiz nights. The Caprice bar has been recommended, as has Rock's with its three plasma screens showing Sky Sports. There are discos and live music in some hotels (including Hasenstall – previously Tiffany's – in the Silberhorn). The cinema often shows English-language films.

OFF THE SLOPES ★★★★☆
Good for a relaxing time
With its unbeatable scenery and pedestrian-friendly trains and cable car (there's a special, though pricey, pass for pedestrians), Wengen is a superb resort for those who want a completely relaxing holiday. It's easy for mixed parties of skiers and non-skiers to meet up for lunch on the mountain. There are some lovely walks, and ice skating and curling are popular with reporters. Several hotels have health spas. Excursions to Interlaken and Bern are possible by train, as is the trip up to the Jungfraujoch (see the Grindelwald chapter). Helicopter flights from Männlichen have been recommended.

Wengen

561

Interactive resort shortlist builder at www.wtss.co.uk

Zermatt

A magical combination of nearly everything you could want from a ski resort, both on and off the slopes

£115
RESORT PRICE INDEX

RATINGS

The mountains

Extent	★★★★
Fast lifts	★★★★★
Queues	★★★
Terrain p'ks	★★★★
Snow	★★★★
Expert	★★★★
Intermediate	★★★★
Beginner	★★
X-country	★
Restaurants	★★★★★
Schools	★★★
Families	★★

The resort

Charm	★★★★★
Convenience	★★
Scenery	★★★★★
Eating out	★★★★★
Après-ski	★★★★★
Off-slope	★★★★

NEWS

For 2008/09 an extensive new beginner area (Wolli) opened at Leisee, just above Sunnegga, with a little cable car linking the two. A special cheap lift pass is available too.

A new 120-person restaurant has opened atop the Klein Matterhorn. Snowmaking was also increased – the resort is one of the first to trial an all-weather system that works at higher temperatures.

For 2009/10 a third stage will be added to the modern gondola from Zermatt up to Schwarzsee via Furi, taking you up to Trockener Steg in 20-25 minutes without changing lifts.

➕ Wonderful, high and extensive slopes in four varied areas

➕ Spectacular high mountain scenery, dominated by the Matterhorn

➕ Charming, if rather sprawling, old mountain village, largely traffic-free

➕ Reliable snow at altitude

➕ World's best mountain restaurants

➕ Extensive helicopter operation

➕ Nightlife to suit most tastes

➕ Smart shops

➕ Linked to Cervinia in Italy

➖ Main lifts may be a long walk, or a crowded bus or taxi ride from home

➖ Not ideal for beginners, despite recent efforts to improve matters

➖ One of Europe's priciest lift passes

➖ Slow train up to Gornergrat annoys some people, but can be avoided

➖ Some lift queues at peak periods

➖ Annoying electric taxis in 'car-free' streets detract from ambience

➖ Not cheap, and can be pricey

➖ Not much skiing to be done in really bad weather

You must try Zermatt before you die. Few places can match its combination of excellent advanced and intermediate slopes, reliable snow, magnificent scenery, Alpine charm and mountain restaurants with superb food and stunning views.

Zermatt has its drawbacks – see the long list above. But for us, and for virtually all our reporters, these pale into insignificance compared with its attractions (especially as recent investment has ensured the mountains are better connected). It comes close to matching perfectly our notion of the ideal winter resort and is one of our favourites – one of us regularly takes his holiday here.

THE RESORT

Zermatt started life as a simple farming village, developed as a mountaineering centre in the 19th century, then became a winter resort. Summer is still as big as winter here.

The village is essentially car-free, but not traffic-free – electric buggies operating either as hotel shuttles or as public taxis zip around the streets. Residents can drive up to Zermatt, but the rest of us must park at Täsch (or more distant Visp) and arrive by train. At Täsch there's a big underground car park (SF11 a day), and you can wheel luggage trolleys on to the trains.

Like all resorts, Zermatt attracts a wide range of people, but it's noticeable that the clientele is not only well heeled but also very international and relatively elderly, for what is quite a sporty resort.

VILLAGE CHARM ★★★★★
Old and new in harmony
The village is a mixture of ancient barns, chocolate-box chalets, grand 19th-century hotels and modern buildings, most in traditional style but some decidedly funky. It sprawls along both sides of a river, mountains rising steeply on each side.

Arriving at the station, it all seems very towny, especially if there is no snow on the ground. The centre doesn't have the relaxed, rustic feel of other car-free resorts, such as Wengen and Saas-Fee. The main street running away from the station is lined with luxury hotels, restaurants, banks and glitzy shops. The electric taxis are intrusive, especially at busy times.

So does it deserve 5 stars? On the whole, yes. At quieter times and in

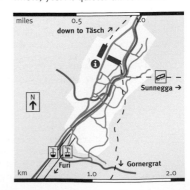

↑ Better than your average park bench view, and this is only the Klein Matterhorn – the little spike in the middle. The lift station to its left is Trockener Steg

SNOWPIX.COM / CHRIS GILL

KEY FACTS

Resort	1620m
	5,310ft

Zermatt only	
Slopes	1620-3820m
	5,310-12,530ft
Lifts	32
Pistes	183km
	114 miles
Blue	16%
Red	58%
Black	26%
Snowmaking	33%

Zermatt-Cervinia-Valtournenche combined	
Slopes	1525-3820m
	5,000-12,530ft
Lifts	57
Pistes	313km
	194 miles
Blue	22%
Red	60%
Black	18%
Snowmaking	33%

quieter parts, the place is magical. The oldest, most charming part of the village has narrow lanes and old wooden barns with slate roofs, many of them supported on stone 'legs'.

CONVENIENCE ★★★★★
Lifts at opposite ends
Staying in Zermatt almost inevitably involves long walks or bus rides: accommodation is widely spread, and the lifts are widely separated.

You arrive at a fair-sized square at the north end of the resort, where you find ranks of shuttle, taxis and horse-drawn sleighs to ferry you to your lodgings. You can use these to get to the ski lifts as well, but there is also a ski-bus service that skirts the town, along the river. This is now free, but inadequate, and many people resort to taxis (12F for up to four people, we are told). Hence our 2-star rating.

The cog railway to the Gornergrat sector starts from near the main station. The Sunnegga underground funicular for the Rothorn sector is a few minutes' walk away, but the lifts to Furi for the Glacier and Schwarzsee areas (and the link to Cervinia) are at the opposite end of the long village. Walking from the station to the Furi lifts can take 20 minutes. Snow is left on the ground, of course, but is not reliably gritted, so walks can be hazardous as well as tiring.

Staying near the lifts to Furi means you can beat the crowds at the major lift queue black spot, and is more

convenient for the slopes in general now that there's a gondola connection from Furi to Riffelberg and Gornergrat. But being near the Gornergrat and Sunnegga railways, near the station end of the main street, is more convenient for most shops, bars and restaurants. Some accommodation is up the steep hill across the river in Winkelmatten – you can ski back to it from all areas, and it has its own reliable bus service.

SCENERY ★★★★★
On a grand scale
The unmistakeable Matterhorn is not visible from central parts of the village – if you want the famous view from your balcony, stay on the east side of the village, or at the south end – but once you are on the slopes its unreal profile dominates the views. The cable car trip up to the Klein Matterhorn opens up vast panoramas, as well as close-up glacier views.

THE MOUNTAINS

Practically all of the slopes are above the treeline – the runs served by the Sunnegga funicular are the main exception. A single piste map (in a handy quick-folding size) covers both Cervinia's and Zermatt's slopes fairly clearly, and lists recommended 'ski safari' routes of either 10,500m/34,450ft or 12,500m/41,000ft vertical.

The yellow runs shown in each sector, and all those on the Stockhorn, are now called 'itinéraires' on the piste map. The term is not explained on the map – ridiculous. Before 2006/07, they were described as 'ski runs' and defined as protected (from avalanches we presume), marked but not prepared or patrolled. On our March 2008 visit we spotted one sign on a yellow run saying it wasn't patrolled. Check the situation if skiing alone.

We have been impressed by recent service improvements: polite and helpful lift staff; big boards at the bottom of each sector indicating which lifts and pistes are open in all sectors; useful announcements in English on the train and some cable cars; and free tissues at most lift stations.

EXTENT OF THE SLOPES ★★★★☆
Beautiful and varied
Zermatt's piste map divides the slopes into several sectors and markets some as 'paradises'. We think this is bizarre, so here we drop 'paradise' and divide the slopes into four main sectors.

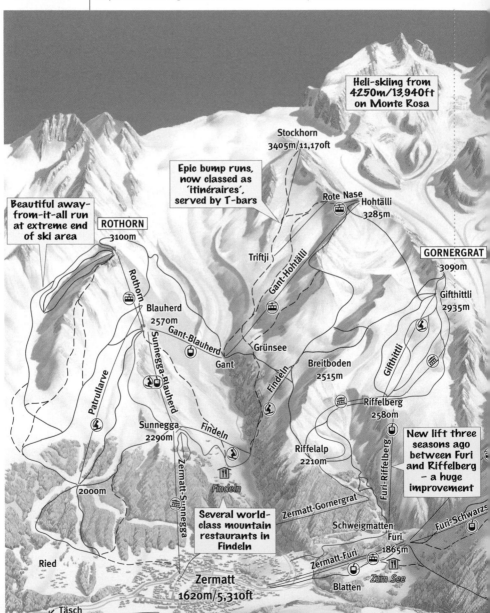

Heli-skiing from 4250m/13,940ft on Monte Rosa

Stockhorn
3405m/11,170ft

Epic bump runs, now classed as 'itinéraires', served by T-bars

Rote Nase   Hohtälli
3285m

Beautiful away-from-it-all run at extreme end of ski area

ROTHORN
3100m

Triftji

Gant-Hohtälli

GORNERGRAT
3090m

Rothorn

Blauherd
2570m

Gant-Blauherd

Grünsee

Gifthittli
2935m

Sunnegga-Blauherd

Gant

Findeln

Breitboden
2515m

Gifthittli

Patrullarve

Riffelberg
2580m

Sunnegga
2290m

Findeln

Findeln

New lift three seasons ago between Furi and Riffelberg – a huge improvement

2000m

Zermatt-Sunnegga

Riffelalp
2210m

Furi-Riffelberg

Findeln

Several world-class mountain restaurants in Findeln

Zermatt-Gornergrat

Schweigmatten

Furi-Schwarz

Ried

Zermatt-Furi

Furi
1865m

Furi-Schwarz

Zermatt
1620m/5,310ft

Zum See

Blatten

Täsch

Zmutt

The **Rothorn** sector is reached by an underground funicular to Sunnegga starting by the river, not far from the centre of the village. A hybrid chondola goes from there to Blauherd, where a cable car goes up to Rothorn.

The second main area, **Gornergrat**, is reached from Zermatt by cog railway trains that take 30 or 40 minutes to the top – arrive early to get a seat on the right-hand side and enjoy the fabulous views. It can be a long journey if you have to stand.

There are several links between Rothorn and Gornergrat, via two lift stations in the Findel valley (below the Findelgletscher). From Rothorn you have a choice of a piste to Gant or a piste or an itinerary to a point below Findeln. From Gornergrat it's a piste to Gant or itineraries to either point – note that the one to below Findeln is rather tricky – and the alternative chair ride down is steep enough to have one reporter paralysed with fear.

The third major sector is the super-

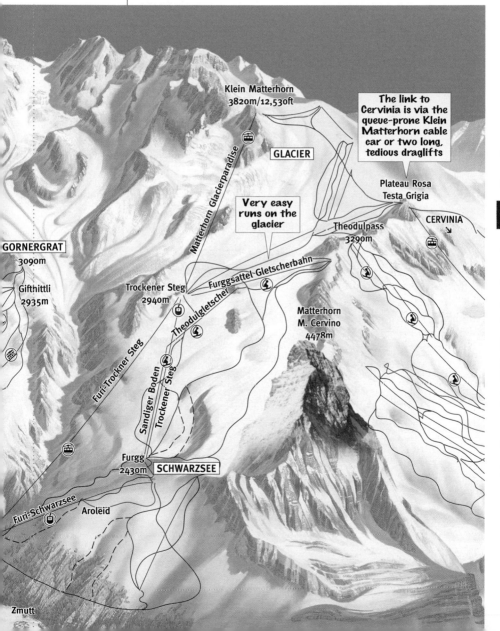

Klein Matterhorn
3820m/12,530ft

The link to Cervinia is via the queue-prone Klein Matterhorn cable car or two long, tedious draglifts

GLACIER

Plateau Rosa
Testa Grigia

CERVINIA

Very easy runs on the glacier

Theodulpass
3290m

GORNERGRAT
3090m

Matterhorn Glacierparadise

Gifthittli
2935m

Trockener Steg
2940m

Furggsattel-Gletscherbahn

Theodulgletscher

Matterhorn
M. Cervino
4478m

Furi-Trockner Steg

Sandiger Boden

Trockener Steg

Furgg
2430m **SCHWARZSEE**

Furi-Schwarzsee Aroleid

Zmutt

high **Glacier**. The established route up to the focal point of Trockener Steg is a two-stage cable car via the lower junction of Furi. Above Trockener Steg a third cable car makes a spectacular ascent to Klein Matterhorn. When you arrive, you walk through a long tunnel, to emerge on top of the world for the highest piste in Europe. This area links to Cervinia – make sure you have an appropriate pass, and your passport.

But there is now an alternative viable route to Trockener Steg: the gondola to Schwarzsee will from the coming season be extended by a third stage. Tricky call: the cable cars will be quicker unless you hit a queue at Furi.

The Gornergrat and Glacier sectors are linked by a gondola between Riffelberg and Furi via Schweigmatten – you can ski down to that point from Gornergrat.

Distinct from the Glacier sector is the small but worthwhile **Schwarzsee** area at the top of the second stage of the aforementioned gondola via Furi.

There are pistes back to the village from all sectors – though some can be closed or tricky due to poor snow conditions. They can be hazardous at the end of the day, due to crowds and speeding skiers – particularly the black from Furgg. (Much better to enjoy it early in the day, and ride the gondola down to Furi at close of play.)

FAST LIFTS ★★★★★
Huge improvements

All of Zermatt's four sectors are now well-connected by fast chairs, gondolas or mountain railways. And another new gondola is planned for Schwarzsee for 2009/10.

QUEUES ★★★☆☆
Main problems being solved

Zermatt has improved its lift system hugely in recent years, eliminating major bottlenecks. Our 2009 reporters are generally positive, but problems remain – two bottlenecks in particular.

The Klein Matterhorn cable car has queues much of the time (up to an hour mid-morning; quieter in the afternoon). There may be queues for the cable cars up to Trockener Steg, too – though the burden will now be shared with the gondola via Schwarzsee. One regular reporter recommends jumping the Glacier lift queues once in your holiday by splashing out 200 francs a head for a

OFF-PISTE RUNS FROM THE ACCESSIBLE TO THE EPIC

Zermatt offers a wide variety of off-piste runs for all abilities, from off-piste beginner to expert. And if the runs reached from the lift system aren't enough, heli-skiing is available (and popular).

The 'itinéraires' (see 'The mountains' earlier in this chapter) marked in yellow on the piste map (and by broken black lines on our map) open up a lot of ungroomed terrain. If you love long mogul pitches, those between Stockhorn and Triftji are the stuff of dreams. From the top of the Stockhorn draglift there's a steep run (usually with big moguls) back down. Or you can carry on down further to the older Triftji T-bar that goes up to Rote Nase and serves a wide, long face that can be another vast mogul field. Being north-facing and high, the snow in the whole Stockhorn-Triftji area keeps in good condition long after a new snowfall. The 'itinéraires' carry on down from the Triftji T-bar to Gant, but snow quality can deteriorate on this lower part. And be warned: this whole area does not normally open until February (sometimes not until March, because of insufficient snow). There are two wonderful 'itinéraires' from Rothorn, with spectacular views. But they need good snow-cover to be really enjoyable. At Schwarzsee there are a couple of steep north-facing gullies through the woods.

Away from the marked runs, there are marvellous off-piste possibilities from the top lifts in each sector, but they are dangerous, because of rocky and glacial terrain; guidance is essential. Stockhorn is a great starting point; descending towards Gant, one special run goes down 'the lost valley'; going in the other direction, there is an excellent descent to the Gornergletscher, ending at Furi (but see warning below about the end of the glacier). In the Schwarzsee sector there are many good slopes, including 'innru waldieni', right underneath the Matterhorn, reached from the Hörnli T-bar.

Zermatt is the Alps' biggest heli-skiing centre; at times the helipad has choppers taking off every few minutes. The classic run is from over 4250m/13,940ft on Monte Rosa and descends over 2300m/7,550ft vertical through wonderful glacier scenery to Furi; it is not steep, but getting off the end of the glacier can be tricky and involve walking along narrow rocky paths above long drops or side-stepping down steep slopes, depending on the amount of snow around (we've encountered both).

And there are lots of ski touring opportunities, too, including some among stunning glacial scenery.

Now that the onward cable car to Gornergrat from Hohtälli has been removed, the top section of piste from there can get dangerously busy ('awful crowds on a narrow red that was bumped by mid-morning').

The lower runs to the valley get horribly crowded at the end of the day. But you can always dally in a restaurant or two along the way, to let the pressure ease.

TERRAIN PARKS ★★★★
One of Switzerland's best

Gravity Park situated next to the Furggsattel six-seat chair is one of Switzerland's best winter parks. (It moves up to Plateau Rosa in the summer so that it can stay open 365 days a year.) There is a nicely integrated 120m/390ft-long super-pipe that sits next to an array of kickers, rails, a quarter-pipe, a wall ride and a new mail box and tree jib. The park is set up nicely so that you can choose either a kicker or rail line, and try several hits in a row. It is a short park, so you'll be doing a lot of laps (on a fast chair) during the day. Check www.matterhornparadise.ch for details.

SNOW RELIABILITY ★★★★
Generally good

Zermatt has rocky terrain and a relatively dry climate. But it also has some of the highest slopes in Europe, and quite a lot of snowmaking. Three of the four sectors go up to over 3000m/9,840ft, and the Glacier area has summer skiing. There are loads of runs above 2500m/8,200ft, many of which are north-facing, guaranteeing decent snow except in freak years.

Snowmaking machines serve some of the pistes, on all four areas, from above 3000m/9,840ft right down to resort level. Coverage is gradually increased each season – the runs to resort level were extremely well maintained during our March 2008 visit. Piste grooming is excellent.

FOR EXPERTS ★★★★
Head off-piste

There is some great off-piste when conditions are right – see our feature panel – but Zermatt doesn't get huge snowfall, so you can't always count on it, particularly early in the season. There are few challenging pistes. The handful of black runs marked on the piste map are not worthy of their classification; the one with the

↑ The long red run from Rothorn to Gant has views like this for much of its length. But beware mega-queues at the bottom – best to do it early in the day

SNOWPIX.COM / CHRIS GILL

20-minute heli-lift to Plateau Rosa incorporating a close-up tour of the Matterhorn – 'fantastic; one of the highlights of my life'.

The second bottleneck is Gant in the Findel valley – especially the old four-seat gondola to Blauherd. Half-hour waits are common here in high season. The gondola is a slow ride, too, though you may be compensated by seeing herds of chamois on the slopes below. If you are crossing between sectors you can avoid Gant by using the new Sunnegga-Breitboden chairlift, but that doesn't help if you want to ski the lovely long red run from Rothorn past Fluhalp.

The high-speed quad from Furgg has been a bottleneck, but the new top stage of the gondola to Trockener Steg should sort that out.

You may find standing room only on the Gornergrat train – but there will be another one along in 24 minutes. We love getting the 8am train with the lifties and restaurant staff. It arrives at the top just as they drop the rope to open the pistes, and you have the slopes to yourself for an hour or two.

LIFT PASSES

Zermatt

Prices in SF

Age	1-day	6-day
under 16	36	175
16 to 19	60	298
20 to 64	71	350
over 65	66	322

Free under 9

Beginner no deals

Notes

Covers all lifts on the Swiss side of the border; half-day passes and single-ascent tickets on some lifts also available

Alternative passes

International for Zermatt and Cervinia; International-Aosta for Zermatt and Cervinia plus 2 days in Val d'Aosta; Peak Pass for pedestrians

boarding

Boarders in soft boots have one big advantage over skiers in Zermatt – they have much more comfortable walks to and from the lift stations! Even so, there aren't many snowboarders around. The slopes are best for experienced freeriders and there's a world-class terrain park above Trockener Steg on the glacier. There is, however, an excellent little beginner area at Blauherd, complete with moving carpet lift, which we've seen many beginner snowboarders having lessons on. The main lifts are boarder-friendly: train, funicular, gondolas, cable cars and fast chairs, and there aren't too many flat bits. Stoked is a specialist school.

steepest pitches (Blauherd-Patrullarve) is also very wide. That's one of the consequences of making their toughest regularly skied runs 'itinéraires' (see under 'The mountains' earlier in this chapter).

FOR INTERMEDIATES ★★★★
Mile after mile of beautiful runs
Zermatt is ideal for adventurous intermediates. Many of the blue runs tend to be at the difficult end of their classification. Reds vary – some are tough, some ought to be blue. There are very beautiful reds down lift-free valleys from both Gornergrat (Kelle) and Hohtälli (White Hare) to

Breitboden – we love these first thing in the morning, before anyone else is on them. The steepest part of Kelle has been reclassified black, but an easier red variant now bypasses it. From Breitboden you can go on down to Gant, or to Riffelalp on a run that includes a narrow wooded path with a sheer cliff and magnificent views to the right. The 5km/3 mile Kumme/Tufternkumme run, from Rothorn itself to the bottom of the Patrullarve chair, also gets away from the lift system and has an interesting mix of straight-running and mogul pitches (but it gets a lot of sun and lacks snowmaking).
In the Glacier sector the reds

THE WORLD'S BEST MOUNTAIN RESTAURANTS ★★★★★

Even reporters who don't normally stop long for lunch usually succumb to temptation here. The choice of restaurants is enormous, the food usually excellent, the small hut-based places very atmospheric (some with spectacular views), the table service friendly (if over-worked). It is impossible to list here all those worth a visit. It is best to book; check prices are within your budget first! The mountain restaurants are included in the tourist office restaurant directory.

Below Sunnegga, down at Findeln, are several attractive, expensive, rustic restaurants sharing a great Matterhorn view. Chez Vrony (967 2552) is one of our favourites; we've had wonderful spicy fish soup, wild mushroom risotto, salmon pasta, great desserts. We had one report of poor service last year – and certainly it does get stretched at times – but otherwise we get a stream of endorsements. We and readers have also enjoyed the Adler (967 1058), where the food is 'simple but wholesome'. This year we have an enthusiastic report on the Findlerhof (967 2588) – 'great inside and out, lovely food'. And another on the Paradies (967 3451) – 'excellent food, super-friendly service'. Further up the Findel valley, in a beautiful, isolated situation off the run from Rothorn, Fluhalp (967 2597) is popular, often with live music on the terrace).

On Gornergrat, the Kulmhotel (966 6400) at the top has both self- and table-service restaurants; we had two good table-service meals on our 2008 visit, with excellent food and good service. At Riffelalp, the Alphitta (967 2114) has several cosy rustic rooms for bad-weather days and does 'great -value rösti' (no credit cards though). The Chämi-Hitta, lower down on the run to Furi, is another cosy spot with 'friendly service'.

Up above Trockener Steg, 'friendly' Gandegghütte (607 8868) is mainly notable for its stunning views of the glacier. The hotel at Schwarzsee (967 2263) is right at the foot of the Matterhorn, with staggering views and endless variations of rösti. Down the hill from here, Stafelalp (967 3062) is a regular reader favourite – glorious position, 'excellent food; friendly, prompt service'. At Furi, the Restaurant Furri (966 2777) is 'welcoming', and does 'ace rösti'.

On the way back to the village, Zum See (967 2045) is a charming old hut with Matterhorn views and the reputation of being Zermatt's best mountain restaurant ('fabulous tuna carpaccio') – we've certainly eaten well there.

SCHOOLS

Swiss
t 966 2466

Stoked
t 967 7020

Summit
t 967 0001

European Snowsport
t 967 6787

Almrausch
t 967 0808

AER
t 967 7067

Prato Borni
t 967 5115

Classes (Swiss prices)
5 days (10am to 3.30
with lunch break)
SF335

Private lessons
SF170 for 2hr for 1 or
2 people

GUIDES

Alpin Center
t 966 2460

CHILDCARE

Kinderparadies
t 967 7252
Ages from 3mnth;
9am-5pm

**Kinderclub Pumuckel
(Hotel Ginabelle)**
t 966 5000
Ages from 30mnth

Snowflakes (Stoked)
t 967 7020
Ages from 4; 9am-12
noon

**Nico Kids Club
(Schweizerhof hotel)**
t 966 0000
Ages from 2 to 8;
8.30-6pm; Sun-Fri

Snowli Village (Swiss)
t 966 2466
Ages 4 to 5: SF425
for 5 days

Private babysitters
List at tourist office

Ski school
From age 6; 5 full
days incl. lunch SF378
(Swiss prices)

served by the fast quad chair from Furgg are gloriously set at the foot of the Matterhorn. The Furggsattel chair from Trockener Steg serves more pistes with stunning views, notably the 1100m/3,610ft-vertical Matterhorn piste – a red that is more blue in gradient for most of its considerable length. It is classified red because of a short, steep pitch near the end, which a lot of less confident intermediates struggle on. It is often closed though, due to a lack of snowmaking.

For timid intermediates, the best runs are the blues from Blauherd on Rothorn, and above Riffelberg on Gornergrat, and the runs between Klein Matterhorn and Trockener Steg. Of these, the Riffelberg area often has the best combination of good snow and easy cruising, and is popular with the schools. Blauherd gets afternoon sun, but the snowmaking means that heavy, slushy snow near the bottom is more likely than bare patches.

In the Glacier sector most of the runs, though marked red on the piste map, are very flat and represent the easiest slopes Zermatt has to offer, as well as the best snow. The problem here is the possibility of bad weather.

Even an early intermediate can make the trip to Cervinia, crossing at Theodulpass rather than taking the more challenging Ventina run from Testa Grigia/Plateau Rosa.

Beware the run from Furgg to Furi at the end of the day, because it can be chopped up, moguled in places and very crowded (the only reason it is classified black that we can see, because it isn't very steep). A much more relaxed alternative is to use the beautifully scenic Weisse Perle run from Schwarzsee (the Stafelalp variant is even more scenic but has a short uphill and steep downhill sections). Or you can ride the gondola down.

FOR BEGINNERS ★★★★★
Far from ideal
These days the resort makes an effort to cater for beginners – there are beginner areas dotted around on all four sectors, and last season a major new one was developed (with three moving carpets and two rope tows) at Leisee, close to Sunnegga – an excellent facility, by all accounts. And there is now a half-price day pass to get you to and from that area, which is a step forward. All of which has led us to give Zermatt a second star this

year, at last. But it's a real drag for beginners to have to get themselves up the mountain, and – more seriously – the Zermatt slopes as a whole are very challenging for near-beginners, which includes fast learners who are ready to quit the nursery slopes after a couple of days. Of course you can learn to ski here, but given a choice we would still go elsewhere.

FOR CROSS-COUNTRY ★★★★★
Fairly limited
There's a 4km/2.5 mile loop at Furi, 3km/2 miles of trails near the bottom of the gondola to the Glacier area and another 12km/7 miles from Täsch to Randa (don't count on good snow). There are also 'ski walking trails', best tackled as part of an organised group.

SCHOOLS AND GUIDES ★★★★★
Competition paying off
The main Swiss school seems to have improved since competition was permitted, and this year's one report is positive. Stoked snowboard school is generally well regarded by reporters. It is made up of talented young instructors, some of whom are British and all of whom speak good English. Group sizes are said to be small. Summit and European Snowsport are staffed mainly by Brits. We've had positive reports on Summit, but this year's one report is inconclusive.

FOR FAMILIES ★★★★★
Good hotel nurseries
We get precious few reports from families here, which is not surprising given the prices, the general inconvenience of the place and the challenges facing beginners and near-beginners. But, as our margin panel shows, there are plenty of facilities for children and we don't doubt that they are thoroughly well run. The tourist office has a list of babysitters.

GETTING THERE

Air Geneva 240km/150 miles (4hr); Zürich 265km/165 miles (4hr30); Sion 80km/ 50 miles (2hr)

Rail Station in resort

UK PACKAGES

Alpine Answers, Alpine Weekends, Crystal, Crystal Finest, Descent International, Elegant Resorts, Independent Ski Links, Inghams, Interactive Resorts, Interhome, Kuoni, Lagrange, Made to Measure, Momentum, Mountain Tracks, Neilson, Oxford Ski Co, Powder Byrne, Scott Dunn, Simply Alpine, Ski Activity, Ski Expectations, Ski Freshtracks, Ski Independence, Ski Line, Ski Safari, Ski Solutions, Ski Total, Skitracer, Skiweekends. com, Snow Finders, Supertravel, Switzerland Travel Centre, Thomson, VIP, White Roc
Täsch *Interhome*

SMART LODGINGS

Check out our feature chapters at the front of the book.

STAYING THERE

Chalets Several operators have places here; many of the most comfortable are in apartment blocks. VIP have some luxury chalets.

Hotels There are over 100 hotels, mostly comfortable and traditional-style 3-stars and 4-stars, but taking in the whole range. Inghams features a large selection (and has chalets and apartments too).

*****Mont Cervin (966 8888) Biggest in town. Elegantly traditional.

*****Zermatterhof (966 6600) Traditional 'grand hotel' style with piano bar.

*****Omnia (966 7171) Modern, minimalist, central, reached by a lift in a rock, smart fitness centre.

****Coeur des Alpes (966 4080) Smart, modern B&B place at south end of town; relaxed, friendly feel. Pool and fitness facilities visible through glass lobby floor.

****Alex (966 7070) Close to train stations. Repeatedly praised ('food and rooms quite superb'). Pool.

****Ambassador (966 2611) Near train stations. Large pool; sauna. Very popular with readers for 'very good staff, outstanding breakfast, very good dinner' – though it offers no choice.

****Beausite (966 6868) Grand place over the river with Matterhorn views. 'Simply the best hotel we've stayed at – food out of this world.'

****Julen (966 7600) Charming, modern-rustic chalet over the river.

****Matterhorn Focus (966 2424) Super-stylish B&B place designed by Heinz Julen, right by the Matterhorn lifts. 'Exceptionally good.'

****Metropol (966 3566) 'Couldn't have been more friendly and helpful.' 'Great' wellness centre. Pool.

****Monte Rosa (966 0333) Well-modernised original Zermatt hotel in centre; full of climbing mementos.

****Sonne (966 2066) In quiet setting; 'superb' wellness centre.

****Walliserhof (966 6555) Central 'friendly' hotel. Good rooms. Spa.

***Alpenroyal (966 6066) 'Nothing but praise for its comfort, service, food and location' (well out of the centre).

***Atlanta (966 3535) No frills, but 'clean, warm, friendly and serves wholesome food'; close to centre, with Matterhorn views from some rooms.

***Butterfly (966 4166) Near the train stations. 'Very comfortable, friendly, and good five-course meals.'

***Matterhorn Blick (967 2017) Next to the church. 'Extremely welcoming; returning guests treated as friends,' said a 2008 reader on a fourth visit.

Apartments There are lots. We have enjoyed staying in the apartments of the hotel Ambassador (966 2611) several times (with free use of all its facilities such as a pool and a sauna). Ski Solutions has a decent selection; www.zermattapartmentrentals.com and the Vanessa complex (966 3510) have been recommended by reporters.

At altitude There are several hotels on the hill, of which the pick is:

*****Riffelalp Resort (966 0555) At the first stop on the Gornergrat railway; pool, spa, own evening trains. Highly recommended – luxurious, but 'not at all stuffy'.

You can also stay at the top of the railway in the Kulmhotel Gornergrat (966 6400) – an austere building but smart and modern inside with good-value rooms. But at 3100m/10,170ft, there's a risk of altitude sickness.

EATING OUT *****
Huge choice at all price levels

There are over 100 restaurants to choose from: top-quality haute cuisine, through traditional Swiss food, Chinese, Japanese and Thai to egg and chips. There is even a McDonald's. The tourist office produces a directory, with photos. A reader this year makes the point that you pay a lot less at restaurants at the south end of the village, well away from the centre.

One of our favourites is the Pipe – a tiny place with interesting Asian/African/Caribbean fusion dishes, 'still superb' according to a reader this year. We've also enjoyed the Schwyzer Stübli (local specialities and live Swiss music and dancing); good value Mexican and Swiss dishes at the Weisshorn, endorsed by a reader this year ('very good food, friendly service,

Interactive resort shortlist builder at www.wtss.co.uk

ACTIVITIES

Indoor Sauna, tennis, squash, hotel swimming pools (some open to public), fitness centre, climbing wall, bowling, gallery, library, concerts, museums, cinema

Outdoor Ice rinks, curling, sleigh rides, 45km/28 miles cleared paths, snowshoeing, tobogganing, helicopter flights, paragliding, climbing

Phone numbers
From elsewhere in Switzerland add the prefix 027; from abroad use the prefix +41 27

TOURIST OFFICE

t 966 8100
info@zermatt.ch
www.zermatt.ch

shame about the decor'); and decent Thai food at Rua Thai.

Other reader tips this year include: Casa Rustica ('good Swiss food, despite the name'); Klein Matterhorn ('superb food'); and the dear old Whymper-Stube ('great food, very friendly service, reasonable prices'). And tips worth bearing in mind from last year: Nelly's Grotta for 'great food at reasonable prices'; pizzeria Roma for good value. One past reporter suggested walking up to the Olympia Stübli for 'good food in a relaxed atmosphere'. You can also eat up at Othmar's and get home by toboggan.

APRES-SKI ★★★★★
Something for everybody
There's a good mix of sophisticated and informal fun, though it helps if you have deep pockets. Promenading the main street checking out expensive shoes and watches is a popular early-evening activity.

There are lively places to pause on your final descent. On the way back from the Glacier or Schwarzsee sectors there are lots of restaurants below Furi. Hennu Stall blasts out loud music and attracts huge crowds – live bands play most days. 'Possibly my favourite mountain bar of all,' says one fan. For a quieter time, try a cake or tart at Zum See. On the way back from Rothorn, Othmar's Skihütte has great views, and the Olympia Stübli often has live music. The new Snowboat bar (by the Sunnegga funicular) is a small, modern place, with a terrace and lounge bar. Good for a quiet drink.

For a lively bar through the evening you won't beat the Papperla Pub – 'great atmosphere, band inside and heat lamps outside'. The long-established North Wall doesn't get many mentions in reports but still seems to be the ski bum/season-worker favourite. Potters Bar (geddit?) is a relaxed, friendly British pub.

There are plenty of quieter places. Reader tips include the Little Bar (crowded if there are ten people in) and the cosy/cramped Hexen. Of the hotel bars, the Alex has been noted for 'comfy sofas, service and pool table' and the Pollux for 'nice atmosphere and good service'. For cigars, head to the 'super' Havanna bar of the Mont Cervin. The Vernissage is our favourite quiet bar – unusual, stylish and modern, with the projection room for the cinema built

into the upstairs bar and displays of art elsewhere. Heimberg was designed by the same guy and has a good cocktail bar downstairs and a restaurant above. Elsie's famous bar is wood-panelled and atmospheric, and attracts an older crowd, but gets uncomfortably busy early and late.

Later on, the hotel Post complex has something for everyone, from a quiet, comfortable bar (Papa Caesar's) to a lively disco (Broken), live music (Pink) and various restaurants. The T-Bar draws a young crowd for dancing and live bands. At Grampi's, the 'very entertaining' Elton John seems to be still pulling in the crowds – there is a disco downstairs. The Papperla has a nightclub downstairs – 'still heaving at 3.30am', say reporters.

OFF THE SLOPES ★★★★
Considerable attractions
Zermatt is an attractive place to spend time. As well as expensive jewellery and clothes shops, there are interesting places selling food, wine, books and art. It is easy (but costly) for pedestrians to get around on the lifts and meet others for lunch, and there are some nice walks – a special map is available. If the weather is good, the Klein Matterhorn cable car is an experience not to be missed, and there is now a restaurant at the top as well as a viewing platform and an Ice Grotto, with 'incredible carvings'. Be aware that the air is thin up there, though. The Matterhorn Museum in town is worth seeing. You can take a helicopter trip around the Matterhorn (see 'Queues'). There is a cinema, and free village guided tours. For an icy experience, visit (or stay at) the Igloo above Riffelberg.

Täsch 1450m/4,755ft
Täsch, where visitors must leave their cars, is just a 13-minute train ride from Zermatt, so makes a viable base. There are five 3-star hotels charging half the Zermatt price. The Täscherhof (966 6262) – 'fine, comfortable and with a reasonably priced restaurant' – and the Walliserhof (966 3966) – 'a very good option' – have been recommended by past reporters. Täsch is very quiet in the evening, but trains run until 12.30am Monday to Wednesday, and hourly all night from Thursday to Sunday. Taxis can operate up to the edge of Zermatt.

Most people who give it a try find America is pretty seductive, despite the relatively small sizes of its ski areas. What got the US started in the UK market was its (generally) reliable snow, and that remains a key factor. Other factors are the relatively deserted pistes, the quality of accommodation, the excellent, varied resort restaurants, the high standards of service and courtesy, and the immaculate piste grooming. Depending on the resort, you may also be struck by the cute Wild West ambience and the superb quality of the snow. Of course, US skiing does have some distinct disadvantages, too. Read on.

We have organised our American chapters in regional sections – California, Colorado, Utah, Rest of the West and New England.

Most American resorts receive serious amounts of snow – typically in the region of 6m to 12m (or 250 to 500 inches, as they measure it there) in a season. It tends to arrive in more frequent falls than in Europe, so your chances of hitting fresh snow are appreciably higher. And most resorts have serious snowmaking facilities that are used well – laying down a base of snow early in the season, rather than patching up shortages later. There are wide differences in quantity and quality of snowfall, both between individual resorts and between regions – check out our regional introductions.

The classification of pistes (or trails, to use the local term) is different from that in Europe. Red runs don't exist. The colours used are combined with shapes. Green circles correspond fairly closely to greens in France and easy blues in the rest of Europe. American blue squares correspond to blues and easy reds in Europe; the tougher ones are sometimes labelled as double squares, or as blue-black squares. Then there are black diamond runs, which is where things get interesting. Single diamonds correspond fairly closely to European blacks and really tough reds. But then there are multiple diamonds. Double diamond runs are seriously steep – usually steeper than the steepest pistes in the Alps. A few resorts have wildly steep 'extreme' double diamonds, or triple diamonds.

The most obvious drawback to the US is that many resorts have

573

PATROLLED AND AVALANCHE-CONTROLLED OFF-PISTE

One of the great attractions of North American resorts to us is that they have patrolled and avalanche-controlled ungroomed terrain that would be classified as off-piste in Europe. Each resort has a 'ski area boundary'; this may be marked by signs on the trees bordering the trails or there may be a rope running right round the ski area boundary. The 'boundary' may be moved depending on snow conditions, and anywhere within the boundary is known as 'in-bounds' and is patrolled and avalanche controlled. In-bounds terrain includes areas between marked and groomed trails and often big areas of ski-anywhere bowls or steep couloirs (or chutes, to use the local term). In Europe such terrain is normally off-piste, and we recommend you ski it only with a qualified local guide; in North America it is safe to ski it without that expense. North America also has what it calls backcountry, which is the area outside the ski area boundary (and which you are often forbidden to access except through gates placed at various points on the boundary). This is not controlled or patrolled and should be treated like European off-piste and skied only with a guide.

SNOWPIX.COM / CHRIS GILL
← Superb snow, trees all around, non-spectacular scenery, no crowds: the general American formula. Here on Aspen Mountain, the lack of crowds is taken to extremes

slopes that are very modest in extent compared with major Alpine areas. But usually there are other resorts nearby – so if you are prepared to travel a bit, you won't get bored. Roads are good and car hire is cheap (watch out for extra insurance charges, though). But if snow is expected, you will need a 4WD or snow chains (you'll have to buy them – we've yet to find a US rental company that will provide them). It's also true that in many resorts the mountains are slightly monotonous, with countless similar trails cut through the forest. You don't usually get the spectacular mountain scenery and the distinctive high-mountain runs of the Alps. But the forest runs do offer good visibility in bad weather, and unlike in Europe, it's normal to be able to ski in among the trees themselves (or glades as they call them) – great fun in fresh snow.

GREAT GROOMING AND DESERTED SLOPES

Piste grooming is taken very seriously – most US resorts set standards that only the best Alpine resorts seem to be able to match. Every morning you can expect to step out on to perfect 'corduroy' pistes. But this doesn't mean that there aren't moguls – far from it. It's just that you get moguls where the resort says you can expect moguls, not everywhere.

The slopes of most US resorts are blissfully free of crowds – a key advantage that becomes more important every year as the pistes of Europe become ever more congested. If you want to ski quickly and safely with less fear of collisions, head for the States.

Ski schools offer consistently high standards, but work in a way that seems strange to Europeans – and disappointing to many. Your group will often have different instructors from day to day. Your classmates will vary too – people don't sign up for a week, but only for a day or two as they feel the need. This is no doubt partly because lessons are expensive – £80 a day in Vail last season, for example. But at least you don't have to join ski school to get to know the mountain: most resorts offer free guided tours of the area, once or twice a day; and many have 'mountain hosts' on hand to help you find your way. Piste maps are freely available at lift stations, and signposting is generally exemplary.

Childcare, similarly, is impressive but expensive.

Lift passes are expensive, too, especially if you just walk up to the ticket booth and pay the advertised rate. But in many resorts you can save huge amounts by buying in advance through tour operators or websites. Strangely, you can often also save money by buying discounted lift passes from local stores rather than at the official ticket office. Lifts are generally efficient, and queues are orderly and short, partly because spare seats are religiously filled with the aid of cheerful, conscientious attendants who ask 'How are you today?' or urge you to 'Have a nice day' every time you get on a lift. You'll also find that Americans on chairlifts with you will be keen to talk to you on the way – weird to European eyes, but we like it. First-time visitors are surprised that some chairlifts in the States do not have safety bars; even on a chair that has a bar, you will find Americans curiously reluctant to use it, and eager to raise it as soon as the top station is in view. They worry about being trapped, not falling off. The lifts close irritatingly early – often at 3pm or 3.30. That may explain another drawback of America – the dearth of decent mountain restaurants. The norm is a monster self-service refuelling station – designed to minimise time off the slopes.

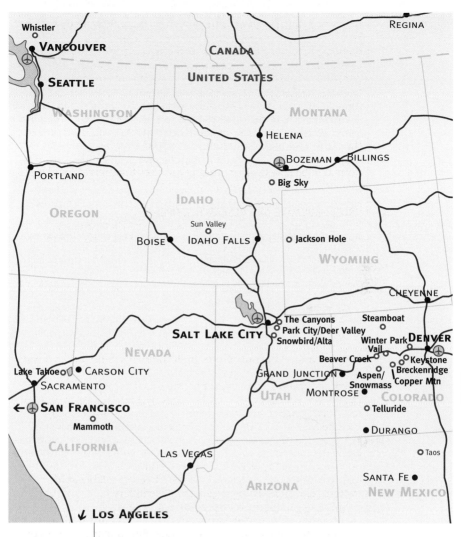

Interactive resort shortlist builder at www.wtss.co.uk

Small restaurants with table service and decent food are rare.

US resort towns vary widely in style and convenience, from cute restored mining towns miles from the lifts to purpose-built monstrosities. Two important things the resorts have in common are good-value, spacious accommodation and restaurants that are reliably good, reasonably priced and varied in cuisine. Young people should be aware that the rigorously enforced legal age for drinking alcohol is 21; even if you are older, carry evidence of age, especially if you look younger than you are.

Crossing the pond is no longer cheap, but eating and drinking when you get there is generally cheaper than in the Alps – the US Resort Price Index ratings in our survey varied from 65 in the cheapest resort (Big Sky) to 95 in the priciest (Aspen and Vail).

In the end, your reaction to skiing and snowboarding in America may depend on your reaction to America. If repeated cheerful exhortations to have a nice day wind you up – or if you like to ride chairlifts in silence – perhaps you'd better stick to the Alps.

California/Nevada

California? It means surfing, beaches, wine, Hollywood, Disneyland and San Francisco cable cars. Nevada means gambling. But this region also has the highest mountains in continental USA and some of America's biggest winter resorts, usually reliable for snow from November to May. What's more, winter holidays here are less expensive than you might expect.

Most visitors head for the Lake Tahoe area. Spectacularly set high in the Sierra Nevada 320km/200 miles east of San Francisco, Lake Tahoe is ringed by skiable mountains containing 14 downhill resorts and seven cross-country centres – the highest concentration of winter sports resorts in the USA. Then, a long way south (more often reached from LA), there is Mammoth.

Each of the three major 'destination' resorts – Heavenly and Squaw Valley in the Lake Tahoe area and Mammoth further south – is covered in its own chapter immediately after this page.

The other main Lake Tahoe resorts (shown on our map) each have an entry in the resort directory at the back of the book. Many are well worth visiting for a day or two, especially the four second-division resorts – Alpine Meadows, Kirkwood, Northstar and Sierra-at-Tahoe. We also enjoyed Sugar Bowl and Mount Rose. You could visit them all by car (best to have a 4WD) from a single base, but a two-centre holiday with some time at the north end of the lake and some at the south would be better. A lift pass covering various resorts around the lake and another valid at seven northern resorts are both available through tour operators (also see www.skilaketahoe. co.uk and www.gotahoenorth.com).

Californian resorts often have the deepest snowfall in North America, which Rockies powder connoisseurs are inclined to brand as wet 'Sierra Cement'. The snow can be heavy – we've had a visit spoiled by rain. But most people find the snow just fine, especially in comparison with what you would expect in the Alps – we've had truly fabulous powder days in all the major resorts here.

Californian resorts don't have the traditional mountain-town ambience that can add an extra dimension to holidays in other parts of the States, particularly Colorado. The recently developed car-free plaza in South Lake Tahoe called Heavenly Village and the pedestrian Village at Mammoth – both linked to the slopes by gondola – haven't achieved a great deal in this respect. But Squaw Valley and Northstar have both developed attractive new base villages. If we were to pick one base for a Tahoe holiday, it would now be Squaw.

Map

To Reno
80
Mount Rose
To Sacramento & San Francisco
Truckee River
TRUCKEE
80
Truckee/Tahoe Airport
Sugar Bowl
Donner Ski Ranch
Diamond Peak
Northstar at-Tahoe
INCLINE VILLAGE
Squaw Valley
TAHOE CITY
Truckee River
STATELINE
Marlette Lake
Alpine Meadows
LAKE TAHOE
1890M
Spooner Lake
50
50
Homewood
Tahoe Queen Shuttle
NEVADA
Daggett Pass 2235m
CALIFORNIA
Emerald Bay
SOUTH LAKE TAHOE
Heavenly
5km / 3 miles
Fallen Leaf Lake
50
Upper Truckee River
Twin Bridges
Echo Summit 2250m
Meyers
Luther Pass 2340m
Grover Hot Springs State Park
Sierra-at-Tahoe
To Sacramento
50
Kirkwood
Carson Pass 2615m

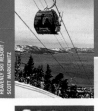

Heavenly

It's unique: fabulous lake and 'desert' views from interestingly varied slopes above a tacky lakeside casino town

£90
RESORT PRICE INDEX

RATINGS

The mountains

Extent	★★★
Fast lifts	★★★★
Queues	★★★★
Terrain p'ks	★★★★★
Snow	★★★★
Expert	★★★
Intermediate	★★★★
Beginner	★★★★
X-country	★★★
Restaurants	★
Schools	★★★★
Families	★★

The resort

Charm	★
Convenience	★
Scenery	★★★★
Eating out	★★★★
Après-ski	★★★
Off-slope	★★

It's all below the treeline – a compelling mix of defined trails and delightful gladed areas ↓

➕ Spectacular setting, with amazing views of Lake Tahoe and Nevada

➕ Fair-sized mountain that offers a sensation of travelling around

➕ Large areas of widely spaced trees, largely on intermediate slopes – fabulous in fresh powder

➕ Some serious challenges for experts

➕ Numerous other worthwhile resorts within an hour's drive

➕ A unique nightlife scene

➕ Good snow record plus impressive snowmaking facilities

➖ South Lake Tahoe, where you stay, is a bizarre and messy place spreading along a busy highway

➖ No trail back to Heavenly Village at the base of the gondola

➖ Gondola vulnerable to wind closure

➖ If the tree skiing is not good, or if you are not up to it, you are mainly confined to easy groomed blues and mogulled blacks

➖ If natural snow is poor, most of the challenging terrain may be closed

➖ Very little traditional après-ski

A resort called Heavenly invites an obvious question: just how close to heaven does it take you? Physically, close enough: with a top height of 3060m/10,040ft and vertical of 1060m/3,480ft, it's the highest and biggest of the resorts set around famously deep, pure and beautiful Lake Tahoe. Metaphorically, it's not quite so close. In particular, anyone drawn to Heavenly by its exceptionally scenic setting is likely to be dismayed by the base town of South Lake Tahoe.

The official line is that Heavenly is a proper ski resort now that it has a gondola from downtown South Lake Tahoe, and the car-free Heavenly Village development around it. Well, not quite. The 'village' is neat, but quiet and small – the general feel of South Lake Tahoe isn't much affected. And many visitors still use the original out-of-town lift bases to avoid the queue-prone gondola.

THE RESORT

Heavenly is at the south end of Lake Tahoe. The base-town – South Lake Tahoe – is primarily a summer resort. We place it in California, but actually it straddles the border with Nevada, and this is what really sets this place apart: its economy is driven by gambling, which Nevada permits.

The central Stateline area is dominated by a handful of high-rise hotel-casinos crammed together on the Nevada side of the line. These brash but comfortable hotels offer good-value accommodation (subsidised by the gambling), swanky restaurants and big-name entertainers. It's bizarre to pick your way between the slot machines in ski gear, carrying skis or board. The rest of the town spreads for miles along US Highway 50, past the small purpose-built Heavenly Village development around the main lift base. There are other lift base areas on both California and Nevada sides of the hill.

Other resorts around the lake are easily visited from a base here. A car is handy to explore them (although buses, some free, are available) and to get to many of the best restaurants, but parking can be expensive.

You can visit Squaw Valley by coach and return by boat across the lake.

NEWS

For 2009/10 a new moving carpet is planned to serve the beginner runs and Adventure Peak activity area at the top of the gondola.

For 2008/09 two black glades, the Pinnacles, were cut in the SkiWays Glades, and a new gladed area, Powderbowl Woods, opened by the chairlift of the same name. The Skyline Trail was improved to make it less flat, and the Stagecoach area gained snowmaking. On the Nevada side, the East Peak Lodge was revamped.

KEY FACTS

Resort	1900m
	6,230ft
Slopes	2000-3060m
	6,570-10,040ft
Lifts	29
Pistes	4,800 acres
Green	20%
Blue	45%
Black	35%
Snowmaking	70%

VILLAGE CHARM ★☆☆☆☆
The highway rules

From a distance the casinos look like a classic American downtown area, which you'd expect to be full of shops and bars. But there's none of that – just the seriously busy and pedestrian-hostile highway. Out along this road are dozens of low-rise hotels and motels (some quite shabby), stores, wedding chapels and so on. The general effect is less dire than it might be, thanks to the camouflage of tall trees. Heavenly Village provides a downtown après-ski focus (basically just one bar), but is otherwise not a great success. It's a pity the ice rink has a huge generator/chiller next to it.

CONVENIENCE ★☆☆☆☆
Gamble on the gondola?

The central area close to Heavenly Village and the gondola looks the obvious place to stay, despite the lack of trails down to it. Some of the casino-hotels are within five minutes' walk of the gondola, but others are a hike away. Much of the cheaper places are literally miles away from here, and better placed for the alternative lift bases – California Lodge, up a heavily wooded slope 2km/1 mile out of South Lake Tahoe, and the more remote Nevada bases, Boulder Lodge and Stagecoach Lodge. There are free shuttle-buses, though these have been criticised in 2009 as 'infrequent and inadequate'. You can ski down at the end of the day to all these bases.

SCENERY ★★★★☆
Surpasses expectations

Many reporters enthuse about the spectacular views over Lake Tahoe, surrounded by splendid mountain scenery. The casinos are a conspicuous part of those views from the lower slopes, though not from above mid-mountain; the long Ridge Run, across the top, is good for lake views. In the other direction the slopes overlook the wild and arid Nevada 'desert'.

THE MOUNTAIN

Practically all of Heavenly's slopes are cut through forest, but in many areas the forest is not dense and there is excellent tree skiing. The trail map gives a good indication of the density of trees, and the classification of nearby trails gives a good idea of steepness. As always in America, this 'off-piste' terrain is avalanche controlled. But it's 'patrolled' only by hollering; since collision with a tree may render you unconscious, don't ski the trees alone.

EXTENT OF THE SLOPES ★★★☆☆
Interestingly complex

The mountain is complicated, and getting from A to B requires more careful navigation than is usual on American mountains (eg it's not obvious from the piste map that it's much better to take the Comet rather than the Dipper chair back from Nevada to the California side). Quite a few of the links between different sectors involve long, flat tracks – one of those, Skyline, was remodelled last season and should now be better.

There is a clear division between the California side of the mountain (above South Lake Tahoe) and the Nevada side.

On the California side there are two main sectors. The steep lower slopes are served by the Aerial Tramway (that is, cable car) and Gunbarrel fast chair from California Lodge. The much more extensive upper slopes beyond are served by four fast chairs out of an elevated valley, reachable from the top of the tram and by the gondola from South Lake Tahoe. The major Sky Express chairlift takes you to the area high-point, and the Skyline trail to the Nevada side, mentioned above.

The Nevada side is more fragmented, but the central focus is East Peak Lodge. Above it is an excellent intermediate area, served by two fast quad chairs, with a downhill

boarding

Heavenly's varied terrain makes a perfect playground for advanced freeriders. Intermediates will have fun too, as there are plenty of gentle powder runs served mainly by chairs. And there are good areas for beginners. Heavenly has several terrain parks and the South Shore Soldiers spring freestyle camps (www. southshoresoldiers.com). There are now beginner camps that run from January to March. Get all your kit at Burton Heavenly, at California lodge; boards, boots and bindings are available to demo for free as well.

LIFT PASSES

Heavenly

Prices in US$

Age	1-day	6-day
under 13	47	282
13 to 18	74	444
19 to 64	86	516
over 65	74	444

Free under 5

Beginner combined lesson/lift pass/ equipment deals

Notes

Prices are those at the ticket window in the resort in high season – reduced prices are available online before your trip and to international visitors who pre-book through a UK tour operator; it is not necessary to buy a complete holiday package to obtain these prices

extension served by the Galaxy chair. From the fast Dipper chair back up, you can access the open terrain of Milky Way Bowl, leading to the seriously steep chutes of Mott and Killebrew canyons, served by the Mott Canyon chair. Below East Peak Lodge are runs down to Nevada's two bases, Stagecoach and Boulder – the latter often quiet because its chairs are slow.

FAST LIFTS ★★★★
California does it better
Most people can spend practically all their time on fast chairs. The Mott Canyon chair is slow, but that's a niche market. The main weakness is the slow chairs up from Boulder Lodge.

QUEUES ★★★★
Gondola up and down
The gondola can have queues to go up in the morning and down at the end of the day – and you'll see signs advising you to get back to the gondola ridiculously early. There's no need – have a beer or two at the bar near the top while you wait for the queue to disappear. Or forget the gondola and use one of the other bases, served by shuttle buses. The gondola also seems prone to closure

because of wind. Recent reporters have had few other problems, often commenting on uncrowded slopes.

TERRAIN PARKS ★★★★★
Splendid for all abilities
Heavenly has something for everyone – all sensibly located on the California slopes. The Groove Park, at the top of the lifts up from California Lodge, has beginner features such as small jumps and boxes for novice park riders. Intermediates should head to Powderbowl Park on the Powderbowl run; this is a great progression area, which has had a good facelift in 2009 with a triple kicker line and new rails, boxes and a wall ride with a unique step-up double coping. High Roller Park, near the top of the Canyon chair, serves expert riders; there are big kicker lines, and all sorts of jibs including an awesome pyramid jib box feature and three-level box, a large metal water pipe and big step-up jump. Below this, at the top of the Powderbowl chairlift, is a beast of a super-pipe with 7m/23ft walls. The Cascade boardercross can be found to the side of the Tamarack chair. The High Roller Nightlife at the California base was not built for 2008/09.

Heavenly

579

SCHOOLS

Heavenly
t 775 586 7000

Classes
3-day (3 x 2¼hr)
learn-to-ski package
(includes equipment
and pass) $425

Private lessons
From $395 for 3hr

CHILDCARE

Day Care Center
t 775 586 7000
Ages 6wk to 6yr;
8.30-4pm; $150
including lunch;
discount if booked
ahead

Ski school
For ages 4 to 13
(snowboarding 5 to
13); full day
(including 5hr of
teaching, equipment,
pass and lunch) $175

UK PACKAGES

*Alpine Answers,
AmeriCan Ski, American
Ski Classics, Crystal,
Crystal Finest, Erna
Low, Funway Holidays,
Independent Ski Links,
Simply Alpine, Ski
Dream, Ski
Independence, Ski Line,
Ski Safari, Ski
Solutions, Skitracer,
Skiworld, Trailfinders,
United Vacations*

SNOW RELIABILITY ★★★★
No worries for intermediates
Heavenly averages an impressive 360 inches per year, but does sometimes need to call on its impressive snowmaking system, which now ensures that most sections are open most of the time. But good natural snow is needed for Mott and Killebrew Canyons to be enjoyable (or even open). There's a useful TV programme at 7.30am, *Another Heavenly Morning*, which covers snow conditions.

FOR EXPERTS ★★★
Some specific challenges
The black runs under the California base lifts – including the Face and Gunbarrel (often used for mogul competitions) – are seriously steep. We've seen lots of people struggling on the top-to-bottom icy bumps. Many of the single diamonds higher up are at the easy end of the range. Ellie's, at the top of the mountain, may offer continuous moguls too, but was groomed and a great fast cruise when we last skied it. SkiWays Glades, to skier's right of that, offer friendly, widely spaced trees, and two trails, the Pinnacles, opened further to the right for 2008/09. On the Nevada side there are some excellent single-diamond glade areas too – some identified on the trail map – plus some really steep stuff. Milky Way Bowl provides a gentle single-diamond introduction to the double-diamond terrain beyond it: the chutes in the otherwise densely wooded Mott and Killebrew canyons are seriously steep and narrow. They are accessed through roped gateways, and are not to be underestimated. The Mott Canyon chair is slow, but you may not mind.

FOR INTERMEDIATES ★★★★
Lots to do
Heavenly is a good intermediate area. The California side offers a progression from the relaxed cruising of the long Ridge Run, starting right at the top of the mountain, to more challenging blues dropping off the ridge towards Sky Deck. Confident intermediates will want to spend time on the Nevada side, where there is more variety of terrain, some longer runs down to the lift bases and more carving space. There are some great top-to-bottom cruises down to Stagecoach Lodge (served by a fast chair) and Boulder Lodge (served by successive very slow

chairs and then the fast Olympic quad). And adventurous intermediates will enjoy exploring the tree runs from the fast Sky chair on the California side and lower down, in a new area of glades off the Powder Bowl chair.

FOR BEGINNERS ★★★★
An excellent place to learn
There's an excellent beginner area at the top of the gondola and others at the California base lodge and Boulder Lodge in Nevada. On the California side there are gentle green runs to progress to at the top of the cable car.

FOR CROSS-COUNTRY ★★★
A separate world
The serious stuff is around the lake – notably at the Spooner Lake: over 80km/50 miles of prepared trails.

MOUNTAIN RESTAURANTS ★
Some improvement maybe?
We have long considered the on-mountain catering grossly inadequate, especially in bad weather. Probably the best choice is the Gunbarrel Grill in Lake View Lodge, which a 2009 reader recommends for its 'excellent buffet for about $25'. East Peak Lodge has been renovated, the menu widened, and with more indoor seating than previously ('nice music too'). The other options consist of outdoor decks serving BBQs and pizzas (hugely unenjoyable in a blizzard, as we can testify) and grossly overcrowded cafeterias, 'I recommend starving, unless you're happy with crowds and stodge' and 'resoundingly awful with almost nowhere to sit indoors', say two reporters.

SCHOOLS AND GUIDES ★★★★
Small groups if you're lucky
Recent reports are positive – this year one couple at different levels had 'excellent' classes in groups of four or fewer. The school's Mountain Adventure clinics are 'well worth it to gain some local knowledge'. Package deals of tuition and lift ticket are worth looking into.

FOR FAMILIES ★★
Hardly heavenly
Heavenly offers various children's programmes and facilities, and Adventure Peak is home to family activities such as tubing. But there are more obvious choices for a family trip.

GETTING THERE

Air San Francisco 320km/200 miles (3hr45); Reno 90km/55 miles (1hr30); South Lake Tahoe, 15min

ACTIVITIES

Indoor Casinos, spas, art galleries, multiplex cinema, museums

Outdoor Lake cruises, snowmobiling, sleigh rides, dog sledding, hot springs, fishing, ice rink, zip-line, snowshoeing, factory outlet shops

Phone numbers
Different area codes are used on the two sides of the stateline; for this chapter, therefore, the area code is included with each number

From distant parts of the US, add the prefix 1. From abroad, add the prefix +1

TOURIST OFFICE

t 775 586 7000
info@vailresorts.com
www.skiheavenly.com

STAYING THERE

Accommodation in the South Lake Tahoe area is abundant and ranges from the huge casinos to small motels.
Chalets UK tour operators run some good catered chalets.
Hotels Of the main casino hotels, Harrah's (775 588 6611) and Harveys (775 588 2411) are the closest to the gondola. Rooms booked on the spot are expensive; packages are cheaper.
****Embassy Suites (530 544 5400) Luxury suites close to the gondola. Huge breakfast spread and après cocktails included.
Inn by the Lake (530 542 0330) 'Posh motel', less convenient but 'big rooms, nice view'. Hot tub, pool.
Rodeway Inn (530 541 7150) Simple place a short walk from the gondola.
Tahoe Chalet Inn (530 544 3311) Clean, friendly, near casinos. Back rooms (away from highway) preferable.
3 Peaks Resort (530 544 4131) Convenient, with large rooms. Pool.
Timber Cove Lodge (530 541 6722) Bland but well run, with lake views from some rooms.
Lakeland Village (530 544 1685) Wide range of 'very comfortable' lodgings.
Apartments Plenty of choice. The Ridge Tahoe condos near Stagecoach Lodge have been recommended. Shuttle to the lifts.

EATING OUT ★★★★
Good value and choice
There's a huge variety. The casino hotels' all-you-can-eat buffets offer fantastic value and variety and there are 'gourmet' choices too – try the Forest Buffet on the 18th floor at Harrah's and 19 on the 19th at Harveys – 'great steaks'. A 2009 reporter recommends Evans American Gourmet

Cafe ('wonderful fresh food, extensive wine list'). The Brit-style Tudor pub near the Inn by the Lake, serves 'great burgers, steaks and Guinness'.
Other reporter suggestions include Hunan Garden for Chinese and Taj Mahal for Indian, Cecil's for steaks, Nephele's ('good game'), Fresh Ketch at Tahoe Keys Marina ('good fish; went twice and loved it'), Zephyr Cove Resort and Coyote Grill for Mexican fast food. For breakfast, try the Blue Angel or the Driftwood Cafe.

APRES-SKI ★★★
Getting better
The close-of-play scene has looked up in the last few years: there is an Austrian-style umbrella bar near the top of the gondola and Fire+Ice at the foot of it (with an outdoor seating area with fires and heaters). Both get busy. McP's is a locals' hangout directly across from the gondola. It was still operating for 2008/09 but is due to be razed to the ground as part of a planned resort revamp. Whiskey Dick's, on the main highway, has regular live music. Later on, the casinos have shows with top-name entertainers. And you can dance and dine your way across the lake on a paddle steamer.

OFF THE SLOPES ★★
Luck be a lady
If you enjoy gambling, you're in the right place. If you want to get away from the bright lights, try a boat trip on Lake Tahoe, snowmobiling or a hot-air balloon ride. Pedestrians can use the cable car or the gondola to share the lake views. Adventure Peak, at the top of the gondola, has tubing, snow biking, tobogganing and snowshoeing, and the Heavenly Flyer, a zip-line.

Mammoth Mountain

A big, sprawling mountain above a car-oriented, sprawling but pleasantly woody resort, a six-hour drive from Los Angeles

£85
RESORT PRICE INDEX

RATINGS

The mountains

Extent	★★★
Fast lifts	★★★★
Queues	★★★★
Terrain p'ks	★★★★★
Snow	★★★★
Expert	★★★★
Intermediate	★★★★
Beginner	★★★★
X-country	★★★★
Restaurants	★
Schools	★★★★
Families	★★★★

The resort

Charm	★★
Convenience	★★
Scenery	★★★
Eating out	★★★★★
Après-ski	★★★
Off-slope	★

582

NEWS

Commercial flights from Los Angeles to Mammoth resumed in December 2008, after renovations to the airport.

The terrain parks were improved and got more snowmaking. And four new adventure zones were built at the family fun parks.

- ☐ One of North America's bigger ski hills, with something for everyone
- ☐ Good mix of open Alpine-style bowls and classic American wooded slopes
- ☐ Impressive snowfall record
- ☐ Uncrowded slopes most of the time
- ☐ Mightily impressive terrain parks
- ☐ Good views, including more Alpine drama than usual in the US

- ☐ Mammoth Lakes is a rather straggling place with no focus, where life revolves around cars
- ☐ Most accommodation is miles from the slopes – though there are several convenient options
- ☐ Weekend crowds in high season
- ☐ Trail map and signing inadequate
- ☐ Wind can be a problem

Mammoth may not be mammoth in Alpine terms – from end to end, it measures less than one-third of the size of Val d'Isère/Tignes, in area it's more like one-sixth – but it is big enough to amuse many people for a week. It can be a superb mountain for anyone who is happy in deep snow, but is equally suited to families and mixed-ability groups looking for groomed runs.

Thanks to Intrawest, developer/owner of Whistler in Canada, there is now something resembling a village to stay in – a typical Intrawest assembly of lodgings, restaurants and shops. But The Village, as it is called, is small, and a gondola ride from the slopes – most people stay elsewhere, in hotels, condos and houses spread around the vast wooded area that makes up the resort of Mammoth Lakes, and never go near The Village. So forget villages: pick your location carefully, and you can walk to a lift; get a car (and a Californian mindset), and you can enjoy exploring an impressive range of restaurants.

THE RESORT

The mountain is set above Mammoth Lakes, a small year-round resort town that spreads over a wide area of woodland. The drive up from Los Angeles takes over five hours (more in poor conditions); but it is not without interest. You pass through the Santa Monica mountains close to Beverly Hills, then the San Gabriel mountains and Mojave Desert (with the world's biggest jet-plane parking lot) before reaching the Sierra Nevada range.

The Mammoth lift pass also covers June, a small mountain half an hour's drive north, chiefly attractive for its quiet, often deserted slopes. See feature box, later in this chapter.

VILLAGE CHARM ★★
Good first impressions
The place is entirely geared to driving, with no discernible centre – hotels, restaurants and little shopping centres are scattered along the four-lane highway called Main Street and Old Mammoth Road, which crosses it. The

resort buildings are generally timber-clad in traditional style – even McDonald's has been tastefully designed – and are set among trees, so although it may be short on village ambience, the place has a pleasant enough appearance – particularly when under snow. The Village is car-free, and neatly designed, but one reporter tells us the shops are finding life difficult, and some have closed.

CONVENIENCE ★★
Canyon is closest
The town meets the mountain at two lift bases, both a mile or two from most of the hotels and condos.

The major base is Canyon Lodge, with a big day lodge and four chairlifts; there are hotels, condos and individual homes in the area below the lodge. The Village is linked to Canyon Lodge by a gondola, so is a fairly convenient base. The minor base, with a single six-pack, is Eagle Lodge (also known as Juniper Springs, which strictly is the name of the condo development at the base).

Steep, open bowls at the top, descending into trees and gentler terrain at the bottom; ideal, really →

MAMMOTH MOUNTAIN SKI AREA

Mammoth Mountain

Interactive resort shortlist builder at **www.wtss.co.uk**

KEY FACTS

Resort	2425m
	7,950ft

Mammoth only	
Slopes	2425-3370m
	7,950-11,050ft
Lifts	28
Pistes	3,500 acres
Green	25%
Blue	40%
Black	35%
Snowmaking	
	33%

June Mountain only	
Slopes	2290-3075m
	7,510-10,090ft
Lifts	7
Pistes	500 acres
Green	35%
Blue	45%
Black	20%
Snowmaking	none

A road runs along the north fringe of the mountain past an anonymous chairlift base to two other major base areas: The Mill Cafe, with two fast chairs, and Main Lodge, a mini-resort with three fast access lifts and a big day lodge. You can stay here, in the Mammoth Mountain Inn; but who wants to be based four miles from the 50+ restaurants in Mammoth Lakes?

Shuttle-buses run on several colour-coded routes serving the lift bases. Night buses also run via here until midnight. But a car is useful.

SCENERY ★★★☆☆
Impressive up top
The resort has a sheltered, wooded setting below contrasting Alpine style ridges. From the top there are great views into Nevada to the north-east, and of the jagged peaks of the Minarets to the west.

THE MOUNTAIN

The 28 lifts access an impressive area, suitable for all abilities. The highest runs are open, the lower ones sheltered by trees.

Finding your way around is not easy at first. The chairlifts are either named or numbered (the traditional practice was to give them numbers), but the trails are still ill defined: the map shows trails by means of isolated symbols, not continuous lines, and signposting of runs on the mountain is sporadic. On the lower part of the mountain this is mainly an inconvenience. But higher up there are real dangers in poor visibility. The map uses six classifications, including green/black and blue/black – a good idea, but somewhat pointless when you often end up on the wrong trail.

EXTENT OF THE SLOPES ★★★☆☆
Interesting variety
From **Main Lodge** the two-stage Panorama gondola goes via McCoy Station right to the top. There are countless ways down the front of the mountain, which range from steep to very steep – or vertical if the wind has created a cornice, as it often does. Or you can go off the back of the hill, down to **Outpost 14**, whence Chair 14 or Chair 13 bring you back to lower points on the ridge. The third option is to follow the ridge, which curls around and eventually brings you down to the Main Lodge area – though you wouldn't know it from studying the trail map. This route brings you past an easy area served by a double chair, and a very easy area served by the Discovery fast quad.

McCoy Station can also be reached using the Stump Alley fast chair from **The Mill Cafe**, on the road up from town. The fast Gold Rush quad, also from The Mill Cafe, takes you into the more heavily wooded eastern half of the area. This has long, gentle runs served by lifts up from **Canyon Lodge** and **Eagle Lodge** and seriously steep stuff as well as some intermediate terrain on the subsidiary peak known as Lincoln, served by lifts 25 and 22.

FAST LIFTS ★★★★☆
Where it counts
There is plenty of choice from every base: all the main access lifts are fast chairs or gondolas. The Outpost area is the least well served.

QUEUES ★★★★☆
Normally quiet slopes
Mammoth's lifts and slopes are usually very quiet, with few queues even during the busiest periods. The lift

LIFT PASSES

Mammoth Mountain

Prices in US$

Age	1-day	6-day
under 13	41	197
13 to 18	62	298
19 to 64	83	398
over 65	41	197

Free under 7, over 80

Beginner fixed price pass for four lifts only

Notes
Covers all lifts at Mammoth and June Mountains. Discounts for online advanced booking. Afternoon pass available

Alternative pass
June Mountain only

system is fairly impressive, but even that can struggle when the there's an invasion from Los Angeles on fine peak-season weekends. To avoid them, try the blissfully uncrowded June Mountain, half an hour away.

TERRAIN PARKS ★★★★★
Difficult to beat
Mammoth's world-class Unbound terrain comprises no less than seven parks. There are now over 50 jumps and 65 jibs, and three half-pipes in 90 acres of freestyle territory. Main Park, situated above Main Lodge, is huge; everything here is up to pro standard. Kickers in the Boneyard Bonanza range from 18m to 24m (60ft to 80ft) long and border the famous super-duper pipe (183m/600ft long, with 7m/23ft walls) that looms over the car park and dwarfs the super-pipe beside it; it is cut daily. A warm-up mini park on Woolly's run, Disco at Main, has small low-to-the-snow rails and boxes. For intermediate to advanced riders South Park and Forest Trail Park, by the Roller Coaster fast chair, are a real playground. Two treelined itineraries give a choice of rails or kickers, which allow you to hit six or seven obstacles in a row – perfect. There's also a boardercross. The Wonderland beginner park (formerly Family Fun Park) has a new location by Chair 7. It has a fun mini-pipe, various micro-scale rails, boxes and mini-jumps, and has a great atmosphere. The parks can get very crowded on the weekends – try neighbouring June mountain for a quiet and underrated alternative.

SNOW RELIABILITY ★★★★
A long season
Mammoth has an impressive snow record – an annual average of 385 inches, which puts it ahead of major Colorado resorts and about on a par with Jackson Hole. It is appreciably higher than other Californian resorts, and has an ever-expanding array of snow-guns, so it enjoys a long season. The mountain mostly faces roughly north-east; the relatively low and slightly sunny slopes down to Eagle Lodge are affected by warm weather before others. Strong winds are not uncommon on the upper mountain and the snow quality can be affected by these. This is not always a bad thing say reporters: 'powder in interesting places' or 'just like spring snow'. Grooming is generally good, with many slopes kept easily skiable.

FOR EXPERTS ★★★★
Some very challenging terrain
The steep double-diamond chutes strung across the width of the mountain top provide wonderful opportunities for experts. Fortunately for the rest of us there are three or four broad single-diamond slopes, requiring rather less bottle.

There is lots of challenging terrain lower down, too; Chair 5, Chair 22 (the top of which is higher than the very top of Heavenly) and Broadway are often open in bad weather when the top is firmly shut, and their more sheltered slopes may in any case have the best snow. There are plenty of good slopes over the back towards

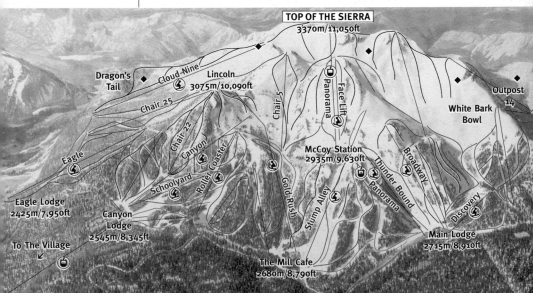

boarding

Mammoth has encouraged snowboarding since its early days. A huge amount has been spent on the terrain parks, and this tends to overshadow just how good the mountain's natural terrain really is. Almost entirely serviced by fast chairs and gondolas, this is a snowboarder's heaven. There are bowls, chutes, tree runs and cliffs dotted around the mountain, something for everybody. Take the Panorama gondola and drop into the back bowls for plenty of powder runs. There are heaps of not-so-steep and wide runs for beginners on the lower parts of the resort. The terrain parks are about the best you will find. Wave Rave snowboard shop has a huge selection of gear.

Outpost 14, too. Many of the steeper trails are short by Alpine standards (typically under 400m/1,300ft vertical), but despite this we've enjoyed some great powder days here.

FOR INTERMEDIATES ★★★★
Lots of great cruising
Although there are exceptions, most of the lower mountain, below the treeline, is intermediate cruising territory and generally flattering.

As you might hope, the six-point trail difficulty scale – which we haven't tried to replicate on our own small trail map – is a good guide to what you'll find on the mountain.

Some of the mountain's longest runs, blue-blacks served by the Cloud Nine Express and Chair 25, are ideal for good intermediates. There are also some excellent, fairly steep, woodland trails down to The Mill Cafe. Most of the long runs above Eagle Lodge, and some of the shorter ones above Canyon Lodge, are easy cruises. There is a variety of terrain, including lots of gentle stuff, at the western extremity of the slopes (the right hand side of the trail map), both on the front side and on the back side.

FOR BEGINNERS ★★★★
Good, gentle slopes
Chair 7 and the Schoolyard Express chair at Canyon Lodge and Discovery Chair at Main Lodge serve quiet,

gentle green runs – perfect progression terrain for novices. Excellent instruction and top-notch piste maintenance usually make progress speedy, delighting reporters.

FOR CROSS-COUNTRY ★★★★
Very popular
Two specialist centres, Tamarack and Sierra Meadows (ungroomed), provide lessons and tours. A 2009 reporter enjoyed an 'excellent outing' to the 30km/19 miles of scenic trails at Tamarack, 'gliding through the forest around mountain lakes'. And there are lots of ungroomed tracks, including some through the pretty Lakes Basin area: 70km/43 miles of trails in all.

MOUNTAIN RESTAURANTS ★☆☆☆☆
Back to base ...
There are only two lunch options on the hill, which can get busy. The newish Top of the Sierra Cafe does a gourmet three-course lunch at weekends, and the Market there has salads and sandwiches. McCoy Station at mid-mountain offers a fair choice and the Parallax table-service restaurant next door is pleasant, with a splendid view from its picture windows. A fair-weather choice is the primitive outdoor BBQ at Outpost 14, on the back of the hill. Most people head for the lift bases. Talons at Eagle Lodge has its fans. The Mill Cafe is 'better than most, with delicious beef

Mammoth Mountain

585

Interactive resort shortlist builder at **www.wtss.co.uk**

JUNE MOUNTAIN: THE WORLD'S QUIETEST SLOPES?

June Mountain, a scenic half-hour drive from Mammoth, is in the same ownership and covered by the lift pass. It makes a pleasant haven if Mammoth is busy. When Mammoth isn't busy, June is quite simply deserted; we've skied run after run without seeing another person.

A double chair goes up from the car park at 2290m/7,510ft over black slopes (often short of snow) to a lodge, June Meadows Chalet. A quad chair serves a gentle blue-run hill, and a double chair goes over very gentle green runs to a quad serving short but genuinely black slopes on June Mountain itself (3100m/ 10,170ft). There are three freestyle areas, a super-pipe and a jib park.

SCHOOLS

Mammoth Mountain
934 2571

Classes
1 day (9.30-3pm)
$109
Private lessons
$150 for 1hr

CHILDCARE

Small World
t 934 2571
Ages newborn to 8yr;
8.30-4.30

Ski school
Takes ages 5 to 12 at
a cost of $140 all day
(9am-3pm)

GETTING THERE

Air Los Angeles
494km/307 miles
(5hr); Reno
275km/175 miles
(4hr15)

UK PACKAGES

AmeriCan Ski, American
Ski Classics,
Independent Ski Links,
Simply Alpine, Ski
Dream, Ski
Independence, Ski Line,
Ski Safari, Ski
Solutions, Skitracer,
Skiworld, Virgin Snow

ACTIVITIES

Indoor Fitness
centres, museum, art
galleries, cinema,
theatre

Outdoor Ice rink,
snow tubing, dog
sledding,
snowmobiling

Phone numbers
From distant parts of
the US, add the prefix
1 760; from abroad,
add the prefix +1 760

TOURIST OFFICE

t 934 2571
800mammoth@
mammoth-mtn.com
www.mammoth
mountain.com

---

sandwiches'. The Yodler (aka Cervinia) at Main Lodge has table service and 'good' Italian food. The Mountainside Grill at the Mammoth Mountain Inn, Canyon Lodge and the Broadway Marketplace are other options.

SCHOOLS AND GUIDES ★★★★
Excellent reports
Feedback on the Mammoth school has been very positive, notably for small classes and patient instruction. And there is a choice of performance classes, such as 'camps' for experts and for women. As is often the case in America though, you may get a different instructor each day.

FOR FAMILIES ★★★★
Family favourite
Mammoth is keen to attract families. The focal point is the Small World childcare centre, with comprehensive facilities for children up to eight years old. Working closely with them is the Woollywood school, based in the Panorama gondola station and offering various tuition packages. There are other kids' schools at the Canyon and Eagle Lodges.

STAYING THERE

A good choice of hotels (none very luxurious or expensive) and condos. The condos tend to be out of town, near the lifts or on the road to them.
***Mammoth Mountain Inn** (934 2581) Good value, but way out of town at Main Lodge. Recently renovated.
***Alpenhof Lodge** (934 6330) Comfortable and centrally located. Shuttle-bus stop and plenty of restaurants nearby.
Westin Monache Resort (934 0400) Condo hotel near The Village gondola, with restaurant, hot tubs and pool.
Quality Inn (934 5114) Good main street hotel with a big hot tub.
Sierra Nevada Rodeway Inn (934 2515) Central, good value. Spa.
Holiday Inn (924 1234) Central location, 'good rooms, cheap bar and an OK restaurant'. Pool.
Apartments The Village Lodge is close to many restaurants and shops; Juniper Springs Lodge is near the Eagle base; both are high-quality places. Other comfortable options are the 1849 Condos (Canyon Lodge area) and the nearby Mammoth Ski and Racquet Club. There's a supermarket in the Minaret Mall, with good discounts.

EATING OUT ★★★★★
Outstanding choice
Mammoth has 50+ restaurants offering a wide choice from typical American to Japanese. There's a local menu guide covering many but not all.

The chalet-style Lakefront in the Tamarack Lodge is one of the best, with great views and 'a real French feel and fabulous food', enthuses a 2009 reporter. Slocums Grill is a popular steakhouse ('excellent meals'). Similarly, Angels has 'good value ribs and steaks'. Chart House serves 'excellent' seafood dishes, and another 2009 visitor liked the 'great salad bar, pizza and pasta' at Giovanni's Italian. For 'good home cooking' the meat loaf or prime rib at the Stove is reportedly worth a try. And we've had excellent dinners at Skadi and Whiskey Creek.

Other possibilities include Shogun for Japanese or Gomez's for Tex-Mex. For a hearty breakfast, try the ... er ... Breakfast Club. LuLu and the Side Door cafe are appealing eateries in The Village. The Parallax at McCoy Station opens for snowcat dinners up the mountain.

APRES-SKI ★★★
Lively at weekends
At the close of play, the Yodler at Main Lodge is still the liveliest spot – a newly renovated chalet (originally transported from Switzerland, so they say) that was briefly renamed Cervinia. (Well, it's quite close to Switzerland ...) Tusks and the Dry Creek bars are other choices at Main Lodge.

Nightlife revolves around a handful of bars, livening up at weekends. The pick of the bunch with reporters are the Clocktower Cellar, Whiskey Creek (stays open late), Grumpy's sports bar and quieter Slocums. In The Village, Hawaiian-style Lakanuki's and the Auld Dubliner Irish bar are worth a look. A new après-ski bus runs from Main Lodge to The Village, connecting with the town buses.

OFF THE SLOPES ★
Mainly sightseeing
There are various outdoor activities, including skating. There are pleasant drives; Mono Lake is 'worth a visit', and the town of Bishop is 40 minutes' drive south. There is factory shopping nearby too, and the World War II centre at Manzanar on the road to Los Angeles is recommended.

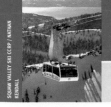

Squaw Valley

The site of the 1960 Winter Olympics has recently become the most compelling base in the Tahoe area, for novices and experts at least

+ Lots of challenging runs and ungroomed terrain
+ Impressive snow record
+ Superb beginner slopes
+ Convenient, pleasant, purpose-built village at the base

− Not for mile-hungry intermediates
− Lifts prone to closure by wind
− Adventurous skiers need guidance to really exploit the area
− Limited range of village amenities

When Intrawest built a neat little pedestrian resort at the base a few years back, Squaw became an attractive 'destination' resort. It can't rival Heavenly for groomed cruisers, but it's now our favourite base in the Tahoe area.

TOP 10 RATINGS

Extent	★★★
Fast lifts	★★★
Queues	★★★★
Snow	★★★★
Expert	★★★★
Intermediate	★★
Beginner	★★★★
Charm	★★★
Convenience	★★★★
Scenery	★★★

KEY FACTS

Resort	1890m	
	6,200ft	
Slopes	1890-2760m	
	6,200-9,050ft	
Lifts		33
Pistes		4,000 acres
Green		25%
Blue		45%
Black		30%
Snowmaking		15%

Phone numbers
From distant parts of the US, add the prefix 1 530; from abroad, add the prefix +1 530

They provide lifts to get you up, but you basically find your own way down ↓

THE RESORT

Squaw is the major resort at the north end of Lake Tahoe. Since construction of the car-free 'Village at Squaw Valley' a few years ago by Intrawest it has been worth considering as a base, but it is still also popular as a day trip from South Lake Tahoe and Heavenly. There are shuttle-buses, and a daily boat. There are other lodgings around the valley, and at Tahoe City.

Village charm For a built-from-scratch development the Village is very successful, although still very small and limited in what it offers. And the older base developments next to it are not unpleasant.

Convenience The Village and adjacent lodgings are at the base of the main lifts. The self-contained, luxurious, conference-oriented Resort at Squaw Creek hotel has its own chairlift into one end of the network.

Scenery There are fabulous views of Lake Tahoe from Squaw Peak.

THE MOUNTAINS

One of the attractions of the area is that the slopes are lightly wooded. There are no trails marked on the mountain map (just lifts that are coloured green, blue or black) and few signs or other aids to route-finding on the ground.

Slopes There are several distinct sectors. A gondola and a big cable car rise 600m/1,970ft to the twin stations of Gold Coast and High Camp (linked by the Pulse gondola). Above them is a wide area of beginner slopes, and beyond that the three highest peaks of the area, with lifts of modest vertical – much the biggest is on Squaw Peak's Headwall six-pack: 535m/1,760ft.

From High Camp you can descend into a steep-sided valley from which the Silverado chair is the return.

Two other peaks are accessed directly from the village. A fast quad serves steep KT-22, a slow triple goes to rather neglected Snow King.

Squaw's cable car runs in the evenings to serve the floodlit slopes (including a 5km/3 mile run to the base area), and terrain parks and the dining facilities at High Camp.

Fast lifts There are fast lifts in each sector, but also slow old chairs.

Queues Few problems are reported, and the slopes are uncrowded.

Terrain parks The main parks are now together at High Camp – the Riviera Park and super-pipe, with intermediate and expert lines, the Belmont for intermediates (also floodlit for night riding) – with new rails and jumps for 2008/09 – and High Camp rail park. There are several peak season parks, when conditions permit. The Papoose area has its own small beginner park.

NEWS

For 2009/10 the High Camp double chair, serving the terrain parks, is due to be upgraded to a triple.

Further improvements are due for the mid-mountain 'Arc at Gold Coast' restaurant, with a new dining area on the ground floor of that building.

For 2008/09 a mid-station was built on the Exhibition lift from the base area. This allows skiing on the bottom half of the run earlier in the season.

Snowmaking was improved, and the main terrain parks were relocated together at High Camp.

UK PACKAGES

AmeriCan Ski, American Ski Classics, Crystal, Funway Holidays, Made to Measure, Simply Alpine, Ski Dream, Ski Independence, Ski Safari, Skitracer, Skiworld, United Vacations, Virgin Snow

TOURIST OFFICE

t 583 6985
squaw@squaw.com
www.squaw.com

Snow reliability An impressive 460 inches on average, plus snowmaking.

Experts The possibilities for experts on KT-22, Squaw Peak and Granite Chief – plus the Silverado valley – are huge, with lots of steep chutes and big mogul fields; many extreme skiing and boarding movies are made here. But at first it is very difficult to identify routes that are safe, and easy to get yourself into tricky spots – to get the most out of the area get a guide.

Intermediates Blue-run skiers have a choice of some lovely cruises in the Emigrant and Snow King sectors and a three-mile top-to-bottom run. But there is not much more groomed cruising, so keen piste-bashers will find the area limited. There is, however, lots of steep blue and easy black terrain in which to develop deep-snow or mogul skills – particularly around the Siberia, Solitude and Granite Chief lifts.

Beginners The Papoose nursery area has a gentle slope served by a double chairlift – a special beginner package, with lift pass, is available. There's a superb choice of easy runs to progress to at altitude.

Snowboarding This is one of the most snowboarder friendly resorts in California. The higher areas are full of steep and deep gullies, cliff drops, kicker building spots and tree runs. And the freestyle areas are great.

Cross-country There are 18km/11 miles of groomed trails at Squaw Creek.

Mountain restaurants The mid-mountain facilities are uninspiring, except in terms of views. Twenty-Two Bistro, near the KT-22 chair, did a 'good tapas lunch' for a 2009 visitor.

Schools and guides The school runs Ski with a Pro adult group lessons hourly. There are specialist workshops.

Families Squaw offers slope-side convenience and a children's on-slope play area at the Papoose base. Squaw Kids takes children from three years.

STAYING THERE

The base village has widened the choice of accommodation.

Hotels The PlumpJack Inn (583 1576) is our favourite – comfortable, stylish, central. The Resort at Squaw Creek (583 6300) offers luxury rooms, an outdoor pool and hot tubs.

Apartments The Village has well-appointed ski-in/ski-out condos.

Eating out For a tiny place, the range of choice in the Village and the nearby older buildings – notably Olympic House – is adequate. The PlumpJack Inn has an excellent restaurant; the Balboa Cafe, run by the same people, also has an impressive menu. More routine places include the Auld Dubliner pub, Fireside (pizza/pasta), Mamasake (sushi), ZenBu (tapas). Dining up the mountain is possible at Alexander's.

Après-ski The Olympic House has several venues. In the Village, the places above mostly function as bars, too: Auld Dubliner is the liveliest. Uncorked at Squaw Valley is a wine bar with live music and weekly wine tastings.

Off the slopes High Camp has an ice rink and other activities. The Trilogy Spa offers a range of body-pampering treatments. Or you can take a paddle steamer cruise across Lake Tahoe.

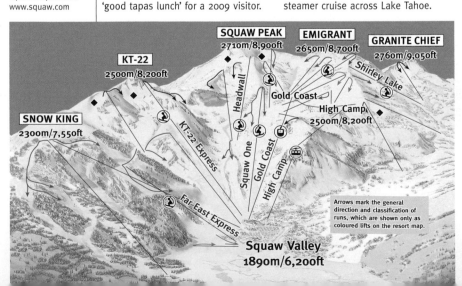

SQUAW PEAK 2710m/8,900ft
EMIGRANT 2650m/8,700ft
GRANITE CHIEF 2760m/9,050ft
KT-22 2500m/8,200ft
Shirley Lake
Headwall
Gold Coast
High Camp 2500m/8,200ft
SNOW KING 2300m/7,550ft
KT-22 Express
Squaw One
Gold Coast
High Camp
Far East Express

Arrows mark the general direction and classification of runs, which are shown only as coloured lifts on the resort map.

Squaw Valley 1890m/6,200ft

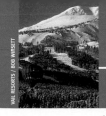

Colorado

Colorado is the most popular American destination for UK visitors. And justifiably so: it has the most alluring combination of attractive resorts, slopes to suit all abilities and excellent, reliable snow – dry enough to justify its 'champagne powder' label. It also has direct scheduled BA flights to Denver (though no longer charter flights).

Colorado has amazingly dry snow. Even when the snow melts and refreezes, the moisture seems to be magically whisked away, leaving it in soft powdery condition. Even in times of snow shortage, the artificial snow is of a quality you'll rarely find in Europe. And like most North American rivals, Colorado resorts generally have excellent, steep, ungroomed terrain that has enormous appeal to the adventurous because you don't need guidance to ski it safely.

The resorts vary enormously. If you want cute restored buildings from the mining boom days of the late 1800s, try the dinky old towns of Telluride or Crested Butte or the much bigger Aspen. Other resorts, such as Aspen's modern satellite Snowmass, major on convenience. Some – such as Vail and Beaver Creek – deliberately pitch themselves upmarket, with lots of glitzy, expensive hotels, while others – such as Breckenridge and Winter Park – are much more down to earth.

There is a cluster of resorts west of Denver that can be combined in a holiday tour by car. You could visit these while staying in cheaper lodging in a valley town such as Frisco.

It's important to be aware that many Colorado resorts are extremely high. As a result, lowlanders going there directly are at risk of altitude sickness, which can put you out of action for days. We now routinely plan our tours starting in one of the lower resorts – or spend a night or two in Denver to get acclimatised.

589

VAIL RESORTS INC / JACK AFFLECK

Colorado does cute – although in this case it's the ersatz Tirolean/ Bavarian cute of central Vail Village ↓

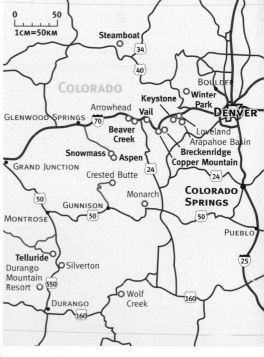

Aspen

Don't be put off by the ritzy image – with a fun, historic town and quiet, extensive slopes, this is America's best resort

RATINGS

The mountains

Extent	★★★★
Fast lifts	★★★★
Queues	★★★★
Terrain p'ks	★★★★★
Snow	★★★★★
Expert	★★★★★
Intermediate	★★★★★
Beginner	★★★★★
X-country	★★★★
Restaurants	★★★
Schools	★★★★★
Families	★★

The resort

Charm	★★★★
Convenience	★★
Scenery	★★★
Eating out	★★★★★
Après-ski	★★★★
Off-slope	★★★★

Our extent rating relates to the whole Aspen-Snowmass area. Aspen alone would rate ★★

590

NEWS

For 2009/10 the Little Nell will gain 26 luxury condos and a new restaurant – an outpost of New York's Il Mulino.

For 2008/09 at Aspen Highlands 18 acres of gladed expert terrain, Canopy Cruiser, opened in the Deep Temerity sector. And Buttermilk gained an Olympic-sized super-pipe. In Aspen town, the rebuilt Limelight Lodge hotel opened. There's also a new luxury coach transfer service from Denver airport.

- ➕ Notably uncrowded slopes
- ➕ Attractive, characterful old mining town, with lots of smart shops
- ➕ Great range of restaurants
- ➕ Excellent Snowmass just up the road
- ➕ Extensive slopes to suit every standard, but ...

- ➖ Slopes split over three separate mountains (four if you count Snowmass), though there's efficient, free transport
- ➖ Expensive, and tending to become more so as cheap places disappear
- ➖ A bit isolated from the rest of Colorado, if you're set on a two-centre trip

Another tour of Colorado in 2008 confirmed that Aspen remains our favourite American resort. It has everything we look for – except, obviously, convenience. Our affection depends heavily on the presence of Aspen Highlands, a little way down the valley, and even more on Snowmass, considerably further down the valley, with its own sizeable and growing village (and covered in a separate chapter). So most days you have to ride a bus; that doesn't worry us, and doesn't seem to worry readers who report on the place – one besotted reporter went for the fifth time last season. (We don't get many reports, and would welcome more – whether you find yourself besotted or not.)

Many rich and some famous guests jet in here, and for connoisseurs of cosmetic surgery the bars of the top hotels can be fascinating places. And the place does seem to be drifting even further upmarket. But, like all other 'glamorous' ski resorts, Aspen is actually filled by ordinary holidaymakers. Don't be put off.

THE RESORT

In 1892 Aspen was a booming silver-mining town, with 12,000 inhabitants, six newspapers and an opera house. But the town's fortunes took a nosedive when the silver price plummeted in 1893, and by the 1930s the population had shrunk to 700 or so, and the handsome Victorian buildings had fallen into disrepair. Development of the skiing started on a small scale in the late 1930s. The first lift was opened shortly after the Second World War, and Aspen hasn't looked back.

Aspen has three mountains. Aspen Mountain is right above the town. Separated from here by a wide valley, and a couple of miles drive from Aspen, are Buttermilk and Aspen Highlands. Buttermilk has no lodgings at the base, but Highlands now has some limited accommodation.

Snowmass, 19km/12 miles away, is covered by the lift pass. It is a proper resort with great attractions as a base for families, in particular, and it gets its own chapter.

All three outlying areas are served by efficient buses from a station near the gondola base.

↑ The town of Aspen sits right beneath Aspen mountain

LIFT PASSES

Four Mountain Pass

Prices in US$

Age	1-day	6-day
under 13	62	300
13 to 17	87	450
18 to 64	96	504
over 65	87	450

Free under 7

Senior over 70: $289 for unlimited period

Beginner included in price of lessons

Notes

Covers Aspen Mountain, Aspen Highlands, Buttermilk and Snowmass, and shuttle-bus between the areas. Savings if you purchase in advance online or through certain tour operators

VILLAGE CHARM ★★★★
Smart old town

Aspen's historic centre – with a typical American grid of streets – has been preserved to form the core of the most fashionable ski town in the Rockies. There's a huge variety of bars, restaurants, shops and art galleries – some amazingly upmarket. Spreading out from this centre, you'll find a mixture of developments, ranging from the homes of the super-rich through surprisingly modest hotels and motels to the mobile homes for the workers. Though the town is busy with traffic, it moves slowly, and pedestrians effectively have priority in much of the central area.

CONVENIENCE ★★
Better by bus

Aspen is very unusual in being a cute old town with a major lift close to the centre: the Silver Queen gondola straight to the top of Aspen Mountain is only yards from some of the top hotels, and the streets running away from the lift base are lined by the restaurants and shops that make Aspen what it is. Downtown Aspen is quite compact by American resort standards, but it spreads far enough to make the free ski-bus a necessity for many visitors staying less centrally. You also need buses to get to the

other mountains, of course. Generally, they work well. But they can get crowded, and you may need to keep an eye on the timetables.

SCENERY ★★★
Beautiful Bells

The views from the upper part of Highlands are the best that Aspen has to offer – the famous and distinctive Maroon Bells that appear on countless postcards. Buttermilk enjoys great views of Pyramid Peak (Colorado's most difficult 14,000ft mountain to climb) and the Maroon Creek valley.

THE MOUNTAINS

Most of the slopes are in the trees. All the mountains have regular, free guided tours, given by excellent amateur ambassadors. The ratio of acres to visitor beds is high, and the slopes are usually blissfully uncrowded. Signposting could be better where runs merge. A reporter found piste classification 'inconsistent' between mountains. Plum TV channel offers slope information.

EXTENT OF THE SLOPES ★★★★
Widely dispersed

Each of the three local mountains is worth a visit – though novices should note that Aspen Mountain has no

Interactive resort shortlist builder at **www.wtss.co.uk**

Highland
Bowl

Loge Peak
356om/11,68oft

Deep
Temerity

Loge Peak

Olympic
Bowl

Steeplechase

Cloud Nine
Bistro

Cloud Nine

Maroon Creek
Valley

Exhibition

ASPEN HIGHLANDS

Golden
Horn

Highlands Village
2450m/8,04oft

ASPEN HIGHLANDS

West Summit
3015m/9,900ft

Cliffhouse
2965m/9,72oft

West Buttermilk

BUTTERMILK

West
Buttermilk
2655m/
8,71oft

Summit

ehack
450m/
,04oft

Panda
Hill

Main
Buttermilk
2400m/788oft

green runs. Much the most extensive mountain in the area is at Snowmass – see separate chapter. Note that our extent rating is based on the total skiable area including Snowmass.

Once you are up the gondola, a series of chairs serves the ridges of **Aspen Mountain**. In general, there are long cruising blue runs along the valley floors and short, steep blacks down from the ridges.

Buttermilk is the smallest, lowest and least challenging mountain, served by a fast quad from the fairly primitive main base lodge. The runs fan out from the top in three directions – back to the base, or down to the slow Tiehack chair, or down to the fast quad at West Buttermilk.

Aspen Highlands consists essentially of a single ridge served by three fast quad chairs, with easy and intermediate slopes along the ridge itself and steep black runs on the flanks – very steep ones at the top. And beyond the lift network is Highland Bowl, where gates give access to a splendid open bowl of entirely double-black gradient.

FAST LIFTS ★★★★
Serving bottom to top
Essentially each mountain relies on one or two key fast chairs or a gondola up to the top stations; the other lifts are slow chairs.

QUEUES ★★★★
Few problems
Major queues are rare on any of the mountains. At Aspen Mountain, the gondola can still have delays at peak times. The alternative is the slow Shadow Mountain chair, with a short uphill walk to reach it. Aspen Highlands is almost always queue-free, even at peak times. The two lifts out of Main Buttermilk sometimes get congested.

TERRAIN PARKS ★★★★★
Some of the world's best
Aspen has a different kind of terrain park on each of its hills. Advanced riders should head to Buttermilk's huge X-Park, home of the Winter X Games until 2010 and designed by renowned shaping experts at Snow Park Technologies. The park stretches over 3km/2 miles and is said to be the longest in the world. There is now a new Olympic-size super-pipe, over 150m/500ft long. The slope-style

KEY FACTS

Resort	2425m
	7,950ft

Aspen Mountain	
Slopes	2425-3415m
	7,950-11,210ft
Lifts	8
Pistes	673 acres
Green	0%
Blue	48%
Black	52%
Snowmaking	31%

Aspen Highlands	
Slopes	2450-3560m
	8,040-11,680ft
Lifts	5
Pistes	1,028 acres
Green	18%
Blue	30%
Black	52%
Snowmaking	11%

Buttermilk	
Slopes	2400-3015m
	7,880-9,900ft
Lifts	9
Pistes	470 acres
Green	35%
Blue	39%
Black	26%
Snowmaking	23%

Total with Snowmass	
Slopes	2400-3815m
	7,880-12,510ft
Lifts	46
Pistes	5,303 acres
Green	10%
Blue	45%
Black	45%
Snowmaking	12%

SCHOOLS

Aspen
t 925 1227

Classes
Full day (5hr) $139,
incl. tax

Private lessons
$449 for 3hr for up to
5 people

There is a huge amount of terrain to explore, which will satisfy all levels of boarder – especially when you include Snowmass (see separate chapter) – and lots of excellent terrain on Aspen Mountain and Highlands. Buttermilk is the least testing of the mountains, with gentle carving runs and freeriding – but it's also home to the most serious terrain park. There are countless good runs, cliff drops and treelines. The hills are free of draglifts, with few flat sections.

course includes a log rail area, big kicker sections, hip jump and box. There is also a separate rail park, with new features popping up every year.

SNOW RELIABILITY ★★★★★
Rarely a problem
Aspen's mountains get an annual average of 300 inches of snow – not in the front rank, but not far behind. In addition, all areas have substantial snowmaking. Immaculate grooming adds to the quality of the pistes, and the light traffic can only help.

FOR EXPERTS ★★★★★
Buttermilk is the only soft stuff
There's plenty to choose from – all the mountains except Buttermilk offer lots of challenges.

Aspen Mountain has a formidable array of double black diamond runs. From the top of the gondola, Walsh's, Hyrup's and Kristi are on a lightly wooded slope and link up with Gentleman's Ridge and Jackpot to form the longest black run on the mountain. A series of steep glades drops down from Gentleman's Ridge. The central Bell ridge has less extreme single diamonds on both its flanks, including some delightful lightly wooded areas. On the opposite side of Spar Gulch is another row of double blacks, collectively called the Dumps, because mining waste was dumped here.

At Highlands there are challenging runs from top to bottom of the mountain. Consider joining a guided group as an introduction to the best of them. Highland Bowl, beyond the top lift, is superb in the right conditions: a big open bowl with pitches from a serious 38° to a terrifying 48°. There are free snowcat rides from the top of the lifts to the first access gate of Highland Bowl, but if these are not operating, it's a 20-minute hike. All the further gates require further hiking.

Left of the bowl, the Steeplechase area consists of a number of parallel natural avalanche chutes, and their

elevation means the snow stays light and dry. The Deep Temerity lift (vertical 520m/1,700ft) adds a useful amount of skiable vertical to these runs and to Highland Bowl. The Olympic Bowl area on the opposite flank of the mountain has great views of the Maroon Bells and some serious moguls. The Thunderbowl chair from the base serves a nice varied area that's often underused.

FOR INTERMEDIATES ★★★★★
Grooming to die for
Most intermediate runs on Highlands are concentrated above the mid-mountain Merry-Go-Round restaurant, many served by the Cloud Nine fast quad chair. But there are good slopes higher up and lower down – don't miss the vast, neglected expanses of Golden Horn, on the eastern limit of the area.

Aspen Mountain has its fair share of intermediate slopes, but they tend to be tougher than on the other mountains. Copper Bowl and Spar Gulch, running between the ridges, are great cruises early in the morning but can get crowded later. Upper Aspen Mountain, at the top of the gondola, has a dense network of well-groomed blues served by the Ajax fast chair. The unusual Ruthie's chair – a fast double, apparently installed to rekindle the romance that quads have destroyed – serves more cruising runs.

The Main Buttermilk runs offer good, easy slopes to practise on, and can be extraordinarily quiet. And good intermediates should be able to handle the relatively easy black runs – when groomed, these are a real blast on carving skis. Buttermilk is also a great place for early experiments off-piste.

FOR BEGINNERS ★★★★★
Can be a great place to learn
Buttermilk is a great mountain for beginners. West Buttermilk has beautifully groomed, gentle, often deserted runs, served by a quad. The

↑ If you're lucky, as we once were, you could have that wide, wide blue run all to yourself; it's Golden Horn, on Aspen Highlands

ASPEN/SNOWMASS / PAUL MORRISON

CHILDCARE

Snow Cubs
t 923 1227
Ages 8wk to 4yr
Grizzlies
t 923 1227
Ages 5 and 6
All-day non-skiing nurseries
Several

Ski school
Ages 7 to 12, $99 per day (9.30 to 3.15, lunch included)

easiest slopes of all, though, are at the base of the Main Buttermilk sector – on Panda Hill. Despite its macho image and serious double diamond terrain, Highlands boasts the highest concentration of green runs in Aspen, served by the fast Exhibition chair.

FOR CROSS-COUNTRY ★★★★
Backcountry bonanza
There are over 65km/39 miles of groomed trails between Aspen and Snowmass in the Roaring Fork valley – the most extensive maintained cross-country system in the US. And the Ashcroft Ski Touring Center maintains around 35km/22 miles of trails around Ashcroft, a mining ghost town. The Pine Creek Cookhouse (925 1044) does excellent food and is accessible only by ski, snowshoe or horse-drawn sleigh. Aspen is at one end of the famous Tenth Mountain Division Trail, heading 370km/230 miles north-east almost to Vail, with 12 huts for overnight stops.

MOUNTAIN RESTAURANTS ★★★
Good by American standards
There aren't many good spots, but they are worth seeking out.
Editors' choice At Highlands, Cloud Nine bistro (544 3063) is the nearest thing in the States to a cosy Alpine hut, with excellent food – thanks to an Austrian chef. Not wildly expensive, either – $30 for two courses.
Worth knowing about On Aspen Mountain there's the Sundeck self-service – about as good as an American self-service restaurant gets – with great views across to Highland Bowl. And there's a satisfactory table-service area, Benedict's. Bonnie's self-service is another option. On Buttermilk the mountaintop Cliffhouse specialises in a Mongolian barbecue stir-fry.

SCHOOLS AND GUIDES ★★★★★
One of the best?
Aspen's school offers a wide variety of specialised (if rather pricey) instruction – mountain exploration groups, off-piste tours, adrenalin sessions, women's groups, and so on. Group classes are usually small and of a high standard. Past reports have been generally positive. Beginner classes sometimes incorporate use of the Ski Doctor (Aspen Club and Spa) – an indoor simulator. Prices are high, but you can save money during specialist weeks and off-peak.

FOR FAMILIES ★★
Choice of nurseries
Aspen caters well for families, with Buttermilk the focus for lessons. Children are bussed to and from the mountain's impressive Fort Frog. And the kids' trail map is a great idea. We get few reports, but the childcare arrangements usually receive excellent reviews. But Snowmass has clear advantages for young families.

STAYING THERE

There's a mixture of hotels, inns, B&Bs, lodges and condos.
Chalets Several UK tour operators have chalets here – some very luxurious.
Hotels There are places for all budgets. Most smaller hotels provide a good après-ski cheese and wine buffet.
★★★★★St Regis Aspen (920 3300) Opulent city-type hotel, near gondola. With a fancy spa facility.

GETTING THERE

Air Aspen 6km/
4 miles (15mins);
Eagle 110km/ 70
miles (1hr45); Denver
360km/225 miles
(4hr45)

Rail Glenwood Springs
(63km/39 miles)

UK PACKAGES

*Alpine Answers,
AmeriCan Ski, American
Ski Classics, Crystal,
Crystal Finest, Erna
Low, Funway Holidays,
Independent Ski Links,
Kuoni, Made to
Measure, Momentum,
Oxford Ski Co, Scott
Dunn, Simply Alpine,
Ski Activity, Ski Dream,
Ski Expectations, Ski
Freshtracks, Ski
Independence, Ski Line,
Ski Safari, Ski
Solutions, Skitracer,
Skiworld, Supertravel,
Trailfinders, United
Vacations, Virgin Snow*

ACTIVITIES

Indoor Club and Spa
(sauna, swimming,
weights, aerobics,
steam, hot tubs);
Recreation Center
(pool, ice rink),
galleries, cinemas,
theatre

Outdoor Snowshoeing,
sleigh rides, ice rink,
snowmobiles,
paragliding, hot-air
ballooning

Phone numbers
From distant parts of
the US, add the prefix
1 970; from abroad,
add the prefix +1 970

TOURIST OFFICE

t 920 7134
intlres@stayaspen
snowmass.com
www.aspensnowmass.
com

*****Hyatt Grand Aspen** (429 9100) A grand place, near the gondola.
*****Little Nell** (920 4600) Stylish, modern hotel right by the gondola, with popular bar. Fireplaces in every room, outdoor pool, hot tub, sauna. Smart new condos due to open here for 2009/10.
*****Jerome** (920 1000) Step back a century: Victorian authenticity combined with modern-day luxury. Several blocks from the gondola.
****Lenado** (925 6246) Smart modern B&B place with open-fire lounge, individually designed rooms.
***Aspen** (925 3441) Central, 'moderate' place, 10 minutes from lifts; comfortable, pool, hot tubs.
***Molly Gibson Lodge** (925 3434) Various room styles, all 'great value'. Pool, hot tub, bar.
***Aspen Mountain Lodge** (925 7650) Small, friendly lodge in a quiet location.
***Limelight Lodge** (925 3025) Newly rebuilt in modern style, moderately priced, central. Pool, hot tubs.
***The Sky** (925 6760) Hip, swanky New York-style hotel in great location by gondola.
St Moritz Lodge (925 3220) Rooms and suites at the west end of town. 'Great staff, lovely hot tub.'
Mountain Chalet (925 7797) Cosy lodge five minutes from gondola. Pool, sauna and fitness room.
Apartments The standards here are high, even in US terms. Many of the smarter developments have their own free shuttle-buses. The Gant, Aspen Square and 'lovely' Aspen Meadows Resort are recommended.

EATING OUT ★★★★★
Dining dilemma

Aspen has an excellent blend of upmarket places and cheaper options – and an easy way to economise in many smarter places is to eat at the bar. Some giveaway magazines include menu guides.

On our last visit we had excellent modern American cuisine at Elevation, and more classic steak-and-seafood stuff at Jimmy's. D19 was strongly recommended for Italian-American dishes. Two places riding the shared-platter wave are Social and DishAspen.

Every year brings a raft of new ventures. This year we're pleased to note a relatively cheap option: Bad Billy's has opened, offering Asian dishes as well as 'burgers and beer'.

Next season sees the re-opening of the much-missed Red Onion, but sadly in refurbished 'upscale steakhouse' form (though with dining until 2am, which can be handy). The big news for next season is the arrival at the Little Nell residences of an outpost of Il Mulino of New York.

Others places worth trying are Piñons for innovative American food, Syzygy with its suave upstairs place and live jazz, Pacifica Seafood and Raw Bar, the basement Steak Pit – a long-established and reliable favourite – Cache Cache for Provençal and Little Annie's.

Cheaper choices receiving favourable past reports include: Bentley's, Mezzaluna, Hickory House and New York Pizzas.

APRES-SKI ★★★★
Lots of options

As the lifts shut, a few bars at the bases get busy – notably Iguana's at Highlands and the revamped Ajax Tavern in Aspen. The Terrace Bar at the Little Nell is a great place for gazing at facelifts.

Later on, wine connoisseurs could try the new Victoria Wine and Espresso Bar. Many of the restaurants are also bars – Jimmy's (spectacular stock of tequila) and Mezzaluna, for example. The J-bar of the Jerome hotel has a traditional feel. Aspen Billiards adjoining fashionable the Cigar Bar has pool. You can get a week's membership of the famous members-only Caribou club.

Venues for late-night dancing and drinking include the Fly Lounge – designed to look like the interior of an aeroplane – the Regal Watering Hole, with nightly DJs, and Club Chelsea.

OFF THE SLOPES ★★★★
Silver service

Aspen has lots to offer, especially if your credit card is in good shape. There are literally dozens of art galleries, as well as the predictable clothes and jewellery shops. There are plenty of shops selling affordable stuff – though a 2008 visitor found them 'disappointing'. Glenwood Springs is worth a visit for its hot-spring outdoor pool. The Aspen Recreation Center at Highlands has a huge swimming complex and an indoor ice rink. Hot-air ballooning is possible too. The best mountain restaurant is awkward for pedestrians to get to.

Beaver Creek

Exclusive and very pricey modern resort with quiet, varied slopes.
Good for a pampered stay or a day trip from Vail

+	The slopes can be very quiet, on weekdays at least
+	Mountain has it all, from superb novice runs to daunting moguls
+	Fast chairlifts all over the place
+	Compact, traffic-free village centre

−	Lacks any Wild West or genuine US town atmosphere
−	Very expensive
−	Disappointing mountain restaurants
−	Not much going on at night

TOP 10 RATINGS

Extent	**
Fast lifts	*****
Queues	*****
Snow	*****
Expert	****
Intermediate	****
Beginner	*****
Charm	**
Convenience	****
Scenery	***

NEWS

For 2009/10 on-mountain signing is due to be improved. More children's adventure glades are planned for Bachelor Gulch.

For 2008/09 a children's ski school opened at the top of the Buckaroo Express gondola. The Osprey (formerly Inn at Beaver Creek) reopened after renovation, and the 210-room spa hotel Westin Riverfront Resort opened in Avon.

The village, with the main Centennial chair going up to the top left and Grouse Mountain peeking up in the centre ↓

'Not exactly roughing it' is the strangely coy slogan of Vail's kid sister resort, discreetly underlining its status as about the smoothest resort in the US. We don't find the exclusive resort village particularly appealing, but the mountain certainly is. We wouldn't dream of visiting Vail without spending a day or two here. A pity that it's impossible to get a decent lunch on the hill.

THE RESORT

Beaver Creek, 16km/10 miles to the west of Vail, was developed in the 1980s and is unashamedly exclusive. The lift system spreads across the mountains to Bachelor Gulch, basically a Ritz-Carlton hotel, and to Arrowhead, a slope-side hamlet that is less pricey than Beaver Creek. Below here is the valley town of Avon, where there are free car parks for day visitors (parking in the resort itself is expensive and limited); you can take a free shuttle to the village or a fast chair up to Bachelor Gulch. A gondola links the Riverfront area of Avon to this chair.

Day trips to Vail, Breckenridge and Keystone (covered by the lift pass) and Copper Mountain are possible.

Village charm The village centres on a small, smart, modern pedestrian area with upmarket shops, open-air ice rink and heated pavements. The choice of bars and restaurants is limited.

Convenience There are top-quality hotels and condos right by the slopes and escalators up from the centre.

Scenery The scenery is pleasantly woody, rather than dramatic.

THE MOUNTAINS

All the slopes are below the treeline, though there are some more open areas. Free mountain tours are held every day at 10am.

Slopes The slopes immediately above Beaver Creek divide into two sectors, each accessed by a fast quad chair – one centred on Spruce Saddle, the other Bachelor Gulch mountain (which links to Arrowhead). Between these are Grouse Mountain and Larkspur Bowl, again with fast quads. Off to the left is another varied sector served, unusually, by two slow chairs.

Fast lifts Fast chairs cover most ground and beginners get their own gondola. But the two chairs at the extreme left of the mountain as you look at it (Rose Bowl and Drink of Water) are 'painfully slow', say reporters.

Queues Queues aren't normally a problem, but improving lift access from the valley seems to be attracting more visitors. One 2008 reporter had 'a 10-minute wait' at the main Centennial chair and a 2009 visitor found it 'busier than Vail at Spring break'. The Cinch chair has also been mentioned as queue-prone.

Terrain parks Park 101 is a small beginners' park, Zoom Room and Lumber Yard have intermediate-level features and the new Rodeo has big hits, for advanced riders. There's a 110m/36oft long half-pipe, off Barrel Stave. Parkology is a park and pipe programme for kids.

Snow reliability An impressive annual snow record (average 310 inches) and extensive snowmaking means you can relax. Grouse Mountain can have thin

KEY FACTS

Resort	2470m
	8,100ft
Slopes	2255-3485m
	7,400-11,440ft
Lifts	17
Pistes	1805 acres
Green	19%
Blue	43%
Black	38%
Snowmaking	36%

LIFT PASSES

See Vail chapter

UK PACKAGES

Alpine Answers, AmeriCan Ski, American Ski Classics, Crystal Finest, Elegant Resorts, Funway Holidays, Kuoni, Made to Measure, Simply Alpine, Ski Dream, Ski Independence, Ski Line, Ski Safari, Skitracer, Skiworld, STC, Supertravel, Trailfinders, United Vacations

Central reservations phone number 496 4500

Phone numbers From distant parts of the US, add the prefix 1 970; from abroad, add the prefix +1 970

TOURIST OFFICE

t 845 9090
bcinfo@vailresorts.com
beavercreek.snow.com

cover (some call it Gravel Mountain). And a 2009 reporter was disappointed with the usually excellent grooming – 'many blue runs were not groomed'.

Experts There is plenty of satisfying single-diamond and seriously steep double-diamond terrain. In the Birds of Prey and Grouse Mountain areas most runs are long, steep and mogulled from top to bottom (but watch the grooming map – when one of these is groomed it makes a great fast cruise, especially the Birds of Prey downhill race course). There are great steep glades on Grouse and at Stone Creek Chutes. Check out the new website too: www.beavercreekextreme.com.

Intermediates There are marvellous long, quiet, cruising blues everywhere you look, including top-to-bottom runs with a vertical of 1000m/3,280ft.

Beginners There are excellent nursery slopes at resort level – served by a short gondola – and more at altitude. And there are plenty of easy longer runs to progress to.

Snowboarding Good riders will love the excellent gladed runs and perfect carving slopes. The resort is great for beginners, too, with special teaching methods and equipment that they claim will help you learn quicker.

Cross-country There's a splendid, mountain-top network of tracks at McCoy Park (over 32km/20 miles), reached via the Strawberry Park lift.

Mountain restaurants Saddle at mid-mountain is the main place – a food court in an airy log building, but it can get very busy. Red Tail Camp is basic; decent barbecues. Spago at Bachelor

Gulch is the best bet for table service.

Schools and guides We've had very good reports over the years.

Families Small World Play School looks after non-skiing kids from two months to six years from 8.30 to 4.30. The area at the top of the Buckaroo gondola has great adventure trails and a new tubing park is due for 2009/10.

STAYING THERE

Hotels Lots of upmarket places, such as the Ritz-Carlton, The Charter and Park Hyatt. The Osprey, Charter and Pines Lodge combine hotel facilities with luxury condo convenience.

Apartments Elkhorn Lodge, Oxford Court, St James Place and SaddleRidge are slope-side condos. For cheaper luxury, consider staying in Arrowhead.

Eating out SaddleRidge is plush and packed with photos and Wild West artefacts. Toscanini, the Golden Eagle Inn, Dusty Boot, and Beaver Creek Chophouse have been recommended. Spago offers fine dining at Bachelor Gulch. You can take a sleigh ride to dine at a swanky log cabin on the slopes. Or try the valley towns; a reader recommends Outback in Avon for 'excellent steaks'. The Eco transit bus runs 24-hour services between Beaver Creek and Avon.

Après-ski Try the Coyote Cafe, Whiskey Elk and McCoy's (live bands).

Off the slopes There are smart boutiques and galleries, an impressive ice rink, bonfire evenings, hot-air balloon rides, dog sledding, and shows and concerts.

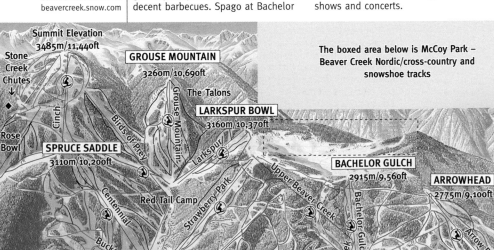

The boxed area below is McCoy Park – Beaver Creek Nordic/cross-country and snowshoe tracks

Breckenridge

A sprawling resort with a cute 'Wild West' core, beneath a wide, varied mountain; increasing amounts of slope-side accommodation

£70
RESORT PRICE INDEX

RATINGS

The mountains

Extent	★★
Fast lifts	★★★
Queues	★★★★
Terrain p'ks	★★★★★
Snow	★★★★★
Expert	★★★★
Intermediate	★★★★
Beginner	★★★★★
X-country	★★★★
Restaurants	★
Schools	★★★★★
Families	★★★★

The resort

Charm	★★★
Convenience	★★★
Scenery	★★★
Eating out	★★★★★
Après-ski	★★★
Off-slope	★★★

NEWS

More luxury condos, One Ski Hill Place, are being built at the Peak 8 base. The 88 ski-in/ski-out lodgings are due to open for 2010/11, as is the Grand Lodge at the Peak 7 base.

The Peak 7 base opened last season, including the Crystal Peak lodge and gondola mid-station – with lodgings, a skier services centre and a table-service restaurant.

- ➕ Local mountains have something for all abilities – good for mixed groups
- ➕ Cute Victorian Main Street, with mainly sympathetic new buildings
- ➕ Plenty of lively bars and restaurants
- ➕ Shared lift pass with four other worthwhile resorts nearby
- ➕ Efficient lifts mean fewer queues
- ➕ Some slope-side accommodation
- ➕ One of the nearest major resorts to Denver; so a short transfer, but ...

- ➖ At 2925m/9,600ft the village is one of the highest you will encounter, with a risk of altitude sickness if you go there directly from the UK
- ➖ Very prone to high winds, affecting particularly the high, exposed advanced slopes
- ➖ On-piste terrain not very extensive, and few long runs
- ➖ Lack of good, central hotels
- ➖ Main Street is a thoroughfare – always busy with traffic

We like the town of Breckenridge a lot – and the slopes too, up to a point. Its drawbacks are non-trivial, though. Some of the expert slopes are exceptionally high (accessed by America's highest lift), and we've found them closed several times. Like many readers, one of us has been affected by altitude sickness here, and now always spends time in a lower resort before hitting Breckenridge; a night or two in Denver is an alternative way to cut the risk. Intermediates more interested in mileage than challenges should plan to explore other resorts (covered by the lift pass) by car or bus.

THE RESORT

Breckenridge was founded in 1859 and became a booming gold-mining town. Old clapboard buildings line much of Main Street and the streets nearby have been well renovated. Small shopping malls and other buildings have been added in similar style. But there are some (rather out-of-place) modern buildings too.

The resort is in the same ownership as Vail, Beaver Creek and Keystone. A multi-day lift ticket covers all these plus Arapahoe Basin. All of them plus Copper Mountain are linked by regular buses (free except for the trips to Vail or Beaver Creek).

VILLAGE CHARM ★★★
A festive treat
The town centre is lively in the evening – particularly at weekends – with lots of people strolling around the shops on their way to or from 100-plus restaurants and bars. Christmas lights and decorations remain throughout the season, giving the town a festive air. This is enhanced by a number of festivals such as Ullr Fest – honouring the Norse God of Winter – and snow sculpture championships.

CONVENIENCE ★★★
Slope life or nightlife
Although there is a lot of slope-side accommodation – more than any other Colorado resort, it is claimed – there is also a fair amount that's inconveniently distant from Main Street and the lift base-stations. Hotels and condominiums are spread over a wide, wooded area and are

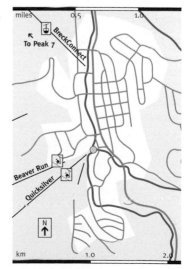

KEY FACTS

Resort	2925m
	9,600ft
Slopes	2925-3915m
	9,600-12,840ft
Lifts	29
Pistes	2,358 acres
Green	14%
Blue	31%
Black	55%
Snowmaking	27%

linked by regular, free shuttle-buses (less frequent in the evening – worth staying centrally if you plan to spend much time in Main Street). There are a couple of supermarkets; one is just behind Main Street, but the other is not in the centre and a long walk if you don't have a car. The new developments taking shape at the bases of Peaks 7 and 8 will increase the ski-in/ski-out options.

SCENERY ★★★
Peak after peak
This is high country; on a clear day above the treeline there are extensive views of Colorado's highest summits – many of which reach 4270m/14,000ft.

THE MOUNTAINS

The slopes are mainly cut through the forest. There is quite a lot of steeper skiing above the treeline; this is prone to closure by high winds.

Signposting is very clear. But surprisingly, the free daily mountain tours from the base of Peaks 8 and 9, disappointed a 2009 visitor ('no orientation, no tips, no local info').

EXTENT OF THE SLOPES ★★
Small but fragmented
There are four sectors, linked by lift

and piste. Two fast chairlifts go from one end of the town up to **Peak 9**, one accessing mainly green runs on the lower half of the hill, the other mainly blue runs higher up. From there you can get to **Peak 10**, with blue and black runs served by one fast quad.

The **Peak 8** area – tough stuff at the top, easier lower down – can be reached by a fast quad from Peak 9. The base lifts of Peak 8 at the Bergenhof can also be reached by the slow Snowflake lift from the suburbs, or by gondola from the fringes of town – where there's ample parking. The long green runs back to town are perfectly satisfactory. The six-pack serving the lower slopes of **Peak 7** can now be accessed from the gondola's new mid-station.

The higher open slopes on Peaks 7 and 8 are accessed by a T-bar – a rarity in these parts – reachable from either base, and by the Imperial fast quad at the top of the Peak 8 lift network. The resort claims a top height of 3960m/13,000ft, but that involves a hike of 45m/150ft vertical at the very top.

FAST LIFTS ★★★
Decent coverage
Breckenridge's gondola and nine fast chairlifts cover all four sectors and provide good access from either end of town – the slow Snowflake chair in between is an obvious exception.

QUEUES ★★★★
Peak times possibly
Most of the time Breckenridge's fast lifts make light work of peak-time crowds. There are few problems outside exceptional times, such as President's Day weekend. But we have received reports of queues for some of the main Peak 8 and Peak 7 lifts at the weekends – '20 to 30 minutes', says a 2009 visitor. The double Chair 6 has been mentioned and the old Snowflake chair that gives access to

boarding

Breckenridge is pretty much ideal for all standards of boarder and hosts several major US snowboarding events. Beginners have ideal nursery slopes and greens to progress to. Intermediates have great cruising runs, all served by chairs. The powder bowls at the top of Peaks 7 and 8 make great riding and can be accessed via the Imperial quad, so avoiding the awkward T-bar (though it is still an important lift – see 'For experts'). Boarders of all levels will enjoy the choice of excellent terrain parks and half-pipes (see 'Terrain parks'). Nearby Arapahoe Basin is another area for hard core boarding in steep bowls and chutes.

Peak 8 for thousands of condo-dwellers, also gets 'lengthy queues' at peak times.

TERRAIN PARKS ★★★★★
Something for everyone
The main focus is Peak 8, with three progressive areas and a couple of pipes. Freeway is one of the best in North America, featuring a series of big jumps, obstacles and enormous championship half-pipe – 'massive, steep, well kept and awesome'. Just above it, Park Lane is an intermediate-level park, with snowmaking. And Trygves has gentle jumps and an introductory pipe for beginners. On Peak 9, Eldorado is a small park, with a half-pipe. There are other parks some years too.

SNOW RELIABILITY ★★★★★
Ample quantities
With its high altitude, Breckenridge boasts a great natural snow record – annual average 300 inches. That is supplemented by substantial snowmaking (used mainly early in the season to form a good base). There are a lot of east- and north-east-facing slopes, which hold snow well. But high winds can remove or spoil the snow, notably on exposed upper runs. Grooming is excellent.

FOR EXPERTS ★★★★
Lots of short but tough runs
A remarkable 55% of the runs are classified black – that's a higher proportion than famous 'macho'

resorts such as Jackson Hole, Taos and Snowbird. And a good proportion are classified as 'expert' (double-diamond) or 'extreme' terrain. But most runs are short – most of the key lifts offer verticals of around 300m/990ft.

Peak 8 is at the core of the tough skiing. The lightly wooded slopes served by Chair 6 are a good place to start – picturesque and not too steep. Below, steeper runs lead further down to the junction with Peak 9. Above, the Imperial quad accesses the double-diamond Imperial Bowl, and the 'extreme' Lake Chutes and Snow White areas. Or you can move to the front face of Peak 8, where the T-bar serves single-diamond runs, the double-diamond Horseshoe and Contest bowls, and a traverse/hike to the steep upper slopes of Peak 7. On the lower, wooded part of Peak 8 is a worthwhile area of single diamonds.

Peak 9's wooded North Slope under Chair E is excellent – shady, sheltered and steep – we've had great runs down Devil's Crotch, Hades and Inferno. Peak 10 has blue-black runs down the central ridge, but more challenging stuff on both flanks. To skier's left is a lovely, lightly wooded area called The Burn.

FOR INTERMEDIATES ★★★★
Nice cruising, limited extent
Breckenridge has some good blue cruising runs for all intermediates. But dedicated piste-bashers are likely to find the runs short and limited in variety. Peak 9 has the easiest slopes.

Breckenridge

601

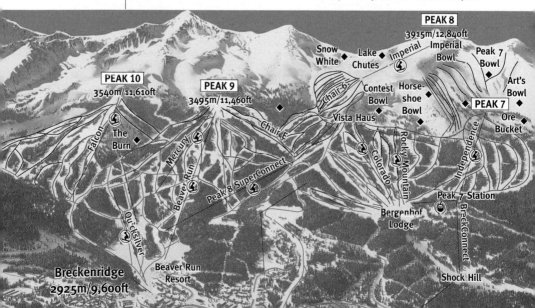

PEAK 8
3915m/12,840ft
Snow White
Lake Chutes
Imperial
Imperial Bowl
Peak 7 Bowl
Art's Bowl
PEAK 10
3540m/11,610ft
PEAK 9
3495m/11,460ft
Chair 6
Contest Bowl
Horse-shoe Bowl
PEAK 7
Ore Bucket
Falcon
The Burn
Mercury
Chair E
Vista Haus
Rocky Mountain
Independence
Beaver Run
Peak 8 SuperConnect
Colorado
Peak 7 Station
BreckConnect
Quicksilver
Bergenhof Lodge
Breckenridge
2925m/9,600ft
Beaver Run Resort
Shock Hill

SCHOOLS

Breckenridge
t 453 3272

Classes
Half day (2½hr) $85
Private lessons
$435 for 3hr for up to 6 people

CHILDCARE

Children's Center, Peak 8 and 9
t +1 888 576 2754
All-day care from 8am to 4.00 for children from age 8wk to 3yr – reservation recommended
Resort sitters
t 513 4445
Mountain sitters
t 477 0024

Ski school
For ages 3 to 12, 9.45 to 3.30 daily ($140 for full day)

GETTING THERE

Air Denver 165km/ 105 miles (2hr15)

It is nearly all gentle, wide, blue runs at the top and almost flat, wide, green runs at the bottom. And the ski patrol is supposed to enforce slow-speed skiing in narrow and crowded areas.

Peak 10 has a number of more challenging runs classified blue-black, such as Crystal and Centennial, which make for good fast cruising. Peaks 7 and 8 both have a choice of blues on trails cut close together in the trees. Adventurous intermediates will also like to try some of the high bowl runs and more gentle gladed runs such as Ore Bucket glades on the fringe of Peak 7 and the runs beneath Chair 6 on Peak 8. For a groomed black try Pika beside the T-bar, says a reporter.

FOR BEGINNERS ★★★★★
Excellent
The bottom of Peak 9 has a big, virtually flat area and some good, gentle nursery slopes. There's then a good choice of green runs to move on to. Beginners can try Peak 8 too, with another selection of green runs and a choice of trails back to town. There is a special beginner package available (see 'Schools and guides').

FOR CROSS-COUNTRY ★★★★
Specialist centre in woods
There are 50km/31 miles of groomed trails in total. Breckenridge's Nordic Center is prettily set in the woods between the town and Peak 8 (served by the shuttle-bus). It has 30km/ 19 miles of trails and 20km/12 miles of snowshoeing trails. A further 20km/ 12 miles of cross-country trails are located at the golf course.

MOUNTAIN RESTAURANTS ★
Not a highlight
Of the self-service places above base level, Peak 9 restaurant is the 'best of a mediocre bunch': 'pretty good and reasonably priced', with 'friendly staff'.

Both Tenmile Station, where Peak 9 meets 10, and the dreary Vista Haus on Peak 8 are food-court operations. But they get nightmarishly busy at weekends. We had hoped that Sevens – a new table-service restaurant at the Peak 7 base lodge would be worth visiting but a 2009 reporter says it's 'small, crowded, noisy, no restrooms; food nothing special'.

SCHOOLS AND GUIDES ★★★★★
Excellent reports
The school gets good reviews. Reporters have praised small classes doing what the class, not the instructor, wants ('you can buy three days of lessons and take them whenever you want', 'friendly, first-class instruction'). The good-value beginner package which includes lessons, equipment rental and lift pass is also highly recommended. Special clinics include women's and telemark. The school's Big Mountain Experience offers guided instruction around Imperial Bowl. There is also a Burton Learn to Ride programme.

FOR FAMILIES ★★★★
Excellent facilities
Past reports on the children's school and nursery have been full of praise for excellent instruction and positive attitudes, combined with lots of fun. The new Mountains of Discovery programme aims to combine teaching and fun on the slopes (for kids aged three to 13 years).

STAYING THERE

A lot of tour operators feature Breckenridge.
Chalets Several tour operators have very comfortable chalets.
Hotels There's a noticeable lack of good places close to Main Street.
★★★★Great Divide Lodge (453 5500) A short walk to the slopes and a bearable walk to Main Street, but dreary. Pool, tub, sauna. 'Good value.'
★★★★Lodge at Breckenridge (453 9300) Stylish luxury spa resort set out of town among 32 acres, with great views. Private shuttle-bus. Pool, tub, steam, sauna and massage.
★★★★Beaver Run (453 6000) Huge, slope-side resort complex with 520 spacious rooms. Pool, hot tubs.
★★★★Barn on the River (800 795 2975) B&B on Main St. Hot tub.
★★★Little Mountain Lodge (453 1969)

Main Street has cute old buildings from gold mining times. But there are some rather out-of-place modern places too →

VAIL RESORTS, INC

UK PACKAGES

Alpine Answers, AmeriCan Ski, American Ski Classics, Crystal, Crystal Finest, Directski.com, Erna Low, Funway Holidays, Independent Ski Links, Inghams, Interactive Resorts, Made to Measure, Neilson, Simply Alpine, Ski Activity, Ski Dream, Ski Expectations, Ski Freshtracks, Ski Independence, Ski Line, Ski McNeill, Ski Safari, Ski Solutions, Skitracer, Skiworld, STC, Supertravel, Thomson, Trailfinders, United Vacations, Virgin Snow **Frisco** *AmeriCan Ski*

ACTIVITIES

Indoor Spas, theatre, museum, galleries, ice rink, recreation centre (pool, tubs, gym, tennis, climbing wall) on the outskirts of town – accessible by bus

Outdoor Horse-drawn sleigh rides, dog sledding, fishing, snowmobiles, snowshoeing, ice rink, hot-air balloon rides

Phone numbers
From distant parts of the US, add the prefix 1 970; from abroad, add the prefix +1 970

TOURIST OFFICE

t 453 5000
breckinfo@vail
resorts.com
www.breckenridge.
snow.com

Luxury B&B near ice rink.
***Village (547 5725) Central. 'Good value with spacious rooms.'
Apartments There is a huge choice of condominiums, many set off the aptly named Four O'Clock run – not the best location for lift/town access. Mountain Thunder Lodge (near the gondola and the supermarket) and Main Street Station (near the Quicksilver lift) are recommended at the luxury end. The Blue Sky condos also opened here recently. A regular visitor also recommends for location, quality and value Village at Breckenridge, Trails End, Corral, One Breckenridge Place and Saddlewood. For a cheaper option try Der Steiermark (Peak 9 base). River Mountain Lodge is praised for 'quality, cost and location'. The Crystal Peak Lodge opened at Peak 7 last season. There are lots of houses to rent, too.

EATING OUT ★★★★★
Over 100 restaurants
There's a very wide range of eating places, from typical American food to fine dining. At peak times they get busy and mostly don't take bookings. The Breckenridge Dining Guide lists the full menu of most places.

A 2009 visitor confirmed the attractions of the Hearthstone (modern American cuisine in a beautiful 120-year-old house): 'excellent; beautifully cooked steak'. Relish has been strongly recommended. For no-nonsense grills-and-fries in a pub ambience, we've enjoyed both the Brewery (famous for its mega 'appetisers', such as buffalo wings, and splendid beers) and the Kenosha steakhouse. Other reader recommendations include: the sophisticated food at Cafe Alpine, Whale's Tail ('great seafood and fish'), Mi Casa ('lively Mexican'), Downstairs at Eric's (classic American), Michael's (extensive Italian menu), Rasta Pasta (pasta with a Jamaican twist), Bubba Gump's (seafood). Extreme Pizza has 'tables made from beautiful Arbor snowboards', and Spencer's (out at Beaver Run resort) is 'excellent both in quality and value'. The Blue Moose does the usual killer breakfasts; Cool River Cafe has some healthier options.

APRES-SKI ★★★
The best in the area
There's not much tea-time animation at the lift bases but the Park Avenue Pub, just off Main Street, and the

---

Brewery were lively on our recent visits. Later on we've enjoyed the Gold Pan saloon (reputedly the oldest bar west of the Mississippi). Reader recommendations for the evenings include the Liquid Lounge and Fatty's sports-bar. Cecilia's serves good cocktails; Burke and Riley's is an Irish bar; Downstairs at Eric's is a disco sports-bar, and 320South (formerly Sherpa & Yeti's) is new.

OFF THE SLOPES ★★★
Pleasant enough
Breckenridge is a pleasant place to wander around, with plenty of souvenir and gift shops. Silverthorne (about 30 minutes away) has excellent bargain factory outlet stores.

Frisco 2765m/9,075ft

Staying in Frisco makes sense for those touring or on a tight budget. It's a pleasant small town with bars, restaurants and good value lodgings. Hotel Frisco (668 5009) is 'comfortable and convenient'. The Lake Dillon Lodge (668 5094) is handy for the bus. Dining recommendations include: Backcountry Brewery, Tuscato (Italian), Blue Spruce Inn ('best food in town, in an old low-ceilinged cabin'), Farley's steakhouse, the Boatyard (pizzeria) and Food Heads World Cafe ('good duck and steak').

Interactive resort shortlist builder at www.wtss.co.uk

Copper Mountain

Great terrain with reliable snow for all ability levels, above a born-again but small and quiet Intrawest resort

✚ Convenient purpose-built resort	▬ Can be long lift queues at weekends
✚ Fair-sized mountain, with good runs for all abilities	▬ Risk of altitude sickness
✚ Good value by Colorado standards	▬ Village rather limited
✚ Few queues on weekdays, but ...	▬ Poor mountain restaurants

TOP 10 RATINGS

Extent	★★
Fast lifts	★★
Queues	★★★★
Snow	★★★★★
Expert	★★★★
Intermediate	★★★★
Beginner	★★★★
Charm	★★
Convenience	★★★★
Scenery	★★★

NEWS

For 2008/09 a new double black diamond glade – Black Bear – opened above East Village. And a new freestyle training facility, Camp Woodward, opened; this indoor-outdoor centre runs courses for improving park and pipe skills.

604

Copper's slopes are some of Colorado's best, and the modern, purpose-built village has become quite a pleasant small resort. Great for an outing from another Colorado resort, or as a base if the budget is tight.

THE RESORT

Rather like the French resorts of the 1960s, Copper Mountain was originally high on convenience, low on charm. Keystone, Breckenridge and Arapahoe Basin are all nearby, and Vail and Winter Park a bit further.

Village charm Intrawest has done a typically thorough job with the modern Village at Copper. The group of wood-and-stone-clad condo buildings with shops, restaurants and car-free walkways and squares, forms the heart of the resort – set just off the I-70 freeway from Denver. Within the limits of its small size, it works well.

Convenience There are two other bases, served by a free shuttle-bus:

East Village at the foot of Copper's steeper terrain and Union Creek at the foot of the easiest runs and beginner area. Each of these is smaller and even quieter than the Village but has accommodation and restaurants.

Scenery There are good views across the high, partly-wooded rolling mountains that typify the Rockies.

THE MOUNTAIN

The area is medium-sized by American standards, and has great runs for all ability levels, with an attractive mix of wooded, gladed and open slopes. Free guided tours are run twice a day.

Slopes The area divides into slopes below Copper Peak and below Union

KEY FACTS

Resort	2955m
	9,700ft
Slopes	2960-3750m
	9,710-12,310ft
Lifts	22
Pistes	2,450 acres
Green	21%
Blue	25%
Black	54%
Snowmaking	16%

UNION PEAK
3750m/12,310ft

Tucker Mountain

COPPER PEAK
3750m/12,310ft

Copper Bowl

Union Bowl

Union Meadows

Spaulding Bowl
3655m/11,990ft

Upper Enchanted Forest

3560m/11,680ft

Excelerator

Timberline

Solitude Station
3485m/11,440ft

American Flyer

3300m/10,830ft

Super Bee

American Eagle

The Village at Copper
2955m/9,700ft

East Village

Union Creek

Cross-country and Snowshoe Center

↑ Copper's high bowls offer ski-anywhere terrain of varied steepness but limited vertical

COPPER MOUNTAIN

UK PACKAGES

Alpine Answers, AmeriCan Ski, American Ski Classics, Crystal, Erna Low, Funway Holidays, Independent Ski Links, Made to Measure, Simply Alpine, Ski Dream, Ski Independence, Ski Safari, Skitracer, Skiworld, Supertravel, Thomson, United Vacations

Central reservations
Call 968 2882; toll-free number (from within the US)
1 888 219 1406

Phone numbers
From distant parts of the US, add the prefix 1 970; from abroad, add the prefix +1 970

TOURIST OFFICE

t 1 866 841 2481
contactcenter@coppercolorado.com
www.coppercolorado.com

Peak. Between the two is Union Bowl. In general, as you look at the mountain the easiest runs are on the right and it gets progressively steeper the further left you go. On the back of the hill are the high Spaulding and Copper Bowls – open slopes, in contrast to the wooded lower runs.

Fast lifts Fast quads depart from the main base area towards each sector; those from Union Creek and all those to the top of the mountain are slow.

Queues Few problems on weekdays, but crowds from Denver cause weekend queues at the main base and the Timberline lift, in particular. The Storm King rope tow can get busy at peak times. You can buy a Beeline Advantage pass to jump most queues.

Terrain parks The main Catalyst park has areas for all abilities, including jumps, jibs, rails, boxes and a quarter-pipe. There's a super-pipe at the base area and a Kidz park and mini pipe (open to learning adults too), plus freestyle zones on the High Point trail. A jib park is available early season.

Snow reliability Height and extensive snowmaking give Copper an early opening date and excellent reliability. Snowfall averages 280 inches a year.

Experts There is a lot of good expert terrain. Spaulding and Copper bowls offer gradients ranging from moderate to seriously steep, but with limited vertical. Don't tackle Union Meadows on your own. The wooded bump runs lower down the left side of the main mountain are much longer. The newish double-diamond Free Fall and Black Bear glades aren't notably steep, just a bit tight in places.

Intermediates There are runs to suit everyone, from top-to-bottom greens on the right of the map through similarly long blues to challenging (usually bumpy) black runs.

Beginners The nursery slopes at Union Creek are excellent, and there are lots

of very easy green runs to graduate to.

Snowboarding Great slopes for all abilities, plus the terrain parks.

Cross-country There are 25km/16 miles of trails through the White River forest.

Mountain restaurants Solitude Station is a dreary food court. The T-Rex Grill has only outside seating. Better options are at the base – JJ's Rocky Mountain Tavern does 'great salads'.

Schools and guides The school offers a wide variety of courses and has a fine reputation, especially for children. 'Friendly, responsive instructors; very small groups', says a recent visitor.

Families The Belly Button childcare facility takes children from two months old and ski school from age three.

STAYING THERE

Hotels and condos There are no hotels. Condos vary a lot in quality and many are not ski in/ski out; exceptions include Copper Mountain Inn, Spruce Lodge (both with outdoor hot tubs) and Copper Junction.

Eating out The CB Grille is praised for the best food in town ('Colorado with Mediterranean flair'). Pizza Carlo, Endo's and JJ's Rocky Mountain Tavern ('excellent bison stew') are popular. The Imperial Palace and Salsa Mountain Cantina have also been mentioned. The Incline Bar & Grill does south-western dishes. Most seasons, sleigh rides take people out to Western-style dinners in tents.

Après-ski At weekends, Endo's Adrenaline Cafe and JJ's Rocky Mountain Tavern (with live music) are popular and Zizzo Ski Bar nightclub gets pumping. But things are pretty quiet during the week.

Off the slopes There's a good sports club with a huge pool, snow tubing, snowmobiling, ice skating and on some Saturdays fire jugglers, street entertainers and fireworks.

Copper Mountain

Interactive resort shortlist builder at **www.wtss.co.uk**

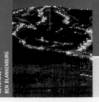

Keystone

A satisfying mountain with plenty of comfortable lodgings spread rather too widely around the valley at the base

NEWS

For 2008/09 the River Run gondola was replaced by an eight-seat version with double the previous capacity and a mid-station quite close to the bottom (handy for avoiding a relatively steep section of blue run near the bottom). The bottom station was moved into the village for easier access. A new skier bridge will connect the slopes to the gondola for 2009/10.

At Arapahoe Basin, the Black Mountain Lodge gained a new sun deck and introduced Full Moon dinner evenings. And parking and shuttle bus services were improved.

+ Good mountain with something for everyone

+ Huge night-skiing operation

+ Other nearby resorts on lift pass

+ Plenty of good condominiums

− Scattered resort, with few conveniently placed lodgings

− No village atmosphere except in small River Run development

− Risk of altitude sickness

Keystone's slopes are quite extensive and varied, but there isn't a proper village at the foot of them. Condos are scattered over a wide area, and the nearest thing to a 'village' is the limited River Run development with its handy new gondola. We prefer to stay elsewhere and make day trips to Keystone's slopes.

THE RESORT

Keystone is a sprawling resort of condominiums spread around a partly wooded valley floor. It is owned by Vail Resorts, and the lift pass covers Vail, Beaver Creek and Breckenridge as well as Arapahoe Basin (see the end of this chapter). Copper Mountain is also nearby.

Village charm River Run, at the base of the main access gondola, is the nearest thing to a conventional ski resort village, with condo buildings, a short main traffic-free street and square and a few restaurants, bars and shops. A second lift base area half a mile to the west, Mountain House, is much less of a village. Another mile west is Lakeside Village, which is not a village at all but a hotel and condo complex, weirdly lacking animation, beside a lake – a huge natural ice rink.

Convenience The resort has no clear centre and is divided into seven 'neighborhoods'. Some are little more than groups of condos, while others have shops, restaurants and bars. And there's only one basic supermarket at River Run. Free, efficient buses link all the component parts.

Scenery Keystone is surrounded by national forest, which covers most of the mountains that overlook it.

THE MOUNTAINS

By US standards Keystone offers extensive slopes both in the forest and above it.

Slopes Three wooded mountains form Keystone's local slopes. Lifts depart from Mountain House and River Run to the peak above the resort, Dercum Mountain. Its front face has Keystone's biggest network of lifts and runs. From the top you can drop over the back down to lifts up the next hill, North Peak. Or you can ride the Outpost gondola directly to the shoulder of North Peak. Beyond North Peak is the third peak, The Outback. It's a simple network, and finding your way around is no problem.

Keystone has the biggest floodlit skiing operation in the US, covering Dercum Mountain top to bottom up to 8.30pm on most nights.

Fast lifts The new gondola (see 'News') has doubled capacity out of River Run and most chairs are fast.

Queues Reporters generally praise quiet slopes but there can be queues for the Outback Express and the slow Wayback chair is a bottleneck. Dercum's front face can get congested at peak times where runs 'funnel' into each other.

Terrain parks The A-51 terrain park is huge, with features for all levels including a super-pipe and half-pipe; it has its own chairlift and is floodlit several nights a week.

Snow reliability Keystone doesn't get as much snow as its neighbours (average 230 inches), but shortage is rarely a problem. It has one of the world's biggest snowmaking systems.

Experts There is a lot of steep ungroomed terrain, but some forest runs are indistinct glade runs requiring guidance to be tackled safely, while the open higher ones are accessed by hiking (from all three peaks) or snowcat ($225 with guides and lunch; $5 for a ride but no guide on Outback). Be aware that the bowls close at 1.30pm. There are also straightforward bump runs to be done on North Peak. You should try

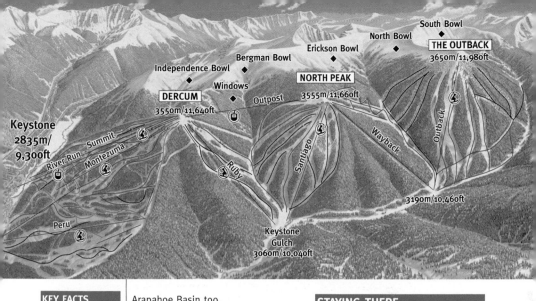

Keystone
2835m/
9,300ft

South Bowl

North Bowl

Erickson Bowl

THE OUTBACK
3650m/11,98oft

Bergman Bowl

Independence Bowl

Windows

NORTH PEAK

DERCUM
3550m/11,64oft

Outpost

3555m/11,66oft

Wayback

Outback

River Run Summit
Montezuma
Ruby

Santiago

3190m/10,46oft

Peru

Keystone
Gulch
3060m/10,04oft

KEY FACTS

Resort	2835m
	9,300ft
Slopes	2835-3650m
	9,300-11,980ft
Lifts	20
Pistes	3,148 acres
Green	19%
Blue	32%
Black	49%
Snowmaking	22%

UK PACKAGES

*Alpine Answers,
AmeriCan Ski, American
Ski Classics, Crystal,
Erna Low, Funway
Holidays, Independent
Ski Links, Simply
Alpine, Ski Dream, Ski
Independence, Ski
Safari, Skitracer, United
Vacations*

Central reservations
phone number
Call 496 4500; toll
free number (from
within the US) 1 877
753 9786

Phone numbers
From distant parts of
the US, add the prefix
1 970; from abroad,
add the prefix +1 970

TOURIST OFFICE

t 496 2316
keystoneinfo@
vailresorts.com
www.keystone.snow.
com

Arapahoe Basin too.

Intermediates Keystone has lots to
offer. The front face of Dercum
Mountain itself is a network of
beautifully groomed blue and green
runs through the trees. The Outback
and North Peak also have easy
cruising and some steeper blues.
Some of the blacks are groomed, and
are tremendous fun early in the day.

Beginners There are good nursery
slopes at the top and bottom of
Dercum Mountain, and excellent long
green runs to progress to.

Snowboarding Keystone is ideal for
beginners and intermediates, with
mainly chairlifts and gondolas, good
beginner areas and cruising runs.
Expert riders will love The Outback.

Cross-country There are 16km/10 miles
of groomed trails and 56km/35 miles
of unprepared trails.

Mountain restaurants The table-service
Alpenglow Stube (North Peak) is a
delightfully cosseting place (you are
given slippers to replace ski boots)
and one of our favourites in the US:
it's expensive but the fixed-price lunch
is a bargain at $32. The alternatives
are much less appealing (the best of
them, Timber Ridge Food Court next to
the Alpenglow was 'crowded and
expensive' says a 2009 reporter).

Schools and guides As well as the
normal lessons, there are bumps, race
and various other advanced classes.
Reporters praise very small groups and
'good' private lessons.

Families Excellent, with programmes
tailored to specific age groups,
dedicated children's teaching areas
and organised kids' nights out.

STAYING THERE

Regular shuttles operate from Denver
airport. You can cut costs and visit
several resorts by staying in Dillon,
10km/6 miles away.

Hotels There isn't a great choice but
they're all of a high standard.

Apartments There are thousands to
choose from. Some of the best are at
River Run (Lone Eagle, Timber Run,
Red Hawk and River Run have been
praised). The Mountain House area is
also slope-side and has a mixture of
luxury and budget options. All other
condos are a bus ride from the lifts.

Eating out Disappointing: it lacks the
range of options you get in most US
resorts. You can eat up the mountain.

Après-ski The Goat Tavern is the 'only
lively bar' and has a restaurant.

Off the slopes There are plenty of
activities, including a spa centre, ice-
skating, tubing and indoor tennis.

Arapahoe Basin

3285m/10,78oft

This small but exceptionally high area,
on the lift pass and a short free bus
ride away, makes a great day out. Pick
your day, though: a weekday (for
empty slopes) in good weather (top
half of the mountain is above the
treeline) after a snowfall (the steeps
need it). A handful of slow chairs serve
the 690m/2,26oft vertical front face,
and one the 335m/1,100ft vertical
Montezuma bowl. Both offer varied
slopes including serious double-
diamonds. The mid-mountain Black
Mountain Lodge serves 'good food'.

Snowmass

Aspen's modern satellite – with impressively varied and extensive slopes, and a smart new Base Village taking shape

TOP 10 RATINGS

Extent	★★★★
Fast lifts	★★★★★
Queues	★★★★
Snow	★★★★★
Expert	★★★★★
Intermediate	★★★★★
Beginner	★★★★★
Charm	★★
Convenience	★★★★
Scenery	★★★★

NEWS

For 2009/10 the Viceroy condo hotel, with a big spa, bar and restaurant, is due to open as the focal lodging at Base Village – where five restaurants and more shops opened for 2008/09.

Also in 2008/09 a fast quad replaced the Sheer Bliss double chair. A big table-service restaurant opened at Sam's Knob.

The slopes of Snowmass are a key part of the attraction of nearby Aspen as a destination. As a base, Snowmass has obvious appeal for families wanting great green runs on their doorstep; its appeal is starting to broaden as more shops and restaurants open at the new Base Village – but don't expect miracles.

THE RESORT

Snowmass is a modern, purpose-built resort, with low-rise buildings set alongside the gentle home slope. Within these buildings is Snowmass Village Mall. Further down the hill, the new Base Village continues to grow.
Village charm The new Base Village is adding a bit of style to what is a rather plain modern resort.
Convenience Much of the lodging is ski-in/ski-out and Snowmass Village Mall has a small cluster of shops and restaurants. The new Base Village is equally convenient. Efficient free bus services (crowded at times) link Snowmass with Aspen's mountains and town – the one to Aspen runs to 2am (small charge after 4.30pm).

Scenery There are wide, long views from the high-points, but not a great deal of drama.

THE MOUNTAIN

Snowmass is big by US standards – almost 8km/5 miles across, with the biggest vertical in the US. Most of the slopes are in the forest; higher ones are open or only lightly wooded.
Slopes Chairlifts and a gondola diverge from the base to go up to the two extreme high-points of Elk Camp and Sam's Knob. Links higher up go to the two sectors in the middle, High Alpine and Big Burn, where a draglift goes to the high-point of the whole lift system; a new fast quad this year has improved the link between them.

ELK CAMP 3450m/11,320ft
HIGH ALPINE 3590m
The Cirque 3815m/12,510ft
BIG BURN 3610m/11,830ft
SAM'S KNOB 3240m/10,630ft
Hanging Valley
Elk Camp
Cafe Suzanne
Alpine Springs
Sheer Bliss
Big Burn
Coney Glade
Sam's Knob
Ullrhof 3005m
Gondola
Village
Two Creeks
Two Creeks 2470m/8,100ft
Snowmass 2565m/8,420ft

| Resort | 2565m |
| | 8,420ft |

Snowmass only

Slopes	2470-3815m
	8,100-12,510ft
Lifts	24
Pistes	3,132 acres
Green	6%
Blue	50%
Black	44%
Snowmaking	7%

See Aspen chapter for statistics on other mountains – star rating for extent includes them all

Hanging Valley Wall is a beautiful and challenging area ➔

ASPEN/SNOWMASS / HAL WILLIAMS

Snowmass

609

Interactive resort shortlist builder at **www.wtss.co.uk**

Fast lifts Most of the key lifts are fast (see above), including from Two Creeks – nearer Aspen, and with free slope-side parking. But there are still a couple of long, slow chairs that can be cold in midwinter.

Queues Any problems can usually be avoided. A February 2008 reader noted short queues for the Cirque draglift. The home slope gets very crowded.

Terrain parks Snowmass has three good freestyle areas. The main park is now on Sam's Knob, with a super-pipe and over 30 features for advanced riders. There are separate intermediate and beginners' parks.

Snow reliability With 300 inches a year plus snowmaking, it's good.

Experts There's great terrain, although the steep runs tend to be short. Consider joining a guided group as an introduction. Our favourite area is around the Hanging Valley Wall and Glades – beautiful scenery and steep wooded slopes. The other seriously steep area is the Cirque, reached by draglift from Big Burn to the area's highest point. From here, the Headwall is not terrifyingly steep, but there are also narrow, often rocky, chutes – Gowdy's is one of the steepest. The runs funnel into a pretty, lightly wooded valley.

Intermediates Excellent – the best mountain in the Aspen area. All four sectors have lots to offer. Highlights include: the top slopes on Big Burn – a huge, varied, lightly wooded area, including the Powerline Glades for the adventurous; long, top-to-bottom cruises from Elk Camp and High Alpine; regularly groomed single-black runs from Sam's Knob. Long Shot is a glorious, ungroomed, 5km/3 mile run, lost in the forest and ending at Two Creeks, and well worth the short hike from the top of Elk Camp.

Beginners In the heart of the resort is a broad, gentle beginners' run. An even easier slope (and less busy) is the wide Assay Hill, at the bottom of Elk Camp. There's also a beginner area served by three lifts, at Elk Camp Meadows, at the top of the Elk Camp gondola. From Sam's Knob there are long, gentle cruises back to the resort.

Snowboarding A great mountain, whatever your boarding style.

Cross-country Excellent trails between here and Aspen – see Aspen chapter.

Mountain restaurants There are some decent places worth seeking out. Gwyn's High Alpine is an elegant table-service restaurant serving above-average food. And it now faces competition from the big new Sam's Smokehouse at Sam's Knob. And Up4Pizza on Big Burn is a 'little gem', says a 2009 visitor.

Schools and guides We've had mixed reports: 'Good' mogul classes, but frequent changes of instructor (sadly, not uncommon) 'completely destroyed' the confidence of one 2008 visitor.

Families Snowmass is a family-friendly resort. The Treehouse adventure centre at Base Village is a very impressive facility and there's a dedicated Family Zone on the mountain.

STAYING THERE

Most accommodation is self-catering. **Hotels** The focal hotel is the huge Silvertree (923 3520) with excellent top-floor Brothers' Grille restaurant and pools. The Viceroy (270 8440) is opening at Base Village for 2009/10.

Apartments Capitol Peak and Hayden Lodge are new luxury condos at Base Village. Tamarack Townhouses and Crestwood Condos are popular.

Eating out The choice is widening. As well as the excellent Brothers' Grille, recent recommendations are Il Poggio (Italian), Artisan and Butch's Lobster Bar. Junk, Liquid Sky and Buchi (Japanese) are new.

Après-ski The liveliest spot early on is the Cirque. But Sneaky's Tavern is a new option at Base village.

Off the slopes There's tubing on Assay Hill, snowshoe trails, snowcat rides and dog sledding.

UK PACKAGES

Alpine Answers, AmeriCan Ski, American Ski Classics, Crystal, Simply Alpine, Ski Dream, Ski Independence, Ski Safari, Supertravel

Phone numbers
From distant parts of the US, add the prefix 1 970; from abroad, add the prefix +1 970

TOURIST OFFICE

t 920 7134
intlres@stayaspen snowmass.com
www.aspen snowmass.com

Steamboat

The home of Champagne Powder™, with a convenient slope-side base and a working cattle town a 10-minute bus ride away

TOP 10 RATINGS

Extent	★★★
Fast lifts	★★★
Queues	★★★★
Snow	★★★★
Expert	★★★
Intermediate	★★★★
Beginner	★★★★★
Charm	★★
Convenience	★★★
Scenery	★★★

NEWS

For 2008/09 more than $1 million was spent improving the snowmaking system, and nearly 400 acres are covered. Also for 2008/09 a mini terrain park was built on Lil' Rodeo slope.

Base area developments are under way, with various buildings demolished during summer 2008. Reconstruction has begun, with One Steamboat Place in Gondola Square due to open for 2009/10. It will offer ski-in/ski-out lodging and new ski pass and ski school offices.

- ➕ Excellent easy runs
- ➕ Famed for its gladed terrain
- ➕ Good snow record
- ➕ Table-service mountain restaurants
- ➕ Plenty of high-quality slope-side lodgings at reasonable rates
- ➕ Town has some Western character

- ➖ Town is a drive from the slopes
- ➖ Modern base 'village' is sprawling and being redeveloped
- ➖ Not enough runs to amuse keen intermediates for a week unless you're prepared to try glades
- ➖ Not a huge amount of challenging terrain – some of it is a hike away

Steamboat's mountain may not match some of its competitors for extent, but it's one of the best for powder fun among the trees and for families. The lift-base village is currently no beauty, and part of it was demolished before the 2008/09 season, with some reconstruction ready for 2009/10. But it's best to stay there, and plan on just the occasional foray to the unremarkable 'cattle town' of Steamboat Springs. The resort was fairly recently taken over by Intrawest (of Whistler fame) and is changing rapidly. We'll wait till the reconstruction is complete before making another visit.

THE RESORT

The resort village is a 10-minute bus ride from the old town of Steamboat Springs. The place is relatively isolated, but you could combine it with resorts west of Denver, from Winter Park to Vail. The recently expanded local airport allows more flights and has improved accessibility.
Village charm The resort village is modern and sprawling. And the old town can be a bit of a disappointment. It may be a working cattle town, but the Wild West isn't much in evidence. The wide main street is lined with bars, hotels and shops in a mixture of styles, from old wooden buildings to concrete plazas.
Convenience Some lodgings are up the sides of the piste, but many are a free bus ride away. Near the gondola there are a few shop- and restaurant-lined multi-level squares, some of which are receiving a much needed revamp over the next few years.
Scenery There are extensive views over rolling hills and the wide Yampa Valley.

THE MOUNTAINS

Steamboat's slopes are prettily set among trees.
   We've had complaints about signposting in the past, so we welcome the installation of a new signage system. Maybe they should put up more signs about the danger of tree wells (unstable hollows that form around the bases of trees when low branches prevent snow from filling in and creating snowpack around the trunk). Two people died in separate incidents two seasons ago by suffocating after falling into tree wells and being covered in snow while skiing intermediate blue trails in the Morningside Park area.
Slopes The gondola from the base rises to the low peak of Thunderhead. Beyond it are lifts to Storm Peak and Sunshine Peak – the latter offering a broad area of blue runs served by a fast quad. On the back of the hill is the Morningside Park area, with a slow chair back up to the high-point of Mt Werner, also accessing some of the top runs on the front side. Below these is an area served by the Pony Express fast chair. There are free daily mountain tours at 10.30am, or you can ski with 1964 Olympic medallist Billy Kidd (now Steamboat's Director of Skiing) at 1pm when he's in town.
Fast lifts Fast chairs serve each area, but there are still a few slow ones too.
Queues Queues form for the gondola first thing, but they move quickly (and can be avoided by using chairs instead). But we now get few other complaints except at the busiest periods: 'Even on a busy holiday weekend we never waited more than

Resort	2105m
	6,900ft
Slopes	2105-3220m
	6,900-10,570ft
Lifts	18
Pistes	2,965 acres
Green	14%
Blue	42%
Black	44%
Snowmaking	13%

10 minutes,' said a recent reporter.

Terrain parks There were four last season. The 12-acre Mavericks park includes rails, boxes, rainbows and a super-pipe. Rabbit Ears is for beginners and Sunbeam for intermediates. For 2008/09 a mini park was built on the beginner Lil' Rodeo slope and may be again in 2009/10.

Snow reliability The term Champagne Powder™ was invented here, so it's no surprise to find that, despite a relatively low altitude, Steamboat has an excellent snow record. With a 10-year annual average of almost 350 inches, that's almost as much as the Colorado leader, Winter Park. There is snowmaking from top to bottom, too.

Experts The main attraction is the challenging terrain in the glades. A great area is on Sunshine Peak below the Sundown chair. Morningside Park and the Pony Express area also have excellent gladed runs. Three steep chutes are easily accessed via the lift back from Morningside, and a short hike gets you to the tree runs of Christmas Tree Bowl. For bumps, try the runs off Four Points or the Sundown chair. Many runs are of limited vertical; try Valley View for a longer black run to the base. You can also go snowcat skiing nearby (see

www.steamboatpowdercats.com).

Intermediates Much of the mountain is ideal, with long cruising blue runs. Morningside Park is a great area for easy black as well as blue slopes – and 'lovely ungroomed terrain in the trees' (but see the warning about tree wells above). The Sunshine area is very gentle. Some of the black runs are regularly groomed, and 'much enjoyed' by reporters. Keen intermediates will find the mountain limited in extent, but given fresh powder it offers a great introduction to tree skiing.

Beginners There's a big nursery area, the Headwall, at the base of the mountain, which had a total revamp two seasons ago, including chair upgradings and moving carpets being lengthened to make it easier for beginners. Lots of easy trails offer good progression – some of the blues are quieter and more relaxing than the greens, which include many cat tracks with steep drops at the side. The Sunshine area is particularly suited to families skiing together.

Snowboarding There's a good learning area (see above), gentle slopes to progress to and you can get around using chairlifts and the gondola. For experienced riders, riding the glades in

Steamboat

Mt Werner 3220m/10,570ft
Morningside Park
Christmas Tree Bowl
Storm Peak 3160m
Sunshine Peak 3165m
Sunshine
Four points
Sundown
Rendezvous Saddle
Pony Express
Storm Peak
Thunderhead 2770m
Gondola
Thunderhead
Christie Peak

Steamboat
Ski Time Square
Gondola base
2105m/6,900ft

UK PACKAGES

*Alpine Answers,
American Ski Classics,
Crystal, Crystal Finest,
Erna Low, Funway
Holidays, Independent
Ski Links, Interactive
Resorts, Made to
Measure, Simply
Alpine, Ski Dream, Ski
Independence, Ski Line,
Ski Safari, Skitracer,
Skiworld, Supertravel,
Thomson, United
Vacations, Virgin Snow*

**Central reservations
phone number**
879 0740

Phone numbers
Calling long-distance,
add the prefix 1 970;
from abroad, add the
prefix +1 970

TOURIST OFFICE

t 879 6111
info@steamboat.com
www.steamboat.com

STEAMBOAT SKI & RESORT
CORPORATION / LARRY PIERCE

The base village is
modern and sprawling
and lacks charm ↓

fresh powder is unbeatable.

Cross-country A free shuttle takes you to 14km/8 miles of groomed tracks at the Touring Center. There are five centres offering a total of 166km/103 miles of trails in the area.

Mountain restaurants There are food courts and table-service restaurants at Thunderhead and Rendezvous Saddle – better than the American fast-food norm, though peak-time crowds can be a problem. A recent reporter comments, 'One downside is the lack of restaurants/huts on the Pony Express/Storm Peak side of the mountain – none except for the very small Four Points Hut.'

Schools and guides Reports are very positive: 'very good in every respect', writes one visitor.

Families Arrangements are exceptional, winning awards from American magazines; there's even evening entertainment. Kids under 12 ski free with a parent or a grandparent buying a pass for at least five days. There's a similar deal for equipment rental.

STAYING THERE

A fair number of UK tour operators feature Steamboat.

Chalets There are some catered chalets run by UK tour operators.

Hotels The Steamboat Grand (871 5050) is the best of the smart hotels at the base (not ski-in/ski-out but with a slope-side ski valet). The Sheraton (879 2220) has had mixed reports; the slope-side Ptarmigan Inn (879 1730) is 'friendly, comfortable and convenient'; and the Inn at Steamboat is small, characterful and good value. Downtown has lots of cheap and cheerful chain hotels and motels.

Apartments There are countless condos, many with good pools and hot tubs, all on a free bus route and some offering their own shuttles. Luxury, well-located places include Antlers, Dulany, Ptarmigan House, Torian Plum, Bronze Tree and Ironwood. A bit lower-priced are Kutuk, Ski Inn and La Casa. Further from the slopes but with their own shuttles are the luxurious Eagle Creek and Canyon Creek and cheaper Timber Run, West and Yampa View.

Eating out There are over 70 bars and restaurants. Pick up a dining guide booklet to check out the menus, or visit www.steamboat-dining.com. You can dine in three restaurants up the mountain. Reader recommendations at the base area include the Tugboat Grill and Pub ('great food, good service and lively atmosphere'), Cafe Diva, the Ore House (steaks), the Montaña (Tex-Mex). The Tugboat is in the demolition area (see 'News'), but will be operating next season. In downtown Steamboat Springs there is quite a wide range of options. Try Antares or Mahogany Ridge for Asian fusion cuisine, Old West Steakhouse, or the Cottonwood Grill for its 'fabulously tasty Pacific Rim cuisine', and Cugino's for Italian. Reporters also recommend the 8th Street Steakhouse with its communal barbecue ('great fun, good food'). For a budget meal, head for the Double Z (pronounced 'Zee', of course) or Johnny B Goods diner for burgers.

Après-ski The base lodge area is livelier than the old town in the evening. At close of play the big Slopeside Grill is popular. The Bear River Bar has a comedy club, and the Tugboat has live music and dancing. The Old Town Pub in the town is 'great for beer and a game of pool'. There's a nightlife trail map – presumably for the ultimate bar crawl.

Off the slopes Getting to Thunderhead restaurant complex is easy for pedestrians. Visiting town is, too. The Strawberry Park Hot Springs are 'a great experience – lovely and relaxing'. Snowmobiling, ice climbing, tubing, hot-air balloons, sleigh rides and dog sledding are also possible.

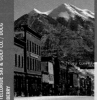

Telluride

Cute old town, smart new Mountain Village, slopes to suit all. What more could you want? More terrain, that's all

✚	Charming restored Victorian mining town with a Wild West atmosphere
✚	Slopes for all, including experts
✚	Dramatic, craggy mountain scenery – unusual for Colorado

▬	Isolated location
▬	Despite expansion, still small
▬	Mountain Village a little quiet
▬	Limited mountain restaurants

We love the old town of Telluride and always enjoy its scenic, varied slopes; but despite recent expansion of its expert terrain, the overall extent is still limited. It makes the place difficult to recommend for a holiday except in combination with another resort – which means travelling some distance.

TOP 10 RATINGS

Extent	★★
Fast lifts	★★★★
Queues	★★★★★
Snow	★★★★
Expert	★★★★
Intermediate	★★★
Beginner	★★★★★
Charm	★★★★
Convenience	★★★★
Scenery	★★★★

NEWS

For 2008/09 a new quad chairlift was built on the back of the summit ridge, opening up 50 acres of expert terrain in Revelation Bowl, accessing another expert chute on the front side and taking the lift system 100m/330ft higher.

There are new hotels and restaurants at Mountain Village, and in the town the classic New Sheridan hotel reopened after a complete renovation.

THE RESORT

Telluride is an isolated resort in south-west Colorado. It first boomed when gold mining took off here.
Village charm The town's old red-brick and timber buildings give it great Wild West charm. But the place has also attracted more upmarket shops and restaurants; a lot of celebrities have plush holiday homes here now too.
Convenience Telluride is still friendly and small-scale, with a smartly developing slope-side base above it – Mountain Village. The two are linked by gondola that runs until midnight. The Village has condos, hotels, several restaurants and shops clustered conveniently around the main lifts.
Scenery The craggy mountain scenery is more Alpine than Colorado-style, with dramatic views.

THE MOUNTAINS

There is something for everyone here, mostly below the tree-line.
Slopes From the town you can ride chairs to access the steep stuff directly above, or a gondola to a lower point on the lip of the main bowl. Mountain Village has lifts up that bowl, while the Sunshine chair accesses an almost separate hill for novices.
Fast lifts Fast chairs cover the main bowl above Mountain Village, slow ones the steep slopes above the town.
Queues These are rarely a problem.
Terrain parks There are three parks. The advanced Hoot Brown park has a super-pipe and all the features you could dream of. There's a newly revamped intermediate park at the top of the Polar Queen Express and a beginner park off the Ute Park lift.

KEY FACTS

Resort	2665m
	8,750ft
Slopes	2665-3830m
	8,750-12,570ft
Lifts	18
Pistes	1,700 acres
Green	23%
Blue	36%
Black	41%
Snowmaking	12%

Palmyra Peak

Giuseppe's

Revelation Bowl ↘ 3830m/12,570ft 365om

Hike-to ↙ 3600m/11,810ft

Black Iron Bowl

Gold Hill 14

Prospect Bowl

Ute Park

3315m

Palmyra 5

3280m

Station St Sophia 3210m

Village 4

Sunshine 10

Telluride 2665m/ 8,750ft

Coonskin Base 2660m/8,730ft

Mountain Village 2910m/9,540ft

Big Billie's 2790m/9,160ft

↑ Main Street is classic Western mining-town stuff, complete with classic central hotel (newly revamped last year)

TELLURIDE SKI AND GOLF COMPANY/ GEORGE HUEY

UK PACKAGES

Alpine Answers, AmeriCan Ski, American Ski Classics, Funway Holidays, Made to Measure, Simply Alpine, Ski Dream, Ski Freshtracks, Ski Independence, Ski Safari, Ski Solutions, United Vacations

Central reservations
Toll-free number (from within the US)
1 800 778 8581

Phone numbers
From distant parts of the US, add the prefix 1 970; from abroad, add the prefix +1 970

TOURIST OFFICE

t 728 6900
info@
tellurideskiresort.com
www.tellurideskiresort.
com

Snow reliability With an average of 309 inches of snow a year and some snowmaking, reliability is good, but there have been some slow starts; it gets a different weather pattern from that of the resorts further north.

Experts The black and double-black bump runs down from Giuseppe's towards town are classic tests, and there are steep gladed runs from all along the ridge between Giuseppe's and the Gold Hill chair. This accesses some truly challenging terrain, including the treeless Revelation Bowl off the back side. There is also steep terrain reached by hiking from Prospect Bowl chair. Helitrax runs a heli-skiing operation.

Intermediates The area's limited extent means keen piste-bashers could get bored after a couple of days. But there are ideal blue cruising runs with great views from the top down to Mountain Village (including the aptly named See Forever). The Prospect Bowl lift accesses some great intermediate terrain, with dozens of rolling pitches through the trees – a very relaxing and pretty area. More challenging are some of the bumpy double-blues from the Apex and Palmyra chairs. Some of the blacks above the town get groomed – worth catching if you can. The blue Telluride Trail back to town though is a narrow, tricky catwalk.

Beginners There are ideal runs below Mountain Village, and splendid long greens served by the Sunshine chair.

Snowboarding The lift system means it is easy to get about, and the terrain parks offer plenty of scope.

Cross-country The beauty of the area makes it splendid for cross-country – both in the valley and at altitude, with 30km/19 miles in total.

Mountain restaurants Given the size of the area, with Mountain Village at the bottom of the main slopes, it's not surprising options are limited. Alpino Vino sounds cool – a new cosy hut on the summit ridge, with great views, 'gourmet sandwiches' and a selection of fine wines. Gorrono Ranch has a bar and terrace, live music and a BBQ.

Schools and guides As well as lessons, the school offers backcountry guiding.

Families Mountain Village has an activity centre and a nursery. The school takes children from aged three.

STAYING THERE

Telluride is tricky to get to from the UK, involving two or three flights or a long 540km/335 mile drive from Denver. Packages fly into nearby Montrose or the tiny Telluride airport (prone to closure by the weather).

Hotels In town, The New Sheridan is actually old but newly renovated – a classic Main Street hotel. Hotel Columbia and Camel's Garden Hotel and Spa are upmarket places. In Mountain Village, the Lumière and the Capella are new luxury hotels – both with spa facilities. Peaks Resort has the renowned Golden Door Spa.

Apartments Try the Aspen Ridge, Ice House or Bear Creek Lodge condos.

Eating out There are over 50 places in town; a couple of the best include the Cosmopolitan in the hotel Columbia and Honga's Lotus Petal (Asian cuisine). The Marmotte is an elegant old place, with a French influence. Allred's, at the top of the gondola has spectacular views and is open for gourmet dining in the evenings. In Mountain Village, the Hop Garden is a new bar and grill. For fine dining, try the new Onyx at the Capella resort.

Après-ski Après-ski revolves around the bars. Mountain Village has some new venues: the Hop Garden has speciality beers and live music on the terrace and there's the Suede (hotel Capella) and the Little Bar (hotel Lumière) to try. In town, the most popular bars are the X-Cafe, the lively Last Dollar, New Sheridan with its 19th-century bar, and Fly Me to the Moon Saloon.

Off the slopes Activities include: dog sledding, horse riding, snowshoeing, ice skating, snowmobiling and glider rides. There are some good walks, concerts at the historic Sheridan Opera House and cinema at the Nugget.

Vail

A vast, swanky resort with some very swanky hotels at the foot of one of the biggest (but also busiest) ski areas in the States

£90
RESORT PRICE INDEX

RATINGS

The mountains

Extent	★★★★
Fast lifts	★★★★★
Queues	★★
Terrain p'ks	★★★★★
Snow	★★★★★
Expert	★★★★
Intermediate	★★★★★
Beginner	★★★
X-country	★★★
Restaurants	★★
Schools	★★★★★
Families	★★★★

The resort

Charm	★★★
Convenience	★★★
Scenery	★★★
Eating out	★★★★★
Après-ski	★★★
Off-slope	★★★

➕ One of the biggest areas in the US – great for confident intermediates, especially

➕ The Back Bowls are big areas of treeless terrain – unusual in the US

➕ Fabulous area of ungroomed, wooded slopes at Blue Sky Basin

➕ Largely traffic-free resort centres, very pleasant in parts – but ...

➖ Resort is a vast sprawl; and a lot of redevelopment is going on

➖ Slopes can be crowded by American standards, with serious lift queues

➖ Inadequate mountain restaurants

➖ Blue Sky Basin and the Back Bowls may not be open in early season; warm weather can close the Bowls

➖ Expensive

We always enjoy skiing Vail; it's a big mountain with a decent vertical, and Blue Sky Basin adds hugely to its attractions. But it is far from being our favourite American mountain. In an American resort you expect the runs to be pretty much crowd-free – and in any resort, these days, you expect 20-minute lift queues to be a thing of the past. In these respects, Vail disappoints.

When the budget runs to a swanky billet in Vail Village, we're happy enough with the resort, too: there is no denying it is a pleasant enough place to wander around in the evening. But we're not enthusiastic about its pseudo-Tirolean style, and the rest of the huge resort – almost four miles long – is much less appealing. In the end, we reckon Vail can't compete with more distinctively American resorts based on old mining or cowboy towns.

THE RESORT

Vail is an enormous resort, stretching along the I-70 freeway running west from Denver. Beaver Creek, 16km/10 miles away, is covered by the lift pass and is easily reached by bus. A short drive over Vail Pass gets you to Breckenridge and Keystone – both owned by Vail Resorts and covered by the lift pass. Copper Mountain is also nearby.

VILLAGE CHARM ★★★☆☆
No real identity
Standing in the centre of Vail Village, surrounded by chalets and bierkellers, you could be forgiven for thinking you were in the Tirol – which is what Vail's

founder, Pete Seibert, intended back in the 1950s. But Vail Village is now just one part of a multi-base resort, built mostly in anonymous modern style.

CONVENIENCE ★★★☆☆
There's always the bus
The vast village benefits from a free and efficient bus service which makes choice of location less than crucial. But the most convenient – and expensive – places to stay are in mock-Tirolean Vail Village, near the Vista Bahn fast chair, or in functional Lionshead, near the gondola – an improving area now that the smart Arrabelle at Vail Square complex has opened. The downside of all the rebuilding work that is going on

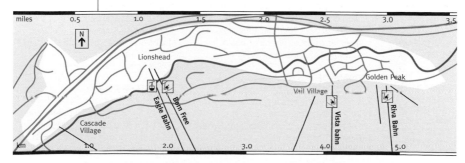

Weekly news updates and resort links at www.wtss.co.uk

↑ The front side of Vail's mountain has trails cut between dense clumps of trees. And you can just see I-70 in the centre right of this pic
TANYA BOOTH

NEWS

though, is that some parts still resemble a building site. There is a lot of accommodation further out – the cheapest tends to be on the far side of the I-70.

SCENERY ★★★☆☆
Unusual for America
Vail's main mountain is densely wooded on the front side. But go over the ridge and the bowls at the back are splendidly wide and mainly open – unusual for America.

THE MOUNTAINS

You get a real sense of travelling around Vail's mountains – something missing in many smaller American resorts. Some of the runs (especially blacks) are overclassified and we've had mixed reports on trail signposting. There are free mountain tours and separate tours of Blue Sky Basin starting at 11am every day.

EXTENT OF THE SLOPES ★★★★☆
Something for everyone
Vail has one of the biggest areas of slopes in the US (only recently overtaken by Big Sky/Moonlight Basin). They can be accessed via three main lifts. From Vail Village, the Vista Bahn

fast chair goes up to the major mid-mountain focal point, Mid-Vail; from Lionshead, the Eagle Bahn gondola goes up to the Eagle's Nest complex; and from the Golden Peak base area just to the east of Vail Village, the Riva Bahn fast chair goes up towards the Two Elk area.

The front face of the mountain is largely north-facing, with well-groomed trails cut through the trees. At altitude the mountainside divides into three bowls – Mid-Vail in the centre, with Game Creek to the south-west and Northeast Bowl to the, er, north-east. Lifts reach the ridge at three points, all giving access to the **Back Bowls** (mostly ungroomed and treeless) and through them to the **Blue Sky Basin** area – mostly ungroomed and wooded, with a 'backcountry' feel that the rest of Vail lacks.

The slopes have yellow-jacketed patrollers who stop people speeding recklessly. You can test equipment at the Vail Sports Demo Center.

FAST LIFTS ★★★★★
Plenty of them
Recent investment means there are lots of fast lifts on both sides of the mountain. All three of Blue Sky Basin's lifts are fast chairs.

KEY FACTS

Resort	2500m
	8,200ft
Slopes	2475-3525m
	8,120-11,570ft
Lifts	32
Pistes	5,289 acres
Green	18%
Blue	29%
Black	53%
Snowmaking	7%

LIFT PASSES

Colorado

Prices in US$

Age	1-day	6-day
under 13	61	366
13 to 64	97	582
over 65	87	522

Free under 5

Beginner included in price of lessons

Notes

Covers all Vail, Beaver Creek, Breckenridge and Keystone resorts, plus Arapahoe Basin; prices quoted are ticket window prices; there are advance purchase discounts and substantial additional reductions for international visitors who pre-book through a UK tour operator (it is not necessary to buy a complete holiday package to obtain these prices)

QUEUES ★★★★★
Can be bad

Vail has some of the longest lift lines we've hit in the US, especially at weekends because of the influx from nearby Denver. Most of our reporters experience some lines. Mid-Vail is a bottleneck that is difficult to avoid; 20-minute waits are common. At peak times it's possible to queue for 45 minutes here. The Northwoods chair is another notable hot-spot and the Eagle Bahn gondola can have 'queues of up to 20 minutes virtually all day'. But other reporters have been luckier ('occasional' queues and 'only 10 minutes maximum wait at the bottom'). One visitor was more upset by the unreliability of some lifts: 'We were stuck on the Game Creek chair twice for up to 30 minutes at −28°C.'

TERRAIN PARKS ★★★★★
Three to fly between

There are three parks, all named with an aviation theme. The Flight School park is used by the ski school and is aimed at novices. It is adjacent to the big pro park, has its own entrance and is accessible by the Riva Bahn fast chair. There is a nice mini-pipe – great for learning. Intermediates should head up the Eagle Bahn gondola or Born Free chair from Lionshead to the Aviator park. Medium-sized kickers and rails will prepare you to step up to the Fly Zone on Golden Peak. This big pro park is accessible by the Riva Bahn fast chair. The park is home to various high-profile events and is often in the top ten in terrain park lists and polls. There are over 40 features, including a huge triple-jump line, a quarter-pipe, and a log rail park – all built in nice fluid lines. The pipe boasts 5.5m/18ft walls, and it is 130m/425ft long. A water tank feature, new super dome and big wall ride are now signature features of the park.

SNOW RELIABILITY ★★★★★
Excellent, except in the Bowls

As well as an exceptional natural snow record (average 348 inches), Vail has extensive snowmaking, normally needed only in early season. Both the Back Bowls and Blue Sky Basin usually open later in the season than the front mountain. Blue Sky is largely north-facing (and wooded) and keeps its snow well, but the Bowls are sunny, and in warm weather snow can deteriorate to the point where they are closed or a traverse is kept open to allow access to Blue Sky Basin. Grooming is excellent.

FOR EXPERTS ★★★★
Transformed by Blue Sky Basin

Vail's Back Bowls are vast areas, served by four chairlifts and a short draglift. You can go virtually anywhere you like in the half-dozen identifiable bowls, trying the gradient and terrain of your choice. There are interesting, lightly wooded areas, as well as the open slopes that dominate the area. Some 87% of the runs in the Back Bowls are classified black but are not particularly steep, and they have disappointed some of our expert reporters. The snow can deteriorate rapidly in warm, sunny weather.

Blue Sky Basin has much better snow than the Back Bowls and some great adventure runs in the trees – some widely spaced, some very tight, some on relatively gentle terrain, some quite steep. All the runs funnel into the same run-out so you can't get lost.

On the front face there are some genuinely steep double black diamond runs, which usually have great snow; they are often mogulled, but they are sometimes groomed to make wonderful fast cruising. The fast Highline lift – on the extreme east of the area – serves three runs. Prima Cornice, served by the Northwoods Express, is one of the steepest runs

boarding

The terrain is about as big as it comes in America. Beginners will enjoy the front side's gentle groomed pistes, ideal for honing skills and serviced by fast chairlifts. But beware of flat areas, especially at the top of the Wildwood and Northwoods lifts. The back bowls will keep most riders busy for days when the snow is right. Blue Sky Basin is definitely worth checking out, with its acres of natural trails, gladed trees and cornices. There are three terrain parks too. The Vail Sports Demo Center at the Patrol Headquarters summit will help if you have any issues with your board, or want to demo the latest gear. There are plenty of specialist shops in town, as well as good snowboard school facilities, with adult-specific courses.

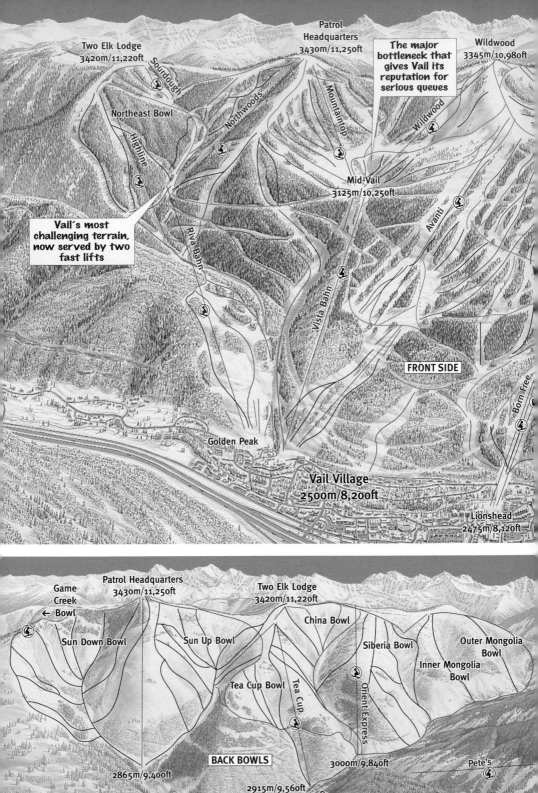

Two Elk Lodge
3420m/11,220ft

Sourdough

Patrol
Headquarters
3430m/11,250ft

The major
bottleneck that
gives Vail its
reputation for
serious queues

Wildwood
3345m/10,980ft

Northeast Bowl

Northwoods

Mountaintop

Wildwood

Highline

Mid-Vail
3125m/10,250ft

Avanti

Vail's most
challenging terrain,
now served by two
fast lifts

Riva Bahn

Vista Bahn

FRONT SIDE

Born Free

Golden Peak

Vail Village
2500m/8,200ft

Lionshead
2475m/8,120ft

Game
Creek
Bowl

Patrol Headquarters
3430m/11,250ft

Two Elk Lodge
3420m/11,220ft

China Bowl

Sun Down Bowl

Sun Up Bowl

Siberia Bowl

Outer Mongolia
Bowl

Inner Mongolia
Bowl

Tea Cup Bowl

Tea Cup

Orient Express

2865m/9,400ft

BACK BOWLS

3000m/9,840ft

Pete's

2915m/9,560ft

Skyline

Blue Sky Basin

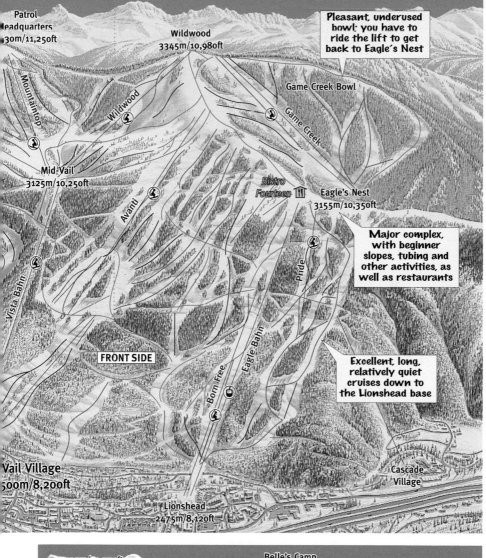

Patrol Headquarters
3430m/11,250ft

Wildwood
3345m/10,980ft

Pleasant, underused bowl; you have to ride the lift to get back to Eagle's Nest

Wildwood

Game Creek Bowl

Game Creek

Mountaintop

Mid-Vail
3125m/10,250ft

Avanti

Bistro Fourteen

Eagle's Nest
3155m/10,350ft

Major complex, with beginner slopes, tubing and other activities, as well as restaurants

Pride

Vista Bahn

FRONT SIDE

Born Free

Eagle Bahn

Excellent, long, relatively quiet cruises down to the Lionshead base

Vail Village
2500m/8,200ft

Cascade Village

Lionshead
2475m/8,120ft

3525m/11,570ft

Belle's Camp
3500m/11,480ft

Pete's Bowl

Earl's Bowl

Earl's

Pete's

Skyline

BLUE SKY BASIN

Orient Express

3000m/9,840ft

China Bowl

Tea Cup Bowl

2915m/9,560ft

↑ The back bowls are largely open, ungroomed terrain, and you can ski wherever you like

VAIL RESORTS, INC / JACK AFFLECK

CHILDCARE

Small World
t 754 3285
Ages 2mnth to 6yr;
8am to 4.30; $109
per day; reservations
recommended

Ski school
Ages 3 to 12; full day
including lift pass and
lunch from US$139;
teens $159 per day

GETTING THERE

Air Eagle 55km/
35 miles (45mins);
Denver 195km/
120 miles (2hr15)

UK PACKAGES

*Alpine Answers,
AmeriCan Ski, American
Ski Classics, Crystal,
Crystal Finest, Elegant
Resorts, Erna Low,
Funway Holidays,
Independent Ski Links,
Inghams, Interactive
Resorts, Kuoni, Made
to Measure,
Momentum, Neilson,
Simply Alpine, Ski
Activity, Ski Dream, Ski
Expectations, Ski
Independence, Ski Line,
Ski Safari, Ski
Solutions, Skitracer,
Skiworld, STC,
Supertravel, Thomson,
Trailfinders, United
Vacations, Virgin Snow*

on the front side of the hill.

If the snow is good, try the back-country Minturn Mile – you leave the ski area through a gate in the Game Creek area to descend a powder bowl and finish on a path by a river – ending up at the atmospheric Saloon. Go with a local guide.

FOR INTERMEDIATES ★★★★★
Ideal territory
The majority of Vail's front face is great intermediate territory, with easy cruising runs. Above Lionshead, especially, there are excellent long, relatively quiet blues – Born Free and Simba both go from top to bottom. Game Creek Bowl, nearby, is excellent, too. Avanti, underneath the chair of the same name, is a nice cruiser.

As well as tackling some of the easier front-face blacks, intermediates will find plenty of interest in the Back Bowls. Some of the runs are groomed and several are classified blue, including Silk Road, which loops around the eastern edge, with wonderful views. Some of the unpisted slopes make the ideal introduction to powder skiing. Confident intermediates will also enjoy Blue Sky Basin's clearly marked blue runs and trying the easier ungroomed runs there.

FOR BEGINNERS ★★★
Good but can be crowded
There are fine nursery slopes at resort level and at altitude, and easy longer runs to progress to. But they can be rather crowded.

FOR CROSS-COUNTRY ★★★
Go for Golden
Vail's cross-country areas (17km/11 miles) are at the foot of Golden Peak and at the Nordic Center on the golf course. There are also 10km/6 miles of snowshoe trails.

MOUNTAIN RESTAURANTS ★★
Surprisingly poor
Vail's mountain restaurants are disappointing for such a big, upscale resort. The major self-service restaurants can be unpleasantly crowded from 11am to 2pm.
Editors' choice The table-service Bistro Fourteen (754 4530) at Eagle's Nest – an airy room doing good food at not exorbitant prices.
Worth knowing about There are self-service places at several major lift junctions. Two Elk is a huge, airy place that many visitors find satisfactory; but it can get very crowded. Go to Wildwood Smokehouse for BBQs, and to Buffalo's for 'sandwich and soup combos'.

SCHOOLS AND GUIDES ★★★★★
Among the best in the world
The Vail-Beaver Creek school generates many glowing reports: 'excellent'; 'the best ski lesson I've ever had'. Class sizes are usually small: 'never more than four in the group lesson', says a recent reporter. You can sign up for lessons on the mountain. SK Immersion is a new 'focused learning' programme that targets strength and technique, while working on alignment.

FOR FAMILIES ★★★★
Good all round
The comprehensive facilities for small children look excellent, and we've had good reports on the school. The main children's centre is at Golden Peak and there are splendid areas with adventure trails and themed play zones. There's even a special kids' cafe area at Mid Vail. Family Night theatre and dinner events are held at Adventure Ridge.

STAYING THERE

There's a big choice of packages to Vail. It's easy to organise your own visit, with regular airport shuttles.
Chalets Several UK tour operators offer catered chalets. Many are out of the centre at East Vail or West Vail or across the busy I-70 freeway.
Hotels Vail has a fair choice of hotels, though nearly all are expensive. Check online for the best deals.
★★★★★Vail Cascade A resort within a resort – lots of facilities and a chairlift right outside.
★★★★★Sonnenalp Very stylish,

↑ Vail Village is the nicest part of this enormous resort and a good (though expensive) place to stay

VAIL RESORTS, INC / JACK AFFLECK

welcoming, central Bavarian-style place. Large spa and splendid piano bar-lounge.

*****Lodge at Vail Right by the Vista Bahn. Some standard rooms small. Huge buffet breakfast. Outdoor pool/spa. Recommended by a reporter.

****Marriot Mountain Resort Also owned by Vail Resorts, near the Eagle Bahn gondola. Impressive spa facilities.

****Manor Vail Resort At Golden Peak. Suites with sitting area, fireplace, kitchen and terrace. Hot tub and new pools. Refurbished for 2008/09.

****Plaza Hotel and Club Good position in Vail Village; smart rooms and suites. Pool, spa and fitness centre.

***Evergreen Lodge Between village and Lionshead. Recently refurbished. Outdoor pool, sauna and hot tub. Sports bar. 'Excellent value for money and spacious rooms.'

Apartments There's a wide range from standard to luxury. The Racquet Club at East Vail has lots of amenities. At Vail Village, Mountain Haus is central and high quality. Vail Cascade Resort and Spa is good value, including breakfast and use of the hotel's leisure facilities. And Manor Vail might be a preferred family choice – it's beside the children's ski school. Good value places at Lionshead include: Village Plaza Inn, Vantage Point, the Antlers, Enzian, Westwind and Vail 21.

EATING OUT *****
Endless choice

Whatever kind of food you want, Vail has it – but most of it is expensive.

Fine-dining options include the Wildflower (in the Lodge), Centre V (French-inspired; in the Arrabelle at Vail Square), the Tour (modern French) and Ludwig's (in the Sonnenalp). For Alpine ambience try the Alpenrose II and Pepi's in the hotel Gramshammer.

For more moderate prices, we've found Blu's 'contemporary American' food satisfactory; Billy's Island Grill does steaks; and Campo de Fiori is an excellent Italian. Bart & Yeti's is good for local ales and no-frills, hearty American food. The Chophouse at Lionshead serves seafood and steaks. Reader recommendations include Lancelot at Vail Village for steaks and seafood, Bagali's Italian Kitchen for pizza, May Palace (Chinese) and Nozawa (Asian) in West Vail, Sapphire (seafood), Montauk (seafood), the Bistro at the Racquet Club, Los Amigos ('decent Mexican fare', 'very family-friendly'), Russell's, Vendetta's, Pazzo's ('great pizzas and very good value') and Sweet Basil at Vail Village ('delicious food; good atmosphere').

APRES-SKI ***
Fairly lively

Lionshead is said to be quiet in the evenings; but Garfinkel's has a DJ, sun deck and happy hour. The Red Lion in the village centre is 'cheap and good fun' with live music, big-screen TVs and huge portions of food. The George models itself on an English-style pub. Pepi's is also popular and Los Amigos is lively at four o'clock. The Tap Room in the Vista Bahn building is a relaxed woody bar.

You can have a good night out at Adventure Ridge at the top of the gondola. As well as bars and restaurants, there's lots to do on the snow – though a reporter reckons the tubing hill is no match for Keystone's.

OFF THE SLOPES ***
A lot to do

Getting around on the free bus is easy, and there are lots of activities to try. The factory outlets at Silverthorne (over Vail Pass) are a must if you can't resist a bargain.

Winter Park

A radical alternative to the run of Colorado resorts, for those more interested in snow and space than in après-ski amusements

£80
RESORT PRICE INDEX

RATINGS

The mountains

Extent	★★★
Fast lifts	★★★★
Queues	★★★★
Terrain p'ks	★★★★★
Snow	★★★★★
Expert	★★★★
Intermediate	★★★★
Beginner	★★★★★
X-country	★★★★
Restaurants	★★★
Schools	★★★★★
Families	★★★★

The resort

Charm	★★
Convenience	★★★
Scenery	★★★
Eating out	★★
Après-ski	★
Off-slope	★

NEWS

A shop and four new restaurants, including a Japanese and a Belgian, opened in the 'village' base area during 2008/09. And a bucket-lift was installed to transfer day visitors between car park and 'village'.

For 2009/10 the Colorado Ski Train that ferried Denver residents to and from the ski area for the day has been axed by the new owners.

And new development is on the back burner for the moment.

KEY FACTS

Resort	2745m
	9,000ft
Slopes	2745-3675m
	9,000-12,060ft
Lifts	25
Pistes	3,060 acres
Green	8%
Blue	36%
Black	56%
Snowmaking	10%

+ The best snowfall record of all Colorado's major resorts

+ Good terrain for all abilities

+ Quiet on weekdays

+ Leading resort for teaching people with disabilities to ski and ride

+ Largely free of inflated prices and ski-resort glitz

− 'Village' at the lift base is still very limited – dead in the evening

− Town is a bus ride away and lacks the usual shops and restaurants

− Trails tend to be either easy cruises or stiff mogul fields

− Some tough terrain liable to closure by bad weather

Winter Park's ski area – developed for the recreation of the citizens of nearby Denver, and still owned by the city – is world class. Now there is the prospect of a world-class resort at the base, too: Intrawest (developers of resorts such as Whistler) is in the first phase of a massive expansion plan.

But things are happening more slowly than was originally hoped, presumably because of the economic situation. For the present, there's only a small, very quiet 'village' at the base and most lodging, shops and restaurants are a bus ride away. If that doesn't matter to you, Winter Park is well worth considering. Some of our reporters rate it their favourite Colorado resort, partly because it makes a refreshing change from the ski resort norm.

THE RESORT

Winter Park started life in the 19th century: when the Rio Grande railway was built, workers climbed the slopes to ski down. One of the resort's mountains, Mary Jane, is named after a legendary 'lady of pleasure', who is said to have received the land as payment for her favours. Until last season the railway still played an important part in depositing Denverites on weekends, but the service has now been axed. By road, the approach is distinctly Alpine, crossing the Continental Divide at Berthoud Pass (3450m/11,320ft). Don't plan on driving over in the dark. The resort is much lower, but high enough for a risk of altitude sickness. Having a car makes day trips to Denver and to resorts such as Copper Mountain, Breckenridge and Keystone possible.

You can stay at the small new 'village' being built at the base of the slopes or in the town of Winter Park, an efficient shuttle-bus ride away.

VILLAGE CHARM ★★
Old or new?

Most accommodation is in spacious condos scattered around either side of US highway 40, the road through the town of Winter Park. Drive into the

town at night, and the neon lights make it seem like a real ski resort town – but in the cold light of day it's clear that the place doesn't amount to much, though the locals are 'friendly'. It even lacks a proper supermarket – the nearest is a drive or bus ride away at Fraser.

Stylish lodgings have been developed at or near the foot of the slopes, including a car-free mini-resort known as The Village at Winter Park Resort. But as yet it's very small, though shops, bars and restaurants are opening slowly. Confusingly, an area between the mountain and the town is known as Old Town.

CONVENIENCE ★★★
Walk or ride

If you stay in the 'village' it's a stroll to the slopes. Shuttle-buses run between the town and the lift base, and the hotels and condos also provide shuttles.

SCENERY ★★★
See the Continental Divide

You are almost on the Continental Divide here, with views of the rolling hills in the other direction from the top of Parsenn Bowl.

↑ Early morning cruising on perfectly groomed corduroy is the norm here

WINTER PARK RESORT

LIFT PASSES

Winter Park Resort

Prices in US$

Age	1-day	6-day
under 13	48	234
over 13	92	468

Free under 6
Seniors no deals
Beginner included in price of lessons

Notes
Multi-day prices quoted are advance-purchase prices; special deals for disabled skiers

UK PACKAGES

Alpine Answers, AmeriCan Ski, American Ski Classics, Crystal, Directski.com, Erna Low, Funway Holidays, Independent Ski Links, Inghams, Interactive Resorts, Made to Measure, Simply Alpine, Ski Dream, Ski Independence, Ski McNeill, Ski Safari, Ski Solutions, Skitracer, Skiworld, Supertravel, Thomson, United Vacations, Virgin Snow

THE MOUNTAINS

There's a good mix of terrain that suits all abilities – when it's all open. There are guided tours at 10am and 1pm ('hosts invaluable', says a reporter). Route finding can be tricky in places.

EXTENT OF THE SLOPES ★★★
Interestingly divided

Winter Park's ski area is big by US standards. There are five distinct, but well-linked, sectors. From the main base, a fast quad takes you to the peak of the original **Winter Park** mountain. From there, you can descend in all directions. Runs lead back towards the main base and over to the **Vasquez Ridge** area on the far right, served by the Pioneer fast quad.

You can also descend to the base of **Mary Jane** mountain, where four chairs up the front face serve tough runs; other chairs serve easier terrain on the flanks. From here you can head for the **Parsenn Bowl** on the Panoramic Express chair for intermediate terrain above and in the trees. From Parsenn, conditions permitting, you can hike for up to half an hour to access advanced and extreme terrain at **Vasquez Cirque**. You can return to Parsenn Bowl using the Eagle Wind chair, saving a long run-out to the Pioneer lift.

FAST LIFTS ★★★★
Adequately covered

Fast chairs have slowly replaced old lifts, though a few slow ones remain.

QUEUES ★★★★
Quiet during the week

During the week the mountain is generally quiet. However, the Zephyr Express can get busy at peak times: 'Get up the mountain before 9am to avoid queues,' says one reporter; 'Wait an hour after lift starting times,' says another. There have traditionally been weekend crowds and queues but these may be less of a problem now that the Ski Train has been axed.

TERRAIN PARKS ★★★★★
Parks for all standards

The flagship Rail Yard park, with 30 features including big jumps, jibs, boxes, a host of variously shaped rails and quarter-, half- and super-pipes, is enough to challenge most experts. It runs down much of the front of Winter Park mountain for 1280m/ 4,200ft. Halfway down it crosses a bridge so that those on the Village Way green run can cross the park safely. At the bottom are the huge features of Dark Territory, open to pass holders only (you need to pay $20, sign a waiver and watch a safety video to get one). For those who prefer smaller hits, there are two parks for intermediates nearby: Dog Patch and Dog Patch East. There's also a beginner-intermediate park, Kendrick, on the Jack Kendrick green run, plus a Starter park for beginners under Prospector Express. Check them out at www.rlyrd.com.

623

Winter Park

Interactive resort shortlist builder at **www.wtss.co.uk**

boarding

There is some great advanced and extreme boarding terrain and a high probability of fresh powder to ride. The different levels of park (see 'Terrain parks') make Winter Park even more attractive to all levels of freestyler. The resort is also an ideal beginner and intermediate boarder area, with excellent terrain for learning. A good school provides classes for all levels, including learning to jump and ride rails.

SNOW RELIABILITY ★★★★★
Among Colorado's best

Winter Park's position, close to the Continental Divide, gives it an average yearly snowfall of 355 inches – the highest of any major Colorado resort. Snowmaking covers a lot of Winter Park mountain's runs.

FOR EXPERTS ★★★★
Some hair-raising challenges

Mary Jane has some of the steepest mogul fields, chutes and hair-raising challenges in the US. On the front side is a row of long black mogul fields that are quite steep enough for most of us. There are some good genuine blacks on Winter Park mountain, too.

Some of the best terrain is open only when there is good snow and/or weather – so it's especially unreliable early in the season. The fearsome chutes of Mary Jane's back side – all steep, narrow and bordered by rocks – need a lot of snow and are accessed by a control gate. Parsenn Bowl has superb blue/black gladed runs and black-diamond gladed runs on the back side down to the Eagle Wind chair. Vasquez Cirque, the least reliably open area, has excellent ungroomed expert terrain but not much vertical before you hit the forest.

FOR INTERMEDIATES ★★★★
Choose your challenge

From pretty much wherever you are on Winter Park mountain and Vasquez Ridge you can choose a run to suit your ability. Most blue runs are well groomed every night, giving you perfect early morning cruising on the famous Colorado 'corduroy' pistes. Black runs, however, tend not to be groomed, and huge moguls form. If bumps are for you, try Mary Jane's front side. If you're learning to love them, the blue/black Sleeper enables you to dip in and out.

Parsenn Bowl has grand views and several gentle cruising pistes as well as more challenging ungroomed terrain. There are blue and blue-black runs and glades here, offering a nice range of gradients. It's also an ideal place to try powder for the first time. But when it's actually snowing you are better off riding lower lifts, sticking to the powdery edges of treelined runs for better visibility.

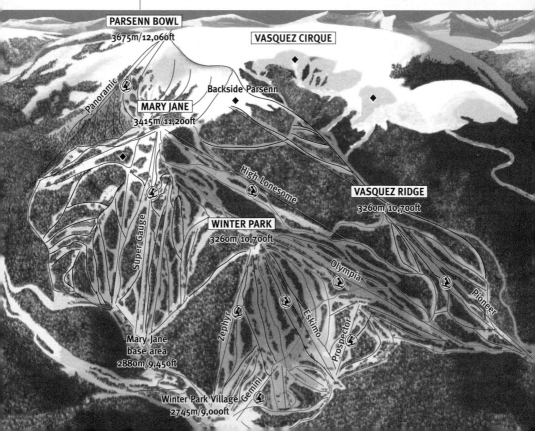

PARSENN BOWL
3675m/12,066ft

VASQUEZ CIRQUE

Backside Parsenn

Panoramic

MARY JANE
3415m/11,200ft

High Lonesome

VASQUEZ RIDGE
3260m/10,700ft

Super Gauge

WINTER PARK
3260m/10,700ft

Olympia

Pioneer

Zephyr

Eskimo

Prospector

Mary Jane
base area
2880m/9,450ft

Winter Park Village
2745m/9,000ft

Gemini

SCHOOLS

Winter Park
t 1 800 729 7907

National Sports Center for the Disabled
t 726 1540
Special programme for disabled skiers and snowboarders

Classes (Winter Park prices)
Half day (2½hr) $69
Private lessons
$359 for 3hr for 1 to 3 people

CHILDCARE

Wee Willies
t 1 800 420 8093
Ages 2mnth to 6yr; $95 per day; 8am to 4pm

Ski school
Takes ages 3 to 17 ($115 per day including lift ticket and lunch)

GETTING THERE

Air Denver 165km/ 105 miles (2hr15)

Rail Denver, Sat and Sun only

ACTIVITIES

Indoor Fitness clubs, hot tubs, museum

Outdoor Ice rink, snowshoeing, snow biking, snowmobiling, snowcat tours

Central reservations toll-free number (from within the US) 1 800 979 0332

Phone numbers From distant parts of the US, add the prefix 1 970; from abroad, add the prefix +1 970

TOURIST OFFICE

t 1 303 316 1564
winterpark@ winterparkresort.com
www.skiwinterpark. com

The blue-black Hughes is a great thrash home at close of play.

FOR BEGINNERS ★★★★★
About the best we've seen
Discovery Park is a 25-acre dedicated area for beginners, reached by a high-speed quad and served by two more chairs and a tow. As well as a nursery area and longer green runs, it has an adventure trail through trees. And the Sorensen Park learning zone at the base area is good too. There are lots of long green runs, but some are perilously close to being flat.

FOR CROSS-COUNTRY ★★★★
Lots of it
There are several different areas nearby (none actually in the resort) with generally excellent snow, totalling over 200km/125 miles of groomed trails, as well as backcountry tours.

MOUNTAIN RESTAURANTS ★★★
Some good facilities
The highlight is the Lodge at Sunspot, at the top of Winter Park mountain. This wood and glass building has a welcoming bar with a roaring log fire and table- and self-service sections – but it gets very busy. Lunch Rock Cafe at the top of Mary Jane does quick snacks and has a deli counter, and there is a self-service (with 'limited choice', says a 2009 reporter) at Snoasis, by the beginner area. Otherwise, it's down to the bases. The Club Car at the base of Mary Jane offers table service and a varied menu.

SCHOOLS AND GUIDES ★★★★★
Very good reports
A recent reporter with a school party said, 'I would like to stress how good, helpful and flexible the ski school is.' 'Three people in our group had lessons, and the improvement in all was quite startling to see,' said another visitor. As well as standard classes there are ideas such as Family Private (for different abilities together) and themed lessons such as bumps, women-only and telemark clinics.

FOR FAMILIES ★★★★
Some of the best
The Children's Center at the base area houses day-care facilities, taking kids from two months to six years and is the meeting point for children's classes, which have their own areas.

STAYING THERE

Chalets A few are available.
Hotels There are a couple of hotel/ condo complexes with restaurants and pools near, but not in, the new Village.
***Iron Horse Resort 'Wonderful; ski-in/ski-out, great restaurant'.
***Winter Park Mountain Lodge Inconveniently positioned across the valley from the lifts; 'best to pay extra for newer deluxe room'.
Apartments There are a lot of comfortable condos, including the slope-side Zephyr Mountain Lodge and Fraser Crossing/Founders Pointe. In or on the way to town, Beaver Village, Winter Park Townhomes, Sawmill Station, Red Quill Village, Meadowridge and Crestview Place have been recommended.

EATING OUT ★★
A real weakness
There isn't the range of places you get in most 'destination' resorts. For 'fine dining' you have to drive 8 miles to Devil's Thumb Ranch. Get hold of the giveaway Grand County menu guide. In town, reporters are keen on Deno's (seafood, steaks etc), New Hong Kong ('excellent' Chinese), Gasthaus Eichler (German-influenced food), Shipwreck Landing North ('food is the best in Winter Park; the craic is great'), Carlos and Maria's (Tex-Mex), Fontenot's (Cajun) and Hernando's (pizza/pasta). Or try the Crooked Creek Saloon, a drive away at Fraser, for good atmosphere and typical American food.

APRES-SKI ★
If you know where to go ...
At close of play, there's action at the main lift base at the Derailer Bar ('the best and cheapest') and Doc's Roadhouse, and at the Club Car at the base of Mary Jane – but reporters are disappointed at how early they close. The Cheeky Monk serves 'good Belgian beer'. Later on, Deno's, the Wild Creek Brewery and the Winter Park Pub are the main hot spots. The Moffat Station micro brewery has good beer.

OFF THE SLOPES ★
Mainly the great outdoors
Reporters are enthusiastic about the floodlit tubing at Fraser, skating at the base area rink and snowmobiling to the Continental Divide. The Silverthorne factory outlet stores are 90 minutes away.

Winter Park

Interactive resort shortlist builder at **www.wtss.co.uk**

Utah

'The Greatest Snow on Earth' is Utah's marketing slogan. And it's true that some Utah resorts do get huge amounts of snow – usually light, dry powder – and if you like the steep and deep, you should at some point make the pilgrimage here. Don't be put off by thinking its a 'dry' Mormon state – getting alcohol has never been a problem and the laws were greatly relaxed in July 2009, making it much like any other US state. But boarders beware: two of its top resorts don't allow snowboarding.

The biggest dumps fall at Alta (which bans boarding) and Snowbird. Their average of 500 inches of snow a year (twice as much as some Colorado resorts) has made them the powder capitals of the world.

Park City, 45 minutes' drive away, is the main 'destination' resort of the area, and a sensible holiday base; upmarket Deer Valley (which bans boarding) is next door; and The Canyons is only a short drive away.

Although only a few miles from Snowbird/Alta as the crow flies, these resorts get 'only' 300 to 350 inches of snow. There are separate chapters on these five resorts. We spent a week in Park City in 2008, and it virtually never stopped snowing. Every day we had fresh, knee-high powder and we never made it to Alta or Snowbird: the

access road to them was often closed but there was no need to go because the snow on the three local mountains was awesome.

Other Utah resorts worth visiting include Brighton and Solitude. They get similar amounts of snow, but it gets tracked out less quickly because the resorts attract far fewer experts. The main claim to fame of Sundance is that it's owned by Robert Redford; it gets 320 inches of snow a year. It was unknown Snowbasin (400 inches), well to the north, that hosted the Olympic downhill events in 2002. Powder Mountain (500 inches), a bit further north, is aptly named. A few seasons ago the resort started all-day guided snowcat tours, which were so popular that in 2008/09 the available terrain was increased to 2,000 acres. There is more about these resorts in the resort directory at the end of the book.

Until July 2009 the sale and consumption of alcohol was tightly controlled in Utah, the Mormon state. Until then, to get a drink in bars and clubs dedicated to drinking (as opposed to restaurants) you had to pay a fee to become a member or be the guest of a member. At some places you had to order food in order to get an alcoholic drink. These rules have now been scrapped. There are still differences between bars and restaurants, but effectively you don't need to worry about them, and as long as you are over 21 (and can prove it – eg by showing your passport) you should have no problem getting alcoholic drinks between 10am and midnight or 1am. The amount of spirits allowed in a drink has been increased too.

TOURIST OFFICE

Ski Utah
www.skiutah.com

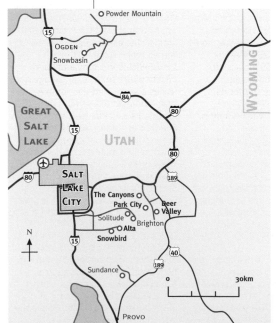

Alta

Cult powder resort linked to Snowbird but with less brutal architecture and a friendlier, old-fashioned feel

➕ Phenomenal snow and steep terrain mean cult status among experts (there's great beginner terrain, too)

➕ Linked to Snowbird, making it one of the largest ski areas in the US

➕ Ski-almost-to-the-door convenience

➖ 'Resort' is no more than a scattering of lodges – not much après-ski atmosphere, and few off-slope diversions

➖ Limited groomed runs for intermediates

Alta and Snowbird are the powder capitals of the world (the snow here is as plentiful, frequent and light as it comes), and their combined area is one of the biggest in the US. Strangely, many locals we meet are still either Alta or Snowbird devotees (the ski areas were separate until 2001/02) and never ski the other area. Madness (unless you're a boarder, in which case Snowbird is your only option – boarding is banned in Alta). On balance, we'd choose to stay in Alta – it has a friendlier feel and less brutal architecture.

TOP 10 RATINGS

Extent	★★★
Fast lifts	★★★★
Queues	★★★
Snow	★★★★★
Expert	★★★★★
Intermediate	★★★
Beginner	★★★
Charm	★★
Convenience	★★★★
Scenery	★★★

NEWS

For 2009/10 the Albion Day Lodge is due to have a revamp of its exterior.

KEY FACTS

Resort	2600m
	8,530ft
Alta and Snowbird combined area see Snowbird	
Alta only	
Slopes	2600-3200m
	8,530-10,500ft
Lifts	11
Pistes	2,200 acres
Green	25%
Blue	40%
Black	35%
Snowmaking	2%

UK PACKAGES

AmeriCan Ski, Simply Alpine, Ski Dream, Skitracer

THE RESORT

Alta sits at the craggy head of Little Cottonwood Canyon, 2km/1 mile beyond Snowbird and less than an hour's drive from downtown Salt Lake City. Both the resort and the approach road are prone to avalanches and closure: visitors can be confined indoors for safety.

Village charm Where once there was a bustling and bawdy mining town, there is now just a strung-out handful of lodges and parking areas.

Convenience Life revolves around the two separate lift base areas – Albion and Wildcat – linked by a bi-directional rope tow along the flat valley floor. There are about a dozen places to stay, all convenient for the lifts.

Scenery Alta is recognised for its impressively rugged scenery and challenging, sparsely wooded ridges.

THE MOUNTAINS

Alta's slopes are lightly wooded, with some treeless slopes. Check out the Snowbird chapter for the linked slopes. Unlike most US resorts, Alta's trail map does not differentiate between single and double black diamond trails – a bad idea we think.

Slopes The dominant feature of Alta's terrain is the steep end of a ridge that separates the area's two basins. To the left, above Albion Base, the slopes stretch away over easy green terrain towards the blue and black runs from Point Supreme and from the top of the

Sugarloaf quad (also the access lift for Snowbird). To the right, above Wildcat Base, is a more concentrated bowl with blue runs down the middle and blacks either side, served by the fast two-stage Collins chair. The two sectors are linked at altitude, and by a flat rope tow along the valley floor.

Fast lifts Fast chairs depart from each base; another forms the link with Snowbird's ski area.

Queues The slopes are normally uncrowded, but the fast Collins lift is said to be increasing numbers on the Wildcat side, with 'everybody skiing top to bottom, making it impossible to load at the mid-station'.

Terrain parks There isn't one.

Snow reliability The quantity and quality of the snow – an average 500 inches a year – and the northerly orientation put Alta in the top rank.

Experts Even before the Snowbird link Alta had cult status among local experts, who flocked to the high ridges after a fresh snowfall. There are dozens of steep slopes and chutes.

Intermediates Adventurous intermediates who are happy to try ungroomed slopes and learn to love powder should like Alta, too. There are good blue bowls in both Alta and Snowbird and not-so-tough blacks to progress to. But if it is miles of perfectly groomed piste you are after, there are plenty of better resorts.

Beginners Timid intermediates and beginners will be very happy on the gentle lower slopes of the Albion side. But it's hard to recommend such a

↑ There are a couple of restaurants up the mountain, but many people ski down to the bases for lunch
ALTA SKI AREA

Phone numbers
From distant parts of the US, add the prefix 1 801; from abroad, add the prefix +1 801

TOURIST OFFICE

t 359 1078
info@alta.com
www.alta.com

narrowly focused resort to beginners.
Snowboarding Boarding is banned (but guided snowcat boarding is available in nearby Grizzly Gulch).
Cross-country There's a 5km/3 mile groomed track.
Mountain restaurants There's one in each sector of the slopes, offering mainly fast food. Alf's on the Albion side has 'fast service' and serves 'great chilli in bread bowls'. The 'nice, light and airy' Watson Shelter on the Wildcat side has self-service and table-service sections. Several lodges at the base do lunch.
Schools and guides The ski school specialises in powder lessons – though there are regular classes, too.
Families Day care for children from two

months is available at the Children's Center at Albion Base.

STAYING THERE

None of the hotels is luxurious in US terms but most get booked up by repeat visitors; unusually for the US, most operate half-board deals, with dinner included.
Hotels The venerable Alta Lodge (742 3500) has comfortable rooms and an atmospheric bar, and has developed a cult following in the US by serving a limited dinner menu at shared tables, in two sittings, instead of enlarging its dining room. Ingenious. Rustler Lodge (742 2200) is more luxurious, with a big outdoor pool, but impersonal. The comfortable, modern and conveniently located Goldminer's Daughter (742 2300) and the basic Peruvian Lodge (742 3000) are cheaper. The Snowpine Lodge (742 2000) has a sauna and is 'convenient, comfortable and friendly' but rather 'old-fashioned'.
Eating out It is possible, but eating in is the routine.
Après-ski This rarely goes beyond a few drinks in one of the hotel bars. The Goldminer's Daughter has the main après-ski bar, with pool table etc.
Off the slopes Few options other than snowshoeing, a sightseeing trip to Salt Lake City, or the Cliff spa at Snowbird.

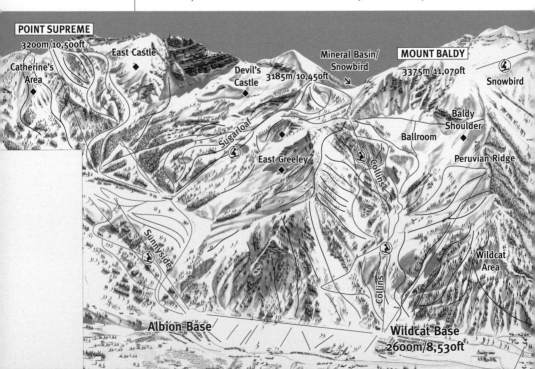

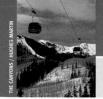

The Canyons

The fourth biggest ski area in the US and still growing, with a small resort developing at the base of the slopes on the edge of Park City

- ➕ Relatively extensive area of slopes for all abilities
- ➕ Modern lift system with few queues
- ➕ Convenient (but soulless) purpose-built resort developing at the base
- ➕ Very easy access to Park City and Deer Valley ski areas

- ➖ Snow on the many south-facing slopes affected by sun
- ➖ Many runs are short
- ➖ Few green runs suitable for those progressing from nursery slopes
- ➖ Resort village limited for après-ski, dining and off-slope diversions

The Canyons has the potential to become the most extensive ski area in the US (and already claims it is the fourth biggest). It has eight linked mountains and anyone having a holiday in Park City should plan to spend some time here. Whether it makes sense to stay in the village at the base is another question.

TOP 10 RATINGS

Extent	★★★
Fast lifts	★★★
Queues	★★★★
Snow	★★★★
Expert	★★★★
Intermediate	★★★★
Beginner	★★
Charm	★★
Convenience	★★★★
Scenery	★★★

NEWS

For 2008/09 a new fixed-grip quad and a blue run opened; these make access from the Dream area to the base of the Tombstone lift easier. The grooming fleet was increased by 25% and snowmaking by 30%. And more glade skiing was created on Peak 5.

For 2009/10 the luxurious Dakota Mountain Lodge is due to open, complete with its own gondola.

THE RESORT

The Canyons has been transformed over the past decade or so. The area of the slopes has doubled, and a car-free village built at the base.

Village charm The village now has a few shops, some restaurants and some bars as well as accommodation (although there is still quite a lot of building going on). But it isn't a very appealing place to spend time – it lacks character and soul – and we would much rather stay in the centre of Park City.

Convenience Staying at the base is convenient for The Canyons but not especially for the other local Park City and Deer Valley slopes. If you stay in Park City, regular shuttle-buses run to the car park below The Canyons village, from which you get a cabriolet lift up to the village (beware: this lift shuts at 5.30pm; after that you need to catch a resort bus down).

Scenery A series of broad, long ridges are separated by valleys and most of the area is fairly densely wooded.

THE MOUNTAINS

The Canyons gets its name from the valleys between the nine mountains that make up the ski area.

Free daily mountain tours start at 10.30am, and there's a First Tracks programme twice a week where former Olympic medallists guide you around the slopes before they officially open.

Slopes Red Pine Lodge, at the heart of the slopes, is reached by an eight-seat gondola from the village. From here you can move in either direction across a series of ridges and valleys. Runs come off both sides of each ridge and generally face north or

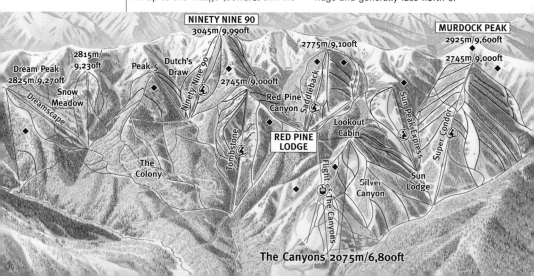

NINETY NINE 90
3045m/9,990ft

MURDOCK PEAK
2925m/9,600ft

2775m/9,100ft

2815m/9,230ft

2745m/9,000ft

Dream Peak
2825m/9,270ft

Peak 5

Dutch's Draw

Dreamscape

Snow Meadow

Ninety Nine 90

2745m/9,000ft

Red Pine Canyon

Saddleback

Sun Peak Express

Super Condor

Lookout Cabin

RED PINE LODGE

Tombstone

The Colony

Flight of The Canyons

Silver Canyon

Sun Lodge

The Canyons 2075m/6,800ft

↑ The Dreamscape area is often blissfully quiet and has easy ungroomed slopes to try as well as the blue groomed trails

THE CANYONS

KEY FACTS

Resort	2075m
	6,800ft
Slopes	2075-3045m
	6,800-9,990ft
Lifts	18
Pistes	3,700 acres
Green	10%
Blue	44%
Black	46%
Snowmaking	6%

UK PACKAGES

AmeriCan Ski, American Ski Classics, Funway Holidays, Simply Alpine, Ski Dream, Ski Safari, Skitracer, Skiworld, United Vacations

Central reservations
Call 1 866 604 4171 (toll-free from within the US)
Phone numbers
From distant parts of the US, add the prefix 1 435; from abroad, add the prefix +1 435

TOURIST OFFICE

t 649 5400
info@thecanyons.com
www.thecanyons.com

south. Most runs are quite short (less than 500m/1,500ft vertical), with some long, quite flat run-outs. If you return to the resort from the Sun Lodge area, you need to take the Towin rope tow, which some reporters find awkward.
Fast lifts The core of the lift system either side of Red Pine Lodge consists of fast quads, but the left-hand third of the trail map has no fast lifts.
Queues The gondola can be busy at peak times. And a recent reporter complained of queues for the key Tombstone fast chair.
Terrain parks There are six natural half-pipes (marked on the trail map). The main terrain park is on Upper and Lower Respect trails, served by the Sun Peak chair, and includes jumps, boxes and rails. The beginners' Progression park is just above here.
Snow reliability Snow here is not the best in Utah. It gets as much on average as Park City (350 inches) and more than Deer Valley. But the south-facing slopes suffer in late-season sun.
Experts There is steep terrain all over the mountain. We particularly liked the north-facing runs off Ninety Nine 90, with steep double black diamond runs plunging down through the trees. We had a great time here on our last visit after fresh snow. A short hike from the top accesses some fine powder runs even days after a snowfall. There is also lots of double diamond terrain on Murdock Peak (a 20-minute hike from the Super Condor lift). Runs off the Peak 5 chair are more sheltered.
Intermediates There are groomed blue runs for intermediates on all the main sectors except Ninety Nine 90. Some are quite short, but you can switch from valley to valley for added interest. From the Super Condor and Tombstone fast chairs there are excellent double blue square runs. The Dreamscape area can be blissfully

quiet, and is great for experiments off-piste to play in powder. Getting back from here you ski through The Colony – a development of huge £5 million homes for the super-rich.
Beginners There are good areas with moving carpets up at Red Pine Lodge. But the run you progress to is rather short and gets very busy.
Snowboarding Except for the flat run-outs from many runs, it's a great area, with lots of natural hits. Canis Lupus is a mile-long, natural half-pipe with numerous obstacles. 'Fantastic fun,' says a 2009 visitor.
Cross-country There are prepared trails on the Park City golf course (20km/12 miles) and the Homestead Resort course (12km/7 miles).
Mountain restaurants The Red Pine Lodge is a large, attractive building with a busy cafeteria, a table-service restaurant and big deck. Reporters found the Sun Lodge 'much quieter and more relaxing'. The table-service Lookout Cabin has wonderful views. The Dreamscape and Tombstone Grill snack huts offer simple food outdoors.
Schools and guides As well as group and 'good' private lessons, there are special clinics. Children's classes are for ages four to 14.
Families There's day care in the Grand Summit Hotel for children from six weeks to six years.

STAYING THERE

Hotels The luxurious Grand Summit and Silverado Lodge both have a pool and hot tub. And the Dakota Lodge is due to open for 2009/10 (see 'News').
Apartments The Escala (with pool and hot tubs) and Westgate Resort and Spa are pricey and luxurious. Of the cheaper places Timberwolf condos have been recommended; other options include Bear Hollow, Hidden Creek, Red Pine and Sundial.
Eating out The Cabin restaurant, in the Grand Summit, serves eclectic US cuisine; Smokie's in the village is more casual. There are snowcat sleigh rides to dinner in a yurt (tent), and the Red Pine Lodge does a BBQ on Saturdays, with a C&W band and dancing.
Après-ski The Cabin Lounge in the Grand Summit has live entertainment, and Smokie's is good for après-ski.
Off the slopes There's snowshoeing, dog sledding, hot-air ballooning, a factory outlet mall and Salt Lake City and Park City nearby.

Deer Valley

Top of the Ivy League of US ski resorts: it promises, and delivers, the best ski and gastronomic experience – we love it

TOP 10 RATINGS

Extent	★★
Fast lifts	★★★★
Queues	★★★★
Snow	★★★★
Expert	★★★
Intermediate	★★★★
Beginner	★★★★
Charm	★★★
Convenience	★★★★
Scenery	★★★

NEWS

For 2008/09 a new cabin seating 40-45 guests replaced the old Cushing's Cabin at the top of Flagstaff Mountain. And Empire Canyon Lodge was revamped to create more seating upstairs. The snowmaking from the base to the top of the Carpenter and Silver Lake Express lifts was also improved, and five snowcats in the piste grooming fleet were upgraded again.

For 2009/10 the 11-storey, luxurious, slope-side St Regis hotel is due to open complete with its own funicular.

KEY FACTS

Resort	2195m
	7,200ft
Slopes	2000-2915m
	6,570-9,570ft
Lifts	22
Pistes	2,026 acres
Green	24%
Blue	43%
Black	33%
Snowmaking	28%

+ Immaculate piste grooming, good snow record and lots of snow-guns

+ Good tree skiing

+ Brilliant free black-diamond tours

+ Many fast lifts and no queues

+ Good restaurants and lodgings

– Relatively expensive

– Small area of slopes

– Mostly short runs of less than 400m/1,310ft vertical

– Quiet at night – though Park City is right next door

Deer Valley prides itself on pampering its guests, with valets to unload your skis, gourmet dining, immaculately groomed slopes, limited numbers on the mountain – and no snowboarding. But it also has some excellent slopes, with interesting terrain for all abilities, including plenty of ungroomed stuff.

The slopes of Deer Valley and Park City are separated by nothing more than a fence, but it seems likely to be permanent, given Deer Valley's ethos. Any skier visiting the area should try both; for most people, Park City is the obvious base – but there are some seductive hotels here at mid-mountain Silver Lake.

THE RESORT

Just a mile from the end of Park City's Main Street, Deer Valley is overtly upmarket – famed for the care and attention lavished on both slopes and guests. But it remains unpretentious. **Village charm** There is no village as such; though the Silver Lake area is somewhat of a mid-mountain focus. **Convenience** The lodgings – luxurious chalets and swanky hotels – are scattered around. **Scenery** The scenery is not without its attractions: from Bald Mountain there are extensive views to Park City.

THE MOUNTAINS

The slopes are varied and interesting. Deer Valley's reputation for immaculate grooming is justified ('the best I have ever seen', says a reporter) but there is also a lot of exciting tree skiing – and some steep bump runs, too. There are free mountain tours for different standards. We went on two three-hour black-diamond tours in 2008 and they were both brilliant, taking us through fresh powder in the trees that we would never have found on our own. The leader of one was an airline pilot five days a week and a guide at Deer Valley for two (not a bad life!). Reporters praise these tours, too. There's a First Tracks tour at 8am. **Slopes** Two chairs take you up to Bald Eagle Mountain, just beyond which is

the mid-mountain focus of Silver Lake Lodge. You can ski from here to the isolated Little Baldy Peak, served by a gondola and a quad chairlift, with mainly easy runs to serve property developments there. But the main skiing is on three linked peaks beyond Silver Lake Lodge – Bald Mountain, Flagstaff Mountain and Empire Canyon. The top of Empire is just a few metres from the runs of the Park City ski area. **Fast lifts** There are fast quads everywhere; the three main peaks have nine. **Queues** Waiting in lift lines is not something that Deer Valley wants its guests to experience, so it limits the number of lift tickets sold. **Terrain parks** The TNT (Tricks 'n' Turns) park on Empire Canyon offers rails, jumps and boxes. **Snow reliability** As you'd expect in Utah, snow reliability is excellent, and there's plenty of snowmaking too. **Experts** Despite the image of pampered luxury there is excellent expert terrain on all three main mountains, including fabulous glades, bumps, chutes and bowls. And the snow doesn't get skied out quickly. The Ski Utah Interconnect Tour to Alta starts here (see the Park City chapter). **Intermediates** There are lots of superbly groomed blue runs. **Beginners** There are nursery slopes at Silver Lake Lodge as well as the base, and gentle green runs to progress to. **Snowboarding** Boarding is banned.

Silver Lake is a convenient spot for lunch with, unusually for an American ski area, a choice of good places to eat ➔

UK PACKAGES

AmeriCan Ski, Made to Measure, Simply Alpine, Ski Dream, Ski Independence, Ski Safari, Skitracer

Central reservations
Call 645 6538.

Phone numbers
From distant parts of the US, add 1 435; from abroad, add the prefix +1 435

TOURIST OFFICE

t 649 1000
skierservices@
deervalley.com
www.deervalley.com

Cross-country There are prepared trails on the Park City and Homestead Resort golf courses and lots of scope for backcountry trips.

Mountain restaurants The best in Utah. There are attractive wood-and-glass self-service places at both Silver Lake (delicious lamb stew and turkey chilli on our 2008 visit) and the base lodge. The grill restaurant at Empire Canyon Lodge is consistently recommended, and the tiny Gondola Grill on Little Baldy Peak is 'great for burgers and views'. For a bit of a treat, try the Stein Eriksen Lodge (including an excellent, good value, all-you-can-eat buffet), the Goldener Hirsch or the Royal Street Café table-service restaurant at Silver Lake Lodge.

Schools and guides The ski school is doubtless excellent; book in advance.

Families The Children's Center gives parents complimentary pagers. It accepts children aged between two months and 12 years.

STAYING THERE

A car is useful for visiting other nearby Utah resorts, though Deer Valley, Park City and The Canyons are all linked by efficient shuttle-buses.

Hotels The Stein Eriksen Lodge and the Goldener Hirsch are two of the plushest hotels in any ski resort.

Apartments There are many luxury apartments and houses to rent. Reader recommendations include Ridgepoint, Royal Plaza and The Woods at Silver Lake – and Aspenwood and Boulder Creek at Snow Park (cheaper).

Eating out Of the gourmet restaurants, the Mariposa is the best. We enjoyed both the all-you-can-eat Seafood Buffet (it's not just seafood) and a 'Fireside Dining' evening at the Empire Canyon Lodge: four courses, each one served at a different fireplace. It's held three nights a week.

Après-ski The Lounge of the Snow Park Lodge at the base area is the main après-ski venue, with live music. Then there's Main Street in Park City.

Off the slopes Park City has lots of shops, galleries etc. Salt Lake City has concerts, sights and shopping. Balloon rides and snowmobiling are popular.

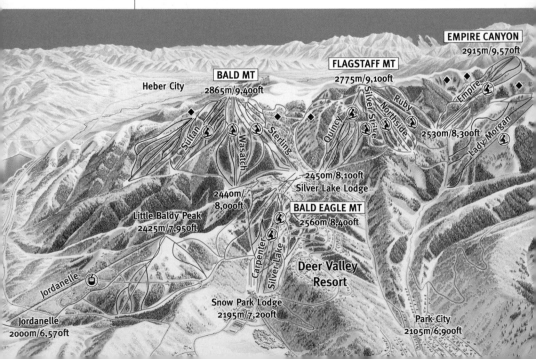

Park City

Stay near the cute and lively old Main Street and visit the three local mountains plus some further afield for a varied holiday

£85
RESORT PRICE INDEX

RATINGS

The mountains

Extent	★★★
Fast lifts	★★★
Queues	★★★★
Terrain p'ks	★★★★★
Snow	★★★★
Expert	★★★★
Intermediate	★★★★
Beginner	★★★★
X-country	★★★
Restaurants	★★
Schools	★★★★
Families	★★

The resort

Charm	★★★
Convenience	★★
Scenery	★★★
Eating out	★★★★★
Après-ski	★★★
Off-slope	★★★

NEWS

For 2008/09 an additional fast quad, Crescent, was installed. It goes from Resort Base to the top of King Con Ridge and seems to have relieved pressure on the Pay Day lift. And there was more glading and snowmaking 25% of the trails are now covered.

For 2009/10 the new High West whisky distillery and saloon is due to open in one of Park City's historic buildings near the Town Lift.

Many of the runs are short but the Eagle super-pipe was used in the 2002 Winter Olympics and is consistently one of the finest-shaped pipes in the world →

- ➕ Entertaining, historic Main Street, convenient for slopes
- ➕ Lots of bars and restaurants make nonsense of Utah's Mormon image
- ➕ Easy to visit other resorts – Deer Valley and The Canyons (covered by area pass) are effectively suburbs

- ➖ Away from Main Street, town is an enormous sprawl and lacks charm
- ➖ Most lodgings involve driving or bussing to Main Street and slopes
- ➖ Runs tend to be rather short
- ➖ Snowfall record comes nowhere near that of Alta, Snowbird et al

Park City has clear attractions, particularly if you ignore its sprawling suburbs and stay near the centre to make the most of the lively bars and restaurants in Main Street. And it's an excellent base for touring other resorts.

Deer Valley is separated from Park City's slopes only by a fence between two pistes, and by separate ownership with different objectives – all very strange, to European eyes. The Canyons is only a little further away, and reached by free buses. These areas are covered by the Three Resort Pass.

Then there are the famously powdery resorts of Snowbird and Alta, less than an hour away by car or bus. Even the Olympic downhill slopes of Snowbasin are within easy reach by car (and by special privately run buses).

THE RESORT

Park City is about 45 minutes by road from Salt Lake City. It was a silver mining boom town and at the turn of the 19th century it boasted a population of 10,000, a red-light area, a Chinese quarter and 27 saloons.

VILLAGE CHARM ★★★
A colourful past

Careful restoration has left the town with a splendid historic centrepiece in Main Street, now lined by a colourful selection of bars, restaurants, art galleries and shops, many quite smart but some touristy souvenir places.

New buildings have been tastefully designed to blend in smoothly. But away from the centre (where most of the lodging is) the resort is an amorphous sprawl and still expanding. Traffic congestion can be bad, especially at weekends.

CONVENIENCE ★★
Depends on your base

The slow Town chairlift goes up to the slopes from Main Street, but the main lifts are on the fringes at Resort Base; there are lodgings out there but most are a bus ride away.

Deer Valley, The Canyons and Park City are linked by free shuttle-buses,

KEY FACTS	
Resort	2105m
	6,900ft
Slopes	2105-3050m
	6,900-10,000ft
Lifts	16
Pistes	3,300 acres
Green	17%
Blue	50%
Black	33%
Snowmaking	15%

which also go around town and run until fairly late but we found it a pain waiting for buses on our 2008 visit. A car is useful (especially for visiting ski areas outside Park City).

If you're not hiring a car, pick a location that's handy for Main Street and the Town chair or the free bus.

SCENERY ★★★☆☆
Gently undulating ridges
In contrast to Park City's sprawling mass below them, the rounded mountain ridges have a modest and gentle presence.

THE MOUNTAIN

Park City Mountain Resort consists mostly of blue and black trails cut through the trees, with easier runs running along the ridges and the valleys between. The more interesting terrain is in the lightly wooded bowls and ridges at the top.

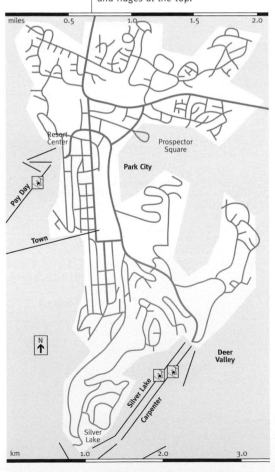

Reporters have enjoyed the 'excellent' free mountain history tours of the slopes – looking at the area's silver mining heritage – that take place at 10am every day. A long floodlit intermediate run and a beginner run are open until 7.30pm.

It is much cheaper to buy lift passes in advance than on the spot.

EXTENT OF THE SLOPES ★★★☆☆
Bowls above the woods
The ski area is much bigger than Deer Valley but a bit smaller than The Canyons. Most of the easy and intermediate runs lie between Summit House and the base area, and are spread along the sides of a series of interconnecting ridges. Virtually all the steep terrain is above Summit House in a series of ungroomed bowls, and accessed by the McConkey's six-pack and the old Jupiter double chair.

FAST LIFTS ★★★☆☆
Now two from the base
Two fast chairlifts whisk you up from Resort Base and others beyond take you to Summit House. But there are a few slow lifts on the highest slopes.

QUEUES ★★★★☆
Peak period crowds
It can get pretty crowded (on some trails as well as the lifts) at weekends and in high season. Pay Day lift from Resort Base used to have big queues. But the new fast quad (see 'News') seems to have eased this problem. You can pay extra for a Fast Tracks pass to jump queues on six main lifts.

TERRAIN PARKS ★★★★★
Among the best in the world
There are four terrain parks here to suit all levels. The vast number of kickers, rails and pipes are maintained daily, and rank among the best in the world. Jonesy's park, located under the Bonanza lift, features a slew of pro-standard jumps and rails for advanced riders only. The Pick 'N' Shovel park, accessible via the Three Kings lift, is the beginner park and features six jumps and 20 rails and fun boxes. The King's Crown park, on the northern slope overlooking the resort, is of intermediate standard with kickers, rails, butter boxes and a quarter-transfer feature. And a Ball Tap, which is a giant bowling ball shaped jib, is now a signature feature in the park. The Eagle super-pipe that was used for

LIFT PASSES

Park City

Prices in US$

Age	1-day	6-day
under 13	52	312
13 to 64	83	498
over 65	56	336

Free under 7

Beginner no deals

Notes

Covers all lifts in Park City Mountain Resort, with ski-bus; day passes are window rates; 6-day prices are advance-purchase prices; additional discounts if purchased in advance with lodging

Alternative passes

Three Resort International Pass covering Park City, The Canyons and Deer Valley available through selected tour operators

boarding

It was not until 1996, when Park City won its Olympic bid, that the resort lifted its ban on snowboarding. Since then it has steamrollered ahead to attract the snowboarding community by building some of the best terrain parks in the world. And Park City has some great ungroomed terrain as well: the higher bowls offer treelined powder runs and great kicker-building spots. Beginners will have no trouble on the lower slopes, all serviced by fast chairlifts. But beware: at weekends and peak season it can get very crowded, especially in the terrain parks. Three-hour group intermediate freeride clinics are offered daily at 1pm.

the 2002 Winter Olympics is consistently one of the finest-shaped pipes in the world. And the Pay Day jib park opens until 7.30pm with a host of floodlit rails and boxes.

SNOW RELIABILITY ★★★★
Not quite the greatest on Earth

Utah is famous for the quality and quantity of its snow. Park City's record doesn't match those of Snowbird and Alta, but an annual average of 350 inches is still impressive, and ahead of most Colorado figures. Snowmaking covers about 15% of the terrain.

FOR EXPERTS ★★★★
Lots of variety

There is a lot of excellent advanced and expert terrain at the top of the lift system. It is all marked as double diamond on the trail map, but there are many runs that deserve only a single-diamond rating – so don't be put off. McConkey's Bowl is served by a six-pack and offers a range of open pitches and gladed terrain; we've had some great runs here on each of our visits. The slow, old Jupiter lift accesses the highest bowls, which include some serious terrain – with narrow couloirs, cliffs and cornices – as well as easier wide-open slopes. We had some enjoyable runs though fresh snow in lightly wooded terrain by heading right at the top of the lift, then skiing down before hiking became necessary. But if you are prepared to hike, you can find fresh powder most of the time – turn left for West Face, Pioneer Ridge and Puma Bowl, right for Scott's Bowl and the vast expanse of Pinecone Ridge, stretching literally for miles down the side of Thaynes Canyon.

Lower down, the side of Summit

Park City

635

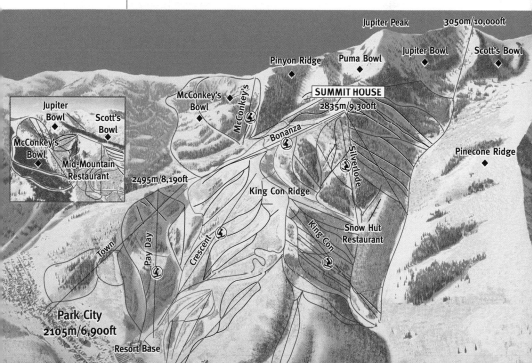

SCHOOLS

Park City
t 1 800 227 2754

Classes
1 3hr day $85

Private lessons
$130 for 1hr

CHILDCARE

Signature 3
(run by ski school)
t 1 800 227 2754
Ages 3½ to 5;
$160 per day,
includes ski tuition,
lunch (max class size
is 3)

Guardian Angel
t 783 2662
Babysitting service

Ski Town Sitters
t 487 9262
Babysitting service

Ski school
The school offers
classes for ages 6 to
14, 9am-3pm, $210
per day including
lunch (max class size
is 5)

House ridge, serviced by the Thaynes and Motherlode chairs, has some little-used black runs, plus a few satisfying trails in the trees. There's a zone of steep runs towards town from further round the ridge. And don't miss Blueslip Bowl near Summit House – so called because in the past when it was out of bounds, ski company employees caught skiing it were fired, and given their notice on a blue slip.

Good skiers (no snowboarders, due to some long flat run-outs) should not miss the Utah Interconnect – see feature panel. Park City Powder Cats offers snowcat skiing and Wasatch Powderbird Guides heli-skiing.

FOR INTERMEDIATES ★★★★
OK for a day or two
There are blue runs served by all the main lifts, apart from Jupiter. The areas around the King Con high-speed quad and Silverlode six-pack have a dense network of great (but fairly short) cruising runs. There are also more difficult trails close by, for those looking for a challenge.

But there are few long, fast cruising runs – most trails are around 1 to 2km/0.5 to 1 mile, and many have long, flat run-outs. The Pioneer and McConkey's chairlifts are off the main drag and serve some very pleasant, often quiet runs. The runs under the Town lift have great views of the town.

FOR BEGINNERS ★★★★
A good chance for fast progress
Novices start on short lifts and a beginners' area near the base lodge. Classes graduate up the hill quite quickly, and there's a good, gentle and wide 'easiest way down' – the three-and-a-half-mile Home Run – clearly marked all the way from Summit House. It's easy enough for most to manage after only a few lessons. The Town chair can be ridden down.

FOR CROSS-COUNTRY ★★★
Some trails; lots of backcountry
There are prepared trails on both the Park City golf course (20km/12 miles), next to the downhill area, and the Homestead Resort course (12km/7 miles), just out of town. There is lots of scope for backcountry trips.

MOUNTAIN RESTAURANTS ★★
Standard self-service stuff
The Mid-Mountain Lodge is a picturesque 19th-century mine building which was heaved up the mountain to its present location near the bottom of Pioneer chair. The food is standard self-service fare but most reporters prefer it to the alternatives. The Summit House has chilli, pizza, soup and 'good hot chocolate'. The Snow Hut, a 'cosier' log building that usually has an outdoor grill, gets good reviews from reporters. 5-Way Cafe is a coffee house in a yurt (tent) halfway down the Bonanza chairlift. There are more options down at Resort Base ('A delicious salad bar and top-quality fresh fish,' said a recent reporter).

SCHOOLS AND GUIDES ★★★★
Good reports
A recent reporter's husband had a good private lesson – 'the instructor tried to take him to as much of the scarce powder as possible'. We have received positive reports of snowboard lessons: 'Tuition the best I've had, but over $120 an hour for private lessons,' says a recent visitor. 'Excellent,' said the daughter of a recent reporter, who was given a detailed record of her achievements in a small two-day class and was riding blue runs by the end.

FOR FAMILIES ★★
Well organised
There are a number of licensed carers. The ski school takes children from age three and a half. Book in advance.

THE UTAH INTERCONNECT

Good skiers prepared to do some hiking should consider this excellent guided backcountry tour that runs four days a week from Deer Valley to Snowbird. (Three days a week it runs from Snowbird, but only as far as Solitude.) When we did it (a few years back, starting from Park City) we got fresh tracks in knee-deep powder practically all day. After a warm-up run to weed out weak skiers, we went up the top chair, through a 'closed' gate in the area boundary and skied down a deserted, prettily wooded valley to Solitude. After taking the lifts to the top of Solitude we did a short traverse/walk, then down more virgin powder towards Brighton. After more powder runs and lunch back in Solitude, it was up the lifts and a 30-minute hike up the Highway to Heaven to north-facing, treelined slopes and a great little gully down into Alta. How much of Alta and Snowbird you get to ski depends on how much time is left. The price ($250) includes two guides, lunch, lift tickets and transport home.

GETTING THERE

Air Salt Lake City 55km/35 miles (1hr)

UK PACKAGES

Alpine Answers, AmeriCan Ski, American Ski Classics, Crystal, Crystal Finest, Funway Holidays, Independent Ski Links, Made to Measure, Momentum, Simply Alpine, Ski Activity, Ski Dream, Ski Independence, Ski Line, Ski Safari, Ski Solutions, Skitracer, Skiworld, Thomson, United Vacations, Virgin Snow

ACTIVITIES

Indoor Park City Racquet Club (tennis, racquetball, swimming pool, hot tub, gym); Silver Mountain Sports Club and Spa (pools, hot tubs, sauna, steam room, tennis, racquetball, gym); other fitness clubs, spa treatments, museum

Outdoor Ice skating, snowmobiles, sleigh rides, hot-air ballooning, snowshoeing, snow tubing, winter fly fishing

Phone numbers
From distant parts of the US, add the prefix 1 435; from abroad, add the prefix +1 435

TOURIST OFFICE

t 649 8111
info@pcski.com
intl@parkcityinfo.com
www.
parkcitymountain.com
www.parkcityinfo.com

STAYING THERE

We prefer to stay near Main Street and its bars and restaurants, but most accommodation is in the sprawling suburbs. These, such as Kimball Junction, are convenient and cheap (but soulless) if you have a car and want to try different resorts daily.
Hotels There's a wide variety, from typical chains to individual little B&Bs.
*****Park City (200 2000) Swanky all-suite place on outskirts, better placed for golf than skiing. Pool, sauna.
***Park City Peaks (649 5000) Decent rooms, 'service and prices of meals good', 'food adequate', indoor-outdoor pool and 'fab hot tub', but out of town. We stayed here in 2008 and thought it adequate.
***Yarrow (649 7000) Adequate, charmless, 'cheap' base, a 15-minute walk from Main Street. Pool, hot tub. 'Good service; friendly, helpful staff.'
Silver King (649 5500) De luxe hotel/condo complex at base of the slopes, with indoor-outdoor pool.
Washington School Inn (649 3800) 'Absolutely excellent' historic inn with 'fantastic service', say reporters. In a great location near Main Street.
Best Western Landmark Inn (649 7300) At Kimball Junction. Pool.
Chateau Apres Lodge (649 9372) Near the slopes: comfortable, faded, cheap.
Apartments There's a big range. The Townlift studios near Main Street and Park Avenue condos are both modern and comfortable, and the latter has a pool and hot tubs. Silver Cliff Village is adjacent to the slopes and has spacious units and access to the facilities of the Silver King Hotel. Other ski-in/ski-out recommendations from reporters are Silver Star and Snowflower. Blue Church Lodge is a well-converted 19th-century Mormon church with luxury condos and rooms.

EATING OUT *****
Lots of choice

There are over 100 restaurants. Our favourites are Wahso (Asian fusion), 350 Main (new American) and Riverhorse – in a grand, high-ceilinged first-floor room with live music. Zoom is the old Union Pacific train depot, now a trendy restaurant owned by Robert Redford (we've had mixed reports – from 'our best meal' to 'mediocre and overpriced'). Chez Betty is small with 'excellent food' – expensive though. Other reporter

recommendations include Fuego Bistro & Pizzeria, Cisero's and Grappa (Italian), Chimayo ('south-western-with-a-twist'), Bangkok Thai, Wasatch Brew Pub ('good steaks', 'best value'), Squatters (a micro brewery, out of town a bit; 'good atmosphere' and 'you can buy six tasters on a ski'), Bandit's Grill ('good value'), the 'excellent' Eating Establishment, No Name Saloon ('brill buffalo burgers') and Butcher's Chop House ('great prime rib and steaks'). There are lots of Tex-Mex places: Zona Rosa and El Chubasco have been praised. See Deer Valley for other options.

APRES-SKI ***
Better than you might think

As the slopes close, Legends is the place to head for at Resort Base. Pig Pen in the ice skating plaza was recommended by a reporter. The Bad Ass Coffee Shop in town is highly rated. The Wasatch Brew Pub makes its own ale. JB Mulligans, O'Shuck's and No Name Saloon are lively, and there's usually live music and dancing at weekends. For clubs, try Harry O's and Cisero's.

OFF THE SLOPES ***
Some things of interest

There's a factory outlet mall at Kimball Junction. Backcountry snowmobiling, balloon flights and trips to Nevada for gambling are popular. You can learn to ski jump or try the Olympic bob track at the Olympic Park down the road – 'worth the effort'. There's Robert Redford's Sundance Film Festival in January and a 10-day Winterfest celebration of the 2002 Olympics in February. There are lots of shops and galleries. Salt Lake City is easily reached and has some good concerts, shopping and Mormon heritage sites.

Snowbird

A powder-pig paradise linked to neighbouring Alta; with big concrete and glass base buildings that remind us of Flaine

TOP 10 RATINGS

Extent	★★★
Fast lifts	★★★★
Queues	★★★
Snow	★★★★★
Expert	★★★★★
Intermediate	★★★
Beginner	★★
Charm	★
Convenience	★★★★★
Scenery	★★★

NEWS

In 2008/09 the Tram Club was remodelled ('think earth tones, leather sofas, less concrete', they say), with lots of TV and projection screens and a new outdoor bar. The Aerie Sushi bar at the Cliff Lodge was also renovated.

KEY FACTS

Resort	2470m
	8,100ft

For Snowbird and Alta combined area

Slopes	2365-3350m
	7,760-11,000ft
Lifts	24
Pistes	4,700 acres
Green	25%
Blue	37%
Black	38%
Snowmaking	12%

Snowbird only

Slopes	2365-3350m
	7,760-11,000ft
Lifts	13
Pistes	2,500 acres
Green	27%
Blue	38%
Black	35%
Snowmaking	21%

- **+** Quantity and quality of powder snow unrivalled
- **+** Link to Alta makes one of the largest ski areas in the US
- **+** Fabulous ungroomed slopes, with steep and not-so-steep options
- **+** Slopes-at-the-door convenience

- **−** Limited groomed runs for intermediates
- **−** Tiny, claustrophobic resort 'village'
- **−** Stark concrete Bauhaus architecture
- **−** Very quiet at night

There can be few places where nature has combined the steep with the deep better than at Snowbird and next-door Alta. The two resorts' combined area is one of the top powder-pig paradises in the world. So it is a shame that Snowbird's concrete, purpose-built 'base village' is so lacking in charm and ski resort ambience. Boarders are banned from Alta's (but not Snowbird's) slopes.

THE RESORT

Snowbird lies 40km/25 miles from Salt Lake City in Little Cottonwood Canyon – just before Alta. Both the resort and (particularly) the approach road are prone to avalanches and closure: visitors are sometimes confined indoors for safety.

Village charm The resort buildings are mainly block-like and lack any semblance of charm.

Convenience The resort area and the slopes are spread along the road on the south side of the narrow canyon. The focal Snowbird Center (lift base/shops/restaurants) is towards the eastern, up-canyon end. All lodgings are within walking distance and most are ski-in/ski-out. There are shuttle-buses, with a service to Alta.

Scenery Snowbird's setting is rugged and rather Alpine. Hidden Peak's lofty heights give impressive views.

THE MOUNTAINS

Snowbird's link with Alta forms one of the largest ski areas in the US.

There are free mountain tours at 9am and 10.30 each day: 'It was quite adventurous, taking some of us down double-black-diamond territory at one point,' says a recent visitor. The nursery slopes are floodlit three evenings a week.

Slopes The north-facing slopes rear up from the edge of the resort. Six access lifts are ranged along the valley floor, the main ones being the 125-person cable car (the Aerial Tram) to Hidden Peak, the Peruvian Express quad and the Gadzoom fast quad. To the west, in Gad Valley, there are runs ranging from very tough to very easy. Mineral Basin, behind Hidden Peak, has 500 acres of terrain for all abilities, but can be badly affected by sun.

Fast lifts The key lifts are fast. One of two fast quads in Mineral Basin forms the link with Alta.

Queues The big problem has always been the cable car, with queues of up to an hour at times. But the Peruvian Express chair provides an alternative way to the top (via Mineral Basin and then the Mineral Basin Express chair).

Terrain parks There is one for all levels, containing rails, hits and a box, plus a 100m/330ft super-pipe.

Snow reliability Snowbird and Alta average 500 inches of snowfall a year – twice as much as some Colorado resorts and around 50% more than the nearby Park City area. There's snowmaking in busy areas.

Experts The trail map is liberally sprinkled with double black diamonds, and some of the gullies off the Cirque ridge – Silver Fox and Great Scott, for example – are exceptionally steep and frequently neck-deep in powder. Lower down lurk the bump runs, including Mach Schnell – a great run straight down the fall line through trees. There is wonderful ski-anywhere terrain in the bowl beneath the high Little Cloud chair, and the Gad 2 lift opens up attractive tree runs. Fantastic go-anywhere terrain under the High Baldy traverse is controlled by gates. Mineral Basin has more expert terrain.

(though there are In Alta).

Mountain restaurants It's the Mid-Gad Lodge self-service cafeteria or back to one of the bases. The table-service Forklift and Rendezvous have been recommended by reporters.

Schools and guides The school offers a range of lessons and clinics – such as women-only and Big Mountain. A recent visitor was 'highly impressed' with her private lessons.

Families Camp Snowbird takes children aged 12 and under. The 'kids ski free' programme allows children (six and under) to ski for free with an adult ($15 a day for the Tram).

Backcountry tours and heli- and cat-skiing are offered.

Intermediates The winding Chip's Run on the Cirque ridge provides the only comfortable route down from the top. For adventurous intermediates wanting to try powder skiing, the bowl below the Little Cloud lift is a must. There are some challenging runs through the trees off the Gad 2 lift and some nice long cruises in Mineral Basin. But the groomed runs don't add up to a lot.

Beginners There is a nursery slope next to Cliff Lodge and the Mountain Learning area part-way up the hill. But progression to longer runs is not easy. Beginners should learn elsewhere.

Snowboarding Competent freeriders will have a wild time in Snowbird's powder (though a reporter complains of 'flat sticky spots where you have to walk'). Alta bans boarders.

Cross-country No prepared trails

STAYING THERE

Hotels There are several lodges and smaller condo blocks. Cliff Lodge (a huge concrete building) and The Lodge at Snowbird were built in the 1970s and renovated a few years ago; both are convenient and have pools and hot tubs, but they lack charm. Reporters tell of 'friendly but amateurish staff' in both.

Eating out Cliff Lodge and Snowbird Center are the focal points. The 'fine dining' Aerie in the Cliff Lodge gets mixed reviews. Readers recommend the Steak Pit in Snowbird Center.

Après-ski Après-ski is a bit muted. The Tram Club and El Chanate Cantina are lively as the slopes close. But a recent visitor complained that many places close early.

Off the slopes Apart from spas in the various lodges, there's ice skating, ice climbing, snowshoeing, snowmobiling.

Snowbird

639

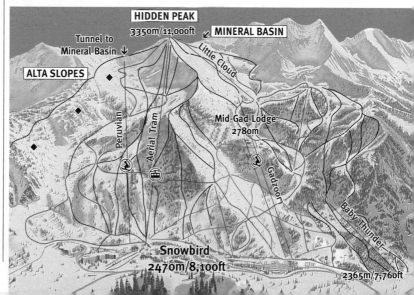

HIDDEN PEAK
3350m/11,000ft
MINERAL BASIN
Tunnel to Mineral Basin
Little Cloud
ALTA SLOPES
Peruvian
Aerial Tram
Mid-Gad Lodge 2780m
Gadzoom
Baby Thunder
Snowbird 2470m/8,100ft
2365m/7,760ft

Rest of the West

This section contains detailed chapters on just two resorts – Jackson Hole and Big Sky. Below are notes on these and various other resorts in different parts of the great chain of mountains that stretches from Washington in the north to New Mexico in the south.

The resorts of Washington state and Oregon are covered in our resort directory/index at the end of this book. We visited Oregon last season, but our exploration was hampered by poor early-season snow. However, if you want to try somewhere largely undiscovered by fellow Brits as yet, it is worth considering. Of the major North American specialists, only Ski Dream and AmeriCan Ski feature Oregon resorts. The major resorts are **Mt Hood** (which has three separate areas of slopes: Mt Hood Meadows, Mt Hood Skibowl and Timberline) and **Mt Bachelor.** These get extended entries in the resort directory/index.

Sun Valley, Idaho, was America's first purpose-built resort, developed in the 1930s by the president of the Union Pacific Railway. It quickly became popular with the Hollywood movie set and has managed to retain its stylish image and ambience; it has one of our favourite luxury hotels. Also in Idaho is the USA's newest purpose-built resort – **Tamarack**, two hours north of Boise. But the company developing the resort hit financial problems and the place closed in early March 2009. When and whether it will reopen for winter operations was unclear when we went to press.

Jackson Hole in Wyoming is a resort with an impressive snow record and equally impressive steep slopes. Jackson is the nearest there is to a town with a genuine Wild West cowboy atmosphere. A 90-minute drive from Jackson over the Teton pass (slower if you go by excursion bus) brings you to **Grand Targhee**, which gets even more snow. The slopes are usually blissfully empty, and are much easier than at Jackson. The main Fred's Mountain offers 1,500 acres and 610m/2,000ft vertical accessed from a central fast quad. One-third of smaller Peaked Mountain is accessed by a fast quad, while the rest – over 1,000 acres – is used for guided snowcat skiing.

About four hours north of Jackson, just inside Montana, is **Big Sky**, with the biggest ski area and one of the biggest verticals in the US. When we visited, we were very impressed – particularly by the lack of crowds. From Big Sky you might visit **Bridger Bowl**, a 90-minute drive away. It boasts broad, steep, lightly wooded slopes that offer wonderful powder descents after a fresh snowfall.

A long way south of all these resorts, **Taos** in New Mexico is the most southerly major resort in America, and because of its isolation it is largely unknown on the international market. There's a small chalet-style base village with a handful of lodges; the adobe town of Taos, home to many famous artists and writers over the years, is 29km/18 miles down the road. There's some good terrain for all standards, but the ski area is best known for steep, challenging terrain, some of which you have to hike to.

JACKSON HOLE MOUNTAIN RESORT / TRISTAN GRESZKO

The West doesn't come any wilder – though the elk are in fact in their national refuge, near Jackson, Wyoming →

Big Sky

Now America's biggest linked ski area, with extraordinarily quiet slopes; unappealing modern resort village, though

£65
RESORT PRICE INDEX

NEWS

For 2008/09 at Moonlight Basin a new expert trail, Timberwolf, opened. At Big Sky, a series of three ziplines opened – you fly through the forest at up to 40kph/25mph; the whole trip lasts two hours and costs $59. Work was done to improve unloading on the Swift Current chair to make it easier for beginners.

The gondola out of the village has been removed and plans to replace it have been put on the back burner for the moment.

+ Ski area is slightly bigger than Vail, with the bonus of a big vertical by US standards

+ By far the quietest slopes you will find in a major resort, anywhere

+ Among the cheapest for eating and drinking too

+ Excellent snow record

+ Wide range of runs for all abilities

+ Some comfortable slope-side accommodation, but ...

− Many condos are spread widely away from the lift base

− Base area lacks charm, though things are improving, slowly

− Resort amenities are limited, with little choice of nightlife

− Tiny top lift accessing the most testing terrain is prone to queues

− Remote location

Big Sky is renowned for its powder, steeps and big vertical. Since the resort buried the hatchet with next-door Moonlight Basin and agreed a joint lift pass, they have been able to boast the biggest linked ski area in the US. They should also be boasting the world's least crowded slopes – we and our reporters have been astonished by the lack of people. Between them, they get an average of around 2,500 people a day on their slopes. So that's about two acres each.

We have no idea how they make this arrangement work financially. We're happy to take advantage of it while it lasts – and to put up with staying in the seriously flawed resort village (especially because eating and drinking is so cheap). But if ambling around in the evening soaking up the mountain village atmosphere is part of your holiday, forget it.

THE RESORT

Big Sky is set amid the wide open spaces of Montana, one hour from the airport town of Bozeman. The resort has been purpose-built at the foot of the slopes on Lone Mountain and Andesite Mountain. The main focus of development is Mountain Village, at the lift base. Bridger Bowl ski area is an easy day trip by car.

VILLAGE CHARM ★
No particular style

Mountain Village is a hotchpotch of buildings in different styles set vaguely around a traffic-free central plaza and bordered by car parks and service roads. Over the next decade a new pedestrian village will take shape if all goes to plan. The first stage of this, Village Center, opened two seasons ago. There are three hotels, a handful of bars and restaurants, a variety of shops and some slope-side condos. The French-style underground Mountain Mall has shops and access to many of the bars and restaurants and some of the lodging.

CONVENIENCE ★★★★
Generally fine

There is some accommodation within walking distance of the lifts. Outlying condos and chalets are served by lifts to the slopes, others by free buses.

SCENERY ★★★
The lone ranger

Lone Mountain is Big Sky's signature peak, its distinctive summit rising over 1000m/3,280ft above the village and Andesite Mountain's wooded slopes. From the top, there are panoramic views of Montana and Yellowstone.

THE MOUNTAINS

Taking Big Sky and Moonlight Basin's slopes together, they cover a big area (5,512 acres) spread over two linked mountains, with long runs for all abilities. There are free mountain tours at both Big Sky and Moonlight. It is cheapest to buy tickets just for the area you are staying in and to buy a Lone Peak Ticket (substantially more expensive) only for days you intend to ski both Big Sky and Moonlight.

KEY FACTS

Resort	2285m
	7,500ft

Big Sky only	
Slopes	2070-3400m
	6,800-11,160ft
Lifts	21
Pistes	3,812 acres
Green	14%
Blue	26%
Black	60%
Snowmaking	10%
Big Sky and Moonlight Basin combined	
Slopes	2070-3400m
	6,800-11,160ft
Lifts	26
Pistes	5,512 acres

LIFT PASSES

Big Sky-Moonlight Basin Interconnect

Prices in US$

Age	1-day	6-day
under 18	73	438
18 to 69	93	528
over 70	83	498

Free under 11

Beginner first half-day lesson includes Big Sky lift pass

Notes
Covers the lifts in Big Sky and Moonlight Basin

EXTENT OF THE SLOPES ★★★★
The most extensive in the US

Lone Mountain provides the resort's poster shot, with some seriously steep, open upper slopes. From Mountain Village a fast quad goes to mid-mountain (the gondola has been removed – see 'News'). From there you can get to the Lone Peak chair, which takes you up to the Lone Peak Tram – two 15-person gondola cabins, operated as if they were a cable car. This leads to the top and fabulous 360° views. The Dakota triple chairlift serves Lone's south face and its steep bowls and glades. But a couple of reporters have found the area prone to closure due to avalanche risk. Lone Mountain's lower slopes are wooded and varied, as are those of **Andesite**

Mountain, which has less vertical, but three of the fast lifts, including one from Mountain Village. From various points on Lone Mountain you can head down to the **Moonlight Basin** slopes, which start with a slow chair from Moonlight Lodge. Runs from the top of that lead to the Six Shooter fast chair which, together with the slow Lone Tree quad near the top, serves nearly all Moonlight's wooded, largely easy intermediate terrain. The Headwaters lift at the top serves expert-only runs.

FAST LIFTS ★★
Needs some more
There are five fast quad chairs, but many of the chairs are still old triples and doubles.

Andesite has great cruising runs, although the vertical isn't huge

ANDESITE
268om/8,8ooft

Southern Comfort

Ramcharger

ThunderWolf

Mountain
Village
2285m/
7,500ft

2o70m/6,8ooft
Lone Moose Meadows

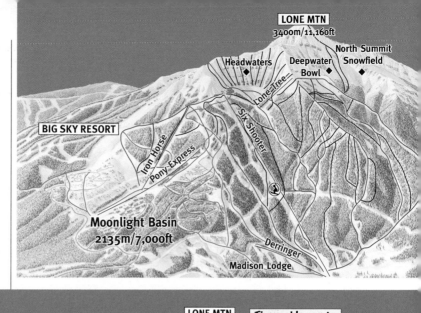

LONE MTN
3400m/11,16oft

Headwaters ◆

Deepwater
Bowl ◆

North Summit
Snowfield ◆

Lone Tree

Six-Shooter

BIG SKY RESORT

Iron Horse

Pony Express

Moonlight Basin
2135m/7,000ft

Derringer

Madison Lodge

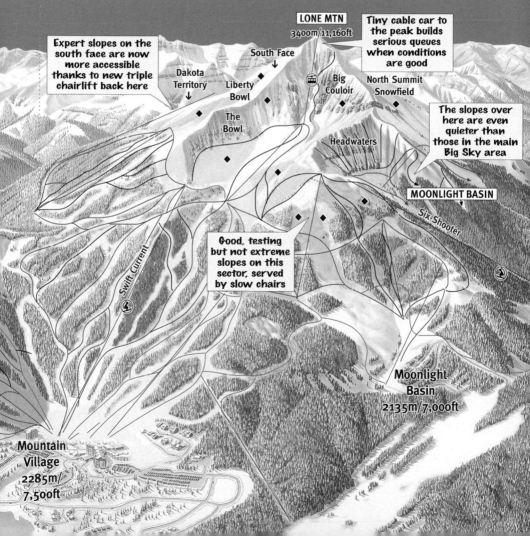

LONE MTN
3400m/11,16oft

Tiny cable car to
the peak builds
serious queues
when conditions
are good

Expert slopes on the
south face are now
more accessible
thanks to new triple
chairlift back here

South Face
↓

Dakota
Territory

Liberty
Bowl
↓

Big
Couloir

North Summit
Snowfield ◆

The
Bowl

Headwaters

The slopes over
here are even
quieter than
those in the main
Big Sky area

MOONLIGHT BASIN

Six-Shooter

Good, testing
but not extreme
slopes on this
sector, served
by slow chairs

Swift Current

Moonlight
Basin
2135m/7,000ft

Mountain
Village
2285m/
7,500ft

Weekly news updates and resort links at www.wtss.co.uk

↑ The slopes are by far the quietest you'll find in any major resort. It isn't unusual to have a whole trail to yourself
TANYA BOOTH

SCHOOLS

Big Sky
t 995 5743

Classes
Half day (2½hr) $67
Private lessons
$235 for 2hr for 1 to 2 persons

QUEUES ★★★★★
Only for the Tram
The tiny Tram still attracts queues on powder days and in peak season. Queues are rare otherwise. But there are still a lot of slow lifts.

TERRAIN PARKS ★★★★
Plenty of choice
Ambush on Andesite is an advanced park, with big jumps, rails, boxes, slides and super-pipe, served by the Ramcharger fast quad. Lone Mountain has Swifty park for intermediates and a natural half-pipe by the Swift Current lift and a beginner park by the Explorer chair. There is also a small beginner park as part of the Family Fun Zone near the base. The Zero Gravity park at Moonlight has boxes, rails, jumps, jibs and hits. There is also a beginner park by the Pony chair at Moonlight.

SNOW RELIABILITY ★★★★★
No worries here
Snowfall averages 400+ inches – more than most resorts in Colorado. Grooming is good, too.

FOR EXPERTS ★★★★
Enough to keep you amused
All of the terrain accessed from the Tram is single or double black diamond. The steepest runs are the Big Couloir on the Big Sky side and the North Summit Snowfield on the Moonlight side. For both, you are required to have a partner to ski with, an avalanche transceiver and a shovel.

We'd recommend a guide, too. There are easier ways down, though – Liberty Bowl is easiest (stay left for the best snow that the prevailing wind blows in). Marx and Lenin are a little steeper. The Dakota Territory has 212 acres of black-diamond glades, chutes and high bowls, to skier's right of Liberty Bowl – served by a triple chairlift. Lower down, the Lone Peak Triple, Challenger and Shedhorn chairs also serve good steep terrain. There are some excellent gladed runs, especially on Andesite. In the Moonlight sector the Headwaters is the biggest challenge – but it gets windblown and you may have to pick your way through rocks at the top. The further you hike to skier's left the steeper the couloirs. There are some good gladed runs lower down.

FOR INTERMEDIATES ★★★★
Great deserted cruising
The bulk of the terrain on both mountains is of intermediate difficulty (including lots of easy blacks). The main complaint we have is that they don't seem to groom any blacks – which means that you can't hurtle down them taking advantage of the lack of people. But there is lots of excellent blue run cruising served by fast chairs and with few others on the runs – Ramcharger, Silver Knife and Thunder Wolf on Andesite, Swift Current on Lone Mountain and Six Shooter in the Moonlight sector. Several wide, gentle bowls offer a good introduction to off-piste. And there are some good easy glade runs such as Singlejack on Moonlight and The Congo on Andesite. In general the groomed blues in Moonlight are easier than those in Big Sky, especially the ones served by the Lone Tree chair. Adventurous intermediates could try Liberty Bowl from the top of the Tram; but be prepared for a rocky, windswept traverse between wooden barriers at the top to access the run.

FOR BEGINNERS ★★★★★
Ideal – lots of lovely greens
Go to Big Sky rather than Moonlight. There's a good, recently improved nursery area at the base of the

boarding

The terrain has lots of variety, with few flats. Experts will enjoy the steeps and the glades, freestylers the good terrain parks, and novices the easy cruising runs served by chairlifts. We have a recent report of 'excellent' instruction.

CHILDCARE

Lone Peak Playhouse
t 995 5847
Ages 6mnth to 8yr;
8.30 to 4.30;
from $80 per day; or
from $127 per day
incl ski school

Ski school
Ages 4 to 14; 9.15 to
3.45; $142 per day

GETTING THERE

Air Bozeman 70km/
45 miles (1hr15)

UK PACKAGES

*AmeriCan Ski, Simply
Alpine, Ski Dream, Ski
Independence, Ski
Safari*

ACTIVITIES

Indoor Solace Spa
(massage, beauty
treatments), fitness
centres in hotels

Outdoor Snowmobiles,
snowshoeing, sleigh
rides, tubing, horse
riding, fly fishing,
ziplines, visiting
Yellowstone National
Park

Central reservations
Call 995 5000; toll-
free number (from
within the US) 1 800
548 4486

Phone numbers
From distant parts of
the US, add the prefix
1 406; from abroad,
add the prefix +1 406

TOURIST OFFICE

Big Sky
t 995 5000
info@bigskyresort.com
www.bigskyresort.com
Moonlight Basin
t 993 6000
resort@
moonlightbasin.com
www.moonlightbasin.
com

Explorer chair. There are long, deserted greens to progress to from those lifts and on Andesite.

FOR CROSS-COUNTRY ★★★★
Head for the Ranch
There are 87km/54 miles of trails at Lone Mountain Ranch, and more at West Yellowstone.

MOUNTAIN RESTAURANTS ★
Back to base for lunch?
Big Sky's one option is the Pinnacle on Andesite. There's a table-service area, offering the 'standard burgers, stews and grills', a large terrace and live music at weekends. In Moonlight there's the Headwaters Grill at Madison. Otherwise, it's back to base.

SCHOOLS AND GUIDES ★★★★
Good reputation
The Big Sky school has a good reputation. A 2009 reporter's private lesson was 'a good mix of technical and guiding'. And a 2008 visitor praised beginner snowboard classes: 'friendly, excellent tuition'.

FOR FAMILIES ★★★★
Usual high US standard
Lone Peak Playhouse in the slope-side Snowcrest Lodge takes children from age six months to eight years and will take them to and from ski school ('perfection', says a reporter). Babysitters are available with 48 hours' notice. Children 10 years and under ski free. There's a Kids' Club in the Huntley Lodge and snow garden at the base. Moonlight Kids takes kids from eight months to eight years.

STAYING THERE

Hotels There's not much choice.
★★★★**Summit** (995 5000) Best in town; central, slope-side, good rooms, outdoor hot-pool with good views.
★★★**Huntley Lodge** (995 5000) Big Sky's original hotel; central, part of Mountain Mall, outdoor pool, hot tubs, saunas. 'Enormous breakfasts.'
The Lodge at Big Sky (995 7858) Five minutes' walk to slopes, run a shuttle at peak times. Indoor pool, indoor/outdoor hot tubs.
★★★**Rainbow Ranch** (995 4132) Five miles south of resort. Luxury riverside rooms and cabins. Recommended.
Apartments The good-value Stillwater condos have been recommended, along with Village Center, Arrowhead,

Snowcrest, Big Horn, Black Eagle and, way out of town, Powder Ridge and Lone Moose. Check location carefully.

EATING OUT ★★★
A fair choice for a small place
Recommendations include: Huntley Dining Room (smart restaurant, 'huge bowls of pasta'); The Peaks in the Summit for lots of choice; The Cabin (fish and steaks); Bambu (Asian fusion); Andiamo ('proper Italian cuisine, stylish surroundings'); Chet's (giant burgers, sandwiches); Whiskey Jack's (burgers, beers, 'good Tex-Mex'). Down in the valley Buck's T-4 is popular with carnivores and has 'a phenomenal wine list'. They'll fetch you from your condo. Rainbow Ranch, also in the valley, has been highly recommended for 'fine dining'. Moonlight dinners and live music are available at a backcountry lodge.

APRES-SKI ★
Limited but entertaining
There are a few places to try; most with regular live music. Chet's bar is 'entertaining', and also has pool. The Carabiner in the Summit and Whiskey Jack's are popular. The Black Bear can be lively.

OFF THE SLOPES ★★
Mainly the great outdoors
There's snowmobiling, snowshoeing, sleigh rides, a floodlit tubing hill, ziplines, visiting Yellowstone National Park (highly recommended by a reporter), treatments at the Solace Spa; the Huntley Lodge pool etc is open to all for a fee.

Moonlight Basin

2135m/7,000ft
There's not much at Moonlight base except a few condos and cabins and the impressive Moonlight Lodge – spacious and log-built, with high ceilings and beams. The bar at the Lodge is lively as the slopes close, and the Timbers restaurant there gets good reviews. But when we visited a couple of years back we were disappointed by the spa, and our nearby condo was poorly maintained. Maybe the Cowboy Heaven Cabins spread up the hillside are better. We had an enjoyable dinner ('delicious burgers' says a 2009 visitor) a drive away at what is now the Headwaters Grill, at Madison base area.

Jackson Hole

Touristy 'Wild West' town, big, exciting slopes and a rapidly changing base village; in some eyes, the best the US has to offer

£75
RESORT PRICE INDEX

RATINGS

The mountains

Extent	★★★
Fast lifts	★★★
Queues	★★★
Terrain p'ks	★★★
Snow	★★★★
Expert	★★★★★
Intermediate	★★
Beginner	★★★
X-country	★★★★
Restaurants	★★
Schools	★★★★
Families	★★★★

The resort

Charm	★★★
Convenience	★★★
Scenery	★★★
Eating out	★★★★★
Après-ski	★★★★
Off-slope	★★★

NEWS

The new Tram (cable car) to Rendezvous Mountain opened in December 2008; it is not big, but has more than double the hourly capacity of the old tram.

The temporary double chairlift, East Ridge, installed to access the summit while the cable car was built, will stay in place for now – but only as a backup.

+ Some real expert-only terrain and one of the US's biggest verticals

+ Jackson town has an entertaining Wild West ambience

+ Unspoiled, remote location

+ Excellent snow record and even more snow (and quiet slopes) 90 minutes away at Grand Targhee

+ Some unique off-slope diversions

+ The town is only 15 minutes from the airport, but ...

− The town is also 15 minutes from the slopes – though the lift-base Teton Village offers an increasingly attractive range of places to stay

− Low altitude and sunny orientation mean snow can deteriorate quickly

− Intermediates wanting groomed cruises will find the area very limited, especially in fresh snow

− Getting there from the UK involves at least one stop and plane change

With its wooden sidewalks, country-music saloons and pool halls, tiny Jackson is a town determinedly playing up the Western thing for the entertainment of summer visitors to Yellowstone – great fun, if you like that kind of thing.

Among those who like steep slopes covered in deep powder or big bumps, Jackson Hole enjoys cult status. Many American mountains have steep runs that you can't find in Europe except by going seriously off-piste, but Jackson just has more than most (and an almost Alpine vertical). It gets a lot of snow – few places get more – but one reporter this year was disappointed to find the snow deteriorated quickly. Well, yes: it can; see above. Better luck next time, JR.

With a double-capacity cable car and a bunch of smooth, upmarket hotels at the base, plus a table-service restaurant on the mountain, Jackson Hole has changed a lot in the last few years. Many locals will tell you the place is losing its soul, going soft, selling out. Maturing nicely, we'd say.

THE RESORT

The town of Jackson sits at the south-eastern edge of Jackson Hole – a high, flat valley surrounded by mountain ranges, in north-west Wyoming. Jackson gets many more visitors in summer than in winter, thanks to the nearby national parks. The slopes are a 15-minute drive or $3 bus ride north-east. At the base is Teton Village, which has developed a lot over the last few years, with an increased choice of bars, restaurants and hotels – some of these notably upscale. We are told the expansion is starting to attract a wider range of visitors too, including more families. There are places between town and village, including lots of homes and condos to rent at very attractive rates.

A popular excursion by car or daily bus is over the Teton pass to the smaller resort of Grand Targhee, which gets even more snow (and keeps it better, with gentler, shadier slopes). See the Rest of the West introduction.

VILLAGE CHARM ★★★
All in cowboy style

To amuse summer tourists the town strives to maintain its Wild West flavour. It has lots of clothing and souvenir shops, as well as upmarket galleries appealing to second-home owners. In winter it's all a bit quiet. There's an efficient free town bus, and visitors praise the friendly and helpful locals. Teton Village isn't actually a village, but is not unpleasant.

CONVENIENCE ★★★
Stay at the slopes or nearby

Teton Village now seems the obvious place to stay – some of the lodgings are ski-in/ski-out, and many are almost so. Cheap condos a short drive away also make sense, given a car.

SCENERY ★★★
It's wild out west

The dramatic and rugged Teton mountains are impressive; they surround Jackson, rising abruptly from the flat valley floor.

We told them they should have gone for a proper jumbo cable car, but the price was too high – so you may still meet queues to get up the hill →
JACKSON HOLE MOUNTAIN RESORT

THE MOUNTAINS

Most of the slopes are below the treeline, but one of the attractions of the place is that most of the forest is not dense. Trail classifications are accurate: our own small map does not distinguish black from double black diamond runs, but the distinction matters – 'expert only' tends to mean just that. There are complimentary tours daily.

EXTENT OF THE SLOPES ★★★
One big mountain, one small
The main lifts out of Teton Village are the Bridger gondola and new cable car, the Tram. This takes you up 1260m/4,130ft to the summit of **Rendezvous** mountain – an exceptional vertical for the US. It can be very cold and windy at the top, even when it's warm and calm below. To the right looking up, fast quads access **Apres Vous** mountain, with half the vertical of Rendezvous and mostly much gentler runs. Between these two peaks, the Bridger gondola goes up over a broad mountainside split by gullies, and gives speedy access to the Thunder and Sublette quad chairs, serving some of the steepest terrain on Rendezvous, and the Casper Bowl triple, from which you can traverse over to the Apres Vous area.

Snow King is a separate area right by Jackson town. There's a good choice of short, steep slopes. Locals use it at lunch time and in the evenings (it's partly floodlit).

FAST LIFTS ★★★
Few at mid-mountain
Fast lifts access both mountains; but slow chairs rule higher up, encouraging descent to the base.

QUEUES ★★★
Bigger capacity but ...
With increased capacity on the Bridger gondola and the arrival of a bigger Tram last season, you'd have thought long queues at the base were history, along with the old Tram – and some recent reporters found just that. But we've had one report this year of 20-minute waits for the Tram mid-week in January. One tip to avoid queuing on powder days is to head for Apres Vous and 'great first tracks in the Saratoga Bowl'. But the Teewinot chair, which also serves the beginner area, may now generate queues at peak periods – perhaps another sign of the resort's changing character?

KEY FACTS

Resort	1925m
	6,310ft

Jackson Hole	
Slopes	1925-3185m
	6,310-10,450ft
Lifts	12
Pistes	2,500 acres
Green	10%
Blue	40%
Black	50%
Snowmaking	6%

Grand Targhee	
Slopes	2260-3005m
	7,410-9,860ft
Lifts	5
Pistes	2,100 acres
(plus 600 acres	
served by snowcat)	
Green	7%
Blue	74%
Black	19%
Snowmaking	none

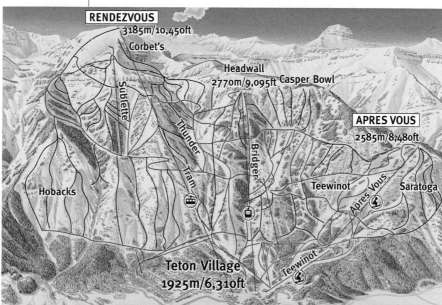

RENDEZVOUS
3185m/10,450ft
Corbet's
Sublette
Headwall
2770m/9,095ft Casper Bowl
Thunder
Tram
Bridger
APRES VOUS
2585m/8,480ft
Hobacks
Teewinot
Apres Vous
Saratoga
Teton Village
1925m/6,310ft
Teewinot

LIFT PASSES		
Jackson Hole		
Prices in US$		
Age	1-day	6-day
under 15	51	288
15 to 64	87	492
over 65	55	312

Free under 6 (Eagle's Rest and Teewinot lifts only)

Beginner ticket for Eagle's Rest and Teewinot lifts ($12)

Notes
Covers all lifts in Jackson Hole; half-day ticket available

Alternative passes
Grand Targhee; Snow King Mountain

Jackson Hole is a cult resort for expert snowboarders, as for skiers. It's not bad for novices, either, with the beginner slopes served by a high-speed quad chair. But intermediates not wishing to venture off the groomed runs will find the resort limited. Two terrain parks and a super-pipe provide the freestyle thrills. There are some good snowboard shops, including the Hole-in-the-Wall at Teton Village.

TERRAIN PARKS ★★★☆☆
Head for the Rodeo
The main Rodeo Grounds terrain park by the Teewinot chair (Apres Vous), has jumps and rails, music and a 137m/450ft long super-pipe. Dick's Ditch is a natural pipe and there's a mini park for novices. But you really come to Jackson for the steeps and deeps of the freeriding.

SNOW RELIABILITY ★★★★☆
Deep snow, strong sun
The claimed average of 460 inches of snow is much more than most Colorado resorts claim. But the base elevation is relatively low for the Rockies, and the slopes are fairly sunny – they basically face south-east (Apres Vous more like south). You may find the steep lower slopes, like the Hobacks, in poor shape, or even shut, and the higher slopes can be affected too. The flanks of some ridges have a more northerly orientation, and of course trees can be helpful. Locals claim that you can expect powder roughly half the time. Don't assume early-season conditions will be good.

FOR EXPERTS ★★★★★
Best for the brave
For the good skier or boarder who wants challenges without the expense of hiring a guide to go off-piste, Jackson is one of the world's best resorts. Rendezvous mountain offers virtually nothing but black slopes. The

routes down the main Rendezvous Bowl are not particularly fearsome; but some of the alternatives are. Go down the East Ridge at least once to stare over the edge of the notorious Corbet's Couloir. It's the jump in that's special; the slope you land on is a mere 50°, they say.

Below Rendezvous Bowl, the wooded flanks of Cheyenne Bowl offer serious challenges, at the steep end of the single black diamond spectrum. If instead you take the ridge run that skirts this bowl to the right, you get to the Hobacks – a huge area of open and lightly wooded slopes, gentler than those higher up, but still black.

Corbet's aside, most of the steepest slopes are more easily reached from the slightly lower quad chairs. From Sublette, you have direct access to the short but seriously steep Alta chutes, and to the less severe Laramie Bowl beside them. Or you can track over to Tensleep Bowl – pausing to inspect Corbet's from below – and on to the less extreme (and less chute-like) Expert Chutes, and the single-black Cirque and Headwall areas. Casper Bowl often has good powder and the Crags is an area of bowls, chutes and glades reached by hiking – both are accessed through gates. Thunder chair serves more steep, narrow, fairly shady chutes. Again, the lower part of the mountain here offers lightly wooded single black diamond slopes.

The gondola serves terrain not

JACKSON HOLE MOUNTAIN RESORT
You may be able to make out some of the many condos at the base, partly hidden by trees. The lift base and its cluster of hotels are at the extreme right. Apres Vous is out of shot, to the right →

SCHOOLS

Jackson Hole
t 1 800 450 0477

Classes
Full day (5½hr) $120
Private lessons
Half day (3hr) from
$370

CHILDCARE

Kids' Ranch
t 1 800 450 0477
Wranglers: ages
6mnth to 2yr; 9am-
4pm; $140 per day
Rough Riders: ages 3
to 6; 9am-3pm;
includes skiing; $143
per day
Little Rippers: ages
5-6; 9am-3pm;
includes boarding;
$210 per day

Ski school
Explorers: ages 7 to
14; 9.00-3.30; $140
per day

GETTING THERE

Air Jackson 20km/
15 miles (45mins)

without interest for experts. In particular, Moran Woods is a splendid, under-utilised area. Even Apres Vous has an area of serious single blacks in Saratoga bowl – usually very quiet.

The gates into the backcountry access over 3,000 acres of amazing terrain, which should be explored only with guidance. You can stay out overnight at a backcountry yurt. There are some helicopter operations.

FOR INTERMEDIATES ★★★★★
Exciting for some
There are good cruising runs on the front face of Apres Vous, and top-to-bottom quite gentle blues from the gondola. But they don't add up to a great deal of mileage, and you shouldn't consider Jackson unless you want to tackle the blacks. It's then important to get guidance on steepness and snow conditions. The steepest single blacks are steep, intimidating when mogulled and fearsome when hard. The daily grooming map is worth consulting.

FOR BEGINNERS ★★★★★
Fine, up to a point
There are good broad, gentle beginner slopes. The progression to the blue Werner run off the Apres Vous chair is gradual enough and the mid-mountain blues on the Casper Bowl chair are reached via the chairs from the beginner area. But few other runs will help build confidence.

FOR CROSS-COUNTRY ★★★★
Plenty of scenic choices
The Saddlehorn Activity Center at Teton has 17km/11 miles of trails and organises trips into the National Parks. And there is lots of groomed trails in the surrounding National Parks.

MOUNTAIN RESTAURANTS ★★★★★
Bridger blossoms
We've always complained about Jackson's on-mountain eateries. But the smart development at the top of the Bridger gondola, opened two years back, is one we're keen to try. A couple of reporters have already approved the table-service Couloir ('excellent elk pasta'). The self-service Rendezvous has separate areas serving soups and salads, Asian dishes, grills etc. Both have great views of the Headwall and outdoor decks as well as indoor seating. And there's a simpler Headwall Pizza and

Deli option. The restaurant at the base of the Casper chairlift does a good range of self-service food. There are simple snack bars at four other points on the mountain.

There are some excellent lunching alternatives at the base, particularly in the smarter hotels.

SCHOOLS AND GUIDES ★★★★
Learn to tackle the steeps
The school is highly regarded. A 2009 visitor ranks it as 'one of the best in the US', enjoying 'another couple of fun and instructive days'. As well as the usual lessons, there are also special types on certain dates. The four-day Steep and Deep Camp (pre-booking required) was 'carefully matched to ability, good value and a maximum five in each group'.

Backcountry guides can be hired – Rendezvous Ski Tours has been recommended for exploring the backcountry from Teton Pass.

FOR FAMILIES ★★★★
Adventures on the Ranch
The area may not seem to be one ideally suited to children, but there are enough easy runs. The 'Kids' Ranch' facilities are good, including regular pizza parties in the evenings. There are classes catering for ages 3 to 17.

STAYING THERE

Teton Village is convenient, Jackson has the atmosphere; bear in mind that some town hotels are far from central.
Hotels Because winter is low season, prices are low.
TETON VILLAGE
★★★★★Four Seasons Resort (732 5000) Stylish luxury, with art on the walls, superb skier services, health club, an exceptional outdoor pool, perfect position just above the base.
★★★★Teton Mountain Lodge & Spa (734 7111) Very comfortable. Good indoor and outdoor pool and fitness centre. 'Decent dinner.'
★★★★Snake River Lodge & Spa (732 6000) Smartly welcoming and comfortable, with fine spa facilities.
★★★★Terra (739 4000) Smart, boutique 'eco' hotel, with rooftop pool and hot tub. Spa. Due for extension in 2009/10.
★★★Alpenhof (733 3242) Tirolean-style, with varied rooms ('small by American standards'). Good food, lively bar. Pool, sauna, hot tub.
★Hostel (733 3415) Basic, good value.

Weekly news updates and resort links at www.wtss.co.uk

ACTIVITIES

Indoor Fitness centres, swimming, tennis, library, concerts, wildlife art and other museums

Outdoor Snowmobiles, snowshoeing, sleigh rides, dog sledding, hot springs, snow kite boarding

UK PACKAGES

Alpine Answers, AmeriCan Ski, American Ski Classics, Crystal, Funway Holidays, Independent Ski Links, Inghams, Made to Measure, Momentum, Scott Dunn, Simply Alpine, Ski Activity, Ski Dream, Ski Freshtracks, Ski Independence, Ski Line, Ski Safari, Ski Solutions, Skitracer, Skiworld, Supertravel, Trailfinders, United Vacations

Phone numbers
From distant parts of the US, add the prefix 1 307; from abroad, add the prefix +1 307

TOURIST OFFICES

Jackson Hole
t 733 2292
info@jacksonhole.com
www.jacksonhole.com

JACKSON TOWN
****Wort (733 2190) Comfortable, central, above the lively Silver Dollar Bar. Hot tub.
****Rusty Parrot Lodge (733 2000) Stylish place with a rustic feel. Small, busy. Hot tub. 'Food, service as good as ever' this year.
***Lodge at Jackson Hole (739 9703) Western-style place on outskirts. Comfortable mini-suite rooms, and free breakfast. Pool, sauna, hot tubs. Shuttle to the slopes.
***Parkway Inn (733 3143) 'Friendly and helpful owners, convenient, with free transport to Teton Village.'
**Forty Niner Inn and Suites (733 7550) Central, good value.
**Trapper Inn (733 2648) Friendly, good value, fairly central. Hot tubs.
BETWEEN THE TWO
*****Amangani Resort (734 7333) Hedonistic luxury in isolated position way above the valley.
****Spring Creek Ranch (733 8833) Exclusive retreat; cross-country on hand. Hot tub.
Apartments There is lots of choice at Teton Village (Cody House is 'superb') and better value places a mile or two away. Surprisingly little in and around Jackson town. Love Ridge and Snow King are 'good value'.

EATING OUT ★★★★★
A wide range of options
Jackson offers a range of excellent dining options. To check out menus, get hold of the local dining guide.

Most of the best bets at Teton Village are in the hotels. Il Villaggio Osteria at the new hotel Terra has a good choice of Italian and seafood dishes – two 2009 reporters enjoyed 'great food and service' there. Options at the Four Seasons include the Peak. The Alpenhof Bistro does seafood.

In Jackson town there is more choice. The Blue Lion is small, with 'intimate dining areas, traditional menu and friendly service'. Burke's Chop House is an 'above average' steakhouse that also serves 'great cocktails'. Similarly, downstairs at the Million Dollar Cowboy does 'wonderful steak' and good wines. The Snake River brew-pub – not to be confused with the expensive Snake River Grill – does 'good pizza' and a great range of beers. Thai Me Up has 'attentive service and good food', Bon Appe Thai does 'fantastic (and hot) authentic curries' and the cute log cabin

Sweetwater serves 'good elk and buffalo'. The Merry Piglets is 'a terrible name but a great Mexican restaurant'. Stone Table does South American dishes as well as tapas and Bubba's BBQ does 'fantastic' food despite the rustic surroundings. The 'saloons' (see 'Après-ski') also serve hearty meals.

There are several places out of town to try too, such as the stylish Grill at Amangani or Calico (Italian).

APRES-SKI ★★★★
Amusing saloons
The renowned Mangy Moose is the focus of après-ski activity at Teton Village – a big, happy place, often with live music – though a January visitor this year found it lacking animation. But there are quieter bars for a relaxed drink.

In Jackson the various saloons will regularly have music and sometimes dancing, in a good old Wild West atmosphere. The two famous places are the Million Dollar Cowboy Bar, featuring saddles as bar stools and a stuffed grizzly bear, and the Silver Dollar around the corner – less tacky and more subdued; there may be ragtime playing as you count the 2032 silver dollars inlaid into the counter. There's also the Shady Lady and the quieter Virginian saloon – a popular locals' hang-out. The Rancher is a huge pool-hall. For a Sunday night out of town, the Stagecoach Inn at Wilson and its band shouldn't be missed for a lively blue grass swing and western night.

OFF THE SLOPES ★★★
'Great' outdoor diversions
Yellowstone National Park is 100km/62 miles to the north. You can tour the park by snowcat or snowmobile with a guide; numbers are now restricted to reduce pollution. Some visitors really enjoy the park; we were distinctly underwhelmed (largely because of the noise and fumes from the snowmobiles and driving everywhere in convoy). The National Elk Refuge, with the largest elk herd in the US, is next to Jackson and across the road from the National Museum of Wildlife Art. Reporters recommend both. In town there are some 40 galleries and museums and various shops, including a number of outlets for Western arts and crafts. Shopping discounts can be gained by joining the Jackson Hole Ski Club ($30).

New England

You go to Utah for the deepest snow, to Colorado for the lightest powder and swankiest resorts, to California for big mountains and low prices. You go to New England for ... well, for what? Extreme cold? Rock-hard artificial snow? Mountains too limited to be of interest beyond New Jersey? Yes and no: all of these preconceptions have some basis, but they don't give the full picture.

Yes, it can be cold: one of our reporters recorded –27°C, with wind chill producing a perceived –73°C. Early in the season, people routinely wear face masks to prevent frostbite. It can also be warm – another reporter had a whole week of rain that washed away the early-season snow. The thing about New England's weather is that it varies – rather like England's. The locals' favourite saying is: 'If you don't like the weather, wait two minutes.'

New England doesn't usually get much super-light powder or deep snow to play in. But the resorts have big snowmaking installations, designed to ensure a long season and to help the slopes to 'recover' after a thaw or a spell of rain. They were the pioneers of snowmaking technology; and 'farming' snow, as they put it, is an art form and a way of life – provided the weather is cold enough. Many of the resorts get impressive amounts of natural snow too – in some seasons.

The mountains are not huge in terms of trail mileage (the largest,

Killington, is one of the few resorts in these pages to get only ✱ for extent of slopes). But several have verticals of over 800m/2,620ft (on a par with Colorado resorts such as Keystone), and most have over 600m/1,970ft (matching Breckenridge), and are worth considering for a short stay, or even for a week if you like familiar runs. For more novelty, a two- or three-centre trip is the obvious solution. Most resorts suit snowboarders well, and many have more than one terrain park.

You won't lack challenge – most of the double black diamond runs are seriously steep. And you won't lack space: most Americans visit over weekends, which means deserted slopes on weekdays – except at peak holiday periods. It also means the resorts are keen to attract long-stay visitors, so UK package prices are low.

But the big weekend and day trip trade also means few New England resorts have developed atmospheric resort villages – just a few condos and a hotel, maybe, with places to stay further out geared to car drivers. New England is easy to get to from Britain – a flight to Boston, then perhaps a three- or four-hour drive to your resort. And there are some pretty towns to visit, with their clapboard houses and big churches. You might also like to consider spending a day or two in Boston – one of America's most charming cities. And you could have a shopping spree at the factory outlet stores that abound in New England.

We cover two of the most popular resorts on the UK market in the chapters that follow – a long chapter on **Killington**, a short one on **Stowe**. But there are many other small areas, too, shown on the map and covered in our directory at the back of the book. Consider renting a car and visiting several resorts.

Jay Peak ○
Sugarloaf ○
87 | 89
VERMONT
Smugglers' ○
Notch ○
Stowe
91
BURLINGTON
Black Mountain ○
Sunday River ○
MAINE
Mad River Glen ○
●**MONTPELIER**
Bolton ○
Mountain
○ Bretton Woods
Mount Cranmore ○
Sugarbush ○ 89
Loon ○
Mountain
○ Attitash
LEWISTON ●
7
Waterville ○
Valley
Pico ○ Suicide Six
PORTLAND
4 | 4
RUTLAND ○ **Killington**
93
95 N
7
○ Okemo
89 ●**CONCORD**
● **DOVER**
91
○ Bromley
NEW
○ Stratton
HAMPSHIRE
● **PORTSMOUTH**
○ Mount Snow
○ Haystack
● **KEENE**
● **MANCHESTER**
0   20   40
BATTLEBORO
3 | 93
NASHUA ●
km

Killington

New England's leading resort, in most respects; good slopes, great après-ski, no real village – for the moment, at least

£70
RESORT PRICE INDEX

RATINGS

The mountains
Extent	★
Fast lifts	★★★
Queues	★★★★
Terrain p'ks	★★★★
Snow	★★★
Expert	★★★
Intermediate	★★★
Beginner	★★★★
X-country	★★★
Restaurants	★
Schools	★★★★
Families	★★★★

The resort
Charm	★
Convenience	★
Scenery	★★★
Eating out	★★★★★
Après-ski	★★★★
Off-slope	★

NEWS

For 2008/09 a fast quad replaced the fixed-grip quad from Bear Mountain base to Skye Peak. The chair accesses a new all-natural terrain park, The Stash, built in partnership with Burton (see 'Terrain parks') like the one in Avoriaz, France.

Also on Skye Peak, a green run – the Great Eastern – was created from the top down to the Skyeship base and the Gateway trail extended. These runs and The Stash gained snowmaking.

At Snowshed, a moving carpet replaced a draglift in the nursery area.

➕ The biggest mountain in the east, matching some Colorado resorts

➕ Lively après-ski, with lots of bar-restaurants offering happy hours and late-night action

➕ Excellent nursery slopes

➕ Comprehensive and very effective snowmaking

➕ Good childcare, although it's not a notably child-oriented resort

➖ No resort village yet: restaurants, hotels and condos are widely spread, mostly along the five-mile access road – a car is needed

➖ Crowds on weekends

➖ New England weather – highly changeable, and can be very cold

➖ The trail network is complex

➖ Terminally tedious for anyone who is not a skier or boarder

It's difficult to ignore Killington. It claims to have the largest mountain, largest number of quad chairs, largest grooming fleet and longest season in the eastern US, and the biggest snowmaking installation in the world. (It tries to be the first resort in the US to open, in October, but often shuts again shortly afterwards.) It also claims to have America's longest lift and longest trail (a winding 16km/10 miles) and New England's steepest mogul slope (Outer Limits – average gradient 46%). These things may matter if your choice of destination is limited to those in the eastern US. In the general scheme of things, they count for very little. Killington is a minor resort, chiefly of interest if you find yourself within driving distance at a time when conditions look good.

THE RESORT

Killington is an extraordinary resort, especially to European eyes. There is no resort village in the usual sense. Most of its hotels and restaurants are spread along a five-mile approach road. The resort caters mainly for weekend visitors who drive in from the east-coast cities. There have been long-term plans to develop the area around the lift base, but those seem to be on hold for now.

Outings to Pico are possible – a separate little mountain next-door in the same ownership, perhaps one day to be linked to the Ramshead sector of Killington's slopes.

VILLAGE CHARM ★
What village?
In Killington, the nearest thing you'll find to a focus is the occasional set of traffic lights with a cluster of shops; the main area is a concentration of buildings along a two-and-a-half mile stretch of the access road. The car is king; but there's also a free day-time shuttle-bus service around the base areas and lodgings. Beyond this it costs $2.

CONVENIENCE ★
Still no proper base
Staying near the start of the access road leaves you well placed for the Skyeship gondola station on the main highway leading past the resort. There are lodgings around the lift base, but little else – most restaurants are way down the access road.

SCENERY ★★★
Plenty of trees
The scenery is unremarkable, but Killington Peak gives an uninterrupted view of classic Vermont – heavily wooded, rolling mountains.

THE MOUNTAINS

Runs spread over a series of wooded peaks, all quite close together but giving the resort a basis for claiming to cover six mountains – or seven if you count Pico. An impressive number of runs and lifts are crammed into a modest area. To some extent the terrain on each sector suits a different ability level. But there are also areas where a mixed ability group would be happy, and there are easy runs from top to bottom of each peak.

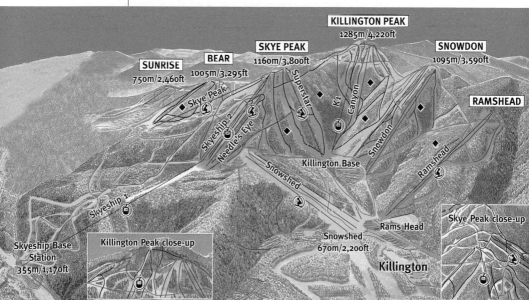

LIFT PASSES

boarding

A cool resort like Killington has to take boarding seriously, and it does. There are terrain features scattered around the area, with lots of interest for all levels, and parts of the mountain have been reshaped to cut out some of the unpleasant flats on green runs. There are excellent beginner slopes, and plenty of friendly (ie slow-loading) high-speed chairlifts – and the Killington school offers the Burton Learn to Ride programme; instruction just for first-time boarders. Several big-name board events are held here, and the terrain parks just get bigger and better.

Some runs of all levels are left to form bumps; there is half-and-half grooming on selected trails; and terrain features – ridges etc – are created. There are also gladed forest areas, not patrolled, where you pick your own line. They come in single and double black diamond and blue grades. We found them great fun.

The result of all this is a complex network of runs. Signposting has been improved recently and there are free guided tours to help you find your way around.

EXTENT OF THE SLOPES ★★★★★
Complicated

The Killington Base area has chairs radiating to three of the six peaks – **Snowdon**, **Killington** (the high-point of the area) and **Skye** – the last also accessible by a gondola starting beside US Highway 4 or by the new fast quad from Bear. Novices and families head for the other main base area, which has two parts: Snowshed, at the foot of the main beginner slope, served by several parallel chairs; and Ramshead, just across the road up to

Killington Base, where there's a Family Center at the foot of the entirely gentle **Ramshead** mountain, with extensive nursery slopes.

The two remaining peaks are behind Skye Peak; they can be reached by trails from Killington and Skye, but each also has a lift base accessible by road. **Bear Mountain** is the experts' hill, served by two quad chairs (one fast) from its mid-mountain base area. The sixth 'peak', **Sunrise**, is a slight blip on the mountainside, with a short triple chair up from the Sunrise Village condos.

FAST LIFTS ★★★★★
Where they are most needed

The proportion of fast lifts to the whole ski area is now quite high; there are still some slow chairs around, but they are mainly on the quieter back of the mountain. Fast chairs or gondolas cover the key locations. The new fast quad from Bear Mountain to Skye Peak has reduced the ride time to five minutes there and provided a smoother link between the two sectors.

KEY FACTS

Resort	670m
	2,200ft
Slopes	355-1285m
	1,170-4,220ft
Lifts	24
Pistes	1,215 acres
Green	28%
Blue	33%
Black	39%
Snowmaking	59%

Killington

653

SCHOOLS

Killington
t 1 800 923 9444
Learn to ski clinics
(including lift pass,
equipment and use of
Discovery Center)
1 2hr lesson $125

Classes
One 2hr group lesson
$60
Private lessons
$105 for 1hr

CHILDCARE

t 1 800 923 9444
Friendly Penguin Day Care
Ages 12wk to 6yr;
$100 a day
First Tracks
Ages 2 to 3; 8.30-
4.00; $130 a day;
includes skiing
MiniStars/Lowriders
Ages 4 to 6; 8.30-
3.00; $130 a day;
includes skiing

Ski school
'Superstars' for ages
6 to 12 and
'Snowzone' for ages
13 to 18 ($130 for a
full day incl. lift pass
and lunch)

UK PACKAGES

*American Ski Classics,
Crystal, Directski.com,
Independent Ski Links,
Inghams, Made to
Measure, Simply
Alpine, Ski Dream, Ski
Independence, Ski Line,
Ski McNeill, Ski Safari,
Ski Solutions, Skitracer,
Skiworld, Thomson,
Trailfinders, Virgin
Snow*

GETTING THERE

Air Boston 260km/
160 miles (3hr)

QUEUES ★★★★
Weekend crowds
Killington gets a lot of weekend and holiday business, which means queues and crowded slopes can be a problem. There may be long waits for the main access lifts. At other times the slopes and lifts are likely to be quiet.

TERRAIN PARKS ★★★★
Follow the Bear
The main freestyle areas are near Bear Mountain, on the back of Skye Peak. There are separate sections along the Bear Claw and Dream Maker trails, served by the new Skye Peak quad. Between them is the new eco-park 'The Stash', which incorporates 34 wooden and natural features – including tree jibs and log rides. (Visitors to Avoriaz in France may think this sounds familiar: there is another Stash there, in the Lindarets valley.) There is also a super-pipe and urban-style rail park near the base. Timberline on Ramshead has small to medium elements, including a mini park. Kids have their own park and pipe classes. There's also an early season park on Killington Peak and a small park at Pico.

SNOW RELIABILITY ★★★
Good if it's cold
Killington has a good snowfall record (average 250 inches) and a huge snowmaking system that seems to receive regular upgrades. But even that is no good if temperatures are too high to operate it. East coast weather is erratic; conditions can change rapidly and it's not unusual to experience extreme cold and rain in one day. Grooming is adequate.

FOR EXPERTS ★★★
Some challenges
The main areas that experts head for are Killington Peak, where there is a handful of genuine double-diamond fall-line runs under the two chairlifts, and Bear mountain. Most of the slopes here are single blacks, but Outer Limits, under the main quad chair, is a double diamond, claimed to be 'the steepest mogul slope in the east'. We suspect there are steeper runs at Stowe and Smugglers' Notch, in fact. There are two or three worthwhile blacks on Snowdon and Skye, too. The designated glades on Skye, Snowdon and Bear are also worth seeking out if you're lucky enough to hit powder.

FOR INTERMEDIATES ★★★
Limited extent
There are lots of easy cruising blue and green runs all over the slopes, except on Bear mountain, where the single blacks present a little more of a challenge for intermediates. Snowdon is a splendid area for those who like to vary their diet, and Skye has some longer runs. There's a blue-classified gladed area on Ramshead. One reporter enjoyed an outing to Pico but complained that the blue run down was more difficult than some blacks.

FOR BEGINNERS ★★★★
Lots of lovely greens
The facilities for complete beginners are excellent. The Snowshed home slope is really one vast nursery slope served by three chairlifts and a very slow draglift. Ramshead also has excellent gentle slopes and novices can progress to the long green run from Skye Peak to the Skyeship base. The school runs separate Learn to Ski and Ride programmes just for first-time skiers and boarders.

FOR CROSS-COUNTRY ★★★
Two main options
Extensive loops are available at two specialist 'resorts' – Mountain Meadows, down on US Highway 4, and Mountain Top Ski Touring, just a short drive away at Chittenden.

MOUNTAIN RESTAURANTS ★
Bearable base lodges
As usual on a small American hill, there is very little refreshment on the mountain. Killington Peak Lodge is the only real option. There is a warming hut at Northbrook station on Skye Peak where you can get soups, and areas are provided if you wish to bring your own food, but most people use the base lodges. These are generally food courts, serving the typical grills, burgers and salads. K-1 lodge seems to have the best choices, including the Mahogany Ridge pub and deli.

SCHOOLS AND GUIDES ★★★★
Improving your strengths
The philosophy of the Killington school is to build on your strengths, and it seems to work for most people. Beginners start and finish their day in a dedicated building with easy chairs, coffee, videos and help with fitting equipment. Speciality clinics include mogul weekends and park classes.

↑ You get a clear picture here of the front slopes of Skye Peak and Killington Peak, with Snowdon and Ramshead on the right

KILLINGTON RESORT

ACTIVITIES

Indoor Massage, fitness centre, outdoor pool, hot tub, sauna (all at Killington Grand Hotel); Spa at the Woods; theatre, cinemas, bowling, at Rutland; climbing wall at Snowshed base

Outdoor Ice rink, snowshoeing, snowmobile tours, sleigh rides

Central reservations phone number
Call 1 800 621 6867 (toll-free from within the US)

Phone numbers
From distant parts of the US, add the prefix 1 802; from abroad, add the prefix +1 802

TOURIST OFFICE

t 422 3333
info@killington.com
www.killington.com

FOR FAMILIES ★★★★
Fine in practice
Ramshead is the focal point for families. There are gentle nursery slopes, accessed by moving carpets, and a couple of 'play' zones. The Family Center there is home to the kids ski school and Penguin day care facility. It takes kids from 12 weeks and will introduce them to skiing from age two years. Classes are small – guaranteed groups of three or five. There is also a family dining area.

STAYING THERE

There is a wide choice of places to stay. As well as hotels and condos, there are a few chalets.
Hotels There are a few places near the lifts, but most are a drive or bus ride away, down Killington Road or on US4.
****Grand Resort (422 5001) Swanky resort-owned place at Snowshed, with outdoor pool, spa and health club.
***Inn of the Six Mountains (228 4676) Couple of miles down Killington Road; smart rooms, good pool and spa. Shuttle-bus to the slopes.
**North Star Lodge (422 4040) Well down Killington Road. Good value. Pool and shuttle-bus to the slopes.

EATING OUT ★★★★★
You name it
There are all sorts of restaurants spread along the Killington Road, from simple pizza or pasta through to 'fine dining' places. Many of the places in the Après-ski section serve food – be aware, though, that most bars do not allow children. The local menu guide is helpful. Cedar's at the Inn of the Six Mountains does fine American cuisine with an International flair, and offers a special children's menu. Alternatives include the Grist Mill for steaks and

seafood, Choices, Hemingway's and Charity's. Peppino's is the place for Italian dishes and Wally's is a family-friendly diner.

APRES-SKI ★★★★
The beast of the east
Killington has a well-deserved reputation for a vibrant après-ski scene; many of its short-stay visitors are clearly intent on making the most of their few days (or nights) here.

There are bars at the base lodges – the Long Trail at Snowshed has a good range of beers – but keen après-skiers head down Killington Road to one of the lively places scattered along its 8km/5 mile length. From 3pm it's cheap drinks and free munchies, then in the early evening it's serious dining time, and later on the real action starts (and admission charges kick in).

The nightlife centres around several well-established bars, most with live music. Leading the way is the popular Wobbly Barn, a famous live-music place that still claims to be one of the US's best après-ski venues. Other lively options include the train-themed Casey's Caboose and Charity's – with an interior apparently lifted from a late-19th-century Parisian brothel. The Pickel Barrel caters for a younger crowd, with theme nights. The Outback complex has something for everyone, from pizzas and free massages to disco and live bands.

OFF THE SLOPES ★
Rent a car
If there is a less amusing resort in which to spend time off the slopes, we have yet to find it. Make sure you have a car, as well as a supply of good books. Factory outlet shopping at Manchester is recommended (a 45-minute drive).

Stowe

Classic, charming Vermont town, some miles from its small but serious – and improving – area of slopes on Mount Mansfield

Extent	★
Fast lifts	★★★
Queues	★★★★
Snow	★★★
Expert	★★★
Intermediate	★★★★
Beginner	★★★★
Charm	★★★★
Convenience	★
Scenery	★★★

➕ Cute tourist town in classic New England style

➕ Some good slopes for all abilities, including serious challenges

➕ Few queues

➕ Excellent cross-country trails

➕ Great children's facilities

➖ Slopes a bus ride from town

➖ Slopes limited in extent

➖ New England weather – highly changeable, and can be very cold

➖ Slow chairlifts in main sector

➖ Weekend queues

➖ Lacks après-ski animation

Stowe is one of New England's cutest little towns, its main street lined with dinky clapboard shops and restaurants. Its mountain, 10km/6 miles away, is another New England classic: something for everyone, but not much of it. A new upscale hotel now offers an attractive slope-side base, right by the gondola.

NEWS

For 2008/09 the long-awaited Stowe Mountain Lodge luxury hotel complex and Spruce Camp day lodge opened at Spruce Peak – beside the gondola. Both buildings incorporate new restaurants and shops.

656

THE RESORT

Stowe is a small town that's a popular spot for tourists year-round. The slopes of Mount Mansfield, Vermont's mainly wooded highest peak, are a 15-minute drive away.

Village charm Stowe is chocolate-box pretty; it has quaint clapboard buildings, bijou shops and more 3- and 4-diamond hotels and restaurants than any other place in New England except Boston.

Convenience Much of the lodging is along the road between the town and the slopes – though you can now stay at the swanky new Stowe Mountain

Lodge, right by the lifts. One 2009 visitor complains of lots of stairs to reach the Mt Mansfield slopes. There's a good day-time shuttle-bus service, but a car is useful.

Scenery Trees and glades define the rolling East Coast scenery – viewed best from the top of Mount Mansfield.

THE MOUNTAINS

There are two main sectors, linked by gondola at base level. Free daily mountain tours.

Slopes The main Mansfield sector, served by a trio of chairlifts from Mansfield base lodge, is dominated by

KEY FACTS

Resort	475m
	1,560ft
Slopes	390-1135m
	1,280-3,720ft
Lifts	13
Pistes	485 acres
Green	16%
Blue	59%
Black	25%
Snowmaking	90%

UK PACKAGES

American Ski Classics, Crystal, Crystal Finest, Directski.com, Independent Ski Links, Made to Measure, Simply Alpine, Ski Activity, Ski Dream, Ski Independence, Ski Line, Ski McNeill, Ski Safari, Skitracer, Skiworld, Virgin Snow

Central reservations phone number
Call 1 800 253 4754 (toll-free from within the US)

Phone numbers
From distant parts of the US, add the prefix 1 802; from abroad, add the prefix +1 802

TOURIST OFFICE

t 253 3000
info@stowe.com
www.stowe.com

STOWE MOUNTAIN RESORT

By some margin, it's the cutest ski resort in New England ↓

the famous Front Four – a row of double black diamond runs. But there is plenty of easier stuff, too. An eight-seat gondola serves a second part of this sector. The Spruce Peak sector has the main nursery area at the bottom. A fast quad heads up to mid-mountain, and another serves the upper slopes. There is a backcountry link with Smugglers' Notch from the top.

Fast lifts Although fast lifts serve each area, some slow chairs remain in the main sector.

Queues The area is largely queue-free mid-week, but there may be weekend queues for the key lifts. Improvements at Spruce Peak have helped there.

Terrain parks Stowe has three terrain parks and a super-pipe: one is for beginners near the gondola base, the others (on Mansfield) are best suited to advanced users. An early/late season rail park is sometimes built.

Snow reliability This is helped by snowmaking on practically all the blue (and some black) runs of the main sectors, and on all of Spruce Peak. Grooming is generally excellent.

Experts The Front Four and their variants on the top half of the main sector are steep, narrow and a real challenge (if they are open); there are others nearby. There are various gladed areas.

Intermediates The usual New England reservation applies: the terrain is limited in extent; there's also a shortage of ordinary black runs (as opposed to double-diamonds).

Beginners The nursery slopes at Spruce Peak are excellent. There are also splendid long green runs to progress to in the main sector, down to Toll House base.

Snowboarding Stowe attracts many snowboarders. Beginners learn on special customised boards at the dedicated centre on Spruce Peak. There's also a special resort website: www.stowked.com.

Cross-country There are excellent centres scattered around (including one at the musically famous Trapp Family Lodge) – 150km/93 miles of groomed and 100km/62 miles of

backcountry trails form the largest network in the eastern US.

Mountain restaurants The Cliff House, at the top of the gondola, has table service. Next best is Midway Cafe near the base of the gondola.

Schools and guides We lack reports on the school, but semi-private lessons are available (up to three in a group). The Stowe Toys Demo Centre is the place to try out the latest equipment, with instruction.

Families Facilities are excellent; the nursery takes children from age 13 months to three years.

STAYING THERE

There are hotels in and around Stowe itself and along the road to the slopes, some with Austrian or Scandinavian names and styles.

Hotels Spruce base now has the luxury Stowe Mountain Lodge, with pool and wellness centre. And the smart Inn at the Mountain, at Toll House, offers slope-side accommodation. Other popular choices are 1066 Ye Olde England Inne (despite the appalling name), the Stowehof Inn, Green Mountain Inn, the Stowe Inn and the Golden Eagle with a pool and hot tub.

Apartments There is a reasonable range of condos available for rent.

Eating out There are restaurants of every kind. The Whip in the Green Mountain Inn, Gracie's, the Shed (basic pub food), Trattoria La Festa and the Solstice at the Stowe Mountain Lodge are a good selection.

Après-ski Rather muted, but there's a choice. The Matterhorn, Shed and Rusty Nail (live music, dancing) on the access road are popular. The Hourglass Bar at Stowe Mountain Lodge serves rare wines, cocktails and beers.

Off the slopes Stowe is a pleasant place to spend time off the slopes – at least if you like shopping. There's also the Vermont Ski Museum and a good cinema. A trip to Burlington's shopping mall and a tour (with samples) of Ben & Jerry's ice cream factory just down the road are other possibilities. There is snowmobiling and dog sledding.

Canada

More British skiers and snowboarders go to Canada than to the US. In many ways it combines the best that the US has to offer – good service, a warm welcome, relatively quiet slopes, good lift systems with lots of fast lifts, frequent dumps of snow, great grooming and a high standard of accommodation – with more spectacular scenery and lower prices. It also has the advantage that you can get direct flights to its main airports without having to change planes and go through customs part-way through your journey. There are charter flights as well as direct Air Canada and British Airways flights.

If Canada – well, western Canada at least – has one central attraction, it is snow. In an average year, you can expect much better snow than in the Alps – and not only good conditions on the pistes but frequent fresh falls to provide the powder you dream of. And, as in the States, there is lots of steep terrain within resort boundaries, which is therefore avalanche protected and safely skiable without guidance. If you really want untracked powder and are feeling flush, there is nothing to beat western Canada's amazing heli-skiing and snowcat skiing operations. The east is different: expect snow and extremes of weather, much like in New England. The main attraction of Québec for us is the French culture and unique ambience, plus the advantage of a shorter flight time. In both east and west, lifts close much earlier than in Europe – as early as 3pm in some cases.

Increased air fares mean that Canada is no longer as cheap a holiday as it was; package prices start at around £700 for a week in Banff (no meals included). But eating and drinking is cheap; all Canadian resorts were near the bottom of our Resort Price Index league table.

The Canadian people are another attraction. They share the American service culture but have a sincerity in putting it into practice that our reporters appreciate. In the west you'll also find spectacular scenery quite unlike what you generally find in the US. You may also see an impressive range of wildlife, especially in the Rockies and the interior of British Columbia.

Note that the legal age for buying and consuming alcohol is 18 in Alberta and Québec, 19 in British Columbia, and the law is strictly enforced; carrying your passport as evidence of age is a good idea even if you are well over the required age.

One of the great attractions of the Rocky Mountain resorts, and particularly Lake Louise, is the grand scenery ↓

658

Western Canada

For international visitors to Canada, the main draw is the west. It has fabulous scenery, good snow and a wonderful sense of the great outdoors. The big names of Whistler, Banff and Lake Louise capture most of the British market, but there are lots of good smaller resorts that more Brits are now starting to explore. You can have a great trip by renting a car and combining two or more of these, perhaps with a couple of days on virgin powder served by helicopters or snowcats as well.

The three big resorts mentioned above and seven of the smaller ones get their own write-ups in this section.

Whistler is plenty big enough to amuse you for a whole holiday. Most visitors to Banff or Lake Louise, a half-hour drive apart, will spend time at both (and could also fit in day trips to Kicking Horse and Panorama).

But none of the others has enough terrain to keep a keen piste-basher amused for a week or ten days without skiing the same runs several times. So we'd suggest that if you want variety, you combine two or more on one holiday. Even if you don't want to drive, it is easy to combine, say, Sun Peaks with Whistler, Big White or Silver Star (and the latter two with each other) using regular buses between them.

New for this edition is a chapter on Revelstoke – which has grown in the last two years from a small local hill with just one lift to the resort with the biggest vertical in North America.

Places that don't get a full chapter that you might also consider for a longer tour include Jasper (which you can reach via the spectacular Icefields Parkway drive from Lake Louise), Apex, Red Mountain and Kimberley – these all have entries in the resort directory.

A few seasons ago we spent two weeks driving from Whistler to Banff, calling in at lots of smaller resorts on the way. It was a fantastic trip; for eight days in the middle it did not stop snowing, we had day after day of dry, light powder, and the variety of slopes and resorts made for great contrasts throughout the trip.

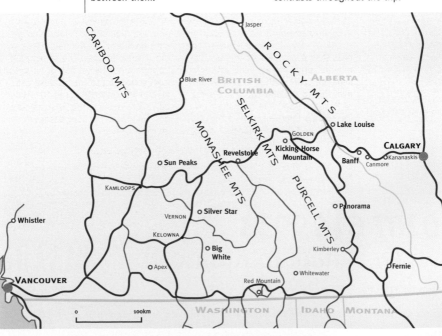

Banff

A major summer resort amid spectacular National Park scenery, with varied ski areas a bus ride from town – including Lake Louise

£75
RESORT PRICE INDEX

RATINGS

The mountains
Extent	★★★
Fast lifts	★★★★
Queues	★★★★
Terrain p'ks	★★★★
Snow	★★★★
Expert	★★★★
Intermediate	★★★★
Beginner	★★★
X-country	★★★★
Restaurants	★★★
Schools	★★★★
Families	★★★★

The resort
Charm	★★★
Convenience	★
Scenery	★★★★
Eating out	★★★★★
Après-ski	★★★
Off-slope	★★★★★

NEWS

For 2009/10 at Sunshine Village, the Mountain Lodge is being extended to include 30 luxury eco-friendly rooms. At Mt Norquay, there are plans to improve the terrain park.

For 2008/09 Mt Norquay built a boardercross area beside the terrain park and increased night skiing to twice a week.

+ Spectacular high-mountain scenery – quite unlike the Colorado Rockies

+ Excellent snow and long season at main local area, Sunshine Village

+ Lots of touristy shops, restaurants and bars

+ Good-value lodging because winter is the area's low season

− Main ski area is a 20-minute bus ride out of town

− You'll probably want to ski Lake Louise too – 45 minutes away

− Most lifts/runs are of limited vertical

− Can be very cold (−30°C or less)

− Banff lacks ski resort atmosphere – though it's not an unattractive town

Huge numbers of British skiers and boarders go to Banff. Price has been a key factor in putting it on the map. Package costs have crept up, but most visitors are still delighted with what they find – particularly the majestic scenery plus the standard Canadian assets of welcoming locals and low on-the-spot prices.

Banff is nothing like your typical ski resort. We enjoy its restaurants and bars, but the daily commuting to Sunshine Village and Lake Louise is a pain. The alternative is to stay a few nights mid-mountain at Sunshine Village and a few at Lake Louise (you'll find Watts at the Chateau, Gill at the lovely Post). Lake Louise also has the advantage of being much closer to Kicking Horse, which makes a great day trip (see separate chapters for Louise and Kicking Horse).

THE RESORT

Banff is a big summer resort with two ski areas nearby. Norquay is a tiny area of slopes overlooking the town. Sunshine Village, its base station 20 minutes' drive from Banff, is a much bigger mountain; despite the name, it's not a village (it has just one hotel at mid-mountain) nor is it notably sunny. Most visitors buy a three-area pass that also covers Lake Louise, 45 minutes' drive away – dealt with in a separate chapter. Bus excursions are available to the more distant resorts of Panorama and Kicking Horse and the smaller (and closer) resort of Nakiska, and day trips for heli-skiing and boarding are offered locally.

VILLAGE CHARM ★★★
Pleasantly touristy
Banff consists basically of a long main street connecting the 'downtown' area – a small network of side roads built in grid fashion, lined with clothing and souvenir shops aimed at summer visitors – with a large area of hotel and condo lodgings. The buildings are low-rise and some are wood-clad. The town is pleasant enough, but it's essentially a modern tourist town, without the character of the classic American cowboy or mining towns.

CONVENIENCE ★
Sprawling town, outlying slopes
Banff is a sprawling place, and many of the lodgings (even on the main Banff Avenue) can be quite a way from the downtown area. A car can be helpful here, especially in cold weather. But there are plentiful taxis.

To get to the slopes there is an efficient, regular bus service that picks up from all the main hotels – free with the Tri-area lift pass. The buses pick up from a number of hotels, so getting from your hotel to the lift base can take much longer than the advertised time. For Sunshine this is 20 minutes, but then there is a long access gondola to ride.

SCENERY ★★★★
Distinctive and dramatic
Banff National Park offers spectacular scenery, and the town's setting is dramatic. Sunshine's Lookout mountain is on the Continental Divide, with wide views into British Columbia.

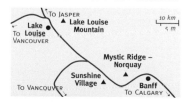

661

KEY FACTS

Resort	1380m
	4,530ft

Norquay, Sunshine and Lake Louise, covered by the Tri-area pass

Slopes	1630-2730m
	5,350-8,950ft
Lifts	26
Pistes	7,748 acres
Green	23%
Blue	39%
Black	38%
Snowmaking	24%

Norquay only

Slopes	1630-2135m
	5,350-7,000ft
Lifts	5
Pistes	190 acres
Green	20%
Blue	36%
Black	44%
Snowmaking	85%

Sunshine only

Slopes	1660-2730m
	5,440-8,950ft
Lifts	12
Pistes	3,358 acres
Green	20%
Blue	55%
Black	25%
Snowmaking	none

THE MOUNTAINS

The Sunshine Village slopes are set on the Continental Divide – the watershed between the Pacific and the Atlantic – and as a result get a lot of snow. Most of the slopes above the village are above the treeline. Although there is a wooded sector served by the second section of the gondola, and some lightly wooded slopes higher up, in bad weather you're better off at Lake Louise or Norquay. The season goes on until May.

Norquay is a much smaller area of quiet, wooded slopes. But it's worth a visit, especially in bad weather or as a first-day warm-up.

There are good, free mountain tours led by friendly volunteer hosts.

EXTENT OF THE SLOPES ★★★
Lots of variety
The main slopes of **Sunshine Village** are not visible from the base station: you ride a gondola to Sunshine Village itself, with a mid-station at the base of Goat's Eye Mountain.

Goat's Eye is served by a fast quad rising 580m/1,900ft – much the most serious lift on the mountain. Although there are some blue runs, this is basically a black mountain, with some genuine double diamonds at the extremities (including the 'backcountry' Wild West area).

Further up at Sunshine Village, lifts fan out in all directions, with short runs back from Mount Standish and longer ones from Lookout Mountain. Lookout is right on the Continental Divide. From the top here experts can pass through a gate and hike up to more extreme terrain.

Many people ride the gondola down at the end of the day. But the 2.5km/1.5 mile green run to the bottom is a pretty cruise. If you go down while the lifts are running, you

can take the Jackrabbit chair to cut out a flat section, but the run gets crowded and is much more enjoyable if you delay your descent a bit. The Canyon trail is a fun alternative for more advanced skiers and riders. Though the lower part is marked black, it's not steep – just a bit narrow and twisty in places.

The slopes at **Norquay** are served by a row of five parallel lifts and have floodlit trails twice a week.

FAST LIFTS ★★★★
Sunshine has it sorted
At Sunshine, most sectors of the slopes have fast chairs, the main exception being the stoppage-prone Wawa chair. Norquay is so small that lift speed is hardly an issue, but it does have one fast chair.

QUEUES ★★★★
Sunshine can get busy
Many visitors are day-trippers from cities such as Calgary – so the slopes are fairly quiet during the week. Public holidays and weekends at Sunshine have provoked past complaints of long queues; it gets busy. But 2009 reporters visiting in March and April (including Easter) had no major problems. Even when busy, queues generally move quickly, and there are effective singles lines so you can jump the queue if in a hurry. On busy weekends, we're told the trick is to arrive at the gondola by 9am.

TERRAIN PARKS ★★★★
Park – and ride ...
At Sunshine, the Rogers terrain park on Lookout Mountain has 21 main features. These include medium to large 15m/50ft kickers and a host of rails and boxes, including a whale tail box, banked C box and whopping 12m/40ft hand rail ('great fun'). A newer section, Grizzly, has more

boarding

Boarders will feel at home in Banff, and there is some excellent freeriding terrain. Natural features are part of the appeal, with ledges, jumps and tree gaps aplenty. Delirium Dive, Silver City and Wild West are controlled off-piste playgrounds. A transceiver, probe, shovel and companion are required in all three. Not for the faint hearted, they are steep and deep. But Sunshine also has some flat areas to beware of, where scooting or walking is required (such as the green run to the base – see notes in main text on avoiding the worst of this), and the blue traverse on Goat's Eye is tedious. A trip to Lake Louise's Powder Bowls is a must for freeriders. There are specialist snowboard shops in Banff: Rude Boys, Rude Girls and Unlimited Skate & Snow.

Tri-area lift pass

Prices in C$

Age	1-day	6-day
under 13	27	237
13 to 17	57	448
18 to 64	80	504
over 65	65	448

Free under 6

Beginner lift, lesson and rental package

Notes

Day pass is for Sunshine only; 3-day-plus pass covers all lifts and transport between Banff, Lake Louise, Norquay and Sunshine Village; prices include 5% GST tax

Sunshine Village mainly offers high, open slopes with reliable snow ↓

features; its 'pièce de resistance' is a 7m/24ft long by 1.2m/4ft high box, painted by local artists. There is also a big, advanced park at Norquay, designed by Jeff Paterson – head park designer for Triple Crown events. Gap jumps, tabletops, rails and boxes litter the park, which also boasts a good-sized half-pipe and new boardercross. The park is now floodlit twice a week from January to March. There is a special park-only pass. There's another park at Lake Louise.

SNOW RELIABILITY ★★★★
Excellent

Sunshine Village claims '100% natural snow', a neat reversal of the usual snowmaking hype. In a poor snow season, some black runs can remain rocky (especially those on Goat's Eye), but the blues are usually fine. 'Three times the snow' is another Sunshine slogan – a cryptic reference to the fact that the average snowfall here is 360 to 400 inches (depending on which figures you believe) – as good as anything in Colorado – compared with a modest 140 inches at Lake Louise and 120 inches on Norquay. But we're told the Sunshine figures relate to

Lookout, and that Goat's Eye gets less. At Norquay there is snowmaking on all green and blue pistes. Late-season snow on Sunshine is usually good (we've had great April snow there).

FOR EXPERTS ★★★★
Pure pleasure

Sunshine has plenty of open runs of genuine black steepness above the treeline on Lookout, but Goat's Eye is much more compelling. It has a great area of expert double black diamond trails and chutes, both above and below the treeline. The slopes are rocky and need good cover, and the top can be windswept. The double-diamond runs at skier's left reportedly hold their snow better than the rest of the mountain.

There are short, not-too-steep black runs on Mount Standish. One more challenging novelty here is a pitch known as the Waterfall run – because you do actually ski down over a snow-covered frozen waterfall. But a lot of snow is needed to cover the waterfall and prevent it reverting to ice. Also try the Shoulder on Lookout Mountain; it is sheltered, tends to accumulate powder and has been deserted

Banff

663

Interactive resort shortlist builder at **www.wtss.co.uk**

664

whenever we've been there; access involves a long traverse that can be tricky and is poorly marked.

A popular backcountry route follows the back of the Wawa ridge, through a river valley ('great fun – tight turns in the trees of the river bed'); a guide is essential, of course.

Real experts will want to get to grips with Delirium Dive and Silver City on Lookout Mountain's north face and the Wild West area on Goat's Eye (with some narrow chutes and rock bands). For all three you must have a companion, an avalanche transceiver, a probe and a shovel – and a guide is recommended. It is probably best to book in advance and rent your transceiver and shovel in Banff (you can't in Sunshine). We tried Delirium in a group with the ski patrol, who provided equipment, and the scariest part was the walk in, along a narrow, icy path with a sheer drop (protected by a flimsy-looking net).

Norquay's two main lifts give only 400m/1,310ft vertical, but both serve black slopes, and the North American chair accesses a couple of serious double-diamond runs.

Heli-skiing is available from bases outside the National Park in British Columbia – roughly two hours' drive.

FOR INTERMEDIATES ★★★★
Ideal runs
Half the runs on Sunshine are classified as intermediate. Wherever you look there are blues and greens – some of the greens as enjoyable (and pretty much as steep) as the blues. We particularly liked the World Cup Downhill run, from the top of Lookout to the Village. All three chairs on Mount Standish are excellent for building confidence, provided you choose a sensible route down. The slow Wawa chair gives access to the

Goat's Eye has some great steep terrain – single and double black diamond runs and an extreme zone. But it's very rocky and windswept and needs a lot of snow to be enjoyable

GOAT'S EYE
2600m/8,530ft

Goat's Eye

Delirium Dive ◆◆

Wild West ◆◆

1660m/5,440ft

2020m/6,630ft

Wolverine

Gondola

If it's snowing hard, visibility is usually best on the easy runs in the trees around here and on the long run down to the bottom of the gondola

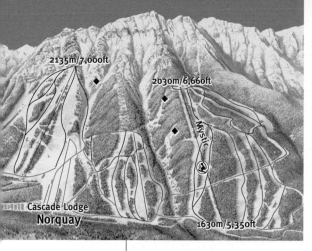

2135m/7,000ft

2030m/6,660ft

Mystic

Cascade Lodge
Norquay

1630m/5,350ft

blue runs down Goat's Eye are good cruises too, some of them with space to indulge in fast carving.

The Mystic Express quad at Norquay serves a handful of quite challenging treelined blues and a couple of blacks that are sometimes groomed, and great fun.

FOR BEGINNERS ★★★☆☆
Pretty good terrain

Sunshine has a good area at the Village, served by a moving carpet. And there are great, long green runs to progress to – notably Meadow Park. Norquay has a good small nursery area with a moving carpet and gentle greens served by the Cascade chair.

Banff is not the ideal destination for a mixed party of beginners and more experienced friends. The beginners are likely to want familiar surroundings, while the more experienced will want to travel.

Wawa Bowl and Tincan Alley ('great first blues'). This area also offers some shelter from bad weather. There's a delightful wooded area under the second stage of the gondola served by Jackrabbit and Wolverine chairs. The

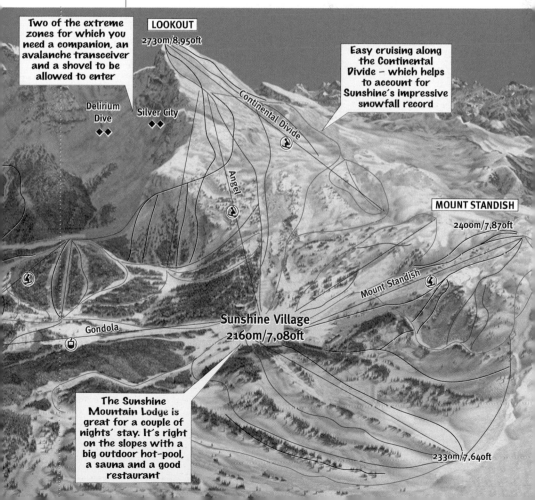

Two of the extreme zones for which you need a companion, an avalanche transceiver and a shovel to be allowed to enter

LOOKOUT
2730m/8,950ft

Continental Divide

Delirium
Dive
♦♦

Silver City
♦♦

Angel

Easy cruising along the Continental Divide – which helps to account for Sunshine's impressive snowfall record

MOUNT STANDISH
2400m/7,870ft

Mount Standish

Sunshine Village
2160m/7,080ft

Gondola

The Sunshine Mountain Lodge is great for a couple of nights' stay. It's right on the slopes with a big outdoor hot-pool, a sauna and a good restaurant

2330m/7,640ft

SCHOOLS

Ski Big 3
t 760 7731

Banff-Norquay
t 760 7716

Sunshine Village
t 1 877 542 2633

Classes (Big 3 prices)
3 days guided tuition
of the three areas
C$285 incl. tax

Private lessons
Half day (3hr) C$387,
incl. tax, for up to 5
people

CHILDCARE

Tiny Tigers (Sunshine)
t 1 877 542 2633
Ages 19mnth to 6yr;
8.30-4.30

Kid's Place (Norquay)
t 760 7709
Ages 19mnth to 6yr;
9am to 4pm

Childcare Connection
t 760 4443
Childminding in guest
accommodation

Ski school
Takes ages 6 to 12 (3
days C$285, incl. tax
and lunch)

GETTING THERE

Air Calgary 140km/
85 miles (1hr45)

FOR CROSS-COUNTRY ★★★★
High in quality and quantity
It's a good area for cross-country.
There are trails near Banff, around the
Bow River, and on the Banff Springs
golf course. But the best area is
around Lake Louise. Altogether, there
are around 80km/50 miles of groomed
trails within Banff National Park.

MOUNTAIN RESTAURANTS ★★★
Quite good
With a mini-resort at mid-mountain,
Sunshine offers better options than
usual in North America. Best is the
Sunshine Mountain Lodge – the table
service in the recently revamped
Chimney Corner Lounge gave 'prompt
service and good food' for a 2009
visitor. The Day Lodge offers three
different styles of food on three floors
– the table service in the top-floor
Lookout Lounge has great views and
does a buffet.
   At Norquay, the big, stylish, timber-
framed Cascade Lodge is excellent – it
has table- and self-service restaurants.

SCHOOLS AND GUIDES ★★★★
Some great ideas
Each mountain has its own school. But
recognising that visitors wanting
lessons won't want to be confined to
just one mountain, the resorts have
organised an excellent Club Ski and
Club Snowboard Program – three-day
courses starting on Sundays and
Thursdays that take you to Sunshine,
Norquay and Lake Louise on different
days, offering a mixture of guiding and

instruction, and fun social events. In
the past we've received rave reviews
about it from reporters. But a 2008
visitor had mixed experiences: 'our
advanced group had a perfect balance
of skills training and guidance, but the
rest of our party had an instructor who
spoke little and gave virtually no
specific skills training'. All abilities are
catered for, including beginners. A
2008 reporter did five days of the
Performance Clinic at Sunshine and
found the instructors 'excellent: they
picked up your mistakes and
encouraged you; my class size was
never more than four'.

FOR FAMILIES ★★★★
Excellent choices
There are various school and activity
programmes for all ages. Some lodges
have family lounges, with games and
TVs. We've had good reports of the
school: 'kind and friendly instructors'
and 'very accommodating; my boy is
now a tremendous skier'. All three
resorts offer childcare. The Tiny Tigers
Ski and Play programme introduces
youngsters to the slopes.

STAYING THERE

A huge amount of accommodation is
on offer; as well as hotels and self-
catering, there are catered chalets.
Hotels Summer is peak season here,
with generally lower prices in winter.
★★★★★Fairmont Banff Springs (762
2211) A late-19th-century, castle-style
property, well outside town (with no

← The Banff Springs hotel – like Chateau Lake Louise, originally part of a chain of Canadian Pacific Railway hotels, built to attract travellers

STUART MCWILLIAM

UK PACKAGES

Alpine Answers, AmeriCan Ski, American Ski Classics, Canadian Affair, Crystal, Crystal Finest, Directski.com, First Choice, Frontier, Funway Holidays, Independent Ski Links, Inghams, Kuoni, Made to Measure, Neilson, Simply Alpine, Ski Activity, Ski Dream, Ski Independence, Ski Line, Ski McNeill, Ski Safari, Ski Solutions, Skitracer, Skiworld, Supertravel, Thomson, Trailfinders, United Vacations, Virgin Snow

ACTIVITIES

Indoor Film theatre, museums, galleries, swimming pools (one with water slides), gym, squash, weight training, bowling, hot tub, sauna, climbing wall

Outdoor Swimming in hot springs, ice rink, sleigh rides, dog sledding, snowmobiles, ice walks, ice fishing, helicopter tours, snowshoeing

Phone numbers
From distant parts of Canada, add the prefix 1 403; from abroad, add the prefix +1 403

TOURIST OFFICE

Banff
t 762 4561
info@SkiBig3.com
www.SkiBig3.com
www.skibanff.com
www.banffnorquay.com

shuttle-bus – you have to use taxis). It's virtually a town within itself – 2,000 beds, over 40 shops, several restaurants and bars, a nightclub and a superb spa (which costs extra).
****Fox (760-8500) Newish place near downtown Banff. Hotel rooms and suites, with a restaurant, fitness area and an unusual 'cavern' style hot pool.
****Rimrock (762 3356) Spectacularly set, out of town, with great views and a smart health club. Luxurious.
****Banff Park Lodge (762 4433) Best-quality, central hotel, with hot tub, steam room and indoor pool.
****Banff Caribou Lodge (762 5887) On the main street, slightly out of town. Wood-clad, individually designed rooms. Very good Red Earth Spa centre, 'excellent' restaurant and bar. Repeatedly recommended by reporters.
***Buffalo Mountain Lodge (762 2400) Less convenient but 'beautiful location and excellent dining room'. Hot tub.
***Irwins Mountain Inn (762 4566) On Banff Avenue: 'good location and excellent value', says a 2009 visitor.
***High Country Inn (762 2236) 'Great: big rooms, pool, hot tub and sauna, easy walk to centre.'
**Homestead Inn (762 4471) Central, cheap, good-sized rooms.
Apartments Don't expect luxury – but there are some decent options. The Banff Rocky Mountain Resort is set in the woods on the edge of town, with indoor pool and hot tubs. Families have recommended the Douglas Fir resort ('kids loved the water slides') – though it's 'a bit out of town'.
At altitude The newly extended Sunshine Mountain Lodge (277 7669) makes a very welcoming, comfortable base at Sunshine Village. Luggage is delivered while you ski. Rooms vary in size, with some smart new ones due to open for 2009/10. Big outdoor hot-pool. Sauna. Good restaurant. Guests can get on the slopes half an hour before people coming up the gondola.

EATING OUT ★★★★★
Lots of choice
Banff boasts over 100 restaurants, from McDonald's to fine dining in the Banff Springs hotel.

The award-winning Maple Leaf Grille has fine seafood and steak dishes on the menu, and over 600 different wines to choose from. We've enjoyed the designer-cool Saltlik – good game, steak and fish. Chilli's at the new Fox hotel is worth a look.

Of the dozens of places that readers recommend, popular spots are Aardvark ('very good pizza'), Giorgios ('good and unpretentious'), Magpie & Stump ('lively', but busy Mexican, with Wild West decor, 'serves beer in jam jars') and Earl's. The Old Spaghetti Factory is a good family choice ('excellent service'). The Bison has 'excellent quality food' and live music. And for traditional burgers and ribs try the Keg, Bumper's, Wild Bill's or Tony Roma's ('rack of ribs to die for').

APRES-SKI ★★★☆☆
Night on the town is best
There's little tea time après-ski because the town is a drive from the slopes. Mad Trapper's Saloon at the top of the Sunshine gondola is the best bet during the close-of-play happy hour, but it gets crowded. In town later, the two main live music venues are the Rose & Crown and Wild Bill's – country and western style, perhaps with line dancing. The Elk and Oarsman has a lively sports bar. For a traditional pint of beer though, head for the St James's Gate Irish pub. There are a couple of good nightclubs.

OFF THE SLOPES ★★★★★
Lots to do
Banff has lots to do off the slopes. There are various outdoor activities, such as snowshoeing, dog sledding, skating and snowmobiling. Ice canyon walks are popular – notably Johnson Canyon, and there's wildlife to see. For less active pursuits, shopping and soaking in the spas and hot springs are popular – the Red Earth Spa at the Caribou Lodge has the works and is open until 8pm. There are sightseeing tours and several museums. Some reporters have enjoyed evenings in Calgary watching the ice hockey. A 2009 reporter enjoyed a good day out in Canmore.

Interactive resort shortlist builder at **www.wtss.co.uk**

Big White

*It's not big by Euro-resort standards, but it's certainly white.
There are few places to match it for learning to ski powder*

➕ Great for learning to ski powder

➕ Slopes quiet except at weekends and holidays

➕ Convenient, purpose-built village with high-quality, good-value condos; good for families

➕ Very friendly staff; good for families

➖ Visibility can be poor, especially on the upper mountain, because of snow, cloud or freezing fog

➖ Few off-slope diversions – and isolated without a car

➖ Limited après-ski

TOP 10 RATINGS

Extent	★★★
Fast lifts	★★★★
Queues	★★★★★
Snow	★★★★★
Expert	★★★
Intermediate	★★★★
Beginner	★★★★
Charm	★★
Convenience	★★★★
Scenery	★★★

KEY FACTS

Resort	1755m
	5,760ft
Slopes	1510-2320m
	4,950-7,610ft
Lifts	16
Pistes	2,765 acres
Green	18%
Blue	54%
Black	28%
Snowmaking	
	In terrain park

'It's the snow' says the Big White slogan. And as slogans go, it's spot on. If you want a good chance of skiing powder on reasonably easy slopes, put Big White high on the shortlist. If you want a suntan (or lively après-ski, or extensive steep bowls and chutes), look elsewhere; but if you are an intermediate looking to learn to ski powder or try gladed skiing for the first time, there can be few better places. Consider combining it with another BC resort such as Silver Star or Sun Peaks for variety.

THE RESORT

Big White is a rapidly growing, purpose-built resort less than an hour from Kelowna airport. Silver Star (see separate chapter) is around two and a half hours away and under the same ownership; twice-a-week transfers make a two-centre holiday easy and you can also just go for the day.

Village charm The village is rather spread out but attractive in wood and stone, with a family-friendly traffic-free centre. Reporters remark on the large number of 'friendly and happy' Aussie workers that the resort recruits for the season.

Convenience Much of the place is ski-in/ski-out and with accommodation in smart modern condos, some very luxurious.

Scenery Trees fill the views wherever you look; and near the top of the mountain the trees usually stay white all winter and are known as 'snow ghosts'; they make visibility tricky in a white-out but are great fun to ski between on clear days.

THE MOUNTAINS

Much of the terrain is heavily wooded. But the trees thin out towards the summits, leading to almost open slopes in the bowls at the top. There's at least one green option from the top

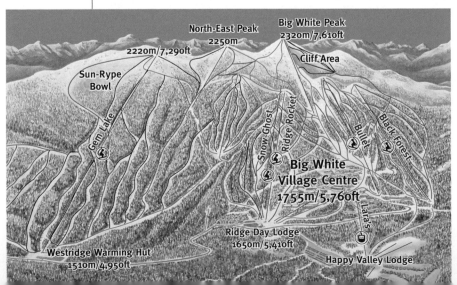

North-East Peak
2250m

Big White Peak
2320m/7,61oft

2220m/7,29oft

Cliff Area

Sun-Rype Bowl

Gem Lake

Snow Ghost

Ridge Rocket

Bullet

Black Forest

Big White Village Centre
1755m/5,76oft

Lara's

Ridge Day Lodge
1650m/5,41oft

Happy Valley Lodge

Westridge Warming Hut
1510m/4,95oft

For 2008/09 Kelowna airport (56km/35 miles away) was improved to take bigger planes (including transatlantic flights). The kids' day care centre was expanded, and the Globe tapas bar, along with several shops, opened in the resort.

For 2009/10 Carvers restaurant, in the Inn at Big White, with food inspired by Indian cuisine, will have Tuesday evening Bollywood nights with Indian-style buffets and belly dancing.

of each lift, but the one from Gem Lake is narrow and can be tricky and busy. In general, the easiest slopes are on the right as you look at the mountain (including some very easy glade skiing) and get steeper the further left you go.

Slopes Chairs run from points below village level to above mid-mountain, serving the main area of wooded beginner and intermediate runs above and beside the village. A T-bar and four chairs serve the higher slopes. Quite some way across the mountainside is the Gem Lake fast chair, serving a range of long top-to-bottom runs; with its 710m/2,330ft vertical, this lift is in a different league from the others. 'Snow hosts' (highly praised by reporters) run twice-daily guided ski tours. The signposting and piste map are both good.

Fast lifts The lifts out of the village and the Gem Lake lift to the top are all fast. But the other upper lifts are tediously slow.

Queues Queues are very rare.

Terrain parks Served by a double chair and by Big White's first snowmaking, the excellent Telus park includes a half-pipe, boardercross, rails and hits

for all levels. It is floodlit Thursday to Saturday evenings – and is highly praised by reporters.

Snow reliability Big White has a reputation for great powder; average snowfall is about 300 inches, which is similar to many Colorado resorts. One reporter points out that most slopes face south-west to south-east and the snow can suffer in periods of sunshine; but on both our visits, it has snowed practically non-stop and we hardly saw the sun.

Experts The Cliff Area at the top right of the ski area is of serious double black diamond pitch; the runs are short, but you can ski them repeatedly using the Cliff chair. Sun-Rype bowl at the opposite edge of the ski area is more forgiving. There are some long blacks off the Gem Lake chair and several shorter ones off the Powder and Falcon chairs. There are glades to explore and bump runs too.

Intermediates The resort is excellent for cruisers and families, with long blues and greens all over the hill. Good intermediates will enjoy the easier blacks and some of the gladed runs too. There is marvellous easy skiing among the trees in the Black

↑ The trees near the top of the mountain are called 'snow ghosts' because they usually stay white all winter

BIG WHITE SKI RESORT, BC / GAVIN CRAWFORD – QUICK PICS

UK PACKAGES

Alpine Answers, AmeriCan Ski, American Ski Classics, Canadian Affair, Frontier, Independent Ski Links, Made to Measure, Simply Alpine, Ski Dream, Ski Freshtracks, Ski Independence, Ski Line, Ski Safari, Skiworld

Central reservations
Call 765 8888; toll-free (within Canada) 1 800 663 2772
Phone numbers
From distant parts of Canada, add the prefix 1 250; from abroad, add +1 250

TOURIST OFFICE

t 765 3101
bigwhite@bigwhite.com
www.bigwhite.com

BIG WHITE SKI RESORT, BC / BIG WHITE SKI

The village is rather spread out but attractive and with a cute, family-friendly traffic-free centre →

Forest area (which we loved when it was snowing) and among the snow ghosts (see 'Scenery'), which we loved when it was clear. Some of the blues off the Gem Lake chair are quite steep, narrow and challenging.

Beginners There's a good dedicated nursery area in the village and lots of long easy runs to progress to.

Snowboarding There's some excellent beginner and freeriding terrain with boarder-friendly chairlifts and few flat areas to worry about.

Cross-country 25km/16 miles of trails.

Mountain restaurants There aren't any – it's back to the bottom for lunch.

School and guides We receive rave reviews from reporters for both adult and children's lessons – and for the free mountain tours.

Families The excellent Kids' Centre takes children from 18 months. Evening activities are organised too.

STAYING THERE

There's an increasing range of packages to Big White including Canada specialist Frontier Ski and North America specialists AmeriCan Ski and Ski Independence.

Hotels The White Crystal Inn receives

better reviews from reporters than the Inn at Big White.

Apartments Condo standards are high. We stayed at Stonebridge and loved it – big rooms, central, well furnished, private hot tub on the balcony. Reporter recommendations include Towering Pines ('superb, huge lounge, private hot tub'), Black Bear and (a bit less luxurious) Eagles and Whitefoot Lodge.

Eating out We had good meals in the Copper Kettle in the White Crystal Inn and the Kettle Valley Steakhouse at Happy Valley ('superb food, amazing choice of wines', says a recent visitor). Reporters also recommend Snowshoe Sam's ('imaginative food'), and Swiss Bear in the Chateau Big White.

Après-ski The atmospheric Snowshoe Sam's has a DJ and live entertainment; try its trademark alcoholic gunbarrel coffee. Raakel's Ridge in the Hofbrauhaus has live music and dancing. The Snow Ghost Lounge in the White Crystal Inn has 'live music some nights and impressive malt whiskies'.

Off the slopes Happy Valley has ice skating, snowmobiling, tubing, dog sledding, sleigh rides and snowshoeing. There are two spas.

Fernie

Lots of snow and lots of steeps – best explored with a guide; a choice of convenient base lodging or a drive from Fernie town

£75
RESORT PRICE INDEX

RATINGS

The mountains
Extent	★★★
Fast lifts	★
Queues	★★★★
Terrain p'ks	★★
Snow	★★★★★
Expert	★★★★★
Intermediate	★★
Beginner	★★★★
X-country	★★★
Restaurants	★
Schools	★★★★
Families	★★★★

The resort
Charm	★★
Convenience	★★★★
Scenery	★★★
Eating out	★★★
Après-ski	★★★
Off-slope	★★

NEWS

For 2008/09 snowmaking was increased in the Timber Bowl chair area. More glades were cut in the KC Chutes, Cedar Ridge, Currie Glades and Stagleap areas, and more lines were cut in Mitchy Chutes. New boxes and rails were added to the Rail Park. The Bear's Den fast food kiosk was upgraded.

- ✚ Good snow record, with less chance of rain than at Whistler (and less chance of Arctic temperatures than at resorts up in the Rockies)
- ✚ Great terrain for those who like it steep and deep; good for confident intermediates too
- ✚ Snowcat operations nearby
- ✚ Some good on-slope accommodation available, but ...

- ▬ Mountain resort is very limited
- ▬ Access to many excellent runs is a slow business, involving slow lift rides and long traverses
- ▬ After a dump it can take time to make the bowls safe
- ▬ Limited groomed cruising
- ▬ Awful trail map and on-mountain signposting
- ▬ No proper mountain restaurants

Fernie has long had cult status among Alberta and British Columbia skiers. It now attracts quite a few British visitors, and the reports we get are almost all positive. Like us, reporters are impressed by the adventurous nature of the skiing – it's mostly steep and ungroomed, with a lot of lightly wooded slopes (not common in Europe). Curiously, it's now quite a good resort for novices, too – it's intermediates who don't want to give the ungroomed terrain a go who need to look elsewhere. The resort village is convenient but small and nothing special. Fernie town, a couple of miles away, has few of the usual tourist trappings, but makes an amusing change from the resort norm.

THE RESORT

Fernie Alpine Resort is set a little way up the mountainside from the flat Elk Valley floor and a couple of miles from the little town of Fernie. Outings to Kimberley are possible; a coach does the trip every week – the drive takes about 90 minutes.

VILLAGE CHARM ★★
Unpretentious small town
A slope-side resort has grown from very little in the past few years, but there's still not much there except convenient lodging and a few restaurants, bars and small shops. It is quiet at night. There's much more going on in the town of Fernie, which is named after William Fernie – a prospector who discovered coal here and triggered a boom in the early 1900s. Much of the town was destroyed by fire in 1908, but some buildings survived. It is primarily a place for locals, not tourists. There are some lively bars, decent places to eat and good outdoor shops. It is down to

Typical Fernie terrain: steep and not-so-steep ungroomed slopes on wooded slopes. Fernie town is in the wide valley below ➔

We have been complaining for years about the dreadful piste map and inadequate on-mountain signposting. A repeat visit in 2007 showed us that nothing had changed. For 2008 there were apparently new larger maps and signs at base level, but readers' reports make it clear that route finding is still a serious challenge. Finding some of the black runs is almost impossible without a guide, and you can easily end up in tight trees on slopes of triple-diamond steepness – as we did on an earlier visit. On our last visit, on one day we skied with an instructor and on another with Kathy Murray, who runs the Steep and Deep camps (see 'Schools and guides'). They took us to runs that are marked on the map but that we'd never have found. Accessing them normally entails long traverses through the trees; there might be a sign at the start (often high up in a tree), but once you set off, there are no further clues about where to go or when to start heading down. Locals don't use the piste map, and when asked about it and the signposting, they just shrug their shoulders or laugh. If you want to explore the best of Fernie's steep terrain, join a Steep and Deep camp or take a guide.

earth rather than charming, and reporters' reactions to it vary: 'I liked the way it felt like real Canada and enjoyed staying in a town with some history,' said one. 'The flip side of being a real town is having a real highway run through it,' said another. Most stress the friendliness of the locals.

CONVENIENCE ★★★★
Base lodging or bus ride

There is accommodation at the resort or in town. Buses between the town and the mountain run at half-hourly intervals at peak times and cost C$3 one way (they are free in the evenings and run every half an hour until 2am). Each hotel has specific pick-up times, although we have a report that the service is unreliable, and a recent visitor found the information on routes 'inadequate'.

SCENERY ★★★
The rocky ridges are impressive

Fernie's two main peaks, Grizzly and Polar, are part of the steep-sided Lizard Range. They provide an impressively rocky backdrop. There are good views across the Elk Valley too.

THE MOUNTAINS

Fernie's 2,500 acres pack in a lot of variety, from superb green terrain at the bottom to ungroomed chutes (that will be satisfyingly steep to anyone but the extreme specialist) and huge numbers of steep runs in the trees. Quite a few runs go directly down the fall line.

EXTENT OF THE SLOPES ★★★
Bowl after bowl

What you see when you arrive at the lift base is a trio of impressive mogul slopes towering above you. These excellent black runs exemplify one of the weaknesses of Fernie's lift system: to get to them you must ride lifts way off to the left or right, and then make long traverses – a slow business. The slow Deer chair approaches the foot of these slopes, but goes no further. It's there to serve the main green-run slow-skiing zone.

On the right, **Lizard Bowl** is a broad snowfield reached by the slow Elk quad then the fast Great Bear quad. Above this is the short Face Lift. The dreadful rope tow that rarely runs. The Face Lift is the best way into **Cedar Bowl** and to Snake Ridge beyond it, but you can still traverse into the lower parts of both Lizard and Cedar Bowls when the Face Lift isn't working. The Haul Back T-bar brings you out of Cedar. There is a mini-bowl between Lizard and Cedar, served by the Boomerang chair.

Off to the left, the Timber Bowl fast quad chair gives access to **Siberia Bowl** and the lower part of **Timber Bowl**. But for access to the higher slopes and to **Currie Bowl** you must take the White Pass quad. A long traverse from the top gets you to the steeper slopes on the flanks of Currie (our favourite area). From there you have to go right to the bottom (unless you head over into Lizard Bowl) and it takes quite a while to get back up for another go.

There are free tours in groups of different abilities, but only on blue and green runs. For the steeper, deeper stuff you need to pay (see 'Schools and guides') – we strongly recommend you do so early in your stay, to help you find your way around and get the most out of your holiday (see the 'Why you need a guide' feature panel). A reporter recommends

KEY FACTS

Resort	1065m
	3,490ft
Slopes	1065-1925m
	3,490-6,320ft
Lifts	10
Pistes	2,504 acres
Green	30%
Blue	40%
Black	30%
Snowmaking	2%

boarding

Fernie is a fine place for good boarders (and there are a lot of local experts here). Lots of natural gullies, hits and endless off-piste opportunities – including some adrenalin-pumping tree runs and knee-deep powder bowls – will keep freeriders of all abilities grinning from ear to ear. But there's a lot of traversing involved to get to many of the best runs – hard work in fresh snow and bumpy later. The main board shops, Board Stiff and Edge of the World, are in downtown Fernie, the latter with an indoor skate park to use while your board gets tuned. It's not a brilliant place for freestylers – the terrain park has gone; replaced by a smaller rail park – for which you'll need a special pass (see 'Terrain parks'). And faint-hearted intermediates should stay away.

LIFT PASSES

Fernie

Prices in C$

Age	1-day	6-day
under 13	26	157
13 to 17	56	334
18 to 64	79	472
over 65	63	378

Free under 6

Beginner rental, pass and tuition deals

Notes

Prices include taxes; half-day pass available

chatting to the locals: 'If you are a good skier, they will be delighted to show you the best runs.'

FAST LIFTS ★
A poor show
There are only two fast chairs, serving opposite ends of the mountain. And only one of them goes up from the resort base area. Slow chairs and a couple of draglifts elsewhere make getting around the mountain a slow process.

QUEUES ★★★★
Not usually a problem
Queues are generally rare unless there are weekend crowds from Calgary or heavy snow keeps part of the mountain closed. But people complain about the slow chairlifts, and about breakdowns on one or two.

TERRAIN PARKS ★★
Just a rail park
Fernie no longer builds a traditional park. Instead, there is a patrolled rail park beside the Great Bear Express –

you'll need a special pass (C$5 per day) and to sign a waiver to use it. The park was expanded for 2009 and new rails and boxes of various sizes, for all levels, were added.

SNOW RELIABILITY ★★★★★
A key part of the appeal
Fernie has an excellent snow record – with an average of 350 inches per year, better than practically all of Colorado. But the altitude is modest: rain is not unknown, and in warmer weather the lower slopes can suffer. Too much snow can be a problem, with the high bowls prone to closure – we've had reports of them being shut all week. Snowmaking has been increased and now covers most of the base area. Piste grooming has also been increased; we were impressed with it on our most recent visit and so are most reporters.

FOR EXPERTS ★★★★★
Wonderful – but get a guide
The combination of heavy snowfalls and abundant steep terrain with the

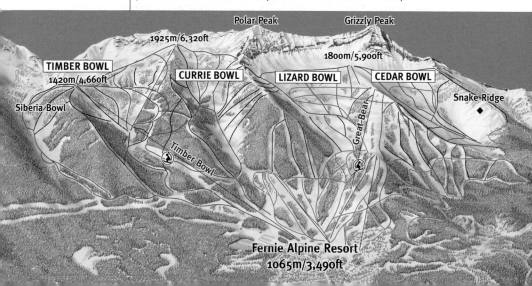

Fernie Alpine Resort
1065m/3,490ft

Good skiers who relish off-piste should consider treating themselves to some cat skiing (where you ride snowcats instead of lifts); there are several operations in this area. Island Lake Lodge (423 3700) does three-, four- or seven-day all-inclusive packages in a cosy chalet 10km/6 miles from Fernie, amid 7,000 acres of spectacular bowls and ridges. It has 36 beds and four cats. In a day you might do 10-15 powder runs averaging 500m/1,640ft vertical, taking in all kinds of terrain from gentle open slopes to some very Alpine adventures. You can do single days on a standby basis; we managed this once and loved it, but our second attempt failed. One visitor picked up a late-season bargain with Powder Cowboy (422 8754). It has two cats accessing 6,000 acres, 60km/37 miles from Fernie. 'Absolutely superb; best day's skiing we have ever had.' Fernie Wilderness Adventures (423 6704) has three cats accessing 3,000 acres, and reports have been positive.

shelter of trees makes this a superb mountain for good skiers, so long as you know where you are going. To get the most out of the terrain we strongly recommend getting guidance early in your holiday (see feature panel).

There are about a dozen identifiable faces offering genuine black or double black slopes, each of them with several alternative ways down. Pay attention to the diamonds: the singles are usually pretty tough, and the doubles are serious. Even where the trail map shows trees to be sparse, expect them to be close together, and where there aren't any, expect alder bushes unless there's lots of snow. There are a couple of areas where you can do laps fairly efficiently, but mostly you have to put up with the long traverse-descent-runout-lift-lift cycle on each lap (see 'Extent of the slopes').

There are backcountry routes you can take with guidance (some include an overnight camp) and snowcat operations in other nearby mountains – see feature panel. A regular reporter especially enjoyed exploring Fish Bowl, a short hike outside the resort boundary from Cedar Bowl.

FOR INTERMEDIATES **
Getting better
When we first visited, years ago, only the green and blue runs on the lower mountain were groomed. But on our most recent visit a few runs from the top were also groomed, including some great blue cruisers down Lizard Bowl – easily reached using the fast quad. But it doesn't add up to much, and if you are not happy to try some of the easier ungroomed terrain in the bowls and glades, we'd recommend you go elsewhere. For the adventurous willing to give the powder a go, though, Fernie should be on your shortlist.

FOR BEGINNERS ****
Surprisingly, pretty good
There's a good nursery area served by two lifts (a moving carpet and a drag), and the lower mountain served by the Deer and Elk chairs has lots of wide, smooth trails to gain confidence on. But the green runs from the top of the mountain are usually cat-tracks, which nonetheless have tough parts to them.

FOR CROSS-COUNTRY ***
Some possibilities
There are 14km/8 miles of trails marked out in the forest adjacent to the resort. In the Fernie area as a whole there are around 50km/30 miles of tracks (including some on the fairways of the Fernie golf course).

MOUNTAIN RESTAURANTS *
One small sit-down place
Lost Boys Cafe is a small place with good views at the top of the Timber Express chairlift. It has a basic, limited menu and gets mixed reviews – but 'the chilli is lovely – huge portions', says a recent visitor. Bear's Den at the top of the Elk chair is an open-air fast-food kiosk that was upgraded for last season. Most people head back to base for lunch. The ancient Day Lodge is a no-frills place serving salads and burgers ('friendly with good service'), Snow Creek is handy for the nursery slopes, has 'comfy sofas by an open fire' and does 'great nachos and wraps'. Kelsey's is popular for burgers, soups and the like. On Sundays you can try the brunch at the Lizard Creek ('you won't eat for the rest of the day').

SCHOOLS AND GUIDES ****
Highly praised
Reporters praise the school, which seems to achieve rapid progress – no doubt partly because groups are often very small. But we received a mixed

GETTING THERE

Air Calgary 340km/210 miles (4hr15)

UK PACKAGES

Alpine Answers, AmeriCan Ski, American Ski Classics, Canadian Affair, Canadian Powder Tours, Chalet Group, Crystal, Frontier, Independent Ski Links, Inghams, Interactive Resorts, Kuoni, Made to Measure, Simply Alpine, Ski Dream, Ski Freshtracks, Ski Independence, Ski Safari, Skitracer, Skiworld, Snoworks, Virgin Snow

SCHOOLS

Fernie
t 423 4655

Classes
Half day (2hr) C$93
(incl. taxes)

Private lessons
C$251 (incl. taxes) for
2hr for up to 5 people

CHILDCARE

Telus Resort Kids
t 423 2430
Age 19mnth to 6yr;
8.30 to 4.30

Ski school
For ages 5 to 12
(C$108 per day, incl.
taxes and lunch)

ACTIVITIES

Indoor Museum,
galleries, Aquatic
Centre, fitness centre,
ice rink, cinema,
curling, climbing wall,
brewery tour

Outdoor Sleigh rides,
snowmobiling, dog
sledding, snowshoe
excursions, walking

**Central reservations
phone number**
Call 1 877 333 2339
(toll-free from within
Canada)

Phone numbers
From distant parts of
Canada, add the
prefix 1 250; from
abroad, add the prefix
+1 250

TOURIST OFFICE

t 423 4655
info@skifernie.com
www.skifernie.com

report of private instruction last year:
'Our friends had two lessons, with
different instructors; the first one was
excellent, the second was poor.'

There are several programmes to
help you get the best out of the
mountain. The Steep and Deep camps
have had good feedback; it is a two-
day programme (C$289) where you get
technique tips while exploring steep
terrain – a great way to get to know
the mountain. There is also a
Mountain Guide programme (C$149 a
day) where you are guided around the
groomed and ungroomed runs but not
given any coaching. 'First Tracks'
(C$189) gets you up the mountain at
8am for two hours – a recent reporter
was delighted with this: 'He took us to
an untracked bowl and invited us to
rip it up!'

FOR FAMILIES ★★★★
Good day care centre
There's a day care centre in the
Cornerstone Lodge. A recent reporter's
son was 'very happy' there – 'the staff
were friendly and efficient'. There are
also 'Kids' Activity Nights' for children
aged six to 12. And there's a
Wilderness Adventure Park where kids
ski past cut-outs of bears and wolves.

STAYING THERE

Fernie is increasingly easy to find in
tour operator brochures.
Chalets Some UK tour operators run
chalets. Beavertail Lodge at the resort
is run along chalet lines and has
received several rave reviews: 'The
best chalet I have ever stayed in; food
equal to a Michelin-starred restaurant.'
Canadian Powder Tours has a chalet in
town and includes guiding by the
owners: 'Food excellent. I am a novice
off-piste but had a brilliant time.'
Hotels and condos There's a wide
choice, some impressively comfortable.
AT THE RESORT
****Lizard Creek Lodge** Best ski-in/
ski-out condo hotel – 'excellent and
beautifully decorated', says a recent
visitor. Spa, outdoor pool and hot tub.
****Snow Creek Lodge** Similar to the
Lizard Creek Lodge. 'Fantastic and
extremely convenient.'
***Wolf's Den Mountain Lodge** 'Simple
but comfortable', say reporters. Indoor
hot tub, small gym. At base of slope.
Cornerstone Lodge Condo hotel – 'very
clean, modern and well equipped'.
Griz Inn Sport Hotel Condo hotel with

good facilities. Pool.
Timberline Lodges Very comfortable
condos a shuttle-ride from the lifts.
Alpine Lodge B&B praised by a
reporter – 'welcoming and convenient'.
IN OR TOWARDS TOWN
****Best Western Fernie Mountain
Lodge** Next to golf course near town.
Recommended by reporters. Pool, hot
tub, fitness room. But a 30-minute bus
ride to the slopes.

EATING OUT ★★★
Better choice in town
At the base, there isn't a huge choice.
The restaurant of Lizard Creek Lodge
has had mixed reports: 'excellent
Alberta tenderloin and lobster', 'food
variable' say two reporters. Gabriella's
does cheap and cheerful Italian, and
lots of readers have enjoyed it.
Kelsey's (part of a chain) serves
standard, reliable steaks, burgers,
soups etc. The Corner Pocket has
moved from the Grand Central Hotel in
Fernie town to the Griz Inn.

In the town of Fernie, there are
quite a few options. Reporter
recommendations include the
expensive Old Elevator (a converted
grain store; 'excellent service; the
salmon and elk were delicious'),
Jamochas (a coffee house that does
meals), Curry Bowl (various Asian
styles; 'great meal'), Mojo Rising
(Cajun food) in the Royal hotel, Rip'n
Richard's Eatery (south-western food
and a lively atmosphere), Yamagoya
('great sushi') and the Sawai Thai. El
Guapo, in the Edge of the World board
shop, does 'tasty, very cheap' Mexican.

APRES-SKI ★★★
Have a beer
During the week, the resort bars are
pretty quiet later on. In town, the bars
of the Royal hotel are popular with
locals. Other recommendations are the
Park Place Lodge Pub ('service, prices
and atmosphere were excellent'). The
resort offers BBQs at the mid-
mountain Bear's Den on Fridays, with
a torchlit descent to follow.

OFF THE SLOPES ★★
Get out and about
There is a walking tour of historic
Fernie and visits to the Art Station (old
railroad station). You could take in an
ice hockey game. There's a pool at the
Aquatic Centre in town. But the main
diversion is the great outdoors.

Kicking Horse

One of Canada's newest resorts: only a few lifts, but great powder at the top, and a fledgling village at the base

+	Great terrain for experts and some for adventurous intermediates	−	Resort village still small and quiet
+	Big vertical served by a fast lift	−	Gondola has no mid-station, so you may have to ski crud lower down
+	Splendid mountain-top restaurant	−	Few groomed intermediate runs

TOP 10 RATINGS

Extent	★★★
Fast lifts	★★★
Queues	★★★★
Snow	★★★★
Expert	★★★★
Intermediate	★★★
Beginner	★★★
Charm	★★
Convenience	★★★★
Scenery	★★★

NEWS

For 2008/09 31 acres of new gladed skiing were introduced off Redemption Ridge. Hidden Nuggets is a series of new natural terrain features for freestyle fun.

In 2000/01 a new gondola from the base area to high, powder-filled bowls – previously heli-skiing country – opened. In 2002 came a new quad chairlift serving more high slopes. Since then there have been no new lifts but a small resort village at the base has been built and there are some cute places to stay. But there's not much to do except drink, eat and sleep once the lifts have closed. It's good for a short stay though or a day trip from Banff or Lake Louise.

THE RESORT

Eight miles from the logging town of Golden, Kicking Horse has grown much more slowly than was originally envisaged and is still in its formative days. Daily Powder Express buses run from Banff and Lake Louise – 2008/09 cost was C$87 including a lift pass.
Village charm The first phase of a resort village at the lift base now has several lodges, a few restaurants and bars, a ski shop and a general store. The town of Golden has no real charm.
Convenience Golden is spread-out beside the transcontinental highway and we prefer to stay at the mountain.
Scenery The scenery is not without drama; three distinctive ridges offer good views of the crags, chutes and glades – especially from Eagle's Eye.

THE MOUNTAINS

The lower two-thirds of the hill are wooded, with trails cut in the usual style. The upper third is a mix of open and lightly wooded slopes, with scores of ways down for experts through the bowls, chutes and trees.
Slopes The eight-seat gondola to Eagle's Eye takes you to the top in one stage of 1150m/3,770ft vertical. It serves two bowls and CPR Ridge, which separates them. If you want to stay high, you can repeat-ride the slow chair to the slightly higher peak of Blue Heaven. But most of the high slopes lead you below this chair, and with no mid-station on the gondola you have to make the full descent – and the snow conditions on the lower slopes may be poor. Two chairlifts from near the base serve the lower runs that formed the original ski area. There are free mountain tours.
Fast lifts Just the gondola.
Queues We've had reports of serious weekend queues for the gondola in the last two seasons: one reporter had a 50-minute wait on a Sunday. Problems seem to arise if for some reason the gondola stops for a while; queues build quickly at busy times. During the week though it's quiet and problems are rare.

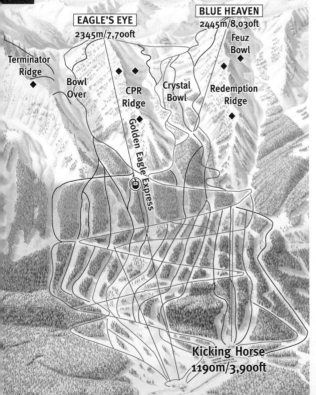

↑ Choose your route and enjoy the powder – that's what Kicking Horse is all about. Eagle's Eye is on the ridge

KICKING HORSE RESORT

KEY FACTS

Resort	1190m
	3,900ft
Slopes	1190-2445m
	3,900-8,030ft
Lifts	5
Pistes	2,750 acres
Green	20%
Blue	20%
Black	60%
Snowmaking	Some

UK PACKAGES

Alpine Answers, AmeriCan Ski, Bramble Ski, Canadian Affair, Crystal, Frontier, Independent Ski Links, Kuoni, Made to Measure, Neilson, Simply Alpine, Ski Dream, Ski Freshtracks, Ski Independence, Ski Safari, Skitracer, Skiworld

Central reservations
Call 439 5424
Phone numbers
From distant parts of Canada, add the prefix 1 250; from abroad, add the prefix +1 250

TOURIST OFFICE

t 439 5424
guestservices@kicking horseresort.com
www.kickinghorse resort.com

Terrain park There's a small park on the lower slopes and 'hidden' features (marked on the trail map) such as half-pipes and log jibs in Bowl Over.
Snow reliability An average of 275 inches of snow a year is not enough to put the resort in the top flight, but it's not far off. The top slopes usually have light, dry powder but the lower ones may have crud and thin cover.
Experts It's advanced skiers and riders who will get the most out of the area. From CPR Ridge, drop off to skier's right through trees or to skier's left through chutes – there are endless options. You can also hike to Terminator Ridge (often closed due to avalanche danger). The chair to Blue Heaven opens up easier ski-anywhere terrain back into Crystal Bowl and access to the wide (and less tracked out) Feuz Bowl via steep treeless chutes. The lower half of the mountain has short black runs cut through the woods, some with big moguls. There is heli-skiing nearby.
Intermediates Adventurous intermediates will have a fine time learning to play in the powder from Blue Heaven down to Crystal Bowl. Most of it is open, but you can head off into trees if you want to. There is very little groomed cruising, though there is a top-to-bottom 10km/6 mile winding green run. Timid intermediates should go elsewhere.
Beginners We can't imagine why a UK-based beginner would come here, but the beginner slopes are fine.
Snowboarding Freeriders will love this powder paradise.
Cross-country Loops of 25km/16 miles plus skating trails at Dawn Mountain; a 5km/3 mile loop on the golf course.
Mountain restaurants The Eagle's Eye at the top of the gondola is Canada's best mountain restaurant – excellent food and service in stylish log-cabin surroundings with splendid views. The

Heaven's Door yurt (tent) in Crystal Bowl serves snacks; many people lunch at one of the lodges at the base.
Schools and guides Two reporters booked group lessons, and each was the only pupil: 'excellent' was the verdict from both. Another joined a free mountain tour and again was the only one. Yet another took an avalanche safety course that 'was worth every penny; truly memorable'.
Families The school teaches children from the age of three.

STAYING THERE

There are smart, quite large condo-style lodges on the slopes. But we'd choose to stay in one of three much more captivating places (each personally run by the owners and with about 10 rooms and outdoor hot tubs) a short walk away – described below.
Hotels The log-built Vagabond Lodge features a fabulous first-floor living room and comfortable, traditional-style rooms. Copper Horse Lodge has spacious but more austere rooms in modern styles. Highland Lodge has lovely hardwood furniture from India, a welcoming sitting room and a cosy, woody bar. In Golden, one reader has stayed at the Auberge Kicking Horse B&B twice ('good – and good value').
Apartments The Whispering Pines town homes were 'the most luxurious ski lodgings we've had', said a reporter. The 'luxurious' Selkirk apartments have also been recommended.
Eating out Eagle's Eye at the top of the gondola opens at weekends ('the finest of fine dining, with prices to match'). Ronnie's Local Hero pub in Highland Lodge does 'well-priced' modern Canadian cooking with a Scottish flavour. Corks in Copper Horse Lodge does 'excellent food and friendly service'. Kuma is a sushi bar. Peaks Grill is a big restaurant in Glacier Lodge. In Golden, Kicking Horse Grill, Eleven22 and the out-of-town Cedar House are highly rated.
Après-ski Quiet. As a 2009 visitor says, 'It's a great resort if your idea of après is a meal, a drink and bed.' The liveliest place as the lifts close is reportedly Ronnie's Local Hero with its deck, blazing outdoor fireplace and music. In Golden the Mad Trapper and Golden Taps are lively bars.
Off the slopes There is snowmobiling, snowshoeing, dog sledding, tubing and an outdoor ice rink.

Lake Louise

Stunning views and the biggest ski area in the Banff region, with some good places to stay but no real village

£75
RESORT PRICE INDEX

RATINGS

The mountains

Extent	★★★
Fast lifts	★★★★
Queues	★★★★
Terrain p'ks	★★
Snow	★★★
Expert	★★★★
Intermediate	★★★★
Beginner	★★★
X-country	★★★★★
Restaurants	★★
Schools	★★★★
Families	★★★★

The resort

Charm	★★★
Convenience	★
Scenery	★★★★
Eating out	★★
Après-ski	★★
Off-slope	★★★★

NEWS

For 2008/09 the old Ptarmigan quad was replaced; the new chair is more efficient and comfortable, but is still slow.

And a serious terrain park was re-opened, following removal of the jumps the previous season. Further park improvements are due for 2009/10.

➕ Spectacular high-mountain scenery, in a largely unspoilt wilderness

➕ Large ski area by local standards

➕ Snowy slopes of Sunshine Village within reach (see Banff chapter)

➕ Lots of wildlife around the valley

➕ Good value for money

➖ 'Village' is just a few hotels and shops, quiet in the evening

➖ Local slopes a short drive from the 'village', Sunshine much further

➖ Snowfall record modest

➖ Can be very cold, and the chairlifts have no covers

If you care more for scenery than for après-ski action, Lake Louise is worth considering for a holiday. We've seen a few spectacular mountain views, and the view from the Fairmont Chateau Lake Louise hotel of the Victoria Glacier across the frozen Lake Louise is as spectacular as they come: simply stunning.

Even if you prefer the more animated base of Banff, you'll want to make expeditions to Lake Louise during your holiday. It can't compete with Sunshine Village for quantity of snow, but it's an interesting mountain. And from the slopes you get a distant version of that stunning view.

THE RESORT

Lake Louise is small, but it's a resort of three distinct parts. First, there's the splendid lake itself overlooked by the huge Fairmont Chateau Lake Louise hotel. Then there's Lake Louise 'village' – a spacious collection of hotels, condos, petrol station, liquor store and a few shops a couple of miles away in the valley bottom. Finally, a mile or two across the valley, there's the lift base station.

You'll probably want to sample the usually better snow of Sunshine Village, 45 minutes away (buses on certain days only). Bus trips run to the more distant resorts of Kicking Horse and Panorama, subject to demand, and there are heli-skiing day trips.

VILLAGE CHARM ★★★
Low key and relaxed
The 'village' has no focus other than a small shopping mall, but it's a quiet and relaxing place. Up at the lake, it's all about the setting: the scenery provides the charm, and somehow the scale of the giant hotel seems perfectly appropriate.

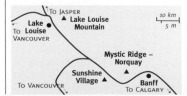

CONVENIENCE ★
Lake or village, not slopes
Most lodging is around the 'village'. Buses run every half hour to the ski area. Staying up at the Chateau, or near it, just means a longer bus ride. If you need to resort to taxis, they are said to be 'ridiculously expensive'.

SCENERY ★★★★
Splendid lakes and mountains
Lake Louise itself is in a spectacular setting beneath the Victoria Glacier. Tom Wilson, who discovered it in 1882, declared: 'As God is my judge, I never in all my exploration have seen such a matchless scene.' Neither have we. And it can be appreciated from many of the rooms of the hotel on the lake shore. And there are grand views of other peaks and glaciers, including Canada's Matterhorn lookalike, Mount Assiniboine, from the ski area.

THE MOUNTAINS

There's an attractive mixture of high, open slopes, low trails cut through forest and gladed slopes between the two. There are good free guided tours at 10am and 1.15pm. Louise is known for fiercely low temperatures; we've luckily escaped them on recent visits.

When conditions are poor, the ski patrol may erect temporary signs at the start of some blue runs indicating black difficulty – an interesting development.

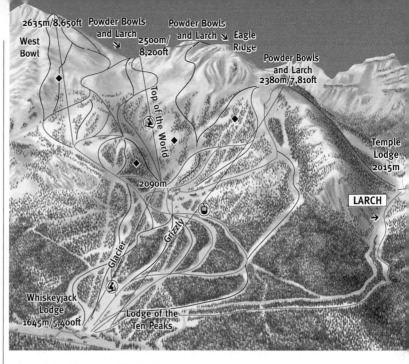

KEY FACTS

Resort	1645m
	5,400ft

Sunshine, Norquay and Lake Louise, covered by the Tri-area pass

Slopes	1630-2730m	
	5,350-8,950ft	
Lifts		26
Pistes	7,748 acres	
Green		23%
Blue		39%
Black		38%
Snowmaking		24%

Lake Louise only

Slopes	1645-2635m	
	5,400-8,650ft	
Lifts		9
Pistes	4,200 acres	
Green		25%
Blue		45%
Black		30%
Snowmaking		40%

EXTENT OF THE SLOPES ★★★★★
A wide variety
The Lake Louise ski area is a fair size by North American standards – it ranks sixth in skiable area – but is quite modest by Alpine standards; a good intermediate could ski the groomed trails in a day or two.

From the base area you have a choice of a fast quad to mid-mountain, followed by a six-pack to the top centre of the **Front Side** (or South Face), or the gondola direct to a slightly lower point off to the right side. From both, as elsewhere, there's a choice of green, blue or black runs (good for a group of mixed abilities who want to keep meeting up). In poor visibility, the gondola is a better option, as the treeline goes almost to the top there. Or you can stay on the lower part of the mountain using the chairs. From mid-mountain on the left, the long Summit draglift takes you to the high point of the area.

From here or the top chair you can go over the ridge and into the **Powder Bowls** – almost treeless, shady and mainly steep (though there are easy ways round the steep parts). From the top of the gondola, the Ptarmigan area is more wooded. From below the bowls you can take the Paradise lift back to the top again or go on down to Temple Lodge, base station of the Ptarmigan chair back to the main mountain and a fast chair to the separate **Larch** area. Its lift-served vertical is a modest 375m/1,230ft, but the sector has pretty wooded runs of all levels. From Temple Lodge there's a long green path back to the base area.

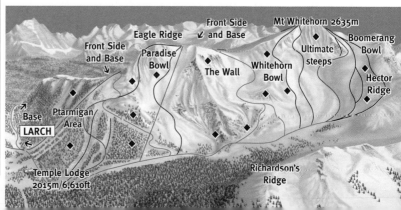

↑ Sunny slopes above the base area, and majestic scenery beyond

SNOWPIX.COM / CHRIS GILL

LIFT PASSES

Tri-area lift pass

Prices in C$

Age	1-day	6-day
under 13	26	237
13 to 17	55	448
18 to 64	80	504
over 65	55	448

Free under 6

Beginner lift, lesson and rental package

Notes

Day pass is for Lake Louise only; 3-day-plus pass covers all lifts and transport between Banff, Lake Louise, Norquay and Sunshine Village; prices include tax

FAST LIFTS ★★★★
Beware the cold rides
There is gondola and fast chair access to most of the slopes on the Front Side, and to Larch. The few slow lifts serve steep slopes where your descent may take some time, so the lift ride time is bearable. Reporters regularly complain of extremely cold rides.

QUEUES ★★★★
Not unknown
Half of the area's visitors come for the day from nearby cities, such as Calgary, so there can be queues for some lifts at weekends and public holidays ('but still only five minutes', say 2009 visitors). More of a problem can be busy pistes and breakdowns. Even the new Ptarmigan chair does not seem to be immune: 'We experienced a 25-minute stoppage,' says one reporter.

TERRAIN PARKS ★★
It's back, but smaller
To much local discontent, the park was closed in 2008, after the resort's owners deemed man-made jumps too dangerous. The good news, though, is that the park was back last season and is due to be further improved for 2009/10. As previously, it is situated below the Glacier Chair on the front

side and features 15 different rails, boxes and six moderate jumps. It isn't as progressive and advanced as before, but the resort says it's 'an excellent place to go to have fun and practise your skills'.

SNOW RELIABILITY ★★★
Usually OK
Lake Louise gets around 140 inches a year on the Front Side, which is not a lot, and nowhere near as much as Sunshine Village down the road (see Banff chapter). The front side faces south-west, which is not good; but the Powder Bowls face north-east, and Larch about north. Snowmaking covers 40% of the pistes. Grooming is fine.

FOR EXPERTS ★★★★
Widespread pleasure
There are plenty of steep slopes. On the Front Side, as well as a score of marked black-diamond trails in and above the trees, there is the alluring West Bowl, reached from the Summit drag – a wide, open expanse of snow outside the area boundary. Because this is National Park territory, you can in theory go anywhere and there's a great sense of exploration among the trees lower down. But outside the boundaries there are no patrols and, of course, no avalanche control. A guide is essential.

Inside the boundaries, the Powder Bowls area offers countless black mogul/powder runs. From the Summit drag, you can drop into The Ultimate Steeps (if it is open), directly behind the peak – a row of exceptional chutes almost 1km/0.5 miles long. Starting from the blue Boomerang trails, you can also access much tamer, wide, open slopes in Boomerang Bowl.

The Top of the World six-pack takes you to the very popular Paradise Bowl/ Eagle Ridge/Quadra Ridge area, also served by its own triple chair on the back side – there are endless variants here, ranging from comfortably steep single diamonds to very challenging double diamonds. The seriously steep slope served by the Ptarmigan quad chair has great gladed terrain and is a good place to beat the crowds and find good snow. The Larch area has some steep double-diamond stuff in the trees. And with good snow cover, the open snowfields at the top are great for those with the energy to hike up. Heli-skiing is available outside the National Park.

boarding

Lake Louise is a great mountain for freeriders, with all the challenging terrain in the bowls and glades. The two sides of the mountain mean there is ample space at this sometimes very crowded resort. Get up early and head to the Powder Bowls first thing for some epic fun. Ask a local or hire a guide to get the best out of the bowls, as there is often great terrain only a short hike away. Beginners will have fun on the Front Side's blue and green runs. But there's a T-bar at the base area and beware of the vicious Summit button lift (top left looking at the trail map). Also avoid the long green run through the woods from Larch back to base. This is tedious for skiers, but a nightmare for boarders. Freestylers will be happy to know that the terrain park has been restored to something like its former glory, jumps and all, after a year or two out of commission.

SCHOOLS

Ski Big 3
t 760 7731

Lake Louise
t 522 1333

Classes (Big 3 prices)
3 days guided tuition of the three areas
C$285 incl. tax

Private lessons
Half day (3hr) C$387, incl. tax, for up to 5 people

CHILDCARE

Telus Play Station & Daycare
t 522 3555
Ages 18 days to 6yr; 8.30-4.30

Ski school
Takes ages 6 to 12 (3 days C$285, incl. tax and lunch)

UK PACKAGES

Alpine Answers, AmeriCan Ski, Canadian Affair, Crystal, Crystal Finest, First Choice, Frontier, Funway Holidays, Independent Ski Links, Inghams, Kuoni, Made to Measure, Neilson, Simply Alpine, Ski Activity, Ski Dream, Ski Independence, Ski Line, Ski Safari, Skitracer, Skiworld, Supertravel, Thomson, Trailfinders, United Vacations, Virgin Snow

FOR INTERMEDIATES ★★★★
Some good cruising

Almost half the runs are classified as intermediate. But from the top of the Front Side the blue runs down are little more than paths in places, and there are very few blues or greens in the Powder Bowls. Once you get part-way down the Front Side the blues are much more interesting. And when groomed, the Men's and Ladies' Downhill black runs are great fast cruises on the lower half of the mountain. Juniper in the same area is a varied cruise. Meadowlark is a beautiful treelined run to the base area – to find it from the Grizzly Express gondola, first follow Eagle Meadows. The Larch area has some short but ideal intermediate runs – and reporters have enjoyed the natural lumps and bumps of the aptly named blue, Rock Garden ('never had so much fun; really away from it all'). The adventurous should also try the blue Boomerang run – which starts with a short side-step up from the top of the Summit drag – and some of the ungroomed Powder Bowls terrain.

FOR BEGINNERS ★★★
Some long greens

Louise offers first-timers a 'discover skiing or boarding' package that includes a lift pass, with a day or half-day tuition. There is a decent nursery area near the base, served by a short T-bar. You progress to the gentle, wide Wiwaxy (a designated and policed 'slow ski zone'), Pinecone Way and the slightly more difficult Deer Run or Eagle Meadows. The greens in the Powder Bowls and in the Larch area are worth trying for the views, though some do contain slightly steep pitches and can get busy ('our beginner was very nervous trying the Saddleback Bowl').

FOR CROSS-COUNTRY ★★★★★
High in quality and quantity

It's a very good area for cross-country, with around 80km/50 miles of groomed trails in the National Park – plenty of scenic stops needed. There are 14km/9 miles of excellent trails in the local area and at Lake Louise itself. An alternative is the secluded Emerald Lake Lodge, 40km/25 miles away and with some lovely trails.

MOUNTAIN RESTAURANTS ★★
Good base facilities

There is now only one proper hut on the mountain, as the Whitehorn Lodge no longer opens in winter. The Temple Lodge near the bottom of Larch and the Ptarmigan chair is a rustic style building with table- and self-service restaurants, but can get 'unpleasantly' crowded. Most people eat at the base, where there are big-scale facilities. Whiskyjack Lodge has reopened the World Cup Alpine Room, now offering fixed-price, 'high quality' buffet lunches. The Lodge of the Ten Peaks is a hugely impressive log-built affair with various eating, drinking and lounging options including the Great Bear Room self-service.

SCHOOLS AND GUIDES ★★★★
More positive reports

Our 2009 reports on the school are encouraging, both for adult and for children's classes: 'excellent private lessons'; 'great instructor who worked hard to make sure everyone in our mixed-ability group learnt new stuff'; 'the children made good progress and enjoyed themselves'. Be aware though that your instructor may change from day to day – a common system in North America. See the Banff chapter for details on the excellent three-day, three-mountain Club Ski and Club Snowboard Program.

↑ Believe it or not, there are several named runs through these trees in the Ptarmigan area, above Temple Lodge
SNOWPIX.COM / CHRIS GILL

GETTING THERE

Air Calgary 195km/ 120 miles (2hr30)

ACTIVITIES

Indoor Mainly hotel-based pools, saunas and hot tubs

Outdoor Ice rinks, walking, swimming in hot springs, sleigh rides, dog sledding, snowmobiling

Phone numbers
From distant parts of Canada, add the prefix 1 403; from abroad, add the prefix +1 403

TOURIST OFFICE

t 522 3555
info@skilouise.com
www.skilouise.com
www.SkiBig3.com

FOR FAMILIES ★★★★
Fairly positive
The resort is keen to attract families and has decent school and childcare facilities. The Minute Maid Wilderness Adventure Park is a kids' learning area at the base. The school gets good reviews and now offers a fun learning programme for teenagers.

STAYING THERE

You might like to consider a two-centre holiday, combining Lake Louise with, say, Banff or Kicking Horse.
Hotels Summer is the peak season here. Prices are much lower in winter.
★★★★★Fairmont Chateau Lake Louise (522 3511) Grand monster with 500 rooms and seven restaurants in a fantastic setting with stunning views over frozen Lake Louise to the glacier beyond; shops, pool, hot tub, sauna.
★★★★Post (522 3989) Small, relaxed, comfortable Relais & Châteaux place in the village, with excellent restaurant (huge wine list), pool, hot tub, steam room. Avoid rooms on railway side.
★★★Lake Louise Inn (522 3791) Cheaper option in the village, with pool, hot tub and sauna. Various suites. 'Comfortable, convenient and good breakfasts.'

★★★Deer Lodge (522 3991) Charming old hotel next to the Chateau. 'Small rooms, but helpful staff; good food.' 'Amazing' roof-top hot tub.
Apartments Some are available but local shopping is limited. The Baker Creek Chalets (522 3761) are a popular retreat for a traditional 'log cabin, log fire, isolation and wildlife' experience.
At altitude Skoki Lodge (253 6888) is a charming log cabin, 11km/7 miles on skis from Temple Lodge. Built in the 1930s, it sleeps 22. Reports welcome.

EATING OUT ★★
Limited choice
The Post hotel's restaurant has repeatedly impressed us and reporters with its ambitious food and excellent service – 'exceptional, if expensive', 'stunning lunch', 'very welcoming'. The Fairview Dining Room at the Chateau is also top-notch. For something cheaper, the Timberwolf Cafe at the Inn and the Outpost at the Post are recommended. And a 2009 reporter had an 'excellent' meal at the Num-ti-Jah Lodge near Bow Lake, about 30-minutes drive away.

APRES-SKI ★★
Lively at teatime, quiet later
At close of play there is some action in the main base lodge but the hub is the Kokanee Kabin, which has live music most weekends, outdoor fire and terrace. Later on, things are fairly quiet. Try the Glacier Saloon, the Explorer's Lounge in the Lake Louise Inn or the Outpost Pub in the Post hotel.

OFF THE SLOPES ★★★★
Beautiful scenery
Lake Louise makes a lovely, peaceful place to stay for someone who does not intend to hit the slopes but enjoys the great outdoors. The lake itself makes a stunning setting for walks, snowshoeing, cross-country skiing and ice skating. A reporter highly recommends the Wilson Icefield discovery tour – a helicopter flight, snowshoe walk and lunch ('barbecue with superb steaks'). There are lots of attractions around the Banff area too (see that chapter for more). Banff also has good touristy shopping.

Lake Louise is near one end of the Columbia Icefields Parkway, a three-hour drive to Jasper through National Parks – one of the world's most beautiful drives.

Panorama

A purpose-built Intrawest resort with an unusual mountain –
not many lifts, but a sizeable area and an impressive vertical

+ Car-free village with some slope-side lodgings, plus a lower part
+ Fair-sized ski area with big vertical
+ Runs are usually deserted

− Not many easy cruising runs
− Snowfall record not impressive by high local standards
− Quiet, even lifeless village

TOP 10 RATINGS

Extent	**★★**★★★
Fast lifts	**★★★**
Queues	**★★★★★**
Snow	**★★★**
Expert	**★★★★**
Intermediate	**★★★**
Beginner	**★★★★**
Charm	**★★**
Convenience	**★★★★**
Scenery	**★★★**

NEWS

For 2008/09 the beginner area was extended and a new moving carpet installed to replace a rope tow.

The Showoff terrain park was revamped and moved to a better position under the Mile One Quad. And 'learn to ski' packages were introduced.

Panorama's vertical of 1220m/4,000ft is one of the biggest in North America, and it has some excellent terrain for experts and adventurous intermediates. It's good for beginners, too. But timid intermediates may find themselves confined to the rather limited lower mountain.

THE RESORT

Panorama is a small, quiet, purpose-built resort above the lakeside town of Invermere in eastern British Columbia, about two hours' scenic drive south-west of Banff. Lodging is concentrated mainly in two car-free areas.

The resort also runs day trips to Lake Louise and Kicking Horse (given a demand).

Village charm Accommodation at the foot of the main slopes is quite attractive, centred around a hot-pool complex and skating rink and with a lovely mountain backdrop. But the 'lower village' where most of the lodging resides lacks character or life.

Convenience The best place to stay for ski-in/ski-out convenience is the 'upper village'. The 'lower village' is linked to it and to the slopes by a bucket lift that runs until 10pm.

Scenery Panorama's tall slopes are heavily wooded, and there are good views from the mountain.

THE MOUNTAINS

The slopes basically follow three ridges, joined at top and bottom. Almost all of the terrain is wooded. Helpful handwritten boards at the lifts show trail conditions. Free tours of the mountain run twice daily. Night skiing is offered Thursday to Saturday.

Slopes From the upper village, a fast quad goes over gentle slopes to mid-mountain, and above it another fast quad serves both intermediate and expert slopes. Then a slow quad takes you to the summit. From here there are long blue and black runs down various ridges and two expert bowls.

Fast lifts Most people spend their time on only four lifts, of which two are fast – so a high proportion.

Queues We get no reports of queues, but the Sunbird triple chair is said to be prone to breakdowns.

Terrain parks The main Showoff park is 1km/0.5 mile long and now has a new position under the Mile One Quad. You can hit ten to 12 features in a row, with jumps, boxes and rails. There is a small, novice park by the Toby lift, floodlit until 9pm.

Snow reliability Annual snowfall is low by local standards (188 inches – about half the Fernie figure). But 40% of trails are covered by snowmaking.

Experts There are genuine black runs scattered all over the mountain, and some expert-only areas. At the very top of the mountain and accessed through a gate is the Extreme Dream

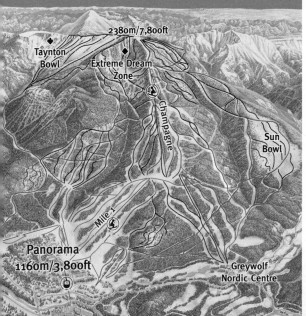

238om/7,8ooft

Taynton Bowl

Extreme Dream Zone

Champagne

Sun Bowl

Mile 1

Panorama
1160m/3,800ft

Greywolf Nordic Centre

↑ There's now quite a range of lodgings in the upper village, at the foot of the slopes

PANORAMA MOUNTAIN VILLAGE

KEY FACTS

Resort	1160m
	3,800ft
Slopes	1160-2380m
	3,800-7,800ft
Lifts	9
Pistes	2,847 acres
Green	20%
Blue	55%
Black	25%
Snowmaking	40%

UK PACKAGES

AmeriCan Ski, Canadian Affair, Frontier, Inghams, Simply Alpine, Ski Dream, Ski Independence, Ski Safari, Snoworks

Central reservations
Call 342 6941

Phone numbers
From distant parts of Canada, add the prefix 1 250; from abroad, add +1 250

TOURIST OFFICE

t 342 6941
paninfo@intrawest.com
www.skipanorama.com

Zone – seriously steep trails with cliffs and tight trees. Off the back of the summit is Taynton Bowl – excellent, varied terrain; some open areas, some lightly and some more densely forested areas; very few people; best snow on the hill. It is almost all classed as double diamond, but it really isn't worryingly steep. But doing laps is a slow business – a long blue cruise run-out, then three lifts (one slow). RK Heli-Skiing is based in the village and specialises in one-day sessions for first-time heli-skiers.

Intermediates For adventurous intermediates the terrain is excellent – there are easy blacks all over the mountain, some of them regularly groomed. The black View of 1000 Peaks has fabulous views but can be a bit tricky in parts. Both this and the blue run from the top are long for North America (up to 3.5km/2 miles). Sun Bowl is a good introduction to a powder bowl and Millennium (black running into blue) is a great roller coaster. But the less confident may find all this uncomfortably challenging. The blues in the centre of the area are gentler but they don't add up to a lot. Adventurous intermediates should consider a day's heli-skiing.

Beginners Beginner packages are available through the school. There are a couple of lifts and new moving carpet serving a quiet, gentle nursery area. There are good, longer runs to progress to on the Mile 1 fast quad.

Snowboarding There is good steep terrain and tree runs for expert freeriders. The main lifts are all chairs, and beginners have several good long green runs to practise on.

Cross-country There are 20km/12 miles of trails starting at the Nordic Centre.

Mountain restaurants The only real choice on the slopes is the Elkhorn Cabin, a tiny, charming old mountain hut (complete with roaring log fire)

that could almost be in the Alps. Reserve a table for the C$17 two-course lunch.

Schools and guides The ski school generally gets glowing reports. 'The private lessons were very professional, good value and included a free lunch,' says a 2009 visitor. There are various specialist programmes too.

Families There is quite a lot for families, including the outdoor pool and kids' themed nights. The school runs Snowbirds for three to four year olds, and the Adventure Club for kids from 5 to 14. Wee Wascals is the childcare centre, taking children from 18 months to five years. Evening babysitters are also available.

STAYING THERE

The better places are the newer ones in the upper village.

Hotels Earl Grey Lodge is a smart, central, six-bedroom, log-built place.

Apartments The Ski Tip Lodge is the best located in the resort, beside the Mile High Quad. The slope-side Panorama Springs has a big outdoor hot-pool and sauna. The 1000 Peaks Summit and 1000 Peaks Lodge are comfortable and spacious. It's best to stock up on groceries in Invermere.

Eating out There are a few options. At the top end is Greys (at the Earl Grey Lodge), with its excellent fixed menus. Chopper's Landing has 'good menus and a relaxed, friendly atmosphere'. Alternatives include the Wildfire Grill (seafood) and the Great Hall (pasta and pizza). The ski school organises BBQs at the Elkhorn Cabin (see 'Mountain restaurants'), followed by a torchlit descent. There's a horse-drawn wagon ride to enjoy chilli around a campfire. The town of Invermere is worth an evening out – there's a bus once each evening. Try Angus McToogle's, Portabellas or Strands.

Après-ski This revolves around the Crazy Horse Saloon (Pine Inn), which has live music, and the Alpine style Jackpine pub (Horsethief Lodge). Ski Tip Lodge is popular as the lifts close.

Off the slopes The hot-pool facility – with thermal baths, a swimming pool, slides and a sauna – is excellent, but it gets rather taken over by kids. There is dog sledding, snowmobiling, ice fishing, snowshoeing and skating. The Wolf Education Centre and Bavin Glassworks ('quirky handmade glass jewellery') are worth visiting.

Revelstoke

New resort rapidly acquiring cult status for its steep terrain; shame it's so remote and without a proper village yet

- ➕ Fabulous, steep, ungroomed terrain
- ➕ Great cat- and heli-skiing
- ➕ Stunning views over frozen Columbia river
- ➕ Good-value lodging in town

- ➖ Very remote location
- ➖ Not much intermediate terrain
- ➖ Revelstoke town unremarkable and a 15-minute drive away
- ➖ Resort base village still being built

TOP 10 RATINGS

Extent	★★★
Fast lifts	★★★★★
Queues	★★★★★
Snow	★★★★★
Expert	★★★★★
Intermediate	★★
Beginner	★
Charm	★★
Convenience	★
Scenery	★★★★

NEWS

For 2008/09 the gondola was extended down from the Day Lodge to the Village, the Ripper fast quad chair opened, and the size of the ski area doubled. The first accommodation at the base opened in Nelsen Lodge in March 2009.

Until 2007/08 Revelstoke was a small hill for locals served by one short lift. But a gondola and two fast chairs have transformed it into a resort with the biggest vertical in North America and around 3,000 acres of slopes, more than many Canadian rivals. Its terrain is mostly ungroomed and steep; if you enjoy adventure skiing, put it on your shortlist. Consider combining it with other resorts as a 2- or 3-centre holiday. The first stage of a resort village at the base opened in 2009, but for now the best place to stay is Revelstoke town.

THE RESORT

Revelstoke is remote. Getting there from the UK involves two flights to get to Kelowna or Kamloops followed by a three-hour drive. Or it's a drive of five or six hours from Calgary, or seven or eight hours from Vancouver; and that's in good weather. The Village at the base of the gondola will be a building site for the next few years. Better to stay in Revelstoke town for more choice of lodging and restaurants.

Village charm The town is the standard North American grid pattern with a mix of unremarkable old and new buildings. It's very much a locals' working town rather than a resort.
Convenience The mountain is a 15- to 20-minute drive away. Last season there were five ('unreliable') buses to and from the mountain each day.
Scenery The views over the partly frozen Columbia river are stunning, as are the towering peaks rising up around the slopes.

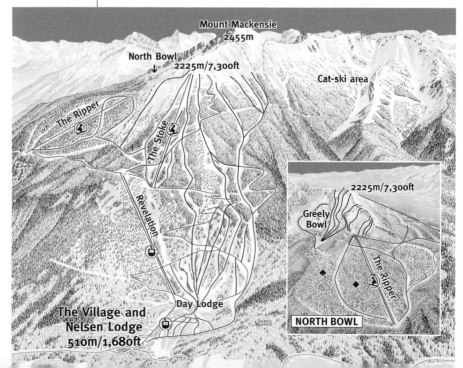

Mount Mackensie
2455m

North Bowl
2225m/7,300ft

Cat-ski area

The Ripper

The Stoke

Revelation

2225m/7,300ft

Greely Bowl

The Ripper

Day Lodge

NORTH BOWL

The Village and Nelsen Lodge
510m/1,680ft

↑ There are great views over the partly frozen Columbia river

REVELSTOKE / DOUG MARSHALL

KEY FACTS

Resort	510m
	1,680ft
Slopes	510-2225m
	1,680-7,300ft
Lifts	4
Pistes	3,031 acres
Green	10%
Blue	42%
Black	48%
Snowmaking	none

UK PACKAGES

Canadian Affair, Crystal, Frontier, Momentum, Powder Skiing in North America, Ski Freshtracks, Ski Safari, Skiworld

Phone numbers
From distant parts of Canada add the prefix 1 250; from abroad use the prefix +1 250

TOURIST OFFICE

t 837 0087
info@ revelstoke
mountainresort.com
www.revelstoke
mountainresort.com

THE MOUNTAINS

A gondola takes you from the Village or the Day Lodge mid-station to mid-mountain, from which you can reach both the fast quads. The trail map marks black runs, but there's no single/double diamond differentiation. And reporters remark that lots of the runs are much longer than they appear from the map. Free mountain tours leave at 10am and 1pm. Be prepared for extreme cold (–41°C with wind chill on our December visit; –27°C on a reporter's March visit) – though obviously it's not always this cold.

Extent Its 3,031 acres make it bigger than most other Canadian resorts. It also has over 2,200 acres of cat-skiing, accessed directly from the slopes.

Fast lifts All three main lifts are fast.

Queues We have no reports of queues. Trails are quiet too.

Terrain parks There isn't one.

Snow reliability They claim an average of 480 to 720 inches a year – up there with Alta and Snowbird.

Experts Experts are flocking to Revelstoke. On skier's left, there are long top-to-bottom black runs such as Pitch Black and Snow Rodeo, some of which turn into steep blues on the lower slopes and many of which are often groomed. On skier's right, North Bowl (reached by a long traverse) is a huge area of ungroomed, ski-anywhere, steep terrain. In between are several big areas of glades with nicely spaced trees. Then there's cat-skiing – we did a fabulous day of this among the trees, hitting fresh powder everywhere when the main ski area was windswept; book up well in advance as they have only one cat (which holds 12 people). There's heli-skiing right from the base too.

Intermediates Most blues are steepish and suit adventurous intermediates best. The Ripper chair accesses the easiest blues. And there's a 15km/9.5 mile long blue/green run from top to bottom. But the intermediate terrain doesn't add up to much (the claimed 42% gives a misleading impression). The mountain suits experts best.

Beginners Stay away. We didn't see any on our visit.

Snowboarding There's fabulous freeriding terrain but lots of flats to negotiate, especially at the entry to and exit from North Bowl.

Cross-country There are 22km/14 miles of groomed trails.

Queues Not an issue.

Mountain restaurants The Day Lodge serves good food but gets packed. A small hut at the top of the gondola does soup, snacks and hot drinks. The new Nelsen Lodge at the base will have a restaurant.

Schools and guides The ski school programme is designed to help people progress from the groomed runs to the ungroomed and backcountry.

STAYING THERE

Hotels The first stage of Nelsen Lodge at the base opened in March 2009, but the area will be a building site for the next few years. Revelstoke has several motels and a few more charming B&Bs and hotels. We stayed at the Courthouse Inn (837 3369), which was friendly and did a great breakfast. A reporter enjoyed the Inn on the River (837 3262) with 'great views over the river from both our suite and the hot tub'. The Regent Inn (837 2107) dates from the 1920s and is central, with bar, restaurant, hot tub and sauna.

Eating out There are a few good coffee shops in town ('The Modern is the best,' says a reporter). Dining options include Woolsey Creek ('fine dining'), Zala's ('nice halibut, pizzas'), Bad Paul's ('family-friendly, huge portions') and Kawakubo ('awesome sushi'). Nelsen Lodge promises 'Asian fusion'.

Après-ski Try the Village Idiot, Last Drop (comfy sofas, log fire; in Powder Springs Inn) and River City (music, pool; in Regent Inn) – and the local Mt Begbie beers. The Cabin has a bowling alley, and Traverse is a strip club.

Off the slopes The Aquatic Centre is good, with pools, hot tubs, sauna, steam (free ticket from some hotels).

Silver Star

Tiny, car-free, purpose-built village designed to resemble a Victorian-era mining town, with slopes for all standards

➕ Atmospheric purpose-built village

➕ Very family-friendly

➕ Some good runs for all abilities

➕ Excellent cross-country skiing

➖ Tiny village with little choice of bars and restaurants; very quiet at night

➖ Limited choice of accommodation

➖ Ski area not huge

TOP 10 RATINGS

Extent	★★★
Fast lifts	★★★★
Queues	★★★★★
Snow	★★★★
Expert	★★★★
Intermediate	★★★
Beginner	★★★★
Charm	★★★
Convenience	★★★★★
Scenery	★★★

This quiet, family-friendly resort has a tiny traffic-free centre resembling a 19th-century mining town. There are slopes to suit everyone, and it's easy to combine a stay here with one at Big White, which has the same owners.

THE RESORT

Silver Star is a small resort, purpose-built since the 1980s right on the slopes. Big White (see separate chapter) is around two and a half hours away and under the same ownership; twice-a-week transfers make a two-centre holiday easy and you can also just go for the day.
Village charm The village has brightly painted Victorian-style buildings with wooden sidewalks and pseudo gas lights. It's a bit Disneyesque but works surprisingly well.

Convenience The centre is compact and car-free. Ski-in/ski-out chalets are dotted in the trees too.
Scenery The views from Silver Star's summit are predominantly woody, over gently rolling mountains.

THE MOUNTAINS

The mountain has trees going right to the top and three main linked faces. Free tours are offered twice a day.
Slopes The mainly south-facing Vance Creek slopes around the village have largely easy intermediate runs served

687

NEWS

For 2009/10 a boardercross and a beginners' terrain park with 12 rails and boxes are planned, both on Vance Creek. Firelight Lodge, a luxury 44-unit condo complex, is due to open, as is a new pizzeria.

For 2008/09 Kelowna airport (one hour away) was improved to take bigger planes (including transatlantic flights). A Swiss style restaurant, Isidore's, opened in the 'village' for evening dining only.

KEY FACTS

Resort	1610m
	5,280ft
Slopes	1155-1915m
	3,790-6,280ft
Lifts	12
Pistes	3,065 acres
Green	20%
Blue	50%
Black	30%
Snowmaking	none

UK PACKAGES

AmeriCan Ski, Canadian Affair, Frontier, Made to Measure, Ski Dream, Ski Independence, Ski Line, Ski Safari, Skiworld

Central reservations
Call 558 6083; toll-free (within Canada) 1 800 663 4431
Phone numbers
From distant parts of Canada, add the prefix 1 250; from abroad, add +1 250

TOURIST OFFICE

t 542 0224
info@skisilverstar.com
www.skisilverstar.com

by a six-pack, which starts below the main village. From there you can reach the Silver Woods area of north-east-facing, mainly intermediate slopes and glades, served by a high-speed quad. The top of the Vance Creek area links to the Putnam Creek face on the back side, which has lots of steep black and double-black trails, mostly with big moguls, served by a fast quad. But you can stick to easier alternatives too. There are some flattish areas, including the link with the back side.

Fast lifts There's one for each sector.

Queues We've no reports of queues.

Terrain parks The 16-acre Telus park on the Vance Creek side has tabletops, hips, fun boxes, rails, wall rides, an Aerial Training Site with big air jumps and a half-pipe. A beginner park and a boardercross are due for 2009/10.

Snow reliability Silver Star gets an average of 276 inches a year, not in the top flight but not far off.

Experts Putnam Creek has a dense network of single and double black diamond runs plunging through the trees, many of them mogul runs – 'in a league of its own' says a 2009 visitor. The runs to the left as you ride up the chair are north-facing and keep their snow well. There are some short blacks on the Vance Creek side, too.

Intermediates Vance Creek has mainly easy cruising runs. Silver Woods has lovely runs cut through the trees and easy blue gladed runs amid the trees themselves. Putnam Creek also has excellent blue cruising – we especially liked Gypsy Queen and Sunny Ridge. Good intermediates will appreciate the two black runs they groom daily (look on the boards for which they are).

Beginners There's a nursery area by the village with a moving carpet and long easy green runs to move on to.

Snowboarding There's a T-bar at the top of the Putnam side, but the other lifts are all chairs. Several flattish areas make life difficult though.

Cross-country Cross-country is big; they claim 'The Best Nordic Skiing in North America'. There are 105km/65 miles of trails, some at altitude.

Mountain restaurants The small atmospheric Paradise Camp on Putnam Creek, is popular and 'has good snacks and drinks'.

Schools and guides The ski school has a good reputation. A 2009 reporter said, 'My wife was a beginner and, after three half-days, was skiing blue runs with great confidence.'

Families Star Kids takes children aged five and under. 'Our children loved it,' said a recent reporter.

STAYING THERE

It is mainly specialist North American operators who come here, such as Frontier Ski and Ski Independence.

Hotels Silver Star Club Resort has three separate properties including the Vance Creek right in the village centre.

Apartments The Snowbird and new Firelight Lodges are the best in town, both ski-in/ski-out with private hot tubs. Other recommendations include Chilcoot Lodge, Creekside, Grandview, Pinnacles and renting one of the attractive houses in the woods.

Eating out A 2009 reporter praises the new Isidore's, Bulldog Grand Cafe and Long John's Pub in the Lord Aberdeen Hotel with mining theme decor.

Après-ski It's very quiet. But the Club Saloon and Den Bistro and Bar may be lively and have live entertainment.

Off the slopes There's a pretty natural ice rink on a lake, a nearby tubing hill and horse-drawn sleigh rides.

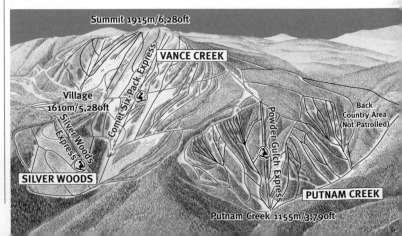

Summit 1915m/6,280ft
VANCE CREEK
Comet Six-Pack Express
Village 1610m/5,280ft
Silver Woods Express
SILVER WOODS
Powder Gulch Express
Back Country Area (Not Patrolled)
PUTNAM CREEK
Putnam Creek 1155m/3,790ft

Sun Peaks

Attractive car-free village at the foot of three linked mountains with varied slopes including some unusual easy groomed glade runs

+ Great terrain for early intermediates
+ Excellent glades
+ Slopes very quiet during the week
+ Good for families

− Village may be too small and quiet for some tastes
− Ski area modest by Alpine standards

TOP 10 RATINGS

Extent	★★★
Fast lifts	★★
Queues	★★★★★
Snow	★★★★
Expert	★★★
Intermediate	★★★★
Beginner	★★★★
Charm	★★★
Convenience	★★★★
Scenery	★★★

NEWS

For 2008/09 new glades for all levels opened in the Lonesome Fir area, accessed from the Sundance Express lift. Snowmaking was increased and the grooming fleet improved. A new bridge was built at Orient Ridge, allowing ski-in/ski-out access to East Village.

Sun Peaks has sprung from the drawing board since the mid-1990s. It now has a friendly, attractive small village and a fair amount of varied terrain – enough for three or four days, say. We suggest combining it with resorts such as Whistler, Silver Star or Big White on a two- or three-centre trip.

THE RESORT

Until 1993 Sun Peaks was Tod Mountain, a local hill for the residents of nearby Kamloops. Since then the ski area has been expanded and a small (smaller than many reporters expect), attractive resort village developed. There are regular transfers to other resorts such as Whistler – making a two-centre trip easy.

Village charm The low-rise pastel-coloured buildings have a vaguely Tirolean feeling to them. It's a pleasant place to stroll around and very family-friendly. The traffic-free main street is lined with lodgings, restaurants and shops, including a smart art gallery, a chocolate shop and a few coffee bars.

Convenience Much of the accommodation is ski-in/ski-out.

Scenery The slopes are pleasantly wooded and Mt Tod's modest summit looks south over gently rolling and gladed terrain.

THE MOUNTAINS

There are three linked mountains but the links to and from Mt Morrisey from the other two are roundabout and flattish. Free guided tours are run twice a day (9.15 and 1pm) and at 1pm you can ski for free with former Olympic champion and Canada's Female Athlete of the 20th Century Nancy Greene when she's in town (don't miss it – she is great fun!). At the top of all main lifts there is a board with the grooming conditions of the pistes in that area.

Slopes With almost 3,700 acres of skiable terrain, Sun Peaks is the second biggest ski area in British Columbia (Whistler is the biggest) – but it's not big by Alpine standards.

One lift goes from the centre of the village to mid-mountain on Sun Peaks' original ski hill, Mt Tod. This has mainly black runs, but there are easier blues and greens. Many of Mt Tod's steepest runs are served only by the slow Burfield quad (there's a mid-station that allows you to ski the top runs only). Also reached from the village centre, the Sundance area has mainly blue and green cruising runs. Both Sundance and Tod have some great gladed areas to play in (12 of them marked on the trail map).

Mt Morrisey is reached by a long green run from the top of Sundance and has a delightful network of easy blue runs with trees left uncut in the trails, effectively making them groomed glade runs that even early intermediates can try.

Fast lifts The three distinct sectors are each served by a high-speed quad. The other lifts are painfully slow.

Queues Weekdays are usually very quiet; it's only at peak weekends that

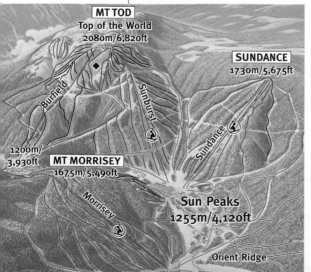

MT TOD
Top of the World
2080m/6,820ft

SUNDANCE
1730m/5,675ft

Burfield

Sunburst

Sundance

1200m/
3,930ft

MT MORRISEY
1675m/5,490ft

Morrisey

Sun Peaks
1255m/4,120ft

Orient Ridge

KEY FACTS

Resort	1255m
	4,120ft
Slopes	1200-2080m
	3,930-6,820ft
Lifts	11
Pistes	3,678 acres
Green	10%
Blue	58%
Black	32%
Snowmaking	3%

UK PACKAGES

AmeriCan Ski, American Ski Classics, Canadian Affair, Erna Low, Frontier, Made to Measure, Simply Alpine, Ski Dream, Ski Freshtracks, Ski Independence, Ski Line, Ski Safari, Skitracer, Skiworld

Phone numbers
From distant parts of Canada, add the prefix 1 250; from abroad, add the prefix +1 250

TOURIST OFFICE

t 578 5474
info@sunpeaksresort.
com
www.sunpeaksresort.
com

you might find short queues.

Terrain parks There are three levels of park on Sundance – advanced with rails, jumps, jibs and fun boxes, plus intermediate and beginner areas. But there is no half-pipe.

Snow reliability Sun Peaks gets an average snowfall of 220 inches a year: not in the top league but better than some. The snow can suffer on the lower part of Mt Tod's south-facing slopes, especially later in the season.

Experts Mt Tod has most of the steep terrain and you can ski some good (but short) steep and gladed runs without descending to the bottom by riding the Burfield quad from its mid-station, and the Crystal and Elevation chairs. Some of the blacks on Mt Morrisey (such as Static Cling) have steep mogul sections, too.

Intermediates This is great terrain for early intermediates, with the easy and charming groomed glades of Mt Morrisey, lovely swooping blues on Sundance and the long 5 Mile run from Mt Tod. More adventurous intermediates can also tackle the easier glades (such as Cahilty) and blacks (such as Peek-A-Boo).

Beginners There are nursery slopes right in the village centre, with long easy greens to progress to.

Snowboarding Boarders can explore the whole mountain. But beware the flat greens to and from Mt Morrisey.

Cross-country 40km/25 miles of trails.

Mountain restaurants The Sunburst Lodge is the only option and gets busy; its cinnamon buns are highly recommended. The Umbrella Cafe at the Morrisey base serves hot soup and sandwiches and 'has the best toilets on the mountain'. And it's easy to return to a village restaurant for lunch – Mountain High Pizza is 'great value'; Bento's Day Lodge has 'a good range of basic hot food and drinks'.

Schools and guides A recent visitor

chose private lessons and 'found the instruction second to none and worth every cent'. Another reporter had a 'fantastic instructor' and was the only person in a group lesson. Her kids 'were happy', too, but her husband found that his lesson (with five others) was 'more like a guided tour'.

Families The playschool takes children from age 18 months and the ski school children from three years.

STAYING THERE

There's a lot of self-catering accommodation as well as hotels.

Hotels Nancy Greene's Cahilty Lodge is a friendly and comfortable ski-in/ski-out base and you get the chance to ski with her and husband Al Raine (former Canadian ski team coach): 'It was great fun skiing with Nancy and Al; good rooms – a very welcoming hotel,' says a reporter. The ski-in/ski-out Delta Sun Peaks Resort (outdoor pool and hot tub) in the village centre is 'luxurious with lovely rooms' and 'really good food'. We've enjoyed staying at both. Fireside Lodge has 'excellent facilities'. Heffley Boutique Inn is family run and 'comfortable'.

Apartments Delta Residences are 'luxurious, ski-in/ski-out and bang in the centre of the village'. Condos at Crystal Forest are 'fully equipped, well designed and tastefully decorated'; other well-positioned condos include McGillivray Creek, Forest Trails, Snow Creek Village and Timberline Village.

Eating out For a small resort, there's a good choice of restaurants. Reader recommendations include Powder Hounds ('friendly and efficient service', 'varied menu'), Steakhouse ('good honest steaks' but 'patchy service'), Servus (more sophisticated food – 'recommended'), Chopstixx ('good Japanese and Thai food but service is slow'), Bella Italia ('good meal') and Mantles in the Delta Sun Peaks ('excellent quality dining').

Après-ski Bottoms, Masa's and Macker's Sports Grill are the main après-ski bars. At weekends MackDaddy's nightclub in The Delta can get lively – 'noisy revellers spilling out at 3am'. There are fondue evenings with torchlit descents and winter bonfires.

Off the slopes You can choose from skating, tubing, tobogganing, snowmobiling, dog sledding, snowshoeing and sleigh rides.

Whistler

North America's biggest mountain, with terrain to suit every standard and a big, purpose-built, largely car-free village

£75
RESORT PRICE INDEX

RATINGS

The mountains

Extent	★★★★
Fast lifts	★★★★★
Queues	★★★
Terrain p'ks	★★★★★
Snow	★★★★
Expert	★★★★★
Intermediate	★★★★★
Beginner	★★★
X-country	★★★
Restaurants	★★
Schools	★★★★★
Families	★★★★

The resort

Charm	★★★
Convenience	★★★★
Scenery	★★★
Eating out	★★★★★
Après-ski	★★★★
Off-slope	★★★

Whistler is justifiably famous for the huge amount of steep skiing available in its high bowls; there's a lot of easy cruising too ↓

- ➕ North America's biggest, both in area and vertical (1610m/5,280ft)
- ➕ Good slopes for most abilities, with an unrivalled combination of high open bowls and woodland trails
- ➕ Good snow record
- ➕ Almost Alpine scenery
- ➕ Attractive modern village at the foot of the slopes, with car-free central areas and lively après-ski
- ➕ Good range of village restaurants (but long waits where you can't book)

- ➖ Proximity to Pacific Ocean means a lot of cloudy weather, and rain at resort level is not unusual
- ➖ Inadequate lift system; long lift queues and crowded runs can be a big problem – especially in peak periods and at weekends
- ➖ Winter Olympics likely to mean some good slopes above Creekside will be closed to the public for much of the 2009/10 season
- ➖ Mountain restaurants are mostly functional (and overcrowded)
- ➖ Resort restaurants oversubscribed

Whistler is unlike any other resort in North America. In some respects – the scale, the scenery, the crowds – it is more like an Alpine resort. But it follows the North American pattern in offering excellent snow and a lot of woodland runs, as well as the high bowls and glaciers that evoke the Alps.

All things considered, the mountain is about the best that North America has to offer, and for us a visit here is always a highlight of the season (except for the crowds). But we'll admit that we are generally lucky with the weather, and haven't had to put up with much rain at resort level – a real hazard. And we time our visits to avoid peak periods and weekends, when queues and overcrowding can be horrendous.

Whistler is hosting many events during this year's 2010 Winter Olympics. In preparation, the resort has made huge investments in infrastructure and base area facilities; but it's the new record-breaking Peak 2 Peak gondola connecting its two mountains that has been hitting the headlines (see 'News').

Whistler's two mountains were at last connected at mid-mountain for 2008/09: the 28-person Peak 2 Peak gondola runs between Whistler's Roundhouse Lodge and the Rendezvous Lodge on Blackcomb in 11 minutes. The lift spans 4.4km/2.7 miles with a capacity of over 2,000 people per hour in each direction.

New rails were built in the terrain parks and the super-pipe was improved. More luxury condos opened at Creekside and several new resort restaurants opened.

The 2010 Vancouver Winter Olympics takes place from 12 to 28 February and the Paralympics from 12 to 21 March. The Alpine and Nordic skiing, bobsleigh etc events will be held in Whistler.

KEY FACTS

Resort	675m
	2,210ft
Altitude	650-2285m
	2,140-7,490ft
Lifts	38
Pistes	8,171 acres
Green	18%
Blue	55%
Black	27%
Snowmaking	7%

THE RESORT

Whistler Village sits at the foot of its two mountains, Whistler and Blackcomb, a scenic 113km/70 mile drive from Vancouver on Canada's west coast. Whistler started as a locals' ski area in 1966 at what is now Whistler Creek (aka Creekside). Whistler Village, a 10-minute bus ride away, was developed in the late 1970s and Upper Village around the base of Blackcomb Mountain, a 10-minute walk from Whistler Village, in the 1980s.

VILLAGE CHARM ★★★
High rise but tasteful
The three main centres are all traffic-free. The architecture is varied and, for a purpose-built resort, quite tasteful – but it is all a bit urban, with lots of blocks approaching 10 storeys high. There are also many chalet-style apartments on the hillsides.

CONVENIENCE ★★★★
Peak 2 Peak makes a difference
Now that the new Peak 2 Peak gondola is in place, Whistler Village, Upper Village and Creekside are all equally convenient – you can easily access both mountains by taking a maximum of three lifts,

Whistler Village has most of the bars, restaurants and shops, and two gondolas (one to each mountain). But some reporters find the central area around Village Square noisy in the early hours. A pedestrian bridge over an access road links the main centre to newer Whistler North, further from the lifts, making a huge car-free area of streets lined with shops, condos and restaurants.

Upper Village is much smaller and quieter. So is Creekside, which has been revamped and expanded and will

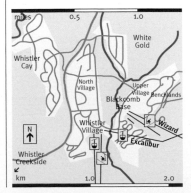

play an important role in the Olympics, with many of the Alpine events finishing above here.

There is a free bus between central Whistler and Upper Village, but it can be just as quick to walk. Some lodging is a long way from the centre and means taking (inexpensive) buses or taxis. Some hotels have free buses, which will pick you up as well as take you to restaurants and nightlife.

SCENERY ★★★
Almost Alpine
There are splendid views of the deep Fitzsimmons Creek valley from both mountains – and especially from the new Peak 2 Peak gondola (which goes right across it – the two gondolas with glass floors are particularly spectacular). The upper slopes give good views to coastal sounds, high open bowls, glaciers and ridges.

THE MOUNTAINS

Whistler and Blackcomb together form the biggest area of slopes, with the longest runs, in North America.

Many reporters enthuse about the mountain host service and the 'go slow' patrol – some find the latter 'over zealous', but crowded slopes, especially on the runs home, mean they're often needed; we approve. Piste maintenance was 'quite shocking' says a 2009 visitor and some blues and greens 'get mogulled quickly'.

EXTENT OF THE SLOPES ★★★★
The biggest in North America
Whistler Mountain is accessed from Whistler Village by a two-stage, 10-person gondola that rises over 1100m/3,610ft to Roundhouse Lodge at mid-mountain. Or you can use two fast quads – if they are running (see feature panel opposite).

Runs down through the trees fan out from the gondola: cruises to the Emerald and Big Red chairs and longer runs to the gondola mid-station.

From Roundhouse you can see the jewel in Whistler's crown – magnificent above-the-treeline bowls, served by the fast Peak and Harmony quads. The bowl beyond Harmony is now served by the Symphony fast quad. The bowls are mostly go-anywhere terrain for experts, but there are groomed trails, so anyone can appreciate the views. Roundhouse is also where you catch the new Peak 2 Peak gondola to

LIFT PASSES

Whistler/Blackcomb

Prices in C$

Age	1-day	6-day
under 13	46	243
13 to 18	76	404
19 to 64	89	473
over 65	76	404

Free under 7

Beginner lift, lesson and rental deal

Notes

Covers Whistler and Blackcomb mountains; prices include sales tax

---

transfer to Blackcomb Mountain.

A six-seat gondola from Creekside also accesses Whistler Mountain.

Access to **Blackcomb** from Whistler Village is by an eight-seat gondola, followed by a fast quad. From the base of Blackcomb you take two consecutive fast quads up to the main Rendezvous restaurant. From there you can go left for great cruising terrain and the Glacier Express quad up to the Horstman Glacier area, or right for steeper slopes, the terrain park or the 7th Heaven chair. The 1610m/5,280ft vertical from the top of 7th Heaven to the base is the biggest in North America. A T-bar from the Horstman Glacier brings you (with a short hike) to the Blackcomb Glacier in the next valley – away from all lifts. You can catch the new Peak 2 Peak gondola to Whistler Mountain from Rendezvous.

Fresh Tracks is a deal that allows you to ride up Whistler Mountain (at extra cost) from 7.15, have a buffet breakfast and get to the slopes as they open – very popular with many reporters. Free guided tours of each mountain are offered at 11.30.

FAST LIFTS ★★★★★
Can't cope with the crowds

The resort has more fast lifts than any other in north America. Gondolas provide the main access, with lots of fast chairs to both tops. But they need updating: amazingly to European eyes, all the fast chairs are quads – with no six-packs or eight seaters that are now common in the Alps.

QUEUES ★★★ ★★
An ever-increasing problem

Whistler has become a victim of its own success. At peak periods (eg Christmas and New Year) and weekends when people pour in from Vancouver queues can be 'horrendous'. There are displays of waiting times at different lifts, which readers generally find useful.

Some reporters have signed up with the ski school just to get lift priority. Others have visited Vancouver at the weekend to avoid the crowds.

The routes out of Whistler Village in the morning can be busy (we had a report last season of a queue of more than 200 metres for the gondola to Blackcomb). Creekside is less of a problem, but gets lengthy queues at weekends. Some of the chairs higher up also produce long queues: the Harmony quad, especially, is no longer up to the job (even the singles line can take ages), and the Emerald chair often has queues. And we had a report of a 45-minute wait for the Peak chair on a Sunday in early January. We have several reports of lift closures – a March 2007 visitor noted the Peak Chair open 'only once during eleven days', and a 2008 visitor said that 'on powder days, it wouldn't open until 11.30'. Another reader found the Fitzsimmons and Garbanzo quads 'rarely open', despite queues for the gondola. Visiting outside peak season may not help – we found some lifts, including the gondola to Blackcomb, were kept closed during a visit in early

Whistler

HOW WHISTLER NEEDS TO IMPROVE

We get lots of reports on Whistler. Nearly all of them heap praise upon the excellent varied terrain and many other aspects of the resort such as the ski school, the après-ski, the quality of village restaurants and the value for money. But an increasing number of them are now complaining about drawbacks that the resort could do something about – mainly to do with overcrowding. Here's a shopping list of improvements that we (and reporters) would like the resort to make:

* Replace outdated fast quads with six- and eight-packs to eliminate some of the appalling peak period queues (see 'Queues'), and build extra runs to cope with the extra people there would be at the top of those lifts

* Restrict the number of day tickets sold (as Lech and Deer Valley do) to prevent serious overcrowding (on pistes as well as lifts) at weekends and peak periods

* Open the lifts till later. Closing at 3pm or 3.30pm until end-Feb is ridiculous

* Open lifts that currently are too often kept shut when there are queues elsewhere – eg the Fitzsimmons chair from the base of Whistler

* Groom more runs more of the time

* Build a new lift with a mid-station up from Creekside to Whistler Peak that could stay open when it's windy and that would allow access to the lower half of the Peak to Creek run without going all the way to the top

* Encourage more restaurants to open, both on and off the mountain

December. Crowds on the slopes, especially the runs home, can be annoying, too.

TERRAIN PARKS ★★★★★
World class for all abilities
The terrain parks had a $40,000 injection to produce new obstacles for 2008/09. There's a good rating system based on size (S, M, L, XL). Novices should begin in the Terrain Garden on Blackcomb. It features small rails and rollers to get a feel for airtime and improve your control. For the S-M line hit the Habitat park by the Emerald chair on Whistler Mountain. Initiate yourself on a host of rails, boxes, medium kickers and a hip. The M-L Nintendo park is huge, but is usually the busiest and is by the Catskinner chairlift on Blackcomb. Step-up jumps, hips, tabletops, rails, boxes: this park will suit most intermediate to advanced riders. Pros and very confident freestylers should hit the Highest Level Park (part of the

One of our favourite runs is behind the mountain away from all the lifts on the Blackcomb glacier – over 1000m/3,280ft vertical to the Excelerator chair

Fabulous, usually deserted, ungroomed slopes are reached by climbing Spanky's Ladder and dropping over the back

New Peak 2 Peak gondola means you no longer have to ski to the village to switch between mountains

Great blue and green cruising, but beginners should beware of some steeper sections on the greens

BLACKCOMB

Horstman Hut
2285m/7,490ft

7th Heaven

Blackcomb Glacier

Horstman Glacier

Rendezvous Lodge
1860

Glacier

Crystal Hut

Jersey Cream
1645m

Solar Coaster

Glacier Creek

Peak 2 Peak

Flute Bowl

Excelerator

1130m

Wizard

Excalibur

Blackcomb Base

Nintendo park); the fact that you need to sign a waiver, wear a helmet and buy a special pass indicates the size of the obstacles here. The super-pipe in Blackcomb is more than 137m/450ft long with 5m/16.5ft high walls, and it's shaped daily. From Thurs to Sat evenings the super-pipe and a mini jib park on Blackcomb are floodlit; the same pass will get you into both. There is also a boardercross on Blackcomb ('lots of fast, flowing corners; excellently groomed').

SNOW RELIABILITY ★★★★
Excellent at altitude
Snow conditions at the top are usually excellent – the place gets an average of over 400 inches of snow a year (that's way more than Colorado resorts). But because the resort is low and close to the Pacific, the bottom slopes can have poor snow and be slushy – leading people to 'download' from the mid-stations, especially in late season.

Symphony Express lift (new in 2006) makes the Flute Bowl area much more accessible – with blue runs and easy glades as well as expert terrain

The classic high bowls that first gave Whistler cult status among expert skiers in the 1980s and 1990s

WHISTLER MOUNTAIN
2180m/7,160ft

Rhapsody Bowl   Piccolo

Flute Bowl

Symphony

Symphony Bowl

Glacier Bowl

The Peak

Whistler Bowl

West Bowl

Bagel Bowl

2 Peak

Roundhouse Lodge
1850m

Harmony

Emerald

1595m

1425m

Big Red

The 1530m/5,020ft vertical Peak to Creek runs are excellent in good snow

Whistler Village

Garbanzo

Raven's Nest
1300m

Take the gondola from 7.15am for uncrowded fresh tracks skiing and a buffet breakfast

1005m

Creekside

Fitzsimmons

These runs are to be the 2010 Winter Olympic downhill and Super G courses

Creekside
650m/2,140ft

Whistler Village
675m/2,210ft

Whistler has world-class terrain parks as well as epic terrain for freeriders: bowls with great powder and awesome steeps, steep gullies, tree runs, and shedloads of natural hits, wind lips and cliffs. Get up early if you fancy cutting first tracks, however. There are mellow groomed runs ideal for beginners, too, and the lifts are generally snowboard-friendly; there are T-bars on the glacier, but they're not vicious and any discomfort is worth it for the powder. The resort is fast gaining as big a reputation for its summer snowboarding facilities and camps on the glacier as for its winter snowboarding. The resort's specialist school will teach riders how to ride piste, pipe, park and powder according to your level. Specialist snowboard shops include Showcase and Katmandu Boards.

FOR EXPERTS ★★★★★
Few can rival it
Whistler Mountain's bowls are enough to keep experts happy for weeks. Each has endless variations, with chutes and gullies of varied steepness and width. The biggest challenges are around Flute, Glacier, Whistler and West Bowls – you can literally go anywhere in these high, wide areas.

Blackcomb's steep slopes are not as extensive as Whistler's, but some are more challenging. From the top of the 7th Heaven lift, traverse to Xhiggy's Meadow for sunny bowl runs. If you're feeling brave, go in the opposite direction and drop into the extremely steep chutes down towards Glacier Creek, including the infamous 41° Couloir Extreme (which can have massive moguls at the top), Secret Bowl and the very steep Pakalolo couloir. Our favourite runs are the also serious, but less frequented, steep bowls reached by a short hike up Spanky's Ladder, after taking the Glacier Express lift. You emerge after the hike at the top of a huge deserted area with several ways down; best to have a guide.

Both mountains have challenging trails through trees. The Peak to Creek area offers 400 acres below Whistler's West Bowl to Creekside.

There's also backcountry guiding, cat-skiing and heli-skiing available by the day. A 2009 reporter had 'two incredible days' with Powder Mountain cat-skiing ('thoroughly recommend it, though it was hard to go back to the crowds afterwards'). Other recent reporters used Coast Range mountain guides ('top-quality guides and superb skiing') and found the heli-skiing 'expensive but a great experience'. We recommend the two-day Extremely Canadian clinic (see 'Schools and guides') for getting the most out of the in-bounds steep terrain.

FOR INTERMEDIATES ★★★★★
Ideal and extensive terrain
Both mountains are an intermediate's paradise. In good weather, good intermediates will enjoy the easier slopes in the high bowls.

One of our favourite intermediate runs is down the Blackcomb Glacier, from the top of the mountain to the bottom of the Excelerator chair over 1000m/3,280ft below. This 5km/3 mile run, away from all lifts, starts with a two-minute walk up from the top of the Showcase T-bar. Don't be put off by the sign that says 'Experts only'. You drop over the ridge into a wide bowl; traverse the slope to get to gentler gradients – descend too soon and you'll get a shock in the very steep double-diamond Blowhole.

You are guaranteed good snow on the Horstman Glacier too, and typically gentle runs. The blue runs served by the 7th Heaven chair are 'heavenly on a sunny day', as a reporter put it. Lower down there are lots of perfect cruising runs through the trees – ideal when the weather is bad.

On Whistler Mountain, the ridges and bowls served by the Harmony and Symphony quads have lots to offer – not only groomers but excellent terrain for experiments off-piste. The Saddle run from the top of the Harmony Express lift is a favourite with many of our reporters, though it can get busy. The blue Highway 86 path, which skirts West Bowl from the top of the Peak chair, has beautiful views over a steep valley and across to the rather phallic Black Tusk mountain. The green Burnt Stew Trail also has great views.

Lower down the mountain there is a vast choice of groomed blue runs, with a series of fast chairs to bring you back up to the top of the gondola. It's a cruiser's paradise – especially the aptly named Ego Bowl. A great long run is the fabulous Dave

Whistler and Blackcomb
t 904 8134

Classes
3 days Ski Esprit
C$362 (incl. taxes)

Private lessons
Half day (3hr) from
C$355

Extremely Canadian
t 938 9656

GUIDES

Whistler Guides
t 938 9242

CHILDCARE

Whistler Kids
t 1 800 766 0449
Ages 18mnth to 4yr;
from 8am; non-skiing;
C$109 per day (incl.
taxes)

Ski school
Offers Adventure
Camps for ages 3 to
12 and Teen Ski
programmes for ages
13 to 18 (C$579 incl.
taxes for 5 days)

Murray Downhill all the way from mid-mountain to the finish at Creekside (though this is likely to be closed for large parts of the 2009/10 season because it is the Olympic men's downhill course). Although it is classed black, it's a wonderful fast and varied cruise when it has been groomed. There is also the 7km/4.4 mile long blue Peak to Creek run to try (great if it has been groomed recently – check before setting off).

FOR BEGINNERS ★★★★★
OK if the sun shines
Whistler has excellent nursery slopes by the mid-station of the gondola, as does Blackcomb at the base area. Both have facilities higher up too.

The map has a guide to easy runs, and slow zones are marked. On Whistler, there are some gentle runs from the top of the gondola. Their downside is other people speeding past. You can return to base by various chairs or continue on greens.

On Blackcomb, there are green runs from the top to the bottom. The top parts are particularly gentle, with some steeper pitches lower down.

In general, greens can be trickier than in many North American resorts – steeper, busier and on the lower mountain in less good condition. 'Our tentative beginner found it hard to move around with confidence because of the varying steepness of green runs,' says a reporter.

Another serious reservation is the weather. Beginners don't get a lot out of heavy snowfalls, and might be put off by rain.

FOR CROSS-COUNTRY ★★★★★
Picturesque but low
There are over 32km/20 miles of cross-country tracks around Lost Lake, starting by the river, on the path between Whistler and Blackcomb. But it is low altitude here, so conditions can be unreliable. A specialist school, Cross-Country Connection (905 0071) offers lessons, tours and rental. Keen cross-country merchants can go to the Whistler Olympic Park and its 55km/34 miles of trails (some 20 minutes away by car).

MOUNTAIN RESTAURANTS ★★★★★
Overcrowded
The main restaurants sell decent, good-value food but are charmless self-service stops with long queues.

They're huge, but not huge enough. 'Seat-seekers' are employed to find you space, but success is not guaranteed. The piste map advises eating before 11.30am or after 1pm.

Blackcomb has the Rendezvous, mainly a big (850-seat) self-service place but also home to Christine's, a table-service restaurant that is the best on either mountain. Glacier Creek, at the bottom of the Glacier Express, is a better self-service place. But even this (1,496 seats) gets incredibly crowded. Whistler has the Roundhouse (1,740-seat); Steep's Grill is its unremarkable table-service refuge.

Reporters generally prefer the smaller places, but they're still packed, unless you time it right, and may be closed in early and late season. On Blackcomb, Crystal Hut (great waffles) and Horstman Hut are tiny, with great views. On Whistler, Raven's Nest, at the top of the Creekside gondola, is a small and friendly deli/cafe. Reporters like the Chic Pea near the top of the Garbanzo chairlift: 'great Naan bread sandwiches and Chick Pea stew'. Harmony Hut, at the top of the Harmony chair, specialises in stews and cider. You can, of course, descend to the base – table-service Dusty's at Whistler Creek has been praised.

SCHOOLS AND GUIDES ★★★★★
A great formula
Ski Esprit groups run for three, four or five days and combine instruction with showing you around the mountains – with the same instructor daily. Many of our reporters have joined these groups (usually small), and all reports are glowing. There are various specialist clinics and snowboard classes – a 2009 reporter recommends the Supergroup classes (maximum of three in a group): 'ended up just my wife and me – overall very pleased'.

Extremely Canadian specialises in guiding and coaching adventurous advanced intermediates upwards in Whistler's steep and deep terrain. A lot of its coaches compete in freeride and skier-cross competitions. We have been with them several times and they really are great. And reporters have said, 'I would never have found some of the runs we were taken on' and 'they really push you'. They run two-day clinics three times a week.

Backcountry day trips or overnight touring are available with the Whistler Alpine Guides Bureau.

GETTING THERE

Air Vancouver 135km/85 miles (2hr15)

UK PACKAGES

Alpine Answers, AmeriCan Ski, American Ski Classics, Canadian Affair, Cold Comforts Lodging, Crystal, Crystal Finest, Elegant Resorts, Erna Low, First Choice, Frontier, Funway Holidays, Independent Ski Links, Inghams, Interactive Resorts, Kaluma, Kuoni, Made to Measure, Momentum, Neilson, Oxford Ski Co, Scott Dunn, Simply Alpine, Ski Activity, Ski Dream, Ski Expectations, Ski Freshtracks, Ski Independence, Ski Line, Ski Safari, Ski Solutions, Skitracer, Skiworld, STC, Supertravel, Thomson, Trailfinders, United Vacations, Virgin Snow

FOR FAMILIES ★★★★☆
Impressive

Blackcomb's base area has the slow-moving Magic chair to get children part-way up the mountain. Whistler's gondola mid-station has a splendid kids-only area. A reporter found the staff 'friendly, and instilled confidence'.

The Children's Adventure Park on Blackcomb features a Magic Castle, terrain features and 'colourful characters'. One reporter enthused about 'climb and dine', where children spend a few fun hours at the Great Wall climbing centre (see 'Off the slopes'), including a meal, while parents go out to eat.

STAYING THERE

A lot of British tour operators go to Whistler and some run catered chalets.
Hotels There is a wide range, including a lot of top-end places.
★★★★★Fairmont Chateau Whistler (938 8000) Well run, luxurious, at the foot of Blackcomb. We've stayed there several times and love it. Consistently recommended by reporters. Excellent spa with pools and tubs. The Gold floor is expensive and cosseting.
★★★★★Westin Resort & Spa (905 5000) Luxury all-suite hotel at the foot of Whistler mountain next to the lifts, with pools and hot tubs.
★★★★★Four Seasons (935 3400) Luxury hotel five minutes from Blackcomb base, but with ski valet service at the base. Unremarkable public areas but good food. Good fitness/spa facilities.
★★★★★Pan Pacific Mountainside (905 2999) Luxury, all-suite, at Whistler Village base. Pool/steam/hot tub. Recommended by a 2009 reporter.
★★★★Crystal Lodge (932 2221) 'Comfortable, friendly, convenient'; in Whistler Village. Pool/sauna/hot tub.
★★★★Sundial Boutique (932 2321) One and two bedroom suites. 'Great

for groups and families, excellent location in Whistler Village.' Hot tubs.
★★★Lost Lake Lodge (932 2882) 'Excellent' place: studios and suites, out by the golf course. Pool/hot tub.
★★★Glacier Lodge (932 2882) In Upper Village. 'Big rooms, quiet area, recommended.' Pool/hot tub.
★★★Tantalus Resort Lodge (932 4146) In Whistler Village. 'Fine.' Shuttle service to lifts. Hot tub.
★★★Whistler Village Inn & Suites (932 4004) 'Great location, good sized rooms and enough breakfast to keep you going all morning.' Hot tub/sauna.
Apartments There are plenty of spacious, comfortable condominiums. Price tends to be dictated by location – ski in/ski out condos are pricier than those a shuttle ride from the lifts.

EATING OUT ★★★★★
Good but crowded

Reporters are enthusiastic about the range, quality and value of places to eat but there aren't enough restaurant seats to meet demand. You have to book well ahead (one 2009 reporter 'booked two months in advance and still couldn't get a table before 9pm at the Rimrock'), even to eat in bars; but a lot of places won't take bookings for small groups so you have to queue.

At the top of the market, the Rimrock Cafe near Whistler Creek serves 'outstanding seafood and game' and has several different small areas which makes it feel more intimate than many Whistler restaurants; we had a fabulous meal there last season. In Whistler Village, we've had several excellent meals at Araxi ('superb', 'excellent service', say reporters) and Il Caminetto di Umberto (classy Italian; 'excellent food, worth the price').

Good mid-market Whistler Village places include the Keg ('great value' steak and seafood), Mongolie (Asian), Teppan (Japanese) and Kypriaki Norte ('excellent duck'). Reporters also suggest Bocca (Italian: 'home-made pasta', 'inexpensive'), the Bearfoot Bistro (European, 'the best gourmet restaurant, a stellar wine list'), Sushi Village ('impressive quality for quite a simple place'). A 2009 visitor rates 21 Steps ('excellent varied menu') and the pricey Rick's Grill ('seafood and steak').

In Village North the good-value Brewhouse (steaks, burgers, ribs etc) has good microbrews and a lively atmosphere, Caramba has 'good Mediterranean food at reasonable prices'. Hy's Steakhouse has 'melt in your mouth' steaks. Sushi-Ya and Quattro (Italian) are good.

In Upper Village, options are limited. Thai One On is 'excellent'; Monk's Grill has 'good steaks'.

There are plenty of budget places, including the après-ski bars below. The Old Spaghetti Factory in Whistler Village serves 'good pasta'.

APRES-SKI ★★★★
Something for most tastes
Whistler is very lively. Popular at Whistler are the Longhorn (with a terrace), Brewhouse, Garibaldi Lift Company ('the tables are full by 3pm'),

Dubh Linn Gate Irish pub and Tapley's. Merlin's is the focus at Blackcomb base. Dusty's is the place at Creekside – good beer, loud music.

Later on, Buffalo Bill's is lively and loud, and the Amsterdam Cafe is popular. Tommy Africa's, Maxx Fish, the Savage Beagle, Garfinkel's and Moe Joe's are the main clubs. Try the Mallard bar in Chateau Whistler and the Crystal Lounge for a quieter time.

OFF THE SLOPES ★★★
Quite a lot to do
Meadow Park Sports Centre has a full range of fitness facilities. There are several luxurious spas and an eight-screen cinema. Reporters recommend walks around the lake and the Great Wall Underground climbing centre. Ziptrek Ecotours offers tours on ziplines and suspension bridges through the forest between Whistler and Blackcomb mountains – 'great fun' says a reporter. You can also do ATV/snowmobile trips and dog sledding. Excursions to Squamish (for eagle watching) and to Vancouver are easy. And non-slope users can get around the mountain easily (don't miss the Peak 2 Peak gondola for great views).

Whistler

Interactive resort shortlist builder at **www.wtss.co.uk**

For us the main attraction of skiing or riding in eastern Canada is the French culture and language that are predominant in the province of Québec. It really feels like a different country from the rest of Canada – as, indeed, many of its residents want it to become. It is relatively easy to get to – only a six-hour flight from the UK, compared with a 10-hour flight for western Canada.

Tremblant is the main destination resort and is one of the cutest purpose-built resorts we've seen (though it is now in danger of being spoiled by expansion). The other main base is Québec city, which dates from 1608 and is full of atmosphere and Canadian history. Slopes of the main resorts are small, both in extent and in vertical drop, and the weather can be perishingly cold in early and midwinter (one reporter experienced –42°C in February). But at least this means that the extensive snowmaking systems, common to all the resorts, can be effective for a long season. Be prepared for variable snow conditions, and don't go expecting light, dry powder – if that's what you want, head west.

NEWS

Le Massif: the resort has begun a C$230-million investment project that will include new accommodation and expansion of the ski area. A new 150-room hotel at Baie-Saint-Paul is due to open for 2009/10, and there are plans to add new lifts, trails, and a mid-mountain restaurant.

For 2008/09 a third peak was opened, Mont à Liguori. Four new gladed runs were created in the main area and an easy glade developed especially for children.

There are lots of ski and snowboard areas in Ontario – Canada's most populated province – but most of them are tiny and cater just for locals. For people heading on holiday for a week or more, eastern Canada really means the province of Québec. The province and its capital, Québec city, are heavily dominated by the French culture and language. Notices, menus, trail maps and so on are usually printed in both French and English. Many ski area workers are bilingual or only French-speaking. And French cuisine abounds. The Frenchness of it is one of the big attractions for us.

The weather is very variable. Hence the snow, though pretty much guaranteed by snowmaking, can vary enormously in quality. When we were there one April, we were slush skiing in Tremblant one day and rattling along on a rock-hard surface in Mont-Ste-Anne the next.

The main destination resort is **Tremblant** (covered in the next chapter), about 90 minutes' drive from Montreal. The other main place to stay for easy access to several ski areas is **Québec city**. Old Québec, at the city's heart, is North America's only walled city and is a World Heritage site. Within the city walls are narrow, winding streets and 17th- and 18th-century houses. It is situated right on the banks of the St Lawrence river. In January/February there is a famous two-week carnival, with an ice castle, snow sculptures, dog-sled and canoe races, parades and balls. But most of

the winter is low season, with good-value rooms available in big hotels.

There are several ski areas close to Québec city. The biggest and most varied is **Mont-Ste-Anne**, 30 minutes away and with accommodation of its own. It extends to only 465 acres – easily skied in a day by a good skier. A gondola takes you to the top, and slopes lead down the front (south) and back (north) sides. The views over the ice floes of the St Lawrence river are spectacular.

Stoneham is the closest resort to Québec city, around 20 minutes away. It also has its own small village with accommodation and an impressive base lodge. It is a small area, with 325 acres of terrain spread across three linked peaks. The resort offers top-class terrain parks and a half-pipe, and will be hosting the Snowboarding Freestyle World Championships in 2013. It is very sheltered, in a sunny setting protected from wind, and suits families well, with mainly intermediate and beginner terrain. Dual-mountain lift passes are valid for use at Mont-Ste-Anne too. **Le Massif** is around an hour away from Québec city and is a cult area with locals. It is in a UNESCO World Biosphere Reserve and is just metres from the St Lawrence river. The views of the ice floes are stunning, and you feel you are heading straight down into them when you are on the pretty, treelined trails. The area of slopes, though small, has the largest vertical in the east – 770m/2,530ft. There are also 34 acres of off-piste.

INTRAWEST

Tremblant

Cute, purpose-built, traffic-free village with a real French Canadian feel, at the foot of a very small area of slopes

£80
RESORT PRICE INDEX

TOP 10 RATINGS

Extent	★
Fast lifts	★★★★★
Queues	★★★
Snow	★★★★
Expert	★★
Intermediate	★★★
Beginner	★★★★
Charm	★★★★
Convenience	★★★★
Scenery	★★★

NEWS

For 2009/10 a new eight-seat gondola is due to link the Versant Soleil area with the centre of the village. A new casino is also due to open.

Work has begun on a new top-to-bottom green run for Versant Soleil which will open this area up to beginners, but it may not be ready until the 2010/11 season.

KEY FACTS

Resort	265m
	870ft
Slopes	230-875m
	750-2,870ft
Lifts	13
Pistes	631 acres
Green	17%
Blue	33%
Black	50%
Snowmaking	
	1037 guns

+ Charming, purpose-built core village

+ Good snow reliability with extensive artificial backup

+ Some good runs for all abilities

− Very limited area for piste-bashers

− Can be perishingly cold in midwinter

− Weekend queues and overcrowding

− Some reports of poor service

Tremblant is eastern Canada's main destination resort and attracts quite a lot of Brits. But for keen piste-bashers the limited slopes don't really match the appeal of the cute and lively little core village, built in traditional style and with typical thoroughness by Intrawest.

THE RESORT

Tremblant has been transformed from a locals' hill to being eastern Canada's leading destination ski resort. Intrawest (which also owns Whistler and several other North American resorts) developed a purpose-built village in the style of old Québec.
Village charm Buildings in vibrant colours line narrow, cobbled, traffic-free streets and squares, and it has a very French feel to it. More recent expansion on the edge is not so cute.
Convenience The village is compact but there is a regular, free ski-bus and a local town service for C$2.25. We have some reports of poor service ('not up to usual North American standards', said two separate recent reporters) and extreme cold (−42°C in February, said one reporter).
Scenery There are good views over the village and a 14km/9 mile lake on the South Side. The North Side overlooks National Park wilderness.

THE MOUNTAINS

In its small area, Tremblant has a good variety of pleasantly wooded terrain.
Slopes A heated gondola from the

village takes you to the top of the so-called South Side (really south-west facing and so good for the afternoon sun). From here you can drop over the back onto the North Side (which is really north-east facing and gets the morning sun). A high-speed quad brings you back and there are two other chairs to play on here plus the slow Edge lift which accesses another summit, serving mainly expert terrain. On the South Side you can go right back to town on blue or green runs, or use two high-speed quads to explore the top and bottom halves. The Versant Soleil area is more directly south-facing and has mainly black and tree runs with one top-to-bottom blue. Free mountain tours go twice daily.
Fast lifts Most of the lifts are fast.
Queues At weekends there can be queues, but they tend to move quickly. We found crowds on the main run back to the village more of a problem.
Terrain parks On the South Side is the 30-acre Adrenaline park and half-pipe for advanced riders. A pass costs C$15. There's a beginner park on the North Side. Helmets are compulsory in both parks. The school offers freestyle classes.
Snow reliability Canada's east coast

STATION MONT TREMBLANT

The top of the South Side and the Grand Manitou restaurant. Over the ridge is the North Side and views over the National Park wilderness →

UK PACKAGES

Alpine Answers, American Ski Classics, Crystal, Crystal Finest, Erna Low, Frontier, Independent Ski Links, Inghams, Kuoni, Neilson, Simply Alpine, Ski Dream, Ski Independence, Ski Safari, Ski Solutions, Skitracer, Skiworld, STC, Thomson, Trailfinders, Virgin Snow

Central reservations phone number
Call 0800 028 3476 (UK number)

Phone numbers
From distant parts of Canada, add the prefix 1 819; from abroad, add the prefix +1 819

TOURIST OFFICE

t 1 514 876 7273
info_tremblant@
intrawest.com
www.tremblant.ca

---

doesn't get as much snow as western Canada does, but around 75% of the trails are covered by snowmaking. Grooming is excellent.

Experts Half the runs are classified black, but we found many of them did not deserve their grading. There are steep, top-to-bottom bump runs on the North Side and great gladed tree runs off the Edge lift. The Versant Soleil area has more black runs and some tough runs in the trees. But the gladed runs really need decent snow, preferably fresh, to be much fun.

Intermediates Both North and South Sides have good cruising, and we found the North Side less crowded. There are blue runs in the trees as well as on groomed trails.

Beginners The 2-acre beginner area is excellent, and there are long, easy, top-to-bottom greens to progress to. There are plans to open up the Versant Soleil to beginners with a new green piste (see 'News').

Snowboarding The slopes are good for beginners, but better boarders can't count on fresh natural snow to play in. A specialist shop, Adrénaline, runs a Burton learn-to-ride programme. And there are good terrain parks.

Cross-country There are around 65km/40 miles of trails, some at the top of the mountain, with great views.

Mountain restaurants The main Grand Manitou restaurant has good views and decent food, but can get crowded. Many people go back to town.

Schools and guides Past reporters praised the school: 'good instructors and both children made progress'. However, a 2008 visitor found that the two ski instructors their daughter had

---

were 'not up to the usual North American standard'.

Families The Kids' Club offers day care from ages one to six years. There's a children's adventure area on the Nansen trail.

STAYING THERE

There's no shortage of packages from the UK.

Hotels and condos The luxurious Fairmont Tremblant ('one of the best hotels I have ever stayed in') and the condos in the Place St Bernard, the Tour des Voyagers and the Chouette have been recommended by readers.

Eating out Try the Forge, Ya'ooo Pizza Bar, Shack, Casey's, Spag & Co, Windigo, Plus Minus (but it's 'very expensive', says a recent visitor) and the Loup Garou at the Fairmont. Fat Mardi's (steaks and seafood) has a kids' menu.

Après-ski The Forge is good as the slopes close, and the Shack brews its own beer, as does La Diable in the Residence Inn.

Off the slopes The Aquaclub La Source pool complex resembles a lake set in a forest, but reporters complain it's expensive (C$15 for three hours). For adults only, the 'excellent' Spa Scandinavie offers sauna, steam room, outdoor hot tubs and waterfalls. You can also go hiking, ice climbing, horse riding, ice skating, curling, snowshoeing, tubing, snowmobiling, dog sledding and on sleigh rides. You can visit Montreal (highly recommended by reporters), and you can take a helicopter charter with a scenic stop on top of a mountain.

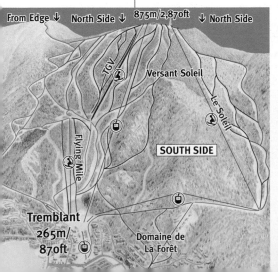

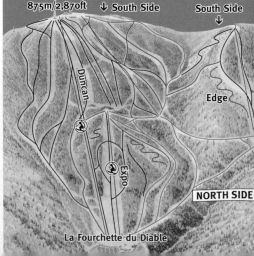

Spain

It's dangerous to generalise about Spanish resorts – which is why we don't provide the lists of ➕ and ➖ points that we do for other second-division countries. There are now some well-equipped Pyrenean resorts with fine, snow-sure slopes that compare favourably with mid-sized places in the Alps. Two resorts are certainly not downmarket – Sierra Nevada (see below) and Baqueira-Beret (see next chapter) are both frequented by Spanish royalty. Winter sports are becoming more popular with the prosperous Spanish themselves, and as a result many of the smaller resorts are continually improving.

UK PACKAGES

Sierra Nevada *Crystal, Independent Ski Links, Thomson*
Formigal *Crystal, Neilson, Skitracer, Thomson, White Roc*

The general ambience of Spanish resorts is attractive – with eating, posing and partying taken seriously.

Sierra Nevada (2100m/6,890ft) is in the extreme south of Spain, near Granada (a must-see, and much quieter than in summer), with views to the Atlas mountains in Morocco.

The hub of the resort is Pradollano, a stylish modern development with shops and a few restaurants and bars set around traffic-free open spaces.

Most of the accommodation is in older, less smart buildings set along a road winding up the steep hillside. A two-stage chairlift also goes up the hillside, with red runs back down to the main lift stations at Pradollano.

From Pradollano an eight-person gondola and parallel 14-person one go up to Borreguiles, at the heart of the 87km/54 miles of slopes. Here there are excellent nursery slopes, and lifts going up to the broad upper slopes beneath the peak of Veleta, where there is also a terrain park. There are three identifiable sectors, well linked, with a good range of intermediate and easy runs but not a lot for experts.

It can get very busy at weekends and queues can develop for quite a lot of slow old lifts, especially the chair up the village slope. The home run can get crowded too.

Sierra Nevada can have good snow years when the Alps has bad, and vice versa. Most slopes face north-west, but some get the afternoon sun. And when the wind blows, as it does, the slopes close; there are no trees.

There is a group of worthwhile resorts in the western Pyrenees, between Pau and Huesca.

Formigal now claims to be the largest ski area in the Spanish Pyrenees (137km/85 miles of runs), having expanded last year. It is a

favourite with experts for its 38 black runs – though many of them could be red. Recent developments include four freeride areas, heli-skiing and snowcat skiing and boarding, a second terrain park and revamped restaurants.

The village, of solidly built apartment blocks, is on the east side of the Tena valley, while all the slopes are on the west side, spreading over a series of side-valleys with north- and south-facing treeless slopes served by 21 lifts. So ski-in/ski-out this is not. The whole thing is really set up for motorists, who can park at one of four lift bases. Sextas, the first and the nearest to the village, has a smart day lodge and eight-seat chair.

Although the top station is only 2250m/7,380ft, Formigal has a justified reputation for wind. If it gets too bad you can slip down to **Panticosa**, about 10km/6 miles away and under the same ownership. It has also seen some modernisation, and the 35km/22 miles of runs offer something for everybody in a more sheltered environment. Thermal baths and two 4-star hotels opened last year. A 2009 reporter recommends staying in Panticosa and driving to Formigal to ski and enjoyed the low prices compared with France.

Candanchu and nearby **Astún**, with almost 80km/50 miles of pistes between them, are popular on the Spanish market. They offer a wide range of lodging set in some of the Pyrenees' most stunning scenery. Both resorts have some tough runs.

The other main group of Spanish resorts is just east of Andorra. The 60km/37 miles of runs at **La Molina** are linked to those of **Masella**, over the mountain, via a gondola and six-pack. The whole area, called Alp 2500 offers 128km/79 miles of slopes.

TOURIST OFFICES

Sierra Nevada
www.cetursa.es
Formigal and Panticosa
www.aramon.co.uk
www.formigal.com
Candanchu/Astún
www.astun.com
La Molina
www.lamolina.com

Baqueira-Beret

Spain's leading winter resort, with high, extensive, north-facing slopes; for Spanish animation, though, stay down the valley

TOP 10 RATINGS

Extent	★★
Fast lifts	★★
Queues	★★★★
Snow	★★★
Expert	★★★
Intermediate	★★★★
Beginner	★★
Charm	★★
Convenience	★★★
Scenery	★★★

KEY FACTS

Resort	1500m
	4,920ft
Slopes	1500-2510m
	4,920-8,230ft
Lifts	33
Pistes	108km
	65 miles
Green	7%
Blue	51%
Red	34%
Black	8%
Snowmaking	
	549 guns

BAQUEIRA -BERET TOURIST OFFICE

It's a wide area of slopes (wider than our trail map shows) and you get a real feeling of travel ↓

- **+** Compact modern resort
- **+** Reasonable snow reliability
- **+** Some good off-piste potential
- **+** Lots of good intermediate slopes
- **+** Friendly, helpful locals

- **−** Drab blocks dominate the main village, which lacks atmosphere
- **−** Resort is not cleverly laid out, and traffic intrudes
- **−** Still lots of old, slow lifts

Baqueira is in a different league from other resorts in the Spanish Pyrenees – a smart, family-oriented resort with a wide area of slopes that gives a real feeling of travel. It attracts an almost entirely Spanish clientele (which regularly includes their royal family), so don't count on English being spoken.

THE RESORT

Baqueira was purpose-built in the 1960s and has its fair share of drab, high-rise blocks.

Village charm The central area is clustered below the road that runs through to the high pass of Port de la Bonaigua, while the main lift base is just above it. But up the steep hill from the main base are some newer, smaller-scale stone-clad developments. At the very top is an alternative chairlift into the slopes. Overall though, the place lacks atmosphere.

Convenience The most convenient base is close to the main lifts, but the village is small enough for location not to be too much of an issue. There is a lot of accommodation spread down the valley, and big car parks with road-train shuttles up to the lift base.

Scenery The resort is flanked by broad lightly wooded but bleak slopes.

THE MOUNTAINS

There is an extensive area of long, mainly intermediate runs, practically all of them on open, treeless slopes and facing roughly west.

Slopes The slopes are split into three distinct but well-connected areas – Baqueira, Beret and Bonaigua. From the base station at Baqueira, a fast quad, which you ride with skis off, and a parallel 9-seater gondola take you up to the nursery slopes at 1800m/ 5,910ft. Fast chairs go on up to Cap de Baqueira. From here there is a wide variety of long runs, served by chairs and drags – including a long black down to Orri. From several points you can descend into the Bonaigua sector, leading to the summit of the Bonaigua pass. Beyond the pass is an expanding area of slopes served by a fast quad.

From the opposite extremity of the Baqueira sector at Orri a triple chair takes you off to the Beret sector, where a series of more-or-less parallel chairs serve mainly blue and red runs. A fast quad from Beret accesses a fourth sector at Blanhiblar, with red and blue pistes and an itinerary. All main lift bases are accessible by road.

Fast lifts There are a few fast chairs dotted around, but it's not a highlight.

Queues Weekdays are quiet and the gondola seems to have dealt with weekend queues. The Blanhiblar sector is always quiet.

Terrain park In the Beret area.

Snow reliability Most of the slopes are above 1800m/5,910ft and there is extensive snowmaking, but afternoon sun is a problem in spring. We've had mixed reports of the grooming.

Experts Experts will find few on-piste

For 2008/09 access to Baqueira 1500 was improved, with a new road and car park quite near the centre. The gondola from the village centre was extended to start from there, and there's a new skier services building. Two new 5-star hotels also opened. Some lower slopes were improved to make them easier. And 14 new snow-guns were installed.

UK PACKAGES

Crystal Finest, Scott Dunn, Simply Alpine, Ski Miquel

Phone numbers
From abroad use the prefix +34

TOURIST OFFICE

t 973 639010
viajes@baqueira.es
www.baqueira.es

challenges, but there are extensive off-piste opportunities all over the area. And there are four ungroomed itinerary runs including the steep and narrow Escornacrabes, from the top of Cap de Baqueira. Cheap heli-lifts are available.
Intermediates It's excellent, with lots of good long runs such as the 4km/2 mile blue from Tuc deth Dossau and some classic reds such as Muntanyó down to Port de la Bonaigua and Mirador above town. Less daring intermediates will enjoy the Beret and Bonaigua areas best.
Beginners The nursery slopes at the top of the gondola are good but the blues there can be a bit tough. Beret has an excellent nursery slope and gentler blues.
Snowboarding The main nursery slopes are served by a draglift and moving carpets. Experienced freeriders have plenty of chair-served off-piste.
Cross-country There are 7km/4 miles of trails between Orri and Beret.
Mountain restaurants All run by the lift company, the huts are said to be 'lacking in number and variety, and very smoky'. The self-service places at Beret, and the table-service place at 1800m have been recommended. You can also get table service at Cap del Port (at the Bonaigua pass), at Baqueira 2200 and at Beret.
Schools and guides A reporter 'highly

recommends' the Baqueira British Ski School – which offers a cheaper rate for guiding only and added snowboarding tuition last year.
Families There's a nursery next to the Montarto hotel at the base area, which takes children from 3 months to two-and-a-half years, but lack of spoken English is a problem. Ski school classes start from age four and there are snow gardens in each sector.

STAYING THERE

Chalet Ski Miquel has a catered chalet.
Hotels The 4-star Montarto (973 639001) is recommended, and the 5-star Rafael La Pleta (973 645550), just above the village has 'spacious rooms, wonderful service'. The Parador (973 640801) down the valley in Arties and the 2-star Husa Vielha (973 640275) in Vielha, 15km/9 miles away, have been recommended.
Eating out The more interesting restaurants are down the valley in Salardu (Bar Gris is 'excellent'), Arties and Vielha. Reporters have enjoyed the local tapas bars.
Après-ski There are pubs and discos down the valley. Pacha, in the main village, gets going late.
Off the slopes Pool and spa facilities are available in some hotels. Vielha has a sports centre and ice rink.

Baqueira-Beret

705

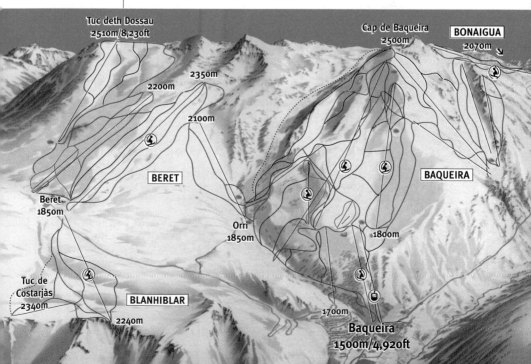

Finland

- Peace, quiet and Lapp charm
- Ideal terrain for cross-country
- Reliable snow for a long season
- Some very short airport transfers
- Good for families and beginners

- Can be bitterly cold (and dark)
- Small ski areas lacking challenge
- Mainly dull hotels and food
- Quite expensive
- Draglifts are the norm

For skiers with no appetite for the hustle and hassle of Alpine resorts in high season – perhaps especially for families – escape to the white silence of Lapland can be an attractive alternative. Finland has the lion's share of Lapland and we are getting more reports on it than we used to – on Levi, especially. The resorts are rapidly developing both their ski areas and facilities – see 'News'. Of the resorts covered here, only Ruka and Iso-Syöte are south of the Arctic Circle.

NEWS

In Levi a new hotel, Koutalaki, is due to open for 2009/10, and a major expansion project is due to begin on the hotel Levitunturi – 30 more rooms and a vast new spa centre are to open in summer 2010. Last season the hotel Sokos and six more restaurants opened.

At Ruka a new pedestrian village is taking shape at the foot of the slopes – the Ruka Village hotel and suites is due to open for 2009/10.

A kids' nursery area that opened last season will be improved. And more features are planned for the mini-terrain park.

In Iso-Syöte for 2009/10 a moving carpet is due to replace a T-bar as part of a revamped children's area.

In Pyhä the terrain park built last season will be further improved, as will snowmaking facilities.

For 2008/09 a new blue run opened on the northern slopes as an adventure route for kids.

In Ylläs a beginner tow was added for 2008/09.

The Arctic landscape of flat and gently rolling forest punctuated by many lakes and the occasional treeless hill is a paradise for cross-country skiing. Weather permitting, it also offers good beginner and intermediate downhilling, albeit on a small scale.

The resorts usually open a few runs in late November. For two months in midwinter the sun does not rise – at least, not at sea level. Most areas have floodlit runs. The mountains do not open fully until mid-February, when a normal skiing day is possible and Finnish schools have holidays that usually coincide with ours – a busy time. Finland comes into its own at the end of the season, with friendlier temperatures and long daylight hours. Understandably, Easter is extremely popular, and the slopes are crowded.

Conditions are usually hard-packed powder or fresh snow from the start of the season to the end (early May).

The temperature can be extremely variable, yo-yoing between zero and minus 30°C several times in a week. Fine days are the coldest, but the best for skiing: it may be 10 to 15 degrees warmer on the slopes than at valley level. 'Mild' days of cloud and wind are worse, and face masks are sold.

The staple Finnish lift is the T-bar. Ruka has some chairs, Levi has two gondolas and Ylläs one. Pistes are wide and well maintained, with good nursery slopes. The Finns are great boarders and consider their terrain parks far superior to those in the Alps; super-pipes are increasingly common.

None of the areas has significant vertical by alpine standards, and in some cases it is seriously limited.

There are few mountain restaurants – but you are never far from the base, with its self-service restaurants. The ski areas also have shelters or 'kotas' – log-built teepees with an open fire and a smoke hole – where you can eat a snack.

Ski school is good, with English widely spoken. All ski areas have indoor playrooms for small children, but they may be closed at weekends.

Excursions are common – husky-sledding, snowmobile safaris, a reindeer sleigh ride and tea with the Lapp drivers in their tent. Reporters are generally very enthusiastic about these off-slope adventures.

Hotels are self-contained resorts, large and practical rather than stylish, typically with a shop, a cafe, a bar with dance floor, and a pool and sauna with outdoor cooling-off area. Hotel supper is typically served no later than seven, sometimes followed by a children's disco or dancing to a live band. Finns usually prefer to stay in cabins, and tour operators offer the compromise of staying in a cabin but taking half-board at a nearby hotel. Cabins vary, but are mostly well equipped, with a sauna and drying cupboard as standard.

The main resorts are Levi and Ylläs, respectively 17km/10 miles north and 50km/31 miles west of Kittilä, which has charter flights from Britain.

Ylläs mountain has two gateways, both 4km/2 miles from the mountain. The minor one is Ylläsjärvi near the Sport Resort Ylläs base, the major one Äkäslompolo near the Ylläs-Ski base. Development is taking place at both. Äkäslompolo has 330km/205 miles of cross-country trails, transforming it from awkward sprawl to doorstep ski resort of limitless scope. From the lift base trails fan out around the mountain, across the frozen lake and away through the endless forest.

Ylläs is the largest downhill ski area, with 460m/1,510ft vertical. Lifts and pistes on two broad flanks of the mountain give plenty of scope for novices. Second- and third-week skiers will rapidly conquer the benign black runs. We've had a good report of the ski school in 2009 too. Ylläs has a welcoming mountain-top restaurant.

The Äkäs cabins at Äkäslompolo are reportedly 'excellent' but meals at the Äkäs hotel (016 553000) 'very average'. Dining out is limited but Julie's ('pizzas and Lapp dishes') and Poros ('more upmarket', 'very good') are recommended.

Levi generates most of our reader reports. It is a purpose-built village of hotels and cabins at the foot of its slopes. The 44 runs are mostly intermediate level and served by lots of drags. Buses run to/from the lifts. There are 'excellent' terrain parks and 230km/143 miles of cross-country trails. Levi's biggest hotel, Levitunturi (016 646301) is starting a major expansion project, which will include a huge new spa facility. The Sokos hotel opened this year and the Levilheto apartments (403 120200) are recommended. The Hollo Poro complex offers lodging, restaurants and bars. Of the facilities mentioned by reporters, the hotel itself is a 'good, convenient base'; the new Kultainen Poro restaurant is a fine dining place and the Pihvipirtti does a 'good fish buffet'; the Wanha bar is also praised. There are dozens of other eateries: six new places opened this year. And Olivers Irish Bar is 'very lively'.

Ruka lies 80km/50 miles south of the Arctic Circle, close to Kuusamo airport and the Russian border, in a region known for snow. The ski area, on two sides of a single low hill (Ruka East and Ruka West), has a mixture of open and forest terrain, 20 lifts (including one six-pack and four other chairs), and 20km/12 miles of pistes, most are floodlit, with snowmaking. There are runs of all colours, but none is steep and the vertical is a very modest 200m/66oft. There are terrain parks and the ski school has received good past reports.

The cross-country scope is vast:

they advertise 500km/310 miles, of which 40km/25 miles are floodlit.

The atmosphere at the resort and on the slopes is upbeat – with live music in the Monomesta bar and sun terraces outside the Piste, very popular in spring. Hotels include the Rantasipi Rukahovi (08 85910), only 50m/160ft from the slopes, and the Royal Ruka (08 868 6000), the resort's flagship property. The first lodging at the new pedestrian village is due to open this year. There is good cabin lodging; most of it requires use of the ski-bus. Decent restaurants include Riipinen, Vanha Karhu, and Kalakeidas. A new ice rink opened last season.

Pyhä, 150km/93 miles north-east of Rovaniemi, has seven lifts (two arc chairs) and 12 runs. The vertical is only 280m/920ft and there is no steep terrain, but it has good off-piste. The best powder runs are on both sides of a long T-bar on the north slope. There's 170km/106 miles of cross-country. The Hotel Pyhätunturi (016 856111) is at mid-mountain.

Iso-Syöte, 150km/93 miles south of the Arctic Circle and 140km/87 miles from Oulu airport, is Finland's southernmost fell region – but it receives the most snow in the country. Catering mainly for families, it suits beginners and intermediates since, of its 15 pistes (covering 20km/12 miles), there are only two black runs. However, there is a freeride area among the trees. The runs are short, with the longest 1200m/3940ft and a maximum vertical of less than 200m/660 feet. Seven runs are floodlit at night. There's a terrain park, new children's area with reindeer rides, snow tubing, tobogganing and 120km/75 miles of cross-country trails. Accommodation is mainly hotels and cabins, including the Iso-Syöte hotel (0201 476400) at the top of the slopes (pool, sauna).

Interactive resort shortlist builder at **www.wtss.co.uk**

UK PACKAGES

Ylläs Crystal, First Choice, Inghams, Inntravel, Kuoni, Neilson, Skiworld
Levi Crystal, Crystal Finest, First Choice, Inghams, Kuoni, Neilson, Simply Alpine, Skiworld
Ruka Crystal, First Choice, Inghams, Simply Alpine, Skiworld, Thomson
Pyhä Crystal, First Choice, Simply Alpine
Iso-Syöte Crystal, First Choice, Simply Alpine, Thomson

Phone numbers
From abroad use the prefix +358 and omit the initial '0' of the phone number

TOURIST OFFICES

Levi
www.levi.fi
Ylläs
www.yllas.fi
Ruka
www.ski.ruka.fi
Pyhä
www.ski.pyha.fi
Iso-Syöte
www.syote.fi

Norway

+ One of the best places in Europe for serious cross-country skiing
+ The home of telemark – plenty of opportunities to learn and practise
+ Freedom from the glitz and ill-mannered lift queues of the Alps
+ Impressive terrain parks
+ Usually reliable snow conditions throughout a long season

− Very limited downhill areas
− Very basic mountain restaurants
− Booze is prohibitively taxed
− Scenery more Pennine than Alpine
− Après-ski that is either deadly dull or irritatingly rowdy
− Short daylight hours in midwinter
− Highly changeable weather
− Limited off-slope activities

NEWS

In Tryvann, all three children's areas are to be improved. The Radisson SAS hotel complex opened last season, with four pools and six restaurants.

At Beitostølen, a new lodging and retail centre is due to open in 2009/10. Last season, two new restaurants opened.

In Geilo last season, 95 slope-side chalets, Havsdalsgrenda, opened; the Highland hotel gained a spa.

At Voss for 2008/09 a new terrain park was built at Tråstolen, and the Storastova hut on Slettafjellet was revamped. An après-ski bar opened.

For downhillers who fancy a change from the usual ski-resort glitz, Norway could be just the place. For families with young children, in particular, it can make sense; you'll have no trouble finding junk food to please the kids – the mountain restaurants serve little else. Speaking for ourselves, any one of our first three ▬ points is enough to make us pause. Add together all our negative points, and you can count us out. One reporter ticks us off for this 'narrow-minded view'. But his main addition to our plus points is the fact that he can be in Lillehammer four hours after taking off from Edinburgh. Four hours after taking off from Gatwick, we can be in Megève or Chamonix. Hmmm, tricky …

There is a traditional friendship between Norway and Britain, and English is widely spoken.

For the Norwegians and Swedes, skiing is a weekend rather than a special holiday activity, and not an occasion for extravagance. So at lunchtime they tend to haul sandwiches out of their backpacks as we might while walking the Pennine Way, and in the evening they cook in their apartments. Don't expect a tempting choice of restaurants.

The Norwegians have a problem with alcohol. Walk into an après-ski bar at 5pm on a Saturday and you may find young men already inebriated – not merry, but incoherent. And this is despite – or, some say, because of – prohibitively high taxes on booze. Restaurant prices for wine are ludicrous, and shop prices may be irrelevant – Hemsedal has no liquor store. Our one attempt at self-catering there was an unusually sober affair as a result. Other prices are generally not high by Alpine standards.

Cross-country skiing comes as naturally to Norwegians as walking; and even if you're not very keen, the fact that cross-country is normal, and not a wimp's alternative to 'real' skiing, gives Norway a special appeal. Here, cross-country is both a way of

getting about the valleys and a way of exploring the hills. What distinguishes Norway for the keen cross-country skier is the network of long trails across the gentle uplands, with refuges along the way where backpackers can pause for refreshment or stay overnight. More and more Norwegians are taking to telemarking, and snowboarding is very popular – local youths fill the impressive terrain parks at weekends.

For downhill skiing, the country isn't nearly so attractive. Despite the fact that it is able to hold downhill races, Norway's Alpine areas are of limited appeal. The most rewarding resort is **Hemsedal**, covered in the next chapter.

Just 20 minutes from the centre of Oslo on a spur of the underground system is **Tryvann** (150m/490ft), a small area popular with the locals. The train arrives near the top station (525m/1720ft) on Holmenkollen. The main slopes – with a vertical of 380m/1,250ft – are served by two drags and two chairs, one of them fast. Two drags serve a separate nursery slope. There's a good terrain park, half-pipe and boardercross. The whole area has snowmaking. The slopes are floodlit most evenings – and are busier then than in the day. The area has day lodge facilities and a couple of cafes.

The site of the 1994 Olympics, the little lakeside town of **Lillehammer**, is not actually a downhill resort at all. The slalom events were held 15km/9 miles north at Hafjell (230m/750ft) – 'excellent' buses run to/from there. This is a worthwhile little area with a vertical of 830m/2,720ft, 15 lifts (including an eight-person gondola) and 33km/21 miles of pistes. The downhill and super-G races went to Kvitfjell, about 35km/22 miles further north, developed for the purpose. It's steeper but smaller – 18km/11 miles of pistes. Families have a dedicated area, with a children's snow garden. Hafjell's Quality Hotel (61 274000) is a 'comfortable and friendly' base. Town facilities are limited and quiet, but a reporter recommends Woody's bar.

Norway's other widely known resort is **Geilo** (800m/2,620ft). This is a small, quiet, unspoiled community on the railway line from Bergen to Oslo. It provides all the basics of a resort – a handful of cafes and shops around the railway station, a dozen hotels more widely spread around the wide valley, children's facilities and a sports centre.

Geilo is a superb cross-country resort. As the Bergen-Oslo railway runs through the town it is possible to go for long tours and return by train.

Geilo is very limited for downhillers. The 32km/20 miles of piste are spread over two small hills – one, Geilolia, a bus ride away from Geilo, with a good, informal hotel, a restaurant at its foot and a pizzeria on the mountain. This area has a six-pack link to the family beginners' zone. None of the runs is really difficult. There are two good terrain parks and a super-pipe.

Clearly the best hotel, and one of the attractions of staying in Geilo, is the Dr Holms (032 095700) – smartly white-painted outside, beautifully furnished and spacious inside, with spa facilities and bar/cafe. This is the après-ski centre, but prices are steep. The resort is quiet in the evening, but the main hotels provide entertainment.

On the edge of the beautiful Jotunheimen National Park, about 225km/140 miles north-west of Oslo, lies the small resort of **Beitostølen** (750m/2,460ft). The slopes are best suited to beginners and early intermediates. Confident intermediates and experts will prefer the Alpine Centre, 6km/4 miles away, where they will find blacks, moguls and off-piste.

There's a good terrain park and over 300km/186 miles of cross-country.

A long way north of the other resorts is **Oppdal** (550m/1,800ft), with more pistes than any of its rivals (55km/34 miles). The total vertical is 790m/2,590ft, but this is misleading – most runs are short. Three of the lifts are chairs. There are two terrain parks.

There are slightly more extensive slopes at **Trysil** (460m/1,510ft), off to the east, on the border with Sweden, and the runs are longer (up to 4km/2 miles and 685m/2,250ft vertical). Well suited to families, it has a fast lift to the nursery area and gentle runs to progress to. There's now a six-pack, and the children's areas are being improved – the best is beside the new Radisson hotel complex (see 'News') and will have more lifts for 2009/10. There are good blues to progress to and the ski school has had positive feedback. The runs here are all around the conical Trysilfjellet, some way from Trysil itself – though there are some lodgings at the hill. A connecting lift serves lodging at Fageråsen and there's a shuttle-bus at Høyfjellssenter. Nightlife is lively – the Låven and Ski-pub'n are popular hangouts.

In complete contrast to all of these resorts is **Voss** (50m/160ft), a sizeable lakeside town quite close to the sea. A cable car links the town to the slopes on Hangur and Slettafjell, with a total of 40km/25 miles of 'well groomed' pistes. Queues aren't normally a problem. There's a fast quad from Bavallan and a children's area at the base there. There's also a new terrain park. The ski school is 'very accommodating' with 'excellent', small classes. And there are 20km/12 miles of cross-country trails. Hotels are of a high standard, and suit families quite well: Fleischer's (520500) is reportedly 'comfortable'. The spectacular Flåm railway is a notable excursion.

UK PACKAGES

Lillehammer *Directski. com, Neilson, Ski McNeill*
Geilo *Headwater, Inntravel, Neilson*
Beitostølen *Neilson*
Voss *Inghams*

Phone numbers
From abroad use the prefix +47

TOURIST OFFICES

Tryvann
www.tryvann.no
Lillehammer
www.lillehammerturist.no
Geilo
www.geilo.no
Beitostølen
www.beitostolen.com
Oppdal
www.oppdal.com
Trysil
www.skistar.com
Voss
www.vossresort.no

Hemsedal

The best place for an Alpine skiing holiday in Norway; just be sure that's what you want (check out the previous chapter)

➕ Impressive snow reliability because of northerly location

➕ Increasing amounts of convenient slope-side accommodation

➕ Extensive cross-country trails compared to the Alps

➕ Some quite challenging slopes, and hills with a slightly Alpine feel

➕ Excellent children's nursery slopes

➖ Not much of a village

➖ Limited slopes

➖ Exposed upper mountain prone to closure because of bad weather

➖ Weekend queues

➖ Limited on-mountain dining

➖ No liquor store for miles

➖ Après-ski quiet during the week and rowdy at weekends

TOP 10 RATINGS

Extent	★★★★★
Fast lifts	★★★
Queues	★★★★
Snow	★★★★
Expert	★★
Intermediate	★★★★
Beginner	★★★
Charm	★★
Convenience	★★
Scenery	★★

KEY FACTS

Resort	640m
	2,100ft
Slopes	670-1450m
	2,200-4,760ft
Lifts	22
Pistes	43km
	27 miles
Green	41%
Blue	25%
Red	18%
Black	16%
Snowmaking	60%

710

Hemsedal's craggy terrain is reminiscent of a small-but-serious Alpine resort. Most people not resident in Scandinavia would be better advised to go for the real thing, but if you like the sound of Norway, Hemsedal is the place for downhill skiing. Go after the February school holidays, if possible.

THE RESORT

Hemsedal is both an unspoiled valley and a village, also referred to as Trøym and Sentrum ('Centre') – a mile or two across the valley from the slopes, where you can also stay. The place is geared mainly to weekenders arriving by car or coach. But there is a ski-bus linking all parts and floodlit paths to/from the centre. The lift pass also covers smaller Solheisen, up the valley. Geilo is an hour away.

Village charm There's not much to do the charming: Sentrum is little more

than a small area of apartment/hotels, shops, a garage, a bank and a couple of cashpoints that might be empty by evening. Note the absence of a liquor store. But the focus seems to be shifting towards practical slope-side development, with chalet-style buildings and new amenities that suit families well.

Convenience Sentrum is a bus ride from the slopes, but more lodgings seem to open every year close to the base. The new Alpin Lodge has brought a self-contained centre of apartments, restaurants and shops

Totten
1450m/4,760ft

Tinden
1350m

Røgjin
1325m

Fjellet
1125m

940m

Veslestølen

Skarsnuten

670m/2,200ft

Hemsedal
Skisenter

Fjellandsby

Hemsedal
640m/2,100ft

↑ Hemsedal is big on terrain – we doubt this shot does justice to the current parks

HEMSEDAL TURISTKONTOR / ØYSTEIN SAGABRÅTEN

NEWS

For 2008/09 the new slope-side Alpin Lodge, with 30 new apartments, skier services centre, parking, restaurants, and shops opened below the nursery area. A draglift takes you up to the main lifts. A new green run goes back to the base from below the Skarsnuten lift, bypassing the busy home run.

Children's facilities continue to develop; Gaupeland is a new supervised day care and snow garden.

More lodging opened at Skarsnuten.

UK PACKAGES

Inntravel, Neilson, Simply Alpine

Phone numbers
From abroad use the prefix +47

TOURIST OFFICE

t 320 55030
info@hemsedal.com
www.hemsedal.com

beside the nursery slopes. You can also stay further up the hill at Skarsnuten – a pleasantly woody separate area, linked to the main network by its own lift and red run.
Scenery The views from Hemsedal's Tinden and Totten peaks are a little more Alpine and rugged in nature than is usual in Norwegian resorts.

THE MOUNTAINS

Hemsedal's slopes pack a lot of variety into a small space. They are shaded in midwinter, and can be very cold.
Slopes Most of the best slopes are reached by fast lift, so you can pack a lot of runs into the day. There's night skiing four times a week, until 9pm.
Fast lifts Of the four fast chairs, experts get the eight-pack. A few awkward draglifts remain though.
Queues Hemsedal is only a three-hour drive from Oslo, the capital, leading to weekend crowds and queues for the main access lifts. Otherwise it is quiet. Closure of the exposed upper lifts by wind produces crowds lower down.
Terrain parks There are two good parks on the lower Tinden slopes, including pipes of various sizes. The main park has the usual array of features plus a new big-air bag. There's also a beginner park, floodlit on some evenings.
Snow reliability The combination of latitude, altitude and orientation makes for good snow. Snowmaking now covers over half the slopes.
Experts There is quite a bit to amuse experts. Several black pistes of 450m/1,480ft vertical, some with moguls, are reached by the eight-seat chair or the adjacent steep T-bar from the base. There are wide areas of gentler off-piste terrain served by drags.

Intermediates Mileage-hungry piste-bashers will find Hemsedal's runs very limited. There are quite a few red and blue runs to play on, but the difference in difficulty is slight.
Beginners Beginners have a separate, gentle nursery area. There are splendid long green runs – but they get a lot of traffic, some of it very fast. Some long blues and reds also suit novices.
Snowboarding There is plenty of freeriding terrain, and some pistes are suitable for carving. The parks are popular and there's a boardercross.
Cross-country By Alpine standards there is lots to do – 120km/75 miles of prepared trails in the valley and forest and (in late season) 90km/56 miles at altitude. There is a special trail map. Most of the trails are a few miles down the valley at the Gravset centre and 12km/7 miles of them are floodlit.
Mountain restaurants The one functional self-service mountain restaurant is basic, but has a newish menu and sun terrace. The Hollvin at the base has been recently revamped.
Schools and guides We lack recent reports; past feedback has been good.
Families The resort caters well for families; the kids' nursery slopes at the lift base keep growing and Gaupeland (or Lynx) is a new child-friendly learning and fun area for three- to six-year olds.

STAYING THERE

Most of the accommodation is in apartments, varying widely in convenience for the slopes. Some catered chalets are available.
Hotels The best hotel is the Skogstad (320 55000) in Sentrum – comfortable, but its bar and nightclub may be noisy at weekends. The hotel Skarsnuten (320 61700), on the mountain, is stylishly modern. UK tour operators use some of the other valley hotels.
Apartments The Alpin Lodge opened this year, with 30 apartments built in chalet-style. Alternatives are the Tinden and Alpin apartments, a walk from the lift base.
Eating out The choice is improving. Lodgen bar and restaurant is new at the Skisenter. The Oxen is a popular steakhouse in town.
Après-ski It's minimal in the week, rowdy at weekends and holidays.
Off the slopes Diversions include dog sledding, tobogganing, activity centre (with bowling) and snowmobiling.

+ Snow-sure from December to May
+ Unspoiled, beautiful landscape
+ Uncrowded pistes and lifts
+ Vibrant (but regimented) après-ski
+ Excellent cross-country and good range of off-slope activities

− Limited challenging downhill terrain
− Small areas by Alpine standards
− Lacks the dramatic peaks and vistas of the Alps
− Short days during the early season

Sweden's landscape of forests and lakes and miles of unspoiled wilderness is entirely different from the Alps' grandeur and traffic-choked roads. Standards of accommodation, food and service are good, and the people are welcoming, lively and friendly. There are plenty of off-slope activities, but most of the downhill areas are limited in size and challenge. Sweden appeals most to those who want an all-round winter holiday in a different environment and culture.

NEWS

In Vemdalen: for 2008/09 a new six-pack opened at the Klövsjö area. A new mountain restaurant opened at the top of Mt Skalsfjället at Vemdalsskalet. And a children's activity centre and moving carpet have been built at Vemdalsskalet. Björnrike has a new children's centre too.

At Sälen, several restaurants were expanded.

Holidaying in Sweden is a completely different experience from a holiday in the Alps. The language is generally incomprehensible to us and, although virtually everyone speaks good English, the menus and signs are often written only in Swedish. The food is delightful, especially if you like fish and venison. And resorts are very family-friendly. It is significantly cheaper than neighbouring Norway, but reporters still complain that wine, spirits and traditional Swedish restaurants are very expensive (burgers and beer are less so).

One myth about Swedish skiing is that it is dark. It is true that the days are very short in December and early January. But from early February the lifts usually work from 9am to 4.30pm and by March it is light until 8.30pm. Most resorts have some floodlit pistes.

On the downside, downhill slopes are limited in both challenge and extent and the lift systems dominated by T-bars. But there is lots of cross-country and backcountry skiing.

Après-ski is taken very seriously – with live bands from mid- to late-afternoon. But it stops suddenly, dinner is served and then the nightlife starts. There is plenty to do off the slopes: snowmobile safaris, ice fishing, dog sled rides, ice climbing, saunas galore and visiting local Sami villages.

The main resort is **Åre** (which has its own chapter). **Sälen** is the largest winter sports area – and is made up of four separate sets of slopes totalling 144km/89 miles of piste. Most slopes are very gentle, suiting beginners and

early or timid intermediates best. Lindvallen and Högfjället are vaguely linked by a lift and a long cross-country slog, and Tandålen and Hundfjället by lift. There's also a bus service between them.

Vemdalen has three main areas of slopes linked by buses with a total of 45km/28 miles of pistes. A joint lift pass serves them all, there are no queues and T-bars dominate. Björnrike is great for families, beginners and early intermediates, with nine lifts and mainly gentle pistes. There is a hotel right on the slopes, built in modern style. Vemdalsskalet has more advanced intermediate terrain, with nine lifts and a terrain park. The Högfjällshotell at the base is large, dates from 1936 and prides itself on its après-ski with live entertainment. Klövsjö/Storhogna has 12 lifts, mainly easy green runs but three blacks and a hotel and apartments at the base.

Riksgränsen, above the Arctic Circle, is an area of jagged mountain peaks and narrow fjords. The season starts in mid-February and ends in June – when you can ski under the midnight sun. There are only six lifts and 21km/13 miles of piste. But there is some good off-piste and heli-skiing.

Björkliden, also above the Arctic Circle, is famous for Scandinavia's largest cave system. You can go snowshoeing in the caves and there are also several cross-country trails.

Ramundberget is a small, quiet, ski-in/ski-out family resort. It gets lots of snow and has 22km/14 miles of mainly easy or intermediate pistes.

UK PACKAGES

Vemdalen *Neilson*

TOURIST OFFICES

www.visitsweden.com
Sälen
www.skistar.com
Vemdalen (Björnrike, Vemdalsskalet)
www.skistar.com
Riksgränsen
www.stromma.se/en/ Riksgransen
Björkliden
www.bjorkliden.com
Ramundberget
www.ramundberget.se

Åre

Sweden's best slopes, strung out along a frozen lake above a small but charming town and with lots of non-skiing activities

+ Cute little town centre
+ Good snow reliability
+ Good for intermediates and novices
+ Extensive cross-country trails
+ Excellent children's facilities
+ Lively après-ski scene
+ Lots of off-slope diversions

− Lots of T-bars
− Exposed upper mountain prone to closure because of bad weather
− High winds detrimental to snow conditions
− Few expert challenges

TOP 10 RATINGS

Extent	★★
Fast lifts	★
Queues	★★★★
Snow	★★★
Expert	★★
Intermediate	★★★★
Beginner	★★★★
Charm	★★★
Convenience	★★★
Scenery	★★★

NEWS

For 2008/09 two chairlifts in the central sector of the ski area were revamped to increase capacity and the children's area at Åre Bjornen was expanded.

Åre has the biggest area of linked slopes in Sweden and some of its most challenging terrain. But it suits beginners, intermediates and families best. It has a dinky little town centre and a long area of slopes set along a frozen lake.

THE RESORT

Åre is a small town but Sweden's main ski resort.

Village charm The centre is made up of old, pretty, coloured wooden buildings and some larger modern additions. When we were there the main square had a roaring open fire to warm up by.

Convenience As well as lodgings in town, there is lots spread out along the valley, with a concentration in the Duved area.

Scenery The resort sits along the shoreline of a huge, long lake, frozen in the winter months.

THE MOUNTAINS

The terrain is mainly beginner and intermediate tree-lined slopes, with a couple of windswept bowls above.

Slopes There are two main areas (linked by an 'infrequent' shuttle-bus).

The largest is accessed by a funicular from the centre of town or by a six-pack or cable car a short climb above it. This takes you to the hub of a network of runs and (mainly) T-bars that stretches for 10km/6 miles from end to end. The cable car is often shut because it goes above the treeline to the top of the slopes (known as the 'high zone'), which often suffers from howling gales. A gondola also accesses the high zone from a different point. You can get back on-piste right into the town square. A separate area of slopes is above Duved and served by a high-speed chair. There are several floodlit slopes, open different nights. Signposting can be 'confusing till you get used to it; language doesn't help'.

Fast lifts The central area has fast lifts to the top, but old T-bars predominate.

Queues In high season there can be ('orderly and polite') queues for some lifts. But 2009 reporters saw none.

Terrain parks There's a boardercross

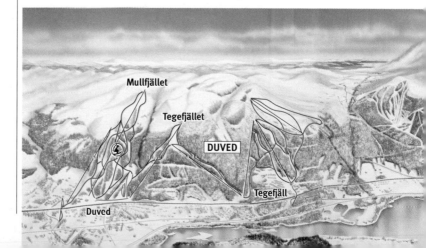

course, a half-pipe and a big terrain park, plus two parks for novices.

Snow reliability Snow reliability is good from November to May. But high winds can blow fresh snow away. They also mean that artificial snow is often made wet so that it doesn't blow away and it compacts to a hard, icy surface.

Experts Experts will find Åre's slopes limited, especially if the high zone is closed. If it is open, there is a lot of off-piste available and guides to take you there, including an 8km/5 mile run over the back, accessed by a 15 minute hike or a snowmobile tow (which costs extra). The piste map shows 10 avalanche zones to be wary of. On the main lower area the steepest (and iciest when we were there) pistes are in the Olympia area. There are also steep black and red runs back to town.

Intermediates The slopes are ideal for most intermediates, with pretty blue runs through the trees. Because they tend to be more sheltered, the blue runs also often have the best snow. You can get a real sense of travelling from hill to hill on the main area. The snowmobile tow to the top services some gentle off-piste, and there are great views and a cafe at the top.

Beginners There are good facilities, both on the main area and at Duved.

Snowboarding There's good varied terrain but most lifts are draglifts.

Cross-country There's 74km/46 miles of prepared cross-country trails and three times as much unprepared. Some trails are floodlit.

Mountain restaurants There are some good ones. Our favourite was the rustic Buustamons Fjällgärd, in the woods near Ullådalsområdet. A 2009 visitor liked the free open air barbecue

fires on the slopes: 'Buy some sausages at the supermarket and have an alfresco meal.'

Schools and guides The ski school has a good reputation and a reporter was impressed with his private lesson.

Families There are four special children's areas, and kids under eight years old get free lift passes if wearing helmets. There are plans to start a kindergarten that takes children from the age of two for 2009/10.

STAYING THERE

Neilson is the only major UK tour operator to offer packages to Åre.

Hotels The best central hotel is the charming old Diplomat Åregården. The slope-side Tott has good spa facilities, views and 'friendly, efficient staff'. The Holiday Club by the lake and Renen in Duved are popular with families. The central Åre Torg is a budget option.

Apartments There are plenty of cabins and apartments; reporters have recommended the ones at Åre Fjällby.

Eating out Werséns in town is good. A 2009 visitor recommends Madonna di Campiglio (pizzas) and the Japanese restaurant in the Bygget.

Après-ski Après-ski is lively. The Fjällgården on the slopes, the Tott and the Åregården are packed from 3pm and have live bands. Later on, the Country Club and Bygget also have live bands and there are plenty of bars for a quiet drink – including the Black Sheep at Åre Fjällby, which is decorated like a British pub.

Off the slopes Lots to do, including dog or reindeer sled rides, skating, ice fishing, tobogganing, ice driving, ice climbing and snowmobiling. There's also the longest zipline in Europe.

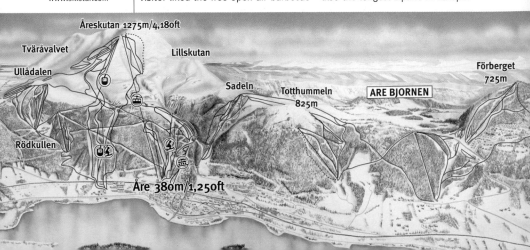

Bulgaria

Bulgaria has traditionally attracted beginners and early intermediates looking for a jolly time on a tight budget. Standards have been low. But Bansko's arrival on the scene has raised the bar for Bulgarian resorts (see separate chapter).

Two years ago one of our reporters summed-up her stay in Borovets thus: 'Skis: old and well used. Ski school: easily arranged, no shortage of English speakers. Hotels: modern, clean, over-heated. Staff: mostly operating scams to relieve you of cash. Food: in the resort, good standard stuff; on the mountain, rubbish. Bars: all a bit quiet. Bulgarians: mainly miserable. Conclusion: you get what you pay for – and next time we will be paying a lot more to get a lot more.' Which more or less reflects the general tone of the few reports we receive on the 'old' pre-Bansko Bulgarian resorts. Sadly, but perhaps not surprisingly, we have received none this year.

But maybe things are looking up. The installation of Bulgaria's first six-pack at **Pamporovo** is a sign that the resort continues to work on the quality of its offering.

The resort is strictly for beginners and very unadventurous intermediates, with mostly easy runs. Others will find the limited area of short runs rather inadequate, despite the two new slopes. The slopes are pretty and sheltered, with pistes starting at a high point of 1925m/6,320ft and cutting through pine forest. The ski schools are repeatedly praised – instructors are patient, enthusiastic and speak good English, and class sizes are usually quite small. The main hotels are in a purpose-built village in an attractively wooded setting slightly away from the slopes – there is a shuttle-bus. The 5-star hotel Pamporovo has had the best reports, but the food there has not. There is a handful of lively bars and discos.

Borovets has more to offer, with 58km/36 miles of slopes. The resort is a collection of large, modern hotels in a beautiful wooded setting, with bars, restaurants and shops housed within them. There is a small selection of quirkier bars, shops and eating places.

A long gondola rises over 1000m/3,280ft to reach both the small, high, easy slopes of Markoudjika – where a new quad replaced a draglift this year – and the longer, steepish Yastrebets pistes. The runs are best for good intermediates. The resort is not ideal for novices: nursery slopes are crowded, and the step from easy Markoudjika to testing reds is a big one. There is night skiing and 35km/22 miles of cross-country.

Queues may form for the gondola at peak times. The gondola is also said to be prone to closure by wind. Grooming is erratic.

The ski school is generally well regarded but past reports have complained of large classes. Most reporters stay at the Rila or the Samokov hotels – both huge. The Lion has been recommended. There are lively bars catering well to an '18-30' type crowd – Buzz is said to be best. Tour operator reps organise pub crawls, folklore evenings etc. Excursions to the Rila monastery or Sofia by coach are interesting.

Bansko

The future of eastern European skiing – or so it seemed in 2004. Bansko still sets the pace, but some of the gloss is wearing off.

TOP 10 RATINGS

Extent	★☆☆☆☆
Fast lifts	★★★★★
Queues	★★★
Snow	★★★
Expert	★★
Intermediate	★★★★
Beginner	★★★
Charm	★★
Convenience	★★
Scenery	★★★

NEWS

Development of smart new hotels and apartments around the base area continues. The Florimont hotel, casino and spa complex opened for 2008/09.

But the planned ring road for the resort to ease congestion was not finished for last season, and there's no word on the likely completion date.

Snowmaking has been increased recently and the area now claims 100% cover.

BANSKO SKI AREA

On-mountain facilities are well above the norm for eastern Europe ↘

+ Bulgaria's best mountain

+ Lots of fast lifts on the mountain

+ Picturesque town at the base

+ Smart new or renovated hotels

+ Low prices

+ Friendly, helpful locals

+ Cheap and very cheerful traditional restaurants all over the town

– Long gondola ride up to the main lift base – and long queues at the morning peak

– Limited slopes by Alpine standards

– Long airport transfers; poor roads

– Few off-slope diversions

– Lots of building going on and half-finished buildings around

When it first opened fully in 2004, Bansko seemed to show what eastern Europe had to offer, given proper investment (more than £20 million spent on smart lifts and snowmaking). Since then, readers have continued to report favourably on the small ski area. But the bed-base continues to expand (many apartments selling to Brits), the access gondola cannot cope with peak morning demand, and parts of the base area still resemble a building site.

THE RESORT

Bansko is an old town, set on a flat valley floor in the scenic Pirin National Park, that has been catapulted into the 21st century by installation of modern lifts on its slopes and construction of a lot of new lodgings, many near the base of the new access gondola to the slopes. Last season the resort took a further step forward by hosting World Cup women's downhill and Super-G races.

Village charm The town looks no great beauty on the outskirts. But head into the central square and the town reveals a quiet and charming heart, with architecture straight out of Disney's *Beauty And The Beast*. There are few outward signs of commercial tourism here except for hotels, which nestle between homes, shops, restaurants and churches.

Convenience The town centre is a fair walk from the gondola base – some hotels run shuttle-buses to/from the lift – but a more convenient hub is developing rapidly at the base, including upmarket hotels and apartments. The downside is that construction is still in progress, with all that that entails.

Scenery The Pirin National Park is noted more for its flora and fauna than for dramatic scenery.

THE MOUNTAINS

Until 2003/04, the draglifts and pistes in the Pirin National Park were accessible only by army jeeps and minibuses up a tortuous 12km/7 mile road. Now an eight-seater gondola ferries skiers to Bunderishka. There is a blue piste back to the town, with snowmaking and floodlighting.

Slopes From Bunderishka two successive fast quad chairs take you up mainly north-facing slopes to the high point of the area. From there you

KEY FACTS

Resort	990m
	3,250ft
Slopes	990-2600m
	3,250-8,530ft
Lifts	24
Pistes	70km
	43 miles
Blue	350%
Red	45%
Black	35%
Snowmaking	100%

UK PACKAGES

*Balkan Holidays,
Crystal, Directski.com,
First Choice,
Independent Ski Links,
Inghams, Neilson,
Simply Alpine, Ski
McNeill, Skitracer,
Thomson*

TOURIST OFFICE

www.banskoski.com

can ski down reds or blues to Shiligarnika, or a red followed by the Tomba black to Bunderishka. There are also a few slopes near the mid-station of the gondola – served by a newish quad and draglift. A 2008 visitor found the slopes quiet and 'well groomed' but was disappointed to find some pistes not open, including the Tomba black. The resort map shows a chair going up to the right of Bunderishka and a long red run back down. This has not worked for several years so is not shown on our map.

Fast lifts Apart from a few draglifts, most lifts are fast chairs.

Queues The gondola can suffer long queues at peak times. A 2008 visitor 'gave up early in the week and drove to the top of the gondola'; then he discovered he could ride the gondola well before its official opening time.

Terrain parks There's a half-pipe and a terrain park near the top.

Snow reliability The resort now claims snowmaking covers all of the pistes. Together with good grooming (by Bulgarian standards) and north-facing slopes, this means more reliable snow than the Bulgarian norm.

Experts There are no challenging pistes – the one black ought to be red. But there is some good tree skiing and one reporter enjoyed some good off-piste with a ski instructor.

Intermediates Good medium-to-difficult reds come straight down the face from the top, and varied blues go round to skier's right. All in all, there are four or five ways down the 900m/2,950ft vertical of the main area.

Beginners The nursery slopes near the top of the gondola are good, with little through traffic. There are blue runs served by draglifts at the top of the mountain and the long ski road down to town is gentle and easy.

Snowboarding Varied, but limited. A reporter in his second week on a board approved and the few draglifts can be avoided.

Mountain restaurants A fair sprinkling, including some modern ones with outdoor bars (but not enough seating). The char-grills they serve are said to be good value. The Platoto near the top is our reporters' favourite.

Schools and guides Both the main Ulen school and the Pirin 2000 school have received positive feedback from our most recent reporters ('very good and flexible tuition').

Families There's a nursery area up the mountain. The kindergarten takes children from four to seven years old.

STAYING THERE

Hotels There are newish hotels around the gondola station, including the swanky new Florimont with its own casino. The traditional-style 5-star Kempinski Grand Arena has 'excellent facilities'. Pirin near the town square and the Strazhite, near the gondola have had good reviews in the past. All these have pools and some spa/fitness facilities.

Eating out Reporters enthuse about the town's many mehanas (traditional inns) with roaring fires, real Bulgarian food and good wine.

Après-ski There are lively bars at the gondola base and new ones keep opening. Popular venues are the Lion pub, B4 and Amigos, and the bowling alley at the hotel Strazhite. The hotel Florimont has bars and a nightclub.

Off the slopes Excursions to the Rila monastery and trips across the border into Greece are possible. Some hotels have good spa centres and there's an ice rink.

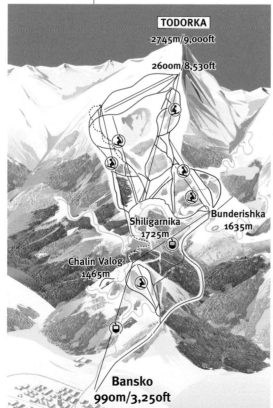

TODORKA
2745m/9,000ft

2600m/8,530ft

Shiligarnika
1725m

Bunderishka
1635m

Chalin Valog
1465m

Bansko
990m/3,250ft

➕ Cheap packages, and extremely low prices on the spot

➕ Interesting excursions and friendly local people

➕ Good tuition, keen instructors

➖ Primitive facilities – especially mountain restaurants and toilets

➖ Uninspiring food

➖ Very limited slopes – of no interest to anyone other than novices

Romania sells mainly on price. On-the-spot prices, in particular, are very low. Provided you don't have unreasonably high expectations, you'll probably come back from Poiana Brasov content. It allows complete beginners to try a ski holiday at the absolute minimum cost, and to have a jolly time in the evenings without adding substantially to that cost.

We admit it's some years since we visited, and we rarely get reports from readers – if you go, please let us know what you find.

Romania's main resort – and now the only one featuring regularly in UK package programmes – is **Poiana Brasov** (1030m/3,380ft). It is a short drive above the city of Brasov in the Carpathian mountains, about 120km/75 miles (on alarmingly rough, slow roads) north-west of the capital and arrival airport, Bucharest.

The resort is purpose-built, but not designed for convenience: the hotels are scattered about a pretty, wooded plateau, served by regular buses and cheap taxis. The place has the air of a spacious holiday camp, but with some serious-sized hotels – some right by the lifts.

The slopes are extremely limited – approximately 14km/9 miles of pistes in total. They consist of decent intermediate tree-lined runs of about 750m/2,460ft vertical, roughly following the line of the main cable car and gondola, plus an open nursery area at the top. There are also some nursery lifts at village level, which are used when snow permits. Night skiing is also available. The resort gets weekend crowds from Brasov and Bucharest, and queues can result, but in the week there are few problems.

A key part of the resort's appeal is the friendly and effective teaching.

Hotel standards are higher than you might expect. The linked Bradul (0268 407330) and Sport (0268 407330) hotels are handy for the lower nursery slopes and for one of the cable cars, and look smart after refurbishment. Guests in both have use of the Sport's sauna/hot tub/fitness room. Looking ahead, a new Radisson hotel with over 180 luxury rooms, restaurant, bars and smart spa facility is due to open during 2010.

Après-ski revolves around the hotel bars and nightclubs – plus outings to rustic barns for barbies with gypsy music, and to the bars and restaurants of Brasov. With cheap beer and very cheap spirits on tap, things can be quite lively. Off-slope facilities are limited; there is a good-sized pool, and bowling. An excursion to nearby Bran Castle (Count Dracula's home) is also popular.

UK PACKAGES

Poiana Brasov *Balkan Holidays, Inghams, Neilson, Transylvania Live*

Phone numbers

From abroad use the prefix +40 and omit the initial '0' of the phone number

TOURIST OFFICE

www.poiana-brasov.com

✳ **Want to keep up to date?**

Our website has weekly resort news throughout the year, and you can register for our monthly email newsletter – with special holiday offers, as well as resort news highlights.

Find out more at:

www.wtss.co.uk

Slovenia

- ✚ Good value for money
- ✚ Beautiful scenery
- ✚ Good beginners' slopes and lessons
- ▬ Limited, easy slopes on the whole
- ▬ Mainly slow, antiquated lifts
- ▬ Uninspiring food, though improving

Slovenia offers good value for money 'on the sunny side of the Alps'. The main resorts are popular with economy-minded British and Dutch visitors and with visitors from neighbouring Italy and Austria, giving quite a cosmopolitan feel.

Slovenia is a small country bordering Italy to the west and Austria to the north. The first state to break away from Yugoslavia, Slovenia managed to escape the turmoil that engulfed the Balkans. There is a positive feel to the resorts and a warm and hospitable welcome. Prices are low.

The main resorts are within two-and-a-half hours' bus ride of the capital, Ljubljana. The ski areas are small, but have improving lift systems and few queues. Ski schools are high quality and cheap, reputedly with good English. Hotel star ratings tend to be a trifle generous, but standards of service and hygiene are high.

Kranjska Gora (810m/2,660ft) is the best-known resort, a pretty village not far from the borders with Austria and Italy and dominated by the Julian Alps. The Lek, Kompas and Larix hotels – with pools – are the best for slope-side convenience. There are 30km/19 miles of mainly intermediate slopes, rising up to 1570m/5,150ft. Challenges are largely confined to the World Cup slalom run. Snow reliability is not good, despite improved snowmaking. The lifts are rather antiquated (mostly T-bars), but queues are rare, except on local holidays. There are 40km/25 miles of cross-country.

Vogel (1535m/5,040ft), in the beautiful **Bohinj** basin, has the best slopes and conditions in the area. The 18km/11 miles of slopes are reached by a cable car up from the valley. There's a collection of small hotels and restaurants at the base. Pistes of varying difficulty run from the high point at 1800m/5,910ft back into a central bowl with a small beginner area. When conditions permit, there is a long red run to the bottom cable car station. For a change of scene, **Kobla**, with 23km/14 miles of wooded runs, is a short bus ride away. There are 13km/8 miles of cross-country.

Bled, with its beautiful lake and fairly lively nightlife, is an attractive base. Its local slopes are very limited, but free (with lift pass) buses run to Vogel (20km/12 miles) and Kobla (a bit nearer).

Slovenia's second city, **Maribor** (265m/870ft), in the north-east, is 6km/4 miles from its local slopes – the biggest ski area in the country, with 40km/25 miles of runs, 20 or so lifts (including a new six-pack for 2008/09) and 36km/22 miles of cross-country. Some slopes are floodlit for night skiing and snowmaking has been improved recently. The area lift pass also covers Kranjska Gora. There are several atmospheric old inns serving good, Hungarian-influenced food. And the 4-star Arena hotel opened at the slopes last season.

❄ **Want a shortlist shortcut?**

Our website will build a shortlist for you: you specify your priorities and the system will use our resort ratings to draw up a personal shortlist – confined to one area or country, if you like.

Find out more at:

www.wtss.co.uk

Scotland

- Easy to get to from northern Britain
- It is possible to experience perfect snow and stirring skiing
- Decent, cheap accommodation and good-value packages
- Mid-week it's rarely crowded
- Extensive ski-touring possibilities
- Lots to do off the slopes

- Weather is extremely changeable and sometimes vicious
- Snowfall is erratic, to say the least, and pistes can be closed through lack of snow
- Slopes limited; runs mainly short
- Queueing can be a problem
- Little ski resort ambience and few memorable mountain restaurants

Conditions in Scotland are unpredictable, to say the least. If you live nearby and can go at short notice when things look good, the several ski areas are a tremendous asset. But booking a holiday here as a replacement for your usual week in the Alps is just too risky.

For novices who are really keen to learn, Scotland could make sense, especially if you live nearby. You can book instruction via one of the excellent outdoor centres, many of which also provide accommodation and a wide range of other activities. The ski schools at the resorts themselves are also very good.

Most of the slopes in most of the areas suit intermediates best. But all apart from The Lecht offer one or two tough or very tough slopes.

Snowboarding is popular and most of the resorts have some special terrain features, but maintaining these facilities in good nick is problematic. The natural terrain is good for free-riding when the conditions are right.

Cairngorm is the best-known resort, with 12 lifts and 37km/23 miles of runs. Aviemore is the main centre (with a shuttle-bus to the slopes), but you can stay in other villages in the Spey valley. The slopes are accessed by a funicular from the main car park up to Ptarmigan at 1100m/3,610ft.

Nevis Range is the highest Scottish resort and has 11 lifts in addition to the long six-seat gondola accessing the slopes and 35km/22 miles of runs on the north-facing slopes of Aonach Mor. There are many B&Bs and hotels in and around Fort William, 10 minutes away by shuttle.

Glenshee boasts 21 lifts and 40km/25 miles of runs, spread out over three minor parallel valleys and some natural quarter-pipes. Glenshee remains primarily a venue for day-trippers, though there are hotels, hostels and B&Bs in the area.

Glencoe's more limited slopes (seven lifts, 20km/12 miles of runs) lie just east of moody Glen Coe itself. You have to ride a double chairlift and a button lift to get to the main slopes, including the nursery area. The isolated Kings House Hotel is 2km/1 mile away.

The Lecht is largely a novices' area, with 13 lifts and 20km/12 miles of runs on the gentle slopes beside a high pass, with a series of parallel lifts and runs above the car parks. With a maximum vertical of only 200m/660ft, runs are short. There's extensive snowmaking, a terrain park, and a day lodge at the base. The village of Tomintoul is 10km/6 miles away.

FURTHER INFORMATION

The VisitScotland organisation runs an excellent website at: ski.visitscotland.com

t 0845 22 55 121
info@visitscotland.com

720

Japan

+ Reliable deep powder snow in Hokkaido resorts, lift-served
+ Exotic atmosphere, fabulous food
+ Polite and gracious locals
+ Night skiing is the norm, allowing a long ski day if you want one

− The language barrier
− It's a long way – around 6,000 miles and you have to change planes
− Lack of off-slope diversions
− Snowfall can go on for weeks in Hokkaido resorts

KEY FACTS

Niseko	
Vertical	958m
	3,140ft
Lifts	38
Pistes	48km
	30 miles
Green	30%
Blue	40%
Black	30%

Rusutsu	
Vertical	595m
	1,950ft
Lifts	19
Pistes	37
Green	30%
Blue	40%
Black	30%

Furano	
Vertical	950m
	3,115ft
Lifts	10
Pistes	25km
	16 miles
Green	40%
Blue	40%
Black	20%

Although it is roughly the same size as the British Isles, Japan has hundreds of ski resorts. Several UK tour operators feature Japanese resorts, going to places on the northern island of Hokkaido that have developed something like cult status with keen skiers and riders from Australia, in particular. The reason? Snow – huge and reliable falls of powder snow.

In these remote parts of Japan, hardly anything is written in English and no English-language media are available (except websites). Going independently sounds like hard work; but presumably going with a tour operator is not.

You fly in to Sapporo (about two hours by bus from Rusutsu and a bit longer to Niseko or Furano), via Tokyo or Osaka. As you are travelling such a great distance you might want to combine your skiing with a stay in Tokyo or (preferably) Kyoto.

Niseko is made up of three areas of slopes – Grand Hirafu (Hirafu and Hanazono), Annupuri and Niseko Village (formerly Higashiyama) – with a total of 38 lifts covered by a single pass. The three are linked, but not as efficiently as you might wish. There are modern lifts, but also some old single chairs on upper slopes.

The most popular and most easily accessible area, Grand Hirafu, is open from 8.30am to 9.00pm, thanks to what is one of the world's largest – and most heavily used – night skiing operations.

Niseko has a well-deserved reputation for powder snow, which falls almost constantly from December to the end of February. Skiing waist-deep powder is an everyday occurrence. Clearly, this will suit some holiday skiers and not others. Niseko does offer groomed runs, but you can get those closer to home, and get a tan while you ski them. The snow does stop sometimes, and when it does the powder gets tracked out quickly. But it's usually not too long before another snowstorm marches in across the Sea of Japan from Siberia, and the powder returns. The terrain is not steep, disappointing some experts.

The lack of sun has not proved a deterrent to Australians, who now come in their thousands. For them,

721

← There are lots of resorts on the main island of Honshu; only the better-known ones are shown on our map. But the best snow is on Hokkaido

UK PACKAGES

Niseko *Crystal, Crystal Finest, Mountain Tracks, Ski Dream, Ski Independence, Ski Safari, Skitracer, Skiworld*
Rusutsu *Crystal, Ski Independence, Ski Safari, Skitracer*
Furano *Mountain Tracks, Ski Independence, Ski Safari, Skitracer, Skiworld*
Hakuba *Skiworld*

More information
To really get to grips with the resorts on offer in Japan, spend some time delving into this site: www.snowjapan.com

TOURIST OFFICES

Niseko
www.nisekotourism. com
www.niseko.ne.jp/en/ index.html
Hirafu
www.grand-hirafu.jp/ winter/en/
Niseko Village
t 0136 44 1111
www.niseko-higashiyama.co.jp
Annupuri
t 0136 58 2080
www.cks.chuo-bus. co.jp/annupuri/english. php

Rusutsu
t 0136 46 3331
www.rusutsu.co.jp
Furano
t 0167 22 5777
www.furano-kankou. com/english
www.skifurano.com

guaranteed powder and reasonable costs have been an unbeatable combination. For UK-based travellers, the cost is higher: from around £1,600 for a week or £2,300 for a 10-day two-centre holiday.

There are several modern ski-in/ski-out hotels (but little else) at the bases. The Hilton Niseko Village at the foot of the slopes is among the best, with spectacular views from most of the rooms and its own spa and onsen (see below). Or you can stay in the atmospheric little town of Hirafu where there are now some impressive modern apartments alongside traditional pensions and lodges, raising accommodation standards well above the norm for the simple country town. The lift bases are well serviced by shuttle-buses.

While there isn't a lot to do outside of ski, eat and drink in Hirafu, the Australian influx means that the little town makes up for its lack of sophistication with a vibrant nightlife and plenty of variety in the way of bars, restaurants and tiny underground-style clubs. There are now a few very upmarket restaurants in town and several chic bars. And an igloo-style Ice Bar is dug out of a snowdrift each year, complete with icicles on the roof and a real bar selling all manner of cocktails.

Rusutsu is about an hour from Niseko, and makes a viable day trip;

or you could combine the two in a two-centre holiday. The slopes, over three interlinked mountains, are more limited, but offer slightly more challenge. The snow here can be as good as in Niseko (though it doesn't fall in quite the same quantity), and it doesn't get tracked out so quickly. There's also a good terrain park and half-pipe. The pivotal, self-contained Rusutsu Resort Hotel complex offers a wide choice of good restaurants plus all sorts of other facilities – bars, shopping mall, swimming, wave pool and onsen.

One of the main alternatives to these two on Hokkaido is **Furano** – one of the more famous resorts within Japan, capable of hosting World Cup events and offering a tad more vertical than Niseko, at 955m/3,130ft over two linked sectors. It is five to six hours from Niseko and Rusutsu, so not within day-trip range. This is a resort where you can either stick to the relatively easy trails or join a guided group to explore off-piste. You can also go with a guided group to the lift-served but ungroomed Asahidake mountain (a live volcano, around an hour away). One of the most comfortable hotels is the New Furano Prince, a free five-minute ride on the resort shuttle from the main base and a 10-minute bus ride from town; again it has great views and its own onsen.

The largest ski area in Japan is on the main island of Honshu: **Shiga Kogen**, comprising 21 interlinked resorts and a huge diversity of terrain covered by one lift ticket. It was the site of several major events in the 1998 Winter Olympics.

Hakuba is also handy to reach by train if you find yourself in Tokyo and don't have time for the trip to Hokkaido. It is a group of 10 resorts accessing more than 200 runs amid the rugged peaks of Japan's 'Alps'.

THE ONSEN EXPERIENCE

Onsen are complexes of hot baths to soak in, showers and communal volcanic thermal pools; they are a key part of Japanese culture and a major part of après-ski. All onsen are basically set up in the same way: men and women shower and bathe in their separate areas. Then, if they wish, they can congregate to soak and have a drink in a communal thermal pool, which more often than not will be outside and surrounded by snow.

Australia

- ✚ Offers skiing and boarding during the European summer
- ✚ Most of the resorts offer upmarket slope-side accommodation
- ✚ Snowcat skiing offered in a couple of resorts

- ➖ It's a long way from Britain
- ➖ Mountains rather low and slopes rather limited by Alpine standards
- ➖ Day lift passes are very expensive – up to £50 per day

Even more than New Zealand, Australia offers resorts that are basically of local interest, but that can amuse people with other reasons to travel there – escaping a European summer to catch up with those long-lost relatives, say.

The major resorts are concentrated in the populous south-east corner of the country, between Sydney and Melbourne, with the largest in New South Wales (NSW) – in the National Park centred on Australia's highest mountain, Mt Kosciusko (2230m/ 7,320ft), about six hours' drive south of Sydney. It costs A$27 a day just to enter the Kosciusko National Park. Skiing has been going on here since the early 1900s – as it has in the next-door state of Victoria.

The season generally runs from early June to mid-October. In the last few years there have been major dumps in early July or even June, but August and September remain the most reliable months.

Thredbo, established in 1957, is a sophisticated, upmarket Alpine-style village in NSW. It hosted the only World Cup race event held in Australia, thanks to a vertical of 670m/2,200ft.

Thredbo is rather like a small French purpose-built resort – user-friendly, and mostly made up of modern apartments, many new luxury ski-in/ski-out chalets, and lodges run by clubs. There are many upmarket chalets for rent, too. Originally Thredbo had an Austrian flavour but this has now given way to lively, modern, casual-elegant bars and restaurants, increasing numbers of very smart architect-designed apartments and a pedestrian mall with good shopping and sculptures. It's a steep place, with some stiff climbs. Road access is easy.

The slopes, prettily wooded with gum trees, rise up across the valley from the village, served by a regular shuttle-bus through the resort. Snowmaking now covers all major slopes top to bottom. When the big falls arrive conditions can be as good as anywhere, but it's rarely cold enough for powder to last for more than a few hours. The runs are many and varied. The dozen lifts include three fast quad chairs, and the trails include Australia's highest (2035m/6,680ft) and longest (6km/ 4 miles). The blacks are not steep – except for the challenging Golf Course and parts of Funnelweb, named after Australia's most poisonous spider; but on the higher lifts there are off-piste variants, including a beautiful guided backcountry tour to Dead Horse Gap, with transport back to the resort provided. There are now three distinct terrain parks and the slopes are also dotted with natural terrain features.

There is an attractive pedestrian mall with good shopping and some high-class restaurants both on and off the mountain. An impressive sports training complex is open to the public, with an Olympic-size pool.

On the other side of the mountain range is the large **Perisher** resort complex, with a pass covering 50 lifts and six base stations – more than anywhere else in Australia – but a vertical of less than 430m/1,410ft. The main area is Perisher/Smiggins, where lifts and runs – practically all easy or intermediate – range over three lightly wooded sectors. The resort is reachable by road, or by the Skitube, a rack railway that tunnels up from Bullocks Flat and goes on to the second area, **Blue Cow/Guthega**, where the slopes offer more challenges.

Perisher Blue is doing its best to catch up with Thredbo by upgrading hotels and building more facilities. The resort is very spread out and has no

UK PACKAGES

Perisher *Ski Dream*

TOURIST OFFICES

Thredbo
www.thredbo.com.au

Perisher Blue
(for Perisher,
Smiggins, Blue Cow,
Guthega)
www.perisherblue.
com.au

Charlotte Pass
www.charlottepass.
com.au

Selwyn Snowfields
www.selwynsnow.
com.au

Mount Hotham
www.hotham.
com.au

Falls Creek
(for Falls Creek and
Mt McKay)
www.fallscreek.com.
au

Mt Buller
www.mtbuller.com.au

Mt Buffalo
www.mtbuffalochalet.
com.au

central focus except for one cavernous base facility full of shops and eateries, and while a sophisticated pedestrian village has been widely talked about, the project has stalled. Perisher has more ski-in/ski-out accommodation than Thredbo, although it does appeal more to the masses, with its shopping-mall-style village centre filled with every manner of shop, bar and fast food restaurant. Its main advantage over Thredbo is its snow, thanks to its position further within the mountain ranges and its higher altitude. For this reason it is one of the few resorts offering a first tracks programme, as it is actually worth rising early here after a big snowfall. There is a super-sized terrain park at Blue Cow.

Many on a budget stay in the lakeside town of Jindabyne, a half-hour drive from both Thredbo and Perisher, with a lively youth-oriented nightlife scene. There are also some upmarket chalets on the road up to Thredbo.

From Perisher, a snowcat can take you on an 8km/5 mile ride to the isolated chalets of Australia's highest resort, **Charlotte Pass** (1760m/5,770ft), with five lifts but only 200m/660ft vertical and 50 hectares of terrain – the entire ski field can be seen from most of the lodges. People visit the Pass more for its charm and Alpine beauty than for the skiing although it is popular with families and beginners. The major hotel is the historic and turreted Kosciusko Chalet, a good spot for romantic weekends. Mt Kosciusko is easily reached on cross-country skis.

If you want to learn to ski among the gum trees at the lowest price, **Selwyn Snowfields** is the place. Its lift tickets cost much less than those of major ski fields, especially in low season. Selwyn has 12 lifts across 45 hectares, of which 80% is beginner or intermediate, plus snow tubing and tobogganing, and is about an hour from Cooma, near Jindabyne.

In Victoria, resorts are not as high as in NSW but many have good snow.

Mount Hotham has a justified reputation for snow, bills itself 'the powder capital of Australia' and offers free snowcat skiing on its best slopes. Some of Australia's most exclusive hotels are being built here in a bid to turn Hotham into a year-round destination. It is an eight-hour drive from Sydney, and a four-hour drive from Melbourne. (The airport 20 minutes' drive from Hotham does not currently have commercial flights.) Hotham's 13 lifts serve a complete range of runs, with plenty of variety, and free cat skiing on the more powdery slopes. The longest run is 2.5km/1.5 miles, and there is more consistently steep terrain here than anywhere else in Australia. There are snow kiting lessons and snowshoe tours, and this is the only place in the country to offer dog sledding.

The village is built along the top of a ridge, with the slopes below it. The focus is Mount Hotham Central, with apartments, shops, a few good restaurants and the White Mountain Spa. Hotham Heights Chalets is a nest of upscale multi-storey buildings. You can also stay 15 minutes' drive away at Dinner Plain – cool chalets and the new Japanese-inspired Onsen Retreat and Spa set prettily among gum trees. There are also a number of restaurants and bars here, and cross-country trails.

For $A125 with a valid lift pass you can take a six-minute helicopter ride to ski at nearby **Falls Creek** – the most Alpine of Australia's resorts, completely snow-bound in winter. There are snowcats from the car park, which is now overlooked by Australia's newest large luxury retreat, the Quay West Resort & Spa. There are 18 lifts, though the area is smaller than Mount Hotham's and the runs are mostly intermediate. There are extensive terrain park features. Falls Creek also has a lavish spa to rival Mt Hotham's, and is always adding to the number of funky architect-designed lodges. For some, the big attraction at Falls Creek is being able to access Australia's steepest skiing on the adjacent **Mt McKay** – 365m/1,200ft vertical of true black-diamond terrain. Guided snowcat rides ($A69) are worth the trip.

The other Victorian resort of note is the isolated peak of **Mt Buller**. Only a three-hour drive from Melbourne, this place is a magnet for old money, which has financed a proper sophisticated resort village with a luxury hotel, a pampering spa, Australia's highest cinema complex and even a university campus. Draped around the mountain are 25 lifts – the largest network in Victoria. There are fees to enter and to park overnight.

Mt Buffalo is worth visiting mainly to stay in the historic Mt Buffalo Resort, with its dramatic views over the craggy Victorian Alps. The Chalet is done up in true 1930s style.

New Zealand

- For Europeans, more interesting than summer skiing on glaciers
- Huge areas of off-piste terrain accessible by helicopter
- Some spectacular scenery, as seen in *The Lord of the Rings* movies

- Limited on-mountain restaurants – though these are being upgraded
- Half-hour-plus drives from accommodation up to the ski areas
- Highly changeable weather
- No trees

The number of keen Kiwi skiers and boarders kicking around the Alps gives a clue that there must be some decent slopes back home – and indeed there are. The networks of lifts and runs are rather limited. But the heli-skiing around the Mt Cook region on the South Island is definitely worth writing home about. For Europeans already spending a lot to travel to New Zealand, the extra cost of a day or two's heli-drops around the Methven area is well worthwhile.

There are resorts on both North Island and South Island. The main concentration on South Island is around the scenic lakeside resort of Queenstown – see next chapter.

As in the northern hemisphere, the season doesn't really get under way until midwinter – mid or late June; it runs until some time in October. Mount Hutt aims to open first, in late May, and disputes the longest-season title with Whakapapa and Turoa, which in 2008 stayed open until November 16 with a 5m snow base.

Skiing at almost every New Zealand ski resort involves at least a half-hour drive from a nearby town – usually below the snowline – to the ski field itself. Coach transfers from the hotels and towns to the ski fields are generally well organised. The ski field will have a base lodge, usually with a restaurant and a cafeteria, equipment rental and one or two shops, as well as the main lifts. The only on-snow accommodation is in smart apartments at Cardrona on the South Island, and some private lodges at the base of Whakapapa on the North Island.

In what follows, we describe the most prominent resorts (apart from Queenstown and its mountains), but there are other possibilities.

Any of the major resorts is worth a day or two of your time if you're in the area and the conditions are right. But if your credit card is also in good condition, don't miss the heli-skiing; even if you're no expert off-piste, with powder skis it's a doddle, and tremendously satisfying.

Methven Heliski or Wilderness Heliski (03 302 8108) offer the longest and most spectacular runs. Both are operated by the same company, Alpine Guides (based at Mt Cook), but fly to different regions. The cost for about five runs averaging 1000m/3,280ft vertical each is NZ$875. There are several other companies operating on South Island. Harris Mountains Heli-ski (03 442 6722), operating out of Queenstown and Wanaka, caters mainly for the large Japanese market, and the three-run days (NZ$775) are generally very easy skiing, with long waits between lifts. Alpine Heli-ski (03 441 2300), based in Queenstown, was started by a breakaway group from the major Queenstown operation, Southern Lakes Heliski (03 442 6222). Alpine's prices start at NZ$759 for three runs; Southern offers two-, four-, six- and eight-run packages ranging from NZ$675 to NZ$1035, or NZ$1399 to NZ$1490 for a private charter. Both Alpine and Southern are more amenable than Harris Mountains to exciting skiing. Try to leave the arrangements loose, to cope with the changeable weather.

An alternative adventure is to fly by plane to ski down the Tasman Glacier. For two gentle 10km/6 mile schusses down the length of the glacier the cost is high – about NZ$1,175 starting from Queenstown or Christchurch. The main draw is the immense grandeur of the place, along with the flights. If you're a good skier, you will find the Clarke Glacier eight-run day out of Queenstown with Southern Lakes

KEY FACTS

Whakapapa/Turoa

Altitude	1630-2300m	
	5,350-7,550ft	
Lifts		23
Pistes	1050 hectares	
	2,590 acres	
Blue		25%
Red		50%
Black		25%
Snowmaking		some

Mount Hutt

Altitude	1405-2085m	
	4,610-6,840ft	
Lifts		4
Pistes	365 hectares	
	900 acres	
Green		25%
Blue		50%
Black		25%
Snowmaking		
	42 hectares	
	104 acres	

Treble Cone

Altitude	1200-1960m	
	3,940-6,430ft	
Lifts		5
Pistes	550 hectares	
	1,360 acres	
Green		10%
Blue		45%
Black		45%
Snowmaking		
	50 hectares	
	124 acres	

Cardrona

Altitude	1670-1895m	
	5,480-6,220ft	
Lifts		7
Pistes	320 hectares	
	791 acres	
Green		25%
Blue		55%
Black		20%
Snowmaking		some

Snow Park

Altitude	1530m	
	5,020ft	
Lifts		1
Snowmaking		100%

Heliski more satisfying, though more expensive. There is an extensive range of ski touring on offer through Alpine Guides (03 302 8108) as well, from NZ$1695 for two people for three days in the Arrowsmith Ranges.

Snowboarding is very popular in New Zealand, and most of the major resorts have special terrain parks.

New Zealand's biggest resorts are on the slopes of the active volcano Mt Ruapehu, which has occasionally erupted in recent years, leaving the slopes black with volcanic ash. Mt Ruapehu is within four hours' drive of both Auckland and Wellington.

The two ski fields, Whakapapa (pronounced Fukapapa) and Turoa, are in the same ownership and have recently had a NZ$30 million upgrade. The two fields, about an hour's drive apart, offer exciting skiing and wide open slopes on a larger scale than found on the South Island.

Whakapapa, New Zealand's largest ski field with 550 hectares of terrain and over 30 trails, is located on the north-facing slopes. It offers a vertical of 670m/2,200ft served by 14 lifts including three fast lifts. Next to the base lodge is an extensive and self-contained beginners' area, Happy Valley, with half-a-dozen rope tows, a chairlift and snowmaking that allows this section to open early in the season. The resort's lifts and runs range across craggy terrain made especially interesting because of the twists, turns and drops of the solidified lava on which it sits. The ski field is in fact divided by an ancient

lava flow, and the terrain features many cliffs and unexpected breaks along with wide open cruisers and challenging off-piste. There is also a mix of deep gullies, superb natural half-pipes for snowboarders and narrow chutes. There are six mountain restaurants including New Zealand's highest cafe at 2020m/6,630ft.

Accommodation is mostly 6km/4 miles away at Whakapapa village, and the best middle-of-the-road property is a motel named the Skotel. There is on-snow accommodation at the base. A complete anomaly in this area of rustic lodges is the Grand Chateau, a hotel in the classic style of the 1920s, with high ceilings, sweeping drapes over picture windows and marble floors. It has undergone major renovations and extensions in recent years and is highly recommended.

Worth knowing about is the hike to Mt Ruapehu's fizzing Crater Lake. Ask a ski patroller for directions or, better, talk them into taking you on a guided trip. This involves about a half-hour (500m/1,640ft) hike up from the top of the highest T-bar, and then a long traverse across a large flat tundra-like area. A few lefts and rights and you are staring into the mouth of a volcano. Awesome views and neighbouring volcanos give this area an other-worldly feel.

Turoa has an impressive 720m/2,360ft vertical – the biggest in Australasia, over 500 hectares of terrain and plenty of backcountry. The longest run is 4km/2.5 miles. Along with a snazzy new cafe and base

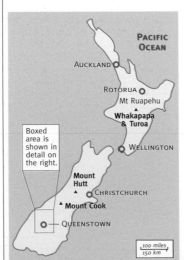

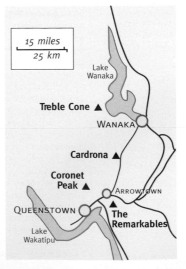

lodge, a new six seater chairlift debuted in 2007 opening up far more advanced terrain. There's plenty of lift-served off-piste scope away from the gentle intermediate runs, plus the chance to ski on the Mangaehuehu Glacier. Accommodation is 20 minutes away in the funky and lively town of Ohakune.

The South Island has 19 ski areas, including seven club fields. **Mt Hutt**, an hour west of Christchurch in the northern part of the island, has a 670m/2,200ft vertical and some of the country's most impressive, consistently steep, wide-open terrain – all within view of the Pacific Ocean. On a clear day you can even see the sandy beaches in the distance beyond the patchwork Canterbury plains – in fact it often snows on the beaches here. The lift system is half the size of Whakapapa's but recently it was totally upgraded and rearranged. The main area is an open bowl with gentle terrain in the centre and the steeper terrain up higher, ringing the ski field.

Mt Hutt has an impressive modern base lodge, including a spacious, welcoming cafe and brasserie with a glorious outdoor terrace, plus a well-stocked rental shop.

Mt Hutt Heliskiing operated by the Alpine Guides team (03 302 8401) offers one run on the North Peak for NZ$175 or three runs in the Mt Hutt backcountry for NZ$475. The heli-pad is right in the car park – just book in at the heli-hut or take the NZ$79 one-way heli-taxi to the ski field.

There is no accommodation on-mountain – most people stay in the little town of **Methven**, where there are several comfortable up-market B&Bs as well as motels. The very British South Island capital of Christchurch, 90 minutes away, is also an option.

About six hours' drive south of Christchurch is the quiet lakeside town of Wanaka, which is also 90 minutes from Queenstown, and there are two resorts accessible from here.

Treble Cone, 20km/12 miles from Wanaka, has more advanced slopes than any other NZ ski area, plus the advantage of a better lift system. To encourage beginners it started offering free skiing on all beginner lifts during the 2009 season. In area, the ski field comes second only to the North Island fields. Three new runs were added in 2006. There are backcountry ski tours, the only ones out of a resort in NZ,

offering powder runs in Treble's back bowls. Back on the ski field, there are two well-maintained intermediate trails, one 3.5km/2 miles, the other 2km/1.2 miles. Both on the main flank and off to the side in Saddle Basin there are long natural half-pipes which are great fun when snow is good, as well as smooth, wide runs for cruising. Treble Cone is reached by a long and winding dirt track that adds to the excitement, although the new owners are planning a gondola from the valley. The ski field offers stunning views across Lake Wanaka, with snow-capped Alpine-style peaks in the distance. There's a good cafe at the lift base with an enormous sun deck.

Cardrona, 34km/21 miles from Wanaka, is famous for its dry snow and is popular with families due to its superior childcare and teaching facilities. The terrain is noted for its well-groomed, flattering cruisers. But there are some serious if short chutes, and the middle basin, Arcadia, has hosted the New Zealand Extreme Skiing Championships. The total vertical is a modest 390m/1,280ft. Millions have been poured into the resort by its family owners over the past few years, resulting in a large base area focused around an odd clock tower. Cardrona is big on terrain features: it has the southern hemisphere's biggest half-pipe and biggest park – 1.2km/0.75 mile long– plus two other parks.

There's a bar and brasserie-style restaurant, a noodle bar with sun deck overlooking the nursery slopes, large rental facility and a licensed childcare centre, plus 15 modern apartments at the base. Learners are looked after well, with three moving carpets.

Snow Park – a dedicated terrain park across the valley from Cardrona – is really making waves and attracting the cream of international freeriders. Two super-pipes, a quarter-pipe, big kickers and more than 40 rails, hits and jumps including NZ's first triple jump line, are all spread across a 24 hectare field and served by one fast quad. An impressive proper restaurant, the Woolshed, has now been built, along with accommodation.

Nearby, at 1500m/4,920ft, is New Zealand's only cross-country ski area, the **Waiorau Snow Farm**, a beautiful place with 55km/34 miles of what the owners claim are the best-prepared and most varied trails in the world.

UK PACKAGES

Wanaka *American Ski*

Phone numbers
From abroad use the prefix +64 and omit the initial '0' of the phone number

TOURIST OFFICES

Whakapapa
t 07 892 3738
info@mtruapehu.com
www.mtruapehu.com

Mount Hutt
t 03 302 8811
service@mthutt.co.nz
www.nzski.com

Treble Cone
t 03 443 7443
info@treblecone.com
www.treblecone.co.nz

Cardrona
t 03 443 7341
info@cardrona.com
www.cardrona.com

Snow Park
t 03 443 9991
info@snowparknz.com
www.snowparknz.com

Waiorau Snow Farm
t 03 443 0300
info@snowfarmnz.com
www.snowfarmnz.com

Interactive resort shortlist builder at **www.wtss.co.uk**

Queenstown

A lively lakeside year-round resort, famous for its adrenalin-rush activities and well placed for a range of South Island resorts

- ➕ For Europeans, more interesting than summer skiing on glaciers
- ➕ Huge heli-skiing areas
- ➕ Lots to do off the slopes, especially for adrenalin junkies
- ➕ Lively town, with good restaurants
- ➕ Grand views locally, and the spectacular 'fjord' country nearby

- ➖ Slopes (in two separate areas locally) are a drive from town
- ➖ Limited lift-served slopes
- ➖ Highly changeable weather
- ➖ No trees, so skiing in bad weather is virtually impossible

RATINGS

The mountains

Extent	★
Fast lifts	★★★
Queues	★★★
Terrain p'ks	★★★★
Snow	★★
Expert	★★★
Intermediate	★★★
Beginner	★★★
X-country	★
Restaurants	★
Schools	★★★
Families	★★★

The resort

Charm	★★
Convenience	★
Scenery	★★★★
Eating out	★★★★★
Après-ski	★★★★
Off-slope	★★★★★

KEY FACTS

Resort	310m
	1,020ft

The Remarkables	
Slopes	1580-1945m
	5,180-6,380ft
Lifts	7
Pistes	220 hectares
	545 acres
Green	30%
Blue	40%
Black	30%
Snowmaking	
	25 acres

Coronet Peak	
Slopes	1230-1650m
	4,040-5,410ft
Lifts	7
Pistes	280 hectares
	690 acres
Green	20%
Blue	45%
Black	35%
Snowmaking	
	203 guns

If you want a single destination in New Zealand – as opposed to visiting a few different mountains on your travels – Queenstown is probably it, especially if you can cope with the cost of a few heli-drops. Although the resorts of North Island are impressive, the Southern Alps are, in the end, more compelling – and their resorts are free of volcanic interruptions.

From Queenstown you have a choice of the two local ski areas – Coronet Peak and The Remarkables – plus the option of an outing to Cardrona and Treble Cone, perhaps with a few nights in the up and coming lakeside town of Wanaka. You can fly to Queenstown from Sydney, Brisbane and Melbourne.

THE RESORT

Queenstown is a winter-and-summer resort on the shore of Lake Wakatipu. (There is a map of the area in the chapter on New Zealand.) No fewer than 173 operators offer every kind of adventure activity, from bungee jumping to river surfing.

The local slopes of Coronet Peak and The Remarkables are described here. There are two others within driving distance – Treble Cone and Cardrona, at least 90 minutes away, near Wanaka – a much quieter town in another beautiful lakeside setting. Cardrona also has some on-mountain lodgings. See the New Zealand introduction.

VILLAGE CHARM ★★
Get a piece of the action
The town itself is no great beauty – it has a very commercial feel; it is now a hotbed of property development. But in recent years much effort has been put into smartening up the place, with such additions as the classy Steamer Wharf, many new lakeside luxury apartments and swanky hotels. The town has a lively, relaxed feel, with more than 160 licensed bars and cafes, some good restaurants, and lots of touristy clothes shops alongside designer boutiques.

CONVENIENCE ★
Definitely not slope-side
Both Coronet Peak and The Remarkables are about a 30-minute drive from Queenstown.

SCENERY ★★★★
Remarkable maybe?
The lakeside setting is splendid, with views to the peaks of the aptly named Remarkables range beyond.

THE MOUNTAINS

At each base area you'll find a mini-resort – a ski school, a ski rental shop, a functional self-service restaurant.

Each area has something for all abilities of skier or boarder, with off-piste opportunities as well as prepared and patrolled trails. They use the American green/blue/black convention for run classification. Both mountains have Burton Learn To Ride systems, designed to turn beginners into life-time riders.

The Remarkables, true to their name, are a dramatic range of craggy peaks visible across the lake from some parts of Queenstown. The slopes, appealing mainly though not exclusively to families and beginners, are tucked in a bowl right behind the largest visible peak, a 45-minute drive from town by smart shuttle bus.

Boarding is popular in New Zealand, and although the two mountains close to Queenstown don't seem to have quite such a hold on the boarding market as Cardrona (see New Zealand introduction), they have everything you need, including equipment and tuition. You needn't go anywhere near a draglift, and there are no flats to worry about except on the lowest green at The Remarkables and a few lower dips to watch in the Rocky Gully area of Coronet.

Coronet Peak, about 25 minutes' drive from Queenstown, is a far more satisfying mountain for intermediates and above. There is a big new day lodge at the base.

EXTENT OF THE SLOPES ★☆☆☆☆
Perfectly formed
At **The Remarkables**, two chairs go up from the base, a fast quad serving easy runs and a slow one that accesses mainly long, easy runs plus a couple of black chutes. The Shadow Basin chair leads to steeper terrain, including three hike-accessed, expert-only chutes that drop down to Lake Alta, and the Homeward Run – a broad, fairly gentle, unprepared slope down to the resort access road, where a shuttle-truck takes you back up.

At Coronet Peak, again, there are three main chairlifts, including a fast quad that accesses practically all the runs, and a six-seater installed in 2005 that opened up much more terrain. The main mountainside is a pleasantly varied intermediate slope, full of highly enjoyable rolling terrain that snowboarders adore, though it steepens near the bottom. The main trail down the face of the mountain is 1.8km/1.1 miles long. A novice trail was added a few seasons ago. A fourth lift, a T-bar, serves another intermediate area to one side. There is also a dedicated beginner area, with drags. It's now level with the day lodge terrace – great for kids. There's night skiing at weekends.

FAST LIFTS ★★★☆☆
They exist
Coronet Peak has two fast chairs that serve most slopes. The Remarkables has a fast quad.

QUEUES ★★★☆☆
It depends
Coronet and The Remarkables can suffer a little from high-season crowds – there are certainly enough beds locally to lead to queues at peak times. But these aren't normally a major worry.

TERRAIN PARKS ★★★★☆
The Remarkables rules
Coronet Peak has two half-pipes but The Remarkables is now the big competitor in the park market with its spectacular mountain-top super-pipe, the trendy new 1km/0.5 mile long

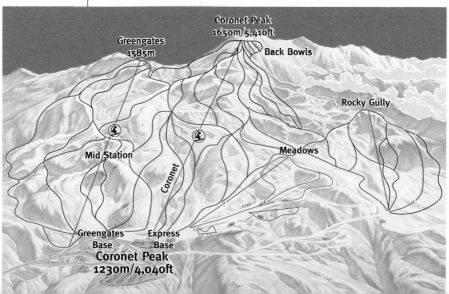

Coronet Peak
1230m/4,040ft

Greengates
1585m

Coronet Peak
1650m/5,410ft

Back Bowls

Rocky Gully

Mid Station

Coronet

Meadows

Greengates
Base

Express
Base

↑ It's quite normal to have decent snow on the slopes, but snowless valleys below. This is the base of Coronet Peak
WWW.NZSKI.COM / MILES HOLDEN

Stash natural terrain area designed by Burton (as in Avoriaz), plus two huge 30m/100ft wide parks, one for beginners. These features have transformed the resort and attracted a whole new market of jibbers.

SNOW RELIABILITY ★★
Good overall, but unpredictable
The New Zealand weather is highly variable, so it's difficult to be confident about snow conditions – though the mountains certainly get oodles of snow. The South Island resorts are at the same sort of latitude as the Alps, but are much more influenced by the ocean; fortunately, their ocean is a lot colder than ours. Coronet tends to receive sleet and/or rain even when it's snowing in The Remarkables. But Coronet Peak now has snowmaking on practically all its intermediate terrain.

FOR EXPERTS ★★★
Challenges exist
Both areas have quite a choice of genuinely black slopes. Coronet's Back Bowls is a seriously steep experts-only area, and there are other black slopes scattered around the mountain. The main enjoyment comes from venturing off-piste all over the place. The Remarkables' Shadow Basin chair serves some excellent (if short) slopes. And The Remarkables' hike-up expert chutes are truly world-class.

FOR INTERMEDIATES ★★★
Fine, within limits
There's some very enjoyable intermediate skiing in both areas – appreciably more at Coronet, where there are also easy blacks to go on to.

FOR BEGINNERS ★★★
Excellent
There are gentle slopes at both areas, served by rope tows, and longer green runs served by chairs. The Remarkables sun deck overlooks the beginner area. And many other diversions if you decide it's a drag.

FOR CROSS-COUNTRY ★
Limited
There is a short loop around a lake in the middle of The Remarkables area, but the only serious cross-country area is near Cardrona (see New Zealand intro).

MOUNTAIN RESTAURANTS ★
Er, what mountain restaurants?
In such small areas, restaurants above base level don't really make sense – though Coronet now has Heidi's Hut offering simple fare. Both areas have a simple cafeteria at the base, and Coronet now has a fancy restaurant too. The Remarkables cafeteria has a big sunny deck and is regularly visited by the local parrots (keas).

SCHOOLS AND GUIDES ★★★
All the usual classes
The schools are well organised, with a wide range of options, including 'guaranteed' beginner classes.

FOR FAMILIES ★★★
Look good
Either mountain is fine for families. At both resorts there are nurseries and clubs for children aged from two to five years old. There's also a wide range of kids' activities on offer each day. The Queenstown nursery takes younger children all day.

STAYING THERE

There are lots of big luxury hotels – all either new or refurbished – built to meet the big summer demand.

Hotels Some hotels are quite some way from central Queenstown. In town they range from the very simple to the glossily pretentious Millennium (03 441 8888), the new 19-room-only Queenstown Park Boutique Hotel, the five-star Sofitel (03 450 0045) and the exquisite, cool Spire (03 441 0004). Also highly regarded are the luxury Chalet Queenstown B&B, the Commonage Villas, the Alta apartments and The Rees Apartment Hotel on the lake. Two of the best-value places to stay are the Heritage Hotel (03 442 4988) or the Mercure Grand Hotel St Moritz (03 442 4990).

EATING OUT ★★★★★
Lots of choice

We're told there are now over 160 bars and restaurants – a quite astonishing figure. Restaurants include Chinese, Italian, Malaysian, Japanese – you name it, Queenstown has it. The lakeside Steamer Wharf complex has some good spots: the new Atlas is the place to go from breakfast or until late and the Boardwalk is the place to go for seafood (or the Wai). Breakfast at Joe's Garage is a must. A dining experience with a difference is the Bath House, located in a 1911 Victorian bath house on the lake shore. Solero Vino has delicious Mediterranean food and a rustic bar. Halo restaurant is newish and serves up delicious organic meals with vegan options. The Bunker does excellent local cuisine such as Bluff oysters and lamb. Gantley's, in a historic home a little way out of town, is a classic restaurant with the most expensive wine list in the area.

At the other end of the scale, pizza-lovers crowd into The Cow, a cosy barn-like place where you sit on logs around a fire waiting for tables. Lone Star offers straight but satisfying American-style food.

APRES-SKI ★★★★
Lively little town

Queenstown has a good range of bars and clubs that stay open late, with disco or live music. The best upmarket bars are Bardeaux, Barmuda and Dux de Lux, an excellent brew-pub in a stone cottage. 12Alt, opened in March 2009, is the town's first true gay-friendly bar. Winnebagos is very lively and has a roof that slides back to the night sky to allow the hot and sweaty dance floor a blast of fresh air and even fresh snow. There's a small upmarket casino in the plush Steamer Wharf, and Skycity Casino in the mall. The Steamer Wharf also contains Minus Five, an ice bar, and The Boiler Room for 80s music. There's duty-free shopping in the mall opposite.

OFF THE SLOPES ★★★★★
Scare yourself silly

There are lots of scary things to do – see the feature box below. To the west is the spectacularly scenic 'fjord country', and you can go on independent or guided walks. The sightseeing flights by plane or helicopter are to be preferred to the slow bus ride – weather permitting. The Skyline gondola rises 400m/1,310ft above Queenstown for a great view; try a spin down the public go-cart track, too. Cruise the lake on an historic steamship or go wine tasting. Arrowtown is interesting for a quick visit – it's a cute, touristy old mining town where you can kit yourself out to go panning for gold or enjoy excellent food and boutique brews in the Arrow Brewing Company, new in 2009. The Winter Festival, in early July, is an annual 'action-packed week of mayhem'.

UK PACKAGES

AmeriCan Ski, Kuoni, Ski Dream

Phone numbers
From abroad use the prefix +64 and omit the initial '0' of the phone number

TOURIST OFFICE

The Remarkables and Coronet Peak
t 03 442 4640
snowcentre@nzski.com
www.nzski.com

GET THAT ADRENALIN RUSH

The streets of Queenstown are lined by no fewer than 173 activity operators offering various artificial thrills. We've sampled just a few.

AJ Hackett's bungee jump at Kawarau Bridge is where this crazy activity got off the ground, as it were. The Shotover Jet Boat experience is less demanding – whizzing along the rocky river in a boat that can get along in very shallow water, passing very close to cliffs and trees. Fly By Wire involves swinging through a canyon on a cable propelled by a fan engine on your rear. The whitewater rafting takes you over some exciting rapids. One route even passes through a tunnel excavated in the gold-mining days.

+ Varied terrain and excellent off-piste
+ Cheap local prices

- Remote and inaccessible, even from Buenos Aires
- Very little English spoken

Argentina's two main resorts are of sharply contrasting character and a long way apart physically as well. Go to San Carlos de Bariloche for the cultural experience and the intermediate piste skiing, and go to Las Leñas for the best and most extensive off-piste terrain in the southern hemisphere. We combined Las Leñas with Chilean resorts on our visit – something we'd recommend.

KEY FACTS

Las Leñas

Slopes	2240-3430m
	7,350-11,250ft
Lifts	13
Pistes	27
Green	8%
Blue	23%
Red/Black	69%

Bariloche (Catedral)

Slopes	1030-2180m
	3,380-7,150ft
Lifts	38
Pistes	120km
	75 miles
Green	15%
Blue	75%
Red/Black	10%
Snowmaking	25 acres

UK PACKAGES

Las Leñas *Ski Dream, Skitracer, Skiworld*

TOURIST OFFICES

Las Leñas
www.laslenas.com

Bariloche
www.
catedralaltapatagonia.
com/invierno
www.bariloche.com

Cerro Castor
www.cerrocastor.com

Argentina lies on the eastern, rain-shadowed side of the Andes, a recipe for dry, light powder at high altitudes throughout a season that lasts from June to October.

The premier resort is **Las Leñas**, built by Frenchmen in the 1980s when pyramid architecture ruled. It dominates a white wilderness, miles from civilisation; the nearest major airport is Mendoza 400km/250 miles away (Malargue is much nearer but has few scheduled flights).

But be warned: gales and blizzards can close most of the resort down for days, especially during late July and early August. Mid-August to mid-September is the best time to visit.

A dozen lifts serve a few groomed slopes, and freestylers can rip it up in the terrain park and half-pipe. But the real attraction is for experts: an antiquated double chair called El Marte opens up 270° of ski-anywhere off-piste terrain (plus a couple of pistes) – from gentle slopes suiting powder novices to couloirs and cliffs for the brave. But before you are allowed to venture into the great off-piste, you have to stop at a mountain-top hut where a local asks you to enter your name and passport number, and sign a document in Spanish releasing the resort from all responsibility for you. He then sticks a coloured tag, valid for a week, on your clothing, which allows you to venture where you like.

But venture not without a guide. We saw snowboarders precariously perched on top of 100m/330ft cliffs and skiers riding under dodgy-looking cornices. The place is vast and you need to know where you are going. Our recommendation would be to book a week with the Whistler-based

ski school Extremely Canadian, which specialises in steep and deep terrain and runs trips to Las Leñas every year (see www.extremelycanadian.com). We went with them and had a great time. There's good snowcat-skiing too.

The smartest hotel is the 5-star Pisces, with pool, hot tub, sauna and gym. Escorpio is a 4-star option. There are a few bars and clubs and a casino.

San Carlos de Bariloche has almost nothing in common with Las Leñas, except that it is Argentina's only other international winter sports option. Founded in 1903 by Swiss and German immigrants, it is a substantial resort town with a cheerful lifestyle, and is still influenced by the Swiss-German culture. The smart Llao Llao Resort and Spa, on a bluff above the lake, has a pool, sauna and fitness centre. The Edelweiss offers top-quality facilities in the town centre.

The slopes are at Catedral, 20 minutes by shuttle-bus. They are well below the treeline, and good-quality snow cannot be guaranteed. The runs, which are cut through the forest, face east as protection from the prevailing westerlies and suit intermediates best, though there is some good off-piste. There's a terrain park and half-pipe. It's best to avoid August, which is the Argentinian society choice and therefore prone to long queues.

Cerro Castor, the most southerly city in the world, is a remote outpost just 195m/640ft above sea level. The Beagle Strait off Tierra del Fuego is famously windy, but winter is the calmest period and conditions are often surprisingly good. It has a small ski area with 19 runs but a vertical drop of 770m/2,530ft. The British team trained here in the run-up to the Turin Winter Olympics.

Chile

+ One of the most varied options for the European summer
+ The Andes are spectacular
+ Good snow records
+ Good local food and wine

- It's a long way from Britain
- By Alpine standards, the ski areas are small and resorts lack character
- Little English spoken outside hotels
- Nightlife is limited

If you want to carry on skiing or boarding in our summer, Chile is a good choice. It's a long way to go (it took us 36 hours from leaving home to arriving at our first hotel on our visit) and the ski areas are small; but if you combine visits to at least two resorts with, say, a tour of Chile's wine areas or a visit to the Atacama desert, it can make a varied and compelling holiday.

KEY FACTS

Valle Nevado/La Parva/El Colorado

Slopes	2430-3670m
	7.970-12,040ft
Lifts	43
Pistes	113km
	70 miles
Green	14%
Blue	30%
Red	42%
Black	14%

Portillo

Slopes	2450-3310m
	8,040-10,860ft
Lifts	14
Pistes	1,200 acres
Green	10%
Blue	35%
Red	35%
Black	20%

Termas de Chillán

Slopes	1600-2700m
	5,250-8,860ft
Lifts	13
Pistes	35km
	22 miles
Green	22%
Blue	41%
Red	31%
Black	6%

Lying in the path of the prevailing winds off the Pacific, the Chilean Andes are ideally located to catch all the snow that's going, resulting in truly dramatic falls in good years. In such a long narrow country, conditions vary considerably from north to south. In general, the season starts in mid-June and finishes in early October (mid-July to mid-September is the best time to visit). The ski areas are small in comparison with big Alpine resorts (a keen piste-basher could ski all the pistes in an area in a day) but there's a lot of off-piste available. Adventurous skiers and boarders should sign on for the well-run heli-ski operations, both for the spectacular flights over 5000m/16,400ft peaks and the remote powder fields. We'd recommend visiting two or three ski areas as you are travelling so far.

Valle Nevado (just 60km/37 miles from Santiago), La Parva and El Colorado form the biggest area of linked pistes and are known as the Tres Valles (Chile's equivalent of the Three Valleys). **La Parva** is condoville for the capital's elite, a collection of apartments occupied mostly at weekends, while **El Colorado** offers a scattering of accommodation around a shabby base station. Both are linked to **Valle Nevado**, a high-rise, wood-clad tourist development in the mode of Les Arcs, not surprisingly as it was designed by the Chilean architect Eduardo Stern after he'd worked in France and on the Les Arcs project. The best hotel is called Valle Nevado and has the best restaurant, the Fourchette d'Or which serves delicious international food and excellent breakfasts. Puerta del Sol is the mid-market option and 3 Puntas the budget choice. All three offer half-board packages and you can generally eat dinner at a restaurant in a different hotel if you like. There is a small communal outdoor pool, a few shops, hotel bars and a nightclub.

Valle Nevado is ski-in/ski-out and has a network of well-groomed, mainly intermediate pistes served by 11 lifts including the Andes Express (Chile's only high-speed chair). There is no Tres Valles lift pass – you pay extra on a day that you want ski another resort.

Portillo, 164km/102 miles from Santiago, consists of little more than the startlingly bright yellow Hotel Portillo, set beside the potholed main road from Chile to Argentina. It was built in the 1940s and owned and run by the Chilean government until they sold it to two Americans in 1962. It is now run by Henry Purcell (the nephew of one of the Americans) and his son Michael (aka Miguel). Service is impeccable, with 550 staff (mostly long-serving – the head waiter has been there over 40 years) serving a maximum of 450 guests. The traditional public rooms are handsomely furnished with polished wood and leather. And there's a huge outdoor hot pool to relax in after coming off the slopes.

The hotel and a lake in front of it stand between two unconnected areas. Turn right for the El Plateau double chair to Tio Bob's, the only mountain restaurant. Then drop into the rocky jaws of Garganta, the challenging black run back to base, or sweep down the friendly blue. The Laguna quad chair, on the other side of the hotel, accesses the Juncalillo piste, the

Hotel Portillo was built in the 1940s and behind its brash exterior are lovely, old-fashioned public rooms furnished with polished wood and leather →

DAVE WATTS

UK PACKAGES

Valle Nevado *AmeriCan Ski, Crystal, Crystal Finest, Kuoni, Momentum, Scott Dunn Latin America, Ski Safari, Skiworld*
Portillo *AmeriCan Ski, Crystal, Kuoni, Momentum, Scott Dunn Latin America, Ski Dream, Ski Safari, Skiworld*
Pucón *Snoworks*
Termas de Chillán *Momentum, Scott Dunn Latin America, Ski Safari*

TOURIST OFFICES

Valle Nevado
www.vallenevado.com
Portillo
www.skiportillo.com
Termas de Chillán
www.skichillan.cl

longest in the resort. But to stick to the groomers – and there are few of them (you could ski them all in a couple of hours) – is to miss the point. Portillo has radical terrain on both sides of the mountain, but the first challenge is the unique Va et Vient slingshot lifts. Skiers ride on linked buttons, four or five abreast, blasting upwards at high speed to a treacherously steep landing point. From the top of Roca Jack, the longest of the four slingshots, a high traverse, leads to a series of chutes. When the lake is frozen, skiers can take the steep powder slopes down to the shore and skate back to the hotel. To get the most out of the area you need a guide (and you need to be prepared to hike from the top of the lifts). Good off-piste skiers should consider going on former World Freeskiing Champion, Chris Davenport's, Ski with the Superstars week here – see www.steepskiing.com.

Termas de Chillán is Chile's leading ski and spa resort, in a forested setting and with a small network of lifts under twin volcanoes, which provide the thermal water and mud for the spa. You can ski all day and then enjoy a relaxing soak and a variety of spa treatments (including being coated in volcanic mud) to get rid of the aches and pains.

The resort is around 80km/50 miles from the railway station at Chillán, a small town four hours by train to the south of Santiago (or you can fly to Concepción 195km/121 miles away).

The biggest and best hotel is the ski-in/ski-out 5-star Gran. This is also home to the main spa, two restaurants, a casino and a conference centre. The cosier, chalet-style Pirimahuida is 10 minutes' drive down

the valley in Las Trancas. And there are slope-side apartments, a shop and a rustic Club Haus restaurant.

The top of the El Tata T-bar at 2700m/8,860ft is the starting point for the wonderful, away-from-all-the-lifts top-to-bottom of the mountain Golf Alto run – at 13km/8 miles long and with a vertical drop of 1100m/3,610 feet it is South America's longest piste. It is rolling, undulating and interestingly varied with some narrow sections and some where you need to schuss to get up the incline beyond. As well as 33 largely intermediate pistes (which we skied in three hours or so), there is off-piste (best in September, when there is spring snow normally). For freestylers, there's a terrain park with half- and quarter-pipes, jumps and a fun box. As well as downhill skiing there is cross-country, snowmobiling and dog sledding.

Like Termas de Chillán, **Pucón**, on the eastern shore of Lake Villarrica, was developed as a summer resort. The present lift system was installed between 1988 and 1990 and serves limited terrain for all standards. The climb up to the crater, which requires skins and crampons, takes between two and four hours from the top of the lifts, but it's worth it for the awesome close-up of molten lava. The Gran Hotel Pucón, built in 1934 on the lake shore, is the best place to stay.

Cerro Mirador is Chile's most southerly snow-zone, located 8km/5 miles outside Punta Arenas in the Magellanes National Reserve. It has wooded runs and dramatic views over the Magellan Straits. But it is tiny, with just 11 pistes accessed by a double chair and a T-bar. There is no on-mountain accommodation.

REFERENCE SECTION

Ski businesses 736

Tour ops, agents, etc

Ski retailers 741

Resort directory / index 742

735

SKI BUSINESSES

This is a list of ski businesses including all the holiday operators and ski travel agents we know about.

360 Sun and Ski
Family holidays in Les Carroz, French Alps
Tel 0870 068 3180

Action Outdoor Holidays
All-inclusive holidays in the French Alps
Tel 0845 890 0362

Albus Travel
St Anton specialist
Tel 01449 711952

Alpharooms.com
Ski travel agent
Tel 0871 911 0030

Alpine Action
Chalets in Les Trois Vallées
Tel 01273 466535

Alpine Answers
Ski travel agent + tailor-made holidays
Tel 020 7801 1080

Alpine Club
Chalets in St-Martin-de-Belleville
Tel +33 630 226215

Alpine Life
Catered chalet in Saas-Fee
Tel 0780 198 2645

Alpine Ski and Golf Company
Chalets in Les Houches and Chamonix
Tel 07791 147106

Alpine Weekends
Weekends in the Alps
Tel 020 8944 9762

Alps Accommodation
Accommodation in Samoëns and Les Carroz
Tel +33 688 655070

Alpsholiday
Apartments in Serre-Chevalier
Tel +33 492 204426

Altitude Holidays
Catered chalet and in-resort services in Le Grand Massif
Tel 0870 870 7669

AmeriCan Ski
North America specialist plus undiscovered gems in France
Tel 01892 511894

American Ski Classics
Holidays in major North American resorts
Tel 0870 242 0623

Aravis Alpine Retreat
Renovated Alpine farmhouse in St Jean-de-Sixt (La Clusaz) for bespoke groups by arrangement
Tel 020 8748 6057

Ardmore Educational Travel
Group and school trips
Tel 01628 826699

Balkan Holidays
Holidays in Bulgaria, Slovenia, Romania and Serbia
Tel 0845 130 1114

Barrelli Ski
Chalets in Champagny, Chamonix and Les Houches
Tel 0117 940 1500

Belvedere Properties
Luxury chalets in Méribel and Verbier
Tel 01264 738 257

Bigfoot Travel
Hotel, self-catered and catered chalet holidays in the Chamonix Valley
Tel +33 450 530063

BoardnLodge.com Ltd
Catered and self-catered holidays in Europe
Tel 020 3239 8181

Borderline
Specialist in Barèges
Tel +33 562 926895

Bramble Ski
Chalets in Verbier and Kicking Horse
Tel 0871 218 0988

Canadian Affair
Holidays in Canada
Tel 0141 248 6777

Canadian Powder Tours Chalet Holidays
Chalet holidays in Western Canada
Tel +1 250 423 3019

Catered Ski Chalets
Ski travel agent
Tel 020 3080 0202

Chalet Bezière
Chalet in Samoëns
Tel +33 450 905181

Chalet Chocolat
Chalet in Morzine
Tel 01872 580814

The Chalet Company
Catered chalets in Morzine
Tel 0871 717 4208 / +33 450 796840

Chalet Entre Deux Eaux
Chalet in Morzine
Tel +33 450 37 47 55

Chalet Espen
Chalet in Engelberg
Tel +41 41 637 2220

Chalet Famille
Chalet in Morzine
Tel 0870 068 3456

Chaletfinder.co.uk
Ski travel agent
Tel 01453 766094

Chalet la Forêt
Chalet in Chamonix
Tel 0754 557 5277

The Chalet Group
Chalet accommodation in Europe and Canada

Chalet Gueret
Luxury chalet near Morzine
Tel 01884 255437

Chalet Kiana
Self-catered chalet in Les Contamines
Tel 07968 123470

Chalet Number One
Chalet in Ste-Foy
Tel 01328 823667 / +33 479 064755

Chalet Snowboard
Snowboard holidays in Morzine
Tel 020 8133 4180

Challenge Activ
Chalets and apartments in Morzine
Tel 0871 717 4113 / +33 450 790307

Chamonix.uk.com
Apartment holidays in central Chamonix
Tel 01224 641559

Le Chardon Mountain Lodges Val d'Isère
Upmarket chalets in Val d'Isère
Tel 0845 092 0350

Chez Michelle
Self-catering apartment in Samoëns
Tel 01372 456463

Chill Chalet
Accommodation in Paradiski
Tel +33 614 611437

Club Europe Schools Skiing
Schools trips to Europe
Tel 0800 496 4996

Club Med
All-inclusive holidays in 'ski villages'
Tel 0845 3676767

Cold Comforts Lodging
Whistler specialist
Tel 0800 881 8429 / 020 7993 8544

Collineige
Chamonix valley specialist
Tel 01483 579242

Connick Ski
Chalet with in-house ski school in Châtel
Tel +33 450 732212 / +33 607 131537

Contiki Holidays
Holidays for 18-35s
Tel 0845 075 0990

Cooltip Mountain Holidays
Chalets in Méribel
Tel 01964 563563

The Corporate Ski Company
Event management company
Tel 020 8542 8555

Crystal
Major mainstream operator
Tel 0871 231 2256

Crystal Finest
Ski holidays to Europe and North America
Tel 0871 971 0364

Descent International
Luxury chalets in France and Switzerland
Tel 020 7384 3854

Ski businesses

736

Weekly news updates and resort links at **www.wtss.co.uk**

Directski.com
Holidays in Europe and North America
Tel 0800 201 205

Elegant Resorts
Luxury ski holidays
Tel 01244 897333

Elevation Holidays
Holidays in the Austrian Alps
Tel 0845 644 3578

Erna Low
Self-catering holidays in the Alps and North America
Tel 0845 863 0525

Esprit Ski
Families specialist in Europe
Tel 01252 618300

Exodus
Cross-country skiing holidays
Tel 0845 863 9600

Family Friendly Skiing
Family specialist in the Three Valleys – in-house nannies
Tel +33 450 327121

Family Ski Company
Family skiing holidays in France and Switzerland
Tel 01684 540333

Ferme de Montagne
Luxury chalet hotel in Les Gets
Tel 0800 072 3069

Finlays
Catered chalets in Val d'Isère, Courchevel and Paradiski; short breaks in France and Switzerland
Tel 01573 226611

First Choice Ski
Major mainstream operator
Tel 0871 664 0130

Flexiski
Weekends and corporate events in Europe
Tel 020 8939 0861

Friendship Travel
Holidays for singles 25 to 60
Tel 0871 200 2035

Frontier Ski
Holidays in Canada and Alaska
Tel 020 8776 8709

Funway Holidays
US and Canada programme
Tel 0844 557 0770

Haig Ski
Chalet with guiding near Morzine
Tel +33 450 811947

Hannibals
Holidays in Serre-Chevalier
Tel 01233 813105

Headwater Holidays
Cross-country skiing holidays
Tel 01606 720199

High Mountain Holidays
Holidays in Chamonix
Tel 01993 775540

Holiday in Alps
Chalets and apartments in the French Alps
Tel 01327 828239

Huski
Chalet holidays in Chamonix
Tel 08000 971 760

Ifyouski.com
Ski travel agent
Tel 0844 371 7733 / 0844 371 7734

Iglu.com
Ski travel agent
Tel 020 8542 6658

Independent Ski Links
Ski travel agent + accommodation, packages and tailor-made holidays in Europe and N America
Tel 01964 533905

I Need Snow
Ski travel agent
Tel 020 8123 7817

Inghams
Major mainstream operator
Tel 020 8780 4447

Inntravel
Holidays in the snow
Tel 01653 617941

Inspired to Ski
Holidays with tuition in France
Tel 07885 630340

Interactive Resorts
Catered chalets worldwide
Tel 020 3080 0202

Interhome
Apartments and chalets in Europe
Tel 020 8780 6633

Interski
Group holidays with tuition in Italy
Tel 01623 456333

Italian Safaris
Italian ski specialists and multi-resort safaris
Tel +39 347 348 5757 / 07930 902590

James Orr Heli-ski
Heli-skiing packages in Canada
Tel 01799 516964

Jeffersons Private Jet Holidays
Luxury holidays by private jet
Tel 020 8746 2496

Just Skiing
Courmayeur specialist plus La Thuile and Cervinia, also in the Italian Alps
Tel 01202 479988

Just Slovenia
Accommodation in Slovenia
Tel 01373 814230

Kaluma Ski
Holidays in the Alps
Tel 0870 442 8044

Karibuni
Short-break chalet holidays in La Clusaz
Tel 01202 661865

Kuoni
Worldwide trips
Tel 01306 742500

Kwik Ski
Ski travel agent
Tel 0800 655 6300

Lagrange Holidays
Ski holidays in Europe
Tel 020 7371 6111

The Last Resort
Catered chalet and self-catered apartments in the Aravis ski region
Tel 0800 652 3977

Leisure Direction
Self-drive holidays to the French Alps and the Pyrenees
Tel 0844 576 5504

Le Ski
Chalets in Courchevel, Val d'Isère and La Tania
Tel 01484 548996

Made to Measure Ski
Wide variety of tailor-made holidays
Tel 01243 533333

Mark Warner
Chalet hotel holidays in big-name resorts
Tel 0871 703 3881

Marmotte Mountain Adventure
Chalets in Chamonix Valley
Tel +33 682 891523

McNab Snowsports
Snowboarding holidays worldwide
Tel 0141 416 3828

Meije Tours
Accommodation in La Grave
Tel +33 476 799246

Meriski
Chalet specialist in Méribel
Tel 01285 648510

MGS Ski Limited
Hotel and apartments in Val Cenis
Tel 01603 742842

Momentum Ski
Tailor-made and ski weekend specialists
Tel 020 7371 9111

Mountain Action
Chalet in St Martin de Belleville
Tel 0871 717 4213

Mountain Beds
Tailor-made holidays, mainly in Verbier
Tel 020 7924 2650

A Mountain Chalet
Chalet in La Rosière
Tel +33 479 065738

Mountain Heaven
Catered and self-catered accommodation in France and Switzerland
Tel 0151 625 1921

Mountain Lodge
Chalet hotel in Les Crosets, Portes du Soleil
Tel 0845 1271750

Mountainsun Ltd
Chalets in Europe
Tel 07941 196517

Mountain Tracks
Off-piste courses, hut to hut ski touring and avalanche awareness programmes
Tel 020 8123 2978

Neilson
Major mainstream operator
Tel 0845 070 3460

Nick Ski
Catered chalet in La Tania
Tel +33 673 436769

Ski businesses

737

Interactive resort shortlist builder at **www.wtss.co.uk**

Norwegian Wood Travel
Holidays in Norway
Tel 01562 67707

Optimum Ski
Chalet in Villaroger, part of Les Arcs ski area
Tel 0131 208 1154 /
+33 479 069126

The Oxford Ski Company
Chalets and hotels in Europe and North America
Tel 0870 787 1785

Peak Leisure
Chalet in Ste-Foy
Tel 0870 760 5610

Peak Retreats
Holidays to traditional French Alps resorts
Tel 0844 576 0123

Peak Ski
Chalets in Verbier
Tel 01442 832629

PGL Ski
Specialist in school group holidays and holidays for teenagers
Tel 08700 551551

Powder Byrne
Luxury hotel holidays in Europe
Tel 020 8246 5300

Powder Skiing in North America Limited
Heli-skiing holidays in Canada
Tel 020 7736 8191

Powder White
Chalets in big-name resorts
Tel 020 8877 8888

Première Neige
Catered and self-catered holidays in Ste-Foy, with nanny service
Tel 0870 383 1000

Pure Alpine Holidays
Ski and tennis holidays
Tel 01273 778006

Purple Ski
Chalet holidays in Méribel
Tel 01885 488799

PV-Holidays.com (Pierre & Vacances)
Apartments in France
Tel 0870 0267 145

Ramblers Holidays
Mostly cross-country holidays
Tel 01707 331133

Reach4theAlps
Holidays in the French Alps
Tel 0845 680 1947

Richmond Holidays
Holidays for all members of the church family
Tel 020 3004 2661

Ride & Slide
Chalets in Morzine
Tel +33 450 388962

Rocketski.com
Club hotels and chalets in France and Italy
Tel 01273 810777

Rude Chalets
Holidays in Morzine, Avoriaz and Chamonix
Tel 0870 068 7030

Scott Dunn Latin America
Tailor-made holidays to South America
Tel 020 8682 5030

Scott Dunn Ski
Luxury chalet and hotel holidays
Tel 020 8682 5050

Silver Ski
Chalet holidays in France
Tel 01622 735544

Simon Butler Skiing
Holidays with ski instruction in Megève
Tel 0870 873 0001 /
01483 212726

Simply Alpine
Chalets and apartments in Europe and N America
Tel 023 9279 8901

Ski 2
Specialists in Champoluc (Monterosa) and San Cassiano (Sella Ronda)
Tel 01962 713330

Ski Activity
Holidays in big-name resorts
Tel 01738 840888

Ski Addiction
Chalets and hotels in the Portes du Soleil
Tel +33 450 733983

Skialot
Chalet in Châtel
Tel 0780 156 9264 / 0845 004 3622

Ski Alpage
Chalet in St-Martin-de-Belleville
Tel +33 479 089228

Ski Amis
Catered chalet and self-catered holidays in the French Alps
Tel 020 7692 0850

Ski Basics
Catered chalets in Méribel
Tel 01225 429378

Ski Beat
Chalets in the French Alps
Tel 01243 780405

Ski Blanc
Chalet holidays in Méribel
Tel 020 8502 9082

SkiBound
Schools division of First Choice
Tel 01273 244531

Skibug
Catered chalets in La Plagne
Tel 020 8886 0271

Ski Chamois
Holidays in Morzine
Tel 01302 369006

Ski Collection
French self-catering 3- and 4-star apartment specialist
Tel 0844 576 0175

Ski Cuisine
Chalets in Méribel
Tel 01702 589543

Ski-Dazzle
Chalet holidays in Les Trois Vallées
Tel +33 479 001725

Ski Deep
Chalets in La Tania and Le Praz
Tel 01483 722706 / +33 479 081905

Ski-direct.co.uk
Ski travel agent
Tel 0844 553 3501

Ski Dream
Major operator to worldwide destinations, specialising in North America
Tel 0845 277 3333

Ski Etoile
Chalets, hotels and apartments in Montgenèvre
Tel 01952 253252

Ski Europe
Ski travel agent
Tel 01350 728869

Ski Expectations
Ski travel agent + chalets and hotels in Europe, the USA and Canada
Tel 01799 531888

Ski Famille
Family holidays in Les Gets and Morzine
Tel 0845 644 3764

Ski France
Packaged and tailor-made holidays and accommodation in France
Tel 0845 862 1121

Ski Freedom
Chalets in Verbier, Champéry and Zinal
Tel 01442 263377

Ski Freshtracks
Holidays for Ski Club of GB members
Tel 0845 458 0784 / 020 8410 2022

Ski Hame
Catered chalets in Méribel and La Tania
Tel 01875 320157

Ski Hillwood
Austrian family holidays
Tel 01923 290700

Ski Hiver
Chalets in Peisey (Paradiski)
Tel 020 8144 3680

Skiholidayextras.com
Cheap deals on ski extras (passes, hire, lessons)
Tel 0870 787 3402

Ski-in.co.uk
Apartment and chalet in Serre-Chevalier
Tel 01630 672540

Ski Independence
USA, Canada, Japan, France, Switzerland and Austria
Tel 0845 310 3030

Skiing Austria
Accommodation in Austria
Tel 020 8123 7817

Ski La Cote
Catered chalet holidays in the Portes du Soleil
Tel 01482 668357

Ski Line
Ski travel agent + chalet holidays in Europe and North America
Tel 020 8313 3999

Ski Link
Courchevel specialist
Tel 0871 218 0174

Ski Magic
Chalet holidays in La Tania
Tel 0151 677 2317

Ski McNeill
Ski travel agent + packages and tailor-made flexible trips to Europe
Tel 0870 6001359

Ski Miquel Holidays
Small but eclectic programme
Tel 01457 821200

Ski-Monterosa Ltd
Monterosa (Alagna) specialist
Tel 0151 353 2317

Ski Morgins Holidays
Chalet holidays in Morgins
Tel 01568 770681

Ski Morzine
Accommodation in Morzine
Tel 01932 837639

Skiology.co.uk
Chalets in Les Carroz
Tel 07894 758535

Ski Olympic
Chalet holidays in France
Tel 01302 328820

Ski Peak
Specialist in Vaujany
Tel 01428 608070

SkiPlan Travel Service
Schools programme
Tel 0870 241 4499

Ski Power
Chalets in La Tania and Courchevel 1650
Tel 01737 306029

Ski Rosie
Luxury catered chalet in Morgins and self-catered apartments in Châtel
Tel +41 24 477 7677

Ski Safari
Tailor-made specialist to Canada, USA, Switzerland, Chile and Japan
Tel 01273 224060

Ski Soleil
Chalet and apartments in La Plagne
Tel 020 3239 3454

Ski Solutions
Tailor-made holidays
Tel 020 7471 7777

Ski Supreme
Holidays to France
Tel 0845 194 7541

Ski Surf
Ski travel agent
Tel 020 8731 2111

Skitopia
Hotels and chalets in the French Alps
Tel 01209 860002

Ski Total
Chalet holidays in Europe
Tel 01252 618333

Skitracer.com
Ski travel agent + holidays in Europe, Canada and America
Tel 020 8600 1668

Ski Travel Centre
Ski travel agent
Tel 0141 649 9696

Ski businesses

739

Interactive resort shortlist builder at **www.wtss.co.uk**

Ski-Val
Catered chalets in France and Austria
Tel 01822 611200

Ski Verbier
Specialists in Verbier
Tel 020 7401 1101

Ski Weekend
Weekend and ten-day holidays
Tel 01392 878353

Ski Weekender
Ski weekend specialist in La Clusaz
Tel 01202 661865

Skiweekends.com
3- and 6-day holidays to The Three Valleys and the Chamonix Valley
Tel 01992 532270

Ski with Julia
Hotels, catered and self-catered chalets in Verbier
Tel 01386 584478

Skiworld
European and North American programme
Tel 08444 930 430

Ski Yogi
Hotels and catered chalets in Italy
Tel 01799 531886

Sloping Off
Schools holidays
Tel 01273 648200

Snowbizz
Family ski specialist in Puy-St-Vincent
Tel 01778 341455

Snowcard Insurance Services
Winter sports insurance
Tel 01327 262805

Snowcoach
Holidays to Austria and France
Tel 01727 866177

SnowCrazy
Chalets in La Rosière, Les Arcs, Ste Foy and La Plagne
Tel 01342 302910

Snow Finders
Ski travel agent + holidays to Europe and N America
Tel 01858 466888

Snowfocus
Chalet in Châtel
Tel 01392 479555 / +33 450 732863

Snow Hounds
Ski travel agent
Tel 01243 788487

Snowlife
Catered chalet in La Clusaz
Tel 01534 863630

Snowline
Catered chalets in France with childcare
Tel 0844 557 3118

Snoworks
Holidays with ski courses
Tel 08701 225549

Snowpod
Serviced apartments with a twist in Tignes
Tel 07881 725062

Snowscape
Weekly and flexible trips to Austria
Tel 08453 708570

Snowstar Holidays
Tignes specialist in catered chalets
Tel 020 8133 8411

SnowYourWay.com
Valloire and Valfréjus (Maurienne) with transport provided
Tel 0870 760 6448

Snowy Pockets
Chalet and apartment holidays in Arosa
Tel 01707 251696

Solo's
Singles' holidays, ages 25 to 69
Tel 0844 815 0005

La Source
Chalet and other accommodation in Villard-Reculas (Alpe-d'Huez)
Tel 01707 655988

Stanford Skiing
Megève specialist
Tel 01603 477471

Star Ski Chalets
Chalets in Morzine
Tel +33 679 181401

STC
Tailormade holidays in Europe and North America, specialising in Austria
Tel 01483 771222

Sugar Mountain
Chalet in Morzine
Tel +33 450 749033

Supertravel
Upmarket European and North American holidays
Tel 020 7962 9933

Susie Ward Alpine Holidays
Upmarket accommodation in Châtel
Tel +33 675 819196

Switzerland Travel Centre
Specialists in Swiss resorts
Tel 020 7420 4900

Ted Bentley Chalet Holidays
Luxury chalet holidays in Nendaz
Tel 01934 820854

Teletext Holidays
Travel agency
Tel 0808 201 4444

TheWhiteChalet.com
Chalet in Argentière
Tel +33 450 542284

Thomson Ski
Major mainstream operator
Tel 0871 971 0578

Trail Alpine
Chalet in Morzine
Tel 0870 750 6560

Trailfinders
North American programme
Tel 0845 050 5900

Transylvania Live
Holidays in Romania
Tel 0808 101 6781

UCPA
All-inclusive budget trips to France
Tel +33 892 680 599

United Vacations Ski USA & Canada
US and Canada programme
Tel 0844 499 2229

Val d'Isère A La Carte
Specialists in Val d'Isère hotels and self-catering holidays
Tel +33 629 894457

Vanilla Ski
Chalet in Seez (near La Rosière and Les Arcs)
Tel 01932 860696

VIP
Chalets in Val d'Isère, Méribel and Zermatt
Tel 0844 557 3119

Virgin Snow
Holidays to America and Canada
Tel 0844 557 3962

White Roc
Weekends and tailor-made hotel holidays; luxury chalets/apartments with hotel services
Tel 020 7792 1188

YSE
Chalet holidays in Val d'Isère
Tel 0845 122 1414

SKI RETAILERS

Here we list ski equipment shops – all these shops stock this guidebook.

SOUTH-WEST ENGLAND

Devon Ski Centre
Oak Place, Newton Abbot
Tel 01626 351278

Skate and Ski
104 High Street, Staple Hill,
Bristol
Tel 0117 970 1356

Snow & Rock
Units 1-3 Shield Retail Ctre,
Link Road, Filton, Bristol
Tel 0117 914 3000

Team Ski
37 High East Street,
Dorchester, Dorset
Tel 01305 268035

Westsports
Market House, Marlborough
Rd, Old Town, Swindon
Tel 01793 532588

SOUTH-EAST ENGLAND

Alpine Room
71-73 Main Road, Danbury
Tel 01245 223563

Mountain High
41 Reading Road,
Pangbourne, Berkshire
Tel 0118 984 1851

Ski Bartlett
1-2 Rosslyn Parade, Uxbridge
Road, Hillingdon, Middlesex
Tel 020 8848 0040

Snow & Rock
188 Kensington High Street,
London
Tel 020 7937 0872

Snow & Rock
4 Mercer Street, Covent
Garden, London
Tel 020 7420 1444

Snow & Rock
4 Grays Inn Road, London
Tel 020 7831 6900

Snow & Rock
5th floor, Harrods, 87-135
Brompton Rd, London
Tel 020 7173 6476

Snow & Rock
Sporting Club, 38-42 King's
Road, London
Tel 020 7589 5418

Snow & Rock
47-51 William Street, London
Tel 020 7256 3940

Snow & Rock
99 Fordwater Road, Chertsey
Tel 01932 566886

Snow & Rock
The Boardwalk, Port Solent,
Portsmouth, Hampshire
Tel 023 9220 5388

Snow & Rock
Unit 1 Davidson Way, Rom
Valley Way, Romford, Essex
Tel 01708 436400

Snow & Rock
54-55 Market Street, Brighton
Tel 01273 827660

Two Seasons
28-30 Castle Street, Kingston
Tel 020 8974 8973

Two Seasons
28/9 Northbrook St, Newbury
Tel 01635 41011

MIDDLE ENGLAND

Element
39 Pelham St, Nottingham
Tel 0115 947 2672

Lockwoods Ski Shop
125-129 Rugby Road,
Milverton, Leamington Spa
Tel 01926 339388

Mountain High
Tower Court, Hornes Lane,
Princes Risborough, Bucks
Tel 01844 274260

Snow & Rock
14 Priory Queensway,
Birmingham
Tel 0121 236 8280

Two Seasons
Unit 3-4, Number 1 Fletcher
Gate, Nottingham
Tel 0115 950 1333

Two Seasons
229-231 Wellingborough
Road, Northampton
Tel 01604 627377

Two Seasons
32 Princes Walk, Grosvenor
Centre, Northampton
Tel 01604 603737

Two Seasons
15 Pump Street, Worcester
Tel 01905 731144

Two Seasons
64 Lower Precinct, Coventry
Tel 024 7663 0020

Two Seasons
32-34 Mill Lane, Solihull
Tel 0121 705 5544

Two Seasons
26 Bakers Lane, Lichfield
Tel 01543 411422

Two Seasons
Unit 1C Regents Court,
Leamington Spa
Tel 01926 888169

Two Seasons
43-47 High Street, Leicester
Tel 0116 262 5855

Two Seasons
Unit 126 North Mall, The
Westfield Centre, Derby
Tel 01332 343284

Two Seasons
213-217 Broad Street Mall,
Reading
Tel 01189 588222

EASTERN ENGLAND

Snow & Rock
Hemel Ski Centre, St Albans
Hill, Hemel Hempstead
Tel 01422 235305

Snow & Rock
97 London Road, St Albans
Tel 01727 848102

SnowFit
2 Cucumber Lane, Brundall,
Norwich
Tel 01603 716655

Two Seasons
5, Christ Lane, Cambridge
Tel 01223 362832

Two Seasons
16 Westgate, Peterborough
Tel 01773 312184

NORTHERN ENGLAND

Freetime Climb + Ski
1 2 Market Street, Carlisle
Tel 01228 598210

Glide & Slide
5/7 Station Road, Otley
Tel 01943 461136

Sayers
66 High St, Yarm, Cleveland
Tel 01642 785423

Snow & Rock
Sheffield Ski Centre, Vale
Road, Parkwood Springs,
Sheffield
Tel 0114 275 1700

Snow & Rock
Princess Parkway, Princess
Park, Didsbury, Manchester
Tel 0161 448 4444

Snow & Rock
Unit 6, Trafford Way, Trafford
Quays, Manchester
Tel 0161 746 1010

Snow & Rock
Metro Park West, Gibside
Way, Gateshead
Tel 0191 493 3680

Snow & Rock
Unit 1 Eastham Point, New
Chester Road, Eastham,
Wirral
Tel 0151 328 5500

SCOTLAND

Craigdon Mountain Sports
61-65 High Street, Inverurie,
Highland
Tel 01467 625855

Craigdon Mountain Sports
5 St Andrew's Street,
Aberdeen
Tel 01224 624333

Craigdon Mountain Sports
25-29 Kinnoull Street, Perth
Tel 01738 831006

Craigdon Mountain Sports
78 Academy Street, Inverness
Tel 01463 248600

NORTHERN IRELAND

Macski
140 Lisburn Road, Belfast
Tel 028 9066 5525

REPUBLIC OF IRELAND

The Great Outdoors
Chatham Street, Dublin 2,
Ireland
Tel +353 1679 4293

Snow & Rock
Unit 3.2-4.2, Dundrum Town
Centre, Dublin 14, Ireland
Tel +353 1292 4700

Ski Retailers

741

Interactive resort shortlist builder at **www.wtss.co.uk**

This is an index to the resort chapters in the book; you'll find page references for about 400 resorts that are described in those chapters. But you'll also find brief descriptions here of another 700 resorts, most of them smaller than those we've covered in full.

Key

⬆ Lifts
➤ Pistes
◢ UK tour operators

49 Degrees North USA
Inland area with best snow in Washington State, including 120-acre bowl reserved for powder weekends.
1195m; slopes 1195–1760m
⬆ 5 ➤ 780 acres

Abetone Italy
Resort in the exposed Appennines, less than two hours from Florence and Pisa.
1390m; slopes 1390–1900m
⬆ 25 ➤ 50km

Abtenau Austria
Sizeable village in Dachstein-West region near Salzburg, on large plain ideal for cross-country.
710m; slopes 710–1260m
⬆ 6 ➤ 10km

Achenkirch Austria
Unspoiled, low-altitude Tirolean village close to Niederau and Alpbach. Beautiful setting overlooking a lake.
930m; slopes 930–1800m
⬆ 7 ➤ 25km
◢ Ramblers

Adelboden 491

Les Aillons-Margériaz France
Traditional village near Chambéry. Nicely sheltered slopes. .
1000m; slopes 1000–1900m
⬆ 20 ➤ 40km

Alagna 450
Small resort on the eastern fringe of the Monterosa Ski area.

Alba 483
Trentino village with a small, quiet area.

Alberschwende 213

Albiez-Montrond France
Authentic old French village in Maurienne valley with panoramic views. Own easy slopes and close to other ski areas.
1500m; slopes 1500–2200m
⬆ 13 ➤ 67 hectares
◢ Lagrange

Alleghe Italy
Dolomite village near Cortina in a pretty lakeside setting close to numerous areas.
980m
⬆ 24 ➤ 80km
◢ Interhome

Les Allues 316
Rustic village on the road up to Méribel.

Alpbach 120

Alpe-d'Huez 234

Alpe-du-Grand-Serre France
Tiny resort near Alpe-d'Huez and Les Deux-Alpes. Good for bad-weather days.
1370m; slopes 1370–2185m
⬆ 19 ➤ 55km

Alpendorf Austria
Outpost of St Johann im Pongau, at one end of an extensive three-valley lift network linking via Wagrain to Flachau – all part of the Salzburger Sportwelt area. Good cruising, intermediate runs.
850m; slopes 800–2185m
⬆ 64 ➤ 200km
◢ Skiing Austria

Alpenglow USA
Alaskan ski resort.
762m; slopes 2500–3900m
⬆ 4 ➤ 320 acres

Alpine Meadows USA
Squaw Valley's neighbour has similar, lightly wooded terrain, with runs of all classifications and an impressive snow record, but a modest total vertical. The slopes are lightly wooded, with broad open runs between glades. The base sits in a broad bowl, with excellent beginner slopes. The resort boundary is open – expeditions require guidance. There is no resort in the European sense of the word, but there's lots of lodgings close by in lakeside Tahoe City.
2085m; slopes 2085–2635m
⬆ 13 ➤ 2400 acres

Alps Resort South Korea
Korea's most northerly, snow-reliable resort, about five hours from Seoul. ⬆ 5

Alta 627

Alta Badia 461

Altenmarkt Austria
Unspoiled village, well placed just off the Salzburg-Villach autobahn for numerous resorts including snow-sure Obertauern and those in the Salzburger Sportwelt.
855m; slopes 855–2130m
⬆ 23 ➤ 150km
◢ Made to Measure, Skiing Austria

Alto Campoo Spain
Barren, desolate place near Santander, with undistinguished slopes, but magnificent wilderness views.
1650m; slopes 1650–2130m
⬆ 13

Alt St Johann Switzerland
Old cross-country village with Alpine slopes connecting into Unterwasser area near Liechtenstein.
900m; slopes 900–2260m
⬆ 19 ➤ 60km

Alyeska USA
Alaskan area 60km/37 miles from Anchorage, with luxury hotel.
75m; slopes 75–1200m
⬆ 9 ➤ 785 acres
◢ Frontier, Ski Dream

Aminona 501
Purpose-built resort in the Crans-Montana network.

Andalo 479
Trentino village not far from Madonna.

Andelsbuch 213

Andermatt 493

Andorra la Vella 102

Angel Fire USA
Intermediate area near Taos, New Mexico. Height usually ensures good snow.
2620m; slopes 2620–3255m
⬆ 5 ➤ 455 acres

Les Angles France
Attractive resort with one of the best ski areas in the Pyrenees. Pretty, tree-lined, mostly easy skiing.
1600m; slopes 1600–2400m
⬆ 18 ➤ 40km
◢ Lagrange, Ski Collection, Ski France, Skiholidayextras. com

Ankogel 114

Annaberg-Lungötz Austria
Peaceful village in a pretty setting, sharing a sizeable area with Gosau. Close to Filzmoos.
775m; slopes 775–1620m
⬆ 33 ➤ 65km

Annupuri 721
One of the three interlinked ski areas of Niseko.

Antagnod 424
Weekend day-tripper area on the road up to Champoluc, above Aosta valley. No village.

Anthony Lakes USA
Small area in Oregon with just one chairlift and two beginner lifts.
2165m; slopes 2165–2435m
⬆ 3 ➤ 21 trails

Anzère 495

Aosta 424
Historic working valley town with a gondola up to the mountain resort of Pila.

Aosta valley 424

Apex Canada
Small, friendly, rather isolated resort, well worth stopping off here for a night or two on a tour of western BC resorts. Modern, purpose-built slope-side base with some accommodation and a few bars and restaurants. The slopes suit confident intermediates upwards best. There are some steep, narrow double black diamond runs in the trees, wonderful single diamond Wildside glades, great cruising blues which adventurous intermediates will love but more timid ones might freeze on. There are also excellent beginner slopes and runs to progress to. There's an ice-skating trail through the woods, floodlit at night.
1575m; slopes 1575–2180m
⬆ 4 ➤ 1112 acres
◢ AmeriCan Ski, Frontier, Ski Dream, Ski Safari

Aprica Italy
Ugly, straggling village between Lake Como and the Brenta Dolomites, with bland slopes and limited facilities.
1180m; slopes 1180–2310m
⬆ 24 ➤ 40km

Arabba 461

Aragnouet-Piau France
Purpose-built mid-mountain satellite of St-Lary, best suited to families, beginners and early intermediates.
1850m; slopes 1420–2500m
⬆ 18 ➤ 80km

Arapahoe Basin 606
Small, exceptionally high day-skiing area near Keystone.

Araucarias Chile
Exotic area in central Chile, around and below a mildly active volcano in the Conguillio National Park.
1500m
⬆ 4 ➤ 350 hectares

Arcalis 102

Les Arcs 244

Ardent 253
Quiet hamlet with quick access to Avoriaz.

Åre 713

Arêches-Beaufort France
Secluded little village 25km/16 miles from Albertville, with mostly intermediate terrain on two areas 3km/2 miles apart. The slopes of both Les Saisies and Les Contamines are less than 25km/16 miles away.
1080m; slopes 1080–2300m
⛷ 15 ⛴ 50km

Argentière 258
Village beneath Chamonix's Grands Montets.

Arinsal 105

Arizona Snowbowl USA
Small but interesting ski area just outside the pleasant town of Flagstaff. Worth a visit if en route to the nearby Grand Canyon in winter. Low snowfall despite the high altitude is a drawback.
slopes 2690–3290m ⛷ 4

Arnoldstein / Dreiländereck
Austria
One of several little areas overlooking the town of Villach.
68om; slopes 680–1455m
⛷ 7 ⛴ 10km

Arolla Switzerland
Tiny village in pretty riverside setting south of Sion. Main attraction is heli-skiing. Wonderful descents from 3800m/12,470ft. Recommended for day trips.
2000m; slopes 2000–2890m
⛷ 6 ⛴ 47km

Arosa 496

Arrowhead 597
Slope-side hamlet next to Beaver Creek.

Artesina Italy
Purpose-built Piedmont resort south of Turin, lacking character and atmosphere. Part of Mondolé ski area with Prato Nevoso.
1300m; slopes 1320–2100m
⛷ 25 ⛴ 90km

Ascutney Mountain USA
Family resort in Vermont 60km/37 miles from Killington, 200km/124 miles from Boston.
⛷ 6 ⛴ 200 acres

Asiago Italy
Sizeable resort close to Verona, but at low altitude and with limited vertical.
1000m; slopes 1000–1380m
⛷ 17 ⛷ Exodus

Aspen 590

Attitash USA
One of the biggest ski areas in eastern US. Uncrowded slopes. Lodging in nearby North Conway, and other New Hampshire areas close by.
slopes 180–715m
⛷ 12 ⛴ 280 acres

Au 213

Auffach Austria
Small, quiet, attractive old village with the longest, highest, sunniest runs in the Wildschönau area.
875m

Auris-en-Oisans 234
Quiet hamlet linked to Alpe-d'Huez.

Auron France
Pleasant, family-oriented and recently redeveloped village with varied, sheltered, intermediate slopes; a stark contrast to nearby Isola 2000. Good choice of mountain restaurants.
1600m; slopes 1150–2450m
⛷ 21 ⛴ 135km
⛷ Ski France, Skiholidayextras.com

Auronzo di Cadore Italy
Sizeable village that's a cheaper base for visiting Cortina. Its own slopes are of negligible interest.
865m; slopes 865–1585m
⛷ 5 ⛴ 7km

Aussois France
Charming rustic working village near Modane in the Maurienne valley. Small but interesting south-facing ski area, good for intermediates and families.
1500m; slopes 1500–2750m
⛷ 11 ⛴ 55km
⛷ AmeriCan Ski, Peak Retreats

Autrans France
Major cross-country village, close to Grenoble. Two limited areas of downhill slopes.
1050m; slopes 1050–1710m
⛷ 16 ⛴ 19km

Avon USA
Small town only a couple of miles from Beaver Creek. Inexpensive base from which to ski Beaver Creek, Vail and Breckenridge.
⛷ AmeriCan Ski, Ski Line

Avoriaz 1800 253

Axamer Lizum 140

Axams 140
Quiet village in Innsbruck area.

Ax-les-Thermes France
Sizeable spa village near Font-Romeu and Andorra. Gondola access to the ski area above Bonascre. Mostly fast chairlifts, serving an expanding area of intermediate slopes.
1400m; slopes 1400–2400m
⛷ 19 ⛴ 75km

Bad Gastein 123

Badger Pass USA
Base for 350 miles of superb backcountry touring in Yosemite National Park. Spectacular views.
2195m; slopes 2195–2435m
⛷ 5 ⛴ 90 acres

Bad Hofgastein 123
Relaxed and spacious spa resort in the Gastein Valley.

Badia 461
Roadside village that used to be called Pedraces, linked via La Villa to the Alta Badia and Sella Ronda.

Bad Kleinkirchheim 126

Banff 661

Bansko 716

Baqueira-Beret 704

Barboleuse 555
Quiet base for skiing the Villars slopes.

Bardonecchia Italy
A sizeable old railway town, lacking classic mountain charm but with market-town character and set in a beautiful, wide valley, near the entrance to the Fréjus road tunnel. There are two separate areas of moderately interesting slopes either side of town – both a free bus ride away – which are usually quiet but overcrowded when weekenders pour in from Turin. The snow record isn't particularly good, but there is now extensive snowmaking on the larger sector. There is little challenge for experts, but virtually the whole area is good for intermediates. For boarders there are a lot of awkward draglifts to cope with. Accommodation is almost all in hotels, and as a working town it lacks the usual après-ski. The Three Valleys can be reached via a gondola from Orelle.
1310m; slopes 1290–2750m
⛷ 21 ⛴ 100km
⛷ Alpine Answers, Crystal, Erna Low, First Choice, Interhome, Neilson, Thomson

Barèges 413

Bariloche 732

Les Barzettes 501
Smaller base along the road from Crans-Montana.

Bayrischzell Germany
Bavarian resort south of Munich and close to Austrian border.
800m; slopes 1090–1563m
⛷ 25 ⛴ 40km

Bear Mountain USA
Southern California's main area, in the beautiful San Bernardino National Forest region. Full snowmaking.
slopes 2170–2685m
⛷ 12 ⛴ 195 acres

Bears Town South Korea
Modern resort with runs cut out of thick forest. Biggest resort near Seoul (only an hour's drive), so it can get very crowded. English-language website at www. bearstown.com ⛷ 9

Bear Valley USA
Resort in northern California, between Lake Tahoe and Yosemite.
2010m; slopes 2010–2590m
⛷ 10 ⛴ 1280 acres

Beaulard Italy
Little place just off the road between Sauze d'Oulx and Bardonecchia.
1215m; slopes 1215–2120m
⛷ 6 ⛴ 20km

Beaver Creek 597

Beaver Mountain USA
Small Utah area north of Salt Lake City, too far from Park City for a day trip.
2195m; slopes 2195–2680m
⛷ 3 ⛴ 525 acres

Beitostølen 708

Belleayre Mountain USA
State-owned resort near Albany, New York State. Cheap prices but old lifts and short runs.
775m; slopes 775–1015m
⛷ 7 ⛴ 170 acres

Bellwald Switzerland
Traditional Rhône valley resort near Fiesch, Riederalp and Bettmeralp. Part of the Goms Valley region.
1600m; slopes 1600–2560m
⛷ 5 ⛴ 31km

Ben Lomond Australia
Small intermediate/beginner area in Ben Lomond National Park, Tasmania, 260km/162 miles from Hobart.
1450m; slopes 1460–1570m
⛷ 6 ⛴ 14 hectares

Berchtesgaden Germany
Pleasant old town close to Salzburg, known for its Nordic skiing but with several little Alpine areas nearby.
550m

Bergün Switzerland
Traditional, quiet, unspoiled, virtually traffic-free little family resort on the rail route between Davos and St Moritz. 5km/3 mile toboggan run.
1375m; slopes 1400–2550m
⛷ 5 ⛴ 23km

Berkshire East USA
Resort in Massachusetts, southern New England, near the Mohawk Trail.
slopes 165–525m
⛷ 5 ⛴ 200 acres

Berwang 227
Unspoiled village in the Zugspitz Arena.

Bessans France
Old cross-country village near Modane well placed for touring Maurienne valley resorts.
1710m; slopes 1740–2200m
⛷ 2 🚡 3km

Besse France
Charming old village built out of lava, with purpose-built slope-side satellite Super-Besse. Beautiful extinct-volcano scenery.
1050m; slopes 1300–1850m
⛷ 22 🚡 45km
✉ Lagrange

Bethel USA
Pleasant, historic town very close to Sunday River, Maine. Attractive alternative to staying in the slope-side resort.

Le Bettex 305
Small base above St-Gervais, with links to Megève.

Bettmeralp Switzerland
Central village of the sizeable Aletsch area near Brig, high above the Rhône valley, amid spectacular glacial scenery. Reached by cable cars from the valley.
1955m; slopes 1900–2870m
⛷ 35 🚡 99km

Beuil-les-Launes France
Alpes-Maritimes resort closest to Nice. Medieval village which shares area with Valberg.
1450m; slopes 1400–2100m
⛷ 26 🚡 90km

Bezau 213
Village in the Bregenzerwald region.

Biberwier 227
Limited little village with a small area of its own. Best as a quiet base from which to access the Zugspitz area.

Bichlbach 227
Smallest of the Zugspitz villages with very limited slopes of its own. Suitable as an unspoiled base for visiting the rest of the area.

Bielmonte Italy
Popular with day trippers from Milan. Worthwhile on a bad-weather day.
1200m; slopes 1200–1620m
⛷ 13 🚡 20km

Big Mountain USA
See Whitefish – name changed in 2007.
✉ AmeriCan Ski

Big Powderhorn USA
Area with the most 'resort' facilities in south Lake Superior region – and the highest lift capacity too. The area suffers from winds.
370m; slopes 370–560m
⛷ 10 🚡 250 acres

Big Sky 641
Big White 668
Bischofshofen Austria
Working town and mountain resort near St Johann im Pongau, with very limited local runs and the main slopes starting nearby at Muhlbach (Hochkönig area).
545m; slopes 545–1000m
⛷ 1 🚡 2km

Bivio Switzerland
Quiet village near St Moritz and Savognin, with easy slopes opened up by a few lifts.
1770m; slopes 1780–2560m
⛷ 4 🚡 40km

Bizau Austria
Area in the Bregenzerwald region north-west of Lech.
680m; slopes 680–1700m
⛷ 6 🚡 24km

Björkliden 712
Björnrike 712
Black Mountain USA
New Hampshire area with lodging in nearby Jackson.
⛷ 4 🚡 143 acres

Blatten Switzerland
Mountainside hamlet above Naters, beside the Rhône near Brig. Small but tall Belalp ski area, with larger Aletsch area nearby. Recently installed six-pack.
1320m; slopes 1320–3100m
⛷ 9 🚡 60km

Bled 719
Blue Cow 723
Blue Mountain Canada
Largest area in Ontario, with glorious views of Lake Huron. High-capacity lift system and 100% snowmaking.
230m; slopes 230–450m
⛷ 15 🚡 275 acres
✉ Ski Dream

Blue River Canada
Base of world-famous Mike Wiegele heli-ski operation in Cariboo and Monashee mountains.

Bluewood USA
Particularly remote area even by American north-west standards. Worth a visit if you're in Walla Walla.
1355m; slopes 1355–1725m
⛷ 3 🚡 530 acres

Bogus Basin USA
Sizeable area overlooking Idaho's attractive, interesting capital, Boise. Limited accommodation at the base.
1760m; slopes 1760–2310m
⛷ 8 🚡 2600 acres

Bohinj 719

Bois-d'Amont France
One of four resorts that make up Les Rousses area in Jura region on the Franco-Suisse border.
1050m; slopes 1120–1680m
⛷ 40 🚡 40km
✉ Lagrange

Boi Taull Spain
A typical Pyrenean resort set high above the Boi Valley, close to the stunning Aigues Tortes National Park. Good intermediate terrain. Recently installed fast quad.
slopes 2020–2750m
⛷ 15 🚡 44km

Bolognola Italy
Tiny area in Macerata region near the Adriatic Riviera.
1070m; slopes 1070–1845m
⛷ 7 🚡 5km

Bolton Valley USA
Resort near Stowe with mostly intermediate slopes.
465m; slopes 465–960m
⛷ 6 🚡 155 acres

Bonneval-sur-Arc France
Unspoiled, remote old village in the Haute Maurienne valley with many of its slopes at high altitude. Pass to neighbouring Val d'Isère is closed in winter.
1800m; slopes 1800–3000m
⛷ 11 🚡 25km

Bons 288
Rustic, unspoiled old hamlet linked to Les Deux-Alpes.

Boreal USA
Closest area to north Lake Tahoe town, Truckee. Limited slopes, best for novices.
2195m; slopes 2195–2375m
⛷ 9 🚡 380 acres

Bormio 426
Borovets 715
Bosco Chiesanuova Italy
Weekend day trippers' place near Verona. A long drive from any other resort.
1105m; slopes 1105–1805m
⛷ 18 🚡 20km

Bosco Gurin Switzerland
Highest ski area in Ticino. The only German-speaking village in the Italian canton.
1500m; slopes 1500–2400m
⛷ 6 🚡 30km

Les Bottières 373
La Bourboule France
Spa and cross-country village with the Alpine slopes of Le Mont-Dore nearby. Spectacular extinct-volcano scenery.
850m; slopes 1050–1850m
⛷ 41 🚡 80km
✉ Lagrange

Bourg-d'Oisans France
Pleasant valley town on main Grenoble-Briançon road. Cheap base for visits to Alpe-d'Huez and Les Deux-Alpes.

Bourg-St-Maurice 244
French valley town with a funicular to Les Arcs.

Bovec Slovenia
Town near the small area of Kanin on the Italian border.
✉ BoardnLodge

Boyne Highlands USA
Area with impressive, high-capacity lift system for weekend Detroit crowds. Fierce winds off Lake Michigan a major drawback.
225m; slopes 225–390m
⛷ 10 🚡 240 acres

Boyne Mountain USA
Resort popular with weekend Detroit crowds. Not as windy as sister resort Boyne Highlands.
190m; slopes 190–340m
⛷ 12 🚡 115 acres

Bozel France
Small town that, in good snow conditions, you can ski down to off-piste from Courchevel and catch a bus back. Also near access road for Champagny-en-Vanoise (which has a gondola up to the La Plagne ski area).
860m

Bramans France
Old cross-country village near Modane. Well placed for touring numerous nearby resorts such as Val Cenis and Valloire.
1230m
⛷ 1 🚡 3km

Bramberg Austria
Village near Pass Thurn (Kitzbühel area). Shares odd area with Neukirchen – the only valley lift is in Neukirchen.
820m; slopes 820–900m ⛷ 2

Brand Austria
Family resort with small, low area. Linked to Burserburg ski area since 2007/08 via a high altitude cable car across a dividing valley.
1050m; slopes 1050–1920m
⛷ 13 🚡 50km
✉ Pure Alpine, STC

Les Brasses France
Collective name for six traditional hamlets with some of the closest slopes to Geneva, but best known for cross-country.
900m; slopes 900–1600m
⛷ 14 🚡 50km

Braunwald Switzerland
Sunny but limited area near Zurich, a funicular ride above Linthal. Newish combi-mix lift.
1300m; slopes 1300–1905m
⛷ 8 🚡 32km

Breckenridge 599
Bregenzerwald 213
Brentonico Italy
Little resort just off Verona-Trento motorway.
1160m; slopes 1160–1520m ⛷ 16

Bressanone Italy
Valley town 20 minutes by free ski-bus from the lift base of Plose.
565m

La Bresse France
Largest resort in the northerly Vosges mountains near Strasbourg. Three separate downhill areas (with a lot of snowmaking), but also extensive ski de fond and lots of other activities.
900m; slopes 900–1350m
⛷ 26 🚡 62km

Briançon 360
Part of the Grand Serre Chevalier region, but with own ski area.

Brian Head USA
Utah area south of Salt Lake City, too far from Park City for a day trip.
2925m; slopes 2925–3445m
⛷ 10 🚡 500 acres

Brides-les-Bains 316
Quiet spa town in valley below Méribel.

Bridger Bowl 640

Brigels–Andiast Switzerland
In the same valley as Laax/ Flims. Access from two sunny villages. Mostly red runs.
1300m; slopes 1100–2415m
⛷ 7 🚡 75km

Brighton USA
Brighton is linked with Solitude in the valley next to Alta and Snowbird. Total acreage is half that of Alta/ Snowbird, but is fair by general US standards. This valley attracts fewer people so the powder doesn't get tracked out in hours, as it does over the hill. Brighton has four fast chairs, including one serving the resort's maximum vertical of 530m/ 1,740ft on Clayton Peak. This and the slightly lower Mt Millicent are almost all expert terrain, but other lifts serve a wide spectrum of runs. The resorts' boundaries are open, and there are excellent backcountry adventures to be had. There are four terrain parks. Accommodation is in the slope-side Brighton Lodge and some cabins.
2670m; slopes 2665–3200m
⛷ 15 🚡 2250 acres
📧 AmeriCan Ski

Brixen 193
Grossraum village that shares slopes with Söll and Ellmau.

Bromley USA
New York City weekend retreat, reputedly the warmest place to ski in chilly Vermont.
595m; slopes 595–1000m
⛷ 9 🚡 300 acres

Bromont Canada
Purpose-built resort an hour east of Montreal, with one of the best small areas in eastern Canada, popular for its night skiing.
slopes 405–575m
⛷ 6 🚡 135 acres
📧 AmeriCan Ski

Bruck am Grossglockner
Austria
Low beginners' resort, but could suit intermediates looking for a small, quiet base from which to visit nearby Zell am See.
760m

Brundage Mountain USA
Remote, uncrowded Idaho area with glorious views across the lake towards Hell's Canyon. Mostly intermediate slopes. Also has a snowcat operation.
1760m; slopes 1760–2320m
⛷ 5 🚡 1300 acres

Bruneck Italy
Town with gondola link into the Plan de Corones/Kronplatz area. Italian name is Brunico.

Brunico Italy
Town with gondola link into the Plan de Corones/Kronplatz area. German name is Bruneck.

Bruson 543
Relaxing respite from Verbier's crowds.

Brusson 424
Cross-country village in the Aosta valley.

Les Bugnenets–Savagnieres
Switzerland
Very small area in the Jura mountains, north of Neuchatel. Short runs served by drag lifts. Valid with the Valais Ski Card.
slopes 1090–1440m
⛷ 7 🚡 30km

Bukovel Ukraine
Ukraine's second highest resort with major expansion scheme underway.
slopes 900–1370m
⛷ 14 🚡 50km

Burke Mountain USA
Uncrowded, isolated family resort in Vermont with mostly intermediate slopes. Great views from the top.
385m; slopes 385–995m
⛷ 4 🚡 130 acres

Bürserberg Austria
Undistinguished valley town linked to Brand since 2007/08, via a high altitude cable car across a dividing valley.
900m; slopes 1035–1850m
⛷ 13 🚡 50km

Cairngorm 720

Caldirola Italy
Genoese weekend day-tripper spot in a remote region off the motorway to Turin.
1010m; slopes 1010–1460m
⛷ 3 🚡 5km

Cambre-d'Aze France
Quiet ski area in the Pyrenees with few British visitors. Good beginner and intermediate terrain. Forms part of the Neiges Catalan (10 resorts on one pass).
1640m; slopes 1640–2400m
⛷ 17 🚡 35km

Camigliatello Italy
Tiny area on the foot of the Italian 'boot' near Cosenza. Weekend/day-trip spot.
1270m; slopes 1270–1750m
⛷ 4 🚡 6km

Campitello 483
Linked to the Sella Ronda, with quick connections to the interesting Arabba section.

Campitello Matese Italy
The only slopes near Naples. Surprisingly large area when snowcover is complete. Weekend crowds.
1440m; slopes 1440–2100m
⛷ 8 🚡 40km

Campo di Giove Italy
Highest slopes in L'Aquila region east of Rome.
1070m
⛷ 6 🚡 23km

Campodolcino Italy
Valley town with new funicular up to the fringe of Madesimo's slopes.
1070m; slopes 1545–2880m
⛷ 6 🚡 8km

Campo Felice Italy
Easiest resort to reach from Rome, off Aquila motorway. One of the better lift systems in the vicinity.
1410m; slopes 1520–2065m
⛷ 14 🚡 40km

Campo Imperatore Italy
One of the best of many little areas east of Rome in L'Aquila region.
1980m
⛷ 8 🚡 20km

Canazei 483
Sizeable and lively rustic village in the Sella Ronda's most heavily wooded section of mountain.

Candanchu / Astún 703

Canillo 109
Small, quiet village linked to Soldeu.

Canmore Canada
Old frontier town on the way to Nakiska/Fortress, well placed for touring the region and an attractive alternative to staying in Banff.

Cannon Mountain USA
One of several small New Hampshire resorts scattered along the Interstate 93 highway; a ski area and nothing more. High, steep mountain by eastern standards.
605m; slopes 605–1260m
⛷ 9 🚡 165 acres

The Canyons 629

Cardrona 725

Carezza 483
Dense network of short lifts close to Val di Fassa, previously called Passo Costalunga.

Les Carroz-d'Arâches 294
An attractive, spacious village on the road up to Flaine.

Caspoggio Italy
Attractive, unspoiled village north-east of Lake Como, with easy slopes (and more at nearby Chiesa).
1100m; slopes 1100–2155m
⛷ 8 🚡 22km

Castelrotto Italy
Picturesque village west of Sella Ronda circuit with small sunny Alpine area and good cross-country trails.
1060m

Castel S Angelo Italy
Tiny area in Macerata region near Adriatic Riviera.
805m
⛷ 4 🚡 2km

Castle Mountain Canada
Remote resort south of Calgary. Good proportion of intermediate and advanced terrain. Newish area on Haig Ridge provides more beginner and intermediate terrain.
1410m; slopes 1410–2270m
⛷ 5 🚡 250 acres

Catedral (Bariloche) 732

Cauterets 413

Cavalese 479
Unspoiled medieval town in Val di Fiemme.

Caviahue Argentina
Mountain village at the foot of the Copahue Volcano. 357km/222 miles from Neuquén City.
1645m; slopes 1645–2045m
⛷ 8 🚡 37km

The Cedars Lebanon
The largest of Lebanon's ski areas, 130km/80 miles inland from Beirut. Good, open slopes with a surprisingly long season. New hotel and gondola in 2008/09.
1850m; slopes 2100–2870m ⛷ 6

Ceillac France
Tight cluster of rustic old buildings near Serre-Chevalier. Not far from the highest village in Europe, St-Veran.
1600m; slopes 1600–2450m
⛷ 7 🚡 25km

Celerina 532
Quiet village with links to St Moritz's slopes.

Cerkno Slovenia
Modern, family resort 50km/31 miles from Ljubljana. Lifts include three fast chairs.
900m
⛷8 ⛷ 18km

Cerler Spain
Very limited, purpose-built resort with a compact ski area similar to that of nearby Andorra's Arinsal.
1500m; slopes 1500–2630m
⛷ 18 ⛷ 61km

Le Cernix France
Hamlet near Megève where Les Saisies' slopes link to those of Crest-Voland. Uncrowded retreat.
1250m; slopes 1150–1950m
⛷45 ⛷ 80km

Cerrato Lago Italy
Very limited area near the coastal town of La Spezia.
1270m; slopes 1270–1890m
⛷ 5 ⛷ 3km

Cerro Bayo Argentina
Limited area amid stunning scenery 10km/6 miles from La Angostura, and 90km/56 miles from San Carlos de Bariloche.
slopes 1050–1780m
⛷ 12 ⛷ 200 hectares
🚡 Snoworks

Cerro Castor 732

Cerro Mirador 733

Cervinia 428

Cesana Torinese Italy
Little Italian village linking the Sauze d'Oulx, Sestriere and Sansicario side of the Milky Way to the Clavière, Montgenèvre side.
1350m

Le Châble 543
Small village below Verbier.

Chaillol France
Cross-country base on the edge of the beautiful Ecrins National Park, near Gap. Small Alpine area, lots of snowmakers.
1600m; slopes 1450–2000m
⛷ 10

Chamois Italy
Small area above Buisson, a few miles down the road from Valtournenche (near Cervinia) - worth a look on bad-weather days.
1815m; slopes 1815–2270m
⛷ 9 ⛷ 20km

Chamonix 258

Champagny-en-Vanoise 339
Charming village linking to the La Plagne network.

Champéry 498

Champex-Lac Switzerland
Lakeside hamlet tucked away in the trees above Orsières. A nice quiet, unspoiled base from which to visit Verbier's area.
1470m; slopes 1470–2220m
⛷ 4 ⛷ 25km

Champfèr 532
Village just outside St Moritz on the way to the Corvatsch lifts.

Champoluc 450
Unspoiled village at one end of the Monterosa Ski area.

Champorcher Italy
Small village south of Aosta valley with tall but narrow ski area, mostly red runs on open slopes, with one black through the trees to the lift base at Chardonney.
1430m; slopes 1430–2500m
⛷ 5 ⛷ 21km

Champoussin 498
Quiet mountainside village in the Champéry area.

Chamrousse France
Functional family resort near Grenoble, with good, sheltered slopes. Chairlifts and a cable car from three bases (1650, 1700 and 1750) serve largely beginner and intermediate slopes.
1650m; slopes 1400–2255m
⛷ 24 ⛷ 92km
🚡 Crystal, Erna Low, Lagrange, Ski Collection, Ski France, Skiholidayextras.com, Thomson

Chandolin 539

Chantemerle 360
One of the main valley villages making up the big resort of Serre-Chevalier.

Chapa Verde Chile
60km/37 miles north-east of Rancagua and 145km/90 miles from Santiago.
1200m; slopes 1200–2500m
⛷ 4 ⛷ 1200 hectares

Chapelco Argentina
Small ski area with full infrastructure of services 19km/12 miles from sizeable town of San Martin de Los Andes. Accommodation in hotels 11km/7 miles from the slopes.
slopes 1250–1980m
⛷ 10 ⛷ 140 hectares
🚡 Snoworks

La Chapelle-d'Abondance 268
Unspoiled village 5km/3 miles down the valley from Châtel.

Charlotte Pass 723

Château d'Oex Switzerland
Pleasant little valley town that is the main French-speaking component of the shared lift-pass area around Gstaad. Local slopes are pleasant and undemanding but low (La Braye, at the top, is at only 1650m/5,400ft), and not connected to any of the Gstaad sectors – though the local railway makes moving around to other resorts painless. This is where Alpine hot-air ballooning first took off, and it's still a local speciality.
960m; slopes 890–3000m
⛷ 63 ⛷ 250km

Châtel 268

Le Chatelard France
Small resort in remote Parc des Bauges between Lake Annecy and Chambéry.

Chiesa Italy
Attractive beginners' resort with a fairly high plateau of easy runs above the resort.
1000m; slopes 1700–2335m
⛷ 16 ⛷ 50km

Le Chinaillon France
Modern, chalet-style village at base of lifts above Le Grand-Bornand.
1300m; slopes 1000–2100m
⛷ 37 ⛷ 90km

Chiomonte Italy
Tiny resort on the main road east of Bardonecchia and Sauze d'Oulx. A good half-day trip from either.
745m; slopes 745–2210m
⛷ 6 ⛷ 10km

Chsea Algeria
Largest of Algeria's skiable areas, 135km/84 miles south-east of coastal town of Alger in the Djur Djur mountains.
1860m; slopes 1860–2510m ⛷ 2

Chur-Brambruesch
Switzerland
Chur's local ski area a cable-car and gondola ride from the town.
595m; slopes 1170–2200m
⛷ 6 ⛷ 25km

Churwalden Switzerland
Hamlet on fringe of Lenzerheide-Valbella area, linked via a slow chair. Four short local runs served by a quad and steep drag.
1230m; slopes 1230–2865m
⛷ 40 ⛷ 155km

Claviere 327
Small Italian village linked to Montgenèvre (in France).

La Clusaz 273

Les Coches 339
Small, purpose-built village, linked to the La Plagne ski area.

Cogne 424
One of Aosta valley's larger villages. Small area worth a short visit from nearby Pila.

Colfosco 461
Sprawling village next to Corvara at the junction of the Alta Badia and the Sella Ronda circuit.

Colle di Tenda Italy
Dour, modern resort that shares a good area with much nicer Limone. Not far from Nice.
1400m; slopes 1120–2040m
⛷ 33 ⛷ 80km

Colle Isarco Italy
Brenner Pass area – and the bargain-shopping town of Vipiteno is nearby.
1095m; slopes 1095–2720m
⛷ 5 ⛷ 15km

Le Collet-d'Allevard France
Ski area of sizeable summer spa Allevard-les-Bains in remote region east of Chambéry-Grenoble road.
1450m; slopes 1450–2140m
⛷ 10 ⛷ 35km

Collio Italy
Tiny area of short runs in a remote spot between lakes Garda and d'Iseo.
840m; slopes 840–1715m ⛷ 14

Les Collons 543
A collection of chalets below Thyon 2000 in the Verbier area.

Combloux 305
Quiet, unspoiled alternative to linked Megève.

Les Contamines 275

Copper Mountain 604

Le Corbier 373

Corno alle Scale Italy
Small resort in the Emilia Romagna region of the Apennines.
1355m; slopes 1355–1945m
⛷ 9 ⛷ 36km

Coronet Peak 728
Closest area to Queenstown (20 minutes).

Corrençon-en-Vercors France
Charming, rustic village at foot of Villard-de-Lans ski area. Good cross-country, too.
1160m; slopes 1160–2170m
⛷ 25 ⛷ 130km

Cortina d'Ampezzo 434

Corvara 461
Lively village with lots of facilities at the junction of the Alta Badia and the Sella Ronda circuit.

Courchevel 277

Courmayeur 439

Cranmore USA
Area in New Hampshire with attractive town/resort of North Conway. Easy skiing. Good for families.
150m; slopes 150–515m
⛷ 9 ⛷ 190 acres

Crans-Montana 501

Crested Butte USA
Crested Butte has one of the cutest old Wild West towns in Colorado, and the steep, gnarly terrain enjoys cult status among experts. It's a small area, but it packs in an astonishing mixture of perfect beginner slopes, easy cruising runs and expert terrain. Snowfall is modest by Colorado standards, but for those who like steep, ungroomed terrain, if the snow is good, it's idyllic. You can stay there or at the mountain, a couple of miles away, with its modern resort 'village'.
2860m; slopes 2775–3620m
🚡 16 🎿 1208 acres
🚐 AmeriCan Ski, American Ski Classics, Crystal, Funway Holidays, Ski Dream, Ski Safari, United Vacations

Crest-Voland France
Attractive, unspoiled traditional village near Megève and Le Grand Bornand with wonderfully uncrowded intermediate slopes linked to Les Saises and beyond to Praz sur Arly, as part of the new Espace Diamant region.
1035m; slopes 1230–2070m
🚡 84 🎿 175km

Crissolo Italy
Small, remote day-tripper area, south-west of Turin. Part of the Monviso ski area.
1320m; slopes 1745–2340m
🚡 4 🎿 20km

La Croix-Fry 273
Couple of hotels on the pass close to La Clusaz.

Les Crosets 498
Isolated mini-resort above Champéry, on the Portes du Soleil circuit.

Crystal Mountain USA
Area in glorious Mt Rainier National Park, near Seattle. Good, varied area given good snow/weather, but it's often wet. Lively at weekends.
1340m; slopes 1340–2135m
🚡 9 🎿 2300 acres

Cuchara Valley USA
Quiet little family resort in southern Colorado, some way from any other ski area.
2800m; slopes 2800–3285m
🚡 4 🎿 250 acres

Cutigliano Italy
Sizeable village near Abetone in the Appennines. Less than two hours from Florence and Pisa.
1125m; slopes 1125–1850m
🚡 9 🎿 13km

Cypress Mountain Canada
Vancouver's most challenging area, 20 minutes from the city and with 40% for experts. Good snowfall record but rain is a problem.
920m; slopes 910–1445m 🚡 5

Daemyeong Vivaldi Resort
South Korea
One of the less ugly Korean resorts, 75km/47 miles from Seoul. 🚡 10

La Daille 393
Ugly apartment complex at the entrance to Val d'Isère, with lifts into the Bellevarde slopes.

Daisen Japan
Western Honshu's main area, four hours from Osaka.
800m; slopes 740–1120m 🚡 21

Damüls 213
Scattered but attractive village in Bregenzerwald area close to the German and Swiss borders.

Davos 503

Deer Mountain USA
South Dakota area close to 'Old West' town Deadwood and Mount Rushmore.
1825m; slopes 1825–2085m
🚡 4 🎿 370 acres

Deer Valley 631

Les Deux-Alpes 288

Les Diablerets Switzerland
Unspoiled but spread-out village towered over by the Diablerets massif, with two areas of local slopes, plus Glacier 3000. A high-speed quad followed by a slow chair lead up to the red runs of the Meilleret area and the link to Villars. A gondola in the centre of town takes you to Isenau, a mix of blues and reds served by draglifts. From Isenau there's a red run down to Col du Pillon and the cable car to and from the glacier. On Glacier 3000, you'll find blue runs at over 3000m/9,840ft, stunning views and the long, black Combe d'Audon – a wonderful, usually quiet, run away from all the lifts with sheer cliffs rising up on both sides. Snow reliability away from the glacier is not great – especially on sunny Isenau.
1150m; slopes 1115–3000m
🚡 46 🎿 125km
🚐 Alpine Answers, Independent Ski Links, Interhome, Lagrange, Momentum, Neilson, Simply Alpine, Solo's, Switzerland Travel Centre

Diamond Peak USA
Quiet, pleasant, intermediate area on Lake Tahoe, with lodging in Incline Village five minutes' drive away. Its narrow area consists of a long ridge served by one fast chair; there are great lake views from the run along the ridge and from the terrace of Snowflake Lodge. There are black runs off the ridge, but nothing seriously steep.
2040m; slopes 2040–2600m
🚡 6 🎿 655 acres

Dienten 138
Quiet village at the heart of the Hochkönig area.

Dinner Plain Australia
Attractive resort best known for cross-country skiing. Shuttle to Mt Hotham for Alpine slopes. Four hours from Melbourne.
1520m; slopes 1490–1520m

Discovery Ski Area USA
Pleasant area miles from anywhere except Butte, Montana, with largely intermediate slopes but double-black runs on the back of the mountain – and the chance of seriously good snow. Usually deserted. Fairmont Hot Springs (two huge thermal pools) are nearby. There are plans to extend the ski area on south-eastern side, including a new connecting road from Philipsburg.
1975m; slopes 1975–2485m
🚡 6 🎿 614 acres

Disentis Switzerland
Unspoiled old village in a pretty setting on the Glacier Express rail route near Andermatt. Scenic area with long runs.
1135m; slopes 1150–2830m
🚡 9 🎿 60km
🚐 Interhome, Switzerland Travel Centre

Dobbiaco Italy
Small resort in the South Tyrol. Toblach is its German name.
1250m; slopes 1250–1610m
🚡 5 🎿 15km
🚐 Exodus, Headwater, Ramblers

Dodge Ridge USA
Novice/leisurely intermediate area north of Yosemite. The pass from Reno is closed in winter, preventing crowds.
2010m; slopes 2010–2500m
🚡 12 🎿 815 acres

Dolonne 439
Quiet suburb of Courmayeur.

Donnersbachwald Austria
Small area in the Dachstein-Tauern region.
950m; slopes 950–1990m
🚡 4 🎿 25km

Donner Ski Ranch USA
One of California's first ski resorts, still family owned and operated.
2140m; slopes 2140–2370m
🚡 6 🎿 460 acres

Dorfgastein 123
Quieter, friendlier alternative to Bad Gastein.

Doucy-Combelouvière 404
Quiet hamlet tucked away in the trees at the foot of Valmorel's slopes, linked by easy pistes and a series of draglifts.

Dundret Sweden
Lapland area 100km/62 miles north of the Arctic Circle with floodlit slopes open through winter when the sun barely rises.
slopes 475–825m
🚡 7 🎿 15km

Durango Mountain Resort USA
This is not a resort you would cross the Atlantic to visit – it's a small area even by US standards, and won't amuse most non-beginners for more than a day or two. Directly above the resort is a steepish slope with a slow double chair off to the right serving gentle green runs. All link to the shady mountainside that forms the main part of the area, served by a row of three chairs with a vertical of not much over 350m/1,150ft. Snowcat skiing is said to operate from the top. The heart of the resort is Purgatory Village, a modern, purpose-built affair. Evening options in the 'village' are extremely limited. The city of Durango has a historic district and is worth a look.
2680m; slopes 2680–3300m
🚡 11 🎿 1200 acres
🚐 AmeriCan Ski

Eaglecrest USA
Close to famous Yukon gold rush town Skagway. Family resort famous for its ski school.
365m; slopes 365–790m
🚡 3 🎿 640 acres

Eben im Pongau Austria
Part of Salzburger Sportwelt Amadé area that includes nearby St Johann, Wagrain, Flachau and Zauchensee. Village spoiled by the autobahn passing through it.
855m; slopes 855 2185m
🚡 100 🎿 350km

Egg 213
Biggest village in Bregenzerwald, with a small ski area at Schetteregg.

Ehrwald 227
Friendly, relaxed, pretty village with several nicely varied areas, notably the Zugspitz glacier. Poor bus services, so a car is desirable.

747

El Colorado / Farellones 733
Area connected to the Valle Nevado ski area.

Eldora Mountain USA
Day-visitor resort with varied terrain (including plenty of steep stuff) close to Denver Boulder (45min by regular scheduled bus). All forest trails, but with some good glade areas. Crowded at weekends, and all the chairs are slow.
2795m; slopes 2805–3230m
🚡 12 ⛷ 680 acres

Elk Meadows USA
Area south of Salt Lake City, more than a day trip from Park City.
2775m; slopes 2745–3170m
🚡 6 ⛷ 1400 acres

Ellmau 129

Elm Switzerland
One hour from Zürich, at the head of a quiet, isolated, valley. Good choice of runs including a long black to the valley.
1000m; slopes 1000–2105m
🚡 6 ⛷ 40km

Encamp 102

Enego Italy
Limited weekend day-trippers' area near Vicenza and Trento.
1300m; slopes 1300–1445m
🚡 7 ⛷ 30km

Engelberg 510

Entrèves 439
Hotels at the base of the lift up to Courmayeur's slopes.

Escaldes Andorra
Central valley town, effectively part of Andorra la Vella.

Etna Italy
Scenic, uncrowded, short-season area on the volcano's flank, 20 minutes from Nickolossi.
1800m; slopes 1800–2350m
⛷ 5km

Evolène Switzerland
Charming rustic village with own little area in unspoiled, attractive setting south of Sion. Area lift pass gives access to the 4 Valleys.
1370m; slopes 1405–2680m
🚡 7 ⛷ 42km

Faak am See Austria
Limited area, one of five overlooking town of Villach.
560m; slopes 560–800m
🚡 1 ⛷ 2km

Fai della Paganella 479
Trentino village that shares its slopes with Andalo.

Fairmont Hot Springs Canada
Major luxury spa complex ideal for a relaxing holiday with some gentle skiing thrown in.
🚡 2 ⛷ 60 acres

Faistenau Austria
Cross-country area close to Salzburg and St Wolfgang. Limited Alpine slopes.
785m; slopes 785–1000m
🚡 5 ⛷ 3km

Falcade 479
Trentino village south of the Sella Ronda.

Falera 518
Village with access to ski area shared by Flims and Laax.

Le Falgoux France
One of the most beautiful old villages in France, set in the very scenic Volcano National Park. Several ski areas nearby.
930m; slopes 930–1350m

Falkertsee Austria
Base area rather than a village, with bleak, open slopes in contrast to nearby Badkleinkirchheim.
1690m; slopes 1690–2385m
🚡 5 ⛷ 15km

Falls Creek 723

La Feclaz France
One of several little resorts in the remote Parc des Bauges. Popular cross-country base.
1165m

Feldberg Germany
Resort in the Black Forest.
🚡 28 ⛷ 50km

Fernie 671

Fieberbrunn Austria
Atmospheric and friendly Tirolean village, sprawling along the valley road for 2km/1 mile, but mostly set back from the road and railway. Its small but attractive area of wooded slopes is a bus ride away. One sector consists mainly of blue runs, the other mainly of easy reds, all mostly below the treeline. Across a valley are separate lifts going up to the high point of 2020m/6,630ft on Hochhörndl. The addition of a big gondola extended the slopes down to a new valley station and so opened up an off-piste area. Boarder-friendly, hosting major competitions in its terrain park. Village accommodation is in hotels, and there is accommodation at the lift station.
800m; slopes 835–2020m
🚡 11 ⛷ 35m
📧 First Choice, Snowscape, Thomson

Fiesch Switzerland
Traditional Rhône valley resort close to Brig, with a lift up to Fiescheralp (2220m/7,280ft) at one end of the beautiful Aletsch area extending across the mountainside via Bettmeralp to Riederalp.
1050m; slopes 1900–2900m
🚡 36 ⛷ 100km

Fiescheralp Switzerland
Mountain outpost of Fiesch, down in the Rhône valley. At one end of the beautiful Aletsch area extending across the mountainside via Bettmeralp to Riederalp.
2220m; slopes 1900–2870m
🚡 36 ⛷ 99km

Filzmoos Austria
Charming, unspoiled, friendly village with leisurely slopes that are ideal for novices. Good snow record for its height. 'Quiet pistes', 'superb piste preparation' and 'splendid nursery slopes', say reporters.
1055m; slopes 1055–1645m
🚡 12 ⛷ 32km
📧 Inghams, Interhome, Simply Alpine, Skiing Austria, Skitracer

Finkenberg 132
Village between Mayrhofen and Hintertux, linked to the first but not the second.

Fiss Austria
Nicely compact, quiet, traditional village sharing an extensive, sunny area with bigger Serfaus.
1435m; slopes 1200–2700m
🚡 42 ⛷ 160km
📧 Interhome, Skiing Austria

Flachau Austria
Quiet, spacious village in a pretty setting at one end of an extensive three-valley lift network linking via Wagrain to Alpendorf. Flachauwinkl, up the valley, is at the centre of another similarly extensive and impressive lift system. All these resorts are covered by the Salzburger Sportwelt area.
925m; slopes 800–2185m
🚡 64 ⛷ 200km
📧 Interhome, Made to Measure, Skiing Austria

Flachauwinkl Austria
Tiny ski station beside Tauern autobahn, at the centre of an extensive three-valley lift network linking Kleinarl to Zauchensee. Flachau, down the valley, is at one end of a similarly extensive lift system. All these resorts are covered by the Salzburger Sportwelt ski pass that our figures relate to.
930m; slopes 800–2185m
🚡 64 ⛷ 200km

Flaine 294

Flims 518
Long-established resort sharing a huge area with Laax.

Flumet France
Surprisingly large traditional village, the main place from which to ski the sizeable Val d'Arly ski area, now linked through to Les Saisies/ Crest Voland. Close to better-known Megève.
1000m; slopes 1000–2070m
🚡 84 ⛷ 175km

Flumserberg Switzerland
Collective name for the villages sharing a varied area an hour south-east of Zürich. Part of the wider Heidiland region. Mostly red and black runs, served by good network fast lifts.
425m; slopes 1220–2220m
🚡 16 ⛷ 65km

Folgaria 479
Largest of several resorts east of Trento. Old lift system.

Folgarida 479
Small Trentino village, with links to Madonna di Campiglio.

Foncine-le-Haut France
Major cross-country village in the Jura Mountains with extensive trails.
📧 Lagrange

Fonni Gennargentu Italy
Sardinia's only 'ski area' – and it's tiny.
🚡 1 ⛷ 5km

Font-Romeu 413

Foppolo Italy
Relatively unattractive but user-friendly village, a short transfer from Bergamo.
1510m; slopes 1610–2160m
🚡 9 ⛷ 47km

Forca Canapine Italy
Limited area near the Adriatic and Ascoli Piceno. Popular with weekend day-trippers.
1450m; slopes 1450–1690m
🚡 11 ⛷ 20km

Formazza Italy
Cross-country base with some downhill slopes.
1280m; slopes 1275–1755m
⛷ 8km

Formigal 703

Formigueres France
Small downhill and cross-country area in the Neiges Catalanes. There are 110km cross-country trails.
slopes 1700–2350m
🚡 8 ⛷ 19km
📧 Chalet Group

Le Fornet 393
Rustic old hamlet 3km/2 miles up the valley from Val d'Isère, with cable car up to the Col de l'Iseran area.

Forstau Austria
Secluded hamlet above Radstadt–Schladming road. Very limited area with old lifts, but nice and quiet.
930m; slopes 930–1885m
🚡 7 ⛷ 14km

La Foux-d'Allos France
Purpose-built resort that shares a good intermediate area with Pra-Loup.
1800m; slopes 1800–2600m
🚡 52 ⛷ 190km

Frabosa Soprana   Italy
One of numerous little areas south of Turin, well placed for combining winter sports with Riviera sightseeing.
850m; slopes 860–1740m
⛷ 7 ⛷ 40km

Frisco   599
Small town down the valley from Breckenridge.

Frontignano   Italy
Best lift system in the Macerata region, near the Adriatic Riviera.
1340m; slopes 1340–2000m
⛷ 8 ⛷ 10km

Fucine   479

Fügen   Austria
Unspoiled Zillertal village with road up to satellite Hochfügen – part of fair-sized Ski Optimal area, along with Kaltenbach.
550m
🚂 Crystal, Friendship Travel, Interhome, Lagrange, STC

Fulpmes   210

Furano   721

Fusch   Austria
Cheaper, quiet place to stay when visiting Zell am See. Across a golf course from Kaprun and Schuttdorf.
805m; slopes 805–1050m
⛷ 2 ⛷ 5km

Fuschl am See   Austria
Attractive, unspoiled, lakeside village close to St Wolfgang and Salzburg, 30 minutes from its slopes. Best suited to part-time skiers who want to sightsee as well.
670m

Gåla   Norway
Base for downhill and cross-country skiing, an hour's drive north of Lillehammer.
930m; slopes 830–1150m
⛷ 7 ⛷ 20km
🚂 Inntravel, Norwegian Wood Travel

Gallio   Italy
One of several low resorts near Vicenza and Trento. Popular with weekend day-trippers.
1100m; slopes 1100–1550m
⛷ 11 ⛷ 50km

Galtür   144
Charming village near Ischgl.

Gambarie d'Aspromonte   Italy
Italy's second most southerly ski area (after Mt Etna). On the 'toe' of the Italian 'boot' near Reggio di Calabria.
1310m; slopes 1310–1650m ⛷ 3

Gantschier   Austria
No slopes of its own but particularly well placed for visiting all the Montafon areas.
700m

Gargellen   217
Quiet village tucked up a side valley in the Montafon area.

Garmisch-Partenkirchen   416

Gaschurn   217
Village in the Montafon area.

Gaustablikk   Norway
Small snow-sure Alpine area on Mt Gausta in southern Norway with plenty of cross-country. ⛷ 15km

Gavarnie   France
Traditional village and fair-sized ski area, with the longest ski run in the Pyrenees. Grand views of the Cirque de Gavarnie.
1400m; slopes 1850–2400m
⛷ 11 ⛷ 45km

Geilo   708

Gérardmer   France
Sizeable lakeside resort in the northerly Vosges mountains near Strasbourg, with plenty of amenities. Limited downhill slopes nearby include one of almost 4km/2.5 miles. Extensive ski de fond trails in the area.
665m; slopes 750–1150m
⛷ 20 ⛷ 40km
🚂 Lagrange

Gerlitzen   114

Gerlos   167
Inexpensive but fairly snow-sure resort east of the Zillertal, and linked to Zell and Königsleiten.

Gerlosplatte   Austria
Inexpensive but fairly snow-sure area above the village of Krimml, linked to Königsleiten, Gerlos and Zell am Ziller to form a fair-sized intermediate area. 'Good runs, if unchallenging' was the verdict of one 2006 visitor.

Les Gets   301

La Giettaz   305
Tiny village between La Clusaz and Megève.

Gitschtal / Weissbriach   Austria
One of many little areas near Hermagor in eastern Austria, close to Italian border.
690m; slopes 690–1400m
⛷ 4 ⛷ 5km

Glaris   Switzerland
Hamlet base station for the uncrowded Rinerhorn section of the Davos slopes.
1455m; slopes 1455–2490m
⛷ 5 ⛷ 30km

Glencoe   720

Glenshee   720

Going   129
Tiny, attractively rustic village with small local ski area near Ellmau and linked to the huge SkiWelt area.

Goldegg   Austria
Year-round resort famous for its lakeside castle. Limited slopes but Wagrain (Salzburger Sportwelt) and Grossarl (Gastein valley) are nearby.
825m; slopes 825–1250m
⛷ 4 ⛷ 12km

Golden   Canada
Small logging town, the place to stay when visiting Kicking Horse resort 15 minutes away. Also the launch pad for Purcell heli-skiing.

Golte   Slovenia
Ski area in the East Karavanke mountains, above Mozirje. Gondola to the slopes from Zekovec village. Mostly advanced runs.
⛷ 7 ⛷ 18km

Gore Mountain   USA
One of the better areas in New York State. Near Lake Placid, sufficiently far north to avoid worst weekend crowds. Intermediate terrain.
455m; slopes 455–1095m
⛷ 9 ⛷ 290 acres

Göriach   Austria
Hamlet with trail connecting into one of the longest, most snow-sure cross-country networks in Europe.
1250m

Gortipohl   Austria
Traditional village in pretty Montafontal.
920m; slopes 900–2395m
⛷ 62 ⛷ 209km

Gosau   Austria
Family-friendly resort, with straggling village. Plenty of pretty, if low, runs. Fast lifts mean queues are rare. Snow-sure Obertauern and Schladming are within reach.
755m; slopes 755–1800m
⛷ 37 ⛷ 80km
🚂 Skiing Austria

Göstling   Austria
One of Austria's easternmost resorts, between Salzburg and Vienna. A traditional village in wooded setting.
530m; slopes 530–1880m
⛷ 12 ⛷ 19km

Götzens   140

Gourette-Eaux-Bonnes   France
Most snow-sure resort in the French Pyrenees. Very popular with local families, so best avoided at weekends. Recently revamped lifts and slopes.
1400m; slopes 1400–2400m
⛷ 15 ⛷ 30km

Grächen   Switzerland
Charming chalet-village reached by tricky access road off the approach to Zermatt. A small area of open slopes, mainly above the trees and of red-run difficulty, reached by two gondolas – one to Hannigalp (2115m/6,940ft), the main focus of activity with a very impressive children's nursery area. The village has almost a score of hotels, mostly 3-star; most of the accommodation is in chalets and apartments. The sports centre offers tennis and badminton, as well as a natural ice rink.
1615m; slopes 1615–2865m
⛷ 13 ⛷ 40km
🚂 Interhome

Le Grand-Bornand   France
Covered by the Aravis lift pass, and much smaller and even more charming than La Clusaz. The slopes can be accessed from either the outskirts of the village or the satellite village of Le Chinaillon. There are worthwhile shady black runs on Le Lachat, and on the lower peak of La Floria. There are plenty of good cruising blue and red intermediate runs, and also good beginner slopes. And there are extensive cross-country trails in the Vallée du Bouchet and towards Le Chinaillon.
1000m; slopes 1000–2100m
⛷ 37 ⛷ 90km
🚂 AmeriCan Ski, Erna Low, Karibuni, Last Resort, Peak Retreats, Simply Alpine, Ski France, Ski Weekender, Skiholidayextras.com

Grand Hirafu   721
One of the three interlinked ski areas of Niseko.

Grand Targhee   640

Les Granges   244
Hamlet at the mid-station of the funicular up from Bourg.

Grangesises   Italy
Small satellite of Sestriere, with lifts up to the main slopes.

Granite Peak   USA
One of the oldest areas in the Great Lakes region, and now one of the largest. New base village. Good selection of black runs on the upper mountain.
⛷ 7 ⛷ 400 acres

Grau Roig   107
Mini-resort between Pas de la Casa and Soldeu.

La Grave   303

Great Divide USA
Area near Helena, Montana, best for experts. Mostly bowls; plus near-extreme Rawhide Gulch.
1765m; slopes 1765–2195m
⛷ *6* 🚡 *720 acres*

Gresse-en-Vercors France
Resort south of Grenoble. Sheltered slopes worth noting for bad-weather days.
1250m; slopes 1600–1750m
⛷ *13* 🚡 *18km*
✉ *Interhome*

Gressoney-la-Trinité 450
Villages in the Monterosa Ski area.

Gressoney-St-Jean 424
Village in the Monterosa Ski area.

Grimentz 539

Grindelwald 512

Grossarl 123
Secluded village linked to Dorfgastein in the Gastein valley.

Grossglockner area 114

Grosskirchheim Austria
Very limited area near Heiligenblut.
1025m; slopes 1025–1400m

Grouse Mountain Canada
The Vancouver area with the largest lift capacity. Superb city views from mostly easy slopes; night skiing.
880m; slopes 880–1245m
⛷ *11* 🚡 *120 acres*
✉ *AmeriCan Ski, Ski Dream*

Grünau Austria
Spacious riverside village in a lovely lake-filled part of eastern Austria. Nicely varied area, but very low.
525m; slopes 600–1600m
⛷ *14* 🚡 *40km*

Gryon 555
Village below Villars.

Gstaad Switzerland
Despite its exclusive reputation, Gstaad is an attractive, traditional village where anyone could have a relaxing holiday. There are four sectors, covered by a single, confusing map. The largest sector is above Saanenmöser and Schönried, reached by train. Snow-cover can be unreliable except on the Glacier des Diablerets, 15km/9 miles away. Few runs challenge experts. Black runs rarely exceed red or even blue difficulty. There is off-piste potential. Given good snow, this is a superb area for intermediates, with long, easy descents in the major area. The nursery slopes at Wispile are adequate, and there are plenty of runs to progress to. Time lost on buses or trains is more of a problem than queues.
1050m; slopes 950–3000m
⛷ *62* 🚡 *250km*

✉ *Alpine Answers, Interhome, Made to Measure, Momentum, Oxford Ski Co, Ski Weekend, Switzerland Travel Centre, White Roc*

Gunstock USA
One of the New Hampshire resorts closest to Boston, popular with families. Primarily easy slopes. Gorgeous Lake Winnisquam views.
275m; slopes 275–700m
⛷ *8* 🚡 *220 acres*

Guthega 723

Guzet France
A charming cluster of chalets set among a pine forest at Guzet 1400. Three main sectors offer slopes for all levels.
1400m; slopes 1100–2100m
⛷ *14* 🚡 *40km*

Hafjell Norway
Main ski area for Lillehammer.
1250m; slopes 610–2000m
⛷ *12* 🚡 *33km*
✉ *Norwegian Wood Travel*

Haider Alm Italy
Area in the Val Venosta in the South Tyrol close to Nauders. Malda Haider in Italian.
⛷ *5* 🚡 *20km*

Hakuba Happo One 721
European-style resort four hours from Tokyo.

Harper Mountain Canada
Small, family-friendly resort in Kamloops, British Colombia.
1100m; slopes 1100–1525m
⛷ *3* 🚡 *400 acres*

Harrachov Czech Republic
Closest resort to Prague, with enough terrain to justify a day trip. No beginner area.
650m; slopes 650–1020m
⛷ *4* 🚡 *8 runs*

Hasliberg Switzerland
Four rustic hamlets on a sunny plateau overlooking Meiringen and Lake Brienz. Two of them are the bottom stations of a varied intermediate area.
1050m

Haukelifjell Norway

Haus 186
Village next to Schladming.

Haystack USA
Minor satellite of Mount Snow, in Vermont, but with a bit more steep skiing.
580m; slopes 580–1095m
⛷ *26* 🚡 *540 acres*

Heavenly 577

Hebalm Austria
One of many small areas in Austria's easternmost ski region near Slovenian border. No major resorts in vicinity.
1350m; slopes 1350–1400m
⛷ *6* 🚡 *11km*

Heiligenblut 114

Heiterwang 227

Hemlock Resort Canada
Area 55 miles east of Vancouver towards Sun Peaks. Mostly intermediate terrain and with snowfall of 600 inches a year. Lodging is available at the base area.
1000m; slopes 1000–1375m
⛷ *4* 🚡 *350 acres*

Hemsedal 710

Heremence Switzerland
Quiet, traditional village in unspoiled attractive setting south of Sion. Verbier's slopes are accessed a few minutes' drive away at Les Masses.
1250m

Hermagor Austria
Main village base for the Nassfeld ski area in Carinthia.
600m; slopes 610–2000m
⛷ *30* 🚡 *100km*

High King Mountain 138

High One Resort South Korea
Small ski area at the High 1 leisure and golf complex, 250km/155 miles from Seoul by train. 🚡 *21km*

Hintermoos 138
Village in the Hochkönig area.

Hintersee Austria
Easy slopes very close to Salzburg. Several long top-to-bottom runs and lifts means the size of the area is greatly reduced if the snowline is high.
745m; slopes 750–1470m
⛷ *9* 🚡 *40km*

Hinterstoder Austria
A very quiet valley village – neat but not overtly charming – spread along the road up the dead-end Stodertal in Upper Austria. The local Höss slopes are pleasantly wooded, less densely at the top, with splendid views. It's a small area, but has a worthwhile vertical of 1250m/4,100ft, and 450m/1,475ft above mid-mountain. A gondola from the main street goes up to the flat-bottomed bowl of Huttererböden (1400m/4,600ft), where there are very gentle but limited nursery slopes and lifts up to higher points. Most of the mountain is of easy red steepness. The run to the valley is a pleasant red with one or two tricky bits where it takes a quick plunge; it has effective snowmaking.
600m; slopes 600–1860m
⛷ *10* 🚡 *35km*

Hinterthal 138
Village in the Hochkönig area.

Hintertux / Tux valley 132

Hippach 167
Hamlet near a crowd-free lift into Mayrhofen's main area.

Hittisau 213

Hochfügen Austria
See Hochzillertal.
1500m; slopes 560–2500m
⛷ *35* 🚡 *155km*

Hochgurgl 172
Quiet village with connection to Obergurgl's slopes.

Hochkönig 138

Hochpillberg Austria
Hamlet with fabulous views towards Innsbruck and an antique chairlift into varied terrain above Schwaz with good vertical of 1000m/3,280ft. Wonderfully safe for children; all accommodation within two minutes of lift.
1300m; slopes 1300–2100m
⛷ *5* 🚡 *10km*

Hochsölden 190
Satellite above Sölden.

Hoch-Ybrig Switzerland
Purpose-built complex only 64km/40 miles south-east of Zürich, with facilities for families.
1050m; slopes 1050–1830m
⛷ *10* 🚡 *40km*

Hochzillertal Austria
Along with Hochfugen forms the large Ski Optimal area above the valley village of Kaltenbach. Best suited to intermediates – but there is plenty of potential for off-piste too.
1500m; slopes 560–2500m
⛷ *35* 🚡 *155km*

Hohuanshan Taiwan
Limited ski area with short season in high, wild, inaccessible Miitaku mountains. Also known as Mt Hehuan.
3275m ⛷ *1*

Holiday Valley USA
Family resort in New York State, an hour's drive south-east of Buffalo.
slopes 485–685m
⛷ *12* 🚡 *270 acres*

Hollersbach Austria
Hamlet near Mittersill, over Pass Thurn from Kitzbühel, with a gondola up to the Resterhöhe above Pass Thurn.
805m; slopes 805–1000m
⛷ *2* 🚡 *5km*

Homewood USA
Uncrowded area near Tahoe City with the most sheltered slopes in the vicinity. All the slopes are served by slow chairlifts, and the views are as much of an attraction as the slopes. Set right on the western shore of the lake, so access is quick and easy. The notably quiet slopes include plenty of short black pitches as well as cruisers.
1900m; slopes 1900–2400m
⛷ *7* 🚡 *1260 acres*

Hoodoo Ski Bowl USA
Small area in Oregon with short runs and limited vertical of around 300m/980ft. Some 65km/40 miles from Bend (see Mount Bachelor).
1420m; slopes 1420–1740m
▲ 5 ⬥ 800 acres

Hopfgarten 193
Small chalet village with lift link into the Ski Welt area.

Horseshoe Resort Canada
Toronto region resort with high-capacity lift system and 100% snowmaking. The second mountain – The Heights – is open to members only.
310m; slopes 310–405m
▲ 7 ⬥ 60 acres

Les Houches 258
Varied, tree-lined area at the entrance to the Chamonix valley.

Hovden Norway
Big, modern luxury lakeside hotel in wilderness midway between Oslo and Bergen. Cross-country venue with some Alpine slopes.
820m; slopes 820–1175m
▲ 5 ⬥ 14km

La Hoya Argentina
Small uncrowded resort 15km/9 miles from the small town of Esquel.
slopes 1350–2150m
▲ 9 ⬥ 22km

Huez 234
Charming old hamlet on the road up to Alpe-d'Huez.

Hunter Mountain USA
Popular New Yorkers' area so it gets very crowded at weekends.
485m; slopes 485–975m
▲ 14 ⬥ 230 acres
➡ Ski Dream

Hüttschlag Austria
Hamlet in a dead-end valley with lifts into the Gastein area at nearby Grossarl.
1020m; slopes 1020–1220m ▲ 1

Hyundai Sungwoo Resort South Korea
Modern high-rise resort, 140km/87 miles from Seoul. Host to the 2009 World Snowboard Championships. Own English-language web site at www.hdsungwoo.co.kr.
▲ 9

Idre Fjäll Sweden
Collective name for four areas 490km/305 miles north-west of Stockholm.
slopes 590–890m
▲ 30 ⬥ 28km

Igls 140

Iizuna Japan
Tiny area 2.5 hours from Tokyo.
slopes 1080–1480m ▲ 7

Incline Village USA
Large village on northern edge of Lake Tahoe – it is a reasonable stop-off if you are touring.

Indianhead USA
South Lake Superior area with the most snowfall in the region. Winds are a problem.
395m; slopes 395–585m
▲ 12 ⬥ 195 acres

Inneralpbach 120
Small satellite of Alpbach.

Innerarosa 496
The prettiest part of Arosa.

Innichen Italy
Small resort in South Tyrol. San Candido is its Italian name.
1175m; slopes 1175–1580m
▲ 4 ⬥ 15km

Innsbruck 140

Interlaken Switzerland
Lakeside summer resort near Wengen, Grindelwald and Mürren.
➡ Crystal, Kuoni, Simply Alpine, Solo's

Ischgl 144

Ishiuchi Maruyama-Gala-Yuzawa Kogen Japan
Three resorts with a shared lift pass 90 minutes from Tokyo by bullet train and offering the largest ski area in the central Honshu region.
255m; slopes 255–920m ▲ 52

Isola 2000 France
A small, high, purpose-built family resort, a long way south but Nice airport is only 90km/55 miles away. The compact slopes are linked in a horseshoe shape around the resort and most runs are above the treeline. Isola often has snow when other French resorts lack it, but at other times it misses out. There are excellent nursery slopes in the heart of the resort. Accommodation is largely self-catering, much of it slope-side. The après-ski scene is muted, but trips to the Riviera and Monte Carlo are easy.
2000m; slopes 1840–2610m
▲ 22 ⬥ 120km
➡ Erna Low, Lagrange, Leisure Direction, PV-Holidays.com, Ski Collection, Ski France, Skiholidayextras.com, Ski Solutions

Iso Syöte 706

Itter 193
Next to Söll.

Jackson USA
Classic New England village, and a major cross-country base. A lovely place from which to ski New Hampshire's Alpine areas.
➡ Virgin Snow

Jackson Hole 646

Jasná Slovakia
Largest ski area in Slovakia, in the Low Tatras mountains. Big children's area, terrain park, night skiing. Several tough 'freeride zones'.
slopes 1240–2005m
▲ 14 ⬥ 21km

Jasper Canada
Set in the middle of Jasper National Park, this low-key, low-rise little town appeals more to those keen on scenery and wildlife (and cross-country skiing) rather than piste miles. A visit could be combined with a stay in Whistler, Banff or Lake Louise. Snowfall is modest by North American standards and there is lots of steep terrain that needs good snow to be fun. Keen piste-bashers will cover all the groomed runs in half a day. There are excellent nursery slopes. There are 300km/186 miles of cross-country trails. Most accommodation is out of town or on the outskirts and the local slopes are a 30-minute drive. A visitor enthuses: 'Great skiing, no queues anywhere and a lot of fun in the gladed bowl.'
1065m; slopes 1065–2610m
▲ 9 ⬥ 1675 acres
➡ AmeriCan Ski, Canadian Affair, Crystal, Crystal Finest, Frontier, Inghams, Kuoni, Made to Measure, Ski Dream, Ski Independence, Ski Safari, Skiworld, Trailfinders, Virgin Snow

Jay Peak USA
In northern Vermont, near the Canadian border. Crowded at weekends but quiet in the week. Vermont's only cable car takes you to the summit and to views of four US states plus Canada. The only fast chair goes almost as high. It gets a lot of snow (350 inches on average) and has some good runs for advanced skiers and good intermediates – notably 100+ acres of glades. There's good beginner terrain, and there are blue cruisers, too, but they don't add up to a lot. There is slope-side accommodation, mainly in condos.
550m; slopes 550–1205m
▲ 8 ⬥ 385 acres

Jochberg 151
Straggling village, 8km/5 miles from Kitzbühel.

La Joue-du-Loup France
Slightly stylish little purpose-built ski-in/ski-out family resort a few km north-west of Gap. Shares a fair-sized intermediate area with Superdévoluy.
1500m; slopes 1500–2510m
▲ 32 ⬥ 100km
➡ Lagrange, Ski Collection

Jouvenceaux 456
Less boisterous base from which to ski Sauze d'Oulx's terrain.

Jukkasjärvi Sweden
Centuries-old cross-country resort with unique ice hotel rebuilt every December.

June Mountain USA
Small area a half-hour drive from Mammoth and in same ownership. Empty slopes except on peak weekends.
2300m; slopes 2300–3090m
▲ 8 ⬥ 500 acres

Juns 132
Small village between Lanersbach and Hintertux.

Kals am Grossglockner Austria
Village in a remote valley north of Lienz. Now linked by new lifts to Matrei.
1325m; slopes 1325–2305m
▲ 15 ⬥ 110km

Kaltenbach Austria
One of the larger, quieter Zillertal areas, with plenty of high-altitude slopes, mostly above the treeline.
560m; slopes 560–2500m
▲ 35 ⬥ 155km

Kananaskis Canada
Small area near Calgary, nicely set in woods, with slopes at Nakiska and Fortress Mountain.
slopes 1525–2465m
▲ 12 ⬥ 605 acres
➡ Frontier

Kandersteg Switzerland
Good cross-country base set amid beautiful scenery near Interlaken. Easy, but limited, slopes. Popular with families.
1175m; slopes 1175–1900m
▲ 7 ⬥ 14km
➡ Headwater, Inghams, Inntravel, Kuoni, Simply Alpine, Switzerland Travel Centre

Kanin Slovenia
Small area near Bovec, 17km/11 miles from the Italian border, with plans to link with Sella Nevea. Kanin is Slovenia's highest. A visitor was impressed with the quality of the area and particularly enjoyed its 'massive' area of off-piste. There are plans for a lift link to the slopes of nearby Sella Nevea in the next few years.
980m; slopes 1600–2300m
▲ 6 ⬥ 15km

Kappl 144
Small village down the valley from Ischgl.

Kaprun 222
Village near Zell am See with local slopes and convenient access to Kitzsteinhorn glacier.

Les Karellis France
Resort with slopes that are more scenic, challenging and snow-sure than those of better-known Valloire, nearby. six-pack has improved access. 'Great little place for a day out,' says a reporter.
1600m; slopes 1600–2550m
⛊ 17 ⛷ 60km

Kastelruth Italy
German name for Castelrotto.
🚌 Inntravel

Kasurila Finland
Siilinjarvi ski area popular with boarders. ⛊ 5

Katschberg 114

Keystone 606

Kicking Horse 676

Killington 652

Kimberley Canada
This mining town turned twee mock Austro-Bavarian/English Tudor resort enjoys a beautiful setting 2 hours from Banff. The terrain offers a mix of blue and black runs (plus the occasional green) and a vertical of 750m/2,460ft. In addition to the lifts up the front there are two other slow chairs. The mainly forested runs are spread over two rather featureless hills. There are only a few short double diamonds, but classification tends to understate difficulty, and many of the single diamonds are quite challenging. It has a reputation for good powder, although it doesn't get huge amounts by the standards of this region.
1230m; slopes 1230–1980m
⛊ 5 ⛷ 1800 acres
🚌 AmeriCan Ski, Frontier, Inghams, Ski Dream, Ski Safari

Kirchberg 151
Lively town close to Kitzbühel.

Kirchdorf Austria
Attractive village a bus ride from St Johann in Tirol.
640m
🚌 Crystal, Simply Alpine, Skiing Austria, Snowcoach, Solo's, Thomson

Kirkwood USA
Kirkwood is renowned for its powder, and has a lot to offer experts and confident intermediates, but it's limited for intermediates who are not happy to tackle black runs. It makes a great outing from South Lake Tahoe, though heavy snowfall may close the high-level passes to get there. Deep snow is part of the attraction, often reportedly better than Heavenly.
2375m; slopes 2375–2985m
⛊ 12 ⛷ 2300 acres

Kitzbühel 151

Kleinarl Austria
Secluded traditional village up a pretty side valley from Wagrain, at one end of a three-valley lift network linking it via Flachauwinkl to Zauchensee – all part of the Salzburger Sportwelt ski pass area that our figures relate to.
1015m; slopes 800–2185m
⛊ 59 ⛷ 200km
🚌 Interhome

Klippitztörl Austria
One of many little areas in Austria's easternmost ski region near Slovenian border. 'Great little area with pretty tree-lined runs,' says a visitor.
1550m; slopes 1460–1820m
⛊ 6 ⛷ 25km

Klösterle Austria
Valley village at the base of the Sonnenkopf ski area a few km west of the Arlberg pass – and covered by the Arlberg ski pass.
1100m; slopes 1100–2300m
⛊ 10 ⛷ 39km

Klosters 516

Kobla 719

Kolasin 1450 Montenegro
Small ski area on Bjelasica Mountain above the town of the Kolasin, where you stay.
1450m
⛊ 5 ⛷ 20km

Kolsass-Weer Austria
Pair of Inn-side villages with low, inconvenient and limited slopes.
555m; slopes 555–1010m
⛊ 3 ⛷ 14km

Königsleiten 167
Quiet, high resort sharing fairly snow-sure area with Gerlos, now also linked to Zell im Zillertal to form the fair-sized Zillertal Arena area.

Konjiam South Korea
Purpose-built resort 40 minutes north of Seoul. The slopes suit beginners best, and offer the area's longest run at 1.8km. The resort is the first in South Korea to introduce a maximum visitor number to reduce overcrowding on the slopes. The base village has over 400 condos, a restaurant and spa, all tastefully built around small plazas and water features - popular with families.
⛊ 3 ⛷ 11 runs

Kopaonik Serbia
Modern, sympathetically designed family resort in a pretty setting.
1770m; slopes 1110–2015m
⛊ 23 ⛷ 60km
🚌 BoardnLodge

Koralpe Austria
Largest and steepest of many gentle little areas in Austria's easternmost ski region near the Slovenian border.
1550m; slopes 1550–2050m
⛊ 10 ⛷ 25km

Korea Condo South Korea
A single condo complex built some way from the three slopes. ⛊ 2

Kössen Austria
Village near St Johann in Tirol with low, scattered and limited local slopes.
600m; slopes 600–1700m
⛊ 9 ⛷ 25km

Kötschach-Mauthen Austria
One of many little areas near Hermagor in eastern Austria, close to the Italian border.
710m; slopes 710–1300m
⛊ 4 ⛷ 7km

Kranjska Gora 719

Krimml Austria
Sunny area, high enough to have good snow usually. Shares regional pass with Wildkogel resorts (Neukirchen).
1075m; slopes 1640–2040m
⛊ 9 ⛷ 33km

Krispl-Gaissau Austria
Easy slopes very close to Salzburg. Several long top-to-bottom lifts mean the size of the area is greatly reduced if the snow line is high.
925m; slopes 750–1570m
⛊ 11 ⛷ 40km

Kronplatz Italy
Distinctive ski area in South Tyrol, with amazingly efficient lifts from Brunico and San Vigilio di Marebbe. Plan de Corones is its Italian name.
1200m; slopes 1200–2275m
⛊ 32 ⛷ 103km
🚌 Momentum, Neilson

Krvavec Slovenia
Slopes spread across Kalska mountain. Lifts include a gondola.
1450m; slopes 1450–1970m
⛊ 10 ⛷ 35km

Kühtai 140

Kusatsu Kokusai Japan
Attractive spa village with hot springs, three hours from Tokyo.
slopes 1250–2170m ⛊ 13

Laax 518

Le Lac Blanc France
Mini-resort with recently installed first six-pack in the northerly Vosges mountains near Strasbourg. Extensive ski de fond trails.
830m; slopes 830–1235m
⛊ 9 ⛷ 14km

Laces Italy
Village in the Val Venosta in the South Tyrol covered by the Ortler Skiarena pass.

Lachtal Austria
Second largest ski resort in the Styrian region NE of Salzburg.
1600m; slopes 1600–2100m
⛊ 8 ⛷ 29km

Ladis Austria
Smaller alternative to Serfaus and Fiss, with lifts that connect into the same varied ski area.
1200m; slopes 1200–2540m
⛊ 42 ⛷ 160km
🚌 Skiing Austria

Lagunillas Chile
83km/52 miles south-east of Santiago. ⛷ 494 acres

Le Laisinant 393
Tiny hamlet a short bus-ride up the valley from Val d'Isère, with a chairlift up to the Solaise and Le Fornet slopes.

Lake Louise 678

Lake Tahoe USA
Collection of 14 ski areas spectacularly set on California-Nevada border - Heavenly and Squaw Valley best known.
🚌 AmeriCan Ski, Crystal Finest, Independent Ski Links, Skiworld, Supertravel, Virgin Snow

Lamoura France
One of four villages that makes up the Les Rousses area in the Jura.
1120m; slopes 1120–1680m
⛊ 40 ⛷ 40km
🚌 Headwater

Landeck–Zams Austria
Small area in the Tirol region.
816m; slopes 816–2210m
⛊ 7 ⛷ 22km

Lanersbach 132
Attractive village near Hintertux.

Lans-en-Vercors France
Village close to Villard-de-Lans and 30km/19 miles from Grenoble. Highest slopes in the region; few snowmakers.
1020m; slopes 1400–1805m
🚡 *16* 🚠 *24km*

Lanslebourg France
One of the villages that makes up Val Cenis.

Lanslevillard France
One of the villages that makes up Val Cenis.

Laterns-Gapfohl Austria
900m; slopes 900–1785m
🚡 *6* 🚠 *27km*

Lauchernalp-Lötschental
Switzerland
Small but tall slopes reached by cable car from Wiler in the secluded, picturesque dead-end Lötschental, north of Rhône valley. Glacier runs above 3000m.
1420m; slopes 1420–2700m
🚡 *7* 🚠 *33km*

Lauterbrunnen 523
Valley town with rail connection up to Mürren.

Le Lavancher 258
Quiet village between Chamonix and Argentière.

Lavarone 479
One of several areas east of Trento.

Leadville USA
Old mining town full of historic buildings. Own easy area (Ski Cooper) plus snowcat operation. Picturesque inexpensive base for visiting Copper Mountain, Vail and Beaver Creek.

Lech 158

The Lecht 720

Lélex France
Family resort with pretty wooded slopes between Dijon and Geneva.
900m; slopes 900–1680m
🚡 *29* 🚠 *50km*

Las Leñas 732

Lenggries-Brauneck 414

Lenk 491
Traditional village that shares an area with Adelboden and has its own separate slopes.

Lenzerheide Switzerland
The senior partner with Valbella in an extensive area of intermediate slopes in a pretty setting around a lake, all at a decent altitude. The slopes are on the two sides of the valley. The east-facing, morning-sun slopes are mainly fairly gentle. The west-facing slopes have more character, both in skiing and visual terms, including a run on the back of the dramatic peak of the Rothorn. There is considerable off-piste potential.
1470m; slopes 1230–2865m
🚡 *28* 🚠 *155km*
✉ *Alpine Answers, Crystal, Interhome, Made to Measure, Switzerland Travel Centre*

Leogang 179
Quiet village with link to Saalbach-Hinterglemm.

Lermoos 227
Focal resort of the Zugspitze area: a pleasant little village with a small area of shady intermediate slopes. New six-pack for 2006/07.

Lessach Austria
Hamlet with trail connecting into one of the longest, most snow-sure cross-country networks in Europe.
1210m; 🚡 *1*

Leukerbad Switzerland
Major spa resort of Roman origin, spectacularly set beneath towering cliffs, which are scaled by a cable car up to high-altitude cross-country trails. The downhill slopes are on the opposite side of the valley, mainly above the treeline, served by draglifts and of red gradient, though there are a couple of blacks including a World Cup downhill course, which descends from the high, open slopes into the woods. There is also a slightly separate wooded sector served by a couple of chairlifts. A new six-pack replaced three draglifts for 2008/09.
1410m; slopes 1410–2700m
🚡 *13* 🚠 *50km*
✉ *Kuoni, Made to Measure, Switzerland Travel Centre, Thomson*

Leutasch Austria
Traditional cross-country village with limited slopes but a pleasant day trip from nearby Seefeld or Innsbruck.
1130m; slopes 1130–1605m
🚡 *3* 🚠 *6km*
✉ *Headwater, Inntravel, Simply Alpine*

Levi 706

Leysin Switzerland
This is a spread-out village, climbing up a wooded hillside. The lifts are to the east of the village and take you to a pretty mix of mainly red and blue runs. Itineraries from the top of Chaux de Mont provide the best options for experts, along with a heli-operation. There are nursery slopes at village level. The revolving Kuklos restaurant at La Berneuse has stunning views.
1250m; slopes 1300–2200m
🚡 *14* 🚠 *60km*
✉ *Simply Alpine, Switzerland Travel Centre*

Lienz Austria
Pleasant town in pretty surroundings.
675m; slopes 730–2290m
🚡 *17* 🚠 *41km*
✉ *Skiing Austria*

Lillehammer 708

Limone Italy
Pleasant old town not far from Turin, with a pretty area, but far from snow-sure.
1010m; slopes 1030–2050m
🚡 *25* 🚠 *80km*

Lincoln USA
Sprawling New Hampshire town from which to visit Loon mountain.

Lindvallen-Högfjället Sweden
Two of the mountains that make up the four unlinked ski areas of Sälen.
800m; slopes 590–890m
🚡 *46* 🚠 *85km*

Le Lioran France
Auvergne village near Aurillac with a purpose-built satellite above. Spectacular volcanic scenery.
1160m; slopes 1160–1850m
🚡 *24* 🚠 *60km*

Livigno 444

Lizzola Italy
Small base development in remote region north of Bergamo. Several other little areas nearby.
1250m; slopes 1250–2070m
🚡 *9* 🚠 *30km*

Loch Lomond Canada
Steep, narrow, challenging slopes near Thunder Bay on the shores of Lake Superior. Candy Mountain is nearby.
215m; slopes 215–440m
🚡 *3* 🚠 *90 acres*

Lofer Austria
Quiet, traditional village in a pretty setting north of Saalbach with a small area of its own, and Waidring's relatively snow-sure Steinplatte nearby.
640m; slopes 640–1745m
🚡 *14* 🚠 *46km*
✉ *Skiing Austria, STC*

Longchamp 404
Purpose-built resort that shares slopes with Valmorel.

Loon Mountain USA
Small, smart, modern resort just outside Lincoln, New Hampshire. Mostly intermediate runs.
290m; slopes 290–910m
🚡 *10* 🚠 *275 acres*
✉ *Directski.com, Ski McNeill, Virgin Snow*

Lost Trail USA
Remote Montana area, open only Thursday to Sunday and holidays. Mostly intermediate slopes.
2005m; slopes 2005–2370m
🚡 *6* 🚠 *800 acres*

Loveland USA
Exceptionally high and snowy slopes right next to highway I70, just east of the Continental Divide, easily reached from other Colorado resorts, especially Keystone.
3230m; slopes 3230–3870m
🚡 *9* 🚠 *1365 acres*

Luchon France
Sizeable village with plenty of amenities, with gondola (eight minutes) to its ski area at purpose-built Superbagnères.
630m; slopes 1440–2260m
🚡 *16* 🚠 *35km*
✉ *Lagrange*

Lurisia Italy
Sizeable spa resort, a good base for visits to surrounding little ski areas and to Nice.
750m; slopes 800–1800m
🚡 *8* 🚠 *35km*

Lutsen Mountains USA
Largest ski area in between Vermont and Colorado, with panoramic views of Lake Superior, only 3km/2 miles away. Four small linked hills with 95% snowmaking offer surprisingly good and extensive terrain, with something for everyone. Moose Mountain has the biggest vertical (250m/820ft), with cruisers or bumps top to bottom, great views of the lake, and backcountry glade runs. Small close-side village. Good cross-country, snow-shoeing and snowmobiling nearby.
80m; slopes 80–335m
🚡 *9* 🚠 *1000 acres*

Luz-Ardiden France
Spa village below its ski area. Cauterets and Barèges nearby.
710m; slopes 1730–2450m
🚡 *15* 🚠 *60km*

Resort directory / index

Interactive resort shortlist builder at **www.wtss.co.uk**

Macugnaga Italy
A pair of quiet, pretty villages dramatically set at the head of a remote valley, over the mountains from Zermatt and Saas-Fee. Lifts run up to the foot of the Belvedere glacier. A chairlift rises very slowly from the village to Burky, in the middle of the quiet, woody area of gentle runs. There is an excellent nursery slope beside the village and a two-stage cable car going over sunny slopes to the Swiss border. There are good, varied red runs down the 1100m/3,610ft vertical of the top cable car. In the right conditions, off-piste possibilities from the cable car are considerable.
1325m; slopes 1325–2800m
🚡 12 ➚ 38km

Madesimo Italy
Remote valley village, a mix of traditional buildings and piecemeal modern development, north of Bergamo, great for a weekend. From mid-mountain there are pleasant runs to the village, or you can cut across to the open slopes above Motta, equipped with fast quads. The top of the gondola serves the famous Canalone, a long, sweeping, easy black, but classed as off-piste. There is also an off-piste route at 1600m/5,250ft vertical to Fraciscio.
1545m; slopes 1545–2880m
🚡 12 ➚ 60km
📧 *Inghams, Pure Alpine*

Madonna di Campiglio 448
Mad River Glen USA
Mad River Glen is a cult resort with locals, owned for a decade now by a co-operative, with some tough ungroomed terrain, a few well-groomed intermediate trails and old-fashioned lifts – it still has a single-person chairlift (approaching some 60 years of operation). And snowboarding is still banned.
485m; slopes 485–1110m
🚡 4 ➚ 115 acres

La Magdelaine Italy
Close to Cervinia, and good on bad-weather days.
1645m; slopes 1645–1870m
🚡 4 ➚ 4km

Maishofen Austria
Cheaper place to stay when visiting equidistant Saalbach and Zell am See.
765m

Malbun Liechtenstein
Quaint user-friendly little family resort, 16km/10 miles from the capital, Vaduz. Limited slopes and short easy runs.
1600m; slopes 1595–2100m
🚡 6 ➚ 21km

Malcesine Italy
Large summer resort on Lake Garda with a fair area of slopes, served by a revolving cable car.
1430m; slopes 1430–1830m
🚡 8 ➚ 12km

Malga Ciapela Italy
Resort at the foot of the Marmolada glacier massif, with a link into the Sella Ronda. Cortina is nearby.
1445m; slopes 1445–3270m
🚡 8 ➚ 18km

Malga Haider Italy
Small area in Val Venosta, close to Austrian border. Haideralm is its German name.
🚡 5 ➚ 20km

Mallnitz 114
Mammoth Mountain 582
Manigod France
Small valley village, sharing quiet, wooded slopes with La Clusaz - over the Col de la Croix-Fry. 'Fantastic, place to avoid the crowds,' says a visitor.
1100m ➚ 132km

Marble Mountain Canada
Tiny area in the Humber Valley on the island of Newfoundland, near the charming town of Corner Brook and Gros Morne National Park. Good snow record by east coast standards. Splendid base lodge, and some slope-side lodging. Blomidon Cat Skiing operates nearby.
85m; slopes 10–545m
🚡 5 ➚ 175 acres
📧 *Frontier*

Les Marecottes Switzerland
Small area near Martigny. Valid with the Valais Ski Card.
1100m; slopes 1775–2200m
🚡 5 ➚ 25km

Maria Alm 138
Charming village at one end of the Hochkönig area.

Mariapfarr Austria
Village at the heart of one of the longest, most snow-reliable cross-country networks in Europe. Sizeable Mauterndorf-St Michael Alpine area and Obertauern area are nearby.
1120m
🚡 5 ➚ 30km

Mariazell Austria
Traditional Styria village with an impressive basilica. Limited slopes.
870m; slopes 870–1265m
🚡 5 ➚ 11km

Maribor 719
Marilleva 479
Small Trentino resort linked with Madonna di Campiglio.

Le Markstein France
Long-standing small resort in the northerly Vosges mountains near Strasbourg, which has hosted World Cup slalom races. Extensive ski de fond trails.
slopes 770–1270m 🚡 10

Masella Spain
Friendly Pyrenean village linked with slopes of La Molina to form the Alp 2500 area. Weekend crowds.
1600m; slopes 1600–2535m
🚡 31 ➚ 121km

La Massana 102
Les Masses 543
A hamlet below Les Collons in Thyon sector of the Verbier ski area.

Le Massif 700
Matrei in Osttirol Austria
Large market village south of Felbertauern tunnel. Mostly high slopes, now linked to Kals on the other side of the hill.
1000m; slopes 1000–2400m
🚡 15 ➚ 110km
📧 *Skiing Austria*

Maurienne Valley France
A great curving trench with over 20 winter resorts, ranging from pleasant old valley villages to convenience resorts purpose-built in the 1960s.

Mauterndorf Austria
Village near Obertauern with tremendous snow record.
1120m; slopes 1075–2360m
🚡 10 ➚ 35km

Maverick Mountain USA
Montana resort with plenty of terrain accessed by few lifts. Cowboy Winter Games venue – rodeo one day, ski races the next.
2155m; slopes 2155–2800m
🚡 2 ➚ 500 acres

Mayens de Riddes Switzerland
Hamlet at the base of lifts on the back of Verbier's Savoleyres sector, more often referred to as La Tzoumaz.
1500m
📧 *Interhome*

Mayens-de-Sion Switzerland
Tranquil hamlet off the road up to Les Collons – part of the Verbier area.
1470m

Mayrhofen 167
Méaudre France
Small resort near Grenoble with good snowmaking to make up for its low altitude.
1000m; slopes 1000–1600m
🚡 10 ➚ 18km

Megève 305
Meiringen 520
Melchsee-Frutt Switzerland
Limited, but high and snow-sure bowl above a car-free village. Family-friendly.
1920m; slopes 1080–2255m
🚡 11 ➚ 32km

Mellau 213
Les Menuires 312
Merano 2000 Italy
Small ski area just outside Merano, with main lift base at Falzeben above Avelengo/Hafling.
2000m; slopes 2000–2240m
🚡 7 ➚ 40km
📧 *Simply Alpine*

Méribel 316
Métabief-Mont-d'Or France
Twin villages in the Jura region, not far from Geneva.
900m; slopes 880–1460m
🚡 22 ➚ 42km

Methven 725
Nearest town/accommodation to Mt Hutt.

Mieders 210
Mijoux France
Pretty wooded slopes between Dijon and Geneva. Lélex nearby.
1000m; slopes 900–1680m
🚡 29 ➚ 50km

Mission Ridge USA
Area in dry region that gets higher-quality snow than other Seattle resorts but less of it. Good intermediate slopes.
1390m; slopes 1390–2065m
🚡 6 ➚ 300 acres

Misurina Italy
Tiny village near Cortina. A cheap alternative base.
1755m; slopes 1755–1900m
🚡 4 ➚ 13km

Mittenwald 414
Mittersill Austria
Valley-junction village south of Pass Thurn. A gondola runs from Hollersbach up to the Resterhöhe sector above Pass Thurn.
790m; slopes 1265–1895m
🚡 15 ➚ 25km

Moena Italy
Large village between Cavalese and Sella Ronda resorts, ideally located for touring the Dolomites area.
1180m; slopes 1180–2515m
🚡 24 ➚ 35km
📧 *Interhome*

La Molina 703
Mölltal Glacier 114
Molveno Italy
Lakeside village on edge of Dolomites, with a couple of lifts - but mostly used as a base to ski nearby Andalo.
📧 *Simply Alpine*

Monarch USA
Wonderfully uncrowded area, a day trip from Crested Butte. Great powder. Good for all but experts.
3290m; slopes 3290–3645m
⛷ 5 ⛏ 800 acres

Monesi Italy
Southernmost of the resorts south of Turin. Close to Monaco and Nice.
1310m; slopes 1310–2180m
⛷ 5 ⛏ 38km

Le Monêtier 360
Quiet little village with access to Serre-Chevalier's slopes.

La Mongie 413

Montafon 217

Montalbert 339
Traditional village with direct access to the La Plagne network.

Mont Blanc Canada
Small locals' hill near Tremblant, with only 300m/980ft of vertical and no resemblance to the Franco-Italian item.
⛷ 7 ⛏ 36

Montchavin 339
Attractive village on the fringe of La Plagne.

Mont-de-Lans 288
Low village near Les Deux-Alpes.

Le Mont-Dore France
Attractive traditional small town, the largest resort in the stunningly beautiful volcanic Auvergne region near Clermont-Ferrand.
1050m; slopes 1350–1850m
⛷ 18 ⛏ 42km

Monte Bondone 479
Trento's local hill.

Monte Campione Italy
Tiny purpose-built resort, spread thinly over four mountainsides. 80% snowmaking helps to offset the low altitude.
1100m; slopes 1200–2010m
⛷ 16 ⛏ 80km

Monte Livata Italy
Closest resort to Rome, popular with weekenders.
1430m; slopes 1430–1750m
⛷ 8 ⛏ 8km

Monte Piselli Italy
Tiny area with the highest slopes of the many little resorts east of Rome.
2100m; slopes 2100–2690m
⛷ 3 ⛏ 5km

Monte Pora Italy
Tiny resort near Lake d'Iseo and Bergamo. Several other little areas nearby.
1350m; slopes 1350–1880m
⛷ 11 ⛏ 30km

Monterosa Ski 450

Mont Gabriel Canada
Montreal area with runs on four sides of the mountain, though the south-facing sides rarely open. Two short but renowned double black diamond bump runs. ⛏ 9

Montgenèvre 327

Mont Glen Canada
Least crowded of the Montreal areas, so a good weekend choice.
680m; slopes 680–1035m
⛷ 4 ⛏ 110 acres

Mont Grand Fonds Canada
Small area sufficiently far from Québec not to get overrun at weekends.
400m; slopes 400–735m ⛷ 4

Mont Habitant Canada
Very limited area in the Montreal region but with a good base lodge. ⛏ 3

Mont Olympia Canada
Small, two-mountain area near Montreal, one mostly novice terrain, the other best suited to experts. ⛏ 6

Mont Orford Canada
Cold, windswept lone peak (no resort), worth a trip from nearby Montreal on a fine day.
slopes 305–855m
⛷ 8 ⛏ 180 acres

Mont-Ste-Anne 700

Mont-St-Sauveur Canada
Perhaps the prettiest resort in Canada, popular with Montreal (60km/37 miles) day trippers and luxury condo owners.

Mont Sutton Canada
Varied with some of the best glade skiing in eastern Canada, including some for novices. Quaint Sutton village nearby.
⛷ 9 ⛏ 175 acres

Moonlight Basin 641
Quiet area of slopes linked to Big Sky, Montana.

Morgins 498
Chalet resort just on the Swiss side of the Portes du Soleil circuit.

Morillon France
Valley village with a gondola link up to its purpose-built satellite and the Flaine network.
700m
🚠 Altitude, AmeriCan Ski, Chalet Group, Erna Low, Lagrange, Peak Retreats

Morin Heights Canada
Area in the Montreal region with 100% snowmaking. Attractive base lodge. ⛷ 6

Morzine 331

Les Mosses Switzerland
Peaceful resort and area, best for a day trip from Villars or Les Diablerets. There's a terrain park, a few chalet-style hotel-restaurants, shops and a rather fine church. Recent visitors recommend its quiet slopes and great views. There are only draglifts to access the mainly red and blue runs. Lunch is mostly at valley level – the Bivouac in the Relais Alpin hotel is recommended by a reporter, or try the Buvette de l'Arsat or the self-service Drosera. Les Mosses prides itself on the number of activities on offer – such as ice-diving, a natural ice rink and an international dog-sled racing course.
1500m; slopes 1500–2200m
⛷ 13 ⛏ 40km

Mottaret 316
Purpose-built but reasonably attractive component of Méribel.

Mottarone Italy
Closest slopes to Lake Maggiore. No village – just a base area.
1200m; slopes 1200–1490m
⛏ 25km

Les Moulins Switzerland
Village down the road from Château d'Oex with its own low area of slopes, part of the big Gstaad lift-pass area.
890m; slopes 890–3000m
⛷ 67 ⛏ 250km

Mount Abram USA
Small, pretty, tree-lined area in Maine, renowned for its immaculately groomed easy runs.
295m; slopes 295–610m
⛷ 5 ⛏ 170 acres

Mountain High USA
Best snowfall record and highest lift capacity in Los Angeles vicinity – plus 95% snowmaking. Mostly intermediate cruising.
2010m; slopes 2010–2500m
⛷ 12 ⛏ 220 acres

Mount Ashland USA
Arty town in Oregon renowned for Shakespeare performances. Tiny ski area best for experts run by local charity.
1935m; slopes 1935–2285m
⛷ 4 ⛏ 200 acres

Mount Bachelor USA
Extinct volcano in Oregon with a big ski area and runs on all 360° of slopes, served by 11 lifts including seven fast chairs. Higher elevation means better chance of good snow than many other resorts in north-west USA and average annual snowfall of 370 inches is more than any major Colorado resort. The front faces roughly north and has good groomed cruising and beginner terrain lower down, and the west side has steeper runs including blacks through the trees. After a fresh snowfall and in spring snow, the steep terrain on the back south-facing face is the place for experts to head, with steep double diamond terrain on top of the front side too (the top 400m/1,310ft vertical or so is open with trees below that level). There's no lodging at the base. We stayed 30 mins away at smart Sunriver Resort – with a big lodge with bar and restaurant, accommodation in chalets in the grounds and an excellent spa. There's lots of lodging in the attractive small town of Bend (also 30 mins away and served by free shuttles to and from the mountain), which prides itself on its restaurants and local microbreweries.
1920m; slopes 1755–2765m
⛷ 11 ⛏ 3680 acres
🚠 AmeriCan Ski, Ski Dream

Mount Baker USA
Almost on the coast near Seattle, yet one of the top resorts for snow (averages 600 inches a year). Plenty of challenging slopes. Known for spectacular avalanches.
1115m; slopes 1115–1540m
⛷ 9 ⛏ 1000 acres

Mount Baldy Canada
Tiny area, but a worthwhile excursion from Big White. Gets ultra light snow – great glades/powder chutes. A lift and ten runs were added in 2006/07.
slopes 1705–2150m
⛷ 2 ⛏ 150 acres

Mount Baldy USA
Some of the longest and steepest runs in California. Only an hour's drive from Los Angeles so a day trip is feasible, but 20% snowmaking and antiquated lifts are major drawbacks.
1980m; slopes 1980–2620m
⛷ 4 ⛏ 400 acres

Interactive resort shortlist builder at **www.wtss.co.uk**

Mount Baw Baw Australia
Small but entertaining intermediate area in attractive woodland, with great views. Closest area to Melbourne (150km/93 miles).
1450m; slopes 1450–1560m
7 35 hectares

Mount Buffalo 723

Mount Buller 723

Mount Dobson New Zealand
Mostly intermediate slopes in a wide, treeless basin near Mt Cook, with good snow-cover. Accommodation in Fairlie, 40 minutes away.
1610m; slopes 1610–2010m
3 990 acres

Mount Falakro Greece
Area two hours' drive from Salonica in northern Greece; almost as big as Parnassos, uncrowded and with good views. Now with a fast quad.
1720m
8 22km

Mount Hood Meadows USA
The biggest and most varied ski area on Mt Hood in Oregon served by 11 lifts including five fast quads. Good beginner area, intermediate cruising, single black diamond runs in the centre of the main ski area and a big area of double black diamonds roped off and entered through gates. Up to six terrain parks, depending on snow conditions. No accommodation at the base – stay at Timberline (see separate entry) half an hour away or Government Camp (near Mt Hood Skibowl, which also gets its own entry) 20 minutes away.
1635m; slopes 1375–2225m
11 2150 acres
Ski Dream

Mount Hood Skibowl USA
Small area of mainly tough gladed runs, offering the steepest and most extreme slopes in the Mount Hood area. Claims to be America's largest night skiing area with nearly all the green and blue and a lot of the blacks open until 10pm or 11pm every night. Two floodlit terrain parks, two tubing hills, snow bikes and kids' and adults' snowmobiles. Just below Timberline ski area (see separate entry) – can stay there or in Government Camp at the foot of Skibowl's slopes, a sizeable settlement with a choice of lodgings and restaurants. Other local ski area is Mt Hood Meadows – see separate entry.
1075m; slopes 1075–1530m
7 960 acres

Mount Hotham 723
Mount Hutt 725
Mount Lemmon USA
Southernmost area in North America, close to famous Old West town Tombstone, Arizona. Reasonable snowfall.
2500m; slopes 2500–2790m
3 70 acres

Mount McKay 723

Mount Pilio Greece
Pleasant slopes cut out of dense forest, only 15km/9 miles from the holiday resort of Portaria above town of Volos. 'Very small and disorganised,' says a reporter.
1500m 3

Mount Rose USA
Much the highest base elevation in the Tahoe area – a good 600m/1,970ft above the lake – and with an annual snowfall average of 400 inches you can generally depend on great snow. The last few years have seen big changes here: a second six-pack, and the relocation of the quad it replaced to open up the Chutes – a shady bowl mainly of serious double diamond gradient. This bowl separates the front face of the mountain, with a row of blue and easy black runs to the base, from a wider, gentler, lightly wooded area known variously as East Bowl or Slide Bowl. Both have a lot to offer, especially for someone staying in Heavenly who may be finding the groomed stuff monotonous and the ungroomed stuff too challenging.
2520m; slopes 2410–2955m
6 1200 acres

Mount Shasta Ski Park USA
Californian resort 300 miles N of San Francisco.
4 425 acres

Mount Snow USA
A one-peak resort, with a long row of lifts on the front face (two fast quads among them) serving easy and intermediate runs of just over 500m/1,640ft vertical. There's a separate area of black runs on the north face – including a couple of short but serious double blacks – served by a pair of triple chairs. And on the opposite side a small area of intermediate runs above Carinthia base, accessed by a third fast quad. Mount Snow is reputed to have some of the best terrain parks in the east. Accommodation at the base includes a Grand Summit hotel.
580m; slopes 580–1095m
19 590 acres

Mount Spokane USA
Little intermediate area outside Spokane (Washington State).
1160m; slopes 1160–1795m
5 350 acres

Mount St Louis / Moonstone Canada
Premier area in Toronto region, spread over three peaks. Very high-capacity lift system and 100% snowmaking.
13 175

Mount Sunapee USA
Area in New Hampshire closest to Boston; primarily intermediate terrain.
375m; slopes 375–835m
10 230 acres

Mount Vermio Greece
Oldest ski base in Greece. Two areas in central Macedonia 60km/37 miles from Thessaloniki. Barren but interesting slopes.
slopes 1420–2000m 7

Mount Washington Resort Canada
Scenic area on Vancouver Island with lodging in the base village. Impressive snowfall record but rain is a problem.
1110m; slopes 1110–1590m
6 970 acres
Frontier

Mount Washington Resort USA
This resort was formerly called Bretton Woods (Director of Skiing a certain Bode Miller) and is one of several small resorts in New Hampshire scattered along the Interstate 93 highway. The slopes here are on a single mountain face, but it is highly rated, particularly by families, who relish the top-to-bottom easy trails on the main peak, Mt Rosebrook. There is a good mix of terrain, with West Mountain consisting mainly of double diamond slopes. Snowmaking is comprehensive. There's a 150m/500ft half-pipe. Four of the nine lifts are fast. There are a few places to stay near the base, with the grand old Mount Washington hotel five minutes away and plans for a new pedestrian village.
480m; slopes 480–940m
9 435 acres

Mount Waterman USA
Small Los Angeles area where children ski free. The lack of much snowmaking is a drawback.
2135m; slopes 2135–2440m
3 210 acres

Mühlbach 138
Village in the Hochkönig area.

Mühltal Austria
Small village halfway between Niederau and Auffach in the Wildschönau. No local skiing of its own.
780m; slopes 830–1900m
29 42km

Muhr Austria
Village by Katschberg tunnel well placed for visiting St Michael, Badkleinkirchheim, Flachau and Obertauern.
1110m

Muju Resort South Korea
Largest area in Korea and with a fair amount of lodging. Though it is the furthest resort from Seoul (four hours south) it is still overcrowded.
14

Mürren 523
Mutters 140
Myoko Suginohara Kokusai Japan
A series of small resorts two or three hours from Tokyo, which together make up an area of extensive slopes with longer, wider runs than normal for Japan. *15*

Naeba Japan
Fashionable resort with lots of accommodation two hours north of Tokyo. Crowded slopes.
900m; slopes 900–1800m 30

Nakiska Canada
Small area of wooded runs between Banff and Calgary, with emphasis on downhill speed. Unreliable snow, but state-of-the-art snowmaking and pancake-flat grooming.
1524m; slopes 1525–2215m
4 230 acres

Nasserein 200
Quiet suburb of St Anton.

Nassfeld Ski Arena 114
Nauders Austria
Spacious, traditionally Tirolean village tucked away only 3km/2 miles from the Swiss border and almost on the Italian one. Its slopes start 2km/1 mile outside the village (free shuttle-bus) and are mainly high and sunny intermediate runs spread over three areas. There is lots of snowmaking. The area is not ideal for experts, though there is a lot of off-piste terrain. It's not ideal for complete beginners either – the village nursery slopes are some way out. There are five cross-country trails amounting to 40km/25 miles in all.
1400m; slopes 1400–2850m
25 115km
Skiing Austria

Nax Switzerland
Quiet, sunny village in a balcony setting overlooking the Rhône valley. Own little area and only a short drive from Veysonnaz. Handful of red and blue runs.
1300m ♦ 6

Nendaz 543
A sizeable family resort linked in to the Verbier ski area.

Neukirchen Austria
Quiet, pretty beginners' resort with a fairly snow-sure plateau at the top of its mountain.
855m; slopes 855–2150m
♦ 14 ♦ 35km
▬ Crystal

Neustift 210

Nevegal Italy
Weekend place near Belluno, south of Cortina.
1030m; slopes 1030–1650m
♦ 14 ♦ 30km

Nevis Range 720

Niederau Austria
Chalet-style village, the main resort in the Wildschönau and a favourite with beginners and early intermediate skiers. Quite spread out, but few hotels are more than five minutes' walk from a main lift.
830m ♦ 27
▬ Directski.com, First Choice, Inghams, Neilson, Ski McNeill, Skiing Austria, Skitracer, Thomson

Niederdorf Italy
Cross-country village in South Tyrol. Villabassa is its Italian name.

Niseko 721

Niseko Village 721
One of the three interlinked ski areas of Niseko.

Nockberge Innerkrems Austria
Area just south of Katschberg tunnel.
1500m; slopes 1500–2300m
♦ 10 ♦ 33km

Nordseter Norway
Cluster of hotels in deep forest north of Lillehammer. Some Alpine facilities but best for cross-country.
850m; slopes 1000–1090m
♦ 2 ♦ 2km

Norefjell Norway
Norway's toughest run, a very steep 600m/1,970ft drop. 120km/75 miles north-west of Oslo.
185m; slopes 185–1185m
♦ 10 ♦ 23km

La Norma France
Traffic-free, purpose-built resort near Modane and Val Cenis. Readers report 'good atmosphere, no high-rise blocks, pistes mostly easy except for Crêtes' and 'uncrowded at half-term, good for kids, low prices for pass, school, rentals'.
1350m; slopes 1350–2750m
♦ 18 ♦ 65km
▬ AmeriCan Ski, Erna Low, Interhome, Lagrange, Peak Retreats, Ski France, Skiholidayextras.com

Norquay 661
Banff's quiet local hill.

North Conway USA
Attractive factory-outlet-shopping town in New Hampshire close to Attitash and Cranmore ski areas.
▬ Virgin Snow

Northstar-at-Tahoe USA
Classic US-style mountain, with runs cut through dense forest and a pleasant new base village that is still growing. The whole area is very sheltered and good for bad-weather days. A gondola and a fast quad go up to a lodge at Big Springs, only 16om/52oft above the village. From this point three fast chairs radiate to serve a broad bowl with some short steep slopes at the top, with easier blue runs lower down and around the ridges. From the ridge you can access the Backside, a steeper bowl with a central fast quad chair serving a row of easy black runs and there are more black runs with a modest vertical of 390m/1,280ft on Lookout Mountain.
1930m; slopes 1930–2625m
♦ 17 ♦ 2655 acres
▬ American Ski Classics, Funway Holidays, Ski Dream, United Vacations

Nôtre-Dame-de-Bellecombe France
Pleasant 'very French' village spoiled by the busy road. Inexpensive base from which to visit Megève, though it has fair slopes of its own. Queues and slow lifts can be a problem now it is linked to Les Saises. Free bus to/from Crest Voland.
1150m; slopes 1035–2070m
♦ 84 ♦ 175km
▬ AmeriCan Ski, Erna Low, Lagrange, Peak Retreats

Nova Levante 479
Trentino village close to Bozen/Bolzano.

Nozawa Onsen Japan
Spa village with good hot springs three hours from Tokyo. The runs are cut out of heavy vegetation.
500m; slopes 500–1650m ♦ 21

Nub's Nob USA
One of the most sheltered Great Lakes ski areas (many suffer fierce winds). 100% snowmaking; weekend crowds from Detroit. Wooded slopes suitable for all abilities.
275m; slopes 275–405m
♦ 8 ♦ 245 acres

O2Resort South Korea
Korea's first winter sports resort to be built up the mountain. The resort is located in Gangwon province, which receives the most snowfall in Korea. Facilities include condo and youth hostel accommodation, a golf course, a fitness centre, a spa and restaurants. The ski area is suitable for all levels, and includes a 3.2km long run. There is also a kids' park and toboggan area.
1420m ♦ 16 runs

Oberammergau 414

Oberau Austria
Pretty village, most central of those forming the Wildschönau region – but least convenient for the slopes.
935m
▬ Inghams, Interhome, Neilson, Skiing Austria

Obereggen 479
Tiny resort close to Bozen/Bolzano.

Obergurgl 172

Oberjoch-Hindelang Germany
Small, low-altitude resort, particularly good for beginners.
850m; slopes 1140–1520m
♦ 12 ♦ 32km

Oberlech 158
Car- and crowd-free family resort alternative to Lech.

Oberndorf Austria
Quiet hamlet connected to St Johann's area.
700m
▬ Lagrange

Oberperfuss 140

Obersaxen-Mundaun-Lumnezia Switzerland
Several quiet villages above Ilanz, in the Vorderrhein Valley, have a sizeable area of mainly red and blue runs on four linked mountains. The main lifts are fast chairs. Recommended by a reporter.
1300m; slopes 1200–2310m
♦ 18 ♦ 120km

Oberstaufen Germany
Three small areas: Steibis; Thulkirchdorf and Hochgrat. Within an hour of Friedrichshafen.
600m; slopes 860–1880m
♦ 30 ♦ 45km

Oberstdorf 414

Obertauern 177

Ochapowace Canada
Main area in Saskatchewan, east of Regina. It doesn't get a huge amount of snow but 75% snowmaking helps.
♦ 4 ♦ 100 acres

Ohau New Zealand
Some of NZ's steepest slopes, with great views of Lake Ohau 9km/6 miles away (where you stay). 320km/200 miles south of Christchurch.
1500m; slopes 1425–1825m
♦ 3 ♦ 310 acres

Okemo USA
Family-oriented resort with worthwhile and nicely varied area. The slopes on Okemo mountain are largely intermediate or easy – though there are a dozen black runs and a couple of short double black diamonds. The runs on the next-door mountain, Jackson Gore, are still being developed, but there is a base development, including the Jackson Gore Inn – a hotel to complement the many slope-side condos arranged neatly around the base of the main restaurant. On-mountain restaurants are better than the US norm, especially if you count the options at Solitude village, a secondary lift base area.
345m; slopes 345–1020m
♦ 18 ♦ 624 acres

Oppdal 708

Orcières-Merlette France
High, convenient family resort a few km north-east of Gap, Merlette being the ugly, purpose-built ski station above the village of Orcières (1450m/4,760ft). Snow-sure beginner area. Slopes have a good mix of difficulty spread over several mountain flanks, and have been recently expanded – a process that culminated with the opening of a cable car up to almost 3000m/9,840ft on Roche Brune.
1850m; slopes 1850–2725m
♦ 29 ♦ 85km
▬ Lagrange, Ski Collection, Ski France, Skiholidayextras.com

Ordino 102

Orelle France
Village in the Maurienne with access by gondola to Val Thorens in the Trois Vallées. High, exposed slopes better suited to confident intermediates.
▬ Peak Retreats

Oropa Italy
Little area just off the Aosta–Turin motorway. An easy change of scene from Courmayeur.
1180m; slopes 1200–2390m
15km

Les Orres France
Friendly modern resort with great views and varied intermediate terrain, but the snow is unreliable, and it's a long transfer from Lyon.
1550m; slopes 1550–2720m
23 62km
Lagrange, Ski Collection, Ski France, Skiholidayextras.com

Orsières Switzerland
Traditional, winter resort near Martigny. Close to Grand St Bernard resorts, including Champex-Lac. Well-positioned base from which to visit Verbier and the Chamonix valley.
900m

Ortisei 468
Charming market town in Val Gardena with indirect links to the Sella Ronda circuit.

Oslo Norway
Capital city with cross-country ski trails in its parks. Alpine slopes and lifts in Nordmarka region, just north of city boundaries.

Otre il Colle Italy
Smallest of many little resorts near Bergamo.
1100m; slopes 1100–2000m
7 7km

Ötz Austria
Village at the entrance to the Ötz valley with an easy/intermediate ski area of its own and access to the Sölden, Kuhtai and Niederau areas.
820m; slopes 820–2200m
10 25km

Oukaimeden Morocco
Slopes 75km/47 miles from Marrakech with a surprisingly long season.
2600m; slopes 2600–3260m
7 15km

Ovindoli Italy
One of the smallest areas in L'Aquila region east of Rome, but it has higher slopes than most and one of the better lift systems.
1375m; slopes 1375–2220m
9 10km

Ovronnaz Switzerland
Pretty village set on a sunny shelf above the Rhône valley, with a good pool complex. Limited area but Crans-Montana and Anzère are close.
1350m; slopes 1350–2080m
8 30km

Owl's Head Canada
Steep mountain rising out of a lake, in a remote spot bordering Vermont, away from weekend crowds.
7 90 acres

Oz-en-Oisans 234
Attractive old village with satellite at the lifts into Alpe-d'Huez.

Pajarito Mountain USA
Los Alamos area laid out by nuclear scientists. Atomic slopes too – steep, ungroomed. Open Fridays, weekends and holidays. Fun day out from Taos.
2685m; slopes 2685–3170m
6 220 acres

Pal 105
Prettily wooded mountain linked with slopes of Arinsal.

Palandöken Turkey
Varied skiing area, transformed by three big hotels, overlooking the Anatolian city of Erzurum.
slopes 2150–3100m 4

Pampeago 479
Trentino area convenient for a trip from Milan.

Pamporovo 715

Panarotta Italy
Smallest of the resorts east of Trento. It is at a higher altitude than nearby Andalo, so it is worth a day out from there.
1500m; slopes 1500–2000m
6 7km

Panorama 683

Panticosa Spain
Charming old Pyrenees spa village near Formigal with sheltered but limited slopes.
1500m; slopes 1500–2220m
15 34km
White Roc

Paradiski 337

Park City 633

Parnassos Greece
Biggest and best-organised area in Greece, 180km/112 miles from Athens and with surprisingly good slopes and lifts. 'The Mykonos of winter and very crowded at weekends,' says a reporter.
slopes 1600–2300m
9 14km

Parpan Switzerland
Pretty village linked to the large intermediate area of Lenzerheide.
1510m; slopes 1230–2865m
37 155km

Partenen 217
Traditional village in the Montafon.

La Parva 733
Area linked with Valle Nevado, 50km/31 miles east of Santiago.

Pas de la Casa 107

Passo Costalunga 483
Dense network of short lifts close to Val di Fassa, now called the Carezza area.

Passo Lanciano Italy
Closest area to Adriatic. Weekend crowds from nearby Pescara when the snow is good.
1305m; slopes 1305–2000m
13

Passo Rolle Italy
Small group of lifts either side of the road over a high pass just north of San Martino di Castrozza.

Passo San Pellegrino 479
Little ski area south of the Sella Ronda, in Trentino.

Passo Tonale 454

Pass Thurn 151
Road-side lift base for one of Kitzbühel's ski areas.

Pebble Creek USA
Small area on Utah-Jackson Hole route. Blend of open and wooded slopes.
1920m; slopes 1920–2530m
3 600 acres

Pec Pod Snezku
Czech Republic
Collection of hamlets spread along the valley road leading to the main lifts and the very limited ski area.
770m; slopes 710–1190m
10 9km

Peisey 244
Small village linked to Les Arcs.

Peisey-Vallandry 244
Group of small villages linked to Les Arcs and the Paradiski area.

Pejo 479
Trentino resort near Madonna.

Penitentes Argentina
Inaugurated in 1979, 180km/112 miles from Mendoza. Accommodation at the base.
10 300 hectares

Perelik Bulgaria
New development aiming to link Pamporovo with Mechi Chal. Construction of the first lodgings is planned for 2008, but it's not clear when the planned 12 lifts and 28km/17 miles of pistes will be open.

Perisher / Smiggins 723

Pescasseroli Italy
One of numerous areas east of Rome in L'Aquila region.
1250m; slopes 1250–1945m
6 25km

Pescocostanzo Italy
One of numerous areas east of Rome in L'Aquila region.
1395m; slopes 1395–1900m
4 25km

Pettneu Austria
Beginners' resort with an irregular bus link to nearby St Anton.
1250m; slopes 1230–2020m
4 15km

Petzen Austria
One of many little areas in Austria's easternmost ski region near the Slovenian border.
600m; slopes 600–1700m
5 16km

Peyragudes-Peyresourde
France
Small Pyrenean resort with its ski area starting high above.
1000m; slopes 1600–2400m
15 37km
Lagrange, Ski France, Skiholidayextras.com

Pfelders Italy
Resort near Merano in the South Tyrol covered by the Ortler Skiarena pass.
4 5km

Pfunds Austria
Picturesque valley village with no slopes but quick access to several resorts in Switzerland and Italy, as well as Austria.
970m

Phoenix Park South Korea
Golf complex with 12 trails in winter. Two hours (140km/87 miles) from Seoul.
slopes 650–1050m 9

Piancavallo Italy
Uninspiring yet curiously trendy purpose-built village, an easy drive from Venice. 'Not for piste-bashers and experts but highly suitable for beginners and intermediates,' says a reporter.
1270m; slopes 1270–1830m
17 45km

Piani delle Betulle Italy
One of several little areas near the east coast of Lake Como.
730m; slopes 730–1850m
6 10km

Piani di Artavaggio Italy
Small base complex rather than a village. One of several little areas near Lake Como.
875m; slopes 875–1875m
7 15km

Piani di Bobbio Italy
Largest of several tiny resorts above Lake Como.
770m; slopes 770–1855m
10 20km

Piani di Erna Italy
Small base development – no village. One of several little areas above Lake Como.
600m; slopes 600–1635m
5 9km

Piau-Engaly France
User-friendly St-Lary satellite in one of the best Pyrenean areas.
1850m; slopes 1700–2500m
20 40km

Piazzatorre Italy
One of many little areas in the Bergamo region.
870m; slopes 870–2000m
⛷ 5 ⛷ 25km

Pichl 186
Hamlet outside Schladming, with lifts into two of the local areas.

Pico USA
Low-key little family area (no resort village) close to Killington.
605m; slopes 605–1215m
⛷ 9 ⛷ 160 acres

Piesendorf Austria
Cheaper, quiet place to stay when visiting Zell am See. Tucked behind Kaprun near Niedernsill.
780m
⛷ 3 ⛷ 3km

Pievepelago Italy
Much the smallest and most limited of the Appennine ski resorts. Less than 2 hours from Florence and Pisa.
1115m; slopes 1115–1410m
⛷ 7 ⛷ 8km

Pila 424
Purpose-built mountain resort linked by newly-upgraded gondola to the historic valley town of Aosta. Limited but varied, snow-sure terrain. Uncrowded, flattering slopes, good for beginners. Highly praised by recent reporters.

Pinzolo 479
Trentino resort near Madonna.

Pitztal Austria
Long valley with good glacier area at its head, accessed by underground funicular.
1250m; slopes 880–3440m
⛷ 19 ⛷ 87km
🚄 Interhome, Skiing Austria

Pla-d'Adet France
Limited purpose-built complex at the foot of the St-Lary ski area (the original village is further down the mountain).
1680m; slopes 1420–2450m
⛷ 32 ⛷ 80km
🚄 Lagrange

La Plagne 339

Plan de Corones Italy
Distinctive ski area in South Tyrol, with amazingly efficient lifts from Brunico and San Vigilio di Marebbe. Better known by its German name, Kronplatz.
1200m; slopes 1200–2275m
⛷ 32 ⛷ 103km

Plan-Peisey 244
Small development with link to Les Arcs.

Plose Italy
Varied area close to Bressanone, with the longest run in the South Tyrol.
560m; slopes 1065–2500m
⛷ 11 ⛷ 40km

Poiana Brasov 718

Pomerelle USA
Small area in Idaho on the Utah–Sun Valley route.
2430m; slopes 2430–2735m
⛷ 3 ⛷ 300 acres

Pontechianale Italy
Highest, largest area in a remote region south-west of Turin. Day-tripper place.
1600m; slopes 1600–2760m
⛷ 8 ⛷ 30km

Ponte di Legno 454
Attractive sheltered alternative to Passo Tonale.

Pontresina Switzerland
Small, sedate, sunny village with one main street, rather spoiled by the sanatorium-style architecture. All downhill skiing involves travel by car or bus, except the single long piste on Pontresina's own hill, Languard. It's cheaper to stay here than St Moritz.
1805m
⛷ 56 ⛷ 350km
🚄 Switzerland Travel Centre

Port-Ainé Spain
Small but high intermediate area in the Spanish Pyrenees near Andorra. Lifts include a six-pack; eponymous 3-star hotel at base.
1975m; slopes 1650–2440m
⛷ 8 ⛷ 44km

Port del Comte Spain
High resort in the forested region of Lleida, north-west of Barcelona. The slopes spread across three linked sectors: El Sucre, El Hostal and El Estivella.
slopes 1700–2400m
⛷ 15 ⛷ 40km

Porté Puymorens France
Little-known Pyrenean area close to Pas de la Casa in Andorra. Plans to link the two are now moving forward with the opening in 2005 of the first lift on the French side of Pas de la Casa.
slopes 1600–2600m
⛷ 13 ⛷ 45km

Porter Heights New Zealand
Closest skiing to Christchurch (one hour). Open, sunny bowl offering mostly intermediate skiiing – with back bowls for powder.
1340m; slopes 1340–1950m
⛷ 5 ⛷ 200 acres

Portes du Soleil 349

Portillo 733

Powderhorn USA
Area in west Colorado perched on the world's highest flat-top mountain, Grand Mesa. Sensational views. Day trip from Aspen.
2490m; slopes 2490–2975m
⛷ 4 ⛷ 300 acres

Powder King Canada
Remote resort in British Columbia, between Prince George and Dawson City. As its name suggests, it has great powder. Plenty of lodging.
880m; slopes 880–1520m
⛷ 3 ⛷ 160 acres

Powder Mountain USA
Massive Utah area sprawled over six ridges, an hour and a quarter's drive from Salt Lake City. An ample 2,800 acres is lift served, a mix of mainly north-facing slopes with enough green, blue and black runs to satisfy all abilities. You access the rest by snowcat or snowmobile tow, buses and hiking. It is the abundance of intermediate freeride terrain that makes it special. You can also stay in Ogden, 32km/20 miles away.
2100m; slopes 2100–2740m
⛷ 7 ⛷ 5500 acres

Pozza di Fassa 483
Pretty Trentino village with its own slopes.

Pragelato Italy
Inexpensive base, linked by cable car to Sestriere. Its own area is worth a try for half a day.
1535m; slopes 1535–2700m
⛷ 6 ⛷ 50km
🚄 Kuoni, Neilson, White Roc

Prägraten am Grossvenediger Austria
Traditional mountaineering/ski touring village in lovely setting south of Felbertauern tunnel. The Alpine ski slopes of Matrei are nearby.
1310m; slopes 1310–1490m
⛷ 2 ⛷ 30km

Prali Italy
Tiny resort east of Sestriere – a worthwhile half-day trip.
1450m; slopes 1450–2500m
⛷ 7 ⛷ 25km

Pralognan-la-Vanoise France
Unspoiled traditional village overlooked by spectacular peaks. Champagny (La Plagne) and Courchevel are close by.
1410m; slopes 1410–2355m
⛷ 14 ⛷ 30km
🚄 Erna Low, Lagrange, PV-Holidays.com, Ski France, Skiholidayextras.com, Ski Independence

Pra-Loup France
Convenient, purpose-built family resort with an extensive, varied intermediate area linked to La Foux-d'Allos.
1500m; slopes 1500–2600m
⛷ 32 ⛷ 83km
🚄 Lagrange, Leisure Direction, Ski Collection, Ski France, Skiholidayextras.com

Prati di Tivo Italy
Weekend day-trip place east of Rome and near the town of Teramo. A sizeable resort by southern Italy standards.
1450m; slopes 1450–1800m
⛷ 6 ⛷ 16km

Prato Nevoso Italy
Purpose-built resort with rather bland slopes. Part of Mondolé ski area with Artesina.
1500m; slopes 1500–1950m
⛷ 25 ⛷ 90km
🚄 Thomson

Prato Selva Italy
Tiny base development (no village) east of Rome near Teramo. Weekend day-trip place.
1370m; slopes 1370–1800m
⛷ 4 ⛷ 10km

Le Praz 277
Aka Courchevel 1300 – the lowest and most attractive of the Courchevel resorts.

Les Praz 258
Quiet hamlet 4km/2 miles from Chamonix.

Praz-de-Lys France
Little-known snow-pocket area near Lake Geneva that can have good snow when nearby resorts (eg La Clusaz) do not.
1500m; slopes 1200–2000m
⛷ 23 ⛷ 60km
🚄 Lagrange, PV-Holidays.com

Praz-sur-Arly France
Traditional village in a pretty, wooded setting just down the road from Megève. Newly linked slopes to Notre Dame de Bellecombe and beyond to Crest Voland/Les Saises, to form the Espace Diamant.
1035m; slopes 1035–2070m
⛷ 84 ⛷ 175km
🚄 Lagrange, Leisure Direction, Ski France, Skiholidayextras.com

Predazzo 479
Small, quiet place in Trentino near Sella Ronda resorts.

Premanon France
One of four resorts that make up Les Rousses area in Jura region.
1050m; slopes 1120–1680m
⛷ 40
🚄 Lagrange

La Presolana Italy
Large summer resort near Bergamo. Several other little areas nearby.
1250m; slopes 1250–1650m
⛷ 6 ⛷ 15km

Les Prodains 253
Village at the foot of the cliffs on which Avoriaz sits.

Pucón 733
Ski area on the side of the active Villarrica volcano in southern Chile, 800km/500 miles south of Santiago. Lodgings are at Pucón village, 30 minutes away from the slopes.

Puigmal France
Resort in the French Pyrenees with accommodation in nearby villages.
1830m; slopes 1830–2700m
⛷ 12 ↗ 34km

Puy-St-Vincent 350

Pyhä 706

The French Pyrenees 413

Pyrenees 2000 France
Tiny resort built in a pleasing manner. Shares a pretty area of short runs with Font-Romeu. Impressive snowmaking.
2000m; slopes 1750–2250m
⛷ 32 ↗ 52km

Québec City 700

Queenstown 728

Radium Hot Springs Canada
Summer resort offering an alternative to the purpose-built slope-side resort of Panorama.
slopes 975–2155m
⛷ 8 ↗ 300 acres

Radstadt Austria
Interesting, unspoiled medieval town near Schladming that has its own small area, with the Salzburger Sportwelt slopes accessed from nearby Zauchensee or Flachau.
855m; slopes 855–2185m
⛷ 100 ↗ 350km

Ragged Mountain USA
Family-owned ski area in New Hampshire.
⛷ 9 ↗ 200 acres

Rainbow New Zealand
Northernmost ski area on South Island. Wide, treeless area, best for beginners and intermediates. Accommodation at St Arnaud.
1440m; slopes 1440–1760m
⛷ 5 ↗ 865 acres

Ramsau am Dachstein Austria
Charming village overlooked by the Dachstein glacier. Renowned for cross-country, it also has Alpine slopes locally, on the glacier and at Schladming.
1200m; slopes 1100–2700m
⛷ 18 ↗ 30km

Ramundberget 712

Rauris Austria
Small village in a quiet, dead-end valley south-east of Zell, about 25km/16 miles by road. Across the valley road from the village are nursery draglifts and a gondola accessing intermediate slopes with a vertical of 1250m/4,100ft. 'Well groomed slopes, few queues and worth a day or two's visit from Zell,' says a reporter.
950m; slopes 950–2200m
⛷ 8 ↗ 30km
📧 *Crystal, Neilson, Simply Alpine, Skiing Austria, Thomson*

Ravascletto Italy
Resort in a pretty wooded setting near Austrian border, with most of its terrain high above on an open plateau.
920m; slopes 920–1735m
⛷ 12 ↗ 40km

Reallon France
Traditional-style village, with splendid views from above Lac de Serre-Ponçon.
1560m; slopes 1560–2115m
⛷ 6 ↗ 20km

Red Lodge USA
Picturesque Old West Montana town. Ideal for a combined trip with Big Sky or Jackson Hole.
1800m; slopes 2155–2860m
⛷ 8 ↗ 1600 acres
📧 *AmeriCan Ski*

Red Mountain Resort Canada
Area renowned for its steep and deep powder, eight hours east of Vancouver, 3km/2 miles from Rossland, a sleepy old mining town. The main mountain is Granite, a conical peak with more or less separate faces of blue, black and double-black steepness. Next-door Red Mountain itself is half the size. There is an increasing amount of green and blue runs to warm up on, but it's the black and double-black stuff that dominates, and is the real attraction. The tough stuff is marked on the map but not on the mountain; and it's mostly in trees, with cliffs and gnarly narrow bits, so you need a guide.
1185m; slopes 1185–2075m
⛷ 6 ↗ 1685 acres
📧 *AmeriCan Ski, Frontier, Ski Dream, Ski Freshtracks, Ski Independence, Ski Safari, Skiworld*

Red River USA
New Mexico western town – complete with stetsons and saloons – with intermediate slopes above.
2665m; slopes 2665–3155m
⛷ 7 ↗ 290 acres

Reichenfels Austria
One of many small areas in Austria's easternmost ski region near the Slovenian border.
810m; slopes 810–1400m

Reinwald Italy
Resort near Merano in the South Tyrol covered by the Ortler Skiarena pass.

Reit im Winkl Germany
Southern Bavarian resort, straddling the German–Austrian border. Winklmoos ski area is best suited to intermediates.
750m; slopes 750–1800m
⛷ 7 ↗ 40km

The Remarkables 728
Three bleak basins 45 minutes from Queenstown.

Rencurel-les-Coulumes France
One of seven little resorts just west of Grenoble. Unspoiled, inexpensive place to tour. Villard-de-Lans is the main resort.

Reschenpass Austria
Area in the Tirol, but only just – it's right on the Swiss border, and it includes two small resorts in Italy – Schöneben and Haider Alm (this bit of Italy is German-speaking). Nauders is the main resort.
1520m
⛷ 7 ↗ 28

Rettenberg Germany
Small resort near Austrian border.
750m; slopes 820–1650m
⛷ 15 ↗ 40km

Reutte Austria
500-year-old market town with many traditional hotels, and rail links to nearby Lermoos.
855m; slopes 855–1900m
⛷ 9 ↗ 19km

Revelstoke 685

Rhêmes Notre Dame 424
Unspoiled village in the beautiful Rhêmes valley, south of Aosta. Courmayeur and La Thuile within reach.

Riederalp Switzerland
Pretty, car-free village perched high above the Rhône valley. Access by cable car or gondola from the valley village of Mörel near Brig. A reader reports 'friendly locals, stunning views, no crowds, not much après'.
1900m; slopes 1900–2870m
⛷ 36 ↗ 99km
📧 *Made to Measure*

Rifensberg 213

Rigi-Kaltbad Switzerland
Resort on a mountain rising out of Lake Lucerne, with superb all-round views, accessed by the world's first mountain railroad.
1440m; slopes 1195–1795m
⛷ 7 ↗ 9km

Riihivuori Finland
Small area with 'base' at the top of the mountain. 20km/12 miles south of the city of Jyväskylä. ⛷ 5

Riksgränsen 712

Riscone Italy
Dolomite village sharing a pretty area with San Vigilio. Good snowmaking. Short easy runs.
1200m; slopes 1200–2275m
⛷ 35 ↗ 40km

Risoul / Vars 352

Rittner Horn Italy
Resort near Merano in the South Tyrol covered by the Ortler Skiarena pass.
⛷ 3 ↗ 15km

Rivisondoli Italy
Sizeable mountain retreat east of Rome, with one of the better lift systems in the vicinity.
1350m; slopes 1350–2050m
⛷ 7 ↗ 16km

Roccaraso Italy
Largest of the resorts east of Rome – at least when snow-cover is complete.
1280m; slopes 1280–2200m
⛷ 12 ↗ 56km

Rohrmoos 186
Suburb of Schladming, with vast area of nursery slopes.

La Rosière 355

Rossland Canada
Remote little town 5km/3 miles from cult powder paradise Red Mountain.

Rougemont Switzerland
Cute rustic hamlet just over the French/German language border near Gstaad, with worthwhile local slopes and links to Gstaad's Eggli sector.
991m; slopes 890–3000m
⛷ 62 ↗ 250km

Les Rousses France
Group of four villages – Les Rousses, Premanon, Lamoura and Bois d'Amont – in the Jura mountains, 50km/31 miles from Geneva airport.
1120m; slopes 1120–1680m
⛷ 40 ↗ 40km
📧 *Lagrange*

Ruka 706

Russbach Austria
Secluded village tucked up a side valley and linked into the Gosau-Annaberg-Lungotz area. The slopes are spread over a wide area.
815m; slopes 780–1620m
⛷ 33 ↗ 65km

Rusutsu 721

Saalbach-Hinterglemm 179

Saalfelden Austria
Town ideally placed for touring eastern Tirol. Extensive lift networks of Maria-Alm and Saalbach are nearby.
745m; slopes 745–1550m
⛷ 3 ↗ 3km

Saanen Switzerland
Cheaper and more convenient alternative to staying in Gstaad – but much less going on.
slopes 950–3000m
⛷ 62 ⛰ 250km

Saanenmöser Switzerland
Small village with rail/road links to Gstaad. Scenic and quiet local slopes, with good mountain restaurants (Horneggli and Kübelialp are recent recommendations).
1270m; slopes 1270–3000m
⛷ 67 ⛰ 250km

Saas-Almagell Switzerland
Compact village up the valley from Saas-Grund, with good cross-country trails and walks, and a limited Alpine area.
1670m; slopes 1670–2400m
⛷ 8 ⛰ 12km

Saas-Fee 527

Saas-Grund Switzerland
Sprawling valley village below Saas-Fee, with a separate, small but high Alpine area.
1560m; slopes 1560–3200m
⛷ 7 ⛰ 35km

Saddleback USA
Small area between Maine's premier resorts. High slopes by local standards.
695m; slopes 695–1255m
⛷ 5 ⛰ 100 acres

Sahoro Japan
Ugly, purpose-built complex on snowy northern Hokkaido island, with a limited area.
610m; slopes 610–1030m
⛷ 8 ⛰ 15km
🚌 Club Med

Les Saisies France
Traditional-style cross-country venue, surrounded by varied four-mountain Alpine slopes. Now part of Espace Diamant. Easy runs, but some lift queues at peak times.
1650m; slopes 1035–2070m
⛷ 84 ⛰ 175km
🚌 AmeriCan Ski, Erna Low, Lagrange, Leisure Direction, Peak Retreats, Ski Collection, Ski France, Ski Independence, Skiholidayextras.com

Sälen 712

Salt Lake City USA
Underrated base from which to ski Utah. 30 minutes from Park City, Deer Valley, The Canyons, Snowbird, Alta, Snowbasin. Cheaper and livelier than the resorts.
🚌 AmeriCan Ski

Salzburg-Stadt Austria
A single, long challenging run off the back of Salzburg's local mountain, accessed by a spectacular lift-ride from a suburb of Grödig.
425m

Samedan Switzerland
Valley town, just down the road from St Moritz. A run heads back to base from Corviglia-Marguns.
1720m; slopes 1740–2570m
⛷ 56 ⛰ 350km

Samnaun 144
Shares large ski area with Ischgl.

Samoëns 358

San Bernardino Switzerland
Pretty resort south of the road tunnel, close to Madesimo.
1625m; slopes 1600–2525m
⛷ 8 ⛰ 35km

San Candido Italy
Small resort in the South Tyrol. Innichen is its German name.
1175m; slopes 1175–1580m
⛷ 4 ⛰ 15km

San Carlos de Bariloche 732

San Cassiano 461
Quiet village linked via the Alta Badia to the Sella Ronda circuit.

Sandia Peak USA
The world's longest lift ride ascends from Albuquerque. Mostly gentle slopes; children ski free.
slopes 2645–3165m
⛷ 7 ⛰ 100 acres

San Grée di Viola Italy
Easternmost of resorts south of Turin, surprisingly close to the Italian Riviera.
1100m; slopes 1100–1800m
⛰ 30km

San Martin de los Andes Argentina
Sizeable town with accommodation, 19 km/12 miles from the Chapelco ski area.

San Martino di Castrozza 479
Trentino village south of Val di Fassa.

Sansicario 456
Small, stylish resort in the Milky Way near Sauze d'Oulx.

San Simone Italy
Tiny development north of Bergamo, close to unappealing Foppolo area.
2000m; slopes 1105–2300m
⛷ 9 ⛰ 14km

Santa Caterina Italy
Pretty, user-friendly village near Bormio, with a snow-sure novice and intermediate area.
1740m; slopes 1740–2725m
⛷ 8 ⛰ 25km

Santa Cristina 468
Quiet village in Val Gardena on the periphery of the Sella Ronda circuit.

Santa Fe USA
Interesting area only 15 miles from beautiful Santa Fe town. A tree-filled bowl with a good variety of terrain crammed into its small area. Ideal stopover en route from Albuquerque airport to Taos.
3145m; slopes 3155–3680m
⛷ 7 ⛰ 550 acres

Santa Maria Maggiore Italy
Resort south of the Simplon Pass from the Rhône valley, and near Lake Maggiore.
820m; slopes 820–1890m
⛷ 5 ⛰ 10km

San Vigilio di Marebbe Italy
Pretty village in South Tyrol with lifts on two mountains, one being the quite impressive Plan de Corones / Kronplatz.
1200m; slopes 1200–2275m
⛷ 31 ⛰ 103km

San Vito di Cadore Italy
Sizeable, alternative place to stay to Cortina. Negligible local slopes, though.
1010m; slopes 1010–1380m
⛷ 9 ⛰ 12km

Sappada Italy
Isolated resort close to the Austrian border below Lienz.
1215m; slopes 1215–2050m
⛷ 17 ⛰ 21km

Sappee Finland
Resort within easy reach of Helsinki, popular with boarders and telemarkers. Lake views. ⛷ 7

Sarnano Italy
Main resort in the Macerata region near Adriatic Riviera. Valley village with ski slopes accessed by lift.
540m
⛷ 9 ⛰ 11km

Le Sauze France
Fine area near Barcelonnette, sadly remote from airports.
1400m; slopes 1400–2440m
⛷ 23 ⛰ 65km

Sauze d'Oulx 456

Savognin Switzerland
Pretty village with a good mid-sized area; a good base for the nearby resorts of St Moritz, Davos/Klosters and Laax.
1200m; slopes 1200–2715m
⛷ 10 ⛰ 80km
🚌 Crystal, Pure Alpine, Switzerland Travel Centre

Scheffau 193
Rustic village not far from Söll.

Schia Italy
Very limited area of short runs – the only ski area near Parma. No village.
1245m; slopes 1245–1415m
⛷ 7 ⛰ 15km

Schilpario Italy
One of many little areas near Bergamo.
1125m; slopes 1125–1635m
⛷ 5 ⛰ 15km

Schladming 186

Schnalstal Italy
Valley and high ski area, in the Dolomites near Merano. Val Senales is its Italian name.
3210m; slopes 2110–3210m
⛷ 12 ⛰ 35km

Schöneben Italy
Area in the Val Venosta in the South Tyrol, close to Austrian border and Nauders.
1520m
⛷ 7 ⛰ 28km

Schönried Switzerland
A cheaper and quieter resort alternative to staying in Gstaad.
1230m; slopes 890–3000m
⛷ 67 ⛰ 250km
🚌 Interhome

Schoppernau 213
A scattered farming community, one of two main areas in Bregenzerwald northwest of Lech.

Schröcken 213
Bregenzerwald area village near Lech.

Schruns 217
Pleasant town at the heart of the Montafon region.

Schüttdorf 222
Ordinary dormitory satellite of Zell am See.

Schwarzach im Pongau Austria
Riverside village with rail links. There are limited slopes at Goldegg; Wagrain (Salzburger Sportwelt) and Grossarl (Gastein valley) are also nearby.
600m

Schwarzenberg 213

Schwaz Austria
Valley town beside the Inn with a lift into varied terrain shared with the village of Pill and its mountain outpost, Hochpillberg.
540m; slopes 540–2030m
⛷ 6 ⛰ 10km

Schweitzer USA
Excellent family-friendly resort in northern Idaho, 85 miles from Spokane (Washington state) and 45 miles from Canada. Area of slopes on a par with places like Keystone and Steamboat. Lifts include two fast quads and a six pack. A reader who went there from Fernie preferred Schweitzer; he reports 'nice condo blocks at the base, terrain for all levels including black chutes and glades at the top, fresh tracks all day'.
1220m; slopes 1229–1950m
⛷ 10 ⛰ 2900 acres
🚌 AmeriCan Ski

Schwemmalm Italy
Resort near Merano in the South Tyrol covered by the Ortler Skiarena pass.
⛷ 5 ⛰ 18km

Scopello Italy
Low area close to the Aosta valley, worth considering for a day trip in bad weather.
slopes 690–1700m
🚡 6 ⬆ 35km

Scuol Switzerland
Year-round spa resort close to Austria and Italy, with an impressive range of terrain.
1250m; slopes 1250–2800m
🚡 15 ⬆ 80km
✉ Switzerland Travel Centre

Searchmont Resort Canada
Ontario area with modern lift system and 95% snowmaking. Fine Lake Superior views.
275m; slopes 275–485m
🚡 4 ⬆ 65 acres

Sedrun 493
Charming, unspoiled old village on the Glacier Express rail route close to Andermatt. Fine terrain amid glorious scenery; covered on Gotthard Oberalp lift-pass.

Seefeld Austria
Traditional Tirolean style, upmarket resort, with a large, pedestrian-only centre. The slopes, on the outskirts, are served by a regular free shuttle-bus. Gschwandtkopf is a rounded hill of 300m/980ft vertical and intermediate runs on two main slopes. Rosshütte is more extensive, and has a terrain park and half-pipe. There is a cable car across to the separate peak of Härmelekopf. Seefeld's cross-country trails are some of the best in the Alps.
1200m; slopes 1200–2100m
🚡 25 ⬆ 38km
✉ Crystal, Inghams, Interhome, Lagrange, Neilson, Simply Alpine, Skiing Austria, Thomson

See im Paznaun 144
Small family-friendly area in the Paznaun Valley, near Ischgl.

Le Seignus-d'Allos France
Close to La Foux-d'Allos (which shares large area with Pra-Loup) and has own little area, too.
1400m; slopes 1400–2425m
🚡 13 ⬆ 47km

Seis Italy
German name for Siusi.

Sella Nevea Italy
Limited but developing resort in a beautiful setting on the Slovenian border (there are plans to link to Kanin). Summer glacier nearby.
1140m; slopes 1190–1800m
🚡 11 ⬆ 8km

Sella Ronda 461

Selva / Val Gardena 468

Selvino Italy
Closest resort to Bergamo.
960m; slopes 960–1400m
🚡 9 ⬆ 20km

Selwyn Snowfields 723

Semmering Austria
Long-established winter sports resort set in pretty scenery, 100km/62 miles from Vienna, towards Graz. Mostly intermediate terrain.
1000m; slopes 1000–1340m
🚡 5 ⬆ 14km

Les Sept-Laux France
Improving family resort near Grenoble. Modern lift system – 90% of lifts having been replaced in recent years. Pretty slopes.
1350m; slopes 1350–2400m
🚡 21 ⬆ 120km
✉ Mountain Heaven, Simply Alpine

Serfaus Austria
Charming traffic-free village (with underground people-mover to get you to the lifts) at the foot of a long, narrow, relatively snow-sure ski area, linked to Fiss. There are few challenging slopes for experts, but it is a good area for touring. Most of the area is ideal for intermediates and the nursery slopes are good. Most of the slopes are above the treeline, and with good snowmaking the area is fairly snow-sure, despite the sun. The 60km/37 miles of cross-country trails include very pretty loops at altitude. It's virtually unknown in the UK – a lack of English speakers may be a drawback.
1430m; slopes 1200–2750m
🚡 53 ⬆ 185km
✉ Crystal, Crystal Finest, Inghams, Interhome, Skiing Austria

Serrada Italy
Very limited area near Trento.
slopes 1250–1605m 🚡 5

Serre-Chevalier 360

Sesto Italy
Dolomite village off the Alta Val Pusteria, surrounded by pretty little areas. Sexten is its German name.
1310m; slopes 1130–2200m
🚡 31 ⬆ 50km

Sestola Italy
Appennine village a short drive from Pisa and Florence with its pistes, some way above, almost completely equipped with snowmakers.
900m; slopes 1280–1975m
🚡 23 ⬆ 50km

Sestriere 475

Seven Springs Mountain USA
Pennsylvania's largest resort.
slopes 220–2995m
🚡 18 ⬆ 494 acres

Sexten Italy
Dolomite village off the Hochpustertal, surrounded by pretty little areas. Sesto is its Italian name.
1310m; slopes 1130–2200m
🚡 31 ⬆ 50km

Shames Mountain Canada
Remote spot inland from coastal town of Prince Rupert and with impressive snowfall record. Deep powder.
670m; slopes 670–1195m
🚡 3 ⬆ 183 acres

Shawnee Peak USA
Small area near Bethel and Sunday River renowned for its night skiing. Spectacular views. Mostly groomed cruising.
185m; slopes 185–580m
🚡 5 ⬆ 225 acres

Shemshak Iran
Most popular of the three mountain resorts within easy reach of Tehran (60km/37 miles). 'Plenty of untracked lines and bumps; lifts get quite busy,' says a reporter.
3600m; slopes 2550–3050m
🚡 7

Shiga Kogen 721
Largest area in Japan.

Showdown USA
Intermediate area in Montana cut out of forest north of Bozeman. 50km/30 miles to the nearest hotel.
2065m; slopes 2065–2490m
🚡 4 ⬆ 640 acres

Sierra-at-Tahoe USA
A Colorado-style resort, with runs cut on densely wooded slopes. It claims an impressive average of 420 inches of snow. The slopes are spread over two flanks of Huckleberry Mountain, above the base lodge, and West Bowl, off to one side – 'As a boarder the whole mountain was excellent,' says one visitor. The fronts of both offer good intermediate cruising plus some genuine single diamond blacks. The backside of Huckleberry has easier blue and green slopes. This is a natural day trip for those staying in South Lake Tahoe.
2210m; slopes 2025–2700m
🚡 10 ⬆ 2000 acres

Sierra Nevada 703

Sierra Summit USA
Sierra Nevada area accessible only from the west. 100% snowmaking.
2160m; slopes 2160–2645m
🚡 8 ⬆ 250 acres

Sierre 539
Not a ski resort but the hub of the Coeur du Valais region of which the Val d'Anniviers is a part.

Silbertal 217
Low secluded village in the Montafon area.

Sillian Austria
A gondola and two fast quads serve this varied area in Austria's Hochpustertal region.
1100m
🚡 6 ⬆ 45km

Sils Maria 532
Pretty lakeside village, linked to the St Moritz Corvatsch slopes.

Silvaplana 532
Pretty lakeside village near St Moritz.

Silver Mountain USA
Northern Idaho area near delightful resort town of Coeur d'Alene. Best for experts, but plenty for intermediates too.
1215m; slopes 1215–1915m
🚡 6 ⬆ 1500 acres

Silver Star 687

Silverthorne USA
Factory outlet town on main road close to Keystone and Breckenridge. Good budget base for skiing those resorts plus Vail and Beaver Creek.
✉ AmeriCan Ski

Silverton USA
Expert-only area in southern Colorado that used to be heli-ski country. Served by one lift. Avalanche transceiver, shovel and probe compulsory.
3170m; slopes 3170–3750m 🚡 1

Sinaia Romania
Dreary main-road town with a modest, open area of slopes. Recent investment in new lifts, included a gondola.
795m; slopes 795–2030m
🚡 10 ⬆ 20km

Sipapu USA
Great little New Mexico area, with mostly treelined runs. Snow unreliable, but 70% snowmaking. Nice day out from Taos when conditions are good.
slopes 2500–2765m
🚡 4 ⬆ 70 acres

Siusi 468
Village west of the Sella Ronda circuit; Seis in German.

Siviez 543
A quieter and cheaper base for Verbier's Four Valleys circuit.

Sixt-Fer-a-Cheval 294
Traditional village near Samoëns.

Sjusjøen Norway
Cluster of hotels in deep forest close to Lillehammer. Some Alpine facilities but better for cross-country.
885m; slopes 1000–1090m
🚡 2 ⬆ 2km
✉ Exodus, Inntravel

Ski Apache USA
Apache-owned area south of Albuquerque noted for groomed steeps. Panoramic views. Nearest lodging in charming Ruidoso.
2925m; slopes 2925–3505m
🚡 11 ⬆ 750 acres

Ski Cooper USA
Small area close to historic Old West town of Leadville. Good ski/sightseeing day out from nearby Vail, Beaver Creek and Copper Mountain.
slopes 3200–3565m ⛰4

Ski Windham USA
Two hours from New York City and second only to Hunter for weekend crowds. Decent slopes by eastern standards.
485m; slopes 485–940m
⛰7 ⛷ 230 acres

Smugglers' Notch USA
French-style purpose-built family resort with sympathetic instructors, comprehensive childcare, child-friendly layout and long, quiet, easy runs. There are varied and satisfying slopes, spread over three hills, with a worthwhile vertical of 800m/2,610ft. It's a great area for beginners, but mileage-hungry intermediates should go elsewhere. Snowboarding is encouraged, and there are three impressive terrain parks and an Olympic-size super-pipe.
315m; slopes 315–1110m
⛰8 ⛷ 1000 acres
⇥ *Ski Dream*

Snowbasin USA
Underrated hill, usually with very good snow. No base village, but a worthwhile day out from Park City. The crowd-free slopes cover a lot of pleasantly varied terrain. This is a great mountain for experts – the Grizzly Downhill course drops 885m/2,900ft and is already claimed to be a modern classic. Between the race course and the area boundary is a splendid area of off-piste wooded glades and gullies. Middle Bowl is great terrain for the adventurous, with a complex network of blues and blacks. You have to stay in one of the towns of Ogden on the Salt Lake plain in the backwater of Huntsville.
1965m; slopes 1965–2865m
⛰12 ⛷ 2820 acres

Snowbird 638

Snowbowl (Arizona) USA
One of America's oldest areas, near Flagstaff, Arizona, atop an extinct volcano and with stunning desert views. Good snowfall record.
2805m; slopes 2805–3505m
⛰5 ⛷ 135 acres

Snowbowl (Montana) USA
Montana area renowned for powder, outside lively town of Missoula. Intermediate pistes plus 700 acres of extreme slopes. Grizzly Chute is the ultimate challenge.
1520m; slopes 1520–2315m
⛰4 ⛷ 1400 acres

Snowmass 608

Snow Park 725

Snow Summit USA
San Bernardino National Forest ski area near Palm Springs. Lovely lake views. 100% snowmaking. High-capacity lift system for weekend crowds.
2135m; slopes 2135–2500m
⛰12 ⛷ 230 acres

Snow Valley USA
Area quite near Palm Springs. Fine desert views. High-capacity lift system copes with weekend crowds better than nearby Big Bear.
2040m; slopes 2040–2390m
⛰11 ⛷ 230 acres

Sochi Russia

Solda Italy
Small resort in South Tyrol.
1905m; slopes 1905–2625m
⛰10 ⛷ 40km

Sölden 190

Soldeu 109

Soldier Mountain USA
Family resort in Central Idaho; backcountry snowcat tours.
slopes 1770–2195m
⛰4 ⛷ 670 acres

Solitude USA
Smart, car-free mini-village linked with Brighton in the valley next to Alta and Snowbird. Most (not all) of the slopes are easy or intermediate, including a wide area served by the one fast quad. When open, the top lift accesses lots of steeps in Honeycomb Canyon, on the back of the hill, with a short quad to bring you back to the front face. Headwall Forest and Eagle Ridge also have good blacks. The resorts' boundaries are open, and there are excellent backcountry adventures to be had. Two fast quads replaced old chairs out of the resort for 2008/09.
2490m; slopes 2435–3200m
⛰14 ⛷ 2250 acres
⇥ *AmeriCan Ski, Ski Safari*

Söll 193

Solvista USA
Child-oriented resort close to Winter Park. Low snowfall record for Colorado.
2490m; slopes 2490–2795m
⛰5 ⛷ 250 acres

Sommand France
Purpose-built base that shares area with Praz-de-Lys.
1420m; slopes 1200–1800m
⛰22 ⛷ 50km

Sonnenkopf Austria
Ski area above Klösterle a few km west of the Arlberg pass – and covered by the Arlberg ski pass. 'Uncrowded, gentle runs, interesting off-piste,' says a reporter.
slopes 1100–2300m
⛰9 ⛷ 30km

Sorenberg Switzerland
Popular weekend retreat between Berne and Lucerne, with a high proportion of steep, low runs.
1165m; slopes 1165–2350m
⛰18 ⛷ 50km

South Lake Tahoe USA
Tacky base for skiing Heavenly, with cheap lodging, traffic and gambling.

Spindleruv Mlyn
Czech Republic
Largest Giant Mountains region resort but with few facilities serving several little low areas.
715m; slopes 750–1310m
⛰16 ⛷ 25km

Spital am Pyhrn Austria
Small village near Hinterstoder in Upper Austria, a bus ride from its limited intermediate slopes at Wurzeralm. From the valley station a 3km/2 mile funicular goes up to a mid-mountain col with several restaurants and nursery slopes. Lifts and runs go off from here in several directions over pleasantly wooded intermediate terrain; the blues are tough, so transition from the nursery slopes is not easy. On the flat Teichlboden there are cross-country loops. The local lift pass also covers the slopes at Hinterstoder, a short drive away.
650m; slopes 810–1870m
⛰8 ⛷ 14km

Spittal an der Drau Austria
Historic Carinthian town with a limited area starting a lift-ride above it. A good day trip from Bad Kleinkirchheim or from Slovenia.
555m; slopes 1650–2140m
⛰12 ⛷ 27km

Spitzingsee Germany
Beautiful small lake (and village) an hour from Munich.
⛰18 ⛷ 25km

Splugen Reinwald Switzerland
Small intermediate area south of Chur.
1455m; slopes 1455–2215m
⛰7 ⛷ 30km

Sportgastein 123
Remote, high ski area at the top of the Badgastein valley.

Squaw Valley 587

Stafal 450
Tiny, isolated village, with good access to the Monterosa Ski area.

St Andra Austria
Valley-junction village ideally placed for one of the longest, most snow-sure cross-country networks in Europe. Close to the Tauern pass and to St Michael.
1045m

St Anton 200

Starhill Resort South Korea
Purpose-built resort formerly called Cheonmasan, 30km/19 miles north-east of Seoul. ⛰8

Stari Vrh Slovenia
About 30 minutes from Ljubljana airport. A reader who lives there says: 'Runs range from a never-groomed black and three interesting reds to a winding blue virtually from top to bottom.' Recently installed heated six-pack.
slopes 580–1200m
⛰5 ⛷ 12km

Stary Smokovec Slovakia
Spa town in the High Tatras mountains, with three small areas – Tatransky Lomica is the biggest. Funicular railway and snowmaking facilities.
1480m; slopes 1000–1500m
⛰8 ⛷ 4km

St Cergue Switzerland
Limited resort in the Jura mountains, less than an hour from Geneva and good for families with young children.
1045m; slopes 1045–1700m
⛰7 ⛷ 20km

St Christoph 200
Small village on Arlberg pass above St Anton.

St-Colomban-des-Villards 373

Steamboat 610

Ste-Foy-Tarentaise 369

Steinach Austria
Pleasant market town in picturesque surroundings, just off the autobahn up to the Brenner Pass, south of Innsbruck. Small area of slopes on Bergeralm, with gondola access to nursery and other slopes up at 1600m, and toboggan run as well as pistes back to the bottom. Extensive snowmaking. Night skiing.
1050m; slopes 1050–2200m
⛰5 ⛷ 25km

Stevens Pass USA
A day trip from Seattle, and accommodation 60km/37 miles away in Bavarian-style town Leavenworth. Mostly intermediate slopes, with long expert runs on backside. Busy at weekends Jan to March.
1235m; slopes 1235–1785m
⛰14 ⛷ 1125 acres

St-François-Longchamp 404
Sunny, gentle slopes linked to Valmorel.

St Gallenkirch 217
Village in the Montafon valley.

St-Gervais   305
Small town sharing its ski area with Megève.

St Jakob am Arlberg   200
Village near St Anton.

St Jakob in Defereggen Austria
Unspoiled traditional village in a pretty, sunny valley close to Lienz and Heiligenblut, and with a good proportion of high-altitude slopes.
1400m; slopes 1400–2520m
🚡 *9* 🚠 *34km*

St Jakob in Haus   Austria
Snowy village with its own slopes. Fieberbrunn, Waidring and St Johann are nearby.
855m; slopes 855–1500m
🚡 *8* 🚠 *16km*

St-Jean-d'Arves   373

St Jean d'Aulps   France
Small village in Portes du Soleil area, not part of main circuit but with its own interesting slopes consisting of two small areas - Domaine Chèvrerie and Domaine Grande Terche.

St-Jean-de-Sixt   France
Traditional hamlet, a cheap base for La Clusaz and Le Grand-Bornand (3km/2 miles to both).
960m
✉ *Karibuni, Last Resort*

St-Jean-Montclar   France
Small village at the foot of thickly forested slopes. Good day out from nearby Pra-Loup.
1300m; slopes 1300–2500m
🚡 *18* 🚠 *50km*

St Johann im Pongau   Austria
Bustling, lively working town with its own small area. An extensive three-valley lift network starts 4km/2 miles away at Alpendorf, linking via Wagrain to Flachau – all part of the Salzburger Sportwelt ski pass area.
650m; slopes 800–2285m
🚡 *64* 🚠 *200km*
✉ *Skiing Austria*

St Johann in Tirol   Austria
Friendly valley town, an attractive place for beginners and leisurely part-timers – keen piste-bashers will ski all the local slopes in a day and need to go on to explore nearby resorts covered by the Kitzbüheler Alpenskipass as well. There is nothing here to challenge an expert. The main access lift is a 10-minute walk from the centre. It gets more snow than neighbouring Kitzbühel and the SkiWelt, and also has substantial snowmaking. Given good snow, St Johann is one of the best cross-country resorts in Austria – trails total 275km/171 miles.
650m; slopes 670–1700m
🚡 *17* 🚠 *60km*

St Lary Espiaube   413
St-Lary-Soulan   413

St Leonhard in Pitztal   Austria
Village beneath a fine glacier in the Oetz area, accessed by underground funicular.
1250m; slopes 1735–3440m
🚡 *12* 🚠 *40km*

St Luc   539

St Margarethen   Austria
Valley village near Styria/ Carinthia border, sharing slopes with higher Katschberg.
1065m; slopes 1075–2210m
🚡 *14* 🚠 *70km*

St Martin bei Lofer   Austria
Traditional cross-country village in a lovely setting beneath the impressive Loferer Steinberge massif. Alpine slopes at Lofer.
635m

St-Martin-de-Belleville   371

St Martin in Tennengebirge   Austria
Highest village in the Dachstein-West region near Salzburg. It has limited slopes of its own but nearby Annaberg has an interesting area.
1000m; slopes 1000–1350m
🚡 *5* 🚠 *4km*

St-Maurice-sur-Moselle France
One of several areas near Strasbourg. No snowmakers.
550m; slopes 900–1250m
🚡 *8* 🚠 *24km*

St Michael im Lungau Austria
Quiet, unspoiled village in the Tauern pass snowpocket with an uncrowded but disjointed intermediate area. Close to Obertauern and Wagrain.
1075m; slopes 1075–2360m
🚡 *25* 🚠 *105km*

St Moritz   532

St-Nicolas-de-Véroce   305
Small hamlet in the Megève network.

St-Nicolas-la-Chapelle   France
Small village close to larger Flumet, in the Val d'Arly.
1000m; slopes 1000–1600m
🚡 *10* 🚠 *40km*

St-Nizier-du-Moucherotte   France
Unspoiled, inexpensive resort just west of Grenoble with no lifts of its own. Villard-de-Lans is the main resort.

Stoneham   700

Stoos   Switzerland
Small, unspoiled village an hour from Zürich. Overcrowded at weekends. Magnificent views of Lake Lucerne.
1300m; slopes 570–1920m 🚡 *9*

Storlien   Sweden
Small family resort amid magnificent wilderness scenery, one hour from Trondheim, 30 minutes from Åre.
600m; slopes 600–790m
🚡 *7* 🚠 *16km*

Stowe   656

St-Pierre-de-Chartreuse France
Locals' weekend place near Grenoble. Unreliable snow.
900m; slopes 900–1800m
🚡 *14* 🚠 *35km*

Stratton   USA
Something like the classic Alpine arrangement of a village at the foot of the lifts: a smart, modern development with a car-free shopping street. The slopes are mostly easy and intermediate, with some blacks and some short double-black pitches, spread widely around the flanks of a single peak, served by modern lifts. Stratton calls itself the 'snowboarding capital of the east', with no fewer than five terrain parks. The Suntanner Park has a super-pipe.
570m; slopes 570–1180m
🚡 *14* 🚠 *660 acres*

Strobl   Austria
Close to St Wolfgang in a beautiful lakeside setting. There are slopes at nearby St Gilgen and Postalm.
545m; slopes 545–1510m
🚡 *8* 🚠 *12km*

St-Sorlin-d'Arves   373

St Stephan   Switzerland
Unspoiled old farming village at the foot of the largest sector of slopes in the area around Gstaad. Upgraded chairlift for 2006/07.
995m; slopes 950–3000m
🚡 *67* 🚠 *250km*

Stubai valley   210

Stuben   200
Small, unspoiled village linked to St Anton.

St Veit im Pongau   Austria
Spa resort with limited slopes at Goldegg; Wagrain (Salzburger Sportwelt) and Grossarl (Gastein valley) are nearby.
765m

St-Veran   France
Said to be the highest 'real' village in Europe, and full of charm. Close to Serre-Chevalier and the Milky Way. Snow-reliable cross-country skiing.
2040m; slopes 2040–2800m
🚡 *15* 🚠 *30km*

St Wolfgang   Austria
Charming lakeside resort near Salzburg, some way from any slopes, best for a relaxing winter holiday with one or two days on the slopes.
540m; slopes 665–1350m

🚡 *9* 🚠 *17km*
✉ *Crystal, Inghams, Simply Alpine, Skitracer, Thomson*

Sugar Bowl   USA
Exposed area north of Lake Tahoe. The first Sierra Nevada area to be developed, next to the railway from the Bay area to Truckee (and so away from the lake); but with five fast quads, there is nothing antique about it now. Sugar Bowl claims a huge average snowfall of 500 inches a year. We were impressed by the varied terrain, including lots of genuine black and double diamond runs from the higher lifts as well as good cruising; the single-black Silver Belt is rated by an experienced American reader as his favourite run in the US. There is lodging at the base in The Inn, and a small development of condos is under way at the Mt Judah base, near the smart day lodge.
2100m; slopes 2100–2555m
🚡 *8* 🚠 *1500 acres*

Sugarbush   USA
Fast-developing resort, midway between Killington and Stowe, and one of the physically larger ski areas in the east. Its runs spread over broad mountainsides rather than being cut close together. The main sector is an extensive bowl below Lincoln Peak, with lifts up to six points on the rim; a long up-and-over chairlift accesses the Mt Ellen area – smaller, but with more altitude and more vertical (795m/2,600ft). The easy runs are confined to the lower slopes; higher up, the direct runs are seriously steep. Most accommodation is in the historic village of Waitsfield, but a village is developing at the base.
480m; slopes 450–1245m
🚡 *16* 🚠 *508 acres*
✉ *Ski Safari*

Sugarloaf   USA
Maine resort that has a much better-developed village at the base than most small New England resorts. The mountain is fair-sized by local standards, but a keen piste-basher could ski it out in a day or two. With 86om/2,82oft it claims the biggest continuous vertical in New England, and there is something for everybody, with genuine steeps up around and above the treeline and gentle terrain lower down in the woods. The resort has a super-pipe and a terrain park.
430m; slopes 405–1290m
🚡 *15* 🚠 *1410 acres*
✉ *American Ski Classics, Ski Dream*

Sulden Italy
Small resort in South Tyrol. Solda is its Italian name.
1905m; slopes 1905–2625m
⬆ 10 ⬆ 40km

Summit at Snoqualmie USA
Four areas – Summit East, Summit Central, Summit West and Alpental – with interlinked lifts. Damp weather and wet snow are major drawbacks.
slopes 915–1645m
⬆ 24 ⬆ 2000 acres

Sun Alpina Japan
Collective name for three ski areas four hours away from Tokyo. ⬆ 21

Sundance USA
Robert Redford-owned, tastefully designed family resort set amid trees in snow-sure Utah. It's a small, narrow mountain but the vertical is respectable, the setting beneath Mt Timpanogos is spectacular and there is terrain to suit all abilities. The lower mountain is easy-intermediate, served by a quad chair, the upper part steeper: one triple chair serves purely black slopes, the other blue and black trails. There are 17km/11 miles of cross-country trails, of varying difficulty, in a separate area just beyond the downhill slopes.
1860m; slopes 1860–2515m
⬆ 4 ⬆ 450 acres
✈ American Ski, Ski Dream, Ski Safari

Sunday River USA
One of the more attractive resorts in the East, four hours from Boston, best for intermediate cruisers. Condos cluster at the three main lift bases at the eastern end of the mountain. The slopes spread across eight peaks, each basically served by one lift, with links from one to the next. But it's a small area. The western sector has far fewer lifts and runs than the eastern end, where most of the lifts, as well as most of the beds, are concentrated. Only four of the chairs are fast quads but queues are not a problem – midweek, the resort is very quiet. Cross-country is big around here. Sunday River was one of the pioneers of snowmaking, and over 90% of its trails are served by it.
245m; slopes 245–955m
⬆ 18 ⬆ 667 acres
✈ American Ski Classics, Ski Dream, Ski Independence, Ski Safari

Sunlight Mountain Resort USA
Quiet, small area 10 miles south of Glenwood Springs. Varied terrain with some serious glades. A reader who included it in a tour of Colorado thought it 'well worth a visit for the day'.
2405m; slopes 2405–3015m
⬆ 3 ⬆ 470 acres

Sun Peaks 689

Sunrise Park USA
Arizona's largest area, operated by Apaches. Slopes are spread over three mountains; best for novices and leisurely intermediates.
2805m; slopes 2805–3500m
⬆ 12 ⬆ 800 acres

Sunshine Village 661
One-hotel mountain station in Banff's ski area.

Sun Valley 640

Suomu Finland
A lodge (no village) right on the Arctic Circle with a few slopes but mostly a ski-touring place.
140m; slopes 140–410m ⬆ 3

Superbagnères France
Little more than a particularly French-dominated Club Med; best for a low-cost, low-effort family trip to the Pyrenees. Said to have good off-piste if the snow is good.
1880m; slopes 1440–2260m
⬆ 16 ⬆ 35km
✈ Lagrange

Super-Besse France
Purpose-built resort amid spectacular extinct-volcano scenery. Shares area with spa town of Mont-Dore. Limited village.
1350m; slopes 1300–1850m
⬆ 22 ⬆ 43km
✈ Lagrange

Superdévoluy France
Purpose-built but friendly family resort in a remote spot near Gap, with huge tower blocks plus traditional chalets. Sizeable intermediate area shared with La Joue-du-Loup.
1450m; slopes 1450–2450m
⬆ 23 ⬆ 100km
✈ Crystal, Erna Low, Lagrange

Super Espot Spain
Small area on the eastern edge of the Aigues Tortes National Park, close to the valley town of Sort.
slopes 1500–2500m
⬆ 8 ⬆ 28km

Supermolina Spain
Dreary, purpose-built satellite of Pyrenean resort of La Molina, with a reasonable sized area of its own and linked to the slopes of Masella to form an area called Alp 2500.
1700m; slopes 1600–2535m
⬆ 31 ⬆ 121km

Les Sybelles 373

Tahko Finland
Largest resort in southern Finland. Plenty of intermediate slopes in an attractive, wooded, frozen-lake setting.
⬆ 9

Tahoe City USA
Small lakeside accommodation base for visiting nearby Alpine Meadows and Squaw Valley.

Talisman Mountain Resort Canada
One of the best areas in the Toronto region, but with a relatively low lift capacity. 100% snowmaking.
235m; slopes 235–420m ⬆ 8

Tamsweg Austria
Large cross-country village with rail links in snowy region close to Tauern Pass and St Michael.
1025m

La Tania 378

Taos 640

Tärnaby-Hemavan Sweden
Twin resorts in north Sweden, offering downhill, cross-country and heliskiing. Own airport.
slopes 465–1135m
⬆ 13 ⬆ 44km

El Tarter 109
Relatively quiet, convenient alternative to Soldeu.

Tarvisio Italy
Interesting, animated old town bordering Austria and Slovenia. A major cross-country base with fairly limited Alpine slopes.
750m; slopes 750–1860m
⬆ 12 ⬆ 15km

Täsch 562
The final road base on the way to car-free Zermatt.

Tauplitz Austria
Traditional village at the foot of an interestingly varied area north of Schladming. Readers have found 'wonderful snow, plenty of good off-piste, friendly locals', and 'varied runs, good lift system, few queues, spectacular scenery'.
900m; slopes 900–2000m
⬆ 18 ⬆ 40km

Telluride 613

Temù Italy
Sheltered hamlet near Passo Tonale. Worth a visit in bad weather.
1155m; slopes 1155–1955m
⬆ 4 ⬆ 5km

Tengendai Japan
Tiny area three hours by train and bus from Tokyo. One of Japan's best snow records, including occasional powder.
920m; slopes 920–1820m ⬆ 4

Termas de Chillán 733

Termignon France
Traditional rustic village 6km/4 miles down the Maurienne valley from Lanslebourg and the slopes of Val Cenis, to which it is linked. The local slopes are limited and served by slow lifts, but have the advantage of being extremely quiet.
1300m; slopes 1300–2500m
⬆ 6 ⬆ 35km
✈ Peak Retreats

Terminillo Italy
Purpose-built resort 100km/62 miles from Rome with a worthwhile area when its lower runs have snow-cover.
1500m; slopes 1500–2210m
⬆ 15 ⬆ 40km

Thollon-les-Mémises France
Attractive base for a relaxed holiday. Own little area and close to Portes du Soleil.
1000m; slopes 1600–2000m
⬆ 19 ⬆ 50km

Thredbo 723

Three Valleys 382

La Thuile 477

Thyon 2000 543
Mid-mountain resort above Veysonnaz in the Verbier ski area.

Tignes 384

Timberline (Palmer Snowfield) USA
Fair-sized area of largely intermediate slopes served by six lifts including four fast quads on Mt Hood in Oregon. Average snowfall 300 to 400 inches, comparable with Colorado's best. Also has a summer skiing area (closed in winter season) on Palmer glacier. Six terrain parks – something for all standards. Can ski down two ungroomed and unpatrolled trails to Mt Hood Skibowl area – see below. Timberline Lodge at mid-mountain is a splendidly atmospheric place built of huge logs and beams as part of a work creation programme in the 1930s Depression and opened by President Roosevelt in 1937. Huge central fireplace, comfy armchairs and sofas, historic original art on the walls, excellent 'fine dining' Cascade restaurant, snacks at first-floor balcony of Ram's Head Bar overlooking the lobby, creaky old bedrooms, outdoor pool and hot tub, sauna. A great place to stay while skiing all three of Mt Hood's ski areas (see also Mt Hood Meadows and Mt Hood Skibowl). We loved it on our 2008/09 season stay.
1800m; slopes 1510–2600m
⬆ 6 ⬆ 1430 acres

Toblach Italy
Small resort in South Tyrol.
Dobbiaco is its Italian name.
1250m; slopes 1250–1610m
🚡 5 🎿 15km

Togari Japan
One of several areas close to
the 1998 Olympic site.
Nagano, 2hr30 from Tokyo.
slopes 400–1050m 🚡 9

Torgnon Italy
Small resort off the road up
to Cervinia, good for bad-
weather days. Some good
cross-country loops.
1500m; slopes 1500–1965m
🚡 7 🎿 6km

Torgon Switzerland
Old village in a pretty wooded
setting, with a connection to
the Portes du Soleil. Still
some steep draglifts.
1150m; slopes 975–2275m
🚡 209 🎿 650km
✉ Interhome

Le Tour 258
Charming, unspoiled hamlet
at the head of the Chamonix
valley.

La Toussuire 373

Trafoi Italy
Quiet, traditional village in the
Val Venosta in the South Tyrol
covered by the Ortler Skiarena
pass.
1570m; slopes 1570–2550m
🚡 4 🎿 10km

Treble Cone 725
Tremblant 701
Trentino 479
Troodos Cyprus
Ski area on Mt Olympus, a
70-minute drive from Nicosia.
Pretty, wooded slopes and
fine views.
slopes 1730–1950m
🚡 4 🎿 5km

Tröpolach Austria
Small village at base of access
gondola for Nassfeld ski area.
610m; slopes 610–2195m
🚡 30 🎿 100km

Trysil 708
Tryvann 708
Tschagguns 217
Village in the Montafon valley.

Tsugaike Kogen Japan
Sizeable resort four hours
from Tokyo, three hours from
Osaka. Helicopter service to
the top station.
800m; slopes 800–1700m 🚡 26

Tulfes Austria
Hamlet on mountain shelf
close to Innsbruck, with small
main area above the trees
and long runs back to base.
920m; slopes 920–2305m
🚡 7 🎿 20km

Turoa 725
Turracherhöhe Austria
Tiny, unspoiled resort on a
mountain shelf, with varied
intermediate slopes above
and below it. A good outing
from Bad Kleinkirchheim.
1765m; slopes 1400–2200m
🚡 11 🎿 30km

Tyax Mountain Lake Resort
Canada
Heli-skiing operation in the
Chilcotin mountains –
transfers from Whistler or
Vancouver.

La Tzoumaz Switzerland
Hamlet at the base of lifts on
the back of Verbier's
Savoleyres sector, sometimes
referred to as Mayens de
Riddes.
1500m

Uludag Turkey
Surprisingly suave, laid-back,
well-equipped, purpose-built
resort near Bursa, south of
Istanbul.
1750m; slopes 1750–2322m
🚡 14 🎿 15km

Unken Austria
Traditional village hidden in a
side valley. Closest slopes to
Salzburg.
565m; slopes 1000–1500m
🚡 4 🎿 8km

Untergurgl 172
Valley-floor alternative to
staying in Hochgurgl or
Obergurgl.

Unternberg Austria
Riverside village with trail
connecting into one of the
longest, most snow-sure
cross-country networks in
Europe. St Margarethen
downhill slopes close by.
1030m

Unterwasser-Toggenburg
Switzerland
Old but not especially
attractive resort 90 minutes
from Zürich. Fabulous lake
and mountain views. The
more challenging half of the
Toggenburg area shared with
Wildhaus.
910m; slopes 900–2260m
🚡 19 🎿 60km

Uttendorf-Weiss-See Austria
Astute alternative to crowded
Kaprun when the snowline is
high.
805m; slopes 1485–2600m
🚡 9 🎿 18km

Vail 615
Valbella Switzerland
Convenient but ordinary
village sharing large
intermediate Lenzerheide
area.
1540m; slopes 1230–2865m
🚡 37 🎿 155km

Valberg France
Large Alpes-Maritimes resort
(bigger than better-known
Isola 2000) close to Nice.
1650m; slopes 1430–2100m
🚡 26 🎿 90km

Val Cenis France
Two quiet villages –
Lanslebourg and Lanslevillard
– in a high and remote part of
the Maurienne valley. Lifts go
from base stations in and
between the two villages –
the main one a gondola
starting near Lanslevillard.
Above mid-mountain is a
good range of open runs.
Below mid-mountain all the
runs are prettily wooded.
Most of the runs are north-
facing, and there is
snowmaking on the home
runs. There is ample off-piste
and a few bump runs for
experts, and cruises of up to
1400m/4,590ft vertical for
intermediates. Lanslevillard
has excellent nursery slopes,
and there are extensive cross-
country trails at Bessans.
Connected to the slopes of
nearby Termignon from
2008/09.
1400m; slopes 1300–2800m
🚡 27 🎿 125km
✉ AmeriCan Ski, Crystal, Erna
Low, Lagrange, MGS, Peak
Retreats, Ski France,
Skiholidayextras.com,
Snowcoach, Thomson

Val d'Anniviers 539
Val di Fassa 483
Val d'Illiez 498
Peaceful, unspoiled village
near Champéry in the Portes
du Soleil.

Val d'Isère 393
Val Ferret Switzerland
Old climbing village near
Martigny, with spectacular
views. Own tiny area.
1600m
🚡 3 🎿 20km

Valfrejus France
Small and unusual modern
resort on a narrow, shady
shelf in the Maurienne valley
– built in the woods, with the
slopes higher up above the
treeline. The focus is Plateau
d'Arrondaz, with steep, open
slopes above, offering
genuine bumpy blacks with
excellent snow (snowmaking
on the lower runs is urgently
required, though). There's a
natural terrain park, and good
off-piste is available above
the main plateau. The nursery
slopes are at mid-mountain
and village levels.
1550m; slopes 1550–2740m
🚡 13 🎿 65km
✉ AmeriCan Ski, Erna Low,
Lagrange, Peak Retreats, Ski
Collection, Ski France,
Skiholidayextras.com,
SnowYourWay.com

Val Gardena 468
Valley area of Selva, Ortisei
and Santa Cristina – part of
the Sella Ronda circuit.

Valgrisenche 424
Vallandry 244
Family-friendly satellite of Les
Arcs. For package holidays
see Peisey-Vallandry.

Valle Nevado 733
Valloire France
Friendly, bustling old
mountain village free of
through-traffic in winter and
sharing with Valmeinier the
most extensive slopes in the
Maurienne region, spreading
over three sectors. The Sétaz
sector generally has the best
snow and the toughest
slopes. The broad, open,
west-facing slopes of Crey du
Quart offer a choice of routes
to link to the Valmeinier
valley. Snow on most of the
slopes is affected by the sun,
but there is a lot of
snowmaking. The gondolas
can have queues in the
morning peak. Experts will
find the area limited: the area
from Crey du Quart down into
the Valmeinier valley has
some decent off-piste if the
snow is good. The vast
majority of the slopes are
ideal for intermediates. There
are nursery slopes at village
level and up the mountain.
1430m; slopes 1430–2595m
🚡 33 🎿 150km
✉ AmeriCan Ski, Crystal, Erna
Low, Lagrange, Leisure
Direction, Peak Retreats,
PV-Holidays.com, Ski France,
Skiholidayextras.com, Ski
Independence, SnowYourWay.
com

Vallorcine 258
Quiet backwater village on
road between Chamonix and
Switzerland, now linked to
Balme area above Le Tour.

Vallter 2000 Spain
Small resort on the far eastern
fringes of the Pyrenees, close
to the Costa Brava.
slopes 1960–2535m
🚡 10 🎿 420 acres

Valmeinier France
Quiet, old mountain village
with a modern purpose-built
satellite where most people
stay. Shares with Valloire the
most extensive slopes in the
Maurienne region, spreading
widely over three mostly
sunny sectors.
*1500-1800m; slopes 1430–
2595m*
🚡 33 🎿 150km
✉ Crystal, Erna Low,
Lagrange, Leisure Direction,
Peak Retreats, PV-Holidays.
com, Ski Collection, Ski France,
Skiholidayextras.com, Ski
Independence, Snowcoach

Valmorel	404
Val Senales	Italy

Valley near Merano in South Tyrol.
3210m; slopes 2110–3210m
⛷ 12 🚠 35km

Val Thorens	406
Valtournenche	428

Cheaper alternative to Cervinia.

Vandans	217

Sizeable working village in the Montafon area.

Vars	352

Large, convenient purpose-built resort linked to Risoul.

Vasilitsa	Greece

Resort in northern Greece, in the Pindos range, offering 'very good intermediate skiing', according to reports.
1780m ⛷ 8

Vaujany	234

Tiny village in the heart of the Alpe-d'Huez ski area.

Las Vegas Ski Resort	USA

Tiny area formerly known as Lee Canyon, cut from forest 50 minutes' drive north-west of Las Vegas. Quite high, but limited snowmaking. Cafe and rental shop at the base. Top resort designers Ecosign have produced a development plan multiplying the size of the area and taking the top height up to 3120m.
2595m; slopes 2595–2855m
⛷ 4 🚠 200 acres

Velka–Raca	Slovakia

Small resort near Oscadnica, with a modern lift system, including a 'chondola'.
630m; slopes 630–1050m
⛷ 6 🚠 14km

Vemdalen	712
Vemdalsskalet	712
Venosc	France

Captivating tiny village of cobbled streets, ancient church and craft shops with fast gondola to Les Deux-Alpes.
🚌 *Peak Retreats*

Vent	Austria

High, remote Oztal village known mainly as a touring base, with just enough lift-served skiing to warrant a day trip from nearby Obergurgl.
1900m; slopes 1900–2680m
⛷ 4 🚠 15km

Ventron	France

Small village near La Bresse in the northerly Vosges mountains near Strasbourg, with more ski de fond than downhill terrain.
630m; slopes 900–1110m
⛷ 8 🚠 15km

Verbier	543
Vercorin	539
Verditz	Austria

One of several small, mostly mountain-top areas overlooking the town of Villach.
675m; slopes 675–2165m
⛷ 5 🚠 17km

Vex	Switzerland

Major village in unspoiled, attractive setting south of Sion. Verbier slopes accessed nearby at Mayens-de-l'Ours.
900m

Veysonnaz	543

Little, old village within Verbier's Four Valleys network.

Vichères–Liddes	Switzerland

Limited area near to Martigny. Part of the Grand St Bernard region, including Val Ferret and Champex-Lac. Valid with the Valais ski Card.
1350m; slopes 1350–2270m
⛷ 4 🚠 15km

Vic-sur-Cère	France

Charming village with fine architecture, beneath Super-Lioran ski area. Beautiful extinct-volcano scenery.
680m; slopes 1250–1850m
⛷ 24 🚠 60km
🚌 *Lagrange*

Viehhofen	Austria

Cheaper place to stay when visiting Saalbach. It is 3km/2 miles from the Schönleiten gondola, and there is a run back to the village from the Asitz section.
860m ⛷ 1

Vigla-Pisoderi	Greece

The longest run in Greece (over 2km), in an unspoiled setting 18km/11 miles from the town of Florina in the north.
1600m ⛷ 5

Vigo di Fassa	483

Best base for the Fassa valley.

La Villa	461

Quiet Sella Ronda village.

Villabassa	Italy

Cross-country village in South Tyrol. Niederdorf is its German name.

Villach-Dobratsch	Austria

One of several small, mostly mountain-top areas overlooking the town of Villach.
900m; slopes 980–2165m
⛷ 8 🚠 15km

Villar-d'Arêne	France

Tiny area on main road between La Grave and Serre-Chevalier. Empty, immaculately groomed, short easy runs, plus a couple of hotels.
1650m

Villard-de-Lans	France

Unspoiled, lively, traditional village west of Grenoble. Snow-sure, thanks to snowmaking.
1050m; slopes 1160–2170m
⛷ 29 🚠 130km
🚌 *AmeriCan Ski, PV-Holidays. com*

Villard-Reculas	234

Rustic village on periphery of Alpe-d'Huez ski area.

Villaroger	244

Rustic hamlet with direct links up to Arc 2000.

Villars	555
Villeneuve	360

One of the main valley villages making up the big resort of Serre-Chevalier.

Vipiteno	Italy

Bargain-shopping town close to Brenner Pass.
960m; slopes 960–2100m
⛷ 12 🚠 25km

Virgen	Austria

Traditional village in a beautiful valley south of the Felbertauern tunnel. Slopes at Matrei.
1200m

Vitosha	Bulgaria

Limited area of slopes and a few widely scattered hotels, 22km/14 miles from Sofia, leading to crowds at weekends. The slopes are north-facing and have a decent snow record.
1810m; slopes 1515–2290m
⛷ 12 🚠 29km

Vogel	719
Vorarlberg	212
Vorderlanersbach	132

Village with access to Mayrhofen's ski area.

Voss	708
Vuokatti	Finland

Small mountain in a remarkable setting, surrounded on three sides by lots of little lakes. Good activity base. ⛷ 8

Wagrain	Austria

A towny little resort at the centre of a lift system that is typical of many in Salzburgerland – spreading widely across several low, partly wooded ridges. Flachau and Alpendorf/St Johann are at its extremities, and all these resorts are covered by Salzburger Sportwelt lift pass that our figures relate to. It's pleasant without being notably charming, and though it's a compact place the main lift bases are still a good walk apart. The slopes – wooded at the bottom, open higher up – are practically all easy/intermediate stuff, but cover a huge area almost 15km/9 miles across. The lift system is impressive, with a lot of

fast chairs and gondolas. Despite the altitude, most of the upper slopes are fairly open. Some get too much sun for comfort, and snow reliability is not a strong point.
850m; slopes 850–2190m
⛷ 64 🚠 200km

Waidring	Austria

Quiet valley village north of Kitzbühel, with nursery slopes on the doorstep and a powerful gondola (with big car parks) on the outskirts going up to Steinplatte – an area of mainly gentle open slopes which is also accessible from Germany. Impressive lift system with two six-packs and four quads, but still prone to weekend queues. Slopes face north, and there is extensive snowmaking.
780m; slopes 1230–1860m
⛷ 8 🚠 25km

Waiorau Snow Farm	725
Wald im Pinzgau	Austria

Cross-country village surrounded by Alpine areas – Gerlos, Krimml and Neukirchen – and with Pass Thurn also nearby.
885m
⛷ 55 🚠 155km

Wanaka	725
Warth	213

Bregenzerwald area village near Lech.

Waterville Valley	USA

Compact New Hampshire area with runs dropping either side of a broad, gentle ridge rising 615m/2,020ft above the lift base. A couple of short but genuine double black diamond mogul fields, but most of the slopes are intermediate. The village is a Disneyesque affair a couple of miles away down on the flat valley bottom.
600m; slopes 600–1215m
⛷ 12 🚠 255 acres

Watles	Italy

Village in the Val Venosta in the South Tyrol covered by the Ortler Skiarena pass.
⛷ 3 🚠 18km

Weinebene	Austria

One of many gentle little areas in Austria's easternmost ski region near the Slovenian border. No major resorts in the vicinity.
1560m; slopes 1560–1835m
⛷ 5 🚠 12km

Weissbach bei Lofer	Austria

Traditional resort between Lofer and Saalfelden. It has no slopes of its own, but it's well placed for touring the Tirol. Kitzbühel, Saalbach, St Johann and Zell am See are nearby.
665m

Weissensee Naggeralm
Austria
Little area in eastern Austria and the location of Europe's largest frozen lake, which is used for all kinds of ice sports, including ice-golf.
930m; slopes 930–1400m
🎿 5 ⬆ 6km

Weisspriach Austria
Hamlet on snowy pass near Obertauern that shares its area with Mauterndorf and St Michael.
1115m; slopes 1115–2050m
🎿 5 ⬆ 30km

Wengen 557

Wentworth Canada
Long-established Nova Scotia area with largest accessible acreage in the Maritime Provinces. Harsh climate ensures good snow-cover despite low altitude.
55m; slopes 55–300m
🎿 6 ⬆ 150 acres

Werfen Austria
Traditional village spoiled by the Tauern autobahn, which runs between it and the slopes. Good touring in the Dachstein West region.
620m

Werfenweng Austria
Hamlet with the advantage over the main village of Werfen of being away from the autobahn and close to the slopes. Best for novices.
1000m; slopes 1000–1835m
🎿 10 ⬆ 25km
🚠 Thomson

Westendorf 220

Whakapapa / Turoa 725

Whistler 691

Whitecap Mountains Resort
USA
Largest, snowiest area in Wisconsin, close enough to Lake Superior and Minneapolis to ensure winds and weekend crowds.
435m; slopes 435–555m
🎿 7 ⬆ 500 acres

Whiteface Mountain USA
Varied area in New York State 15km/10 miles from attractive lakeside resort of Lake Placid. 93% snowmaking ensures good snowcover. Plenty to do off the slopes.
365m; slopes 365–1345m
🎿 10 ⬆ 211 acres

Whitefish Mountain Resort
USA
Formerly known as Big Mountain, and set close to the Canadian border and to Montana's Glacier National Park. This place has revamped its image, and at least one of our reporters (who now makes an annual pilgrimage) rates it as simply the best. Lots of redevelopment is taking place, both on and off the slopes. Its 3,000 acres

embrace a wide range of slopes that are not only impressively snowy but also blissfully devoid of people. There's easy cruising in dense forest around the base area, and steeper stuff higher up on 'gladed' slopes. There are two 'excellent' terrain parks. There is accommodation at the base and you can also stay in the small town of Whitefish, a few miles away.
1370m; slopes 1370–2135m
🎿 12 ⬆ 3000 acres
🚠 Ski Dream, Ski Safari

White Pass Village USA
Closest area to Mt St Helens. Remote and uncrowded during the week, with a good snowfall record. Some genuinely steep, expert terrain, as well as intermediate cruising.
1370m; slopes 1370–1825m
🎿 5 ⬆ 635 acres

Whitewater Canada
Renowned for powder (40% off-piste), food ('excellent day lodge' says a reporter) and weekend party atmosphere. Accommodation in the historic town of Nelson or a great day out from nearby Red Mountain Resort.
1640m; slopes 1640–2040m 🎿 3
🚠 Frontier, Ski Dream

Wildcat Mountain USA
New Hampshire area infamous for bad weather, but one of the best areas on a nice day. Lodging in nearby Jackson and North Conway.
slopes 600–1250m
🎿 4 ⬆ 225 acres

Wildhaus Switzerland
Undeveloped farming community in stunning scenery near Liechtenstein; popular with families and serious snowboarders. Shares its slopes with Unterwasser.
1050m; slopes 900–2260m
🎿 19 ⬆ 60km

Wildschönau Austria
The dramatic-sounding brand name adopted by a group of attractive small resorts in the Tirol – Niederau, Oberau and Auffach.
830m; slopes 830–1905m
🎿 26 ⬆ 70km
🚠 Simply Alpine

Willamette Pass USA
Set in national forest near beautiful Crater Lake, Oregon. Small area of varied slopes. Gets an average of 430 inches of snow a year – that's up there with Utah.
1560m; slopes 1560–2035m
🎿 6 ⬆ 550 acres

Williams USA
Tiny area above the main place to stay for the Grand Canyon.
slopes 2010–2270m
🎿 2 ⬆ 50 acres

Willingen Germany
Resort in Sauerland, east of Düsseldorf.
🎿 16

Windischgarsten Austria
Large working village in Upper Austria with cross-country trails around and downhill slopes at nearby Hinterstoder and Spital am Pyrhn.
600m

Winterberg Germany
Resort in Sauerland, east of Düsseldorf.
🎿 18

Winter Park 622

Wolf Creek USA
Remote area on a pass of the same name, with 'the most snow in Colorado' – 465 inches a year. One-third of the terrain is standard American trails through the trees; two-thirds is 'wilderness', served by a single lift. Great stop en route between Taos and Telluride. Stay in Pagosa Springs to the west, or South Fork to the east.
3140m; slopes 3140–3630m
🎿 6 ⬆ 1600 acres
🚠 AmeriCan Ski

Wolf Mountain USA
Utah cross-country area close to Salt Lake City. Powder Mountain and Snowbasin are nearby Alpine areas.
🎿 3 ⬆ 100 acres

Xonrupt France
Cross-country venue only 3km/2 miles from nearest Alpine slopes at Gérardmer.
715m
🚠 Lagrange

Yangji Pine Resort South Korea
Modern resort an hour (60km/37 miles) south of Seoul, with runs cut out of dense forest. Gets very crowded. 🎿 6

Ylläs 706

Yong Pyong Resort
South Korea
The first of South Korea's dozen recently developed resorts, also known as Dragon Valley. 200km/125 miles east of Seoul, close to the east coast. Self-contained purpose-built resort village is centred on 200-room Dragon Valley Hotel. Modern lifts serve a small, mainly wooded slope area, with snowmaking on all its runs. English web site at www.yongpyong.co.kr.
750m; slopes 750–1460m
🎿 15 ⬆ 20km

Zakopane Poland
An interesting old town 100km/62 miles south of Kraków on the Slovakian border. Mostly intermediate slopes, branded as 14 small and fragmented sectors. Recently reported to have renovated its 70-year-old cable car.
830m; slopes 1000–1960m
🎿 20 ⬆ 10km
🚠 Interhome

Zao Japan
Big area with unpredictable weather, 4 hours from Tokyo by train. Known for 'chouoh' – pines frozen into weird shapes. Hot springs.
780m; slopes 780–1660m 🎿 42

Zauchensee Austria
Purpose-built resort isolated at the head of its valley, at one end of big three-valley lift network linking it via Flachauwinkl to Kleinarl – all part of the Salzburger Sportwelt ski pass area that our figures relate to. A reader reports 'attractive, compact village, shops limited to ski kit, no nightlife, dining only in hotels, relatively easy family-friendly skiing'.
855m; slopes 800–2185m
🎿 64 ⬆ 200km
🚠 Ski Hillwood

Zell am See 222

Zell im Zillertal 167
Sprawling valley town with slopes on two mountains.

Zermatt 562

Zillertal Austria
Valley of ten ski resorts, of which the most well known is Mayrhofen.

Zinal 539

Zug 158
Tiny village with Lech's toughest skiing on its doorstep.

Zugspitz Arena 227

Zuoz Switzerland
An unspoiled village in a sunny setting just down the valley from St Moritz, with gentle slopes at village level and some more challenging runs higher up.
1715m; slopes 1720–2465m
🎿 5 ⬆ 15km
🚠 Inntravel

Zürs 158
High, smart but soulless village on road to Lech.

Zweisimmen Switzerland
Limited but inexpensive base for slopes around Gstaad, with its own delightful little easy area too.
965m; slopes 950–3000m
🎿 67 ⬆ 250km